Leadership
in NONPROFIT
ORGANIZATIONS
A REFERENCE HANDBOOK

Leadership in NONPROFIT ORGANIZATIONS

A REFERENCE HANDBOOK

2

Kathryn A. Agard

Grand Valley State University

EDITOR

$SAGE | reference

Los Angeles | London | New Delhi
Singapore | Washington DC

For information:

SAGE Publications, Inc.
2455 Teller Road
Thousand Oaks, California 91320
E-mail: order@sagepub.com

SAGE Publications Ltd.
1 Oliver's Yard
55 City Road
London EC1Y 1SP
United Kingdom

SAGE Publications India Pvt. Ltd.
B 1/I 1 Mohan Cooperative Industrial Area
Mathura Road, New Delhi 110 044
India

SAGE Publications Asia-Pacific Pte. Ltd.
33 Pekin Street #02-01
Far East Square
Singapore 048763

Printed in Mexico

Library of Congress Cataloging-in-Publication Data

Leadership in nonprofit organizations: a reference handbook / edited by Kathryn A. Agard.
   v. cm.
Includes bibliographical references and index.
ISBN 978-1-4129-6886-7 (cloth)
  1. Nonprofit organizations—Management. 2. Leadership. I. Agard, Kathryn A.

HD62.6.L413 2011
658.4'092—dc22   2010019999

10 11 12 13 14 10 9 8 7 6 5 4

Publisher:	Rolf A. Janke
Acquisitions Editor:	Jim Brace-Thompson
Assistant to the Publisher:	Michele Thompson
Developmental Editor:	Diana Axelsen
Reference Systems Manager:	Leticia Gutierrez
Reference Systems Coordinator:	Laura Notton
Production Editor:	Jane Haenel
Editorial Assistant:	Marlene Corrado
Copy Editors:	Patricia Sutton, Jacqueline Tasch
Typesetter:	C&M Digitals (P) Ltd.
Proofreader:	Penny Sippel
Indexer:	Joan Shapiro
Cover Designer:	Candice Harman

CONTENTS

VOLUME ONE

Part V continues in Volume Two

VOLUME TWO

PART VIII. ETHICS AND SOCIAL RESPONSIBILITY IN THE NONPROFIT WORLD

55

Selection, Functions, Structure, and Procedures of the Nonprofit Board

Barbara A. Metelsky

North Carolina State University

Nonprofit organization governance is not "one size fits all." There is no ideal board size, simple formula for board composition, a definitive board member job description, perfect committee structure, or a best way to run a board meeting (Robinson, 2006). While every nonprofit must have a board of directors, board size and composition, board job descriptions and committee structures, and board meeting processes vary because nonprofit organizations are different. They have different missions and unique histories and are at different stages in their organizational life cycle. They are various sizes, have diverse organizational structures, and change over time, resulting in different organizational needs. Therefore, this chapter does not profess to be the ultimate or authoritative word on the topics it covers; that is, recruiting and selecting the board, board job descriptions and board agreements, board committee structures, and board meeting processes. Rather, its intent is to provide an overview of each topic and suggest references for further information on these important governance issues.

Recruiting and Selecting the Board

Board members are the volunteer leaders of a nonprofit organization. When selected carefully, board members bring valuable resources to nonprofits, which can be capitalized on to advance the organization's mission. These resources include knowledge, skills, specialized expertise, personal and professional contacts, and financial resources.

The recruitment and selection of board members should be undertaken in a thoughtful and deliberate manner. First,

optimal board size and desired composition should be determined based on an assessment of organizational needs. It is import to re-examine these factors on a regular basis because as the needs of a nonprofit organization changes, its board of directors should change as well.

Board Size

Board size is established by the nonprofit and is typically specified in its bylaws. Outside entities may play a role in determining board size. State laws, for example, define the minimum allowable number of board members (Independent Sector & BoardSource, 2009). External authorities such as government agencies or funders may also influence board size by establishing requirements for stakeholder group representation on the boards of nonprofits they support.

Nonprofit boards vary significantly in size ranging from fewer than 5 to more than 60 members. The average board has 16 members (Ostrower, 2007). Larger boards allow for increased diversity and greater representation of constituent and stakeholder groups bringing new ideas and important perspectives to board deliberations. A large board can provide more community connections that broaden the organization's networks and enhance its social capital and fundraising capacity. Nonprofits with few or no staff members may benefit from a larger working board, which supports its operations in addition to fulfilling its governance role. However, large boards can be more difficult to manage, may make decision making more challenging, and can diffuse responsibility. Members of large boards may be underused, leading to dissatisfaction and resignations.

Conversely, small boards are typically less time consuming to manage and can be more efficient in decision making. Members of small boards may feel more connected to each other and to the organization and may have a clearer sense of their personal impact on the advancement of the organization's mission. However, when a board is too small, its work may be negatively impacted. Small boards mean less diversity of ideas and fewer community connections. Members of small boards may burn out when there are too few members to carry out their responsibilities.

Therefore, when determining board size, nonprofit leaders should consider the organization's needs and balance the benefits and challenges that come with boards of varying sizes. To learn more about the impact of nonprofit board size on nonprofit governance and organizational effectiveness, consult the following sources: Bradshaw, Murray, and Wolpin (1992); Golden and Zajac (2001); Miller, Weiss, and MacLead (1988); O'Regan and Oster (2005); Ostrower (2007); and Provan (1980).

Composition

Decisions about board composition should be based on a nonprofit organization's needs as well as its strategic direction. The board governance committee should determine what knowledge, skills, expertise, contacts, and resources are needed to advance the organization's current work and realize its desired future. Consideration should be given to: (a) personal attributes, (b) diversity and representation, and (c) the chief executive officer's role on the board.

Many boards find it helpful to complete a matrix to assess current board composition as compared to desired board composition. This identifies gaps, which the board seeks to fill through its recruitment process. For further information on board composition matrices, including examples, see Dambach, Davis, and Gale (2009) and Robinson (2008).

A nonprofit's bylaws can be used to assure board diversity by specifying composition requirements (Robinson, 2008). It is important to include composition mandates placed on the organization by external groups, for example, consumer representation mandated by a funder or membership representation required by the organization's charter.

Personal Attributes

Personal attributes include a board member's or prospective member's skills, professional knowledge, personal qualities, and experience. Such attributes can be drawn on to make the board and the nonprofit organization more effective. While some personal attributes are likely to advance the work of any nonprofit (e.g., good communication skills); other personal attributes may be particularly well suited to meet a specific organization's needs (e.g., Spanish language skills).

Desirable board member skills include facilitation, consensus building, and networking. Beneficial professional knowledge varies from organization to organization and includes law, community organizing, accounting, public relations, research, medicine, real estate, education, and finance. Desirable personal qualities in board members are passion for the organization's mission and a sense of humor; good board members are hard working, good listeners, risk takers, ethical, and well-organized. Experience on other boards and personal experience as a consumer of services can also be valuable attributes (Robinson, 2008).

Diversity and Representation

The demographics of our nation and our communities are changing rapidly. Nonprofit boards should reflect the diversity of the community in which it is situated and of the people it serves. Board service provides "an important opportunity for community participation" (Daley & Marsiglia, 2001, p. 290), bringing new knowledge, enhanced creativity, and essential community perspectives to board deliberations. When assessing diversity and community representation, boards should consider factors beyond race and gender, including ethnicity, language, age, socioeconomic status, religion, sexual orientation, and ability status.

While the benefits of nonprofit board diversity are touted by many, a recent study (Ostrower, 2007) found that boards are largely homogeneous. In regard to race, on average, 86% of board members are white, non-Latino; 7% are African American or black, and 3.5% are Latino/Latina. Medians demonstrate even greater homogeneity; 96% white, and 0 for African Americans or blacks and Latinos/Latinas. Clearly, board membership does not reflect the diversity of our nation.

The picture for gender diversity is dramatically different. On average, 94% of boards include women, and overall, women are almost equally represented. However, there are gender differences related to board size and nonprofit type. The larger the nonprofit board, the smaller the percentage of female members. Education, cultural, and human services boards have the largest percentages of female board members (Ostrower, 2007).

In addition, the board members of larger and wealthier nonprofits come predominately from elite groups (Ostrower, 2007). This supports the findings of Widmer (1987) who reported that minority board members, like their white counterparts, were not typically representative in terms of socioeconomic status of the communities being served.

Finally, most boards are composed of members between the ages of 36 and 65. On average, only 16% of board members are over age 65, and 7% are under the age of 36 (Ostrower, 2007). This signifies a serious underutilization of the time and talents of the senior and young adult segments of the population.

These findings give rise to "basic questions about the ability of many boards to truly represent and respond to the diversity of the public they serve" (Ostrower, 2007, p. 18). The most ethical groups and often the most successful nonprofits are led by those who directly benefit from the organization's programs (Robinson, 2008). "To do their best work, anti-poverty agencies need poor people among the leadership, arts organizations should include artists, and groups that serve the disabled should include those with disabilities . . . on the board" (Robinson, 2008, p. 13).

It is important to remember, however, that simply placing diverse people on the board is insufficient. Research has shown that diverse board members are often marginalized (Widmer, 1987). Instead, diverse members must be welcomed, have their voices heard and opinions valued, and play leadership roles. For further information on diversity and representation in nonprofit boards see BoardSource (1999), Brown (2002), Daley (2002), Gottlieb (2005), and Siciliano (1996).

Chief Executive Officer

Some nonprofits, particularly larger ones that have adopted more corporate-like governance structures, have also adopted the practice of making the organization's chief executive officer a voting member of the board. Ostrower (2007) found that 33% of survey respondents include the CEO as a voting board member. Boards should carefully consider the ramifications of this practice, including the potential for conflicts of interest. CEOs should consider whether voting rights might place them in a difficult position with all or some board members over contentious votes. Most important, state laws should be checked to ensure that this practice is not prohibited.

In the event a board chooses to have its CEO serve on the board, the CEO should not serve as board chairperson. This separation of roles is a key internal control and accountability mechanism (Independent Sector & BoardSource, 2009). Decisions regarding the CEO's board member status should be specified in the organization's bylaws.

Recruitment

Once the board's optimal size and desired compositional mix have been determined, the board governance committee can turn its attention to the identification, cultivation, and selection of prospective board members. When the board makes its selections, the final step in the recruitment process takes place, that is, the election of new members.

Identifying Prospects

Boards often view the recruitment process as a once a year task. However, the identification of board prospects should be an ongoing effort led by the governance committee with assistance from other board members and the chief executive officer. Prospective board members can be found among people already associated with the organization, such as committee members, volunteers, donors, and the people the organization serves. Professional associations, service organizations, and other nonprofits such as the Chamber of Commerce, League of United Latin American Citizens, Society for Human Resource Management, Urban League, American Bar Association, and Junior League are other sources of potential board members. Faith institutions including churches, mosques, synagogues, and temples as well as educational institutions of all levels are also good sources for recruiting board members.

In addition, board-matching services are offered in some communities by voluntary action centers, community foundations, nonprofit resource centers, and the United Way. A national online board-matching service is provided by Boardnet USA (www.boardnetusa.org). Caution should be taken when recruiting certain groups of people. Board members often first approach friends and others they know. Recruiting friends may be appropriate if friends are passionate about the organization's mission and possess knowledge, skills, and abilities the board needs (Robinson, 2008). However, recruiting friends to the exclusion of undertaking broader recruitment efforts often leads to a board that is less diverse.

Another trap some boards fall into is focusing their recruitment efforts on people who are wealthy or well-connected. These individuals may have no interest in your organization and may already be spread too thin by service on numerous boards. On the other hand, if wealthy and well-connected people are known to be passionate about an organization's cause or have expressed interest in its work, they should be considered for board service (Robinson, 2008).

Recruitment Techniques and Prospect Cultivation

A wide range of techniques can be used to recruit new board members. Recruitment techniques include inviting prospects to attend a board meeting or organization event, arranging organization tours, conducting informal meetings and formal interviews, and completing an application form. The recruitment techniques an organization elects to use will depend in part on its organizational culture as well as time and financial constraints.

The cultivation of board member prospects is a key part of the recruitment process. Cultivation is used to assess what the prospective board member can contribute to the organization and to determine what he or she will need from the organization to be successful. The cultivation process should also be used to help prospects new to board service understand the roles and responsibilities of board members and to aid all prospects in understanding the specific requirements for service on the organization's board. It is important to be clear and up front about how much time a board member can expect to spend fulfilling board duties and what the organization's fundraising and personal giving expectations are. It is helpful to share copies of the organization's board job description or an example board agreement. (These documents are described in the next section of this chapter.) In addition, potential conflicts of interests should be explored with the prospective board member. Discuss how the board handles conflicts of interest and share the organization's conflict of interest policy.

Finally, cultivation is about relationship building and as such should be a personalized and affirming process. Whatever the outcome, it is important for the prospective board member to come away feeling positive about the organization.

Selecting and Electing New Board Members

A nonprofit's bylaws should specify the organization's process for selecting and electing new board members. Self-perpetuating boards are solely responsible for the selection and election of its members. In membership organizations, the members typically vote for the board and may even elect board officers. In nonprofits established by government entities, for-profit organizations, or other nonprofits, these external bodies may have the authority to nominate board members or to appoint individuals to fill designated board seats (Dambach et al., 2009).

If the board has approached the recruitment process in a strategic manner and has identified diverse prospects with attributes that will help the organization advance its mission, the selection of new board members should be relatively uncomplicated. The governance committee should use its previously developed board composition matrix to determine which prospective board members, individually and as a group, are best suited to help the organization reach its short- and long-term goals. If the role of board member is not the right fit for a particular prospect, consideration should be given as to whether this individual might support the organization in some other way.

When inviting prospects to join the board, it is important to make them feel needed and wanted. Let candidates know why they were selected and how the board believes they will benefit the organization. For prospects who accept an invitation to join the board, draft a board agreement. The agreement should be finalized and signed after the board vote appointing the person to the board. For further information on board recruitment, see Create the Future (n.d.) and Gottlieb (2003).

Board Job Descriptions and Board Agreements

Board job descriptions and board agreements are important documents that communicate expectations about board service between prospective and current board members and the nonprofit organization. They play an important role in the recruitment of new board members, in evaluating board members, and when necessary in removing individuals from the board.

Board Job Descriptions

As with job descriptions for staff members, the main purpose of a board job description is to provide an overview of duties. Board job descriptions also set expectations for performance, provide a basis for evaluation, and can be used to support the firing of ineffective board members (Robinson, 2008). Research has shown that clear board job descriptions play a role in helping nonprofits carry out their missions (Bradshaw, Murray, & Wolpin, 1992).

Job descriptions should be developed for the position of board member and for each board officer position. Most board job descriptions include a list of generic responsibilities tied to traditionally defined roles. Good board descriptions, however, should go beyond a listing of generic duties. They should be customized to reflect the specific expectations of service on your nonprofit organization's board.

A generic board member job description should include: (a) a position overview, (b) a list of position responsibilities, and (c) an outline of performance expectations. The description may also specify known or anticipated time commitments. The generic position should then be customized as previously discussed. See Appendix A for a generic board member job description.

Job descriptions for board officer positions should also be created. Officer positions vary from board to board. Some common board officer positions are: chairperson or president, vice chairperson or vice president, treasurer, and secretary. Board officer job descriptions should delineate the specific responsibilities of the respective positions. The following provides an overview of the key duties for these common officer positions, which may be incorporated into their respective job descriptions.

Chairperson

The board chairperson is a member of the board, serves as its chief volunteer officer, and is responsible for the board's activities. The chair works collaboratively with other board members to govern the organization and works in partnership with the chief executive officer to provide leadership. Key duties include (a) ensuring that the board meets its legal obligations, (b) serving as a role model for other board members, (c) supporting the CEO with key functions and serving as a sounding board, (d) developing or providing input into board agendas and running board meetings, (e) appointing committee chairpersons, (f) overseeing board officer transition, and (g) representing the organization and serving as a spokesperson as needed.

Vice Chairperson

The vice chairperson assumes the board chairperson's duties in the chair's absence. Key responsibilities include: (a) performing the chairperson's role when the chair is unavailable, including running board meetings; (b) chairing a major board committee; (c) assisting the chair with board officer transition planning; and (d) performing special assignments delegated by the chair or assigned by the board.

The board vice chairperson is often the successor to the board chairperson. However, making this position an automatic successor to the presidency is not advised because some excellent vice chairpersons do not have the knowledge, skills, and abilities necessary to lead the board.

Treasurer

The board treasurer provides leadership regarding the board's fiscal oversight role. Key duties include (a) chairing the finance committee, (b) providing a finance report at board meetings, (c) assisting with budget development and presenting the budget to the board, (d) ensuring that financial controls are in place and are being properly executed, (e) overseeing the wise investment of excess revenues, and (f) participating in the selection of an auditing firm.

Secretary

The board secretary is responsible for keeping a record of all board action. Key responsibilities include: (a) taking of board meeting minutes, (b) disseminating meeting agendas and minutes, (c) maintaining all board records, and (d) providing a notice of board meeting and committee meetings as required. In cases where staff support is available to complete all or some of the above responsibilities, the secretary is responsible to oversee that they have been completed in a thorough, accurate, timely, and confidential manner. For further information on and examples of board member and board officer job descriptions see Dambach et al. (2009), McNamara (n.d.), and Robinson (2008).

Board Agreements

Like board job descriptions, board agreements also outline board member responsibilities, both generic and specific. In addition, board agreements spell out what board members can expect from the nonprofit organization. These reciprocal agreements are more detailed, thereby lessening the likelihood of a misunderstanding regarding expectations. They hold both the board member and the organization accountable (Robinson, 2008).

The following provides an example of reciprocal responsibility statements related to the board's fiscal oversight role:

Board member responsibility: I accept fiduciary responsibility for the organization. I will monitor the organization's financial status and oversee its fiscal soundness and integrity.

Organization responsibility: Timely, accurate, and complete financial statements will be distributed to the board member. The board member will receive training to read and interpret our financial statements.

Board agreements are excellent tools for board recruitment because they provide prospective members with an understanding of what will be required of them and what the organization will provide to them in return. Like board job descriptions, the best board agreements are personalized. For example, a board agreement for a new board member who is a certified public accountant (CPA) might specify that the board member agrees to serve on the board's finance committee. Conversely, the agreement would spell out the organization's commitment to the board member; for example, sponsoring the board member's annual attendance at a nonprofit accounting conference.

In addition to reciprocal responsibilities, board agreements should specify the board member's term, committee assignments, and board leadership positions as applicable. Board agreements may also include ethics or conflict of interest statements. Board agreements should be signed and dated by the board member, board chairperson, and chief operating officer of the organization. For further information on board agreements, see Robinson (2008). Sample board agreements can be found on the websites of BoardnetUSA (www.boardnetusa.org) and BoardSource (www.boardsource.org).

Board Committee Structures

Board committees facilitate the work of the board. Committee structures vary from nonprofit to nonprofit but typically include standing committees and task forces. When designing a board committee structure, care should be taken to ensure that (a) the board has a sufficient number of members and the necessary expertise to carry out the committees' respective assignments, (b) the organization has the capacity to support the committees' work, and (c) procedures are put in place to make sure that board committee work advances the work of the full board rather than usurps its responsibilities.

Standing Committees

Standing committees are a permanent part of the organization's governance structure. They are specified in the organization's bylaws, which also outline their major responsibilities. Common standing committees include governance, executive, finance, audit, and fundraising. Other standing committees may include program, personnel, marketing, and community relations. When deciding which standing committees should be part of a nonprofit's governance structure, consideration should be given to the type, extent, and duration of the board's anticipated involvement; that is, policy focused, extensive, and ongoing versus supportive, limited, and one time or episodic. In addition, creating a committee structure that parallels staff responsibilities should be avoided (Dambach et al., 2009; Holland, 2006).

Governance

The governance committee or board development committee is considered by many to be the board's most important committee. Its role is to strengthen the board's own effectiveness. The committee is responsible for addressing board composition, the recruitment of board members, board orientation and training, board leadership development, the evaluation of individual board members, and the assessment of the board's performance. Its duties also include the ongoing evaluation of board structure, processes, and guiding documents such as the organization's bylaws and board policies (Dambach et al., 2009).

Executive Committee

The executive committee is typically composed of the board officers and is chaired by the board chairperson. The organization's chief executive officer usually serves as an ex-officio member unless the CEO is also an officer of the board. The executive committee is empowered to handle routine board matters and address crisis situations that arise between board meetings. If the executive committee is authorized to act on behalf of the full board, details regarding committee membership, authority, and functions should be outlined in the organization's bylaws (Dambach et al., 2009). Executive committee action should be presented to and ratified by the full board at its next meeting.

Not all nonprofit organizations have executive committees. The boards of new nonprofits and small organizations do not typically need them. In addition, some larger nonprofits choose not to have an executive committee to prevent other board members from being underused or feeling unneeded (Dambach et al., 2009). More important is the concern that the executive committee may become a de facto board.

Finance Committee

The finance committee is responsible for fiscal oversight and is typically chaired by the board treasurer. Committee functions include working with the chief executive officer to prepare the organization's annual budget, monitoring income and expenses, ensuring that the organization's financial practices meet applicable state and federal law, establishing financial controls, overseeing the organization's investments, and ensuring the timely and accurate completion of the Internal Revenue Service (IRS) Form 990, 990-EZ, or 990-PF, as applicable (Block 2001; Dambach et al., 2009).

Audit Committee

Not all nonprofits have outside audits conducted. But for some nonprofits—for example, nonprofits that receive more than $500,000 in federal funds—audits are mandated by law. Many nonprofits use their finance committees to oversee the organization's audit requirements. However, the 2002 passage of the Sarbanes-Oxley Act and the IRS 990 requirement to specify whether a specific committee is charged with overseeing the audit and the selection of the audit firm has led many nonprofits to establish a distinct audit committee. Separate finance and audit committees provide a check and balance for the organization (Independent Sector & BoardSource, 2009).

Fundraising Committee

The fundraising or resource development committee is typically responsible for setting annual fundraising goals and assisting with the development of fundraising plans. The committee may also examine and make recommendations about alternative fundraising strategies. In addition, committee members may be involved with the solicitation of donations and in planning or conducting special events (Block, 2001).

Task Forces

Many boards are moving to more flexible board committee structures, which can be accomplished through the increased use of task forces. Task forces are appointed to address a specific issue or complete a specific assignment over a limited period of time. Once their assigned task has been completed, they are disbanded (Dambach et al., 2009). Task forces can be established for a wide range of purposes. Examples include reviewing staff salary structures and benefit packages, doing strategic planning, designing a public relations campaign, or overseeing the search for a new chief executive officer.

Task forces provide a number of benefits beyond their flexibility. They can provide board members with substantial opportunities for engagement without the long-term commitment required for service on standing committees. Task force work can capitalize on the knowledge, skills, and abilities of individual board members. They can also provide opportunities for new board members to take on leadership roles.

Committee Membership

Board committees are chaired by a member of the board, who is typically appointed by the board chairperson. Board standing committees are generally composed exclusively of board members and may be provided with staff support (Dambach et al., 2009). The chief executive officer or another senior staff member may serve as an ex-officio member of a committee; for example, the organization's finance director may be appointed to serve as an ex-officio member of the board finance committee. In some nonprofits, committee members may include volunteers, consumers, or patrons of the organization's services, representatives from the community, donors, or staff members. This is a more common practice for board task forces and for organizational rather than board committees.

Brown and Iverson (2004) studied nonprofit organizations' strategic orientation and how their governing boards are correspondingly structured to match their orientation. Miles and Snow's typology of strategy was used to categorize nonprofits into strategic types. Brown and Iverson found that "prospectors" emphasized innovative programs and encouraged experimentation by staff. These nonprofits had broader committee structures and on average included members representing more than two constituent groups per committee. "Defenders" used fewer innovative strategies; instead, they emphasized the maintenance of well-defined and efficient services. These nonprofits typically had fewer board committees and committee members.

Brown and Iverson (2004) note that some nonprofits deliberately structure their governance committees to facilitate their organization's strategic philosophies. They suggest that nonprofits must adapt committee structures to their particular circumstances and should consider how their governance structures enable or prevent them from implementing their desired strategy.

For further information on board committee structures, see The Committee Series by BoardSource (www.boardsource.org).

Board Meeting Practices

The practices boards use to run meetings impact board effectiveness and efficiency. Board meeting practices include meeting frequency, length, methods, and who attends meetings. It also includes agendas, meeting processes, and board minutes. These practices vary from organization to organization and are determined in part by state laws, the specific needs of the organization, and preferences of board members.

Meeting Frequency, Length, Methods, and Attendees

The frequency of board meetings and their length, the methods board members use to meet, and the people who attend meetings all play an important role in effective governance. Boards should carefully consider these important practices and establish related board policies as appropriate.

Meeting Frequency

The frequency of board meetings varies from organization to organization. Many boards meet 10 to 12 times a year; others meet bimonthly, quarterly, or less frequently. In general, board meetings should be held when there is substantive business or strategic or generative work to accomplish. Other factors, however, should be considered when determining the frequency of board meetings. They include state laws, funder requirements, organizational life cycle, and board turnover. Most important, a board should meet with enough frequency to fulfill its fiduciary role.

State laws specify the minimum number of times a board must meet annually (Independent Sector & BoardSource, 2009). Government funders may mandate board meeting frequency. Some funders use meeting frequency as an indicator of board involvement; a common consideration in funding decisions.

Board meetings also serve an affiliative function; that is, they help board members to feel a part of the organization. Therefore, the boards of new nonprofits may need to meet more often to allow board members to get to know one another. In addition, when there has been significant turnover on the board, it may be advisable to conduct more frequent meetings for a period of time to foster group cohesiveness.

However, boards should avoid meeting for meeting's sake. Meetings that primarily or exclusively focus on information sharing are generally unproductive. Such meetings are a source of frustration for board members, which can lead to resignation. Fewer, focused, and productive meetings are recommended. When fewer meetings are warranted, efforts must be made to ensure that board members stay informed and connected between meetings. Alternative methods of information sharing such as mailing reports, sending e-updates, or posting information to a web-based board information portal can be used to keep the board apprised of ongoing activities and issues that do not require board input or action. When such information sharing mechanisms are used, procedures should be put in place for the timely distribution of information. In addition, board job descriptions and board culture should convey the expectation that board members will review materials disseminated between meetings.

Meeting Length

Meeting length should reflect the amount of time necessary to conduct the business at hand and to provide the board with opportunities for strategic and generative thinking (Chait, Ryan, & Taylor, 2005). Conducting lengthier bimonthly or quarterly meetings on a regular basis or scheduling an occasional extended meeting may be more productive than shorter monthly meetings. Longer meetings when structured appropriately allow more time for deliberation on complex issues.

When determining meeting length, time should be allotted for board socialization and networking purposes. In addition, holding an occasional event with an exclusively social purpose can strengthen the board's working relationship. Finding the right balance between work and social activities is important. The balance will vary from nonprofit to nonprofit and will change over time.

Meeting Methods

Consideration should also be given to the meeting methods boards use; for example, face to face and audio- or videoconference. Some boards are turning to alternatives to the traditional face-to-face board meeting, particularly when board members are geographically disbursed. Others may elect to use alternative methods to save time or money. However, facilitating and participating in alternate mode meetings can be challenging. A board should weigh the pros and cons of each method when deciding how it will meet.

State laws regulate whether nonprofit boards may use alternative meeting mechanisms. Some states require that board meetings be held with all board members meeting in the same place at the same time (Independent Sector & BoardSource, 2009). Therefore, nonprofits must determine if state law precludes them from conducting meetings via other means.

Meeting Attendees

Board meetings should be attended by all board members. The nonprofit's chief executive officer also typically attends each meeting. Staff members or other individuals acting in an advisory capacity may be invited to participate. Membership organizations may allow members to attend all or some of its board meetings. Under certain circumstances, state sunshine laws may require board meetings to be open to the public (Independent Sector & BoardSource, 2009).

When staff members attend board meetings, care should be taken to assure that staff members do not take over meetings and that staff opinions do not replace board deliberation, resulting in "rubber stamping." Finally, regardless of who is present at a board meeting, only board members have voting rights. This includes the CEO if she or he also serves as a member of the board.

Agendas, Meeting Processes, and Board Minutes

The substantive matter of board meetings and the processes used to conduct and record meetings influence board performance and ultimately the board's ability to advance the organization's mission (Axelrod, 2005). Therefore, nonprofit organizations should establish procedures for the development of board agendas, meeting processes, and the taking of board minutes designed to improve the board's efficiency and effectiveness.

Agendas

Agendas shape both the focus and process of board meetings. The primary purpose of board meetings is to make decisions around issues that impact organizational mission. However, board meetings too often consist of a series of reports resulting in little or no substantive work being conducted. Board agendas can address this problem by specifying what issues the board should focus its attention on during the meeting and what decisions need to be made (Robinson, 2008). Board agendas also play a key role in effective meeting management. When used appropriately, they help to keep meetings on track and on time. This reduces frustration over wasted time, which is a major factor in board member resignations.

In nonprofit organizations that have paid staff members, agendas are often drafted by the chief executive officer in consultation with the board chairperson. In organizations without staff, the responsibility for agenda development typically falls to the board chairperson or to the board executive committee. Regardless of who takes the lead in developing the agenda, the entire board should be consulted for input on agenda items.

Agendas may follow one of several format variations that include: traditional, consent, and strategic activities, resource planning, and operations. The following provides a description of these agenda types:

Traditional. The traditional agenda uses this common pattern: (a) review the agenda, (b) vote on minutes from the prior meeting, (c) present and discuss committee reports, (d) discuss old business and take action as needed, (e) discuss new business and take action as needed, (f) conduct an executive session as needed, and (g) schedule the next meeting. Some boards end with an evaluation of the meeting, which provides an opportunity for board self-assessment and organizational learning (Inglis & Weaver, 2000). Although this agenda format is widely used, it has a number of limitations. Most significant, this format often results in the board spending most of its time hearing reports and discussing operational issues, leaving little time for the performance of board's fiduciary and strategic responsibilities (Stoetz & Raber, 1994, as cited in Inglis & Weaver, 2000) and generative work (Chait et al., 2005).

Consent. An alternate agenda format designed to counteract the limitations of the traditional agenda is the consent agenda. This agenda combines routine and noncontroversial action items, which do not require board deliberation, into one overarching item for board approval. Its purpose is to prevent the board from spending time reviewing, discussing, and approving matters for which a consensus already exists, thus leaving the board more time for deliberation on substantive matters (Renz, n.d.). Consent agenda items must be sent to the board in advance of the meeting. Board members must be provided with sufficient supporting documentation to determine whether discussion is needed. If one or more board members wish to discuss the item, it must be removed from the consent agenda (Renz, n.d.). Consent agendas are followed by agenda items that require board deliberation and decision making. These matters should be listed on the agenda in priority order (Dambach et al., 2009).

Strategic Activities, Resource Planning, and Operations. Inglis and Weaver (2000) developed an alternative agenda format and board agenda tool based on findings from Inglis, Alexander, and Weaver's (1999) study of nonprofit boards. Their agenda focuses the board's work around three major categories: strategic activities, resource planning, and operations. Feedback from some board members who adopted this format reported an improved focus on agenda items related to board roles, better discussions, and enhanced communication (Inglis &Weaver, 2000).

Regardless of the agenda format that a board elects to use, it is important that (a) proposals for board action are identified before the board meeting, (b) board members are informed of the issues that will come before them, and (c) information needed to inform decision making is distributed in advance of the meeting (Dambach et al., 2009). In addition, agenda items should be limited to several high-priority issues. The amount of time spent on each should be commensurate with their relative importance and the complexity of the decisions to be made.

Meeting Processes

The board must enact meeting processes that facilitate the effective and efficient functioning of the board as well as meet applicable laws. Key meeting processes include: achieving a quorum, setting deliberation and decision-making procedures, and evaluating meetings.

Quorum

A quorum is the minimum number of voting board members who must be present at a meeting for business can be legally transacted. Typically, the organization's bylaws specify the percentage of board members present that constitutes a quorum. State laws define minimum quorum requirements. However, a board may be stricter about its own requirements and should establish its quorum at the highest level of attendance it can reasonably expect to achieve (Flynn, 2004; Independent Sector & BoardSource, 2009).

Before the board meeting begins the board chairperson or secretary should determine if a quorum is present. If the quorum requirement cannot be met, the meeting must be cancelled, and no action can be taken. In cases where one or more board members are delayed and a quorum is expected, the board must delay the start of the meeting until a quorum has been reached.

Deliberation and Decision-Making Procedures

The board chairperson is responsible for facilitating meetings. The chair establishes the tone and pace of the meeting. She or he fosters discussion and deliberation and ensures that board decision-making processes, as stipulated in the organization's bylaws or policies, are followed. Many nonprofit boards have adopted the use of *Robert's Rules of Order* (Roberts, 2000) to manage meetings. The book, first published in 1876, was developed to serve as a guide for the use of parliamentary procedures in meeting bodies or ordinary societies.

Nonprofits are not required to employ Robert's rules. Given their complexity, boards often find them challenging to use. In addition, their tendency to prematurely shut down dialogue necessary for effective decision making makes their value for use by nonprofit boards questionable. Other boards use a consensus process for decision making. A consensus process encourages discussion and deliberation leading to a broader range of potential solutions. A traditional consensus model allows one board member to block a decision when he or she strongly disagrees. A modified consensus model allows for a majority vote when full consensus cannot be reached (Robinson, 2008). Consensus decision making requires a board chairperson with strong facilitation skills and can be time consuming. However, the benefits of a consensus process can easily outweigh these challenges (Robinson, 2008).

Regardless of the specific decision-making procedures selected, it is most important that boards create a "culture of inquiry" that fosters healthy debate (Axelrod, 2007). The norms of a culture of inquiry include "the capacity to explore divergent views in a respectful rather than adversarial manner" (p. 1). This does not mean, however, that conflict should be avoided. Productive conflict is necessary to foster generative communication among nonprofit board members (Jameson & Metelsky, 2009), which leads to generative governance through the reframing of issues that come before the board (Chait et al., 2005).

Executive Sessions

When the board needs to discuss confidential issues, it holds an executive session, a meeting or part of a meeting that is held without staff. Typically, all board members are present. Others who have information that is pertinent to the discussion may be invited to join the meeting. The meeting minutes should document that an executive session was held and the topics of discussion. However, details of the discussion and decisions made should not be recorded except in separate confidential board minutes. The organization's bylaws or board policies should outline the procedures for calling and conducting executive sessions (Dambach et al., 2009; Masoka, 2009).

Reasons for conducting executive sessions include: (a) performance evaluations and compensation decisions regarding the chief executive officer (CEO), (b) annual meetings with the auditor, (c) serious conflicts among board members, (d) reports by a management consultant, and (e) investigations into concerns about the CEO (Dambach et al., 2009; Masoka, 2009). When the issue to be discussed involves the CEO, he or she is excluded from the meeting. If the CEO is a voting member of board, she or he has the legal right to be present (Masoka, 2009).

Some boards choose to hold executive sessions several times a year or set aside part of each meeting for an executive session. This provides board members with regularly scheduled time to discuss sensitive matters and reduces the anxiety of CEOs and staff who expect bad news from executive sessions (Masoka, 2009).

Evaluating Meetings

To ensure that board members remain engaged and satisfied with board service, it is important to evaluate board meetings. Meeting evaluation is the responsibility of the governance committee, which typically works with in partnership with the board chairperson to review evaluation results and recommend changes as needed (Dambach et al., 2009). Meeting evaluation can be conducted as part of an annual board assessment. However, more frequent evaluations are suggested. Some boards evaluate each of their meetings.

Meeting evaluations may be conducted informally or formally. Informal methods include setting aside time at the end of each meeting for the board to discuss what worked and what didn't or having governance committee members follow up with individual board members by phone or e-mail a few days after a meeting. More formal mechanisms include paper or web-based surveys (Dambach et al., 2009). Formal interviews of board members that include an assessment of board meetings may be conducted as part of the board's annual performance review.

Decisions regarding how often to evaluate board meetings and in what manner feedback should be obtained will depend in part on time and costs. In times of board or organizational transition and when dissatisfaction with board meetings and board progress is expressed, evaluation should take place more frequently and in a more comprehensive manner. For further information on effective board meeting practices, see Herman and Renz (2000).

Meeting Minutes

Meeting minutes are the official record of what transpired at a board meeting. They identify when the meeting was held and who attended, and they provide an overview of what was discussed. Most important, minutes document actions taken by the board. The taking of minutes is typically the role of the board secretary. However, some nonprofit organizations delegate the task of taking minutes to a staff member. Regardless of who takes them, the legal nature of board minutes requires that careful attention is taken to ensure their thoroughness and accuracy. All board members have the responsibility to review the board minutes and address any errors or omissions.

The content and format of meeting minutes varies somewhat from organization to organization, largely because of organizationally defined expectations and individual preferences. Elements considered as essential for inclusion in quality board minutes are (1) the organization's name, (2) the date and location of the meeting, (3) the time the meeting began, (4) the names of the board members in attendance as well those who were absent (noting excused absences), (5) whether a quorum was present or not, (6) the names of staff members or guests in attendance, (7) reports or documents presented, (8) the motions made and who made them, (9) a brief overview of major discussions including dissenting opinions, (10) conflicts of interests on votes before the board and how the board member with the conflict handled the situation, (11) the outcome of votes taken, (12) the names of board members who dissented or abstained from the vote, (13) items for future action, and (14) the time the meeting ends (Flynn, 2004).

Minutes do not need to be word for word accounts of what transpired; however, the recording of decisions alone is insufficient for legal purposes. Minutes should document key discussion points and opinions for and against the matter under consideration. They should provide enough detail to make them readily understood, even by those who were not in attendance. However, minutes should not include the names or direct quotes related to debates to allow board members to engage in serious dialogue without fear of personal liability (Flynn, 2004).

Board minutes should be prepared and distributed to the full board for review prior to its next meeting. Ideally, they should be sent to board members shortly after the meeting date while meeting details are still fresh in the minds of attendees. The timely completion and review of minutes allows for their revision as necessary before they are voted on by the board at the following meeting. Once the minutes have been approved, they should be signed and dated by the board secretary and chairperson. Minutes should be placed on file and maintained in the organization's permanent archives.

In addition to their role as a legal document, board minutes can serve other important organizational purposes that include providing a history of the organization, serving as a mechanism for institutional memory, sharing information, fostering organizational learning, and supporting the orientation or new board members. The use of minutes for these additional purposes may require the recording of additional information, changes to traditional formats, editing, compiling data culled from the minutes, and analyzing minutes over a specific period of time. For further information on board meeting minutes, consult BoardSource (n.d.); Dambach et al. (2009); and Keenen (2007).

Summary

As noted at the start of this chapter, nonprofit organization governance is not "one size fits all." While there is no ideal board size, simple formula for board composition, a definitive board member job description, perfect committee structure, or a best way to run a board meeting (Robinson, 2008), nonprofit practice and research have led to the identification of best and evidence-based practices. It is important for nonprofit practitioners to stay abreast of such practices and informed on new legislation and regulations that may impact board decision making about these important issues.

Several organizations whose publications have been cited in this chapter are excellent sources for keeping up-to-date on these and other governance topics. They include: BoardSource (www.boardsource.org), Independent Sector (www.independentsector.org), and the Center on Nonprofits and Philanthropy of the Urban Institute (http://www.urbaninstitute.org/center/cnp/index.cfm).

Two peer-reviewed scholarly journals, *Nonprofit Management and Leadership* and *Nonprofit and Voluntary Sector Quarterly,* are highly regarded sources for the latest research on nonprofit governance and boards. *Voluntas: The International Journal of Voluntary and Nonprofit Organizations,* which has a global focus, is another highly valuable scholarly journal.

Finally, a number of practitioner publications provide the latest information on issues impacting nonprofit governance. They include: *The Chronicle of Philanthropy* (http://philanthropy.com), *The Nonprofit Quarterly* (www.nonprofitquarterly.org), and the *Philanthropy Journal* (http://www.philanthropyjournal.org).

References and Further Readings

Axelrod, N. R. (2005). Board leadership and development. In R. D. Herman & Associates (Ed.), *The Jossey-Bass handbook of nonprofit leadership and management* (2nd ed., pp. 131–152). San Francisco: Jossey-Bass.

Axelrod, N. R. (2007). *Culture of inquiry: Healthy debate in the boardroom.* Washington, DC: BoardSource.

Block, S. R. (2001). Board of directors. In J. S. Ott (Ed.), *Understanding nonprofit organizations: Governance, leadership, and management* (pp. 15–37). Boulder, CO: Westview Press.

BoardSource. (1999). *Perspectives on nonprofit board diversity.* Available from http://www.boardsource.org/Knowledge.asp?ID=2.291

BoardSource (n.d.). *Board meeting minutes.* Available from http://www.boardsource.org/Knowledge.asp?ID=1.207

Bradshaw, P., Murray, V., & Wolpin, J. (1992). Do nonprofit boards make a difference? An exploration of the relationships among board structure, process, and effectiveness. *Nonprofit and Voluntary Sector Quarterly, 21*(3), 227–249.

Brown, W. A. (2002). Racial diversity and performance of nonprofit boards of directors. *The Journal of Applied Management and Entrepreneurship, 7*(4), 43–57.

Brown, W. A., & Iverson, J. O. (2004). Exploring strategy and board structure in nonprofit organizations. *Nonprofit and Voluntary Sector Quarterly, 33*(3), 377–400.

Chait, R., Ryan, W. P., & Taylor, B. E. (2005). *Governance as leadership: Reframing the work of nonprofit boards.* Hoboken, NJ: John Wiley.

Create the Future (n.d.). *Developing a board recruitment plan.* Available from http://www.createthefuture.com/developing.htm

Daley, J. M. (2002). An action guide for nonprofit board diversity. *Journal of Community Practice, 10*(1), 33–54.

Daley, J. M., & Marsiglia, F. F. (2001). Social diversity within nonprofit boards: Members' views on status and issues. *Journal of the Community Development Society, 32*(2), 290–309.

Dambach, C. F., Davis, M., & Gale, R. L. (2009). *Structures and practices of nonprofit boards* (2nd ed.) (Governance Series 6). Washington, DC: BoardSource.

Dector, A. (Ed.). (2007). *Diversity in governance: A toolkit for inclusion on nonprofit boards.* Ontario, Canada: The Maytree Foundation.

Flynn, O. (2004). *Meet smarter: A guide to better board meetings.* Washington, DC: BoardSource.

Golden, B. R., & Zajac, E. J. (2001). When will boards influence strategy? Inclination x power = strategic change. *Strategic Management Journal, 22*(12), 1087–1111.

Gottlieb, H. (2003). *Recruiting your organization's first board.* Available from http://www.help4nonprofits.com/NP_Bd_RecruitingStartupBoard_Art.htm

Gottlieb, H. (2005). *Board diversity: A bigger issue than you think.* Available from http://www.help4nonprofits.com/NP_Bd_Diversity_Art.htm

Herman, R. D., & Renz, D. O. (2000). Board practices of especially effective and less effective local nonprofit organizations. *The American Review of Public Administration, 30*(2), 146–160.

Holland, T. P. (2006). Strengthening board performance. In R. L. Edwards, & J. A. Yankey (Eds.). *Effectively managing nonprofit organizations.* Washington, DC: NASW Press.

Independent Sector & BoardSource. (2009). *The principles workbook: Steering your board to good governance and ethical practice.* Available from http://www.nonprofitpanel.org

Inglis, S., Alexander, T., &Weaver, L. (1999). Roles and responsibilities of community nonprofit boards. *Nonprofit Management and Leadership, 10*(2), 153–167.

Inglis, S., & Weaver, L. (2000). Designing agendas to reflect board roles and responsibilities. *Nonprofit Management and Leadership, 11*(1), 65–77.

Jameson, J. K., & Metelsky, B. A. (2009). *The performance of governance among nonprofit boards of directors:*

Communication strategies that promote or impede generative discussion. Paper proposal accepted for presentation at the 4th Annual INGRoup Conference, Colorado Springs, CO.

Kennen, E. (2007). *How to take meeting minutes: Sample of board of directors meeting minutes.* Available from http://non-profit-governance.suite101.com/article.cfm/how_to_take_meeting_minutes

Masoka, J. (2009). *Should the board hold executive sessions?* Available from http://www.blueavocado.org/content/should-board-hold-executive-sessions

McNamara, C. (n.d.). *Sample job descriptions for members of boards of directors.* Minneapolis, MN: Authenticity Consulting, LLC. Available from http://www.management help.org/boards/brdjobs.htm#anchor321357

Metelsky, B. A., & Jameson, J. K. (2009, November). *Nonprofit board communication: "Let's give them something to talk about."* Paper presented at the 38th annual conference of the Association for Research on Nonprofit Organizations and Voluntary Action, Cleveland, OH.

Miller, L. E., Weiss, R. M., & MacLeod, B. V. (1988). Boards of directors in nonprofit organizations: Composition, activities, and organizational outcomes. *Nonprofit and Voluntary Sector Quarterly, 17*(81), 81–89.

O'Regan, K., & Oster, S. M. (2005). Does the structure and composition of the board matter? The case of nonprofit organizations. *The Journal of Law, Economics, & Organizations, 21*(1), 205–227.

Ostrower, F. (2007). *Nonprofit governance in the United States: Findings on performance and accountability from the first national representative study.* Washington, DC: The Urban Institute. Available from http://www.urban.org.url.cfm?ID=411479

Provan, K. G. (1980). Board power and organizational effectiveness among human services agencies. *The Academy of Management Journal, 23*(2), 221–236.

Renz, D. (n.d.). *Consent agenda.* Kansas City, MO: Midwest Center for Nonprofit Leadership. Available from http://bsbpa.umkc.edu/mwcnl/board%20resources/Consent%20Agendas.pdf

Roberts, H. M. (2000). *Robert's rules of order* (10th ed.). Reading, MA: Perseus.

Robinson, A. (2006). *Great boards for small groups: A 1-hour guide to governing a growing nonprofit.* Medfield, MA: Emerson and Church.

Siciliano, J. (1996). The relationship of board member diversity to organizational performance. *Journal of Business Ethics, 15*(12), 1313–1320.

Widmer, C. (1987). Minority participation on boards of directors of nonprofit human services agencies: Some evidence and suggestions. *Nonprofit and Voluntary Sector Quarterly, 16*(4), 33–44.

56

DIFFERENCES IN BOARDS BASED ON THE SIZE, AGE, AND TYPE OF THE ORGANIZATIONS

RIKKI ABZUG

Ramapo College of New Jersey

In considering nonprofit boards and research about them, as with most organizational structures, there is a tension between those scholars and followers who wonder why there are so many different forms of governance and those who wonder why there are so few. Clearly, this is partially a matter of perspective—how few is few?—but it is also a subject of interest to the social/managerial scientist. Under what conditions do organizational structures such as nonprofit boards come to look so alike? Under what other conditions do these same structures come to differentiate? As the title of this chapter suggests, we will be most interested in exploring how a nonprofit organization's size, age, and function/type help us to understand and predict the different (and similar) kinds of governing boards we find. This chapter will proceed as follows: We first explore the reasons nonprofits have boards, and why we should care about their composition. Next, we lay out the various kinds of differences that may exist across boards—this will first entail a review of what is mandated and what has evolved to become similar and quite diverse across boards. Then, we will explore how nonprofits themselves differ by age, size, and type/function, finally exploring if and how those differences impact variations in boards. We restrict our inquiry to boards of U.S. nonprofits but note that differences in boards across countries and cultures are a fascinating, if understudied, phenomenon.

Why Boards?

When folks think about the good—and sometimes, although rarely, the bad—work that nonprofits do, they're likely to associate that work with either the people on the front lines or the people at the top. Media coverage of disasters often includes reporting about volunteers and staffers of nonprofit relief and recovery organizations handing out water bottles, kitchen staples, clothing, and so on to needy recipients. Direct appeals and press releases sent out from nonprofits usually include the thoughts and words of the executive director, or maybe the chairman of the board. However, the rest of the board, and in some cases the whole of the board, remains somewhat separate from the public presence of the organization. Sure, the board is named in the annual report and maybe even on a page of the website, but the public persona of the nonprofit is most usually embodied by the executive director or particularly charismatic or personable staffers or volunteers. So what is this background board, why is it needed, who belongs, and why should we care about who is on it?

To answer that question, it may be useful to first think about what happens when something goes wrong organizationally. In the public or governmental sphere, when something goes awry in an agency, such as an office of disaster management, food safety, or child welfare, a director may be implicated. So, when a situation is bobbled, a member is caught in an illegal act, or a plan or proposal is deemed unworkable, it is often the director who is brought to task. In the end, however, if enough—or very powerful—agencies fail and enough directors are admonished and replaced, ultimate blame may fall on the elected officials who were responsible for the appointments. When that occurs, and local and national history is replete with examples of exactly these scenarios, general elections provide the public with an organ to exercise their supreme ownership of the process and therefore the offending agencies. The buck stops there—with the electorate. If organizational transformation is deemed necessary, the public, through their vote, can accomplish that change.

The government/public example stands in contrast to the example of the business corporation gone bad. Small businesses—usually sole proprietorships and closely held corporations—provide a starting and simplified example. When something is amiss in a small business, say, a "mom and pop store," the legal, financial, and finally governance responsibility lies with the actual business owners. This is the best argument for organizational incorporation. Although both unincorporated and incorporated business owners are ultimately liable, only the incorporated business owners are liable only up to the amount of financing that they have put into the business. This allows the small business owner and family to remain solvent and personally protected even though, in their role of business owners, they remain responsible and accountable.

This process is somewhat attenuated in the case of the large publicly traded corporation. In cases of corporate wrongdoing, such as disastrous strategic alliances, thoughtless expansions, and witless or offensive layoffs, the Chief Executive Officer (CEO) and his (it's almost always "his") strategic management team are only the first line of defense. The CEO is hired by and sometimes hires and serves the board of directors. The corporate board of directors, itself, nominally includes elected shareholder (owner) representatives whose overarching interest is in protecting the organization's stockholders. However, bad behavior by boards—including, but not limited to overly cozy relationships with unchecked CEOs, obscene CEO pay packages, even insider trading—can be further addressed. Disgruntled slates of underrepresented stockholders, relative outsiders with very deep pockets, or even leveraged management teams can battle for ultimate governance control of a publicly traded organization, where active takeover markets exist.

The nonprofit governance story is different again. Whereas public/government organizations ultimately answer to a voting public and for-profit corporations answer to classes of owners, the nonprofit organization answers to neither. Nonprofit organizations, either unincorporated or incorporated by the states, run by either executive directors/CEOs or hands-on boards of trustees, are neither owned nor elected/appointed. They operate under the auspices of their board of directors/trustees and answer, organizationally, to that body alone. States can revoke incorporation, the Internal Revenue Service (IRS) can deny or terminate tax exemption, yet a nonprofit can continue to operate as an unincorporated association accountable only to its board of directors (if it has one).

Now, nonprofits often need public resources in the form of donations, volunteers, or even goodwill in order to thrive, but the buck ultimately stops with the board of directors. For this reason, the nonprofit board of directors is a particularly interesting and study-worthy body. Who sits on these boards and the differences and similarities between boards in the sector, then, tells us a lot about the distribution of certain kinds of organizational power in the United States. Without voters and shareholders as an ultimate check on power, nonprofit boards may be seen to have even greater leeway to determine organizational trajectories than other organizational governance bodies. Who wields this power and through what structures are questions of interest for scholars in and out of the nonprofit sector. We start our inquiry with the question of how variable this structure and practice of ultimately unchecked power really is.

What Is the Same About All (U.S.) Boards?

All U.S. nonprofit corporations are legally obligated (like all corporations) to have a board of directors. Note that this is not necessarily an obligation for unincorporated associations, although it may well be best practice. Unlike all U.S. corporations, however, most nonprofits are not incorporated in Delaware but rather are usually incorporated in the state in which they were founded and as a result are subject to state (nonprofit) incorporation law. Fifty different state incorporation laws mean 50 different statutes dictating forms and functions of nonprofit boards. So while all boards of nonprofit corporations are legally mandated, the mandates may differ state by state. Let us not overstate nor understate these differences, however. It is worth briefly exploring 50 different laws to determine the commonalities and room for difference across nonprofit boards. According to BoardSource (1999), "Several states have statutes concerning some variation of these duties, which can be used in court to determine whether a board member acted improperly. These standards are usually described as the duty of care, the duty of loyalty, and the duty of obedience":

> *Duty of care* describes the level of competence that is expected of a board member and is commonly expressed as the duty of "care that an ordinarily prudent person would exercise in a like position and under similar circumstances." This means that a board member has the duty to exercise reasonable care when he or she makes a decision as a steward of the organization.

Duty of loyalty is a standard of faithfulness; a board member must give undivided allegiance when making decisions affecting the organization. This means that a board member can never use information obtained as a member for personal gain but must act in the best interests of the organization.

Duty of obedience requires board members to be faithful to the organization's mission. They are not permitted to act in a way that is inconsistent with the central goals of the organization or the laws that govern nonprofit activities. A basis for this rule lies in the public's trust that the organization will manage donated funds to fulfill the organization's mission.

Some of the similarities we find in nonprofit state incorporation law can be attributed to only two common sources for most of the states' laws:

(1) the 1952 Model Nonprofit Corporation Act (MNPCA), promulgated by the American Bar Association (ABA) and currently adopted (with amendments) in twelve states and the District of Columbia, and (2) the ABA's 1988 Revised Model Nonprofit Corporation Act (RMNPCA), closely related to, or adopted by, the law of twenty-six states. (Malamut, 2008, p. 8)

These common sources nevertheless allow for slight but meaningful differences as state laws have evolved.

In one instance, according to a 1999 BoardSource e-book, perhaps the definitive guide to nonprofit organization self-starters, every state has different regulations that determine the minimum size of the board. The website Legalzoom.com confirms that most states require a three-director minimum, but some states require only one, including California, Colorado, Delaware, Georgia, Iowa, Kansas, Michigan, Mississippi, Nevada, New Hampshire, North Carolina, Oklahoma, Oregon, Pennsylvania, Virginia, and Washington. The website continues,

Every non-profit corporation must have a president, treasurer and secretary. In some states, one person can hold every office. In others, one person can hold up to two offices, but cannot be both the president and the secretary. The states where one person may hold every office include: Arkansas, Delaware, Florida, Georgia, Iowa, Illinois, Hawaii, Kansas, Kentucky, Maine, Massachusetts, Michigan, Minnesota, Mississippi, Missouri, Nevada, New Hampshire, New Jersey, North Carolina, Ohio, Oklahoma, Oregon, Pennsylvania, South Carolina, Texas, Utah, Virginia, and Wyoming.

In California, for instance,

You must have at least one director for your nonprofit public benefit corporation; you must state the number of directors in either the articles of incorporation or the bylaws of your nonprofit public benefit corporation; directors do not have to reside within California, nor do they have to be of a certain age; and under California law, no more than 49 percent of a board of directors may be interested persons. An interested

person is a director who provides nondirector services to the nonprofit public benefit corporation and is paid for the services rendered. The law also extends to cover any close relative of the director. (Citizen Media Law Project, n.d.-a)

Contrast that to Florida's much briefer rules: "You must have at least three directors, age eighteen or older, for your nonprofit corporation; directors do not have to reside within Florida, nor do they have to be of a certain age" (Citizen Media Law Project, n.d.-b), or the curious case in Michigan, whereby, "directors may be sixteen or seventeen years old, but the nonprofit corporation then faces certain requirements on quorum and the articles of incorporation" (Citizen Media Law Project, n.d.-c).

Legal Responsibilities and Beyond

It is interesting to note that the BoardSource (1999) e-book, counsels that beyond the legal requirement of all nonprofits to have a board, the board "is responsible for the ultimate governance of the organization and has legal, fiduciary, and ethical responsibilities . . . the board holds the ultimate decision-making powers for the organization," which is a clear suggestion of similarity (p. 5). However, a few lines later, the BoardSource e-book continues, "Although boards have specific legal responsibilities, there is also room for each board to define its roles and area of focus based on where the organization is in its life cycle" (p. 5). Underscoring this theme of board variation, the e-book continues, "The answers to the next few questions are 'It depends.' The board's composition, role, and frequency of meetings all depend on what the board needs to do—for this organization at this point in time [emphasis in original]" (p. 6). We will look further into how type and time (age) of organization help determine the board's makeup, function, and practices, after first highlighting the ways (beyond legal) that boards can vary.

What Kinds of Nonlegal Differences Distinguish Boards?

Board Composition

According to Ostrower and Stone (2006), board composition has dominated the growing nonprofit board literature at least since 1987, when Middleton (1987) first surveyed the research literature. As Abzug and Simonoff (2004) have argued, in the nonprofit realm, there is a literature that assumes that when the right components are assembled, be they compositional or structural, organizational effectiveness will follow. As such, who sits on a board does matter (Ostrower & Stone, 2006), and boards that "look" different might perform differently. So just how and in what ways are boards composed differently?

Demographic Differences

Certainly boards look different as a result of demographic composition. A large literature suggests that board and organizational legitimacy in demographically diverse environments may be related to relative demographic diversity in board composition (see, e.g., Abzug and Simonoff, 2004). Reviewing the extant literature, Abzug and Simonoff (2004), and Ostrower and Stone (2006) all seize on gender, race and ethnicity, and class as key demographic differences of board members. Both metastudies review scores of individual studies that either look to understand the factors behind these board demographic differences or posit ways in which these differences impact governance and organizational practices.

Professional/Occupational/Expertise Differences

Yet, demographic differences are not the only potential differences in board composition. Indeed, Abzug (1996) has divided the board composition literature into, at least, the studies of board demographic composition (focusing on ascriptive characteristics and board members' professional or occupational prestige) and status attributes (focusing on achievement and elite characteristics). As such, boards can be racially homogenous yet widely diverse in terms of educational achievement. Alternatively, board members can be ethnically and gender-wise diverse, yet strikingly similar in terms of the quality and quantity of their networks. In a 1987 survey of the extant literature on board composition, Middleton underscores the point that the important boundary-spanning functions of boards are often performed through the interorganizational linkages that board members' organizational and community affiliations provide. She notes, therefore, that the "composition of nonprofit boards is a particularly important aspect from which to examine interorganizational linkages" and that as a result, there are two perspectives from which to look at composition (Middleton, 1987, p. 144). One perspective is the diversity of external organizations represented on the board, and the second is the range of social group memberships of the board. Both perspectives lead to compositional differences among boards and suggest that there are numerous ways to measure the heterogeneity of nonprofit boards.

Board Structure

As noted above, board composition studies have dominated much of the recent research on boards of directors, but they have not entirely crowded out studies focusing on the other ways that boards differ and their consequences. Even in their early reviews and studies, Middleton (1987) and Abzug and Simonoff (2004) recognized that board structural differences might also be important as characteristics. Indeed, degree of hierarchy, democratic nature, officer and committee setup, even board size, might all influence the way that opinions get expressed and decisions are reached by boards. Middleton (1987) makes an explicit connection between board compositional diversity and structural diversity when she states that "the structure of the board—that is, its officer positions and committee—also influences the degree to which diverse opinion are expressed" (p. 148). Middleton further notes that boards may differ based on how well they have developed their formal structure as well as their use of that structure in decision making. This leads us to yet another way in which boards may differ—practices and policies.

Board Functions/Roles

While broad governance policies and practices are either laid out in or implicit in state law that codifies the standards and functions of the governance role, within those broad mandates are many avenues for differentiation. Again, a whole literature has developed to explore differences in board practices. Some studies seek to understand differences in the likelihood of boards' success in achieving their prescribed responsibilities, whereas others focus on the differences in how boards interpret their responsibilities. Some of the earlier studies in this vein sought to delineate different types or categories of boards based on their different roles/functions. So, for example, in a 1990 book, Mathiasen suggested that boards, over their lifecycles, took on one of three forms: organizing board, governing board, and institutional board. In 1992, Wood suggested that boards have three operating styles: (1) ratifying or rubber-stamping executive's policies, (2) corporate or working with organizational executives, and (3) participatory or operating independently of executives. In delineating different nonprofit board roles, almost all of the studies seek to center the variations in the relationship between the board and the CEO/ED.

In summary, while boards may share similar legal mandates as well as compositional, structural, and functional forms, they may also differentiate in ways both subtle and stark along all of these dimensions. Predicting how similar versus how different boards may become is the theme of the next sections of this chapter.

Independent Variables

As Abzug and Simonoff (2004) note, we care deeply about differences in board structure, composition, and function/role because, as Middleton (1987) has suggested, these are all important factors determining organizational internal relations, environmental mediation, and quality of governance. As such, these board differences may be construed as dependent variables, leaving us to consider what, then, predicts/explains how boards got this way (Abzug & Simonoff, 2004).

The question before us is the extent to which the board variation described in detail above is based on, determined by, or correlated to the organizational characteristics of size, age, and type. Researchers of all organizations are well advised to consider these characteristics before making sweeping generalizations about patterns in any organizational structure. Practitioners may also find that beyond providing prescriptions for best practice, these characteristics also provide structural limits and boundaries.

Size of Organizations

In a 1988 study, Aldrich and Marsden stated that of all organizational characteristics, size is "the most important correlate of diversity in organization structure" (p. 373). Indeed, in 1976, Kimberly did a meta-analysis of all previous organizational studies that sought to explore the relationship between organizational size and organizational structure; he found more than 80 scholarly studies up until that point. Conveniently, for our work on nonprofits, Kimberly found that the most common measure of size in the literature is the number of employees—a measure with relevance for third-sector organizations. Kimberly's meta-analysis found that most studies of size and structure found size to be exogenous—causing other variables (for instance, structure) to assume particular values. In the end, the value of Kimberly's early work in informing our own is his notion that there are three basic levels of analysis in which size may be important. Most relevant for us is the first, primarily internal, level, which draws attention to implications of size for transactions within the organization—governance, in the present case.

This leads us to generalized organizational theory, which holds that the greater the number of employees, the greater the problem of social control and finds a generalized positive relationship between size and formalization. From this, we might expect that smaller nonprofit organizations, especially, perhaps, those underneath the $25,000 budget IRS reporting threshold, might have different internal/governance structures than larger organizations. Also, we might expect that the organization (perhaps a university or a hospital) that employs thousands of people may need to be governed differently from the organization (perhaps a start-up cultural or preservation society) that has just hired its first professional executive director.

Age of Organizations

Closely tied, theoretically, to size of organizations as a contextual variable is age of organizations. A large degree of the explanatory power of age of organizations is likely tied up with increasing size of organizations over the life cycle. Yet, age exerts its own independent predictive power. Much of the research on the effect of age as an independent variable can be traced to pioneering work by Stinchcombe (1965), who, noting the unique problems of new and young organizations, laid the theoretical groundwork for the liability of newness concept. In a well-known

study, Stinchcombe has argued for the importance of time imprinting on organizations, beyond the impact of age itself. He argued that the founding blueprints of organizations are heavily dependent on environmental influences at that time and shape organizational internal structures. Johnson (2003) has expanded that theme, suggesting that founders act as cultural entrepreneurs who draw on temporally available organizational repertoires and genres to animate new enterprises. These repertoires and genres may then influence the organization's structures over time. In the case of nonprofit boards, researchers have sought evidence for a mythical "golden age of trusteeship" before the world wars and a more dynamic sectoral growth engine from the 1960s civil rights era forward (Abzug & Simonoff, 2004; Hall, 1992). Putting this altogether, we can argue that it is not just young or old organizations that might share common internal/governance structures, but particularly, old organizations all founded around the same time or young organizations all recently founded.

Type of Organizations

Along with the difficult-to-separate concepts of size and age, other contextual characteristics of organizations have been shown to be predictive. We next focus on one of the consistently most studied. The dean of organizational strategy researchers, Michael Porter (1981) has long argued for the importance of "industry" in predicting firm performance. Much scholarship has followed in this vein, thus anointing "industry" or "organizational type" as an independent variable with tremendous predictive power. Theorists of nonprofits have picked up on this theme by using National Taxonomy of Exempt Entities (NTEE), IRS designation, or subsector categorizations in place of industry designation. Whichever way organizational type is delineated, its predictive power over everything from performance to internal structure has been well documented. Indeed, Abzug and Simonoff (2004) argue that industry, as both arena of negotiation of normal practices and arbiter of competition for revenue, will be a prominent predictor of board structure and composition. Again, we may not be surprised to find board compositional or structural differences between organizations that, say, use volunteer labor to provide food and shelter to homeless families in local communities and organizations that hire scores of curators, preservationists, and security guards to enable the public's exposure to great works of art. It is probably not a big stretch to imagine that the boards of local YMCAs and YWCAs may look rather different from the boards of local symphony orchestras or rape crisis centers. Organizational diversity comes in many flavors, and so we might expect board diversity to follow.

In sum, much past organizational research has pointed to the predictive power of organizational size, age, and type on internal organizations structures. Our next step is to present the results of the studies that have looked at the predictive power of these characteristics on the demographic, structural, and procedural differences in boards outlined above.

What We Know About the Role of Size, Age, and Type of Nonprofit Organizations Regarding Differences in Boards

Our foremost finding, repeated over and over, is that there is no "one size fits all" board, even when holding contextual variables constant. Although some patterns have emerged over time, as we discuss below, the overwhelming empirical finding is that boards find individual compositions, structures, practices, and policies to best suit their environments, missions, and visions. When they don't, organizational failure sometimes follows, except, of course, when it doesn't.

Size, Age, and Type of Nonprofit and Board Composition

The largest historical study of nonprofit boards of trustees, the "Six Cities" Project administered by Yale University's Program on Nonprofit Organizations (PONPO), concluded that, for our purposes, the important influence of time period (age) and industry/subsector cannot be overstated in understanding differences in nonprofit governance (Abzug & Simonoff, 2004). Specifically, Abzug and Simonoff (2004) conclude that (a) "boards of trustees, as boundary spanners, were more gender and racially diverse in later time periods than in the earliest time period," suggesting that younger organizations in current times may well start out with more demographically diverse board members; and that (b) industries (organizational types) that are less closely aligned with the public sphere's concerns for social justice (such as Junior Leagues and elite cultural organizations) would exhibit less demographically diverse boards. Ostrower and Stone (2006, pp. 615–616) sum up a host of smaller scale studies with the observations that "organizational size and field of activity are two apparent sources of . . . variation, with women more likely to serve on the boards of smaller and less prestigious nonprofits;" "boards are overwhelmingly white," and "studies consistently find that trustees are drawn from higher socioeconomic groups." Their review of studies clearly points to prestigious art boards as preserves of board members with elite affiliations, along with United Ways, in comparison to YMCAs or YWCAs. Still, a consistent theme that runs through the Ostrower and Stone (2006) review is that

in terms of understanding board heterogeneity, we will need to expand our research to include additional types of institutions. In particular, we know very little about boards of smaller, community-based organizations. While such boards may be similar to those of larger organizations, they may also be radically different in some way, forcing us to rethink and refine current assumptions. (p. 624)

We can discern any number of hypotheses about particular ways that size, age, and type (industry) of organization might influence or covary with gender, age, race/ethnicity, professional/occupational identity, or even eliteness of board members, as the research in this field is quite nascent. We might also suggest that variables such as location—region of the country or urban/rural setting—may also play a predictive role in board composition. We also have every reason to believe that these same independent variables might also covary with the structures of nonprofit governance.

Size, Age, and Type of Nonprofit and Board Structure

Although there are many prescriptive volumes on setting up/structuring nonprofit boards, little empirical research has explored the variations in these structures. Perhaps, the prescriptive literature has been so successful that there is so little variation in structure as to make the topic relatively uninteresting to the research. Alternatively, the few studies may be a signal that the field is ripe for the researcher. For instance, looking at the structural variable of board size, Abzug and Simonoff (2004) concluded that health, Junior League, and community foundation boards tended to be relatively small compared with culture, United Way, and higher education boards, which tended to be larger. This suggests that there may be very interesting board and board committee structure variation by organization size, age, and type, if only researchers were to look. We might be curious to know, for instance, if boards of larger organizations are both larger and have more committees than boards of comparatively smaller organizations. Would boards of financially larger organizations be similarly structured to boards of organizations that are large in terms of employees or clients served? Do boards of "younger" organizations have more newfangled committee and other structures than "older" organizations, which have been consistently structured for decades, if not centuries? What other board structures are both variable across organizations and of great enough import to warrant systematic study. Further research in this field will help to answer these questions. In the meantime, we turn to other ways in which boards differ—in this case, role and function—and the ways that size, age, and organizational subsector might influence that difference.

Size, Age, and Type of Nonprofit and Board Function/Role

So how do organizations come to differ in nonprofit board role/function? If we narrow board function/role to the relationship between the board and the CEO/executive director, we have some historical studies to guide our comprehension. In terms of board function/role as defined by the board/CEO relationship, Ostrower and Stone (2006) report that past research suggests these relationships vary by age of organization, where younger nonprofits are more likely to be dominated by the board; and size of the nonprofit, where larger nonprofits are likely to be dominated by their CEOs. However, we are still awaiting an influx of studies that try to contextualize the function/role differences in boards that we have seen prescribed in the practitioner-oriented literature. So, for example, we will look forward to studies that explore how organizational size, age, and type covary with board policies (adoption of codes of conduct, conflict of interest, term-limits, etc.), board practices (number and scheduling of meetings, hands-on versus policy-setting activity, financial and executive oversight activity, etc.), and even board roles (rubber stamping, policy setting, talking heads, etc.). While we expect diversity across organizations, we also expect to find at least some patterns that may be dictated by organizational size, age, and type.

Who Decides?

Now we know that boards can be quite diverse—or starkly similar—in their demographics, professional/occupational/expert makeup, policies, practices, and roles, based at least in part on the organization's size, age, and occupation. But who gets to put the pieces together and opt for that diverse (or homogenous) board that does or does not reflect or adapt to the organization's environment? While boards come together in many ways, the literature on life cycle (see, e.g., Mathiasen, 1990, and Wood, 1992) suggests that the two main starting points for composing a board are the founding board members themselves and/or the executive director/CEO. Nonprofit boards are usually considered "self-perpetuating" in that they can legally opt out of voter-determined democratic transitions of power, favoring, instead, direct board member replacement. Many nonprofit boards have nominating committees designed to determine board personnel needs, then recruit, appoint, and orient new board members, all within the confines of the board itself. Such self-perpetuating boards may be interested either in direct replication or in purposeful diversity (and all shades in between). In the instance of direct replication, nominating committees or other board structures designed to accomplish similar tasks may replace outgoing board members such that new board members come to look very much like extant board members. The similarities can be based on, at least, demography—all female boards driven by mission to remain all-female—or profession/occupation/expertise—medical personnel board members of health organizations may opt to recruit more medical personnel board members as terms expire. Alternatively, boards may be interested in

diversifying their ranks, demographically based on changing communities, clients, or even funder expectations, or by profession/occupation/expertise, based on changes in legal and task environments. In any case, the current board determines the composition of the future board, with the size, age, and type of organization playing a limiting role. The self-perpetuating board can also be the genesis of board policies, practices, and roles that conform or not to prevailing organizational size, age, and industry norms.

Yet, again, depending on the organization's size, age, and type, a self-perpetuating board may not be so empowered as to replace itself. For many nonprofit organizations, board development begins and ends with a relatively powerful executive director. Whether through founding by a strong executive or through crisis or peaceful transition to a strong executive, many nonprofit organizational boards are constructed to support, defend, or protect the director. Even in these cases, the executive director can choose to keep a board relatively homogeneous based on demographics, expertise/skills, or even loyalty to the director. Or the executive director can decide, based on outside demands, to diversify the board to best suit him- or herself or the organization's environment. The executive director, as a result of the influence of community, consultant, or funder, may also initiate board policy, practice, or role transition. All of this director-initiated activity may still be delimited by exigencies of the organization's size, age, or industry/subsector. Board diversity or its opposite, then, can come out of a self-perpetuating board, or even more likely, out of a motivated executive director.

Further Prescriptions for the Care and Feeding of the Nonprofit Board

To the extent that an organization's board is diverse—relative to other organizations, relative to the communities in which it resides, relative to itself years earlier—how can those diverse voices/opinions be harnessed to work together for the good of the organization and the community/population that it serves? Obviously, the organization must consider in which ways the board is diverse—whether demographically or professionally/occupationally/expertise-wise. As with any diverse group, diverse nonprofit boards may not be diverse on all dimensions. Board chairs, executive directors, nominating committees, board development committees, or anyone else responsible for board orientation can start a board member's orientation with that which all board members should share—a passion for the mission. For no matter how diverse the board, its work should be dominated by what brought them together in the first place—the care and feeding of the organizational mission. The conscientious board leader will find a way to balance the shared organizational goals of the diverse board members with each one's unique perspective/stance and skills/expertise. Team-building exercises should be proportional to individual contributions by divergently situated board members depending on the needs of the organization. Yet again, some of those very needs may be a product of the organization's size, age, and/or industry/subsector.

Summary

We end where we began. Nonprofit boards may be seen as strikingly similar; research suggests the dominance of prescriptive models, limited legal mandates, and relative racial homogeneity, for instance. They can also be quite different in terms of their composition, structure, and function, although research on all but composition is sparse. The responsibility for some of these differences may come down to the self-perpetuating boards themselves or empowered executive directors. Some of the differences may, indeed, be based on the size, age, and type of organization in question, although much more research needs to be done before we will feel comfortable identifying empirically robust patterns beyond the "no one size fits all" admonition.

References and Further Readings

Abzug, R. (1996). The evolution of trusteeship in the United States: A round-up of findings. *Nonprofit Management and Leadership, 7,* 101–111.

Abzug, R., & Simonoff, J. S. (2004). *Nonprofit trusteeship in different contexts.* Hants, UK: Ashgate.

Aldrich, H. E., & Marsden, P. V. (1988). Environments and organizations. *Handbook of Sociology, 361–392.*

BoardSource, (1999). *Starting a nonprofit organization.* BoardSource E-Book series. Available from www.boardsource.org

Citizen Media Law Project. (n.d.-a). *Forming a nonprofit corporation in California.* Available from http://www.citmedialaw.org/legal-guide/california/forming-nonprofit-corporation-california

Citizen Media Law Project. (n.d.-b). *Forming a nonprofit corporation in Florida.* Available from http://www.citmedialaw.org/legal-guide/florida/forming-nonprofit-corporation-florida

Citizen Media Law Project. (n.d.-c). *Forming a nonprofit corporation in Michigan.* Available from http://www.citmedialaw.org/legal-guide/michigan/forming-nonprofit-corporation-michigan

Hall, P. D. (1992). Cultures of trusteeship. In P. E. Hall, *Inventing the nonprofit sector and other essays on philanthropy, voluntarism, and nonprofit organizations* (pp. 135–206). Baltimore, MD: The Johns Hopkins University Press.

Johnson, V. (2003). *Unpacking the "organizational imprinting hypothesis": Cultural entrepreneurship in the founding of the Paris Opera* (Working Paper Series). New York: Columbia University, Center on Organizational Innovation. Available from http://www.coi.columbia,edu/pdf/oih)vj.pdf

Kimberly, J. A. (1976). Organizational size and the structuralist perspective: A review, critique, and proposal. *Administrative Science Quarterly, 21*(4), 571–597.

Legalzoom.com. (2009). *Managing a non-profit corporation.* Available from https://www.legalzoom.com/nonprofits guide/manage-non-profit.html

Malamut, M. (2008). Summary of sources of state nonprofit incorporation laws. *National Parliamentarian.* Available from http://www.michaelmalamut.com/articles/2008q2_-_sources_of_nonprofit_laws.pdf

Mathiasen, K. (1990). *Board passages: Three key stages in a nonprofit board's life cycle.* Washington, DC: National Center for Nonprofit Boards.

Middleton, M. (1987). Nonprofit boards of directors: Beyond the governance function. In W. W. Powell (Ed.), *The nonprofit sector: A research handbook* (pp. 141–153). New Haven, CT: Yale University Press.

Ostrower, F., & Stone, M. M. (2006). Governance: Research trends, gaps, and future prospects. In W. W. Powell & R. Steinberg (Eds.), *The nonprofit sector: A research handbook* (2nd ed., pp. 612–628). New Haven, CT: Yale University Press.

Porter, M. E. (1981). The contributions of industrial organization to strategic management. *Academy of Management Review, 6*(4), 609–620.

Stinchcombe, A. L. (1965). Social structure and organizations. In J. G. March (Ed.), *Handbook of organizations* (pp. 142–193). Chicago: Rand McNally.

Wood, M. M. (1992). Is governing board behavior cyclical? *Nonprofit Management and Leadership, 3,* 139–163.

57

BOARD AND STAFF LEADERSHIP ROLES

Theoretical Perspectives

THOMAS G. FUECHTMANN
DePaul University

The title of this article implies at least three things: (1) that board and staff have different roles in the nonprofit organization setting, (2) that some theory or theories exist to explain the difference, and (3) that both board and staff have a role in organization leadership. Since other articles in this publication deal explicitly with executive leadership in the nonprofit setting, the focus here will be essentially on the board's leadership role in the board–staff relationship.

Intuitively, it is generally assumed that board and staff have different responsibilities, but the difference between those functions may not be always clear in experience. In many smaller *workgroup* organizations, the board itself has to pitch in and do the work of a small or even nonexistent staff. In that case, the same people function as both board and staff. But even in some larger, and presumably more sophisticated, organizations, the board seems to function as a kind of supermanager—duplicating the work of staff (presumably at a higher level) or inserting itself obtrusively in staff work by micromanaging. In effect, distinct lines between board and staff responsibilities become blurred.

At the other extreme, in trying to avoid micromanaging, the board may take a principled hands-off approach, seeing its function as merely hiring a CEO and giving that position free rein. In such a case, the board may run a very real risk of abdicating its responsibility, not only for the organization's effectiveness but also even for its legitimacy and acceptance by the public. The end result of this minimalist approach to the board's role can be disastrous, both for the

organization itself and for the people it was created to serve. A classic example, though by no means the only one in recent years, is the United Way in the early 1990s. When its national director was dismissed for financial impropriety, the organization lost millions of dollars in donations, its credibility with donors, and the ability to serve the people depending on it for service.

The problem for understanding board and staff roles poses two questions: (1) how to determine distinct roles for board and staff so that each has a clear job description; and (2) once the difference is clear, how to engage board and staff in complementary fashion for organization leadership. Both questions are important.

On the first question, the most important theoretical work on defining and delimiting the board's job description has been done by John Carver in his development of *policy governance*. Governance, says Carver, is the clear responsibility of the board and is the foundation concept for its job description. In an extensive series of books, articles, and media presentations from 1979 on, Carver has articulated a theoretical model of policy governance. The key publication is *Boards That Make a Difference: A New Design for Leadership in Nonprofit and Public Organizations*, now in its third edition (2006).

Theoretical work on the second question is more the focus of writing and consulting by associates of BoardSource, a resource for information, consulting, training, and leadership development for board members of nonprofit organizations. Getting board and staff to function as a *leadership* team is the theme of *Governance as*

Leadership: Reframing the Work of Nonprofit Boards by Richard P. Chait, William P. Ryan, and Barbara E. Taylor (2005). All three authors have extensive careers as nonprofit administrators, authors, and consultants. In their view, delineating the roles and responsibilities of board and staff may be a good place to start, but it does not ensure board effectiveness. Rather than the roles and structures for board and staff interaction, they focus instead on "modes of managing and leading" (p. 27).

The two questions above—(1) about the job definitions of board and staff, and (2) about the actual collaboration of board and staff in effective leadership—provide the framework for this article. The work of John Carver deals with the first question, the work of Chait, Ryan, and Taylor with the second. These two works can provide a foundational starting point for understanding board and staff relations at a more theoretical level. The presentation of their theories here will use extensive quotations from the two books to let the authors speak as much as possible in their own voices.

Board and Staff: Determining Different Roles

For John Carver (2006), the problem with nonprofit organization leadership is confusion about the role of the board. He is hardly modest about the intention of his work:

> This book is not about making incremental improvements in boards. . . . My intent is to explain a compelling logical, philosophically founded yet completely practical approach to every governing board's job, one that makes it impossible ever to think of boards the same way again. (p. 6)

The key to distinguishing the functions of board and staff is the concept of governance. In the nonprofit setting, the purpose of governance is to "ensure, usually on behalf of others, that an organization achieves what it should achieve, while avoiding those behaviors and situations that should be avoided" (Carver 2006, pp. xvii–xviii). Governance is the ultimate responsibility of the board, while the responsibility of the staff is management. In developing a theory of governance, John Carver provides a powerful and useful framework for delineating the distinct responsibilities of board and staff.

Rather than seeing the nonprofit board's job as a function of *management*, Carver sees it first and fundamentally as one of responsibility for *ownership*. In the case of a public equity corporation, it is clear that the shareholders are the ultimate owners of the organization, with the role of the board being to represent the shareholders and to be accountable to them for the financial effectiveness of the firm. But when we ask the question, who owns the nonprofit organization, the answer may be less immediately obvious. Carver argues that in the nonprofit setting, it is the community being served that is the ultimate stakeholder.

The nonprofit board exercises *moral ownership* on their behalf and is accountable to that community for the effectiveness of the organization.

The ownership question is indeed theoretical in nature, but it has very practical consequences. Two examples from empirical research and case study illustrate the importance of taking seriously the question of moral ownership.

Example 1. In a study of 12 nonprofit organizations in New York and Connecticut, Judith Millesen (2005) asked the question, to whom is the board accountable? The president of one small social service organization said "the board was accountable to 'no one'" (p. 12). Only three of the organizations could provide a coherent answer. But in those cases where the board recognized its accountability to a community outside itself, that sense of moral ownership led the board to recognize its governance obligation on behalf of its clients and to explicitly include their interests in its decision making. In one instance, a board opted to continue a money-losing program (over the objection of a board member) because it was so critical for the community "owners" of the organization (p. 12).

Example 2. In a classic article, "Why Are We Replacing the Furniture When Half the Neighborhood Is Missing?" Gus Newport (2005) points out the organizational wisdom in a question phrased by a foundation trustee on a site visit to consider a grant to a community organization:

> On seeing a map of the area, one of the trustees inquired what all the dark spaces were. "Abandoned lots" was the reply.
>
> The trustee's response: "We come out here to replace some worn furniture when half of the neighborhood is missing?" (p. 36)

The question led to a far more in-depth assessment of the needs of the community based on interviewing and listening to residents themselves. As a consequence, community voices were included on the board and an action agenda formulated that enlisted both city and pro bono professional support for a whole new urban plan. What was the result?

> To date, vacant lots have been transformed into over 440 new homes, a town common, gardens, urban agriculture, parks and playgrounds, and 500 housing units have been rehabbed. (Newport, 2005, p. 38)

In this case, the organization's board did more than simply listen to its community owners. It transformed the organization itself, with spectacular results.

Carver (2006) says, "The importance of the owners-to-board link is so great that the proper board job is best described as ownership one step down rather than management one step up" (p. 6). The board's real job is to make sure that the organization is achieving the purpose for which it was created, that is, to be always focused on the following questions: What is this organization for? What difference does it make? (p. 90). In terms of program planning, it should be asking, why are we doing this, rather than, how can we do it? Getting this principle right helps the board understand its relationship to staff. Even though they may be volunteers, board members are there not merely to *help* the staff, but to "own the business" (p. 25).

In Carver's model, the board exercises governance over the organization through its control over and articulation of *policy*. Every organization begins with a set of values and perspectives, which the board translates into action through policy directives. The board's policy work presents "the most powerful lever for the exercise of leadership" (Carver, 2006, p. 41). Carver says,

> Directing an organization can be like rearing a child. Controlling every behavior is a fatiguing and impossible charge. Inculcating the policies of life is far more effective, and . . . it is the only serviceable approach in the long run. (p. 42)

If it wants to "lead the parade," the board must take responsibility for setting its own agenda rather than simply reacting to staff initiatives. The board's work of policymaking is both "preliminary and predominant" (Carver, 2006, p. 46). The focus on policy allows the board to direct the organization by its focus on the implementation of values rather than the details of administration. This essential job design for the board allows it to control what goes on inside the organization, while remaining outside the arena of staff work. Carver acknowledges that "policymaking does not constitute all of a board's job" (2006, p. 47). But it is the central function that gives the work of the board both power and coherence.

Carver insists that serious policy work must be stated explicitly, clearly, and briefly. It should not be buried in dusty policy manuals but must be constantly updated and readily available in the board's continual agenda setting. Further, in order for policies to actively guide the board's leadership, they must be logically related and consistent. Carver conceives of policies at successively more specific levels, using the image of a set of nested mixing bowls (Figure 57.1). The larger scope policy statements are on the outside, containing and controlling more specific policies on the inside.

Second, Carver (2006) posits that all board policymaking can and should be categorized under one of four global headings: (1) "Ends"—the stated purpose of the organization, what results it intends to achieve, for whose benefit, and at what cost; (2) "Executive Limitations"—the boundaries—both of ethics and prudence—within which the staff is expected to employ means to accomplish the organization's purpose; (3) "Board-Management Delegation"—the manner in which authority is delegated to the executive and staff of the organization and the manner in which executive performance is reported and evaluated; (4) "Governance Process"—the board's own self-governance—specifying how it represents the ownership, disciplines itself, and exercises leadership in the organization. In the model, all board policies fall into one of these categories. Together, they can be graphically represented in what Carver calls the

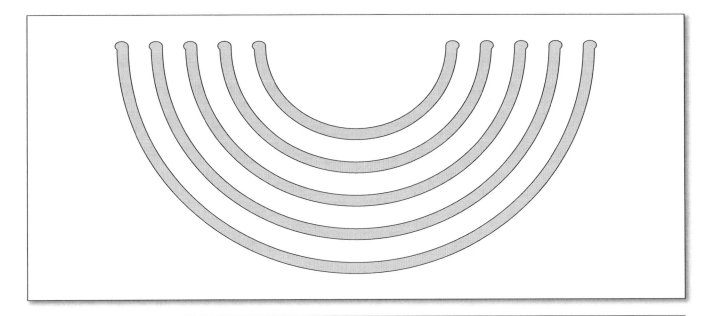

Figure 57.1 A Nested Set of Policies

SOURCE: Carver, 2006, p. 63.

NOTE: Smaller issues fit within larger issues, as smaller bowls fit within larger ones. The entire set can be controlled by handling only the outermost bowl.

"policy circle" (see Figure 57.2). For Carver, "*policy development is not an occasional board chore but its chief occupation* [italics in original]" (p. 72). By being proactive on the broadest issues, the board is able to avoid the critical governance mistake of merely reacting to events or staff initiatives and reports. Through its articulation of and ongoing dialogue about policy, the board actually *leads* the organization.

Ends

"The most important work of any governing board is to define and redefine the reason for organizational existence" (Carver, 2006, p. 79). This is a far more demanding and all-inclusive task than simply saying the board should support the organization's mission. In Carver's model, focusing on the organization's purpose is a perpetual obligation—one that permeates everything the board does. The global ends statement articulates the fundamental purpose of the organization, the results by which it makes a difference in the world. This statement may differ from the traditional mission statement. It is more technical in nature by specifying organizational results in terms of cost, benefits, and beneficiaries. Important in Carver's thought is that the "ends" statement does not include the means by which the ends are

to be accomplished but focus clearly and only on the results to be expected from the organization's action. Carver also insists that his concept of the ends or means distinction is different from the language of "goals and objectives" because those terms can be applied to either means or ends. Likewise, the term *strategy* typically includes both ends and means. Ends are results; everything else—programs, services, even staff morale—are means and should be excluded from this policymaking area.

The board's perpetual focus on ends, on achieving results, flows from its moral ownership obligations. It must be constantly in touch with the external environment of the organization, taking a viewpoint outside and above the organization itself. The board must resist the "captivating allure of organizational events and issues," which can occupy the board's full attention. "The ends concept prevents righteous busyness from becoming just as meaningful as results, or perhaps more so" (Carver 2006, p. 85).

The board's work of evaluation is founded on its articulation of *ends* policies. When the board knows what it wants to achieve, it is then able to ask whether the organization's activities are successful or not. In the business context, results based on profit and loss are theoretically much easier to evaluate; business programs either make money or they don't. In the nonprofit

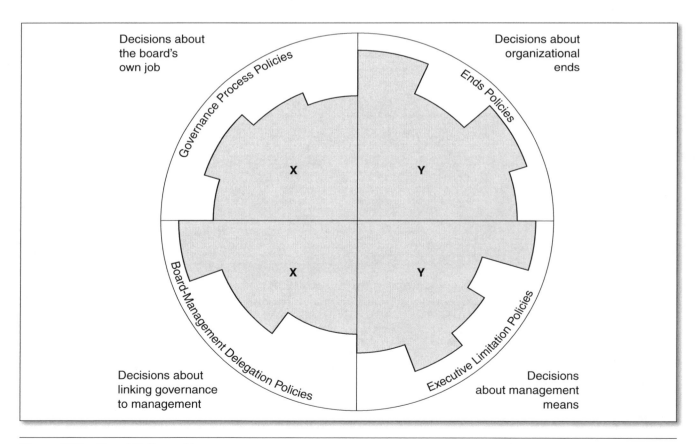

Figure 57.2   Board Policymaking
SOURCE: Carver, 2006, p. 74.

arena, evaluation is typically more difficult conceptually, since the market (even though it may play a strong role in such nonprofits as hospitals or educational institutions) is not the final factor in judging whether or not a program or service is worthwhile. Ultimately, the board has to answer the simple questions: "What did we want to accomplish? Are we achieving it?" (Carver, 2006, p. 110).

Executive Limitations

The second quadrant on Carver's policy circle deals with the board's relationship to the work of the organization's staff. From the governance perspective, this area is frequently problematic. Boards may easily find their attention and agenda largely dictated by staff issues and operations, reacting to a staff report or opining on operations questions that a timid staff "kicks upstairs" to the board. Sometimes the board can't resist the temptation to spend time on an issue that appeals to a particular board member's expertise or indulge in the "enticing complexity of operations" (Carver, 2006, p. 116). Or the board can go to the opposite extreme, deciding that it should simply stay out of the way and let the CEO and staff do their jobs. In effect, the board becomes an unthinking rubber stamp for everything the staff does.

From the governance perspective, the board must have control over staff operations. At the same time, the board must be free from the complexity of staff operations. Carver's solution for this nagging dilemma is to simplify the board's task through policymaking. The board, he says, should establish explicit boundaries, dictated by ethics and prudence, which the staff must not overstep. Rather than prescribe any specific means, the board leaves the staff free to employ its own creativity and ingenuity in developing programs and activities. Further, the staff is free to manage those activities as long as they stay within the limits set up by the board.

This approach, perhaps paradoxically, assigns a great degree of freedom to the staff—what Carver (2006) calls the *irony of delegation*. The most positive approach a board can take toward its subordinates' means is verbally negative. Conversely, the most negative approach is prescriptive and positive. Telling a subordinate how to do a task automatically eliminates all other methods. Telling a subordinate how not to do it leaves open all other possible methods (p. 122). Delegation within limits empowers the staff to use their creativity and innovation while ensuring real accountability. The message to the CEO and staff is "'Go till we say stop,' rather than 'Stop till we say go'" (p. 132).

Such an executive limitations policy may still leave the board with areas of concern. Carver encourages the board to identify and make explicit its "worry list" and explicitly verbalize those concerns in a second level of more narrow, explicit policy statements. He (2006) cites one

board member who described her "heartburn strategy: I determine what's bothering me, see if the policy covers it, put it in writing" (p. 281).

Board-Executive Relationship

In this third quadrant of the policy circle, Carver (2006) deals with the structural relationship between the board and CEO. The actual title of the position (president, supervisor, executive director) is immaterial; he is focusing technically on the CEO function. It might seem that, with all the power Carver's model assigns to the board, the CEO emerges in a relatively weaker role. Such an impression would be totally wrong. Carver says, "A powerfully designed CEO position is a key to board excellence" (p. 154). The title of his chapter asserts the principle, "Strong Boards Need Strong Executives" (Carver, 2006, chap. 6).

Accountability, says Carver, "is the responsibility that accumulates upward" (2006, p. 158). The CEO's accountability to the board has two key features. (1) From the CEO's point of view, the position is accountable to the board *as a body*. The relationship with *individual* members of the board—including the board chair—is that of colleagues, working on a common task. (2) From the board's point of view, "the CEO is accountable for no less than the entire product and behavior of the organization. . . . For most official purposes, the board has only one employee, the CEO" (p. 159). The job description of the CEO, then, becomes quite simple. The CEO is expected simply to accomplish two things: (1) to achieve the ends (results) expected by the board, and (2) not to violate the executive limitations policies prescribed by the board (p. 161).

The working relationship between a strong board and a strong CEO is one of *teamwork*. When the board and CEO understand and respect each other's job definitions, they can each accomplish their respective roles with the support, but without the intrusion, of the other party. The CEO does not expect the board to make executive decisions for him by inviting the board to become involved in the "how" of staff operations. (This does not prevent the CEO from informally calling on the expertise of individual board members for information or advice.) On the other hand, if the board is solidly grounded in its responsibility to make policy, it can ask the CEO for help and support in developing policy options for its consideration and ultimate decision making. When the board and CEO each know what they are supposed to do, both sides are freed up to work in harmony and to help each other. A smooth running organization needs both a strong board and a strong executive.

Board Self-Governance

The policy governance model is fundamentally a redesign of the board's job. That demands a job description for the board itself. "A board that cannot govern itself cannot hope to govern an organization" (Carver, 2006, p. 185). Delineating the board's own self-governance is the task of the fourth policy quadrant. The first assumption here is that the board is responsible for its own behavior. It cannot depend on a CEO (no matter how talented and capable) either to keep the board motivated and engaged or to provide the board with an agenda. The CEO is not the board's babysitter, responsible for providing it tasks to spend time on. The board must take responsibility for managing itself, and making its own value contribution to the organization through specific *board products*. Carver identifies three specific *core products* for which the board is accountable: (1) linkage to the ownership, (2) explicit governing policies, and (3) ensurance of satisfactory organizational performance (Carver, 2006, p. 199). These compose the three essential board obligations, which cannot be delegated.

Linkage to Owners

"Ownership," says Carver (2006), "constitutes the origin of board accountability" (p. 196). It has already been asserted above that the board is there, not just to help run things, but to "own the business." The first obligation of the board is to identify and connect with the organization's principal stakeholders. That group may be easily identifiable as a specific set of people, for example, the members of a country club or trade association. Or the ownership may be more widespread and diverse, for example, the population of a school district or the listening area of a public radio station. What is at stake here is not simply the legal ownership as defined in law but a wider and more encompassing moral ownership. Ownership should not be confused with the organization's funders who give through either private donations or service contracts. "The test for ownership is not with whom the board makes a deal, but whom the board has no right not to ignore" (p. 188). Nor should ownership be confused with the board's relation to staff because "the board's trust relationship with owners supersedes its relationship with staff" (p. 188). However specific or obscure the ownership may be, "the more board members agree on whose behalf they are serving, the more powerful their rule as board members will feel" (p. 187).

Explicit Governing Policies

The central intention of the Carver model is to create a governance system based on explicit policies. Articulating those policies in the four quadrants of the policy circle is a core and quintessential board product. Part of the board's policymaking in self-governance should include the board's own written acknowledgment of this obligation. In the policy governance model, the board should perpetually be busy about policy. Failure in this respect constitutes a failure in the board's own accountability.

Ensuring Organizational Performance

The board must be continually focused on results. The board is not responsible for the staff's job, but it is responsible for monitoring and evaluating the staff's work product against the criteria and expectations the board has determined.

For Carver, the obligation to produce these three core products constitutes the essential elements of the board's job description. Anyone familiar with the nonprofit sector may immediately ask, what about fundraising as part of the board's job description? For Carver, this task is optional. It can be included in the board's stated obligations if the board so chooses, depending on the nature of the organization. The same is true for other such tasks as advocacy in the political arena. Carver's preference is to keep such "optional" tasks out of, or at least to a minimum in, the board's own job description. The more items that are included, the greater the risk of diluting attention to the board's core governing responsibilities (Carver, 2006, p. 207).

The third edition of *Boards That Make a Difference* is filled with often helpful examples of policy statements from organizations employing the policy governance model, as well as accolades from nonprofit executives and board members. Carver acknowledges that the model has drawn criticism, especially for its alleged rigidity and inflexibility. Indeed, Carver (2006) devotes a whole chapter in the third edition to responding to criticisms of his policy governance model, insisting that it has proved workable in practice for a wide range of organizations (chap. 12).

In any case, the Carver model provides the most comprehensive theoretical answer to our first question, how to determine distinct roles and responsibilities for board and staff. For Carver, the first principle for leadership in nonprofit organizations is to understand that board and staff each have a different job and that clarifying the board's job as governance is critical to understanding the role of staff in accomplishing the organization's mission.

Board and Staff: Modes of Leadership

The next question is, given their distinct roles, how to ensure that board and staff function coherently and complementarily for organization leadership?

Chait, Ryan, and Taylor (2005) agree with Carver that "the nonprofit sector has a board problem. Frustration with boards is so troubled and widespread that *board* and *troubled board* have become almost interchangeable" (p. 11). But they disagree with Carver on where to locate the problem. The board's job description, they say, is a good enough point of departure for new boards or inexperienced trustees. However, it does not explain the frustration of talented and experienced board trustees with the governance process as they experience it. Nor does it explain the failure of organizations to make use of the expertise of individual board members, either when they convene in board meetings or in less official (but still important) collaboration with staff outside the board setting proper. Confusion about roles and responsibilities, they say, is an "inadequate diagnosis" for explaining the problem.

> Governing is too complicated to reduce to simple aphorisms, however seductive, like "boards set policies which administrators implement" or "boards establish ends and management determines means." (Chait et al., 2005, p. 5)

The task and structure approach ultimately is unsatisfactory as a prescription for effective board action: "Can any of us name the job where we succeeded by focusing diligently on our job description?" (Chait et al., 2005, p. 24). In effect, the BoardSource authors argue, not so much that Carver's theory of governance is wrong but that it fails to provide an adequate guide to organization leadership on the part of the board.

The analysis begins with two observations. First, nonprofit managers in recent decades have gone to school and learned how to become *leaders*. "The transition from nonprofit administrators to organization leaders" (Chait et al., 2005, p. 3) is one aspect of a profound change in nonprofit organization dynamics. The corollary is that nonprofit boards no longer exercise leadership but have become more like managers (p. 4). The net result is that real governance has moved from the boardroom to the executive office. There is little worthwhile work, then, for trustees to do. The remedy, argue the authors, is to rethink governance in terms of leadership.

The approach in the work of the BoardSource associates is more behavioral and experiential in tone than Carver's approach. It is based on the best practices observed in a variety of organizations and articulated in numerous conversations. The result is a "framework"—if not exactly a full theory—of organizational behavior. The key concept is that governance happens in three modes and that all three are required for governance to rise to the level of organizational leadership:

> Type I—The *fiduciary mode*, where organizations are concerned primarily with the stewardship of tangible assets
>
> Type II—The *strategic mode*, where boards create a strategic partnership with management
>
> Type III—The *generative mode*, where boards provide a less recognized but critical source of leadership for the organization (Chait et al., 2005, pp. 6–7)

The graphic expression of this concept is a triangle—which needs all three sides to be complete (see Figure 57.3). "*When trustees work well in all three of these modes, the board achieves governance as leadership* [italics in original]" (Chait et al., 2005, pp. 6–7).

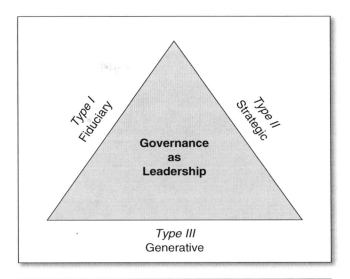

Figure 57.3 Governance as Leadership: The Governance Triangle

SOURCE: Chait, Ryan, and Taylor, 2005, p. 7.

Type I: Fiduciary Mode

Fiduciary work is the fundamental substratum of trusteeship. It involves the duties of loyalty and care that board members owe the organization to ensure that its assets are protected and resources used effectively, that the organization stays faithful to its mission, that it acts lawfully and ethically, and that board members avoid any personal benefit and act in the best interest of the organization and those it serves. In the era since the Sarbanes-Oxley legislation focusing on the private sector, nonprofit boards have become much more attentive to issues of financial accountability and integrity in their fiduciary oversight.

The board's fiduciary responsibility is often understood as the duty of a watchdog—to make sure nothing bad happens. This type of governing is indeed essential, but when a board sees its duties exclusively in Type I mode, it runs the risk of becoming trapped in a narrow mental rut. The Type I board devotes itself almost exclusively to watching for what can go wrong. Its meetings and its work are typically a response to initiatives by the staff—reports, budgets, program reviews. This kind of work is essential, but if that is all the board does, its focus is "to prevent trouble rather than promote success" (Chait et al., 2005, p. 19). That is hardly a prescription for leadership.

Yet there is within the Type 1 fiduciary mode real possibility for creative initiative and leadership. The key difference is that the board must go beyond *oversight*, the typical Type 1 attitude, to *inquiry*—which pushes into new territory. The following are some examples of the different kind of questions a board might ask in the fiduciary mode are (Chait et al., 2005, p. 38):

Oversight Questions	Inquiry Questions
Can we afford it?	What's the opportunity cost?
Is the budget balanced?	Does the budget reflect our priorities?
Is it legal?	Is it ethical?

Type I thinking is critically important, but for a board to act exclusively in this mode has its dangers. The risk is a bureaucratic routinization of tasks that can lead to boredom and jeopardize the board's own exercise of the very fiduciary responsibility it is trying to realize. In short, Type I thinking must be complemented by other modes.

Type II: Strategic Mode

It is not enough for an organization to make the trains run on time; it must be certain that the tracks point to a destination worth arriving at. The organization governed by Type I thinking may know what it's doing and even do it well. But in the competitive nonprofit environment of recent decades, it is a fallacy to think that simply good intentions and even doing good works will ensure long-term success. Chait, Ryan, and Taylor (2005) comment on the switch in thinking that has occurred in recent decades:

> The dominant "theory" was that success depended more on the organization's self-evident virtues and unique purposes than on a carefully crafted strategy. Financial support was an act of faith and charity, not a response to an inspired strategy. Then circumstances changed. (p. 62)

Today any organization pursuing a grant or seeking donations is pretty much forced to provide its fundraisers a strategic plan to carry along in their briefcase as they knock on doors or develop a website.

The problem, though, as many organizations have discovered (and many corporations as well!) is that strategic plans don't always work. "For many nonprofit boards that have embraced formal strategic planning, one overarching concern has arisen: the organization's strategic plan is neither strategic nor a plan" (Chait et al., 2005, p. 57). The plan may simply sketch a blue-sky vision that has few earthly underpinnings. It may fail to deal with necessary changes to the organizational infrastructure—"people, policies, programs budgets, incentives, and facilities" that must be integrated into making the plan work (p. 58). The plan may ignore the strategic drivers that are critical for getting results. Sometimes trustees may be presented a plan devised by management into which they have had little input; in effect they are asked to buy into other people's ideas, leaving them feeling disenfranchised. Some plans

may not account for the pace of change, leaving plans irrelevant to the real environment. In short, organizations may experience "the rise and fall of strategic planning"—the title of Henry Mintzberg's book on the subject (1994). An organization may find value in an annual strategic planning retreat to write or revise the requisite strategic plan, but simply having a plan does not ensure organizational success.

Rather than having a plan, the board must learn to *think strategically*, not just once a year at the annual retreat but all the time. "Strategic thinking should not be treated as heavy artillery or a last-ditch measure deployed only at times of crisis. It is in fact most useful when honed through continuous use" (Chait et al., 2005, p. 64). The board is actually well situated at the top of the organization for the kind of big picture, big idea thinking that should inform the strategic planning process. It may well be easier for the board to imagine a new organizational scenario than it is for top managers, whose day job is implementing the status quo.

> In fact, as smart generalists, the board's capacity to see the panorama more clearly than the pixels underscores a central tenet of Type II governance: boards are better suited to think together than to plan together, to expand the essence of a great idea rather than elaborate the details of a plan. (Chait et al., 2005, p. 66)

Indeed, until the organization learns to use *ideas* rather than *plans* as the "drive motors of strategy, the full range of trustees' talents will be vastly underutilized" (Chait et al., 2005, p. 68).

This Type II governance calls for a different relationship between the board and management than the Type I oversight mode. Here, board and staff develop a strategic partnership, like the teamwork of partners in a doubles tennis match (Chait et al., 2005, p. 69). This Type II mode of governance has implications for how the board goes about its work. The board structure must reflect the focus on ideas, not just organizational functions. Task forces may be created to deal with questions that cut across the domain of the board's functional committees (e.g., finance, development). For example, instead of asking, "How can we maintain market share?" the board might consider, "Are we in the right markets?" Or instead of, "How much debt capacity do we have?" the board might ask the more fundamental question, "Where do we want to invest (or disinvest)?" (Chait et al., 2005, p. 75).

Board meetings should not be forced into ritualized agendas but allow time for thinking aloud with the CEO about questions of this type. Board information and communications need to stretch the board's attention beyond the confines of the organization itself, engaging with the ownership and the environment. Finally, this type of governance offers opportunity for engagement of the board in actually implementing the strategy, employing individual board members' expertise in such arenas as contract negotiation, political advocacy, or fundraising.

Type III: Generative Mode

Most boards will have some familiarity with operating in the fiduciary and strategic modes. They probably will have less experience in the generative mode—the operating style that offers the most potential for true leadership at the board level. Trustees typically do generative thinking in their "day jobs," where they take it for granted as a requisite for leadership success. But board work frequently does not provide trustees with the opportunity for creative leadership in typical board settings. Describing this mode and offering some help for how to do it at board level constitute perhaps the most important contribution of the BoardSource approach.

Board members are usually familiar with such organizational processes as "mission setting, strategy development, and problem solving" (Chait et al., 2005, p. 80). But a fourth process, of generative thinking, is actually more powerful:

> Generative thinking precedes and—more to the point, it *generates* the other processes. . . . A prior, unexamined cognitive process generates the moral commitments that missions codify, the goals that strategies advance, and the diagnoses that problem solving addresses. (Chait et al., 2005, pp. 80–81)

The generative thinking process constitutes the "fuzzy front end" of how "big hairy ideas" get conceived and become the drivers for continually moving an organization forward. This is the kind of thinking that is essential for leadership in the governance process. But, assert the authors, boards do very little of it because "most boards are not organized and equipped to do generative work" (Chait et al., 2005, p. 92).

Determining if and locating where generative thinking takes place in an organization is a powerful predictor of the organization's operating style and aptitude for success. A 2 × 2 column table plotting trustee versus executive engagement identifies four characteristic profiles (see Figure 57.4).

The ideal profile is in Quadrant II—where both trustees and executives are highly engaged in the generative mode, resulting in collaborative leadership. In Quadrant I, only the trustees are highly engaged, resulting in "governance by fiat." Quadrant IV identifies the opposite case, where generative leadership is situated with the executive, and trustees are effectively displaced and absent from real governance. Quadrant III identifies the situation where nobody is in charge, leaving organizational leadership to staff or whoever will step forward.

Boards are ideally positioned for generative leadership. They have the power. They have the breadth of perspective. And they are situated at the "edge" of the organization, close

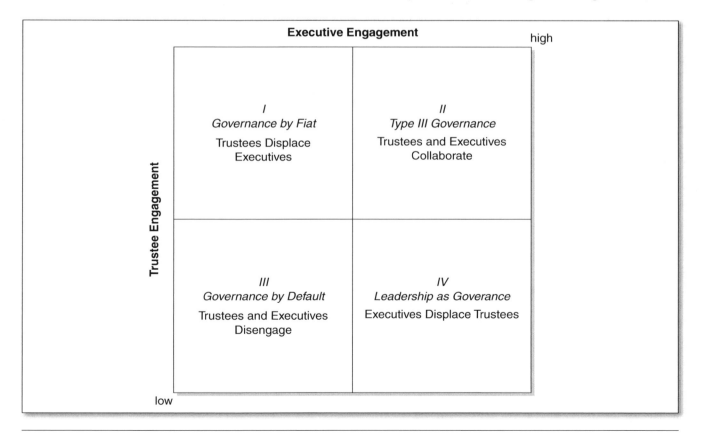

Figure 57.4   Generative Thinking: Four Scenarios
SOURCE: Chait, Ryan, and Taylor, 2005, p. 98.

enough to understand its inner workings but connected to the outside environment and the "ownership" (to borrow a phrase from Carver). The question is, *how* to do it?

The final third of *Governance as Leadership* provides real world examples of the Type III mode of governance, as well as consultant suggestions and exercises for implementing the generative mode. This story from a social service organization shows how the board worked with executives, not just to adopt a proposed *solution* but to understand the *problem*:

> The stated problem was voluntary turnover of staff. The technical solution proposed was to increase compensation. The board discussed the pluses and minuses of many pay plans—across-the-board versus merit pay, signing bonuses versus retention bonuses, individual rewards versus group rewards. But after deliberating in a generative mode, the problem turned out to be how to create a "great place to work" for professional staff. In the end, quality of work life, not money, was the decisive factor. (Chait et al., 2005, p. 108)

For a board to work in this fashion requires robust dialogue, not groupthink. "Type III governance posits that great minds think differently, and that discussions are enriched by multiple perspectives" (Chait et al., 2005, p. 125). From their consulting experience, the authors propose a number of techniques to push the board to think in the generative mode and to make use of board resources as "working capital" (chap. 7).

"But generative work without strategic or fiduciary work, can lapse all too quickly into self-absorbed navelgazing" (Chait et al., 2005, p. 181). Boards function best and provide the most effective leadership when they engage creatively in all three modes. Again, a real world example can provide an illustration. The case involves the loan of 21 Monet paintings by the Boston Museum of Fine Arts to the Bellagio Casino in Las Vegas. (The case was reported by Edgers, 2004.) See Chait et al., 2005, pp. 109–110. Chait and associates note that in coming to its decision to loan the paintings, the museum board considered questions from all three perspectives (pp. 109–110):

Type I Governance: Are the paintings travel worthy? What are the insurance and security arrangements? Are there any bequest-related restrictions on travel or venues? How long a loan period? How much will Bellagio pay? How and where will the MFA's name appear?

Type II Governance: Will the absence of the Monets affect MFA patronage? How will the association with the Bellagio and Las Vegas affect the MFA's image and reputation? Should the MFA sponsor "tie-in" events in Boston or Las Vegas? What can the MFA accomplish with the income from the Bellagio?

Type III Governance: What will we do or not do if the price is right? Should we loan art to the highest bidder? Should we display art where the masses already are? Do MFA masterworks "belong" in neon-light, pop-culture, for-profit venues? How conservative or iconoclastic an institution do we wish to be?

The case illustrates the principle that all three modes of thinking are essential for the board to arrive at a decision in which it can have confidence that serious questions have not been overlooked.

This is governance as leadership in partnership with the executives. "The CEO still stands as *the* leader of the organization and still provides leadership for the board" (Chait et al., 2005, p. 181). But "the less an organization depends on a lonely and heroic leader, the more leadership and the better governance the organization will have" (p. 181).

Future Directions

Both Carver's policy governance model and Chait, Ryan, and Taylor's modes of operating model have been used effectively in consulting. For the policy governance model, there is extensive work on implementation (see Carver, 2002, 2006; Carver & Carver, 2009; Carver & Charney, 2004). The theory itself is well articulated. The most productive direction for future research is the kind of empirical testing done by Judith Millesen (2005), cited above. The Carvers' writings include numerous illustrations from their consulting work, but it would be helpful to have some elaborated case studies of organizations that have successfully implemented the model as well as those that tried and failed.

The Chait, Ryan, and Taylor framework would likewise benefit from empirical case study analysis, perhaps emerging from the extensive consulting work of BoardSource. Ultimately it will be the stories—both of success and of failure—that will help to improve the collaborative and creative leadership of board and staff in nonprofit organizations.

References and Further Readings

American Bar Association Committee on Nonprofit Corporations. (2002). *Guidebook for directors of nonprofit corporations* (2nd ed.). Chicago: Author.

American Bar Association Coordinating Committee on Nonprofit Governance. (2005). *Guide to nonprofit governance in the wake of Sarbanes-Oxley*. Chicago: Author.

BoardSource. (2005). *The source: Twelve principles of governance that power exceptional boards*. Washington, DC: Author.

BoardSource. (2007). *Exceptional board practices: The source in action*. Washington, DC: Author.

Carver, J. (2002). *John Carver on board leadership*. San Francisco: Jossey-Bass.

Carver, J. (2006). *Boards that make a difference: A new design for leadership in nonprofit and public organizations* (3rd ed.). San Francisco: Jossey-Bass.

Carver, J., & Carver, M. M. (2006). *Reinventing your board: A step-by-step guide to implementing policy governance*. San Francisco: Jossey-Bass.

Carver, J., & Carver, M. M. (2009). *The policy governance model and the role of the board member: A Carver policy governance guide* (Rev. ed.). San Francisco: Jossey-Bass.

Carver, M., & Charney, B. (2004). *The board member's playbook: Using policy governance to solve problems, make decisions, and build a stronger board.* San Francisco: Jossey-Bass.

Chait, R. P., Ryan, W. P., & Taylor, B. E. (2005). *Governance as leadership: Reframing the work of nonprofit boards.* Hoboken, NJ: John Wiley & Sons.

Dambach, C. S. (2009). *Structures and practices of nonprofit boards* (2nd ed.). Washington, DC: BoardSource.

Edgers, G. (2004, February 15). Art fans take a Vegas vacation. *Boston Globe*, pp. N1, N4.

Grace, K. S. (2009). *The nonprofit board's role in mission, planning, and evaluation* (2nd ed.). Washington, DC: BoardSource.

Greenfield, J. M. (2009). *Fundraising responsibilities of nonprofit boards* (2nd ed.). Washington, DC: BoardSource.

Hopkins, B. R. (2009). *Legal responsibilities of nonprofit boards* (2nd ed.). Washington, DC: BoardSource.

Ingram, R. T. (2009). *Ten basic responsibilities of nonprofit boards* (2nd ed.). Washington, DC: BoardSource.

Lang, A. S. (2009). *Financial responsibilities of nonprofit boards* (2nd ed.). Washington, DC: BoardSource.

Millesen, J. (2005). Who "owns" your nonprofit? *Nonprofit Quarterly, 12*(4), 10–14.

Mintzberg, H. (1994). *The rise and fall of strategic planning: Reconceiving roles for planning, plans, planners.* New York: Free Press.

Newport, G. (2005). Why are we replacing furniture when half the neighborhood is missing? *Nonprofit Quarterly, 12*(4), 32–38.

Oliver, C. (2009). *Getting started with policy governance: Bringing purpose, integrity and efficiency to your board's work.* Hoboken, NJ: John Wiley & Sons.

Pointer, D. D., & Orlikoff, J. E. (2002). *The high performance board.* San Francisco: Jossey-Bass.

58

Philanthropic Leadership at the Community Level

Mary B. Mc Donald

University of San Diego

Philanthropy takes on many forms in a community including individual giving, corporate giving, charitable bequests, and foundation grantmaking. Contributions in 2008 can be used to illustrate the presence and strength of each of these forms. According to "Giving USA," the annual survey of giving patterns in the United States, total giving was estimated at more than $300 billion, with the total divided among individual giving at 75%, foundation grantmaking at 13%, charitable bequests at 7%, and corporate giving at 5% (http://www.givingusa .org). As is traditionally the case, individual giving was the greatest source of charitable dollars in 2008, with individual philanthropists directly supporting the mission and programs of specific nonprofits and causes. This form of giving most directly represents a donor's preference for the use of a donated dollar, in that the donor selects a nonprofit, a program, or a cause and gives the money to that effort directly.

Foundations, on the other hand, are institutions that manage private funds dedicated to public purposes and direct the majority of those funds through grants to nonprofit organizations (Prewitt, 2006, p. 356). There are two kinds of grantmaking foundations: the private foundation and the community foundation, each governed by a different set of Internal Revenue Service (IRS) rules. Both kinds of foundations traditionally facilitate their work through managing a collective pool of funds that have been donated, earned from investments, or granted to the foundation for mission-related activities. These funds are then distributed on behalf of the original donors in respect to the foundation mission and personal preference, in many cases through donor-advised accounts. In addition to the traditional fund-managing and grantmaking roles, foundation activities include convening key community stakeholders, collaborating within and across sectors, and building nonprofit partner capacity. Studies have found differences in the mix of activities conducted by an individual foundation, but research generally agrees that foundations are exercising leadership at the community level (Center for Effective Philanthropy, 2008; Fairfield & Wing, 2008; Foundation Center, 2007; Ostrander, 2007; Ostrower, 2006). Given this prevalence of foundation leadership, nonprofit leaders within a community may not be aware of or understand the power inherent in acquiring knowledge of the processes of foundations in developing and exercising leadership strategies.

Why Would Nonprofits Care?

Understanding how foundations lead communities is extremely important to the success of nonprofits in the United States for a number of reasons. For one, foundations are a source of a good deal of money. In 2008, the more than 75,000 foundations operating in the United States granted an estimated $45.6 billion (Lawrence & Mukai, 2008, p. 1). The amount of money contributed to the nonprofit sector by foundations has been found to bring significant influence to bear on nonprofits (Gronbjerg & Martell, 2000). Therefore, successful nonprofits look to foundations for this support and strategically must acknowledge the influence that accompanies those resources.

A second reason understanding foundation leadership is important is that it includes different activities, norms, structures, and roles. Often, individual foundations choose their activities based on the foundation's individual circumstances, such as the foundation type or its organizational values, those underlying institutional principles that govern a foundation's relationships with various constituencies. To relate to foundations successfully requires a nonprofit professional to understand how these different institutional circumstances impact the choices foundations make. Certainly, foundations are viewed often as unique. "Once you have seen one foundation" goes the popular adage, "you have seen one foundation" (Ostrower, 2006, p. 510). While that is true, foundations have important institutional similarities, and in those are clues to deciphering the leadership style of an individual foundation. Foundations, for example, are private institutions defined by their mission and the requirements of their tax-exempt status. These private institutions all have missions that call them to serve the "greater good" in their activities and to meet the requirements of tax exemption (such as to distribute their earnings for charitable purposes rather than to shareholders).

Differences between foundations become apparent when one compares foundations by type. Consider, for example, the case of private versus community foundations. Private foundations, such as the W. K. Kellogg Foundation, are generally established through the endowed gift of a single source and, therefore, focus on the wishes of the founding donor. Community foundations are legally classified as public charities and operate by both raising and distributing money to specific geographies based on the wishes of a diverse group of donors with unique personal causes and unique community needs. It is also important for nonprofit leaders to consider a foundation's size and institutionalized values to ensure congruency with requests for funds and participation at roundtable discussions. Those values are often operationalized in the attitudes and perceptions of foundation leaders (Ostrower, 2006). A prudent nonprofit professional understands these differences and uses that understanding in all foundation relations.

There is a third reason for nonprofits to understand foundation leadership. The expectations foundations have regarding nonprofits are changing, related to the pressure within the philanthropic community for accountability and effectiveness. These same expectations are recently evidenced in Requests for Proposals (RFPs) from government, foundations, and other funders. Although there is a lack of clarity about the meaning of *effectiveness*, it is generally accepted that there is pressure on foundations to be both accountable and transparent in their activities. Foundations transfer this emphasis to their grantees, with calls for nonprofits to use data to demonstrate need, to track progress toward goals, and to measure impact. Foundations now often make accountability an expectation for grantees in priorities and grantmaking. There are differences in how foundations approach accountability and effectiveness (Ostrower, 2007; Sowa, Coleman, &

Sandfort, 2004). Understanding how foundations view effectiveness in their work will give nonprofit professionals critical insight in approaching foundations for support and anticipating the extent to which accountability will be required in their work.

This chapter discusses how foundations lead in communities and then offers realistic strategies for nonprofits to use as they access foundation leadership through grant awards and collaboration related to foundations. Before this discussion can occur, however, we need a definition of leadership.

Leadership: A Transactional/ Transformational Approach

In writings about philanthropic leadership and the role of foundations, phrases like *foundation effectiveness* and *adaptive or strategic leadership* often appear (Bernholz, Fulton, & Kasper, 2005; Center for Effective Philanthropy, 2007; Ostrower, 2006). These phrases represent common themes such as the relationship between the leader (i.e., the foundation) and the follower (i.e., the grantee) or the practices of leadership, which include negotiated work as opposed to collaborative work. Transformational leadership is a framework that effectively articulates the range of leadership styles and activities. This concept is familiar to professionals from a variety of backgrounds and provides an appropriate framework for the discussion of philanthropic leadership because it is accepted by those who write about philanthropy and is familiar to the trustees and other volunteer professionals who make up philanthropic leadership.

First defined by James MacGregor Burns (1978), the fundamental principle is that there are two categories or styles in the way people (or organizations) lead: transactional and transformational. Transactional leaders influence and lead through direct exchange, in that the leader and the follower exchange one thing for another. Leaders exchange something of value that they possess or control with followers in exchange for a particular outcome or service. For a foundation, this might be that the foundation gives money to a grantee to accomplish certain goals. The exchange is the money for the program. Transactional leaders often define the work based on negotiated work plans or contracts. When the work is completed (or not), leaders award the followers with tangible (e.g., money) or intangible (e.g., praise, additional work) rewards or with punishment (e.g., penalties, consternation), concluding the transaction (Rowold & Rohmann, 2009). The traditional philanthropic functions such as fiscal management and fund distribution (including all the grantmaking and management functions) could be viewed as transactional.

A transformational leadership style, on the other hand, is not based on transactions. The relationship between leaders and followers is more engaged. Central to the style is the mutual development of vision and action. Transformational leaders influence followers toward action that is collectively developed rather than action that is basically a transfer of resources. Transformational leaders solicit followers' ideas, encourage creativity, and instill high standards and deep convictions (Bass, 1997). Transformational leadership is strategic and is characterized by leveraging resources and adapting goals to circumstances and opportunities.

Neither leadership style is the "right one" for all organizations in all situations. Transformational leaders who are committed to building vision do not necessarily do so to the detriment of making effective investment decisions or managing an efficient grant portfolio. The two styles can exist together in a foundation, with the transformational leadership enhanced by the transactional functions (Bass, 1997; Burns, 1978), or a foundation might have only one style. Clearly, a foundation cannot be effective in leading a community if the fiscal and fiduciary transactions are not performed in a flawless manner. There is, however, increasing awareness in the philanthropic community that using both styles builds innovation, creativity, sustainability, and impact over time (Bernholz et al., 2005; Center for Effective Philanthropy, 2007; Ostrower, 2006; Walden, 2006).

Transformational activities include convening diverse stakeholders, collaborating with government and business, partnering with grantees around innovative strategies, or advocating for public policy positions. Auspos, Brown, Kubisch, and Sutton (2009) uncovered six "civic roles for philanthropic organizations' engagement in communities," using as a case study Living Cities, a "consortium of financial organizations, private foundations and private sector organizations . . . working . . . to improve distressed neighborhoods in 23 cities" (p. 135). These various roles can be viewed as transformational in nature and can be used to illustrate how foundations can successfully lead in a community. The six roles identified in the case study were the following:

1. Convening and leveraging diverse networks of relationships

2. Developing local data and plans for community change

3. Leveraging new resources on behalf of the community

4. Mobilizing political will

5. Framing new messages and communicating strategically

6. Generating and testing new ideas and building and sharing knowledge

For foundations, transformational roles are often classified as direct charitable activities. The Foundation Center (2007) conducted a study of 900 of the top 3,000 foundations in the United States in terms of giving (in 2005), focused mainly on independent and family foundations.

The results, as reported in "More Than Grantmaking: A First Look at Foundations' Direct Charitable Activities," illustrate the importance foundations place on direct charitable activities. First, different types of foundations are involved in direct charitable activities, and the level of support for such activities varies. According to the Foundation Center, a quarter of the independent and family foundations surveyed conduct direct charitable activities (and programs) and "spending ranges from a small fraction of their overall charitable administrative expenses to more than 25 percent for about one in four" (Foundation Center, 2007, p. 6). Second, the size and the type of the foundation influenced the involvement in these activities. Half of the surveyed foundations that make grants of $10 million or more indicated that they conduct direct charitable activities, and community foundations reported far higher levels of participation in these activities (61%) than independent or corporate foundations. Third, three fifths of the reporting independent and family foundations indicated that their involvement in direct charitable activities has increased in the last 5 years, and three fourths predicted that the "practice is becoming more widespread" (Foundation Center, 2007, p. 5).

The increase of nongrantmaking activities is viewed by many in the foundation world as a move toward effectiveness (Bernholz et al., 2005; Center for Effective Philanthropy, 2007; Ostrower, 2006). Gwen Walden (2006) of the California Endowment identified convening, training, advocacy, strategic communications, nontraditional investment strategies and leveraging as activities that are transitioning foundations from "grantmaking to changemaking" (p. 30). Many philanthropic leaders measure a foundation's effectiveness by the success of those it funds (Bernholz et al., 2005; Center for Effective Philanthropy, 2007).

Philanthropic Transformational Leadership

In *On the Brink of New Promise,* Bernholz et al. (2005) laid out a blueprint for the activities of philanthropic leaders. They emphasized the community context of foundations, describing dynamic and fluid forces for change such as changing demographics, technology, economics, and institutional roles. The authors asserted that philanthropy needs to be engaged in community as proactively strategic rather than as reactive participants. Community philanthropy was defined as "the practice of catalyzing and raising resources from a community on behalf of a community, . . . including affinity across geography, issues, and identity" (Bernholz et al., 2005, p. 1). Given that definition, the leadership role these authors describe could be assumed by any foundation that asserts impact on particular issues, a particular geography, or a particular group.

Bernholz et al. (2005) challenged foundations to adopt two core values. The first value is to be transformational leaders and the second to be strategic in that effort. To be transformational leaders, foundations cannot act as the "community ATM" (Rosenberg, 2009). This metaphor is used to describe foundations that respond to financial needs as requests come to them: direct grantmaking. The increasing pressure for effectiveness is moving foundations to expand their activities to a change-making role, one of transformational leaders. And along with it, grantees are finding varying strategies and success.

Attitudes and Perceptions

Foundations are embracing the effectiveness, transformational challenge with varying attitudes and perceptions. Using survey data collected from 1,192 staffed, grantmaking foundations, a team from the Urban Institute developed a typology for grouping foundations based on their attitudes and perceptions of effectiveness. Reviewing this research gives a clear framework for understanding the variation of foundation values and behaviors. It is valuable because it moves beyond the traditional grouping of foundations to one based on their views and values related to foundation effectiveness. Foundations were asked to report what they viewed as important to achieving effectiveness, and then, they were grouped based on their responses to questions measuring effectiveness components and approaches. The scales and the views and activities associated with them are as follows (Ostrower, 2006, pp. 511–512):

- *Proactive orientation:* Foundations that measure high on this scale view proactivity as important and make grants for foundation-designed initiatives, using measurable outcomes as an important grantmaking criterion. They believe it is important to engage in activities beyond grantmaking to increase impact, focus on root causes, collaborate, and seek out social needs.
- *Technical assistance/capacity building:* Foundations that measure high on this scale view technical assistance and capacity building as important and support that work. They also provide nonfinancial technical assistance in areas that include board development, strategy and planning, fundraising, communications, technology, and hosting grantee convenings.
- *Social policy/advocacy:* Foundations that rank high on this scale believe that influencing social policy is important to being effective. They award grants to support advocacy and place a high value on social change.
- *Internal staff development:* Foundations that rank high on this scale provide opportunities for training and development in use of computers and/or technology, internal management, and grantmaking.

The foundations were then clustered into four groups according to how they ranked on the four scales. The distribution of foundations across these groups is an indication of the range of attitudes and perceptions among the responding foundations. One group of 313 foundations (29%) rated all four areas as high. A second group included those foundations that ranked relatively high on the proactivity and social policy scales, but not on the management/technical assistance or internal staff development scales. There were 296 foundations (28%) in this group.

The third group was comprised of foundations that ranked high on the proactivity and internal staff development scales, but not on the social policy or management/technical assistance scales. There were 230 foundations or 22% in this group. The fourth group included 224 foundations (21%) that ranked all four scales low.

Once foundations were grouped, similarities and differences were analyzed both within and between the groups. Reviewing these similarities and differences can give a nonprofit professional useful insight into the attitudes and behaviors of foundations. For example, consider a foundation that views all four areas (proactivity, social policy, management technical assistance, and internal staff development) as important to their foundation effectiveness. The research found that such a foundation (high in all areas) believed it was important to publicize the foundation and its work to be effective and that strengthening other organizations was an important goal of their grantmaking. Nearly half of these foundations believed that ethnic or racial diversity of board and staff was an important criterion in grantmaking decisions, and a high percentage make investments or do not because of social, political, or environmental practices. A high percentage of foundations that rated all four areas as highly important to foundation effectiveness were found to have used evaluation in their grantmaking, to have conducted a strategic plan, to be involved in communication activities, and to have participated in collaboration. Foundations that rated some or all of these activities as important to effectiveness are leading as transformational leaders. Foundations that were low in all areas were less likely to hold these types of attitudes or practice these types of behaviors. If a foundation sees their effectiveness as being determined by the transformational attitudes and behaviors measured by this study, a nonprofit professional can expect pressure to partner with the foundation in a transformational manner. To be successful with such a foundation will require more than a well-written proposal.

Although foundation professionals find activities beyond grantmaking to be important and an increasing part of the grantee/foundation relationship, nonprofit professionals question whether the activities are successful (Center for Effective Philanthropy, 2007). In an effort to determine what assistance is being given beyond grants and to measure the effectiveness of that effort, the Center for Effective Philanthropy conducted a survey with nonprofit organizations and their experience with certain foundations as well as surveys and interviews with foundation program staffs and boards. The research found that foundation staff members believe that assistance beyond grants is important for impact and goal achievement; they "know little about the actual results of the assistance they provide" (Center for Effective Philanthropy, 2007, p. 6). In addition, the majority of grantees (of a large foundation) receive no assistance, and those that do generally just get two or three types of assistance beyond grants, which according to those surveyed is not effective. To provide comprehensive assistance requires a significant investment on the part of the foundation, yet it was reported that assistance embedded in a set of supports provides the most positive experiences.

Transformational Leadership: Why Foundations Lead as They Do

The leadership theory and the research presented in this chapter can be synthesized as follows:

- Individual foundations take on different roles in communities, and those differences include the foundation's involvement with views of effectiveness, relationship to grantees, and leadership activities.
- Transactional and transformation leadership styles exist in community philanthropy as a continuum and are selected by foundations in communities based on the foundation's size, type, and the attitudes and perceptions its leaders hold about effectiveness.
- Transformational activities can often include networking and leveraging resources and relationships across diverse groups, generating and sharing knowledge, and using data to articulate needs, monitor progress, and measure impact.
- Transformational activities are promoted as a strategy to strengthen foundations' capacity to adapt and lead in dynamic environments.
- Transformation activities can often bring foundations to expect grantees to use data to demonstrate need, to measure progress, and to report impact.
- Direct charitable activities, support beyond a grant, takes time and resources.

Given these realities, why does a foundation choose a particular leadership style? Certainly, choosing a style has both organizational benefits and risks. If the philanthropic leadership is transactional, a foundation has the benefit of a high level of control. The foundation leadership (including board, staff, and donors) determine how money will be managed and distributed. The leadership decides what is important and what will be done with foundation money. This style of leader controls the organization's "message," the focus and priority of issues, and the assessment of efforts. A transactional leader also has the ultimate authority for quality. This leader negotiates an exchange of resources for services and continues or discontinues those efforts based on the criterion of that particular foundation. Moving to a transformational style risks the loss of this exclusive control by inviting others, including grantees, to share in leading the vision and the work.

Sharing exclusive control often means putting the foundation's name and credibility on the line and can mean supporting weak partners or those who are not able or willing to support shared vision or priorities. For a foundation to lead exclusively through grantmaking, in a transactional style, puts a high level of trust in the foundation's capacity to act individually. A foundation may be in that position because of the amount of money the foundation has to grant based on its priorities or because the priorities are precise or unique, making collaboration arguably irrelevant. Increasingly, single institutions are less likely to have the resources to act independently in communities. Communities are dynamic, and community needs are often interrelated. Independent action can be risky for many foundations, whereas for others, it is a realistic and successful approach.

The range in leadership styles ultimately means that nonprofit professionals cannot guess how any one foundation approaches its leadership in a community. Guessing is not the road to success in foundation relations. Success waits at the intersection of styles. Success lives when nonprofits and foundations match.

Leadership Strategies for Nonprofit Professionals

Just as a foundation's relationship with grantees reflects a leadership style, a grantee's relationship with a foundation equally reflects a style. In a transactional relationship, the grantee views the foundation as a funder, a contracting institution. Generally, the nonprofit views the foundation as the leader and itself as the follower. The foundation leadership (board and staff) assess need and determine areas of focus. The foundation may put out an RFP or call for proposals, to which the nonprofit would respond. Even if it does not use an RFP or call for proposals, the foundation will have funding priorities, focus areas, or interests that are used to make fund distribution decisions. Whatever approach is used, the foundation selects and funds the work, and the nonprofit conducts and reports the work. In a transformational relationship, the grantee is not necessarily a follower. Depending on the activities of the foundation, a grantee might be called on to determine needs (through a convening, for example) or to collaborate with others around programs or initiatives. This is a very different role for a nonprofit, and not all are ready or interested in relating to foundations in this way for two reasons. One, the nonprofit may believe that it does not have the organizational capacity—staff or other resources—to be involved in community collaboration or collective visioning. The second reason is that the nonprofit may not consider community leadership that is transformational a priority. In measuring the components of organizational effectiveness, these nonprofits would not rate high on the four scales: proactive orientation, technical assistance/capacity building, social policy/advocacy, and internal staff development (i.e., as noted in Ostrower, 2006). Also, a nonprofit needs to come to clear terms about the power dynamic that traditionally exists between those that give money (foundations) and those that ask for it (nonprofits). This dynamic is, in many cases already described, old and ineffective in the age of philanthropic effectiveness and stands in the way of successful grantmaking impact (Orosz, 2007). To be successful, the nonprofit needs to find foundations that lead with a style that matches its style of following. To find these foundations requires a strategic process, conducted with thought and intention.

Strategy as a vehicle to drive organizational excellence developed in organizational leadership in the last 40 years. Any number of models and tools are dedicated to the theory and practice of strategic planning for nonprofits. Generally, those are beyond the scope of this writing except in the most basic of form (see Allison & Kaye, 1997, and Bryson, 1995, for a thorough treatment of strategic planning). That basic form is this: The actions of nonprofits must be based in the context of the world in which their mission lives. For nonprofits to be successful with foundation relationships, they need to ground both their strategy and intention in a contextual process. They need a strategy as defined in the strategic organizational studies and framed as an intentional process. In his book, *The Nonprofit Strategic Revolution,* David La Piana (2008) defined strategy as a "coordinated set of actions toward an end to creating and sustaining a competitive advantage" (p. 32). La Piana describes strategic thinking and positioning as an ongoing activity. It is, for example, a thoughtful assessment of a nonprofit and its context, creating significant information for the nonprofit's leadership to use in priority- and strategy-setting decisions. Strategies for foundation relations are the result of a contextual assessment of the nonprofit and its mission, values, and resources. This assessment is done within the community environment and includes all foundations involved in community philanthropic efforts, their resources, and their leadership style. The strategic assessment needs to be completed as a part of the nonprofit's strategic planning to "chart the course" and then used in any and all decisions related to foundation relations. The assessment process includes a "strengths/weakness/opportunity/threats" analysis of both the internal and the external context of the nonprofit and, as such, can be conducted using a series of three steps. Knowing the unique nature of foundation leadership, the key is to systematically take the time and focus to analyze both the challenges and opportunities available in the nonprofit and foundation relationships.

Step 1: Know Your Organization

The first step is to thoughtfully consider the nonprofit's mission. In this step, a nonprofit conducts a systematic review of the mission and values of the organization and considers the alignment of current programming to that mission and values. This is an internal and an external assessment, in that information is gathered from both "inside and outside" the organization. What is this nonprofit? Why does it receive a tax exemption? To conduct such an assessment, the nonprofit leadership needs, first, to revisit the mission and values of the organization to ensure that all leadership understands and agrees with the definition of the mission and values. Then, a good deal of data must be used to discern how the mission and values are currently being articulated in services or advocacy or policy depending, of course, on the mission itself. A thoughtful assessment includes an honest consideration of the governance system. What is the role of the board of directors? Next, what are the systems that define the operations of the nonprofit? All systems must be considered including human resources (including volunteers), fiscal management, consumer outreach, and service delivery. Where does the money go? For example, are there funds going to support community collaboration? One looks in this assessment for evidence of leveraging of funds or diversity of funding that comes through partnerships or mutual service delivery.

In this stage, deficiencies can appear. How capable is the nonprofit of delivering data about these systems? Organizational capacity issues can surface at this step, and those are important if a nonprofit aspires to seek funding from a foundation that requires data beyond what the nonprofit can provide. Also, aligned to mission and values, the nonprofit must realistically review service delivery. Who are they serving, and to what extent do those individuals match the organizational mission? Multiple-year data need to be viewed to determine trends. In this stage, the nonprofit also needs to assess how it relates to its consumers/clients/patients. A foundation that is transformational in leadership will look for nonprofits that consult and involve consumers in service delivery design. Such a foundation will look for evidence that the nonprofit seeks out information from consumers about the effectiveness of programming. Some might look for consumer representation on the board of directors or on an advisory committee. The nonprofit needs to be thoughtful about the consumer relationship and be able to provide a rationale for that relationship based on organizational mission. Once this information is gathered, the strengths and weaknesses of each of the systems must be assessed.

Step 2: Know the Community and the Context

Knowing the community requires a nonprofit to assess a number of relationships. First, there needs to be a clear definition of the community it serves as a nonprofit first related to it. The nonprofit's community can be defined by a number of things, such as geography, ethnicity, gender, or other items. Consider the local scope of Every Woman's Place in Muskegon, Michigan, an empowerment organization for women, youth, and children (everywomansplace.org), versus the larger community of the American Association of Retired Persons (AARP). The community for Every Woman's Place is defined by geography, and for AARP, community is defined by age and membership. In all cases, a nonprofit needs to define its community before it can presume to build a relationship with a foundation.

Second, driven by the community definition, the nonprofit must gather significant data about that community. What is going on in the community? Economic and political data are important. Trends are enormously important so data from multiple years must be gathered. Other comparative data may also be important for comparison such as data from different geographies, different constituent groups, or different program types. Data from national sources such as the U.S. Census prove a good source for demographics. Other national sources can found through a simple search of the Internet. Local data can often be found from those sources based on county or zip code.

Third, data must also be gathered through focus groups and interviews with key informants such as foundation leaders, donors to the nonprofit, and other community leaders. How does the nonprofit decide who needs to be interviewed? The choice is based on the mission and value review conducted in the first step and on the assessment of the economic and political context conducted in this step. Who are the critical people, and what are the essential organizations that determine the nonprofit's context? Questions in the interviews are strategic in nature. They address the strengths and weaknesses of the nonprofit as well as the opportunities and threats to constrict or expand services. It is important in this step to consider the foundations that operate in the nonprofit's community. What is their leadership style, defined by their mission, values, and grantmaking patterns? Are they engaged in direct charitable activities, and how do they define effectiveness?

The nonprofit also must consider what role the foundations have played in the strategic position of the nonprofit. Have foundations just been funders? To what extent has the nonprofit engaged with foundations or in community collaboration? If the nonprofit prefers a transactional relationship where funding is traded for programming, this can be affirmed at this step, and certain foundations can be found that prefer that to a transformational approach. This assessment produces the information needed to select foundation strategies that work.

Step 3: Act as Foundation Partners

In this step, a nonprofit sets a strategic direction. If the nonprofit decides to partner with a foundation that is transformational in style, the nonprofit needs to prioritize community engagement, internal capacity, and communication.

The nonprofit's strategic direction needs to provide resources including time and funding for the professional and board leadership to be involved in community collaboration. This could include interagency initiatives or community coalitions. Foundation leaders or core constituents need to be involved in the nonprofit's strategic planning, and internal systems need to accommodate timely data collection and effective program evaluation. Finally, the nonprofit's communication must be transparent and must accommodate the foundation's need to focus on impact and effectiveness.

With a clear understanding of internal strengths and external opportunities, the nonprofit leadership can select the foundations that have a matching strategic direction. Thoughtful direction comes from such an understanding.

Summary

Nonprofit professionals are successful when they recognize the diversity in foundations and understand the extent to which foundation leadership in communities is driven by foundation type, size, attitudes, and perceptions. Beyond that recognition is the need for nonprofits to assess their own organization and its leadership style and then to relate to foundations that are a match in expectations and style. A nonprofit can "win" a grant by delivering a program. Ultimately, however, the nonprofit succeeds when, in a strategic and thoughtful manner, it matches its capacity with foundations. Whether a foundation is transformational or transactional, it will look for nonprofits that can deliver through understanding. That is why and how successful nonprofit professionals relate to foundations in communities.

References and Further Readings

Allison, M., & Kaye, J. (1997). *Strategic planning for nonprofit organizations: A practical guide and workbook.* New York: John Wiley.

Auspos, P., Brown, P., Kubisch, A., & Sutton, S. (2009). Philanthropy's civic role in community change. *The Foundation Review, 1*(1), 135–145.

Bass, B. (1997). Does the transactional-transformational leadership paradigm transcend organizational and national boundaries? *American Psychologist, 52,* 130–139.

Bernholz, L., Fulton, K., & Kasper, G. (2005). *On the brink of new promise: The future of U.S. community foundations.* Retrieved May 10, 2009, from http://www.blueprintrd .com/text/foc_FINALfutureofcommunity_complete.pdf

Bryson, J. (1995). *Strategic planning for public and nonprofit organizations.* San Francisco: Jossey-Bass.

Burns, J. M. (1978). *Leadership.* New York: Harper & Row.

Center for Effective Philanthropy. (2007). *More than money.* Retrieved May 15, 2009, from http://www.effective philanthropy.org/images/pdfs/CEP_More_than_Money .pdf

Center for Effective Philanthropy. (2008). *Beyond the rhetoric.* Retrieved May 15, 2009, from http://www.effective philanthropy.org/images/pdfs/CEP_Beyond_the_Rhetoric .pdf

Fairfield, K., & Wing, K. (2008). Collaboration in foundation grantor-grantee relationships. *Nonprofit Management & Leadership, 19*(1), 27–44.

Foundation Center. (2007). *More than grantmaking: A first look at foundations direct charitable activities.* Retrieved May 14, 2009, from http://foundationcenter.org/gainknowledge/research/pdf/dca_2007.pdf

Giving USA. (2009). *U.S. charitable giving estimated to be $307.65 billion in 2008.* Retrieved June 20, 2009, from http://www.givingusa.org/press_releases/gusa/GivingReaches 300billion.pdf

Gronbjerg, K. A., & Martell, L. (2000). Philanthropic funding of human services: Solving ambiguity through the two-stage competitive process. *Nonprofit and Voluntary Sector Quarterly, 29*(Supplement), 9–40.

La Piana, D. (2008). *The nonprofit strategy revolution: Real-time strategic planning in a rapid-response world.* St. Paul, MN: Fieldstone Alliance.

Lawrence, S., & Mukai, R. (2008). *Foundation growth and giving estimates* (Foundations Today Series). New York: Foundation Center.

Orosz, J. (2007). *Effective foundation management.* New York: AltaMira Press.

Ostrander, S. (2007). Innovation, accountability, and independence at three private foundations funding higher education civic engagement, 1995–2005. *Nonprofit Management & Leadership, 18*(2), 237–253.

Ostrower, F. (2006). Foundation approaches to effectiveness: A typology. *Nonprofit and Voluntary Sector Quarterly, 35*(3), 510–516.

Ostrower, F. (2007). The relativity of foundation effectiveness: The case of community foundations. *Nonprofit and Voluntary Sector Quarterly, 36*(3), 521–527.

Prewitt, K. (2006). Foundation. In W. W. Powell & R. Steinberg (Eds.), *The non-profit sector: A research handbook* (pp. 355–377). New Haven, CT: Yale University Press.

Rosenberg, V. (2009). *Interview with Mary Mc Donald concerning the Michigan 3D Project.* Grand Haven: Council of Michigan Foundations.

Rowold, J., & Rohmann, A. (2009). Relationships between leadership styles and followers' emotional experience and effectiveness in the voluntary sector. *Nonprofit and Voluntary Sector Quarterly, 38*(2), 270–286.

Sowa, J., Coleman, S., & Sandfort, J. (2004). No longer unmeasureable? A multidimensional integrated model of nonprofit organizational effectiveness. *Nonprofit and Voluntary Sector Quarterly, 33*(4), 711–728.

Walden, G. I. (2006). When a grant is not a grant: Fostering deep philanthropic engagement. In *State of philanthropy 2006: Creating dialogue for tomorrow's movements.* Washington, DC: National Committee for Responsive Philanthropy.

59

LEADING NONPROFIT PARTNERSHIPS WITH GOVERNMENT

RAMYA RAMANATH

Grand Valley State University

O ur understanding of how nonprofit organizations (NPOs) relate to government has come a long way in that we now know that the nature of interactions between the two are not just diverse but vary over time and among different fields of service. This diversity and complexity in relations between the two is expressed in a vast array of typologies developed by various nonprofit scholars over the years (Ramanath & Ebrahim, in press). These typologies inform us that relations between NPOs and government agencies, whether federal, state, or local, may be cooperative, complementary, adversarial, confrontational, or even co-optive. Of particular concern to this chapter are predominantly cooperative relations between NPOs that are contracted by government to deliver social services. The recent preponderance of such partnership arrangements in areas such as child abuse prevention, day care, mental health, employment and training, nursing care, prison alternatives, youth development, and numerous other social service innovations begs examination of how such contractual relationships could be best managed. Are there management styles and leadership traits that are particularly conducive to navigating a nonprofit's service-delivery partnership with government?

To address this question, the chapter begins by outlining the factors that have contributed to the increasing complexity in NPO-government interactions including interactions of a contractual nature. The chapter then moves to uncovering the meaning of the term *partnerships* in NPO-government interactions. We then examine some of the key dilemmas for nonprofits in public service provision. These issues include board governance, managing finances, documentation, and reporting requirements while maintaining

staff morale, maintaining mission effectiveness and sustaining outcomes over the long run, and retaining an advocacy voice. The details presented in this chapter draw on research conducted by various nonprofit scholars and practitioners including work of the chapter author in such interrelated areas as nonprofit governance, nonprofit-government relations, accountability and collaborative leadership.

Dynamics of Nonprofit-Government Interactions: A Complex Ecosystem

Applying the analogy of an "ecosystem" is an effort to build a broad conceptual framework for understanding NPO-government interactions (Ramanath, 2005, p. 47). In a general sense, an ecosystem refers to organisms and the interconnected environment in which they function. The dictionary definitions of the term include "a biological community of interacting organisms and their physical environment" (*Compact Oxford English Dictionary*, 2003). My usage of the term is solely intended to highlight the progressively complex nature of NPO-government interactions. Like a rainforest or a coral reef, the institutional environment of NPOs is posited as emerging and evolving from relatively less to more complex forms, from sparse to more densely populated, and from low to higher degrees of interconnectedness between the components in its habitat (Ramanath, 2005, p. 47). As an ecosystem evolves, over time, into a more interconnected system of organisms so does the very composition of the species (NPOs and government organizations and all other members in a policy field, such as in health, housing, or education) that constitute it. This evolution in NPO-government relations (in the United States) is briefly reviewed in the paragraphs that follow.

The nonprofit sector in the United States predates formation of the republic. For much of its early years, it operated nearly independently of financial support from the state. Fire departments, schools, orphanages, and hospitals, for instance, primarily relied on private donations, endowment income, and in-kind help. This reliance on private charity was largely a reflection of policy preferences of the time in that the young government was expected to play a minimalistic role in social service provision and voluntarism, and mutual help was hailed as a panacea for most social issues except for those related to child protection, the care of the mentally ill, and juvenile care where state and local governments played a leading role (Smith & Lipsky, 1993, p. 71). In all other areas, private charity played a crucial role. Individual donors, volunteers, members, and beneficiaries of services demanded accountability and effectiveness, but what they sought from the nonprofit was, as Brinkerhoff and Brinkerhoff (2002, p. 8) note, primarily tangible benefits, such as services and value-based benefits. This general expectation from individual donors and others has not changed, but what has changed is the number of "species" that now populate the environment of NPOs and the accountability requirements imposed by each on a nonprofit organization. The values and the effectiveness of nonprofit organizations are not merely assessed by beneficiaries, members, and individual donors but by the government and other oversight agencies, by foundations, the media, and by the public at large. Among the more critical and dominant members of the habitat of NPO-led human service provision is the government at the federal, state, and, increasingly, at the local level.

Government and nonprofit organizations have been working together to produce services since colonial times, but what is new, as Smith and Lipsky (1993) state, "is the *norm* of looking to nonprofits to provide human services, and the substantial dependence of government on the sector [italics in original]" (p. 5). This rise in government as a major player in the NPO environment is attributable to a host of factors many of which are traced to the 1960s and the 1970s when NPOs alongside for-profit players began to be looked on as agents of government as part of a nationwide effort to expand the American welfare state. This fundamental change in the pattern of relationship between government and private sector was labeled by Salamon (1981) as creation of a "third party government." The period, in fact, witnessed the fastest growth in the U.S. nonprofit sector. Nonprofits were perceived as partners to rather than substitutes for government.

Involvement of nonprofit organizations in service delivery was (and continues to be) justified on grounds that it would infuse public service delivery with much needed flexibility, commitment, and cost effectiveness. NPOs

were credited with their capacity to "build the networks of trust and reciprocity" (Boris, 1999, p. 3), were perceived as relatively autonomous from political parties, and were expected to be less bureaucratic and more innovative and function as vital instruments for generating social capital and participation to allow democratic societies to function effectively. The shift toward greater NPO-government interaction was further justified on grounds of what Salamon (1987), in a later work, described as "voluntary failure" in that the voluntary nonprofit sector for reasons of philanthropic insufficiency, particularism, paternalism, and amateurism falls short in its ability to effectively deliver social services independently. Government is, in comparison, more efficient with raising and distributing funds and formulating policies that benefit large portions of the public and is proficient at redistributing resources to correct inequities and negative externalities (Young, 2001). As such, government and nonprofit organizations can complement one another in delivering social services. This rise in the "contracting regime" (Smith & Lipsky, 1993, p. 43) not only spurred growth in nonprofits but also "lured a new heavyweight into the human services ring, namely, for-profit firms, including not only a pioneering group of human services for-profits but also several large, well financed, and diversified corporations" (Frumkin & Andre-Clark, 2000, p. 145). This competition from large business firms poses many challenges for human service NPOs, most notably of increasing operational efficiency.

The optimism over NPO-government dependencies of the 1980s gave way to a heavy dose of skepticism under the Reagan administration when federal spending on most social services was cut. Funding responsibilities were reallocated between levels of government, that is, from federal to the state as was the organization of some responsibilities between government programs. In the process, nonprofit organizations were left to rely on state and local funding, and private charity, as before, was called on to fill the gap. Advocacy NPOs, such as the Independent Sector and the OMB Watch (Office of Management and Budget Watch, www.ombwatch.org), mobilized to address concerns about decreases in funding. These years were, interestingly, marked by growth in the nonprofit sector as a whole: The number of employees in all nonprofit organizations increased by 1 million from 1982 to 1987 (Independent Sector, 2001) and private contributions to the sector doubled between 1980 and 1990. NPOs, particularly those involved in employment and training, community health, and social services, were the hardest hit by Reagan-era government cutbacks and in response employed new methods of fundraising and sought new funding sources including Medicaid, fees-for-service, community fundraising campaigns, such as the United Way, and other income-generating activities.

More intentional relationships among the government, private, and the nonprofit sectors have grown in recent years alongside a call for more cooperation not only between nonprofit organizations and government but also between coalitions and collectives of NPOs that are encouraged to work together to achieve greater efficiency and effectiveness in program delivery. Snavely and Tracy (2000) identify a series of federal initiatives, such as the Department of Housing and Urban Development's Continuum of Care program, Access to Jobs program of the Transportation Equity Act of the 21st Century, the Welfare to Work program, and the Personal Responsibilities and Work Opportunities Reconciliation Act of 1996—all of which require NPOs to collaborate with one another and across sectors to deliver services on behalf of government.

Public service delivery recently expanded to include religious organizations among the list of those contracted to deliver assistance. Despite their long-term involvement in human service delivery, the "charitable choice" provision stirred debate and discussion on the pros and cons of public service provision by faith-based organizations (FBOs). Section 104 of the Personal Responsibilities and Work Opportunities Reconciliation Act of 1996 contains a special section that "allows States to contract with religious organizations, or to allow religious organizations to accept certificates, vouchers, or other forms of disbursement" (Personal Responsibility and Work Opportunity Reconciliation Act, 1996, p. 2105) quite like other nonprofit providers but without limiting the religious character of these organizations and without impinging on the religious freedom of the recipients of program assistance. Recent evidence on the administrative and programmatic infrastructure supporting implementation of government grants and contracts has been varied primarily because organizations that make up the faith-based sector are so varied. What holds true for a larger faith-based nonprofit organization, such as the Salvation Army or the Catholic Charities, may not hold true for smaller-sized faith-based NPOs. While the Bush administration of 2001 vociferously supported involvement of religious organizations in social service provision, there was little concrete thought given to how these programs would be administered among the wide and varied range of faith-based participants. A good number of faith-based groups, particularly local congregations and small-sized faith-based NPOs, lack sufficient experience and infrastructure to fulfill government funding requirements (Campbell, 2008; Chaves, 2004).

It is, admittedly, in response to concerns over capacity that intermediary nonprofit organizations of a great variety sprouted across the developmental landscape. State norms and procedures are transmitted to faith-based nonprofit organizations through the medium of intermediary nonprofits who serve vital bridging and buffering roles (Ramanath, 2007). Effective intermediaries are found to share the faith-based values of the NPOs and are powerful members of the "local social order" within which faith-based nonprofits operate (Fligstein, 2001). These intermediary nonprofits are

yet another species to have emerged as key players in the ecosystem of NPO-government interactions.

Despite these sophisticated policy developments and a long history with NPO-led delivery, the number of people in need of human services shows no signs of falling. As public funding will decrease or at best remain unchanged, nonprofit organizations will be called on to ever greater degrees to serve as partners with the state, with businesses, and with other nonprofit organizations. This may be a tall order for many NPOs, for the environment surrounding their governance and management has grown more complex, denser, and more interconnected. The ever expanding pie of providers of social services, the increasing competition among nonprofit organizations and among nonprofits and for-profits, mounting pressures on nonprofits to demonstrate greater accountability and performance evaluation, dire need for building capacity for greater NPO-led political advocacy, and demands of greater operational efficiency including building capacity to engage staff time in managing a partnership—all carry with them great risks and challenges for nonprofit social service agencies. How must the leader of such a nonprofit manage the complex ecosystem such that a strategic balance is struck between capacity, support, mission, and values? Before the chapter addresses these tensions, the following section reviews the concept of partnerships as it applies to NPO-government interactions.

The Meaning of Partnerships in NPO-Government Interactions

Over the last 2 decades, federal, state, and local governments have developed a variety of interorganizational arrangements with nonprofit organizations to deliver human services. Such arrangements between governments and nonprofits could range from simple networking (described as partnerships with loose linkages between organizations), which lie at one end of the continuum, to partnerships that are fully "collaborative" (Cigler, 1999, pp. 88–89). Cigler distinguishes partnerships based on the complexity of their purpose, the intensity of linkages between members, and the extent of formality in agreements reached. Cigler defines collaborative partnerships as those that entail strong linkages between members and have a specific purpose that is both complex and long-term in nature.

Koebel, Steinberg, and Dyck (1998, pp. 48–52) propose a taxonomy of public-private partnerships based on the extent of power sharing among partners. They build their taxonomy on what they identify as three critical dimensions: the extent to which decision making is shared, the duration of the agreement, and the division of responsibilities across partners. Standardized public services can be provided through partnerships with little power sharing through competitive or preferred contracting. Even when the government writes up a service provision contract with a chosen nonprofit because of its special efficiency or in the absence of alternate providers, Koebel et al. (1998) point out that there indeed could be elements of a "true partnership," that is, of greater power sharing among partners. This may happen because (a) the nonprofit may have discretion over the terms of the contract or (b) the nonprofit may have discretion over implementation and as such could demand a renegotiation of the terms. Greater degree of power sharing is achieved through franchise provision (where government creates or adopts a particular program that can be provided through multiple providers). Where greater uncertainty exists over program requirements (perhaps due to variations in local contexts), fuller power sharing among partners is required.

Smith and Lipsky (1993, p. 224), in contrast, describe NPO-government contractual relationship in social service provision as inherently tipped to the side of the government such that "governments tend to have the upper hand" (p. 224). They argue that over time "government priorities and controls increasingly structure the procedures and priorities of nonprofit providers" (p. 206). Grønbjerg (1993) writes that the manner in which contracts operate "creates a world of uncertainty and ambiguity that easily lends itself to goal displacement and may compromise the nonprofits themselves, their missions, and funder objectives" (p. 261). Sanger (2003) finds that some NPOs may cherry-pick their clients so that performance measures are easily met (p. 37). Bernstein (1991) similarly refers to contractual delivery as "this ongoing, messy process of accommodation and affirmation" wherein the NPOs find ways to manipulate numbers and show positive outcomes to retain their grantee status (p. 178). Her research finds that nonprofit managers often play the "game" and tend to cope and manage the stress and conflict entailed in meeting numerical targets by concentrating their efforts and energies on the client, that is, the intended beneficiary (p. 433).

In line with DeHoog (1990), Brown and Troutt (2004) place the responsibility for successful contractual relationship (and hence a "true" partnership) squarely in the hands of government. They note that within the ranks of government, the political regime must ensure that funding to the program is stable and predictable so that planning is possible and a trustworthy relationship can develop between the NPO and government agencies involved. Program officers in government must be knowledgeable; creative; willing to share a clearly articulated, common mission; diligent in their accountability duties; and willing to enforce standards while respecting the independence and expertise of organizations. Brown and Troutt (2004) conclude that "a participatory process with significant input from the sector [nonprofit sector] into the design of standards, contract terms, and accountability criteria minimizes organizational stress and contributes to a trusting, collaborative, long-term relationship in which both parties can work together smoothly to fulfill a common mission" (p. 25).

Are there measures that nonprofit leaders may put into practice to help build true partnerships and more importantly to help safeguard the organizations' interests as it goes about fulfilling its contractual obligations? The following section will outline some of the key issues in nonprofit governance and the measures that may be taken to effectively lead the nonprofit organization through the game of partnering with government.

Dealing With the Perils and Pitfalls of the "Contracting Regime"

The leader of a nonprofit organization unlike the leader of a government or of a private for-profit enterprise faces special challenges in management. Leaders of nonprofit organizations have a social change mission: a mission that demands balancing values with ambition, greater relevance and impact with efficiency, and technical competency with the ability to inspire (Smillie and Hailey, 2001, p. 133). "Nonprofits," as Frumkin and Andre-Clarke (2000) note, "must create value within operational and environmental constraints that are at once more complex than those faced by corporations and more opaque then those confronted by government" (p. 160). In addition to these hefty demands on a nonprofit leader, is the demand for his or her critical ability to manage partnerships with a range of stakeholders many of whom place competing demands and expectations on the organization. A key member of this stakeholder group, as reviewed in an earlier section, is the government. How is one to negotiate these responsibilities and the inherent tensions such that the mission of the nonprofit toward its client community and its members is served?

Prior to the onset of what is popularly described as the *contracting regime*, NPOs relied primarily on a pool of dedicated, passionate workers; on endowed income; and on individual and in-kind contributions (Smith & Lipsky, 1993). This was the case for many social service nonprofit agencies prior to the 1960s. As Smith and Lipsky describe, "simply put, they were striving to accomplish group purposes" (p. 186). Many nonprofits today, in contrast, must engage with the government to both protect and to expand their financial base. Following the 1960s, many NPOs were indeed founded in response to the availability of government funds. The very decision of seeking funds through contractual arrangements is one that the board and the executive director must weigh carefully. In their pursuit of continued survival and stability, nonprofit organizations are likely to seek opportunities such as those afforded by a government contract. Government funding is often considered the most stable source of revenue for nonprofits. Scholars have, however, deduced a multitude of issues and tensions that can and do arise when NPOs choose to cooperate with the state.

It is worth noting that partnership with government may not be every NPO's cup of tea. A careful, detailed assessment of how an NPO's mission and capacity aligns with the intent of a government grant or contract is critical at the board of director's and the wider organizational level. While some NPOs may categorically decide not to seek government funds, still others may legitimately cite shortages of time, money, and staff to enter and manage such contracts. Some NPOs, for instance, are created in opposition to governmental priorities and would, on principle, not seek working with government. Willingness or otherwise to engage in partnerships with government is additionally related to the nature of client's needs, as well as the perceptual frames and past experiences of its founding members and staff (Ramanath, 2005). Gazley and Brudney (2007) note that, despite great similarity in goals between the two sectors, there is greater reluctance and fear among NPO executives than among their government counterparts to engage in partnership arrangements (p. 411). Such reluctance or proclivity to partner with government is related more to "concerns about internal capacity and mission, rather than external factors such as statutory pressure" (p. 411).

In detailing the issues involved in cooperative relations with government, this chapter focuses on service delivery partnerships wherein a government agency, whether at the federal, state, or local level, funds an NPO by way of a direct grant or a contract. Most scholarship on NPO-government relations, as Smith (2000, p. 183) notes, is focused on direct government funding in the form of grants or contracts. However, it must be kept in mind that government contributes to nonprofit revenues in a variety of ways comprising fees and third-party payments, tax credits and deductions, tax-exempt bonds, and regulations that stimulate NPO service provision. The chapter does not address these other forms of contributions but, instead, focuses on the most extensive yet competitive form of government funding to nonprofit human service providers, namely, through the medium of direct government grants and contracts.

Choosing to Apply for a Government Grant or Contract: The Role of Boards

First and foremost is the very composition and role of the board of an NPO. Public funds demand creation of structures and processes that are akin to the board of a business enterprise. The bureaucracy of public service delivery and the desire to maintain financial stability may consume executive leadership to such an extent that the NPO may be mired in a "subsidy trap." This occurs, according to Brooks (2000), when NPOs that receive a large portion of their revenues from government sources structure their organizations to continue receiving government support. Administrative requirements of managing grants can thus dictate, for instance, the extent to which the board is involved in resource development activities. This can be risky, for it means that board engagement is minimized and

a considerable proportion of resource development activities rests in the hands of the executive of the NPO. NPOs that do rely on government funding find the executive director in the powerful position of being able to self-appoint the board. Smith and Lipsky (1993) find that the boards of government-sponsored agencies "are less affluent than were board members of traditional agencies, in part because they are not expected to contribute their own money to an organization funded primarily by government" (p. 77). Unlike traditional charities and new community organizations, government-sponsored agencies are those set up in direct response to government funding and as such rely wholly and almost exclusively on government funding (Smith & Lipsky, 1993).

Although not involved in direct fund development, NPOs with heavy reliance on government funding may attract board members with connections with high profile political leaders that are able to help with key negotiations and contract renewal. Thus, not all board and executive leadership changes required of and brought about by reliance on government funding are necessarily "bad." What the chief executive of an NPO must keep in mind is that heavy reliance on a singular source of funding creates room for a board that plays a limited role in fund development. Akingbola (2004, p. 455) finds that some nonprofits may become so dependent on government funding that they are forced to "close shop" when government funding dries up. Private fundraising efforts must be pursued simultaneously such that the perils of a subsidy trap are minimized and the board feels vested in such areas as strategic planning, committee involvement, and resource development. In their research on nonprofit social service agencies, Hodge and Piccolo (2005) find that "agencies that encourage board involvement in planning, for example, appear to be less vulnerable and will be more likely to deliver services over a greater period of time" (p. 184).

Board-level assessment of an NPO's willingness and ability to enter a contractual arrangement with government entails, among other aspects, an honest assessment of its capacities to handle the reporting and accountability requirements of a grant or contract. The following section covers how such demands may best be managed by an NPO.

Reporting and Accountability Requirements

The growth in public social welfare expenditures over the last 4 decades has brought with it new and heightened demands on nonprofit organizations to demonstrate their effectiveness in both financial and programmatic areas. These reporting and accountability pressures are not exclusively felt by the nonprofit sector but "are part of a larger trend across the service provision sector, affecting both public agencies and private providers" (Christensen & Ebrahim, 2006, p. 196). Nonprofit organizations can be accountable on multiple levels: upward, lateral, and downward. *Upward accountability* implies accountability to individual and institutional donors and oversight agencies and is enforced to ensure that the resource distributed to a nonprofit is used for the earmarked purpose, and this is monitored through reporting, auditing, and other evaluation and monitoring activities. Such reporting and evaluation, it is found, can interfere with a nonprofit's obligations to its lateral and downward constituents. *Lateral constituents* include an NPO's responsibility to itself, comprising its answerability to its own mission and externally to its key stakeholders. *Downward accountability*, on the other hand, implies its accountability to its clients and beneficiaries. The two latter forms of accountability are, as Christensen and Ebrahim (2006) point out, "more often a result of felt responsibility" and are realized through less formal methods than is upward accountability (p. 196).

Why is discussion of various accountabilities critical to our discussion of leading NPO-government contractual partnerships? Najam (1996) states that nonprofit organizations must internalize the complex layers of accountability demands so that they can "begin creating mechanisms and organizational structures that are equally accountable to their patrons, their clients, and to their own selves" (p. 352). These new demands on nonprofit organizations require that executives develop new skill sets and mediate reporting requirements with government funders and furthermore create a staff culture that both appreciates and finds value in the bureaucracy of a contractual relationship. The executive must, as Smith and Lipsky (1993) note in their influential research, "identify measurable stages of client progress, design improved record keeping systems, and insist that staff keep better records, track client success, and summarize client outcomes in ways that satisfy sponsors (and, it is to be wished, aid the agency in improving performance)" (p. 81).

Christensen and Ebrahim (2006) are more optimistic and find that the demands of upward accountability need not necessarily stifle mission achievement in an NPO. They suggest a host of strategies that nonprofit organizations may choose to implement to better balance various levels of accountabilities listed above, as follows:

1. Enhanced communication between funders and recipients (i.e., between program officers in government and between NPOs) are critical to helping balance various levels of accountability. They find that upward accountability (in the case of this chapter, to government) is likely to be perceived onerous by NPO staffs if they do not see any value to such reporting for their own decision-making processes and activities. If upward accountability is to be satisfactorily realized, then mechanisms must be negotiated and must be mutually planned such that they are beneficial to the NPO and the clients they are seeking to serve.

2. Internal activities, such as staff meetings and community training (lateral accountability measures), appear to result in improving other levels of accountability. In other words, if staff members view reporting and evaluation on

mission achievement as part and parcel of their job profiles, the demands of upward accountability to a funder such as the government will be more easily realized.

3. Staffs in NPOs typically do perceive downward and lateral accountability as their fundamental means to realize NPO missions. As such, executive feedback on their performance in these areas is critical to help maintain staff morale in the face of high reporting requirements. Christensen and Ebrahim (2006) note, "The implication for funders interested in long-term outcomes is that while upward mechanisms are oriented primarily to the measurement of outcomes, downward and lateral mechanisms can enable the achievement of those outcomes (and mission)" (p. 207).

The following section discusses how plans to enter and manage the details of contractual delivery must go hand in hand with discussions about how best to sustain desirable program outcomes over the long run.

Sustaining Outcomes

Government funding of a nonprofit organization is not intended to go in perpetuity. NPOs contracted by the government are supposed to take ownership and maintenance of programs when funding draws to a close. Contract renewals, while desirable for an NPO's budgetary stability as well as staff, client, and program retention, may not happen. Such uncertainty is particularly true for service areas where the extent of interdependence between government and nonprofits is yet to be fully accepted by government (health care being a notable exception). A majority of NPOs are working in areas that are yet to be embraced enthusiastically as part of government policy. Such NPOs need to prepare for the reality that government priority could change. Such changes may be a response to a variety of different pressures that governments themselves face such as having to meet newly identified needs, reallocate funds in response to budgetary shortfalls, and associated program cutbacks.

Akingbola (2004) points to the difficulty that a nonprofit may face in "sustaining and developing competencies it has acquired through the focus of government funding on specific services" (p. 462). This is particularly true of term limited contracts because unless renewed, the NPO would find it challenging to retain staff beyond the contractual period. This may result in less training dedicated to staff due to uncertainty in retaining the contract and even cause attrition of critical staff. Nonprofits tend to shy away from developing continuous improvement plans when government contracts fail to see beyond term limits. Shediac-Rizkallah and Bone (1998) inform us that NPOs need to pay attention to three sets of factors when entering into any type of funding arrangement with an institutional donor: project design and implementation, organizational setting, and broader community environment. Some of these factors, they note, are more amenable to control by program staff than are others. Aspects such as the extent of community involvement in program planning and implementation, training community members to maintain the program independently, choosing an organizational base for the program or program components, and cultivating and nurturing program champions and advocates—are all critical components to sustenance that program staff can well control.

This stated, the possibility of sustaining program or project outcomes beyond government funding is intricately tied to the motivations that guide the very choice of seeking government grants and the extent to which leadership in close coordination with the program staff (in both the NPO and government) are vested in implementing the program to realize quality community-level outcomes. This is well summarized by Shediac-Rizkallah and Bone (1998, p. 105) when they state that the process of sustainability is unlikely to be significantly facilitated until funders and policymakers alter their funding practices (i.e., programs must be driven by the needs of communities rather than by those of donor agencies and experts); unlikely unless designed with local capability in mind; unlikely for long-term sustainability unless enough resources are allocated to yield initial success; and lastly, unlikely unless allocating resources to cover the maintenance and recurrent costs of existing programs or services with a proven track record rather than making investment decisions that are biased toward spending on new programs.

A final key concern is that of maintaining an advocacy voice through the various stages of a grant or contract, that is, from the stage of design to implementation and beyond.

Policy Advocacy

NPOs play an advocacy role in all types of relations with government. Najam (2000, p. 391), for instance, identifies advocacy not as a relationship type but a function of NPO-government relations. As such, Najam (2000) draws a distinction between activist and persuasive advocacy. In a similar vein, Lewis (2001, pp. 44–56) distinguishes between a radical and liberal view of civil society and associates each with two different forms of advocacy. While the radical view is commonly associated with outright revolution, the liberal, more dominant, view is characterized by an emphasis on incremental reform of government (with careful negotiation, balance, and harmony). Although the lines between the two forms of advocacy are highly blurred, advocacy of the liberal kind is more prevalent in the human service provision in the United States. Much policy change and programmatic negotiations take place behind closed doors and are thus more cooperative than confrontational.

Advocacy is an umbrella term and lobbying is one among other forms of advocacy. Berry and Arons (2003) draw the distinction between administrative and legislative lobbying. While all nonprofits that deliver social services do engage in administrative lobbying in that they seek to influence agency administrators who may in turn transmit client needs to legislators, few engage with legislators directly (i.e., few, if any, lobby). Public charities face restricted lobbying regulations in that the Internal Revenue Service (IRS) limits their ability to lobby beyond a "substantial" degree (for a detailed discussion on the history of NPO lobbying regulations, see chapter 5, Berry & Arons, 2003, pp. 47–65). The result of the regulation is that far too many NPOs are intimidated by the ambiguity of the restriction and refrain from being involved in the governmental process altogether. The hesitation to lobby the legislature is particularly acute for those that receive government funding and thus fear "biting the hand that feeds them" (Schmid, 2003). Salamon (1995) disagrees and finds, instead, that government financial support and the extent of political and advocacy activity is positively correlated. Government funds, he finds, increase the extent of political activity and thus are beneficial for NPOs that desire being politically active.

Besides NPO ignorance and widespread fear to influence the governmental process, some NPOs cite budget, time, and capacity as important constraints to participation in policy advocacy. Some reject advocacy as a mission or limit the extent of their advocacy citing paucity of funds. It is, for instance, reasonable to expect NPOs with larger budgets, more staff, and more volunteers to engage more extensively in advocacy and political activity. Larger organizations with greater political leverage can alter the power parity and using various strategies and tactics, can make the government dependent on its services (Ramanath & Ebrahim, in press).

Berry and Arons (2003), however, argue that "the reality of tight resources should not become an excuse for inaction" (p. 163). Developing an advocacy agenda, they note, must be treated as an incremental process wherein as an NPO grows or as government grants and contracts increase in proportion to revenues, managing relations with government will loom larger in NPO activities. They suggest a series of steps that NPOs may undertake to better manage relations with government. These include (a) allocating staff whose exclusive responsibility is to build relations with government, (b) developing lobbying as an everyday task rather than as an activity that is only undertaken in the face of a grave threat or emergency, and (c) building a database of valuable information that is strategically packaged and can be used by a government agency. Berry and Arons note that "having an agency utilize an organizations [NPO's] data base is the optimum position for an interest group" (p. 164). Small NPOs could furthermore form coalitions to enhance their political voice and may further collaborate with nonprofit intermediaries (explained in an earlier section) that are comparatively well established, are better networked, and could potentially help overcome capacity shortfalls. Schmid,

Bar, and Nirel (2008) advocate for the use of volunteers who unlike directors of NPOs, "can be more assertive and persistent in negotiations with policy makers" (p. 597). Many volunteers, they note, have substantial professional experience and are well connected with key personnel in government agencies "which they can use to promote the organization's political activity and espoused goals" (p. 597).

What is lost to many nonprofit organizations is that advocacy could take numerous forms that range from sending newsletters and annual reports to local, state, and federal policymakers to inviting them to events and informal visits, to periodically visiting them and occasionally recognizing them, and to engaging in legislative lobbying. NPOs, without doubt, play a vital role as social service providers. Irrespective of the form of advocacy, engagement with policymakers is of critical importance to all NPOs including those that receive a large proportion of their resources from government. It is certainly possible to argue that engagement in service delivery, by itself, is a means to influence public policy. What is being emphasized here is the need to negotiate the terms and conditions of the contract and to continually keep lines of communication with government, alive.

Failure on the part of an NPO to engage in advocacy is a failure not merely to exercise influence on government but also amounts to losing the opportunity to educate one's clientele about the workings of government and instilling a spirit of civic and political engagement and hence strengthening democratic ideals (Berry & Arons, 2003). This is a vital loss for all nonprofit organizations and may compromise their mission in the long run. Government is, after all, a vital source of funding for NPOs contributing up to 20% to the revenues of non-health-related NPOs in the United States and a far larger percentage to the revenues of human service providers (Berry & Arons, 2003, p. 8). In Berry and Arons's (2003) study sample of 59 public charities, government support made up 33% of the revenues of the participating organizations. This "underestimates the true level of assistance since some of the income that nonprofits count under services are fees paid through government programs" (p. 10). Berry and Arons forcefully argue that "the poor and other disadvantaged constituencies certainly do not have the discretionary income to join interest groups" (p. 8). As such, registered 501(c)(3)s, that is, NPOs, must take the primary responsibility of representing the underrepresented in the halls of government.

Summary

Leaders in governments, businesses, and nonprofit organizations are increasingly aware that they are least likely to address, let alone solve, complex social problems on their own. Government at the federal, state, and more importantly at the local level has come to occupy a decisive position in the ecosystem of NPO delivery of human services.

For several NPOs that deliver services to low-income individuals and families, the government acts more as a complement than as an adversary and looks to NPOs to deliver mainstream, critical services under its directives. This nature of interaction between the two has brought about significant displacement, substitution, and realignment in nonprofit activities over time. While initial debates and discussions centered on the pros and cons of NPO-government interaction, more recent discussions focus on how best to tackle the new, more variegated and dense environment surrounding management of NPO partnerships with government agencies.

Pressure both from within and without an NPO to enter cooperative arrangements with government agencies is indeed a formidable challenge for any leader. It is particularly demanding on a small or medium-sized NPO that wishes to expand its financial base while also improving the coverage and effectiveness of its services. Despite the complexity of the work, the game of managing partnerships can indeed be played and played such that a healthy balance is struck between capacity, support, mission, and organizational values. Drawing on empirical and theoretical work of a variety of scholars, this chapter discussed some of the key issues that must be dealt with prior to and in course of such service delivery. When considering grant or contract funding from a government agency, board members should be mindful of raising questions and concerns in such areas as mission alignment, autonomy, resource parity, culture for service delivery, size, leadership style, real and opportunity costs, the crafting of terms and conditions of agreement, and in monitoring intended outcomes. The level of board involvement in each of these arenas may differ depending on the complexity of the partnership and the type of NPO, yet their role in leading discussions and debates on how a potential grant or contract may impact organizational performance is critical. The director on his or her part must shoulder the responsibility of creating and sustaining an organizational culture that values and sees the bureaucracy of reporting and evaluation as an opportunity to improve staff performance and maintain morale and hence improve client outcomes. The time limits of contracts and the variability in the political environment demands that NPOs give serious consideration to sustenance of effective program outcomes. This may be achieved by involving communities in program planning and implementation, training community members to promote program maintenance, choosing an organizational base for the program or program components, and nurturing community-wide advocates for program continuation.

A final key consideration is the need for retaining an advocacy voice within the NPO, that is, a voice that persistently speaks on behalf of the needs of its underrepresented clientele. This may be achieved through multiple means including forming coalitions to enhance political voice, collaborating with nonprofit intermediaries that are comparatively well established, are better networked, and could serve as vital bridging and buffering agents with government. Other scholars advocate for the use of experienced, well-networked volunteers who unlike directors of NPOs can unreservedly negotiate with policymakers and serve as champions for contract renewal or favorably negotiate terms and conditions of a grant or contract.

Despite a host of issues and dilemmas that NPOs are likely to face in service delivery with the state, it is important for leaders to recognize that financial dependence on government funds, even to a large extent, does not have to translate to organizational (NPO) dependence. Deliberate steps may be taken to maintain a strategic balance. This chapter is a modest attempt to summarize some of the key steps that leaders of NPOs can take to achieve the common end of delivering public good through contractual relations with the state.

References and Further Readings

Akingbola, K. (2004, Summer). Staffing, retention, and government funding. *Nonprofit Management and Leadership, 14*(4), 453–465.

Bernstein, S. R. (1991). *Managing contracted services in the nonprofit agency: Administrative, ethical, and political issues.* Philadelphia: Temple University Press.

Berry, J. M., & Arons, D. F. (2003). *A voice for nonprofits.* Washington, DC: Brookings Institution Press.

Boris, E. T. (1999). Nonprofit organizations in a democracy: Varied roles and responsibilities. In E. T. Boris & C. E. Steuerle (Eds.), *Nonprofits & government: Collaboration and conflict* (pp. 3–29). Washington, DC: Urban Institute Press.

Brinkerhoff, J. M., & Brinkerhoff, D.W. (2002). Government-nonprofit relations in comparative perspective: Evolution, themes and new directions. *Public Administration and Development, 22,* 3–18.

Brooks, A. C. (2000). Public subsidies and charitable giving: Crowding out, crowding in, or both? *Journal of Policy Analysis and Management, 18*(3), 451–464.

Brown, L. K., & Troutt, E. (2004). Funding relations between nonprofits and government: A positive example. *Nonprofit and Voluntary Sector Quarterly, 33*(5), 5–27.

Campbell, D. (2008, November). *Do faith-based initiatives spur enduring local partnerships? A post-initiative analysis.* Paper presented at the annual meeting of the Association for Research on Nonprofit Organizations and Voluntary Action, Philadelphia, PA.

Chaves, M. (2004). *Congregations in America.* Cambridge, MA: Harvard University Press.

Christensen, R. A., & Ebrahim, A. (2006). How does accountability affect mission? The case of a nonprofit serving immigrants and refugees. *Nonprofit Management and Leadership, 17*(2), 195–209.

Cigler, B. A. (1999). Conditions for the emergence of multicommunity collaborative organizations. *Policy Studies Review, 16*(1), 86–102.

Compact Oxford English Dictionary. (2003). Oxford University Press. Retrieved July 30, 2009, from http://www.askoxford.com/dictionaries/compact_oed/?view=uk

DeHoog, R. H. (1990). Competition, negotiation, or cooperation: Three models for service contracting. *Administration & Society, 22*(3), 317–340.

Fligstein, N. (2001). Social skill and the theory of fields. *Sociological Theory, 19*(2), 105–125.

Frumkin, P., & Andre-Clark, A. (2000). When missions, markets, and politics collide: Values and strategy in the nonprofit human services. *Nonprofit and Voluntary Sector Quarterly, 29*(1), 141–163.

Gazley, B., & Brudney, J. L. (2007). The purpose (and perils) of government-nonprofit partnership. *Nonprofit and Voluntary Sector Quarterly, 36*(3), 389–415.

Grønbjerg, K. A. (1993). *Understanding nonprofit funding: Managing revenues in social services and community development organizations.* San Francisco: Jossey-Bass.

Hodge, M. M., & Piccolo, R. F. (2005). Funding source, board involvement techniques, and financial vulnerability in nonprofit organizations: A test of resource dependence. *Nonprofit Management and Leadership, 16*(2), 171–190.

Independent Sector. (2001). Employment in the nonprofit sector. In *Nonprofit almanac: Facts and figures.* Retrieved July 20, 2009, from http://www.independentsector.org/PDFs/npemployment.pdf

Koebel, T. C., Steinberg, R., & Dyck, R. G. (1998). Public-private partnerships for affordable housing: Definitions and applications in an international perspective. In C. T. Koebel (Ed.), *Shelter and society: Theory, research, and policy for nonprofit housing* (Chap. 3, pp. 39–69). New York: State University of New York Press.

Lewis, D. (2001). *The management of non-governmental development organizations: An introduction.* London: Routledge.

Najam, A. (1996). NGO accountability: A conceptual framework. *Development Policy Review, 14*(4), 339–354.

Najam, A. (2000). The four-C's of third sector-government relations: Cooperation, confrontation, complementarity, and co-optation. *Nonprofit Management and Leadership, 10*(4), 375–396.

Personal Responsibility and Work Opportunity Reconciliation Act, Pub. L. No. 104-193, 110 Stat. 2105 (1996).

Ramanath, R. (2005). *From conflict to collaboration: Nongovernmental organizations and their negotiations for local control of slum and squatter housing in Mumbai, India.* Unpublished doctoral dissertation, Virginia Polytechnic Institute and State University, Blacksburg, VA. Retrieved July 30, 2009, from http://www.ipg.vt.edu/papers/Dissertation_Ramya_Ramanath.pdf

Ramanath, R. (2007, November 14). *Buffering organizational identity in public service delivery: The case of ten small-sized faith-related community organizations and a local capacity building intermediary organization in Grand Rapids, Michigan.* Paper presented at the annual meeting of the Association for Research on Nonprofit Organizations and Voluntary Action (ARNOVA), Atlanta, Georgia.

Ramanath, R., & Ebrahim, A. (in press). Strategies and tactics in NGO-government relations: Insights from slum housing in Mumbai. *Nonprofit Management and Leadership.*

Salamon, L. M. (1981). Rethinking public management: Third-party government and the changing forms of public action. *Public Policy, 29*, 255–275.

Salamon, L. M. (1987). Partners in public service. In W. W. Powell (Ed.), *The nonprofit sector: A research handbook* (Chap. 6, pp. 99–117). New Haven, CT: Yale University Press.

Salamon, L. M. (1995). *Explaining nonprofit advocacy: An exploratory analysis.* Paper presented at the Independent Sector Spring Research Forum, Alexandria, Virginia.

Sanger, M. (2003). *The welfare marketplace: Privatization and welfare reform.* Washington, DC: Brookings Institution Press.

Schmid, H. (2003). Rethinking the policy of contracting out social services to nongovernmental organizations: Lessons and dilemmas. *Public Management Review, 5*, 307–323.

Schmid, H., Bar, M., & Nirel, R. (2008). Advocacy activities in nonprofit human service organizations: Implications for policy. *Nonprofit and Voluntary Sector Quarterly, 37*(4), 581–602.

Shediac-Rizkallah, & Bone, L. R. (1998). Planning for the sustainability of community-based health programs: Conceptual frameworks and future directions for research, practice and policy. *Health Education Research, 13*(1), 87–108.

Smillie, I., & Hailey, J. (2001). *Managing for change: Leadership, strategy and management in Asian NGOs.* London: Earthscan.

Smith, S. R. (2000). Government financing of nonprofit activity. In E. T. Boris & E. Steuerle (Eds.), *Nonprofit and government: Collaboration and conflict* (Chap. 5, pp. 177–210). Washington, DC: Urban Institute Press.

Smith, S. R., & Lipsky, M. (1993). *Nonprofits for hire.* Cambridge, MA: Harvard University Press.

Snavley, K., & Tracy, M. B. (2000). Collaboration among rural nonprofit organizations. *Nonprofit Management and Leadership, 11*(2), 145–165.

Young, D. R. (2001). Third party government. In J. S. Ott (Ed.), *Nature of the nonprofit sector* (Chap. 30, pp. 365–368). Boulder, CO: Westview Press.

60

WHAT NONPROFIT LEADERS SHOULD KNOW ABOUT BASIC ECONOMIC PRINCIPLES

ALVIN KAMIENSKI

North Park University

It is likely no coincidence that Adam Smith's (1776) *The Wealth of Nations*, considered by many the origin of modern economics, was published the same year a fledgling nation issued its Declaration of Independence, which asserted, "we hold these truths to be self-evident, that all men are created equal, that they are endowed by their Creator with certain unalienable Rights, that among these are Life, Liberty and the pursuit of Happiness" (Armitage, 2007, p. 56). These documents serve as evidence of the contemporary philosophical thinking in the late 18th century, ideals that further fashioned our current understanding of basic economic principles:

- All acts are *rational.*

  People seek to maximize happiness—also known as utility.

  Businesses seek to maximize profits.

- Resources used to achieve those ends are perpetually *scarce.*
- Decisions are made so that *new benefits exceed new costs.* Every decision involves choice concerning how to best use and distribute those precious gifts.

Yet it has become common practice to substitute the pursuit of happiness with greed and economics with finance. The task of large, publicly traded for-profit companies—the fiduciary responsibility—is to create wealth for its shareholders. Because 87% of sales in the United States are generated by these firms, the vast majority of our time focuses on the actions of those profit-oriented firms (McConnell, Brue, & Flynn, 2009). However, from an employment perspective, only 1 in 5 Americans is employed by these firms (Nickels, McHugh, & McHugh, 2005). Yet on any given evening's national or even local nightly newscast, the focus of the day's business events will more often than not have an eye toward these large financially focused organizations.

One goal for this chapter, and an altruistic charge to undergraduate students, is to return the focus of economics back to its origins. The definition of economics traces its etymology to the Greek *oikonomos*, which refers to the concepts of care or stewardship of the resources that a household (or a nation) has with which to provide for its dependents (Singer, 1991). For example, take two large companies, a nonprofit, such as Habitat for Humanity, and a publicly traded for-profit, such as Microsoft. Microsoft may contribute to the happiness of consumers by providing software to make run our computers. But it made its investors even happier by earning $17.7 billion in profits in 2008, paying out $4 billion in dividends (Microsoft, 2008). Habitat for Humanity, driven by social welfare to improve community well-being, sought to make its customers happy by providing housing for the underprivileged. In so doing, they succeeded in earning a $59 million profit in 2007, all of which was reinvested (Habitat for Humanity, 2007). To say that Microsoft is ignorant of economics is untrue; but Habitat for Humanity in its efforts to provide care seems more aligned to *oikonomos* and the true spirit of the origins of the discipline of economics.

Keeping in mind care as a driving principle in economics, those who study economics in its native form agree that economic efforts are driven by the desire to be efficient across two dimensions:

1. *Productive efficiency*—production should use the smallest amount of scarce resources, output needs created with the least inputs possible.

2. *Allocation efficiency*—when successful at productive efficiency, businesses keep prices low and produce more output. Consumers can afford to purchase the optimal mix of goods and services to create happiness.

How Nonprofits Are Affected

Nonprofits, while exempt from taxation, are not exempt from the basic principles of economics. However, there are two particular dimensions above to which a nonprofit modus operandi may differ significantly. First, it must be dispelled that nonprofit organizations are not interested in profit. On the contrary, while their missions may not be driven by the profit motive, the ability to retain a portion of annual income for the purposes of reinvestment and self-sufficiency is tantamount for sustainability (McDonald, 2007). Indeed, the church that cannot adequately retain some funding for future use will likely find that divine intervention is less reliable than a profit orientation.

The difference then is in the amount or degree of profit that they may seek. It is unlikely that a nonprofit and its stakeholders would accept the $4.55 billion profit that Exxon Mobil posted in the first quarter alone of 2009; nor would they accept the $1.427 billion dollar loss posted by the Ford Motor Company during that same time period (Exxon Mobil, 2009; Ford Motor Company, 2009). Rather, they may be more oriented toward, as Herbert Simon called it, a *satisficing* approach (1957). Under this method, the nonprofit sets a reasonable profit target that is consistent with the expectations of its key constituents, including its board, management, employees, and customers.

The second significant difference is the way in which nonprofits fill the gaps left by allocation inefficiencies. When considering the market for services such as legal counsel, one recognizes that service providers are highly educated professionals whose market values command fees that exceed several hundreds of dollars per hour. The prices of these services are prohibitive to those who cannot afford them, and thus, those people and society as a whole experience less happiness. This creates an opportunity whereby an individual or an organization can provide services pro bono. So what would underlie a lawyer's willingness to accept submarket rates for services rendered? The answer is provided by the third economic principle, *marginalism*. That lawyer recognizes that her happiness in life is greater when benefits exceed costs. She might lose $500, the opportunity cost of one hour of her time providing council for free, but her recognition of the intangible benefits—the positive feeling of aiding a fellow person, the smile on that client's face, or the knowledge that justice can be served—must exceed the chance to bill someone else who could afford her

time. In that way, respecting the definition of economics as rooted in care, the pursuit of happiness for one person can and will include the betterment and happiness of another, which in turn creates a human condition that is perpetually advancing due to rational, self-interested behavior. It is this particular facet that makes nonprofit a necessity in every economic system.

Why This Study Is Important to Undergraduates

Recent employment trends indicate that an increasing number of young professionals are choosing to pursue careers in nonprofit management (Tschirhart, Reed, Freeman, & Anker, 2008). As the lines between managing for-profit and nonprofit businesses converge, it is imperative that undergraduate students have at least a cursory knowledge of the economic principles that are so regularly embraced in the larger business sector. As the world of business evolves to include more overt attention to issues of business ethics and justice, as evidenced by the emergence of the triple bottom line—people-social, planet-environmental, and profit-stakeholders—the undergraduate student who articulates the sense of caring embedded in the original concept of economics is in a unique position to succeed (Grisham, 2009). If embraced by future leaders, this balanced, analytical perspective of marginal benefits exceeding marginal costs may permeate both for-profit and nonprofit organizations in an implicitly conjoined pursuit of the enhancement of societal well-being.

The Circular Flow

Now that the basic principles of economics are understood—rationality, scarcity, and marginalism—it is imperative to describe how the participants in economics—*businesses*, *consumers*, and the *government*—come together. The buying and selling of goods, services, and resources in return for cash flows exist in an environment of mutual interdependence. These interactions and transactions are articulated in the circular flow shown in Figure 60.1.

In a limited summary of key interactions, people proffer their labor resource in exchange to businesses who use that input in conjunction with other resources—such as raw materials—to produce the products and services that consumers can buy using the wages paid to them by these producers. Each of the two parties is interlocked in a relationship where both acknowledge each other's motive, profit making for the business and the pursuit of happiness for the consumer. Each arrow in the diagram represents the flow of both a tangible item, for example, a product such as a cheeseburger or a resource such as labor, as well as a monetary flow, for example, consumer expenditures or wages.

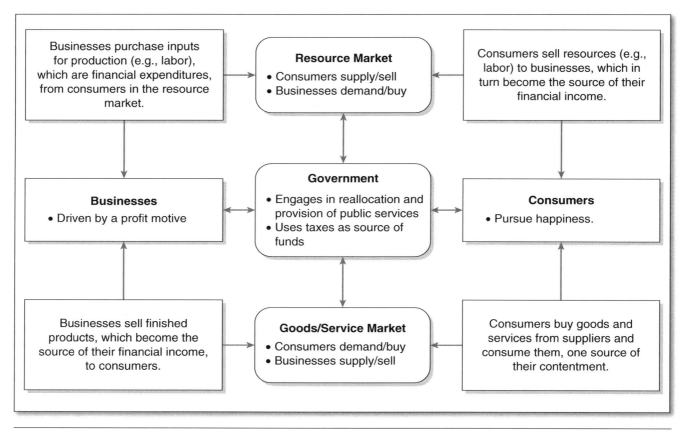

Figure 60.1   The Circular Flow

The key takeaway in reflecting on the circular flow is to realize the need for symbiosis between the participants. In a competitive, reasonably free market system as exists currently in the United States, there can be few interactions as desirable as a person going to work at a job he or she enjoys and getting paid a wage that allows him or her to consume products that both sustain and entertain, saving a bit of the income for future use and paying reasonable taxes to a government that provides infrastructure, defense, health care, and education.

How Nonprofits Are Affected

Nonprofits exist within the businesses box. The role of all businesses is to create and sell, at a profit, products and services by purchasing the appropriate mix of resource inputs. This may not always bode well for social well-being as if left unchecked, firms would pursue only profitable activities. The nonprofit then serves as a socially oriented organization correcting for the shortfalls of the market. The response from firms in the nonprofit space, such as the American Red Cross, was to be expected in the wake of Hurricane Katrina; on the other hand, one would not predict with equal certainty that the investors of firms who produced the pumps, cleaning supplies, heavy machinery, and food stuffs consumed by the Red Cross would allow those firms to act with equal selflessness. The government in recognition of the critical space nonprofit organizations occupy intervenes to reinforce the role of caregiving in the profit-oriented marketplace by adjusting the flows in the circular flow.

As evidence of its desire to encourage the formation of nonprofits, the government provides an exemption from corporate taxation. For the nonprofit, the arrow representing cash flows between businesses and the government is unidirectional. The government provides flows in the form of grants and direct support to the nonprofit but does not demand tax flows in return. Salvaging these tax funds allows the nonprofit to invest a greater percentage of its revenue in the provision of its services while concurrently providing an incentive for entrepreneurship (Auteri, 2003). Business operators interested in investor returns and in social returns find the government a willing partner in the formation of new opportunities to create wealth—defined more broadly than financially.

The second principle that affects the nonprofit organization is the redistribution of income. Many nonprofits track and monitor the percentages of their income by sources, especially in regards to government funding (Luksetich, 2008). Given the fiscal policies of our government, the nonprofit is affected within the circular flow by being able to access governmental funding with the consumer as the second tier conduit. When broken into deciles, in 2006, it was estimated that greater than 50% of the annual income in the United States accrued to the highest income-earning households, while less than 4% of income accrued to the lowest 20% of households (U.S. Census Bureau, 2007). With its progressive tax system, the United States engages in a practice of taxing higher income earners and redirecting those monies to the lesser earners. These inflows represent additional sources of consumption expenditures that may enable targeted populations to consume additional goods and services. The nonprofit organization can fill gaps in market systems by providing critical goods and services in exchange for a modest revenue stream that flows from the government first through the consumer and ultimately back to the nonprofit business. This indirect revenue stream increases the funding nonprofits receive from the government and provides more opportunities for sustainability.

The Macroeconomic Environment

To the three key economic principles—rationality, scarcity, and marginalism—have been added the interdependence of the three key constituents: businesses, consumers, and the government. It is now important to frame the larger context in which nonprofit businesses operate. Macroeconomics is generally defined as an examination of the economy as a whole and primarily attributable to the operations of a nation such as the United States (Samuelson & Nordhaus, 2004). By aggregating and estimating all the economic interactions, macroeconomics interests itself in issues such as output, income, employment, prices, and production as a whole.

While the study of macroeconomics is a wonderful endeavor, especially in light of an ever-globalizing business environment, there are two facets of macroeconomics that have policy implications that are of extreme relevance to nonprofit organizations. First off, it should be noted that in the context of the U.S. economic system, researchers have identified three common goals: *growth, full employment,* and *price-level stability* (McConnell et al., 2009). Three aggregate measures of macroeconomics help to determine if these three goals are being met: gross domestic product (GDP), the unemployment rate, and the consumer price index (CPI), respectively. Collectively, they can determine the overall economic conditions in the domestic economy, which in turn will affect the policy decisions that are made to attempt to stimulate or curb economic growth. Table 60.1 presents a summary of common conditions seen among these relationships.

When in a recessionary environment, expansionary *fiscal policy* infers increases in governmental spending on items such as schools, infrastructure, and defense, and it is often accompanied by a reduction in taxation. These measures are intended to remand money for consumption back to consumers and to provide additional revenue sources to businesses that can be used to hire workers. Both of these elements existed in President Obama's 2009 American Recovery and Reinvestment Act (Fremstad, 2009). Conversely, when in an inflationary environment, contractionary policies, the inverse of expansionary policy—increases in taxes and decreases in government spending—are implemented. These types of policies led to the balancing of the budget during the Clinton administration (Elmendorf, Liebman, & Wilcox, 2001).

The above actions are those taken by the executive and legislative branches of the government. Additionally, there is a partnership of the Federal Reserve System (also known as "the Fed"), the central bank of the United States, with the *monetary policy* that creates a flexible yet stable monetary supply to fuel both consumption and expansion. In concert with expansionary fiscal policy, the

(T) Data Measured	Direction	Economic Environment	Traditional Fiscal Policy	Traditional Monetary Policy
Gross domestic product growth	Declining			
Unemployment	Rising	Recessionary	Expansionary	Easy money
Consumer price index	Declining			
Gross domestic product growth	Rising			
Unemployment	Declining	Inflationary	Contractionary	Tight money
Consumer price index	Rising			

Table 60.1 Macroeconomic Measures and Traditional Policy Outcomes

Fed will adjust its target interest rates to spark economic activity in what is termed an *easy money* policy. When the desire is to stimulate growth, the Fed will take actions, primarily lowering its key target interest rate, to make money more available to consumers and businesses alike. Conversely, in concert with a desired reduction in economic growth, the Fed will employ a *tight money* policy in which the key target interest rate will be raised to provide a disincentive to borrowing and spending and an incentive to savings.

How Nonprofits Are Affected

Nonprofit organizations are highly affected by operations in the macroeconomy as well as by the policies that correspond. In times of economic stagnation, the first likelihood is that nonprofits will suffer as it relates to their ability to fund raise. Research has shown that for every 100 points gained in the Standard & Poor's 500 Index, approximately $600 million is lost in philanthropy (Indiana University Center on Philanthropy & Giving USA Foundation, 2009). However, these funding shortfalls from the private sector may be somewhat offset by new spending by the government sector. However, historically these monies are allocated for infrastructure projects that are highly correlated with employment (Bateman & Taylor, 2007). Thus, social and human service agencies are likely to not see substantial portions of these increases in government spending. It may also come to pass that monies originally earmarked for human service spending are allocated toward other projects in the short-term as states and the federal government respond to the decrease in their tax inflows. The likelihood, then, is that the nonprofit will be adversely affected in periods of slowed economic growth.

Alternatively, expansionary fiscal policy is often coupled with easy monetary policy accompanied by a lowering of interest rates. So while sources of annual operating or fundraising capital may diminish in the short run, sources of debt capital are generally much easier to access and at substantial interest expense cost savings. But nonprofits must be cautious not to rely too heavily on borrowing as potential donors may not be interested in paying for interest expense.

The opposite is often true during a period of quickened economic growth accompanied by the contractionary fiscal policy and tight monetary policy. The growth of wealth to consumers is a likely boon as it was estimated in 2009 that every 100-point increase in the Standard & Poor's 500 Index creates $1 billion in new philanthropic giving (Indiana University Center on Philanthropy & Giving USA Foundation, 2009). However, decreases in government spending, increases in income taxes, and relatively higher interest rates are all conditions that will make it increasingly difficult for the nonprofit to sufficiently diversify its funding sources.

Private, Public, and Quasi-Public Goods and Services

To review, economics is primarily concerned with how its three key principles—rationality, scarcity, and marginalism—are codependent between the three major constituents—business, consumers, and the government—within the overarching context of the fiscal and monetary policies that accompany a nation's macroeconomic environment as measured by GDP, unemployment, and the price level. Delving deeper into economic issues germane to the nonprofit, the analysis shifts to issues traditionally considered microeconomic. The commonly held definition of *microeconomic* is the study of a particular economic entity, such as an industry (also known as an assembly of similar producers competing for the same customers), a particular business, or an individual household (McConnell et al., 2009). Microeconomics analyzes and attempts to predict the ways that these smaller organisms behave within the larger context, taking into account its unique constraints, capabilities, and access to resources.

Within microeconomics, we look at more specific issues such as the types of products or services a company produces and how its properties determine the ways in which that company can be successful. It is important to define the two dimensions that further define the things we consume. The two dimensions relevant to all goods are rivalry and excludability. *Rivalry* is akin to competing for purchase. Since resources are scarce and output limited, there is a limited supply available for consumption. When a unit is purchased by one party, it reduces the likelihood that subsequent units will be available to be consumed by others. In essence, one person's consumption may preclude another's. This consequence of scarcity serves to limit the amount of potential societal well being that emanates from consumption as there is always a hard cap on the amount of goods and services that can be consumed and the benefits from them will always accrue only to a limited number.

The second dimension of all goods is *excludability*. Within a market system, as opposed to systems rooted in socialism, consumption is an option accessible only to those with both the willingness (or desire) and the ability (or money) to purchase. It is more than likely that a large proportion of consumers would like, or are willing, to be surrounded by luxury goods, such as big homes with expensive décor; however, a much smaller fraction of those willing have the monetary ability to acquire those comforts. The fact that price can be a barrier to purchasing is the excludability dimension of a product. Similar to rivalry, excludability limits the amount of happiness available in the system as the benefits of such consumption, whether conspicuous or otherwise, accrue to a limited portion of the population.

The combination of rivalry and excludability are the fundamental characteristics of the *private goods* within the market system. Examples of these abound and the range includes everything imaginable that can be bought from the dollar store to the grocery store to the department store and beyond. Goods and services for which the opposite is true are classified as *public goods*. For these goods and services, one person's consumption does not limit the prospect for another, thus eliminating rivalry; simultaneously, the pricing of these items are in essence free—or indirectly so—thus eliminating price as an excludable dimension. Examples of these would include things such as public sidewalks, a Fourth of July fireworks display, and a disaster alert system. Consumers pay for these indirectly through taxes; no one is asked to provide explicitly for his or her provision nor is anyone prevented from participating fully in her or his benefits.

The final classification of goods and services are those considered to be *quasi-public* goods. These types of goods or services are those for which the producers could be either from government entities or from the private sector. This market is primarily occupied by service providers as most do not primarily engage in the construction of physical goods but are active in the provision of services such as public safety, child care, and education. Even those goods for which the government does play a significant role in production, such as roads and bridges, a portion of the labor may be provided by government employees but a high proportion will also be subcontracted to the private sector.

How Nonprofits Are Affected

While there is no specific provision that prevents nonprofit enterprises from producing goods or services in either the private, public, or quasi-public markets, a high percentage of these firms will be found operating in the quasi-public space. Table 60.2 shows examples of industries that occupy each space.

From above, it can be inferred that many more offerings exist in markets where providers could be for-profit, nonprofit, or governmental. The key takeaway for the undergraduate student is to recognize there are a multitude of career options available in nonprofit settings where the business models and challenges require the same skills and acumen as necessary in traditional for-profit settings.

There is one particular nuance associated with the provision of public goods that often affect nonprofit operations. When products and services are available at no cost—the lack of excludability—then consumers can reap the benefits of use without contributing any financial support for production. In many ways, this can be positive. For example, as it relates to the tourism trade, travelers to our country should expect to be protected by the law enforcement officials that American taxpayers support. In absence of this safety, our economy, specifically the travel and tourism sector, would suffer. In other ways, this can be

	For-Profits	Nonprofits	Government
Private goods & services	Electronics Automobiles Airplanes		
	Entertainment Media Consumer products		
Quasi-public goods & services	Education Medical care Road construction Counseling services Child care Legal counsel		
Public goods			National defense Sidewalks

Table 60.2 Examples of Firms in Public, Private, and Quasi-Public Markets

a negative, a scenario referred to as the free rider problem (Gerber & Wichardt, 2009). There has been much debate and discussion regarding this issue.

Demand

Thus far, we have covered rationality, scarcity, and marginalism; business consumers and the government; fiscal and monetary policies, GDP, unemployment, and the price level; and private, public, and quasi-public goods and services. But no textbook including economics would be complete without a discussion of supply and demand. *Ceteris paribus* (holding all else constant), the analysis will stay at the microeconomic level and use the example of a private, nonprofit enterprise competing in the market for elementary school students, a tuition-based private elementary school. Before proceeding, it is helpful to remember that this entity, while not interested in maximizing its total profit intake, is interested in satisficing. The initial focus will be on the revenue, or demand, side of this nonprofit school's business.

Demand is demonstrated as a quantified expression of a consumer's willingness and ability to purchase a good or service at a particular price. Let's assume for the time being that this school is the only private elementary school in a neighborhood. Assume also that there are free public schools as well in the market. If a poll was conducted of the citizenry that asked, How many children would you be willing to send to the private school if the tuition were as follows, then Table 60.3 shows the responses of the entire local population.

The most traditional presentation of demand, as expressed in Table 60.3, is the demand curve shown in Figure 60.2 in which the law of demand can be seen: As price falls, the quantity demanded for a good or service increases.

Price (annual tuition)	Quantity Demanded (number of students)
$10,000	0
$9,000	200
$8,000	400
$7,000	600
$6,000	800
$5,000	1,000
$4,000	1,200
$3,000	1,400

Table 60.3 Firm Demand for Private Elementary School

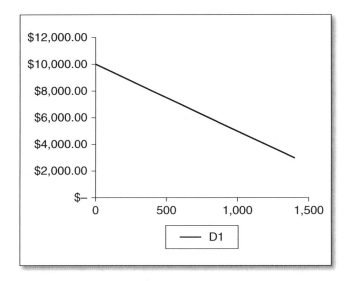

Figure 60.2 Firm Demand Curve for Private Elementary School

Determinants of Demand

Figure 60.2 shows the combination of quantities of goods and services demanded allowing price as the only variable, ceteris paribus. There are many other nonprice factors that can increase or decrease the overall demand. Changes in these conditions create a new set of quantities demanded for the same prices. Figure 60.3 depicts these possibilities.

The major reasons that these shifts could occur are as follows:

1. *Income.* When the income of consumers increases, they become more willing and able to spend money. Let's assume a household has an income earner who gets a pay raise. This household that traditionally sent its children to the public school might now enroll them in the private school. Thus, demand for a private elementary school would shift from D1 to D2. When income declines, the opposite would be true, and demand would shift from D1 to D3.

2. *Preferences.* When trends in consumer tastes change, demand will also change. Let's assume a report is released by an independent agency that infers that private school education will add 20 years to a life span, help a person lose weight, and make a person more money. Even with the same income, if consumers see new benefits in consumption, then their willingness to purchase increases, and demand shits from D1 to D2. If the report contained the opposite, the inverse would be true, and demand would shift from D1 to D3.

3. *Number of buyers.* If more people come to a marketplace, the likelihood of consumption, based on this increase in the volume of purchasers, will increase demand. Let's suppose new families move into the

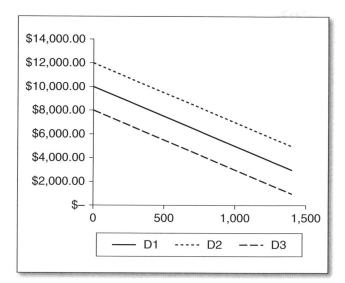

Figure 60.3 Demand Curves for Private Elementary School

school's neighborhood. Within this new population, there will be more consumers who rationally perceive happiness to come through a private education, and thus, demand will shift from D1 to D2. If there is a flight of the population from the community, again the opposite occurs, and demand would shift from D1 to D3.

4. *Prices of related goods and services.* Consumption decisions are not made in a vacuum. Consumption of one good often necessitates the consumption of another. All collegiate students understand when purchasing education that there are correlated expenditures. The undergraduate is intimately aware of the financial burdens of paying for the room, board, and textbooks that accompany university attendance. The levels of prices of these complementary goods can have a significant impact on consumer willingness and ability to buy that core product or service. Let's assume that the prices of textbooks dramatically increase for the family considering sending their child to private school. This increase in correlated costs leaves less household income to purchase tuition. This will have a negative effect on demand for elementary education and cause demand to shift from D1 to D3. If, on the other hand, a private elementary school bundles textbooks in with tuition, then this may have a positive impact on demand and shift the demand curve from D1 to D2.

There is another set of circumstances under which the prices of related goods and services applies, and that is for goods that are considered as substitutes to the core product. Substitutes are not competitors but rather products, which function to provide alternate paths to happiness. For now, let's move our example to preschool. Parents might have two major choices as it relates to

their young child's daily activities. They may be concurrently in the market for a preschool in which they are comparing two schools (School A and School B) as well as evaluating a daycare facility that is noncurricular and purely social. School A and School B would be competitors to each other while the daycare facility would be a substitute.

With this substitute relationship in effect, the family leaning toward either School A or School B will find itself reevaluating its options based on pricing changes by the daycare facility. If the facility raises its rates, then the family is more likely to send their child to a preschool thus increasing the demand for preschool and shifting the demand curve from D1 to D2. Conversely, if the daycare center lowers its prices, then parents who were considering preschool are much more likely to switch to daycare, driving down demand from D1 to D3.

Supply

If demand is an expression of consumer willingness and ability to consume certain quantities of goods or services at a variety of prices, then supply is the correlated microeconomic analysis of supplier willingness to produce a certain quantity of goods and services across those ranges of prices. Ceteris paribus, the analysis will stay at the microeconomic level and use the example of a private nonprofit competing in the market for elementary school students. Reflecting back, it must be recalled that this enterprise is not necessarily interested in profit maximization but is indeed in being modestly profitable. The firm spends its energies thinking not only about revenues but also about the cost it can control as it purchases the inputs necessary to educate its students. In its budgeting and planning processes, the school considers two major types of expenses—variable and fixed costs. *Variable costs* are those whose levels are dependent on the quantity of output, while *fixed costs* are independent of the quantities produced. For example, variable costs for a school would include teacher salaries and fixed costs would include the building's rent.

Let's assume again for the time being that this school is the only private elementary school in a neighborhood. Assume also that there are free public goods, or public schools, as well in the market. If you were able to interview the management of the private school and ask, How many children would you be willing to educate if the tuition were as follows? then Table 60.4 shows the responses of the entire local population.

The most traditional presentation of supply, as expressed in Table 60.4, is the supply curve shown in Figure 60.4 in which the law of supply can be seen: As price rises, the quantity supplied of a good or service increases.

Price (annual tuition)	Quantity Supplied (number of students)
$10,000	1600
$9,000	1400
$8,000	1200
$7,000	1000
$6,000	800
$5,000	600
$4,000	400
$3,000	200

Table 60.4 Firm Supply for Private Elementary School

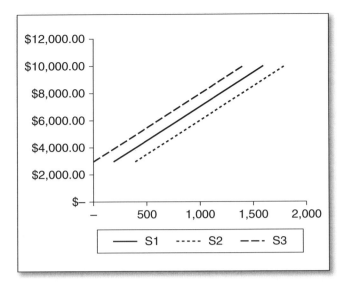

Figure 60.5 Supply Curves for Private Elementary School

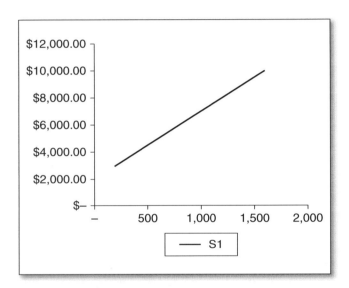

Figure 60.4 Firm Supply Curve for Private Elementary School

Determinants of Supply

As with demand, supply shows the combination of quantities of goods and services supplied allowing price as the only variable, ceteris paribus. There are many other nonprice factors that can increase or decrease the overall supply. Changes in these conditions create a new set of quantities supplied for the same prices. Figure 60.5 depicts these possibilities. The major reasons that these shifts in supply could occur are as follows:

1. *Resource prices.* Every firm, whether for-profit or nonprofit, begins with an analysis of its costs, especially those controllable, variable costs. The firm's output may be heavily reliant on the levels of the prices of the resources it purchases in production. For example, if the available pool

of teachers available for hire is predominantly younger, less experienced, and less specialized, those teachers may command a lower wage rate in the market. The firm realizes it can hire more teachers without increasing its costs and can expand its student enrollment capacity thus moving supply from S1 to S2. If, on the other hand, these young teachers organize in a unionlike assembly and mandate a certain wage that is higher than the wage rate the school is willing to pay, then the school will respond by hiring fewer teachers and thus allowing fewer students to enroll. As a result, supply would shift from S1 to S3.

2. *Number of sellers.* Similar to the logic that applied to the number of buyers as related to demand, if more producers come to a marketplace, then the likelihood of consumption, based on this increase in the volume of producers, will increase supply. Let's suppose that other firms seeing a lack of competitors move into the neighborhood of the new school. Within this new population of producers, there will be more organizations who can educate children, and thus, supply will shift from S1 to S2. If these new firms eventually decide to close their doors and exit the community, the opposite occurs and supply would shift from S1 to S3.

3. *Taxes and subsidies.* In general, a consumer is only interested in the total acquisition cost of the good inclusive of any taxes required to be paid upon purchase. The consumer will be relatively indifferent to the allocation of a good's cost versus taxes, choosing to simplify and lump both costs together in considering whether to buy or not. As such, taxes serve to raise the total acquisition cost of an item. Let's assume that states chose to tax students who attend private elementary schools. This would have the effect of making private elementary schools more costly in aggregate. Businesses view these taxes analogous to costs in terms of the impacts they have on their customers. Thus,

just as when resource prices rise, so taxes have the effect of lowering supply and shifting the curve from S1 to S3. Conversely, if that tax is removed, then the supply curve would shift back to S1 from S2.

The issue of subsidies is one that can have a positive impact for both producers and consumers alike. A subsidy is a form of nonrevenue financial support, such as a government grant, or, more broadly classified, it could also appear in the form of a charitable donation. Incoming subsidies have the effect of lowering the overall costs of production and allowing the producer to bring a larger volume of products to market at a lower overall price. Thus, a subsidy would move the supply curve from S1 to S2, and the elimination or reduction of a subsidy would move the supply curve from S2 to S1. This issue is germane to nonprofit organizations and will be discussed further below.

Equilibrium

Keep in mind the true goal of economics—care for all people by being as efficient as possible with the scarce resources we have to work with (productively efficient) so that as much happiness as possible can be created for the greatest number (allocably efficient). If achieved, then the old adage of "waste not, want not" can be applied. Using the data from our private elementary school in Tables 60.3 and 60.4, this is visually represented in economics as the equilibrium point of supply and demand as pictured in Figure 60.6.

The equilibrium point would be at the intersection of the demand curve, D1, and the supply curve, S1. At the point where tuition is $6,000 per year, consumers interested in sending their children to private elementary school would be willing, in aggregate, to send 800 students,

which is the same number of students the school would be willing to educate at that same price. Thus, no household is left wanting to send its children, and no seats in the classroom sit empty.

How Nonprofits Are Affected

When it comes to supply and demand, the laws of both reasonably apply universally to both the for-profit and nonprofit firm. For example, this has been witnessed as true in industries such as higher education where there has been an increase of for-profit players, such as the University of Phoenix, which have entered the space and profited by using a low-cost approach and stealing students away from more costly nonprofit schools (Ruch, 2001). The application of supply and demand is also seen in the market for public elementary education through the growth of the charter school market where both for-profit and nonprofit players have entered into a quasi-public space and been allowed to compete using government funding as a subsidy to its operations (Stoddard and Corcoran, 2007). In any case, the fundamental principles apply but many changes in the environment can have significant impacts to the nonprofit.

For example, the fact that nonprofits are not subject to corporate taxes has a positive influence on the numbers of sellers, which can increase the quantities of nonprofit services available and lower costs to consumers. Subsidies, as provided to firms such as biotechnology companies, can have the effect of lowering production costs and thus lowering the eventual costs of prescription medication to consumers. The undergraduate student needs to be aware of the universality of supply and demand and should pay particular attention to changes in the business environment, keeping an eye open to changes in policies that may influence consumer behavior or facilitate competitive advantages for the nonprofit producer.

Summary

Throughout the course of this chapter, the major goal has been to show how the basic principles of economics, and especially its origins in care, apply to nonprofit organizations. The key takeaways are as follows:

1. Everyone acts rationally. For people, this means self-interested decision making with an eye on pursuing happiness. To a for-profit business, this means to maximize profit. But for the nonprofit that also seeks profit, the question is, how much profit?

2. Resources are scarce and must be used wisely.

3. Decisions are made by all in a manner that expects more goods to be returned than is spent in its discovery.

4. Efficiency in the use of resources is tantamount to creating as much output as is feasible. With a greater quantity of

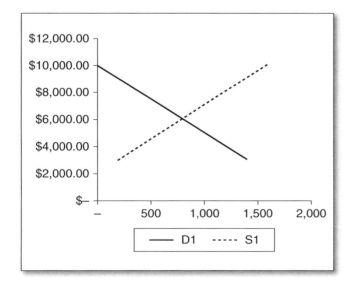

Figure 60.6 The Equilibrium Point of Supply and Demand

goods and services available, there is a greater chance to improve the overall well-being of society as a whole.

5. Business, consumers, and the government are dependent on one another as each engages in the exchange of resources and money flows to achieve its relevant goals.

6. All people and businesses operate in a larger macroeconomic context where each must be aware of and agile in responding to changes in fiscal and monetary policies that are likely to be enacted in response to changes in prices, employment, and growth.

7. Goods and services can either be public, private, or quasi-public and produced by for-profits, nonprofits, the government, or, commonly, some combination of all three.

8. Demand is an expression of consumer willingness and ability to purchase a good or service at various prices. Supply is an expression of producer willingness and ability to produce a good or service at various prices. There are many nonprice factors.

9. The equilibrium of supply and demand is a most desirable outcome as it is a demonstration of the system's ability to be efficient, creating the most amount of happiness with the least amount of waste.

10. Undergraduate students need to appreciate the universality of economic principles so as to be sensitive to how changes in the environment may affect relevant parties in the system.

References and Further Readings

Armitage, D. (2007). *The Declaration of Independence: A global history*. Cambridge, MA: Harvard University Press.

Auteri, M. (2003). The entrepreneurial establishment of a nonprofit organization. *Public Organization Review, 3,* 171–189.

Bateman, F., & Taylor, J. (2007). Does the distribution of new deal spending reflect an optimal provision of public goods? *Economics Bulletin, 3,* 1–5.

Elmendorf, D. W., Liebman, J. B., & Wilcox, D. W. (2001). *Fiscal policy and social security policy during the 1990s* (Working Paper No. 8488). Cambridge, MA: National Bureau of Economic Research (NBER).

Exxon Mobil Corporation. (2009, May 5). *Form 10-Q.* Retrieved June 1, 2009, from http://sec.gov

Ford Motor Company. (2009, May 8). *Form 10-Q.* Retrieved June 1, 2009, from http://sec.gov

Fremstad, S. (2009). *The tax provisions in the American recovery and reinvestment act.* Washington, DC: Center for Economic and Policy Research (CEPR).

Gerber, A., & Wichardt, P. (2009). Providing public goods in the absence of strong institutions. *Journal of Public Economics, 93,* 429–439.

Grisham, T. (2009). Leading sustainability. *World Review of Entrepreneurship, Management and Sustainable Development, 5,* 42–55.

Habitat for Humanity. (2007). *Form 990.* Retrieved June 1, 2009, from http://guidestar.org

Indiana University Center on Philanthropy & Giving USA Foundation. (2009). *Giving USA 2009: The annual report on philanthropy for the year 2008* (54th ed.). Glenview, IL: Giving USA Foundation.

Luksetich, W. (2008). Government funding and nonprofit organizations. *Nonprofit and Voluntary Sector Quarterly, 37,* 434–442.

McConnell, C., Brue, S., & Flynn, S. (2009). *Economics.* New York: McGraw-Hill/Irwin.

McDonald, R. (2007). An investigation of innovation in nonprofit organizations: The role of organizational mission. *Nonprofit and Voluntary Sector Quarterly, 36,* 256–281.

Microsoft Corporation. (2008, July 31). *Form 10-K.* Retrieved June 1, 2009, from http://sec.gov

Nickels, W., McHugh, J., & McHugh, S. (2005). *Understanding business.* New York: McGraw-Hill/Irwin.

Ruch, R. S. (2001). *Higher Ed, Inc.: The rise of the for-profit university.* Baltimore, MD: Johns Hopkins University Press.

Samuelson, P., & Nordhaus, W. (2004). *Macroeconomics.* New York: McGraw-Hill/Irwin.

Simon, H. A. (1957). *Models of man: Social and rational.* New York: John Wiley.

Singer, K. (1991). Oikonomia: An inquiry into beginnings of economic thought and language. In M. Blaug (Ed.), *Aristotle (384–322 BC).* Brookfield, VT: Ashgate.

Smith, A. (1776). *An inquiry into the nature and causes of the wealth of nations.* New York: Modern Library.

Stoddard, C., & Corcoran, S. P. (2007). The political economy of school choice: Support for charter schools across states and school districts. *Journal of Urban Economics, 62,* 27–54.

Tschirhart, M., Reed, K., Freeman, S., & Anker, A. (2008). Is the grass greener? Sector shifting and choice of sector by MPA and MBA graduates. *Nonprofit and Voluntary Sector Quarterly, 37,* 668–688.

U.S. Census Bureau. (2007). *Income, poverty and health insurance coverage in the United States: 2007.* Retrieved June 1, 2009, from http://www.census.gov/prod/2008pubs/p60–235.pdf

U.S. Department of Health and Human Services. (2005). *Medicaid drug price comparisons: Average manufacturer price to published prices* (OIG Publication No. OEI-05–05-00240). Washington, DC: Author. Available from http://www.oig.hhs.gov/oei/reports/oei-05–05–00240.pdf

61

WHEN THINGS GO WRONG

Leadership and the Problem of Unintended Consequences

TIMOTHY O'BRIEN AND GIANFRANCO FARRUGGIA

North Park University

This chapter will examine the phenomenon of unintended consequences and how nonprofit leaders might consider managing them. We will look at *unintended consequences* as defined by Robert K. Merton; *systems theory*, specifically complex adaptive systems; *complex responsive processes*, which provide insights about how new knowledge is created; *sensemaking*, which provides insights as to how we use perceptions to manage and make decisions; and the *learning organization* and the role of *strategic planning*. These areas of understanding collectively form both context and methodology that nonprofit leaders can consider when unintended consequences occur or in making efforts to avoid the occurrence.

Unintended Consequences

The "law of unintended consequences" (also known as unforeseen consequences) states that any purposeful action will be the source of some unintended consequences. When one reviews this topic, one cannot avoid reviewing the seminal work of Robert K. Merton, a foremost sociologist who wrote on this very subject during his time at Harvard University. In fact, the author and subject matter have had such an impact that Mongardini and Tabboni (1998) edited an entire textbook on the subject and its offshoots.

Merton's work strongly suggests that one go beyond "the ready solution provided by ascribing uncontemplated consequences of action to the inscrutable will of God or Providence or Fate" (1936, p. 894). These considerations of

a "higher power" or destiny also imply that the inability to foresee consequences shouldn't automatically be associated with personal undesirability or that onlookers' views should be "axiologically negative" (p. 895). Further highlights presented by Merton deal with consequences being "those elements in the resulting situation which are exclusively the outcome of the action . . . which would not have occurred had the action not taken place" (p. 895). Merton further delineates these into consequences based on and dealing with individuals and consequences for others by way of social structures, culture components, and society.

A clear message regarding collective action is provided by Merton: Don't assume that it uncompromisingly entails purpose that is unambiguously explicit. Furthermore, "it must not be inferred that purposive action implies 'rationality' of human action (that a person always uses the objectively most adequate means for the attainment of their end)" and that "rationality and irrationality are not to be identified with the success and failure of action, respectively" (1936, p. 896). When Merton turns his attention to the "action" component of the subject matter, he differentiates between unorganized and formally organized action. Unorganized action "refers to actions of individuals considered distributively out of which may grow . . . [formally organized actions] when like-minded individuals form an association in order to achieve a common purpose" (p. 896). Furthermore, consequences that are unintended may be a result of either unorganized or organized action. Additionally, Merton warns of two pitfalls: the first being the difficulty of establishing the extent to which consequences may reasonably be ascribed to undeniable actions and the second involving the problem of determining the tangible rationale of a specified action. Additionally, this is further complicated with "discriminating between rationalization and truth in those cases where apparently unintended consequences are *post facto* declared to have been intended" (p. 897). Moreover, Merton indicates that a recurrent basis for error is removed if it is recognized that the involved features in unanticipated consequences are merely features and that none alone serves to explain any solid case.

Merton (1936) makes a very simple yet quite insightful and discerning statement regarding knowledge: "Lack of knowledge is the *sole* barrier to a correct anticipation" (p. 898). He goes on to categorize various factors related to unintended consequences: (1) knowledge, (2) error, (3) domineering interest, and (4) public predictions, which are explored below.

Knowledge

For knowledge, conjectural associations referenced in behavioral sciences are called on by stating, "the set of consequences of any repeated act is not constant but there is a range of consequences, *any one of which may follow the act in any given case*" and that it's "impossible to predict with certainty the results in any particular case" (Merton, 1936, p. 899). The results of this issue are that actions permit a varying array of unexpected results and that one may generally say consequences are surprising when a precise comprehension of many particulars is needed for even a forecast that is highly estimated. Merton does distinguish lack of knowledge from ignorance. The "ignorance factor" is augmented by life's demands that very often require us to act with assurance even though the information on which we base our action is incomplete. Frank Knight (as cited in Merton, 1936, p. 900) indicates that we usually act on "opinion and estimate" to which Merton adds, "Immediate action of some sort, will usually involve ignorance of certain aspects of the situation and will bring about unexpected results." Just a little over 70 years ago (and certainly applicable today), Merton stated, "In our present economic order, it is manifestly uneconomic behavior to concern ourselves with attempts to obtain knowledge for predicting outcomes of action to such an extent that we have practically no time or energy for other pursuits" (1936, p. 900). This issue of knowledge results in laying the groundwork for potentially unforeseen results and effects, or the lack of knowledge opens us up to potentially researching a subject matter, topic, or issue to such an inexhaustible end that it becomes never ending.

Error

Error (also referred to as mistake, blunder, inaccuracy, miscalculation), Merton explains,

may intrude itself . . . in any phase of purposive action: we may err in our appraisal of the present situation, in our inference from this to the future objective situation, or our selection of a course of action, or finally in the execution of the action chosen. (1936, p. 901)

Merton indicates that a frequent erroneous belief often involves assuming that an action that has previously led to a desired result will continue to do so and that this conjecture is often fixed in habit and pragmatism. It is specifically these actions that have previously led to certain ends that become automatic through ongoing recurrence that fail to recognize that success is not certain at all times in all conditions and circumstances. Merton goes on to further delineate a range of errors: "simple neglect (lack of systematic thoroughness in examining the situation) to pathological obsession where there is a determined refusal or inability to consider certain elements of the problem" (1936, p. 901). Merton ends his discussion of this type of error by highlighting that emotions lead to situational alterations and events that unavoidably stir up unexpected consequences.

Domineering Interest

Domineering interest "excludes the consideration of further or other consequences of the same act" and the "immediacy of interest may range from physiological needs to basic cultural values" (Merton, 1936, pp. 901–902). Merton further explores conventional economics in which individuals employ resources for profitability to render societal returns and gains "by an invisible hand to promote an end which was not part of [the] intention (Adam Smith as cited in Merton), may serve as an example of economic interest leading to this sequence" (1936, p. 902). Merton further indicates that self-interested action is not adverse to a thorough examination of successful achievement and additionally states that satisfying interests demands impartial situational investigation. Merton further indicates that domineering interests tend to bring about failure to engage in necessary computations and generate an emotive predisposition that may result in failure in other areas of interest. Merton (p. 903) ends this issue by stating that "due to the fact that when a system of values enjoins certain *specific* actions, adherents are not concerned with the objective consequences of these actions but only with the subjective satisfaction of duty well performed."

Public Predictions

Public predictions are characteristically human and stand in the way of successful forecasting and preparation. Merton states that such "predictions of future social development are frequently not sustained precisely because the prediction has become a new element in the concrete situation thus tending to change the initial course of developments" (1936, pp. 903–904). Merton further indicates that this eventuality often explains social actions emerging in unanticipated tendencies and assumes considerable significance for communal planning.

Merton's Conclusion

This review entailed "one fundamental social process. It would take [the reader] too far afield . . . to examine exhaustively the implications of this analysis for social prediction, control and planning" (Merton, 1998, p. 296). The intent was to direct the reader's attention to go beyond merely consigning unanticipated consequences to the realms of theology and exploratory philosophy. A little over 60 years later, Merton (1998, p. 296) still asks the following questions: "How does the phenomenon of unintended and unanticipated consequences come about? How are we to think about its recurrence in every domain of society, culture, and civilization?"

Considering that Merton's work essentially describes human collective action, we might pursue some contemporary organizational theories to shed light on how nonprofit leaders might approach the phenomenon of unintended consequences. Next, we will examine systems theory to set the context; we will also examine the learning organization (Senge, 2006) in order to understand the role of learning and adaptation. Another closely related theory is complex responsive processes (Stacey, 2002), which theorizes how knowledge is created through the process of interaction and "sensemaking" (Weick, 2001), which provides insight on how our perceptions are formulated. All of these theories provide useful points of view that nonprofit leaders can use to effectively perform management functions in unstable environments.

Systems Theory

Systems theory is a transdisciplinary phenomenon. Systems exist in the natural sciences as well as in the social sciences. Edgar Schein (1980) defines a *system* as something that is composed of regularly interacting or interrelating groups of activities. It could be anything from a single organism to an organization to a society. Systems theory was derived in the field of biology in the 1920s. It was developed to explain the interrelatedness of organisms in an ecosystem (Bateson, 1979). In this era, scientists began to question the Newtonian mechanistic view of the world. Interrelatedness of organisms to their environment generated a more dynamic understanding about how the world actually works. If we consider humans in the same light, then we begin to recognize that there are dynamic forces at work that create great complexity as humans interact with their environment and form ways to organize into groups for collective, purposeful action. The concept

of a system depends on a web of relationships, and organizations can be viewed as achieving their intended purpose through dynamic interactions with their environment. "The systems view of man links him again to the world he lives in, for he is seen as emerging in that world and reflecting its general character" (Laszlo, 1972, p. 79). Unintended consequences can be viewed as an outcome of this dynamic interaction.

Complex Adaptive Systems

Organizational theorists have come to understand that human organizations are complex adaptive systems and can be studied as such to understand organizational behavior, structure, and outcomes. Living organisms are complex adaptive systems. A complex adaptive system has been defined as complex in that it is diverse and made up of multiple interconnected elements and as adaptive in that it has the capacity to change and learn from experience (Holland, 1995). Organizational theorist Edgar Schein (1980) describes organizations as complex social systems that cannot be studied using reductionist methods but need to be studied as a whole. Peter Senge (2006) defines *systems thinking* as the primary driving force of organizational learning. His conceptual framework recognizes that all human endeavors are systems and are bound together by interrelated actions. Although a significant element of organizational management is related to limiting risk, systems thinking recognizes that, due to the complexity of our interrelatedness, complete limitation of risk is not possible. In this case, unintended consequences are normative. This fits with Merton's understanding that "it is manifestly uneconomic behavior to concern ourselves with attempts to obtain knowledge for predicting outcomes of action to such an extent that we have practically no time or energy for other pursuits" (1936, p. 900). The complexity of our organizational life does not allow for perfect prediction—only for thoughtful planning and developing an enhanced ability to learn, interacting effectively with our environment.

In relating complex adaptive systems to human organizations, Vogelsang (2002) includes the following concepts:

- *Agents evolve with schemata.* Agents act with each other creating and re-creating schemata (assumptions, expectations, values, habits) that organize their relations at the local level. This is a continual process of evolving understanding.
- *Global patterns of relationship emerge.* As agents interact locally, they generate complexity and variety and create global patterns of interacting: rituals, structured relationships, communication systems, and operating values.
- *Coevolution occurs at the edge of chaos.* Complex adaptive systems operate at "boundary regions" near the edge of chaos where frozen components of order melt, and the agents in the system coevolve in order to survive and optimize themselves in a changing environment.

- *System evolution is based on recombination.* In every interaction, the agents enact historic patterns with slight or major variations. The agents recognize the patterns, experience the difference, and choose to reconstruct them or construct new patterns. The system generates novelty without abandoning the best elements of the past. The system is flexible and open to learning in order to evolve while maintaining consistency with its purpose, values, rituals, and relationships (schemata).
- *No one point of control exists.* For a complex adaptive system to survive, it must cultivate variety, but one cannot direct the variations. One can only influence the rules, relationships, and choices made in interactions while being influenced by others.

The dynamism of the environments within which we interact provides ample opportunity for unintended consequences to take place. This leads us to an attempt to try to understand how we might predict outcomes. The better we are at prediction, the better our ability to mitigate risk and provide stability. This ability to predict, however, might provide us with a false sense of stability and control. If we recognize that control can sometimes be elusive, we can then create organizations that are built as open systems. Morgan (1997, p. 45) describes organizational evolution in terms of an open system: "The more unpredictable the industry, the more open the management system should be in order to allow the level of self-organizing and open communications that is needed in order to innovate." We might conclude then that unpredictability is an entry point to innovation. We innovate to survive and grow. This places the phenomenon or unintended consequences in a different light. It might be considered an opportunity to learn and innovate.

Complex Responsive Processes

Another organizational theory that provides insight into the phenomenon of unintended consequences is one presented by Ralph Stacey (2002). Stacey's theory is based on the question, What if human interaction is analogous to the abstract interaction modeled by complex adaptive systems? Stacey asserts that knowledge is actually *created* through "complex responsive processes" where meaning is created in human interaction. Knowledge is not something that can be stored; it is created in the living present. If we consider that a primary task of management is to manage the creation of knowledge, this knowledge is thought of as residing inside of individual heads, in tacit form. This creates a situation where management's primary task is to retain employees and to use methods of encouragement, such as empowerment. Management is also charged with "extracting" knowledge from individuals and converting it into explicit knowledge that can be stored and manipulated thus creating value for the organization. If, however, we consider knowledge creation from the perspective of complex

adaptive systems, management's role shifts from control to persuasion and facilitation of the interactions that create new knowledge.

Stacey proposes that we move on from systems thinking (Senge, 2006), toward an understanding that knowledge arises in complex responsive processes of relating, that knowledge itself is continuously reproduced and potentially transformed. He states that knowledge cannot be managed because knowledge is a participative self-organizing process. He describes *human agency* as the processes of interaction between humans that perpetually construct themselves as continuity and potential transformation. He describes causality in nature: Nature is unfolding already enfolded forms. This is described as *formative teleology*. Given this context, we will next examine key theories that can provide the context for leadership and unintended consequences, namely, learning organizations.

Learning Organizations

Senge's (2006) model of learning organizations is segmented into three levels: (1) practice (what you do), (2) principles (guiding ideas), and (3) insights and essences (the state of being of those with high levels of mastery in the discipline). These levels of understanding apply to all of the disciplines in his learning organizational model. He also identifies three distinct stages of learning:

1. *New cognitive capacities.* People see new things and can speak in a new language. This opening stage allows people to see more clearly their own and others' assumptions and the actions and consequences of both. At this early stage, they struggle to translate new cognitive and linguistic competencies into new actions. Behavior starts to change, but old assumptions, values, and rules are still in place.

2. *New action rules.* Old assumptions loosen in response to cognitive insights derived in stage one. People begin to experiment with action rules to see what they yield and may develop new language to produce new action. They are still unable to string together new rules when under stress.

3. *New values and assumptions.* People can string together rules that reflect new action values and operating assumptions. This stage provides adaptation to new rules and operating assumptions. At this stage, people can apply new rules under stress and ambiguity.

This sequence of change according to Senge begins with the *cognitive shift,* a coming to know something, where understanding and language development leads the developmental process allowing rules, behaviors, values, and assumptions to change. Strategic planning can be the place where this cognitive shift takes place. We will address the role of strategic planning later in this chapter.

Senge then develops five disciplines in the learning organization model:

1. *Personal mastery.* We continually clarify and deepen our personal vision, focus our energies, develop patience, and attempt to see reality objectively. He calls personal mastery the spiritual foundation of the learning organization. This foundational element seems to lay the groundwork for the other disciplines.

2. *Mental models.* Deeply ingrained assumptions, generalizations, and images influence how we understand the world and how we take action in it. Mental models are of particular importance in understanding how we might approach unintended consequences. We need to have a more explicit understanding of our own mental models to evaluate them and change them as we move into new circumstances, or realities. Cognition or new understanding will be the catalyst in our efforts to change our mental models.

3. *Building shared vision.* Unearthing shared pictures of the future assumes that we already have a vision of the future. The shared vision dimension helps to develop the relationships in which new knowledge is created based on emerging reality.

4. *Team learning.* This discipline provides synergy, where groups of people benefit from the idea that the total is greater than the sum of its parts. Members of a group enter into dialogue. The group can then enter into thinking together. A part of this is to arrive at an understanding of what patterns of interaction undermine learning.

5. *Systems thinking.* Such thinking recognizes that all human endeavors or organizations are systems bound by invisible fabrics of interrelated actions that often take years to fully play out their effects on one another. This is a conceptual framework to provide an understanding of how to make patterns clearer and to help us to see how to change them effectively.

Senge's model leads the reader to this fifth discipline as a key to leadership and organizational life in the 21st century. We can interact effectively with our environment only if we have an understanding of our organization's place and function within that environment and an understanding of the dynamic interaction of the people that comprise the organization as well as the people and organizations that comprise the environment within which interactions take place.

Sensemaking

Sensemaking provides a framework for understanding learning based on action and experience—in community. This theory provides an understanding about collective perceptions. Sensemaking involves placing stimuli into some kind of framework. It can be defined as a recurring cycle comprised of a sequence of events occurring over time. Individuals form unconscious and conscious anticipations and assumptions, which serve as predictions of future events. Subsequently, individuals experience events that may be discrepant from predictions. These events trigger a need for explanation and correspondingly for a process through which interpretations and discrepancies are developed. Sensemaking might then be considered as the way that unintended consequences are discovered.

Sensemaking has a lot to do with expectations. Whenever expectations are disconfirmed, some kind of ongoing activity is interrupted. Sensemaking is grounded in both individual and social activity. The process of sensemaking happens when human situations are progressively clarified, but this clarification often works in reverse. We make sense of events in retrospect. Sensemaking is less about discovery (implicit knowledge) than it is about invention (knowledge in action). Sensemaking highlights invention that precedes interpretation. It is a very active process as opposed to the inactive process of interpretation.

Sensemaking carries with it the notion that reality is an ongoing accomplishment that takes form when people make retrospective sense of the situations in which they find themselves and their creations.

The properties of sensemaking are

- *Grounded in identity.* Identities are constituted out of the process of interaction. The concept of self is created through interaction with others. Self-concept is an agent of its own creation even though it is created through interaction and is based on human needs, such as

  self-enhancement,

  self-efficacy (desire to perceive oneself as competent and effective),

  self-consistency (desire to sense and experience coherence and continuity).

- *Retrospective.* All perception is memory. We are aware of what we have done, never of doing it. Retrospective sensemaking is an activity with many different meanings that may need to be synthesized. Too many meanings (not too few) cause confusion, not ignorance. We remember meaningful lived experiences. Time itself exists in two forms: duration or the stream of experience and discrete segments.

- *Enactive of sensible environments.* Sensemaking is an active process of ongoing codetermination tied to relating rather than results. Weick (2001) gives us the example of newcomers to an organization to illustrate this property of sensemaking.

    Newcomers are first flooded with surprises. Hermeneutics then help the newcomer gloss over surprises and as routines develop and meaning becomes fixed by the organization's culture, facticity develops as things become taken for granted. Functional theories become more useful, interdependent activities of the newcomer and others have evolved, and along with them, the referents and accounts that are given when a moment in the process of evolving is frozen. People seem to need the idea that there is a world with pre-given features or ready-made information, because to give up this idea is to fall into idealism, nihilism or subjectivism. Either there is an absolute ground or everything falls apart. (Weick, 2001, p. 35)

- *Social.* An organization is a network of intersubjectively shared meanings that are sustained through the development and use of common language and everyday social interaction. Sensemaking is never solitary because what a person does internally is contingent on others. Social contact is mediated through discourse.
- *Ongoing.* There are no absolute starting points, no self-evident, self-contained certainties on which we can build because we always find ourselves in the midst of complex situations that we try to disentangle by making then revising provisional assumptions. Weick (2001) illustrates this by discussing the value of off-site meetings that focus and crystallize meanings in organizations. They are focal points for different streams of ongoing activity. The concept of *interruption* is defined as a signal that important changes have occurred in the environment (interruption of the expectation and in the flow of events).
- *Focused on and by extracted cues.* Extracted cues are simple, familiar structures that are seeds from which people develop a larger sense of what may be occurring. These cues are context dependent or based on particularities related to who is speaking, the relevant aspects of the speaker's biography, current purposes and intent, setting, relationship between speaker and hearer, and so on. The social context is crucial for sensemaking because it binds people to actions that they then must justify. The context provides norms and expectations that constrain explanations. Any point of reference will do because it stimulates a cognitive structure that leads people to act with more intensity, which in turn creates a material order in place of a presumed order. Context, while a necessary aspect of sensemaking, is not content specific.
- *Driven by plausibility rather than accuracy.* The criterion of accuracy is secondary. Sensemaking is about embellishment and elaboration of a single point of reference or extracted cue, knowing just enough and no more.

The notions that Weick (2001) provides about how we make sense of the world follow some of the patterns that form the matrix of a learning organization. The learning process is essentially done in community (codetermined) in service of creating the future.

If we consider human organizations as complex adaptive systems that continually learn and evolve through the interaction of the agents that comprise those organizations, the questions become, How might we rethink the idea of unintended consequences? What are our assumptions and what methods might leaders employ to understand and manage this seemingly chaotic phenomenon? What is the real task of

the learning organization? If our understanding of what knowledge is and how it is created is informed by these theories, what is the best approach to leading our organizations?

The next step in our inquiry is to understand the methodology that many nonprofit organizations use to vision, plan, and turn their vision into reality: strategic planning. Based on years of practical experience and the executive leadership of the authors, the following is offered for leaders of nonprofit organizations as a way of reducing the possibility of unintended consequences.

Strategic Planning

Strategic planning in its purest form is deceptively simple and is broken down into the following areas: (1) getting organized, (2) situational analysis, (3) setting direction, (4) refinement and plan adoption, and (5) implementation (Barry, 2001). Bryson (2004, p. xii) defines it as a "disciplined effort to produce fundamental decisions and actions that shape and guide what an organization . . . is, what it does, and why it does it." There are noted benefits (the "whats" and "whys") to strategic planning. One very important benefit is problem solving and refining results by maintaining focused momentum. Another significant benefit is committed communicative teamwork that influences circumstances to reduce, to the extent possible, unintended consequences.

Getting Organized

Barry (2001, p. 24) describes this step as "lay[ing] out a planning process that results in a good plan, builds commitment, and uses people's time well . . . [to not] result in wasted time, frustration, and low-quality." This process involves (1) noting why planning is necessary for a nonprofit organization and any concerns voiced by various stakeholders, (2) selecting a leader or steering group to maintain the organization's planning pathway, (3) determining if there is a need for external assistance, (4) outlining a fitting organizational planning process, and (5) getting key stakeholders' procedural commitment and dedication.

Situational Analysis

Barry (20011997, p. 36) describes this step as "tak[ing] a hard look at your organization and the world in which you operate, and then identify[ing] key issues or choices regarding your organization's future . . . [to] result in a clear, common understanding of your organization's situation as well as a clear definition of the strategic issues and choices the organization faces." This analysis involves (1) gathering indispensable background data and information for discussions of the nonprofit organization's position and circumstances, (2) having discussions on organizational history, recent progress, purpose and cause, strengths, weaknesses, opportunities, and challenges, and (3) getting concurrence on the most critical matters relating to the organization's potential.

Setting Direction

Barry (2001, p. 52) describes this step as "sort[ing] through [identified] issues, reach[ing] general agreement on the best direction for your organization, and develop[ing] a . . . strategic plan . . . [that] describe[s] what your organization intends to accomplish over the next few years, as well as how you will begin to accomplish those goals." This planning can use the following four approaches:

- *Critical issues.* Use logical ordering with the most essential issues being discussed first followed by the subsequent issues until all issues are addressed.
- *Scenario.* Develop various alternative futures of the nonprofit organization's appearance followed by paramount scenario selection, and determine the transition to the preferred future.
- *Goals.* Set several major targets or guidelines by having organizational departments or divisions plan for the achievement or contribution to the goals.
- *Alignment.* Or get organizational parts to work in sync for mission accomplishment by determining the alignment of its purpose, its programs, and its resources.

Refinement and Adoption

Barry (1997, p. 70) describes this step as "solicit[ing] comments [from groups or people to] make needed improvements in your plan . . . [to] fine-tune . . .[it] into a plan that is right on the mark." It is highly recommended that stakeholder groups or people be given adequate time for review and frank comments that involve (1) plan overview, (2) general reaction to the plan, (3) what is liked about, problematic with, flaccid about, or omitted from the plan, (4) unambiguous thoughts for plan improvement, and (5) where perils are in the plan.

Implementation

Barry (1997, p. 72) describes this step as "implement[ing] the plans developed in Steps 1–4, monitor progress, make midcourse corrections, and periodically update the plan." This component involves delegation of responsibilities and establishing of timelines for the execution of each major plan goal, strategy, or task. Six guidelines are offered for proper implementation: (1) Practice good work in steps 1 through 4 to greatly help with plan implementation, (2) render strategic plan into annual work plans and budgets, (3) be attentive on the large goal, (4) pay attention to variations and alterations, (5) keep stakeholders and associates apprised of the plan, and (6) monitor the plan's progress. This implementation phase ends with what Bryson (2005, p. 191) calls a "prelude to a new round of strategic planning."

Relationship Between Strategic Planning and Unintended Consequences

How does this five-step strategic planning process relate to unintended consequences? Recall Merton's statement regarding knowledge: "Lack of knowledge is the *sole* barrier to a correct anticipation" (1936, p. 898). In its simplest form, strategic planning deals with (1) laying the groundwork for potentially unforeseen results to bring about knowledge, (2) the reduction of error and mistakes, (3) benefiting organizational and societal interests, and (4) predictions for social development and planning. These relationships are further embedded in considerations made by McLaughlin (2006): (1) Rethink fundamental assumptions about need, (2) conduct future scans for the purposes of institutional learning and presentation of opportunities, and (3) accept the need for survival and the larger context in which nonprofit organizations operate. McLaughlin (2006, p. 61) indicates that the "solution is to break the chore down into manageable parts, . . . business conditions that exist outside of the organization's day-to-day control." All in all, unintended consequences should be viewed as normative and given consideration for their existence in the ongoing operations of nonprofit organizations.

Strategic planning is in essence a method that can be used to facilitate knowledge creation and develop learning capacities. The method provides the opportunity for communal reflection on the history and meaning of the organization. It provides a way for people to enter into conversations that go beyond day-to-day, task-focused conversations. It allows for reflection on the meaning of those tasks enabling movement from task to vision.

The strategic planning process is where we can explore our evolving understanding of the organization, including creation of contingencies that might address unintended consequences. We do this in relational, complex responsive processes as developed by Stacey (2002). The chaotic nature of rapidly changing environments within which we operate can be recognized and plans created even if we don't have perfect knowledge of the consequences of our actions. We don't know what the unintended consequences might be, but we do know that they exist and that our best approach is to actively and intentionally create a learning organization poised to deal with them as they emerge. We recognize the organization as a complex adaptive system that is open to its environment and where new knowledge is continually being created. Strategic planning methodology is therefore not simply a way to vision the future and create action steps to achieve; it is a way to create awareness of the complex factors that currently exist and open the way for communal learning and development. Given the increasing complexity of nonprofit organizations, the learning organization, recognizing itself as a complex adaptive system, places priority and great urgency on obtaining a broad knowledge of the system (environment) and effectively responding to emerging phenomena.

It is unfortunate that many organizations undertake a strategic plan with the idea that it is an obligation or expectation of funders, board members, and other constituents, but they do not leverage the learning opportunities that lie at its heart. Strategic planning is not where we discover the way forward, it is the way that we create the future—through recognition of learning as a primary value and with the understanding that knowledge is not a commodity but a dynamic reality. Unintended consequences, by definition, might not be recognized during this process, but by fostering learning, the organization is better adapted to recognize them and respond effectively.

Although the strategic planning model seems linear, it allows for and is actually designed to accommodate the reality of idea emergence. Senge's work provides context for organizational learning. Developing an understanding of ambiguity, complexity, and chaos can help to provide context for people who enter into strategic planning and allow us to work within a framework that permits all these realities to be a part of the fabric of the effort. Developing an understanding of how we learn and how we make sense of our environment and each other can help us through the disorderly aspects of group process and emergent knowledge creation. The theories provide a context for our work. Recognition of chaotic conditions, uncertainty, and ambiguity, as well as an understanding of human intelligence, does not directly answer the questions at hand, but together they provide a different set of lenses that we can look through when seeking our future. All of these conditions also provide us with the idea that unintended consequences are always a part of our landscape. We cannot escape them in a world of great complexity. All we can do is develop our collective capacity to learn and adapt. This calls for nonprofit leaders to foster a climate of trust and openness where learning and innovation are emphasized and rewarded.

Summary and Future Directions

Management research has questioned the validity of strategic planning and found that the presumed linear progression from analysis to objectives to action and results is more fanciful than factual (Bolman & Deal, 1997). While this does not speak well for the validity of strategic (or any other) planning, the authors go on to speak about the symbolic and human interaction importance of planning. Plans themselves provide means for the interaction that creates consensus or shared vision and symbolize the organization's efforts toward creating a sustainable future. Although there might not be the linear progression that seems to be an inherent expectation in planning, the process creates an explicit set of assumptions and agreements which in and of themselves provide milestones for tracking progress. Without long-term plans, most organizations are rudderless and simply reacting to environmental changes without a set of comparative markers. Healthy organizations should be constantly challenging their operating norms and assumptions (Morgan, 1997), and it is those norms and assumptions that are reviewed in a strategic plan. The organization becomes one that has a learning orientation. When a strategic plan is developed, it represents the consensus of the organization's stakeholders, and organizational structures and activities are redirected toward the new strategies. The plan itself presents to all who are involved a symbol of what the organization values. With this directional approach, nonprofit leaders are providing the best possible approach to managing the unknown.

References and Further Readings

Barry, B. W. (2001). *Strategic planning workbook for nonprofit organizations* (Rev. ed.). St. Paul, MN: Amherst H. Wilder Foundation.

Bateson, G. (1979). *Mind and nature: A necessary unity.* New York: Ballantine.

Bolman, L., & Deal, T. (1997). *Reframing organizations: Artistry, choice and leadership.* San Francisco: Jossey-Bass.

Bryson, J. M. (2004). *Strategic planning for nonprofit organizations.* New York: John Wiley & Sons.

Bryson, J. M. (2005). The strategy change cycle—an effective strategic planning approach for nonprofit organizations. In R. D. Herman (Ed.), *The Jossey-Bass handbook of nonprofit leadership & management* (pp. 171–198). San Francisco: Jossey-Bass.

Holland, J. (1995). *Hidden order: How adaptation builds complexity.* Reading, MA: Helix Books.

Laszlo, E. (1972). *The systems view of the world.* New York: George Brazillier.

McLaughlin, T. A. (2006). *Nonprofit strategic positioning: Decide where to be, plan what to do.* New York: John Wiley & Sons.

Merton, R. K. (1936). The unanticipated consequences of purposive social action. *American Sociological Review, 1*(6), 894–904.

Merton, R. K. (1998). Afterword—unanticipated consequences and kindred sociological ideas: A personal gloss. In C. Mongardini & S. Tabboni (Eds.), *Robert K. Merton & contemporary sociology* (pp. 295–318). New Brunswick, NJ: Transaction.

Mongardini, C., & Tabboni, S. (1998). *Robert K. Merton & contemporary sociology.* New Brunswick, NJ: Transaction.

Morgan, G. (1997). *Images of organization.* Thousand Oaks, CA: Sage.

Schein, E. (1980). *Organizational psychology.* Englewood Cliffs, NJ: Prentice Hall.

Senge, P. (2006). *The fifth discipline: The art and practice of the learning organization.* New York: Doubleday.

Stacey, R. (2002). *Complex responsive processes in organizations: Learning and knowledge creation.* New York: Routledge.

Vogelsang, J. (2002). *Futuring: A complex adaptive approach to strategic planning.* San Francisco: Support Center for Nonprofit Management.

Weick, K. (2001). *Making sense of the organization.* Malden, MA: Blackwell.

62

LEADING COLLABORATION

Creating Strategic Alliances and Restructuring via Mergers, Acquisitions, and Integration

H. LUKE SHAEFER, MARIAM DELAND, AND THEODORE R. JONES
University of Michigan School of Social Work

Nonprofit leaders often lament that resources have become scarcer in recent years, making it harder to keep their organizations financially stable. At the same time, organizational leaders as well as funders such as federated appeals and charitable foundations have become increasingly concerned with the effectiveness of the services provided by the sector from direct human services to health to the arts. Is there a great deal of redundancy in what programs are offered? Are programs ineffective because they exist in a vacuum and fail to work in tandem with other related services in the community? These and other related concerns regarding the effectiveness and the efficiency of services have driven a growth in interest in strategic collaborations in the nonprofit sector. Collaborations can take many different forms: short-term partnerships between nonprofits and businesses, long-term resource sharing between agencies to lower fixed costs, or even organizational mergers or acquisitions. Strategic collaborations can make nonprofits more efficient. They can also help them serve their target populations better. Collaborations can thus be a powerful strategic tool for leaders of the sector.

It is important to be clear, however, that collaboration is not a silver bullet. In some cases, collaborative initiatives can provide no benefit at all and at worst may actually distract organizations from their missions. Partnering organizations may clash due to conflicting interests or cultures. In other cases, organizations have incentives to engage in collaboration in name only.

This chapter offers an introduction to collaboration within the nonprofit sector. It begins by discussing the context. Why are so many nonprofits interested in building collaborations? The chapter continues by discussing the two key strategic rationales for pursuing collaborative partnerships: to improve organizational efficiency or to improve the effectiveness of programs. From there, it continues by discussing the many different types of collaborations and the challenges that nonprofit leaders face in building successful partnerships. Throughout the chapter, real examples of nonprofit collaborations are highlighted. Many of these examples come from Michigan, where the authors have been conducting a study on this topic. In the end, this chapter concludes that collaboration can be an important tool for lowering an organization's fixed costs or improving its effectiveness. However, making collaborations successful can be difficult, and so such initiatives should be entered into with the strategic goals clearly articulated and with knowledge of the many roadblocks that can get in the way.

The Context: Shrinking Resources or a Growing Sector?

Are we truly in the midst of a period of shrinking resources in the nonprofit sector? If we examine just the economic crisis of 2008 and 2009, this may be the case. However, if we consider the past two decades, the answer is an unequivocal no. In fact, all the evidence suggests that the sector has grown at an unprecedented rate over the past 15 years. Among those nonprofit groups that must report to the Internal Revenue

Service (those with gross receipts of $25,000 or more—sometimes called *public charities*), between 1995 and 2005 inflation-adjusted total revenue exploded from $653 billion to $1.1 trillion, more than a 50% increase. This growth was stronger in some subsectors than others but was spread widely. Human services organizations saw their total inflation-adjusted revenue jump from $92 to $132 billion while funding for the arts, culture, and humanities grew from $12.6 to $21 billion during the same period. (Most nonprofit monetary estimates are taken from *The Nonprofit Almanac 2008* by Wing, Pollak, & Blackwood, 2008.)

Most funding sources grew during this time. Private charitable contributions grew particularly fast, as Americans became significantly more generous, giving a greater proportion of national income and more per capita to charity than ever before. Assets in the sector grew similarly so that by 2005 public charities in the United States controlled roughly $2 trillion in assets. Far from shrinking or even holding steady, the nonprofit sector has grown at an unprecedented rate over the past 2 decades, greatly increasing its place in the national economy and society as a whole.

Still, many nonprofit leaders have legitimate reasons to believe that resources are scarcer now than in the past. Their concerns may be driven by the economic crisis of 2008 and 2009 during which all indications are that nonprofits—at least in direct health or human service provision—have experienced a serious growth in demand for services, while very likely seeing a decline in resources most likely driven by declines in state government funding. However, many sector leaders began voicing feelings of scarcity long before the 2008 to 2009 economic crisis. Thus, it is unlikely that the economic crisis is singularly driving these perceptions, and other factors must be considered. One such factor is that this growth in resources available to nonprofits has led to equal growth in expenses. Perhaps most importantly, the nonprofit workforce grew from 11.1 million in 1998 to 13 million in 2005, outpacing the rest of the U.S. workforce during that period. Total nonprofit wages grew to $470 million in 2005, making up roughly 8% of total national wages. Just as total revenue has grown, so have expenses, leading nonprofit leaders to feel as though resources have largely been stagnant over the past 2 decades. Still another cause for feelings of scarcity is the funding structure faced by most nonprofits, which must raise resources from an uncertain pool of private donations, foundation grants, and state and federal contracts. Any change in one of these funding environments can affect an organization's budget, leading to a great deal of uncertainty.

While these factors are most likely drivers of funding anxiety, the most important cause may be the growth in the number of organizations competing for funding in recent decades. While revenues available to nonprofits exploded in the late 1990s, so did the number of organizations. Just among public charities, the number of these organizations grew by more than 66% from 187,000 in 1995 to 311,000 in 2005. When total resources are divided among the total number of organizations, it is clear that there has been virtually no growth in total revenue per organization during this period! And this does not count growth in religious congregations, which also compete for private charitable dollars.

What has spurred the remarkable growth in nonprofit organizations since the early 1990s? It is likely that this growth is a direct result of the growing revenue streams available to nonprofits. As standard economic theory suggests is the case with any competitive market, as demand grows, so will supply. As American society has demanded more opportunities to spend their income in the nonprofit sector—either through charitable contributions or through fees for service, more providers have entered the market in an attempt to capture those dollars.

Is this growth in the number of agencies good for the sector? Indeed, the nonprofit sector was founded in part on a value of pluralism and freedom. Nonprofits can address the needs of minority stakeholders in ways that governments often cannot. Thus, Americans count on a "vibrant nonprofit sector as a guarantor of their liberties and a mechanism to ensure a degree of pluralism" (Salamon, 1999, p.14). Unfortunately, a by-product of this pluralism is that nonprofits often continue to exist, even when they do not effectively address the needs that spurred their creation. Thus, a possible cost to the value of pluralism within the sector is the well-being of those whom the sector serves. As Bradley, Jensen, and Silverman (2003) write of the nonprofit sector, "small outfits can't possibly achieve scale efficiencies. If organizations with similar missions merged or shared assets, they'd reduce their costs significantly, which would free up more funds for creating social benefits" (pp. 100–101). Thus, has been born the main rationales for strategic collaboration.

Strategic Reasons for Collaboration: Improving Effectiveness, Maximizing Efficiency

A joint undertaking such as collaboration carries with it rewards as well as risks and should be entered into with great deliberation by all involved parties. At the outset, those involved should always engage in negotiations that will clearly establish the strategic aims of the shared venture and the responsibilities of all involved. Otherwise, organizational partnerships often collapse under the weight of poor planning and unclear expectations.

These negotiations should seek to clearly establish each party's value proposition for pursuing the joint venture. That is to say, what is in it for them. Clearly identifying these value propositions allows for each party to determine the perspective costs and benefits of the partnership and can give insight into the probability of success or failure of the venture. Once each organization has effectively communicated their value proposition, all parties must collectively weigh the pros and cons of the partnership. While the reasons for pursuing collaboration are many, Austin

(2004) contends that they can be categorized into two strategic aims: effectiveness gains and efficiency gains.

Effectiveness Gains

Effectiveness gains refer to improvements in an organization's ability to serve its target population either through improved or expanded services. Becoming more effective in delivering programs or services to an organization's target population is a main strategic reason to engage in collaboration. A collaboration with another nonprofit, for-profit, or government agency might enable an agency to access resources it otherwise could not. Often these are monetary resources, but they may also include the specialized skills of other organizations, access to potential customers, or access to information. Another effectiveness gain comes in the form of nonprofits pairing complementary services that are more effective in concert than they would be separately. For example, in Flint, Michigan, a coalition of area agencies combating homelessness through a wide range of services from prevention programs to shelters have paired up in a *continuum of care* through which they hope clients may be better served because of greater communication and synergy of services. Other types of effectiveness gains can come in the form of eliminating redundant services from a service system that allows for the reallocation of resources in the form of funds, space, and personnel to other initiatives, in effect, bolstering the overall effectiveness of the nonprofit.

When seeking to identify collaborations that may improve effectiveness, organizations should ask how their services could be improved through partnership with other entities. How will the organization's target population be made better off through a proposed joint initiative? How will a proposed partnership further the organization's efforts in pursuit of its mission?

Efficiency Gains

Efficiency gains may result from collaborations as well. Efficiency gains revolve mostly around cost savings that can be realized through partnerships. Organizations may choose to share some of the fixed costs of operations, such as administrative services, sharing space or major resources, or even the sharing of key personnel. When seeking such efficiency gains through partnership, the key question that each party must ask is how tasks currently being done could be done at lower cost through partnership with other entities. This often results in the more efficient use of existing resources. Nonprofit organizations often underutilize key resources. How often does the large community room go empty? Could one copier or printer easily serve the needs of two offices rather than one? How many days a week is the agency's bus sitting in the parking lot? Identifying untapped potential of existing resources is the key to success.

Joint investment in a new resource (such as a gymnasium, exhibit space, or magnetic resonance imaging [MRI] machine)—and the resulting diffusion of risk—can be an attractive form of the efficiency gains that accrue from these types of partnerships. Nonprofit managers often face difficult choices when making decisions about significant organizational investments. Will the capital investment be successful or will the money be lost? Will the nonprofit be able to derive maximum value from the use of the equipment in relation to the capital outlay, or will the piece of equipment go underutilized? Partnerships allow all parties involved in a venture to share these risks, minimizing the detrimental effect of a failed investment to any one agency.

Efficiency: A Means to Improve Effectiveness

While the two main strategic goals of nonprofit collaboration can be defined as efficiency gains or effectiveness gains, in truth, the final goal of any such initiative comes down to effectiveness gains. Efficiency gains are useful only to the degree that they can lead to increased effectiveness. Reducing the fixed costs of administrative services means that more resources can be reallocated to other programs. Every dollar saved by sharing accounting services by the local YMCA can be reallocated to mentoring or recreation programs for youth. Jointly purchasing a major piece of equipment means that cost savings can go toward serving the agency's target population. Sometimes organizations get caught up in efforts to become more efficient for efficiency's sake. However, any change done in the name of increased efficiency should translate into direct improvements in the service delivery for the target population. Otherwise, they have offered no strategic benefit whatsoever. If your organization is looking to undertake some efficiency improvements, a key question is, what will happen to the cost savings? How will they benefit your target population and further your mission? If they do not further the organization's mission, then they have no strategic value at all.

Exploring Different Types of Collaboration

Collaborations take numerous forms, pairing nonprofits with other nonprofits, with for-profit businesses, or with government agencies. They may be short-term or long-term initiatives. They may seek to lower the costs and maximize the use of organizational resources, or they may focus on leveraging the resources of partnering organizations to better serve a common target population. This section details some of the different forms such ventures can take, offering real-life examples.

Collaborations Between Two or More Nonprofit Agencies

As discussed previously, organizations often seek to improve the efficiency or the effectiveness of their programs by partnering with other nonprofit agencies. They might seek to reduce overhead by sharing administrative costs thus freeing up more resources to be spent on programs. If multiple organizations in the same community have complementary or even substitutable missions and work with the same target population, there may be a potential benefit for them to work together. Reorganizing services so that there is less duplication can free up resources for other programs. It is also possible that through working together, nonprofits can be more effective than they can be apart. Depending on the specific strategic goal of the initiative, interorganizational partnerships in the nonprofit sector may take the form of partnering in service delivery in the short-term or long-term, in sharing of resources, or in organizational mergers or acquisitions.

Long-Term Partnering in Service Delivery

An important type of collaboration between nonprofit organizations involves the pairing of services either for a short-term project or for long-term initiatives. Such partnerships can often expand the reach of all those involved. For example, an agency that provides tutoring services to at-risk youth might want to collaborate with an agency that provides preventative health exams for the same population. By pairing the two services within the same after-school program, both agencies may reach a broader population than they could apart. In this example, the programs offered by the two agencies are complementary: They build on each other instead of competing.

In an alternative scenario, two tutoring programs in the same community might realize they are providing essentially the same type of service. In the absence of collaboration, these programs might be considered substitutes and would likely compete for the same funding or even the same students. Through interorganizational negotiations, however, they might agree to a specialization of services that benefits themselves and their clients. *Agency A* might agree to focus their tutoring on reading skills while *Agency B* focuses on math skills. Or *Agency A* might target their programs to junior high students while *Agency B* focuses on high school–age youth. Through partnership, it is possible that both organizations can expand their reach through specialization and in doing so better meet the needs of their target population.

Sharing of Space or Resources

A very practical type of collaboration occurs when two or more nonprofit organizations agree to share space or resources. Two nonprofits can often cut costs by pooling resources. Often, organizations must purchase key resources but do not use them to full capacity. If organizations purchase them cooperatively, they can share the costs and better use the resources to their full capacity. Austin (2004) offers the example of two hospitals in the same community jointly purchasing an MRI machine. By partnering in this purchase, they can share the tremendous fixed cost (purchase price of roughly $2 million) while taking better advantage of the low marginal cost of each use of the machine. In another example, more than 40 arts organizations in southeast Michigan created an online *sharing resource clearinghouse*, in which agencies can trade specialized services with one another. Through this system, nonprofits are able to trade access to resources such as the graphic design expertise of one organization or the bus-and-driver housed in another. Pooling these resources has enabled participants to reduce these costs while also using their existing assets more fully.

Sharing space often means renting, purchasing, or building one space for use by multiple organizations. In the case of Temple Beth Emeth, a Jewish Reform synagogue, and St. Clare's Episcopal Church in Ann Arbor, Michigan, two independent religious congregations have co-owned the same worship space since 1976, making it one of the first such collaborations between two faith communities from different religions. While the effort began as a way to cut the fixed costs of both congregations, the partnership has become its own statement of sorts by the two bodies. Another example of this is the *one-stop shop* model of social service delivery. In recent years, social service providers have borrowed from retailers who are cohoused in shopping malls by building a space where numerous human service providers can colocate. Beyond the obvious efficiency advantages of jointly owned space, this may also expand the reach of participating organizations and help with interorganizational streamlining of programs.

In all of these cases, partnering agencies need to clearly define the expectations for all involved parties. The primary purpose of these types of ventures should always be improved efficiency—meaning that the partnership lowers the participants' costs and allows them to reallocate resources elsewhere. Unfortunately, in some cases, these types of collaborations do not succeed in this goal. This will be discussed in more detail below in the challenges section.

Organizational Mergers

Finally, when multiple organizations provide the same type of services or provide complementary services, a merger may be in the strategic interests of both. The goal of such a merger would be to combine resources, pool funding, and/or increase the organizations' ability to achieve their collective mission. Recent research suggests that mergers and acquisitions are becoming more common, especially as agencies seek out ways to reduce their costs (Jacobs, 2008). Although the process of merging organizations is complicated and delicate, many believe that this is a promising way to increase the effectiveness of the nonprofit sector (Bradley et al., 2003). This argument holds that having multiple organizations with similar missions in the same geographical area lowers the ability of each agency to be effective and wastes resources, hurting the agencies' shared target population.

In one example of a successful organizational merger, the Rare Foundation and Winning Futures determined that their missions were very similar (to inspire youth through connections with successful adults) and they had overlapping programs. Thus, in an effort to cut fixed agency costs and free up more resources for services, the two merged, creating one organization that could better pursue its mission. In New Orleans, Louisiana, a movement is underway to encourage collaboration between nonprofits. Part of this movement included the merger between the Center for Nonprofit Resources and the Greater New Orleans Community Data Center, to create The Greater New Orleans Nonprofit Knowledge Works. Previously, these organizations were providing similar services and competing for funding sources. Now they have merged and are better able to assist in the capacity building of the nonprofit sector in their community.

When considering a merger or acquisition, all involved parties must consider the legal implications. Mergers are much more complicated than other forms of collaboration. For example, mergers typically require the formal approval of the board. In such a case, the collaboration should be discussed at several meetings before a vote of the board is taken (Jacobs, 2008). Mergers may also require a vote of the members of the organization (Jacobs, 2008). In this case, it would also be important to inform the members of the possibility of the merger to give them time to consider their votes. Finally, and most importantly, mergers or acquisitions may have financial implications. Can the merged entities access the endowment of one of the original organizations? Will an important funder approve a grant that was awarded to one or the other following a merger? How does the merger affect the new entities' tax status? These are all key issues that must be addressed.

Partnerships Between Nonprofit and For-Profit Firms

It is also becoming increasingly popular for nonprofit agencies to collaborate with for-profit enterprises. Indeed, in their seminal book *Forces for Good* (2008), Crutchfield and Grant suggest that collaboration with the for-profit sector is a key practice of successful nonprofits. Such relationships seek to be mutually beneficial. Some of the benefits can be similar to collaborations between nonprofit organizations. For example, collaborations might involve cost-cutting measures or information sharing, as discussed above. However, more often, businesses and nonprofits collaborate for different reasons. Such relationships can be based on fundraising goals or collaboration on an area of shared interest for both entities.

Fundraising Relationship

Often, for-profit firms seek to partner with nonprofits in efforts to give back to the community or donate to a specific cause. While for-profits often have altruistic motives for this type of collaboration, they also have a powerful incentive to publicly appear responsive to community needs. It is critical to remember that such partnerships allow for-profit entities to benefit from a nonprofit's brand, enhancing their credibility. Thus, nonprofit leaders should be aware that the relationship is not one-sided in these partnerships. Indeed, nonprofits should be careful to partner with for-profit organizations that are worthy of their "seal of approval" because a nonprofit's "brand" is its greatest asset. It should avoid partnering with entities that will detract from that brand. For example, an environmental justice organization should avoid partnering with a known polluter, unless it is on a venture to reduce that firm's pollution (discussed later on).

The most common type of venture-involved partnerships is fundraising efforts. This might be as simple as a firm asking employees to donate to the nonprofit organization via payroll deduction. In other cases, this might involve more complex collaborations involving major fundraising events, corporate matching of donations, or long-term ongoing donations of money or materials. Austin (2004) highlights a new type of partnership in which nonprofits purchase corporate endorsements of their websites, allowing a firm to place its logo on the nonprofit's website. This can be a very lucrative arrangement with almost no costs, as long as the for-profit firm does not detract from the nonprofit's brand.

Often agencies are brought together by interest in a common issue, such as a for-profit art supply company and a nonprofit that promotes art programs at inner-city schools. The arts supply company has an altruistic motive for this partnership—promoting the arts—and a business motive—increasing its consumer base. Other times, the owner or CEO of a business may have an interest in a particular social issue. This was the case when a former CEO of the clothing manufacturer American Eagle Outfitters decided to partner with Jumpstart, a program that helped prepare low-income youth for preschool and early education, among other things. The CEO was drawn to this issue because as a young immigrant child, he had trouble reading and wanted to give other children a better chance (Austin, 2000). Nonprofit managers, for their part, can foster these types of relationships so that one-time donations can turn into long-term relationships. They should seek out for-profit firms that may have similar interests.

Partnership on a Project

In some cases, nonprofits and for-profit firms may have very different strategic interests for jointly pursuing a project. Crutchfield and Grant (2008) highlight the example of the nonprofit Environmental Defense, which partnered with McDonald's to help the fast-food chain reduce its food packaging and make it more environmentally friendly. This eventually led to a reduction in packaging waste of 150,000 tons within 10 years. While Environmental Defense's primary objective was to reduce product waste, McDonald's primary objective was to reduce food costs. Different incentives can lead to the same goal.

Collaborations between nonprofits and for-profits can also be designed to allow one or both parties to benefit from the knowledge and skills of the other. Many agencies are finding ways to collaborate that are mutually beneficial. This can involve collaborating on projects that benefit the community or sharing information in ways that help both agencies meet their goals. Austin (2004) highlights the example of Starbucks Coffee Company's work with Cooperative for American Relief Everywhere (CARE). Through this partnership, Starbucks was able to learn ways to start community projects in some of the coffee-growing communities that the company wished to assist. In turn, Starbucks promoted CARE in its stores and sold special bags of coffee to benefit CARE. Both agencies benefited from the expertise of the other.

Nonprofits and Government Relationships

There is a great deal of collaboration between government agencies and nonprofits. Nonprofit agencies can partner with local, state, or federal government agencies. There are different types of nonprofit-government collaborations, such as programs funded by competitive government contracts, government grant-funded programs, or nonprofit agencies that are funded, at least in part, by government agencies, such as public universities. Most often, though, these types of partnerships usually take the form of government grants and programs in which nonprofit agencies deliver services specified and paid for through government. Such partnerships are a key source of funding, especially in the human services, where government funding makes up over a third of organizational revenue.

In comparison to the types of collaborations detailed in the previous section, these types of relationships should not be characterized as partnerships between equals. Indeed, almost always, they are contractual relationships for services. While they can be critical in expanding the ability of nonprofits to serve their target population, they can also put limits on the activities of agencies, as government sets the parameters of service delivery. Thus, nonprofits should think strategically about the consequences of these types of arrangements. While such relationships have the ability to expand the scope of services offered by an organization, they can also create barriers for the organization by limiting whom they can serve and how they can serve them. For example, as executive director of the Community Self-Determination Institute in Watts, California, Aqeela Sherrills made the decision that the million-plus dollars in government funding his agency was receiving was detracting from the organization's mission to spread peace in urban war zones. Thus, the organization greatly reduced its funding but returned to services that members felt better served their target population.

Challenges to Collaboration

Strategic collaboration can yield great benefits to nonprofit organizations, increasing their effectiveness or improving their efficiency. Numerous challenges, however, can present barriers to success, even in the best-laid plans. Often, strategic partners will not see eye to eye on all things. In this case, involved parties must be cognizant that disagreement and divergent viewpoints can lead to fissures in the relationship and ultimately to the collapse of the collaboration. Some of the barriers to success revolve around divergent organizational cultures and organizational identities, joint ventures entered into at a funder's behest, divergent interests in the collaboration, and threats to reputation and branding.

Organizational Culture and Identity

Most scholars agree that organizations can have distinctive cultures. Some are hierarchical and bureaucratic. Others are free-flowing and horizontally structured. Some are more results focused, by any means, while others tend to be focused more on processes. Often organizational cultures of partnering entities may be dissimilar to each other, creating barriers to effective communication and a high risk of conflict. Often stark differences in culture can lead one entity to feel disrespected by the other. Or it can lead to role confusion. If one entity had a very free-flowing meeting style and the other used structured agendas, this could even make the process of learning about conflicting cultures difficult.

Organizational identity is a powerful phenomenon. Nonprofits compete with private companies for employees not on the basis of salaries but instead on the basis of mission and organizational identity. The uniqueness of a nonprofit's cultural identity can be compromised by working with a partner with a dissimilar cultural identity, creating protective feelings amongst a nonprofit's employees that their organization is losing a special aspect of itself. Interorganizational communication may become compromised as feelings of animosity and distrust manifest and ultimately interfere with the effective relationship building that is essential to the success of any collaboration.

When conducting strategic negotiations at the outset of a partnership, participating entities must also use the time period to assess the similarities and dissimilarities in organizational culture each will bring to the joint undertaking. Does one nonprofit promote a relaxed atmosphere for their employees to work while another nonprofit promotes a professional view that their employees should exercise a measure of formality in all interactions? Does one nonprofit have a leadership structure that encourages employees to take independent initiative, while another operates in a more rigid environment that borders on micromanagement? Identifying these differences and assessing their importance early on can be the key in ensuring that they do not inhibit the chance for success. In some cases, organizations may decide that the barriers to success are too great.

Funder-Driven Collaboration

Often collaboration is *funder-driven*, meaning, for instance, the government, the United Way, or a foundation will require that nonprofits work together. These funders will make collaboration a condition for funding, often in the name of improved effectiveness. Funders located in a community often can see redundancies in services or areas in which entities working together can be more effective than when they work apart. They may then require those receiving grants to collaborate with each other. This can be highly useful, as it causes organizations to partner in ways they often would not do otherwise. However, it is important to remember that these types of collaborations are not driven by the organizations. Thus, they may suffer from the other roadblocks listed in this section. Further, the partnering entities may see no incentive to collaborate in more than only name, leading to ineffectual partnerships.

Competing Interests

As previously discussed, nonprofits entering collaboration with another nonprofit, a for-profit firm, or government should make sure that all participating parties clearly identify and communicate their value proposition. This means they should be clear about their main interests and incentives for participating in the initiative. Often, organizations have multiple interests for engaging in an initiative. In the Environmental Defense and McDonald's partnership discussed previously (as related in Crutchfield & Grant, 2008), McDonald's had at least three obvious interests in the partnership: (1) to reduce its costs by reducing its food packaging, (2) to reduce its waste and positively impact the environment, and (3) to appear to its customers and possible customers to be positively impacting the environment. Of these three interests, Environmental shared only one. Thus, it is often possible for partners to find common ground, even when all of their interests do not align. However, parties with interests that are too divergent may want to assess their ongoing or proposed partnerships. In one example, university researchers and nonprofits often partner in the evaluation of programs. However, if the organization is only interested in seeing "good" results and not interested in objective evaluation, the researchers may want to demure. Their interests in the collaboration are likely too divergent.

Assessing potential parties' interests for engaging in collaboration—those clearly stated and those not so clearly stated—is a critical step to avoiding the barriers to effective joint venture. For instance, if a nonprofit is collaborating with a for-profit company because the nonprofit is in vital need of resources, while the for-profit company seeks to expand its customer base, what can be supposed about how the collaboration would operate? Could it potentially spell a differentiation of power to the advantage of the for-profit firm? Differentiation of interests is not a deal breaker when it comes to institutional collaboration. It is instead an inducement for prior planning to bring divergent interests in line in service to a common goal.

Protecting the Brand

Finally, all nonprofits should be particularly aware that their reputation or their *brand* is their chief asset. A nonprofit's brand is sacrosanct because it directly affects its ability to fund raise and generate popular support within its target community and in the community at large. Collaborations carry with them the very real possibility of damaging a nonprofit's reputation and ultimately its ability to perform its underlying mission. For example, if a national animal rights organization announced a joint initiative to stop animal testing in partnership with a major poultry production company, then what would be the probable adverse reaction from some funders? In another example, a nonprofit may be approached about a fundraising partnership by a for-profit firm that has recently suffered from some bad press and is looking to repair its image. The nonprofit's leaders should be particularly wary of this type of relationship, even if it promises substantial financial rewards, because it may negatively affect its organization's brand in the long-term. The risk of a potential collaboration to a nonprofit's reputation is the weightiest countermeasure to a potential collaboration's value.

Five Key Guidelines to Successful Collaboration

Entering into collaboration with another agency can be a little bit like choosing a spouse. Even under perfect conditions, finding the right partner can prove tough. Even if you do find "the one," there is planning to do, and the clearer expectations are, the better. Making such a commitment requires more thought and planning than casual dating. Similarly, entering into a strategic partnership with another organization requires clear communication, clear expectations, and plenty of planning. Partners may have different expectations about what they hope to get out of the arrangement. If they align, that's great. If they compete, this may be a red flag. Thus, to help foster the best possible partnership, it is helpful to start by addressing some key issues early on in the process. Such an exercise can help identify possible barriers to success, helping the relationship develop in a more positive way. The following are some general guidelines that may help an agency determine whether collaboration is in their best interest.

Clearly Define the Purpose of Any Proposed Collaboration

An organization considering a strategic partnership must begin by clearly identifying the purpose of the initiative. Your agency needs to understand its purpose for collaboration in order to find the best fit. What is the strategic goal of the proposed initiative? Generally, how long would it last (short-term or long-term), and how will success be measured? Identifying at the very beginning the reasons for a collaboration—and the strategic outcomes that partners hope to achieve—are critical to ensuring that an agency begins down the right path. If organizations begin negotiations before these are well specified, it may result in a great deal of lost effort.

Identifying the Right Partner

Once your agency has clearly articulated its strategic goals, an organization must consider whether a proposed partner is the right one for their agency. Most important, it must consider the potential impact of the partners in question on its *brand*, or reputation. As previously discussed, for nonprofits (and perhaps even for-profits), an organization's brand is its most important asset. It captures the way that others perceive the agency. Whenever one agency partners with another, the brand of each is impacted. This impact can be positive or negative. Thinking about this ahead of time can cut down on future headaches.

Choosing the partner means taking the time to consider organizations that you might want to collaborate with and brainstorming the effect of such partnerships on the brand of your agency. For example, if your agency promotes use of green energy sources and you are interested in a corporate fundraising collaboration, consider the implications of collaborating with a car manufacturing company versus an organic food company. In some cases, the car manufacturer may be a good partner—perhaps if the partnership is a strategic initiative to find ways to cut down on polluting emissions of factories or increase fuel efficiency in cars. However, a traditional fundraising relationship between the organization and the car company might diminish the nonprofit's brand. On the other hand, partnering with the organic food company might actually reinforce the nonprofit's brand.

It is important, beyond questions of the brand, to research potential partners and assess whether your agency and they can work well together. Does the organization seem to have a culture that will mesh well with your own? Are they known for living up to commitments? Or have they had experiences where they did not fulfill their obligations? A whole host of organizational issues often get in the way of what would appear to be an obvious fit between agencies. Such issues are not often deal breakers. In fact, early identification of major differences in organizational cultures can help leadership teams address these differences and make the partnership a fruitful one.

Clearly Articulate the Interests of Both Entities

The first guideline requires your agency to identify and clearly articulate the reasons that it wants to enter into a strategic partnership. Once your agency has found a partner, it is time to dig a little bit deeper into your agency's own motivations, and into those of your agency's potential partner. Both agencies need to spend time clarifying the incentives, both primary and secondary, for its organization. Both agencies should benefit

from the collaboration, but it is important to remember that both agencies have different reasons for wanting to collaborate. On its own, your agency needs to spend some time articulating the things that it hopes to gain from the collaboration and its motivation for it (your organization's value proposition). Finally, your agency needs to list the things that (1) it is willing to give up to further the initiative and (2) what things are not negotiable. Your organization's partnering agency should do the same. Once you have done this, both agencies need to spend time discussing these interests. Putting this information on the table ahead of time can help in identifying possible conflicts of interest.

At the very worst, some agencies may have malevolent intentions for engaging in collaboration. More than one "merger of equals" has resulted in one organization swallowing up another in an effort to gain its resources and eliminate a competitor. Nonprofit leaders should be aware that these types of situations do exist and should look out for partners who may not have the best intentions. Further, if a nonprofit determines that a proposed joint undertaking is only of greater benefit to itself but has the real possibility of being financially destabilizing to its fellow partner, then it has an ethical duty to warn the other nonprofit of this possibility.

It is important to remember that agencies exist for different reasons. For-profits exist to make money. Nonprofits exist to fulfill their mission. Governments exist to serve the people and provide vital services. Even in collaborations between nonprofit agencies, agencies have different missions to fulfill. Collaboration happens in the overlap of interests. When the interests of two or more agencies can be served by the same means, you have grounds for collaboration.

Assess the Costs and Benefits

At this point, your agency should know why they want to collaborate, who they want to collaborate with, and what they hope to gain. Thus, it is time to explicitly outline the costs and benefits of a proposed venture and determine whether a proposed undertaking is in the best interests of your agency. Sometimes costs and benefits are not exactly clear. Thus, it is necessary for your agency to take plenty of time to think this through. For example, your agency might be considering sharing space with another agency in order to save money. The money your agency saves would allow your agency to start a new program. However, your agency may find that the new location would not be accessible to your agency's clients. Another question is the extent to which the collaboration will take up the time of your agency's staff. What are the costs in terms of staff time? What effect will this collaboration have on organizational culture? How will it affect your organization's autonomy? If your partner has government grants, will this impose restrictions on what you can do? Will a for-profit firm hinder your ability to serve a vulnerable population.

Perhaps the for-profit firm will help you raise 50% of your organization's budget, on the condition that your agency give up your agency's needle exchange program that serves homeless drug users. This is a substantial cost if this is a core service that your agency believes in.

A critical analytic tool for spelling out the costs of a joint venture is to identify its opportunity costs. Economists suggest the true cost of something is not just what you pay for it, but what you give up to get it. The opportunity cost of college, for example, is what you could have done with your time otherwise. For some individuals, such as LeBron James, the professional basketball player, the opportunity cost of college is too high. He would lose money by attending college. (For most of us, of course, college is a great investment and the opportunity costs are low.) The true cost of collaboration is the alternative of what you could have done with those resources instead: perhaps a partnership with another agency, perhaps a different program. Weighing the opportunity costs is critical to making sure you have made a good investment.

Spell Out Responsibilities of Both Parties

A successful partnership must be carefully executed. Sometimes, agencies carefully go through the planning stages, but fail to properly execute the collaboration. For this reason, collaborations often end up in limbo. Setting out responsibilities and creating a timeline can help to ensure that this is collaboration in more than only name.

Both parties need to work together to explicitly state the responsibilities that each has. If the responsibilities are lopsided (one has far more than the other), then this should raise a red flag. Next, partners should create a time line in which milestones are to happen and identify who is responsible for doing the work. This process can be simple, as in cases of collaboration on a project, or complex, as in collaboration between a government body and a nonprofit agency. Be sure to take sufficient time to decide which partner will do what and how it will get done.

Finally, like any relationship, prepare for the unexpected. Both partners must be committed to the process and yet be flexible. They must be willing to meet the needs of the other but must not sacrifice their own needs. Successful collaborations are carefully crafted and require a lot of work, but if your agency finds the right partner and makes the right preparations, it gives the relationship the best start possible.

Future Directions

Many social entrepreneurs—individuals with innovative ideas and the drive to make them happen—hope to start a new nonprofit organization. With a new or energized approach, it seems like the obvious choice to begin a new organization. The United States is often called a *nation of joiners*. But perhaps just as true is that we are a *nation of starters*. There is much in the history of the nonprofit sector to support such a choice. Indeed, the whole history of the sector is one of people who have seen social problems and worked to fix them. Today, however, the sector is bigger than ever. In the midst of resources that are growing at an unprecedented rate (with the exception of the 2008–2009 economic crisis), there are more organizations than ever before. Thus, anyone thinking of starting an organization is obligated to look at the system of organizations in their community serving that target population. How many are there? How effective are they? Would it be possible to work through an existing organization? If not, why? And how would a new entity serve the target population better?

This is not to say that a new venture is not the right way to go. In some cases, it will be. However, no matter what, the nonprofit sector is moving toward a path of closer collaboration across organizations. Thus, any new effort should see itself as a part of a *system of services* and seek to complement—and even strengthen—services already being provided. Using the guidelines discussed above and being aware of many of the challenges that pose barriers to successful collaboration, nonprofit leaders can work to develop an ever stronger sector through strategic, meaningful, and effective collaborations.

References and Further Readings

Austin, J. A. (2000). Strategic collaboration between nonprofits and businesses. *Nonprofit and Voluntary Sector Quarterly, 29*(1), 69–87.

Austin, J. A. (2004). Institutional collaboration. In D. R. Young (Ed.), *Effective economic decision-making by nonprofit organizations* (pp. 149–166). New York: Foundation Center.

Bradley, B., Jensen, P., & Silverman, L. (2003). The nonprofit sector's $100 billion opportunity. *Harvard Business Review, 81*(5), 94–103, 130.

Crutchfield, L. R., & Grant, H. M. (2008). *Forces for good*. San Francisco: Jossey-Bass.

Jacobs, J. A. (2008). Mergers: Easier (and harder) than you think. *Associations Now, 4*(8), 33–36.

Salamon, L. M (1999). *America's nonprofit sector: A primer* (2nd ed.). New York: Foundation Center.

Wing, K. T., Pollak, T. H., & Blackwood, A. (2008). *The nonprofit almanac 2008*. Washington, DC: Urban Institute.

63

Major Social Change Theories That Nonprofit Leaders Should Know

Agnes Meinhard

Ryerson University

Seldom in the history of humanity has either the pace or variety of change been greater than that witnessed in the past 3 decades (Homer-Dixon, 2000). The revolution in communication and technology has made the world a smaller and vastly more interconnected place. The ripple effects of this revolution extend to the very structure of our society:

- Increases in life expectancy through medical advances and vast migrations of people have contributed to significant demographic shifts in Western societies. These shifts pose new challenges to governments and nonprofit organizations in particular.
- One of these challenges is a growing clash of values between upholding individual rights and civil liberties on the one hand and a demand for greater adherence to more "traditional" religious and cultural values on the other. Nonprofit organizations often find themselves caught in the middle.
- With more rapid communication and transportation capabilities, global competition and trade agreements are shifting production around the world thus affecting millions of lives.
- Advances in technology have made many jobs obsolete, creating major employment, welfare, and educational challenges. The gap between rich and poor continues to grow, even in Western countries (Dunn, 2003).
- Paradoxically, despite these strides in technology, famine, drought, and disease are still endemic in much of the world and often made worse by the displacement of people from rural to urban settings and the destruction of environmental ecosystems.

These changes have implications not only for businesses and corporations but also for nonprofit organizations many of which serve the poor, the displaced, and the diseased. In addition, accompanying these major societal transformations is a general philosophical shift that leans toward adopting the "corporate model" as the gold standard for efficiency in both public and nonprofit sector organizations, irrespective of its degree of applicability and relevance (Meinhard, Foster, & Berger, 2004; Rice & Prince, 2000). This has led to demands on nonprofit organizations to adopt more efficient businesslike practices, even as they are coping with all the other changes.

It is not surprising then that the challenge of navigating an organization in times of rapid and multifaceted change may seem staggering to the people within. With so many things happening simultaneously, it is difficult to know where to focus, to understand what is critical, and to be aware of the opportunities and resources that may be available. Much like first-time parents, leaders can be overwhelmed by the barrage of new information and the struggle to determine what is most important. However, their sense of being consumed by these details can be significantly reduced if given a lens through which to see what is critical and tools with which to confront the new challenges. In this chapter, various lenses are offered to help leaders navigate change: a wide-angle one to understand the broader context of the challenges they face and a telescopic one to focus on those aspects of the external and internal environments that are critical to their organizations. While there is no "magic bullet" to make organizational transformations easy and painless, the research and theories presented here will enhance understanding of the complexities involved and help leaders move forward in the context of their organizations' missions.

Many societal observers have noted that change is constant and that the human species is quite adept at accommodating to the demands of a changing environment (Wheatley,

1992). Our very presence on this planet today attests to our adaptability as a species. And yet, as individuals, we have all experienced reluctance—and even failure—to change. How many times have we balked at work directives that require us to change? How often do we cringe at the thought of learning yet another new task or software system? How many well-intentioned resolutions to change certain personal habits have we made that we have failed to keep? So although at a species level we display admirable adaptability, at an individual level, we portray a degree of reluctance to and difficulty with change. This is especially true today with the ceaseless bombardment of new technologies. The pace of technological change is relentless, yet our human capacity to absorb new technology is limited (Homer-Dixon, 2000). This individual reluctance toward change and our limited absorption capabilities have implications in organizational settings. Recent studies serve to illustrate how difficult it is to guide organizations through successful transformations; an estimated 60% to 80% fail to achieve their goals (Champy, 1995; Kotter, 1995). And yet on a species level, organizations, just as humans, have adapted to changing environments mostly through a process of replacement; organizations no longer serving the needs of their environment die only to be replaced by new, better fitting organizations (Hannan & Freeman, 1989).

Some organizations do, however, engage in substantial change processes that are successful and result in significant restructuring to the benefit of the organization. These transformations may have resulted from small, incremental steps taken over a number of years, or they may have been the result of planned, radical strategies (Kotter, 1995). The following sections present theories and empirical observations that elucidate why change is so difficult and provide guidelines for consideration before embarking on organizational transformations.

Conceptual Model

The conceptual model presented in Figure 63.1 visually illustrates the complex and integrative dimensions of leadership and organizational change, positioning it within the

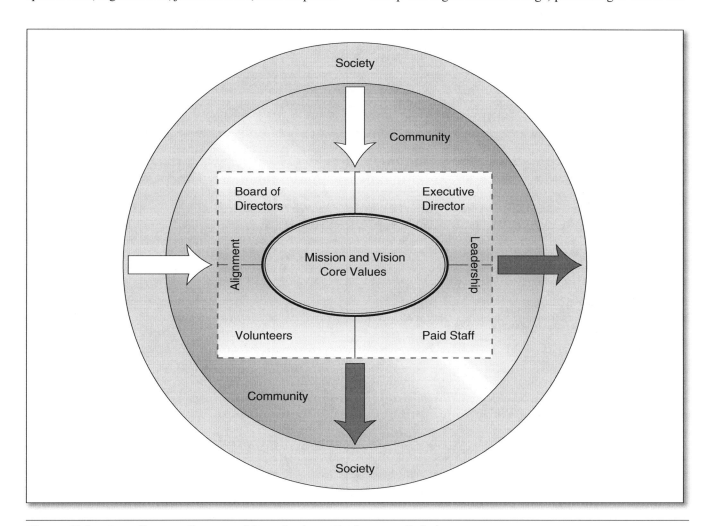

Figure 63.1   Open Systems Concept of Organization—Environment Relations

NOTE: The author gratefully acknowledges input from personal discussions with Peter Elson in conceptualizing this figure.

fundamental context of the relationship of nonprofit organizations to their immediate community and society at large.

The outer ring represents society-at-large—those social, economic, political, legal, and technological forces that influence trade agreements, domestic and foreign policies, the degree of inequality and poverty in society, and the technological changes that so often drive productivity expectations. This macrosocietal ecosystem interacts in a dynamic fashion with the communities in which nonprofit organizations function—found just inside the outer ring in the diagram. Community, in this case, is not limited to a geographically contained neighborhood; rather, it is used in its broadest sense, as a community of people and organizations that are in immediate contact with the focus organization regardless of their geographic location. For example, large organizations operate within a provincial or state and national or international community while others serve virtual communities over the Internet, but still, most nonprofit organizations are small to medium in size and operate at a local level. This section thus represents the external stakeholders, including funders, clients, collaborators, and the interests of the general public. Otherwise known as the *domain environment* (Daft, 2001), it defines the dynamics that influence access to scarce resources (competition or collaboration with other organizations) and the political, social, economic, and technological context of the organization.

The inner rectangle with the broken lines represents the open system character of the nonprofit organization and its own dynamic relationship with society and community. The premise is that as open systems, nonprofit organizations are both affected by and in turn influence their community and society. This interaction between the organization and its environment is depicted by two sets of arrows. The white arrows indicate community and societal inputs affecting the organization; the dark arrows represent outputs from the organization to the community and society.

At the very center of the organization, depicted by the oval, is the core of the organization (Thompson, 1967) expressed through its vision and mission. It is a manifestation of both the internal soul of the organization and the public good it provides to community and society. Surrounding this core are the four major internal stakeholder groups—the board of directors, the executive director, paid staff members, and volunteers—each with their own roles in the fulfillment of the organization's mission. In larger organizations, staff and volunteers are distributed in different organizational departments or subunits that have to be aligned in order to efficiently fulfill the organization's mission. The organization as a whole has to be in tune with its environment, positioning its vision and mission in relationship to the needs (present or future) of its stakeholders, the community, and the society it serves. Organizational change is basically a realignment of the organization's structure—technical, political, and cultural

(Tichy, 1983)—to meet the changing demands of its environment. Leadership is a fundamental prerequisite to the creation of a supportive climate for change. In a nonprofit organization, formal leadership manifests itself at the board of directors and the executive director levels. Leadership also is found throughout the organization including paid staff and volunteers. The extent to which an organization is adaptable and flexible and undertakes ongoing planning, asset-based development, training, and organizational learning, will determine its success. Leadership, alignment, and adaptation capacities all interact with each other and play key roles in the dynamics of organizational change.

Organizations and Their Relationship to the Environment

As open systems, nonprofit organizations are dependent on their environments for survival. They import human, financial, technical, and natural resources, such as volunteers, skilled labor, knowledge, and donations or grants, from the environment to produce a product or provide a service of value to the community and/or society (Katz & Kahn, 1966). Therefore, the organization is dependent on its environment both for its resources and for the consumption of its services or products (Pfeffer & Salancik, 1978). If resources are not available or if the organization's outputs are not valued, the organization will be unable to sustain itself. Together, the resource suppliers and the service consumers constitute the organization's niche (Hannan & Freeman, 1989).

The first challenge a newly formed organization faces when trying to gain a foothold in a particular niche is to establish its legitimacy, in other words, to convince both internal and external stakeholders that it can reliably carry out its mission (Stinchcombe, 1965). It does this by reinforcing behaviors that are successful and dropping those that do not work. Thus, during its formative years, a nonprofit organization, whether it is a hospice, an artists' cooperative, or an environmental watchdog, establishes a pattern of operations and a nexus of relationships that is best suited for its niche. This process of institutionalizing organizational beliefs, culture, structure, patterns of behavior, and networks of relationships predisposes organizations to powerful forces of inertia that over time make it difficult for them to change (DiMaggio & Powell, 1983; Hannan & Freeman, 1989).

This is borne out by statistics recording the survival rates of organizations. Whether they are for-profit or nonprofit, 5-year survival rates hover around the 20% range (Aldrich, 1979). Referring to this phenomenon as the *liability of newness*, organizational researchers have hypothesized both internal, or organizational, and external, or environmental, causes to account for this. According to Stinchcombe (1965), internal causes stem from a lack of organizational knowledge and inadequate core competencies on the one hand and problems of coordination and poor socialization on the other. External reasons include a lack of or tightly controlled resources, financial or other, and competition from other organizations. Although these pressures are particularly strong during the founding process, they can occur at any time in an organization's life cycle.

Greiner (1972) identified various stages of organizational growth with each culminating in a crisis that has to be resolved through some kind of organizational change. The first stage of growth, *a time of creativity*, culminates in a *crisis of leadership*. The entrepreneurial, creative leader is not generally a competent manager, and management becomes more important as an organization grows. This crisis of leadership is resolved by finding a competent manager-leader to provide clear direction to the organization. The second stage of growth, *a time of direction* under the new management, culminates in a *crisis of autonomy*. As an organization grows, it is impossible for one person to control all aspects of operation, and too much centralized control leads to dissatisfaction. More autonomy is needed in the organization. The crisis is resolved through delegation of power to individual units. However, this third stage of growth, *the delegation* stage, precipitates its own problems and leads to a *crisis of control*. Although decisions can now be made autonomously, organizational actions must be coordinated. This fourth stage of growth, *coordination,* requires more rules and regulations and reporting protocols to ensure that all the units of an organization are working together toward a common goal. The proliferation of rules and regulations and reporting requirements leads to the well-known *crisis of too much red tape*. This crisis can be addressed by increasing collaboration among organizational units through multifunctional teams and a matrix structure. Greiner did not identify a crisis for the last growth stage, *collaboration*, but Daft (2001) added the *crisis of revitalization*, which occurs when an organization has elaborated a final, stable structure. Each of the crises identified above defines a specific aspect of one or more of the four broader reasons for failure hypothesized by Stinchcombe (1965): lack of knowledge, inadequate competencies, problems of coordination, and poor socialization. Failure to negotiate any one of these crises can lead to an organization's demise.

Recent longitudinal research in several Western countries suggests that most for-profit organizations do not exhibit significant growth over their lifetimes (Aldrich & Ruef, 2006). In the United States, only about 15% of firms added significant numbers to their workforce. Although there have been no similar investigations of nonprofit organizations, it is safe to assume that the rate of growth would be even lower in the nonprofit sector. Thus, while there may be some internal pressures for change even in small nonprofit organizations—many nonprofits do undergo a crisis of leadership—most of the pressure for change would come from the external environment.

The external pressures identified by Stinchcombe (1965) relate to inaccessibility or scarcity of resources and high levels of competition in the niche. Each of these conditions leads to environmental uncertainty. Uncertainty about acquiring resources and making a dent in a competitive market is greatest in the early stages of an organization's existence, but whenever there are changes in the niche, even an established organization faces renewed uncertainty. The frequency, predictability, and size of environmental changes and the number of concurrent environmental changes determine the extent of environmental uncertainty; whether the changes occur slowly or rapidly and at regular or irregular intervals and whether many aspects of an organization's environment are changing as opposed to only one or two, all have an impact on the extent of uncertainty faced by an organization.

Researchers have found that certain organizational structures and strategies are more conducive in helping an organization navigate rapidly changing, uncertain environments. Organizations with flatter structures, decentralized decision making, and horizontal as well as vertical communications are more successful than the more rule-bound, centralized "tall" bureaucratic structures. They are more nimble and can undertake the rapid changes necessary to remain relevant in their changing niches (Burns & Stalker, 1966; Lawrence & Lorsch, 1967).

Other researchers have noted that organizations adopt various strategies to neutralize the effects of environmental uncertainty, such as stockpiling, creating new markets, boundary spanning, resource diversification, lobbying government, vertical and horizontal integration, mergers, and even illegal activities (Pfeffer & Salancik, 1978; Thompson, 1967). Overall, a generalist strategy, that is, providing diversified services or products that serve several different niches simultaneously, is more likely to afford an organization protection in times of environmental uncertainty. While one niche may be rapidly changing, stability in the organization's other niches can give the organization the necessary time and organizational slack to undertake the changes needed to reengage in the niche. On the other hand, organizations with specialist strategies, providing only one product or service to a single niche, are less likely to survive changes in their niche. Before they can complete the changes, they will be replaced by new organizations that better serve the changed niche (Hannan & Freeman, 1989).

For the past 3 decades, the environment of the nonprofit sector has become quite volatile, subject to critical ideological and technological changes that have had a pronounced impact on the social, political, and economic climate of the nonprofit sector. Changes in social policies, funding patterns, and accountability demands have thrown many nonprofit organizations into turmoil, threatening their viability and exerting pressure on them to change.

Barriers to Change: The Role of Organizational Paradigms

How nonprofit organizations respond to internal and external pressures to change may affect the course of their development and even their survival. It is generally acknowledged that major organizational change is very difficult. Statistics indicate that the majority of organizations fail to achieve change, and many of them actually do not survive the change process. For example, several studies evaluating the impact of Total Quality Management (TQM) programs found that in at least two thirds of the organizations studied, the hoped-for improvements were not achieved. This was not because TQM is ineffective but rather because the program was poorly implemented (Beer, 2003). Another study noted that about 70% of organizational reengineering attempts fail (Champy, 1995). And Kotter (1995) found that very few efforts at organizational change of any kind were successful. He goes on to say that a major reason for these failures is that change is a multiphase project that requires a considerable amount of time.

Whether or not an organization has sufficient time to implement the changes successfully also depends on the timing of the change. Tushman and Romanelli (1994) found that timing was the strongest predictor of successful change. Organizations undertaking change during relatively stable times are more likely to be successful because change takes time to implement, and when there is no external pressure driving the change, there is time to experiment and evaluate; in stable times, there are usually slack resources available to cushion the disruptive effects of change, and even large scale changes are implemented as a series of small steps, which need time. On the other hand, in times of crises, change has to be rapid, which is very disruptive to the organization. With no time to experiment and evaluate and with little access to slack resources, many organizations do not survive the change process.

Even in stable times, organizational change is strewn with difficulties, so why is it that most nonprofit organizations seem to wait until crisis is upon them before undertaking change (Meinhard & Foster, 1996)? The simple answer is that most nonprofit organizations do not engage in systematic environmental scanning; therefore, they remain unaware of subtle changes occurring in the environment. By the time they realize that they have to do something in response to the changing environment, it is often too late. But this answer does not explain why organizations do not do a better job of environmental scanning and why even those organizations that are alert to environmental trends often do not respond in timely or appropriate ways.

Part of the explanation lies in the concept of organizational paradigms. Paradigm refers to the shared understanding and shared exemplars that emerge in any kind of a social entity to guide behavior (Kuhn, 1993). In organizations, it is a way of doing things, a way of looking at the world that includes beliefs about cause-effect relations and both explicit and tacit standards of practice and behavior (Brown, 1989, pp. 134–135). As the culmination of an institutionalization process that every nonprofit organization goes through to gain legitimacy, the organization's paradigm is the glue that binds its members together, providing a sense of collective identity. It also affords the organization distinctiveness, differentiating it from other organizational actors in its environment (DiMaggio & Powell, 1983). As such, the paradigm serves the organization well; as long as its environment remains stable, the organization will have no difficulty surviving, expanding, and thriving, and in the process, becoming more securely ensconced in its niche. But the very paradigm that garnered the nonprofit organization its legitimacy is often so strong that it inhibits members from perceiving the necessity for change. Much like the *Titanic,* organizations speed ahead in the dark, confident in their course, and complacent in their successes. Even though they realize there may be obstacles out there, few organizations engage in systematic environmental scanning. This leaves them unaware of subtle environmental changes that are often the precursors of dramatic environmental shifts. Thus, they are unprepared when the necessity for change becomes unavoidable.

Paradigms not only place blinders on organizations, inhibiting them from seeing the necessity for change and limiting their solution alternatives, but also they generate powerful inertial forces that resist change. Defining as they do, both the power structure and social networks of organizations, the vested interests of individuals may be threatened by change, invoking resistance, which can slow down the change process, render it inadequate, or stop it altogether.

As long as changes do not involve transforming their essential paradigm, organizations have no problem engaging in fine-tuning, which involves small adjustments to structure or operations, or instituting small, incremental changes, where new units or activities are added. Often, these strategies tend to mask or delay the inevitable necessity for substantial transformations and ultimately place the organization at a disadvantage. Even in times of crises, organizations may rely on "quick fixes" rather than sustainable restructuring. An example of a quick fix is the tendency to downsize across the board in response to funding cuts rather than to engage in strategic restructuring.

In summary, change is difficult because (1) the paradigm provides the frame and the concepts with which to perceive the world, and therefore, it is difficult to recognize new opportunities and to find solutions to new problems; (2) the paradigm defines the power structure in the organization, and thus, it is very difficult to make any changes that will upset those with vested interests in the perpetuation of the paradigm; and (3) the paradigm contains the myths of the culture, and thus, to change the paradigm implies giving up the myths that define the group, and this may presage the dissolution of the group.

Leadership and the Human Dimension of Change

Whereas in the previous section, barriers to change were examined from a macro-organizational and theoretical perspective, the focus in this section is the role of the individual in hindering or advancing change. Humans are the essential elements in all organizations, and although their collective, interactive behavior in the organization is more than just the sum of each individual's activity, an understanding of the complexity of the individual and his or her power to facilitate, delay, or subvert change, is essential for understanding the challenges of change in the organization. There are four stages at which human nature is most likely to affect the change process: (1) during environmental scanning and information gathering, (2) at the initial stage of the change process, (3) during the heart of implementation, and (4) at the closing stages of change. These individual factors are often exacerbated in group settings where the dynamics of group interaction can either increase the resistance to change or provide support for it. The role of the leader is never more telling than during times of transformation when all members of an organization have to be channeled toward its new goals. Each of these four stages presents its own challenges.

During the *environmental scanning stage*, various impediments to perception may prevent individuals from correctly interpreting what is happening in the environment. Pfeffer and Salancik (1978) point out that there are two types of environmental forces acting on the organization: objective forces and perceived forces. *Objective forces* refer to all the environmental forces that impinge on the organization, both general and specific, whether or not they are perceived by organizational actors. No one can really know the objective environment because everything is experienced and interpreted through human senses. Nevertheless, it is there, and it is changing; and although the objective forces are unknowable, organizational actors must remain open to different perspectives and interpretations of what are considered to be "the facts." Misreading the environment can lead to dire consequences, as the Canadian Red Cross Blood Services learned when it continued to ignore and misinterpret signals about the safety of its blood supply. Charged for distributing tainted blood, the Red Cross paid heavy fines and eventually lost its role as Canada's blood supplier (CBC News, 2006, In Depth: Tainted Blood section). The role of the leader is to encourage open expression of opinions in order to attain the fullest understanding of the complexities of both the internal situation and the external environment of the organization. However, as Hinings and Greenwood (1989) point out, there is a danger that disagreements among individuals' interpretations may paralyze the organization and prevent it from pursuing any course of action. Here again, leadership is crucial for assimilating the information, setting a course of action, and defusing disagreements. This can be doubly challenging in nonprofit organizations because of the inherent duality of leadership; the paid executive director leads daily operations, but the volunteer board chair or president is ultimately responsible for the organization's behavior and for providing strategic direction. This duality can create difficulties and conflict; thus, a harmonious relationship between the chief executive and the board of directors is critical to effective leadership in nonprofits (Hermann & Heimovics, 1991).

Resistance is almost reflexive during the *initial stage of the change process*. It is largely driven by individual feelings of insecurity and a fear of the unknown, including fear of changes to the social network; fear of the loss of power, status, or even one's job; and fear of being unable to learn technologies and adapt to new work systems. Resentment caused by these fears is amplified when the necessity for change is not clearly understood by those to be affected. As researchers of organizational change remark, communication at all stages of the change process is a key to success (e.g., Kotter, 1995; Tichy, 1983). This is particularly true of the early stages, which set the tone for the entire process. Therefore, all scholars agree that communicating a clear vision of where the organization must head is essential. But as Lewin (1951, pp. 172–174) suggested in his famous force field theory of change, before embarking on the transformation process, the old understandings and patterns of behavior must be "unfrozen." This means that the vision communicated to organizational members must include valid and relevant information that the old way of doing things is no longer effective and that not changing may jeopardize the organization or even endanger its survival.

Resistance may grow during the *implementation stage* as the impending change becomes more concrete and therefore possibly more threatening. Specific details of the change are questioned. Interaction increases as more people become involved in the change process. What was at first unorganized opposition may become mobilized into coalitions against change. Leaders throughout the organization need to spend time explaining the change, listen to member concerns and involve them in the process, recruit respected colleagues as emissaries for change, create conditions that motivate members to participate in the change process, and ensure an equitable reward structure following the change (Gilley, Dixon, & Gilley, 2008; Kotter, 1995).

Change may also fail in the *closing stages* of the process, what Lewin calls the "refreezing" stage. Even when organizational members have dropped their resistance and have begun the process, they may not follow through. Before the new patterns are entrenched, organizational members may slip back to doing things the old way. This may occur at a conscious level or may not even be realized, as the institutionalized patterns and old habits take over again. The probability of backsliding is compounded in a group setting, where group behavior patterns can reinforce the individual ones. Thus, sustaining the momentum in the latter stages of change is important. The leader must keep the project going through ongoing communications, continued team building, continued removal of barriers, and distribution of fair rewards. The transformation is not complete until the new patterns of behavior are embedded in the organization's culture (Kotter, 1995; Tichy, 1983).

The research of Hinings and Greenwood (1989) is instructive in revealing the various ways in which organizational transformations can be delayed or derailed. Basing their model of change on Lewin's force field theory, they demonstrate that organizational change is seldom the simple linear process of "unfreezing—transforming—refreezing." In fact, some organizations are unable to contemplate major change as they suffer from *inertia*; others may end up with what the authors call *aborted* or *unresolved excursions*. Only a few will experience successful *reorientations* (transformations). Inertia describes organizations whose original paradigm remains coherent throughout, major transformations are not contemplated, and the changes accomplished are only minor adjustments in the organization. Aborted excursions refer to situations in which there has never been a full unfreezing of the original paradigm. Organizational performance declines as uncertainly about the change prevails. Ultimately, the change experiment is aborted and the original paradigm is reinstated. In the case of unresolved excursions, the organization is "locked between the gravitational pulls of competing" paradigms. The old paradigm is no longer coherent, but the new paradigm has not yet been accepted reflecting the tension between the two contradictory sets of ideas. The organization continues operating in conditions of high uncertainty. Even reorientations indicating successful transformations are not always smooth and linear. They occur in one of three ways: (a) by linear progression as depicted by Lewin, where the old paradigm is dismantled, followed by a transformation period, which culminates in the full adoption of the new paradigm; (b) by delayed acceptance, where the dismantling of the old paradigm takes a long time only to be suddenly replaced by the new one; and (c) by oscillations between the old and new paradigms, as expressed in a series of temporary reversals caused by resistance to the dismantling of the old paradigm and incomplete acceptance of the new paradigm. Unlike unresolved excursions, in this scenario, the new paradigm is finally adopted.

In summary, organizational transformation is a multistage process subject to individual shortcomings and resistance that can delay or derail the desired outcome.

Leaders must recognize both internal and external indicators that suggest a need for change, envision the new direction the organization has to take, articulate and communicate the vision, and inspire members to accept and follow it. Each of these tasks requires specific and different skills. Often, these skills are not lodged in a single individual; therefore, another important characteristic of an effective leader is the ability to recognize his or her strengths and weaknesses and delegate appropriately. In addition, an effective leader has to be familiar with all aspects of the organization, know and understand the needs and concerns of its members, match the various organizational tasks with the interests and the abilities of its members, and coordinate the effort.

Organizational Transformation as a Holistic Process

One of the most important and most overlooked aspects of managing organizational transformations is remembering that an organization is a complex system in which the various formal and informal subsystems are intricately interrelated. A change in one part of the organization can have ripple effects throughout the enterprise; thus, a holistic perspective on change is important. For example, in one nonprofit organization, changes in human resource policies at the head office put a severe strain on the branch offices, which were now required to submit more information without a commensurate increase in staffing. The change was introduced without sufficient consideration of the organization-wide implications, and frustrated members in branch offices, many with only volunteer staff, scuttled the project simply through noncompliance. Subsequently, a different system was put in place after broad consultation with all branches. However, valuable time, energy, and goodwill were lost in the abortive first attempt.

Tichy (1983) uses a rope metaphor to underscore the tight interrelationship among the political, cultural, and technical systems of the organization. Thus, even a small change in one system can affect the others For example, the simple introduction of e-mail as its primary form of communication ended up changing the composition, the power structure, and the culture of a national fundraising organization supporting children's educational needs overseas. Many older members, without computer skills or Internet access, gracefully bowed out, making room on the board for younger individuals. Their outlook changed the culture and the strategic direction of the organization. Although in this example the initial technological change was not a major one, its widespread and unexpected repercussions serve as a good illustration of the way in which the various subsystems of an organization are interrelated.

The above examples illustrate the ripple effects a change in one subsystem can produce throughout the organization. However, Tichy (1983) goes further, suggesting that synchronizing the political, cultural, and technological subsystems of an organization is essential to the transformation process: "Ultimately, transforming organizations is a reweaving of the three strands" (Tichy 1983, p. 52) that enhances the process of transformation. Activating the organization's political subsystem helps find the necessary resources (funds, materials, space, staff, volunteers, and time) and support (endorsement, backing, approval, and legitimacy) for the transformation. Implementation requires the activation of the technical system, which includes fostering the exchange of information and organizing into planning and task groups to forward the transformation. It can also involve the realignment of the organization's structure to accommodate other changes. Situating the change in the context of the organization's norms, values, and mission is important to reassure members that its culture will not be weakened. Recognizing and working with the various subcultures and informal friendship networks in the organization helps defuse resistance.

As illustrated in the conceptual model presented in Figure 63.1 at the beginning of the chapter, the organization is totally embedded in its environment. More recent theories of organizational change take a holistic perspective that includes the environment. Based on complexity theory and the application of chaos theory to organizations, this approach eschews the fortress metaphor of organization defending itself against "destructive" forces from the outside, changing only when absolutely necessary. Instead, it offers an alternative view, one that likens an organization to a stream. The stream represents process structures "that maintain form over time, yet have no rigidity of structure" (Wheatley, 1992, p. 15). Water has a need to flow, but the form of the stream changes, at times curving to bypass rocks, at times broadening, at times narrowing. "Structures emerge but only as temporary solutions that facilitate rather than interfere. There is none of the rigid reliance on single forms, on true answers, on past practices" characteristic of organizations (Wheatley, 1992, p. 16).

The organization is part of a complex ecosystem that is in constant, at times chaotic, flux. Leaders should recognize that chaos and complexity are "not problems to be solved but . . . aspects of a process by which living systems adapt, renew, maintain and transcend themselves through self-organization" (Dennard, 1996, p. 495). Indeed, the basic lesson of chaos theory for organizations is that change is constant and that from the chaos of change comes order, which then reverts to chaos again in a continuing pattern. Therefore, organizations should not fear change; rather, they should be open places where people and ideas can mix freely to re-create the organization in synchronization with the environment. The more open an organization is to the outside world, the more easily it will be able to absorb the ideas that are necessary for innovation and renewal. But as evidenced in this chapter, mature organizations cling to their old ways; they are loathe to relinquish the very paradigms that were the keys to their

past successes. According to complexity theory, for mature organizations to transcend and reach this open state, they may need to enter a phase of "creative destruction," dismantling systems and structures that have become too rigid, have too little variety, and are not responsive to the current needs of their environment (Zimmerman, Plsek, & Lindberg, 1998). Although the old is destroyed, in this process, the emphasis is on the word *creative*: creating the potential for innovation and new insights as the organization struggles to renew itself in harmony with its environment.

The role of the leader is to facilitate taking the road toward the fulfillment of the mission by nurturing individual capacity in an atmosphere of free exchange of ideas. One way in which to do this is to increase the organization's capacity for *double-loop learning*; thus, organizational members are constantly questioning the premises of their organizational paradigms, testing them in the context of their changing realities (e.g., Argyris, 1993). By providing courses and seminars, by recruiting people from the outside to create the new core competencies, by involving clients and other stakeholders in planning, leaders can expose organizational members to the new ideas necessary for continual innovation and change.

Summary and Future Directions

If present trends persist, the future of nonprofit organizations will continue to be fraught with uncertainty and change driven by forces from within and without. These forces will need to be aligned with the organization's mission and reconciled with institutional views of the voluntary sector. This chapter has attempted to provide the reader various lenses with which to understand the complexities of organizational change. The lenses focused on internal and external forces that organizations need to be aware of, barriers to successful transformations, and prevailing knowledge about managing transformations. Finally, this chapter highlighted the holistic nature of change not only within the organization but also as part of an ever-changing social and organizational ecosystem. Although recognizing that leadership is important, the emphasis in this chapter was more on what leaders have to be aware of than on how they need to act.

Some of the issues that nonprofit organizations will confront in the coming years are (1) the continuing redefinition of the relationship among the three sectors, especially the governmental one; (2) the proliferation of commercial ventures and the subsequent blurring of boundaries between nonprofit and for-profit sectors; (3) the restructuring of the nonprofit form and the exploration of new roles for voluntary organizations; (4) the increasing "capacity divide" between very large nonprofit organizations and smaller ones; (5) the exploding population diversity in large urban centers and how it affects volunteering; (6) the rate of technological innovation and its implications for volunteering, advocacy, and service delivery; and (7) the impact of heightened security measures on the ability of nonprofit organizations to act in an advocacy capacity.

Building a successful future in the context of nonprofit leadership and change will have a number of common elements: (1) building a diverse portfolio of services and revenue sources, (2) creating community sector networks to identify common issues and build a support system, (3) effectively and efficiently increasing transparency and accountability to internal and external stakeholders, (4) integrating program delivery with support to participate in civil society, (5) harnessing technology to learn from the world and develop staff and volunteers, and (6) increasing access to professional leadership skills through research and development as well as educational programs.

References and Further Readings

Aldrich, H. E. (1979). *Organizations and environments*. Englewood Cliffs, NJ: Prentice-Hall.

Aldrich, H. E., & Ruef, M. (2006). *Organizations evolving* (2nd ed.). Thousand Oaks, CA: Sage.

Argyris, C. (1993). *Knowledge for action: A guide to overcoming barriers to organizational change*. San Francisco: Jossey-Bass.

Beer, M. (2003). Why total quality management programs do not persist: The role of management quality and implications for leading a TQM Transformation. *Decision Sciences, 34*(4), 623–642.

Brown, R. H. (1989). *Social science as civic discourse*. Chicago: University of Chicago Press.

Burns, T., & Stalker, G. M. (1966). *The management of innovation*. London: Tavistock.

Canadian Broadcasting Company (CBC) News. (2006, July 25). *Tainted blood scandal*. Available from http://www.cbc.ca/news/background/taintedblood

Champy, J. (1995). A light that failed. *Across the Board, 32*(3), 27–31.

Daft, R. T. (2001). *Organization theory and design* (7th ed., pp. 130–132). Cincinnati, OH: South-Western College.

Dennard, L. F. (1996). The new paradigm in science and public administration. *Public Administration Review, 56*(2), 495.

DiMaggio, P. J., & Powell, W. W. (1983). The iron cage revisited: Institutional isomorphism and collective rationality in organizational fields. *American Sociological Review, 48*, 147–160.

Dunn, J. R. (2003). *Are widening income inequalities making Canadians less healthy? The health determinants partnership-making connections project*. Available from www.opc.on.ca/english/index.htm

Gilley, A., Dixon, P., & Gilley, J. (2008) Characteristics of leadership effectiveness: Implementing change and driving innovation in organizations. *Human Resource Development Quarterly, 19*(2), 153–169.

Greiner, L. E. (1972). Evolution and revolution as organizations grow. *Harvard Business Review, 76*(3), 37–46.

Hannan, M., & Freeman, J. H. (1984). Structural inertia and organizational change. *American Sociological Review, 49*, 149–164.

Hannan, M. T., & Freeman, J. H. (1989). *Organizational ecology*. Cambridge, MA: Harvard University Press.

Herman, R. D., & Heimovics, R. D. (1991). *Executive leadership in nonprofit organizations* (pp. 317–366). San Francisco: Jossey-Bass.

Hinings, C. R., & Greenwood, R. (1989). *The dynamics of strategic change*. Oxford, UK: B. Blackwell.

Homer-Dixon, T. (2000). Prologue. In T. Homer-Dixon, *The ingenuity gap* (pp. 1–8). Toronto, ON: Alfred A. Knopf.

Katz, D., & Khan, R. L. (1966). *Organizations and the system concept: The social psychology of organizations* (pp. 14–20). New York: John Wiley & Sons.

Kotter, J. (1995). Leading change: Why transformation efforts fail. *Harvard Business Review, 74*(2), 59–67.

Kuhn, T. (1993). *The structure of scientific revolutions* (3rd ed.). Chicago: University of Chicago Press.

Lawrence, P. R., & Lorsch, J. (1967). *Organization and environment*. Boston: Harvard University.

Lewin, K. (1951). *Field theory in social science*. New York: Harper & Row.

Meinhard, A., & Foster, M. (1996, June). *Women's voluntary organizations and the restructuring of Canada's voluntary sector: A theoretical perspective* (Working Paper No. 6). Toronto, ON: Centre for Voluntary Sector Studies, Ryerson University.

Meinhard, A., Foster, M., & Berger, I. (2004). *The process of institutional isomorphism in Ontario's voluntary sector*. Paper presented at the annual conference of the Administrative Sciences Association of Canada, Quebec City, Quebec.

Pfeffer, J., & Salancik, G. (1978). *The external control of organizations*. New York: Harper & Row.

Rice, J. J., & Prince, M. J. (2000). *Changing politics of Canadian social policy*. Toronto, ON: University of Toronto Press.

Stinchcombe, A. L. (1965). Social structure and organizations. In J. G. March (Ed.), *Handbook of organizations* (pp. 142–193). Chicago: Rand McNally.

Thompson, J. D. (1967). *Organizations in action*. New York: McGraw-Hill.

Tichy, N. M. (1983). *Managing strategic change: Technical, political, and cultural dynamics*. Hoboken, NJ: John Wiley & Sons.

Tushman, M., & Romanelli, E. (1994). Organization transformation as punctuated equilibrium: An empirical test. *Academy of Management Journal, 34*, 1141–1166.

Wheatley, M. (1992). *Leadership and the new science*. San Francisco: Berret-Koehler.

Zimmerman, B., Plsek, P., & Lindberg, C. (1998). *Edgeware: Insights from complexity science for health care leaders*. Dallas, TX: VHA.

64

PUBLIC POLICY ON TAX EXEMPTIONS FOR NONPROFIT ORGANIZATIONS

MELISSA A. WALKER

Wichita State University

Public policy related to tax exemption defines the broad boundaries of the nonprofit sector. Nonprofit organizations do not pay income tax, property tax, or sales tax on purchases. Government requirements to become exempt capture some but not all charitable practice. The entry begins with an examination of taxation and how government defines charitable activity. A discussion of exemption criteria follows. The entry concludes with an application of exemption requirements to three different types of human services. This illustrates the difficulty of formulating a uniform definition that fits every nonprofit.

Taxation and Nonprofits

By and large, government does not require nonprofits to pay tax on income, property, or sales. Requirements that exempt nonprofits from taxation involve federal, state, and local government. To be recognized as exempt under section 501(c)(3) of the federal income tax code, nonprofits use Form 1024 to apply to the Internal Revenue Service (IRS). After a review that can take up to 6 months, the IRS issues a letter of determination. State requirements usually follow IRS exemption criteria (Bowman & Fremont-Smith, 2006). With respect to property tax, most local governments do not require payment from nonprofits. In most states with sales tax, a nonprofit may apply for a certificate that assures retailers the organization is exempt. Nonprofits do not pay tax on purchases; however, most states require a nonprofit to collect and remit tax on sales made by the organization.

In 2005, 1.4 million nonprofits were registered with the IRS (Wing, Pollak, & Blackwood, 2008). Nonprofits with annual gross receipts under $5,000 and religious organizations are not required to file. Over 500,000 organizations had annual gross receipts of more than $25,000 and were required to file a Form 990 tax return with the IRS. Most states also require nonprofits file a Form 990 each year.

The largest group of exempt entities, public charities, meets the definition of charitable contained in section 501(c)(3) of the IRS tax code (Hopkins, 2009). Section 501(c)(3) exempts religious, educational, scientific, cultural, environmental, health, and human service organizations from federal income tax. These organizations are engaged in activities that benefit the public. Public support (donations from individuals, foundations, and corporations as well as grants from government) is a substantial proportion of total revenue (Wing et al., 2008). Public charities will be the focus here. Henceforth, nonprofits will refer to public charities. A brief description of income, property, and sales tax follows.

Income Tax

Income tax levies profit generated by individuals and corporations. Nonprofits do not pay federal or state income tax. It is likely that a tax on nonprofits' net income (the difference between revenue and expense) would generate a small amount of revenue (Simon, 1987). When nonprofits earn income unrelated to a charitable purpose, proceeds from this activity are taxed at the corporate rate. This is known as the unrelated business income tax, or UBIT.

Property Tax

Property tax is a central resource for local government. A few state and local governments, according to a survey by Leland (1998), require nonprofits to make payments in lieu of taxes (PILOTs) or to provide services in lieu of taxes (SILOTs). In Philadelphia and Pittsburgh, for example, nonprofits that provide health care or education make a PILOT (Steinberg & Bilodeau, 1999). With the exception of PILOTs and SILOTs, most nonprofits are not required to pay property tax.

There are several studies of property tax exemption and nonprofits (Brody, 2002; Brody & Cordes, 2006; Chang & Tuckman, 1990; Dover, 2003; Hansmann, 1987b; Steinberg & Bilodeau, 1999). Does property tax exemption increase the market share of nonprofit organizations? In a study of nonprofit hospitals in Tennessee, Chang and Tuckman (1990) did not find a relationship between property tax exemption and market share. So far, there is no evidence property tax exemption causes charitable organizations to buy more land in a particular locale that does not tax nonprofits (Steinberg & Bilodeau, 1999). Hansmann (1987b) did not find a significant effect on the share of nonprofits in cities with higher property tax rates. Services provided by nonprofits may, in fact, improve a community and raise property values. Dover (2003) found this effect in Toledo, Ohio.

Sales Tax

Sales tax is levied on the purchase of certain goods and sometimes services. It is paid by consumers or end users at the point of purchase. Retailers collect and remit sales tax to state and sometimes also local government. State and local government try to apply the same tax to all private organizations, both for-profit and not-for-profit. In most cases, how nonprofits are treated is simply a matter of whether or not a good (or service) is taxed. If so, all private organizations that sell goods and services not excluded from the tax base must collect and remit sales tax. When there are exclusions of certain goods or some nonprofits are exempt, this adds to the administrative expense of government (Due & Mikesell, 1983; Steinberg & Bilodeau, 1999). It also adds to the administrative costs of private nonprofit and for-profit organizations (Blumenthal & Kalambokidis, 2006).

A state or local government's decision about whether nonprofits must remit tax on sales made by the organization turns on a number of factors. This is more than a matter of whether or not sales tax is levied on a particular good or service. Meeting federal IRS income tax exemption guidelines is usually not enough. When sales are occasional (e.g., sales in conjunction with a special fundraising event), typically, nonprofits are not required to remit sales tax. In this case, the intent of a purchase is to make a donation. Sales characterized as regular, habitual, or integral to a nonprofit's activities are taxable. This is true whether the sale is related to a nonprofit's charitable purpose or unrelated. In the case of regular sales, the intent of a purchase is to acquire a good or service (not to make a donation). States define regular sales in different ways. If sales occur, for example, more than 20 days out of the year, then these sales may be considered regular. When a hospital or museum operates a gift shop or café, tax on sales made must be collected. Some states require child care providers to remit sales tax on fees.

Tax treatment of nonprofits with respect to sales and property illustrates the role of state and local government. State constitutions exempt nonprofits. State statute drawn from legislation and common law encode exemption requirements. Common law defines charitable activity broadly, for example, religious, educational, or scientific, relieving the burden of government (Bowman & Fremont-Smith, 2006). State and federal law are parallel (Bowman & Fremont-Smith, 2006).

In sum, the following applies with respect to income tax, property tax, and sales tax:

1. State government follows federal determination of income tax exemption. Most nonprofits do not pay federal or state income tax.

2. Most nonprofits do not pay local property tax. In some places, hospitals and universities, for example, make payments in lieu of taxes.

3. Most bodies of state and local government do not require nonprofits to pay sales tax on purchases or sales tax on occasional sales. In the case of regular sales, nonprofits are required to collect and remit sales tax.

The degree to which exemption requirements are followed is not known. It would be difficult for state and local government to monitor, for example, every sale involving a nonprofit. The cost of enforcement would likely exceed the value of revenue generated by taxation.

Tax Treatment of Nonprofits

There are many ways to define charitable. One approach is to take into account the beneficiaries of nonprofit activity. When people are in need and services are delivered at no cost, this may signal a charitable purpose. In exchange, government does not require nonprofits to pay tax. However, not all nonprofits exclusively serve individuals of limited means. Nonprofit hospitals, universities, child care centers, recreation programs, and museums serve a range of individuals. This diversity is reflected in ever-evolving exemption criteria.

The federal definition of *charitable* in section 501(c)(3) suggests nonprofits engage in activities that provide a public benefit. This is one of the requirements to obtain federal income tax exemption. When an organization meets this test, the IRS issues a letter of determination. Once a determination is made, donors may deduct charitable contributions to the organization.

At the state and local level, nonprofits are not required to pay income tax or property tax (Bowman & Fremont-Smith, 2006; Brody & Cordes, 2006). State statute often alludes to a public benefit. Requirements for sales tax exemption are more complex. State and local government usually do not require nonprofits to pay sales tax on purchases (Bowman & Fremont-Smith, 2006). The presumption may be that a purchase supports a charitable activity, for example, program supplies or food purchased by a shelter. However, when a nonprofit is regularly (not occasionally) engaged in the sale of a taxable good or service, state and local governments require remittance of sales tax (Bowman & Fremont-Smith, 2006). To do otherwise would reduce sales tax revenue and increase administrative burden. This is a matter of treating all private organizations the same way, particularly when a good or service is provided by both nonprofit and for-profit entities.

To date, there is no single, uniform definition of *charitable*. Statute and regulation usually invoke more than one. The result is a patchwork of public policy and exemption practice (Borek, 2005). One reason for this may be the range of activities and organizations. Nonprofits deliver many different services including health, education, human services, and arts. This confounds development of a uniform definition of charitable. It makes it difficult to define and apply a single exemption criterion to every nonprofit.

The problem of defining charitable activity is likely to continue as the number of nonprofits grows. Between 1995 and 2005, nonprofits registered with the IRS increased 27%; during the same period, accounting for inflation, revenue reported by nonprofits increased nearly 54% (Wing et al., 2008). Rapid growth and the variation in nonprofit pursuits challenge government to precisely define charitable activity.

What Is Charitable?

Exemption requires nonprofits to fulfill a charitable purpose (Hopkins, 2009). However, the word *charitable* can mean many things (Harvard Law Review, 2001). This section explores three concepts central to exemption: (1) public benefit, (2) the nondistribution constraint, and (3) competition. Each rationale could, by itself or in combination, exempt an organization from taxation. In the final segment of this entry, these conceptualizations are applied to three different types of nonprofits. This will illustrate the degree to which exemption policy and practice match.

Public Benefit

Atkinson (1997) observes exemption rests on a normative description of activities considered charitable. Public benefit can be a property of a service. It can be a characteristic of a beneficiary. Nonprofits are expected to engage in activities that benefit the general public. To the extent services are available at no cost or low cost, this may indicate a charitable purpose. There is also an expectation nonprofits will serve people in need, particularly those not served by for-profit or public entities. Weisbrod (1977, 1988) suggests nonprofits arise to supply unmet demand; nonprofits offer services government and markets do not. In so doing, nonprofits reduce the burden of government. In exchange, nonprofits receive a tax subsidy (Simon, Dale, & Chisolm, 2006).

Subsidy

Law and regulation promote charitable activity with an indirect subsidy (Brody, 2002; Brody & Cordes, 2006; Simon et al., 2006). The connection between the public benefit charities provide and the tax subsidy government confers is tenuous. For Atkinson (1997), this is one part tax policy and one part politics.

Presumably, the social benefit nonprofits provide offsets forgone tax revenue. Steinberg and Bilodeau (1999) found studies that estimate the effect of tax exemption have yet to precisely measure the monetary tradeoff. At the federal level, Borek (2005) estimates that the value of forgone tax revenue associated with exemption of nonprofits and the charitable tax deduction for individuals exceeds federal social welfare spending. What is more, tax exemption does not guarantee nonprofits will serve those most in need. For Salamon (1999), there can be voluntary failure. To the extent this is the case, the value to government in lost revenue may indeed be greater than the burden relieved by nonprofits (Borek, 2005; Diamond, 2002).

Finally, with respect to the subsidy argument, nonprofits do not necessarily produce services government would otherwise provide (Steinberg & Bilodeau, 1999). While this may be true of services for individuals who have little money, are severely mentally ill, or have a developmental disability, it is unlikely government will supply, for example, all health care, child care, or recreation demanded by a market. Hospitals, nursing homes, child care programs, and museums engage in activities government does not.

Donations

To the extent a nonprofit relies on donations, its purpose may be charitable. Hall and Colombo (1992) assert tax exemption should be granted when both government and the marketplace fail to provide collective goods. One indication of such a failure is the extent to which an organization depends on donations (i.e., private contributions made by individuals, foundations, and corporations as well as public support provided by government). It is unlikely, Hall and Colombo reason, public support will equal the cost of services. Some services will be undercapitalized. This is a justification for exemption. Hall and Colombo propose when a nonprofit receives at least one third of its total revenue from donations, this indicates both government and market failure. Under these conditions, nonprofits are undercapitalized. This, then, is the threshold Hall and Colombo offer for charitable exemption: when one third of a nonprofit's revenue comes from donations.

Nondistribution Constraint

Another factor is the nondistribution constraint. There are no owners, shareholders, or individuals who benefit. In a nonprofit, any surplus or excess of revenue over expense is reinvested in the organization. There is no distribution of profit to owners or shareholders. Profit is used to fulfill a charitable purpose.

The nondistribution constraint emphasizes nonprofits are not primarily in the business of making money. The mission of a human service organization, for example, is not foremost to generate a surplus. It is to provide a human service (Steinberg, 2006). The 1894 federal income tax act did not regard religious, educational, or charitable organizations as entities primarily engaged in income-producing activities (Diamond, 2002; Scrivner, 1996). For this reason, these organizations were made exempt from federal income tax.

When ordinary contractual mechanisms fail, consumers may regard nonprofits as more trustworthy. The nondistribution constraint reassures consumers unable to judge quality that nonprofits are less likely to engage in opportunism. There is no (or less) profit motive. Where there is contract failure, consumers will regard nonprofits as more trustworthy (Hansmann, 1987a). Steinberg and Gray (1993) observe it would be difficult to measure contract failure. Where is contract failure most likely to occur? in the delivery of hospital care? child care? Are consumers able to judge the quality of these services?

Competition

Hansmann (1981) argues a public subsidy is justified when nonprofits are more efficient and effective than for-profits. Exemption, according to Hansmann, frees capital businesses have that charities lack. Hansmann (1981, 1987a) distinguishes between commercial and donative organizations. Commercial nonprofits depend on fees. Commercial activity should not be the primary focus (Harvard Law Review, 2001). Donative nonprofits are supported by contributions (e.g., private donations made by individuals, foundations, and corporations). Nonprofits that serve the general public (public charities) are considered social benefit or donative organizations (Hansmann, 1987a; Hoyt, 2001; Salamon, 1999). Nonprofits that serve members or entities that pay a fee for services are regarded as commercial (Hansmann, 1987a; Hoyt, 2001; Salamon, 1999).

Subsidizing commercial activity calls into question exemption assumptions that define a charitable purpose. Nonprofits supported by fees deliver a service in exchange for a fee. The general public does not, necessarily, benefit. The beneficiary is the recipient of a service. Fees supply a nonprofit's capital needs. When this is the case, Hansmann (1981, 1987a) advises nonprofits should not be subsidized.

Fees

The largest source of revenue for nonprofits is fees. Health care (Medicare, insurers, patients), education (tuition), human services (Medicaid, insurers, clients), and arts (admission, membership) organizations depend on fees. In 2005, 70% of all revenue generated by nonprofits was fee-for-service or payments (Wing et al., 2008). The proportion of total revenue derived from fees is rising. Private payments to social and legal services increased 80% between 1977 and 1997 (Weitzman, Jalandoni, Lamkin, & Pollak, 2002). In 1997, according to Independent Sector (Weitzman et al., 2002), 71% of social and legal service revenue came from payments made by public (52%) and private sources (18%).

As financial pressure mounts, it is likely nonprofits will engage in more commercial activity, blurring the boundary between nonprofit and for-profit (Weisbrod, 1997). In some cases, both nonprofits and for-profits provide services (e.g., hospitals, clinics, nursing homes, child care, and recreation; Salamon, 1999; Wing et al., 2008). This raises concerns about unfair competition. A tax subsidy gives nonprofits a competitive advantage. Direct competition with for-profits is addressed in state statute. Several court decisions involve industries where nonprofits depend on fees and directly compete with businesses.

Court cases involving hospitals and child care extend exemption criteria. While most general care hospitals are nonprofit, there are also for-profit and some public hospitals (Salamon, 1999). Hospitals depend, as do many health care organizations, on fees (Medicare, insurers, patients). In 1985, the Utah Supreme Court ruled hospitals must deliver community care (Sanders, 1995). The court established six exemption criteria including the extent to which an organization is supported by donations (Steinberg & Bilodeau, 1999). Another fee-based industry where tax exemption has been questioned is child care. A Minnesota Supreme Court decision concerning property taxation of a child care center took into account the surplus (excess of revenue over expense) produced by fees (*Under the Rainbow v. County of Goodhue*, 2007). The court ruled this profit could be taxed; the center should not receive a subsidy by way of exemption.

In light of the varied roles nonprofits play and increased dependence on fees, charitable activity is difficult to define (Weisbrod, 1998). Exemption rests on a normative definition. A subsidy is justified when an organization (1) provides a public benefit, (2) delivers a service that is not provided by for-profits or government, and (3) does not distribute a surplus (excess of revenue over expense or profit) to owners or shareholders (nondistribution constraint). When a nonprofit serves people in need and is supported by donations, there is less ambiguity about meeting exemption requirements. When a nonprofit depends on fees and competes with for-profit business, the degree to which exemption requirements are met is not as clear. When fees generate capital to support a commercial activity, this undermines the subsidy rationale; unfair competition becomes a concern.

A subsidy, or quid pro quo, arrangement allows government to choose which services lessen the public burden (Brody, 2002). In the next section, exemption criteria will be explored in the context of three different types of human services. Each depends on fees. Two services supported by Medicaid benefit individuals who are chronically ill: individuals with a severe mental illness or a developmental disability. This activity generates fees and offers a public benefit. The public benefit associated with a third human service is not as clear. The service is recreation. Beneficiaries are members who pay.

Exemption and Human Services

Human services are a good test of exemption requirements. This is a diverse subsector serving people in need—those who are poor, homeless, jobless, abused, ex-offenders, mentally ill, or have a developmental disability. The National Taxonomy of Exempt Entities (NTEE) also includes youth centers, clubs, scouts, camps, mentoring, and child care in this category.

About one in every three public charities delivers human services (Wing et al., 2008). In number, this is the largest subsector. Most organizations are small. Fees in 2005 accounted for 53% of total revenue; only health (88%) and education (56%) depend more on fees (Wing et al., 2008). Fees are paid by government and other third parties as well as clients themselves. About one third of all human services expense is associated with residential care (custodial, shelter) and one quarter is recreation (Wing et al., 2008).

Mental Illness and Developmental Disability

Health, education, and human services are often reimbursed at a fixed rate for a particular service. Government certifies eligibility. Agencies deliver services and are reimbursed. Nonprofit, for-profit, and some public agencies serve two distinct groups of beneficiaries: (1) individuals who have a severe mental illness or (2) a developmental disability. Severe mental illness can involve bipolar disorder, schizophrenia, or severe depression. Mental health services often include counseling and community support.

A development disability can be autism, Down syndrome, or cerebral palsy. Residential and day treatment as well as respite and in-home care are among services delivered in the community and reimbursed primarily by Medicaid on a fee-for-service basis (Smith, 2006).

The transition from institutional to community care has been facilitated by Medicaid (Vladeck, 2003). Medicaid covers about 60% of the reimbursement rate. To receive the federal portion, state and local governments must appropriate, on average, a 40% match. As long as an individual qualifies, government pays providers to deliver services. An increase in the volume of service will increase the cost to government. From the perspective of providers, fee for service arrangements offer a financial incentive to deliver more services. From the perspective of government, fees can put government at risk when service volume increases (DeHoog & Salamon, 2002). Not all services are covered by Medicaid. For services that are, the fixed reimbursement rate may not cover the actual cost of delivering a particular service. The rate does not necessarily correlate with assessed need or with actual cost. Rate studies set reimbursement rates based on local market conditions. At the state and local level, political will and financial capacity to match the federal share have a lot to do with the availability of funds..

Mental health and developmental disability reimbursements follow a competition prescription (Kettl, 1993). Low rates probably discourage providers from overproduction. When the reimbursement rate does not cover the entire cost of a particular service or when a service is not covered by Medicaid, providers are left to find other ways to pay for it. In some cases, if there is no payer, agencies may not provide a service. To the extent agencies do not serve clients, this effectively rations a service.

How are exemption requirements relevant? Government has chosen two groups of beneficiaries—individuals with developmental disabilities and individuals with a severe mental illness. Arguably, both populations are in need. Since private organizations serve beneficiaries in the community—no longer are these services provided in government-run institutions—the public sector is relieved of the burden of service delivery. So far, it appears organizations that serve these two groups provide services that are in keeping with exemption requirements. What about fees? Do nonprofits have an unfair competitive advantage?

This may be a commercial activity (Hansmann, 1987a; Hoyt, 2001; Salamon, 1999). Reimbursement rates are based on market conditions. This is not a donation. It is a payment made by a third party, in this case government, in exchange for a service. What is more, nonprofit, for-profit, and public organizations deliver services. There may be competition. In 2001, of all Medicaid spending for mental health, 63% went to nonprofits, 26% went to for-profits, and 11% went to public organizations (Bowman & Fremont-Smith, 2006). Nonprofits predominate in delivery of mental health and developmental disability services. However, for-profits are more likely to provide, for example, home care for individuals with developmental disabilities. With respect to this particular service, tax exemption affords nonprofits a competitive advantage. If a nonprofit was required to remit income, property, and/or sales tax to the extent it relies on fees paid by government, presumably this would be the source of the tax.

Recreation

Recreation is another human service that addresses a range of needs. Mentoring programs (Big Brothers Big Sisters) and recreation programs (Boys and Girls Clubs, some Young Men's Christian Associations [YMCAs]) target children in low-income neighborhoods. YMCAs use a sliding-fee scale for membership based on ability to pay. Child care and youth groups including sports clubs and camps are available to anyone who can pay the fee. Unlike developmental disability and mental health, clients rather than government are the primary source of fees. Most recreation is delivered by nonprofits but there are private health clubs and public recreation centers. Dependence on fees and competition could be relevant to determination of tax exempt status.

In 1844, the YMCA began in London. Young men arrived in the city to assume jobs generated by the Industrial Revolution. They lived in tenements and slept over shop floors. One of these young men, George Williams, wanted to provide a safe alternative to the streets. He started a Bible study group. The YMCA began as an evangelical organization open to all Christians.

By the late 1800s, new YMCAs opened across the United States. Each city with a new facility took pride in a series of firsts including the first gymnasium and the first swimming pool. There were hotel-like rooms; rental income became an important source of revenue. Over time, lay volunteers were replaced by paid professionals. By the end of World War II, most YMCAs had begun to admit women. Today, membership is by far the largest source of support.

Earned income is invested in facilities and programs. YMCAs use membership fees to build new facilities (branches) and offer more services. Gymnasiums and pools are expensive. Membership fees cover the cost of new construction as well as the cost of improving existing facilities. With many members, fitness equipment wears out and must be replaced. Fees paid by members also cover the cost of youth services that are free to the community (e.g., afterschool, summer camp, and learn-to-swim programs). Many YMCAs also offer child care and subsidize fees for families of limited means.

The benefits of YMCA services may extend beyond members. Early learning, afterschool programs, summer camp, and fitness centers can contribute to the quality of life in a community. These activities suggest the YMCA has a social purpose. It is not only in the business of making money.

YMCA services may reduce the burden of government. For local government, youth programs may reduce the burden of recreation center expense. To the extent child care and afterschool programs help students do well in school, this could reduce resources the public schools must invest in readiness and learning. Finally, members who participate in fitness programs are less likely to require health care intervention.

So far, it appears YMCAs should qualify for tax exemption. However, for-profit health clubs argue that the tax subsidy YMCAs receive gives these nonprofits an unfair advantage. Nonprofits and for-profits operate in the same market under the same conditions. YMCAs have a financial advantage—not having to pay income, property, or sales tax. The effect of this tax subsidy could put YMCAs in a more profitable position vis-à-vis for-profit health clubs. This may also be true with respect to the delivery of child care, health care, and other services.

With respect to fees—whether private (YMCA memberships) or public (Medicaid)—the tax subsidy that exempt organizations receive from government does not necessarily produce a level playing field. To the degree nonprofits serve individuals who are poor or disadvantaged due to a chronic illness (e.g., severe mental illness or developmental disability), this could mitigate the inequality. The YMCA is prohibited from distributing any profit; surplus must be reinvested in the organization. Even so, a normative definition of charitable activity does not fare well when services depend on fees, do not benefit the general public, and/or do not relieve the burden of government. Since fees are a central resource, this question remains.

Summary

Nonprofits do not pay income tax, property tax, or sales tax on purchases. When organizations meet a normative definition of charitable, government provides a tax subsidy. Taxation of nonprofits involves federal, state, and local governments. State government follows the federal determination of income tax exemption. Most nonprofits are not required to pay local property tax. State and local governments do not require payment of tax on purchases, but nonprofits must remit tax on regular sales.

There are many ways to define charitable. One approach is to take into account the beneficiaries of nonprofit activity. Another is to examine the service(s) delivered. When people who are in need are served at no cost, this could relieve the burden of government. This is a fairly straightforward proposition when an organization relies on donations, but what about fees? Health, education, human service, and arts organizations depend on fees.

Whether payment is made by government or private sources, subsidizing commercial activity calls into question the exemption assumptions that define a charitable purpose. Nonprofits supported by fees deliver a service in exchange for a fee. The general public does not necessarily benefit. The beneficiary is the service recipient. Fees supply a nonprofit's capital needs. Where this is the case, should nonprofits be tax-exempt? receive a subsidy? Given the range of nonprofit activity and dependence on fees, it is likely the definition of charitable and associated exemption requirements will continue to evolve.

References and Further Readings

Atkinson, R. (1997). Theories of the federal income tax exemption for charities: Thesis, antithesis, and syntheses. *Stetson Law Review, 27,* 395–431.

Bittker, B., & Rahdert, G. (1976, January). The exemption of nonprofit organizations from federal income taxation. *Yale Law Journal, 85*(3), 299–358.

Blumenthal, M., & Kalambokidis, L. (2006, June). The compliance costs of maintaining tax exempt status. *National Tax Journal, 59*(2), 235–252.

Borek, C. (2005). Decoupling tax exemptions for charitable organizations. *William Mitchell Law Review, 31*(1), 183–225.

Bowman, W., & Fremont-Smith, M. R. (2006). Nonprofits and state and local governments. In E. T. Boris & C. E. Steuerle (Eds.), *Nonprofits and government: Collaboration conflict* (2nd ed., pp. 181–217). Washington, DC: Urban Institute Press.

Brody, E. (2002). Legal theories of tax exemption: A sovereignty perspective. In E. Brody (Ed.), *Property tax exemption for charities* (pp. 145–172). Washington, DC: The Urban Institute Press.

Brody, E., & Cordes, J. (2006). Tax treatment of nonprofit organizations: A two-edged sword? In E. Boris & E. Steuerle (Eds.), *Nonprofits and government: Collaboration and conflict* (pp. 141–180). Washington, DC: Urban Institute Press.

Chang, C., & Tuckman, H. (1990, June). Do higher property tax rates increase the market share of nonprofit hospitals? *National Tax Journal, 43*(2), 175–187.

Colombo, J., & Hall, M. (1995). *The charitable tax exemption.* Boulder, CO: Westview Press.

DeHoog, R. H., & Salamon, L. (2002). Purchase-of-service contracting. In L. Salamon (Ed.), *The tools of government* (pp. 319–339). New York: Oxford University Press.

Diamond, S. (2002). Efficiency and benevolence: Philanthropic tax exemptions in 19th century America. In E. Brody (Ed.), *Property tax exemption for charities* (pp. 115–144). Washington, DC: Urban Institute Press.

Dover, M. (2003). *The social system of real property ownership: Public and nonprofit property tax exemptions and corporate tax abatements in city and suburb, 1955–2000.* Unpublished doctoral dissertation, University of Michigan, Ann Arbor.

Due, J., & Mikesell, J. (1983). *Sales taxation: State and local structure and administration.* Baltimore, MD: Johns Hopkins University Press.

Gallagher, J. G. (1999, July). *Sales tax exemption for charitable, educational, and religious nonprofit organizations.* Washington, DC: National Council of Nonprofit Associations.

Hall, M., & Colombo, J. (1992). The donative theory of the charitable tax exemption. *Ohio State Law Journal, 52,* 1379–1476.

Hansmann, H. (1981, November). The rationale for exempting nonprofit organizations from corporate taxation. *Yale Law Journal, 91*(1), 54–100.

Hansmann, H. (1987a). Economic theories of nonprofit organization. In W. W. Powell (Ed.), *The nonprofit sector: A research handbook* (pp. 27–42). New Haven, CT: Yale University Press.

Hansmann, H. (1987b, March). The effect of tax exemption and other factors on the market share of nonprofit versus for-profit firms. *National Tax Journal, 40*(1), 71–82.

Harvard Law Review. (2001). Developments in the law: Nonprofit corporations. In S. Ott (Ed.), *Understanding nonprofit organizations: Governance, leadership, and management* (pp. 61–79). Boulder, CO: Westview Press.

Hopkins, B. (2009). *The law of tax-exempt organizations* (9th ed.). New York: John Wiley & Sons.

Hoyt, C. (2001). Tax-exempt organization. In S. Ott (Ed.), *The nature of the nonprofit sector* (pp. 148–151). Boulder, CO: Westview Press.

Kettl, D. F. (1993). *Sharing power: Public governance and private markets.* Washington, DC: Brookings Institution Press.

Leland, P. (1998, November 5–7). *Payments in-lieu-of-taxes (PILOTs) by nonprofit organizations as a source of municipal revenue: Final results from a national study.* Paper presented at Annual Conference of ARNOVA (Association for Research on Nonprofit Organizations and Voluntary Action), Seattle, WA.

Salamon, L. (1999). *America's nonprofit sector: A primer* (2nd ed.). New York: Foundation Center.

Sanders, S. (1995). The "common sense" of the nonprofit hospital exemption: A policy analysis. *Journal of Policy Analysis and Management, 14*(3), 446–466.

Scrivner, G. (1996). Common characteristics in tax litigation affecting nonprofits: Clues to fundamental responses to legal and ethical crisis. Unpublished doctoral dissertation, University of Colorado at Denver.

Simon, J. (1987). The tax treatment of nonprofit organizations: A review of federal and state policies. In W. W. Powell (Ed.), *The nonprofit sector: A research handbook* (pp. 67–98). New Haven, CT: Yale University Press.

Simon, J., Dale, H., & Chisolm, L. (2006). Federal tax treatment of charitable organizations. In W. W. Powell & R. Steinberg (Eds.), *The nonprofit sector: A research handbook* (pp. 267–306). New Haven, CT: Yale University Press.

Smith, S. R. (2006). Government financing of nonprofit activity. In E. Boris & E. Steuerle (Eds.), *Nonprofits and government: Collaboration and conflict* (2nd ed., pp. 219–256). Washington, DC: Urban Institute Press.

Smith, S. R., & Lipsky, M. (1993). *Nonprofits for hire: The welfare state in the age of contracting.* Cambridge, MA: Harvard University Press.

Steinberg, R. (2006). Economic theories of nonprofit organization. In W. W. Powell & R. Steinberg (Eds.), *The nonprofit sector: A research handbook* (2nd ed., pp. 117–139). New Haven, CT: Yale University Press.

Steinberg, R., & Bilodeau, M. (1999, July). *Should nonprofit organizations pay sales and property taxes?* Washington, DC: National Council of Nonprofit Associations.

Steinberg, R., & Gray, B. (1993, Winter). The role of nonprofit enterprise in 1993: Hansmann revisited. *Nonprofit and Voluntary Sector Quarterly, 22*(4), 297–316.

Under the Rainbow Child Care Center v. County of Goodhue, A07–468 (Mnn. Supreme Court 2007). Retrieved 8/11/2008, from http://www.mncn.org/doc/Under%20the%20Rainbow%20v%20Goodhue.pdf

Vladeck, B. (2003, January/February). Where the action really is: Medicaid and the disabled. *Health Affairs, 22*(1), 90–100.

Weisbrod, B. (1977). *The voluntary sector: An economic analysis.* Lexington, MA: Lexington Books.

Weisbrod, B. (1988). *The nonprofit economy.* Cambridge, MA: Harvard University Press.

Weisbrod, B. (1997). The future of the nonprofit sector: Its entwining with private enterprise and government. *Journal of Policy Analysis and Management, 16*(4), 541–555.

Weisbrod, B. (1998). Modeling the nonprofit organization as a multiproduct firm: A framework for choice. In B. Weisbrod (Ed.), *To profit or not to profit: The commercial transformation of the nonprofit sector* (pp. 47–64). Cambridge, UK: Cambridge University Press.

Weitzman, M., Jalandoni, N., Lamkin, L., & Pollak, T. (2002). *The new nonprofit almanac and desk reference.* San Francisco: Jossey-Bass.

Wing, K. T., Pollak, T. H., & Blackwood, A. (2008). *The nonprofit almanac 2008.* Washington, DC: Urban Institute Press.

65

Nonprofit Organization Life Cycles

Dorothy Norris-Tirrell

University of Memphis

Many internal and external factors influence how nonprofit organizations develop and change over time. Some nonprofits ultimately emerge as effective and sustainable organizations while others do not survive beyond initial start-up efforts. A nonprofit organization life cycle model provides a way to understand and shape nonprofit organization evolution, regardless of the mission or programs. Just as humans follow a predictable pattern of development, nonprofit organizations progress through a series of stages as illustrated in the following fictive "Mainstreet Theater" scenario:

In 1987, a once vibrant art deco design theatre changed ownership and was slated to begin showing adult themed movies. Located in the downtown section of a small older city, the Mainstreet Theater became the catalyst for community action. Informal conversations and chance meetings brought neighbors and local business owners together to eventually purchase and renovate the theater for community use. In the first year, the group filed paperwork to become a nonprofit entity in the state of Florida and to receive recognition as a 501(c)(3) tax exempt organization by the IRS and held a successful star-studded fundraising event. The new nonprofit organization submitted grant proposals for foundation and government funding including the U.S. Department of Housing and Urban Development's downtown revitalization program. The active and visible agenda to restore the theater energized residents and local supporters of the arts. In less than a year, volunteers saw that the building was purchased, renovation begun and a summer children's program initiated.

Then at a strategic planning session billed to take the Mainstreet Theater "to the next level"—conflict emerged! Was the theater going be an art film house, a community theater, a company playhouse, or just a location for other contracted programming? The supporters and their motivations were split. Months of meetings, information gathering and choosing sides followed. Finally, the much loved mayor of the community stepped in to mediate. A community playhouse, with a special emphasis on children's afterschool and summer programming was the result. Not everyone was happy with the vision, but all participants felt involved in the process and, for the most part, remained supportive.

Over the next decade or so, staff was hired, two plays a year were produced using volunteer actors with their openings serving as major fundraisers, and the children's programming initiated was well received attracting interns from around the country. After 8 years successful years, the theater's first executive director retired. The board of directors selected a new executive director after a national search process. The new executive revived the idea of a resident theater company, splitting the board of directors and crippling the theater's programs. By 2000, the Mainstreet Theater was in debt and struggling to survive. After consulting with area arts experts and key funders, the board fired the executive but agreed to support the creation of a new nonprofit, The Children's Theatre Group, which would lease the Mainstreet Theater for professional company produced plays, actor workshops and children's programming. The Mainstreet Theater board would continue responsibility for the historic building, which would still be available for use by other nonprofits and community groups. Today, the Children's Theatre Group continues to be successful, and the Mainstreet Theater is a busy community treasure. (Example created by Norris-Tirrell)

While some of the painful details have been left out of this short scenario, the "Mainstreet Theater" is an almost perfect example of a nonprofit organization that moved clearly through the stages of the nonprofit organization life cycle, approached death, and has been revitalized. The life cycle model offers nonprofit decision makers practical insights for planning and for diagnosing their organization's needs, particularly those related to leadership recruitment and development. This chapter begins with an overview of a nonprofit organization life cycle model and its stages. The next section examines the roles and responsibilities of volunteer leaders important at each stage and then discusses strategies for using this knowledge for recruitment and development.

The Nonprofit Organization Life Cycle

The concept of a nonprofit organization life cycle builds on research suggesting that organizations tend to move through humanlike stages of development (Stevens, 2003). These stages include conception or formation where the idea of an organization emerges and takes root, puberty and growth where the organization's stakeholders struggle with developing priorities and internal coordination, adulthood and mastery of the organization's internal and external environments, and finally, old age where choices are made regarding revitalization, atrophy, survival on the margin, or death. The organization life cycle research is part of a larger research theme of organization ecology. Focused mainly on commercial organizations, this research, using a selection and adaptation or environmental vulnerability lens, examines when and why new organizations form and die (see Adizes, 1988; Carroll & Hannan, 2000; Kimberly & Miles, 1980).

The stages of the nonprofit organization life cycle follow an expected pattern, with each stage shaping structure, processes, and outcomes. At each stage, organization leaders face a new set of challenges and opportunities. How the organization weathers the challenges of each stage and transitions from one stage to the next greatly influences the potential for overall success. Importantly, the tactics that produce success in one stage can create frustration and failure in the next.

The nonprofit organization life cycle model is a tool for diagnosing and reframing problems as predictable for a particular stage. Rather than blaming others, the model allows organization leaders to step back and compare their organizations to a prototype facing common challenges at each life cycle stage—to realize that other nonprofit organizations have faced the same issues and transitioned successfully to the next stage. Using the model, nonprofit decision makers can set realistic expectations for behavior and take action to avoid common stage specific pitfalls.

Figure 65.1 represents the "ideal" progression allowing the organization to fully develop as it moves from one stage to the next. In reality, the stages do not necessarily follow this pattern. Organizations can easily repeat stages or experience them out of order. Ending or dissolution can come during the growth stage, before the organization has reached a point that might produce the best success story. Also, not easily seen in the figure is the ongoing influence of the organization's context, particularly the political, social, and economic dynamics that continually shape decision making and implementation. In addition, life cycle stages are not determined by organizational size or age. An older, larger nonprofit can be vibrant and innovative or stagnating and in decline.

The nonprofit life cycle model is intended to be diagnostic, not deterministic. While the indicators in each stage represent common patterns of behaviors and challenges, they are not cast in stone. Each nonprofit organization evolves on its own unique and dynamic path. An overview of each life cycle stage is presented next.

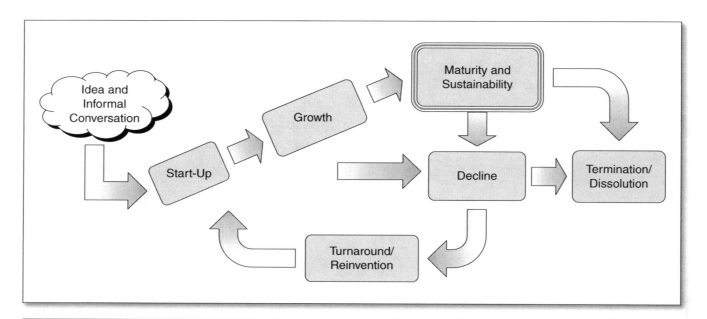

Figure 65.1   Nonprofit Organization Life Cycle Model

Stage 1: Idea and Exploration

In this initial stage, individuals and groups come together around an interest or identified gap. Sometimes one socially minded entrepreneur is the genesis. For example, Mothers Against Drunk Driving was formed by one mother in response to the tragedy of her child's death by a drunk driver. Although some nonprofits are started by government agencies, private firms, or other nonprofit organizations, most nonprofits are the result of great ideas formulated by individuals brought together by shared concern for particular problems or issues. This stage is typically idea focused and evolves through the work of high energy, passionate volunteers.

The founding group formally and informally examines the potential role of a new nonprofit organization. Their time and energy is spent gathering information (such as a market analysis to determine existing nonprofit, for-profit, and government organizations that have similar interests), brainstorming, and developing a broadening set of supporters.

Stage 2: Start-Up and Formation

Once the decision is made to form a new nonprofit organization, the organizers bring together a founding board of directors to create the initial organization mission and purposes. Paperwork, including articles of incorporation and bylaws, must be completed for chartering at the state level and Internal Revenue Service (IRS) recognition as a nonprofit organization (see Publication 557: "Tax Exempt Status for Your Organization" at IRS.gov). States and localities may have other requirements to be addressed prior to beginning operations, which includes hiring staff and implementing fundraising strategies (see your state government webpage for requirements). The formation stage focuses on the creation and approval of the organization's operational structure for governance and decision making, developing initial goals and action steps, and beginning implementation.

Stage 3: Growth and Formalization

In the growth stage, planning and priority setting continue to be emphasized while operational processes are formalized and routinized. Common at this stage is the introduction of new staff and volunteer leaders, either due to an increase in size of the governing body, original participants choosing to step out, or the recruitment of new members. The board of directors begins to diversify and decentralize—potentially moving the organization's priorities away from the originating leader or group's focus. Often, staff is hired at this point because the board realizes the organization cannot reach its goals with volunteers alone. As a result, this stage can be difficult, filled with frustration and unrealized opportunity as the organization appears to be inefficient in rehashing priorities and processes. Just as an adolescent tests boundaries and struggles to identify "what he or she will be when he or she grows up," the nonprofit organization at this stage is verifying its vision, mission, and priorities. If the struggle is not used to advance the organization, failure can result. Many nonprofits dissolve at this point because they cannot find goals and priorities that unite leaders. Others fail because their charismatic leader leaves, and the group has not formed an identity apart from that leader. However, the nonprofits that successfully navigate these pitfalls to establish priorities and operating structures or systems are poised to move to the next stage.

Stage 4: Maturity and Sustainability

The maturity stage is the ideal state of development for any organization. Nonprofit organizations have mastered their environment, found their niche, and are secure in their future existence. They nurture an innovative organizational culture and are respected in their field. As this stage is reached, resources including funding, staffing, and volunteers are diversified and stable while strategies are in place for ongoing planning, evaluation, and quality improvement. Reflecting a healthy and effective nonprofit providing high quality services, organization and program level outcomes are shared with stakeholders and organization purposes assessed and revised with a focus on the future.

Stage 5: Decline

This beginning point of this stage is hard to definitively identify. In the decline stage, the nonprofit has lost its core and energy. Activity and output rather than outcomes and impacts have become the focus. External cues are ignored, and lost is the tenuous balance between "mission and market." Staff is in conflict and morale is low. The organization may now exist in "name only" or on the margin with client or participant numbers decreasing, meeting attendance dropping, leader recruitment difficult, and resources uncertain and constrained. The emphasis of organization decision making is survival with a status quo vision. When faced with a crisis such as creditors demanding money or the board and staff in mutiny, intentional choices must be made about revitalization, atrophy, survival on the margin, or dissolution.

Stage 6: Turnaround/Reinvention

Examples of organizational renewal or turnaround abound. Decisive action is required to move the organization back to viability. This stage often requires the recruitment of new volunteer leaders and hiring of new staff in order to effectively initiate processes for examining and revising the mission, restructuring the organization, and ultimately returning the organization to an earlier life cycle stage. If renewal is not successful, the decision to dissolve the organization remains an option.

Stage 7: Termination/Dissolution

The final stage of the nonprofit organization's life cycle is the least studied and rarest. While for-profit businesses file for bankruptcy at a predictable rate, nonprofits are more likely to end or dissolve because (1) the organization has successfully resolved the problem or issue that it was formed to address or (2) participant stakeholders determine that the current organizational effort has gone as far as it can go. The latter may be the result of bankruptcy, although rare for a nonprofit organization. Often before bankruptcy, the nonprofit goes "underground" with a small board and a savings account waiting for the opportunity to reemerge. The second rationale may lead to merger or acquisition allowing the

nonprofit's mission to continue in a different form. Regardless of what produces dissolution, nonprofit leaders should carefully distribute the organization's assets (typically to a like nonprofit organization) as spelled out in their bylaws and recognize individual effort and share the organization's results broadly.

Using the Life Cycle Model for Leader Recruitment and Development

Each life cycle stage calls for decision makers with a particular set of knowledge and skills. By nature and experience, individuals tend to enjoy taking certain roles more than others. This section identifies the volunteer board member's role at each stage of the nonprofit organization life cycle and then discusses the importance of board member recruitment and development. Table 65.1 summarizes the key board member roles at each stage.

Stage	Challenges	Key Board Roles
The idea	• Converting ideas to action • Mobilizing support	• Maintain commitment to the cause • Understand the market • Follow through
Start-up	• Saying no to extraneous opportunities • Burn out • Excess homogeneity	• Heavily focus on implementation • Set boundaries and priorities • Sustain energy and creativity
Growth	• Competing visions • Demand exceeding capacity • Defining role of board vs. staff	• Continue process orientation • Develop structures, systems and procedures, delegating to staff appropriately • Exercise good judgment
Maturity	• Pitfalls of bureaucratic thinking • Balancing growth vs. stability	• Revisit mission • Scan environment from a futurist focus • Assure resiliency • Build bench
Decline	• Constrained resources • Flagging morale • Protection of status quo	• Risk moving beyond status quo • Stay honest and open in perspective • Be willing to bring in outside views
Reinvention	• Crisis-point mentality	• Use problem-solving orientation • Stay committed to the cause • Restore credibility for key stakeholders
Dissolution	• High emotion	• Plan appropriately/seek expert help as needed • Celebrate • Attend to final tasks: archiving, handling assets, and informing stakeholders

Table 65.1 Life Cycle Stage and Board Roles

The Idea Stage

In the "Mainstreet Theater" scenario offered at the beginning of this chapter, initial leaders came to the table out of personal concern for their community. They were willing to invest their time, expertise, and dollars to solve a problem. The founding group identified a problem and moved quickly to explore a range of solutions ultimately determining that a nonprofit organization could be a useful structure for short- and longer-term goals.

At the idea stage, leaders are challenged to convert their great ideas to actions that can be implemented and to generate the support of others, including potential board members, funding sources, and clients. Since the individuals at the table at the exploration stage cultivated the idea, their commitment is generally very strong. However, as time goes on and action is slow, commitment may wane. Turning great ideas into implementation plans and then successfully taking action requires not only hard work but also expertise often at a level related to the organization's mission.

In addition, the initial first leaders should have an understanding of the new nonprofit organization's competitive market. How many like organizations already exist? Who are local foundations and governments currently funding for this type of work? What is the competition for discretionary spending? The list of potential questions is endless to analyze the potential for success and avoid entering a market that is already overrun with nonprofit organizations competing for resources and volunteers. At this stage, leaders who understand the industry and the market and can also articulate options clearly and in a nonthreatening manner so that a good decision about moving forward (or not) can be made are vital. Sometimes, a good first step for a group with a great idea is to work with an existing nonprofit organization to begin the program. The existing nonprofit can serve as fiscal agent and accept tax deductible donations allowing the newly forming group to test their ideas and develop a base of support prior to beginning the formal organization creation processes. Once the decision is made to move forward, the ability to follow through on obligations and accomplish tasks in a timely way is essential to build and mobilize a team of volunteers and supporters crucial to the next stages.

The Start-Up Stage

At this stage, the founding group becomes the official board of directors with sole decision-making authority and operational responsibility for the new organization. The board members' personal interests or connections to the organization's mission continue to be the focal driver for processes. In the "Mainstreet Theater" scenario, the founding board of directors identified the purchase of the property and building as its first goal, at the same time recognizing that to garner private and corporate donations and to be eligible for possible grant funding, a nonprofit charter from the state and IRS 501(c)(3) recognition were crucial. The group began the tasks of incorporation while planning initial fundraising efforts.

The start-up stage typically brings a long checklist of tasks to complete including filing paperwork, obtaining start-up resources, establishing budgets and bookkeeping systems, and beginning program implementation. Highly motivated board members and other volunteers are needed who will roll up their shirt sleeves and tackle whatever needs to be done. The focus is a strong emotional commitment or passion (and possible zealousness) for the cause. It also brings many new and unplanned opportunities as people and groups discover the new nonprofit organization. The newness of the effort makes it hard to say no and risk the chance of missing out on resources, visibility, or political support. Leaders are needed who can maintain an implementation or "get it done" focus while setting boundaries and priorities. This will allow the group to know when to say yes to the new opportunities that advance the organization's mission and when to say no to the extraneous ones. All too quickly, a highly motivated group can experience feelings of chaos and crisis in the face of few resources and long hours resulting in burn out, even if it is committed to the mission.

Another challenge at this stage is homogeneity of the founding group. Because these individuals tend to be very alike in their experiences and thinking, the founding group may overlook stakeholders, resources, and strategies important to the organization's success. At this stage of the newly forming nonprofit, high energy and creative leaders should encourage exploration of multiple opportunities, bringing new and diverse perspectives to the table, and steady, appropriate progress. Successfully moving forward calls for leaders who can get things done while preserving the enthusiasm and "we can do anything" attitude of the founding group.

The Growth Stage

The growth stage is clearly seen in the "Mainstreet Theater" scenario. Once the initial goal of purchasing the building neared completion, planning was needed for the next steps. The initial strategic planning efforts that resulted in competing visions and desires for the building while painful for those involved was a critical step in developing consensus about the theater's role and building legitimacy for the group in the local, regional, state, and national communities. The process that followed was intentionally inclusive and deliberate, ultimately enlarging financial and community support for the theater. Hiring executive staff that appreciated the process was also the key to setting the groundwork for success.

The biggest roles for board members at the growth stage are to value process and maintain a focus on the organization's mission. The volunteer leaders may begin to feel that they are spending too much time on "administrivia" moving the organization to hire staff. As the board member pool expands, new members are often recruited to bring particular professional expertise to the organization, such as accounting and financial management, real estate, law, and marketing. As new board members join the group and staff is hired, different visions for the nonprofit are likely to emerge. Handling the conflict and tension that is natural to this stage so that creativity is nurtured and personal feelings spared requires leaders to understand the importance of an authentic process orientation. While failure is not uncommon at this stage, handled skillfully, the nonprofit organization can emerge ready to build a successful future. Planning processes define the organization's mission and programming niche that should create a strategic focus for the organization.

Potential demand for taking on new organizational programs continues at this stage while structural and resource capacity for implementation is limited. Nonprofit leaders must appreciate the possibilities that would come with a new direction while exercising good judgment. Leaders must keep their eyes on the mission and vision in assessing suitability for new programs and strategies.

Also, as the organization chart is developed and staff is hired, board members must relinquish the hands-on role that is now delegated to paid personnel and take on new roles. Since much of the focus at this stage is the creation of more sophisticated operational structures, systems, and procedures, determining and clarifying staff versus board roles and responsibilities can be a natural part of the process. Care should be taken to avoid duplication of roles and responsibilities. For example, a nonprofit does not need to hire a professional fundraising staff member charged with a broad range of resource development goals and at the same time appoint a board level committee on fundraising strategy without carefully considering how to avoid overlapping expectations. Some staff and board members may become frustrated with what they view as a bureaucratic approach to formalizing roles. However, clearly delineating responsibilities will result in increased goal achievement and more enjoyable processes to get there. As the board moves from being a support group to accepting responsibility for the organization, its focus is no longer technical expertise and activity coordination but on making informed decisions in an expeditious manner. While actions tend to be more reactive than strategic, this stage needs leaders who are comfortable with changing ideas, appreciative of structures and systems, and able to exercise good judgment to know what opportunities to pursue thus laying the foundation for transitioning to the next stage where governance is the focus.

The Maturity Stage

The "Mainstreet Theater" scenario built into a mature and sustainable nonprofit organization. It strategically involved hundreds of volunteers in restoration, community theater programming, and fundraising. It became a key actor in the community and a site sought after for events throughout the region. This did not happen overnight. It required shared leadership by the board of directors and the executive and constant attention to various stakeholder needs.

When the nonprofit reaches this stage of optimal organizational functioning, the temptation is to rest on its laurels. Increased board size and diversity is common as are systems that allow for board development focused on the role of future vision, accountability, and policy governance. Everything is working well, so why change anything. However, challenges remain that require leadership attention. Too often, what's working takes on a life of its own, leading to the creating of systems and procedures that may preclude change. This tendency for stability is natural but must be balanced with opportunities for growth and change that are required to maintain the organization's vibrancy. The negative implications of these bureaucratic characteristics include a growing overemphasis on rules and procedures, closed decision-making processes, and an emphasis on efficiency. Leaders must measure success against the organization's mission rather than artificial ratios. This stage also requires leaders who continually scan the organization's environment for pertinent information including trends, professional advances, policy changes, and public perception related to the organization's mission and programs—with the understanding that the nonprofit must maintain an "edge" cycling programs in and out based on relevancy and efficacy. To ensure the organization's resilience and prepare an uncertain future, leaders should examine strategies to enhance financial security, such as a diversification of revenue sources, development of a "rainy day" cash reserve, and the creation of an endowment fund.

A final task for leaders at this stage is the development of strategies for developing the organization's next leaders, both staff and volunteer. With a focus on staff, the board may consider an explicit career development plan that identifies employees with potential and invests in their training in preparation for executive level positions. At the same time, the board should be concerned with a leadership path for volunteer leaders. Each nonprofit has a different norm for how leaders are introduced to the organization. Some nonprofits require leaders to have first volunteered at the program or committee level, moving then to a coordinator or chair role before coming to the board of directors. Others have a nominating committee that interviews and orients potential board members before asking them to serve. Whatever strategy is used, leadership sustainability requires intentional planning and ongoing board development through venues such as retreats, readings, short training sessions, and ongoing role modeling by current leaders. Balancing future opportunities with the organization's ongoing sustainability is a hallmark of the mature nonprofit organization.

The Decline Stage

In the "Mainstreet Theater" scenario, the decline stage was a surprise. Although the board of directors knew a year in advance that the executive would be retiring and conducted a national search for her replacement, the group was not prepared for the dissonance in organization visions that resulted quickly after the transition. In the short run, the board members kept their heads in the sand hoping the problem would resolve itself and ignoring the many individuals and groups who were either withdrawing their participation and support or challenging the change in policies. The "wait it out" strategy led to an organization facing debt. When board members started resigning in protest, the remaining leaders called in past leaders and supporters to plan for next steps.

No nonprofit organization enters the decline stage willingly. Instead, denial is more typical. While certainly noticing that resources are growing more constrained, key leaders have left, and the morale of staff and volunteers is flagging, leaders often have explanations for these issues and seek strategies for protecting the status quo awaiting everything to return to the previous state, regardless of how successful it was. For example, at this stage many nonprofits are tempted to spend organizational reserves to meet operating budgets allowing denial about the severity of the problems to continue. This urge should be resisted until options for the organization's future are clarified.

The task for leaders then is to step out of that status quo and to think creatively. This requires a certain amount of risk because other board members and staff are going to continue to resist. The opportunity for open and honest dialogue must be created so that everyone has the same information and as much as possible comes to see the same reality. A common need at this stage is to bring in an outside perspective to assist in this process and make appropriate decisions about the next steps of reinvention or dissolution. The outside perspective can be a consultant or evaluator, expert speaker, focus group, visits to model organizations, or a conference. Intentional action is required by leaders to move the organization toward reinvention or dissolution.

The Reinvention Stage

Turnaround for the "Mainstreet Theater" started with financial crisis and ended with a reenvisioned future for the nonprofit organization. The process began with bringing an inclusive group, including past leaders, arts professionals, and funders, to the table to explore the possible futures for the theater. The group gathered information, sought expert advice, and focused on trends to develop the new organization priorities. While the nonprofit mission did not change, the implementation strategies were drastically changed as the board determined its priorities to be the maintenance of the historic building and the use of a Request for Proposal (RFP) process to invite other nonprofits to use the space for children and community programming. The result to date is a vibrant organization using its assets to support the community.

The precursor for this stage is the organization's reaching point of crisis. Leaving this crisis mind-set behind and allowing the organization to move forward with implementation of necessary processes is essential. Often this stage brings new volunteer and staff leadership to the table. Whether new or continuing, leaders must bring a commitment to the mission, the capacity for frank and confrontation dialogue, and the capacity to rethink everything about the organization including major restructuring of management, operations, and finances. Emphasizing a problem-solving orientation, leaders should openly consider all options for moving forward, collecting data, weighing the costs and benefits, and making decisions in the best interests of the clients and the community at large. Throughout the reinvention stage, leaders should work to restore credibility with important stakeholders, such as funders, political and community officials, and corporate executives. This end of this stage is typically a return to late start-up or early growth stage: positioned for positive life cycle progress.

The Dissolution Stage

Whether the result of bankruptcy, merger, or a long, slow decline, the dissolution stage is a highly emotional and difficult point in the nonprofit organization life cycle. Often, months and sometimes years have led up to the decision to end or dissolve the organization. The tasks are simple at this stage: Plan to terminate the organization's operations in accordance with the bylaws and state law. The leader's job is to ensure that these things, including the disbursement of organization assets, happen appropriately and with honor. To ensure that legal and ethical issues are addressed, outside expertise may be useful. Regardless of the reason for dissolution, leaders should take the opportunity to celebrate the results of the organization, inform all stakeholders including clients and funders, and archive the lessons learned from the organization's work. While closing up the organization is difficult and thankless work, the accomplishments of the organization may be important to the history of a given locality. Websites and public or higher education institution libraries are common repositories for historic artifacts and final documents about the organization. The final stage of the nonprofit organization life cycle brings closure to the work and accomplishments of many board members, staff, and volunteers.

Special Circumstances in the Nonprofit Organization Life Cycle

Two circumstances require discussion when thinking about a nonprofit life cycle: (1) the possibility of *founder's syndrome* and (2) the impact of mergers. Both influence organization life cycles in important and unavoidable ways.

As noted earlier, a nonprofit organization can be founded by a visionary individual with a calling for the mission. Founders often have the characteristics of entrepreneurs: high energy, self-determination, urgency. As the organization is formed, its work is intimately intertwined with the founder's vision. Her or his legacy can and should be great; however, without careful management, a founder can paralyze and eventually strangle the organization's capacity for mission achievement. No matter how long the founder remains active with the organization, she or he is inextricably linked. Individuals who become involved with a nonprofit organization led by a charismatic founder should carefully consider how and when this leader will separate from the organization. The start-up stage and growth stage bring pressures for the founder to question his or her future role. As the board of directors is expanded and staff is hired, the future of the organization requires real and symbolic "transference of sole organizational ownership" so that shared ownership and interdependence result (Stevens, 2002, p. 80). This type of succession planning is more common in the for-profit corporate world but has an important role in the nonprofit organization.

Dissolution is a common task for nonprofit organizations that merge. Questions include, which organization will give its charter, or will both organizations officially dissolve and obtain a new charter. If only one organization relinquishes its charter, care should be taken in creating processes that integrate the mission, programs, board members, staff, and volunteers of the merging organization into the existing organization. The organization that results is in many ways a new organization, returning to the start-up stage at least for a short time period. Experts including lawyers and estate planners may be very useful for ensuring that the important details are addressed. Organizational experts may be useful in bridging two organizational cultures and merging staff and volunteers. The board members' role in this type of situation is to make sure that the newly merged organization has the resources necessary to succeed and that processes are in place to build a strong infrastructure, begin planning processes to develop shared priorities, and assure stakeholders that the merged organization is on track for success.

Board Recruitment and Development

Understanding the nonprofit organization life cycle allows nominating committees and other leaders to be more aware of the knowledge and skills appropriate at each stage so that they can recruit prospective board members to match their organization's stage of development. Each nonprofit has unique circumstances and characteristics that define its life cycle. The following bullets identify some common leadership attributes and skills needed at each life cycle stage:

- Early stages need individuals who feel rewarded by sharing creativity and enthusiasm while building a sense of belonging.
- The start-up and growth stages provide many opportunities for getting things done thus producing a great feeling of accomplishment.
- The growth stage can bring tension and conflict requiring individuals who do possess the skills to mediate this environment and the temperament to tolerate changing emotions and priorities.
- The maturity stage focuses on stability, so individuals who like "rocking the boat" are often not tolerated; on the other hand, leaders are needed who can present a strong and appropriate rationale for rethinking and change as warranted.
- Reinvention is a sort of revolution, so the leaders are needed who bring passion for the cause and thinking outside of the box—even in the face of others who "love" the status quo.
- At the dissolution stage, new members are not typically brought on to the board—although training new or existing board members regarding responsibilities at this stage continues to be very important.

While a leader with an ideal set of attributes and skills may allow the nonprofit organization to efficaciously move through each life cycle stage and transition to the next, board member recruitment opportunities may not parallel the organization's evolution. Board member terms of office are determined by the organization's bylaws rather than organization transition points. The continuity that a stable board of directors brings is also important to a nonprofit organization. So in addition to recruiting new board members who may bring desirable stage-specific knowledge and expertise, offering training and development opportunities to current board members is an important tactic to ensure that nonprofit leaders have the knowledge and skills needed at a given life cycle stage. Board assessment is a first step determining training and development needs. Regular self-assessment by board members provides baseline information and helps identify transition points. Training and development include a wide range of tactics such as the following:

- *Retreats.* Ranging in length from a half day to several days, retreats provide leaders with the time away from day-to-day obligations to explore issues and opportunities. Deliberate planning is needed to ensure that time is used efficiently and that desired outcomes are achieved. A consultant or facilitator is often useful to keep the group on task.

- *Board orientation sessions.* When new board members join, an orientation meeting is an excellent time to go over the nonprofit's mission, goals, structure, programs, and procedures for how the board operates. This includes board member roles and responsibilities. It is often useful for all board members to attend the orientation annually providing the opportunity for shared understanding of organization mission, vision, priorities, and current status.
- *Strategic planning processes.* Many organizations have 3-, 5-, or 10-year plans. These processes are often extensive and involve as many stakeholders as possible. A regular review and update of the plan is an excellent opportunity for board members to learn more about current organization strengths and weaknesses and to plan how they fit in the organization's future.
- *Short trainings.* Many boards use 10 to 15 minutes at each board meeting to reinforce the board member skills and responsibilities. These trainings should target the needs of the board member's needs at each life cycle stage and can range in focus from consensus decision-making strategies to how to read the organization's financial documents or using the organization's board member section of the webpage.
- *Expert speakers.* Bringing outside speakers to talk with the board about the latest research related to the organization's mission or proposed local, state, or federal legislation that may impact the organization or its clients can be useful at all organization life cycle stages. Research centers, university professors, government officials, foundation program officers, and legislators can be useful in connecting the organization to the bigger picture.
- *Site visits.* Visiting model or high performing organizations can provide leaders with information about options for their organization and new perspective.
- *Conferences.* Conferences sponsored by professional associations or discipline-based societies can be an incredible source of information and opportunity for learning about trends, research findings, successful programming, and operational strategies that can move the organization to the next level.

The transition from one life cycle stage to the next is an important point for assessment and training and development opportunities. Investing in the nonprofit organization's leaders is a simple strategy to encourage new thinking and acting essential to organizational success.

Future Directions

In addition to the internal factors, such as leadership changes that more predictably shape the life cycle evolution of a nonprofit, external factors increasingly have a significant influence. With every economic downturn, the number of nonprofit organization mergers and bankruptcies increases. As foundations and affiliated funders like the United Way look carefully at the resources available and the number of nonprofits serving similar needs in a community, they often encourage formal and information collaboration with a goal toward organizational merger. This reduces the number of nonprofits competing for the same dollars and often increases the scope and depth of services provided to a particular service population. Changes in the availability of government funding or the priorities of foundations also impact the viability of nonprofit organizations. While diversifying the organization's financial base is the easy answer, the results for the nonprofit sector are more complex as more nonprofits are considering social enterprise options and developing new funding sources, such as the low-profit limited liability company (L3C) status. The L3C is a hybrid legal structure that allows profit to be generated for socially beneficial goals. Revenue diversification is more difficult for some types of nonprofits, particularly grassroots organizations with a single focus mission.

Another source of uncertainty is produced by disaster situations including weather-related events, such as Hurricane Katrina. Preparedness for these unanticipated events requires leaders to think through a wide range of issues related to communication, risk management, information systems, and human resources. While planning cannot address every situation, preparation improves the organization's resiliency and overall capacity.

Financial and other vulnerabilities regardless of their causes are an important driver in how nonprofit organizations transition from one life cycle stage to the next. Nonprofit leaders must prepare their organizations for both challenges and opportunities.

Summary

The nonprofit organization life cycle model provides an evolutionary perspective useful for nonprofit leaders. As a prototype, progress through the life cycle represents the many hurdles faced by nonprofit leaders. The stages may occur out of order and may need to be repeated to achieve success. As a diagnostic tool, the model can help nonprofit leaders recognize and address critical junctures in their organization's life cycle. These periods of transition from one life cycle stage to the next are opportunities for nonprofit leaders to assess progress, to reconsider commitment, and to shift priorities as necessary.

The model also highlights the changing roles of nonprofit board members as the organization progresses through each stage. By matching the organization's life cycle demands with the talent and temperament of volunteers, strategic board recruitment as well as training and development activities can prepare the organization for common challenges at each stage and create a context for overall success.

References and Further Readings

Adizes, I. (1988). *Corporate lifecycles: How and why corporations grow, die and what to do about it*. Englewood Cliffs, NJ: Prentice Hall.

Archibald, M. (2007). An organizational ecology of national self-help/mutual-aid organizations. *Nonprofit Voluntary Sector Quarterly, 36*(4), 598–621.

Avina, J. (1993). The evolutional life cycle of nongovernmental development organizations. *Public Administration and Development, 13*(5), 453–474.

Block, S. R. (2003). *Why nonprofits fail: Overcoming founder's syndrome, fundphobia and other obstacles to success*. San Francisco: Jossey-Bass.

Carroll, C. R., & Hannan, M. T. (2000). *The demography of corporations and industries*. Princeton, NJ: Princeton University Press.

Connelly, P. M. (2006). *Navigating the organizational lifecycle: A capacity-building guide for nonprofit leaders*. Washington, DC: BoardSource.

Greiner, L. (1998, May). Evolution and revolution as organizations grow. *Harvard Business Review*, 37–46.

Kimberly, J. R., & Miles, R. H. (1980). *The organizational life cycle*. San Francisco: Jossey-Bass.

Norris-Tirrell, D. (2001). Organization evolution or termination: Mergers of private nonprofit agencies. *International Journal of Public Administration, 24*(3), 1–12.

Simon, J. S., & Donovan, J. T. (2001). *The five life stages of nonprofit organizations: Where you are, where you're going, and what to expect when you get there*. Saint Paul, MN: Amherst H. Wilder Foundation.

Stevens, S. K. (2002). *Nonprofit lifecycles: Stage-based wisdom for nonprofit capacity*. Long Lake, MN: Stagewise.

U.S. Internal Revenue Service. (2008). *Tax exempt status for your organization* (Publication 557). Washington, DC: U.S. Government Printing Office.

66

ROLE OF NONPROFIT LEADERS IN SETTING THE VALUES, VISION, AND MISSION OF THE ORGANIZATION

SALVATORE P. ALAIMO

Grand Valley State University

An executive director (ED), sometimes called a chief executive officer (CEO), of a nonprofit organization is typically the most highly paid and the top hierarchical staff member in the organization. He or she is responsible for leading and managing the organization while ensuring the proper stewardship of resources as expected from a tax-exempt organization held in the public trust. Stephen Covey (1996) tells us,

> Leadership focuses on doing the right things; management focuses on doing things right. . . . Most managers and executives operate within existing paradigms or ways of thinking, but leaders have the courage to bring those paradigms to the surface, identify the underlying assumptions and motivations, and challenge them. (p. 154)

As managers tend to respond to change, leaders initiate and develop the culture for change. Leaders foster a culture for innovation beyond the problem solving of managers. Some maintain that managers focus more on efficiency while leaders focus more on effectiveness (Lynch, 1993).

There are overlapping aspects of leadership and management, however, an effective leader does not necessarily make an effective manager and vice versa. Leadership is defined as "a process whereby an individual influences a group of individuals to achieve a common goal" (Northouse, 2004, p. 3), while management is a discipline and practice involving work specific to the performance of an organization

(Drucker, 1974) typically involving the primary functions of planning, organizing, staffing, and controlling (Fayol, 1916). By combining the responsibilities of leadership and management, an ED is charged with practicing the discipline of managing people and resources through these functions while influencing the staff, board of directors, direct service or administrative volunteers, donors, and members of the community toward a common goal for their organization.

Leadership responsibilities for a nonprofit organization also reside with the board of directors. The board is a group of volunteers ultimately and legally responsible for the governance of the organization. They are charged with ensuring compliance with all national, state, and local laws; setting the mission and ensuring it is carried out; providing advice and counsel to staff; and linking the organization to the external community. The board works toward satisfying these primary goals by fulfilling the three standards of conduct—the *duty of obedience*, the *duty of care*, and the *duty of loyalty* (Axelrod, 2005; Burgess, 1993). The duty of obedience involves acting consistently within the organization's mission, purpose, and applicable laws. The board fulfills the duty of care when it acts in good faith and in the organization's best interests when making decisions by staying informed, asking critical questions, and participating in governance. The duty of loyalty is fulfilled when the organization's interests come first and above individual interests, and it avoids conflict of interest. Some of the specific tasks the board is responsible for include hiring, evaluating, and firing, if necessary, the ED. The ED is hierarchically accountable to the board; however, some suggest that in spite if this line of accountability, more often than not, the ED works more in partnership with the board and even guides the board through "board-centered leadership" (Herman & Heimovics, 1991) to ensure the organization is managed effectively and working toward achieving its mission.

Mission

This common goal that drives the operations of the organization and defines its purpose is the organization's *mission*. The mission of a 501(C)(3) nonprofit organization embodies its primary (charitable) purpose or reason for being (Dym & Hutson, 2005). This primary, charitable purpose allows it to attain tax-exempt status by the Internal Revenue Service (IRS) and places it in the public's trust to carry out that purpose. The mission represents an entrepreneurial idea resulting from a person or group of people determining that a specific need in society has not been sufficiently met or met at all. It serves as the foundation for stakeholders to rally around, as well as a guideline for how the organization will serve the public good (Minkoff & Powell, 2006). The mission is expected to represent the organization's values, philosophy, and ethical standards (Bryson, 2005), as well as the basis for developing strategies, meeting objectives, and measuring performance (Dym & Hutson, 2005). Nanus and Dobbs specifically characterize the mission as "the maximization of the social goods they produce for both society and the people who participate in them" and "the single most important measure of success of nonprofit organizations" (1993, p. 39). It represents a covenant between the organization delivering and those consuming the organization's program(s), goods, or services.

Vision

Another common focus for the organization that drives its operations, helps define its purpose by supporting the mission, and helps charts the course and direction for the organization is the *vision*. The organization's vision describes what successful work toward its mission looks like and typically describes how the organization plans on getting to that point of success. For example, the mission statement of Decatur Cooperative Ministry (DCM), a small transitional housing nonprofit, reads, "Decatur Cooperative Ministry alleviates and prevents homelessness while affirming the dignity of each family" (Decatur Cooperative Ministry, 2009, "Mission and Vision"). The vision statement ("Mission and Vision") describes how the group will successfully carry out that mission

to lead our diverse congregations and community in ending homelessness by

- providing individualized, comprehensive services to homeless families;
- raising awareness and providing education about homelessness and its systemic causes;
- advocating for social justice and long-term solutions to homelessness.

Consensus for the organization's vision is important for successful work toward transitioning the organization from its current to its desired state or condition. The ED is charged with soliciting, encouraging, and rewarding stakeholder input for the organization's vision to gain such consensus and a common focus for moving the organization forward. Some suggest that discussions about the vision, visioning exercises, and the development of vision statements come at the beginning of strategic planning to set the course for the process and the direction for the organization. Others such as Bryson suggest that visioning come later in the process to ensure it is detailed, fully understood by stakeholders, and more likely to be successfully carried out.

Values

A nonprofit organization's mission, strategies, and programs—developed to meet a societal need—are inherently based on *values*. Values embody what the organization stands for and are initially established by the founders. Some examples may include respecting the consumers they serve as unique individuals, social justice, privacy and confidentiality, quality of life, and health and wellness or dignity as mentioned in the DCM mission statement. The ED of a nonprofit demonstrates ethical leadership when he or she imbues the stakeholders and the community in which the ED resides and serves with the values of the organization. *Ethics* are defined as "personal and organizational values transformed into action" (Johnstone & Waymire, 1992, p. 20) or "principles on which decisions as to action should be based, derived from a specific value system" (Beckett & Maynard, 2005, p. 24).

John Dewey, a 20th-century philosopher, stated that "the motive for our action must be supplied from the sense of duty or ideal good" (1900–1901/1991, p. 42). The function of this ideal good is to "transform obstacles into means" (p. 43). The attainment or work toward the organization's mission represents this ideal good. It is the basis for transforming the obstacle of addressing the particular social needs of consumers by determining the means (intervention or service delivery) necessary to attain it. Dewey's description of this transformation includes the steps of defining the present conditions (needs assessment), defining the ideal good (intended results), and then acting to modify the current conditions toward becoming the ideal good (the intervention).

In this transformation is where an organization's values become embedded in its service delivery.

Important Considerations for Setting the Mission, Vision, and Values

Strategic Planning

The original mission, vision, and values of the organization are established by the person or group of people who founded the organization. Missions and visions may not be static as the environment in which the organization operates as well as the needs of the organization's target audience change over time. On rare occasions, missions are rendered obsolete as in the classic case of the March of Dimes, which changed its focus to preventing and curing birth defects after a cure was found for polio, its original focus. The ED, along with the board of directors, is responsible for strategic planning where they periodically revisit the organization's mission, vision, and values. This involves periodically conducting needs assessments for the target population served by the organization to determine if these needs have changed in volume, scope, demographically, economically, or in other areas. It also involves evaluating the organization's overall performance and how well it works toward its mission. Such an assessment must answer how well the organization is currently serving its consumers and fulfilling the promise set forth by the mission. When combining the needs assessment with the organizational evaluation, the organization must determine its ability to either continue to meet the most current needs of its target population or change its operations to meet needs that have changed.

Visions are subject to change, as the future desired state or condition of the organization and its path toward that success also tend to change over time due to the environment and changing consumer needs, or the visionary path may be altered due to the feasibility of its attainment. The original values of the organization as set forth by the founders are likely to remain in place as long as the mission remains relatively the same. However, there are instances where the leadership of the organization fulfills its responsibility to ensure the proper values are part of the organization's culture and ways of working and delivering service. An example might be when an organization realizes it is not inclusive enough when engaging stakeholders, especially based on the target population it serves. So it may adopt a new policy toward more diversity and pluralism to work toward engaging stakeholders more representative of the clientele served.

Resources

The executive director and the board are the central figures for ensuring the organization can successfully work toward its mission. This involves the four major functions of planning, organizing, staffing, and controlling but more specifically ensuring the organization has adequate resources to carry out the mission. Nonprofit organizations are open systems requiring resources from their external environments, so financial resources are not only necessary to carry out the mission, but also they are necessary to remain viable in an increasingly competitive market and ultimately to survive. Therefore, fundraising at some level is typically a key responsibility for an ED and the board of a nonprofit organization. Human resources, including paid staff and volunteers, are necessary to run the administration of the organization and deliver the programs to its target population. The success of the organization's programs is directly linked to the organization's success at working toward its mission. The ED is responsible for ensuring that these human resources, including the board, understand, buy into, and support the organization's mission. Capital, in the form of buildings, facilities, equipment, and other major assets, is a necessary structure for an organization to operate. An ED is charged with making sure the organization has the adequate capital to operate efficiently and effectively and to keep up with technological advances.

Leadership and Organizational Culture

Leaders can have a significant impact on an organization's stakeholders while working through the establishment of and revisiting the organization's mission, vision, and values. This is not exclusively a result of hierarchical position. The organizational culture perspective subscribes to the fact that members' behavior is driven by beliefs, values, and norms rather than simply rules or authority (Ott, 1989). *Organizational culture* has been characterized as comprising shared values, ideas, beliefs, assumptions, norms, artifacts, and/or patterns of behavior (Ott, 1989; Schein, 1992) and defined as

> a pattern of shared basic assumptions that the group has learned as it solved problems of external adaptation and internal integration, that has worked well enough to be considered valid and, therefore to be taught to new members as the correct way to perceive, think and feel in relation to these problems. (Schein, 1992, p. 12)

The culture of an organization is a social construction that is both a product and a process. It's a product when it comes in the form of wisdom accumulated and passed on to others, especially new members of the organization, and it's a process because it gets renewed and recreated (Bolman & Deal, 2003).

The leader of an organization can have profound influence on the organization's culture in many ways. The culture of a nonprofit organization is largely built upon the ED's values, activities, and tasks, which are inculcated in staff and other stakeholders (Hay, 1990). The leader's use of language is a key driver of the enculturation process, as the way values and rules of behavior are communicated, including nonverbal communication, shapes the values and norms of the organization's culture (Bjerke, 1999). A leader can have formal influence based on her or his position and authority (Ivancevich, Szilagyi, & Wallace, 1977) and therefore sets the priorities for the organization. He or she may also have informal influence based on his or her expertise or special skills or talents that are important for the organization, such as an ED with expertise in fundraising or financial management. This influence, especially in the United States, where status is linked to education and knowledge, can garner respect within the nonprofit professional organizations or within the individual's own organization (Berke, 1999).

The issue of accountability has garnered much attention recently in the nonprofit sector, and while it typically is linked to more top-down approaches to management and leadership within the context of meeting goals or objectives, it also has its place in influencing the culture of an organization. If a leader communicates the rules of behavior and the priorities for an organization, this communication has no meaning for an organization's members if there is no accountability for following those rules or satisfying those priorities. Without the proper accountability framework, a leader's voice for an organization becomes rhetoric without any foundation for meaningful action. The leader must provide the organization's members with the level of support and a working environment that enables them to deliver on what they're accountable for. This involves leveraging the creative capabilities of the organization's members, engaging members through the psychological contract of their expectations combined with those of the organization's—aligning members' thoughts, decisions, and actions with their goals and the roles involved in achieving them and helping developing members realize their potential through mentoring and coaching (Kraines, 2001).

Leaders in and of themselves are symbols, and their patterns of behavior and leadership can be artifacts for the organization that communicate information about the organization's values, guiding beliefs, and ways of doing things (Ott, 1989). This can be especially true for the founding ED of a nonprofit organization who serves as the original, dominant leader that develops the organization based on his or her individual context and perspective and who attracts those who share similar values and beliefs. Schein reminds us that "Founders usually have a major impact on how the group initially defines and solves its external adaptation and internal integration problems" (1992, p. 212). Congruence must exist between the cultural values and operating norms for an organization to be successful (Anthes, 1987). As a result, culture and strategy are linked; impacting an organization's culture will likely influence the organization's strategic direction and ability to achieve its goals and

objectives (Hay, 1990). More specifically, an organizational culture that promotes an environment for employee satisfaction is more likely to enhance productivity and organizational effectiveness (Ostroff & Schmitt, 1993). A leader, even a founder although less likely, can also be the driver for cultural change within an organization, but only if he or she can handle personal and/or professional discomfort that typically comes with the reflection and introspection necessary for effective change (Block, 2005). There remains debate on whether organizational culture can be managed, and there are constraints that include (Nord, 1985)

- life cycles, conflicting interests, a lack of willingness on the part of some actors;
- different salience attached to issues, different meanings, poor communication;
- lack of subordinate development, bad timing;
- a leader getting trapped by his or her own rhetoric; and
- complexity.

There is also debate over whether the leader is managing the culture or the culture of the environment is managing the leader. However, what remains constant is that leaders of organizations can have great influence on their organization's culture and be the catalyst for cultural change through symbolism, modeling behavior, employing appropriate reward systems, and using other strategies or methods. The importance of this influence can be realized in how it can impact the vision, strategy, enacting of values, direction, operations, and organizational performance in a group working toward its mission.

Future Directions

There are several current trends for the environment in which nonprofit organizations operate that will impact and increase the importance of the role of leadership in setting the mission, vision, and values of the organization. First, nonprofits are operating in an increasingly competitive environment that provides an uncertain and finite amount of resources. Some observers claim that within this environment there exist too many nonprofits and the duplication of services. The nonprofits that are more succinct, specific, and effective in establishing missions that address well-established and described societal needs are more likely to get the attention of funders, volunteers, and other resource providers and acquire the necessary resources to remain viable and competitive. The effective communication of an organization's mission, vision, and values through marketing, public relations, and the boundary expansion efforts in the community by the ED and the board will become increasingly important in this area. An effective establishment and the revisiting of the mission, vision, and values of an organization will greatly enhance the likelihood of an effective strategic planning process, which in turn should positively impact the organization's ability to acquire resources and operate efficiently.

Second, nonprofits operate in an environment where there is an increasing call for accountability. This call combined with the increasing accessibility of information and the advent of charity-rating organizations has affected the efforts of nonprofits: They become more efficient and effective. External stakeholders, such as foundations, the United Way, government agencies, and accrediting bodies now seek information that indicates the extent to which nonprofit programs are achieving their intended outcomes as promised in their mission statements. The leaders of nonprofit organizations must recognize that program evaluation is not something extra they do when funds happen to be available, a luxury item, something too nebulous and subjective to engage in, or something they do only when asked by external stakeholders. They must instead build capacity for it and make it an embedded part of the organization's culture and operations, so they develop a culture for continuous improvement. Connecting program evaluation with evaluating the work toward the organization's mission will be increasingly important to the organization's overall success.

Third, the nonprofit sector is continuing to professionalize itself through the many graduate programs in nonprofit studies across the United States. This is raising the bar for the desirable experience and education in potential executive directors. The next wave of EDs must realize the importance of balancing leadership and management to keep stakeholders involved and engaged, acquire the necessary resources, plan for the future, and consume the latest research available in their service delivery area all while modeling behavior and demonstrating fairness, integrity, honesty, openness, and accountability. In this way, EDs now must be "expert generalists" and not just emphasize or focus on their previous area of expertise such as financial management or fundraising. The new job descriptions for EDs are becoming more complex and demanding as the boards hiring them are realizing the value of an ED that can wear many hats and the full breadth of the responsibility for the position. Professional development and the will to learn will play increasingly important parts in the personal and professional growth of EDs as they strive to remain current and knowledgeable about the latest trends, research, methods, and tools for service delivery and the overall management of their organizations.

Fourth, research continues to tell us that board governance remains a challenge for nonprofits. Reasons for this challenge include (1) its being a volunteer position and the misperceptions that go along with the role of the volunteer; (2) a lack of conveying to board members the responsibilities and expectations of serving; (3) a lack of training, other than orientations, for board members; and (4) an increasingly busy society where time demands for board members are hampering their ability to properly commit and engage in their duties and responsibilities to their organizations. The board's role in setting the mission, vision, and values for the organization will be increasingly important for the organization as the starting point for engaging the board members in their primary duties and responsibilities. The board's level of investment and commitment to its organization will be reflected in its role in revisiting the mission and vision through strategic planning and through setting policy for the organization.

Preparing for the Leadership Role

Transformational Leadership

Leading a nonprofit organization is not necessarily linked to a hierarchical position, as the executive director, a board member, an employee, a direct service volunteer, or a client or consumer can assume leadership roles depending on the issues and situations the organizations faces and the current environment it operates in. *Transactional leadership* is inherent and cuts across all of these stakeholders when they assume the leadership role, as communicating information, planning, and executing tasks will all likely be part of that role. What is not inherent is what the challenges of leading a nonprofit organization in today's environment often require: *transformational leadership*, which "refers to a process whereby an individual engages with others and creates a connection that raises the level of motivation and morality in both the leader and the follower" (Northouse, 2004, p. 170). This type of leadership tends to the needs of followers for the purpose of maximizing their ability to reach their greatest potential and achieve beyond what is typically expected of them. The success of such transformation relies on the leader's charisma and ability to incorporate his or her vision for influencing followers on a one-to-one basis and the norms and culture on an organizational level.

Transformational leadership is important for focusing stakeholders on the mission of the organization and creating a culture of continuous improvement where (1) individuals view their work as more than responsibilities and tasks by connecting their specific role and performance with the organization's work toward satisfying the mission, (2) individuals strive to meet their goals and improve their performance for the sake of the organization and its mission, and (3) the organization proactively seeks to improve its efficiency and effectiveness for serving its consumers and overall constituency. Some recommended steps for enacting transformational leadership include, but are not limited to

- focusing on individuals, their needs and their roles in the organization's performance and their work toward its mission;
- being conscious of how one's own behavior impacts the needs and desires of other stakeholders and the organization as a whole;

- promoting and instilling intellectual stimulation and development in the organization's stakeholders to move them beyond typical views of their work and roles in the organization's success and provide renewed and enhanced perspectives and value for their work;
- earning trust and respect and gaining integrity by modeling behavior and ensuring behavior matches rhetoric and the messages conveyed to stakeholders; and
- creating a culture that embraces positive change that contributes to the organization's mission and enables the organization to adapt to a rapidly changing environment.

The Multifactor Leadership Questionnaire (MLQ) developed by Bass (1985) is a recommended tool to use for assessing one's leadership on seven factors related to transformational leadership. MLQ forms can be obtained at http://www.mindgarden.com/products/mlq.htm.

Education, Experience, and Professional Development

The nonprofit sector and the world of philanthropy are increasingly professionalizing their personnel, operations, and measures for performance. One important contributing factor to this movement has been the emergence of nonprofit management programs in higher education. There are an estimated more than 100 graduate programs offering courses in nonprofit or philanthropic studies, and approximately 45 of these institutions are members of the Nonprofit Academic Centers Council (NACC) whose mission is to "support academic centers devoted to the study of the nonprofit/nongovernmental sector, philanthropy and voluntary action to advance education, research and practice that increases the nonprofit sector's ability to enhance civic engagement, democracy and human welfare" (Nonprofit Academic Centers Council [NACC], 2009, "Mission & Goals"). NACC provides curricular guidelines for both undergraduate and graduate studies in the nonprofit sector, nonprofit leadership, and philanthropy (NACC, 2007).

Existing and aspiring nonprofit leaders are encouraged to consider and take advantage of the expanding number of higher educational opportunities available and review the NACC curricular guidelines to acquire a foundational understanding of not only what will likely be taught in these programs but also what is expected of nonprofit leaders. The will to learn is an important trait for nonprofit leaders, as the environment they operate in is constantly changing. To remain current and knowledgeable in order to effectively lead a nonprofit organization, leaders must learn about new and innovative methods of service delivery; new legislation that impacts nonprofit organizations; the latest research on issues impacting the organization such as those pertaining to the organization's subsector, size, service delivery niche, personnel, and so on; recommended practices for overall nonprofit management and specific areas such as fundraising, volunteer management, or contract

management as well as the specific professions within an organization such as social work, health care, or performing arts.

The old adage, "there is no substitute for experience," holds true for nonprofit leadership, and we are reminded again here that experience in nonprofit leadership is not necessarily linked to the hierarchical position or role one has in the organization. In fact, sometimes the best way to learn about how an organization operates and to become an effective leader is to start at the bottom. United Parcel Service (UPS) is famous for touting that their executives all started as either drivers or workers in their distribution facilities. As one moves forward in a career and builds a body of work, an individual's portfolio, all of one's experience regardless of the consequences or outcomes contributes to the social construction of who one is as a person and as a leader. Individuals are encouraged to take advantage of opportunities to gain depth and breadth of experience that goes beyond paid employment in a nonprofit organization. She or he can serve on the board of directors of an organization; volunteer in a direct service or administrative capacity; engage in advocacy or lobbying to influence policy; work with community groups to assist with organizing or focusing on specific issues; write articles or editorials for nonprofit trade publications, a local newspaper, or relevant blogs; serve as a research assistant to a professor conducting research on nonprofit sector issues; or take advantage of the American Humanics program that provides internships and leadership opportunities for nonprofit studies students who gain practical experience at local nonprofit organizations while earning their certificates or degrees. Gaining practical experience will enable individuals to bridge theory with practice by connecting concepts learned in school, help build a network of friends and colleagues in the field, expand and enlighten his or her perspectives for nonprofit management, and ultimately better prepare him or her to be an effective nonprofit leader.

An individual's knowledge base will likely not, and should not, encompass just his or her higher education and practical experience. There is an abundance of professional development opportunities that individuals are encouraged to take advantage of that typically complement formal education and work experience. These opportunities may be delivered by specific professionals or groups such as a local Directors of Volunteers in Agencies (DOVIA) for volunteer administrators and managers or a chapter of the Association of Fundraising Professionals (AFP). They may be delivered by a statewide association of nonprofit organizations or by a national organization's annual conference, such as those of the American Evaluation Association (AEA) or the Alliance for Nonprofit Management. These opportunities vary in cost; however, occasionally, scholarships or travel stipends are offered for opportunities not local to your area. These opportunities also provide the benefits of networking with colleagues or kindred groups and some professional groups offer certification in their respective fields.

Managing Ethical Dilemmas

Nonprofit leaders constantly face ethical dilemmas because of competing demands from stakeholders, resource dependency, personal agendas, personality conflicts, poorly communicated expectations, other factors, and simply because nonprofits operate in political environments. For example, an organization is considering applying for a grant that requires program outcomes not relative to its specific programs. Does the organization apply for the grant and then "stretch" its programs and risk drifting from its mission in order to acquire the funds? A board member has a relative who owns a construction company that has offered to build a new wing for the local hospital at a discounted cost. Does the organization take the offer to save its organization money or avoid risking the appearance of conflict of interest and put the job out to open bid? Say an organization has formally evaluated its programs for the first time since it was founded 10 years ago. To whom are the results communicated? Are they shared with existing and potential consumers? How far does the organization go in publishing the results to be transparent?

It seems that almost every day we can read about how leaders in business, government, or the nonprofit sector have behaved unethically. Our behavior as leaders is influenced and judged by who we are and what we do. Ethical leadership requires a balance of consequentialism and an intrinsic motivation to do what is right. There will be times that a leader will act based on the consequences for him or herself as an individual, for stakeholders, and/or for the entire organization such as in obeying the law. While this is important, solely acting out of the potential consequences will likely cause a leader to stray from ethical leadership, which requires acting on what is the right thing to do based on values, doing no harm to others or your organization. For example, obeying the law to the letter may involve highly unethical behavior. The principles for ethical leadership are respect, service, justice, honesty, and community (Northouse, 2004, p. 310). It is not enough for a leader to personally have these values and embody them through her or his actions. It is incumbent on a leader to infuse the culture of his or her organization with them so the stakeholders also adopt them and act accordingly through a sincere, intrinsic motivation. Here is a great opportunity to connect the mission and vision with these values and the overarching values of the organization.

Summary

Nonprofit organizations are established through entrepreneurial ideas by a person or group of people who have determined there is an insufficiently met need in society. Through this establishment, the organization's mission, vision, and values are set. This process typically involves the executive director, the most highly paid and the top hierarchical staff person in the organization and on the board of directors, a volunteer group of people legally responsible for the organization. The mission of the organization defines the organization's purpose and reason for existing and typically conveys the audience the organization serves. The vision describes what the successful work toward the mission looks like and can describe the process to get there, usually from a current state or condition to a desired future one. Values usually drive the establishment of the organization and its mission and vision and help to shape what the organization stands for and deems important. Some examples of values include integrity, treating the whole person, diversity and inclusiveness, holistic care and respecting an individual's rights, and social justice.

The mission, vision, and values are inextricably linked and their establishment, reexamination, revision, and refocus are all important responsibilities of the leadership of the organization, typically the ED and the board of directors. Successful leadership and management of nonprofit organizations require that individuals continually expand their knowledge base, practical experience, professional development to stay abreast of the current research and recommended practices for their field, service delivery niche, and the sector as a whole. It also requires that they employ ethical leadership to do what is right, do no harm, and protect the stakeholders and reputation of the organization. This process will help enable leaders to transform their organization to effectively serve their mission and realize their vision while ensuring their values are understood, represented, and valued. Nonprofit leaders are in an optimum position to impact the culture and operations of the organization to ensure the common focus, investment, commitment and work toward incorporating and satisfying all three as the organization strives to remain fiscally healthy, improve performance, and ultimately satisfy the covenants between the organization and the consumers as inherent in the promise of its mission and the public trust of its tax exempt status.

References and Further Readings

Alaimo, S. (2008). Nonprofits and evaluation: Managing expectations from the leader's perspective. *New Directions for Evaluation, 119*, 73–92.

Anthes, E. W., & Cronin, J. (1987). Organizational issues in nonprofit personnel administration and management. In E. W. Anthes & J. Cronin (Eds.), *Personnel matters in the nonprofit organization* (pp. 13–30). Hampton, AR: Independent Community Consultants.

Axelrod, N. R. (2005). Board leadership and development. In R. D. Herman & Associates (Eds.), *The Jossey-Bass handbook of nonprofit leadership and management* (pp. 131–152). San Francisco: John Wiley & Sons.

Bass, B. M. (1985). *Leadership and performance beyond expectations*. New York: Free Press.

Beckett, C., & Maynard, A. (2005). *Values & ethics in social work*. Thousand Oaks, CA: Sage.

Bjerke, B. (1999). *Business leadership and culture*. Northampton, MA: Edward Elgar.

Block, S. R. (2005). *Why nonprofits fail*. San Francisco: Jossey-Bass.

Bolman, L. G., & Deal, T. (2003). *Reframing organizations: Artistry, choice and leadership*. San Francisco: Jossey-Bass.

Brinckerhoff, P. (2000). *Mission-based management*. New York: John Wiley & Sons.

Bryson, J. M. (2005). The strategy change cycle: An effective strategic planning approach for nonprofit organizations. In R. D. Herman & Associates (Eds.), *The Jossey-Bass handbook of nonprofit leadership and management* (2nd ed., pp. 171–203). San Francisco: Jossey-Bass.

Burgess, B. (1993). The board of directors. In T. D. Connors (Ed.), *The nonprofit management handbook: Operating policies and procedures* (pp. 195–227). New York: John Wiley & Sons.

Carver, J. (2002). *On board leadership*. San Francisco: Jossey-Bass.

Covey, S. R. (1996). Three roles of the leader in the new paradigm. In F. Hesselbein, M. Goldsmith, & R. Beckhard (Eds.), *The leader of the future* (pp. 149–159). San Francisco: Jossey-Bass.

Decatur Cooperative Ministry. (2009). *Mission and vision*. Retrieved March 9, 2009, from http://www.decaturcooperativeministry.org/missionvision.php

Denhardt, R. B., Denhardt, J. V., & Aristigueta, M. P. (2002). *Managing human behavior in public & nonprofit organizations*. Thousand Oaks, CA: Sage.

Dewey, J. (1991). *Lectures on ethics*. Carbondale: Southern Illinois Press. (Original work published 1900–1901)

Drucker, P. F. (1974). *Management: Tasks, responsibilities, practices*. New York: Harper & Row.

Drucker, P. F. (1990). *Managing the nonprofit organization*. New York: HarperCollins.

Dym, B., & Hutson, H. (2005). *Leadership in nonprofit organizations*. Thousand Oaks, CA: Sage.

Fayol, H. (1916). *General and industrial management*. London: Pittman.

Hay, R. D. (1990). *Strategic management in nonprofit organizations*. Westport, CT: Greenwood Press.

Herman, R. D., & Heimovics, D. (1991). *Executive leadership in nonprofit organizations: New strategies for shaping executive-board dynamics*. San Francisco: Jossey-Bass.

Herman, R. D., & Heimovics, D. (2005). Executive leadership. In R. D. Herman & Associates (Eds.), *The Jossey-Bass handbook of nonprofit leadership and management* (pp. 153–170). San Francisco: Jossey-Bass.

Ivancevich, J. M., Szilagyi, A. D., Jr., & Wallace, M. J., Jr. (1977). *Organizational behavior and performance*. Santa Monica, CA: Goodyear.

Jeavons, T. H. (2005). Ethical nonprofit management. In R. D. Herman & Associates (Eds.), *The Jossey-Bass handbook of nonprofit management and leadership* (pp. 204–229). San Francisco: Jossey-Bass.

Johnstone, G., & Waymire, J. V. (1992). *What if . . . a guide to ethical decision making*. Ottawa, ON: Johnstone Training & Consultation.

Kraines, G. (2001). *Accountability leadership: How to strengthen productivity through sound managerial leadership*. Franklin Lakes, NJ: Career Press.

Lynch, R. (1993). *Lead! How public and nonprofit managers can bring out the best in themselves and their organizations*. San Francisco: Jossey-Bass.

Martin, J. (2002). *Organizational Culture: Mapping the terrain*. Thousand Oaks, CA: Sage.

Minkoff, D. C., & Powell, W. W. (2006). Nonprofit mission: Constancy, responsiveness or deflection? In W. W. Powell & R. Steinberg (Eds.), *The non-profit sector: A research handbook* (2nd ed., pp. 591–611). New Haven, CT: Yale University Press.

Nanus, B., & Dobbs, S. M. (1993). *Leaders who make a difference: Essential strategies for meeting the nonprofit challenge*. San Francisco: Jossey-Bass.

Nonprofit Academic Centers Council (NACC). (2007). *Resources: Building NACC members—building the field*. Retrieved June 17, 2009, from http://www.naccouncil.org/resources.asp

Nonprofit Academic Centers Council (NACC). (2009). *Mission & goals*. Retrieved June 17, 2009, from http://www.naccouncil.org/mission.asp

Nord, W. R. (1985). Can organizational culture be managed? In P. J. Frost, L. F. Moore, M. R. Louis, C. C. Lundberg, & J. Martin (Eds.), *Organizational culture* (pp. 187–196). Beverly Hills, CA: Sage.

Northouse, P. G. (2004). *Leadership: Theory and practice* (3rd ed.). Thousand Oaks, CA: Sage.

Ostroff, C., & Schmitt, N. (1993). Configurations of organizational effectiveness and efficiency. *Academy of Management Journal, 36*(6), 1345–1361.

Ott, J. S. (1989). *The organizational culture perspective*. Chicago: Dorsey Press.

Schein, E. (1992). *Organizational culture and leadership*. San Francisco: Jossey-Bass.

ROLE OF NONPROFIT LEADERS IN DATA AND NEEDS ANALYSIS AND ASSESSMENT

TERESA R. BEHRENS

Johnson Center for Philanthropy, Grand Valley State University

For many nonprofit organizations, program evaluation is done to respond to the demands of a funder. Most government and foundation grants include some requirement for reporting on results.

While the specific requirements vary widely, as do the resources provided by the funder specifically for evaluation, there are two forces at work in the nonprofit community that are influencing evaluation requirements (Behrens & Kelly, 2008). One of these is the push for greater accountability and transparency. Because of the tax-privileged nature of nonprofits, the public has a right to ask for an accounting of what has been accomplished with these dollars. Funders are being pushed to become more transparent about their work as well as the results of their grantees.

The other major force is the increasing awareness of the complexity of the environments in which nonprofits work. The mix of funding streams, reporting requirements, restrictions on eligibility for services, and so on, create highly interconnected systems that nonprofits must navigate. From the individual perspective, there is greater awareness of how each individual may confront multiple interrelated challenges of poverty, lack of access to health care or high quality education, and poor employment prospects. No one intervention can address all these needs, but any one intervention may impact other systems. In such an environment, simple indicators of outcomes are unlikely to provide useful information.

The pressure for accountability often pushes nonprofits toward identifying simple measures of outcomes; the system perspective can drive them toward collecting large quantities of data. One overall responsibility of nonprofit leaders is to ensure that *whatever resources are spent on evaluation to meet funders' needs also meet the needs of the organization.*

Much has been written from evaluators' perspectives on assessing whether an organization or program is ready for evaluation. Patton (2008) provides an excellent overview of how evaluation can be conducted to support its use by an organization. Less has been written from the nonprofit leader's perspective on how to be ready to use evaluation effectively.

This chapter will focus on how evaluation, and more broadly, use of data, can be used as part of a continuous learning process to improve nonprofit effectiveness.

Readiness for Evaluation

Much of the writing on readiness for evaluation focuses on what it takes to *do* evaluation. Some of the commonly mentioned characteristics of readiness include the following:

- *Clarity about the purpose of evaluation.* Is the evaluation being done to improve a program (formative) or to reach a determination on whether or not it works (summative)?
- *Resources for evaluation.* Are there sufficient resources of staff time and funding for external consultants to collect the needed data?
- *Attitude toward evaluation.* Does the organizational leadership believe in the value of evaluation?
- *Data systems.* Are there existing data that can be used or is the organization willing and able to create systems to gather data?

- *Program maturity.* Is the program at an evaluable stage? That is, has it been in effect long enough to be able to reasonably expect to see outcomes?

With all of the above criteria met, the nonprofit executive can indeed help to ensure that an evaluation can be technically accomplished. That is, relevant data will be collected at an appropriate time in the course of the program. However, meeting all of these criteria does not ensure that the evaluation will ultimately be useful to the organization; these are necessary but insufficient criteria if the executive is concerned about getting the best return on the evaluation investment.

Readiness to Use Evaluation

Getting the most from evaluation requires that the organization adopt a learning stance, seeking opportunities to learn to do their work better. Senge (1990) popularized the concept of a learning organization in *The Fifth Discipline* in which he argues that the key to organizational success is to be continually learning. In this chapter, we describe how a nonprofit leader can use evaluation in support of being a learning organization.

The Learning Cycle

Figure 67.1 (from Kim & Cory, 2006) presents a fairly common depiction of a learning cycle. There are many different versions of how the learning cycle is described (e.g., "plan, do, act, check"), but the basic concept is the same: Learning involves a continuous cycle of gathering data, making changes based on what is learned, and then observing to see the impact of the changes and making continuing adjustments.

In most discussions about learning, the milestones within the boxes get the most attention. However, as noted in Figure 67.2, the lines—the activities or processes that take place within the organization to get to these stages—are equally important.

To use data and evaluation for learning, the nonprofit leader has to ensure that the processes of reflecting, conceptualizing, operationalizing, and perceiving are being carried out appropriately in the organization. Too often, in the rush to launch programs, these processes are short-circuited. Program development moves from observing a need, to gathering data about the extent of the need, to designing a program, and to implementation in the best tradition of program design. However, a lack of attention to the quality of *how* this work is carried out can lead to less effective programs.

It is the role of the nonprofit leader to ensure the quality of these organizational processes. At the highest level, the leader needs to ensure that the cyclical learning process is seen as valued. Rather than a checklist of things to consider, thinking in cyclical terms suggests that a "checkcircle" of factors to consider may be a more useful model (Figure 67.3).

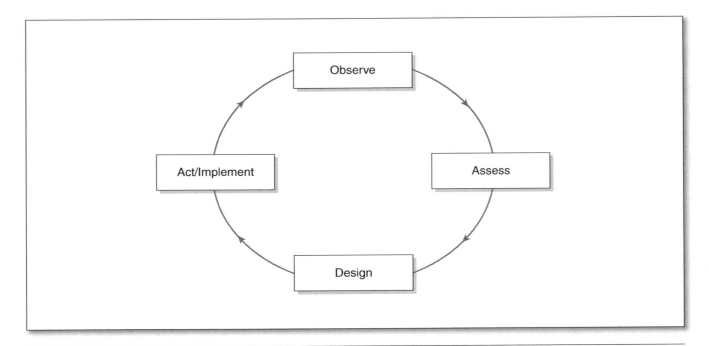

Figure 67.1   The Learning Circle

SOURCE: Kim and Cory, 2006.

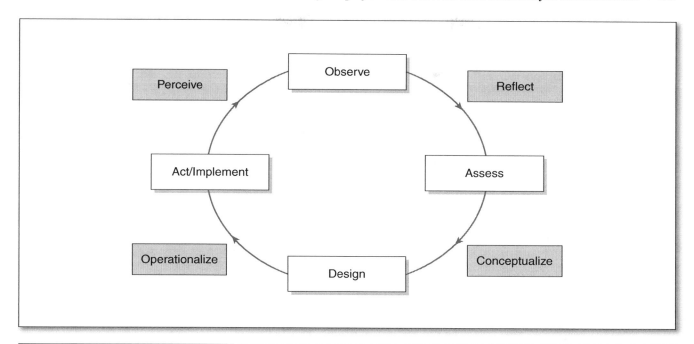

Figure 67.2   Learning Processes

SOURCE: Kim and Cory, 2006.

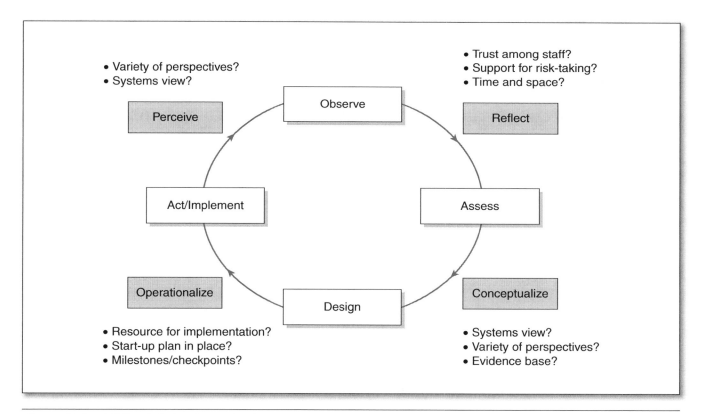

Figure 67.3   A "Checkcircle" for Evaluation Use

SOURCE: Kim and Cory, 2006.

Observe/Reflect

Beginning at the *observe* stage, the leader can improve the quality of reflection on these observations by asking some key questions:

1. *Is there an environment of trust in the organization?* To freely share their observations, staff members must feel that they will not be subject to ridicule, skepticism, or other ways of invalidating their observations. The climate should be one in which each person's observations are taken seriously. An environment where out-of-the-box thinking is encouraged is one in which links and relationships relevant to the issue at hand may be surfaced.

2. *Is there support for risk taking?* Organizational cultures that do not treat mistakes as failures are more likely to foster learning. If the dominant storyline in the organization is "the last person who screwed up got fired," then it is not a climate in which creativity and open dialogue will occur. It has to be OK to acknowledge when things didn't go as planned and to admit it when the emperor is naked. The executive can and should model this behavior.

3. *Do staff members have the time and space for reflection?* Taking time to reflect together is the way to maximize on the diversity of a group and enable the most creative thinking. Nonprofit staff members are notoriously overbooked and busy carrying out their work. Helping to see reflection time as valid and important work time is an important role of leadership. Again, the executive can model the behavior and create an expectation that staff will make these reflection times a priority.

Anyone who has worked in an organization has had the experience of coming out of a meeting and comparing notes about what was *really* happening in the meeting. To have an effective learning environment, these observations and reflections need to take place in front of the group; they need to be part of the meeting. Getting all of the facts on the table—even the "elephant in the room," like the fact that the executive's pet project isn't working—is an essential step before learning can take place. Good facilitation, discussed in more detail below, can make this reflection process a safe environment.

Assess/Conceptualize

At the assess stage, formal information gathering is carried out to determine the scale and scope of the social issue to be addressed. The conceptualization process—the development of a shared understanding of the issues and how to address them—follows from this information gathering. The nonprofit leader can consider the following questions in order to make this conceptualization process effective:

1. *Have we looked at this from a systems view?* The organizational leader often has the broadest perspective on the organization; other staff may have broad understanding of the particular social issues being addressed. Both are necessary to understand how the problems and interventions are conceptualized as part of the existing networks and systems in a community and the capacities of the organization. There are several different facilitation approaches that can help foster this systems perspective. See below for further suggestions.

2. *Do we have a variety of perspectives?* Including the perspectives of program participants, other community and nonprofit leaders and staff, as well as from a variety of internal perspectives, is the key to getting the best information on how alternatives under consideration might be impacted by or have an impact on other parts of the organization or community.

3. *What is the quality of the evidence base being used?* The quality of the conceptualization can be only as good as the assessment information on which it is based. The data should include things such as

   a. What is the problem we are addressing?

      i. What is the scale of the issue? How many people are affected or involved? (Are you trying to house 20 homeless people? 200? 2000?)

      ii. What is the scope of the issue? What is the geographic area you are (or should be) concerned about? (Are the homeless moving among churches in your community? Surrounding communities?)

      iii. Who else is working on the issue? What are they discovering? What data do they have?

      iv. Which is the group you really need to target? (Are the homeless predominantly single men? Women and children? Two-adult families? English speaking?) Are there particular characteristics of this group that you need to take into account, such as cultural beliefs or traditions?

      v. What are the related needs that you should address, either directly or in cooperation with others?

   b. What do we know about what works?

      i. Are there interventions that have been demonstrated to be effective? What does the available research tell you?

      ii. What have others in your area who are addressing this issue tried? What evidence do they have of success?

      iii. What do members of the target group say about what they need?

Using the services to the homeless as an example again, a service provider might offer only emergency shelter; shelter and meals; shelter, meals, and health care; shelter, meals, health care, employment counseling, and so on. Another strategy might be to offer only supportive services and work with another housing provider. Housing families will have different requirements for both space and services than housing single adults. The "right" mix will depend on getting the view from many different parts of the system of services.

Basing decisions on data that are accepted as valid and reliable, rather than on the preferred theories of individuals, is more likely to lead to positive outcomes. A leader with good teaching skills can help the group maintain rigor in the discussion. This also may be one point where bringing in an external facilitator (who may also be the evaluator) may help keep the discussion grounded in the data.

A Word About Standards of Evidence

In the nonprofit world, there are few examples of "proven" approaches to social problems. Proving results requires using randomized experiments. For example, we would randomly assign homeless people to different types of services and track them over time to see what services resulted in the best outcomes. The impracticality of this approach (such as getting enough people assigned to enough different treatments, getting participants to agree to participate, the cost of monitoring the different programs and individuals, and having services that are clearly defined and different from each other) means that doing experiments is typically not the way programs are evaluated. Instead, we look for ways to logically demonstrate that the services provided made a difference. At a minimum, we look for evidence that change actually occurred, meaning that we have "before" and "after" data. Note that before and after data do not prove that the program caused the change, only that there was change. Having a comparison group that is not randomly assigned gives you some additional evidence that the program made a difference, but it is also very feasible that some other difference between the two groups caused change. Logic models, discussed below, have been developed as a way programs can demonstrate the linkages between what was done and what was achieved.

Rather than the "gold" standard of true experimental research, evaluation often relies on something more akin to the legal standard of what a "reasonable person" would believe.

In this assessment and conceptualization phase of the process, one thing to be clear about is what a *system* is. The term is often used loosely (even in this chapter), but there are some key elements that need to be present in order for something to be a system. It has to have parts that work together (in an order that matters) to achieve a purpose. When we speak of *social service systems*, we are often referring to a collection of social service providers who do *not* actually work together. Often, the process of bringing people together to review data and get a shared understanding of the issues is a major intervention in its own right!

Design/Operationalization

Based on all of this information, the leader should ensure that there is a shared understanding of what the initiative or program is seeking to accomplish and what the key strategies for achieving the goals will be. In short, the leader needs to ensure that there is a *theory of change*. A theory of change defines all the building blocks required to bring about a given long-term goal (ActKnowledge, n.d).

Knowlton and Phillips's (2009) book is a good resource for details on how to develop a theory of change, as well as sample logic models, for various types of programs; the web-based tools available at www.theoryofchange.org are also helpful.

If an external evaluator will be used, this is the ideal point at which to engage them. There are several advantages to bringing the evaluator into the conversation at this point. First, their professional advice on the clarity of the program goals and logic model can be used to the best advantage. Second, if the evaluation design is developed along with the program, there is an opportunity to build evaluation data collection into the other work of the program. Third, opportunities for participative evaluation in which program beneficiaries contribute to shaping the evaluation can be developed. Participative evaluation may result in more relevant data with broader ownership of both the program and the evaluation. Finally, a professional evaluator can also help staff assess the quality of the data on which program design decisions are being made.

As new programs are put in place, the more traditional management questions arise. The role of the leader is to ensure effective operationalization by asking management questions such as the following:

1. *Do we have the resources to implement the program?* The right staff capabilities, technology infrastructure, program space, and referral networks are some of the resource requirements to be considered.

2. *Is there a clear start-up plan?* As anyone who has ever finally received a grant and then said, "Wow. Now what do we do?" knows, a plan for ramping up activity is critical to success. Plans for how resources will be reallocated, how initial participant recruitment will be put in place, and so on, are as important as the plans for how the program will look once it is in place.

3. *Are there milestones or checkpoints?* Clarity about when progress will be assessed is part of the leader's responsibility in operationalization.

At this stage, a logic model can be used to provide a graphic depiction of this detailed view of the program. A logic model is a simple way to connect the dots between activities, the outputs of those activities, the expected outcomes (short- and long-term), and impact that will follow from those outputs. (See Figure 67.4 for a logic model template.) The logic model then provides a guide to the ongoing assessment. Data can be collected over time to assess progress at each stage, from implementation (Are the resources there? Are the activities fully implemented?) through impact (Have we reduced homelessness in our community?).

Assumptions							
Problem Statement			Strategies	Activities	Results		
Problem	Who is affected?	Where is the problem? (place)			Outputs (short-term)	Intermediate-term outcomes	Impacts (long-term)

Figure 67.4   Logic Model Template

Implement/Perceive

The old parable of the blind men and the elephant is a good one to keep in mind when assessing any system. In the parable, each blind man is touching a different part of the elephant and describes the elephant based on that part: "It is like a tree trunk," or "It is like a rope." Our view of any system depends on where we sit in relation to that system. The nonprofit leader is often in a better position to see a broader network than line staff. The executive will also have the authority to make decisions about formal partnerships or other forms of collaboration that might contribute to a more effective program.

These are some key questions to ask about this part of the cycle:

1. *Who else should be involved?* One of the key roles of the nonprofit leader is to ensure that the perceptions of those who have different vantage points are included in any implementation and observation processes.

2. *Who or what other processes interact with this system?* Traditional evaluations will sometimes discuss the "context" of the program or of the evaluation. Thinking more specifically about the systems that are impacted or have an impact on the program being implemented allows a more systematic look at the environment. Sometimes, *unintended* consequences can actually be foreseen if this approach is taken.

This systems analysis is often best accomplished through a formal process with a group that includes representatives from outside the organization and especially representatives of the group that is expected to use and benefit from a program. In the homelessness example,

meal providers, medical service providers, merchants concerned about panhandling, school officials who work with homeless youth, and police are among the groups who might offer valuable perspectives.

There are many formal methods for analyzing systems; Williams (n.d.) has an easy-to-understand website that explains many of these methods. Iman and Williams (2008) provide examples of how different systems approaches were used in many different social programs.

Executive Skills

In summary, the role of the nonprofit executive can be described in four main responsibilities that help to promote continuous learning:

- Creating a "data culture" by demonstrating use
- Creating a climate of trust
- Making time and space to reflect on evaluation findings and other data
- Holding the big picture (systems view)

Technical skills in evaluation can be accessed through an evaluation consultant; the responsibility for use, however, must rest inside the organization. The skills that are needed to carry out the roles above are not the ones taught in traditional management classes. They include skills in teaching, facilitating, and framing good questions.

Teaching skills come into play in working with both staff and board members to understand the learning framework and the systems context for the program. Teaching skills include having a tool kit of ways to convey information to others in ways they can understand it. Sometimes, the leader may actually need to give a presentation to the staff; other times, she might create a setting in which the learning can be more of a process of self-discovery. For example, the executive director could give a presentation on which key partners are for a new program to provide supportive housing, could ask a staff member to research who in the community is doing this work, or could lead a board discussion at which the service providers are placed on a map. In fact, all of the above might be necessary. The executive director can choose what approach is likely to achieve the needed results in the needed time frame if she has some basic understanding of how individual learning takes place.

Facilitating skills, including the ability to carefully construct a meeting agenda, is important in almost every aspect of creating a learning environment. Being able to clearly specify meeting goals and objectives, develop a logical flow of topics, keep the meeting on topic, respond to events and people as the meeting unfolds, and ensure that an accurate record of the meeting is made are among the skills needed. For example, a meeting at which unfavorable data about a program's outcomes are going to be shared can be framed as a learning meeting with objectives to identify what can and should be done differently, to identify what is working well and should be maintained, and to develop a set of lessons to share with the field. Contrast this with a meeting objective of finding out what went wrong (and who is responsible as the unstated objective).

Framing good questions is a skill that is useful to support both productive meetings and effective teaching and learning. Good questions have the following characteristics:

- Cannot be answered with a simple yes or no
- Invite people to think and reflect
- Empower people rather than invite self-defense
- Question assumptions

By posing good questions and teaching others to do the same, a nonprofit leader can also contribute to developing a climate of trust. When questions are asked to achieve understanding rather than to fix blame, it becomes a safe environment to admit mistakes—the first step in being able to learn from them!

There are a number of excellent resources on how to frame good questions (e.g., Marquardt, 2005).

Involving the Board of Directors

Ideally, the culture of learning will extend to the organization's board of directors. Because the board has the ultimate legal and fiduciary responsibility for the organization, board members often have a tendency to focus on the accountability purpose of evaluation rather than the learning uses. This in turn often leads staff to not share the full evaluation results with the board. Bringing the board into the learning process, however, can result in a more effective organization.

One way to reframe evaluation for board members is to emphasize that the goal is not to "prove" success or failure, but to "understand the results." Even board members steeped in a business culture know that if profits are down, you need to get to the root of why they are down to turn it around.

Depending on the nature of the board, there are some strategies that might be used to engage them in the learning cycle:

- Share evaluation results with the whole board in a discussion format—again, posing questions about what was accomplished, what could be done differently, and so on. Clearly marking these discussion sessions as different from the board's decision-making sessions is helpful. For example, if the board usually meets around a table, having a conversation seated in comfortable chairs might signal that this conversation is different.
- Set up an "evaluation" committee of the board. Members of this committee will spend more time learning about the evaluation processes being used and the results. They can then become the spokespeople to the rest of the board.
- Bring in an outside evaluation specialist who can help educate the board about evaluation. In particular, board members are often unclear about the issue of standards of evidence and the difference between summative and formative evaluation. If they become comfortable with these concepts, they may become more comfortable with the use of logic models and other evaluation tools.

Working With Funders

It is unfortunate that each funder has its own evaluation requirements. Government funders at the federal, state, and local levels have different reporting forms and requirements from each other, let alone those of foundations. In general, though, funders have become more attuned to reporting outcomes rather than just numbers served. As with the board of directors, there are different ways in which funders might be involved in evaluation discussions.

In the case of local funders, inviting them into learning conversations as described previously might be a good strategy. Funders who are committed to a particular community are more likely to appreciate the understanding-rather-than-proving framework.

Other funders might provide a form in which you need to report results. Nothing about using this learning framework means that you will not have the numbers to report. In fact, learning requires that you have good data!

Summary

Given the many hats that nonprofit leaders wear, they cannot be expected to become experts in evaluation. The technical aspects of evaluation are in many cases best left to people with special training or expertise and used on a consulting basis. However, the nonprofit executive plays a critical role ensuring that the resources, both financial and human, that are spent on evaluation are put to the best use for the organization for which they are responsible, not just for the purposes of the funder.

References and Further Readings

ActKnowledge. (n.d.). *Theory of change: Introduction.* Retrieved July 27, 2009, from http://www.actknowledge.org/theoryofchange/toconline.html

Behrens, T., & Kelly, T. (2008). Paying the piper: Foundation evaluation capacity calls the tune. *New Directions for Evaluation, 119,* 37–50.

Iman, I., & Williams, B. (2008). *Systems concepts in evaluation: An expert anthology.* Washington, DC: American Evaluation Association.

Kim, D., & Cory, D. (2006). *It begins here: Organizational learning journey toolkit.* Singapore, Republic of Singapore: Cobee Trading.

Knowlton, L. W., & Phillips, C. C. (2009). *The logic model guidebook: Better strategies for great results.* Thousand Oaks, CA: Sage.

Marquardt, M. J. (2005). *Leading with questions: How leaders find the right solutions by knowing what to ask.* San Francisco: Jossey-Bass.

Patton, M. Q. (2008). *Utilization-focused evaluation* (4th ed.). Thousand Oaks, CA: Sage.

Senge, P. (1990). *The fifth discipline.* New York: Doubleday.

Williams, B. (n.d.). *Bob Williams.* Retrieved July 22, 2009, from http://users.actrix.co.nz/bobwill

68

Culture, Climate, and Social Context in Nonprofit Organizations

Audrey Barrett

San Diego City College

Taking a look at what goes right or wrong in a nonprofit organization often prompts a conversation about organizational context. Unfortunately, the dialogue typically only starts during the postmortem analysis undertaken after a major ethical breach. During such a time, an organization's members will closely examine the incident, and in high profile cases, the community at large will also get involved through media reports, blog posts, and case analysis. The result of these analyses often yields succinct explanations for the most egregious behavior by nonprofit organizations. The explanation typically sounds something like "it was the culture of the organization that allowed this to happen." It sounds reasonable, end of the story, right? For most people, yes, the cultural explanation brings closure to the story and they can move on to the next topic of interest. However, for current and aspiring nonprofit leaders, the story has just begun.

Individuals in leadership roles who invest the time to gain a deeper understanding of the omnipotence of organizational social context (or organizational climate and culture) will find themselves better prepared to create, maintain, and lead healthy nonprofit organizations. Without an adequate understanding of organizational climate or culture, many well-intended leaders have led organizations to their demise, made news headlines for major ethical breeches of conduct, or quietly left their executive positions as bewildered failures. If these "failed" leadership attempts had taken the following two golden rules under advisement, their outcomes may have been different: (1) Hard work and good intentions to promote a leadership initiative that does not resonate with the existing culture of an organization will almost always fail, and (2) working within the established culture of an organization, no matter how negative the effect of the existing culture, provides the most likely route to successful leadership change. Thus, a comprehensive understanding of organizational culture serves as an important knowledge base for organizational leaders.

Nonprofit leaders have reasons unique to the third sector to attend to the culture of their organizations through knowledge, assessment, and continuous learning. These reasons are different from those for the for-profit and government sectors and are directly tied to the organization's sustainability. Ethics and the perception of being an ethical organization play a vital role to nonprofit agencies as nonprofits rely largely on donor funding to remain viable and to fulfill their missions. If an ethical breech occurs in a nonprofit agency, the funding streams can become very scarce or disappear completely. Thus, as the culture of an organization has an effect on its members' behavior and their behavior constitutes the ethics and ethical image of an organization, an understanding of organizational culture and its role on ethical behavior serve as critical knowledge for the leaders of nonprofit organizations to possess.

This chapter seeks to provide readers with an understanding of the concepts of organizational climate and organizational culture. Gaining a true understanding of these notions requires recognition that becoming fluent in the culture of an organization facilitates opportunities for positive change and protects against ethical failures, mission drift, and other ineffective practices. To that end, various conceptualizations of organizational context throughout this chapter introduce the reader to the theoretical complexity and rich history behind terms used so often but rarely understood. The chapter discussions culminate with the introduction of two premiere scholarly works on nonprofit ethics and a push for the reader to apply their understanding of organizational context within their current social settings. Without a doubt, understanding how to harness the power of organizational context shapes your skills as a leader and provides some of the tools necessary to solve social problems. This chapter aims to serve as a primer to advance the knowledge of an aspiring or current nonprofit leader to help accomplish many important leadership tasks.

Understanding Organizational Climate, Culture, and Social Context

Are Organizational Climate and Culture the Same Thing?

Already in this chapter the terms *organizational climate* and *culture* have been used interchangeably along with a third term, *social context*. This presentation may falsely give the impression that the three terms represent an identical concept. However, the following serves as a better way to conceptualize these three related terms. Using an analogy, organizational climate and culture represent adopted siblings, and their shared surname is social context. Stated more specifically, social context represents a broad term that has recently entered the academic literature, and it describes the environment within which an organization's members operate. The use of this term in the literature has sought to unify the camps of scholars who rally behind either research on climate or research on culture. Climate and culture represent specific terms each with a long history in the academic literature. Notably, while a great deal of overlap exists between the two terms, prior to the push by modern scholars to unify the concepts through the study of social context, the majority of the literature has existed in two "silos": research on climate and research on culture. The next sections of this chapter provide a historical overview of climate and culture with a discussion of their relevance to current and aspiring nonprofit leaders. These sections serve to provide knowledge of the historical differences in understanding, measuring, and effecting organizational climate and culture. Acquiring such a knowledge base can facilitate a broader depth of understanding and provide a common language for integrating the concepts. Increasing the complexity of one's understanding can perhaps most importantly increase the capacity for assessing and shaping the behavior within one's organization.

Understanding Organizational Climate

Notable literary and scholarly works since the mid-1800s have explored the human dimension of organizations. This exploration indicates the first recognition that the underlying values of organizations affect workers and that a socialization process occurs in the workplace. Examining the human element developed into a specialized branch of organizational study with the social context of organizational life as its focus. This branch became known as organizational climate. Thus, organizational climate represents one of the first widely studied concepts to address the social context in organizations and, as such, represents an older term than culture related to organizational behavior.

Definitions of Climate

A multitude of definitions for organizational climate provide different perspectives on an organization's membership and the organization's capacity to change. Some scholars identified climate as a relatively enduring quality of the organizational environment experienced by individuals that influences the behavior of its members. Meanwhile, others indicate that climate can be managed or altered within a relatively short scope of time. Clearly, differences exist within the definitions, but most academics include within their conceptualization an element of perception. For example, climate is the way individuals perceive the personal impact of their work environment or is related to the psychological environment in which the behavior of individuals occurs.

The study of these definitions and the research that supports the multifaceted understanding of climate over the decades yields the following amalgamated definition: Organizational climate consists of the *visible attributes of an organization's values as interpreted, in a shared manner, by multiple members* of the organization. Distinct from but related to organizational culture, climate functions with significantly more malleability than culture. Change in organizational climate, may, over time, produce a change in organizational culture, and within a single organization, multiple (even contradictory) climates may exist.

History of Climate and the Emergence of Organizational Culture

The notion of organizational climate as a discipline emerged from the field of psychology, and scholars in this area essentially sought to study and understand the way individuals describe and perceive the environment of their organization (Verbeke, Volgering, & Hessels, 1998). Researchers' drive to delve further into the study of climate served to satisfy their need to understand what environmental influences in an organization affected the motivation and behavior of its constituents (Reichers & Schneider, 1990).

Ultimately, the study of organizational climate split and evolved in two directions: research on climate and research on culture. Some scholars maintained the original pursuit of climate research while new interest in organizational culture rapidly took hold among other researchers. Following this split, a notable division occurred between researchers about which of the two concepts composed the most relevant aspects of organizational life and which served as more valuable on a number of levels (academic, fiscal, personnel management, organizational change, and leadership, among others). This divisiveness in the literature still remains, as articulated by researchers who advocate keeping the concepts of climate and culture distinct and independent of each other. However, a growing number of researchers laud the benefits of understanding climate and culture as reciprocal and reinforcing concepts that may benefit from mutual study. To gain a better understanding of the distinctions and similarities between climate and culture, a review of the most common definitions and the history of organizational culture is necessary.

Understanding Organizational Culture

The notion of culture has its roots primarily in the field of anthropology. Scholars studying indigenous peoples used largely qualitative methods to gain insight into tribal practices, mores, values, and specific artifacts of culture. The study of organizational culture emerged from the initial studies of organizational climate when the business field became interested in measuring and understanding the human side of organizations. In the 1980s, organizational culture became a popular research interest and yielded multiple best-selling books. These early researchers often adopted the qualitative research methodologies, typically used by anthropologists, to gain insight into the culture of organizations. Organizational culture often serves as the reference for *unwritten rules* in organizations, rules that new members must learn and obey (or risk being ostracized), and that fully acculturated members do not violate.

Definitions of Culture

Researchers from the 1950s described culture as a transmitted pattern of values, ideas, and other symbolic systems that shape behavior. Moving from a definition of general culture to the specifics of organizational culture, Schein (2004, p. 17) provides one of the most frequently cited definitions:

> a pattern of shared basic assumptions that was learned by a group as it solved its problems of external adaptation and internal integration, that has worked well enough to be considered valid and, therefore, to be taught to new members as the correct way to perceive, think, and feel in relation to those problems.

Schein's work highlights the key components most researchers agree on regarding organizational culture while Cooke and Szumal (1993) note that most definitions of culture share a common theme "organized around the behavioral expectations and the normative beliefs of

individuals in an organization" (p. 1301). The Ethics Resource Center (2007, p. 9) gets right to the heart of applied culture by including in their definition the comment that ethical culture "sets norms for employee behavior and tells employees how things really work in the organization."

Reviewing the existing definitions of culture yields some insight into the incredible strength a culture maintains over an organization's members. Some researchers hypothesize that members of an organization invest a fair amount of energy into making sense of their organization's culture. This level of investment makes sense as the organizations people belong to typically provide financial means or fulfill personal satisfaction needs. Thus, we can assume the level of investment in organizations is high; therefore, the potential power of the culture over our behavior to sustain these needed connections is also high.

The study of these definitions and the research that supports the multifaceted understanding of culture over the decades yields the following amalgamated definition of organizational culture: a singular and *pervasive set of values and beliefs shared by the members of an organization.* New members of the group receive socialization to acculturate them into the highly homeostatic values and beliefs. Culture exists as distinct from but related to climate, and while multiple climates may exist within an organization, solely one culture reigns.

Only One Culture per Organization but Multiple Climates Can Exist; Why the Discrepancy?

The discussion of climate stated that multiple climates can exist within a single organization, while culture was identified as a singular force throughout the whole organization. To help understand these concepts, imagine an overriding culture directing the behavior of the organization as a whole, while various climates exist within each department of the organization (e.g., within the accounting department vs. within the marketing department vs. within the food service department). Weather patterns provide an easy analogy for this discussion. During the season of summer in the United States, it can simultaneously rain in the Rocky Mountains and be sunny throughout the Midwest. In this example, summer is analogous to culture, while rain and sunshine are analogous to climate. There is one season with multiple expressions of acceptable seasonal weather. To extend this example, we can further illustrate some of the confines of culture.

The weather expressions in our example, while varied, all present as within the acceptable tolerance of the season. Culture and climate share a similar relationship. Just as one wouldn't expect snow and freezing rain during the summer, one also wouldn't see a Wall Street investment banker wearing shorts to a business meeting. Behavior that is outside the norms of the culture typically only occurs once due to the strength of the culture within the organization and the homeostatic tendency of organizations to rebalance. If the Wall Street banker wore shorts to his meeting, it might be his last meeting as he may be fired as a result. Or perhaps, he would wear them as an outward expression of disdain for the predominant culture if he was planning to quit his job. In other words, it takes extreme circumstances to see behavior that flows against the cultural norms, and those who violate the norms are often punished or leave the organization of their own accord.

As the weather example highlights, multiple climates may exist within an organization. Researchers have studied these varying climates within organizations to identify clusters of persons sharing common perceptions. Stated another way, climate research has evolved into research with a particular referent. Examples of this include the study of climate *for* service, *for* safety, *for* ethics, or *for* the adoption of best practices. These types of studies examine climate as the shared perceptions of an organization's environment. Recognizing that different climates use and maintain distinct characteristics for accomplishing certain tasks can serve nonprofit leaders well. Depending on the nature of an organization, a nonprofit leader may wish to shape the organization's climate differently. The judgment would be based on the identified best practices for that particular climate type to best accomplish the organization's mission.

To provide a balanced history in this chapter, it serves as important to note that the writings of theorists who identify multiple cultures occurring within a single organization do constitute some of the literature. However, upon closer examination of the studies indicating this assertion, one can easily reclassify the multiple culture types into subclimates. Framing the work in this manner, the few theorists who claim multiple cultures exist within a single organization ultimately lend strength to the theory that organizations may have multiple climates but only one culture. For the purposes of this chapter, the understanding of culture as enduring and solitary within an organization and climate as more variable, with the ability for multiple climates to coexist, shall be used. This definition represents the most popular view in the literature, and it is the basis for introducing an integrated notion of social context.

Summary of Climate and Culture Definitions

As noted, climate and culture exist as related concepts with similar definitions. Thus, a summary of the information presented thus far may be helpful to the reader. Research on the subject of organizational climate evolved first and much earlier, but it was surpassed in popularity by research on organizational culture in the late 1980s. The study of climate and culture exists with great disparities within their definitions, and scholars exist on all sides who advocate alternately for merging the concepts, keeping them distinct, and for evolving them into an integrated approach with a new name. The level of disagreement may cause distress and confusion for the novice reader on this topic.

However, out of the chaos, clarity will flow as scholars discuss, debate, and move the conversation forward. Kuhn (1996) emerged as among the first to recognize the ferocity with which scientists and researchers hold on to what they identify as "known" or traditionally supported—even when confronted with overwhelming evidence to the contrary. Considering Kuhn's ideas, scholars can recognize the current state of confusion as progress, because the prior clarity only remained by virtue of rigid definitions and boundaries. Growth and advancement of the field will occur as researchers add to the body of knowledge through multilevel research, unrestrained by historical confines. Ultimately, the field will gain a greater understanding of the social context and the ethical dimension of organizations.

One can already note the progress achieved within a relatively short time frame (150 years or especially the last 3 decades) as the field of organizational behavior and an understanding of social context was first speculated about and then nurtured into an established field of study. The fact that an understanding of climate, culture, and the terminology to describe them has thoroughly been integrated into the lexicon of executive managers and academic scholars alike serves as readily observable evidence of this progress.

Knowledge Is Power: Why Understanding Differences in How to Measure an Organization's Social Context Matters

Scholars describe organizational climate and culture throughout the literature as among the most powerful constructs researchers can use to understand the human (expressive and communicative) component of organizations. However, in spite of this stated power, limited agreement exists about how to best define, measure, and apply knowledge regarding these important concepts. The next sections of this chapter provide a brief introduction to evaluating research studies and to quantitative and qualitative research methodologies. This information serves to inform the reader prior to discussing differences in measuring climate and culture within an organization and introducing two research works on nonprofit organizational ethics. The following statistical overview represents a minimum knowledge base for nonprofit leaders, and it provides a common background of understanding for the discussions in the coming sections of this chapter.

Reports of research and supposed best practices are often available an arm's reach away as most people readily have Internet access via a computer or smart phone. This easy availability presents the opportunity for accessing an incredible amount of information about any given subject 24 hours a day. Great, right, but with so much available, how do we evaluate the quality of the material we access? It serves as an important question when one considers that research often factors into program decisions, funding decisions, and grant decisions. As such, it is imperative that the research we use to inform our decisions is statistically sound.

Nonprofit leaders must possess the ability to evaluate the information they obtain, and that is presented to them. This means acquiring an understanding of basic statistical practices in order to perform due diligence when considering material that could affect the organization. Without adequate knowledge, nonprofit leaders place themselves at the mercy of those who publish studies and research. The next paragraphs provide essential information regarding five important topics to consider when evaluating research: (1) the sampling process used, (2) the statistical validity, (3) the statistical reliability, (4) the funder of the research, and (5) the source of the publication.

When considering the sampling techniques of a study, the questions you should ask include the following: (1) Did the researcher take steps to ensure an adequate size sample was gathered to support the claims made in the report? (2) Was the sample representative, meaning, did the sample make efforts to ensure its demographic characteristics were a close match to the population at large? (3) Was the sample randomly selected, meaning, everyone had an equal chance of being included? If any of these strategies were not used or not disclosed, it raises a warning flag about the quality of the study and the meaningfulness of its claims.

Statistical validity and reliability of research usually come in the form of a numerical value for quantitative research and a statement for qualitative research. *Validity* refers to the quality of a study measuring what it claims to measure. Multiple types of validity exist, although a discussion of them is beyond the scope of this chapter. *Reliability* refers to the ability of an instrument or survey to obtain the same results over and over again with repeated use of the research instrument.

To gain an appreciation for why validity and reliability are important, imagine that you take a math exam and receive an A grade. If the test is a reliable measure of your math ability, then taking the exam again would result in another A grade. If the math exam is not reliable, then you would be likely to get any grade, not the A that is reflective of your true ability. This example also relates to validity. If the math exam is not a valid test, then the grade you receive would not actually reflect your math ability. Thus, the grade would be irrelevant because the test was invalid. Stated another way, using a test of learning styles to determine math ability would produce a false result because a learning styles test is not a valid math test. From these examples, you can see it is essential that instruments measure what they claim to measure (are valid) and that they will achieve the same result every time (are reliable).

When a study does not indicate statistical validity or reliability, the ability of the research to show claims about the results is reduced. Alternately, when statistical validity

and reliability are demonstrated, a study can indirectly bring about changes in the way we address social problems. This is *evidence-based practice* in action: New research results prompt a change in the way social services are provided. As a nonprofit leader, the importance of being able to critically evaluate research and make determinations about its relevance to your organization's mission can be an important part of your role. Consider the following.

Imagine you determine statistically sound research results indicate a need to revamp the programs offered by your nonprofit organization. How do you deliver this information to your staff when they have spent years (sometimes decades) providing services in a manner now determined to be less effective by the new research report? This is when an understanding of your organization's culture will serve you well and help to ease a naturally difficult task.

To communicate necessary—but unwelcome—information and pave the way for changes with the least amount of resistance, you must understand organizational culture and its influence over people. Due to the high level of investment people naturally have in their work, research that contradicts what has been done in the past often is not welcome. You'll hear people express their angst about change and their level of investment through comments such as "but we've always done things this way." Without an adequate understanding of culture, organizational leaders can view employees who make these comments as stubborn. This view can bring about a battle of wills with the leader enforcing change that the staff resists evermore fervently. This represents a lose-lose situation for the organizational leader, the staff, and the people who receive services through your agency.

Instead, if as a leader you recognize resistance as a natural expression of investment and commitment, you can help ease the transition to a new way of providing services and turn a challenging scenario to a win-win situation for everyone. A leader might make the connections for the staff between a new behavior or process and the mission of the organization. By reminding the individual of their emotional commitment to the higher goals of the nonprofit, and then linking with a plan on how to achieve those lofty goals in a new way, the transition to a new way of working should gain acceptance more easily. This example depicts how situations can be handled in a respectful manner by skilled leaders. The plan as outlined is often certainly easier said than done, but the positive outcome it yields is worth the effort on all levels.

Returning to the evaluation of research, when making judgments about credibility, take a moment to note the funding source for the research and the type of publication where it is published. Knowing the source of funding can raise important questions or allay concerns about potential biases in the results. Consider this comparison and determine which study has a greater risk of being biased: a study funded by federal grants and conducted by researchers from multiple universities about a new medication versus research conducted by a pharmaceutical company to test a new medication it produces. While both studies may be valid, the pharmaceutical company conducting its own research has an inherent conflict of interest that must be considered as the results of the study are evaluated. This demonstrates why as the consumer of research you must ensure the needed steps to ensure quality steps were taken by the researchers and be aware of potential conflicts or biases. Considering the funding source can be a good place to start.

This segues perfectly to the final point about research: the type of publication. Research studies published in a peer-reviewed journal have the highest credibility standing because other experts in the field have reviewed and critically evaluated the study prior to accepting it for publication. This means potential conflicts of interest, poor methodology for studying the subject, and other problematic research studies have likely been eliminated from consideration for publication. Compare how you might view a study published in a journal that requires this level of a review process versus a brochure created by the person or entity conducting the research. The brochure or non-peer-reviewed publication lacks the previously described expert vetting process and therefore must be more carefully evaluated by you, the consumer.

The pharmaceutical company example extends well to highlighting this point. A report about the medication study conducted by the pharmaceutical company and published in a brochure created by the pharmaceutical company holds far less credibility than the federally funded medication study conducted by scientists from multiple institutions and published in a peer-reviewed journal, such as the *Journal of the American Medical Association* (JAMA). Attending to the credibility of research and reports that relate to your organization can help you adopt new programs as appropriate and avoid following scientifically unsupported trends when they are not warranted.

Awareness of the five factors described in the preceding paragraphs helps you to evaluate research whether you are an undergraduate studying a paper's topic or a nonprofit leader making program decisions or preparing for a grant application. Bringing the discussion of research evaluation back to the study of organizational climate and culture, the next sections discuss the differences in measuring climate and culture and introduce the notion of overt and covert expressions of organizational context. An understanding of these differences serves as important to the nonprofit leader for appropriately knowing how to assess and shape your organization to best achieve its mission.

Measuring Climate and Culture and Introduction to Types of Research

Researchers have historically measured climate through quantitative methods and culture via qualitative methods.

However, a review of the literature indicates that qualitative, quantitative, and mixed-methodological studies of both organizational climate and culture exist. This may raise the question, what is the difference between a quantitative and qualitative research study, and why does a nonprofit leader need to know? The following serves as a brief introduction to the two primary types of research. The interested reader may wish to extend their knowledge of the five points previously described and the two types of research through an introductory statistics course or review of a statistics textbook. Understanding statistics will provide you with an invaluable edge in whatever career path you pursue.

Quantitative research refers to observable or measurable things that can be counted. Quantitative measures assign values to responses, for example, on a survey or questionnaire. The numerical values are then used to compute statistical results. Quantitative studies offer numerous pros to busy nonprofit executives wishing to assess their organization. A quantitative survey instrument often can be generated online and distributed via e-mail. This makes the process of gathering surveys, tallying results, and computing final answers easier and less time-consuming than extensive interviews, which are the hallmark of qualitative research (described in the next section).

The necessity of fixing your response represents the primary complaint about quantitative measures. For example, if a survey question reads, "On a scale of one to four, how satisfied are you with your current employment position," some people feel uncomfortable being forced to *quantify* their response. These individuals would prefer a qualitative assessment where their responses can be open-ended and *qualified*. For example, someone may wish to answer, "I am satisfied with my job, but I'd like a longer lunch hour." The nuance of that response can be captured in a qualitative interview and must be condensed to a numerical answer in a quantitative assessment.

You may have gathered some understanding of qualitative research from the description of quantitative research. Examples of qualitative research include an in-depth case study of one person or organization, interviews with open-ended questions, and phenomenological research, which aims at understanding the unique experience of someone. Qualitative studies attend to the nuance in the response of the person or group being studied and provide a forum for expressing that thought completely.

The pros of qualitative research include the completeness of results from the individuals who participate. The cons include difficulty getting large numbers of people to participate and the lengthy process of analyzing the results. These cons weigh heavily against nonprofit organizations when contemplating what type of assessment tools to use as nonprofit organizations typically have little time or financial resources to allocate to a lengthy assessment process.

The results of qualitative studies also can present significant challenges for making data-based decisions as a result of the assessment. Consider reporting the results from a quantitative survey where the same questions are asked of all people and their numerical responses can be averaged and reported versus reporting results from a qualitative survey with open-ended questions. If 15 people were surveyed with an open-ended question, you may well have 15 very different responses. This makes reporting and using qualitative data very difficult.

Both types of research serve a valuable role depending on the task you are trying to accomplish. Often, a mixed-methodological approach combining some quantitative and qualitative assessment is best. For example, when using a mixed-methods approach, you might choose to interview key people within an organization at the beginning of your study (qualitative assessment) and then develop a survey instrument to gather data from many people (quantitative assessment). In this manner, you collect comprehensive data and maximize the advantages offered by both research methodologies.

Thinking about quantitative and qualitative research reminds nonprofit leaders to attend to both the overt and covert signs of their organizations' cultures. By focusing solely on either manifestation, nonprofit leaders can miss early indicators of problems in time to make course corrections. Imagine, as a nonprofit leader, you are planning an organizational assessment to gain insight into the culture of your agency. You must consider the time required to complete the evaluation, who will participate, who will oversee the evaluation (someone internal or a third party), and what will the information be used for once gathered. These questions, along with ensuring one attends to both the overt and covert elements of the culture, represent an important part of planning the assessment process.

Consider the following example where only the overt signs of culture are measured. A nonprofit agency conducts an organizational ethics assessment and concludes that the organization is soundly ethical and adheres to the best practices related to ethics. Three months after the assessment, a major ethical breech occurs, and the nonprofit agency finds its story on the front page of the local newspaper. What happened? How could the assessment have missed the ethical risk factors within this organization? By focusing only on the observable, this ethics assessment used an audit format to check off a list of "best practices," and thus, the powerful covert elements of the culture were missed. The checklist contained items such as, does the organization have a code of ethics, are annual employee ethics trainings held, do employees pledge to behave ethically, and are key policies in place, such as a conflict of interest policy and a gift acceptance policy? While the items on the checklist represent best practices related to ethics, the presence of these policies and procedures mean nothing if the culture of the organization does not support its intent. The checklist approach relies on the assumption that policies and procedures are upheld and adhered to by the members of the organization. In our case example, this

assumption was incorrect. The ethics assessment declared a state of ethical health, then 3 months later the true state of the agency played out in the ethical breech.

No matter how well written or how many trainings an agency offers on ethics, if policies and procedures exist in conflict with the culture of an organization, they are rendered ineffective. In the example discussed here, the daily practices of middle and senior management were in complete defiance of the code of ethics, and these individuals were not held accountable for their actions. In fact, because performance (ethical or not) was rewarded in this organization, sometimes violating the code of ethics actually was encouraged due to the performance outcome. Given that the lack of discipline for violating stated ethical standards was common knowledge within the organization, a culture of unethical behavior flourished.

This organization had the observable signs of being an ethical organization, but the covert cues contained within the culture were stronger and led the individuals to their demise via a major ethical scandal. Stated another way, by members attending only to the overt signs of an organization's culture and overlooking potentially critical information contained within the nuance of daily practice, an organization is placed at great risk for ethical problems. The strongest example of covert cultural cues within this organization included the history of undisciplined ethical breaches by management. As noted, this indirectly communicated to the rest of the staff that ethical misbehavior is acceptable within the culture—even though it conflicts with the formal code of ethics. In a case like our example, the organization's code of ethics is worth little more than the paper it is written on. Consider the fact that Enron had a code of ethics. Enron provides an excellent case study of how the overt cultural signs of an organization can conflict with the cultural cues that depict what is truly acceptable within the organization.

The preceding section highlighted how a seemingly thorough assessment of evidenced-based practices can yield an incorrect result. The next section reviews the current status of the scholarly literature on nonprofit ethics and discusses two premiere works in the field. These two empirical studies show both a strong emphasis on culture in the assessment process and in the recommendations for strengthening organizations. This emphasis represents an evolution from prior nonprofit assessment recommendations that used the checklist approach and attended only to the overt (or observable) elements of culture.

Empirical Work in Nonprofit Ethics

While a significant body of practitioner-focused research composes the third-sector literature, a paucity of empirical work exists overall and even less within the narrow field of nonprofit ethics assessment. The field presents as ripe with research opportunities for the motivated scholar, and a deeper discussion of this important issue is presented in

Chapter 93 of this volume. Two important works constitute the bulk of the available literature discussing nonprofit ethics: The *National Nonprofit Ethics Survey* conducted by the Ethics Resource Center (2008) and *The Nonprofit Ethics Survey: A Contextual Approach* (Barrett, 2008). The embryonic state of the field is evident simply by the recency of these two empirical works. However, both contribute in complementary and meaningful ways to the tools and knowledge important to leaders of nonprofit organizations.

The National Nonprofit Ethics Survey

The *National Nonprofit Ethics Survey* (NNES) published in 2008 provides a snapshot view of third-sector ethics based on survey data gathered through telephone interviews with employees of nonprofit organizations. The key findings of this report serve as a means for shifting the background information provided in this chapter from the theoretical to the practical by clearly identifying the impact of organizational culture on the ethical behavior of nonprofit employees. The key findings of the NNES indicate the following trends.

First, compared to the business and government sectors, the third sector has the highest percentage of organizations that rate as having a "strong ethical culture" per the survey interpretations. Additionally, more nonprofit organizations use an effective ethics compliance program—a characteristic the NNES shows as critical to organizational ethical health. In fact, the NNSE indicates in another key finding that "a well implemented [compliance] program and a strong ethical culture essentially eliminate misconduct and increase reporting [of violations] to 100 percent" (Ethics Resource Center, 2008, p. viii).

This means that students preparing for a career in nonprofit leadership must recognize the importance of structural elements, such as formal ethics programs, within their organizations. Skilled and knowledgeable leaders must ensure the ethics programs within their organizations are appropriately targeted, meaning different programs for different levels of employees and management, and that the ethical principles emphasized as important to the organization are consistently applied and enforced at all levels of the organization.

The second key finding communicates the power of culture on ethics within the organization as this chapter has discussed. As noted, the nonprofit sector reported the highest number of organizations with strong ethical cultures. However, the numbers have begun to decline (as compared to prior surveys conducted by the Ethics Resource Center), and the strength of those cultures has also decreased. This indicates a need for proactive leadership to identify the cause of these changes and the downward trend of scores. Aspiring nonprofit leaders may enter a workforce with characteristics more like the traditional business environment than the nonprofit sector if this trend does not reverse.

Nonprofit organizations rely on ethical behavior and the perception of being ethical organizations for their viability.

Thus, the time to identify and remedy the cause is limited. Students entering the field as executive directors, founders, and program managers must be willing to advocate for the health of the organizations they serve. Without the maintenance of strong ethical health, the organizations will likely suffer, if not fail, thus leaving the social need they were designed to fill unmet or increasing the burden on other similar agencies.

The third key finding indicates that midsized organizations have the greatest risk for experiencing an ethical lapse, and the number of midsized nonprofit organizations composing the nonprofit sector is growing. And the final key finding discussed here relates to how governance issues and perceptions of power within an organization affect the ethical health of nonprofit agencies. The NNES found that when comparing boards of directors across the three economic sectors, nonprofit boards of directors have the greatest impact on the perceptions of their employees both good and bad. While that authority can be harnessed and used to positively shape the ethical tone of the organization, the NNES also shows that within nonprofit organizations when employees perceive the board of directors, not the executive director, as the leader of the organization, there was a more than 20% greater reporting of misconduct and a more than 20% decrease in the belief that their organization has strong ethical leadership. This again serves as critical knowledge for nonprofit leaders so that employee perceptions of authority can be managed through good communication practices and transparency.

The concise nature of the NNES, the fact that its data set extends back several years, and that the survey has the funding and support to continue going forward makes it a must read for knowledgeable nonprofit leaders. Arming oneself with facts and information about the general trends related to third-sector ethics serve as a navigational guide in a world of limited resources and endless need.

The full report of the NNES and smaller reports of nonprofit data collected by the Ethics Resource Center through their "National Business Ethics Surveys" in prior years serve as excellent primers for nonprofit leaders. The trends over time and the easily digestible format of the reports allow nonprofit leaders to (1) understand some of the invisible forces of culture that may be at work within their organizations and (2) avoid placing themselves at risk for an ethical breech. The reports also provide practical information for building a strong ethical culture and identifying potential areas of risk. The NNES can provide a sector-wide overview to be used in complement with specific organizational information provided by the "Nonprofit Ethics Survey" described in the next section.

The Nonprofit Ethics Survey

Barrett's *Nonprofit Ethics Survey*, also published in 2008, provides an empirically supported survey tool for nonprofit organizations to conduct an organizational level ethics assessment. The information collected via the survey provides the leadership of a nonprofit organization with a data-based place to assess and understand the current status of their organization. The survey exists in a user-friendly online format that offers confidential assessment, easy data collection, and a comprehensive report of survey results.

The opportunity to compare results across levels of the organization serves as a key feature of the "Nonprofit Ethics Survey." All members of the organization respond to the same questions about ethics within the organization, which allows for a comparison of results by level. Thus, an organization can take note if discrepancies exist between the way the board members view the ethical workings of the organization and the perceptions line staff hold about the organization. Unidentified discrepancies set the stage for ethical lapses in behavior. Thus, while it may initially be painful for organizational leaders to recognize that ethical issues exist within the organization, it serves as far better to identify and correct them internally than to learn about them on the front page of the morning newspaper.

A proactive and informed nonprofit leader has the opportunity to synergistically combine the information provided by these two important pieces of nonprofit literature and truly shape and/or maintain the ethical health of his or her organization. Both the report and the survey instrument are available online. Please see the chapter's reference section for additional information. The survey can be accessed free of charge at www.sandiego.edu/npresearch.

Opportunities to Apply Your Knowledge of Social Context Now

The traditional process of acquiring an education often presents students with lots of theory and few opportunities to practice what has been learned. This pattern will continue if you've read this chapter or similar works as part of a class assignment and allow the learning to stop with the completion of your assignment (e.g., writing a paper, engaging in a class or online discussion with peers, or answering essay questions about the material). However, the subject of organizational behavior and social context affords nearly endless opportunities to immediately apply what you have learned. Taking time to practice and apply what you've learned through this reading will greatly increase your understanding of these concepts and help to develop your skills as a leader. The next paragraphs outline some immediate opportunities students have to apply their knowledge of organizational social context.

During college many students choose to join various clubs and organizations. These groups provide opportunities to see the dynamics and strength of organizational social context at work. Consider the cultural differences between social sororities and fraternities as compared to subject or service organizations by conducting your own observational study. Attend a recruitment meeting for Phi Delta Epsilon, the coed international premed fraternity, and a similar meeting for one of the social sororities or fraternities on your campus. You will see the culture of each organization being communicated to the new potential members from the first moment of contact. Some examples of communicating the cultural norms include the type of recruitment announcement (e-mails, posters, word of mouth), time of the meeting and location, what attire the current members of the organization wear at the recruitment meeting (casual, formal, displaying the organization's logo or name), the formality of the meeting (following Robert's rules of order, using a whistle to call attention, or being quiet until everyone settles in their seats and pays attention to the speaker), and how the selection criteria for joining the organization is shared (do they provide a list of required characteristics like minimum grade point average [GPA] and community service hours or a list of events where you'll be observed but without knowledge of what the organization is actually seeking). All of these elements initiate the process of communicating the culture or social context of each organization to new potential members. The new recruits then respond to the culture by either attempting to learn more and shape their behavior to fit into the culture or by recognizing their authentic selves don't fit into the culture. In the latter, an individual may make the choice not to get involved or perhaps decide to what degree to get involved.

The method of attending a meeting of an organization unfamiliar to you to practice applying your cultural observational skills can be effective. Trying to identify overt and covert examples of an organization's culture for groups you already belong to can be more challenging. As a member of a particular organization, you are often already entrenched and schooled in its norms and thereby blind to the overt or covert signs of the culture because it just feels "normal." This makes practice more difficult especially if you are new to the concepts of social context.

Opening your eyes and mind to messages about social context can be very helpful in understanding the dynamics of what happens in an organization and with practice can help you shape the direction of decisions to best serve the organization's mission. Over time, learning to assess the social context of organizations will occur automatically as you enter new environments. This can serve you in all aspects of life as it allows you to connect better with people. Noting the cultural cues when you walk into an office or agency for an internship or job interview can provide you with opportunities to show the interviewer how you would be a good match for the organization.

Summary

The discussion of social context throughout this chapter and the introduction of empirical tools and reports to assess and understand organizational culture provide a foundational knowledge base for the aspiring leader. To solidify the connection for yourself between theory and practice, try to apply the concepts within the organizational contexts currently available to you.

As this chapter has discussed, organizational climate and organizational culture constitute two concepts integral to assessing and understanding the contextual elements of organizational behavior. An overview of their definitions and evolutionary roots and an examination of their areas of confluence and divergence have been explored and provide a useful backdrop for understanding the ethical behavior of nonprofit organizations. Understanding these definitions along with a basic knowledge of how to evaluate research prepares you for a successful and rewarding career able to shape the dynamics of organizations you lead to best achieve their missions. Nonprofit leaders well versed in their understanding of organizational culture and open to the practical applications introduced by the two empirical works presented will likely find themselves better equipped to lead organizations with strong ethical health. As an effective leader in every setting, apply the knowledge you have acquired from this chapter to your everyday contexts and strive to be a lifelong learner in your chosen field.

References and Further Readings

Barrett, A. (2008). *The nonprofit ethics survey: A contextual approach.* Doctoral dissertation, University of San Diego, 2008. *Dissertation Abstracts International, A 69*(5), 149–155. Available from http://www.sandiego.edu/npresearch

Cooke, R. A., & Szumal, J. L. (1993). Measuring normative beliefs and shared behavioral expectations in organizations: The reliability and validity of organizational culture. *Psychological Reports, 72,* 1299–1330.

Ethics Resource Center. (2007). *National business ethics survey* (Report). Arlington, VA: Author.

Ethics Resource Center. (2008). *National nonprofit ethics survey: An inside view on nonprofit sector ethics* (Report). Arlington, VA: Author.

Kuhn, T. S. (1996). *The structure of scientific revolutions* (3rd ed.). Chicago: University of Chicago Press.

Reichers, A. E., & Schneider, B. (1990). Climate and culture: An evolution of constructs. In B. Schneider (Ed.), *Organizational climate and culture* (1st ed., pp. 5–39). San Francisco: Jossey-Bass.

Schein, E. H. (2004). *Organizational culture and leadership* (3rd ed.). San Francisco: Jossey-Bass.

Verbeke, W., Volgering, M., & Hessels, M. (1998). Exploring the conceptual expansion within the field of organizational behaviour, organizational climate, and organizational culture. *Journal of Management Studies, 35*(3), 303–329.

69

MARKETING ISSUES

Who Is the Customer?

CHRIS HUIZENGA

North Park University

One idea that all nonprofit leaders, board, and staff members need to embrace about the basic nature of customers is that people want to believe in and be a part of something greater than themselves.

> The market for something to believe in is infinite. We are here to find meaning. We are here to help other people do the same. Everything else is secondary.... [Your customers] want to believe in you and what you do. And they'll go elsewhere if they don't. (MacLeod, 2008)

People need to believe in something. A nonprofit's constituents must believe that the organization aligns its efforts to its mission and that it will do so as effectively and efficiently as possible using honest practices. Here, the role of marketing in the nonprofit sector becomes the development, maintenance, and enhancement of the organization's public perception, building and reinforcing the belief and trust that sustains it and gives it purpose.

If the old adage that "perception is reality" holds true, then it is imperative that the organization's marketing efforts first communicate truth, integrity, and trust to its constituents in all it does. In doing so, it can shape their beliefs and reinforce their trust in the organization, justifying its place in the universe and thereby supporting the reasons why it deserves to exist. Considering MacLeod's insight, marketing's role is to protect your customer's beliefs, managing perceptions while enhancing and building its reputation in a broken, busy world. Without organizational integrity, there is no reason to believe in your group and therefore no justification for your existence.

Ultimately, nonprofit marketing has to connect with, resonate with, and inspire its constituents. Unless you truly understand your relationship with your customers and honestly know the beliefs they hold about your group, you are lost. You must learn as much as you can about your different customer segments: their age, where they live, what they do for a living, their income level, what they like, what they don't like, their interests, and so on, using this information to develop the customer relationship and to connect the organization's mission and strategy to your customer's expectations.

Communicating Your Mission

The mission is the organization's reason for being. Knowing the mission will help align resources to strategies and will essentially direct the decisions of the board and staff as well as the decisions of the other customers. Everyone who has a stake in the organization, be they staff, board members, donors, volunteers, or beneficiaries, should have at least a general sense of why it exists, and the best way to do that is with a clear mission.

There is a danger in too broadly describing a mission. Too often, marketers see mission statements so incredibly vague that they may as well read, "we exist to provide the public with this, that, and the other thing." It's a decent start, but we need to unpack this a little bit. Are your services really for the entire public? If you work for a government agency, then the answer may be yes. But even then, you have to break down the definition of *public*. Are you looking at customers in a particular neighborhood, a particular socioeconomic status, those receiving a particular service? You must keep in mind that you cannot exist for everybody without doing so at the expense of somebody, so you need to start by identifying your various types of customers.

Identifying Your Customer Types

The organization has to identify the markets that would have the most stakes in the mission. Keep in mind that a nonprofit organization can have several types of customers, all with different types of stakes and interests in the same mission. Customers can generally be narrowed down to the following types: internal, external, service, and referral sources.

Internal Customers

Often, the internal customer is overlooked in the marketing plan, but his or her interest and involvement in the organization has tremendous impact on the fulfillment of its mission. The board of directors has a customer interest in the organization because they are the ones ultimately responsible for moving the mission forward, even more so than the executive director. The board members choose whether or not to serve the organization in this role, exchanging their time and finances, assuming legal risk for the organization, and so on—all in an attempt to serve the group and its other constituents. The organization's staff, from the executive director down to staff and volunteers, can also be considered customers. This group makes a conscious decision to work for the organization. Many of the nonprofit's employees choose to invest their time and talents into that specific organization because the mission and the work resonate with their personal values and beliefs. In much the same way, volunteers are internal customers because they also believe in the mission and view the giving of their time and talents as an investment in something bigger than themselves (Brinkerhoff, 2002).

External Customers

This group consists of individuals and entities that support the organization financially or through some other asset gift, such as bequests or endowments. Nonprofit organizations can receive monetary assistance from government grants to conduct work that the government would otherwise have to provide itself but does not because it is less expensive to outsource the work to the nonprofit organization. Foundations, similarly, support various nonprofits that have missions and goals that closely align with their values. Some organizations offer memberships, exchanging certain benefits (often in the form of discounts, members-only material or services, etc.) to those individuals or organizations in exchange for some type of service. Some of these organizations are set up as professional associations, and if they are large enough, they can support memberships to other organizations in the form of chapters or charters (Brinkerhoff, 2002).

Service Clients

Many people automatically know this group as the primary customer as they are the ones receiving the services of the organization. Typically, this is the group that the mission statement identifies (Brinkerhoff, 2002). This group, while primary, can most times be broken down into segments that need to be communicated to in different ways and/or be engaged differently from one another. For example, a church may well consider its primary customer to be its regularly attending congregation, with secondary customers being visitors. While the overall mission may be to teach church doctrine to its members, it will have to do it in various ways that accommodate each segment of its overall population to be effective in carrying out the mission. Some church bodies may have a sizable family population and therefore various customer segments. To carry out its mission of teaching doctrine, the leadership may set up youth programs for the various age groups, and in our example here, the leaders may set up programs to teach children of kindergarten through high school age and even college groups. The church may recognize a need then to establish a service for young adults or groups for married couples, singles, empty nesters, and senior citizens. Each of these groups has demographics unique to them and separate from the other groups, and yet they each are considered part of the church's primary customer. As uniquely different groups, they will have characteristics that are true and uniquely definitive of their group, and as such, those demographics must be considered when the time comes to communicate with and market to each segment. Furthermore, the church in this example must consider visitors (its secondary customers) and again identify and segment that population and consider from there how best to strategically communicate with those groups.

Referral Sources

Some of the most powerful allies for a nonprofit organization are the entities that refer others to your organization. These sources could be responsible for sending more donors or new partner organizations to your organization. For example, primary care physicians often refer their patients to specialty practitioners when the need arises for their patients. Without these referrals, margins for the health system would suffer and missions would come to a screeching halt. Referrals are the lifeblood of almost any organization. Identifying the referral sources in your own organization is crucial. Once you are able to identify the various customers, you have to segment and quantify them (Brinkerhoff, 2002).

Segment and Quantify the Markets

Segmenting the various markets your organization works with is crucial to helping you understand how to craft the marketing message across various groups. Taking another look at our earlier example of the church and its primary customer segments, it is safe to say that it should not use the same type of marketing to appeal to youth as it would to senior citizens. What connects and resonates with one group may not appeal to the other, even if they have a common interest. Similarly, the marketing your organization does to reach donors will attempt to connect with their values in a completely different way than it would with service customers. This may sound obvious, but it is unfortunately common with many nonprofit organizations.

To properly segment your customers, identify the different constituency groups that make up your organization's customers. Develop profiles for each group in a way that adequately represents the primary characteristics of that group. Then, develop measures of segment attractiveness based on how closely the wants and needs of this particular group align with the mission of your organization. Keep in mind that while your organization wants to serve all of your various customer segments, in order to manage and track an efficient and effective marketing campaign, you will not be able to cater the same message to every single group.

There are certain truths and characteristics within any market segment. For starters, each segment is mutually exclusive, meaning that one group is not like any other. While there may be some similarities, there are clearly defined differences between segments. Segments display a level of *customer life cycle*, meaning that there is a certain point in the lives of that group where they simply do not need your organization. Consider it a type of event horizon in which the segment finds itself above or below a certain line where it does not make logical sense for them to seek your organization's service or for your organization to pursue them as a customer. Segments are measurable, meaning that its demographics can be quantified or categorized and can be averaged out to create a "picture" of the group's dynamics that would be mostly true of everyone in that segment. Furthermore, *segments are reachable*, meaning that there is a way to connect with them. Consider a nonprofit organization that serves adults that cannot read. Developing marketing collateral full of text or pointing this segment toward the organization's website would do little good, and thus, other media avenues or referral sources have to be pursued. Granted—this is but one customer segment for this organization. Other customer segments exist, necessitating more relevant tactics. Consider your segment, consider your organization's goal, consider

what will resonate with this group, and determine what action this customer segment should take; what do they believe, and what do you want them to do? This scenario requires thinking in broader terms than simply "marketing." It requires thinking in terms of communication goals. Segments are sustainable yet variable and changing, meaning that there is a staying power to a group or its condition. However, you must be sure that marketing plans are fluid to manage changes in the internal or external environments. Segments respond and act to needs and wants in ways that are unique to their groups (Brinkerhoff, 2002).

Your Target Customers

When developing strategic marketing plans, your organization should consider the primary target markets and look at each of those individually. Consider your strategic positioning with each group by identifying its values, providing a call to action, and developing a marketing mix for each target market. Look at secondary segments that contribute to the organization but require less weight for targeting and marketing dollars.

What Are Their Values?

It is terribly difficult for a person to change his or her values or beliefs. While individuals may like and welcome new ways of doing something (for example, communicating), the methods by which they do it are more apt to change (for example, texting friends as opposed to calling them). The value in communicating has not changed so much as the method with which it is done. Values and beliefs drive messages that connect, resonate, and inspire (Brinkerhoff, 2002).

Some values are *functional*, which essentially satisfies the questions, what will this thing or service do for me? Will it do what I want it to do? How well will it do it? Other values are *social*. Is there a social benefit in using this service? For example, if that service happens to be a membership in an organization, is there a social benefit? If it's a professional association, will that membership advance your career? If it's a family membership in the Young Men's Christian Association (YMCA), will your family befriend other families? Some values are *emotional* in nature: What is the emotional reward for participating with an organization? For example, donors may give financial support to an organization that works with sick children in third world countries because there is an emotional value for them in knowing that their support helps to provide health care, food, clean water, and education to children halfway around the world. In much the same way, many employees and volunteers choose to work for a particular organization based mostly on its mission. For them, the value is in knowing that their time and talents are being invested in something meaningful to them. *Epistemic* values primarily satisfy a desire for knowledge. A lot of museums and zoos rely on fulfilling this value for customers. For example, the Smithsonian Institution with its 19 museums satisfies the epistemic need for knowledge for millions of visitors interested or curious about American history, just as the Lincoln Park Zoo in Chicago provides knowledge about animals. Some values are *conditional*, meaning that sometimes a customer's choice is based on circumstance. Many of the nation's poor and hungry, for example, would rather not go to community kitchens for food, but their condition and proximity to the kitchen's location dictate their choice in using this service (Clow & Kurtz, 2004).

The Strategic Customer-Centric Marketing Plan

The marketing plan built around an organization's needs will ultimately fail. Everything the organization does, its very reason for existing, rests with the wants and needs of the customer. Therefore, keep the marketing plan customer-centric and be mindful that the plan will account for the various target markets identified earlier. Your organization's marketing plan must justify and support your organization's reason to exist and ultimately shape the belief of the constituents into something favorable.

When working with customer-centric marketing (Andreason & Kotler, 2007), consider the market you'll communicate with. Where are these people, and what are they like? What are their current perceptions, needs and wants, and will those variables change by the time your organization implements the strategy? How satisfied are the customers with the service your organization has provided? What do they believe to be true about the brand?

There are three distinct purchase phases wherein the nonprofit organization will interact and communicate with its various customers: the prepurchase, consumption, and postpurchase phases. During the prepurchase phase, the role of the marketer is to reduce the purchase risk for the customer, which, for example, could be to put a potential donor's mind at ease so she or he is more trusting of the organization and is therefore more likely to give a gift. It could be to increase the probability of receiving a donation. The marketer has to develop the corporate image while building brand equity and increasing awareness of the organization and its mission to any one of its customer segments. In the consumption phase, the marketer needs to enhance customer satisfaction and, at the same time, reinforce the brand in such a way that the customer repeats the desired behavior whether that is to give another gift or to reinforce the abandonment of a negative action. In the postconsumption phase, the marketer has to work to stimulate positive word of mouth among customers and reinforce positive repeat behavior (Clow & Kurtz, 2004). These individuals must also work to close *brand gap*, which is the distance between what the customer holds true about the brand and what the marketer wants the customer to believe. Brand

gap starts when clients determine their perception of the organization, based on the lead marketing messages, is inaccurate. If the message does not align with the deliverable goods or services, then all the clever marketing in the world will be ineffective. The clients will think the organization is lying and that has to be experienced only once for them to never trust the organization again, to go to the competitors, to withhold their gifts, to reject the program meant to support their rehabilitation or to help them learn to read, and to tell others how much that organization let them down.

The Marketing Cycle

Marketing is not a one-time event. Rather, it is an ongoing process. It is continual, constantly working to improve, connect, and reconnect with customers using improved methods to reinforce the organization's relevance over and over again. Market cycles are exactly that: cyclical. You never launch a marketing campaign once and expect to achieve your goal. Marketing is relationship management, requiring frequent communication. Your organization has to remind customers that it's there, listening to them, changing if it has to, and offering them something in return for choosing your organization. The first step in the marketing cycle is (as discussed earlier) market definition and segmentation: knowing your target audience. Remember that the wants and needs of markets change continually, and the marketer has to constantly reexamine and redefine market segments. Marketers must do research and ask all the questions. Next, the marketer compiles and presents his or her findings so that the service design can be altered in such a way that it fits the wants and needs of the customer. The organization that refuses to change to accommodate its customers will lose them. From this point, the marketer helps her or his organization set their price or understand the value of the organization among its constituents. If the customers do not perceive the value, they will simply go or give elsewhere. From here, the marketer can promote and distribute the marketing message, but the job is far from over. She or he then has to evaluate the effectiveness of the campaign to see if the work produced is meeting the goals and supporting the mission. Once a proper evaluation has been performed, it is time to start all over again using the data gathered to sharpen and adjust the next marketing plan (Brinkerhoff, 2002).

The Integrated Marketing Mix

Many organizations now use an integrated marketing mix to promote their messages. While not every component of the traditional marketing mix has to be used for the organization's marketing efforts to be effective, most organizations will at least use a combination of components. For instance, most organizations will use direct mail as their primary method for distributing their messages, in the form of mailed letters, invitations to events, newsletters, holiday greetings, invoices, and so on. Advertising (print, radio, billboards, etc.) remains a strong component in most organizational portfolios, but advertising on a massive scale is very expensive, and the results are often difficult to track, whereas direct marketing tends to give better results per dollar spent and makes tracking campaign results easier. Building and maintaining a website is a given, considering that a vast majority of donors visit the organization's site before making the decision to support the group and its mission, mainly because websites give more information than is typically available in other formats. Caution: The content on the website has to engage, connect, and resonate with the primary customer segments, and it has to change. Websites have to virtually live, breathe, grow, change, mature—they have to give the impression that the organization itself is active and involved. Websites are the virtual embodiment of the physical organization, and if the site is stale and unchanging, then that will be people's impression of the organization: lifeless, tired, boring, and ineffective.

Every organization must also be prepared to incorporate public relations (PR) into its marketing mix. Depending on your group's niche in the nonprofit world, your organization may or may not always need PR. Keep in mind that PR is not just for crisis management, though that is one aspect of it. Think of PR more as the organization's representation to the news media. The news media can be an organization's best friend or its worst enemy, but they're more often like the great aunt who seldom visits—and every time she does, she wants to hear how you're doing, what's going on, what happened, what you did (or are doing), and so on. Using a PR team internally or hiring a PR firm can be the difference between whether or not your organization will make the news and *how* it'll make the news. Leverage public relations as an instrument to tell your organization's story to the world, and remember that your customers are listening to (and often believing) what the news media are telling them.

Some organizations are sizable enough to have a community relations (CR) team, which is the company's representation to the community and business leaders. Some groups need the immediate community's support more than others, and some groups need favorable government relations in order to move their mission forward. For example, a hospital's leaders may want to add a wing for treating cancer patients but they face concern from the neighbors in the community about construction traffic and noise during the building. The CR team can help maintain favorable connections and reassure community leaders of the treatment center's benefits as well as ease tensions with neighbors.

Remember that nonprofits have internal customers as well, and those internal customers often interact and engage with external customers. Therefore, it is imperative that marketers help everyone organization-wide understand that everyone is on the marketing team. The directors, staff, and volunteers are the culmination of all strategic marketing efforts. These individuals send a message about the organization's brand when engaging with donors, clients, prospects, community leaders, and the public. Just as a tattoo brands its owner, so these representatives brand the organization and vice versa through correlation.

Developing and Using Marketing Collateral

Marketing collateral should be of the absolute highest quality. Marketing is often the first item on the chopping block when it comes to scaling back the budget. When events such as a recession or an industry-wide decrease in demand for a product or service happen, organizations pull back on their marketing and promotion because they are trying to be budget conscious. But what they are not being is strategy focused. When your group's competitors back off on their marketing, they leave a void. Suddenly, the odds of your group's message getting lost in the marketplace vanish. Competing messages subside. There is no longer as much talk in the marketplace about the types of services your organization or its competitors provide. Your group's customers will probably not notice that there is less being said—but they will notice when they hear something about what they want or if they hear something that connects and resonates with their beliefs. Nonprofit leaders have to be bold and demand that marketing should not be taken off the table for the sake of the budget. Rather, they should demand and work toward more effective and efficient marketing. Pulling back on marketing when funds are falling short is like firing all the salespeople of a department store until sales increase.

The organization has to connect with the customers. A marketing team has to continue to press its key messaging on the mission, focusing on and connecting with the various targets that make up the customer base. The messaging has to be to the point, communicating the message using attractive design and providing references for the audience, sources for more information, and the crucial call-to-action (What do you want the customer to do now that they've heard your message?). Your marketing team has to be careful to avoid a lot of things that don't make sense for the customer. Consider their point of view when crafting the message and factoring it into the integrated marketing mix. Avoid industry jargon, asking for money outright, giving history lessons, using out-of-date materials, and otherwise boring the customer with information they do not want. Cut down on brand confusion by tying everything together in the integrated mix with a common look and feel to help maintain a consistent brand (Brinkerhoff, 2002).

Branding and the Customer

Many people think of branding as a logo, identity, service, or product the organization produces. It is not. "A brand is a person's gut feeling about a product, service or organization. . . . It's not what you say it is. It's what *they* say it is" (Neumeier, 2003). In today's environment, the best way to build the brand is by building the trust that customers have toward the organization, since trust is the underlying factor in most purchasing decisions. Trust comes about when an organization proves its reliability to its customers and delights them with service by exceeding customer expectations.

Branding differentiates your organization from your competitors' in the minds of the customer. What do you want to be known for? Who are you, what do you do, and why do you matter? There are nine basic market positions that organizations typically aim for when branding: *best selling, only, best known, easiest, most complete, fastest, most powerful, newest,* and *most affordable.* The nonprofit organization that is successful at branding will have differentiated itself from similar organizations by focusing on purposely being different, by being innovative in its creative marketing approach, and by engaging with the customer in the marketing process with dialogue. Without the customer, without the conversation, without the brand, there is no tribe, and marketing today is all about building tribes around the brand (Neumeier, 2003).

The purpose of branding in the nonprofit realm is to convince more people to continually support the organization with larger gifts over the course of time or to encourage more volunteers to give their time in increasing increments or to maintain highly qualified and efficient staff who work more and more effectively and move the mission forward or to encourage more foundations to give more next year over this past year . . . on and on. But none of that will happen if the perceived trustworthiness of the organization diminishes—if the brand is tainted. Therefore, protecting the brand means engaging the customer. As MacLeod (2008) puts it, "the future of brands is interaction, not commodity. It's not something you buy, but something you participate in. . . . A brand is not a thing, but a place." If customers are participants of the brand, then organizational leaders and marketers are really stewards of a brand that, for all intents and purposes, is actually owned by the customer. A nonprofit's brand equity is determined by its customers' belief in its value.

Engaging the customer means your organization's staff must be a willing recipient of brutal truth. The members must engage and ask. Only 1 of every 25 customers with a complaint actually takes the time to complain. The rest start looking elsewhere to get what they want. To them, the brand lost its value when they lost their trust (Neumeier, 2003).

Social Media and the Power of Groups

Remember: Marketing has to connect, resonate, and inspire. And the only way it can do that and show that it is doing it, is through messages engaging the customer. Social media, such as Facebook, MySpace, Twitter, and others, have altered the way people connect with one another. Many marketers have begun to leverage groups on sites such as Facebook because they recognize a common thread among the people there or because it is one place where individuals can wear a virtual tattoo of sorts by becoming a "fan" or joining a group that follows particular products, causes, events, missions, or brands and thus can be an influencer on those the individual is connected with. Entire groups spring up on these social sites that connect college alumni, breast cancer survivors, fans of television shows, church (small groups), marathon runners, and so on. The thing about social media is that marketing people have to be careful not to label it "marketing," even though we as marketers are the ones working the hardest to leverage it. Instead of wrapping social media into the typical marketing mix and leveraging market, we should *lead* and lead with an idea the group supports and demands. The group already has an interest and perhaps even a mission to change something. All the entire group needs is a way to communicate and someone to lead—which brings up an interesting thought about leadership and tribes and missions: "Leadership is service for the sake of the led. It is not about having your own way. It is about promoting an idea for the betterment of a group" (Achievement, n.d., "Desmond Tutu"). If that is true, then marketers have to adjust their mental role and look at their responsibilities as something more than just "marketing." Marketers have a responsibility to become thought leaders and encouragers.

Keep in mind that these groups, these *tribes*, will not follow an organization's message on a social medium simply because the organization has a Facebook page. Marketers have to lead the tribe with an idea, a belief. And even then, the tribe may not like your group's idea and will want to go in a new direction. It will be up to the executives and the board whether or not to follow the direction of the group. As leaders, marketers are responsible for guiding the tribe in the right direction.

Social media will continue to evolve. Marketers must leverage the relationships social media have helped create by rallying the tribe to action. When the idea or story behind the cause is interesting, it engages, and it spreads. Marketers have to empower the organization's constituents to have impact, helping the tribe transform its shared interests into passionate goals, providing tools for the nonprofit to tighten their communications, and leveraging the organization to grow and gain new members on behalf of the cause. The power of the tribe is that it can and will change or adapt to get what it wants with or without your organization.

Therefore, marketers as leaders must be somewhat flexible to the wants of its constituents, anticipating the shifts within the market before they happen (Godin, 2008). Leaders must help their constituents believe and trust in the organization.

Track It

Marketing is not just creative play at work—it is a social science that requires as much research as it does creative tinkering. Marketing should always follow strategy, and strategy is born out of understanding derived from research. Market research is essentially a study of human belief and behavior. There is a very real danger in overlooking the decision-making processes of your organization's constituents, and an organization risks alienating those it both serves and relies on if it ignores or fails to comprehend trends. You will only start to understand once your organization purposely makes outcome measurements a priority, but then, it must leverage and use the data to plot strategy.

Most nonprofit organizations do not like doing this. In fact, even in the for-profit realm, many marketers cannot adequately explain the financial return on investment the company has made. Although the financial understanding of marketing outcomes is important, the compiled data are often vague and do not always paint a true picture of cause-and-effect, especially because the integrated marketing mix has made it such that any one or a combination of any parts of the mix could have been responsible for generating the customer response. At best, financial results are vague. There are, however, nonfinancial indicators of how much impact the marketing is having on your organization's various customer segments, such as social indicators, which show the organization's impact at large. For example, one organization's mission may be to deter children in the community from joining gangs. After a marketing campaign aimed at children is launched, a social indicator of the marketing success would be the number of gangs in the area or the number of gang-related incidents in that same area. Another method is to use result measures to track the effectiveness of marketing. Here, marketers would measure tangible outputs in terms of organizational objectives. For example, a health care system with several primary care locations conducts a mailing to residents that are new to the service area. The mailing includes a phone number with a tracking extension unique to this campaign. The number of patient appointments made with that tracking extension would be measured against the cost of the campaign (Anthony & Young, 2003).

There are a variety of methods to go about research and tracking. A more hands-off approach is to gather the data from secondary sources, such as trade associations or research journals. However, simple surveys can reveal quite a lot of useful data. Some samples of common marketing surveys include customer loyalty and satisfaction, brand recognition or name testing, advertisement tracking, brand equity, buyer-decision process, positioning, and segmentation (to determine demographic, psychographic, and behavioral characteristics). However, simply reading customer-initiated feedback (such as formal or anonymous e-mails or phone calls) can be quite enlightening. There are some, such as Neumeier, who consider effective research to be done by simply observing your customers at all levels of interaction with your organization and its deliverable goods or services. "Focus groups were invented to focus the research; not *be* the research. The secret to audience insight is unobtrusive observation" (Neumeier, 2003).

The bottom line here is that although you may not like tracking, donors are becoming evermore demanding on how their money is being spent. Tracking the effects of the marketing components is crucial to understanding what is working, what is not, what shows promise, what needs to be done away with, and what connected with customers.

Summary

All of humankind is on a quest for meaning, for something to believe in. "As social animals," says MacLeod (2008), "we are happiest when we feel we belong to something much larger than ourselves. A faith. A movement. A tribe. A noble calling. A purpose-idea." Humanity's search for purpose and reason is what compels us to support organizations with high callings like educating inner-city children, feeding the hungry, fighting disease in third world countries, promoting culture through fine arts, sharing faith, or providing immediate aid to a city devastated by natural disaster. The purpose-idea drives our reason "why." We are here, we act—because we believe the state of things as they currently are can be continually improved. Human beings do not demand that things stay as they are. As people, as customers, we are all on a never-ending endeavor for change. As such, the unquenchable thirst for change begets the need to champion an idea that we can identify with and believe in.

The challenge for marketing and communications in the nonprofit sector is to purposely listen to the voices of those nonprofits serve while fighting our own urges to speak. The organization must be more concerned about the interests of its constituents than it must be about its own infamy; pride and narcissism must never lead the conversation. Nonprofit marketing must be used to connect an idea to a person's beliefs, to resonate with his or her values, and to inspire him or her to take action. As nonprofit leaders and marketers, we are really agents of change, as much servants as we are caretakers of a noble idea.

References and Further Readings

Achievement. (n.d.). *Desmond Tutu*. Retrieved April 10, 2009, from http://www.achievement.org/autodoc/page/tut0int-4

Andreason, A. R., & Kotler, P. (2007). *Strategic marketing for non-profit organizations* (7th ed.). Burlington, MA: Elsevier.

Anthony, R. N., & Young, D. W. (2003). *Management control in nonprofit organizations* (7th ed.). Boston: McGraw-Hill/Irwin.

Brinkerhoff, P. C. (2002). *Mission-based marketing: Positioning your not-for-profit in an increasingly competitive world.* Hoboken, NJ: Wiley.

Carnegie, D. (1937). *How to win friends and influence people.* New York: Simon & Schuster.

Clow, K. E., & Kurtz, D. L. (2004). *Services marketing: Operation, management, and strategy.* Cincinnati, OH: Atomic Dog.

Colvin, G. (2008). *Talent is overrated: What really separates world-class performers from everybody else.* New York: Portfolio.

Fortini-Campbell, L. (2001). *Hitting the sweet spot: How consumer insights can inspire better marketing and advertising.* Chicago: Copy Workshop.

Gladwell, M. (2002). *The tipping point: How little things can make a big difference.* Boston: Back Bay Books.

Gladwell, M. (2008). *Outliers: The story of success.* New York: Little, Brown.

Godin, S. (2003). *Purple cow: Transform your business by being remarkable.* New York: Portfolio.

Godin, S. (2007). *The dip: A little book that teaches you when to quit (and when to stick).* New York: Portfolio.

Godin, S. (2008). *Tribes: We need you to lead us.* New York: Portfolio.

Heath, C. (2007). *Made to stick: Why some ideas survive and others die.* New York: Random.

Levine, R., Locke, C., Searls, D., & Weinberger, D. (2000). *The cluetrain manifesto: The end of business as usual* [Nonmusic Sound Recording]. New York: Simon & Schuster.

MacLeod, H. (2008). *Ignore everybody: And 39 other keys to creativity.* New York: Portfolio.

McLuhan, M. (1996). *The medium is the massage: An inventory of effects.* San Francisco: HardWired.

Medina, J. (2008). *Brain rules: 12 principles for surviving and thriving at work, home, and school.* Seattle, WA: Pear Press.

Neumeier, M. (2003). *The brand gap: How to bridge the distance between business strategy and design.* Indianapolis, IN: New Riders.

Port, M. (2009). *Think big manifesto: Think you can't change your life (and the world)?* Hoboken, NJ: Wiley.

Roam, D. (2010). *Back of the napkin: Solving problems and selling ideas with pictures.* New York: Portfolio.

70

ROLE OF NONPROFIT LEADERS IN MARKETING, POSITIONING, AND PUBLIC RELATIONS

ROBERT SHALETT

Johnson Center for Philanthropy, Grand Valley State University

For one to say that marketing is no longer a dirty word in a nonprofit organization is to state the obvious. True, not long ago, the nonprofit marketing function often doubled as part of the role of the public affairs or public relations persons or departments. But today, marketing is out of the closet in the light of day and relied on more than ever by nonprofits that are increasingly stretched and asked to increase and diversify non-dues revenue streams.

How can this be? Nonprofits are mission-driven organizations, not concerned with budgets and bottom lines. True marketing at its best is a predatory activity. This runs counter to the spirit of many nonprofits.

While some may think that marketing is a necessary evil that has corrupted the sanctity of those with Internal Revenue Service 501(c)(3) and 501(c)(6) status, nonprofit marketing is here to stay. Successful nonprofit leaders recruit marketing professionals to promote their mission-driven programs, to work with their media functions, and to increase their reserves.

General Marketing Technique and Terminology

Marketing is a combination of planning, creativity, data analysis, and selling. While sometimes an organization can get lucky with a million-dollar idea, most of the success stories have at least some element of these components.

That said, one must not forget to respond to observations, and when appropriate, go with your gut.

Although professional marketers talk of a rigorous science to marketing, many of the key concepts are straightforward and common sense. I've listed a few common marketing actions and philosophies:

- *Return on investment (ROI).* This is a simple analysis of expense versus revenue. Did the cost of the direct mail campaign (printing, postage, list rental, etc.) generate more revenue than a total of the expenses? What is the break-even point?
- *Source codes.* To complete an accurate ROI analysis, one must track what generated the sale. This is typically implemented with a source code on the order form, with coded customer call-in phone and fax numbers, and through web transactions. (Take note: Never let the collection of the source code data hinder the customers' transactions. Keep your eye on the ball to ensure a completed transaction!)
- *SWOT analysis.* To determine your direction, a critical part of your planning should be a strengths, weaknesses, opportunities, and threats (SWOT) analysis. If your organization plans to develop a publication, for example, take the time to consider these four characteristics of the product:

  By strengths. Why is your organization uniquely qualified to offer this product?

  By weaknesses. In reference to topic and content, is the publication part of a crowded field?

  By opportunities. Is there a gap or a niche that this new product fills?

By threats. Is this a time-sensitive publication? Does the subject matter have a short shelf life? Can customers get this content for free somewhere else?

- *Four, five, and six Ps.* You may have heard of the Ps of marketing. While marketing projects can be broken down in various ways, the Ps seem to have the most fame:

  Product. A tangible or intangible product or service

  Promotion. Advertisements, direct mail pieces, billboards, radio spots, bumper stickers, and so on

  Packaging. The carrier of your product. Is your packaging easy to mail? Is it environmentally friendly? Is it part of the product itself?

  Price. How much you sell your product for

  Planning. Your strategy for success

  Public. Your targeted audiences

- *Marketing planning.* As part of strategic planning, marketing planning takes into account mission, goals, SWOT analysis, budget (expenses and projections), and evaluation. Marketing plans can focus on a specific product, service or event, or an entire organization.
- *The 80/20 rule.* This is a simple but powerful rule of thumb whose origins are credited to an Italian economist at the turn of the last century.

In marketing, the 80/20 rule suggests that the top 20% of anything generates 80% of your business. For example, on a restaurant menu, 20% of the listed entrées account for 80% of the orders. A total of 20% of your members use 80% of your services. And 20% of your product line generates 80% of your sales. When you focus on that 20%, your marketing becomes more effective. Don't forget to use the 80/20 rule for controlling expenses. A total of 20% of your efforts could be going out the window. What activities do you and your staff spend both time and money completing without reaching 80% of your audience?

- *Recency, frequency, and monetary value (RFM).* This is another method of determining your best customers and capitalizing from them. The theory is that your best customers are the following:

  The most recent (R). Who attended your last event? Who purchased subscriptions last month? These are active and engaged customers. Reach out to them and offer them something else. They are a likely buyer or participant.

  The customers that have the most interactions the most frequently (F). Which of your customers bought a book 2 weeks ago, subscribed to your newsletter last week, and bought a T-shirt yesterday? Who attended every brown-bag discussion group you held last quarter? Who visits your website every day? These are your "bread and butter," your loyal supporters. Don't forget them! They will lead you to your goal—and offer new ideas and feedback.

  The big buyers (M). Who spent the most money in your bookstore? Who sent the largest donations? These customers have a budget for your activities. Know their budget cycles and time you outreach to them.

- *Segments and demographic profiles.* To better know your audience, the key is to break down its characteristics into segments. By doing this, you can tailor your organization's message increasing your chance of reaching the members of the audience. Applied to your lists and your audience, common segments include these traits:

  Gender

  Geography (often zip codes)

  Age

  Workplace

  Past purchases (does not need to be an actual purchase)

  Membership categories (as determined by your group)

- *Target.* Who is your audience (primary, secondary, and tertiary)? Determining your target audience is not as easy as it seems. Are your customers buying with their own money or with their employer's? Is your target an individual or a large institution? Who is the decision maker there?
- *Benefit.* An effective message or promotion *must* include the benefit. Why should I buy or participate? How will this benefit me as a consumer?
- *Call to action.* How can I order? When is the event? How do I register? What number do I call? What is the mailing address? *Essentially,* what next step do you want your target to take? Don't forget this!

Other Good Rules to Remember

Word of Mouth

Whether it is called *viral* marketing, *buzz* marketing, or *one-to-one* marketing (Peppers & Rogers, 1998), keep in mind that word of mouth is the most effective marketing method. There are differentiations between buzz, viral, and one-to-one philosophies, but at the core of each is a desire to unleash word-of-mouth marketing and build relationships.

How did you find a favorite restaurant? What about your hair stylist? Use testimonials and "bring-a-friend" offers in your promotional campaigns to maximize on the power of word of mouth.

Make Your Customers Bigger

The one-to-one marketing philosophy by Peppers and Rogers expounds on the purpose and power of the one-to-one marketing theory (Peppers & Rogers, 1998). Acquiring new customers is expensive and tricky to project. Implementing a turnkey response for your customers will help you to integrate a one-to-one marketing program in your organization. For example, if your group is an accrediting organization, you should consider selling your members the preparation materials for the test. This is also sometimes referred to as *one-stop shopping.*

One-to-one marketing programs are very effective for nonprofits. This type of relationship building strengthens the members' sense of ownership with the organization.

An engaged and active membership base is extremely important to the future of your organization.

Make It Easy for Your Customers

When selling, make it as easy as possible for the member or customer to complete the transaction. Your organization's online registration process should have as few clicks as possible. You should be able to accept payments by as many methods as possible (within reason). You should have one toll-free number to handle as many of your constituencies' concerns as possible. Your staff should be trained to direct queries to the proper person who knows the answer.

Make It Stick

Stickiness keeps your customers coming back. What is stickiness? A loyalty program in which five card punches gets you a free cup of coffee. Airline mileage programs are also loyalty programs. Given two consistent prices and times, wouldn't you opt for the flight that gives you 500 more points toward a free flight? Stickiness can also create a much stronger pull. For example, if your organization is an accrediting organization and your members need or use this process for job advancement, they have nowhere else to turn. Consider developing a certificate program for your educational programs. Your attendees aren't the only ones who will benefit.

Planning

Strategic, business, media, and marketing planning are perhaps the most important and misunderstood functions of successful nonprofit leaders. Planning can be tedious, redundant, and off the mark. However, not planning is a terrible option. Consider driving a tour bus with paid tourists without a map, reservations, or ideas for destinations or time frames, using a credit card for funding.

Granted, many groups function successfully without more than a budget, but this is not advised. One would no doubt find suitable lodging, food, and entertainment for the tourists, but many pitfalls and expenses can be avoided with proper planning. The following definitions can apply to an organization, department, event, product line, or individual product. There is some overlap to these different plans:

Strategic plan. Generally, strategic planning is at the direction of a board or the executive leadership. Strategic (or long-term) plans are usually for between 5- and 10-year time frames. Their intent is to focus the direction of the organization while using the organization's mission and budget.

Business plan. A business plan can also be written to guide for multiple years. A business plan comes out of the strategic plan and uses the organization or individual project budget to forecast success or failure.

Media plan. A media plan directly addresses your organization's communication efforts. This involves print, television, radio, and Internet. It should work in conjunction with the strategic and marketing plans.

Marketing plan. A marketing plan is derived from the strategic plan and usually a business plan (see Box 70.1). The marketing plan can also be organization-wide or product or service specific. It is an analysis of sales strategies and promotions, underscoring the reason to buy.

These are definitions of traditional planning as part of for-profit companies. Most of this is completely applicable to nonprofits. However, there are nuances in the differences. The purpose of a for-profit company is to maximize profit. The purpose of a nonprofit is its mission. Keep these differences in mind as you work on your planning.

Box 70.1   Marketing Plan

I. Executive Summary

II. Business Description

   a. Short description of products and services

   b. Elevator speech

   c. Benefits

   d. Unique position statement

   e. SWOT

      i. Strengths

      ii. Weaknesses

      iii. Opportunities

      iv. Threats

(Continued)

(Continued)

III. Current Environment

   a. Overview of current market

      i. Product
      ii. Pricing
      iii. Distribution
      iv. Competition
      v. Challenges
      vi. Trends

   b. Services required by customers

   c. Changes in customer demands

   d. Successful marketing activities

   e. Marketing activities that aren't working

   f. Return on Investment, or ROI

   g. Profit margin

IV. Target Market

   a. Profile

      i. Primary
      ii. Secondary
      iii. Tertiary

         • Geography?
         • Industry?
         • Size?
         • Accessibility?
         • Decision makers?
         • Service gaps?
         • Underserved markets?

   b. Segments (using common characteristics)

   c. What does the customer want?

   d. Does our market segment need to be more specific?

   e. Does our market segment need to be broader?

V. Goals

   a. What do we want to accomplish? By when?

VI. Marketing Strategies

   a. Outline the programs and strategies to reach goals

VII. Tactics

   a. Outline the tasks needed for implementation of each strategy

   b. Outline how they will be measured

VIII. Budget

   a. Revenue projected

   b. Expenses projected

IX. Design

    a. What message do we want to convey?

X. Evaluation

    a. When and how can we determine success?

    b. How can we evaluate before, during, and after?

    c. Course correction?

Other Thoughts on Planning

Fluidity

All plans should be somewhat fluid and adaptable for unforeseen changes, such as those related to the economy, a hot issue, or the weather. Remember that course correction should also allow room for successes. If something works, do it again!

Analysis-Paralysis

As mentioned, planning is a key component to your success. But don't overdo it to the point where you aren't marketing. Sometimes you need to put the boat in the water to see if it floats!

Nonprofit Versus For-Profit

As touched on earlier, is the for-profit approach good for nonprofits? Always remember your organization's mission statement.

Getting Tactical

A major section of your plan is your tactics, your promotional tools. The following is a short list of promotional methods commonly used by nonprofits to get their messages to their audiences.

Direct Mail/Catalog

Although expensive, direct mail still has its place. Effective direct mail can be a postcard reminder for an event, a brochure promoting your organization's products and services, a fundraising letter, a conference program that details the upcoming sessions, and a product catalog that features all of your publications.

If your organization's product line is large enough to create a catalog, you certainly do not have to have only publications or only professional education programs. You can and should mix your organization's products and services.

This is not to say that a publications catalog should devote half its space to a meeting program; however, a list of upcoming meeting dates for the next year could increase the shelf life of your catalog.

Use the piggyback approach as an effective and inexpensive method of reaching customers. Create flyers or stuffers to include in your dues notices or in your outgoing packages. You will save money on postage by already knowing that the recipient is interested in your products and services.

E-mail

Clearly, an inexpensive and quick way to get your message out is e-mail. That said, most professionals today are inundated with e-mail; therefore, your e-mails need to be relevant, strategically timed, and compellingly written with a clear call for action. Take the time to ensure that your subject line is informative with the intent of pulling your recipients in to read more and act.

Definitely, test your e-mail message before sending. Do the links all work? Do the images transfer as intended? You may want to send the test e-mail to more than one e-mail account on various browsers and platforms to properly assess it.

A relevant concern should be the CAN-SPAM Act of 2003. While you may not be in any danger of running afoul of the law, the CAN-SPAM Act has specific rules regarding claims your organization makes in the subject line, where your group gets its e-mail lists, and how it handles requests from recipients to unsubscribe from future e-mails from you. (See http://www.ftc.gov/spam for more and updated information.)

Advertisements

Print

Advertising in periodicals is expensive, creating a high break-even threshold. Additionally, a successful advertising campaign should be sustained for at least 3 months. Also, advertisements are difficult to track to arrive at an accurate ROI.

If your organization has an opportunity to swap an advertisement with another nonprofit, you both can reach new audiences for virtually no cost. Use ads in your own organization's publications to market your events, products, services, and membership benefits.

Online

Along with much educational content, the current trend in advertising is online. This is less expensive, easier to track, and quicker to revise. The best online ads target customers by key words and link to your site.

Telemarketing

Annoying, but in the right market very effective, telemarketing has fallen a bit out of favor. Technologies such as caller ID and a shift to more cell-phone-based systems have hindered telemarketers' ability to get through to the customers. Of course, the "don't call" list has also empowered customers to opt out of telemarketing calls. (Read more at https://www.donotcall.gov.)

Telemarketing does have its place. Specifically, when marketing to institutions, such as hospitals or libraries, your nonprofit may find telemarketing effective. Fundraisers also rely on telemarketing. Work with your staff or outside telemarketing vendor very closely on your campaign. Ensure that the script is short and coherent. Run an initial test to determine if you need to make any changes to the script. Track the effectiveness of your campaign.

Internet

A later section of this chapter will detail Internet communications more closely. However, your Internet presence should be consistent with all your print materials. Ideally, your organization should offer its products and services in a variety of ways including via the Internet.

Media

An effective media, or communications, program does not happen overnight. One must devote considerable time and effort to developing relationships with reporters and writers. Answer their calls within 24 hours—if not sooner—even if you cannot assist them. They work on tight deadlines, so be sensitive to their schedules. After you have a relationship, pitch relevant story ideas for future articles. Reporters may suggest variations on your theme, and you should be open to their suggestions.

What is news to you and your organization—a new publication, an increase in membership, a new publication release—may not be a newsworthy story. What is a newsworthy story? Readers enjoy human interest stories. For example, a story about your organization working with another organization on a grant-funded project is boring. But if you can tell the story of how the child of a single mom benefited from a mentoring program, you'll pull the reader in to want to learn more. Now, if you incorporate ways that others can get involved with your organization for this year's effort—such as volunteering to mentor—then you have a story.

The current climate for newspapers is bleak. Many newsroom staffs have faced cuts in coworkers and resources. The more you can do to help the reporter, the better your success in landing a story. Be sensitive to the fact that many reporters are wearing more than one hat. Don't inundate them with unnecessary and irrelevant press releases or e-mails. This is a quick way to land on a reporter's "pest list."

Data

With the advent of personal computers and web-based data systems, current, accurate, and accessible data are readily available for marketers. Be creative with your existing data. Would your recent conference attendees be interested in your next event? Or would they be interested in your organization's new publication release?

Buying and Selling Lists

Many list vendors and list brokers are ready to help you with your marketing campaign. Ensure that your purchased lists are current. Test with a smaller percentage first. Conversely, your lists may be of interest to other organizations creating another revenue stream for your organization. This would include your members and nonmember customers. Be mindful and respectful of what you do sell. Remember that your competition can "steal" your members if you make this information public.

Internet Communications

The Internet is everywhere in our society today. Whether at work or home, much of your audience shops and works—both personally and professionally—online. Your organization's Internet presence starts with your website. Is it useful for your audience? Can users easily register for a course or quickly find information they seek? Does the design follow your organization's style and brand? Can you track users' actions—what brought them to your website, what are the most popular pages, how long did they visit your site, and on which webpage do users most often leave?

URL

Is your uniform resource locator (URL) easy to remember? Is your "ideal" URL owned by another group? Should you change your URL to a more memorable address?

E-mail

E-mail marketing was detailed earlier. However, an important point to remember is that the goal of your organization's e-mail campaign is to cause the recipient to act. This could mean to register for an event or to purchase something from your nonprofit. These transactions should take place easily and seamlessly on your site or a third party's website.

E-newsletters

More and more groups use e-newsletters instead of hard copy newsletters. This saves time and money on postage and printing. That said, many people will still print your group's newsletter and read the hard copy on the bus, train, airplane, or at home. Ensure that readers can easily print out your e-newsletter (perhaps in a Portable Document Format [PDF]) so that they can read the hard copy later.

A growing trend in e-newsletters is in the formatting itself. Consider offering a series of headlines with blurbs that pull readers to your organization's website if they want to read the entire article. This will help increase your web traffic. Readers may want to participate in other organizational activities while on your site. If you sell advertising on your site, you can charge more for increased web traffic.

Another benefit to pulling readers to your site regards revisions and updates to the article. If the article is on your website, you can make changes or enhancements directly and quickly. If it's in the body of a newsletter, you will be forced to transmit a correction.

Stores and Meeting Registration

Whether it is on your organization's own computer servers or handled by a third party, consider offering an e-commerce function to your website. This could include a store for your publication offerings and the ability for users to register for an event. Ideally, your members could renew or reactivate their membership and update their status.

Meetings

In addition to conference and seminar registration, more groups are offering web-based learning, or webinars. This could be a one-time live event or an event stored on your site that is always accessible. Offer visuals such as video and charts and graphs. Remember: the more interactive, the better. Allow your participants to ask questions.

Social Media Marketing

Social media marketing is online community building through tagging photos or articles, blogging and microblogging, and developing videos for online dissemination. The purpose of social media marketing is promotion, finding your "birds of a feather," and creating a ripple effect to generate exposure and new business. Social media marketing is a fast moving vehicle with the big advantage of being inexpensive. Proceed with caution: Be sure not to mix inappropriate or potentially misunderstood comments or photos with your professional work.

Search Engine Marketing

Search engine marketing is the strategic purchase of certain key words that increase your prominence in users' searches. Pricing models of the packages vary by search engine and by key word. (See http://searchenginewatch.com for in-depth information.)

Search Engine Optimization

Optimization also increases your search engine prominence but by internal means. The strategic use of key words and metatags on your site can work to increase your organization's web traffic. (See http://searchenginewatch.com.)

Membership Marketing

For many nonprofits, membership dues are a key component to their budget revenues. While this is not always the case, many nonprofit organizations offer a membership package that includes reduced fees for products, services, registrations, and in most cases, "free" resources as part of their member benefits' package.

Member Benefits

Part of the marketing professional's job is to help craft and define the member benefit package. As a member of your organization, what will I receive? Many groups offer a newsletter or magazine to inform members of issues in their particular field of interest. Newsletters and magazines are oftentimes an open forum for members to discuss issues affecting the membership.

A national accounting association may have a state legislative roundup of regulatory items that are affecting its industry. A newsletter or magazine is also an excellent source for job hunters and seekers. Newsletters can help to promote and market upcoming events, new publication releases, membership pushes, and other services that membership in the organization may offer. More and more, we are seeing a move to electronic newsletters and magazines because of increasing costs for postage and paper. Many groups have also embraced a more environmentally friendly posture and done away with their "deadwood" magazines and newsletters.

Keep in mind your membership demographic: older or less computer savvy members may want to receive a hard copy publication. Also, members who live in areas who can take advantage of public transportation may also appreciate hard copy periodicals and in fact do most of their reading while on the train or bus. While readers can always print a copy to read while traveling, it may be prudent to offer members their choice of format—print or electronic. Another key point is to know your members. A flashy magazine may not go over well with a group of volunteers. A dull and drab piece won't work for interior designers.

Group Benefits/Affinity Marketing

Many groups have partnered with for-profit companies for member benefit offerings. Popular offerings include affinity credit cards, discounts on rental cars, and insurance packages.

Be careful: Whether your group endorses the product or service or not, your members will see the relationship as such. Do your homework and have legal counsel review contracts before entering any of these arrangements.

Levels of Membership

Members are the lifeblood of many nonprofit organizations. Even if your group does not have members, one should consider an elite, or premier, status category for your customers. This keeps your known buyers, your key contacts, at hand and engaged. Many groups offer various levels of membership; these include some sort of variation of junior, full, and retired or nonpracticing. A few words about each level follows:

- *Junior or entry-level.* Depending on circumstances, these members are often students, those who have not yet completed a board test or certification course or those new to the field. These members usually pay less for membership dues and receive fewer benefits. However, for the future of your organization, these members are very important to court, to engage, and to encourage feedback from as they have the largest dues-paying future for your group.
- *Member.* This is your rank-and-file full-voting member. These members usually pay full price and receive full member benefits, including discounts.
- *Senior members or member emeritus.* These are important members to keep engaged in the work of your organization. They generally pay discounted membership fees and do not receive all the benefits of the general membership.
- *Institutional membership.* This can be a broad category of bulk membership that allows an entire company or department membership and access to member benefits.

Membership Drives

With membership comes a membership season for the following activities:

Recruitment. An effort to target and enlist new members. Some key questions to successful recruitment efforts include asking, Who are your current members? Where do they work, live, or otherwise fit with your organization's mission? What is your current penetration of these members in the universe? That is, of the potential members who could join, how many are signed up to support your organization? As a recruiter for your area's candle-making society, do you know how many candle makers are in your locality?

Retention. An important effort to maintain current membership levels. One important question for successful retention programs is, who is actually paying for the membership? Is it the individual or the individual's employer? If it is the employer, is the membership tied into a budget cycle? Also, concerning retention, it is important to know satisfaction levels of your members. This is most frequently done through an evaluation process, such as a membership survey. Regular surveys of your membership should reveal your home runs as well as your strikeouts. Feedback is important, and you may never hear from your members until it is too late.

Reactivation. This is a secondary effort that reaches out to past members who have lapsed. This category could be defined as a lapse of membership from 6 to 12 months.

Other common and proven membership marketing techniques include adding services (usually opt in) on the dues renewal correspondence to increase revenue. Knowing that word of mouth is best for marketing, many groups find success in a "bring a member" program. Asking your existing members to help in the recruitment effort may be well worth the one-time discount you offer her or him as a long-term strategy.

Most dues renewal efforts are done by regular mail, although one should expect to see—and offer—an online renewal program.

Conferences and Events

Many nonprofit groups produce conferences, seminars, and events as part of their core business. Depending on the organization, these activities are often central to the purpose of the group—the educational mission. Conferences and events can also be major revenue generators—or losers—for your organization.

Some organizations are known by their convenings and nothing else. This is a time to release policy statements, hold press conferences, and launch publications. Often, it is *only* at these meetings where you will have the chance to meet your members and constituents face to face. Whether developing a new seminar or curriculum, you should first ask several questions regarding content and logistics:

- Is our offering unique? Is there direct or indirect competition?
- Can we partner with another group?
- Should our offering be online or an actual gathering?
- Should we hire an outside company to handle the logistics of registration, onsite organization, and promotion?
- Should we hire experts for content development and delivery?
- Are there collateral materials for the attendees?
- How many attendees do we need to break even?

Registration and Logistics

Major meeting reservations should be made months, if not years, in advance to take advantage of discounted facility and housing rates. Be sure to promote future meetings at the current event. Also, publicize on your website, in your written materials, on your dues statements, and so forth.

Do you have the ability to handle your own registration or should you contract a meeting planner?

Planning Committee

Consider creating a committee of experts to help with the conference. Will the programming be developed internally? Will the programming be purchased by a third party? Will you solicit programming from members or consultants? What is your criteria for the solicited programming?

Sponsors and Exhibits

Will you offer sponsorship opportunities to vendors and other nonprofits? How will you recognize them? Be sure to be mindful of the appearance of the relationship of your organization with its sponsors.

Online

Will your meeting be an online webinar? If not, consider offering online highlights either via video or with written reportage.

Affinity or Partner Marketing

By working with other nonprofits, you can maximize your revenue potentials. Depending on the arrangement, you may also be able to cut some expense. Partnerships can be helpful if you are holding your meeting outside of your geographical territory. Consider the benefits of partnering with a local or neighboring group.

Offers

A common offer for registration is an "early bird discount." An advanced deadline will also help you to determine before the meeting if you are going to achieve your attendance goals. If you are behind in your projections, you may want to increase your marketing efforts and, if possible, decrease some logistical expenses, such as meeting rooms and meals.

Another effective conference registration offer is to "bring a friend" or a reduced rate for groups. This works for several reasons: You know the attendee has a budget for professional development, you know that your meeting content is relevant for the registered attendee, and you know that people like to attend events with coworkers and friends. Capitalize on this!

Publishing Programs

Other than meetings, distributing original content is a very common way many nonprofits choose to increase nondues revenues and communicate to the public. Additionally,

publications can help to market your organization as a reference for many more years than would a direct mail piece or advertisement.

Your Expertise

What unique expertise and information can your organization offer to your audience? What will help the members of the audience with their work? Whether this is a technical research report or more hands-on suggestions, you may have something important to offer.

Many organizations have staff writers and committees of members whose purpose is to develop publication projects.

Print or Electronic?

Should you offer your publication in print, online, or both? Print is generally more expensive because of paper and inventory costs.

Print on Demand

In the past, printing was an even more expensive undertaking with minimums for print runs. Today, print-on-demand technology allows organizations the flexibility to print small runs.

Selling

Is this publication for sale? Is it free for members and for sale to nonmembers? Is there a possibility for a sponsored or bulk sale? However you plan, be sure to know your break-even point as a means of determining your format.

Promotion

Catalogs, online bookstores, meeting sales, and direct mail all work best for selling publications.

Spin-offs and Repackaging

Can you use some existing content to repurpose and create a new product? A seminar curriculum could be rewritten as a publication.

New Product Development

Always be cognizant of other publications in your field. This will help you to develop ideas for new products. Consider a questionnaire for your current users or customers asking for feedback and for new product ideas.

Positioning

Positioning and messaging of your organization is key to how you are perceived by your audiences and others. Let's run through some definitions of terms (Leet, 2007):

Strategic message. A set of statements that prompts targeted audiences to take a desired action

Slogan. A single catchy and evocative phrase

Elevator speech. Spoken, not written, elevator speeches are interactive, generally answering the question, who are you or what do you do?

Your Brand

Your brand is bigger than your strategic message. Your strategic message is only words; your brand is your image, your logo, your editorial style, your colors, and your slogans. Branding correctly can be powerful; it can evoke strong feelings about your organization. Strategic messaging should be done internally with your staff and leadership. Branding requires outside surveying and feedback. Some things to remember:

1. Your messaging and branding should come out of your organization's mission statement.

2. After determining your brand and messages, it is important to be consistent. With images, never stretch or resize your logos. Never omit components of your logo to make it fit. Make sure your staff members have access to your organization's logos, style guides, and messages for their daily work.

3. You may have an established logo and message that needs freshening. Rebranding your organization takes a lot of work with a lot of buy-in from your leadership, your staff, and members. You may want to convene a committee or task force to assist in this endeavor.

At this time, I should say that branding and message development is a difficult process to undertake. It's similar to deciding on paint colors or a favorite pizza restaurant: Everyone has an opinion (Leet, 2007).

Getting Involved

Many marketing and communications programs are part of the business schools of universities and colleges. What is an aspiring nonprofit communications professional to do? It is true that the business school has been the home for the marketing and, in many cases, public relations departments.

However, many degrees are now offered in schools of nonprofit management. These programs all likely offer communications, marketing, and fundraising coursework.

An excellent resource for those wanting to follow a career path in the nonprofit sector is the Nonprofit Academic Centers Council (NACC). According to its website (www.naccouncil.org), NACC "is a membership association comprised of academic centers or programs at accredited colleges and universities that focus on the study of nonprofit organizations, voluntarism and/or philanthropy. Established in 1991, NACC is the first group entirely dedicated to the promotion and networking of centers that provide research and education in philanthropy and the nonprofit sector" (www.naccouncil.org, 2010, "Welcome").

Many traditional marketing associations and organizations such as the Direct Marketing Association (DMA), the American Marketing Association (AMA), and the Public Relations Society of America (PRSA) now offer coursework and resources.

A Word to the Leader(s)

Obviously, as a leader of an organization—whether the chief executive officer or a member of the board—you are fairly, or unfairly, judged by the actions of your staff. The nature of communications and marketing campaigns—proactive messaging efforts—is arguably "the face" of the organization. You should be able to trust your staff, of course. But be mindful that the public will judge your performance by the perception of your communications team, more so than by your education, meeting, membership, and fundraising departments.

Be sure that your messaging is on target: serious, when it needs to be; lighthearted, if appropriate; urgent, when necessary. A joke can easily backfire and cause more harm than if you had remained silent.

Be aware of your team's messaging. Like any good leader, let your staff members do their work, but be aware of their activities to avoid any embarrassing surprises.

Future Directions

Be proactive with your communications efforts. Marketing and public relations efforts are not effective if you are timid. In today's information-saturated society, people must hear or see your message several times before it registers. Most importantly, continue to learn more about your audience. One thing is certain: Your audience will change and so should your communications to its members.

References and Further Readings

Leet, R. K. (2007). *Message matters: Succeeding at the crossroads of mission and market.* Saint Paul, MN: Fieldstone Alliance.

Peppers, D., & Rogers, M. (1998). *The one to one fieldbook: A complete toolkit for implementing a 1 to 1 marketing program.* New York: Bantam Doubleday Dell.

71

MARKETING ISSUES

Options, Types, and Targets

JENNA LEIGH RIEDI

University of Wisconsin–Milwaukee

As the title suggests, there are many different ways a nonprofit can communicate to its target audiences, and there are many different target audiences a nonprofit can choose from. The nonprofit board may find itself asking, how do we identify which groups we wish to reach? What kind of message do we wish to relay to these groups? With which of the many marketing options do we reach these groups? No matter how small a nonprofit organization is, it is always a good idea to formulate a marketing plan so that all these questions are answered.

Marketing management has many definitions, but one that seems most fitting for nonprofits is "marketing management is the process of planning and executing programs designed to influence the behavior of target audiences by creating and maintaining beneficial exchanges for the purposes of satisfying individual and organizational objectives" (Andreasen & Kotler, 2008, p. 36).

The unique circumstance for many nonprofits when it comes to marketing is that they are usually marketing intangible items. There are many different avenues a nonprofit can take to market itself and its mission. There are also many different target audiences a nonprofit organization may find itself wanting to reach with its marketing plan. Whether it is to find more donors, gain new members, reach out to potential clients, entice new volunteers or employees, find future cosponsors, or just to gain more name and/or image recognition from the general public, there are many different reasons why a nonprofit board of directors will decide to put together a marketing plan for its organization.

There are actually three different major ways a nonprofit can communication with its target audiences: advertising, personal communication, and public relations (Rados, 1981). Advertising can be either informative or persuasive, is a paid form of communication, and has an identified sponsor. Publicity on the other hand is free, has no identified sponsor, and is strictly informative (Veeder, 1999). The majority of this chapter will focus on advertising and personal communication since publicity is mostly about the relationship an organization has with certain news media, such as newspapers, and less about actively working on a marketing strategy, which involves advertising and personal communication.

Marketing Strategy

Even before a nonprofit should consider which marketing venues it wants to pursue, the organization needs to develop a marketing strategy complete with goals, a budget, and a system of evaluation. For some nonprofits, it may also be beneficial to appoint a marketing subcommittee of the board of directors if one does not already exist. This way, the nonprofit board can appoint to this subcommittee individuals with experience who are already associated with the organization and can also invite to this subcommittee both community members and professionals for more expertise and free advice. Having professionals on a marketing subcommittee will also be advantageous when the nonprofit is looking for media connections during the implementation phase of the marketing plan.

Goals

Four main questions must be answered fully when putting together the goals of a marketing campaign. What does the organization want to accomplish? Whether it is an increase in attendance at events, a desired change in public action or perception, or more donations, the organization needs to define exactly what it is setting out to do with both quantitative and qualitative measures.

Also, the nonprofit ought to fully understand whom it wants to target. In the marketing world, there is a fancy term for this: *market segmentation*. If an organization tries to come up with a marketing strategy that appeals to everyone, it will most likely end up alienating most, if not all, of the target groups. Rather, the nonprofit needs to focus on a few key groups and learn the best way to connect with them (Sargeant, 1999). To get started with picking the segments to target, the nonprofit should first ask itself, who exactly are the major groups of individuals involved in the organization, and second, what are their motivations and unmet desires in relation to the organization (McLeish, 1995).

What is the assessment of the marketplace? A nonprofit needs to consider the outside forces that will affect the campaign. Did a new competitor just enter the scene, how is the economy, has there been any news circulating relating to the organization's mission or programs? Knowledge of the current climate will help a nonprofit prepare itself successfully for the marketing campaign.

What does the organization want to say? It may seem obvious as to the message the organization wants to send to its target audience, but there are some serious things to consider when putting the message together. A nonprofit should identify and then focus on its main points when creating the message. Whatever message the organization decides to go with, it needs to consider the associations the target audiences will make with them (Herron, 1997).

How will the organization measure its success? An evaluation system needs to be put into place before the campaign even gets underway. The nonprofit must decide how it wants to measure its success (or failure), whether it is through tracking dollars, attendance, or the public's reactions. The number and demographic of people the organization wanted to reach should also be measured. There are many ways to evaluate, so the organization should consider all options before moving forward (Herron, 1997).

Budget

A budget for your marketing campaign is vital, especially when assessing the success of the campaign. If a campaign had the goal of attracting 100 new donors above the $1,000 level and succeeded, the nonprofit can celebrate their success, but they also must look at the budget. Sure, they just raised over $100,000, but what if the marketing costs were $80,000? Knowing how much the organization is spending is critical for a marketing campaign to be successful.

When putting a budget together, the nonprofit must not consider only the obvious costs of printing, postage, supplies, and so on. Other costs must also be considered such as staff time, equipment use, and building-use expenses. If the development assistant will now be using 25% of her time on the marketing campaign instead of on her usual fundraising work, this percentage of her salary should show up on the marketing budget.

Evaluation

Before the marketing campaign is underway, the nonprofit should decide what the success measures will be. Does the organization want an increase in memberships, an increase in donations, or just more hits to the website? Once the desired outcome is decided on, the organization should then figure out how it plans to measure this specific outcome.

If increased membership is the target, then the nonprofit should have a tracking system in place that should show the new memberships enrolled each month. This information needs to have been tracked for several months, if not a few years, before the marketing campaign. That way, other factors affecting the new membership numbers can be ruled out. For example, if the organization has tracked the new membership numbers monthly for the last 5 years, it may learn that memberships are high in the month of December because individuals are buying the memberships as gifts or because individuals are trying to donate more at the end of the year for their tax deductions. Knowing this can help a nonprofit not confuse other factors with its marketing campaign's results.

Once a marketing campaign is over, it is always a good idea for the committee and/or those involved to meet and discuss in detail the success (or failure) of the campaign. The end of one campaign should always be the beginning of another in terms of learning. The nonprofit learns from its successes and mistakes and subsequently carries these lessons over to the next marketing strategy.

Marketing Targets

Before a nonprofit decides on which marketing types to use in its marketing campaign, it needs to decide who exactly it is trying to target and why. The difference between trying to reach a prospective donor and a client for the organization's services can be drastic. While the prospective donor may read the local newspaper everyday and drive on the expressway to work, a homeless client may not even know how to read and may not own a car, much less be driving one to work everyday on the expressway. So the nonprofit can try to reach the donor through mailings to his house, having a billboard along the expressway, or putting an ad in the newspaper. To reach the homeless client, the nonprofit can use bus stop signs, radio advertisements, or even the simplest form of marketing: word of mouth.

Ultimately, every nonprofit is different, and the best thing it can do is research the target audience it is looking to reach and find out the best way to get in touch with these individuals. In fact, one list of target groups for a university consisted of 20 separate groups of individuals. This list included obvious groups such as students, staff, and donors as well as groups one may not instantly associate with a university like veterans, corporations, and community college graduates (Fine, 1990). The following is a list of common targets a nonprofit may try to reach to give nonprofit organizations a basis to start from when considering its list of target groups.

Donors

Donors are typically the target nonprofits are looking to reach the most. Every development director has taken part in marketing whether the person realizes it or not. While it is always a great idea to keep trying to build on the existing donor base and add more donors, it is much easier and less expensive for a nonprofit to keep current donors than it is to gain new ones. So the marketing efforts for donors should make sure to focus on both categories of target audiences: current donors and prospective donors.

Most donors are contacted through direct mailing, word of mouth (cultivation), special events, and/or telemarketing. However, there are many other creative ways to reach a prospective donor or to stay connected with a current one. The marketing plan for donors should also take into account the amount of money and resources the current donor already gives (or the amount the nonprofit is looking to receive from a prospective donor). It is highly unlikely a major gift donor will respond well to telemarketing. Major gift donors typically need to be cultivated over time and therefore should be interacted with through face-to-face meetings and phone conversations. Small gift donors can obviously be contacted through all kinds of marketing options since it typically does not take as much time and effort to receive a $15 donation as it does a $15,000 one.

Social media are becoming more popular, especially with younger generations (also known as future major gift donors!). Nonprofits need to use this medium to reach potential donors and use the Internet to make donating practically painless for individuals. While many people just throw their "junk mail" into the recycle bin without giving it a second look, they are very willing to click on a link and look at a website for a few minutes.

Members

Membership organizations not only need to attract members but also need to retain them. Newsletters, sent through mail or over the Internet, are usually the most common communication form chosen for retention. Also, membership organizations legally need to inform their members of the annual meeting since members have a right to attend and vote at this meeting. A nonprofit can market this annual meeting in a positive light, maybe offer some type of incentive such as a social hour before the event. Not only is it a good thing to have a large number of members attend this annual meeting, but also it can be used as a fundraising technique. Asking a person face-to-face for a donation is much more successful than a mass mailing or newsletter, so here is the nonprofit's chance to speak to its members one-on-one, face-to-face, and attempt to get more funding than just the annual membership dues.

It is also a great idea to keep members informed and engaged with updates relating to the nonprofit throughout the year. While mailing a newsletter is a great way to do this, it is becoming more popular for nonprofit organizations to turn to the Internet as a cheap and easy way to stay connected. The nonprofit's website can have a special section for members only where individuals can log in and catch up on the latest happenings of the organization.

Clients/Customers

A nonprofit that directly serves a group of people needs to be able to reach them so that these individuals know about the services that are available to them. Nonprofit organizations also need to stay competitive if their services are also provided by any other organizations in the area. Nonprofits need to market to clients so that these people know there are services available to them if needed. In addition to educating the public about services offered, some nonprofits also need to target these prospective clients for revenue purposes. If the organization charges a fee for services, this is income for the nonprofit, and therefore, it needs to attract more clients to increase revenue to support and even expand programs.

Sometimes reaching clients can be difficult, however. If the nonprofit is a literacy services center that tutors adults in reading and writing the English language, it cannot advertise heavily through print since its potential students may not be able to read the print advertisement. Also, if the nonprofit services the homeless, it can be difficult to reach this population since it is somewhat transient and can be difficult to locate. As with all marketing situations, and clients are no different, the nonprofit needs to focus on and research the target audience and then decide on the best marketing options to reach these people.

Volunteers

For many nonprofits, volunteers are the backbone of the organization, and attracting them and their services is vital for the organization's success. Just as looking for potential employees or customers can be competitive, so can attracting volunteers, especially if there are other nonprofits in the area with a similar mission. Most metropolitan areas in the United States have a volunteers' website that compiles all the opportunities in the area on a database for potential volunteers to search. It is also a good idea for the nonprofit to go to job fairs and have information on all the volunteer opportunities. Even if they are not hiring for paid positions, the individuals at the fair are most likely out of work and looking for something to do, either to just keep busy or to have something to put on their resumes while they are between jobs.

A specific kind of volunteer a nonprofit should always be marketing for is board members. When elections are around the corner for new board members, a nonprofit should really get the word out that there are seats open on the board. Otherwise, only friends of current board members will know about the opportunity, and suddenly, the nonprofit will have only like-minded people on the board. It is crucial for the board to be diverse in order for the nonprofit to remain successful.

In addition to marketing for board members, a nonprofit board can set up a marketing committee that has a few board members, staff, and community members involved. A marketing professional may not be interested in the full responsibility of being a board member, so asking such individuals to sit on a subcommittee is a better way to ensure his or her involvement. This can also save the nonprofit money if it has a volunteer committee of specialists helping with the overall marketing of the organization instead of hiring more staff people or outsourcing to an agency.

Collaborating Agencies

A nonprofit organization may be looking to join forces with another nonprofit or even a for-profit company in order to further its mission. There are many reasons why a nonprofit would want to join with another organization. Some grantmaking organizations request that nonprofits collaborate before they will grant any money. Most likely, the best way for a nonprofit to do marketing in this area is through direct, personalized letters or phone calls to the appropriate contact at the other organization.

Cause-related marketing is becoming increasingly more popular as regular consumers being to feel more altruistic in their purchasing decisions. The concept of cause-related marketing is a worthy one, and if a nonprofit knows what it is doing and is very careful about which for-profit companies it will join with, it can also be an extremely beneficial endeavor. A nonprofit can move both its name and mission into a larger spotlight and also receive a large donation in the process. While there are legal issues to consider, a nonprofit organization definitely needs to do its research on the company it is considering and then make sure to have an extremely detailed contract that spells out everything relating to the campaign, right down to the dates the campaign will start and end as well as the minimum and maximum amounts the for-profit is prepared to give.

Policymakers

In many cases, a nonprofit may want to reach out and communicate with a legislator or policymaker that could help with a particular policy affecting the nonprofit's mission. For example, a puppy mill regulation bill may be on the floor of a state senate, and a local humane society wants this bill to be passed since it means more animals will be protected from abuse and neglect. Legally, however, nonprofits need to be careful about how much money and other resources are spent on lobbying since Internal Revenue Service 501(c)(3) status nonprofits are legally limited on spending in this area.

Therefore, if a nonprofit wishes to get the attention of a legislator, it needs to be creative. One of the most common ways nonprofits handle this is through volunteers. Many nonprofits will have a link on their websites giving volunteers or community members the necessary resources to contact their local representatives. Providing local representatives' contact information, speaking points, templates of letters, or even brochures for volunteers and community members to hand out at the state capital steps are all great ways to spread the word, educate individuals, and put pressure on these politicians to act.

Employees

Just as any regular organization, sometimes a nonprofit needs to attract individuals to join its staff. The nonprofit sector is becoming very competitive when it comes to attracting top employees, so nonprofit organizations need to put a little more time and effort in their recruitment process. The most popular forms of marketing used to attract potential employees are through print media like newspapers and through the Internet on job websites or the nonprofit's own website.

Marketing Options/Types

Print Media

Newspapers, journals, magazines, yellow pages, direct mail, newsletters, flyers, brochures, business cards, bumper stickers, bookmarks, temporary tattoos, et cetera, et cetera!

There are many options when it comes to printed materials in marketing a nonprofit. The options are almost endless if one sits down and brainstorms the possibilities for a mere 15 minutes. Not only can a nonprofit place a traditional advertisement in a newspaper, but also it can send out a press release to have the newspaper run a story on its organization, submit a letter to the editor, or even place an advertisement in the classifieds. The best individual to contact at a newspaper so that the press release is not buried in the pile of hundreds of releases received each day is the department editor and/or the specific reporter that covers the nonprofit's topic. A follow-up call after submitting a release is almost always necessary as well. Beyond newspapers, a nonprofit can place advertisements in journals, magazines, and even the yellow pages.

There are also many different things a nonprofit can print its information on. The true question is whether or not there is a successful return on investment for these endeavors. While it may seem like a good idea to print thousands of bumper stickers to give out at all events, unless people attending the events actually take the stickers and place them on their cars, the nonprofit just wasted that money. A nonprofit should seriously consider which print materials it wants to make and then assess if it will be cost effective for the goals that were set in the marketing strategy.

Direct mailing is usually a big piece of the marketing puzzle for nonprofit organizations. Before a nonprofit considers a direct mailing campaign, it needs to ask a few questions of itself. Who are we? (Is the nonprofit well known and/or have a popular mission?) What is our market? (Is the nonprofit local or national, what kind of people support the organization?) How should we position ourselves? Should we offer something in return? Are we ready for failure or success? Direct mailing can be expensive, especially the first attempt, so a nonprofit needs to assess if it can handle the cost of such a large endeavor (Lautman, 2001). Typically, direct mailing involves purchasing a list from a broker and "cold mailing" individuals, although this does not typically have a worthy success rate. Obtaining one's own mailing list of interested individuals is always ideal, so the nonprofit should constantly be collecting contact information at events, programs, and so on, to build on this list.

What a nonprofit decides to put in its direct mailing piece is extremely important. There are two main groups direct mail pieces are used to target: membership and charitable contributions. The mailing should be focused only on one or the other, so the organization must choose which group it wants to target. There are many factors to be considered in the creation of the mailing: the person signing the letter (CEO or board president? Or someone else?), the length of the letter (more than two pieces of paper double sided is not recommended), if there will be any teasers, what kind of postage will be used, the size and color and font of the letter, the size and color of the paper and envelope, which photographs or graphics will be used, the attitude of the letter, and if there will be an inclusion of a brochure are all issues the organization must consider when putting the mailing piece together (Greenfield, 2001).

Broadcast: Television, Radio

Most small nonprofits do not attempt to advertise on television, and this is mostly due to the cost. However, if a nonprofit plays its card right, it can get a television station to sponsor it through free airtime for a commercial. Even if this happens, the organization still needs all the equipment,

time, and resources to produce a commercial, so this is a marketing option that may not have a high enough return on investment to pursue for a smaller nonprofit organization. Larger nonprofits will see more success in this marketing type because of the higher availability of resources.

There is a cheaper (if not practically free) option for a nonprofit to get on television, and that is through the local stations' news reports and/or morning shows. The organization needs to contact the assignment editor of the local television station with a story or event for the station to cover and offer to have a volunteer or employee come on a show to talk about the event in more detail. It helps if there are visuals the staff person or volunteer can bring. For example, if the nonprofit is an animal shelter, the spokesperson should bring in a cuddly kitten when discussing the large number of cats available for adoption at the shelter. This will go a long way in getting the attention of viewers.

Radio advertisements are much cheaper to both make and buy for airtime. However, the ability to target a specific demographic may be difficult since most radio stations typically will not allow the advertiser to choose the time slot when its commercial will play. In addition to usually not being able to control the time of day or night the commercial airs, the use of public radio is greatly decreasing due to other music providers, such as compact disc players, MP3 players, and websites like Pandora, which all provide music without commercials.

Just as with the local television stations, the nonprofit can attempt to have a radio show host plug its event on air or mention the nonprofit in general. The organization can also try to get a volunteer or staff person on a morning show to explain things in person. The nonprofit organization will most likely want to contact the news or promotions director of the local radio stations to set up this opportunity. Most stations want to know months in advance about these opportunities, so make sure to keep this in mind when planning an event or marketing campaign.

Another option is to call in during a talk show that is discussing a topic relevant to the nonprofit. For example, if a radio talk show host is discussing the increased number of prisoners being released early from the nearby prison, the nonprofit that offers job placement and counseling services for newly released inmates can have a spokesperson call in and talk about the programs the organization offers for these individuals. Obviously, this is much less expensive than producing and paying for a commercial.

Transit: Bus, Bus Stop, Billboards, Subway

A decade ago, many nonprofits would not have considered public transportation as a viable place to market their organizations. However, with the downturn of the economy coupled with citizens being more environmentally aware, people are now more willing to consider public transportation over driving their own vehicles. Therefore, putting advertisements on buses, in buses, at bus stops, in the subway, and so forth, will be noticed more than ever before.

Cost can vary, but some bus companies will guarantee a length of time the advertisement is posted and then after that keep it up until some other company buys the space. Since not many organizations are realizing they can use this type of marketing venue, this can mean months of extra coverage without pay. The downside to using public transportation for marketing is that advertisements placed in these areas generally reinforce only the organization's message through name recognition and do not necessarily move a person to action.

Billboards are still a very popular way to advertise, although somewhat expensive compared to the other options available. Once again, billboards should not be used to call an individual to action but should concentrate on solidifying the organization's name recognition. Since people are driving rather fast and can dedicate only a few seconds, unless it is rush hour, to looking, the billboard content should be easy to process and not have too much print.

Internet: Website, Social Networking Sites, E-mail, Podcasts, Craigslist

The World Wide Web is becoming the most powerful tool for organizations and individuals alike to market themselves. It is almost considered a must for nonprofits to have a website, and most have dedicated a lot of time and energy on making their websites both attractive and usable. There is also the typical use of e-mail in lieu of mailing such things as newsletters and fundraising appeals. Nonprofits can also become creative and decide to post podcasts or list advertisements on sites like Craigslist. The possibilities are endless for ways to market an organization on the Internet. Additionally, there is also a growing trend of using social networking sites to market one's organization. Sites like Facebook, Twitter, LinkedIn, MySpace, Flickr, and YouTube are all becoming the fastest, cheapest, and best ways to reach certain demographics.

These sites can be used to advertise events, inform the public on topics of concern for the nonprofit, post volunteer and job opportunities, and/or to ask for donations. The possibilities for the uses of the many social network sites are endless, and since the vast majority of these sites are free, nonprofit organizations should have a presence on all of them.

Marketing on the Internet also offers a unique ability to easily track the costs of marketing and return on investments through web programs, such as Google adwords and Google analytics. In a matter of a few clicks, a nonprofit can know how many people have visited its website, how many have found the website by searching for certain words, which ones (anonymously) actually explored the website beyond the first page, and who ended up donating or contacting the organization. No other marketing venue can offer this extensive information, especially at such a low cost to the organization.

Telemarketing

Telemarketing unfortunately has a bad reputation because of organizations handling the use of cold calling inappropriately. If done correctly, telemarketing can actually be very successful for a nonprofit organization. It really takes just some serious common sense to make a telemarketing campaign successful. The organization needs to make sure it does its research well. Know the full name of the person on the list and the correct pronunciation of the name before calling. Make sure the people calling are extremely polite and are willing to listen to the prospect if the person has a comment or complaint (Horowitz, 2000).

There is a very good chance the individual on the other line will not agree to donating anything over the phone. This is not a complete loss, however. If this happens, the nonprofit organization's telemarketer should be prepared to ask if the individual would be interested in receiving something in the mail to learn more about the organization. This not only gives the prospect more time and more information to consider giving a gift but also allows the nonprofit to access the individual's contact information to put the prospect on the mailing list. It is also extremely helpful to have the person calling be a volunteer instead of a paid employee. When the person on the other line realizes that the solicitor is a volunteer, he or she is much more likely to be polite and to listen.

Word of Mouth

Sometimes, the best way to reach someone can be as simple as through someone else. A nonprofit should encourage its members, donors, volunteers, and clients to spread the good word and invite their friends, family members, and coworkers to join the organization or attend an event. Being invited to an annual fundraiser by a close friend is much more effective than receiving a mass mailing invitation in the mail.

Word of mouth is also a great way for a nonprofit to attract more clients or customers. Some nonprofits offer services that address delicate issues, so most advertising options normally used to attract clients may be viewed as too evasive or impersonal. If one person comes to the nonprofit for services and has a good experience, the person will be very likely to recommend the organization to family and friends who may need the services as well.

Special Events

Special events are not just for fundraising or recognition purposes. They can also be used for marketing. If a special event is held in a public place, such as a park, the general public will see the activity and may become curious as to what is going on or want to know who had organized the event. All special events should have literature available for people to take with them, whether it is fliers, brochures, magnets, or some other type of further information explaining the organization. This not only is useful for those attending the event but also is great if a bystander drops by and has questions about the event or the nonprofit. All special events should also have an area where people can give their contact information. This information can be used when mailing out the newsletter, doing a direct mailing campaign, or for invitations to other special events.

Special events in themselves may require a lot of marketing to get a high attendance or enough corporate sponsors, and many of the types of marketing options in this chapter will help. In the advertising for the special event, the nonprofit should also make sure to include general information about the organization as well as on how people can donate to the cause. Therefore, not only is the organization pushing for the special event, but also it is doing double duty by inviting the target audience to learn more about the organization and give these people a chance to donate even if they cannot make it to the event.

The key thing to keep in mind about holding a special event, whether to raise funds, thank donors and volunteers, or spread the word about the organization, is that the nonprofit should have everything (or close to everything) paid for through sponsorships. Therefore, no matter how much or, if things do not go well, how little is raised, all the proceeds are profit. It also helps to get corporate sponsors because these for-profits will most likely agree to help promote the event by possibly putting fliers in their stores or offices since it means more attendance that leads to more positive exposure for them.

Cause-Related Marketing

Cause-related marketing is marketing that ties both a for-profit company and its product or service to a cause associated with a nonprofit organization and is meant to attract consumers. The main goal is to increase sales and corporate image while also contributing to the nonprofit (Ptacek & Salazar, 1997). As consumers are becoming more altruistic in their purchasing decisions, companies are cashing in by forming alliances with nonprofits and thus creating a higher demand product since the consumer now feels like they are being charitable by buying the product (Embley, 1993).

Many for-profit companies have marketing budgets larger than a nonprofit's total budget for the year, so this kind of exposure is practically priceless for the nonprofit. Whether it is a national nonprofit pairing up with a large company or a local nonprofit joining forces with a

mom-and-pop store, this kind of relationship can become very beneficial for both parties. Another major benefit is that this is yet another source of funding a nonprofit can consider. With the state of the current economy, nonprofits need to diversify their sources of funding to avoid losing too much money if one source goes under or if the source can no longer afford to give.

However, there are some serious issues for nonprofits that connect themselves with a for-profit business. If the nonprofit does not get a contract that specifies in detail what the for-profit may do with the nonprofit's name and logo, some abuses may occur. There is also the issue of accountability in terms of contracts. A nonprofit should ensure there is a contract between the two organizations, so it can legally pursue the for-profit company for the money owed to it or for damages incurred with improper use of the nonprofit's name and/or logo if such things should occur.

Summary and Future Directions

For a student wishing to get hands-on experience in any avenue of marketing for nonprofits, the best option is to contact a local nonprofit that has a mission of interest and offer to aid the organization in a volunteer capacity. Another way to offer services and gain experience is to ask if the nonprofit has a marketing committee operating through the board. If so, many subcommittees of boards willingly allow community members to participate. This is also a good option if the student is looking for more than just a few months of experience with the nonprofit since committee seats usually have terms.

Additionally, many cities in the United States have an organization that offers a website where many nonprofits post their current volunteer opportunities. Students interested should locate this organization's website that has such a compiled list and see if any postings match the experience he or she is looking for. When contacting a nonprofit organization, keep in mind that many are understaffed and overworked; therefore, it may take more than one e-mail or phone call to get a response. Do not be discouraged. No matter how a student approaches a nonprofit organization with the offer to aid its cause, keep in mind that most nonprofits will be more than happy to have the help!

A nonprofit has many options when it comes to choosing both marketing types and which target audiences it wishes to reach with those marketing options. Having a strong marketing plan that lays out the identified target groups and how they will be reached should be a staple for every nonprofit organization. The nonprofit should have a clear message for each group and should know the outcome it is looking for once the message has been sent. If a clear plan is laid out, there can be success for the organization in getting its message out.

References and Further Readings

Andreasen, A. R. (2005). *Social marketing in the 21st century.* Thousand Oaks, CA: Sage.

Andreasen, A. R., & Kotler, P. (2008). *Strategic marketing for nonprofit organizations.* Upper Saddle River, NJ: Prentice Hall.

Burnett, J. J. (2007). *Nonprofit marketing best practices.* New York: John Wiley & Sons.

Campbell, B. (2000). *Listening to your donors: The nonprofit's practical guide to designing and conducting surveys.* San Francisco: Jossey-Bass.

Connors, T. D. (2001). *The nonprofit handbook: Management.* New York: John Wiley & Sons.

Daw, J. (2006). *Cause-marketing for nonprofits: Partners for purpose, passion, and profits.* New York: John Wiley & Sons.

Drucker, P. F. (2006). *Managing the nonprofit organization: Practices and principles.* New York: HarperCollins.

Embley, L. L. (1993). *Doing well while doing good: The marketing link between business and nonprofit causes.* Englewood Cliffs, NJ: Prentice Hall.

Fine, S. H. (1990). *Social marketing: Promoting the causes of public and nonprofit agencies.* Needham Heights, MA: Allyn & Bacon.

Greenfield, J. M. (2001). *The nonprofit handbook: Fundraising.* New York: John Wiley & Sons.

Herron, D. B. (1997). *Marketing nonprofit programs and services: Proven and practical strategies to get more customers, members, and donors.* San Francisco: Jossey-Bass.

Horowitz, S. (2000). *Grassroots marketing: Getting noticed in a noisy world.* White River Junction, VT: Chelsea Green.

Lautman, K. P. (2001). *Direct marketing for nonprofits: Essential techniques for the new era.* Gaithersburg, MD: Aspen.

McLeish, B. J. (1995). *Successful marketing strategies for nonprofit organizations.* New York: John Wiley & Sons.

McNamara, C. (2002). *Field guide to nonprofit program design, marketing and evaluation.* Minneapolis, MN: Authenticity Consulting.

Ptacek, J., & Salazar, G. (1997). Enlightened self-interest: Selling business on the benefits of cause-related marketing. *Nonprofit World, 15*(4), 9.

Rados, D. L. (1981). *Marketing For non-profit organizations.* Boston: Auburn House.

Reiss, A. H. (2000). *CPR for nonprofits: Creative strategies for successful fundraising, marketing, communications, and management.* San Francisco: Jossey-Bass.

Sargeant, A. (1999). *Marketing management for nonprofit organizations.* Oxford, UK: Oxford University Press.

Self, D. R., Wymer W. W., & Henley, T. K. (2001). *Marketing communication for local nonprofit organizations: Targets and tools.* New York: Hawthorne Press.

Semenik, R. J., & Bamossy, G. J. (Eds.). (1993). *Advances in nonprofit marketing* (Vol. 4). New York: Elsevier.

Veeder, N. W. (1999). *Marketing human services: Selling your services under managed care.* New York: Springer.

Wendroff, A. L. (2003). *Special events: Proven strategies for nonprofit fundraising.* New York: John Wiley & Sons.

72

TRADITIONAL PRINT VEHICLES AND STAKEHOLDER GROUPS

LORA VITEK

American Veterinary Medical Foundation

Charities historically have shortchanged marketing for reasons ranging from cost constraints to the conviction that marketing dollars are better spent on providing services or salaries. Instead of seeing a brand project as an unnecessary expense, a better approach is to regard it as an investment in a long-term asset with demonstrable returns that will bring more resources to bear in providing services, not less (Rogovin & Wilburn, 2007).

Today, many nonprofit organizations are finding overall marketing, including branding, to be a necessary function rather than a luxury and thus becoming a function that development directors and fundraisers are finding to be a large part of their job description rather than ancillary. In fact, the July 2008 report conducted by the American Marketing Association in partnership with Lipman Hearne that included feedback from more than 1,000 nonprofit organizations found that building awareness, generating revenue, branding, and acquiring and retaining members and customers are top marketing priorities for nonprofit organizations. Organizations identified *building awareness* as their leading priority, regardless of size or subsector (Hearne & American Marketing Association, 2008). In today's landscape of increasing numbers of nonprofit organizations and competition along with tighter and more focused guidelines on dollars spent by corporate, foundation, and other sources and with increasing expectations and knowledge on behalf of individual donors, an organization—no matter the size or mission—needs to sear through the clutter and create a voice to succeed.

Traditional print communication vehicles should be one component of an organization's marketing plan to accomplish that voice or awareness. Just as nonprofits have evolved so must traditional methods of print communication. Social media and the Internet have carved themselves a new, seemingly large piece of the puzzle, but that does not mean print vehicles have vanished or do not hold value among stakeholders. Most all nonprofit organizations can find some value in traditional print marketing. So after decades (or more) of honing your marketing strategies, now is not the time to drop the tried and true when social media marketing is still so unproven for your organization (Dreyer & Grant, 2009).

There is much discussion of late about the strong impact social media tools, such as Facebook or Twitter, have on the nonprofit sector. However, long-term results on the real impact they are having on nonprofit fundraising are still to be determined. All of the focus on social media leaves many with the feeling that traditional print media vehicles are doomed.

Getting Started

The fact of the matter is traditional print vehicles, such as annual reports, newsletters, direct mail, brochures, and pamphlets or flyers, will always remain a function of the nonprofit sector—or any sector. The challenge lies in transforming our current thought process and use of these tools to include innovative and creative tweaks to meet any audiences' need or want. At any given point in a specific economic climate or cultural or generational shift, one of these tools might be more resourceful and successful than another. The key is finding out how, when, and why your nonprofit organization can use each of them to garner the best results in your marketing efforts.

As you begin to think about how your nonprofit organization can use traditional print vehicles to both create awareness of your cause and fund raise, one main item that should be kept in mind is *consistency*. Consistency should be the underlying theme throughout your marketing planning process. Your process should first begin by auditing your current marketing and promotional materials. Determine what components have brought you success in your past and current efforts. In most cases, it is neither wise nor efficient to completely start from scratch. Work from your strengths and improve or change the weak areas.

During this audit process, you might consider pooling a small group of your constituents (include staff, board, community, and donors) together to conduct a feasibility study—just to give you some external thoughts or tips in addition to what you already know. You can also find out if the brand or image is clear, concise, and understood by your audience. Next, and probably the most important thing to consider, is to set the goals you would like to achieve when using print materials. Here are a few best practice goals for traditional print vehicles that will apply to almost every nonprofit organization:

1. *Create awareness:* General organizational materials, such as brochures and pamphlets, should be broad enough to provide any reader with enough information to have a basic understanding of your organization and what your program does. Use your organizational logo and photos consistently so that the reader can tie them back to your organization. Select a few key words or messages and your mission.

2. *Fund raise:* Any piece a nonprofit organization creates should have, at the very least, an underlying goal of fundraising. There should be directions for someone to take action, such as, "to make a donation," please send your check to a specific address or please see a specific website link to make a donation. This print piece that ends up in someone's hands might be the only piece the person ever sees, but it might also move him or her enough to give.

3. *Convey an image:* An organization needs to determine, with the assistance of the board and other key stakeholders, what image it wants to convey. Print materials need to be appealing, neat, and not cluttered. Although many people fear that looking too glossy or shiny has a negative impact, you don't want your group to look like a flailing organization that does not have resources or is not with the times—especially if you want to capture attention among the younger generation.

4. *Provide consistency:* As mentioned earlier, consistency is imperative. Make sure all of your traditional print marketing pieces can be connected to one another as well as to your online materials. You do not want to create the impression or confusion that your group is many different organizations.

After taking all this into consideration, your organization must then determine if it is ready to invest in making necessary changes to the traditional print materials or if you do not have materials already, the creation of new vehicles. This does not mean investing many unbudgeted dollars into the process is warranted. Lipman Hearne and the American Marketing Association (2008) found that of the organizations they studied overall marketing budgets were typically 2% to 3% of the organization's overall operating budget, not including salaries and benefits. This percentage decreased with an increase in organizational size. There are cost-effective and efficient ways you can seek. Auditing and redeveloping only one or two of your traditional marketing vehicles will not have the greatest impact and benefits. This has to be an all or none process. Once completed, your organization will find that the investments of time, labor, and budget were well worth spending in building the awareness, meeting fundraising goals, and creating a strong brand and image that can resonate with all types of audiences. And remember, without marketing, programs and services will suffer, donations will drop, volunteers won't know about volunteer opportunities, and there will be low turnout at events (Jones, 2008).

Traditional Print Communication Vehicles

A nonprofit organization's marketing collateral often needs to meet all the target audiences' needs and wants in fewer amounts of materials. As you begin to analyze and determine each piece, consider your target audiences and how you will be able to best communicate your message in broad terms.

Annual Reports

One important lesson nonprofit organizations can take from the corporate sector is the need and importance of an annual report. Having a print piece such as an annual report might actually save you time and effort in the long run. By creating an annual report, your organization can use this as its "go to" document. It might be the one thing you consider handing out to everyone you meet or you may select it to send only to current donors, supporters, and prospects. There are benefits to creating a sharp, eye-catching piece, and that can certainly be done without spending lots of money. To save additional money, consider using a unique design, unique printing features, and full color only on the cover and using a basic layout throughout the interior. Print only a few of the fancier reports for VIPs and consider printing copies of just the interior in-house to send to the general public or for other purposes. You should also post the annual report on your website or consider sending out a special e-mail that directs people to your annual report link on your site. Be sure to save some of the fancier copies to honor special requests and new funder inquiries. It is important to have something such as this piece at the ready to send to anyone at anytime that you are trying to attract to your organization.

Retaining a graphic designer or marketing expert in your community who will volunteer his or her time or charge a nonprofit rate is a wise investment in producing an annual report. You might even have someone on your board with this expertise.

Cover the Basics

An annual report should begin with general information about your organization that includes the mission, vision, values statement, brief programmatic information, and pertinent staff information. Do not assume the reader knows everything about your organization. This section should provide readers with enough support for the rest of their reading and reviewing of photos, highlights, outcomes, and financial information to understand the nature of your organization and what it is trying to accomplish.

Photos

Nonprofit organizations should be taking photos all year-round, at every event and function in which photos are allowed. In addition, a general photo release should be created and signed by everyone featured in the photo. Photos are immensely important to the annual report. The annual report might be the only piece that a donor or constituent receives or even pays attention to all year-round. If this is the case, one swift and effective way to tell a story is through the photos. One tip that blueavocado.org provides is to flip flop how an organization traditionally would select photos. Instead of first selecting photos, this group suggests you first come up with two to four great options; then consider what photos you have or can get that would be relevant to those topics (Board Café, 2009).

Results/Outcomes

As more and more nonprofits are finding out, being able to illustrate programmatic or service outcomes is the key to funding success and sustainability. Outcomes help the reader determine if your organization deserves his or her financial support and if your organization is making a difference.

Highlighting Partnerships

Common buzz words heard today throughout the nonprofit sector are collaboration, media presence, partnerships, and cause marketing. Why not consider highlighting one of your most important partnerships? If a prominent medium source highlighted your organization in a feature during the year—talk about that article or story and be sure

to mention the source. Consider reaching out to that contact again to ask for a quote or usage of the source's logo. If a well-known company chose to cobrand a particular product with your organization's and its own logo, feature that product within the annual report. Consider introducing organizations that are part of a collaboration to deliver programming in your annual report. Highlighting any of the before mentioned offers additional credibility to your organization. If someone picks up the annual report and is not aware of your organization but can associate a positive awareness in someone featured—it has the potential to build a sense of involvement by that reader with your organization or interest because of the relationship.

Financial Information

In many cases, the financial section can be fairly simple since many people will not understand how to read the finer details of a financial statement. Must-haves include end-of-year revenue and expenses and information that provides the reader with the understanding of your organization's financial health. Percentages spent on program, development, and administrative costs are very helpful as you will likely be asked for them later if you do not provide them. This information provided in a pie chart format might be the simplest and most interpretative way to provide that data. In addition, if development or administrative costs tended to be higher for the particular year due to reasons such as a capital campaign, a one-time fundraising effort, or programmatic expansion, be sure to provide explanation.

Needs or a Reason for Action

After all this reading and reviewing—you have captured the reader's attention. Be clear on how someone can act now and what some of the top priority needs are in case they want to further help your organization. The annual report should not overly focus on this, but a half page would be sufficient. This half page can include a wish list or a few sentences that encompass your organization's focus during the upcoming year.

Having only an online annual report will not entice every donor and will not guarantee that it will be read. The annual report certainly can and should also be available online. But having a printed resource such as this establishes a certain level of credibility and professionalism for your organization.

Newsletters

The newsletter can be an effective way to reach all constituents listed on your entire database fairly frequently and as pre- or post-tool; therefore, it is important to be strategic when considering mailing frequency, size, and content.

The Particulars

No matter the size of your organization, producing a quarterly newsletter is sufficient, although three times annually might also serve an organization just as well. Be creative and strategic with why and how you are using your newsletter. Consider spending a few extra dollars on sending this piece to every name listed on your entire database. Since you'll be mailing quarterly, it will be a frequent, consistent vehicle that lands in your constituents' hands. With that said, this is your chance to engage current supporters and excite new ones.

Use the newsletter as a way for someone to contribute. Of course, it is not as effective as a face-to-face request, but nonetheless it's a way to ask. Having a printer insert a copy of your organization's remittance or giving envelope can be done but can sometimes be pricey. Carving out a section or box in your newsletter that directs people where to send a check or how to contribute online is certainly cost effective.

Do not forget to consider your organizational time line. Look at when events are scheduled for the year, the time of year your organization receives its majority of donations, or when your annual appeal is scheduled to drop in the mail. After considering these factors, you might decide to have your newsletter serve as a save-the-date or follow-up for one of these events—a way to save money instead of using a save-the-date card or a great way to use photos to illustrate successful results. The newsletter can serve as a reminder for your annual appeal by first dropping the letter into someone's mailbox and then dropping the newsletter one or two weeks following the appeal. Donors can be recognized through the newsletter. If there is a time of year when most donations are received—you can choose to highlight a few of those partnerships—consider highlighting a corporate donor, foundation supporter, and an individual donor.

Design

Consider first whether this is an in-house or freelance option. In-house designers can be optimal for certain nonprofits organizations. However, the downside might be scheduling amongst their piles of projects within different departments if you are a large organization. If the newsletter is something your staff does in house or is part of the development staff's role, consider consulting a graphic designer only for postage specifics and assistance on how to place particular headings in order for the piece to be self-mailed. It might also be helpful to use the assistance of a graphic designer to create the initial masthead as a template, which you can use for future layouts. A graphic designer, although there might be a fee, can be very beneficial to your organization offering an external perspective as well as expertise in consistency, layout, and other particulars of set up.

A good suggestion on size is a four- or six-page newsletter format folded and sent as a self-mailer. There is no need to use an envelope; this just creates a barrier to someone opening yet another piece of mail. Using at least two colors for print is imperative, four is ideal, and both can be found affordable today.

Finally, a Plan

After taking the particulars and design into consideration, start with a content plan for your newsletter. Most nonprofit organizations use newsletters as a vehicle to create general awareness, inform, and educate others on your cause. Unless you are specifically homing in on a particular market, the following tips will apply:

- Do not solely focus on past happenings. Telling stories only about past events, past programs, awards received, and grants earned does not provide a real opportunity for a reader to take action or guide a reader into formulating some personal interest or involvement in future happenings. There should be balance among highlighting both the past and future.
- Use photos and captions to tell stories. Just as was mentioned in the annual report discussion, first determine the key messages or sentences that are important to your organization and follow with finding photos or scheduling photo sessions that enhance these messages. Photos are great to tell stories but not if they are meaningless or used haphazardly.
- Keep stories short and to the point. Stories that drag on and give too much detail will lose the reader. It is only important to give necessary details that provider the reader with a good insight into your program. Answer only the who, what, when, where, and why of the topic and move on; no one needs a step-by-step account or analysis of an event or program.
- Always require action at the conclusion of each story. Even if you are not looking for a specific need from someone, this provides the opportunity for that person to inquire about more information. There should be both a phone number and an e-mail address to meet any person's preference for communication.

Unfortunately, newsletters can be the area where there are the most haphazard mistakes made by nonprofit organizations. Sandy Rees, Certified Fundraising Executive (CFRE) discusses the eight most common mistakes made in nonprofit newsletters, one being "too long of a letter by the Executive Director on the front page" (Rees, 2009, "The 8 Most Common Mistakes"). Too often, nonprofit organizations pump newsletters with so much useless information simply because they have seen other nonprofit organizations feature a specific section in their newsletters. Be strategic. Consider all the audiences that are reading the newsletter, which likely includes everyone listed in your database: donors, volunteers, prospects, friends, corporate and foundation sponsors, and so forth. This is a very broad audience. Pick a few areas in which you can support this broad interest. Don't be afraid to use some white space. Give the reader a break from content and photos. And finally, be sure to proof all content more than once. Spelling a donor's name incorrectly or having incorrect contact information could be a make or break point in relationships with constituents.

Brochures

Brochures are the vehicle most difficult for targeting a specific audience. In most cases, the brochure that targets donors, volunteers, or the general community will likely not be the same brochure that targets your clients or participants. Brochures are great to carry with you and make many more connections or lasting impressions than you can make by just talking. Every organization should consider minimally a general brochure. The bifold, tripanel brochure, often given the misnomer "trifold," is constructed by folding an 8½ × 11 sheet of paper twice to create three panels on each side. It is the brochure type most commonly used by small business because it can be mailed in a standard #10 envelope (see Digital Concepts for Business, n.d., "Brochure Design Services").

As a nonprofit organization, a general brochure is a wise investment. In addition, you should audit the list of your programs to determine if additional brochures are needed. There might be specific programs that warrant their own brochure. If you have several programs, you might consider several brochures depending on need and budget, or if your program menu is too overwhelming, it might not be cost effective or necessary to create a brochure for each program (see discussion on pamphlets/flyers). Here are a few tips as you determine your brochure needs:

Seek a Printer/Designer for Advice

When investigating all print material options, it is wise to gain expertise from a designer you trust or printer you frequent. If you have a relationship with a designer, he or she might offer price breaks to nonprofit organizations based on the more work you provide. In addition, as this is a common piece of marketing collateral, they will be able to share insight on best practices and will be able to create a very professional piece. Printers might also offer price breaks to loyal or repeat customers. If you do not already have a relationship with a designer, printers typically have in-house designers on staff that can accomplish a job for you or will be able to recommend a designer with whom they have a relationship. There are also many inexpensive services available online to design and print materials that are also of high quality.

Consistency

There should always be a few key pieces that remain consistent across all marketing materials. Examples of those include the organization's logo, mission, and contact information. If you have several brochures, consider carving out the same area in each brochure for putting these components to tie each brochure back to your organization.

Key Messages

Whether you are considering the general brochure or a program brochure, you should take note of your organization's or program's key messages. You do not need to tell your entire history and background in a general brochure. Take the four or five most important details about your organization or program and highlight those. Consider items that are fairly timeless by making general statements. Try to not get too specific with using statistics that are dated. If you are like many nonprofit organizations, you do not have the resources available to have brochures redesigned, edited, or reprinted year after year because the information is outdated. If it is important to have outcomes or statistical information, consider producing in-house a half sheet or quarter sheet that can easily be inserted into brochures that will provide this information to the reader. Or if necessary, consider providing this information on a pamphlet or flyer.

Photos

Besides not outdating content, you want to be cognizant not to outdate photos. Be sure to select photos that represent a broad range of your participant or client base. With photos, you want to make sure you give a clear picture of what your organization does as well as appeal to all of your target markets reading this information. It is so imperative to continually take photos throughout the year at various programs to be able to have a good selection to choose from. Be sure to also have releases signed by all parties in the photos. It is often difficult to go back later and attempt to find people featured in photos to get their approval.

Pamphlets/Flyers

Pamphlets and flyers can be an inexpensive way to supplement some of your general marketing materials, such as annual reports and your general brochure. If you are a larger organization with many programs, these can be helpful to highlight specific programs and are cost effective because you can print them in-house. For any organization, they can be helpful in promoting events or programs that often have date or time changes.

Donor specific pamphlets can also be created. Depending on the demographics of those listed in your database, it might be helpful to create flyers targeted to older donors, younger donors, different ethnicities, or even volunteers. Again, keeping these materials consistent with one another is the key. You can do this by selecting the same logo and mission placement on each pamphlet, using photos in the same location, or applying shapes and borders. Ultimately, pamphlets can be resourceful to your organization because they are inexpensive to reprint often and you can include dated information such as revenues and expenses, quarterly outcomes, or annual numbers served. Most of the time, unless elaborate and needing graphic design expertise, these pieces can also be created by development staff.

Direct Mail

Mail as a single-channel strategy is decreasing, but mail is still so important because the majority of money comes from it. However, other channels can enhance mail because people are operating in more channels today than ever before (Tode, 2009).

This is a great strategy to remember. If everyone had the attitude that direct mail was a completely hopeless vehicle, received too many mailed solicitations or advertisements, and turned to only e-mail communication, then people would eventually begin feeling that same way with e-mail—inundated—and the cycle would likely come back to mail. Many of the vehicles discussed previously in this article are potential direct mail components; therefore, much of this discussion supplements the tips given to those vehicles.

Just as with any traditional print vehicle you are using, an organization must learn to not overuse a tool. This aversion people are having to receiving direct mail, in many cases, has resulted because of the overuse of direct mail and lack of differentiation in materials that nonprofit organizations send. People get bored with receiving the same old solicitation or same old newsletter.

Good direct mail campaigns are well planned out and strategically sent throughout the year. An organization should consider creating a calendar to map out exactly when direct mailings will hit your audiences, what audiences you are targeting with your mailing, when they will occur, what you will be sending, and what goals you hope to achieve. Such goals may include awareness building, solicitation or fundraising, public relations or promotion, and special events. In any case, even when your plan is simply to inform your audience, there should always be an action to take or a way to follow up.

Personalization

No one appreciates a canned direct mail piece. So when it comes to an event invitation or a solicitation mailing, the more personalization the better. Even if your organization has a database of thousands, there are simple ways this can be done. Try to plan your mailing far in advance of the actual drop date. Assign staff, board, and volunteers to add personal notes to those that are addressed to their contacts or even personal notes to people they do not know who might work in the same type of business or live in the same community. By assigning others in the organization to write notes on letters, it further engages people in the process of fundraising or event planning, and it also gives the recipient the notion that an actual person looked at the letter or hand stuffed it before mailing. Try to avoid using computerized signatures and notes as this can have a

greater negative impact than having no one take the time to sign it at all. Take time to also personalize specific areas of content in your mailing. Instead of considering one blanket fundraising appeal, consider a general appeal with a few interchangeable paragraphs that can be used for different constituents: one for secular organizations, one for nonsecular organizations, one for individual prospects, one for volunteers or members, and so on. A small investment of added time can be the determining factor between a successful and unsuccessful mailing.

Size

Be cognizant of the size of your mailing, for it can often result in unnecessary added costs. When sending event invitations and all supplemental pieces, consider the weight of your mailing. Stamp costs can add up and additional postage might not be worth it when something just as effective and attractive can be mailed at the standard postal rate.

Creativity

As discussion around generational differences between recipients and donors has been one of the hot topics in the nonprofit sector of late, consider using different tools or features when coming up with ideas in your direct mail program. Simple adjustments do not have to necessarily exceed your marketing budget. Again, ask for assistance from a graphic designer or printer. There are so many new ways printers can create projects using unique paper or techniques that might not add much cost to your budget. Thinking about companies that currently donate to your organization, representatives that serve on your board, or foundations that are consistent funders, might inspire thoughts of creative ways that they can partner with your organization on direct mail projects. This benefits partner entities because they are also building awareness of their product or service for a group of people, and they are also appearing philanthropic by making the connection with a worthy cause. It might be something as simple as adding a partner's logo to an invitation you are sending or its stamp of approval to a new program you have added to your menu. Partners might even be willing to share a portion of your cost.

Whether or not your organization completely buys into the success that direct mail campaigns are currently having or will have in the future, it remains a piece of the entire puzzle. Discussion around generational differences and ways to communicate will continue to be buzz words used in the nonprofit sector. As it relates to direct mail, you can use this tool as a way to make an initial contact point with a donor, to engage someone, or to cultivate someone further. It is important to remember to include ways that meet any person's communication preferences as people consider further engaging with your organization. For example, you are sending an invitation out for a special event. Your invitation includes ways to purchase tickets online, a link to a site where you are virtually auctioning off five items, and links to your social networking sites while also including a self-addressed envelope and phone numbers for pertinent staff members. By considering many different communication tools and interests, your invitation, although mailed, illustrates your competence with all different types and ages of donors or audiences. You are tapping into their needs rather than considering only the ways that might be the easiest for your organization to field and handle.

Generational Differences

There is so much discussion around communication with different generations among development and marketing professionals in today's nonprofit sector. Four generations are typically discussed:

- *Veterans (also known as Silent and Great generations)*—those born before 1946. They prefer formal communication.
- *Baby boomers*—those born between 1946 and 1964. They place a heavy emphasis on work and successfully climbing the corporate ladder. Their preference is face-to-face interaction, but they have embraced e-mail.
- *Gen Xers*—those born between 1965 and 1980. They enjoy work but are more concerned about work-life balance. They prefer informal communication and rely heavily on e-mail.
- *Millennials (or Gen Yers)*—those born after 1980. Millennials often have different priorities than their Gen X and baby boomer counterparts. Because of their reliance on technology, they think they can work at any time and any place and believe they should be evaluated on work produced—not on how, when, or where they got it done. Their primary tool for communication is technology (Huggins, n.d.; Smith & Stanton, 2008).

For purposes of discussing traditional print marketing interests, grouping veterans with baby boomers and Gen Xers with Millennials presents us with two overall groups that generally have two different interests in communication preferences.

Veterans and baby boomers tend to prefer traditional print methods for communication, such as letters, brochures, and annual reports; there is embracing of e-mail use but nowhere near that of the other two generations. Gen Xers and Millennials prefer communication via e-mail or social networking. The majority of research online in recent years, points to specific strategies and trends for online marketing and using social networking sites. Usage of these tools is increasing at such a fast pace that the interest or emphasis on traditional print vehicles has diminished. However, simply removing these vehicles from your organization's marketing portfolio is not the answer. The truth is, traditional print marketing is and still will be of value in creating awareness and fundraising. People still have yet to see the true impact that these online tools have on long-term fundraising. We know they assist in building

awareness, especially among Gen Xers and Millennials, but we do not yet fully know if these tools have a direct, strong, and sustainable impact on these young groups in generating fundraising dollars.

> The Facebook application Causes, hugely popular among nonprofit organizations seeking to raise money online, has been largely ineffective in its first two years, trailing direct mail, fundraising events and other more traditional methods of soliciting contributions.
>
> Only a tiny fraction of the 179,000 nonprofits that have turned to Causes as an inexpensive and green way to seek donations have brought in even $1,000, according to data available on the Causes developers' site. The application allows Facebook users to list themselves as supporters of a cause on their profile pages. But fewer than 1 percent of those who have joined a cause have actually donated money through that application. (Greenwell & Hart, 2009, "To Nonprofits Seeking Cash, Facebook")

Giving differs by factors other than generation—educational attainment, frequency of religious attendance, and income. To the extent that these differ by generation, they explain the observed difference in giving by people of different generations (Campbell & Company, & Center on Philanthropy at Indiana University, 2008). Motivations do vary by income, race, education, region of the country, and religious attendance but vary little by generation after controls for these other factors are taken into account.

Millennial donors are most likely to be motivated by a desire to make the world a better place. They give consistent with their income, education level, frequency of religious attendance, and marital status (Campbell & Company, & Center on Philanthropy at Indiana University, 2008).

The most important message about communicating is to maintain a balance and understand how to navigate all marketing vehicles available to and used by your constituents. Your organization must show that it has competency and understands the needs of all generational preferences in its community. Just as you seek to find what your audiences' needs and wants are in relation to their giving to your organization, you must also seek their needs and wants in regard to communication forms or tools. Think beyond the use of a specific marketing tool but more deeply to what kind of messages your tools can offer or afford through the more effective means of finding that right communication.

Summary: Keys to Success When Using Any Traditional Print Vehicle

No matter what print vehicle(s) you are choosing to use and no matter what generation your marketing is targeted to, nonprofit organizations need to consider using resources more creatively to be effective. There will continue to be increasing numbers of nonprofits entering the marketplace and new ways to market online via e-mail, and social networking sites will continue to be developed. Nonprofits that can successfully balance the use of all these tools will be the winners in building awareness and in fundraising efforts.

Your organization's ultimate challenge is to find a way to be different, creative, and innovative without breaking the bank. Capabilities of designers and printers continue to evolve. Just as relationship building is a skill nonprofit professionals need when fundraising and building awareness, so is it imperative that this skill translate into building the same relationship by recognizing communication tools that are effective with your audiences.

Branding

If your organization or program is like many and has competitors and limited funding streams, marketing and branding can help ensure your programs are created to provide value to your target audiences. Branding is creating a point of differentiation and awareness where people recognize the name of your organization and what it does. Developing a strategy that will connect your audiences, young and older, to your cause while also being consistent in an overall marketing effort is the key.

The fact of the matter is that traditional print vehicles, such as annual reports, newsletters, direct mail, brochures, and pamphlets or flyers will always remain a function of the nonprofit sector—or any sector. The challenge lies in transforming current human thought processes and use of these tools to include innovative and creative tweaks to meet any audience need or want. At any given point in a specific economic climate or cultural or generational shift, one of these tools might be more resourceful and successful than another. The key is finding out how, when, and why your nonprofit organization can use each of them to garner the best results in your marketing efforts.

References and Further Readings

Andreasen, A. R. (2003). *Marketing research that won't break the bank.* San Francisco: Jossey-Bass.

Andreasen, A. R., & Kotler, P. (2003). *Strategic marketing for nonprofit organizations* (6th ed.). Englewood Cliffs, NJ: Prentice Hall.

Board Café. (2009, May 31). *The secret to a high impact annual report.* Retrieved June 1, 2009, from http://www.blueavocado.org/content/secret-high-impact-annual-report

Brinckerhoff, P. C. (1997). *Mission–based marketing.* Dillon, CO: Alpine Guild.

Campbell & Company, & Center on Philanthropy at Indiana University. (2008, May). *Generational differences in charitable giving and in motivational giving.* Retrieved June 1, 2009, from http:campbellcompany.com

Digital Concepts for Business. (n.d.). *Brochure design services.* Retrieved June 1, 2009, from http://www.dcfb.com

Dreyer, L., & Grant, M. (2009, March 26). *Can social media marketing and traditional marketing coexist?* Retrieved June 6, 2009, from http://www.nten.org/blog/2009/03/26/can-social-media-marketing-and-traditional-marketing-coexist

Greenwell, M., & Hart, K. (2009, April 22). *To nonprofits seeking cash, Facebook app isn't so green: Though popular, "Causes" ineffective for fundraising.* Retrieved June 5, 2009, from http://www.washingtonpost.com/wp-dyn/content/article/2009/04/21/AR2009042103786.html

Hearne, L., & American Marketing Association. (2008, July). *The state of nonprofit marketing: A report on priorities, spending, measurement, and the challenges ahead.* Retrieved June 11, 2009, from http://www.lipmanhearne.com

Huggins, K. (n.d.). *Communicating across generations.* Retrieved June 15, 2009, from http://ezinearticles.com/?Communicating-Across-Generations&id=1733210

Jones, S. (2008, July 4). *Mistakes nonprofits can't afford to make.* Retrieved June 6, 2009, from www.philanthropyjournal.org

Kotler, P. (2003). *Marketing management* (11th ed.). Englewood Cliffs, NJ: Prentice Hall.

Rees, S. (2009, May 27). *The 8 most common mistakes in nonprofit newsletters.* Retrieved June 1, 2009, from http://ezinearticles.com/?expert_bio=Sandy_Rees

Rogovin, P., & Wilburn, R. C. (2007, October 4). *Misconceptions often undermine charity marketing efforts.* Retrieved October 10, 2007, from http://philanthropy.com/premium/articles/v19/i24/24m000302.htm

Smith, W. Stanton. (2008). *Decoding generational differences: Fact, fiction . . . or should we just get back to work.* Retrieved June 6, 2008, from http://www.deloitte.com/assets/Dcom-UnitedStates/Local%20Assets/Documents/us_Talent_DecodingGenerationalDifferences.pdf

Tode, C. (2009, March 2). *Nonprofit marketing direct to donors.* Retrieved June 6, 2009, from http://www.dmnews.com/Nonprofits-marketing-direct-to-donors/article/128052

Vitek Design. (n.d.). *A web-site of good examples.* Available from http://vitekdesign.com/portfolio.php?p=ink

73

MEDIA RELATIONS

Promotion and Crisis Communications

JOSEPH BORRELL

Shippensburg University

M any nonprofit organizations do great work but are little known by the general public. It is not unusual to hear an organization described as a hidden gem or a little known secret. However, in an increasingly crowded nonprofit sphere, successful organizations must create and maintain a higher profile with the public through an organized public communication effort.

Nonprofit organizations have a number of ways to communicate to the public. This chapter covers the basics of writing press releases, newsletters, and annual reports and gives examples of how broadcast and print media can be engaged to share information about the work of a nonprofit. Typical nonprofit uses of online media are surveyed, and techniques to plan for crisis communication situations are also addressed.

Introduction

First, you get a puzzled look, and finally, the person you are speaking with admits that he or she "never heard of it." You are new to your nonprofit but are proud of the work your organization does. Naturally, when off the job, at your church or a party, people ask you what you do. You tell them where you work, but your organization's public profile is so low that most people, even if they happen to pass by your office on a regular basis, do not seem to recognize even the name of your organization.

The clientele and employees of a typical nonprofit are probably already convinced of the good work of an organization. They see it each day, but for the larger community, the good work that a charitable organization does is probably not so well known. Unless your organization is gifted with enormous resources and can pay for advertising, it must, like most nonprofits, rely instead on creative ways to get the organization's name and story out to members of the community, often with the cooperation of journalists who work for the various news outlets. This process of generating public awareness is known as *publicity*. Publicity is the distribution of information or promotional materials through various media in order to attract attention.

The saying goes that "you can never have too many friends" and for nonprofits, having many supporters may be the key to their long-term sustainability. In fact, you can think of the primary functions of a publicity director for a nonprofit as making acquaintances and then telling the story of your organization. In an increasingly competitive nonprofit sector, distinguishing your organization from other groups is imperative. To a local resident, what makes your nonprofit different than the dozens of other nonprofits in your area? Good work on your part will help build organizational credibility in the community, and since fundraising is important for the security of any nonprofit, a good public relations effort on your part can lead to a favorable environment for later fundraising appeals for the organization.

Job Titles and Duties

Modern publicity agents typically prefer being described as a public relations (PR) professional, but different organizations have different titles for this position such as communications director, information officer, publicist, or spokesperson. The job of a public relations director in a nonprofit organization is rarely boring but does require some special skills. Above all, the publicity director for a nonprofit organization must be an effective writer and general communicator.

The ability to tackle a problem from multiple perspectives is critical. For example, you have to have a keen eye for detail to make sure that an official agency communication is punctuated correctly. Simultaneously, you also need to see the broader picture by making sure the general message transmitted through your writing serves the organization's broader goals.

Typical job responsibilities for a public relations or communications director at a nonprofit are to create and edit materials designed for a variety of audiences, work with the local media, conduct research, advise management, organize special events, and serve as a contact for general inquiries about the organization from members of the larger community.

To do the job effectively, a public relations professional must know his or her organization intimately so as to be able to share specific details with individuals outside the organization. A PR director for an organization has only one item to share with outsiders—factual information. If you are questioned and don't know the facts about a particular matter, it is prudent to simply say you have nothing to add at this time or to vow that you will find out more quickly and report back. It is essential that you always maintain a reputation for delivering accurate information as the communications representative of your organization.

Most public relations professionals belong to one of the professional organizations in the field, such as the Public Relations Society of America or the International Association of Business Communicators, both of which feature a formal code of ethics for members to guide their work. These conventions stress truthfulness in all organizational communications and respect—consider it a professional duty—to the larger society when doing publicity for an organization. Simon and Wylie (1994) argue that a good public relations professional even serves as a sort of conscience for his or her organization by making others in the organization aware of how actions may be perceived by the general public or by otherwise monitoring the programs of a charity to make sure these services live up to what the nonprofit has promised.

Cutlip, Center, and Broom (2000, p. 526) list five aims for the public relations efforts at most nonprofit agencies:

1. Gain acceptance of an organization's mission.

2. Develop channels of communication with those an organization serves.

3. Create and maintain a favorable client for fundraising.

4. Support the development and maintenance of public policy that is favorable to an organization's mission.

5. Inform and motivate key organizational constituents (such as employees, volunteers and trustees) to dedicate themselves and work productively in support of an organization's missions, goals, and objectives.

Publicity and the Idea of a Public

To help with this work, public relations professionals use the concept of *a public* as a way to acknowledge all the different audiences served by an organization. Kotler (1982, p. 47) offers this definition of a public: "A distinct group of people and/or organizations that has an actual or potential interest and/or impact on an organization." As an example, Kotler says, think of a college or university and all the groups that have a stake in the success or failure of an institute of higher education. Obviously, students, as the primary client of a college, is an important group to consider, and there are multiple ways that official information is spread to the average student on a campus. However, faculty, alumni, prospective students (such as high school students), trustees, staff, residents of the local community, suppliers, and local government officials also have an interest in a school but may receive different communications and differing amounts of attention from the administration than an enrolled student.

When communicating on behalf of a nonprofit organization, the nature of your message and the type of people you wish to reach dictate your communications approach. Different strategies are called for if your message needs to be distributed broadly and to reach many different publics than if you present a narrower topic that affects just a small portion of the possible audience. In a world where technology has produced many different pathways for a message to be communicated, an effective communicator understands the habits and interests of the various publics he or she interacts with and knows the right ways to reach that particular public or audience.

Professional communicators benefit from systematic research as they gather information about the various publics they serve. For example, it is not unusual to see a PR professional conducting a survey to better understand such issues as the level of local knowledge about your organization, the community's attitude toward your organization, or the general communications needs of a group vital to your organization and the success of its mission. Once you have a good understanding of the audience or publics you want to reach, only then you should start developing communications materials to reach them.

Basic Publicity Tools for the Nonprofit

After learning about the organization and conducting general research, a newly hired PR director needs some basic materials on hand to develop the communications apparatus for a nonprofit. These prepared materials should be completed before beginning to develop professional contacts within the local media community.

The creation of a brochure is a routine task by even the smallest nonprofit since the completed work can be distributed widely in the community and is a standard feature in the reception area of nonprofits across the country. A folded, three-panel brochure printed on both sides of a standard page is the common format since many communities have existing brochure stands that fit this style, and materials in this format can also be arranged to ensure easy mailing to interested parties. While the size of the brochure necessitates brevity in the text, common elements are the organization's logo, which helps to build audience awareness, along with some brief general information about the organization and its mission. For readers who need more information, the organization's contact information including street address, telephone number, operating hours, and website address can be provided.

In addition to producing a brochure, it is advisable to have on hand some other materials, preferably limited to one page, that address other common questions about your organization. Examples are a short history of the organization, one-page biographies of the staff leaders and board members of your organization, and a brief description of your organization's mission.

Next, get a camera. One should be available at all events. Two maxims guide this advice: "A picture is worth a thousand words," and "if an event wasn't photographed, it didn't happen." With a good quality digital camera, you or a trusted volunteer can take pictures of your events and later distribute a courtesy picture to interested parties or local media outlets. However, for annual reports or other materials demanding high quality, it is advisable to hire a professional to take pictures of your board and officers. Pay special attention to legal concerns when photographing people. Individuals being photographed for publicity purposes should sign a release and be clearly identified at the time of the photograph, so you can write quality captions later. It is also of first-order importance to maintain the confidentiality of clients for some types of nonprofits in the human services area.

Remember that word of mouth is an important source of community knowledge about your nonprofit. How well do staff members handle the common ice-breaker questions of where do they work and what does your organization do? There is no reason to avoid working within the organization to develop the answers so that the message various people give about your enterprise is consistent and not simply a repetition of the organization's mission statement. One strategy is to create a short, easy-to-say statement of what your organization does and then work with employees, board members, and volunteers so that they can deliver this message consistently and sincerely (Feinglass, 2005, p. 29). This type of communications approach is sometimes called an *elevator pitch* due to the idea that it can be delivered to a stranger while you find yourself riding in an elevator.

Longer Organizational Publications

Many organizations produce newsletters as an important vehicle for bringing together the many people and activities of the organization into a brief capsule and to serve as a place for announcing future projects. Research shows that readers like newsletters that can be read quickly and feature articles that help the reader do or feel something positive. Newsletters can be done either in paper or in electronic format, preferably both. While printed newsletters cost more to produce and deliver than an e-mailed versions, printed materials have permanence and are more accessible to those outside your organization. While frequency varies, a general rule of thumb is to have an organizational newsletter produced at least a few times a year because a frequent publication schedule keeps outside stakeholders reminded of your current good work.

Obviously, the information found in a newsletter should be error free and the writing style accessible to the general reader. While it may be tempting to produce a newsletter mostly for the benefit of donor development, newsletters can also be an important internal communications device. For example, a newsletter can boost morale by reinforcing your organization's successes and by serving as a public forum to recognize the personal achievements of volunteers and staff.

Annual reports are often required by outside authorities who also may mandate the inclusion of complex financial statements, perhaps prepared by an outside accounting firm. The Better Business Bureau's Wise Giving charity watchdog, for example, requires that the annual report be available to any requester and contain, at a minimum, the organization's mission statement, summary of charitable work, and a list of officers and board members. Some nonprofits spend a good deal of money yearly going well beyond the legal minimums and create high-quality glossy reports that can be mailed to supporters. Naturally, such efforts require photographs and short reports about various aspects of the nonprofit's work in the previous year. All of these efforts typically require planning and support from the organization's public relations officer.

Many organizations take samples of the various printed products that have been recently produced and put them together into a media kit, which then can be given out to journalists. Special attention should be paid to making the kit reflect well on the organization and to keeping the elements together and organized. For example, a solid first impression will be made on a journalist if the organization's logo adorns a durable binding for the printed materials.

A media kit is designed to help a reporter doing a story on your organization and its mission. If appropriate, a personalized media kit that includes personal phone numbers for key contacts in your nonprofit should be given out. Such information greatly aids reporters who work after business hours to finish a story since they can get correct information when facing a publication deadline. A media kit can also include outside materials, such as recent newspaper and magazine clippings about the organization or positive reports about the nonprofit from outside evaluators. Sometimes, materials originally prepared for media kits are also shown to prospective donors See Box 73.1 for tips on writing media communications.

Communicating With the Media

A press release, also known as a news release, is used by an organization to make an announcement. Nonprofits can use a release to announce new programs, personnel changes, or upcoming events. Some news outlets may use the information verbatim over the air or in print, but larger news outlets often will use the information you provide as the basic building blocks for a story produced by a staff journalist, who will adapt the story to fit the style of the outlet.

Beckwith (2006) reports on the conventions for press releases. A release should be typed, double-spaced, heavy on facts (particularly related to the who, what, where, and when questions), use direct quotes from newsmakers, and generally be under 400 words. Press releases should be dated, may indicate when they are to be considered for publication (unless the information is for immediate release), and end with the famous three-pound symbol signs or the journalistic "-30-" symbol. Given how busy media professionals are, a release should have a catchy headline and the first sentence of the text of the release should also be gripping. Poorly written press releases are quite likely to end up discarded.

While the media release is a common first step to getting local media attention, it is not the only way to get your message into the local paper. Some charities have discovered that letters to the editor can affect local opinion. Often written by an officer or director of the charity, such a letter allows a representative to give his or her side of an event. While newspaper editors have final say in deciding on which letters will run, generally speaking, letters to the editor appear without much editing by the newspaper's staff.

Media Relations

A necessary bit of research for gaining local exposure for your organization is to know about potential places for your publicity materials to run. Start by compiling an accurate list of local media outlets including their addresses, fax numbers, and e-mail addresses. While you will lavish more attention on the news organizations in your area that are the most respected and reach the most people, every organization with at least one journalist on staff within reasonable driving distance should be included in your media directory.

Box 73.1   Tips for Writing Media Communications

1. Remember, you are not writing a term paper. Use words that ordinary people use and are understandable to individuals with at most a high school education.

2. Spelling and grammar count. Press releases and websites that have significant errors, even typographic ones, cast a writer and the sponsoring organization in a poor light.

3. Choose active and vivid verbs. Put these types of verbs into sentences of different lengths and also of varying sentence structures.

4. Be careful about being too enthusiastic. For example, media writings that overuse exclamation marks or superlatives (such as super or great) is not professional.

5. Be organized in your copy, and be sure to limit your main points. Keeping your message simple helps busy people to grasp it.

6. It is not necessary to fill up a page. In fact, white space is good since research shows most people just scan, not read, information presented to them.

7. Make sure your writing answers the basic questions a reader may have. For example, if publicizing an event, make sure you cover the basic who, what, when, and where questions.

One of the chief duties of a nonprofit PR person is to serve as the organization's media liaison, so it is wise to know how the newsroom of a local media outlet works. If you want to reach readers of the local newspaper, learn the name and direct phone number of the writer who handles nonprofit or community issues. As you start submitting materials for publication, work to obtain a basic understanding of the paper's submission policies, including the newspaper's deadlines and preferences governing the submission of photographs for publication. If your organization often has events with high profile speakers, consider the scheduling of a press conference or media briefing to gather attention and attendance for your event.

As you gather this information, don't lose sight of the fact that most media outlets are advertising driven since bringing public attention to products and services of companies is what produces revenue for the media, whereas the goal of most nonprofits, hampered by limited resources, is to get free exposure. While a discussion of creating advertisements is beyond the scope of this chapter, it is important to note that enterprising nonprofits may be able to obtain unsold advertising spaces at little or no cost. Through an outright donation to your charity of advertising space as a public service by a media outlet, you might be able to obtain valuable recognition for your organization simply through your contacts in the media community.

For example, many broadcasters reserve time for community organizations through the playing of short 15- to 60-second spots for local nonprofits. Often called *PSAs*, public service announcements at most stations require professional production quality for these messages in line with the station's policies for standard commercials, but smaller stations may help you produce one. Public service announcements generally air during commercial breaks when broadcasters have been unable to sell all of the available time to commercial sponsors.

Traditional Media

Newspapers, although struggling to retain readership, are often the best places to present your message since the newspaper's ability to reach older and more affluent readers is unparalleled. In big cities, a newspaper is put together in the late evening and made available to readers first thing every morning. In smaller cities, it may be distributed in the afternoons or published on a less regular schedule, such as once a week. Stories on the front page get the most attention, and editors will tell you that having an eye-catching picture attached to a story makes a difference in whether that story gets prominent placement.

Radio and television stations feature shorter stories than a typical newspaper and specialize in quick updates. Some stations also broadcast community calendar features that list upcoming local events, including ones held by nonprofits. For local radio stations, mornings are the most important time slot since these hours attract the most available audience. Many radio stations feature short news updates every half hour or so and may use a locally oriented, humorous approach to attract listeners as they start the workday. Getting an upcoming event for your nonprofit mentioned on a high-profile local morning radio show could generate great awareness and turnout for your event.

Of course, understanding your charity's audience and the sensibilities of the local media is your professional responsibility. A breast cancer awareness event would be a natural tie-in for a station with a largely female audience, such as a light rock station, while promoting the same event over a male-focused rock station could be a promotional disaster. Again, it is advisable to do your research before charging off seeking publicity for your nonprofit organization.

For local television stations, their highest levels of viewing are in the early evening. Thus, a story on your nonprofit during the 6 p.m. news will generate the most reaction in the larger community due to the number of people watching. Television news directors love stories that have great visual appeal and that touch viewers on an emotional level. For example, stories about children and animals are often featured since they boost ratings, but be mindful that the flow of television requires that the information presented be kept short in order to fit the technical requirements of viewing and audience expectations for television content.

In some cities, local cable outlets have a public access channel, which can provide some publicity for your nonprofit. For example, many cable systems will use the bottom of one channel to display continuously cycling information about local charities and events they sponsor. In general, such local cable publicity reaches a smaller audience and one that is more geographically concentrated than over-the-air broadcasting or a local newspaper. See Box 73.2 for tips on writing speeches or broadcasts.

Conventions of Working With Journalists

When dealing with your counterparts in the media, be aware that the key to getting good news coverage is to have a story that is interesting to the average reader, viewer, or listener. Naturally, compelling stories are considered by editors and producers as worthy of media coverage when time and space are limited. In terms of newsworthiness, some nonprofits find great value in having a celebrity attached to their cause, especially as a spokesperson. For example, if a local charity with the mission of combating cancer learns that a local sports professional has a spouse who is a cancer survivor, the shared battle can lead to a public partnership that mobilizes community support.

Box 73.2   Tips for Writing Verbal Media Communications
(for Speeches or Broadcasts)

1. Writing a piece that is to be said aloud should be shorter and more informal and conversational than writing that is designed just for reading by the audience.

2. Writing prepared for delivery is double-spaced and paragraphs formatted for easy reading so that the speaker doesn't stumble or have undue pauses in delivery. To be as easy to deliver as possible, symbols are spelled out. For example, use the word "and" instead of & and "at" in place of @.

3. Write a speech or a broadcast piece as if you were talking to just one person, even if it is to be delivered to an audience of thousands.

4. The first sentence or two must grab the audience's attention or it is likely that people will tune out the rest of the presentation.

5. Be careful about using humor. Jokes that appear funny on paper can fall flat when actually delivered and, depending on the situation, may end up offending some audience members.

6. Simplify complex ideas into a form for the spoken situation that is understandable, yet still truthful. Generally speaking, live audiences don't get a second chance to grasp information that they hear or see, so the job of both the writer and presenter is to make complicated information crystal clear for a casually involved audience member.

7. Shorter and simpler talks that have been ruthlessly edited to improve focus will be the most warmly received by the audience.

A nonprofit public relations director needs to plan ahead to manage a nonprofit's major events, such as having a nationally known speaker travel to your organization's annual award dinner. In addition to producing a printed program for the event, coordinating outside press access to the event, or specifying audiovisual equipment to be rented for the night, you may find yourself pressed into helping your organization's executive director edit a speech or even writing the first draft of your board director's dinner comments.

If you have a major event worthy of press coverage, it is advisable to start working with the media 2 months in advance of when you would like to see a story in print or on the air. This lead time can be crucial to determining whether your organization's story will be prominently featured. For example, some broadcast stations plan out crew schedules weeks in advance. Even if your speaker is well known or your event is newsworthy, a television station may not be able to send personnel to cover your gala fundraising dinner on a Saturday night due to the fact that the crew is covering a sports event across town. In a similar vein, some news organizations require feature materials weeks in advance so they can be logged, screened by management, and put into proper format for publication.

A public relations director will strive to treat members of the media with the utmost respect. If the press is not able to give your event the coverage you believe it deserves, a public relations professional does not take it personally. Print and broadcast newsrooms are very busy places, and even in a small community, more events take place than can be reasonably covered. Perhaps the next event or press release you have will get better placement, but if you damage the relationship, you will not be given the opportunity to find out.

Future Directions

Many nonprofit professionals are excited about the explosive growth of the Internet as a way to communicate to the various publics served by a typical nonprofit. New media also offer a way around the journalists and producers who control access to the audience by allowing charities to communicate directly to their stakeholders without these media intermediaries. The ability to tap into a wider audience and receive audience feedback in real time means new media are changing how charities communicate.

In addition, generational differences are apparent when the users of new media are studied. For example, nonprofits report that younger donors are often more comfortable with technology and expect less formality in communications than their parents' generation. Broadening the pool of people interested in your profit, and therefore potential donors, is a key long-term goal for many nonprofits.

Early nonprofit websites simply took materials used for other purposes, such as printed annual reports, and repurposed them for viewing on a computer screen. Today, a good website has become more important than a brochure, and with standard software packages, a website can be put together without computer coding skills or breaking the budget. Sophisticated nonprofit websites have been created expressly for online fundraising purposes, although such efforts generally require help from outside the organization.

At a minimum, from a publicity standpoint, a nonprofit's website should contain a summary of the organization's mission and services. Ideally, the programmatic part of the website will be supplemented with rich media, such as pictures, audio, and video, to give a browser a fuller sense of what the organization does and how well it accomplishes its mission. In addition, the website should have a detailed "about us" section, including the street address of the nonprofit's main office, phone and fax numbers, and an e-mail directory, which can be used by both the general public and by media professionals. A good website also should contain current information about the nonprofit, such as copies of recent press releases and biographical information about the nonprofit's leadership.

Some charities have found the use of blogging to be an effective communications tool. A *blog*, a contraction for web log, can be thought of as an Internet-based column or diary, which may be read and then commented on by readers worldwide. Unlike a column in a newspaper, blog entries can be quite long and may feature audio, pictures, or video to supplement the writing. There are many different blogging providers, but some nonprofits are using Twitter, a short-form blogging service, to reach supporters with timely information.

Online social networks also have great potential for bringing nonprofits together with their supporters. The best known of these social networking sites, Facebook, is very popular on college campuses. Charities have used Facebook to attract supporters and also spur them to donate to their cause. In addition, Facebook allows individuals with common interests to share music, pictures, and notes freely. Of course, nonprofit public relations professionals who use new media need to be careful to both safeguard their personal privacy and maintain the reputation of their employers when working with new media.

While these newer media sites have the potential to increase the amount of two-way communication between a charity and their various publics, simply choosing these technologies without a clear purpose will likely be a poor investment of time. While the low cost of Internet communication, especially compared to the costs of producing and mailing printed materials, has produced explosive growth, resources must be invested in updating these sources of communication and responding to inquiries received from the public through these sources. Ignoring public comments and leaving stale information up on the web can be more damaging to an organization than being absent from the Internet.

Despite the proliferation of communications vehicles, the key decision of media placements needs to be guided by whichever medium most effectively reaches the right public or audience for that message, whether it is via a traditional media outlet, such as a newspaper story, or through the investment of time creating an organizational presence with social media.

Crisis Communications

The relationship between having in place an existing crisis plan and a nonprofit's ability to weather a crisis intact is hard to overstate. A quick look at the headlines gives some examples of what types of crises can occur. Nonprofits have faced the fallout of having a leader being exposed as a criminal, or even worse, having been the site for an act of violence to occur. External events, such as a natural disaster or an accident, also merit a crisis response. Since such unexpected events have the ability to damage your organization's good name and quickly change the public perception of you and your colleagues, a crisis without an appropriate organizational response can impact significantly the long-run ability to carry out the work of your organization. (See Box 73.3 for communication steps to follow in a crisis situation.)

Box 73.3   Steps in a Crisis Communication Situation

1. Involve key departments and outside organizations as you formulate your crisis plan.

2. Have copies of the detailed crisis plan easily available to team members.

3. Practice how you would handle a crisis situation on a regular basis.

4. Designate people who can declare a crisis is occurring and have the power to bring the crisis team together, even if to an emergency location.

5. Make sure the designated spokesperson has the right information available during the crisis. Outgoing information should come only from him or her.

6. The spokesperson must update regularly the media but avoid speculation. In a crisis, just stick to the facts.

7. After the situation resolves, follow up and thank the press, staff, and previous supporters.

8. When the crisis is over, evaluate what happened. Team members should learn from what has happened and modify the plan for when another crisis situation threatens.

SOURCE: Adapted from Neal (2002) and from Newsom and Haynes (2005).

For example, in 1992, United Way of America was rocked by published reports linking its longtime president to wrongdoing and unfair hiring. Despite over a century of service and billions of dollars in community grants, United Way, including local chapters across the country, became linked to the scandal. The national organization installed new leadership, reduced salaries, and expanded outside oversight in the wake of the media-driven fury. Some local organizations went to journalists in their hometowns to denounce the national organization and emphasize their autonomy. Some longtime supporting individuals and organizations even withdrew from the United Way movement. Today, United Way is a very different organization with reduced national impact due to the crisis ignited by an article in the *Washington Post* (Center & Jackson, 1995).

While all scenarios are not able to be forecast, it is important to have a framework that those involved in the nonprofit will follow. Many organizations have a written and detailed crisis communications plan available to staffers at all times (Seeger, 2006). The presence of a plan means that many difficult questions will have been addressed in advance and that employees involved in the situation will know their role in the response. Another advantage of the advance work needed for a plan is that relationships with individuals from organizations outside the nonprofit, such as local government agencies, will be in place and ready to use in other venues and efforts.

One Voice During a Crisis

During a crisis communications event, it is important that information from within the organization transmitted to external audiences be routed through one spokesperson, even if the same message is expressed through different media. This simple rule allows you to stay *on message*, that is, to provide a consistent and considered message and not have conflicting information from your organization getting out. Given her or his natural authority, often the CEO, or executive director, of the organization or board president does this job in a crisis situation, even if the organization has a full-time communications or public relations director.

Inevitably, no one likes to convey bad news and a crisis, especially one caused by a mistake or a crime, produces a tendency for an organization and its employees to withdraw from the public view. Often, a nonprofit's lawyer, fearful of future lawsuits, will urge that no information be shared outside the organization. Naturally, such advice puts the public relations director at the crosshairs of organizational conflict during an already tense situation.

Some organizations have found that an official decision to send a spokesperson out and deliver a "no comment" response in a crisis leads to more damage since inaccurate and more damaging rumors can spread in the vacuum that comes from the lack of official information. It is better that reporters learn negative or damaging information first from you rather than allowing inaccuracies and speculation to be reported without the benefit of a measured and balanced response that only comes when journalists get the other side of the story. Whether directed to give a minimal response or a fuller explanation, a wise spokesperson expresses genuine concern for those affected by the crisis and remains committed to truth telling, even in the middle of a deep crisis. (See Box 73.4 for examples of crisis scenarios.)

Box 73.4   Media Communications and Crisis Scenarios

Consider each of the following potential crises. What would be your initial crisis communication response? What would you do long-term to repair your organization's public standing?

1. A gunman walks into your office and begins shooting.

2. An employee of your nonprofit is arrested for having an inappropriate sexual relationship that developed due to her employment at your nonprofit.

3. After a severe storm, your office collapses and people are trapped in the rubble.

4. Individuals who have recently visited your facility are now sick, so the health department issues a statewide alert mentioning your organization by name.

5. The treasurer of your organization leaves town and thousands of dollars of your nonprofit's accounts cannot be located.

6. Unannounced, an investigative reporter for a local newspaper photographs your charity's CEO while in a public parking lot and then begins to ask embarrassing questions about charity pay and benefits, drawing from information in the public record.

Summary

A nonprofit organization that has a strong and distinctive public image in its community is more likely to be able to secure the resources it needs to fulfill its mission in the long term. Nurturing the public image of your organization is dependent on relationships with local media professionals, which can be grown only over time and must be based on sincerity, openness, and mutual respect. Refining and updating your organization's media materials, especially those involving new media, should be regularly done, especially since these newer electronic outlets give you the opportunity to speak directly to individuals who may be unfamiliar with your organization but in the years ahead could become major supporters of your nonprofit.

References and Further Readings

Aronson, M., Spetner, D., & Ames, C. (2007). *The public relations writer's handbook: The digital age* (2nd ed.). San Francisco: Jossey-Bass.

Beckwith, S. L. (2006). *Publicity for nonprofits.* Chicago: Kaplan.

Bray, I. (2005). *Effective fundraising for nonprofits: Real-world strategies that work.* Berkeley, CA: Nolo Press.

Center, P., & Jackson, A. H. (1995). *Public relations practices: Managerial case studies and problems* (5th ed.). Englewood Cliffs, NJ: Prentice Hall.

Christian, D., Jacobsen, S., & Minthorn, D. (2009). *The AP stylebook.* New York: Basic Books.

Cutlip, S. M., Center, A. H., & Broom, G. M. (2000). *Effective public relations* (8th ed.). Upper Saddle River, NJ: Prentice Hall.

Feinglass, A. (2005). *The public relations handbook for nonprofits.* San Francisco: Jossey-Bass.

Flanagan, J. (2002). *Successful fundraising* (2nd ed.). New York: McGraw-Hill.

Guth, D. W., & Marsh, C. (2000). *Public relations: A value-driven approach.* Boston: Allyn & Bacon.

Hendrix, J. A., & Hayes, D. C. (2007). *Public relations cases* (7th ed.). Belmont, CA: Wadsworth.

Knessel, D. C. (1982). *Free publicity: A step by step guide.* New York: Sterling.

Kotler, P. (1982). *Marketing for nonprofit organization* (2nd ed.). Englewood Cliffs, NJ: Prentice Hall.

Miller, K. M. (2009). *The first one hundred days of your new non-profit marketing job.* Retrieved June 15, 2009, from http://www.NonprofitMarketingGuide.com/first100days

Neal, K. A. (2002). *A primer on nonprofit PR.* Sarasota, FL: Pineapple Press.

Newsom, D., & Haynes, J. (2005). *Public relations writing* (7th ed.). Belmont, CA: Wadsworth.

Seeger, M. W. (2006). Best practices in crisis communications: An expert panel process. *Journal of Applied Communication Research, 34*(2), 232–244.

Simon, R., & Wylie, F. R. (1994). *Cases in public relations management.* Lincolnwood, IL: NTC Business Books.

Wilcox, D. L., & Cameron, G. T. (2006). *Public relations: Strategies and tactics* (8th ed.). Boston: Pearson.

74

ROLE OF NONPROFIT LEADERS IN EVALUATION AND THE USE OF LOGIC MODELS

LISA WYATT KNOWLTON

Phillips Wyatt Knowlton, Inc.

Results are the new imperative in the nonprofit sector. They are what donors seek, funders demand, and trustees expect. And they are increasingly difficult to achieve as seemingly intractable social problems, complex systems, rapid change, and many players fill the landscape. Whether a public, private, nonprofit, or hybrid—results are the brass ring all organizations need to prove their value. They are the most critical and challenging work of leaders, managers, and their teams. Results reflect the change(s) sought whether an absolute measure, such as a decrease in infant mortality, or an increase in literacy. They are also defined by different attitudes, knowledge, and skills. Most people can name their desired results with specificity. It is a taller challenge to explicitly name reliable routes or strategic roadmaps to achieve them. Identifying the sequence and scope of actions that will achieve results can be overwhelming.

Inevitably, the *results imperative* means generating change and change isn't easy to achieve. The resources and processes these efforts require are often underestimated. And under pressure, busyness can overwhelm the ends an organization seeks. In his most recent text, *A Sense of Urgency*, John Kotter (2008) writes that 70% of change efforts fail. Part of Kotter's response is creating a culture with an action bias. Beyond culture and clear expectations, it is also helpful to identify and use potent tools that support performance. Securing results, often by leading social change, is the principal responsibility of the nonprofit sector.

Sector Growth and Pressure

Better tools and practices to ensure change are even more important as the sector continues to experience unprecedented growth. The Urban Institute based in Washington, D.C., documents this expansion of the nonprofit sector. For the period, of 1995 to 2005, nonprofit revenues grew by 77% and total assets by almost 55%. This contrasts with growth in U.S. gross domestic product of 35%. There are now more than 1.4 million nonprofit organizations in the United States (Blackwood, Wing, & Pollack, 2008) whose efforts contribute to civil society. The work of these charitable organizations ranges from arts to education, health care, and human services. Each aspires to improve some element of our social conditions.

These organizations and their leaders take on valuable and very difficult work. As government revenues shrink, the nonprofit sector is expected to be even more effective. In this context, effectiveness requires real and sustainable results. This challenge falls to leaders.

Author's note: The author acknowledges the contributions of Models 1 to 3, cocreated with Cynthia C. Phillips, PhD. Cynthia's comments on a draft of this content were helpful. Thanks also to Battle Creek Unlimited CEO, Jim Hettinger, for sharing about his successful work. And gratitude to Tim for so many reasons, always.

What Leaders Do

Among practitioners and theorists, a common list of responsibilities of every nonprofit leader includes visioning, planning, communicating, learning, and assessing. Leaders make many important decisions; they secure talent, define direction, and allocate resources. An agile, responsive leader also consistently seeks new information and knowledge to use in organizational and personal performance. At the heart of these responsibilities is the essential need to develop and execute strategies.

Strategies Matter Most

Great strategies are the key lever to securing results. A strategy is generally understood as a selected action (or actions) to achieve a clearly named objective. Strategies are the "do" that nets the "get." Nonprofit leaders need new literacy and tools in strategy development. They also need to be willing, as learning leaders, to use inquiry as they pursue organizational performance. Logic models are an emerging and effective tool to support the critical choices in strategy development.

Logic models can be an important tool that describe strategies, organize the relationships among complex pieces, and provide a shared "action map." Most logic models are developed with the active participation of other stakeholders and therefore require leaders who are inclusive. In the political contexts often present for nonprofit organizations, logic modeling can be used to identify and navigate differing opinions about the best way to achieve desired ends.

Capable leaders use the compelling mission of their organizations to attract talent and financial capital while thoughtfully considering best strategies. Strategies are implemented and adapted with a singular intent of making progress toward results. Like a ship's captain, effective nonprofit leaders aim for a specified destination but recognize that course corrections are inevitable.

Choices and Focus

Effective leaders are willing to make tough choices. They consider evidence along with other objective information and make decisions that deliver results. Leaders with a laser-like focus on achievement value alignment of strategies toward results. They also demonstrate an unwavering discipline that keeps people and their work aimed at explicit outcomes. Because they will take risk and understand the importance of communications, they state intended results both internally and externally.

Consider the example of the Lumina Foundation located in Indianapolis, Indiana, which focuses on postsecondary educational achievement. In its broadly disseminated public communications at its website, the Lumina Foundation states its goal: "To raise the proportion of the U.S. adult population who earn college degrees to 60% by the year 2025, an increase of 16 million graduates above current rates" (www.luminafoundation.org/our_work). Underneath this specific result is the belief that education is critical for individual opportunity, economic vitality, and social stability. Through its explicit declaration, the foundation has publicly cited its intended results and is now organizing its operations to achieve them. The CEO, trustees, and staff have put a stake in the sand about their organizational outcomes. Lumina's public statement (although relatively infrequent among foundations) is *not* unusual for the nonprofit sector. The dilemma they share with more than a million peer organizations in the United States is discovery and implementation of the optimal combination of strategies, activities, and tactics that will ensure they reach named results.

Logic models can be integral tools for managing and leading because they take aim at results and specifically describe options to secure them. Models can provoke better thinking. Moreover, they are flexible aids for design, plans, implementation, and evaluation. Employed across these functions, logic models can also support communication and learning. Because of their practical and proven value in the nonprofit sector (including philanthropy) and government, the use of logic models is on the rise.

What Is a Logic Model?

Logic models might be considered equivalent to a recipe, formula, road map, or blueprint. They describe actions that will best yield a desired change. A logic model is a graphic display of specific elements that represent planned work and intended results. At a given point in time, logic models represent a "snapshot" of shared thinking by a group or team. More important, logic models are complementary to, but slightly different from, a logical framework (or logframe)—often used in Europe.

Logic models display important relationships and connections: between parts and the whole, among strategies and results, about *doing* and *getting*. Logic models are not infallible or perfect. They all have some flaws and can vary considerably in both appearance and quality. But logic models do represent an emerging tool (and technique) that have substantial potential if your organization desires better thinking and improved results.

Logic Model Uses and Benefits

Logic models can return significant value to your work. The most important benefit is their potential to clarify and improve thinking—critical to securing results. Many people and organizations in the nonprofit sector find them highly useful for design, plans, managing, and evaluation.

Logic models can

- help determine optimal scenarios through the exploration of options;
- support decisions about resource allocations;
- improve programs by describing strengths, flaws, and gaps in logic;
- recognize corrections and changes in operations over time;
- promote better understanding, consensus, and teamwork;
- define evaluation focus and priorities; and
- increase communication effectiveness with multiple audiences.

In communications alone, logic models have particular utility. During their creation, naturally, a substantial volume of ideas can be exchanged and learning of all kinds can occur in this process. A logic model can offer an efficient way to explain a comprehensive view or a bounded picture of a selected piece in a bigger system. As a "picture," a logic model represents far more than the old saying about "a thousand words." Modeling, which is simply the generation of multiple iterations or versions, has important process benefits included in the list above. The shared efforts of building and then revising models offer a way to include individual contributions and discover promising combinations that result because of the interactions among multiple participants. When capably facilitated, modeling can identify both shared and distinct norms, experiences, training, and knowledge.

Types: Theory of Change and Program

In *The Logic Model Guidebook* (Wyatt Knowlton & Phillips, 2009), Cynthia Phillips and I define two types of models: theory of change and program. Obviously, theories of change and program can be expressed in many ways, but we parse model types in a dichotomy even though their functions and subject matter contents reflect a huge range. Logic models are the architecture or format for particular content.

A theory of change explicates why something might work (a hypothesis). Or it reflects something that does work (a prescription from evidence). A theory of change logic model describes what you will do and your intended results. It provides a high level narration about selected strategies that once deployed will subsequently generate a specified outcome. In Figure 74.1, the two basic elements of a theory of change model are shown.

Program logic models expand the detail of doing and getting. Typically, they include several more elements: resources, activities, outputs, outcomes (short, intermediate-, and long-term) as well as impact. The resources, activities, and outputs comprise the doing. The timed outcomes and impact reflect getting (or results). A program logic model can describe something as simple as a single event, like a parenting seminar, or as complex as a decade-long,

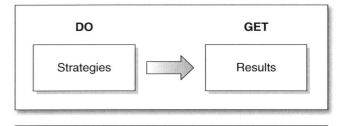

Figure 74.1 Theory of Change Logic Model Elements

SOURCE: Wyatt Knowlton and Phillips, 2009.

multiplayer conservation movement. In philanthropy, an initiative often refers to a portfolio that includes multiple programs, a collaboration of organizations, or a consortium. Figure 74.2 shows the five basic elements of a program logic model. While there is some variation in how these elements are defined and used, the following lexicon reflects common practice.

Resources are the essential inputs to ensure program or organization activities can happen. They are often human, financial, and organizational references. Without these, a program or change effort isn't possible. Sometimes inputs, assets, or capital are used as synonyms for resources. Resources are what any effort needs to begin change work and their continued viability can be an important factor in sustainability.

Activities are specific processes, events, and interventions chosen to compose the program (or initiative). Activities anchor the specific work that will secure changes or results. The choice of activities is absolutely critical in the determination of chances for success. At a "high level," these reflect strategies. Depending on the level of detail, activities can actually range from general actions and processes to tactics.

Outputs generally describe what preceding activities produce. They quantify and qualify what occurs as a result of the designed program (or initiative). In essence, outputs are the yield or production. Outputs help define process indicators for evaluation. They can be used, in part, to determine and inform progress about activities.

Outcomes depend on the combination of the assembly and implementation of resources, activities, and outputs. They also reflect the influence of assumptions and environmental factors (whether named or not). The time spans for short, intermediate, and long-term outcomes are situational and self-defined. These intervals depend largely on context as well as the size and scope of the change effort in play. It is important to be realistic about the relationship between the resources, activities, and likely outcomes.

Impact is synonymous with vision and result. Results are the *end-change* expected from the program or initiative. The results are about the difference that was made. They are most often about people, organizations, and society, for example, less sexism, more enterprise, a dam built, malaria eliminated, or a war ends.

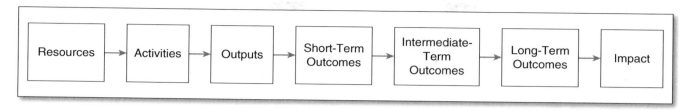

Figure 74.2   Program Logic Model Elements
SOURCE: Wyatt Knowlton and Phillips, 2009.

Explicit Barriers, Facilitators, Assumptions

In addition to the elements here, sometimes program logic models also name the shared assumptions of those creating the model along with environmental barriers and facilitators. For example, if the program logic model is focused on school improvement, then federal legislation like the No Child Left Behind (NCLB) Act of 2001 (Public Law 107-110) might be named as a facilitator because it is an important external factor that influences schools. Similarly, reduced state revenues could be cited as a barrier. A list of assumptions might include statements such as, "We believe all children have the potential to exceed our expectations," and "teaching quality is a weighted factor in student learning." These supplemental elements can help those using the model to better understand context and the lens stakeholders used in the model creation.

How Types Differ

Differentiating between theory of change and program models can be helpful in understanding what each can require as well as their best use. Theory of change models don't reference time, they are independent of it as a simple statement of action relative to result. In this sense, they are "generic." They don't, generally, have much detail and include just a few or short listings of strategies. In contrast, time is important in program logic models—especially since the outcomes are named against a time sequence. The relative level of detail in a program logic model is also greater than a theory of change model. Program logic models include many more elements, specify target audiences, and use a vast array of graphic design options. When considered relative to a theory of change, resources, activities, and outputs are parallel to doing, or strategies. The time-referenced outcomes and impact are the details that constitute getting, or results.

Regardless of which is tackled first, creating both a theory of change and program logic model ensure valuable explication of your work. The model product and its associated processes have important benefits. Both types are best constructed by starting with the end in mind: intended results.

Building Logic Models

The Power of Display

Most people (although not all) are visual learners. It is generally very effective to link concepts, ideas, data, and other information with images. Displaying information in a model can enhance both thinking and learning. Studies (Institute for the Advancement of Research in Education, 2003) have specifically found visual display can support critical thinking, retention, comprehension, and organization. Further, individual and team learning occurs when new information is shared and there is reflection on changes relative to earlier attempts.

Logic models can be powerful when used to communicate because their display often relies primarily on limited text and graphic elements (boxes, arrows, etc.) in contrast to lengthy narrative. However, it is important that models have the benefit of verbal support or presentation because their interpretation is the key to shared understanding.

Engagement and Construction

There can be tremendous value in working with a team or task force in the creation of a logic model and its iterations. The experience of shared construction adds content value to the model. It also promotes healthy group dynamics through an approach that explores varied viewpoints and builds on each other's perspective, experience, and training.

It is best to start with a theory of change model because it is easier to create and requires less detail (see Figure 74.1). To begin, dialogue should focus on inquiry, exploration, and discussion about intended results . . . until shared understanding and agreement is reached. Next, evidence-based strategies, which might achieve results, are listed. These two steps can generate a draft theory of change.

Building a program logic model can be done in many ways, but the sequence of steps my business partner and I have used with success are shown in Figure 74.3.

We begin with the intended impact of the organization or program efforts. The impact describes the vision or "big" end-change sought (Step 1). Once this is named, it is important to consider the outcomes possible to achieve over time (Step 2). Citing the results anchors the intention

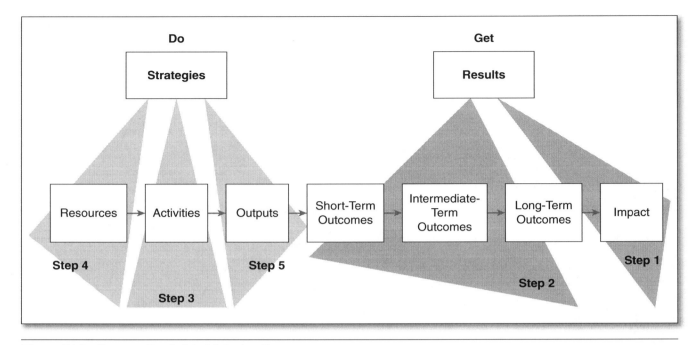

Figure 74.3 Program Logic Model Action Steps

SOURCE: Wyatt Knowlton and Phillips, 2009.

of the work and provides a target of what you hope to achieve. Logically, activities are named next (Step 3) as they are the choice of action(s) you think is necessary to get to the specified results. Once actions are identified, it is possible to describe what inputs or resources (Step 4) are essential to the preceding actions named. Finally, outputs (Step 5) are cited last as they provide a quantitative and qualitative accomplishment of activities.

Models can become more complex and more useful with additional levels of detail. It's important to be aware that most programs and organizations have multiple strategies and multiple outcomes, even if aimed at a single impact. Recall that some program logic models include "extra" elements such as assumptions and external barriers and facilitators. Simply naming these extra elements during the creation process can be helpful since they may generate implications that should be addressed in some adjustment of the model.

A Draft Model

A simple theory of change model for an organization like the Global Food Program might look like Figure 74.4, which has four big strategies to secure its impact of "reduce global hunger."

The program logic model could specify short-, intermediate-, and long-term outcomes, such as new awareness of nutrition, an established food distribution system in Central America, and sustainable agriculture in a region of Africa. And the big four strategies get parsed into activities, resources, and outputs for each one named. Implementation of a food use campaign might be an example of an activity

under the strategy of nutrition education. Resources (for any strategy) might include food donors, staff, facilities, technology, and supportive public policy. And outputs could be the volume of food delivered or seed planted.

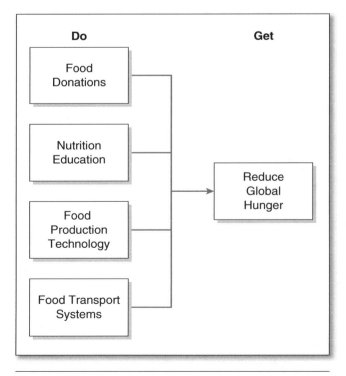

Figure 74.4 Hypothetical Theory of Change for Global Food Program

Quality: Better Models for Better Strategies

Creating a first draft model gets things started, but subsequent critique and revision are important, too. Modeling, which means iterative alternate versions, is essential to model quality. Moving from narrative to display is an inadequate standard. Choices integral to the model content should reflect improvement from one version to the next. This builds credibility for the selected strategies and the whole "scheme" by displaying relationships between elements and their contribution to results.

Challenge of Time

Logic models are never "perfect" for at least two reasons. First, any model or written narrative that represents ideas, concepts, or plans is subject to the passage of time. Over time, conditions as well as knowledge change. Although some facts endure, the dynamic of time ensures that new experiences generate new understanding. What works under current conditions may not work under new ones.

Time and related change are simply and best addressed by employing knowledge. Research, theory, and practice (components of knowledge) are important considerations in determining the quality of logic models. One that relies on evidence has greater chances of success than one without. Most logic models are projections of expected events, planned so their yield (results) are an incremental improvement over past efforts.

Using Knowledge

For example, let's consider this assignment: Create a program logic model for improved Lake Michigan water quality. If we use knowledge, we should be able to build a water quality program model that is *at least* as effective as current practice. We may even be able to generate a model that is more efficient or effective if we are willing to try new, untested innovations. It is highly sensible to rely on retrospective proofs to construct the best possible prospective program plan. In practice, this means I might look at water conservation literature and review recent studies about effective (and failed) water quality programs that mirror a similar context. It might also be important to consider relevant environmental research along with emerging theories about water quality. Through these steps, there is intentional discovery and use of current knowledge, as well as consideration of new approaches.

Finally, it could be a good idea to name what participants believe about what influences water quality, as those perspectives may also color the possibilities of our planned work. The aim, in concept, is to build the best possible program model with what is known (through tested, prior efforts). Sometimes logic models are built to test hypotheses. In these situations, current knowledge may not be available or relevant. These logic models can generate new options through incorporating activities in new combinations and trying ones previously discarded or overlooked.

People and Context Challenges

The second reason models aren't perfect is rooted in their origin. Because individuals and groups create models, they often include the unintended features of their authors. Inevitably, models map our thinking—including our biases, perceptions, assumptions and the social context of any given work group. People and their organizations certainly affect the logic models they build together. Blind spots, myths, "leaps of faith," and vagueness can plague both people and the models they create. Sometimes, errors in models are an unintended mistake. Other times, conscious attempts to use the model to accommodate politics promote a false perception, or intentional persuasion influences elements or relationships among model elements.

Questions for Rigor

Many workplaces welcome questions—some don't. The frequency and depth of inquiry can be an indicator of an organization's learning culture. Leaders who understand and expect accountability welcome questions. They often use inquiry and consider it a way to learn. Rigorous questions can be very helpful in critical thinking that develops better strategies displayed by models. In practice, most experienced management consultants use questions as a way for clients to consider and reconsider their own choices. It may be helpful to remind your colleagues that the questions are about the work, not about them.

In much of the consulting my partner and I do, we actually suggest a *mark-up* process for logic models that mirrors the work done in creating legislation. In this process, inquiry and critique is applied, literally, to the draft logic model in a dialogic exchange. Systematically, you can review a logic model by asking, first, Are the results named clear, plausible, or feasible? Then, ask some questions about outcomes and their relationship to strategies and activities. For example, do the outcomes make sense for the time, resources, and strategies named? Are there other strategies that might be a better combination? Do we have the right staff to implement these strategies? Is there too much or too little in the model for our organization to accomplish? What assumptions does this model suggest we share?

The ultimate judges of logic model quality are those who use them. This question is a reasonable litmus: Did the model do the job it was built to accomplish? From experience, in most circumstances, the work will be far better planned and more likely to achieve success because of the explication, critical thinking, and questions provoked via modeling. There are no substitutes for proven practices, literature, and existing knowledge in the creation of logic models. The best models use these as foundations, then build on this content by engaging diverse experiences, perspectives, opinions, and training of participants.

Logic Models in the Field

Renowned nonprofit, nongovernmental organizations, and U.S. federal agencies use logic models in a range of subject matters and multiple purposes. A small sampling of organizations includes the following:

• The Centers for Disease Control (CDC) uses logic models in most of its program areas and initiatives. For example, its Workforce Health Promotion as well as Heart Disease and Stroke Prevention programs encourage the use of logic models for state-level partners to describe their initiatives. These models later anchor evaluation design and implementation. For each health challenge, the CDC provides a template to jump-start model creation while recognizing each program model is considered unique and that it is distinguished by virtue of the particular culture, conditions, and context it represents.

• The World Bank offers its employees professional development (or continuing education) in monitoring and evaluation. These courses, held in Vienna, Austria, draw professionals from across the globe. The curriculum addresses fundamental concepts and methods of monitoring and evaluation with logic models as a central tool. Government representatives, project teams, nongovernmental organizations, and World Bank staff use models as a way to describe and integrate relationships among performance management, monitoring, and program evaluation. The World Bank employs logic models in a vast range of subjects. One research committee, a few years ago, even used logic models for determining efficiencies in coral reef management and protection.

• United Way of America affiliates use logic models as a standard format for program funding requests and evaluation. United Way organizations from Atlanta, Georgia, to Manchester, New Hampshire, to Portland, Oregon, and in Canada expect nonprofit organization staff to understand and use logic models for the design, planning, improvement, and evaluation of their local program efforts. In 1996, the United Way of America produced and broadly distributed one of the first manuals citing the utility of logic models for evaluation design.

• The David and Lucille Packard Foundation uses logic models inside and outside the organization as a standard practice. Packard staff members use them internally to share draft maps of program designs they think may work and to manage and to evaluate their efforts. They require grantees seeking funds to submit their proposals with a logic model as a key element. Gale Berkowitz, PhD,

director of evaluation, indicates that the "theory of change and logic model(s) are essential components of good programmatic strategy development and management necessary to help us achieve greater impact in our work" (Wyatt Knowlton & Phillips, 2009, p. 99). This foundation is a pioneer in their use of logic models for strategic planning, communication, monitoring, and evaluation.

• The Office of Juvenile Justice and Delinquency Prevention (OJJDP) is a funder for many community and regional nonprofit organizations that provide direct service. In its block grant program, Juvenile Accountability Block Grants (JABG), models describe program design but are also essential to determining measures of progress. Figure 74.5 displays the JABG model. Read from left to right, this display begins with problem and subproblem columns. It provides placeholders for activities that focus on the improvement of systems and programs as well as measures that indicate progress toward results for juvenile delinquency.

Since logic models reflect our mental maps for change, sometimes they appear in public policy discussions and even best-selling books. Thomas Friedman (2008), the highly regarded Pulitzer Prize winner and foreign affairs columnist for the *New York Times,* provides us with a terrific example of a theory of change in his popular book, *Hot, Flat and Crowded.* In a letter equation, Friedman wrote, "REEFIGDCPEERPC<TTCOBCOG." Decoded, he defines a prescription for "a renewable energy system for innovating, generating, and deploying clean power, energy efficiency, resources productivity and conservation is less than the true cost of burning coal, oil and gas" (p. 198). Friedman writes eloquently about U.S. energy challenges, and then, he provides convincing evidence-based remedies. He suggests strategies that can replace the current "Dirty Fuels System" with a "Clean Energy System."

A Logic Model Application in Economic Development

One highly regarded economic development corporation recently used logic models as the centerpiece for self-study. Ultimately, the models and the study provided proof about strategy choices and organizational merit. At the start, the organization's capable chief executive officer wanted to explore what might be appropriate elements of an evaluation system and get a quick look at selected aspects of return on investment. Logic models were generated and used to describe strategies and results. Through the study process, the strategies relied on for several decades were "tested" for value.

Economic development, like other social change is difficult and complicated work. The volume, dynamics, and complexity of variables at play in the attraction and retention of enterprise are immense. Experts agree that even when economic development organizations do all the right

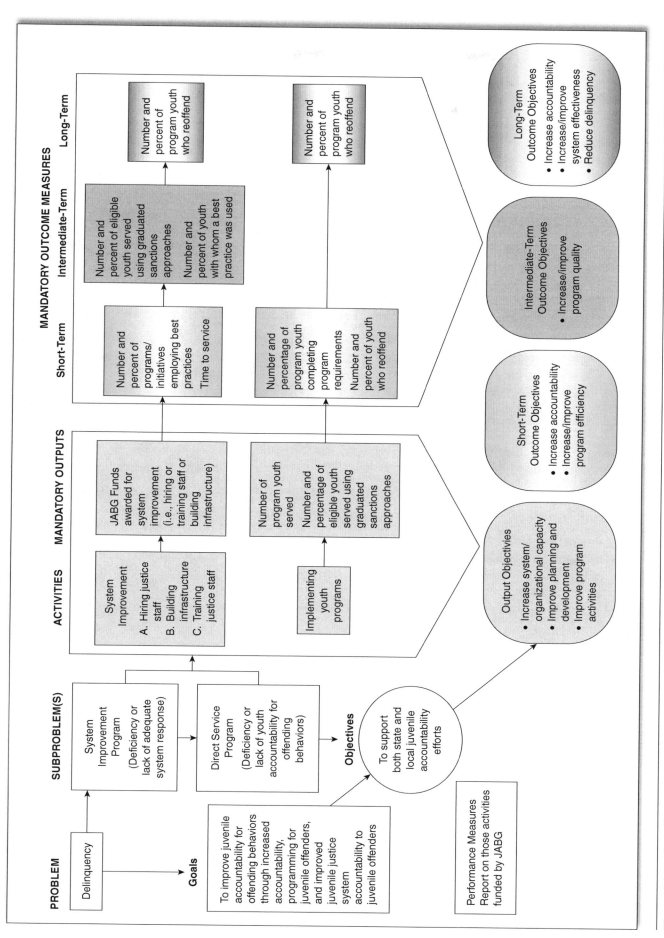

Figure 74.5 Juvenile Accountability Block Grant Logic Model Template

SOURCE: U.S. Office of Juvenile Justice and Delinquency Prevention, 1997.

things well, they may not secure a new or expanded enterprise. However, doing the right things well is requisite to any prospects for success. While the tangibles of roads and sewers and taxes and labor qualifications are obvious, the more subtle challenge of this economic development effort is growing an appetite for how the local community appears to market prospects.

In this application, the local economic development focus is to develop and promote community assets. This reflects its theory of change. While the economic development corporation is a leading and primary agent in this work, it is not alone in what contributes to prospects' perceptions of area assets or limitations. The implicit and explicit interdependencies that establish a "system" are important lenses to view this organization. This *systems view* requires the organization to attend to assets it influences, directly and indirectly. The work controlled most directly by this organization is primarily asset promotion, with some work in asset development. Its "indirect" work is mostly associated with community quality of life (such as improving health care, education, culture). However, these circumstances clearly describe why economic development "progress" means this economic development corporation is also highly dependent on partnerships with other non- and for-profit entities.

The "theory of change" (Figure 74.6) model indicates the focus is to develop and promote community assets. In turn, this development and promotion will yield increases in enterprises (and associated benefits, e.g., growth in wealth). This model indicates the development and promotion work of this economic development organization relies on some preceding conditions, which reflect work inside the community and with partner organizations. Externally, it aims for attraction, creation, expansion, and retention as outcomes. The program logic model (see Figure 74.7) reads left to right. Primary to asset development, this organization's activities include the development of "hard" infrastructure (e.g., roads, airport, facilities, telecommunications) and "competencies" (e.g., e-learning options, workforce development, global connections, and acting as a catalyst for quality of life in the community). Generating local incentives and marketing are essential strategies to asset promotion.

Nearly all of the work in asset promotion is directly influenced by staff while work in asset development has greater dependencies and interaction with other resources. Note that "partnerships" are very prominent and precede these activities as an important input. In fact, they are the intended work strategies as a key platform for all the other strategies named. It is also worth emphasizing that attraction and retention is largely dependent on asset promotion tactics: incentives, responses, and relationships. Asset development involves mostly infrastructure and workforce issues.

These models provided a common platform for inquiry, data collection, and analysis. Evaluation findings were described relative to job growth, taxes, and space utilization. From these data, a reliable construct for return on investment was generated. And using an industry standard multiplier, it was possible to suggest this organization's significant positive effect on area employment rates, family income, schools, local enterprise, and city taxes. The CEO used the models to document both Battle Creek Unlimited's valuable contributions and as a blueprint for future work.

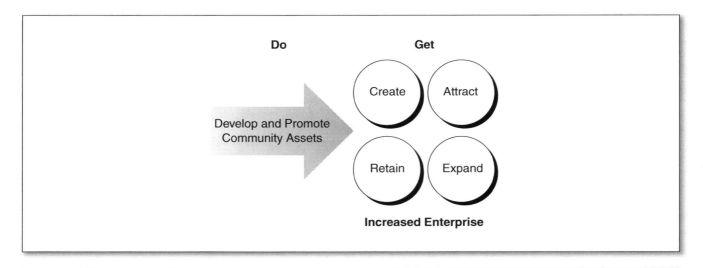

Figure 74.6 Battle Creek Unlimited Theory of Change

SOURCE: Phillips Wyatt Knowlton, 2008. Created by Phillips Wyatt Knowlton, Inc., for the Battle Creek Unlimited program.

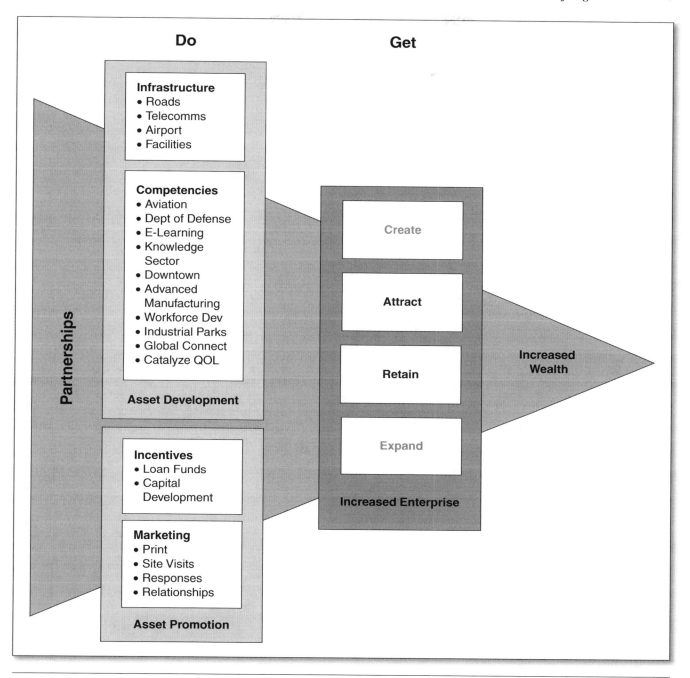

Figure 74.7   Battle Creek Unlimited Program Logic Model

SOURCE: Phillips Wyatt Knowlton, 2008. Created by Phillips Wyatt Knowlton, Inc., for the Battle Creek Unlimited program.

Summary: Logic Models for Leaders

Leaders, through the people and organizations they serve, are invariably expected to deliver results. This requires a panoply of knowledge, skills, and tools. Over the past decade, the United Way of America and the W. K. Kellogg Foundation have helped popularize logic models for evaluation through widely distributed publications. Logic models are now beginning to be recognized as important tools in securing results because they support strategy development.

Current nonprofit practice in choosing strategy often relies on a single individual who prepares a written document, then wide-ranging discussions are held and some direction chosen. When logic models are used, evidence-based versions of the intended work (strategies) and related results are displayed and tested for an optimal combination. External conditions and assumptions are also named. In this way, logic models offer a view of an explicated and cogent whole that can be adjusted based on the experience, training, and knowledge of participants. Field knowledge in the relative subject matter is also a resource. Because most people are visual learners, the graphic display of a logic model avoids the interpretative challenges of lengthy narrative and can be a real-time aid for discovery and learning. The process of modeling engages stakeholders. It has its own yield as diverse opinions and experiences are honored while facilitation forces a review of the best choices designed to secure shared and explicitly named results.

Logic models don't fix a workplace wrought with role confusion, inexperienced staff, loads of politics, or poor implementation. They are not a turnkey remedy for inadequate structure or culture. But they are a potent tool that can focus priorities and communicate complex change. They also assist with alignment and synergy. Most importantly, logic models can help leaders organize and improve choices about the "right work" to achieve results we all need.

References and Further Readings

Blackwood, A., Wing, K., & Pollak, T. (2008). *The nonprofit sector in brief: Facts and figures from the nonprofit almanac 2008: Public charities, giving and volunteering.* Retrieved December 12, 2008, from http://nccsdataweb .urban.org/kbfiles/797/Almanac2008publicCharities.pdf

Buzan, T. (2002). *How to mind map: The thinking tool that will change your life.* New York: Thorsons/HarperCollins.

Chen, H. (2005). *Practical program evaluation: Assessing and improving planning, implementation and effectiveness.* Thousand Oaks, CA: Sage.

Craig, M. (2003). *Thinking visually.* New York: Continuum.

Eriksen, M. (2008, August). *The logic model: A tool to design, implement and evaluate programs.* Retrieved December 18, 2008, from http:www.krevi.dk

Frechtling, J. A. (2007). *Logic modeling methods in program evaluation.* New York: Jossey-Bass.

Friedman, T. (2008). *Hot, flat and crowded.* New York: Farrar, Straus & Giroux.

Hamilton, J., & Bronte-Tinkew, J. (2007). *Logic models in out-of-school time programs: What are they and why are they important.* Available from http:www.childtrends.org

Harrel, A. (1996). Developing a logic model. In *Evaluation strategies for human services programs.* Washington, DC: Urban Institute. Available from http://www.ojp.usdoj.gov/ BJA/evaluation/guide/documents/evaluation_strategies.p3–7 .html

Innovation Network. (2005). *Logic model workbook.* Available from http.//www.innonet.org

Institute for the Advancement of Research in Education. (2003). *Graphic organizers: A review of scientifically based research.* Available from http://www.mirandanet.ac.uk/ vl_blog/?page_id=48

Kane, M., & Trochim, W. (2006). *Concept mapping for planning and evaluation.* Thousand Oaks, CA: Sage.

Kotter, J. (2008). *A sense of urgency.* Boston: Harvard Business Press.

Lohr, L. L. (2003). *Creating graphics for learning and performance: Lessons in visual literacy.* Upper Saddle River, NJ: Pearson Education.

Lumina Foundation. (n.d.). *Lumina strategic plan.* Available from http://www.luminafoundation.org/goal 2025/Lumina Strategic Plan.pdf

Margulies, N. (2005). *Visual thinking: Tools for mapping your ideas.* Williston, VT: Crown House.

McCawley, P. F. (2006). *The logic model for program planning and evaluation.* University of Idaho Extension. Available from http://www.uidaho.edu.extension/LogicModel.pdf

Milstein, B., & Chapel, T. (2007). *Developing a logic model or theory of change.* The Community Toolbox, University of Kansas. Available from http://ctb.ku.edu/tools/en/sub_ section_main_1877.htm

Penna, R., & Phillips, W. (2004). *Outcome frameworks: An overview for practitioners* (1st ed.). Rensselaerville, NY: Rensselaerville Institute.

Renger, R., & Titcomb, A. (2002). A three-step approach to teaching logic models. *American Journal of Evaluation, 23*(4), 493–503.

Rush Project, The. (n.d.). *Learn about utilization logic models.* Available from http://www.researchutilization.org/ logicmodel/learn.html

Taylor-Powell, E., & Henert, E. (2008). *Developing a logic model: Teaching and training guide.* University of Wisconsin Extension. Available from http://www.uwex.edu/ces/pdande

United Way of America. (1996). *Measuring program outcomes: A practical approach.* Available from http://www.live united.org/Outcomes/Resources/MPO/model.cfm

U.S. Office of Juvenile Justice and Delinquency Prevention. (1997). Retrieved October 25, 2007, from http://ojjdp.ncjrs .gov/grantees/pm/logic models.html

W. K. Kellogg Foundation. (2001). *Logic model development guide.* Available from www.wkkf.org/Pubs/Tools/Evaluation/ Pub 3669.pdf

Wyatt Knowlton, L., & Phillips, C. (2009). *The logic model guidebook: Better strategies for great results.* Thousand Oaks, CA: Sage.

75

ROLE OF THE NONPROFIT LEADER IN MANAGING RISK

PAUL CAVANAGH

Seton Hall University

This chapter of the handbook will examine the role of the nonprofit manager in managing risk. Risk management is a traditional function of business management in general. The chapter will first examine the traditional view of risk management in business and then compare that business view with the unique concerns of managing a nonprofit organization. In particular, the chapter will focus on the unique aspects of controlling risk as related to the individuals who receive services from a nonprofit organization. Also, the chapter will focus on the more prominent functions of anticipating risk and risk reduction in the management of nonprofit organizations as compared with a simple insurance model. Finally, we will present an outline for the process of developing a risk management plan.

To consider the nonprofit manager's role in managing risk, we need to examine the traditional business concept of *risk*. The *Merriam Webster Online Dictionary* defines risk as the "possibility of loss or injury." This first definition is supplemented by the insurance related definition: "the chance of loss or the perils to the subject matter of an insurance contract; *also*: the degree of probability of such loss" (http://www.merriam-webster.com/dictionary/risk). This second part of the definition represents the classic, for-profit business concept of risk management: to anticipate and control for the loss of assets of the company. In this business mind-set, the major activities for a manager involve evaluating the cost and probability of loss and using this information to estimate the appropriate level of insurance to protect against such loss. In a traditional business model, loss is a cost of doing business and a company needs to determine what types of loss can be met with normal operating expenses and what types of loss

require an insurance policy (and thus the ongoing cost of an insurance premium).

For example, for a company that manufactures pens, the cost of routine maintenance and repairs of its machinery is considered an inherent cost of business. The company would likely pay for these costs as part of its normal operating expenses. However, a critical failure of its overall assembly line would likely engender a very large expense. Many corporations would consider carrying an insurance policy to protect against such an occurrence. The insurance company will charge a premium based on the expected likelihood of such a fatal failure of the equipment. The cost of the insurance premium is then calculated into the cost of doing business.

Overview of Risk Management in a Nonprofit Organization

In a nonprofit organization, the management of risk entails a wider range of responsibilities. Surely, a nonprofit leader has a fiduciary responsibility to manage and maintain the tangible assets of the organization. But for a nonprofit leader, the responsibility for managing risk neither begins nor ends with the financial resources of the organization. A nonprofit organization, by definition, exists because it is serving some type of public interest. In a majority of instances (61.2%), a nonprofit organization is a public charity providing goods or services that support a chartable mission (National Center for Charitable Statistics, n.d., "Number of Nonprofit Organizations"). "The mission of a nonprofit—the organization's sole reason for existing—is reason enough to devote time and resources to identifying events and circumstances that could make the realization of the mission impossible" (Herman, Head, Jackson, & Fogarty, 2004, p. 33).

At a minimum, the leadership of a nonprofit organization has the responsibilities to anticipate and manage the risks in four broad areas: the lives and safety of the individuals served by the organization, the staff and volunteers that provide the service, the tangible assets of the organization and the intangible assets of reputation, and the integrity of the nonprofit organization. While some of the risks inherent in these four categories are interrelated, we will address each area in turn.

Protecting Those We Serve

A nonprofit organization has a unique responsibility to ensure that neither its collective actions nor inactions causes harm to those who seek the goods or services it provides. The best protection against risk for those who receive services is a well-run nonprofit organization. Such an organization has a clear mission, well-defined goals and objectives, focused policies and procedures, and a competent staff that has been appropriately screened and is effectively trained.

The Role of Good Management

The biggest aspect of risk management in all instances is prevention—anticipating potential risks and developing procedures, policies, and systems to significantly reduce the likelihood that the anticipated risk occurs. In any business, and most especially in a nonprofit organization, the most powerful preventive measure is a well-run organization. *The Handbook of Human Services Management* (Patti, 2008) gives an excellent overview of the best practices approach to nonprofit management. A well-run organization has a clear mission that informs all the stakeholders why the organization exists and what segment or segments of the population are the intended targets for its goods and services. A well-run organization uses some form of formal planning to translate the mission into an annual or multiyear plan with measurable goals and objectives. In turn, the organization has some manner of policy and procedures that inform staff of the regular daily, weekly, and monthly activities that move the organization toward the goals and objectives that will realize the mission.

In a nonprofit organization that takes a proactive approach to managing risk, the annual planning process will include a consideration of how to minimize risk for those who receive the services of the organization. A best practices approach to this is to have a risk assessment committee that is integrated into the planning process. The functions of such a committee are discussed further below. The best planning process may eliminate some risks, but in many instances, the most realistic outcome is a reduction of the likelihood of risk.

Essential in a best practices approach to the ongoing management of risk is a well-designed management information system. This does not necessarily mean the technology that might facilitate the process but the information that is gathered, whether it is via pen and pencil reports or the most sophisticated digital technology. A nonprofit organization has to have a means of observing and measuring whether expected policies and procedures are followed. Then, the information gathered needs to be available to mid- and upper-level management in a timely manner. Perhaps one of the most important components of ongoing risk management is good knowledge about what is and what is not happening as the staff of a nonprofit organization interacts with the individuals and families it serves.

Additionally, a well-managed nonprofit organization needs to cultivate an organizational culture that eliminates the fear of reporting "unpleasant" information. A complicating factor in managing risk is when a nonprofit leader does not learn about a minor incident for which there is an obvious resolution only to have the situation grow to become a major problem. An example might be a caseworker who inadvertently sends a report detailing an individual treatment plan to the wrong person, one who is not the subject of the treatment plan. By doing so, the caseworker has violated laws and policies concerning confidentiality of client information. If this is discovered quickly and reported to supervisors, then remedial actions can be taken. This will allow that any damage to the individual client and any exposure of liability to the agency can be minimized. However, if the caseworker is inclined to hide the mistake, then the potential of the confidential report being shared with a greater number of people rises, and the potential liability and consequences for the agency increase as well.

Staff as an Area of Risk

The actions or inactions of staff members are a concern for any business and especially for any business that provides services to the general public. Nonprofits in particular are oftentimes serving individuals in need. This potential vulnerability raises the issue of risk management efforts concerning clients from a secondary concern in many for-profit businesses to a primary concern in a nonprofit organization. There are three primary areas involved in controlling the risks involved in staff interacting with clients: good hiring practices, including legal screening of applicants; a well-designed organization with adequate resources; and ongoing supervision and evaluation of staff.

Human Resources Management as a Function of Risk Management

A nonprofit manager's main concerns about staff are twofold: that unscrupulous staffers will act in a manner that is damaging to clients, or that those staff members who are unqualified, undertrained, not trained, or overwhelmed may inadvertently act in a manner that is damaging to clients. In either instance, this might involve physical or sexual abuse, intimidation, neglect (in situations of supervision or direct care), violations of confidentially, or theft. The linchpin of risk management as it concerns staff of the agency is good hiring practices. This involves using a best practices approach to human resources planning and implementation. The Pynes (2009) text on *Human Resources Management for Public and Nonprofit Organizations* gives an excellent detailed discussion of this area. In addition, nonprofit leaders should ensure that they have the advice and direction of a human resource professional and/or legal counsel in developing human resource policies.

Of primary concern in hiring staff is an adequate screening process. At a minimum, this involves a well-designed and thorough application form, which requires applicants to provide background information and references. An essential practice in hiring staff is to check the references supplied by the applicant, a step that is too often neglected by nonprofit organizations. While in most instances it is a perfunctory exercise, it is the rare instance when the references do not check out that could save the organization an immeasurable amount of grief.

In an ideal situation, the nonprofit organization will conduct a criminal background check of any staff member who will have contact with clients, and if possible, of all staffers hired by the agency. In many jurisdictions, there are laws or regulations that specify that any staff members that have contact with children or other vulnerable populations (e.g., individuals with developmental disabilities, individuals who are homeless) must have a criminal background check. Currently, there are numerous services available to conduct background checks so that even small nonprofit agencies can afford the process. Whatever screening process will be used should be clearly identified in the material advertising the position. Advertising the screening process serves two functions. It reduces complications of applicants objecting to the process, and it allows applicants who do not want to face this scrutiny to self-screen before ever applying for a position.

Also essential in hiring staff is the obligation of any employer to be fair and nondiscriminatory in their hiring practices. There are a variety of federal laws that prohibit discrimination in hiring and employment practices. An essential resource for information about these regulations is the Federal Equal Employment Opportunity Commission (see http://www.eeoc.gov). In addition, there are many states in which the state laws are more comprehensive than the federal laws concerning nondiscrimination in hiring and employment. A thorough discourse on all the mandates of maintaining a discrimination-free workplace is beyond the scope of this article. However, we can identify two essential characteristics of a discrimination-free workplace: good staff training and well-written and objective job descriptions. As we stress throughout this article, good staff training is a first line of defense in all aspects of risk management. Concerning fair labor practices, it is crucial that all employees who are involved in hiring,

firing, employee evaluation, or discipline are trained in the appropriate and legal approaches to these responsibilities. Related to this is that when hiring, promoting, or evaluating staff, decisions are made in relation to objective criteria grounded in well-written job descriptions. The Hauge and Herman (2006) text on nonprofit employment practices is an excellent resource for further information about this area.

Almost as important as the screening process in hiring is the development of clear and focused job descriptions that identify the primary responsibilities of the job in question and the qualifications of the applicant. Screening staff helps us to limit the likelihood of hiring unscrupulous staff, but another significant concern is staff that is not prepared for the tasks of the job at hand. A best practices approach to human resources management is using a job analysis approach to determine the qualifications for a position. It is then incumbent on the agency to use due diligence to hire individuals with the appropriate qualifications. A corresponding practice is to have a thorough training process for staff to cover the knowledge, skills, abilities, and other characteristics (abbreviated as KSAO) that agencies might not be able to require applicants to have before being hired. For example, an agency serving individuals with a developmental disability may use an applied behavioral analysis (ABA) approach to its treatment planning. Professional staff may be expected to have knowledge and experience with ABA before being hired. However, it is unlikely that this could be a requirement of all entry level staff. In such an instance, the agency needs to have a comprehensive training program to prepare new, nonprofessional hires to support such a treatment approach.

Staff Training

General training and orientation for all employees is an indispensable component of managing the risks that might be related to staff behavior. Such an orientation program needs to identify the particular areas of vulnerability for the population of individuals the agency serves. Additionally, the training needs to specifically identify the types of behaviors that are and are not acceptable in interacting with the clients of the agency. It is also important to communicate this same information to those who receive services from the agency. This is usually done either via client orientation programs or via some type of a printed "client's rights and responsibilities" form. Either way, the key is that those who receive services from the agency are informed about what is and what is not expected in terms of staff behavior. And they are given clear instructions on how and to whom they should report any suspected or direct violations of the behavioral standards.

Risks From "Others Who Receive Services"

Whether already part of a vulnerable population (e.g., children, individuals with a disability) or simply because they are in need of goods or services provided by the nonprofit organization, those seeking services are in a vulnerable state. An area of risk for those seeking services is abuses they may face from other clients engaged with the organization. Plainly, there is a limit to how much an agency can be responsible for concerning the behavior of its clients. However, there are two issues that require the attention of any nonprofit manager: any intimidation or abuse that happens between clients while under the direct supervision of staff of the agency, and the concern that predatory individuals will be attracted to the agency specifically because it serves a vulnerable population.

When providing services, it is incumbent on a nonprofit agency to ensure that those who are inclined to take advantage of others do not have the opportunity to do so while under the care and supervision of the agency. Once again, our primary resource is a well-structured and managed organization. Best practices will be a combination of policy and procedure, organizational structure, and the physical environment of the agency. Clearly written and well-understood policies and procedures, which address staff responsibilities for the supervision and monitoring of the individuals and families receiving services from the agency, is vital.

In the annual and ongoing planning and design of service delivery, nonprofit managers need to consider how and when those who receive services need to wait. Large numbers of individuals or families in a common area awaiting services—whether it is for an initial intake, a scheduled appointment, or between points of service—is a site of potential risk, as well as just poor "customer service." A best practices approach to the management of service delivery is to minimize waiting times when possible. This both produces more satisfied "customers" and reduces the need for large waiting areas. However, it is the nature of life and of human service delivery that at times people will need to wait. Here, it will be important to consider the physical environment. The main considerations are that there is enough space and seating, there are not parts of the waiting area obstructed from view, and that staff has an easy and regular means of viewing the waiting area.

A related area of concern is that predatory individuals might be attracted to an agency specifically because it serves a vulnerable population. It is most obvious with agencies serving children, but it applies to other vulnerable populations as well. The nature of the risks will be different depending on the type of service agency. At a minimum, an agency needs to have some means of controlling access to any buildings used by the agency and a means of knowing who is in the building at all times. As with many issues concerning the protection of those the agencies serve, there is a tension between managing risk and avoiding an approach of Orwellian control that may interfere with the service delivery model. There is no simple answer to this, and reasonable balance must be found on a case-by-case basis.

A good agency should always know who is in its facilities, and likewise, they should know where many clients are going when they leave. Especially, when any child or any individual with some diminished capacity for judgment is returning to a caregiver, the staff needs to ensure that it knows who this individual is. A best practices approach is that information about who might pick up a client (or be waiting at home, etc.) is identified early in a service delivery model, often at the point of intake. Any such procedure needs to identify the necessary actions of staff when there is no identified individual to take over the care of the client. This may involve keeping the client at the agency or in the staff members' care while attempts are made to contact the primary caregiver and/or notify authorities. The key is that these scenarios are considered ahead of time and provisional steps are spelled out in the procedures.

Protecting Staff and Volunteers

All businesses have some level of responsibility to anticipate and minimize risks to their employees. There are legal and regulatory reasons: the U.S. Department of Labor's Occupational Safety and Health Administration would be one source of federal regulations governing employers (see http://www.osha.gov). And there are practical reasons: Sick or injured employees are a cost to a firm. A firm faces the direct costs of lost productivity and/or replacing missing staff. The firm also faces the future costs of higher health, disability, and accident insurance related to the number of claims in a given period.

Nonprofit organizations share all of these same concerns as well as at least one other unique concern. In some nonprofit organizations, staff members face real and unique risks. Examples of this would be individuals working in child or adult protective services, probationary officers, those working with individuals with mental health or behavioral disabilities, and at least some educational settings. Proactive leaders in nonprofit organizations anticipate the potential risks that staff may experience and incorporate preventative measures into the program planning process. Common considerations across all types of service delivery models are that an agency hires appropriate staff and gives them the necessary training and resources. We have already highlighted the importance of a best practices approach to human resources management. Identifying and hiring for the knowledge, skills, abilities, and other characteristics (KSAO) that are required for different positions are as important in protecting staff members as in protecting the individuals and families they serve.

For example, an agency may need to fill a case worker position working with adults with an Axis I mental health diagnosis. They may find a bright, energetic, enthusiastic, and generally competent person to fill the position. However, if this otherwise competent person has neither any formal training in psychology, social work, or human services nor any practical experience in working with adults with a mental health diagnosis, they are exposing the staff member and the client to significant risks. The ideal approach is to hire staff with the KSAOs identified for the position and match that with a structured training program. At a minimum, an agency needs to ensure that they provide the necessary training for staff, particularly if a hire brings commitment and enthusiasm but little applicable training.

A safety concern for staff members in a nonprofit organization is that they have adequate resources to do the job. One important resource is education and training, and that was discussed above. Other resources include such things as sufficient levels of staffing; necessary and sufficient tangible supplies; technology items, such as cell phones and computers; access to technology such as client and referral databases; reasonable physical space to provide services; and transportation or access to transportation. A challenge for nonprofit leaders is determining the necessary and sufficient resources out of a potential infinite wish list of resources.

The Physical Plant

An area of concern that relates to both staff and the individuals the agency serves is the safety of the physical environment of the agency. Materially, this is no different from the liability concerns related to the physical plant of any business. Any business or nonprofit organization wants to have good quality buildings and equipment that are kept in good repair. A best practices approach in any business is to have a risk management survey of the physical plant on some routine basis. In some instances, an annual survey is sufficient; in other cases, it is an ongoing weekly or monthly activity. Such a survey identifies potential risks and develops a plan to remediate the risks, which includes a time line and the responsible staff involved. Risks may be specific physical repairs, such as broken steps or cracked windows. The survey may also identify dangerous situations or procedures. A dangerous situation may be a perfectly intact floor that becomes dangerously slippery when wet. Remediation may involve rubber-backed carpet runners or a complete replacement of the floor. A dangerous practice may be a discovery that keys for agency vehicles are left in an unlocked cabinet accessible to individuals receiving services from the agency. Remediation may involve using a locked cabinet with some limit on who has access to the cabinet and a record of who signs out keys.

Of specific concern for nonprofits is that there is evidence that nonprofits underestimate the need to dedicate financial resources to maintenance and replacement of capital assets, such as buildings and equipment (see Anthony & Young, 2002; and Finkler, 2005). Responsible nonprofit leaders are rightly motivated to see that resources and assets are used to further the mission of the organization. As Anthony and Young argue, however, neglecting adequate funding for capital maintenance and

replacement can save in the short-term but be more costly in the long-term. Two aspects of this are that insurance premium costs will be higher if an insurance underwriter finds the physical plan to be less than safe and premiums will rise if claims are made by staff or clients due to accidents.

Protecting Assets and Resources

Nonprofit leaders, whether they are executives or members of a board of directors, have a fiduciary responsibility to protect the assets of the organization from loss or theft. An asset is anything of sustaining value to an organization. All organizations have tangible assets that are reflected in their financial statements and intangible assets, which may not have direct monetary value, but which are nonetheless of great value to the organization. This section will address risks associated with the tangible assets, and the risks to intangible assets will be addressed in the following section.

It is a joint responsibility of the executives and board members of a nonprofit organization to ensure that the tangible assets of the organization are maintained in a secure manner and used in a fashion consistent with the mission of the organization. Tangible assets include all items of monetary value, which are reflected in the balance sheets of the organization. It is beyond the reach of this chapter to discuss every potential asset of a nonprofit organization. Interested readers are directed to *Financial Management for Public, Health, and Not-for-Profit Organizations* (Finkler, 2005) for a more detailed consideration.

A first responsibility of any nonprofit leader is to institute a process for identifying and managing risks. A first step in this process is knowledge of what assets the organization has. A nonprofit leader needs to be familiar with the traditional financial statements of an organizational entity: the balance sheet, statement of revenue and expenses, statement of changes in net assets, and statement of cash flows. In addition, an organization needs to conduct a regular inventory of its tangible assets. Such an inventory should include an indication of the value of the identified assets. For-profit and particularly manufacturing and retail for-profits do this routinely, driven by a need to understand their inventory related to production and sales. Nonprofits have not traditionally been as vigilant in this regard.

The two main concerns in protecting tangible assets are accidental damage or loss and theft. Assessing what types of loss the organization may experience should be part of the routine assessment of a risk management committee (discussed below). Instrumental in this is using the services of a professional insurance agent or broker who has specific experience in working with nonprofit organizations. A commercial insurance broker, in conjunction with an experienced insurance underwriter, will be able to guide the agency staff (and board members) in determining what types of loss they may face and can recommend remedial actions, which will help reduce the likelihood of loss. A chief component of this is a consideration of *loss history*. A loss history is the recognition of specific losses that the nonprofit has already experienced as well as the types of losses that similar nonprofit organizations have typically experienced.

An important observation is that the insurance broker's—and even more so the insurance underwriter's—main focus will be on taking any and all steps to minimize risk and limit the organization's exposure to any loss that could result in a claim against insurance. In negotiating the terms of insurance policies, nonprofit leaders need to balance the insurance professional's expertise with their own expertise in providing appropriate services. An insurance underwriter might suggest some changes to the organization that would lower risk but at the expense of good practice in delivering services. This is a gray area, which involves intelligent decision making on the part of nonprofit leaders. It is easy for nonprofit managers to resist any suggestions for a change on a claim that a particular approach is necessary for "practice reasons." Conversely, nonprofit leaders cannot give up important aspects of program planning to insurance concerns.

Theft

Theft or misappropriation of agency assets is of a special concern for nonprofit organizations. In addition to the monetary loss, the nonprofit experiences damage to its reputation due to the violation of the trust that the nonprofit will use its assets in service of its mission. It seems that hardly a month goes by without a story about the discovery of some trusted and longtime employee (or volunteer) of a nonprofit having embezzled money—often over a period of many years. While recently there has been great improvement in nonprofit management practices in this regard, this has traditionally been a significant weakness for nonprofit organizations. All nonprofit leaders need to institute a good system of internal financial controls within an organization. The Finkler (2005) text on financial management mentioned above presents a complete consideration of what is necessary. In terms of minimizing the risks of theft and misappropriation, the three key concepts are the segregation of responsibilities, checks and balances, and transparency. Basically, it is important to ensure that for all transactions of receiving, recording, or disbursing assets more than one person is involved. Ideally, there is some rotation of these staff responsibilities so that there is not a situation where one individual has been the sole person "keeping the books" for any great length of time. There should be some redundancy of responsibilities, also rotated, so that multiple eyes review the documentation of the receipt and disbursement of assets. In all instances, members of the finance committee of the board of directors should play some role in reviewing documentation on an ongoing basis. This means actually meeting with the staff and looking at original documents, not just reports given to the board. The advice of an insurance professional and/or

an accountant is well advised in developing a good system of internal controls.

Protecting the Intangible Assets

While we have placed this toward the end of this discussion, this is likely the most important area for the nonprofit leader to consider in his or her assessment of risk management. Intangible assets are those items that do not have an explicit monetary value but nonetheless are of vital importance to the organization. Common intangible assets to all nonprofits are its mission, its reputation, and the training and experience of its staff (human capital). Other intangible assets that many nonprofits may have are such things as cooperative agreements with other organizations, privileged status in receiving government or foundation grants, historical standing in its unique area of service delivery, and historical status in its specific geographic community.

The anchors in this regard for any nonprofit organization are the fraternal twins of mission and reputation.

> A nonprofit's mission is distinct from its reputation. The mission is the helm that guides the nonprofit to its overarching goal. . . . Its *reputation* is the community's collection of beliefs, perceptions, and experiences that either support or refute the values, principles, and worth of the organization in the eyes of the community. (Herman et al., 2004, p. 133)

Nevertheless, if a nonprofit violates, or is thought to have violated, its mission, it will do irreparable damage to its reputation. Likewise, anything which causes damage to a nonprofit's reputation severely hinders its ability to fulfill its mission.

Here, readers come full circle in the discussion of risk management. The central approach to managing risk to the intangible assets of an organization is a well-run organization. A focused and well-articulated mission, a planning process that keeps the mission central to decision making, and an appropriate and aptly trained workforce go a long way toward limiting risks to both mission and reputation. The other characteristic of a nonprofit leader crucial to protecting the value of the organization's mission and reputation is vigilance. Everyday, in the life of a nonprofit organization, there is the potential that staff, volunteers, or board members could make decisions or take actions that damage the mission or reputation of the agency. The nonprofit leader needs to be constantly on the lookout for programmatic and financial decisions that might be leading it astray from its mission. In addition, the nonprofit leader, along with a well-trained staff, needs to be sensitive to actions and situations that might lead to a damaged reputation.

The large events that clearly imperil the organization's reputation are fairly easy to recognize. At least as vital is to discern the minor incidents that *could* lead to a damaged reputation. Minor incidents that are identified and responded to in an appropriate manner can forestall more significant damage. Conversely, minor incidents that are not perceived as important can grow to be unforgiving reputation crises. A well-run organization with a dedication to good customer service is a powerful first step in minimizing risks to the reputation of the organization.

Herman et al. (2004) in their book, *Managing Risk in Nonprofit Organizations*, note that proactive nonprofit organizations need to have a crisis management plan in place *before* a crisis occurs. They recommend that any such plan contain at least three components: a designated spokesperson, generic prepared statements, and written procedures for responding to crises. At least as important in having prepared a crisis management plan is to ensure that staff is aware that such a plan exists and that they have received training in implementing the plan (p. 143). "The manner in which an organization responds to crisis can either instill public confidence or diminish current confidence levels" (Herman et al., p. 143).

A Risk Assessment Committee

It is a joint responsibility of a nonprofit's board of directors and its executives to consider the level of risk management needed by the organization. A best practices approach to this is to have a risk assessment committee as a function of the board. Depending on the size of the organization, this might be a function of the board's finance committee, or it might be a separate standing committee. In either instance, the committee should always be comprised of members of the board and executive staff of the organization. Whether or not other staff, volunteers, or clients serve on the committee, the committee needs a means of gathering their input in the process.

When a risk management committee is initially formed, its first responsibility is to conduct a comprehensive audit of the needs for risk management in the organization. Such an initial overview is best conducted with the guidance of professionals with some experience in conducting such an audit in similar nonprofit organizations. At a minimum, the products of a risk assessment audit will be a written risk management plan and recommendations for the board of directors on policies concerning risk financing and insurance purchasing. A risk management plan "is a document that describes [the organization's] overall philosophy about risk management and discusses specific exposures and related strategies. Such a risk management plan provides a central resource to unify everyone's efforts" (Herman, 2005, p. 27). The risk management plan should become part of the ongoing planning process of the organization and ultimately be reflected in routine policies and procedures. After an initial written risk assessment plan is incorporated, the risk assessment committee will review the plan on at least an annual basis as well as respond to newly identified issues as they arise.

Financing Risk

The possibilities that are available for financing risk are varied and at times quite complicated. Ultimately, the executives and board members of a nonprofit organization need to use the advice of commercial insurance brokers who specialize in nonprofit organizations. The Herman et al. (2004) text gives an excellent overview of the issues involved. The two basic considerations in financing risk are the retention of risk or the transfer of risk. Retention basically means that the nonprofit organization will fund the cost of risk from its own resources and assets. This can be as formal as establishing a captive (in-house) insurance carrier to as informal as a "we'll deal with it as it arises" approach. Clearly, the latter is not recommended as a best practices approach. Most nonprofits expect to fund some losses from their operating budget or savings. The best practices approach is that a risk management plan addresses what type of losses and to what extent losses can be funded in such a manner.

Transferring the financing of risk management expenses involves the cost of loss being funded from outside the organization. The two most common approaches for this are the purchasing of insurance contracts or entering into indemnification contracts. An insurance contract involves an insurance provider agreeing to pay for identified losses in exchange for ongoing premium payments. The organization takes the certainty of the regular cost of an insurance premium in order to avoid the uncertainty of a specific incident of loss. Most organizations will ultimately decide on some mixture of retention and transfer. The most common example of this is that many insurance instruments will designate a "deductible." A deductible is nothing more than a certain amount of loss that the organization "retains" before the insurance policy will take effect.

Indemnification is the process of transferring the costs of risk to another organization but not as an insurance contract. There are numerous examples of indemnity agreements. One example is when an organization contracts with a company to renovate its buildings. The nonprofit may insist on an indemnification agreement with the construction company stipulating that the construction company will pay for any losses due to the construction. An example where the nonprofit provides for the indemnification is when it promises to indemnify volunteer board members to attract the best possible applicants for the board of directors. In this instance, the agency promises to pay for the legal defense of individual board members if they are sued relative to their normal actions and decisions as a member of the board.

As noted above, the issues involved in choosing how to finance risk are complex and require professional guidance.

Our major theme is to identify that it is an essential function of nonprofit leaders to initiate such activities.

Future Directions

While future directions in risk management for nonprofit organizations can be as varied as the many arenas of service delivery they engage in, we can identify two prominent areas of development: technology and environmental issues. Nonprofits, like all organizations, are finding ever-increasing ways of incorporating technology into their business practices and into their means of service delivery. Obviously, as more and more information related to those who receive services is maintained and accessed via technological devices, it raises ever-new issues in how to ensure that the confidentiality of sensitive information is maintained. Of particular note are concerns related to the increasing "portability" of information. Laptops, personal digital assistants (PDAs), wireless networks, and virtual storage of information are all tools that are moving toward the *office-less* office. If anything, many nonprofit organizations are leaders in needing to have staff who are "out in the field" most, if not all, the time. These tools are assisting many organizations in developing low cost and flexible service delivery models, which are exemplary in their field. Nonetheless, these "open networks" not only raise all sorts of issues in how to make necessary information available to staff and clients but also maintain it in a secure manner.

Society is growing evermore aware of environmental hazards and their impacts on our health and well-being in everyday life. There is an infinite range of environmental issues that relate to nonprofit management. Of particular concern to nonprofit leaders is the potential that environmental pollutants might be present in the facilities the organization operates. There is a growing concern that regular cleaning products and poorly maintained heating, ventilating, and air conditioning (HVAC) systems as well as the by-products of numerous methods of construction introduce pollutants in the environment (Meyer, Mannino, Homa, Naeher, & Redd, 1999).

There is also significant suspicion that many of the vulnerable populations that nonprofit organizations service may be even more sensitive to these pollutants than the population at large. It will become increasingly important for nonprofit organizations to have "green committees" looking at all aspects of environmental concerns but with a special consideration of limiting exposures to any toxins in the environment.

References and Further Readings

Anthony, R. N., & Young, D. W. (2002). *Management control in non-profit organizations* (7th ed.). New York: McGraw Hill.

Blackwood, A., Wing, K. T., & Pollak, T. H. (2008). *The nonprofit sector in brief: Facts and figures from the nonprofit almanac 2008: Public charities, giving, and volunteering.* Washington, DC: Urban Institute, National Center for Charitable Statistics.

Federal Equal Employment Opportunity Commission. (n.d.). Retrieved June 23, 2009, from http://www.eeoc.gov/abouteeo/overview_laws.html

Finkler, S. A. (2005). *Financial management for public, health, and not-for-profit organizations* (2nd ed.). Upper Saddle River, NJ: Prentice Hall.

Gramlich, E. M. (1997). *A guide to benefit cost analysis* (2nd ed.). Long Grove, IL: Waveland Press.

Handy, F., & Katz, E. (1998). The wage differential between nonprofit institutions and corporations: Getting more by paying less? *Journal of Comparative Economics, 26*(2), 246–261.

Hauge, J. C., & Herman, M. L. (2006). *Taking the high road: A guide to effective and legal employment practices for nonprofits* (2nd ed.). Washington, DC: Nonprofit Risk Management Center.

Herman, M. L. (2002). Risk management in the nonprofit sector. *Risk Management, 49*(6), 26–31.

Herman, M. L. (2005). Liability exposure and risk management. *Children's Voice, 14*(2), 26–32.

Herman, M. L., Head, G. L., Jackson, P. M., & Fogarty, T. E. (2004). *Managing risk in nonprofit organizations.* Hoboken, NJ: John Wiley & Sons.

Martinez, M. J. (2003). Liability and volunteer organizations: A survey of the law. *Nonprofit Managment and Leadership, 14*(2), 151–169.

Meyer, P., Mannino, D., Homa, D., Naeher, L., & Redd, S. (1999). Every breath we take. *Forum for Applied Research and Public Policy, 14*(4), 43–49.

National Center for Charitable Statistics. (n.d.). *Number of nonprofit organizations in the United States, 1998–2008.* Retrieved March 4, 2009, from http://nccsdataweb.urban.org/PubApps/profile1.php?state=US

Patti, R. J. (Ed.). (2008). *The handbook of human services management* (2nd ed.). Thousand Oaks, CA: Sage.

Pynes, J. E. (2009). *Human resources management for public and nonprofit organizations: A strategic approach* (3rd ed.). San Francisco: Jossey-Bass.

Vanden Berk, K. M. (2003, Winter). Risk management for nonprofit organizations. *Alliance for Children & Families Magazine,* 17–19.

76

USING DATA TO MAKE DECISIONS

JOHN RISLEY

Johnson Center for Philanthropy, Grand Valley State University

The plural of anecdote is data.

Raymond Wolfinger (Polsby, 1984)

One often sees the inverse of the above quotation—the plural of anecdote is *not* data—invoked as a caution to those seeking to use their observations of the world around them to make decisions. The apparent theory behind this inversion of Wolfinger's statement is that what we observe in our daily lives, the anecdotal, does not tell us nearly as much, nor as accurately, as do data. The fact that most readers who are in some way familiar with this quotation likely recognize the "not data" version and not Wolfinger's original is strong testimony for the value most people place on data.

This section will give an overview of data-driven decision making in nonprofit organizations. It will address some key terms and concepts nonprofit leaders and staff should be familiar with when thinking about using data to make decisions for their organizations. The section addresses why this is an important issue for nonprofits to address. Next, the section presents some common barriers to implementing an effective data-driven, decision-making scheme. Following that will be some important issues for nonprofits to remember when practicing data-driven decision making. Finally, some examples are presented of ways in which nonprofit organizations have used data to enhance their decision making.

Why Data-Driven Decision Making Is Important for Nonprofits

In these times, as in all times, nonprofits don't have nearly the resources to address the needs they see in their respective communities. Addressing those needs is a challenge for a nonprofit organization's fundraising, budgeting, staffing, and programming. Cutting across all these aspects of a nonprofit organization is the question of how to decide where to deploy resources in pursuit of the organization's mission. Information is at the heart of all of these decisions. Explicitly deciding which information to consider and how to collect this information is the heart of data-driven decision making. Data-driven decision making can help the three main constituencies of nearly all nonprofits: funders, staff, and clients.

Funders of nonprofits are increasingly looking for information about what their money achieves. As funders, whether public or private, see their money dry up, they want to ensure the money they do have makes a difference. Showing funders that an organization is serious about collecting data and using them to make programming decisions is the key. Presenting success data to funders helps them make decisions on where to invest money. Showing funders that a nonprofit collects and uses data to improve its operations and programs is rapidly becoming an essential part of any funding request.

Nonprofit leaders and staff members need data to drive their decisions because staff time equals money. A nonprofit organization needs to deploy its staff efficiently. One of the most inefficient ways to deploy staff is to have them spending time on programs that do not improve the lives of the nonprofit's clients or community. Data-driven decision making can help nonprofits avoid these inefficiencies.

Clients of nonprofit organizations often have choices on where they go to get services. Using data, nonprofits can show prospective clients that their services are effective. Collecting data also allows clients to have their voices heard in the operation of the programs they use.

Definitions and Related Concepts

What Counts as Data?

As seen above, there is some dispute about whether data are indeed the plural of anecdote. Nonprofit leaders and staff can draw on many anecdotes. They have a wealth of knowledge and experience regarding their communities about what their organizations do, and about how they are (or are not) succeeding. Data-driven decision making seeks a systematic and reliable way to measure and track these successes. Data must be consistently collected and be collected in a time period that allows users to make decisions based on them.

Hiller and Self (2004) offer that "data are records of observations, facts, or information collected for reference or analysis." In their view, data can "take a number of forms, such as transactions, observations, surveys, or interviews. All of these provide data, that is, observations, both quantitative and qualitative, from which inferences may be drawn by means of analysis" (p. 129).

What Is Data-Driven Decision Making?

Keeping those points about data in mind, for our purposes, we will define data-driven decision making in the nonprofit context as the use of systematically collected and analyzed information to inform the allocation of resources (people, time, money) to advance the mission of the organization.

Evaluation

Data-driven decision making is often linked to evaluation—the "process of determining merit, worth, or significance" (Scriven, 2007, p. 1). The important link between evaluation and data-driven decision making is that data must be combined with values, interests, and context. Data, by themselves, do not make decisions. It is the interplay of the data with an organization's values and context that is important.

Logic Model

Logic models are representations of the way a nonprofit organization or program works. The W. K. Kellogg Foundation's guide for logic models defines them as "a picture of how your organization does its work—the theory and assumptions underlying the program. A program logic model links outcomes (both short- and long-term) with program activities/processes and the theoretical assumptions/principles of the program" (2004, p. III).

Common Problems

Data Don't Exist

When data don't exist, it is important to ask how important it is to invest what is needed to obtain these data. Is collecting the data worth the organization's energy, cost, and time? When looking at this question, a nonprofit needs to concentrate on data that will actually *drive* decisions. Some things are nice to know, but knowing them would not change decisions the nonprofit faces. It is best to start at the decision-making end of the continuum and work backward to the data. Ask questions such as, what information, if the leaders had known it, would have led them to make a different decision on planning, programming, or personnel. If a nonprofit still would have invested in a program even knowing certain information, then it is probably not worth it to collect those data.

Data Are in a Difficult to Use Format

This situation usually occurs when data are collected on paper and are stored in different places. Client case files may have lots of data that could help a nonprofit but bringing those data together would entail transferring them from many separate pieces of paper into a central, electronic location.

Others Won't Share Data

Nonprofits should be clear about what data are available to them before deciding to incorporate information into their decision-making system. Many data exist that are not easy to access. School systems, health care organizations, and many government agencies are often reluctant to share data that could help nonprofits make better decisions. This reluctance could be due to legitimate privacy concerns or less legitimate turf protection concerns. Either way, lack of access to data is a frequent problem for nonprofits.

Collecting Data That Are Easy to Measure

A common problem nonprofits face is that decisions about what to measure—about what data to collect—are driven by what is easiest to measure. Typically, process measures or outputs (products produced, meetings held, people trained, people enrolled) are the things that are easiest to count. While this information can be important to know, what is most important is how people and communities being served by the nonprofit are improving. Measures of these outcomes are often much more difficult to develop and collect.

Nonprofits naturally need baseline information—how many people they serve, whom they serve, and the resources they have available in people, time, and facilities. This is common to any type of planning and budgeting. The *data* in data-driven decision making, however, concern information about what is working, what needs are being met, and how outcomes can be better achieved and at lower cost.

Important Aspects

Value of Obtaining Data From Multiple Sources

It is always valuable to get data from more than one source. This is often referred to as *triangulation*. As an example, in the county food security effort outlined below, data were collected from stores to get an idea of what foods were available in certain sections of the county and at what price. People were also asked about the availability and price of food at local stores to determine if their views meshed with the data collected from stores. It turns out that people had concerns about how difficult it could be to get to these stores. These and other concerns greatly affected the accessibility and availability of food.

Don't Need to Be Data Experts

When thinking about data analysis and statistics, nonprofit leaders and staff may begin to get overwhelmed. Most nonprofit leaders know their field, know their community, and know about management of staff and fundraising, but they are not as confident in their data analysis skills. Nonprofit leaders need not be experts in data analysis or statistics. They do need to be able to ask good questions, to be able to accept the limitations of using data to make decisions, and to be able to tap into people around them whom they can consult on these issues.

Organizational Ethic of Continuous Improvement

The most important trait of an organization that uses data to drive decision making is the organizational ethic to continuously improve its work. This can be a difficult mind-set to adopt, especially for an organization that knows it is doing good work and certainly has good intentions.

Example: Food Pantries

Context: Baseline Data

Nearly all data collected by nonprofit organizations can be seen, in some way, to affect decision making. Many times, data, especially when these are data that are collected for the first time, are gathered to get a foundational idea of where things stand for the organization at a particular moment in time. This type of datum is often referred to as *baseline data*. It can be important to collect this type of data set to frame all subsequent data collected that more directly drives decision making for the organization.

An example of this type of baseline data collection involved assessing the food security for citizens in a medium-sized county in the United States. Data were collected to determine the accessibility, availability, and affordability of food within the county. Both quantitative and qualitative data were collected. Data with a geographic aspect were also collected. Therefore, decision makers at nonprofits were able to see how certain needs and existing resources matched up geographically. This is of great use when planning expansion or continuation of existing program sites.

An example of qualitative data collected in this instance that could immediately drive decision making were from a survey question about the various barriers people face when seeking to access food. Fuel prices were particularly high during the period these data were collected. Many people identified the high cost of fuel as a problem for accessing food, especially in rural areas of the county. Therefore, people living in rural areas wanted the food pantries they used to allow for a larger supply of food to be taken during each visit—lessening the number of trips (and fuel costs for the same amount of food secured).

Example: Raising Funds for International Aid

Qualitative Data

Data need not be strictly quantitative. Much value can be derived from qualitative data about the way certain aspects of programs and organizations are conducted. Qualitative data are generally data that are not quantified or assigned a number. This type of datum is often collected through interviews with people. Interview questions yielding qualitative data are open ended in contrast with questions where respondents are given choices for their answers. Open-ended questions have the advantage of allowing for the possibility that the questioner cannot anticipate all the possible responses to each question. Also, often responses to complex questions are not amenable to specific answer choices. In these instances, qualitative data are the only real option for discovering how things actually work. A main drawback for qualitative data is that these cannot be reliably compared with data from other contexts (other people, other projects, other situations). However, if the focus of your decision making is your specific nonprofit program or agency, then qualitative data can be very helpful for your purposes.

Context: Building on Success

A nonprofit agency that raises funds for food security programs (Chianca & Risley, 2005) in the developing world offers a good example of the use of qualitative data to make decisions for a nonprofit. This agency raises funds through volunteer-led community growing projects. Volunteers donate land, materials, and labor to raise, harvest, and sell a crop. The funds secured are then donated to a project in the developing world that helps people secure or maintain food security. These projects include irrigation systems, greenhouses, and other agricultural infrastructure.

The nonprofit coordinating these growing projects wanted to find out how to help all of its growing projects become more successful. The staff members collected data on all the growing projects—the number of volunteers involved, the amount of land dedicated to raising the crops, the type of crops raised, the amount of money raised—using a survey. They then identified several of the best performing projects and conducted more detailed interviews with lead volunteers for these projects. The interviews concentrated on obtaining information from these volunteers on what characteristics made their projects successful. By examining the common success indicators from these interviews, the staff from the nonprofit agency was able to concentrate its support and training for other projects on the things that were most likely to produce more successful projects—and raise more money.

Example: Tax Preparation Assistance

Context: Managing Growth

A nonprofit organization that provides free tax preparation services for low-income individuals and families was experiencing growth in its financial support and was looking to expand the sites where it offered tax preparation counseling. To decide where to place the sites, it used publicly available datum sources to determine the areas of the county it served where lower income people lived, where suitable partner organizations that could house the tax preparation counselors were located, and which potential partners were located near public transportation.

This is an example of using data that are already being collected (usually by a government agency) and are freely available to the public to use. Looking at these data using geographic information system (GIS) mapping allowed the organization to visually examine possible host sites, public transit options, and areas where the target clients are concentrated.

This is a somewhat basic use of data-driven decision making: using data to make planning and programming decisions and using existing data, not data collected by the nonprofit organization itself.

An example of a slightly more involved use of data to drive decisions comes from the same organization (M. Gagen, personal communication, January 12, 2009). In an attempt to learn more about how the organization can expand its number of clients, the nonprofit decided to collect some survey information from them when they came in to have their tax forms completed. The organization wanted to know whom they were reaching. Specifically, where had their clients formerly had their taxes prepared—did they file their own taxes, did they use a commercial tax service, and if so, what did this service cost? By collecting these data, the organization was able to show (to both funders and prospective clients) how much money it was saving the average tax filer it served.

Summary

Data are all around us. They are routinely collected by nonprofit organizations. Putting the data to use in decision making can be tricky. When seeking to implement data-driven decision making, it is important to remember that the actual decisions you are looking to influence should be the main driver of the specific data you collect and use. It is tempting to collect what is easy or to base decisions on data that were already collected by someone else—even if those data do not closely match the decisions you are trying to influence.

This section provided an overview of data-driven decision making in nonprofit organizations. It identified key terms and concepts nonprofit leaders and staff should be familiar with when thinking about using data to make decisions for their organizations; addressed why this is an important issue for nonprofits; presented common barriers to implementing an effective data-driven, decision-making scheme; and presented some examples of ways in which nonprofit organizations have used data to enhance their decision making.

In the next few years, the ubiquity of publicly available data on the Internet will only increase. This will allow nonprofits access to community-level data that will help them discover community needs. Also, the availability of open source software to more easily analyze data should increase. This may be especially useful if free geographic information systems software becomes widely available online.

Part of data-driven decision making is deciding what data to collect. Collecting data can be time consuming, expensive, and sometimes intrusive for a nonprofit's clients. Nonprofits should take care not to collect more data than are necessary. When deciding how many data are necessary, it is important to focus on what are the mission and core goals of the organization.

References and Further Reading

Chianca, T., & Risley, J. (2005). *Organizational evaluation of the Foods Resource Bank.* Kalamazoo: Western Michigan University, Evaluation Center.

Etsy, D. C., & Rushing, R. (2007). *Governing by the numbers: The promise of data driven policymaking in the information age.* Washington, DC: Center for American Progress.

Hiller, S., & Self, J. (2004, Summer). From measurement to management: Using data wisely for planning and decision-making. *Library Trends, 53*(1), 129–155.

Mandinach, E. B., Honey, M., & Light, D. (2006, April). *A theoretical framework for data-driven decision-making.* Paper presented at the annual meeting of the American Educational Research Association, San Francisco, CA.

Polsby, N. W. (1984). The contributions of President Richard F. Fenno, Jr. *PS Political Science and Politics, 17*(4), 778–781.

Sagawa, S., & Jospin, D. (2009). Data-driven decision-making. In *The charismatic organization: Eight ways to grow a nonprofit that builds buzz, delights donors, and energizes employees* (pp. 74–94). San Francisco: Jossey-Bass.

Schalock, R. L., & Bonham, G. S. (2003). Measuring outcomes and managing for results. *Evaluation and Program Planning, 26*(3), 229–235.

Scriven, M. (2007). The logic of evaluation. In H. V. Hansen, C. W. Tindale, J. A. Blair, R. H. Johnson, & D. M. Godden (Eds.), *Dissensus and the search for common ground* ([CD-ROM], pp. 1–16). Windsor, ON: Ontario Society for the Study of Argumentation.

W. K. Kellogg Foundation. (2004). *Using logic models to bring together planning, evaluation, and action: Logic model development guide.* Battle Creek, MI: Author.

Wolk, A., Dholakia, A., & Kreitz, K. (2009). *Building a performance measurement system: Using data to accelerate social impact.* Cambridge, MA: Root Cause.

77

CHALLENGES IN DELIVERING SERVICES USING NEW TECHNOLOGIES

Organizational Capacity and IT Support

ASHIMA SAIGAL

Johnson Center for Philanthropy, Grand Valley State University

Private industry has long recognized information technology's power to reduce costs. By effectively using information technology (IT), companies have increased efficiencies in their management and operations. These efficiencies often lead to an increase in the fiscal bottom line, which is a benefit for the shareholders of the corporation. The technology tools used most often encompass computer hardware, software, and networks, including the Internet.

Technology has a positive impact on the economy and productivity of organizations in the private sector. A report by McKinsey Global Institute reveals that although it is complex and varies across industries, information technology enables and contributes to economic growth (2002). Technology gains have allowed private industries to keep a competitive edge over their rivals, develop new products and services, realize substantial increases in output and productivity, and ultimately provide fiscal savings.

Nonprofit enterprises are increasingly incorporating information technology into their operations. The impetus often comes from other nonprofits, individual donors, foundations, government requirements, and performance and accountability pressures. Those nonprofits seeking to grow and expand have taken a cue from private industry with the goal of achieving comparable efficiency gains and growth in support of their missions.

While there is interest from the nonprofit sector to incorporate information technology into operations, nonprofits struggle with information technology implementation, whether it is for internal operational purposes or for service delivery. The struggles that nonprofits face center on the capacity of the organization or the ability or lack of ability of the organization to integrate technology into their organizations as well as the lack of support from the IT sector.

Organizational Capacity

The capacity of an organization is critical to the capability of nonprofit organizations to implement technology. When looking at organizational capacity, there are three main investments that are the cornerstone of success in information technology implementations in the private sector: infrastructure, human capital, and planning. Throwing more money or resources at an information technology project will not necessarily increase its success if there are no plans. Providing more training for staff will not help an information technology project if there are no infrastructure investments. These three investments are central with each playing an equal role.

The investments translate to both the for-profit and nonprofit sector as being critical for information technology implementation success. The challenge for nonprofits is that these three investments are often in direct conflict with the organization's mission. These next sections delve deeper into each of these investments and uncover the barriers of each for nonprofit organizations.

Infrastructure Investments

Infrastructure investments are meant to provide specific resources for the support of internal functions of an organization. These investments related to information technology may be computer hardware, software, or networking equipment, to name a few. These are the building blocks that form the foundation for the basic information technology requirements of an organization.

For nonprofit organizations, infrastructure investments are lacking for three main reasons: First, organizations are not providing reasonable information technology budgets to support existing and future technology; second, external sources often provide restricted funds, which limit the organizations' ability to fund information technology; and finally, organizations find it difficult to acquire additional funding to support and update their original investments.

First, nonprofit organizations often view investment in infrastructure as shifting focus away from their missions. Nonprofits face a tricky tradeoff between spending on information technology and direct service to clients, making information technology spending a difficult decision. For example, a nonprofit whose mission is to feed the hungry would rather spend money to feed more individuals than on a new computer for which effective implementation could ultimately facilitate even more food. These organizations often have very low or nonexistent information technology budgets and often, when looking to reduce expenses, cut their technology budgets. As noted by a Chief Operating Officer (COO) of a women's organization in conversation with the author about the organization's technology issues, "If we sat down with just the operating budget it could be problematic because sometimes on our really tightest years that is where the CEOs have wanted me to cut." She continued, "Sure you want to cut technology before you cut people, but it hurts just as bad sometimes." This lack of an information technology budget or willingness to cut the budget exemplifies the fact that nonprofits lack interest or sufficient knowledge in allocating dollars for information technology infrastructure investment.

Second, external sources, such as foundations and governmental agencies, demonstrate indifference in building the organizational information technology infrastructure by restricting the amount of money a nonprofit can allocate on its grant application to support administrative capacity or by refusing to allow any capacity support whatsoever. There is little funding to sustain the internal infrastructure of the organization on which programs are built, whereas funding is available and continues to support the programs. These programs rely on a solid infrastructure; thus, a dilemma of supporting the program versus supporting the internal infrastructure continues to manifest.

Finally, organizations struggle to find additional dollars to acquire or support their original investments. This can be through an internal information technology budget, which was previously discussed, which is often lacking, or through external sources, such as foundations or governmental agencies. There are some foundations that will provide funding for technology, but finding them is a challenge, and often, they fund new programs and not existing systems.

Human Capital Investments

Human capital is the human assets of an organization, the skilled workers that keep the organization humming along smoothly. These skilled workers bring a wealth of knowledge and expertise to the organization and contribute to the organization's growth. The skills can be acquired on the job, through life experiences, or through formal education.

The challenges related to human capital fall into two main categories, internal and external. Internal challenges relate often to those individuals who work directly with the organization with a focus on the mission such as social workers, executive director, and development director, to name a few. The external individuals are clients, volunteers, board members, and consultants, those that are external to the organization but have a direct impact on the mission of the organization.

The internal challenges relate to the nonprofit worker. Regardless of how individuals acquire their skills, the majority of nonprofit workers lack technology skills. This requires the organization to invest in its human capital to educate its workforce, which includes volunteers and board members.

The external challenges relate to the client and consultant's skill level. The investments here are for external individuals and may be challenging for the nonprofit to directly influence, but there are ways the nonprofit can have an impact indirectly.

Internal Challenges

Investment in internal human capital remains a challenge. Nonprofits face three key barriers related to the human capital investment. The first two barriers are related to staff members of the organization. First, they are not provided enough time to work with technology, and second, they are often unwilling to use technology. Finally, unrelated to general staff, often information technology professionals are uninterested in working in the nonprofit sector.

Barrier one: Staff time. There are three main issue areas related to staff time: staff training, project management, and information management. Typically, nonprofit organizations do not provide the staff time needed for training, project management, and information management. This section will delve deeper into each of these areas.

First, regarding staff training, most organizations provide little or no time for staff to receive training, and yet most feel that the lack of staff training and expertise are key barriers to successful information technology implementation. The ability to experience and learn through failure is limited and often education is provided only as the staff members work on specific projects. They are also not provided enough formal education or training on information technology thus leaving gaps in their skill set.

Second, regarding project management, many organizations provide little if any time for management or development and implementation of key projects for an organization. Typically, there is no one assigned to lead a project, and if there is someone assigned, they are not provided enough time to truly manage the project. Often, these projects are doomed to failure as no one is in charge to see the project through to effective and successful completion.

Finally, regarding information management, staff is inundated with massive amounts of information, and staffers are challenged to filter relevant information. They often spend many hours cleaning up their e-mail boxes or their files, which takes away from the time they could be spending on the mission of the organization. This frustrates the staff, as well as the management, of the organization. This in turn causes individuals to mistakenly blame the technology for the problems of the organization when in reality it is the massive amounts of information that is causing the problem.

As it is often said in a nonprofit organization, there is never enough time in the day to accomplish all the tasks required. This is truly the case with information technology. Staff never has enough time to receive the training needed, to manage key projects, or to manage the deluge of information that is received.

Barrier two: Staff use of technology. The second internal barrier to the human capital investment relates back to the staff of the organization and its unwillingness to use technology. Most nonprofit organizations have a workforce of educated social workers or teachers. They tend to be very social and focused on connecting with people. Thus, they often are unwilling to use technology because it depersonalizes interactions with clients.

Employees of nonprofit organizations are passionate about the mission but have little technical knowledge or training. Some have even said that they would like to avoid using computers and technology as a whole and prefer working with people, not machines. This disdain of technology can cause problems when an organization is attempting to streamline processes through the use of technology. These individuals may put up barriers and road blocks.

Barrier three: Information technology staffing. Finally, the third internal barrier related to the human capital investment focuses on the nonprofit computer manager and the lack of individuals from the technology professions willing to work in the nonprofit sector.

Those nonprofits that can afford nonprofit computer managers provide little if any formal training. These individuals desire to stay on the cutting edge of technology to remain a desired commodity in their profession (Saidel & Cour, 2003), but nonprofits provide little if any formal training to provide these individuals that opportunity.

Second, for similar reasons, individuals in the technology field do not wish to work in the nonprofit sector. First, the pay is not as high as in the private sector and second, keeping up with technology is more challenging as the nonprofit, typically, does not stay on the cutting edge of technology.

External Challenges

Specifically, internal human capital challenges revolve around the following: having dedicated information technology staff, staff expertise with information technology, and available staff time. Just as there are internal issues, there are some external human capital issues related to the client, volunteers, and external consultants.

Barrier one: Client digital divide. One key external human capital challenge relates to the client's digital divide. There are two main areas where the divide is most pronounced: access to technology and technology education.

Nonprofits often deal with clients who lack access to the technology needed to communicate either with the organization or with individuals at the organization making the use of technology to serve constituents a tough sell for any nonprofit. This is often something that causes nonprofits to put aside the use of technology to serve their client bases.

Another key issue is the lack of education of their client bases. Often, clients seeking assistance from a nonprofit lack the education needed to use the available technology. Some nonprofits work to educate their clients on the use of technology, but if there are physiological needs and safety issues that have not been met as defined by Maslow's hierarchy of needs (www.edpsycinteractive.org/topics/regsys/maslow.html), the client may not be motivated to learn about technology. Basic needs, such as the need for safety and security, will get in the way of client learning.

Two main types of organizations, those that serve the elderly and those serving the mentally or physically handicapped, face particular hurdles. Often, organizations that serve the elderly realize that these individuals have not been introduced to technology and may struggle to help their clients as they now have to teach them about technology. Second, those that work with mentally or physically handicapped also face a potential barrier with lack of accessibility and having to find resources and systems that will work with their client base. These barriers can seem insurmountable, but some can be addressed.

Barrier two: Consultants. Another key external resource related to human capital is consultants. Nonprofits often rely on consultants or contractors to provide support and advice for their information technology usage. There are three main issues related to consultants: First, many nonprofits see consultants as unreliable; second, some nonprofits underutilize external consultants; and finally, often consultants lack knowledge of cultural and gender issues related to nonprofits.

First, in regard to consultants as unreliable, some nonprofits find that consultants do not provide reliable expertise and that it is difficult to find consultants that are professional and affordable. Although consultants can play an important role in the successful implementation of information technology, findings show that the use of consultants varies. Some nonprofits will use contractors to provide tactical implementation of information technology projects, but these contractors frequently do not receive adequate guidance or support from the organizational staff. On the other hand, some nonprofit organizations will use contractors as strategic partners that work in collaboration with the internal information technology staff to implement a project. The challenge comes when the reliance is on the consultant to implement and learn about the organization without the guidance of anyone in the organization and thus leaving the consultant to determine the organization's goals.

Second, in regard to the underutilization of consultants, some nonprofits do not engage consultants because they believe it is too expensive. Often, nonprofits attempt to undertake major initiatives without any guidance or support from an experienced consultant, which could, in the long run, save the nonprofits' resources. But with a short-term focus, nonprofits tend to attempt major projects without experienced help, which often leads to technology projects being ineffectively implemented.

Finally, consultants often lack specific nonprofit knowledge, including that of the specific issues related to culture and gender in an organization. The challenge in finding the right consultant is that they are often focused on the private or public sector and lack knowledge of the issues facing the nonprofit sector.

Barrier three: Volunteers. Challenges related to volunteers are twofold: Volunteers being used within the organization to provide technology support are transient, and volunteers often lack skills to make use of the technology provided by the nonprofit organization.

First, transient support for information technology support may be a hindrance to the nonprofit organization that relies on technology to run its organization. This can cause frustration and problems with staff, and the issue can snowball into major problems. Often, these volunteers lack supervision from anyone in the organization; thus, as with consultants, they will often develop systems that they feel need to be in place rather than those that meet the critical needs of the organization. Often, volunteers work a limited number of hours as they have full-time jobs, which can prevent them from volunteering.

Second, volunteers can lack skills to use the technology provided by the nonprofit organization. Volunteers often cite the mismatch of their skills with an assignment at an organization. The frustration that a volunteer can feel

when he or she is not properly trained or does not understand the needs or requirements of an organization can be a detriment to the organization.

Planning Investments

Even with dollars dedicated to developing information technology infrastructure or providing staff training, organizations often lack a strategic plan on how to effectively spend them. Very few nonprofit organizations have long-term technology plans in place that could help guide the organization in making wise and educated decisions. Some of the key reasons that nonprofits often invest in technology revolve around competition between nonprofits or external pressures. These two key factors often lead to information technology purchases that do not fit strategic needs of the organization. When regarding competition, some nonprofits extend their scope and enhance their services using information technology; other nonprofits may feel pressured to follow their lead, often without the organizations' leaders understanding the ramifications of such an implementation.

Second, external pressures may be another factor that can lead nonprofits to react and enhance their services using information technology through opportunities for new funding or requirements imposed, such as accountability and performance measurements. These external pressures may force the nonprofit to implement technology that does not provide the best solution.

This illustrates the importance of strategic planning—ensuring the use of the right technology for the right purpose. This is evidenced by a story about an African village and a bell. The village invited a delegation of Western technology experts to help the villagers build communication technology. The delegation spoke to the village leader about the plan for a sophisticated information technology station. The village leader listened respectfully, and after hearing all the wonders of modern information technology, he requested a simple bell. Rung once, it is time to gather in the village; rung twice, the well has run dry; and so on. The delegation was shocked. They had not asked first but assumed what was needed. They thought modern technology held all the answers, but they failed to ask the right questions.

Planning provides the organization an opportunity to reflect and ask the right questions, which allows for the alignment of the information technology strategic plan with the overall strategic plan. Without thoughtful deliberation, the nonprofits could implement technology that will not be used effectively or help the organization to be more efficient. Investment in planning is significant to information technology project success, both in the overall information technology planning process and the planning of specific information technology projects. Nonprofit organizations struggle to find balance between tactical and strategic work and often information technology projects are not well planned or managed.

Nonprofit organizations often rely on their information technology staff or contractors to make key planning decisions regarding information technology. Without an experienced decision maker helping to guide the strategic decision-making process, the organization relies on the decisions of information technology staff or contractors who, if not given clear direction, will fall back on their knowledge. Thus, the technology often drives the organization instead of the organization driving the technology.

Most organizations do not tie their information technology strategic plans to their organization's strategic plan. The main dilemma is that organizations lack anyone with technology skills who also has intimate knowledge of the organization. The individual in charge is often a human services person who understands the opportunities offered by technology but struggles with its strategic use. The individual is stuck in a tactical realm following guidelines and benchmarks instead of driving the technology based on the organization's needs.

Finally, information technology projects lack planning or management. Projects start without dedicated staff to manage the project or, worse, a consultant manages the project. Often, those in charge of the project plan do not know what questions to ask, and they rely on consultants to guide or develop systems based on the consultant's skill instead of the organization's needs and requirements.

IT Sector

Support from the IT sector to the nonprofit sector is important to successful implementation of technology. These resources often come from the private sector and include hardware, software, and consultants. As discussed earlier, consultants can be a barrier to effective use of technology but as important are the hardware and software applications that are used within the sector. If the IT sector does not provide these resources to nonprofit organizations, it is likely nonprofit organizations either will have to develop their own products or will do without resources that fit their needs.

Currently, the IT sector supports nonprofits through the use of accounting and donor management software. These software packages currently help the nonprofit sector and are the most effectively used technology within most nonprofit organizations. The areas where nonprofits are struggling relate to the data they collect on their clients, demographics, and usage information. Most nonprofits continue to use homegrown, outdated systems to maintain and manage this information. Often, the systems become a web of various tools to collect and report on data, and work-arounds are developed internally to provide accurately reported data to the leadership of the organization.

Overcoming Barriers

This is not to say the sector has been without success. Through public policy, we have seen an emergence of e-government, which has provided a venue for nonprofits to communicate with their political officials and become more engaged in the political process. Also, an area of technology use for nonprofits that has been quite successful is in the use of accounting and financial management. What has been seen here is a key role that was played by staffs with the needed skills, organizations with the capacity to support the products and the staffs, the type of organizations with the ability to embrace the technology, and an information technology sector with the ability to focus on a need of the sector.

Nonprofits must begin to look at information technology as a strategic tool. Instead of having the technology drive the organization's goals, the goals should drive the technology. The following are some recommendations on overcoming the various barriers presented to nonprofit organizations.

Create baseline budget line items for information technology that support the maintenance and growth of information technology in the organization—nonprofit organizations embrace technology, but the amount of money available for information technology is limited and, too often, a victim of budget cuts. It is critical that organizations build a baseline budget item for information technology to support the growth and maintenance of information technology. Spend the information technology budget throughout the year, not just at the end of the year if money is remaining. Pay for information technology work as you would pay for your utility bills, on a regular basis.

Develop a Technology Committee in Which Board Members, Staff, and Volunteers Can Participate

This committee will provide much of the information technology knowledge that these organizations lack. The committee would provide peer support, recommendations, and guidance to the nonprofit organization. The individuals selected can come from the board and volunteers in the community. The information technology staff of the organization, along with any other technology-savvy individuals, should also be included in this committee. Be sure to incorporate the naysayers in an organization, for they provide unique and differing viewpoints that can help keep the technology from driving the goals.

Use Consultants to Help Support With Their Expertise but Not to Drive Information Technology Projects

A clear vision and focus for consultants will help in the successful implementation of information technology projects in the organization. All projects should be managed and supported by internal staff in the organization, not by an outside consultant. When engaging a consultant, clearly outline the requirements expected of the consultant and those expected of the organization.

Provide Ongoing Continuing Education for All Staff

This particular investment is critical because staff has very little information technology support or education. The importance of education is described well by a human services organization's chief operating officer who stated to the author,

> We are a human service agency, we are not a technology firm and we have non-technical people using a lot of our technology. And if you don't have that bridge between the technology verbiage and usage, to that human service part, you can give them the best instruments in the world but they won't use them and in some instance, won't use them well.

Organizations need to provide information technology education regularly, and this can be accomplished through brown-bag lunches or staff meetings. The education could occur as often as monthly or less frequently, but the key is to provide regular education for staff focused specifically on information technology.

Embed Information Technology Into the Organization's Strategic Plan

Planning is essential to effective use of information technology. When using the strategic plan to drive the requirements of information technology, the projects will align with the organization's goals rather than focus on guidelines and benchmarks. Often, tactics are confused with strategy, but they are different. A tactic is a very specific task to be accomplished, while a strategy is an overarching broader goal, which the tactic supports. It is important to create a tactical plan, but that should be given to the information technology staff to use for implementation. The overall information technology strategy should be embedded into the strategic plan of the organization.

Provide Project Planning and Support for All Information Technology Projects in Organizations

Support and manage every information technology project undertaken by the organization by assigning a key staff person to the project. To ensure successful information technology project implementation, allocate sufficient time and organizational assistance to the individual supporting the project. Organizational assistance can be given through education, such external resources as a team of advisers like the Technology Committee, and organizational leadership. These individuals should have a good understanding of the organization.

Identify Key Measurements for Identifying Success

Knowing your goals and objectives for the project by developing key measurements will help to identify project success and, in the case of failure, with learning what to avoid next time. Drive the measurements by the goals of the organization. For example, the goal of being able to track clients more efficiently could have the measurement of staff spending less time managing client paperwork. These types of measurements will allow the organization to reflect on projects that can be successfully completed internally and those where external support would be beneficial.

Provide Internal Backup for Volunteers

Volunteers can provide much support and help in regard to IT, but day-to-day volunteers should not be working on mission critical applications without backup of staff within the organization. Nothing is worse for an organization than having a volunteer set up a website then leave without providing any information on how to maintain or manage the site. This puts the nonprofit in an awkward position of finding another volunteer, hiring a consultant, or finding staff to uncover the answers.

Hire Staff With an Acumen for Technology

When hiring staff, verify that they have the skill set to learn new technology. This can be done by testing the individual during the hiring process by providing specific tasks to accomplish. These tasks may be simple, such as writing a letter, or more complex tasks, such as updating a website. Whatever the test, make sure that existing staffers are also able to complete the tasks required by new staff. Those not able to complete those tasks should be provided more education.

Always Ask for a Discount

The IT sector is beginning to notice the nonprofit sector, and companies are providing software to the sector for a fee. Many of these companies are offering discounts or purchasing discounts to nonprofit organizations.

Questions to Consider

As noted, nonprofit organizations struggle to use technology effectively. They are lean in usage of technology and lack the resources to provide what is necessary for IT to be effective. The three investments, infrastructure, human capital, and planning, can often stand in the way. It may be necessary for the leader of an organization to decide against a project as the investments are not possible.

The questions in Table 77.1 are intended to help with making decisions related to a specific technology project. There may be additional questions to add to the list, but this list can serve as a starting point. The questions in Table 77.2 are just a sample with examples from a sample organization. Use it as a guide.

Project Description:	
	Answers
Questions related to specific resources that will support internal functions of the organization	
Does the organization have an organization-wide technology budget?	
Does the technology budget include existing and future technology investments?	
Does the organization have the ability to support any new technology investments for this project?	
Questions related to supporting the human assets of the organization	
Does the organization have the ability to provide time and resources for staff and/or volunteers to acquire education?	
Will staff and/or volunteers be learning something new that changes the internal processes of the organization?	
Does the project require a consultant? If so, does the consultant understand the inner workings of the organization and nonprofit organization?	
Questions related to the strategic plan on how to effectively spend the organization's money	
Is this project critical to the strategic direction of the organization?	
Is the project supported by the board?	
What will be done if the project fails?	
Summary	

Table 77.1   Technology Project Planning Questions

Project Description: Develop website that can be updated and managed by staff.	
	Answers
Questions related to specific resources that will support internal functions of the organization	
Does the organization have an organization-wide technology budget?	Yes, the organization has a technology budget for the entire organization.
Does the technology budget include existing and future technology investments?	Yes and no, the technology budget includes the cost of existing technology but not its future cost.
Does the organization have the ability to support any new technology investments for this project?	No, currently the organization is only able to support the existing investments. Any new investments would require additional funding to be found.

Table 77.2   Technology Project Planning Sample

	Answers
Questions related to supporting the organization's human assets	
Does the organization have the ability to provide time and resources for staff and/or volunteers to acquire education?	Yes, staff and board are collaborating on this project. Board will provide the education to the staff and/or volunteers. Additionally, outside training will be provided to staff and/or volunteers.
Will staff and/or volunteers be learning something new that changes the internal processes of the organization?	Yes, the internal processes of the organization will need to change. Staff and/or volunteers will need to develop and design the new processes on updating and maintain the website.
Does the project require a consultant? If so, does the consultant understand the inner workings of the organization and nonprofit organizations?	Yes, an outside training firm will be hired to train staff and/or volunteers on the usage of the new system. The system will also be developed by an outside consulting firm. The consultant does not know the inner workings of the organization nor of nonprofits in general. Staff and/or volunteers will need to educate the consultant.
Questions related to the strategic plan on how to effectively spend the organization's money	
Is this project critical to the strategic direction of the organization?	No, this project is not critical to the strategic directions or goals of the organization.
Is the project supported by the board?	Yes, the board initiated this project and feels it will help them with some short-term goals and other organizational goals.
What will be done if the project fails?	Hopefully, the organization will learn from the mistakes and try to make it work.
Summary	The project has little to do with the organization's strategic goals but is a tactic toward helping to effectively manage our communications. Currently, we have to wait months for website updates to take place and this new system will allow us to make our own changes.

Summary

As Jim Collins in his book *Good to Great* writes about the use of technology in companies that went from being "good" to being "great" companies, "when used right, technology becomes an accelerator of momentum, not a creator of it. The good-to-great companies never began their transition with pioneering technology, for the simple reason that you cannot make good use of technology until you know which technologies are relevant" (Collins, 2001, p. 152). So with this, we know that technology will be a catalyst for taking a company from being good to being great but will not be the sole reason for the transition to a great company. Often, those great companies will not even list technology as a top-10 tool that helped their companies move from being good to great. But it is clear, technology played a role—but that role would not be successful without the investments in infrastructure, planning, and most especially human capital. Technology can also potentially hinder an organization's ability to grow if used ineffectively and without thought.

Both the nonprofit and IT sectors need to increase their capacities. An internal and external change needs to take place for success with IT implementation in nonprofit organizations. Both nonprofits and the IT sector need to increase their capacities, in different ways.

For those interested in being involved in the nonprofit sector as a career, it is important to note that the sector is changing rapidly. Gone are the times when one could set aside technology as a tool and just interact with people. While service to individuals is mission critical to a nonprofit's success, that service will include the use of technology. It would benefit those looking at the sector as well as those in the sector to continue their technology education by taking classes at a community college or adding technology courses to their existing coursework.

Why Important to Undergraduates

The nonprofit landscape as it relates to technology is changing. Many organizations are embracing the use of new technology tools, such as social media tools like Facebook, MySpace, Twitter, and so on, but there are investments that must be made for success. These investments include staff time and resources and possibly actual dollars.

Undergraduates have been exposed to technology both for recreational and academic purposes. It is important that the student understand the gaps that will be found in the nonprofit sector and how those gaps may be filled. Some will require outside help or support, but many are well within the abilities of the newly hired individual. It could be as simple as training existing staff on how to use an existing database system or spreadsheet program, or it could be the more complicated task of being the project manager of a technology project. The skills and training the undergraduate brings to the nonprofit can become an invaluable resource to the organization.

References and Further Readings

Blau, A. (2001). *More than bit players: How information technology will change the ways nonprofits and foundations work and thrive in the information age.* New York: Surdna Foundation.

Collins, J. (2001). *Good to great.* New York: HarperCollins.

Corder, K. (2001). Acquiring new technology: Comparing nonprofit and public sector agencies. *Administration and Society, 33,* 194–219.

Cortes, M., & Rafter, K. M. (2007). *Nonprofits & technology: Emerging research for usable knowledge.* Chicago: Lyceum Books.

Finn, S., Maher, J. K., & Forster, J. (2006). Indicators of information and communication technology adoption in the nonprofit sector. *Nonprofit Management & Leadership, 16*(3), 277–295.

Forester, J. J. (2008). *Southwestern Pennsylvania nonprofit technology survey 2008.* Pittsburgh, PA: Robert Morris University, Bayer Center for Nonprofit Management.

Hackler, D., & Saxton, G. D. (2007, May/June). The strategic use of information technology by nonprofit organizations: Increasing capacity and untapped potential. *Public Administration Review, 67*(3), 474–487.

McKinsey Global Institute. (2002, November). *How information technology enables productivity growth.* San Francisco: Author.

McPherson, R. C. (2007). *Digital giving: How technology is changing charity.* Lincoln, NE: iUniverse.

Saidel, J., & Cour, S. (2003). Information technology and the voluntary sector workplace. *Nonprofit and Voluntary Sector Quarterly, 32*(1), 5–24.

78

LEADING NEW TECHNOLOGY INNOVATION

HEATHER CARPENTER

University of San Diego

Technology is an integral part of all organizations. The majority of nonprofit organizations have a computer with e-mail and access to the Internet and a website. Yet many nonprofit leaders often overlook and underutilize technology within their organizations. This is especially the case with nonprofits that view technology as an administrative component versus an integral and strategic part of the entire organization. Additionally, technology has evolved so quickly in the last 10 years that many nonprofit leaders struggle to make decisions to meet the minimum technology requirements needed to accomplish their programs and missions.

Hackler and Saxton (2007) define six competencies that are critical for strategic technology innovation in nonprofit organizations. These competencies, which are supported by literature, include "(1) information technology (IT) planning; (2) IT budgeting, staffing, and training; (3) Internet and Web site capabilities and use; (4) measuring IT effectiveness; (5) board support and involvement in IT decision-making; and (6) leaders' understanding of the strategic potential of information technology" (p. 474). One additional competency will be explained in this chapter: (7) selecting hardware and software. These seven competencies are the key for nonprofit leaders to lead new technology innovation within their organizations, which impacts nonprofit programs and mission achievement.

IT Planning

Nonprofit technologists (e.g., staff, consultants, nonprofit technology assistance providers) encourage nonprofit managers to integrate technology into the organizational-planning process (Gilbert, 2009), and previous research indicates organizations with Internet access are more likely to engage in technology planning (Hackler & Saxton, 2007). Recent studies show, however, that 63% of nonprofits do not have a formal technology plan (Levine, 2008a), so the majority of nonprofits must overcome a lot of barriers to even begin the technology-planning process. Many of these barriers and/or decisions are capacity related (e.g., allocating time and money to the process). In many cases, nonprofits must shift resources away from programs and services to engage in technology planning (Merkel et al., 2007). Typical technology planning decisions a nonprofit leader must face are, How do I create a technology plan? Should I integrate technology planning into the annual budget planning process for my organization? What should I include in a technology plan? Key studies about nonprofit technology planning and key resources will be used to explain successful technology planning steps.

One group of researchers (Merkel et al., 2007) is helping nonprofits overcome barriers to engage in technological planning. Their participatory research approach empowers nonprofits to take control over the technology planning process. As a result, nonprofits have integrated technology planning into their day-to-day activities. Similar research confirms that when nonprofits engage in technology planning, they are more successful in accomplishing their work (Silverman, Rafter, & Martinez, 2007). Researchers also suggest that nonprofits' obstacles to engage in technology planning could be caused by the few funders that support technology projects and initiatives within nonprofit organizations (Cortez & Rafter, 2007).

Tech Soup (http://www.techsoup.org) and the *Philanthropy Journal* (http://www.philanthropyjournal.com) provide practical how-to articles on technology planning to help nonprofits overcome technology-planning obstacles. These articles state that successful technology planning is achieved when all members of the organization are involved in the planning process. There are also a variety of other technology-planning guidebooks, seminars, and consultants that offer technology-planning assistance to nonprofits.

IT Budgeting, Staffing, and Training

In many cases, large national nonprofits have technology departments and IT support staff working within their organizations, yet small nonprofits (with budgets less than $1 million) struggle with technology innovation (Wing, Pollak, & Blackwood, 2008). Researchers have determined that tech-savvy organizations are more likely to engage in IT budgeting, staffing, and training than smaller organizations (Weill & Aral, 2005). For nonprofit leaders to become proficient in technology, they must make key decisions, such as, How large should my IT budget be? What percentage of my organizational budget should my IT budget be? What line items should I include in the IT budget? Should someone within the organization handle IT, or should I hire an outside consultant to handle our IT needs? How many hours would this person spend on the technology needs in the office? What type of technology training does my staff need? What type of IT training is available? Key studies about nonprofit technology budgeting, staffing, and training as well as how-to resources will be used to help nonprofit managers lead these processes within their organizations.

Budgeting

Studies about nonprofit technology budgeting tend to be broken down into budgeting for capital expenditures, budgeting for discretionary funding, and budgeting for training. The Nonprofit Technology Enterprise Network's (NTEN) staffing survey reported that 93% of nonprofits budgeted for capital expenses, 90% budgeted for discretionary funding, and 53% budgeted for training (Levine, 2008a). While Hackler and Saxton's (2007) study reported (with 2001 data) that 57% of nonprofits budgeted for hardware, 58% budgeted for software, and 36% budgeted for training. Although from completely different data sources and time periods, these two studies may indicate that over time nonprofits increased their technology budgets.

Other studies show the differences in technology budgets between large and small organizations. Small organizations tend to make technology purchases in an ad hoc fashion while larger organizations, as well as organizations that have been in business longer, tend to make more strategic budgeting decisions (Silverman et al., 2007). Researchers also argue there is a cost to nonprofits that do not budget for technology, yet others argue there is a cost to implementing new technologies that organizations may not be ready for (Merkel et al., 2007). Either way, nonprofits still need to budget for technology in a comprehensive manner.

There are some organizations that provide technology budgeting assistance. Tech Soup (http://www.techsoup.org) provides resources for nonprofits to create and maintain an IT budget. NPower (http://www.npower.org) and other IT consultants also provide IT budgeting workshops. The majority of these groups advocate for nonprofits to incorporate IT budgeting into the organizational budgeting process.

Staffing

IT staffing is a challenging issue within nonprofit organizations. One research report stated that 1 in 26 nonprofits has an IT staff person (Levine, 2008b). However, the majority of the respondents in this report had budgets over $1 million, which is not representative of the sector as a whole (Wing et al., 2008). If executive directors do not have the technology expertise, nonprofits often turn to outside consultants, volunteers, or staff members who know something about technology. The staff members are often known as "accidental techies" (Bennett, 2005). An accidental techie takes on the role of managing technology within a nonprofit office without it necessarily being part of his or her regular job description.

The 86% of organizations with budgets under $1 million did not have an accidental techie and instead used friends or volunteers to provide IT support (Hackler & Saxton, 2007). Another study of small nonprofits in the Pennsylvania area found similar results in that nonprofits used volunteers for technology projects. However, researchers that conducted this study were wary about nonprofits involving volunteers in technology projects because volunteers may not always have the technology expertise that is needed for technology-related projects (Merkel et al., 2007). Additionally, 44% of nonprofits with budgets less than $500,000 did not have anyone provide IT support within their organizations (Levine, 2008a).

If nonprofits cannot get technology support from their staff or volunteers, then they can turn to nonprofit technology assistance providers (NTAP), a group that is part of the technology subsector. These support personnel, nonprofit technology assistance providers, circuit riders, and technologists span from technology hardware, software, and support providers to full-time or part-time IT staff within nonprofit organizations. NTEN (http://www.nten.org) is a membership organization whose mission is to support these technologists. NTEN started casually as a group of circuit riders (technology experts that generally travel around to help small grassroots nonprofits with their technology needs) interested in supporting the nonprofits with technology (McInerney, 2007) but over time turned into a formal trade association that caters to many NTAPs and larger nonprofits that can afford to hire full-time technologists. NTEN provides a variety of resources and support to NTAPS but is mainly known for its annual conference with product demonstrations, trainings, and support opportunities.

Additionally, there is also a subset of nonprofit technologists (technologist activists) that provide support to NTAPs, other technologists, and nonprofit staff members through their own smaller nonprofit technology events like Penguin Days (http://www.penguinday.org) that teach nonprofits about free and open source software. However, both these groups tend to be isolated from the majority of nonprofits as confirmed in recent empirical studies (Manzo & Pitkin, 2007). There are NTAPs looking for nonprofits to support and nonprofits looking for NTAPs to support them, yet both groups underutilize one another because they do not venture outside of their respective networks or subsectors or do not know where to find one another.

There are also communication issues between nonprofit staff and NTAPs. Nonprofit workers, especially female workers in the sector, have frustrating experiences working with predominately male technology consultants (Manzo & Pitkin, 2007). Organizations like Aspiration (http://www.aspirationtech.org) provide workshops on how nonprofit staff and NTAPs can communicate effectively and work out their different expectations. Also, researchers and practitioners alike are trying to help nonprofits understand the technology decision-making process (Merkel et al., 2007). Even so, there is a noted disconnect between nonprofit expectations and needs versus NTAP's expectations, and researchers have found that either nonprofits are not aware of all the technology assistance available to them or nonprofits do not find NTAPs helpful (Silverman et al., 2007).

Another way nonprofits can access support for technology is through collaborations and networks. Collaboration and networks are important technology support mechanisms for nonprofits. In fact, the most successful nonprofits were ones that tapped into their networks for technology resources and support (Silverman et al., 2007). Also, partnerships enhanced nonprofits' long-term sustainability efforts and made it so that IT efforts were handled appropriately (Hackler & Saxton, 2007). Similarly, nonprofits that had access to technology had an easier time engaging in collaboration and networks (Clerkin & Gronjberg 2007). In a study of over 2,000 nonprofits in Indiana, 56% of them were involved in collaborations and networks in some capacity.

There are a variety of technology specific networks that nonprofits can access. Some of these networks are limited to nonprofits with certain missions or program focuses; however, these networks tend to connect nonprofits with a plethora of nonprofit technology resources and information. Already mentioned above, NTEN is the largest network of NTAPs, and then, there is the Community Technology Centers Network (http://www.ctcnet.org) that provides resources and support to its member centers across the United States. Community Technology Centers (CTCs) tend to provide computer access to many low-income and underrepresented communities. In recent years, CTCs have struggled financially due to loss of government funding, but the CTC Network continues to provide resources and support to member organizations. Other networks include the National Center for Law and Economic Justice's Low Income Networking and Communications (LINC) Project (http://www.lincproject.org) that did provide support to nonprofits that worked in low-income communities but due to funding issues went out of business and NPower (http://www.npower.org), a network of nonprofits throughout the United States that provides technology training and support to over 4,000 nonprofits. There are also many nonprofit technology-related support networks and groups in cities across the United States. For example, OneNorthwest (http://www.onenw.org) specifically provides technology support to environmental groups in the Seattle area.

Training

Research shows that budget size and number of full-time staff are positively related to whether or not nonprofit staff will receive formal technology training. Additionally, nonprofits that engaged in technology training were more likely to have technology plans (Finn, Maher, & Forester, 2006). NTAPs advocate nonprofits should spend only 30% of their technology budget on hardware and software (http://www.npower.org/training). However, since the majority of nonprofits have budgets under $500,000 (Wing et al., 2008), many do not allocate and, in many cases, may not have sufficient resources to fund staff to participate in technology training programs or conferences. In such situations, online learning is virtually required if any sort of professional development is to occur.

There are many in-person workshops and virtual-training opportunities for nonprofits that want to learn more about nonprofit technology. As mentioned above, the NTEN conference (http://www.nten.org/ntc) is a great opportunity for nonprofits to participate in workshops and gain new skills. However, if nonprofits cannot afford the conference fee, there are other alternatives. Microsoft (http://www.microsoft.com/learning) is a great example of a company that provides on-demand, computer-based training where nonprofit staff can insert a disc and gain training on Windows-based software, such as Microsoft Office. Other training mechanisms include online discussion boards, community social-networking sites, and e-mail listservs (e.g., http://www.techsoup.org/learningcenter/training, http://npower.org/training & http://groups.nten.org/grouplist.htm).

Some researchers have criticized online learning tools in that they provide no opportunity for face-to-face social interaction (Kreijns, Kirschner, & Jochems, 2003). Other research shows, however, that the Internet has proven important for professional development within nonprofit organizations (Finn et al., 2006). As online technology training is still a new phenomenon, there is no research to indicate whether one method (online or in-person) is better than the other.

Internet and Website Capabilities and Use

The earliest nonprofits were on the Internet in the late 1980s (Cravens, 2009); however, the nonprofits that were on the World Wide Web at that time tended to be more technologically savvy. The majority of nonprofits lag way behind. Most nonprofits face many questions about their online presence such as, How interactive should my website be? Is my website "a communications tool, a technical tool, or a strategic tool"? (Hackler & Saxton, 2007, p. 479). What third party websites should I post my nonprofit's information on? Should my organization use an online database? Are my data safe if they are online? What is e-Advocacy (online advocacy), and what sort of tools can I use to perform e-Advocacy? How should I manage my e-mail list? How often should I e-mail my constituents? What types of e-mails should I send? How can I track the e-mail newsletters I send? What's a click-through rate?

NTAPs want to help nonprofits with these decisions, but unfortunately, many nonprofit managers take on more technology projects than they can handle even after the NTAP leaves (Merkel et al., 2007). Current studies of nonprofits' use of the Internet, websites, and the new Web 2.0 infrastructure, as well as how-to sites, will be used to describe how nonprofit leaders make decisions about their online presence.

Internet

Since the Internet has evolved so quickly, studies of nonprofit access to the Internet have become obsolete. Researchers in the past focused on how many or what percentage of nonprofits had access to the Internet. Now, studies focus on nonprofits' use of new Internet capabilities, for example, online advocacy (e-Advocacy) and e-mail marketing efforts (e.g., M & R Strategic Services & Nonprofit Technology Enterprise Network [NTEN], 2008). Empirical research is still lacking in this area. There is an entire market of online software but little research to assess nonprofits' use of this online software.

With limited time and resources, nonprofit leaders must choose the best option. NTAPs are working to provide nonprofit leaders with information, so they can make informed decisions about how to best use the Internet. A few years ago, CompassPoint released a how-to guide for nonprofits to use application service providers (a company or person that provides a technology service over the Internet), the Internet, and online software (Stein & Kenyon, 2004). This guide (p. 10) advises nonprofits to take six steps when selecting an application service provider (ASP):

1. Assemble a team.

2. Define your organizational needs.

3. Search for ASPs and get bids.

4. Apply your search criteria.

5. Check customer references.

6. Sign a contract.

Shortly after this how-to guide emerged, other NTAPs followed suit and provided similar resources about nonprofits' use of the Internet and World Wide Web (e.g., Groundspring.org, 2004; Network for Good, 2008). However, recent how-to resources tend to be directed at teaching nonprofits how to do online fundraising and advocacy rather than at providing a general overview of how nonprofits can best use the Internet.

Websites

In the early 2000s, many nonprofits did not have a website, and those that did were larger organizations (Clerkin & Gronjberg, 2007). For example, educational nonprofits were 7.8 times more likely to have a website than human service and arts or culture and humanity nonprofits. Additionally, organizations in urban areas were more likely to have a website than organizations located in rural areas. Researchers suggest four ways nonprofits can be responsive online: (1) target online content and programs, (2) broaden targeting efforts, (3) balance online efforts and needs of the constituents and stakeholders, and (4) use technology to meet the needs of constituents and the community (Hackler & Saxton, 2007). Scholars believe that website interactivity is tied to organizational performance and connectivity with constituents, and nonprofits are not using the World Wide Web to outreach or connect with their constituents in ways they could be (Kang & Norton, 2004).

Website technology has evolved very quickly. Now, nonprofits can easily update and share their content online. In the past, people had to learn coding to manage their websites. Now, there is open source software and user-friendly interfaces, so any staff member can post information to the organization's website. With this ease come downsides as well. Nonprofits now have to deal with creating and upholding a privacy statement on their websites and be accountable to their donors on how they use this privacy statement. Additionally, more and more software are moving online causing nonprofit leaders to make tough decisions about the safety of their data. Nonprofit leaders also must make decisions about third party websites. Websites like Changing the Present (http://changingthepresent.org) promise to connect nonprofits with new donors and constituents, and some private companies are doing reviews, rankings, and certifications of nonprofits—the Better Business Bureau (http://www.bbb.org/us/charity) and Charity Navigator (http://www.charitynavigator.org), for example. Overall, these sites are receiving mixed reactions from the nonprofit community due to questionable methodology and profiteering from donations.

Web 2.0

Nonprofits are beginning to learn the importance of engaging with stakeholders online. Researchers, consultants, and practitioners advocate for nonprofits to use Web 2.0 technologies to connect with organizational constituents in new ways. Web 2.0 technologies consist of social networking, blogging, and online communities. Beth Dunn (2008), an NTAP, explains how nonprofits can best use Web 2.0 technologies in her presentation *Social Media for Nonprofits: Overview*. Researchers are beginning to measure nonprofits' involvement and interactivity with specific social networking sites (Waters, Burnett, Lamm, & Lucus, 2009). Early findings show nonprofits that participated on the social networking sites did not fully use these sites. For example, few nonprofits actually solicit donations through Facebook, a popular social networking site (http://www.facebook.com), even though the press has recently highlighted the success of nonprofits that use Facebook and Twitter to raise money (Shaer, 2009). There is future potential for nonprofits to use Web 2.0 technologies within their organizations; however, nonprofits must decide on which sites they will participate and how they will manage staff interacting on the Web 2.0 sites.

The Measurement of IT Effectiveness

It was already stated that it is difficult for nonprofits to plan and budget for technology. That, topped by the fact that effectiveness is challenging to define (see Herman & Renz, 2008), makes it equally challenging to define and measure IT effectiveness. Some people use return on investment (ROI)—what the organization gains or loses in order to purchase the technology tool or device—to measure IT effectiveness, yet others use metrics or combine the two methods. There has been a push from funders and the public for nonprofits to show outcomes and measures of their successes. Unfortunately, many nonprofits are not sophisticated enough to use the methods of IT metrics or ROIs to measure their IT effectiveness. Nonprofits think of effectiveness in different terms from funders and NTAPs. Nonprofits define IT effectiveness in terms of success (Silverman et al., 2007), and in assessing this success, nonprofit leaders must ask, what does IT effectiveness look like, and how do we measure it? Academic studies that attempt to define and evaluate nonprofit IT success and how-to documents will be used to describe how nonprofit leaders measure IT success within their organizations.

A study of 28 small nonprofits throughout California found that nonprofit leaders measure the success of their efforts by (1) being able to use the technology, (2) identifying what technology they need to use, (3) being able to change the technology based on their needs, and (4) the people that are using the technology (staff or community)

understanding and/or being receptive to the technology (Silverman et al., 2007). Additionally, in another study, success or effectiveness was measured by staff productivity and number of clients served (Hackler & Saxton, 2007). Moreover, in a third study, nonprofits that took over the technology planning and projects were considered a success (Merkel et al., 2007). These studies confirm there is no one way to measure IT effectiveness or success. Researchers continue to debate about the "divide between organizations that effectively use technology versus those that do not" (Cortez & Rafter, 2007, p. xiii).

This divide argument is part of a larger debate about technology's role in improving performance. Some researchers believe that technology does improve organizational performance (Schneider, 2003; Silverman et al., 2007), yet others believe technology cannot be tied to organizational performance (Clerkin & Gronjberg, 2007). This debate could be linked to the confusion over defining performance and effectiveness within the nonprofit sector.

Technology providers and consultants are addressing the issue of IT effectiveness by teaching nonprofits how to use metrics (the number of visitors on a website or the number of click-throughs in an e-mail). A well-known nonprofit technologist, Beth Kanter (2008), frequently writes about this topic and states the two flaws of using metrics to measure IT effectiveness: First, there are many intangibles in nonprofit technology that are impossible to measure, and second, data are not perfect. Nonprofit managers need to understand these flaws before using any metric or ROI to measure the effectiveness or success of their IT efforts.

Board Support and Involvement in IT Decision Making

There is very little research about board support and involvement in IT decision making because the research that is available on nonprofit boards and governance is focused on general governance practices and board participation. Even with little research on this topic, nonprofit leaders still encounter challenging decisions about involving the board in the IT decision making. Nonprofit leaders must consider, How much do I want my board to be involved in the technology process? Can my board help me with technology decisions? Will my board support my technology decisions? Studies of IT decision making and how-to articles will be used to explain how nonprofits leaders get board members involved in the IT decision-making process.

Researchers believe that board involvement in IT decision making affects whether or not technology will be implemented within organizations. Some boards have more influence over the technology budgeting process than other boards do (Hackler & Saxton, 2007). Also, board support and involvement in IT decision making is linked to organizational culture and values (Manzo &

Pitkin, 2007). If a board does not value technology, then this will trickle down through the organizational culture, and the organization will be less likely to use technology. Researchers encourage nonprofit boards and funders to be more proactive in the nonprofit technology planning and decision-making process (Cortez & Rafter, 2007).

The how-to documents about board involvement in IT decision making appear to be contradictory. On the one hand, NTAPs advocate for board members to take a more proactive role in IT decision making, for example, by creating a technology advisory committee (Peters, 2009). On the other hand, sometimes a nonprofit board is too proactive with IT decision making; for example, they get the organization involved in a technology project that is beyond the organization's capacity (Osten, 2002). There is a delicate balance between having a board involved versus not involved in an IT decision-making process.

Leaders' Understanding of the Strategic Potential of Information Technology

Some studies show that nonprofits are more successful when they incorporate technology planning into their strategic planning process (Silverman et al., 2007). Few nonprofit leaders, however, understand the potential of information technology within their organizations. Like effectiveness, the issue of strategy is a debated topic within the nonprofit sector. Typical decisions a nonprofit leader faces regarding technology strategies are, How can I integrate technology within my organization? How will technology strategy affect my organization? Studies of nonprofit technology use and strategy as well as how-to documents will be used to explain how nonprofits can be more strategic with the information technology within their organizations.

A nonprofit's strategic use of technology can be linked to organizational size and capacity. There is a clear distinction between large and small nonprofits using technology for strategic purposes. Large organizations are more likely to use technology and more likely to find it useful (Cortez & Rafter, 2007). Small organizations that do not use technology in an effective manner often lose funding and support from their constituencies (Schneider, 2003). Researchers found, "unequal access to technology in society at large affects nonprofits' use of technology" (Cortez & Rafter, 2007, p. xv).

The majority of NTAPs value the nonprofits strategically using technology and incorporate the word *strategy* or *strategic* in their how-to publications and workshops. NPower developed Tech Atlas (http://techatlas.org/tools), a set of minimum standards or "nonprofit benchmarks" that nonprofit leaders can follow. Additionally, NTEN's most recent book (Ross, Verclas, & Levine, 2009) covers a range of how-to topics related to a nonprofit's strategic use of technology.

Selecting Hardware and Software

The most challenging decision a nonprofit leader faces is choosing the right hardware or software for his or her organization. Some researchers say these purchasing decisions are influenced by donor or funder preferences (Clerkin & Gronjberg, 2007). Additionally, many nonprofit managers are disappointed about technology products and services because they feel the products are not being developed to meet the needs of nonprofits' specific missions (Manzo & Pitkin, 2007). Research about nonprofits' hardware and software use, how-to documents, and websites will be used to explain how nonprofit leaders' make hardware and software selection decisions.

Hardware

Many hardware selection questions arise for nonprofit leaders, such as, Should we use Macintosh (Mac) or Windows (PC) personal computers? When will we need to replace our computers? How do we network our computers together? When is the right time to replace our server? What type of backup should we purchase or use? What type of telephone system should we use? Should we purchase or lease a telephone system?

Previous research reports that 98% of nonprofit organizations had desktop computers, 59% had laptops (in 2001), and 61% had servers (Hackler & Saxton, 2007). Also, larger organizations and organizations whose income sources were over 50% from the government were more likely to have computers (Clerkin & Gronjberg, 2007). Like hardware use, budgeting for hardware expenses varies by organizational size. Small organizations (income sources under $500,000) budgeted $12,532.50 per year for hardware, and all organizations budgeted $126,278.23 per year (Levine, 2008a).

Organizations such as Tech Soup understand these challenging hardware decisions and provide the *Healthy and Secure Computing Workbook* (http://www.techsoup.org/hsc) that helps managers with their technology hardware planning, implementation, and support decisions. Healthy and Secure Computing (HSC) provides everything from what type of computers nonprofits should have in their offices to how to create a technology inventory.

Software

When it comes to choosing software, the task can be even more daunting. Nonprofit managers' software decisions include, What kind of software do we need on our computers? What kind of support can I get with that software?

Although there is extensive research about nonprofits' computer, e-mail, and website use, there is a dearth of research on nonprofits' use of software. Existing research focuses on nonprofits use of free and open source software (FOSS) around a specific issue area such as disaster relief and advocacy (e.g., Currion, de Silva, & Van de Walle, 2007). Also, as mentioned above, nonprofits are starting to use online software.

There are many NTAPs that guide nonprofits through the software decision-making process. Idealware (http://www.idealware.org) provides nonprofit software reviews. Tech Soup (http://www.techsoup.org) provides articles and information about many types of nonprofit software and discounted software available for purchase. On its website, the Social Source Commons (http://www.socialsourcecommons.org) organization is also attempting to compile a comprehensive list of all the nonprofit software and is providing a variety of mechanisms to sort and find this nonprofit software by type, tags, or keywords.

Summary and Future Directions

Nonprofit leaders face many decisions and challenges when trying to innovate through the use of new technology within their organizations. They use a variety of data sources and resources when considering decisions about technology planning, budgeting, staffing and training and online and web usage, measuring IT effectiveness, board involvement in technology decision making, and the strategic use of technology and hardware and software purchases. Data sources will be used to describe what technology research and resources nonprofit leaders access; as well, recommendations will be made on how nonprofit leaders can better access nonprofit technology research and resources.

Data Sources

There is a dearth of rigorous peer-reviewed research on nonprofits and technology (Cortez & Rafter, 2007), and since technology is quickly evolving, the studies that do exist on nonprofit technology use become obsolete after only a few years. The research that exists comes from two distinct sources: NTAPs and academic researchers.

The NTAP studies tend to have respondents from large organizations (with budgets over $1 million) that can afford technology (e.g., Levine, 2008a, 2008b; Nonprofit Technology Enterprise Network [NTEN] & NPower, 2006). These studies provide real-time information about nonprofits' use of technology and are not outdated as are many of the academic based articles that cover specific subsets of the nonprofit sector, such as health, education, and fundraising, and selected samples of community-based organizations (e.g., Coye & Kell, 2006; Finn et al., 2006; Merkel et al., 2007; Saxton, Guo, & Brown, 2007; Silverman et al., 2007).

The challenge with academic studies is that the data tend to be from a few years prior, even with studies published recently. This is common in the academic publishing process: Academic-based studies become obsolete even

before they are published. Two examples to this fact are the following: Hackler and Saxton's study published in 2007 used data from the "Gift In Kind International 2001 Technology Tracking Study." These authors attempted to synthesize a national sample of nonprofits; however, since the study used data from 2001, it is challenging to assess the relevancy of the data for today's nonprofit leader. Also, the Clerkin & Gronjberg study published in 2007 studied Indiana nonprofits and used data from 2002. Many of these previous studies assessed nonprofits' access to hardware, software, and websites, finding what percentage of nonprofits had computers, a server, a network, a website, and access to the Internet. While this may have been important at the time, this is not the case today. Practically every nonprofit today has computers, access to the Internet, and a website, so now, NTAPs and researchers alike are interested in how nonprofits are using the technology within their organizations. Unfortunately, very few studies covered the topic of nonprofit technology usage until recently.

From these types of data, it is challenging to get an accurate representation of the sector as the majority of nonprofits have budgets less than $500,000 (Wing et al., 2008). The data tend to be skewed toward larger organizations that can afford the technology and have budgets well over $1 million. Technology use appears to be tied to budget size. Several of the studies separated out responders of small and large organizations; however, they did not use a similar scale for classifying small organizations. Some studies included small organizations, which were considered those with budgets less than $1 million; in other studies, small organizations were considered those with budgets less than $500,000. For example, the joint M & R Strategic Services and NTEN's most recent IT staffing survey (2008) specified medium organizations had budgets from $3 million to $5 million, which is a very large span. Given these issues with the academic research studies, some studies were not included in this chapter because they were either outdated or were not representative of the sector; that is, they excluded small organizations (with budgets under $500,000).

It is also important to note another source of data: the "how-to" and practitioner-based technology websites and guidebooks. Academic researchers do not usually cite these sources in reference books, however, these sources were included in this chapter for two reasons. First, since many of the academic studies were outdated, the how-to sources tended to be the most current and up to date. Second, the how-to resources are the types of resources that nonprofit managers are most likely to have access to and use when making technology decisions.

Implications for the Future

Future studies of nonprofit technology should include both practitioner and empirical research. Such future studies will help nonprofit leaders make more informed decisions about the use of new technology to implement strategy and encourage innovation within their organizations. Research papers about nonprofits' use of Web 2.0 and online software are examples of the types of studies needed. More training for nonprofit leaders should also occur and include how nonprofit leaders can begin the process of selecting, managing, using, and evaluating information technology within their organizations, starting, for example, with Tech Soup's Healthy and Secure Computing program (http://www.techsoup.org/hsc) for implementing technology hardware and Idealware (http://www.idealware.org) for implementing software.

References and Further Readings

Bennett, S. (2005). *Accidental techie: Supporting, managing, and maximizing your nonprofit's technology.* St. Paul, MN: Fieldstone.

Clerkin, R. M., & Gronjberg, K. A. (2007). Infrastructure and activities: Relating IT to the work of nonprofit organizations. In M. Cortez & K. Rafter (Eds.), *Nonprofits & technology: Emerging research for useable knowledge* (pp. 3–20). Chicago: Lyceum Books.

Cortez, M., & Rafter, K. (Eds.). (2007). *Nonprofits & technology: Emerging research for useable knowledge.* Chicago: Lyceum Books.

Coye, M. J., & Kell, J. (2006). How hospitals confront new technology. *Health Affairs, 25,* 163–173.

Cravens, J. (2009). *A brief review of the early history of nonprofits and the Internet.* Retrieved March 13, 2009, from http://www.coyotecommunications.com/tech/npo_and_net_history.shtml

Currion, P., de Silva, C., & Van de Walle, B. (2007). Open source software for disaster management. *Communications of the Association for Computing Machinery (ACM), 50*(3), 61–65.

Dunn, B. (2008). *Social media for nonprofits: Overview.* Retrieved June 23, 2009, from http://www.slideshare.net/guestf1e806/social-media-for-nonprofits-overview-presentation

Finn, F., Maher, J. K., & Forester, J. (2006). Indicators of information and communication technology adoption in the nonprofit sector changes between 2000 and 2004. *Nonprofit Management and Leadership, 16,* 277–295.

Gilbert, M. (2008, Winter). The opportunities and dilemmas of technology support organizations. *Nonprofit Quarterly 15*(4).

Groundspring.org. (2004). *Online fundraising handbook: Making the most of the web and email to raise more money online.* San Francisco: Author.

Hackler, D, & Saxton, G. D. (2007, May/June). The strategic use of information technology by nonprofit organizations: Increasing capacity and untapped potential. *Public Administration Review, 67*(3), 474–487.

Herman, R. D., & Renz, D. O. (2008). Advancing nonprofit organizational effectiveness research and theory: Nine theses. *Nonprofit and Voluntary Sector Quarterly, 18,* 399–415.

Kang, S., & Norton, H. E. (2004). Nonprofit organizations' use of the World Wide Web: Are they sufficiently fulfilling organizational goals? *Public Relations Review, 30,* 279–284.

Kanter, B. (2008). *The ROI of social media.* Retrieved March 13, 2009, from http://www.nten.org/blog/2008/01/11/the-roi-of-social-media

Kreijns, K., Kirschner, P. A., & Jochems, W. (2003). Identifying the pitfalls for social interaction in computer-supported collaborative learning environments: A review of research. *Computers in Human Behavior, 19,* 335–353.

Levine, A. (2008a). *Nonprofit IT staffing: Budgets, salaries, training and planning.* Retrieved March 13, 2009, from http://nten.org/research/nonprofit-it-staffing-staffing-levels-recruiting-retention-and-outsourcing

Levine, A. (2008b). *Nonprofit IT staffing: Staffing levels, recruiting, retention and outsourcing.* Retrieved March 13, 2009, from http://nten.org/research/nonprofit-it-staffing-budgets-salaries-training-and-planning

M & R Strategic Services, & Nonprofit Technology Enterprise Network (NTEN). (2008). *2008 eNonprofit benchmarks study.* Retrieved March 13, 2009, from http://e-benchmarks study.com

Manzo, P., & Pitkin, B. (2007). Barriers to information technology usage in the nonprofit sector. In M. Cortez & K. Rafter (Eds.), *Nonprofits & technology: Emerging research for useable knowledge* (pp. 51–67). Chicago: Lyceum Books.

McInerney, P. (2007). Geeks for good: Technology evangelism and the role of circuit riders in IT adoption among nonprofits. In M. Cortez & K. Rafter (Eds.), *Nonprofits & technology: Emerging research for useable knowledge* (pp. 148–162). Chicago: Lyceum Books.

Merkel, C., Farooq, U., Xiao, L., Ganoe, C., Rosson, M. B., & Carroll, J. M. (2007). *Managing technology use and learning in nonprofit community organizations: Methodological challenges and opportunities.* Retrieved March 13, 2009, from http://cscl.ist.psu,edu/public/projects/nexus/publication.html

Network for Good. (2008). *The 2008 online fundraising survival guide: 12 winning strategies to survive & thrive in a down economy.* Bethesda, MD: Author.

Nonprofit Technology Enterprise Network (NTEN), & NPower. (2006). *Technology service provider survey findings.* Retrieved March 13, 2009, from http://nten.org/research/techimpact/research

Osten, M. (2002*). Getting the board on board with technology.* Retrieved March 13, 2009, from http://www.techsoup.org/learningcenter/techplan/archives/page9755.cfm

Peters, C. (2009). *Creating a technology advisory committee at your nonprofit.* Retrieved March 13, 2009, from: http://www.techsoup.org/learningcenter/techplan/page11356.cfm

Ross, H., Verclas, K., & Levine, A. (2009). *Managing technology to meet your mission: A strategic guide for nonprofit leaders.* Hoboken, NJ: John Wiley & Sons.

Saidel, J. R., & Cour, S. (2003). Information technology and the voluntary sector workplace. *Nonprofit and Voluntary Sector Quarterly, 32*(1), 5–24.

Saxton, G., Guo, C., & Brown, W. A. (2007). New dimensions of nonprofit responsiveness: The application and promise of Internet-based technologies. *Public Performance and Management Review, 31*, 144–177.

Schneider, J. A. (2003). Small, minority-based nonprofits in the information age. *Nonprofit Management and Leadership, 13*, 383–399.

Shaer, M. (2009). And now, twitter philanthropy. *Christian Science Monitor*. Retrieved March 13, 2009, from http://features.csmonitor.com/innovation/2009/03/01/and-now-twitter-philanthropy

Silverman, C., Rafter, K., & Martinez, A. (2007). *Successful technology use in small grassroots nonprofits*. Retrieved March 13, 2009, from http://www.usfca.edu/inom/research/INOM-Tech%20Use%20in%20Small%20NPs.pdf

Stein, M., & Kenyon, J. (2004). *The eNonprofit: A guide to asps, Internet services and online software*. San Francisco: CompassPoint Nonprofit Services.

Waters, R. D., Burnett, E., Lamm, A., & Lucus, J. (2009, June). Engaging stakeholders through social networking: How nonprofit organizations are using Facebook. *Public Relations Review, 35*(2), 102–106.

Weill, P., & Aral, S. (2005). *IT savvy pays off: How top performers match IT portfolios and organizational practices* (Working Paper No. 353). Cambridge: MIT Sloan Center for Information Systems Research. Retrieved March 13, 2009, from http://mitsloan.mit.edu/cisr/r-papers.php

Wing, K. T., Pollak, T. H., & Blackwood, M. A. (2008). *The nonprofit almanac 2008*. Washington, DC: Urban Institute.

79

SOCIAL MEDIA
AND ELECTRONIC NETWORKS

JAMES EDWARDS

Johnson Center for Philanthropy, Grand Valley State University

The world for nonprofit organizations, much the same as for their for-profit counterparts, continues to be shaped by technological advances and emerging technologies. For nonprofit leaders, technology change presents both threats and challenges to the daily operations and infrastructure of the nonprofit organization. In the current era of technological change, administrators must wrestle with questions such as whether to use social media, when to upgrade PCs, or when to move staff to laptops or smart phones, among other daily technology decisions. Much of the decision-making processes for these administrators rely on a combination of personal experience with technology and advice from IT staff and finance officers. While it is not possible to provide a specific blueprint for administrators to use in these situations, the purpose of this chapter is to prepare administrators with the necessary foundation from which to make sound decisions about the use of technology.

For the purpose of this chapter, the term *technology* is used interchangeably with the term *information and communication technologies* or *ICTs*. ICTs are described in the literature as modern devices used for the purpose of exchanging, extracting, and retaining information regardless of one's physical location via the Internet, Intranet, and/or the World Wide Web. This term is important as it distinguishes a specific category of technological devices from other devices, and it excludes software lacking the ability to mediate communication.

The expansion and use of ICT in our society is having a profound effect on the way we interact with one another regardless of our age, gender, ethnic background, sexual orientation, or physical location. Interestingly, while this digital culture has the potential to remove barriers to education, employment, health care, housing, and other consumer needs, it also possesses the ability to further marginalize members of our society who have limited or no access to ICTs. Based on a 2009 population estimate of 307 million people in the United States, it is reported that over 227 million people have Internet access. This means that approximately 74% of people in the United States have the ability to participate in education, the process of citizenship, gain employment, seek entertainment, and exchange information and knowledge through the use of technology (Internet World Stats, n.d.). For the remaining 26% of the population, this digital barrier will increasingly represent an inability to fully participate in society. Therefore, it is vital for nonprofit leaders to understand and develop a strategic response to technological change.

Overview of ICT Development in the Nonprofit Sector

In the mid-1960s, computer technology was thought of as an instrument for business or research institutions. The technology of this era consisted of large database storage systems that were designed to automate office processes and to serve as a tool for storing large amounts of financial data and performance information. It was designed for corporations, universities, and large agencies, not for individual users. The corporate or business focus of this period is in contrast to the emphasis on personal devices and personal use prevalent in our current digital culture.

In the 1970s and early 1980s, technology evolved from mainframe computers to affordable PC-based computers.

While this transformation in the size and cost of computers was occurring, the use of ICTs expanded to include educational applications. With the exception of researchers, early adopters of technology in the nonprofit sector began to embrace the use of ICTs from the late 1980s to the early 1990s.

During the 1990s, computers became smaller and faster and supported greater memory at significantly lower prices. These price reductions and simplified operating systems made PC ownership more practical for individuals as well as for nonprofit agencies. In addition to these changes, the Internet became more accessible than ever, and the development of the World Wide Web in the late 1980s provided a range of new possible uses for this technology. This Internet explosion led to the creation of "dot.com" businesses that took advantage of this new technology for the delivery of information, goods, and services to consumers. Billions of dollars were invested into the development, research, and application of these new technologies throughout the world.

For some nonprofit leaders, technology was viewed as a solution to the inefficiencies within their daily operations. As these administrators slowly embraced the use of technology as a way to improve efficiencies within their agencies, staff members often struggled to meet the changing demands of their positions.

Nonprofit technology use often accompanied the adoption of an outcome-driven philosophy that emphasized the use of ICTs to gather, analyze, store, and disseminate outcome information and other mandated reporting requirements attached to program funding. For nonprofits able and willing to enter the digital age at this time, the development of the World Wide Web provided an opportunity to market services beyond their immediate geographic area and to communicate easily with community stakeholders. In a relatively brief period of time, the nonprofit community was irreversibly hurled into the digital age.

In fact, the Princeton Survey Research Associates conducted a study of 203 nonprofit human service organization executives on the use of technology in their organizations. This study found that for most organizations (84%), technology had changed the way they operated over the past 5 years. In this same study, 83% of the executives viewed the use of technology as positively impacting their services. Furthermore, these executives believed that improvements to technological capacities and infrastructure positively changed their agencies' research capabilities, communication abilities, fundraising, and overall daily operations. Additionally, the majority of executives believed their use of technology translated into overall cost savings for the agency (Princeton Survey Research Associates, 2001).

While this study presented a very positive view of technology use among nonprofit human service executives, this perspective was not without its detractors. One quarter of the executives surveyed believed enhancing their technology would not improve their ability to carry out their agencies' mission. While they were positive about the use of technology overall, 29% of the executives feared that increased technology use in their agencies would negatively impact the job performance of their staffs. The implication was that staffers would be distracted from their work by engaging in personal online activities.

This concern and the reality of employee access to resources and entertainment from their desktop PCs, led to the development of common security protocols as well as an explosion of human resource policies and procedures. The incorporation of a new discipline into the nonprofit organization produced communication challenges for some nonprofit leaders. Particularly, early in this relationship, nonprofit leaders' attempts to communicate their organizations' needs to IT professionals, who reframed these discussions within the context of what is possible given the time, money, and software limitations, often created tension and even disappointment when the product did not function as intended. For some organizations, this communication challenge contributed to a slower pace of technology adoption or even an abandonment of technology deployment plans.

In the late 1990s and in early 2000, proponents of increased ICT use in the nonprofit sector including some authors discussed ICT tools, such as e-mail, electronic mailing lists, bulletin boards, chat rooms, and the World Wide Web, as useful in delivering services. Other authors such as Vernon and Lynch (2003) discussed the use of websites to facilitate professional collaboration as well as human service direct practice—similar to what has emerged today through the use of social networking.

The past 10 years have involved the development of increasingly sophisticated data management systems, lower prices for hardware, and the development of competitive *open source* software solutions. Additionally, strategic uses of the World Wide Web and the advent of Social Media and wireless access have changed the landscape of how we disseminate information, consume information, and connect to the world. Recent examples of this change can be seen in the political unrest in Iran that was brought to the attention of the world community—not by the mainstream media—but facilitated through sites like Twitter and YouTube. Similarly, the 2008 U.S. presidential election saw unprecedented use of the World Wide Web to raise campaign funds, deliver messages, and energize a political base. Although many questioned the link between this Internet activity and real votes, on election night, this question was resoundingly answered with the election of President Obama. Most recently, the tragic earthquake in Haiti has shown the power of the mobile device era. Billions of dollars were raised to support relief efforts for the earthquake survivors through the use of text messaging from cell phones, smart phones, and other mobile devices.

So what does this mean for nonprofit organizations and nonprofit leadership? What if any technology should nonprofit organizations embrace?

Planning for Technological Use

Technology-use planning should occur at both the highest level and the lowest levels of the organization. One widely accepted method for nonprofit leaders to address their organizational technological needs is the development of a technology plan. Typical technology plans describe agency policies on technology use, security, and privacy and generally outline the purchase and replacement of technology hardware and software. Technology plans are a good foundational element to address the technology infrastructure needs of the organization. While larger nonprofits typically have a sound technology plan, many small or midsize nonprofits often struggle to develop and maintain a good technology plan.

As an example, in a 2007 interview (Edwards, 2007) with leaders operating 24 nonprofit and government agencies, half of the agencies ($n = 12$) reported not having a technology plan. Of the 12 agencies without a technology plan, only 6 agencies could describe what they believed a technology plan for their agencies would look like. These respondents described their plans as addressing upgrading hardware/software ($n = 4$) and their ICT infrastructure ($n = 2$). Among the agencies with a technology plan, 10 out of 12 respondents described their technology plans as addressing ICT infrastructure ($n = 5$), upgrading software/hardware ($n = 4$), and funding for ICTs ($n = 2$). Two of the 12 agencies with a technology plan did not respond to this question. Additionally, only 2 of the 12 agencies with a technology plan had their board of directors' input into the development of the plan. The vast majority of these agencies acknowledged the influence of ICTs on their services, while struggling to maintain their technology infrastructure. While this small study may not be indicative of all nonprofits, it does raise the question, how are ICTs being integrated into the nonprofit sector?

One criticism of typical technology plans is that they are often constructed at the management level without board involvement and viewed as a support that allows the organization to carry out its mission. This level of technology plan is sufficient for daily operations but is likely to result in an organization that may struggle to understand and incorporate new emerging technologies.

In contrast, having a technology infused throughout the organizational strategic plan allows for incorporating technology use throughout the agency, including communication with the board itself. A plan at this level provides the support and structure for the administrators to begin thinking differently about the use of technology to accomplish the organization's mission. Strategic discussions of technology infusion rather than infrastructure management will set the stage for a management level technology plan.

For example, there is a fundamental difference in a strategic objective to increase the number of mentors available for youth by 50% by May 2011 through the use of enhanced recruitment strategies and stating the following:

increase the number of mentors available for youth by 50% by May 2011 through the use of enhanced recruitment strategies, including the use of social media.

The incorporation of technology into the second statement clearly provides direction for administrators and staff. The second statement also has implications for the staffing needs of the agency and the technology infrastructure. The potential use of social media implies the need for staff with the knowledge and skills to use social media, in addition to a commitment by the agency to ensure access to the technology necessary to use social media (software, hardware, Internet access). Finally, this statement defines a target group of potential mentors as potential consumers of social media.

One challenge to consider is that of how boards and nonprofit leaders, who may have limited experience with technology, will be able to incorporate technology solutions into their planning. One solution is to view understanding the digital culture as another desired skill set within the organization. As leaders routinely assess the skills and attributes of staff and board members, the addition of *digital natives* or *informatics* who can understand and interpret the needs of the organization through a digital lens can keep the organization in touch with technological changes. This is not a new idea, as many organizations have found value in adding the voices of parents, teens, consumers, and so on into the strategic planning process. What the digital native (someone who was born during the digital age) or the informatics will add to this process is a level of technological diversity. Technology inclusion at the highest level of the agency's strategic plan is an important step in leading an organization capable of using technology and responding to emerging technological trends.

The dilemma of how to incorporate technology at every level of the organization is not unique to the nonprofit sector; the field of education and nursing has struggled to increase the use of technology in practice. One solution adopted in nursing was the creation of nursing informatics (NI). To move the field forward in the use of ICTs, nursing has increasingly relied on NIs to support advances in the use of ICTs in practice (Sensmeier, 2009). NIs have practiced formally since the late 1990s. NI programs can be found at Duke University, the University of Illinois, the University of Colorado, and the University of Maryland, among others. The point is that the expansion of NI content in the nursing curriculum is an indication of the level of demand in the profession for nurses possessing both technological skill and skills as a practitioner. Similarly, the demand for technological leadership in nonprofit organizations has become equally pressing.

Introducing New Technology Systems

At the operational level, nonprofit leaders are increasingly under pressure from funding sources to demonstrate meaningful outcomes. In the previous decade, nonprofit leaders focused on the implementation of accounting systems and management systems that captured process information, such as the number of home visits, the number of events, or the number of program participants. It should be noted that for smaller nonprofit organizations, much of this data collecting remains manual. The current trend is to focus on outcomes that show individual, neighborhood, or community benefit from programs and services. This increased reporting sophistication has challenged nonprofits to deploy data capturing tools, that often rely on new technology, to meet these reporting requirements. With each new introduction of technology within the organization, leadership challenges can occur. Additionally, there are often staffers who find themselves either opposed to the change or without the skills necessary to take full advantage of the new technology.

From a management perspective, these new systems make perfect sense. Administrators may struggle to understand why employees are not using the system. One reason commonly cited in the literature that may explain this struggle among employees is the *task to technology fit*. It means systems, no matter how well intended, that require employees to change their daily practices will be met with resistance unless there is a task to technology fit. There are several prominent technology acceptance models described in the literature that provide in-depth analysis of these phenomena. In the interest of simplifying this literature, I will draw on one of the most cited models, the technology acceptance model (TAM) as discussed by Davis (1989). TAM provides two basic criteria for nonprofit leaders to consider through the lens of their employees: (1) Does the employee perceive the new technology to be easy to use? (2) Does the employee perceive the new technology to be useful in carrying out his or her responsibilities?

The two components, *perceived ease of use* (PEU) and *perceived usefulness* (PU), have provided explanatory power in several studies looking at how technology is accepted in nonprofit organizations. If we further examine these components, PEU may be inhibited by the use of passwords that frequently change, screen designs that are difficult to navigate, the lack of sufficient hardware from which to access the system, or time available to learn the system. Additionally, the availability of immediate support, or the lack of support, can have an impact on technology use.

When considering PU, employees may assess whether the system creates efficiency by taking into account whether or not it saves time. Or does it facilitate continued employment? Does it improve service outcomes? Does it generate revenue? Questions of this nature can reflect the staff's struggle to make sense of this systemic change.

Unified Theory of Acceptance and Use of Technology (UTAUT)

The TAM was recently expanded to increase its explanatory power by including elements such as mandated system use and social desirability factors. The expanded model called the *unified theory of acceptance and use of technology* (UTAUT) retains a focus on the two primary concepts of PU and PEU. The concept of PEU, or *effort expectancy*, as it was renamed in the UTAUT model, is mediated by six factors: computer self-efficacy, facilitating conditions, intrinsic motivation or computer playfulness, emotion or level of computer anxiety, objectivity usability, and perceived enjoyment. While all of the six factors of the UTAUT model are important for nonprofit leaders to consider, the concept of computer self-efficacy (CSE) has received significant attention in the literature (Venkatesh, Speier, & Morris, 2002). Table 79.1 describes the UTAUT model and the moderators that contribute to intention to use.

1. Performance Expectancy	
Definition	The degree to which an individual and/or organization believes that using the system will help attain significant rewards
Related terms	Perceived usefulness, extrinsic motivation, job fit, outcome expectations, attitude toward using technology
Moderators	Gender, age, occupation, services provided
2. Effort Expectancy	
Definition	The degree of ease associated with use of the technology
Related terms	Perceived ease of use, complexity, computer anxiety
Moderators	Gender, age, experience with technology

Table 79.1   UTAUT Four Determinants

(Continued)

(Continued)

3. *Social Influence*	
Definition	The degree to which an individual and/or organization perceives that important others believe the technology should be used
Related terms	Subjective norm, social factors, image, social norms, peer dynamics
Moderators	Gender, age, experience, voluntariness, governance, funding sources, competition
4. *Facilitating Conditions*	
Definition	The degree to which an individual believes that an organizational and technical structure exists to support the use of technology
Related terms	Perceived behavioral control, compatibility, trust
Moderators	Age, experience, technology plan, training, technology support

SOURCE: Adapted from S. Taylor, "Technology Acceptance: Increasing New Technology Use by Applying the Right Messages," *Performance Improvement, 43*(2004), 21–23.

Computer Self-Efficacy

CSE is the application of Bandura's (1977) self-efficacy concept to explain the use or lack of computer use. According to the term, self-efficacy refers to an individual's perception of their ability to perform a task or activity. This concept as applied to computer use refers to the individual's perception of his or her ability to use a computer. While the early literature focused on CSE related to general computing, more recent literature discusses the CSE concept in relationship to general computing and specific computing tasks or activities. In other words, because an individual may perceive her or his ability to perform general computing as good (high CSE score), this does not mean that the same individual will also perceive her or his ability to navigate the World Wide Web as good. Because the concept of CSE is influenced by factors such as motivation and technology experience, among other factors, using a specific task measurement has proven to be the more successful way of assessing CSE. For populations that may have limited or no exposure to ICTs, the perception of computer skills and the benefits to be gained from computer use may greatly influence the willingness to participate in computer-related activities.

The point of this theoretical discussion is that because nonprofit sector use of technology will increase in the future, it is crucial that leaders find ways to communicate effectively with employees and other stakeholders in a language that reflects an understanding of how others may view technology use. Considering these questions from the employee perspective will enhance the chances for successful implementation. In fact, the best strategy to increase the effectiveness of a new technology is to incorporate staff and constituents in the design process as early as possible. This strategy provides staff and other users the opportunities to shape the design of the new technology to fit their daily practice. Staff involvement in the early stages of design also facilitates the development of staff *innovators*. Innovators are the one or two personnel who are able to visualize how this new system could positively add to their work experience. Innovators can be influential in helping other staff see the benefits of the new system as well as solving preimplementation problems that could derail the project's success.

In the late 1990s, as educational institutions were working to infuse technology throughout the curriculum, it was often teachers in the role of innovators that influenced their peers to use technology by demonstrating its usefulness in the classroom. These innovators functioned as trainers, coaches, and cheerleaders for teachers struggling to adopt technology into their pedagogy. Similarly, it is important for nonprofit leaders to identify the innovators and harness their talents to improve the likelihood of success for the new system.

Social Media and Social Networking

So far, our discussion has not specified any specific class of ICTs; however, in light of the current climate, it is likely that a significant number of nonprofit organizations are contemplating or have decided to take the plunge into social media and social networking. Because of this reality, a significant portion of the next section has been devoted to this relatively new class of ICTs, which emerged during the Web 2.0 era.

Much as when the World Wide Web was first introduced into the nonprofit sector, there was much enthusiasm around this new technology. As a result of this enthusiasm and because of the apparent success of online businesses, many nonprofits quickly erected their own websites without much consideration for the audience they intended to reach or the actual purpose for the website. In fact, some early nonprofit website creators paid no attention to website accessibility standards so that sites even lacked basic information about the organization, such as e-mail addresses, board of directors' information, and so on. Many of these sites were typically static pages that provided little information to the person opening the webpage. Equally challenging with early nonprofit website use was frequent lack of planning on how the site would be updated or maintained. For employees who accepted the responsibility to update and maintain the agency website, there was typically little formal training and few work hours dedicated to this activity. The result was a website with outdated information about the organization and its services and an employee who felt undervalued and underappreciated.

As an example, in the same study referenced earlier, 24 nonprofit agencies of various sizes were asked a series of questions about their websites. Nineteen of the 24 respondents had a website, 12 of which were stand-alone websites. The primary reason for the development of the agency website was to benefit (in order) consumers ($n = 8$), general public ($n = 8$), staff ($n = 2$), and other professionals ($n = 1$). What is interesting about the agency targeting its consumers is that there was no evidence at the time to support the theory that the agency clients had access to computers or the Internet or possessed the skills necessary to take advantage of web-based resources. While conceptually for these organizations a website made sense, the lack of planning on the purposes for the websites may have led to the agencies' missing their targets.

Similarly, consistent with a website's main target, the agencies described the goal or purpose of a website as a place to provide information about the agency to the public and for potential users of the services. Table 79.2 illustrates the perceptions of the 19 respondents with regard to positive aspects of having a website. The five agencies without a website did not respond to this question.

When asked about the negative aspects of having a website, updating and maintaining the website was most often reported ($n = 8$). Four agencies did not believe there were any negative aspects to having a website. The negative aspects of having a website as reported by the 19 agencies responding to this question are listed in Table 79.3. The five agencies without a website did not respond to this question.

Changing and updating the website was viewed as "easy" especially when this task was performed by staff with professional technology training. For other staffers, training, type of software, and capacity issues influenced their abilities to update and maintain their websites. Interestingly, 6 of the 19 agencies who reported having a website did not respond to this question.

As a follow-up question about the ease of updating the website, agencies were asked who assisted with this function. Of the 14 responses, 8 agencies had on-site assistance and 5 agencies had off-site assistance. Five of the 8 agencies with onsite assistance found changing or updating the website easy. For agencies with offsite assistance, 3 of the 5 agencies viewed changing or updating the website as easy.

When asked what difference the website had made to the agency, the 16 respondents described convenient access for potential consumers ($n = 5$) and greater agency

	Count	*%*
Up-to-date information for potential users	6	32
Community awareness	5	26
Access to services	4	21
Employee and/or volunteer recruitment	2	11
Staff communication	1	5
Other	1	5
Total	**19**	**100**

Table 79.2 Positive Aspects of Having a Website

SOURCE: Adapted from S. Taylor, "Technology Acceptance: Increasing New Technology Use by Applying the Right Messages," *Performance Improvement, 43*(2004), 21–23.

	Count	%
Updating site and maintaining site	8	42
None	4	21
Not enough staff to maintain site	3	16
Other	2	11
Security	1	5
Cost of equipment	1	5
Total	**19**	**100**

Table 79.3 Negative Aspects of Having a Website

SOURCE: Adapted from S. Taylor, "Technology Acceptance: Increasing New Technology Use by Applying the Right Messages," *Performance Improvement, 43*(2004), 21–23.

exposure (n = 4) as noticeable differences. This finding is consistent with the respondents' earlier stated purpose for having a website. Three agencies who reported having a website did not respond to this question. The respondents from these agencies may not have understood the question or did not possess enough information to respond adequately. When asked about what they would like to see in the future, agencies said they would like to see new or redesigned websites, the capacity and ability to keep websites updated, increased client and staff applications, and more agency information available on their sites in the future.

As this study illustrates, much of the early technology use was not always guided by strategic discussions about the best type of technology to use, the goal of its use, and methodology for measuring the effectiveness of this technology. The point here is that as organizations rush to have a presence on Facebook, Twitter, Linkedin, YouTube, Buzz, and other social networking sites, it is important to have defined goals and objectives and a clear understanding of the financial and staff resources necessary to fully use these new media.

Implications of the Digital Divide

While, clearly, Internet use and social media have the potential to reach broad audiences, it is also important for nonprofit leaders to understand which populations may not be online and may be in need of assistance to take advantage of social media and other technologies. For these populations, digital inclusion is not a luxury; rather, it is a necessity for equal and full participation in society.

The Pew Internet & American Life Project, a division of the Pew Research Center, is dedicated to examining the intersection of technology and our communities. As a part of this mission, the Pew Internet & American Life Project (n.d.) has produced over 150 research reports discussing the way technology is shaping our society. A recent Pew Internet & American Life Project report found 44% of Internet users logged on at least once a day. Further, information obtained through the Internet was used to assist in making important decisions for millions of users. The information sought for these major decisions included health information, career information, financial information, educational information, housing information, and consumer information for major purchases. With this new reality, it may be easy to overlook the current digital divide (Pew Internet & American Life Project, n.d.).

The term *digital divide* was first coined by researchers as a way to describe the spread of computer technology in this country and abroad. Over the years, the meaning of the digital divide has been reconceptualized based on changes in the capabilities and portability of ICTs and in response to widespread growth of technology use. The digital divide literature can be categorized into three distinct phases:

1. Access to hardware and software

2. Computer training and literacy skills

3. Social Inclusion

Access to Hardware and Software

Early discussions about the digital divide focused on the gap in computer ownership between wealthy and poor Americans. These early discussions led to the creation of programs designed to move computers into homes, schools, and communities. One common method for increasing exposure to technology was to focus on the introduction of computer systems in kindergarten through 12th-grade education. Some programs distributed laptops to elementary students and teachers. Grants were developed that assisted kindergarten through 12th-grade schools to become physically wired to the Internet as a means to ensure access to technology by children, especially those who otherwise could not afford such technology at home.

In response to the gap in computer ownership, some communities developed community access points, such as public libraries and community centers. According to Hick (2006), the focus on physical access to computers is a simplistic view of the digital divide. Further, Hick observed that computer use became a group activity among the teens in his study. This socializing in connection with computer use adds another dimension to the increasingly complex digital divide issue (Hick, 2006).

Computer Skills/Training

As efforts to distribute computer hardware underwent evaluation, the issue of how ICTs were and were not being used became a focal point of the literature. The digital divide was found to reach beyond the deployment of hardware to include computer-user skill level. The concept of computer self-efficacy (CSE), discussed earlier, became a prominent construct for the investigation into computer-users' or potential users' perception of their ability to use technology.

Similarly, Van Dijk, and Hacker (2003) describe the acquisition of "digital skills" as a significant element in the digital divide concept (p. 316). They define these skills as including the ability to operate the computer, search for information, select information, and use this information. According to Van Dijk and Hacker, computer-skill acquisition can be met only after there is, first, exposure to technology and, second, an opportunity to use technology. In other words, the acquisition of computer skills comes after the recognition of the importance of using the technology and then having physical access to the technology.

Social Inclusion

The latest departure from a focus on hardware and skill level of the computer user in the digital-divide literature has focused on the concept of *social inclusion*. Social inclusion, as it relates to the use of ICTs, refers to the ability of those lacking access to the Internet to participate in the functions of citizenship, access to resources, education, and digital networks through the use of ICTs. In other words, the replication and in some cases the expansion of life roles through the use of ICTs may widen the gap between those with access to digital resources and those without access to digital resources. In this way, access to technology is viewed as more than hardware, software, or skill level but as an essential function for full participation in society.

For example, Horrigan and Rainie (2006) found that nearly 60 million Internet users turned to the Internet for assistance with major life decisions. Additionally, Madden (2006), from a survey of Internet users, found that daily Internet use was associated with positive views of using the Internet to enhance the respondent's employment, seek health information, gain access to information on hobbies, and participate in online shopping. The significance of this trend is that without access to this digital information and participation in digital networks, vulnerable populations are at risk of further disenfranchisement.

Along this same line of theoretical exploration, Bakardjieva (2003) discusses the relationship between diversity and the social uses of ICTs in Canada. This qualitative review highlights the patterns of ICT use for Canadian immigrants and individuals with disabilities. According to Bakardjieva, social uses of the Internet for the immigrant populations consisted of connections with their communities of origin through web-based news outlets and/or participation in culturally similar web-based groups. Further, individuals living with various disabilities perceived the use of the Internet as useful for sharing their experiences and to receive support from people with similar life circumstances.

As our definition of the digital divide continues to evolve, there are important elements for nonprofit organizations to understand; from a direct service perspective, nonprofits should work to ensure that empowerment-oriented services include access to hardware, a provision for skill development, and opportunities for social inclusion. From a marketing perspective, nonprofits must consider the most appropriate medium to reach their target population. For example, to reach young African American professionals as a target audience, sites like blackamericaweb.com or Bebo.com offer better access than MySpace.com. Understanding who is online and where they are likely to be found online is a key strategy for using social media. Finally, nonprofits interested in creating their own social network through the use of social media should view this time as an excellent opportunity to contribute to the digital culture through the use of blogs, Twitter, Facebook, Buzz, and other social medium sites. With a clear strategy and proper resources, nonprofits are in a great position to shape and not just respond to the digital culture.

Technology Use: Policies and Procedures

While not always a popular topic, the exclusion of a section about online ethics would be a major oversight. The unprecedented access to information through the Internet has created a situation where information once private and difficult to obtain has become only a "click away." However, with this power comes responsibility, and often, nonprofits are on the front line of this battle. Members should understand that posting any information online creates the potential for this information to be used by someone else, for purposes not approved by the agency.

Understanding the role of the agency in the community and the mission and values of the agency can aid in the process of developing policies that lead to reasonable use of technology. For example, nonprofits serving populations that may be at risk should avoid the temptation of sharing client success stories online without an in-depth assessment of the risks and benefits of this action—understanding that unintended targets such as abusive partners or others may use the information in unintended ways.

In other situations, nonprofit staff should develop an awareness of the cultural implications of technology use. This means that actions online are not limited to North America or to reaching only individuals who speak English as their first language. Realizing that there are many interested parties for nonprofit communications who reside beyond our borders is an important step.

With regard to the internal operation of the nonprofit organization, it is important to develop and maintain policies that facilitate the safe use of technology for employees. In our digital world, it is often harder to maintain boundaries because of the influence of social media and social networking. Meanwhile, it is impossible to regulate who links to whom or who is a friend or not a friend. Understanding that cyber-bullying may impact the workplace in ways not anticipated is an important step. Further, understanding the implications for e-mail use between staff and consumers or defining who has access to electronic records and what level of access is appropriate become important policy decisions.

Some organizations limit access of employees to certain sites they deem undesirable or potentially disruptive to the workplace. The drawback of this philosophy is that it limits innovation and in turn limits the agencies' ability to respond to changes in ICTs. This is in contrast to theories of innovation. The challenge is to balance innovation at every level, while holding accountable individuals who violate agency policy. For example, some agencies have decided to purchase smart phones, phones designed to help managers communicate more efficiently with one another and their staff. Some of these purchases have not included the text-messaging feature because it is a medium not currently in use within some agencies. This decision may limit innovation in the way staff communicate with one another and does not provide the agency an opportunity to evaluate the effect of text messaging from a cost benefit perspective. The point here is that innovation may occur in areas unexpected; if innovation occurs only from the top down, then the speed at which change occurs may be slowed. To avoid these situations, some nonprofits have created policies that establish technology committees. These committees typically consist of IT professionals, staffers in the role of digital natives and/or innovators, and management team members. These committees can be instrumental in helping the agency maintain ethical operations, while allowing room for bottom-up innovation.

Future Directions

Technology use in the nonprofit sector will, like other areas of our society, continue to expand in the future. What nonprofit leaders can expect is increased sophistication in the type of technologies used and the desired outcomes of this technology use. One factor driving this increasingly focused approach to technology use is the attention nonprofit sector researchers are giving this issue. As early research efforts have focused on opportunities to incorporate technology use into the nonprofit sector, current research efforts have focused on what technologies are being used and the outcomes of this technology use. As the sector develops evidence-based practices for the use of technology, technology adoption decisions will become less controversial and resources will be directed to support this technology use.

A final trend that will continue to affect the nonprofit sector is the increasing use of mobile technology to deliver professional network communications, community messages (global and local), and internal communications. Managing the volume of information directed at the agency and the staff delivered in a format that promotes 24-hour-per-day access will likely be a struggle for nonprofit leaders. This emerging struggle may in fact give rise to new digital management tools designed to sort and prioritize information for delivery and consumption by nonprofit leaders and staff.

Summary

In this digital era, nonprofit leaders are faced with a multitude of decisions with regard to the amount, scope, and depth of their agencies' use of technology. Decisions such as the purchase of desktops versus netbooks or tablets require an organized strategy that is consistent with the mission and values of the organization. Conversations about technology use in nonprofit agencies should begin at the highest level of the organization with input and direction from the end users of the technology. Nonprofit leaders should be cognizant of the skills of staff members and their ability to incorporate technology into their current organizational role. This involves understanding the motivating factors that facilitate the intention to use technology. Additionally, nonprofit leaders should participate in the development of technology-use policies that facilitate ethical use of technology and reflect the diversity of the online community. Finally, defining this era will be the nonprofits' response to the digital divide within and external to the sector. Without attention to the significance of this divide and its impact on the mission of nonprofit organizations, the gains made through strategic community investments may quickly be reversed.

References and Further Readings

Anderson, J. (2008). *Future of the Internet III: How the experts see it*. Retrieved December 22, 2008, from www.pewinternet.org

Bakardjieva, M. (2003, September). What knowledge? Whose fingertips? Negotiating and serving diverse identities through information technology. *Canadian Ethnic Studies, 35*(3), 133–149. Retrieved March 20, 2008, from SocINDEX with full text database.

Bandura, A. (1977). *Social learning theory*. Englewood Cliffs, NJ: Prentice Hall.

Ben Wu, J., & Marakas, G. (2006). The impact of operational user participation on perceived system implementation success: An empirical investigation. *Journal of Computer Information Systems, 46*(5), 127–140.

Berger, C. (2005, September). Interpersonal communication: Theoretical perspectives, future prospects. *Journal of Communication*, 415–447.

Brown, S., Massey, A. P., Montoya-Weiss, M. M., & Burkman, J. R. (2002). Do I really have to? User acceptance of mandated technology. *European Journal of Information Systems, 11*, 283–295.

Chau, P., & Hu, P. (2001). Information technology acceptance by individual professionals: A model comparison approach. *Decisions Sciences, 32*(4), 699–718.

Christensen, C., Horn, M., & Johnson, C. (2008). *Disrupting class: How disruptive innovation will change the way the world learns*. New York: McGraw-Hill.

Corder, K. (2001). Acquiring new technology: Comparing nonprofits and public sector agencies. *Administration & Society, 33*(2), 194–219.

Cuban, L. (2001). *Oversold & underused: Computers in the classroom*. Cambridge, MA: Harvard University Press.

Davies, J. E. (2007). Empowering the next billion. *Economic Self-Reliance Review, 9*(1), 20–25.

Davis, F. (1989). Perceived usefulness, perceived ease of use, and user acceptance of information technology. *MIS Quarterly, 13*(3), 319–340.

Edwards, J. (2007). *Assessing technology acceptance in human service organizations*. Unpublished manuscript.

Fagan, M. H., Neill, S., & Woolridge, B. R. (2004). An empirical investigation into the relationship between computer self-efficacy, anxiety, experience, support and usage. *Journal of Computer Information Systems, 44*(2), 95–104.

Finn, J., & Schoech, D. (Eds.). (2008). Journal of technology in human services [Special issue]. *Journal of Technology in Human Services, 26*(2, 4).

Freddolino, P. (2003). Agency utilization of free Internet web sites. *Journal of Technology in Human Services, 22*(1), 67–73.

Gere, C. (2002). *Digital culture*. London, UK: Reaktion Books.

Hackler, D., & Saxton, G. (2007). The strategic use of information technology by nonprofit organizations: Increasing capacity and untapped potential. *Public Administration Review, 67*(3), 474–487.

Harlow, E., & Webb, S. A. (2003). *Information and communication technologies in the welfare services*. London, UK: Jessica Kingsley.

Hasan, B. (2006). Effectiveness of computer training: The role of multilevel computer self-efficacy. *Journal of Organizational and End User Computing, 18*(1), 50–68.

Hick, S. (2006). Technology, social inclusion and poverty: An exploratory investigation of a community technology center. *Journal of Technology in Human Services, 24*(1), 53–67.

Horrigan, J. B., & Rainie, L. (2006). *The Internet's growing role in life's major moments*. Retrieved July 11, 2007, from www.pewinternet.org

Internet World Stats. (n.d.). Retrieved February 14, 2010, from http://www.internetworldstats.com/america.htm

Karger, H. J., & Levine, J. (1999). *The Internet and technology for the human services*. New York: Longman.

Katerattanakul, P. (2002). Framework of effective website design for business-to-consumer Internet commerce. *INFOR, 40*(1), 57–70.

Madden, M. (2006, April). *Internet penetration and impact*. Washington, DC: Pew Research Center's Pew Internet & American Life Project. Available from http://www.pew internet.org/Reports/2006/Internet-Penetration-and-Impact.aspx

Marakas, G. M., Johnson, R. D., & Clay, P. F. (2007). The evolving nature of the computer self-efficacy construct: An empirical investigation of measurement construction, validity, reliability and stability over time. *Journal of the Association for Information Systems, 8*(1), 16–46.

Martin, S. P., & Robinson, J. P. (2007). The income digital divide: Trends and predictions for levels of internet use. *Social Problems, 54*(1), 1–22.

Pew Internet & American Life Project. (n.d.). Retrieved December 30, 2008, from www.pewinternet.org

Princeton Survey Research Associates. (2001). *Wired, willing and ready: Nonprofit human services organizations' adoption of information technology* (Summary Report). Washington, DC: Independent Sector & Cisco Systems.

Schoech, D., Fitch, D., MacFadden, R., & Schkade, L. (2002). From data to intelligence: Introducing the intelligent organization. *Administration in Social Work, 26*(1), 1–21.

Sensmeier, J. (2009). Alliance for Nursing Informatics statement to the Robert Wood Johnson Foundation initiative on the future of nursing: Acute care, focusing on the area of technology, October 19, 2009. *Computers, Informatics, Nursing, 28*(1), 63–67. DOI 10.1097/NCN.0b013e3181c9017a

Tapscott, D. (1998). *Growing up digital*. New York: McGraw-Hill.

Taylor, S. (2004). Technology acceptance: Increasing new technology use by applying the right messages. *Performance Improvement, 43*(9), 21–23.

Van Dijk, J., & Hacker, K. (2003). The digital divide as a complex and dynamic phenomenon. *Information Society, 19*, 315–326.

Venkatesh, V., Speier, C., & Morris, M. (2002). User acceptance enablers in individual decision making about technology: Toward an integrated model. *Decisions Sciences, 33*(2), 297–316.

Vernon, R., & Lynch, D. (2003). Consumer access to agency websites: Our best foot forward. *Journal of Technology in Human Services, 21*(4), 37–51.

Warschauer, M. (2003a). Social capital and access. *Universal Access Information Society, 2*, 315–330.

Warschauer, M. (2003b). *Technology and social inclusion*. Cambridge: MIT Press.

Zhao, Y., & Frank, K. A. (2003). Factors affecting technology uses schools: An ecological perspective. *American Educational Research Journal, 40*(4), 807–840.

PART VI

LEADING A GRANTMAKING FOUNDATION

80

Role of the Foundation Leader in Defining Grantmaking Areas of Interest and Strategy

Joseph Palus

Indiana University–Purdue University Indianapolis

The pages that follow will examine the role of foundation leaders in setting priorities, defining areas of interest and establishing strategy for employing the foundation's assets in furtherance of its mission. This chapter will (1) set the historical context for the question, (2) discuss key definitional issues, (3) review recent scholarship regarding the roles foundations and their leaders play in society, (4) discuss the definitions of success for foundations as posited by various authors, and (5) survey theoretical considerations relevant to the roles of foundation leaders.

Setting Context: The History of Private Foundations and the Roles of Their Founders

Beginning in the early 20th century, several foundation leaders set forth in their own words the basis on which they defined their priorities and strategies. Critiques of foundation leadership and their strategies have been just as prevalent (and just as early—see Pritchett [1915] for an impassioned and well-reasoned defense against those critiques). The following brief detour into history will survey those founders, both directly and through other authors.

A cursory survey of early 20th-century foundations suggests that defining areas of interest and strategy have always been meaningful exercises. Andrew Carnegie (2002) frames his entire discussion in "The Gospel of Wealth" around exposition of the mechanisms by which an individual of wealth might best make use of Carnegie's advice to "build ladders on which the aspiring may rise" (p. 237). At the core of his work is his assertion that the wealthy should dispose of their wealth for the good of humanity while the person who generated the wealth is still alive. Carnegie did not manage to spend his entire fortune while he was alive. However, he expressed unqualified faith in his chosen trustees to continue to employ his fortune to fulfill his purposes.

As another example, John D. Rockefeller (2004) was abundantly clear about what he sought to accomplish. He noted that the best philanthropy is

> the investment of effort or time or money, carefully considered with relation to the power of employing people at a remunerative wage, to expand and develop the resources at hand, and to give opportunity, for progress and healthful labor where it did not exist before. (p. 684)

Rockefeller's philosophy of the foundation leader's role might best be captured by his assertion that "the only thing which is of lasting benefit to a man is that which he does for himself" (p. 686). To instrumentalize this vision of the best philanthropy, Rockefeller and his successors in philanthropy formed their own principles of grantmaking. These included the following:

- An emphasis on wholesale rather than retail philanthropy (making large grants to a few organizations rather than smaller grants to a larger number of organizations)
- A prohibition against ongoing operating support to organizations not under their direct control (like many foundations today, Rockefeller's foundations mostly funded programs and projects rather than the ongoing expenses of running an organization)
- A prohibition against what we today call restricted gifts (gifts that the organization may use only for a specific purpose prescribed by the grantor)

Excellent historical summaries discuss specific foundations and the foundation field in general. Authors such as Lindemann, Karl and Katz, and McCarthy and Wormser outline similar processes by which foundation leaders defined their areas of interest and strategy. As an example, F. Emerson Andrews (1956) notes that in Simon Guggenheim's initial letter of gift to create the John Simon Guggenheim Memorial Foundation, "a nice balance between direction and freedom is preserved" (p. 90). As an interesting contrast to such lauds, Vanderbilt (1989, pp. 139ff.) outlined a process whereby the Vanderbilt family failed to fulfill its strategy because of its desire to directly control all aspects of both its business and its philanthropy. Other authors have examined the history of community foundations and how they developed strategies and approaches specific to their unique missions of serving the needs of both donors and grantees in the context of a particular community. Foundation history thus provides substantial insight on foundation leaders and their priorities.

Definitional Issues

Before examining the question too much further, let us first define key terms.

Who Is a Foundation Leader?

The definition of a *foundation leader* differs by the type of foundation under discussion. Each type of foundation faces different considerations in terms of grantmaking priorities and strategies. Accordingly, each is potentially accountable to a specific set of leaders:

1. *Independent/family foundations—the role of the board.* Most foundations in the United States today are managed with few or no staff; the leadership of the board of directors in establishing areas of interest and defining strategy is therefore absolutely critical. This is particularly true when the founder of the organization still serves on the board. As the body that is ultimately accountable for everything that the foundation does, the leadership role of any foundation's board of directors (or trustees) is almost

a given. The leadership of the board chair can be particularly important. Yet for independent or family foundations (with or without staff), the leadership of the board is even more critical throughout the life of the foundation. Robert Greenleaf in fact suggested that foundation trustees (or board members) are *the* most important leaders for independent foundations in terms of setting priorities and ensuring effective results. Gersick (2006) discusses the critical role of board members (particularly family members) as a family foundation evolves from board driven to staff driven. He pays particular attention to the role of the founder(s) and the importance of the early decisions those founders make. This highlights one central role of foundation leaders in defining both areas of interest and strategy: By establishing the foundation and its purposes, founders set priorities for its grantmaking for generations to come (if not forever).

2. *Independent/family foundations—the role of the staff.* As in any nonprofit organization, the board of directors has formal authority (and responsibility) for the approval of grants or other foundation actions. However, in those foundations that employ staff, those staff members play a key role in researching, reviewing, and recommending proposed grants to the board. As foundations in the aggregate have become more formalized and more concerned about accountability, professional staff has played an increasingly critical role in each of these areas.

3. *Corporate foundations.* Increasing professionalization in corporate foundations over the last 2 decades has also resulted in increased reliance on staff to carry out priorities, though the board still plays a critical role.

4. *Community foundations.* Community foundation leadership is both rooted and vested in the success of the community that the foundation serves. Accordingly, leadership can shift between board members and staff or between different board members, resulting in different priorities and strategies over time.

5. *Operating foundations.* Operating foundations often manage highly technical and complicated programs. Operating foundation boards may therefore often defer to staff to manage those programs. However, operating foundations also represent a viable option for a donor interested in hands-on philanthropy, so board members—particularly founding board members—may take a more aggressive role in setting priorities and defining strategies.

What Does a Foundation Leader Do?

Regardless of *who* the leaders are or what type of foundation they helm, each foundation leader must undertake a common set of activities with a more or less universal set of objectives and outcomes. Nason (1977) notes that "of the many advantages which foundations offer as a form of philanthropy by no means the least is the opportunity to develop carefully planned and coherent programs" (p. 13).

To establish and manage those programs, foundation leaders must, at a minimum,

- determine whether the foundation's existence will be perpetual or time limited,
- identify its area of interest,
- develop strategies with regard to addressing that area of interest,
- develop guidelines for grantmaking to advance those strategies,
- communicate its grantmaking guidelines to members of the public,
- review and approve or deny requests for grant funding,
- make disbursements to grantees and monitor the use of those funds, and
- manage the organization's assets so that it may continue to make grants.

A foundation that performs these functions might be effective. However, scholars have argued for decades about how best to define that effectiveness. One way to frame the debate revolves around the distinction in the literature between instrumental and expressive giving. Another way to frame the debate revolves around the roles foundations play (and have played) in a democratic society.

With regard to the first distinction, Frumkin (2006) distinguishes between "instrumental purposes, focused on accomplishing a set of defined social objectives . . . [and] expressive goals . . . that have little to do with concerns over the achievement of social outcomes and more to do with the feelings and experiences of the donor" (p. 61); Frumkin further notes the complications in fulfilling the donor's expressive values once the donor has died or disengaged from the organization. While several authors acknowledge this distinction between instrumental and expressive giving, they define it with slight but critical differences. For example, Fleishman (2007) notes that "instrumental giving seeks to achieve particular social aims, while expressive giving reflects a donor's desire to show support for a cause or an organization *without necessarily expecting to achieve a noticeable impact through the grant alone*" [italics added] (p. 47). Brest and Harvey (2008), in contrast, suggest that while expressive values can be used to establish a foundation's priorities, instrumental values must govern the implementation of those priorities.

The most immediate implication of this distinction revolves around potential problems that might arise as the donor's successors either (a) attempt but fail to fulfill the donor's intent, or (b) replace the donor's purposes with their own or with a mix between the donor's purposes and their own. When the family still maintains control over the foundation, the latter result may not necessarily be an unfavorable one. Arguably, the founding donor's family members are best suited to understand and enact the values that the original donor sought to fulfill through his or her giving. Still, the process by which leadership transitions occur (from founder to family or from family to unrelated board and staff members) remains somewhat underexamined. See Gersick (2006)

for one in-depth analysis of this process based on case studies. More broadly, this transition highlights a critical (and yet to be definitively answered) set of questions: Is success for the foundation fulfillment of the donor's intent or impact on society? To the extent that every foundation must struggle with this question, who defines that success? Who is accountable if the foundation is unsuccessful? These questions represent a paradigmatic conceptualization of *agency*, which will be discussed further below.

With regard to Frumkin's question regarding the role of foundations in society, several authors offer discrete sets of roles that foundations might play vis-à-vis both their grantees and the larger society to fulfill their strategy. Fleishman (2007), for example, offers three conceptions. Foundations may embrace some or all of these roles from time to time:

1. *Driver.* According to this conception, foundation strategy revolves around "pursuing specific objectives according to a strategy they develop and whose implementation they guide" (pp. 44ff.). As an example of this approach, Bolda, Saucier, Maddox, Wetle, and Lowe (2006) discuss the role of the Robert Wood Johnson Foundation in capitalizing a new program to provide services for older adults. The emphasis of the program was on partnerships within each of the communities in which programs were established; however, key to the success of those partnerships was the original commitment and drive of the foundation in developing, implementing, and funding the initiative at the outset. Another example of foundations acting as drivers relates to the National Community Development Initiative/Living Cities, a multifoundation, multiyear, and multimillion-dollar comprehensive effort to rebuild neighborhoods in select communities throughout the United States. Through grants and other support since 1991, a range of national foundations have invested over $600 million in the development of buildings and other physical assets to revitalize individual communities. The strategy involved in Living Cities relied on partnerships with local nonprofits that engaged in building homes, commercial space, and other community assets (Living Cities, Inc., 2009), but formation of that strategy arguably rested substantially in the hands of the foundations providing monetary support for the effort.

2. *Partner.* According to this conception of foundation roles, foundation strategy revolves around "shar[ing] control and accountability with the grant-receiving organization" (Fleishman, 2007, p. 9). Ostrander and Schervish (1990) suggest conceiving philanthropic action as a circumstance in which "[d]onors and recipients are both constrained and facilitated by the structure of philanthropy in what they do and how they think . . . [while] . . . reinforcing or changing this structure" (p. 71). Fairfield and Wing (2008) further explore this conception of philanthropy as an ongoing relationship, noting that the power imbalance between funder and recipient render true partnership difficult

but not impossible, as long as the benefits of partnership accrue to each partner and the organizations have built substantial trust between each other.

3. *Catalyst.* Finally, foundations embrace the role of catalyst in the majority of cases, "which involves little active control [by the foundation] and little specific accountability for results on the part of the grantee. The foundations sow seeds and move on, sometimes assessing the consequences of their grants and sometimes not" (Fleishman, 2007, p. 9). Millesen, Strmiska, and Ahrendt (2007) discuss how one community foundation fulfilled this role by "facilitat[ing] a coordinated effort to transform community culture by promoting civic engagement and building social capital in ways that were intended to make the community more self-reliant and less dependent amidst an entrenched civic and economic structure" (p. 2). Other authors such as Hamilton, Parzen, and Brown (2004) note that "[s]ome community foundations are harnessing the power of information by creating new knowledge and introducing new ideas" (p. 5) to generate positive community change.

As organizations focus on the welfare of a particular place and the residents thereof, community foundations in particular must manage relationships with a range of *stakeholders*, as further discussed below. Focusing specifically on community foundations, Graddy and Morgan (2006) offer three roles for these organizations:

1. *Donor services provider.* A community foundation that embraces this role "is primarily positioned to build gift funds by serving financial planners and donors. The mission of the foundation is centered on the donor" (pp. 607–608).

2. *Matchmaker.* Under this conception of the foundation's role, "the mission of the foundation is to match donor's interests with the needs of the community, and considerable attention is paid to developing and maintaining relationships with both constituencies" (p. 608).

3. *Community leader.* For a foundation embracing this role, "the mission of the foundation is centered on responding to, collaborating with, and leading efforts in the community to create policy changes that combat the most significant problems facing the region" (p. 609).

Of course, these are not the only roles that foundations play nor the only ways in which foundation leaders implement strategy or communicate their areas of interest. Alternative conceptions of foundation roles and strategies include the following:

- *Core operating support provider.* Cohen (2007) discusses how certain foundations are exercising leadership by offering unrestricted operating support to grantees rather than restricted grants for specific programs, allowing nonprofit organizations to focus on improving the core services they provide.

- *Responsible investor.* Stetson and Kramer (2008) discuss how foundations are increasingly seeking to align their investment portfolio with the mission of their organization, investing their endowments in companies that further that mission.

- *Drag anchor.* Dowie (2001) suggests that foundations act as drag anchors, "choosing . . . to slow forward motion in order to avoid some perceived obstacle" (p. xxvi).

- *Supporter.* McCarthy (2003) discusses how philanthropy has helped to build civil society over the years by supporting institutions devoted to similar goals.

- *Builder of social capital.* Social capital, according to Robert Putnam (2000), "refers to connections among individuals—social networks and the norms of reciprocity and trustworthiness that arise from them" (p. 19). Easterling (2008) discusses how community foundations, which are both dedicated to and governed by members of the communities in which they operate, are particularly effective in reinforcing social capital, given their "deep and broad knowledge of community issues and community resources [and] . . . personal relationships with leaders from almost every sector of the community" (p. 48).

- *Supplementer of government action.* Sealander (1997) discusses several cases of foundation engagement in public policy work, such as the efforts of the Russell Sage Foundation and the Spelman Rockefeller Memorial, to reform the juvenile justice system in the early 20th century. With reasonably substantial resources but no accountability to voters, foundations can quietly but effectively engage in public policy work to supplement (or influence) government action. For example, Hoffman and Schwarz (2007) discuss foundation engagement with school districts to foster educational reform.

What Is Success in Fulfilling That Strategy?

Defining success is a key role of the foundation leader, both at the board and staff levels. The simplest (but by no means universally accepted) answer to this question is that success is the enactment of donor intent. The questions of what donor intent is and how best to enact it have received intensive and extensive scrutiny over the years. Frumkin (2006) discusses not only the importance of judicial mechanisms to preserve the implied covenant between the donor and his or her successors on the foundation board but also notes the importance of donor intent balanced against the obligations imposed by the nature of philanthropic funds as "public funds being held in trust for public purposes" (p. 315). Hamilton (2001) suggests that effective statements of donor intent offer a clear expression of the values the donor seeks to enact, a benchmark against which to evaluate the effectiveness of grants, and crucial guidance to help succeeding generations of trustees meld their own values with those of the founder. Importantly, he also notes that a statement of donor intent is "work in process, first for the donor, and then for succeeding generations as well" (p. 6). In fact, Hamilton suggests that donor intent is less critical than donor *legacy*, which represents the meshing of the founder's expressive values with those of succeeding generations in a way that honors both. Ylvisaker (1991) asserts that the drift away from donor intent can be corrected through conscious efforts on the part of trustees to pause and reflect on how their current grantmaking both meets current needs and fulfills the donor's legacy. While this represents an admirable aspiration for family philanthropy, the extent to which this approach is realistic is an open question. Wooster (2007) offers a range of examples from history of violations of donor intent (as well as paradigmatic cases of fulfilled donor intent); for example, he discusses the shift in focus away from the Detroit metropolitan area that led to the resignation of Henry Ford from the Ford Foundation board.

Sometimes, a donor actively *refuses* to articulate his intent. Consider John D. MacArthur's (J. D. & C. T. MacArthur Foundation, 1989) refusal to provide instructions as to the direction of the MacArthur Foundation's assets: "I know of a number of foundations where the donors tried to run them from their graves. I have guaranteed the trustees that when I am gone, they can run the show" (p. 12). Smith (2000) takes a very different tack from Hamilton within the context of a discussion of every foundation board's ethical obligations. Interpretation of donor intent, to him, is *the* sacred duty of a board, so future generations have no business blending their own values with the donor's intent. Taking the middle road, Nielsen (2000) cites the broad range of donor intent documents left for boards to interpret (or not) and illustrates the difficulties inherent therein. Fleishman (2007) suggests that donors should actively avoid specificity, suggesting that such specificity could be a sign of donor hubris. Interestingly, he qualifies this point in a later work, noting that donor guidance "provides focus for the grantmaking. Moreover, in many cases—not all—foundation donors bring to their philanthropy the same passion, vision and concentration on results that made them successful in business" (p. 220) Finally, Ostrower (2009) notes that foundations established with limited life spans and with whom the donor is no longer active tend to place a higher emphasis on fulfillment of donor intent as key to their definition of success. Renz and Wolcheck (2009) echo this assertion, noting that "having a living founder is one of the strongest determinants of the lifespan choice of family foundations" (p. 1).

Other common definitions of success include the following:

1. *Impact.* As one example, Lake and colleagues (2000) highlight the efforts of the Kellogg Foundation to shift to "*strategic change making* [Italics in original], [which] put a new emphasis on funding coordinated multisite efforts to solve systemic social problems" (p. 41). In their discussion of strategic philanthropy, Brest and Harvey (2008) assert that "effective grantmaking requires strategies based on clear goals, sound evidence, diligent care in selecting which organizations to fund, and provisions for assessing the results—good or bad" (p. xiii). Billiteri (2007) discusses how best to align the size of the foundation's endowment

with the outcomes that the foundation seeks to produce, highlighting the importance of aligning available resources with the scope of one's efforts.

2. *Enactment of values.* Whitman (2009) suggests that a key aspect of success for foundations relates to their effectiveness in realizing "the specific social values that constitute a foundation's vision of a better world" (p. 305) In some respects, this is indistinguishable from the definition of impact (see above); however, while impact focuses on the external environment, enactment of values arguably focuses at least in part on the foundation itself.

3. *Stronger family relationships.* Gersick (2006) notes that success in grantmaking often leads to an impact not only on the organizations and causes about which the family cares but also on the family itself; a strong grantmaking program often reinforces relationships among family members who serve on the board of the foundation. This is another inward-looking definition of success that nonetheless requires some definition of external success. With regard to family foundations in particular, theories relating to family structure and dynamics are especially relevant. Family dynamics can have a strong effect on board functioning within family foundations. This can in turn affect both the processes and the effectiveness with which grants are made. Research by Wilhelm and colleagues (2008) suggests that parental individual giving has at least some influence on children's giving; if this also holds true for families engaged in foundation philanthropy, we might expect that parental behavior more generally, in addition to family dynamics, may influence the future grantmaking decisions of their children, particularly as the parents cede their governance responsibilities to future generations.

4. *Quality of partnerships.* One final definition of success relates to the quality of community partnerships fostered (and often led) by the foundation; this is particularly relevant to community foundation efforts, as noted by Millesen (2006): "Community foundation board members are committed to playing a leadership role in their communities, whether convening resources, facilitating collaboration, serving as a catalyst, or leading bold initiatives to make the community stronger and more vibrant" (p. 15).

All of these definitions of foundation strategy, foundation leadership, and the roles of foundation leaders in establishing grantmaking areas of interest and strategy are informed by a range of relevant theories, as first noted above:

1. *Agency theory.* The agency problem and its relation to nonprofit finance have received substantial attention in the literature. Key to the definition of the agency problem is the concept of information asymmetry. As Hansmann (1996) notes, "A firm often knows more than its customers about the quality of goods or services that it sells. . . . The firm then has an incentive to deliver a lower-quality

product than it promises" (p. 28). As a result of this information asymmetry between customer (or principal) and agent (or firm), boards and donors (acting as principals) seek to separate implementation of policy from command of resources. Fama and Jensen (1983) note that "a nonprofit is on stronger footing in the competition for survival when it has a decision system that separates the management (initiation and implementation) and control (ratification and monitoring) of important decisions" (p. 344). In part at least, the board of directors represents a mechanism whereby this may be done. Miller (2002) demonstrates that the board may serve to monitor action on behalf of donors and other stakeholders. However, she notes several ways in which board monitoring falls short. For example, she finds that individual board members tend to monitor aspects of the organization that reflect their specific area of expertise rather than those areas that might be most critical to the organization's welfare (p. 447). Within the context of the agency problem, Bebchuk and Fried (2003) discuss the limited ability of for-profit boards of directors to effectively design compensation schemes linked to the performance of the firm; this problem is only greater with a private foundation, for which the definition of success is very much open to debate (as noted above).

2. *Resource dependency theory.* Casciaro (2005) sets forth the main tenets of resource dependency theory: An organization reliant on the resources provided by another party (e.g., government or donors) is likely to adopt behaviors desired by that party. For example, government contracts require the fulfillment of specific conditions and compliance with a bureaucratic structure. Solicitation of ongoing private donations requires continued courtship of donors and a product mix that donors can support. Finally, sale of products or services to outside customers requires ongoing demand for those products. In this regard, resource dependency and agency theory converge: Nonprofit organizations must attract resources to survive and deliver their product, while donors and contractors cannot deliver desired services directly. As Casciaro notes, however, resource dependency theory suffers from a lack of clarity regarding whether the funder has power over or is interdependent with the recipient. Agency theory would arguably support the latter assertion since both the donor and the recipient need something from the other party other than control. In contrast, Froelich (1999) discusses from a resource dependency perspective how donors can skew an organization's activities away from its mission if the organization is unduly dependent on that donor. The challenge is to establish divergent predictions from these theories to determine what is more valuable in explaining behavior. Silver (2004) suggests that while resource dependency theory suggests a relationship in which the foundation has the gold and therefore makes the rules, those rules still function within a *relationship* between grantor and grantee in which each needs something from the other. Building on the work of Ostrander and Schervish

regarding philanthropy as a social relation (as distinct from, among other things, a discrete transaction), Silver demonstrates that small community organizations, in particular, are able to influence the funding priorities of foundations and other grantors, suggesting that Casciaro is correct regarding the incomplete picture of the relationship painted by resource dependency theory.

3. *Stewardship theory.* A different perspective on the principal-agent relationship comes from stewardship theory, which posits that in fact, principals and agents can both be motivated by the same thing—success for the firm. Davis, Schoorman, and Donaldson (1997) note that stewardship theory suggests that organizational success is critical to the utility of the agent, who can be expected to work toward that success under conditions in which he or she is able to do so. Although the disagreement between stewardship theory and agency theory is based on the deepest assumptions about human behavior, at least some empirical work has provided support for predictions based on stewardship theory under certain conditions. Muth and Donaldson (1998) suggest that stewardship theory particularly holds when board members are strongly connected through formal and informal networks. This implies for our purposes here that—in line with network theory—foundation board and staff who are strongly connected will be more likely to act as effective stewards of agency resources than foundation board and staff with few such connections.

4. *Elitist theory and other theories centered around power.* Since Eduard Lindemann's seminal 1936 study of foundation priorities and grantmaking, foundation leaders have been characterized (if not critiqued) as the wealthy and elite within a society working to realize a specific social agenda that advances their own interests. This emphasis on foundations as an instrument of elite influence and power has continued to receive sustained attention. See, for example, works by Karl and Katz (1981) regarding foundation philanthropy intended to influence public policy and by Karl, regarding the role philanthropy plays in reinforcing social hierarchies within a democratic society. Jenkins (2006) makes a more specific assertion, noting that one conception of foundation philanthropy suggests that its purpose is to undercut potential political instability by providing support for more mainstream advocacy groups and thereby marginalizing more extreme voices. More recently, Delfin and Tang (2008) discuss how program-specific grants—given to an organization to support a specific program (often in specific ways)—represent an effort to use a grassroots infrastructure to advance an elitist agenda. Despite the long history of this controversy and the extensive attention it has received—see Arnove (1980) as another example of this line of reasoning—the questions raised in this regard continue to attract significant attention.

5. *Stakeholder theory.* Originally conceptualized by Freeman (1984) as a strategic framework for rethinking

the firm's optimal accountability structure, stakeholder theory advises firms to move beyond maximizing shareholder profit and consider a broader range of organizations and individuals that can help a firm improve its business performance. This includes customers and the community affected by the firm's decisions (Stieb, 2009, pp. 404–405). The question this raises is where to draw the line when identifying the community so affected. Balancing stakeholder interests according to the tenets of stakeholder theory has been demonstrated to become more difficult the more broadly one defines "stakeholders." Yet at least one study has demonstrated that with appropriate limitations to the definition of stakeholder, stakeholder theory yields some powerful predictions. Stakeholder theory is potentially highly relevant to the process whereby foundation leaders set strategic priorities and make grant decisions: How broad a circle of stakeholders should a foundation leader consult prior to establishing policy? How many and which actual and potential grantees should a foundation leader consult to solicit meaningful but non-self-interested feedback? How should a foundation leader balance stakeholder input with donor intent? These questions have been addressed in normative terms to some degree. Still, they warrant further empirical exploration of optimal approaches to defining and incorporating appropriate stakeholders into foundation decision-making processes.

Summary

People are complex and behave in a variety of ways to maximize their utility (or, in more direct terms, to be happy). Foundation giving represents a unique convergence of deeply held individual and shared values with the resources to enact those values in order to be happy. As Brest and Harvey (2008) note, however, resources and values—or in their terms, "money, [and] motivation"—are not enough (p. xiii). Also critical is "a winning strategy." The preceding pages have attempted to provide a broad overview of some of the ways in which foundation leaders establish their priorities and their strategy while highlighting a few of the theories that have proven useful in explaining and predicting how and why foundation leaders do what they do. While foundations have been exposed to intensive and extensive scrutiny over the years from policymakers, foundation insiders, scholars, and advocates much remains unexplored with regard to how foundations operate. The questions raised herein represent only the merest fraction of interesting issues with regard to foundation strategy and operation. Yet compelling answers to these questions may yield important insights into the fundamental nature of philanthropy and of the reasons that some individuals find greater happiness in giving their money away rather than spending it, saving it, or bequeathing it to their heirs.

References and Further Readings

Andrews, F. E. (1956). *Philanthropic foundations*. New York: Russell Sage Foundation.

Arnove, R. F. (1980). *Philanthropy and cultural imperialism: The foundations at home and abroad*. Bloomington: Indiana University Press.

Bebchuk, L. A., & Fried, J. M. (2003). Executive compensation as an agency problem. *Journal of Economic Perspectives, 17*(3), 71–92.

Billiteri, T. J. (2007). *Linking payout and mission: A national dialogue with foundation leaders*. Retrieved February 28, 2009, from: http://www.aspeninstitute.org/sites/default/files/content/docs/pubs/Linking%20Payout%20and%20Mission.pdf

Bolda, E. J., Saucier, P., Maddox, G. L., Wetle, T., & Lowe, J. I. (2006). Governance and management structures for community partnerships: Experiences from the Robert Wood Johnson Foundation's Community Partnerships for Older Adults program. *The Gerontologist, 46*(3), 391–397.

Brest, P., & Harvey, H. (2008). *Money well spent: A strategic plan for smart philanthropy*. New York: Bloomberg Press.

Brilliant, E. (2000). *Private charity and public inquiry: A history of the Filer and Peterson commissions*. Bloomington: Indiana University Press.

Brown, M. C., Karoff, H. P., Goldmark, P., Jones, A. F., Collins, D., McVay, S., et al. (2004). *Just money: A critique of American philanthropy*. Boston: The Philanthropic Initiative Editions.

Carnegie, A. (2002). The gospel of wealth. In A. A. Kass (Ed.), *The perfect gift: The philanthropic imagination in poetry and prose* (pp. 230–244). Bloomington: Indiana University Press.

Casciaro, T. (2005). Power imbalance, mutual dependence and constraint absorption: A closer look at resource dependence theory. *Administrative Science Quarterly, 50*(2), 167–199.

Cohen, R. (2007). *A call to action: Organizing to increase the effectiveness and impact of foundation grantmaking*. Washington, DC: National Committee for Responsive Philanthropy.

Davis, J. H., Schoorman, F. D., & Donaldson, L. (1997). Toward a stewardship theory of management. *Academy of Management Review, 22*(1), 20–47.

Delfin, F. G., & Tang, S.-Y. (2008). Foundation impact on environmental non-governmental organizations: The grantee's perspective. *Nonprofit and Voluntary Sector Quarterly, 37*(4), 603–625.

Donaldson, L., & Davis, J. H. (1991). Stewardship theory or agency theory: CEO governance and shareholder returns. *Australian Journal of Management, 16*(1), 49–65.

Donmoyer, R., & Galloway, F. (2008). An operating foundation's involvement with school reform: A multi-year, mixed methods study of a domestic version of cultural border crossing. In *University Council for Educational Administration: Proceedings from the 2007 UCEA Convention*. Retrieved March 10, 2009, from http://coe.ksu.edu/ucea/2007/Donmoyer_UCEA2007.pdf

Dowie, M. (2001). *American foundations: An investigative history*. Cambridge: MIT Press.

Easterling, D. (2008). The leadership role of community foundations in building social capital. *National Civic Review, 97*(4), 39–61.

Fairfield, K. D., & Wing, K. T. (2008). Collaboration in foundation grantor-grantee relationships. *Nonprofit Management and Leadership, 19*(1), 27–44.

Fama, E. F., & Jensen, M. C. (1983). Agency problems and residual claims. *Journal of Law and Economics, 26*(2), 327–349.

Fleishman, J. (2007). *The foundation: A great American secret*. New York: Public Affairs.

Freeman, R. E. (1984). *Strategic management: A stakeholder approach*. Marshfield, MA: Pittman.

Froehlich, K. A. (1999). Diversification of revenue strategies: Evolving resource dependence in nonprofit organizations. *Nonprofit and Voluntary Sector Quarterly, 28*(3), 246–268.

Frumkin, P. (2006). *Strategic giving: The art and science of philanthropy*. Chicago: University of Chicago Press.

Gersick, K. (2006). *Generations of giving: Leadership and continuity in family foundations*. Lanham, MD: Lexington Books.

Graddy, E. A., & Morgan, D. L. (2006). Community foundations, organizational strategy, and public policy. *Nonprofit and Voluntary Sector Quarterly, 35*(4), 605–630.

Hamilton, R., Parzen, J., & Brown, P. (2004). *Community change makers: The leadership roles of community foundations*. Chicago: University of Chicago, Chapin Hall Center for Children.

Hansmann, H. (1996). *The ownership of enterprise*. Cambridge, MA: Belknap Press/Harvard University Press.

Hoffman, N., & Schwartz, R. (2007). Foundations and school reform: Bridging the cultural divide. In R. Bacchetti, & T. Ehrlich, *Reconnecting education and foundations: Turning good intentions into educational capital* (pp. 107–138). San Francisco: Jossey-Bass.

J. D. & C. T. MacArthur Foundation. (1989). *John D. MacArthur: The man and his legacy*. Retrieved April 20, 2009, from http://www.macfound.org/atf/cf/{B0386CE3-8B29-4162-8098-E466FB856794}/JMCT.PDF

Jenkins, J. C. (2006). Nonprofit organizations and political advocacy. In W. W. Powell & R. S. Steinberg (Eds.), *The nonprofit sector: A research handbook* (2nd ed., pp. 307–332). New Haven, CT: Yale University Press.

Karl, B. D., & Katz, S. (1981). The American philanthropic foundation and the public sphere: 1890–1930. *Minerva: A Review of Science, Learning & Policy, 19*, 236–270.

Lake, K. E., Reis, T. K., & Spann, J. (2000). From grant making to change making: How the W. K. Kellogg Foundation's impact services model evolved to enhance the management and social effects of large initiatives. *Nonprofit and Voluntary Sector Quarterly, 29*(1, Suppl.), 41–68.

McCarthy, K. (2003). *American creed: Philanthropy and the rise of civil society*. Chicago: University of Chicago Press.

Miller, J. (2002). The board as a monitor of organizational activity: The applicability of agency theory to nonprofit boards. *Nonprofit Management and Leadership, 12*(4), 429–450.

Millesen, J. L., Strmiska, K., & Ahrendt, M. (2007). *Economic devastation, renewal and growth: Community foundations as catalysts for change*. Retrieved February 16, 2009, from http://www.progressinitiative.com/cfcatalyst.pdf

Muth, M. M., & Donaldson, L. (1998). Stewardship theory and board structure: A contingency approach. *Australian Journal of Management, 6*(1), 5–28.

Nason, J. (1977). *Trustees and the future of foundations*. New York: Council on Foundations.

Nielsen, W. (2000). The ethics of philanthropy and trusteeship—The Carnegie Foundation: A case study. In W. May & A. L. Soens, *The ethics of giving and receiving: Am I my foolish brother's keeper?* (pp. 96–107). Dallas, TX: Southern Methodist University Press.

Ostrander, S., & Schervish, P. (1990). Giving and getting: Philanthropy as a social relation. In J. Van Til (Ed.), *Critical issues in American philanthropy: Strengthening theory and practice* (pp. 67–98). San Francisco: Jossey-Bass.

Ostrower, F. (2009, February). *Limited life foundations: Motivations, experiences and strategies*. Retrieved March 1, 2009, from http://www.urban.org/UploadedPDF/411836_limitedlifefoundations.pdf

Pritchett, H. (1915). Should the Carnegie Foundation be suppressed? *The North American Review, 201*(713), 554–566.

Putnam, R. (2000). *Bowling alone: The collapse and revival of American community*. New York: Simon & Schuster.

Renz, L., & Wolcheck, D. (2009, April). *Perpetuity or limited lifespan: How do family foundations decide?* Retrieved May 15, 2009, from http://foundationcenter.org/gainknowledge/research/pdf/perpetuity2009.pdf

Rockefeller, J. D. (2004). John D. Rockefeller—The difficult art of giving. In D. Burlingame (Ed.), *Philanthropy in America* (pp. 684–689). Santa Barbara, CA: ABC-CLIO.

Ross, S. A. (1973). The economic theory of agency: The principal's problem. *American Economic Review, 63*(2), 134–139.

Sealander, J. (1997). *Private wealth and public life: Foundation philanthropy and the reshaping of American social policy from the Progressive Era to the New Deal*. Baltimore, MD: Johns Hopkins Press.

Silver, I. (2004). Negotiating the antipoverty agenda: Foundations, community organizations, and comprehensive community initiatives. *Nonprofit and Voluntary Sector Quarterly, 33*(4), 606–627.

Smith, D. H. (2000). Help or respect: Priorities for nonprofit boards. In W. F. May & A. L. Soens, *The ethics of giving and receiving: Am I my foolish brother's keeper?* (pp. 57–71). Dallas, TX: Southern Methodist University Press.

Stetson, A., & Kramer, M. (2008, October). *Risk, return and social impact: Demystifying the law of mission investing by US foundations*. Retrieved February 19, 2009, from http://www.fsg-impact.org/ideas/pdf/TheLawandMissionRelatedInvestingFull.pdf

Stieb, J. A. (2009). Assessing Freeman's stakeholder theory. *Journal of Business Ethics*, 401–414.

Vanderbilt II, A. T. (1989). *Fortune's children: The fall of the house of Vanderbilt*. New York: Quill.

Whitman, J. R. (2009). Measuring social value in philanthropic foundations. *Nonprofit Management and Leadership, 19*(3), 305–325.

Wilhelm, M. O., Brown, E., Rooney, P. A., & Steinberg, R. (2008). The intergenerational transmission of generosity. *Journal of Public Economics, 92*, 2146–2156.

Wooster, M. (2007). *The great philanthropists and the problem of "donor intent"* (3rd ed.). Washington, DC: Capital Research Center.

Ylvisaker, P. (1991). *Family foundations now—and forever?* New York: Council on Foundations.

81

ROLE OF THE FOUNDATION LEADER IN LISTENING TO NONPROFIT ORGANIZATIONS

DIANA SIEGER

Grand Rapids Community Foundation

S ome truths:

- Foundation leaders do not have all the answers.
- Foundation leaders do have access to resources and need to use them wisely.
- Foundation leaders do need to be leaders.
- Foundation leaders do need to care about their communities and the issues they are trying to address.
- Foundation leaders do need to be active listeners.

Charitable foundations have been in existence for more than 150 years (Orosz, 2007) in somewhat the same form found today. Organized philanthropy is an area that has remarkably little written about it. The behavior, norms, and framework of operation are just being codified and documented. Organizations like Grantmakers for Effective Organizations and the Center for Effective Philanthropy (CEP) are examples of organizations providing leadership in this area along with the various Centers for Philanthropy connected to universities around the United States. Two such leaders in this effort at Grand Valley State University's Johnson Center for Philanthropy are its director Kathryn Agard, EdD, and its Distinguished Professor of Philanthropic Studies, Joel Orosz, PhD. Dr. Orosz has written a number of books and articles relating to the operation and issues of foundations.

There is emerging pressure for foundations to demonstrate transparency in their operations and decision making. Legislative and regulatory forces are increasingly examining how foundations operate, how they are financed, and how they grant out the dollars entrusted to them. The role of listening is integral to the operation of *great foundations* that want to make a difference in their communities and in their various areas of focus. Listening is their lifeline, and many foundations understand that and are making positive impact on significant social issues. Those foundations that do not listen provide resources for major initiatives that go nowhere and do not address the key issues in a manner that is effective and sustainable.

Listening to the Nonprofit Sector

This chapter is being written at an interesting yet challenging time. There is a worldwide recession, growing unemployment, a declining economy, and a significant reduction in resources for businesses and for nonprofit organizations. Suffice it to say *everyone* is touched by these sobering conditions.

Now, more than ever before, the people who lead foundations need to *actively listen* and *actively lead*. Leading foundations is not a passive exercise and foundation leaders need to understand that they simply do not have all the answers. The problems experienced today and into the future are quite complicated, and leaders from all sectors of our communities cannot escape that reality. Long-term strategies are needed along with the realization that solutions are not going to be created easily. Further, sustainability in terms of lasting solutions and resources is sorely required.

It is essential for institutions, foundations, corporations, communities, and/or countries to galvanize leadership in ways that are effective in a complex and adaptive environment. Adaptive problems are those complex areas that have taken time to develop and for which there is no clear answer or solution (Heifetz, Kania, & Kramer, 2004). To be successful in resolving these types of issues, sustainable problem solving is essential. Further, no one leader or organization can or should do this alone if results are to be effective and enduring. The leadership needed requires collaborative approaches. Social problems are so very complex and intricate and take years to develop. Just think about poverty for a moment. Is that caused by any one thing? What are the root causes? How does one's point of view shape how one may address this problem?

The nonprofit sector of our society addresses a cross section of issues, causes, and ideas: from the arts to the environment to fulfilling spiritual needs to addressing basic needs to health care to every aspect of human existence. It is a sector that is often misunderstood as its focus is not to make a profit for their owners or investors akin to a for-profit venture but to make a positive impact in our communities and throughout our country. If there is a surplus of funds, it is generally used to address the purpose and mission of the nonprofit organization. Community leaders may think that the sector is not totally accountable, yet nothing could be further from the truth. Transparency in operations, finances, and impact is demanded by the public, and this sector does deliver results.

It is a time for philanthropic leaders, those persons who lead charitable foundations large and small, to reflect more deeply and actively use their collective intellectual capital to problem solve as the sector begins to contract in a time of economic insecurity. *This is the time* for foundation leaders to listen carefully. *This is the time* for foundation leadership to eschew the trappings of position and resources to delve into the knotty issues that are present today and likely will be for some time in the future.

Productive and positive relationships with all sectors are crucial for foundations, and this chapter will highlight the key reasons why this is so. An examination of the origins of charitable foundations will be discussed, in addition to a review of the importance of listening, assessing need and listening, adaptive leadership, the power struggle between foundations and the organizations approaching them for funding, the tangle of paperwork and process, evaluating the performance of foundations, and good grantmaking.

What Are Charitable Foundations?

Charitable foundations are still a mystery to many people who may have a difficult time describing them let alone understanding that there are *various types* of foundations. "The first modern grantmaking charitable foundation in the United States, The Peabody Education Fund, commenced operations in 1867. The pioneering multipurpose foundations arrived early in the twentieth century, with the

establishment of the Carnegie Corporation of New York in 1911 and the Rockefeller Foundation in 1913. After World War II, foundation formation accelerated rapidly" (Orosz, 2007, pp. 20–21).

In 1914, the first community foundation was formed in Cleveland, Ohio, fulfilling the vision of Frederick H. Goff, a community leader who wanted to create a permanent pool of funds. "His vision was to pool the charitable resources of Cleveland's philanthropists, living and dead, into a single, great, and permanent endowment for the betterment of the city. Community leaders would then forever distribute the interest that the trust's resources would accrue to fund 'such charitable purposes as will best make for the mental, moral, and physical improvement of the inhabitants of Cleveland'" (Cleveland Foundation, 2009).

From that time on, communities across the United States started their own community *trusts*, and particularly after 1969, they flourished and are now found around the world from Great Britain to Germany to Japan to countries far and wide.

The distinction between community foundations and private foundations is important. On the most basic level, community foundations receive their support from a multiplicity of sources and generally focus their resources in a specific geographic area. Private foundations derive their support from one source—an individual, family, or corporation, and the causes supported are usually determined by the source of funding (Foundation Center, 2009). Simply put, the most basic difference between community foundations and private foundations is that community foundations need to raise funds while private foundations have received their support as noted above.

There are other types of foundations such as operating foundations and fundraising foundations connected to an institution like a hospital, university, or other nonprofit organization. The latter type generally does not grant funds to other organizations. Rather, they are raising money for the organization to which they are aligned or attached. Private and community foundations are often referred to as *grantmakers* and the organizations they may fund are referred to as *grant seekers*. It has been estimated that there are more than 71,000 grantmaking organizations in the United States (Foundation Center, 2007).

It is also quite likely that foundation staff and other leaders may not understand the roots of organized philanthropy and have not paid enough attention to the very core of what foundations are set in motion to do. As noted by Joel Orosz (2007), "It is a rare foundation employee, indeed, who knows even the most rudimentary facts about the field's rich heritage" (p. 141).

The Role of Listening

There are many skills and abilities that those leading or aspiring to lead foundations need to be successful and effective. Strong problem-solving skills, good understanding of complex systems, and in-depth content knowledge on a variety of issues are just *some* of the skills needed. Another key skill needed is the ability to actively listen.

Active listening requires that the focus is on the speaker, and it is a way to increase understanding on a point of view or topic. It does not suggest that the person listening necessarily agrees with the ideas being conveyed, but it does mean that knowledge and understanding is being sought. It necessitates that leaders listen closely and be able to repeat back what has been stated without showing a bias or an opinion. This helps the person being heard to open up and express themselves freely without fear of retribution or scorn for their ideas, knowledge, and thoughts. It requires patience and an openness that will promote effective communication. It also is a bond of trust that the speaker has with the listener that his or her ideas will not only be heard but also will be carefully considered.

The leader exercising the skill of active listening with an individual or group at the community level or beyond is fairly simple yet requires patience, for the primary goal is to understand an issue or problem. Keeping abreast of what is actually occurring in a broader area and the scope of issues facing a community is exceedingly important to the foundation leader. It is a way for leaders, if they are so inclined, to be responsive to what the community truly needs and means being in touch with and aware of key issues in communities. It is imperative for foundation leaders to *listen very carefully* with the intention of appreciating fully what is being said and again not necessarily agreeing with what is being said or promoted. Listening to the leaders of nonprofit organizations is extremely critical for a foundation that may be trying to address an issue that affects many nonprofits and people. "Foundation grants will profoundly affect a community of people, either directly or indirectly. These people should have a say in how such grants are planned and executed" (Orosz, 2007, p. 115).

But what about the environment in which foundations operate? Is it necessary to fully get the lay of the land prior to launching into funding? Absolutely! While research is crucial, listening to the voices in the community can provide much more than just statistics. Understanding the "environment" is essential when developing initiatives and programs. Their very success depends on the knowledge of the community and its needs.

The following is a scenario that demonstrates the role that a foundation can play in listening to the nonprofit sector:

> The room was quiet and the expressions on the faces of the nonprofit leaders reflected the tough times everyone was experiencing. The Foundation CEO had asked fourteen (14) leaders from area nonprofits to come to a meeting so everyone could simply listen to the stories that were happening everyday. She asked them to spend two hours of their time to talk about the impact of the recession on their respective organizations. It was a time commitment but everyone was there to talk and listen. The comments were constructive and two

themes emerged: the need for effective collaboration and the need for help from the funders in the area of advocacy.

The assumption prior to this listening session could have been that all nonprofits just needed funding. While funding is certainly the top priority, the meeting was held to listen and thus to recognize what other roles foundations could play in the tough times being experienced. Prior to this meeting, when the CEO had proposed holding this session, tremendous caution had been expressed by her staff. She knew, however, that a primary way to learn about the impact of the downturn of the economy—on a sector already overwhelmed and undercapitalized—was to listen.

In the invitation to the listening session, the CEO wrote:

> Some of you may not know me very well and others of you certainly do know me. I am one who seeks good and straightforward information and I am not in anyway suggesting any 'foot in the door' for future funding by asking you to this meeting. I just need to hear firsthand from you what is happening. I don't have any other meetings planned at this point and simply just want to have a decent discussion about how this recession is impacting your organization, the outlook, any predictions from your other funders—governmental, private sources, the community and the like. (Grand Rapids Community Foundation, March 26, 2009)

From this point forward, this foundation leader's plans include crafting a way to call nonprofits together to determine any alignment of mission, programs, and services that could help to reduce overhead costs. She also is bringing her colleagues' foundations together to emphasize the need to advocate for resources beyond the private funding to address the critical social conditions being experienced in the community. Working with public policy officials can be made more compelling by drawing in governmental and other funding sources if the voices of the very sector serving the community can be front and center.

In the meeting summary notes, this foundation official noted the following:

> While funding is desperately needed by all organizations representing all facets of the nonprofit sector, these leaders acknowledged that attention needs to be paid to immediate needs; the long-term view is needed to assure that this community grows and prospers. We found that advocacy for public funding is needed and the Foundation community can be particularly helpful in this regard. The arts need not be pitted against human services and other immediate charitable needs in the community. The sustainability of effective organizations is critical. (Sieger, 2009)

The journey during difficult economic times—and ultimately determining the foundation's role—should be informed by many voices that will be crucial in designing how to move forward. Listening to the nonprofit sector at this time is critical. However, regardless of the economic and social conditions present in the environment, listening is always paramount.

Assessing Need and Listening

There are a variety of ways to collect information regarding issues and areas of focus, or test the temperature of various sectors. All involve listening. Conducting academic research is one way that many foundations search for information to inform decisions and direction. *One critical activity often missing as a foundation scans the landscape* is seeking out information regarding the existing programs that address issues or problems and finding out how effective these efforts are in addressing particular areas of focus. In other words, what is already in existence, and are the programs effective? Financially supporting or developing programs that duplicate existing programs occurs more than it should in some communities. Incomplete information gathering and listening through the lens of "we know what this community needs" create difficult situations and the results are mixed at best.

There are examples of large national foundations that concentrate their attention on particular issue areas. Often, these foundations have carefully crafted a "point of view" by conducting research, hiring content experts, and oftentimes providing planning grants to nonprofits, which may include community foundations. The results of the planning grants may inform the future direction of the theory that the national foundation may have formed for their focus.

When foundations zero in on communities, local nonprofit leaders are influenced by the lure of working with a national or international foundation because of the promise of funding and connection to prestige, which *may or may not* bring greater rewards as time goes on in terms of funding and influence. Certainly, the resources that a large foundation may bring to a community should not be discounted. The very presence of a well-known national foundation can launch effective programs that will provide positive change and be the tipping point in improving the health and welfare of a particular area. The prestige and credibility of the foundation can validate the importance of the issue being addressed.

The successful efforts usually follow a pattern though. When a foundation listens to all voices, seeking to comprehend the culture of a community, this culture once understood can provide the context needed when examining statistics and data. Part of this is discovering what is working already in the community and being aware of efforts that may not provide the results necessary to make a positive, measurable impact.

Another way that the larger private foundations seek out information is through their relationships with one another. There have been occasions when foundations joined together on an issue area and then proceeded with funding and programmatic expertise to zero in on an issue area. There are many examples of these partnerships between and among various foundations. Many times, the power struggle between all parties is also apparent. A good agreement leading to the partnership can assist with any issues occurring between the foundations.

National Example

An example of a successful though short-lived collaboration involves the Charles Stewart Mott Foundation, in concert with the King Baudouin Foundation in Belgium and the German Marshall Fund based in Washington, D.C. A transatlantic fellowship exchange program was initiated in 2000 by these three organizations. This endeavor provided support for five community foundation leaders from the United States to travel to European countries to help develop foundations in those areas each year this program was in operation. Likewise, five European community foundation leaders came to the United States to understand more completely how philanthropy is organized and carried out in this country. It was a successful program but unfortunately ceased operation in 2006 as other priorities were identified by the three funders. However, this effort does provide an example of larger foundations working together to provide resources to carry out good ideas. Many foundations have banded together to address issues such as the environment, the AIDS epidemic, poverty, child abuse and neglect, and much more.

Two Community Level Examples

Meeting Essential Needs

The foundations in the greater Grand Rapids, Michigan, area banded together in 2009 to pool their resources to address the growing immediate needs experienced by individuals and families in the community due to the economic crisis that grips the country and spans the globe. Buffeted by the horrific economic upheaval affecting nearly everyone globally and turning to our own community, charitable foundations are working together as they have in previous situations: creating a pool of funds to help finance organizations that are on the frontline serving people most in need. Listening to all the funders of nonprofit organizations led to the elimination of cumbersome application processes. Further, the decision about where the money is or will be granted rests with the committee of another collaborative effort that has been in existence since 1982. The committee is known as the Essential Needs Task Force (ENTF). The operation of the ENTF these many years has been supported by the Heart of West Michigan United Way, Kent County, and the Kent County Department of Human Services.

So in essence, it is one *collaborative effort* working with another *collaborative effort* trying to respond in a more effective manner. The collaborative funding effort is working hand in hand with the ENTF partnership that has the knowledge and expertise to respond to the many immediate emergency crisis situations that people are facing. This is a tremendous response!

The foundations are leaning on the knowledge of a group of nonprofit and public sector leaders. The funding decisions are turned over to the ENTF leadership team. The group of foundations realized that no one funder or organization can own this issue and address it well and it takes a "community" of funders and service providers to work together. It is simply taking action when it is needed the most.

The Grantmakers for Effective Organizations (2008) noted in its publication *Is Grantmaking Getting Smarter?* that delegating funding decisions "to representatives of recipient communities or grantees" constitutes only 14% of all responses from grantmakers across the country (p. 7). The effort noted above certainly is unique and does demonstrate deeply rooted trust and acknowledgment on the part of foundations in the key organizations focusing on immediate needs.

Arts Organizations Addressing Economic Development

Another example that illustrates how foundations need to be flexible (particularly during difficult economic times) is an effort that is attempting to elevate the importance of the arts in the Grand Rapids, Michigan, area. Besides addressing people's immediate needs and the goal of eliminating homelessness, there is the long-term goal of attracting talent to the community. The integral role that art and public museums, performing arts, theater, and all artistic activities play in terms of the economic development of a community needs to be highlighted.

When the economy of Michigan started to falter in 2001, escalating to an unprecedented level, the goals of the state began to focus on retaining and attracting talent, retraining, and quality education. Many leaders pointed to the role of the arts in attracting people to a community.

It was in this spirit that the foundations called the art organizations together to determine how to effectively promote their importance to the community as well as address the severe financial conditions under which these groups operate. At this juncture, a major marketing effort is underway to elevate the importance of the arts during these trying times to help keep the community vibrant and growing; it is financed by the foundations. Further, plans are being made to determine how the cultural organizations can coordinate some of their activities to streamline operations and reduce the operational expenditures that if not addressed may cause them to close their doors.

Active listening on the part of the foundation leaders will possibly result in the development of effective solutions and ideas. Tearing down the walls between nonprofit leaders and foundation leaders is absolutely essential if communities are going to thrive and grow.

Power Differential Between Foundations and Nonprofit Organizations

As implied in the previous section, a power differential exists between foundations and those nonprofit organizations seeking their funding support. To not acknowledge that would be a sin of omission. The personal bias of this author is that using this *power* to only enhance the very

position of the foundation staff or board leader is wrong. In many cases, the money of a foundation may not have originated from the staff or the board. It may simply not be "their" money, and it is their role to effectively use those funds for the betterment of society. However, power is *good* if used effectively in coordination with others to address key issues. The power of influence and persuasion in developing consensus can lead to crafting a positive result. Misusing this power can only prove harmful and can spiral dangerously out of control.

Joel Orosz referred to the long-time president of the Carnegie Corporation, Alan Pifer, in his book *Effective Foundation Management*. "Pifer pulled no punches in his essay 'Speaking Out,' taking his former foundation field colleagues to task for their arrogance, discourtesy, and timidity" (Orosz, 2007, p. 144). In Alan Pifer's words, as quoted in Dr. Orosz's aforementioned book,

> Above all other aspects of foundation work, I would put the human factor. I mean by this the attitudes and behavior of foundation staff members. If they are arrant, self-important, dogmatic, conscious of power and status, or filled with a sense of their omniscience—traits which the stewardship of money tends to bring out in people—the foundation they serve cannot be a good one. If, on the other hand, they have a genuine humility, are conscious of their own limitations, are aware that money does not confer wisdom, are human, intellectually alive and curious people, . . . the foundation they serve will probably be a good one. In short, the human qualities of its staff may in the end be far more important to what a foundation accomplishes than any other considerations. (Orosz, 2007, p. 144)

Lest community foundations are given a pass, sometimes these *place-based* organizations operate in ways that suggest that they may "know it all" as well. A few years ago, the Community Foundation led by this author wanted to play a more proactive role in the area instead of simply reacting to proposals from area nonprofit organizations. The shift proposed was to focus in predetermined key issue areas and then allocate funding to the community through a request for proposal process. The responsive grantmaking percentage was going to shift to a smaller amount thereby increasing the influence of this foundation's "point of view" on the community and making more resources available to support those viewpoints.

The foundation's board of trustees had a decidedly different opinion! This does note the important role that governance also plays on the operation and the many roles of a charitable foundation. After a lengthy presentation by staff, a robust board discussion ensued with the conclusion that "arrogance" does not trump listening to the good and bad ideas of the nonprofit sector.

The staff and trustees agreed ultimately that responding to the views of the organizations seeking funds was critical and that while the foundation staff was knowledgeable and intelligent, their lenses needed to be more open to all views. This is an important point and one that this foundation continues to value. In fact, while exercising effective and positive community leadership in many areas, listening is seen as a crucial element of the leadership role.

In a report by the Grantmakers for Effective Organizations (2006), a highlighted quote rings so true: "There is a need for a safe space for a dynamic relationship so that grantees are not punished for giving feedback to a funder" (p. 5).

Stewardship

All charitable foundations do play a critical role in being a steward of charitable funds. That means that due diligence must come into play when reviewing requests from nonprofit organizations. While listening has been emphasized as being important, foundations must carefully assess a nonprofit organization's ability to provide the services they purport to deliver, that they are charitable organizations as determined by the Internal Revenue Service, and that their internal operational structures are sound. However, once there are assurances that the funding is directed to programs operated by bona fide nonprofit organizations and that there is a plan on how the money is to be used and accountability is set in motion, listening becomes crucial.

A Word on Adaptive Leadership

In addition to their positive use of power, the most effective foundations are those that work in concert and collaboration with other funders, public entities, nonprofit organizations, and the business sector. This type of leadership brings "listening" to a new level. It means listening for understanding and listening to all viewpoints. Bringing people and organizations together to find solutions to long-term problems is essential and that involves listening.

One of the strategies the Grand Rapids Community Foundation employs is to further this foundation's leadership and that of others in our community to embrace the fact that today's complex problems require intense attention and may result in "messy" work in seeking out ways to address issues. Today's challenges demand and deserve quality bold leadership. Community partners and leaders are needed who understand adaptive leadership and who have the resolve to stay on task in spite of the dangers that Heifetz and Linsky (2002) describe in *Leadership on the Line, Staying Alive Through the Dangers of Leading.* "Adaptive change stimulates resistance because it challenges people's habits, beliefs, and values" (pp. 30–31).

Foundation leaders, through active listening and bold action, understand that the very nature of social problems require long-term strategies and patience. Certainly, finding a cure for cancer has taken decades, and it is no surprise that community problems require a similar long time horizon to address. The concept of adaptive leadership was discussed in Heifetz and Linsky's book (2002), and as noted earlier in this chapter, adaptive problems are those complex areas that have taken time to develop and for which there is no clear answer or solution. To be effective in resolving these types of issues, sustainable problem solving is essential. Further, no one leader or organization can or should do this alone if results are to be effective and ongoing.

If foundations are to do the "good works" in addressing society's problems, then listening is essential along with the fortitude to take action when the time is right. Effective community leadership takes patience, research, time, and tenacity. Many times, the desire arises for swift solutions to problems that have taken years to grow increasingly severe. If the problem is clearly understood and all parties are heard, there is a better chance that sustainable solutions will emerge.

Tangle of Paperwork and Process

Ask any nonprofit staff member what her or his biggest complaint is when approaching a charitable foundation regardless of type, and the answer is immediate and includes

- too much paperwork,
- questions that do not relate to the proposal,
- extensive explanation for proposals that are requesting minimal funding, and
- long response time to the point that the proposal is no longer timely.

The Grants Managers Network noted in its report, "Drowning in Paperwork, Distracted From Purpose," that there are four traits that generally foundations reflect. The first three are *the mystery foundation* where the expectations and priorities are difficult to interpret, the *fickle authority* when the foundation changes direction unpredictably, and the *thinking partner* where the foundation seeks relationships with nonprofits and works with them to develop their proposals and programs (Bearman, 2008, p. 11). The latter can backfire though if the foundation changes focus and potentially drops the nonprofit from funding consideration. The fourth and most desired trait is the *neutral supporter.*

This trait is the most desired in terms of time and effort: Grant seekers appreciate the philosophy of the *neutral supporter,* which sees its role as providing funding and *getting out of the way.* "Nonprofits commented that these funders tend to have clear guidelines, often with a pre-proposal screening process, which make efficient use of the grantseeker's time" (Bearman, 2008, p 11).

The findings from the study that resulted in the Grants Managers Network report are illuminating and should become the core of every foundation's orientation program and refresher training for their staff and board members. From the 10 most important findings, 4 key principles and practices were recommended:

1. *Begin from zero.* Begin with a rigorous assessment of what kind of information is really needed to make grantmaking decisions. Separate basic due diligence requirements from program assessment and treat them differently.

2. *Right-size grant expectations.* Develop a streamlined application and reporting form for small grants, ensure that reporting requirements are congruent with the grant, and store appropriate grantee information so that repeat grantees can provide updates without resubmitting.

3. *Relieve the burden on grantees.* Take advantage of technology, including accepting applications and reports electronically; use reliable sources to verify nonprofit status; when possible, use common applications and reports.

4. *Make communications and grantmaking processes clear and straightforward.* Seek feedback from grantees and applicants; communicate clearly and regularly with grantees (Bearman, 2008).

In a perfect world, certainly the funding relationship between nonprofit organizations and foundations would be responsive and supportive, and listening would occur in both directions. However, there is a factor that many times nonprofit organizations *do not* take into account: the need to *listen* to the very foundation that is being approached for funding. One way of addressing this is by hosting grant workshops that can be done on-site through webinars or other means that encourage interaction with the nonprofit organizations. These sessions may cover grant guidelines and the application process plus general tips for grantwriting. This type of session could provide some useful suggestions for the foundation as well in terms of ease of the application process, understanding the concerns of the nonprofit, and getting a clearer picture of how organizations may collaborate if the opportunity presents itself.

The following is an excerpted blog entry written by this author on the Grand Rapids Community Foundation website (http://www.grfoundation.org/blog/02132009structu.php, February 13, 2009) that relates to urging the applying organization to listen to foundations as well:

I have been writing quite a bit lately about the topic "Listening to Nonprofits." First of all, there are many levels to what seems to be a fairly straightforward topic. We do listen to nonprofits as they are on the frontline of community needs and services in any community.

A foundation that does not listen to nonprofits will not be effective. What is a tough situation, particularly for a community foundation, is when a nonprofit leader contacts me or one of our Program staff requesting a meeting. Now on the face of it, this may seem reasonable *and it is.* However, we do need to be fair and consistent with everyone and we have found that meeting with everyone first is neither efficient nor effective. Other foundations do want nonprofits to meet with them first and then develop a proposal based on the good advice they convey, and many times after *too many* meetings a decision is

rendered. I have an actual example that was relayed to me a year ago by a prominent nonprofit leader in the San Francisco Bay Area who was strung along meeting after meeting over a period of a year with a foundation only to be told that they were not going to be considered. That is a travesty.

What we have developed over years of experience is a way to make sure that when meeting with our nonprofit partners, that the conversation is specific to what the organization needs to address and what funding may be needed. Our pre-application process guides that conversation.

Often the phone calls I receive follow this example:

I just want to meet with you along with _____ (insert volunteer name here) to review how we are doing and pick your brain about what is happening in Grand Rapids and area foundations. We also may want to touch on possible support from the Grand Rapids Community Foundation. I know you'll want to meet with _____ (insert volunteer name here) also because they have always been supportive of the GRCF.

I generally play the voicemail over again to make sure I heard it correctly and yes this does occur quite a bit. Now I understand that people do want to meet with the "President"—I got that—I understand. I am not opposed to be open to talk, listen and strategize. I know that when I receive these calls that it ends up with "so we need your support"—which is fine—which is why we are in business! But there is a more effective and less time consuming route to take.

I cannot stress enough that it is so much better to be forthright about seeking funds. In fact, I venture to say that requesting a "we just want to meet with you to get the lay of the land" session goes the way of needing funding 100% of the time. It just delays the action needed by the applying nonprofit.

In these horrific economic times, organizations want a lifeline—a ray of hope—and oftentimes that means financial support. That is why calls to us have been increasing and we do talk to many people on the phone making inquiries. We guide them to our web site to the place where we have clear instructions on how to apply for funds. This helps so we can review the information, possibly organize a meeting which aids the applying organization structure the conversation to say "this is what we need and why" and for us to give guidance as to next steps and ideas that may or may not involve funding.

Asking for a meeting upfront and not checking our web site delays the process by a few weeks. We are accessible—responsive—and empathetic! We can serve nonprofits much faster and better if our guidelines are followed.

Listening to nonprofits? You bet! Having interested organizations listen to us too? It helps! We understand the dire circumstances that all organizations and people are facing and we are trying our best to reach out to our community. Thanks for "listening" to me!

The Feedback Loop

In recent years, many foundations are trying to evaluate the relationship they have with nonprofits that may or may not have received a grant. Why would foundations do this? Because it is absolutely essential to understand how a major stakeholder may view the operations of a foundation so that improvements can be made, successful practices can be reinforced, and leadership can be strengthened. The nonprofit sector is a large stakeholder for every charitable foundation.

The CEP has created a widely used assessment tool called "the Grantee Perception Report ® (GPR), which provides foundations comparative data on grantee perceptions of key elements of foundation performance" (http://www.effectivephilanthropy.org). The CEP is a nonprofit organization focused on the development of comparative data to enable higher-performing funders. CEP's mission is to provide data and create insight so philanthropic funders can better define, assess, and improve their effectiveness and impact.

The results of this evaluation have helped shape and reshape many foundations' operations and processes relating to the nonprofit sector. The foundation that this author leads has gone through the process of the Grantee Perception assessment twice, and the results have helped in the restructuring of our grant process leading to a more streamlined online application that has reduced the time necessary for the organization applying for funding. A summary of the survey results are on the foundation's website and other foundations have done this as well.

Also, the thought process of the foundation's leader has become more transparent through leading to a blog that has been on the website since January 2006 as well as hosting roundtable sessions with nonprofits on key topic areas and ensuring that trustees and volunteers are integral to the decision-making process for funding. This level of transparency and honesty is highly valued in the nonprofit community and does lead to stronger relationships and ultimately stronger partnerships to resolve knotty issues and problems.

Many times, foundations may use this feedback information to help reshape their grantmaking practices, for example, how they communicate with the nonprofit sector and how much information is needed to make a grant decision. As noted in the report, *Is Grantmaking Getting Smarter?* seeking the perspective of nonprofits is essential for effective grantmaking, "but most grantmakers are slow to adopt this way of working" (Grantmakers for Effective Organizations, 2008, p. 6.). As foundations mature and become more attuned to the needs of the nonprofit sector and the communities that they serve, it is advantageous to lean toward becoming a "learning organization" assessing its results and striving to improve its processes, its programs, and ultimately increasing its impact.

Unique Opportunity

An opportunity presented itself in the early 1990s for Michigan's community foundations that has led to the proliferation throughout the state of committees of primarily high school students making grants, assessing needs, and learning and becoming aware of the many facets of organized philanthropy. Through the generous support and guidance of the W. K. Kellogg Foundation based in Battle Creek, Michigan, community foundations grew their endowments while developing future philanthropists. The Council of Michigan Foundations, acting on behalf the community foundations, wrote a comprehensive plan and proposal to the Kellogg Foundation securing millions of matching fund dollars for community philanthropy.

Nearly 20 years later, most community foundations operate what is commonly known as Youth Advisory Committees (YACs), and these groups use the income earned off the endowments created from the Kellogg grant to replicate the grantmaking process of the host foundation. Teaching young people this skill and craft highlights the basic need to listen to the nonprofit organizations seeking the grants from the YAC. Assessing the needs in the community, understanding what is foremost on the minds of young people, and bringing it together making effective grants are all key activities of these teams. The host foundation is reminded of the importance of being in attunement with the nonprofit sector as the grantmaking process unfolds, and the students are taught how to make good decisions.

The Grand Rapids Community Foundation attracts members to their YAC by promoting the following:

- Participating in a real-life leadership experience in which decisions are made that do have real impact
- Learning about the needs of youth in the community by conducting a survey every 2 years
- Understanding the role of nonprofit organizations in the community by reviewing grant requests
- Gaining decision-making skills and learning how to work as part of a diverse group
- Appreciating the value of service to the community
- Making many new friends who attend different schools and have different backgrounds

The experience for many young people is invaluable, and increasingly, many are making plans to pursue higher education opportunities that will educate them for roles in the philanthropic sector. This is seen as an effective way to introduce future leaders to the role of working with the community to address issues and help create new solutions.

Summary

Charitable foundations need to listen and partner with other organizations, institutions, and for-profit businesses. No longer can foundations "go it alone" as they pursue solutions to society's difficult problems. As the leaders of Grantmakers for Effective Organizations (2008) noted in their report titled *Is Grantmaking Getting Smarter?* "Despite efforts in some foundations to shift to more nonprofit-friendly practices, a pronounced disconnect remains between the ways in which grantmakers are supporting nonprofits and what nonprofits say could contribute most to their success" (p. 6). Listening is one way the disconnection can be eliminated.

In this chapter, the following areas were covered: the importance of relationships with the nonprofit sector, an introduction to the history of charitable foundations, the role of listening, the critical activity of assessing need, the inherent power struggle between the charitable foundation and the nonprofit organization, a brief examination of the notion of adaptive leadership, the sometimes difficult task of moving through the paperwork and application process of foundations, how foundations learn through feedback,

and the opportunity to teach young philanthropists how to involve the nonprofit sector in their decision making.

Listening is critically important to the successful foundation and its partnerships with many stakeholders in communities, throughout regions, and indeed the country. A person seeking a career in the philanthropic sector, generally referring to charitable foundations of any kind, will enjoy the experience of dealing with critical issues, affecting policy while making good grant decisions. There are many opportunities, and it is a field that needs resourceful people with good analytical skills, exceptional listening skills, and an ability to effectively solve problems.

References and Further Readings

Bearman, J. (2008, Fall). Drowning in paperwork, distracted from purpose (Report from Grants Managers Network & Project Streamline). *Grantmakers in the Arts Reader, 19*(3), 5–39.

Cleveland Foundation. (n.d.). *History.* Available from http://www.clevelandfoundation.org/About/History

Foundation Center. (2007). *Highlights of foundation yearbook.* Available from http://foundationcenter.org/gainknowledge/research/pdf/fy2007_highlights.pdf

Foundation Center. (n.d.). *Frequently asked questions.* Available from http://foundationcenter.org/getstarted/faqs

Grand Rapids Community Foundation. (2009, March 26). *[CEO's] Invitation.* Grand Rapids, MI: Grand Rapids Community Foundation.

Grantmakers for Effective Organizations. (2006). *Listen, learn, lead: Grantmaker practices that support nonprofit results.* Washington, DC: Author.

Grantmakers for Effective Organizations. (2008). *Is grantmaking getting smarter? A national study of philanthropic practice.* Washington, DC: Author.

Heifetz, R. A., Kania, J. V., & Kramer, M. R. (2004, Winter). Leading boldly. *Stanford Social Innovation Review,* 21–31.

Heifetz, R. A., & Linsky, M. (2002). *Leadership on the line, staying alive through the danger of leading.* Boston: Harvard Business School Press.

Orosz, J. J. (2007). *Effective foundation management.* Lantham, MD: AltaMira Press.

Sieger, D. (2009, January 9). *Managing in difficult economic times.* Meeting summary notes from the meeting of the Grand Rapids Community Foundation, Grand Rapids, MI.

82

EVALUATION, ACCOUNTABILITY, AND IMPACT OF FOUNDATIONS

ROBERT L. FISCHER

Mandel School of Applied Social Sciences

Foundations play a major role within the nonprofit philanthropic sector and the broader fabric of U.S. society, and this is accompanied by substantial interest in their practices and impacts. Numbering more than 70,000 in the United States, the population of grantmaking foundations grew by nearly three times over the 25-year period from 1981 to 2006 (Foundation Center, 2008). Foundations have dramatically increased their use of evaluation over this period for assessing their internal practices as well as the impact of their grantmaking. Just as individual nonprofits have been required to demonstrate greater accountability for their outcomes, so too have foundations worked to address the basic notion of their own effectiveness and impact in the community. This chapter introduces the concept of foundation evaluation, discusses the variation in its interpretation, and reviews the main approaches to demonstrating the impact of foundations. This topic is of substantial importance because of the vital role that foundations play in society, in providing leadership and funding for the advancement of societal well-being. The accountability of this subsector has implications for its influence in the future and its successful contribution to the betterment of social conditions.

Outcomes Measurement in the Nonprofit Sector

Over the last several decades, there has been an evolutionary change in views of accountability within the nonprofit sector. A previous focus on the type and quantity of services provided, charitable works deemed inherently good, slowly gave way to the assessment of outcomes and the view that donations are like investments. In the mid-1990s, the movement solidified around efforts by national voluntary organizations convened by the United Way of America to adopt a framework for outcomes across the sector (Fischer, 2001). Since that time, it has become common practice for nonprofits to develop program logic models, which clearly spell out the key program activities and how the program activities relate to outputs and outcomes of interest and how nonprofits collect basic outcome data on their services.

This greater need for explicit accountability was echoed by leaders within the nonprofit sector. In a statement to the U.S. Senate Finance Committee in 2005, Brian Gallagher, CEO of the United Way of America, remarked, "Financial accountability is just table stakes. You have to get that right first. But ultimately, the American public should hold our sector accountable for delivering on our missions. . . . To address that concern, I respectfully suggest that nonprofit organizations be asked to report concrete results annually that are tied directly to their missions, not just the level of activity" (Testimony section, p. 3). This view of nonprofit accountability became the predominant position, resulting in wide use of outcome-based funding and reporting requirements by foundation and governmental funders. Over time, questions have been raised about the use of the data produced from these approaches and whether the data are useful to donors (Snibbe, 2006). Some work suggests that high level individual donors may place less value on outcome information produced by nonprofits due to a lack of interest and time and to concerns about the data (Cunningham & Ricks, 2004). At the same time, small donors have been found to be enthusiastic about the nonprofit organizations they give to and the charitable sector in general (Arumi, Wooden, & Johnson, 2005). As such, the use of outcomes in nonprofit accountability approaches is now firmly in place within the sector, and the debate is more about how and when to apply such approaches not whether to apply them.

Following on the heels of a broad expansion of outcomes measurement among nonprofit grantee organizations, it made sense that foundations would begin to look at their own operations in the same vein. On the one hand, more progressive foundations began to see it as a matter of fairness, subjecting grantees to an outcomes approach when they themselves were exempted. Other foundations adopted the practice out of a belief in the knowledge-building potential of evaluation and a sense that they could improve the work of the foundation. As a practical matter, after some period of time advising, persuading, and compelling grantees in the use of such practices, some foundations saw that they now had sufficient capacity to apply these tactics to their operations and that the work of their grantees could feed nicely into the foundation's view of its own impact.

Since the beginning of the new century, there has been increased scrutiny of foundations particularly from the federal government. The U.S. Congress's passage of the Sarbanes-Oxley Act of 2002 included provisions that increased financial reporting requirements for corporations and nonprofits, including foundations and congressional committees, have expressed interest in exploring the tax-exempt status of foundations and such matters as the proportion of their endowments that they translate into grants each year. Further, implementation of the new Form 990 in 2008 by the Internal Revenue Service, resulted in greater requirements and detail on nonprofits' operations,

governance, and compensation practices. This heightened scrutiny speaks partly to the public's understanding of the work of foundations and perceptions about the transparency of their operations. The foundation impact movement, therefore, can be seen as assisting foundations in demonstrating and communicating their work as grantmaking entities within the nonprofit sector.

Foundation Evaluation

The notion of evaluating foundations as to their impact and for the purposes of accountability has been conceived of across numerous domains and organized under a variety of frameworks. One particularly useful framework was offered by the James Irvine Foundation (2005), distinguishing between foundation evaluation focused on program impact and evaluation focused on institutional effectiveness. Program impact is derived mainly from the foundation's direct grantmaking activities, whereas institutional effectiveness relates principally to the foundation's organizational operations, its efficiency, and its relationship with a range of stakeholders. These two dimensions will now be discussed in more detail.

Program Impact

The concept of impact within the evaluation literature has numerous interpretations. However, at its core, impact refers to an influence or effect on an intended target. In the foundation context, there are several aspects associated with this type of impact. Figure 82.1 depicts two hypothesized avenues to foundation impacts. First, this approach would include examination of the type and characteristics of grants that the foundation has made. To the extent that funding

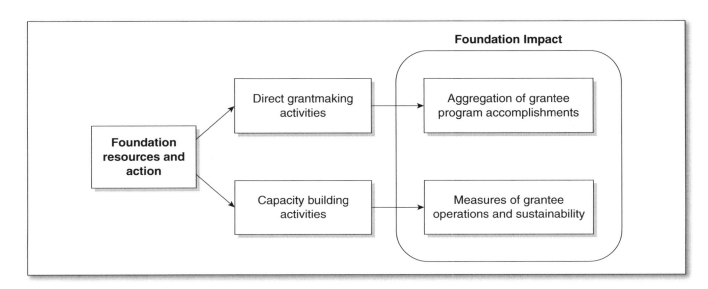

Figure 82.1 Avenues to Foundation Impact

changes the operations of grantees, the individual grants themselves indicate a foundation impact in some sense. Here, impact can be construed as the accomplishments of the grants that were made by the foundation. So, the fact that grant awards resulted in the delivery of services, which in turn brought about changes in the target population, suggests something about a foundation's impact.

Second, impacts may be seen as resulting from a foundation's efforts to promote capacity development within grantees and the grantee community. These impacts could be seen in measures of organizational vitality and efficiency among grantees. Another aspect of impact can also relate to the knowledge accrued through the foundation's work. James Irvine Foundation (2005) refers to this as "(r)esults, learning, and program refinement," and this speaks to the collective impact of a foundation's investments in programs and organizations. These sorts of impacts offer the most generalizable findings, those which can be transferred to application in the experiences of other foundations and in other settings and contexts. In addition, these impacts are often fed back into a foundation's learning cycle and bring about new program approaches as well as enhancement to ongoing strategies.

Institutional Effectiveness

Like nonprofit entities of all types, foundations have an articulated mission, and they undertake a plan to deliver on that mission. The manner in which a foundation undertakes its business through its governance and leadership, its interactions with key stakeholders and customers, and its management and financial practices is all part of the concept of institutional effectiveness. Collectively, these attributes contribute to organizational quality as conceived by scholars such as Peter Drucker and others.

A first area of institutional effectiveness is in the domain of leadership. To the extent that foundations are not only important players as funders but also as community leaders, individual foundations might seek to assess their own leadership role. In examining such leadership in this sense, we might distinguish between activities or efforts and influence. Leadership efforts would include initiatives undertaken by the foundation to inform, educate, and advocate on behalf of needs, issues, or policies. This would include communication campaigns, dissemination of research and practice findings, and convening of potential partners. As to foundation influence as an indicator of leadership, this could include measures of foundation reputation (e.g., citations, media references), engagement in signature initiatives, and success in leveraging resources for initiatives from other funding partners. Some foundations set an objective of being acknowledged as a so-called thought leader within the philanthropic sector, so this dimension of leadership links to this notion.

A second area of effectiveness has to do with how key stakeholders perceive a foundation and how this reflects on the work of the foundation. In this context, foundations may consider who their primary customers or clients are, and what these groups can say about the functioning of the foundation. Assessing effectiveness from the stakeholder perspective can range from the very informal often conducted by foundation staff to the very formal usually administered by a third party. Such a stakeholder feedback approach has been conducted by Grantmakers for Effective Organizations for 168 foundations in the United States (LaFrance Associates, 2008). These grantee perception reports provide the foundation with data on such things as their interactions with grantees, grantmaking process, foundation strategies, and overall performance. The scores generate point-in-time data to assist a foundation in its planning and can also help the foundation monitor its progress over time (Woodwell, 2005).

A third area within the domain of institutional effectiveness is in relation to finance and organization. Inasmuch as foundations are philanthropic entities that collect, invest, and distribute funds, there are many measures of fiscal health that reflect on the operation of the foundation. Measures of investment performance, grantmaking volume, and overhead costs are routinely reported by foundations as measures of their own relative effectiveness. In addition, foundations, like all nonprofits, report on the quality and diversity of staff, the engagement of the board, and progress being made on strategic plans and related initiatives. Collectively, these factors speak to the internal organizational capacity and governance aspects of effectiveness.

Measurement and Interpretation

Beyond the conceptualization of foundation outcomes, there is also the more practical matter of selecting specific measures or indicators of these outcomes, as well as consideration of establishing causality. Though some measures of institutional effectiveness may be relatively straightforward (e.g., return on investment portfolio, stakeholder ratings), for many program strategies the evaluation may require more comparative and rigorous designs drawing on multiple data sources and methods. The power of the randomized control trial to measure causality is an area of consensus; however, it is not uniformly applicable across domains including in foundation work. A range of other designs, many comparative in nature (i.e., quasi-experimental), hold promise as more rigorous approaches to establishing program impact. A number of foundations have invested in multisite or "cluster" evaluation designs as a way to enhance learning. These approaches are attractive in that all sites receive support for some programmatic strategies, and the evaluation is structured with an eye toward cross-site learning, as well as an aggregate assessment of the program benefit. All evaluation strategies involving comparisons over time or between locations provide a stronger basis for foundations to identify the distinct effect of their grantmaking. Such approaches attempt to identify what would have happened in the absence of the program as a baseline for assessing the magnitude of an outcome that was actually observed. In the absence of such designs, extra caution must be exercised in the interpretation of results, especially when making claims about foundation impact, as they may be in part the result of many other forces at work in the community.

Issues for the Field

Despite the marked progress evident among foundations in regard to assessing their impact, there remains much work to be done. In part, additional dialogue is needed across and among foundations so that collectively they are pursuing a shared agenda in this regard. Three issues for consideration are now offered.

Whole More Than the Sum of Its Parts?

Within the outcome measurement framework, the primary focus is on how individual programs convert resources into activities, which then produce program outputs and ultimately desired outcomes for participants. Here, the emphasis is not on the sources of the program funding and other resources but rather on how the program uses them in service of the program mission and objectives. Figure 82.2 depicts a general logic model of foundation impact showing the conceptual linkages from strategy to impact. When looking at the ultimate outcomes, this circumstance leads to an obvious issue of whose outcomes they are. Can both the program and funder (e.g., foundation) lay claim to the same set of outcomes and impacts? Or is the true impact of the foundation found in its broader contribution in terms of leadership and capacity building efforts? No doubt reality lies somewhere in between these two options. Certainly, in practice, foundations claim to varying extents these program outcomes as their own as part of a broader approach to measuring foundation performance (Putnam, 2004). The rigor of the evaluation design undertaken dictates, in part, the ability of a foundation to make these claims in a credible manner.

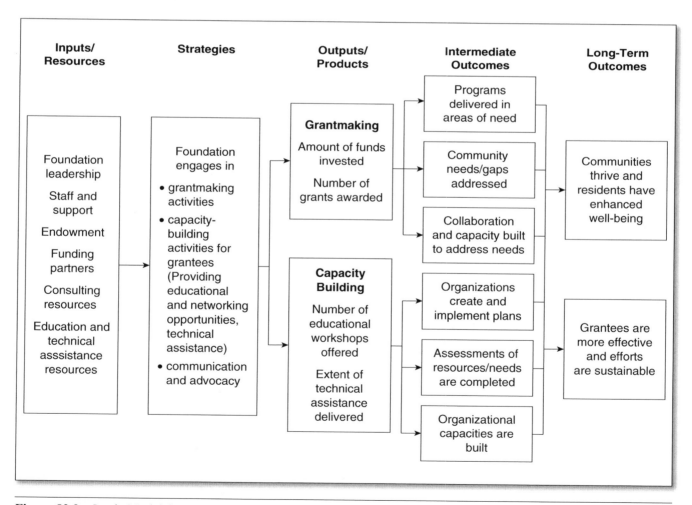

Figure 82.2   Logic Model for Foundation Impact

Data and Common Metrics

At present, there is little consistency in the manner in which foundations assess their own impacts and address issues of accountability. Given the diversity of foundations and their missions and strategies, it is not surprising that they approach the issue of impact in a diverse set of ways. This leads to difficulties in at least two regards. First, it becomes challenging to compare the accomplishments and performance across foundations. This is problematic for donors and those who serve in an oversight role of the foundation community (e.g., federal committees), as well as for the foundations themselves, if they wish to look at their performance relative to their peers. Second, in taking stock of the collective performance of the philanthropic sector, the lack of standard metrics complicates efforts to synthesize data on effectiveness. In dialogues about the societal contribution of foundations, this lack of systematic data results in reliance on disparate information and anecdotes as evidence of benefit.

Use of Findings—So What?

Nonprofits often blame accountability demands on the funder and accept them because the availability of funding is the leverage, motivating them to undertake the efforts. In the foundation world, the leverage aspect is unclear. It may be unfair to assume that foundations would not willingly undertake impact assessment activities, but experience across the nonprofit sector suggests that this may be something all nonprofits share. By looking at the level of participation of foundations in voluntary impact measurement and reporting, we get some sense of this altruistic engagement. In a survey of 77 of the largest U.S. foundations, the Center for Effective Philanthropy (2002) found that the most frequent information used to assess foundation performance in "achieving its social impact and operational goals" (p. 8) was grantee reports and evaluations (72%). The next four most frequent indicators used that related to the foundation's internal effectiveness were administrative costs (37%), investment performance (22%), staff size, caseload, compensation (16%), and use of strategic review (13%). Relatively less frequent were the reported use of measures of foundation influence, such as changes in the field (13%), changes in public policy (12%), peer feedback (9%), and knowledge creation (7%). This pattern of data suggests that foundations rely heavily on their grantees to furnish documentation of the impact of the foundation, as least as recently as 2002 (p. 8).

However, there are a meaningful number of foundations using methods to assess foundation impacts beyond the work of grantees, looking to internal measures of effectiveness and external measures of influence as areas by which they can most closely measure these dimensions. The findings that emerge from these efforts have the capacity to influence not just the grantmaking behavior of foundations but also the program delivery of the grantees to which the data relate. For this to occur, data must be fed back into a decision-making process involving program operators, agency directors, and funders so that an informed dialogue can take place. Learning from successes, as well as failures, is a vital part of making the most of data produced through the evaluation process (Giloth & Gerwitz, 2009).

Future Directions

The area of foundation impact has been the subject of increasing interest over the last decade, and research on this topic has expanded accordingly. However, while much effort on the part of foundations has been directed at promoting effective use of evaluation by their grantees, relatively little attention until recently has been given to the impact of foundations. As the philanthropic community moves forward with this process, there are several areas that will require special emphasis. Three are offered here.

Building Organizational Capacity

The majority of grantees report that they receive no assistance from the foundation beyond the grant itself, but they desire much more. Foundations may need to develop more explicit strategies to promote capacity building among their grantees and prospective grantees. Many foundations recognize nonprofit capacity building as part of their mission and as integral to their success in grantmaking and the success of their grantees in meeting their objectives. As such, foundations should consider opportunities to expand supportive and educational activities for organizations based on the expressed needs of the target entities (Yung et al., 2008). Concurrently, it is incumbent on foundations to examine opportunities for nonprofits to enhance their performance and sustainability through collaborations, mergers, and consolidations. Foundations are well positioned to observe issues of service redundancy and organizational distress, and they can take a leadership role in bringing potential partners together for mutual benefit. As foundations work to increase nonprofit organizational capacity, they must also develop their own capacity in regard to effective governance and management. Foundations with professional staff are often well along the path to achieving their desired capacities, but many foundations have extremely limited internal resources to handle basic functions. If a foundation wishes to be able to assess its own performance over time and be accountable to its stakeholders and the public, it must invest in the internal mechanisms and external relationships to support that work.

Develop Performance Metrics

As the philanthropic sector continues to expand its efforts in the arena of accountability, there will need to be an effort to distill a small set of consistent measures for foundations to use. So rather than have foundations measure everything to varying degrees, the sector should move toward measuring a few things consistently and reliably. This would have the benefit of providing comparable data on foundations to assess the performance of not only individual foundations but also the sector overall. The selection of key indicators is in itself a major undertaking, since particular measures may be preferred by some foundations and not others. Again, this is an opportunity for leadership on the part of the sector from individual foundations and from entities such as the Council on Foundations, Grantmakers for Effective Organizations, and the Center for Effective Philanthropy.

Promote Translational Use of Data, and Create Evidence Base for Field

Related to the discussion of performance metrics, the philanthropic sector has a distinct opportunity to expand the knowledge base about the performance of foundations. Certainly, any one foundation can benefit from data on its own performance, both in terms of informing internal learning and improvement efforts and in demonstrating its impact to stakeholders. In the near term, having all foundations make greater efforts in this regard and make greater use of their own data would be a major boon to the sector. There is a greater opportunity here, as well, to use these data for intrasector learning by sharing data across foundations. Given that it is unlikely that all foundations will have uniformly high performance across all indicators, some foundations may be reluctant to share performance data. However, if the foundation community can work together to make these data more accessible, it is likely to lead to a greater sense of shared mission and promotion of accountability in the long run.

Summary

As key funders and leaders within the nonprofit sector, foundations have a significant role in advancing the pursuit of accountability and improved performance throughout the sector. Over the last 20 years, foundations and other funders have led the charge in bringing enhanced accountability to the programs and organizations they fund. By increasing demands for outcomes measurement and program evaluation, funders have brought about a dramatic increase in the use of outcome assessment methods by nonprofit programs. Now, the burden shifts somewhat to moving the foundation community forward in systematically documenting its distinctive impacts and addressing concerns as to foundations' role in community change. Advancements that have occurred in measuring the organizational effectiveness of foundations as well as program impacts should be continued. With continued attention to this issue, the promise of greater foundation accountability and demonstration of impact will be realized. By integrating such organizational learning into the sector, the societal benefits resulting from the action of foundations will be enhanced and sustained.

References and Further Readings

Arumi, A. M., Wooden, R., & Johnson, J. (2005). *The charitable impulse: Those who give to charities—and those who run them—talk about what's needed to keep the public's trust* (Report from Public Agenda to the Kettering Foundation and Independent Sector). Available from http://www.publicagenda.org/files/pdf/charitable_impulse.pdf

Aspen Institute. (2002, Fall). *Philanthropy: Foundation accountability and effectiveness: A statement for public discussion* [Nonprofit Sector Strategy Group pamphlet]. Washington, DC: Author.

Behrens, T. R., & Kelly, T. (2008). Paying the piper: Foundation evaluation capacity calls the tune. *New Directions for Evaluation, 119,* 37–50.

Buteau, E., Buchanan, P., Bolanos, C., Brock, A., & Chang, K. (2008). *More than money: Making a difference with assistance beyond the grant.* Cambridge, MA: Center for Effective Philanthropy.

Center for Effective Philanthropy. (2002). *Indicators of effectiveness: Understanding and improving foundation performance.* Boston: Author.

Chelimsky, E. (2001). What evaluation could do to support foundations: A framework with nine component parts. *American Journal of Evaluation, 22*(1), 13–28.

Cunningham, K., & Ricks, M. (2004, Summer). Why measure? Nonprofits use metrics to show that they are efficient. But what if donors don't care? *Stanford Social Innovation Review,* 44–51.

Fischer, R. L. (2001). The sea change in nonprofit human services: A critical assessment of outcomes measurement. *Families in Society, 82*(6), 561–568.

Foundation Center. (2008). *Foundation growth and giving estimates: Current outlook.* Available from http://foundationcenter.org/gainknowledge/research/pdf/fgge08.pdf

Gallagher, B. (2005, April 5). *Statement to the United States Senate Committee on Finance.* Available from http://finance.senate.gov/imo/media/doc/bgtest040505.pdf

Giloth, R., & Gerwitz, S. (2009). Philanthropy & mistakes: An untapped resource. *Foundation Review, 1*(1), 115–124.

Huang, J., Buchanan, P., & Buteau, E. (2006). *In search of impact: Practices and perceptions in foundations' provision of program and operating grants to nonprofits.* Cambridge, MA: Center for Effective Philanthropy.

James Irvine Foundation. (2005). *Foundation-wide assessment: An overview.* Retrieved April 10, 2009, from http://www .irvine.org/assets/pdf/evaluation/foundationwide_assessment .pdf

James Irvine Foundation. (2009). *What's the difference? How foundation trustees view evaluation.* Retrieved June 20, 2009, from http://www.fsg-impact.org/ideas/item/trustee_ evaluation_tools.html

Kramer, M., Graves, R., Hirschhorn, J., & Fiske, L. (2007). *From insight to action: New directions in foundation evaluation.* Boston: Foundation Strategy Group (FSG) Social Impact Advisors.

LaFrance Associates. (2008). *Executive summary: Grantee perception report (GPR) subscriber assessment.* Cambridge, MA: Center for Effective Philanthropy.

Ostrower, F. (2004). *Foundation effectiveness: Definitions and challenges.* Washington, DC: Urban Institute.

Patrizi, P. (2006). *The evaluation conversation: A path to impact for foundation boards and executives.* New York: Foundation Center.

Patrizi, P., & Pauly, E. (2004). Field-based evaluation as a path to foundation effectiveness. In M. T. Braverman, N. A. Constantine, & J. K. Slater (Eds.), *Foundations and evaluation: Contexts and practices for effective philanthropy* (pp. 185–200). San Francisco: Jossey-Bass.

Putnam, K. (2004). *Measuring foundation performance: Examples from the field.* Oakland: California HealthCare Foundation.

Snibbe, A. C. (2006, Fall). Drowning in data. *Stanford Social Science Review,* 39–45.

Wisely, D. S. (2002). Parting thoughts on foundation evaluation. *American Journal of Evaluation, 23*(2), 159–164.

Woodwell, W. H., Jr. (2005). *Evaluation as a pathway to learning: Current topics in evaluation for grantmakers.* Washington, DC: Grantmakers for Effective Organizations.

Yung, B., Leahy, P., Deason, L., Fischer, R. L., Perkins, F., Clasen, C., et al. (2008). Capacity building needs of minority health nonprofits. *Evaluation and Program Planning, 31,* 381–392.

83

LEADERSHIP TRAPS FOR THE GRANTMAKER

The Problem of Consistent Positive Feedback

JOEL J. OROSZ

Johnson Center for Philanthropy, Grand Valley State University

It is an article of faith in the worlds of business, politics, and nonprofit organizations that feedback is the leader's friend because it delivers truths that are sometimes painful—but always useful—to those who manage organizations. This feedback, both positive and negative, provides information that allows managers to define areas of strength, identify weaknesses, correct problems, and harness all of these data to the essential task of improving performance in the future. Underlying the high esteem in which feedback is held in these sectors is an assumption that those providing the feedback are reliably reporting their opinions, experiences, and feelings. Whether their feedback is positive or negative, therefore, it is an accurate reflection of their beliefs.

In the highly distinctive world of endowed grantmaking foundations, however, feedback is not regarded as the leader's friend because the information that it delivers is widely regarded as suspect. This assumption is borne out by the fact that the feedback grantmaking foundations receive is overwhelmingly positive: overwhelmingly, in fact, virtually to the point of unanimity. One of two conclusions may be drawn from this tidal wave of positive data. Either foundations and their employees are, like Mary Poppins, "practically perfect in every way," or the data are highly suspect. This entry will take the position that the data are indeed unreliable, analyze the reasons why unreliable feedback data are built into the grantmaking context, and explain how, nonetheless, it is possible to collect sounder data to help endowed grantmaking foundation leaders improve the performance of their employees, their systems, and most importantly, themselves.

Discussion of Theory

The Highly Distinctive Nature of Foundations

Endowed grantmaking foundations occupy a completely distinctive niche among societal organizations in the United States. Alone among society's entities, endowed charitable foundations need not pass any performance test to succeed. In the world of commerce, businesses must pass the market test to survive. They compete with other businesses for customers in the arenas of price, quality, and service. Customers provide feedback through their buying decisions (slumping sales may signal dissatisfaction) and also through comments directed to customer service agents. Customer feedback may be positive, neutral, or negative, but all of it is deemed largely reliable, for customers have no compelling motivation to provide false information. There is a word for businesses that pay inadequate attention to such feedback, and that word is *bankrupt*.

In the world of politics, candidates must pass the test of elections to gain and hold public office. Politicians compete with nominees of other political parties for votes, and feedback thus becomes an invaluable tool for them to understand what the voters value, desire, and dislike. Again, whether voter feedback is positive or negative, politicians consider it to be largely reliable, for political views tend to be strongly held, and this feedback can be measured directly against the results coming from the polls. Politicians who pay insufficient attention to such feedback soon find themselves on the underside of a landslide.

In the world of nonprofit organizations, charity leaders must pass the fundraising test to survive. They compete with other nonprofits for support from clients, corporations, foundations, and individuals. These funders have the option of providing support for any of the approximately 1.5 million nonprofit organizations in the United States, so the competition to raise funds is absolutely fierce. Donors provide feedback by their decisions to fund or not to fund and also by direct comments. Once more, whether positive or negative, the feedback provided is deemed to be reliable, for funders are in a position to evaluate the relative merits of nonprofits and have no strong motivation for obfuscating with regard to their funding decisions. Nonprofit leaders who do not pay close attention to the feedback provided by funders soon find their organizations are not merely not for profit but not long for this world.

Across the commercial, government, and nonprofit sectors, this feedback is often more than just highly reliable; much of it is also objectively measurable. Sales figures, vote tallies, and fundraising campaign dollars can be reliably counted and compared over time. This allows managers to make decisions based on facts, not hunches. In short, feedback allows leaders in all three sectors to effectively manage their organizations.

The Essential Importance of Candid Feedback

So in the three great sectors of society—commercial, governmental, and nonprofit—the tests, respectively, of the market, the electorate, and fundraising provide essential feedback to leaders. There is no question but that the feedback can be the harbinger of brutal tidings, such as bankruptcy in business, lopsided losses in elections, and in the nonprofit realm, organizational failure. For all of its potential harshness, however, the feedback provided by these tests comprises an indispensable tool for leaders and managers. It identifies areas of strength and high-performing employees, thus defining what is working well. Conversely, it fingers areas of weakness and poorly performing employees, thus defining what is working badly or failing outright. This feedback can be used by leaders to build on strengths and correct weaknesses, to reward the better performing and to correct (or terminate) the low-performing employees. Reliable feedback therefore makes organizations better.

Research has demonstrated that employees in high-feedback fields of work generally have a very clear understanding of how they are perceived by their customers and by the general public, while those in *low-feedback* fields

generally have an inflated sense of their own value. In a study conducted by the Joseph and Edna Josephson Institute of Ethics, for example, workers in high-feedback fields, such as teachers, politicians, salespeople, coaches, and sports referees, self-identified levels of honesty, effectiveness, and ethics that were remarkably close to the ratings given to their professions by the general public. On the other hand, workers in low-feedback fields, such as therapists and surgeons, self-identified levels of honesty, effectiveness, and quality much higher than the ratings given to their professions by the general public. The field that suffered the greatest disparity between its inflated self-regard and the low esteem of the general public was that of charitable foundations. For instance, in response to the question, how would you "rate the ethics of foundation trustees or board members . . . , 63% of a sample of grantmakers" answered *excellent* or *very good*, while a mere 12% of the general public gave such high marks. Only 5% of the grantmakers rated the ethics of foundation leaders as *fair* or *poor*, while 36% of the general public rated grantmaker ethics as *fair* or *poor* (and another 4% rated them as *very poor;* see Josephson, 1992, p. 152).

What can account for this huge disconnect in esteem between the employees of endowed charitable foundations and their "customers"? At least four factors account for this gap: (1) the lack of any sort of external test for endowed charitable foundations, (2) the power imbalance between those who make grants and those who seek them, (3) the arbitrary nature of foundation decision making, and (4) the highly concentrated nature of foundation accountability. Each will be examined in turn.

The First Factor: Lack of External Tests

The lack of external tests is a problem completely distinctive to the foundation world. As demonstrated, all other societal institutions must pass tests to survive—all, that is, except endowed grantmaking foundations. An endowed grantmaking foundation need not worry about making a profit nor winning an election nor (community foundations excepted) raising operational funds. An endowed grantmaking foundation, instead, lives off the income produced by the funds comprising its corpus. The endowed grantmaking foundation, therefore, need not be concerned with the opinions of customers, electors, or funders. It is thus insulated from the pressures that other societal organizations feel to meet short-term objectives: profit in the next quarter, a lead in the next poll, or a big gift by next month. In theory, this insulation gives endowed grantmaking foundations great freedom to innovate, to back unpopular causes, and to develop programs that are slow to show concrete results. In practice, most endowed grantmaking foundations exercise this freedom very sparingly or not at all. Jed Emerson, a thoughtful critic of the foundation field, has written: "And I don't understand why people who clearly mean well and want to have an impact with the resources under their control are so hesitant to take some measure of higher value risk" (2006).

The answer to Emerson's question has much to do with aversion to the unfamiliar. This freedom from external tests may liberate foundations to be bold or timid as they choose, but there can be no question that it also insulates the field from beneficial feedback. External tests are treated with such respect by other organizations precisely because they are so consequential to them. If customers become dissatisfied with a company's products or services and nothing is done to address these concerns, profits will wither and the company will go bankrupt. If voters become disillusioned with a politician's policies and nothing is done to address these concerns, poll standings will drop, and the election will be lost. If donors feel a nonprofit has strayed from its mission and nothing is done to assuage their concerns, contributions will dry up, and the organization will soon turn belly up.

For endowed grantmaking foundations, however, no such external test looms on the horizon. The foundation's endowed corpus produces income year in and year out, so there is no fundraising test. There is no public oversight of grantmaking foundations, save for the very minimal financial and legal oversight provided by the Internal Revenue Code, so there is no electoral test. Foundations do have customers—of sorts—in their grant seekers and grantees, but these customers have none of the power of their commercial cousins. Indeed, the situation is inverted, for unlike the commercial sector, in which a number of companies are ferociously competing to win a consumer's business, in the grantmaking world there are a number of customers ferociously competing to win a foundation's grants. Should an individual applicant decide to boycott a foundation it would have no effect, for there are always thousands of other organizations seeking funding. Poor performance on the part of a foundation, therefore, has no practical effect: Chances are, grant seekers will keep asking them for money anyway, and if they decide to look elsewhere, there are plenty of other grant-seeking organizations eager to take their place. So long, therefore, as a private foundation writes checks equal to the minimum 5% of net asset value mandated by the annual payout rule, it hardly matters to them whether they do so with distinction or with marginal competence, for their customers have no practical way to influence their behavior. Endowed grantmaking foundations are thus the only societal institution that can do a lousy job this year and next year get even more money to do an even lousier job, all the while never once receiving a piece of negative feedback about any of their transactions. No external tests, therefore, equals no improvement for foundation leaders.

The Second Factor: The Power Imbalance Between Grantmaker and Grant Seeker

The power imbalance between foundations and their applicants and grantees guarantees that even if feedback occurs, it will be of little value because, regardless of whether positive reviews are merited, all of the feedback will be positive. The key to understanding this dynamic is to comprehend the golden rule in its foundation context, that is, "those who have the gold make the rules." Grant seekers quickly discover that foundation leaders are calling all of the shots. Foundations define their own strategy, set their own priorities, write their own requests for proposals, create their own time lines, devise their own decision-making criteria, and select their own lists of grantees. Those who seek grants literally have only as much impact on any of these decisions as the foundation will allow them to have. While endowed grantmaking foundations often use the rhetoric of *partnership* to describe their relationships with grantees, one would be hard pressed to find any grant seeker or grantee who considered the relationship an equal—or even a reasonably balanced—partnership. While it is true that foundations could accomplish little without their grantees, it is also true that grantees, so far as grantmakers are concerned, constitute little more than interchangeable parts. The oversupply of grant seekers and the undersupply of funding sources mean that even if all of a foundation's current grantees were to go on strike tomorrow, the foundation could find suitable replacements within a few weeks time. Foundations may be nothing without their grantees, but the individual grantees are nothing that foundations cannot replace at the drop of a hat.

Grant seekers and grantees are acutely aware of this power imbalance and exquisitely sensitive to the realization that they are part of a long line of competing organizations happy to take their place should anything go wrong in their relationship with their foundation funder. It becomes a high priority for grant seekers and grantees, therefore, to keep their relationships with foundations—especially those that have already funded them—in the best possible repair. One of their favorite methods of keeping fences mended is to ensure that all communications with the foundation and its employees are unrelentingly upbeat. Program officers' banal observations are therefore promoted to flashes of insight; a routine meeting becomes an epiphany; an offhand foundation suggestion becomes an absolute imperative for action. Program officers are thanked for their generosity, their wisdom, and their genius when, in truth, they have been neither generous nor wise nor even particularly bright.

The consequences of the power imbalance are thus highly deleterious to the field. Grant seekers and grantees understand that the only power they possess is the power to flatter the people who make the decisions. The resulting torrent of unmerited praise skews the entire enterprise, for it devalues the process of feedback. Most foundation employees realize that the grantees and the grant seekers are giving them effusive compliments they have not earned, but the praise is so pleasant that they are loathe to lose it. This is particularly the case if the foundation employee has come from a job in a high-feedback field;

habitually being called a genius is so much nicer than habitually being verbally abused. Most of all, the power imbalance has a pervasively pernicious effect, for it inflates not only the importance of positive feedback, but also it deflates the value of constructive criticism. By rendering any kind of negative feedback so rare, the power imbalance marginalizes constructive criticism, making the rare objection seem to be the work of a crackpot who does not understand the enormous value of the foundation's good works, which, by the way, thousands of other people have seen so clearly and praised so lavishly.

The Third Factor: The Arbitrary Nature of Foundation Decision Making

The arbitrary nature of foundation decision making only intensifies the flood of unearned positive feedback in which the foundation is already wallowing. Endowed grantmaking foundations, for the most part, do not make funding decisions based on subjective and transparent criteria. A strong argument can be made that this is a good thing, for such criteria can easily become too rigid and delimiting. The subjective and secretive funding process used in most foundations, however, creates its own set of problems. Applicants realize that their proposals face a number of hurdles that must be cleared before they can get funded. Typically, program officers must first be convinced of the proposal's value, then the foundation's grants committee, then the foundation's CEO, and then finally, the foundation's board of trustees. That constitutes a lot of moving parts, and since applicants have no way to directly influence most of the decision makers, their response is to do what they can, namely, to smooth things along on a velvet carpet of flattery.

This festival of ardent praise tends to be the most intense around the first gatekeeper, namely, the program officer. In most foundations, program officers are a curious concoction of omnipotence and impotence. The omnipotence comes from the virtually unlimited power of program officers to say no. As the first person to handle most proposals, the program officer can, without consulting anyone else, turn a proposal down flat. It matters not how large or small a request nor if it comes from a humble or august institution; if the program officer says no, then it goes no further. On the other side, the impotence comes from the fact that the program officer typically can approve nothing. No matter how small a request, no matter how obvious its merits, the program officer cannot say yes. He or she proposes, but others higher up the foundation food chain dispose. This odd combination of limitless negative power and a complete dearth of positive power magnifies the arbitrariness of the process.

If, in an organization, a class of employees is endowed with unlimited negative power, it is a safe bet that sooner or later, they will not only use that power but will also come to abuse it. Every grant seeker with any experience has tales to tell of the program officer whose day is made if only he or she can find some picayunish reason to deny a proposal: a slight error in math, a misplaced endnote, or even a stray typing error. Such program officers seem to conceive of themselves as a latter-day Horatius at the bridge, single-handedly preventing a hoard of unworthy proposals from overrunning his or her foundation. In short, they are taking their negative power to an absolute extreme.

Little wonder, then, that applicants and grantees alike dare not breathe a word of critical feedback to the program officer. Here, after all, is a person whose fuse often seems as short as his or her memory seems long and, without question, a person who is always armed with the absolute right to send a proposal straight to the shredder. Because the program officer has no positive powers, flattering will hardly guarantee that a proposal will be funded. Because the program officer has unlimited negative power, however, offending one, even if ever so slightly, is a virtual guarantee of proposal failure. To offer constructive criticism to a grantmaker, therefore, is to take on a fool's errand, while offering praise, no matter how fulsome, is always a wise move.

It must be noted that all of this obsequiousness is a sword that cuts two ways. It obviously inappropriately inflates the egos of foundation employees, while it diminishes, in their eyes, the value of constructive criticism. It has an equally, if not greater, corrosive effect on applicants and grant seekers, for the endless need to praise people who do not deserve the accolades makes grant seekers feel like sycophants and gives rise to resentments that persist even if their project is ultimately funded.

The Fourth Factor: The Highly Concentrated Nature of Foundation Accountability

The highly concentrated nature of foundation accountability has the perverse effect of devaluing the most important feedback foundations can receive, while exalting beyond all proportion feedback of lesser value. In other societal organizations, accountability is widely distributed. For a commercial enterprise, for example, the purchasing decisions of thousands—or even millions—of customers become a major source of accountability. Perhaps, the most illustrative case was that of New Coke, a product launched by the Coca-Cola Company in the 1980s to replace the century-old formula for their flagship soft drink. Consumers reacted negatively, and sales of New Coke, after an initial spike due to people trying it for the first time, rapidly deteriorated. Soon, a grassroots outcry compelled Coca-Cola to reintroduce its old formula, under the banner of Coke Classic. Eventually, New Coke sales collapsed completely, so Coca-Cola quietly withdrew this misbegotten product from the market. Similarly, accountability is widely distributed across the electorate in politics, and among the stakeholders of nonprofit organizations. A museum's patrons, for example, can simply choose not to attend if they dislike a particular exhibition.

Only in endowed grantmaking foundations, once again, is there an exception to this rule of wide accountability. The normal customer system is inverted; instead of foundations competing to serve grantees, the grantees compete with each other to get foundation grants. Applicants and grantees, therefore, exercise no power of accountability over foundations. With no consumer to satisfy, no voter to mollify, and (community foundations excepted) no donors to pacify, accountability in the foundation context shrinks to the handful of people who constitute the foundation's board of trustees. One of the key functions of a board of trustees, of course, is to be the ultimate arbiters of organizational accountability, so it is not a bad thing that a foundation's board is accountable. The problem arises from the fact that they provide the only source of accountability.

The people who work most closely with foundation employees—applicants and grantees—are in the best position to provide the feedback needed to properly assess the employee's—and the foundation's—performance. Yet as has been demonstrated, applicants and grantees compete for the favor of foundation employees and thus fear providing honest feedback. With the people who best know their work effectively muzzled, foundation employees come to realize that out of the hundreds or even thousands of people with whom they work each year only the handful who sit on their foundation's board of trustees truly matter. Others may be dissatisfied with their work or angry with them personally, but they will know better than to say so openly. The only opinions that count are those of board members.

The dysfunctionality of this narrow band of accountability quickly becomes evident. Those who daily witness foundation employees going about their core tasks do not have a voice in the employees' performance review, while people who see only a small portion of the employees' work once a quarter or perhaps only twice a year provide the only oversight. Foundation employees quickly learn that if they can keep the wool pulled over the trustees' eyes, they need not be concerned about any other feedback offered by anyone else. To paraphrase scripture, "If the trustees are for me, who can be against me?"

The High Price of High Praise

As a result, therefore, of the lack of external tests, the power imbalance between foundations and those who depend on them, the arbitrary nature of foundation decision making, and the highly concentrated nature of foundation accountability, all foundation employees live in an unreal and giddy bubble, one in which they can say, "I am practically perfect in every way, and should you doubt me, I can produce all the data required to prove it." Applicants and grantees, however, work in a considerably less idyllic state, one in which they feel forced to mouth the words of praise to program officers who have treated them cavalierly or even poorly. Peter Frumkin (2006) notes this phenomenon,

writing that "few nonprofits are able to express themselves candidly, . . . even if they have major complaints and concerns" (p. 106). Waldemar Nielsen (1972), who was an exemplary program officer himself, went further, writing that although a program officer "may receive public flattery, he is commonly held in private disrespect by those with whom he has professional dealings" (p. 327).

This unhealthy state of affairs underlies many interactions between grantmaker and grant seeker, and it has a corrosive effect on what is ideally supposed to be a working partnership between the funder and the funded. One of the occupational hazards of a long tenure in the field is that, over time, the program officer begins not only to welcome the constant flattery but indeed comes also to expect it, and at the same time, becomes hypersensitive to even a hint of criticism. This description, written in 2007, is just as apt today:

> Thus arose the caricature of the foundation leader, his every move a royal progress, his thirst for fulsome praise unslakable, his aversion to even the mildest criticism absolute. The more out of touch and ineffective he became, the firmer his belief that he was a paragon of effectiveness. He was "large and in charge," the "sage on the stage," and secretly, the butt of every joke whenever applicants (and even grantees) gathered together. (Orosz, 2007, p. 39)

Clearly, foundations pay a huge price for having created the conditions that have led to an excess of praise and a dearth of constructive criticism. But what can be done to reverse, or at least reduce, the doleful effects of this situation? The obvious answer, that of removing the conditions causing the problem in the first place, cannot easily be implemented. No foundation leader is capable of creating an external test, such as the market test, for his or her foundation, nor can the power imbalance between the foundation and those who depend on it be redressed. A bold foundation leader would be capable of creating a less arbitrary decision-making process in any given foundation, one that offered program officers some measure of positive power to counterbalance their negative power, but two things militate against even this modest reform. One is that the negative power program officer model is entrenched by nearly 150 years of tradition in the foundation world and thus is not a simple matter to dislodge or upend. The other is that most foundation CEOs intently avoid rocking any organizational boats; many indeed regard their tenure at the head of an endowed grantmaking foundation as the capstone of their career, which makes it highly unlikely that they will tackle any systemic reforms in foundation management. Foundation leaders are best placed to address the highly concentrated nature of foundation accountability. A 360-degree-performance-review system could be implemented, for example, that would place a significant weight on input from applicants and grantees thus broadening accountability beyond a foundation's small and usually unrepresentative board of trustees. Such an approach is likely to be stoutly resisted by all involved with foundations. Program officers will decry it as a management by popularity contest, foundation officers will declare it too unwieldy, and board members will regard it as an assault on their governance prerogatives. In short, needed reviews to make feedback more representative of actual sentiments will not anytime soon bubble up from within the foundation world.

Yet even if these four factors remain in place and are left unaddressed by the broader foundation field, there are still some things that individual foundations can do to elicit honest feedback. Historically, foundation leaders have been lukewarm about embracing these methods largely because of a sense that such efforts are doomed to failure. First, if the foundation surveyed its applicants and grantees, who would be bold enough—or perhaps foolish enough—to answer honestly, for fear that anything they said that was less than glowing could and would be held against them when they submitted future requests? Second, even if the survey was made anonymous, both applicants and grantees would still self-censor, for fear that foundation employees could divine their identities through the details and context provided in their responses and once more use that knowledge against them. Third, even if that fear of retribution could somehow be laid aside and honest answers could be gathered, the very nature of the two samples to be surveyed all but preordains the answers that would be received. Grantees, since they have received support, would be overwhelmingly positive in their responses, while applicants whose proposals had been declined would be negative in equally overwhelming numbers. So any unfiltered survey would ultimately demonstrate that people who got grants were happy, while those who did not were unhappy. Such a survey is merely an expensive way to grasp the thoroughly obvious. From this last point grows a fourth objection: Every dollar spent surveying applicants or grantees is a dollar that cannot be spent on grants. Why spend precious funds that could go toward meeting the problems of people to do research that would only confirm what was already intuitively obvious?

Discussion of Future Directions

The Futility of Early Attempts in Capturing Candid Feedback

These four criticisms were indeed borne out by some of the early attempts made by individual foundations to survey both their grantees and the applicants they had turned down for funding. Foundations that experimented with direct surveys during the 1980s received responses that were so overwhelmingly positive—even from those organizations they had turned down for funding—that the results were deemed to be virtually worthless. By the 1990s, foundations such as Packard and Kellogg experimented

with a more sophisticated form of surveying, one in which they guaranteed anonymity to their respondents. The results, however, reflected the second critique, for both grantees and rejected applicants feared that if they answered honestly, foundation employees would be able to deduce their identities. As a result, the answers received from both groups were still suspiciously positive, even from those turned down (Orosz, 2000, p. 41). Such results seem to vindicate those who said a search for reliable feedback in the foundation context was as likely to be successful as the search for the Holy Grail.

Efforts to Make the Foundation More Receptive to Candid Feedback

Recently, however, there have evolved improved mechanisms for gathering—and making use of—candid feedback from grantees and rejected applicants alike. Beginning with the creation of the Program on Nonprofit Organizations at Yale University in 1976 and accelerating rapidly during the 1990s, academic centers for the study of philanthropy, volunteerism, and nonprofit management have been established at hundreds of colleges and universities across the United States. As of 2009, according to the Nonprofit Academic Centers Council, 46 of these centers employed full-time directors and faculty and offered regular programs of teaching and research. Such programs as the Center on Philanthropy at Indiana University (http://www.philanthropy.iupui.edu), the Dorothy A. Johnson Center for Philanthropy at Grand Valley State University (http://www.gvsu.edu/jcp), and the Lodestar Center for Philanthropy & Nonprofit Innovation at Arizona State University (http://www.asu.edu/wpp/nonprofit) provide survey designs that could objectively measure the opinions of foundation grantees and applicants. While such academic offerings are certainly an improvement over self-administered surveys, their increasing availability has not, to date, resulted in a ground swell of such research activity. Foundation leaders are usually skeptical of the value of the surveys in the first place, and some regard academic centers as something less than fair brokers, for such centers are themselves grant seekers and staffed by scholars who do not always fully appreciate or understand the complexities and distinctive circumstances of foundation work.

Another important development, this one dating from 1997, moved the field closer to an appreciation of the importance of securing honest feedback. A group of foundation executives and program officers from around the nation coalesced to form Grantmakers for Effective Organizations (GEO, http://www.geofunders.org). Initially, GEO focused on the need for foundations to move beyond the funding of programs to methodical support for the development of strong nonprofit organizations that can devise, administer, and sustain strong programs. GEO quickly expanded its focus to include the central importance of improving the foundations' own "core business." GEO's status of being *of funders, for funders* made foundations more receptive to their advocacy for proactively surveying grantees and applicants to gain useful feedback to improve operations.

The advent of GEO was followed closely by a pair of bottom-up efforts to improve the grantmaker/grant seeker relationship and thus, among other things, enhance the quantity and quality of feedback that grantmakers receive. Both of these initiatives, the GrantCraft program of the Ford Foundation, founded in 2001 (http://www.grantcraft.org), and the Grantmaking School of the Johnson Center for Philanthropy at Grand Valley State University, founded in 2004 (http://www.grantmakingschool.org), seek to train foundation program officers in good practices within the field of grantmaking. It usually comes as a surprise to outsiders to learn that the foundation field, which has been employing program officers in the United States since 1867, has never agreed on fieldwide basic principles of good practice. It usually comes as an even bigger surprise to outsiders to learn that people who will be responsible for wisely choosing grantees and making millions of dollars of grants to them are rarely provided with any training in their craft beyond a rudimentary orientation, instead, being abandoned to a haphazard experience of learning by doing. Given these facts, there is little wonder that the relationship between grantmaker and grant seeker is so fraught with difficulties. Both GrantCraft and the Grantmaking School have defined, in the absence of fieldwide standards, their own sets of good practices, which they impart to program officers through educational programs, publications, and their websites. It is reasonable to believe that, as better-trained program officers percolate up through the infrastructure of the foundation field, communications between them and the grant seekers and grantees will take on a more authentic tone, with honest feedback becoming more the rule rather than the exception.

Candid Feedback Comes of Age: Center for Effective Philanthropy

Contemporaneous with the evolution of GEO, GrantCraft, and the Grantmaking School has been the development of the organization that has, to date, been most successful in improving the quality of feedback from applicants and grantees to foundations, namely the Center for Effective Philanthropy (CEP), located in Cambridge, Massachusetts (http://www.effectivephilanthropy.org). The CEP was conceived in 2001 as a research institute with a mission to provide reliable information to foundations that would allow them to improve their efficiency and effectiveness.

It was not until 2003, when the CEP began to offer foundations their Grantee Perception Report, that the prospect for truly candid and reliable feedback became a reality. The CEP, a neutral third party, guarantees the anonymity of

grantee respondents (foundation employees do not see the raw data) and thus encourages candid responses. As of December 2009, the CEP had generated 173 Grantee Perception Reports for all types and sizes of foundations. The grantees' perceptions of the interactions with foundations during the grantmaking process and the impact of the foundations' actions have provided an eye-opening experience for foundations commissioning the reports. Fully 97% of the participating foundations have made operational changes on the basis of what they have learned from the survey, according to an evaluation conducted by LaFrance Associates, a limited liability company (LLC). Actions taken by the foundations range from major changes in grantmaking strategy to improvements in grantmaking processes and communications with grantees (Center for Effective Philanthropy, n.d., "Grantee Perception Reports"). The *Chronicle of Philanthropy* concluded that the Grantee Perception Reports "have resulted in changes in foundation operations and have fostered frank dialogue between grantmakers and charities, which historically have been wary of speaking out against supporters for fear of losing money" (Wilhelm, 2005, pp. 2–4).

There can be no doubt that the CEP's Grantee Perception Report constitutes a great leap forward in the quest for reliable external feedback in the foundation world. Foundations—for the first time—are able to get unvarnished responses from an uncowed sampling of their customers. The CEP, in 2006, launched a second series of assessments, the Applicant Perception Reports, focusing on the views of applicants whose proposals were declined by foundations, so both successful and unsuccessful requesters can now be heard. As of December 2009, thirty Applicant Perception Reports have been completed by the Center. The constructive data gathered by these reports provide the basis for real foundation improvement (Center for Effective Philanthropy, n.d., "Applicant Perception Reports").

On the other hand, neither the Grantee Perception Report nor the Applicant Perception Report in itself provides a complete solution to the feedback challenge. To date, less than 1/6 of 1% of American foundations have commissioned one or another of the reports. These reports are too expensive for every foundation to pursue, and in any case, the CEP lacks the capacity to conduct them for all of the approximately 80,000 American foundations. Clearly, a less expensive and more accessible way to garner unbiased feedback must be found, perhaps through some sort of joint venture between the CEP and the growing network of university centers for the study of philanthropy.

Paths to Individual Responsibility

Since the institutional leadership of the field of philanthropy has done relatively little to promote candid feedback, it is incumbent on all individuals who work in the field, no matter how low they may be on the organizational chart, to take personal responsibility for securing and using external information. There is a general axiom among program officers that very much holds true: The more time you spend at your desk, the less effective you are as a grantmaker. It is incumbent on grantmaking professionals, therefore, to look beyond the foundation's walls for data and resources to help them improve their performance.

Perhaps the most valuable thing a grantmaker can do is to get, as soon as possible after being hired by the foundation, training in good practices for grantmaking. As previously mentioned, the Grantmaking School and the GrantCraft project of the Ford Foundation provide courses and educational resources that stress the importance of grantmakers' responsiveness to applicants and grantees and promote grantmakers' encouragement of candid feedback. With such training, grantmakers come to realize that the money they are dispensing is not their own; that grantees are partners, not supplicants; that although grantmaking is not a formal profession, it is important to behave professionally; and that humility is an essential personality trait of the most effective grantmakers.

Training is a prerequisite to informed and effective grantmaking, but it is still necessary to get out of the office frequently to maximize personal responsibility. Site visits, in which grantmakers visit the applicant or grantee on his or her own turf, are an important means of keeping in touch, not only with a specific grant seeker but also with developments in the broader field. There are many things that can be done outside of daily foundation responsibilities, as well, such as volunteering for service in nonprofit organizations or serving on their boards of trustees. Such opportunities provide authentic insights into the struggles and successes of a foundation's nonprofit partners and allow the foundation to give unvarnished feedback outside of the supercharged foundation environment. Some foundations will even give employees a sabbatical to go work, for as much as a year, with a key grantee, so they can truly immerse themselves in the reality of their work.

In the end, it is not possible for individual foundation employees to control the way in which their officers and their trustees run their organization. It is, however, not only possible but also imperative for individual employees to take responsibility for being open, approachable, and honest grantmakers. As one of the greatest program officers of all time, Abraham Flexner, once noted, "applicants come to you, psychologically, on their knees. It is your task to help them to their feet" Orosz, 2007 (p. ix).

Summary

The Center for Effective Philanthropy has opened wide the door to honest feedback, and many more foundations should enter. Individual foundations can and should take more vigorous steps to openly court such feedback and to put it to use. Many options are available even to those foundations that find the tools offered by the CEP to be too expensive to use. Tom David (2006) has suggested several practical (and cost-effective) steps foundations can take to solicit useful information, such as convening grantees in retreat settings or at conferences; conducting transparent grantee surveys, focus groups, and phone interviews; distributing mail-back cards; and creating a foundation-wide habit of listening closely to all stakeholders. David further suggests that foundations should actively encourage their staffs to reflect on the data thus collected as well as create group learning forums so that employees absorb the lessons and put them to use. Foundations should publish the results on their websites and in their annual reports and likewise share with their stakeholders and with the broader field the lessons they have learned and the adjustments in practice that they intend to make as a result.

However improvements in soliciting and using honest feedback are achieved, whether by foundation fiat or by individual initiative, it must be done. As legendary Penn State football coach Joe Paterno once remarked, "You are either getting better, or you are getting worse" (Orosz, 2007, p. 42). There is no status quo, only evolution or devolution. Either foundations are making proactive efforts to improve through careful evaluation of external feedback and thoughtful course corrections, or they are getting worse. Foundation leaders need to do more—much more than they have done in the past—to get better, and they need to do so quickly. There is no excuse for organizations with so much freedom and so many resources to behave so arbitrarily and so thoughtlessly toward their customers' needs and wants. Most of all, there can be no justification for the lousy performance that such heedlessness inevitably brings in its train. The benefits of listening carefully to applicants and grantees alike are nicely summarized by the CEP:

> Ultimately, the beneficiaries of better foundation-grantee relationships are not just grantees and foundations, but the people and issues they seek to affect through their work. By working more productively together, foundations and grantees can create more positive social impact. This, after all, is the ultimate goal of both parties. (Bolduc, Buchanan, & Huang, 2004, p. 3)

References and Further Readings

Bolduc, K., Buchanan, P., & Huang, J. (2004). *What nonprofits value in their foundation funders*. New York: Center for Effective Philanthropy.

Center for Effective Philanthropy. (n.d.). *Applicant perception reports*. Retrieved December 6, 2009a, from http://www.effectivephilanthropy.org

Center for Effective Philanthropy. (n.d.). *Grantee perception reports*. Retrieved December 6, 2009b, from http://www.effectivephilanthropy.org

David, T. (2006). Ready, set, learn: The foundation as a learning organization. *Learning*. Retrieved April 4, 2006, from http://www.geofunders.org/Content.aspx?oid=90c322bc-4a8e-45d2-8b5b-3a790c23aa64

Emerson, J. (2006). Foundations: Essential and missing in action. *Alliance Extra*. Retrieved March 10, 2006, from www.allavida.org/alliance/axmar066.html?pnd

Frumkin, P. (2006). Accountability and legitimacy in American foundation philanthropy. In K. Prewitt, M. Dogan, S. Heydemann, & S. Toepler (Eds.), *The legitimacy of philanthropic foundations: U.S. and European perspectives* (p. 106). New York: Russell Sage.

Josephson, M. (1992). *Ethics in grantmaking & grantseeking: Making philanthropy better.* Marina Del Rey, CA: Joseph & Edna Josephson Institute of Ethics.

Nielsen, W. A. (1972). *The big foundations.* New York: Columbia University Press.

Orosz, J. J. (2000). *The insider's guide to grantmaking: How foundations find, fund, and manage effective programs.* San Francisco: Josey-Bass.

Orosz, J. J. (2007). *Effective foundation management: 14 challenges of philanthropic leadership—and how to outfox them.* Lanham, MD: AltaMira Press.

Wilhelm, I. (2005, November 10). Giving charities a voice: Organization offers an unvarnished evaluation. *Chronicle of Philanthropy, 18*(3), 2–4.

84

Ethics and Grantmaking

James Gelatt

University of Maryland University College

Philanthropy is America's most distinctive virtue. . . . [It is] central to our health and survival as a free and open and democratic society. . . . Without [the nonprofit sector] we're a society without a moral compass.

Robert Payton

The issue of ethics has taken on increased importance in the United States, due in large part to the media coverage of companies such as Enron. But ethical issues have been an integral factor in nonprofits almost since their inception. The role of nonprofits in the United States is unique. Nonprofit organizations have played not only a key role in the history of America, but also they have helped define America. We are who we are in part because of nonprofits.

Educational, charitable, civic, religious, and grantmaking institutions represent the most prevalent demonstration of Americans' commitment to the common good. Together, these institutions constitute American philanthropy in its two basic forms—those entities that seek funding in order to provide goods and services to others in need and those entities that were established to award funding to deserving nonprofits in order for them to provide such goods and services. Collectively then, *philanthropy* (from the Greek for "loving others") can be defined (Payton & Moody, 2008) as a

- primary vehicle that people use to put their moral beliefs into practice; and
- voluntary intervention in the lives of others for others' benefit. In this way, philanthropy is innately moral.

Note the link between *philanthropy* and *moral*, or *ethical*. Almost by definition, to be engaged in the field of nonprofit service or grantmaking requires one to act according to ethical standards.

Nonprofits exist because the public decided to create them. What we typically think of as a nonprofit holds legal status from the Internal Revenue Service (IRS)—usually what is called *501(c)(3) status*. Organizations that earn a 501(c)(3) status are eligible to receive tax-deductible contributions. The government has said, Because your organization exists to serve others, we are awarding you with unique status. Persons who contribute to your organization can declare their donations against their income on their income tax forms.

Many grantmaking organizations also hold this 501(c)(3) status. That is true for what are called *private foundations* (usually those with an endowment or "corpus") and *community foundations*, which often serve to pool donations into a coordinated investment and grantmaking entity. As with nonprofit *charitable* organizations, grantmaking organizations are given special tax status in the recognition that they exist to advance the public good.

Nonprofits thus rely on the public's belief in them to survive; in turn, the U.S. public has since colonial times relied on nonprofits for essential services—health care, education, social services (orphanages, for example). Without the public's trust, nonprofits would not exist. And a big part of that trust comes from the public's belief that nonprofits hold themselves to high ethical standards. Warren Buffett commented that "it takes 20 years to build a reputation and five minutes to ruin it. If you think about that, you'll do things differently" (p. 111).

Nonprofits are only as good as the image they project, as we have seen. A few years ago when scandal rocked the United Way both nationally and regionally, the former president of United Way, William Aramony, was found guilty of illegally using over $1 million of United Way's funds for his own personal use. He was sentenced to 7 years in prison. The nonprofit's reputation may be the single most important factor in the nonprofit's ability to carry out its mission, whether that mission is providing services or providing funding for those services. The United Way had enjoyed enormous success. It was backed by the National Football League, ensuring it national visibility and financial support. The United Way's president, William Aramony, was forced to resign after the public learned of his large salary ($460,000 in 1992, plus benefits), his overblown expense account, and his apparent financial misdealings, including the creation of several "spin-off" organizations that received funds intended by donors to go to the public good. Aramony was forced to resign and subsequently was imprisoned. The United Way scandal was not just about one person. It was about the failure of a nonprofit—board and staff alike—to live up to the trust that had been given to it by the public.

Ethics Defined

Let's first review some definitions.

Minkes, Small, and Chatterjee (1999) state that ethics is concerned with prescribing and describing moral requirements and behaviors. There are acceptable and unacceptable ways of behavior. People and organizations exist within a code of ethics. However, this code of ethics is framed by the culture in which the people and organizations exist. In some cultures, it is totally acceptable in a business environment to offer bribes and to accept bribes. In American culture, this behavior is considered unethical. Some organizations think their American code of ethics is the only acceptable behavior and other behaviors, regardless of culture, are unacceptable.

There are two ways of looking at ethics: One way is to determine whether or not something is ethical solely by the consequences of our actions or practices. An action or practice is right if it leads to the greatest possible balance of good. An example of looking at it this way—by examining the consequences—is Utilitarianism. According to Utilitarianism, actions are right in proportion to their tendency to promote happiness or absence of pain. Utilitarianism is committed to the maximization of good. The problem is how does one define *good?*

By comparison, the other way of looking at ethics relates to a sense of duty. It considers factors other than outcomes. Actions are not justified by their consequences. One must consider the importance of *motives*. Those who adhere to this second definition insist on the importance of motives and character. In other words, ethics is based on a set of principles that should be followed and not on the results of our actions.

Both of these definitions apply to philanthropy. Nonprofits, the "charitable" organizations seeking funds or the organizations making financial contributions, are judged externally by how we view their behavior. But what we learned from the Enron debacle was that the appearance of doing good (Enron was viewed as a model corporate citizen)

is not enough. Ethics is also about what people believe including if they believe they have a duty to do what is right.

Ethics and Leadership

Studies of leadership often link leadership with an organization's culture. Edgar Schein, one of the better known authors on leadership and culture (1992), argues that organizational culture and leadership are two sides of the same coin. Leaders establish the organizational culture and then are influenced by it.

If one agrees with that point of view, the implications for leadership are clear:

- It is the responsibility of leadership (and thence management) to create an organizational environment that fosters ethical behavior. That environment is created in part by the establishment and inculcation of values and in setting a clear ethical tone.
- Setting the tone means "walking the walk." To "do as I say, not as I do" just won't cut it.
- Organizational leadership needs to establish clear expectations: which behaviors are expected and acceptable and which are not. Leaders should have an ethical plan in place.

Can ethics be taught? Can nonprofit leaders instill a sense of ethics in making grant awards or fundraising? The organization can teach its employees about the organization's ethical code. Management can give staff clear examples of what is acceptable and help staff to consider real-to-life examples. But the training needs to be accompanied by a modeling of the desired behavior. Internalized ethics is more effective than enforced ethical behavior. One of the ways that culture and ethics are linked is in developing a sense of community within the nonprofit. People are more likely to behave appropriately if they feel a sense of belonging. People are more likely to want to belong if they feel their leaders are behaving in ways that are admirable. If the leader of the nonprofit is more focused on raising funds than on doing good, or more focused on looking good in the grantmaking field than on investing in sound causes, the sense of belonging is likely to suffer. That goes for actions taken and not taken: Doing nothing is the same as doing something. What the organization's leadership doesn't do sends an equally strong message about what is expected and what is tolerated.

An Ethical Framework

It may be useful to see ethics in the larger context of society. Hellriegel, Jackson, and Slocum (1999) provide such a framework in their discussion of ethics. According to this framework, ethics starts with what might be called the *morality* of the individual. Placing the individual in the middle of a set of concentric and ever-widening circles, the next level moves from the "individual" to the "organizational" level. At the organizational level, morality and ethics conjoin. Morals might be said to derive from personal character, whereas ethics exist in a social context in which those morals are applied. In other words, ethics points to standards or codes of behavior expected by the group (the organization, which is essentially a group of people) to which the individual belongs. And it is in this moral/ethical context that ethical issues begin to play out: Although genuine ethics come from a personal value system (morals), it may be possible to *act* ethically without adhering to one's own moral beliefs and value. Such behavior is just that—acting.

An example of this conflict between personal morality and organizational ethics can be found in a book called *On a Clear Day You Can See General Motors* (Wright, 1980). The book describes the experiences of John De Lorean and the other senior executives at General Motors Company (GM) as they developed and sold a car, the Corvair, that they knew was defective—potentially lethally so. The executives decided in the long run it would be cheaper to produce and sell the car and pay for the damages or deaths suffered by people whose Corvairs caught fire. De Lorean says that the people who made this decision strictly on financial and not ethical grounds were in all other contexts good people—husbands, fathers, soccer coaches, community leaders. Somehow, when they left their homes in the morning, they also left behind their personal morality and bought into a skewed sense of what was acceptable behavior. In some ways, De Lorean's actions and those of his colleagues are not so different from those leaders of some grantmaking organizations that abuse the public trust for personal interest or gain. According to an article in *Academic Psychiatry* (Lazarus, 2006), a number of studies have shown that as a result of pharmaceutical industry influence, inaccurate, incomplete, or otherwise biased information based on the results of pharmaceutical-sponsored clinical trials becomes published and accepted by those either in medical school or in practice.

The pharmaceutical example above also demonstrates how ethics and law can conflict. The pharmaceutical industry may not be breaking any law by underwriting research that supports its products. But as a grantmaker, it is certainly stretching the bounds of what would be considered ethical.

Ethics and law can often run counter to one another in the nonprofit sector. In general, grantmaking foundations are prohibited by law from *lobbying*, meaning they cannot directly attempt to influence the passage of legislation. But they are allowed to engage in *advocacy*—that is, encouraging support of a cause that might be under consideration for legislation. The difference is a fine one but one that grantmakers have to appreciate. But take a hypothetical case: Can grantmakers provide support for organizations that do engage in lobbying? What if the grantmaker supports a nonprofit in the environmental field that is comprised of two entities: one, an organization that clearly fits under IRS rules for its educational purposes; and the other, which does not qualify for tax-deductible contributions because it actively supports or fights legislation. The 501(c)(3) entity owns the building and grounds on which the lobbying entity sits. Thus, a grant to one indirectly helps the other.

This is an important distinction to make. The premise of a classic article called "The Four Faces of Social Responsibility" (Dalton & Cosier, 1982) is depicted in Figure 84.1. Here are some examples of how the "four faces" might play out in ethical issues facing nonprofits:

- *Legal/Responsible.* Fortunately, most activities undertaken by nonprofits, both grant seeking and grantmaking, fall into this category.
- *Legal/Irresponsible.* It is legal for grantmaking organizations to pay salaries and expenses for their board members. It may be irresponsible to authorize board members to travel first class, stay in only the best hotels, and charge part of their business space back to the grantmaking organization.
- *Responsible/Illegal.* Suppose your grantmaking organization believes that marijuana when used properly can be a great help to people undergoing chemotherapy for cancer. The law in your state prohibits the use of marijuana. So you award grant funds to a nonprofit that is based in a country where the marijuana laws are not enforced; the nonprofit in turn makes the marijuana available to patients who come to that country.
- *Irresponsible/Illegal.* Fortunately, this too is a rare occurrence in nonprofits although there have been some examples, which are yet to be proved, such as a grantmaking organization awarding funds to entities known to support terrorist activities.

The next level of the concentric rings in the ethical framework proposed by Hielriegel, Jackson, and Slocum (1999) addresses society's role in ethics. Public policy—the making of laws and regulations—tends to follow public opinion—the "will of the people." People decide what is

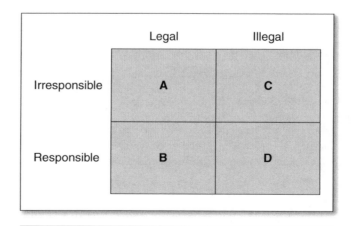

Figure 84.1 Four Faces of Social Responsibility

SOURCE: Dalton and Cosier, 1982.

right or wrong, and what they decide is often reflected in the subsequent passage of laws and the implementation of regulations. As a society, we have decided that corporations should be allowed to set aside a portion of their profits, which go into grants to nonprofits. We have decided that at least some nonprofits should not have to pay property taxes.

Some societal decisions are less clear-cut: Should private foundation grants to abortion clinics or Planned Parenthood be allowed? Should the National Rifle Association Foundation be allowed to target grant funds for programs that teach children and youth about guns?

The final level in the ethical framework (Hielriegel, Jackson, & Slocum, 1999) brings up an important point about ethics. The final level speaks to an overall "system" of ethics—a system within which virtually any ethical decision could be made. What makes ethics and ethical decision making so difficult is that there is no universally accepted system. What is ethical (and legal) in the United States—birth control, for example, or the right to bear arms—might be unethical in some other cultures. There is no consistent agreement on what constitutes ethical behavior even within the United States. Here's an example: The author of this chapter was for several years a consultant to a national grantmaking organization that helped persons with disabilities. The organization both accepted contributions and made grants. Two of the major supporters of the organization were the tobacco industry and the beer industry.

Without the support of those two industries—tobacco and beer—the organization's financial resources would have been cut in half or worse. So the ongoing dilemma within this grantmaking organization was, Should it accept funding from "tainted" sources, from companies that sold products—especially the tobacco companies—that were known to be harmful to people, products that might in fact lead to people becoming disabled?

There was no *right* answer. The answer was a clear *yes* and *no*. That's what makes ethics so difficult. If the answer is black or white, it's probably not an ethical issue in the first place.

Ethical Conduct and Ethical Decision Making

Ethical Conduct

Ethical conduct begins with an atmosphere of trust. The relationship between grantmakers and grant seekers has matured as both parties have become more sophisticated in recent years. Grant seekers take a more businesslike approach. They are better stewards of the funds given to them than might have been the case a generation ago. They understand finance and accounting, sound governance, and strategic planning. Grantmakers, in turn, do more than just give their money away. They become involved in the process, often working with the grant seeker to ensure the

funded project's success. The trust relationship between grant seeker and grantmaker is built on three factors: (1) courtesy, (2) honesty, and (3) responsible management of information (Sievers, 2008).

Unfortunately, the first factor—courtesy—does not always occur in the world of private grantmaking foundations. Staffs among foundations sometimes form their own "club" that is open to colleagues and closed to nonprofit grant seekers. For the relationship to work ethically, the trust needs to begin with common courtesy and civility. The situation is improving, especially among newer grantmakers, such as those who made their fortune in the dot.com boom. Having "made it" on their own, these younger grantmakers tend to be more accessible.

Honesty is also a two-way proposition. Grant seekers walk a fine line: They want to present themselves as competent so that they will be seen as a good investment. But they need to be careful not to "oversell" themselves. Grant seeker honesty also comes up once the project is underway: When the funded project is going awry, with timelines slipping and results at risk, what should the nonprofit staff tell its funder?

The honesty factor is no less tricky for the grantmaker. In many, usually smaller foundations, it can be difficult for the grant seeker to get good information on the foundation's guidelines or funding priorities. Although most of the larger private foundations have published information, what they tend not to say is that sometimes funding decisions are made because certain board members have "pet" projects that get top priority.

This leads to the third trust factor between grant seeker and grantmaker—responsible management of information. In the absence of reliable information, it's human nature to "awfulize"—to imagine the worst case scenario. The nonprofit needs to go out of its way to keep the grantmaker informed—to err on the side of too much information, if anything. The nonprofit should invite site visits by the grantmaker and encourage the grantmaker to meet with those who are being served by the funded project. And in this digital age, there is no reason why grant seekers should not be transparent as well.

Factors That Influence Ethical Conduct

Published research (Rest, 1994) has identified four crucial factors that influence ethical conduct: (1) ethical *awareness*—recognizing that a situation raises ethical issues; (2) ethical *decision making*—determining what course of action is ethically sound; (3) ethical *intent*—identifying which values should take priority in the decision; and (4) ethical *action*—following through on ethical decisions.

Ethical Awareness

Ethical conduct in nonprofit organizations—or any organization for that matter—begins with an acknowledgment that an ethical situation is present. If we are not tuned into ethics generally or do not understand what might constitute an ethical situation, we might "filter" out a situation that in fact should be addressed for its ethical implications. This may mean being aware that what is seen as an ethical situation in one culture may not be seen as such in another. This can be a challenge for grantmaking foundations with an international focus, among them the Ford Foundation, the Bill and Melinda Gates Foundation, and the Kettering Foundation.

My behavior as an employee or board member of a nonprofit starts with my own ethical grounding. It is not only insufficient to say, "I was only following orders" or "it's part of the organizational culture," but also it is being dishonest with oneself. As the example John De Lorean at GM showed, it is easy—and so tempting—to get caught up in the organizational climate, allowing oneself to take actions (or avoid taking actions). Why did it take legal intervention for the United Way to correct a situation that must have been obvious to both staff and board? Why didn't anyone speak up about the way veterans who had been wounded in Iraq were being treated? The answer would seem to have to do with the climate of the time and the desire to follow the leader.

Ethical Decision Making

This is such a significant topic that it will be addressed under its own heading, which follows.

Ethical Intent

Some organizations seem to rely on a code of conduct as a way of identifying what constitutes an ethical situation and how to deal with it. But ethical codes need to emanate from a true commitment to ethics within the organization, led by the organization's top management, and be shared by staff and board throughout.

The MacArthur Foundation (n.d.) seems to have made this kind of commitment to ethical intent, as evidenced by this statement from the foundation:

> The Foundation expects its staff and directors to conduct themselves consistent with the highest ethical standards. The Foundation's policies set forth the expected standards and the procedures to be followed to comply with the policy. The Foundation's Code of Conduct, which emphasizes a number of different policies, is set forth below. No policy can address every conceivable ethical situation. Ultimately, therefore, the Foundation relies on the good judgment, integrity, and honesty of its staff and directors to ensure it addresses all situations in an ethical and legal fashion and in compliance with the applicable policy. ("Code of Conduct")

The MacArthur Foundation's policy goes on to address the standards by which it will interact with its grantees. Here is some of what those standards address:

- The foundation undertakes substantial due diligence to ensure that the proposed grantee organization has the capacity, structure, values, and resources to accomplish the purpose of the grant and that the foundation's grant funds will be used for the intended charitable purpose. Note the inclusion not only of the ability of a grantee to complete the proposed project but also of the values of that grantee.
- Once a grant is made, the foundation does not control the actions of its grantees, yet it continues to have a keen interest in the outcome of the grant and the manner in which grant funds are spent.

The MacArthur Foundation, while acknowledging that it no longer controls the funds once they have been awarded, nevertheless indicates that its continued support is based on a sense of trust that the grantee will operate in an appropriate manner.

Ethical Action

We all find ourselves in situations that at times seem hopeless. And, we all have the choice to do nothing or take action.

Catherine Pulsifer

Ethical decisions need to lead to ethical actions. It does feel sometimes that it would be easier to just let it be and hope the issue will go away. But nonprofits have a unique obligation. It is referred to as *fiduciary responsibility*. A fiduciary responsibility implies a relationship between two or more parties that is based on *trust*. That is why we often call those who serve on nonprofit boards *trustees*. They have been entrusted with the organization's well being and image. They are expected to uphold its values and reflect its ethics in their actions.

Ethical Decision Making

Ethical decision making is at once similar to and distinct from other organizational decision making. The rational decision-making model follows three sequential steps: (1) identify and define the problem; (2) generate alternative solutions to the problem; and (3) select the best solution and implement it. There are several problems with this classic approach:

- It treats decision making and problem solving as the same. Especially as it relates to ethics, there is real risk in waiting until a problem occurs. Nonprofits need to continually monitor the internal and external environment in which they operate to anticipate possible ethical issues and address them before they are blown out of proportion.
- The model assumes that decision making is rational. In fact, what is known about decision making is that it is "bounded" (a term coined by Herbert Simon, 1957) by insufficient information, emotion, office politics, personal agendas, and limited time.

- As a result, most decisions have to be based on the best alternative that nonprofits can come up with at the time. They have to "satisfice"—select an alternative that is not perfect but is "good enough."

In most ethical decisions, there is no single right answer; that's what makes them ethical decisions. Management textbooks often point to Johnson & Johnson Company's (J&J's) decision to pull Tylenol off the shelves in 1982. Someone, or some group of people, substituted real Tylenol with capsules laced with cyanide. Seven persons died from cyanide poisoning as a result. As soon as Johnson & Johnson heard of the problem, the company alerted the public and pulled all Tylenol from store shelves. Johnson & Johnson's prompt actions were laudatory. But the issue was hardly an ethical one. There really was no choice.

The Johnson & Johnson Tylenol case does point out an important aspect about ethics and ethical decision making. J&J's corporate culture, driven by its CEO, was based on honesty and fair practice. In such an organizational culture, the decision to pull Tylenol off the shelves was not only right, it was also logical.

Decision Making in the Nonprofit Sector

Nonprofits present a unique set of ethical considerations. For one, in the for-profit sector, interactions (exchanges) are two-way—consumer-seller. Nonprofits often add a third dimension—nonprofit organization (analogous to the "seller"), recipient of goods or services (the "consumer"), and the grantmaker (the source of funds that makes the exchange possible). All three parties have to be in accord. The grantmaker has to have confidence in the values and capacity of the nonprofit seeking funds. The nonprofit has to have a commitment to the common good; when ethical issues arise, the nonprofit needs to make choices that are consistent with its mission of service. And the recipient needs to earn the trust of the nonprofit. If the recipient abuses the trust of the nonprofit, the nonprofit's image can in turn be damaged.

Checklist for Making Ethical Decisions

The following checklist may be useful as a guide to ethical decision making in nonprofit organizations.

1. *Recognize the ethical dilemma.* The ethical decision-making process starts with candid recognition that an ethical dilemma does in fact exist. That kind of candor is more likely to occur if the culture of the organization—be it grant seeker or grantmaker—does not "shoot the messenger." It is essential that the organization avoid *groupthink*, which occurs when a group makes flawed decisions because of group pressure to conform and not "rock the boat." Groupthink leads to a weakening of "mental efficiency, reality testing, and moral judgment" (Janis, 1972, p. 9).

2. *Get the facts.* Fact-finding need not be an exhaustive process, but it does need to be an honest one. The decision will be doomed to fail if vital information isn't put on the table.

3. *Identify your options.* Here again, identifying options should be unfettered but need not go on indefinitely. Some decision making is stalled by what is called "paralysis by analysis"—the organization spends so much time studying options that the decision never gets made.

4. *Test each option.* Once the list of options has been narrowed, ask, Is it legal? Is it right? Is it beneficial?

5. *Decide which option to follow.* Double-check your decision: How would I feel if my family found out? How would I feel if this matter made the news?

6. *Implement.* Take action but continually evaluate to make sure the course of action makes sense and is working (Donaldson, 1996).

Clearly, the best time to address ethical issues is before an ethical issue arises, using procedures carefully developed, tailored to the organization, and faithfully followed. These procedures include standards of conduct, most broadly described as the nonprofit's code of ethics, and a guarantee and assurance from those within the nonprofit that the standards are supported at the top and met throughout.

Guiding Principles

The following are drawn from two sources—*Understanding Philanthropy* (Payton & Moody, 2008) and *Money Well Spent* (Brest & Harvey, 2008).

- *Seek to do good, but at the least, do no harm.* Goodwill is not enough; it needs to be accompanied by good action. Good actions need to be based on what is sometimes called *systems thinking*—asking the "what if" questions. What are the likely consequences of a proposed action? Will the outcomes reflect the desired goal? Are there possible unintended consequences, and if so, can they be mitigated? Here's an example of unintended consequence: Does providing funds to an individual or nonprofit inadvertently lead to that individual or nonprofit becoming dependent on that support? Doing good and doing no harm means basing organizational decisions on sound evidence, fairness, and accuracy in public pronouncements, and openness to other points of view and other values.

- *Think and act strategically.* For grantmakers, this means recognizing that "saving the world" may be a noble goal but not a realistic one. Grantmakers need to set priorities, determining not only what to fund but also what not to fund. And then, they need to target their grantmaking to reflect those priorities. Thinking and acting strategically also means continual evaluation: Is the grants program making a difference? Should the focus be shifted? Should the grantmaker become more involved in assisting grant recipients?

- *Give all you can.* In the words of noted philanthropist Andrew Carnegie, "The man who dies rich . . . dies disgraced." A corollary of the "give all you can" precept is "give back and pass it on." Most grantmaking entities achieved their wealth from profit-making activities. It only makes good sense to give back to the "community," broadly written, that made wealth possible. "Pass it on" means encouraging others to make a similar commitment to philanthropy. There is more to life than making money, and in the long run, each of us will be judged by who we are, not what we own.

Ethical Case Studies

Each of the following case studies is concerned with the grantmaking side of the equation.

Individual Grantmaking

Although private foundations and corporations get most of the attention, individual giving comprises about three fourths of all giving in the United States. In 2009, for example, individual donations amounted to over $230 billion.

It behooves individuals to make informed decisions. Consider how you would respond to these scenarios:

Scenario #1. You want to contribute to fight cancer. You have been contacted recently by a cancer organization that relies on direct mail and telephone solicitations. How can you determine if the organization operates ethically and merits your support?

Scenario #2. You work for a college whose president prides herself on the college annual campaign for scholarship funds. The president has challenged each of the college departments to have 100% participation by their staff. She has also set fundraising goals for the various departments. As a result, your boss recently held an all-staff meeting in which he suggested that everyone in the department would be demonstrating his or her belief in the college by making the scholarship drive a priority for his or her personal giving. You would like to make your own decisions on where to make your contributions. How might you respond?

Although there are no absolute answers to either question, there are some guidelines that can be followed. Before deciding to make a contribution, one can check with organizations that monitor nonprofits and provide information on them. One of the better sources is Guidestar (http://www2.guidestar.org), whose mission is "to revolutionize philanthropy and nonprofit practice by providing information that advances transparency, enables users to make better decisions, and encourages charitable giving." If the cancer organization that has contacted you is not in Guidestar's database, you might want to think twice about a contribution: If the nonprofit had nothing to hide, why would it not make itself "transparent"?

You can also help nonprofits to hold themselves to ethical standards by asking questions directly: What percentage of their annual budget goes to program costs and what to fundraising? Do they provide an audited annual report? Do they use a fundraising company, and if so, what percentage of dollars raised go to that company? (Note: The Association of Fundraising Professionals Code of Ethics prohibits fundraisers from taking a percentage of funds raised.)

The second scenario is less straightforward. But this much is clear: It is unethical for an employer to coerce employees to contribute to any cause. Individual giving is an individual choice. You might talk with the college's legal counsel or ombudsman, if there is one. You could also recommend that the issue be considered in an all-staff, anonymous survey.

Corporate Giving

Corporate giving is often a gray area in grantmaking. This is because companies tend to see their corporate giving as an extension of their overall marketing and public relations.

Scenario #1. You are the corporate giving officer for your company. The company president has recently decided that the corporate giving should be more closely aligned with profitability. He wants the corporate grants to be made only to nonprofits that are clearly linked to the company's product line. You would prefer that the corporate giving be responsive to community needs. How might you respond to the president's directive?

Scenario #2. Your company has a large international component, and its corporate giving has been expanded to the countries where the company has a large presence. The problem is that some of the nongovernmental organizations (NGOs, the international equivalent of a nonprofit) hold values that run counter to accepted values in the United States. For example, one of the NGOs being considered for grant support does not allow women on its board; nor will it support the education of women.

As with any "sticky" issue, there are no easy answers. But there is a growing body of evidence that a company's corporate social responsibility (CSR) is related to its image and in turn to potential profitability. One idea would be to propose that a portion of every dollar spent on a company product will go toward a charitable cause—heart disease, for example, or the planting of a tree.

The second scenario requires a decision at the top of the company. It may be possible to develop a corporate giving policy that acknowledges and respects different cultures but requires that any NGOs applying for funds agree to standards set within the United States.

Community Foundations

According to the Community Foundations Leadership Team, a community foundation is a tax-exempt, nonprofit, publicly supported philanthropic institution. Its funding comes from many donors to carry out their charitable interests as well as broad-based charitable interests. Community foundations thus both make grants and fund raise to obtain funds that can be turned into grants.

Scenario. You are the development (fundraising) officer for a community foundation. You have developed a close and personal relationship with one of your donors, an elderly person. The donor has started giving you rather expensive gifts in appreciation for your kindness. Is there an ethical dilemma here, and if so, how should you handle it?

There is a dilemma, but as an ethical issue, there are no hard and fast answers. Your community foundation needs a clear policy on the acceptance of gifts. Until one is in place, you should bring this issue to the attention of your CEO, who should in turn bring it to the attention of the board. If the decision is made that expensive gifts are not to be accepted, you need to think of a way to tell the donor without turning the donor off. One suggestion is, ask the donor if you might turn the gifts over to the community foundation, with due recognition to the donor.

Private Foundations

According to the Foundation Center, a

foundation is a non-governmental entity that is established as a nonprofit corporation or a charitable trust, with a principal purpose of making grants to unrelated organizations, institutions, or individuals for scientific, educational, cultural, religious, or other charitable purposes. . . . A private foundation derives its money from a family, an individual, or a corporation. (http://foundationcenter.org/getstarted/faqs/html/foundfun.html, n.d., "Frequently Asked Questions")

Scenario #1. You are on the board of a grantmaking foundation. The board chair wants to direct foundation grants to his college's alumni association. The board chair carries a lot of clout on the board, and it is likely that the other board members will go along with his wish.

Scenario #2. You are a staff person on a grantmaking foundation. The foundation board has decided to make a grant to a nonprofit that supports abortion. You believe that abortion is wrong and immoral and should be illegal. How do you respond?

Scenario #1 should be addressed by a clear code of ethics for the foundation. That code could prohibit grants that have not gone through a review and recommendations by staff. You may not want to "take on" the board chair on this one grant, but you could recommend that the board establish a code of ethics. Contact with the Council on Foundations might provide you with some supporting information on what other foundations have done.

Scenario #2 is more problematic. The short answer is either try to convince your foundation not to get into grants for agencies that support abortion, or begin to look for a job that is a better fit with your values.

Summary

Compared to much of the for-profit sector, nonprofits—both grantmakers and grant seekers—enjoy relatively few government regulations and constraints. Even the appearance of impropriety can be detrimental to philanthropic foundations and charitable organizations. The public relies on the nonprofit sector to use funding for the intended use. Nonprofit organizations have played not only a key role in the history of America, but also they have helped define America. We are who we are in part because of nonprofits.

Nonprofit. Not-for-profit. Independent sector. Third sector. Nongovernmental organization. By whatever name, nonprofits are integral to America's history—and perhaps to its future. Nonprofits are all about philanthropy—literally, the love of humankind. Nonprofits exist because people *choose* to invest some of their disposable income in the form of contributions, dues, gifts in kind, and the like. That is why it is especially important that nonprofits operate ethically.

References and Further Readings

Agarwal, J., & Malloy, D. C. (1999). Ethical work climate dimensions in a not-for-profit organization: An empirical study. *Journal of Business Ethics, 20*(1), 1–14.

Bass, B. M. (2008). *The Bass handbook of leadership: Theory, research, and managerial applications.* New York: Free Press.

Block, P. (1996). *Stewardship: Choosing service over self-interest.* San Francisco: Berrett-Koehler.

Brest, P., & Harvey, H. (2008). *Money well spent: A strategic plan for smart philanthropy.* New York: Bloomberg Press.

Brown, M. N., Giampetro-Meyer, A., & Williamson, C. (2004). *Practical business ethics for the busy manager.* Upper Saddle River, NJ: Pearson Prentice Hall.

Burlingame, D. F. (2004). *Philanthropy in America: A comprehensive historical perspective.* Santa Barbara, CA: ABC-CLIO.

Cahn, S. M., & Markie, P. (Eds.). (2002). *Ethics: History, theory, and contemporary issues.* New York: Oxford University Press.

Capek, M. E. S., & Mead, M. (2006). *Effective philanthropy: Organizational success through deep diversity and gender equality.* Cambridge: MIT Press.

Chait, R. P., Ryan, W. P., & Taylor, B. E. (2005). *Governance as leadership: Reframing the works of nonprofit boards.* New York: John Wiley & Sons.

Crutchfield, L. R., & Grant, H. M. (2008). *Forces for good: The six practices of high-impact nonprofits.* San Francisco: Jossey-Bass.

Dalton, D. R., & Cosier, R. A. (1982, May–June). The four faces of social responsibility. *Business Horizons, 25*(3), 19–27.

Deshpande, S. (1996). Ethical climate and the link between success and ethical behavior: An empirical investigation of a non-profit organization. *Journal of Business Ethics, 15*(3), 315–321.

Donaldson, T. (1996, September–October). Values in tension: Ethics away from home. *Harvard Business Review, 74,* 48–62.

Drucker, P. F. (1992). *Managing the nonprofit organization.* New York: HarperCollins.

Greenleaf, R. K. (1977). *Servant leadership: A journey into the nature of legitimate power and greatness.* New York: Paulist Press.

Gregorian, V. (2004, April 1). Philanthropy should have glass pockets. *Chronicle of Philanthropy,* 43–44.

Hellriegel, D., Jackson, S., & Slocum, J. W. (1999). *Organizational Behavior* (6th ed.). Mason, OH: Thomson South-Western.

Janis, I. L. (1972). *Victims of groupthink.* New York: Houghton Mifflin.

Kidder, R. M. (2009). *How good people make tough choices: Resolving the dilemmas of ethical living* (2nd ed.). New York: Harper.

Lazarus, A. (2006, January–February). The role of the pharmaceutical industry in medical education in psychiatry. *Academic Psychiatry, 30*(1), 40–44.

Lindahl, W. E. (2010). *Principles of fundraising: Theory and practice.* Sudbury, MA: Jones & Bartlett.

Lowenstein, R. (1996). *The making of an American capitalist.* New York: Random House.

MacArthur Foundation. (n.d.). *Code of conduct.* Available from http://www.macfound.org/site/c.lkLXJ8MQKrH/b.938991/k.B58B/Conflicts_of_Interest__Gifts.htm

Mackinnon, B. (2008). *Ethics: Theory and contemporary issues.* Belmont, CA: Cengage Learning.

Minkes A. L., Small, M. W., & Chatterjee, S. R. (1999). Leadership and business ethics: Does it matter? *Journal of Business Ethics, 20*(4), 327–335.

Murphy, P. E. (1988). Implementing business ethics. *Journal of Business Ethics, 7,* 907–915.

Orlikoff, J. E., & Totten, M. K. (2004, April). Conflict of interest and governance: New approaches for a new environment. *Trustee, 75*(4), 15–21.

Payton, R. L., & Moody, M. P. (2008). *Understanding philanthropy: Its meaning and mission.* Bloomington: Indiana University Press.

Rest, J. R. (Ed.). (1994). *Moral development in the professions: Psychology and applied ethics.* Hillsdale, NJ: Lawrence Erlbaum.

Schein, E. H. (1992). *Organizational culture and leadership* (2nd ed.). San Francisco: Jossey-Bass.

Sievers, B. (2008). Both sides now: The ethics of grantmaking and grantseeking. In J. G. Petty (Ed.), *Ethical fundraising: A guide for nonprofit boards and fundraisers* (pp. 247–262). New York: John Wiley & Sons.

Simon, H. A. (1957). *Models of man.* New York: John Wiley & Sons.

Smith, C. A., Organ, D. W., & Near, J. P. (1983). Organizational citizenship behavior: Its nature and antecedents. *Journal of Applied Psychology, 68*(4), 653–663.

Snow, R. M., & Phillips, P. H. (2008). *Making critical decisions: A practical guide for nonprofit organizations.* New York: John Wiley & Sons.

White, D. (2007). *Charity on trial: What you need to know before you give.* Fort Lee, NJ: Barricade Books.

Wilcox, D. M., & Wilcox, W. H. (1997). *Applied ethics in American society.* Fort Worth, TX: Harcourt Brace.

Wright, J. P. (1980). *On a clear day you can see General Motors:John Z. de Lorean's look inside the automotive giant.* New York: Avon Press.

Young, D. R. (Ed.). (2006). *Wise decision making in uncertain times: Using nonprofit resources effectively.* New York: Foundation Center.

PART VII

LEADERSHIP OF NONPROFITS AND THE INDIVIDUAL

85

UNDERSTANDING THE CHARITABLE, PHILANTHROPIC, ALTRUISTIC IMPULSE

PHILIP L. BARCLIFT

Seattle University

Since the rise of sociology as a scholarly discipline in the mid-19th century, the academy has tried to understand the scientific and sociological underpinnings of the philanthropic, or altruistic, impulse. Auguste Comte, generally considered the father of modern sociology, coined the term *altruism*—derived from the Latin word *alter* (other)—in his *Système de Politique Positive* (1851–1854) to designate the totality of what humans do for the benefit of others. Comte recognized that many of our actions—even most of our apparently benevolent ones—are the result of egoism; however, he believed humanity had evolved to the point that most humans could act out of a selfless desire to "live for others," and he wanted a word to signify that desire.

Even though the word *altruism* is normally used as a synonym of *philanthropy* (the love of humans) today, Comte wanted to use it more as a replacement for the Christian notion of *agape*, or selfless love—*caritas* in the Latin, which is roughly transliterated as "charity" in English. He coined this term so that the scientific and philosophical communities could express the notion of living for others without incorporating the theological baggage carried by terms like agape or caritas.

Evolutionary Developments of the Altruistic Impulse

Since research on human altruism initially relied more on Darwin's theory of natural selection than on Comte's sociology, the earliest studies on the altruistic impulse depended predominantly on evolutionary biology and its subdiscipline, sociobiology, for direction. Due in part to the disciplinary bias that guides evolutionary biology, these studies were weighted in favor of natural selection and against Comte's notion of selfless altruism.

Biological organisms survive better when they are stronger, and selfish ones tend to be the strongest, so natural selection will favor the selfish ones. A consensus began to emerge that no organism's altruistic act is really free of selfishness. William Hamilton set the growing consensus into evolutionary doctrine when he concluded that no apparent acts of altruism should be considered unselfish since at their most basic level, the acts were intended to benefit the altruist or the altruist's genetic or social group for transmission into the next generation (Hamilton, 1964).

With that disciplinary bias, evolutionary biologists and sociobiologists tested ways to explain a behavior that looks like Comte's altruism but that works within the more familiar framework of self-interest. They were able to identify four theoretical processes that could account for it: reciprocity, by-product mutualism, group selection, and kin selection or inclusive fitness.

Evolutionary studies benefited from John Nash's *equilibrium theory* in economics. In that theory, Nash argued that the best result would come for the most people if all actors do what is best for themselves *and* for their opponent(s). He showed that even competitors in noncooperative games benefit from cooperating, thereby ensuring greater success over the long-term for each player (Nash, 1950). The implications for evolutionary studies were immediate.

In Robert Trivers's theory of *reciprocal altruism*, he proposed that an organism can benefit from helping unrelated organisms—even organisms of different species—if it perceives the possibility that the other organisms might reciprocate. Trivers's theory depends on two conditions: (1) The two organisms must have the capacity to recognize each other, and (2) the two organisms must exist under conditions in which there is some likelihood of repeated encounters. Applying game theory to his empirical studies, Trivers was able to show that reciprocal altruism could have evolved as a selfish survival mechanism for organisms willing to make short-term sacrifices for long-term gains, just as cooperation in a noncooperative game can achieve mutual, long-term benefits for both competitors, even though cooperation might not benefit either competitor in the short-term (Trivers, 1971; see also Wilkinson, 1990).

By-product mutualism parallels reciprocal altruism except that the actor behaves selfishly and without any consideration of another's fitness benefit. The actor's behavior offers itself fitness benefits, as intended. The fitness benefits that the other organisms might receive are incidental and unintentional. Since there is mutual fitness benefit in the act for both parties, there is benefit for the actor to repeat it. The act of an animal joining a herd—whether of the same or of a different species—is one example. The animal directly benefits itself by joining the herd since it will be safer from predation. Yet by joining the herd, the animal has incidentally made the other members of the herd safer from predation, which was not its intention (Clutton-Brock, 2002).

Group selection, the theory that one organism might sacrifice itself for the benefit of the group to ensure the survival of the group, seems to draw some inspiration from the theories of Charles Darwin himself; however, it contradicts Darwin's belief that natural selection favors the self-interested individual rather than the interests of the group. Darwin (1871) was aware of the group's importance to the individuals' survival and of the role altruism could play in the success of the group. Yet Vero Wynne-Edwards (1962) reversed Darwin's emphasis and put the focus on the group itself in his group selection theory. He thought this theory could explain a pattern of behavior he had observed in various animal populations that used discernible mechanisms to regulate their populations so as not to overexploit their food supplies. Some animals voluntarily sacrificed their opportunities to reproduce in order to ensure that the group would not exhaust its food supply, even though the evolutionary bias is toward reproduction. Based on this insight, Wynne-Edwards asserted that natural selection of groups might explain the survival of the species better than natural selection of individuals does.

Reactions to Wynne-Edwards's theory came swiftly. David Lack (1966) attacked it on the basis that Darwinian mechanisms could explain virtually all of his observations as well as group selection does, and Maynard Smith (1964) and George Williams (1966) attacked it on the basis of a problem they called *free riders*. In a group containing multiple altruists, free riders would invariably arise. Because the altruists were sacrificing themselves for the sake of the group at the same time as the free riders were preserving their own fitness benefits and reaping additional fitness benefits from the altruists' sacrifice, the selfish free riders would have more fitness benefits when the time came for reproduction. Therefore, it would be more likely for the group's selfish traits than for its altruistic traits to survive into the next generation.

Maynard Smith (1964) and George Williams (1966) preferred *kin selection*, the theory that one gene or organism might sacrifice itself for its relatives to ensure that genes with genetic characteristics similar to its own would survive into the next generation. They based their theory on William Hamilton's research on *inclusive fitness*. Hamilton had suggested that altruism could evolve despite the death of the altruist if the degree of the actor's genetic *relation* to the recipient of the act, multiplied by the fitness *benefit* to the recipient, were greater than the *cost* of losing the actor's altruistic gene. This formula came to be called Hamilton's Rule: $RB > C$. If the actor were to sacrifice its life for a relative instead of a stranger, there would be much greater likelihood that the altruistic gene might pass on to the next generation since its relatives share much of the same DNA (Hamilton, 1964).

Kin selection seemed to explain the value or usefulness of generosity between related organisms without suggesting that the acts were selfless. A decade later, sociobiologist Richard Dawkins (1976/1989) would publish a study on such acts called *The Selfish Gene*. He attributed this title both to sociopathic and to altruistic genes, since both are selfish. The genes merely use different strategies to attain their ultimate goal of replicating themselves to some degree in the next generation. As Dawkins saw it, there is no evidence on the genetic level that unselfish altruism can exist. Having stated this verdict, however, Dawkins expressed his surprising conviction that the genes are not the final piece of the altruistic puzzle he sees.

Dawkins (1976/1989) asserted that the human brain has finally evolved to the point that it gives humanity the capacity to transcend the limits of genetic evolution. The dominance of biological explanations of human behavior ended with the emergence of the human mind and cultures. According to his theory, human cultures are transmitted by an evolutionary process of imitation between humans and groups of humans, through which the more useful cultural innovations can survive into the next generation. To give this *unit of cultural transfer* a name, Dawkins coined the word *meme*, from the Greek *mimeme* (to imitate). The transfer of stronger memes makes it possible for the human mind to rebel against its genes through something akin to free will, which liberates the actors' behavior from the biological necessities of survival.

Dawkins showed the limits of evolutionary biology to explain human behavior. Evolutionary biology can identify a genetic predisposition to benefit others when the consequences of that act offer fitness benefits to oneself or to one's group, but it cannot explain how humans move beyond their biological drive for self-survival to perform benevolent acts toward others without regard to the self. Yet a growing body of scholarship shows that many humans *have* acted selflessly for the benefit of others (Piliavin & Charng, 1990). These studies suggest that there is a gulf between the genetic predisposition to act out of self-interest and the impulse to act benevolently toward others without regard for self.

During the 1980s and 1990s, social psychologist Daniel Batson and his research partners moved the study of the philanthropic impulse past the gulf Dawkins had identified without resort to hypothetical memes. Their empirical studies showed that the human capacity for empathy, however it developed, can give rise to altruistic acts that are free of egoistic determinants. For example, by shining a light on the motivational intentions of altruistic acts, using pluralistic models of prosocial motivation rather than focusing on the fitness consequences of the acts, Batson and Shaw (1991) pushed the study of altruism outside "the Eden of egoism" (p. 108). By restricting his studies to the *motivation* of a given act, Batson recasts Comte's theory on altruism and vindicates his optimism.

This restriction yielded new definitions of altruism and egoism: "Altruism is a motivational state with the ultimate goal of increasing another's welfare. Egoism is a motivational state with the ultimate goal of increasing one's own welfare" (Batson & Shaw, 1991, p. 108). Batson and Shaw defined *motivational state* as a goal-directed psychological force. The same force can be applied either to altruism or to egoism. The distinguishing factor is not the strength of the motive; instead, the ultimate goal determines the motive. Since the focus of this definition is the motive rather than the consequences or the perception of consequences of a given act, Batson and Shaw's definition of altruism excludes the demand of self-sacrifice. "Pursuing the ultimate goal of increasing another's welfare may involve cost to the self, but it may also not. Indeed, it may even involve self-benefits and the motivation would still be altruistic, as long as obtaining this self-benefit is an unintended consequence of benefiting the other, and not the ultimate goal" (p. 109).

Batson and Shaw found the key to human altruism in what they called the *empathy-altruism* response. They defined empathy as a set of congruent vicarious emotions, such as sympathy or tenderness, which are directed more toward others than toward self. Empathy creates an attachment between humans and enables them to identify with and to feel emotions that are congruent with—though not identical to—another's emotions. In response to the other's emotional distress, the actor calculates the cost of achieving the altruistic goal and locates the cost that seems least harmful to the self in order to achieve the goal. Batson speaks of "hedonic calculus" in this respect, but he does not find it contradictory to his theory, since the calculus in this equation pertains only to least harm

rather than to greatest personal benefit for the actor (Batson & Shaw, 1991).

To measure this hedonic response, Batson, Duncan, Ackerman, Buckley, and Birch (1981) use a difficulty-of-escape scale. If the cost of escaping the test situation is high, the actor will more likely stay to help the distressed subject; however, if the cost of escaping the test situation is low, the actor will more likely leave than help. However,

if the bystander's motivation is altruistic, his or her goal is to reduce the other's distress. This goal can be reached by helping, but not by escaping. Therefore, the likelihood that the altruistically motivated bystander will help should be independent of the cost of escaping because escaping is a goal-irrelevant behavior. Increasing or decreasing the cost of escaping should remain as high when escape is easy as when it is difficult. (p. 292)

The cumulative result of Batson's studies shifted the tide, such that his erstwhile critic John Dovidio acknowledged, "The burden of proof has now, ironically, shifted to those who argue for universal egoism" (Dovidio, 1991, p. 127).

Repeated studies supported the empathy-altruism hypothesis that empathic arousal will produce altruistic motivations in prosocial behavior. Indeed, an abundance of studies on this hypothesis over the past 3 decades have forged a prominent theoretical footing for it. Many of the behaviors we may have considered the result of reciprocity or group and kin selection might now be attributable to empathy (de Waal, 2008; Dovidio, 1991).

Frans de Waal (2008) observed that it requires a shift in perspective to move an individual "beyond being sensitive to others toward an explicit other-orientation" (p. 285) In addition to the biological mechanisms that help actors perceive and interpret another person's emotional state and that give individuals "an emotional stake" in others' welfare, there are empathic mechanisms that help actors shift to an empathic "other-orientation." Among large-brained species, such as cetaceans, apes, and humans, these mechanisms open the door to "intentionally altruistic altruism," by which the actor studies the dynamics of a situation and looks for a way to benefit another within the perceptible variables. On this level, the altruistic actor is free to choose either to act for self-benefit or to act for another's benefit (p. 292).

Social Developments of the Altruistic Impulse

Much of the data that contextualizes these choices for humans derive from the social institutions and practices that coevolved with the expanding brain. These data inform the humans' choices through culturally constructed windows and through interpretive metaphors that help humans make sense of the data they receive. First among these institutions are the families and communities in which humans live. There is a reason the evolutionary studies of human altruism have devoted so much attention to group and kin selection.

As the human brain expanded sufficiently to support abstract thought and symbolic language, families and communities passed on their histories through songs, stories, and artifacts to help them make sense of their experiences and to bring meaning to their lives (Ricoeur, 1977). Amid these stories, songs, and metaphors, communities became aware of questions they could not answer pertaining to life, death, and human purpose (Dawkins, 2003). While reflecting on these difficult questions, developing cultures began to speak in terms of "sacred things" (Durkheim, 1912/1995) that make demands on human individuals and societies. Early societies began their quest to understand these sacred things with an appreciation of nature forces, divinities, and sanctities. As millennia passed, some societies progressed to notions of pantheism and monotheism.

Social scientists proposed two evolutionary theories to explain the social development of religion and culture. First, sociologist Émile Durkheim (1912/1995) argued that the sense of the sacred was merely a product of human societies and that it most probably—albeit subconsciously—represented the societies themselves. These religious expressions reflected the way societies wanted to be known, both among their members and by people outside their group. To reinforce (or to enforce) these social descriptions, each society established religious rites and "rules of conduct that prescribe how man must conduct himself with sacred things" (p. 38). In this way, all societies developed a set of moral codes and expectations to order their social interactions and to guide them in relation to the sacred.

Second, paleontologist Pierre Teilhard de Chardin, SJ, argued that the human mind (or noosphere) and reflective consciousness had finally evolved to the point that it could at last perceive spiritual realities, which *really do* lie just beyond the mind's senses. The human capacity to detect these spiritual realities led each human society to worship what they could barely sense with the full force of their communal experience. After millennia of experiences with those spiritual realities, human societies began to develop more meaningful constructs to explain their experiences until, finally, these societies were able to interact—however vaguely—with the object of their worship and to perceive in moments of social clarity and of divine revelation the demands that the object of their worship had placed on them (de Chardin, 1959). In this way each society developed a set of moral codes and expectations to order their social interactions and to guide them toward spiritual union with the object of their worship.

Neither of these theories would be especially appealing to more conservative Jews and Christians, who would find a third way to explain the emergence of religion. But the way religion developed is not really the point here. Durkheim and de Chardin both support the growing consensus that cultural practices and institutions coevolved with the human mind. So the greater concern for this study is their observation that early social explorations into the sacred and early attempts to design rites, practices, and moral codes, which could govern worship and social interaction, coevolved with the human mind to provide humans with the cultural data they needed to recognize the benefits of altruistic behavior within their groups.

According to Jonathan Haidt (2007), the primary purpose of the moral systems that coevolved with the mind was to suppress or regulate selfishness, which is what makes social life possible. These moral systems evolved as embedded elements of broader faith systems for the social groups in which they emerged and were able to provide intrinsic reinforcement of the moral system. Every society has formulated a religiously based moral code to regulate selfishness and to promote altruistic behavior toward others. For that reason, social scientists like Haidt have contended that we must study the social impact of religion on the human impulse to behave altruistically.

Henry Allen Moe once contended that "religion is the mother of philanthropy, both conceptually and procedurally" (1961, p. 141). He defended his proposition by looking at the ecclesiastical institutions and legal precedents that fostered the environment for charity (often coerced and frequently enforced in ecclesiastical courts) in the medieval church. This environment gave way to the Elizabethan statutes on charitable uses—in response to ecclesiastical abuses—that permitted citizens to use their money for extra-ecclesiastical charitable causes.

Scholarship supports Moe's observation that institutional developments in Judaism and Christianity inspired American democratic innovations that promoted free association, tax relief for charitable gifts, freedom of expression, and so on, which directly benefited American philanthropy (Payton & Moody, 2008). However, Moe's contention that religion is the mother of philanthropy *conceptually* is overstated. Religion is not the mother of philanthropy. At best, it is philanthropy's big sister, as religion and human altruism coevolved with the emergence of human societies. Still, it is difficult to overstate the influence religion has had on the codevelopment of human altruism.

There are several possible etymologies of the word *religion*. The derivation most scholars accept is the Latin word *religare*, which means "to bind to." The word religion indicates the core reality (realities) or perceived reality (realities) to which we bind ourselves, in which we find value, and by which we assess our values. By this definition, the secular humanist is no less religious than the Evangelical Christian, even though the core realities to which they bind themselves are significantly different. Demerath (2002) noted that even sociology is in this sense a religion to many. The distinguishing characteristics between peoples' varying religious expressions are the core realities to which they bind themselves. In most cases, these core realities are mixed, often inconsistent (e.g., simultaneously altruistic and egoistic) and frequently in competition within us. Yet they shape our systems of value by which we determine where we will use our resources and efforts.

In the United States, roughly 83% of Americans claim to have some religious or spiritual affiliation (Pew Report, 2008). Within the Pew Report's margin of error, a 2008 Gallup poll puts that percentage at 86% (Newport, 2008). Since virtually every spiritual faith tradition in America admonishes its members to behave altruistically (Payton & Moody, 2008), religion and altruism are joined at the hip here.

Regular polling attempts to measure the extent of that connection. A Gallup poll shows that highly religious people worldwide and across religious lines are significantly more likely to donate money (38% highly religious, 29% nonreligious), to donate time (29% highly religious, 18% nonreligious), or to help a stranger (56% highly religious, 49% nonreligious) than nonreligious people. In fact, households in which family members attended religious services regularly contributed 2.48 times more money annually to charitable causes than households in which no family members attended religious services regularly (Pelham & Crabtree, 2008). Since the data also show that "volunteers were more likely than their non-volunteering counterparts to belong to a religious organization (75.6% vs. 58%)" (Saad, 2008), we recognize a strong connection between religion and philanthropy in America.

This connection raises new questions regarding the relationship of religion and altruism among those who claim some affiliation with an organized spiritual tradition. In repeated studies, social scientists have been unable to locate a measure that could fully explain the connection between religion and the philanthropic impulse to which the national polls have pointed for decades. For example, Watson, Morris, and Hood (1984) found an inverse relationship between *extrinsic* religiosity and altruism and a positive relationship between *intrinsic* religiosity and altruism.

Batson's studies supported Watson et al. (1984) on extrinsic religion: He showed that people with extrinsic, or *means*, religiosity tended to use helping others as a means to a selfish end, or they tried to escape the distressful situation altogether. An example of extrinsic religiosity might be found in the ancient Roman Empire, where Jewish and Christian aristocrats made extravagant bequests to the poor in their cities to ensure that their communities would carve *elemosinarius* (Latin for one who is "devoted to the giving of alms") on their gravestones. Giving alms was a means to an ulterior end for them: They wanted to be immortalized in stone. The aristocrats' practice appears to be less about an authentic expression of their faith tradition and more about personal standing in the eyes of their communities (Brown, 2002).

Intrinsic Orientation

Some scholars saw promise in the intrinsic orientation as an explanation of the philanthropic impulse (Watson et al., 1984). However, Batson, Schoenrade, and Ventis (1993)

came to question that orientation as well. In spite of the fact that people with intrinsic, or *end*, religiosity viewed themselves as the most altruistic group, their clinical and field tests with "victims" in distress did not reflect any greater helpfulness. In some tests, people with this orientation offered less help than people with extrinsic religiosity had offered. Batson and his research partners were able to show that people with intrinsic religiosity tended to see their religious expressions themselves as the terminal value, so they had less motivation to help others in distress (Batson et al., 1993). They concluded that neither extrinsic religiosity nor intrinsic religiosity can be shown to incline one to be more altruistic.

A study by Ji, Pendergraft, and Perry (2006), using a massive sampling of 16,000 Evangelical adolescents, confirmed Batson's observations on intrinsic religiosity. Their study suffers methodologically because it does not include a non-Evangelical control group, but its findings are telling. They found that intrinsic religiosity among doctrinally orthodox Evangelical adolescents "is positively related to their holding of altruistic belief, but . . . inversely relate[d] to engagement in altruistic behavior" (p. 171). That is, the more religiously mature these adolescents became in their personal devotional lives, the more likely they were to consider it a virtue to help others, but the less likely they were actually to help others.

There was an extreme example of this phenomenon in ancient Jerusalem. As members of the fledgling church flirted with a form of Christian communism, the whole group forsook private ownership of their possessions and held everything in common (Acts 4:32 [New Revised Standard Version]). A couple named Ananias and Sapphira got swept up in the fervor. They professed great devotion to their new religious tradition and wanted to prove the depth of their faith to others. But they could not bring themselves to give all their possessions to the group, so they told everyone they had done it, while they secretly retained their possessions. Both died of shock when they were found out (Acts 5:1–6).

Their behavior reflects the characteristics social psychologists would identify with intrinsic religiosity. As Rigby and O'Grady noted, "the intrinsic orientation seems to reflect only an increased concern for looking good in society's eyes, for showing the world that one possesses the concern, compassion and tolerance religion advocates" (1989, p. 732). Since there was not an expectation or requirement to give all their goods to the group—seeing that very few other early Christian groups followed this practice—Ananias and Sapphira could have kept their goods. The only other explanation is what Rigby and O'Grady attested of intrinsic religiosity.

Ji et al. (2006) link Evangelical Christians to the intrinsic orientation as well, though not to such an extreme extent. Doctrinal emphasis in Evangelical theology can account for part but not all of the apparent inconsistency the researchers found between the beliefs the adolescents held and their actions in this study. Evangelical theology teaches that the primary act of altruism Christians should offer is not one-to-one direct aid but sharing the gospel with others. They believe they find support for this teaching in Jesus's own words. The resurrected Christ issued his great commission to carry the good news of God's grace throughout the world to make disciples of all nations (Matt. 28:16–20). American Evangelicals have made this charge their central mission as Christ's church. All other charges are subordinate to it. As such, Evangelicals do not see care for the poor as a good in itself; it must lead to evangelism. This conviction might explain why Christians with an intrinsic orientation tended to remain with the victim longer in Batson's studies. Service of the poor is merely one part of a broader mission to share Jesus's message with others so as to make disciples of them. The core of their theological premise gives it an intrinsic orientation, if not hints of an extrinsic one. Their tradition is by no means opposed to direct service, but it subordinates that service to saving souls (Thielicke, 1962/1980). On this basis, their theological presupposition may skew the results of the religiosity orientation studies on Evangelicals, since doctrinal maturity in that tradition tends one more toward evangelism than toward direct service.

Quest Orientation

This doctrinal bias might also explain some of the ambiguity Batson and Ventis (1982) found in their study on the intrinsic orientation within Evangelical populations. Their results were clearer and more promising when they separated intrinsic religiosity from what Batson called a *quest orientation*. Their findings on intrinsic religiosity were consistent with what they had seen before; however, Christians with a quest orientation—those who are more open-minded and freer to question their religious traditions—tended to show less prejudice than Christians from the other religious orientations showed. They also tended to be quicker to offer initial help and to ask more questions of the victim in distress than Christians from the other orientations did. On the other hand, Christians with a quest orientation tended to cease their helpful behavior as soon as the initial crisis was over, whereas Christians with an intrinsic orientation, when they offered their help, tended to stay with the distressed victim longer after the crisis had ended (Batson, Schoenrade, & Ventis, 1993).

Rigby and O'Grady (1989) confirmed Batson's initial findings in their own studies. Batson's quest orientation may provide one key to understanding the relationship between religion and the altruistic impulse. Indeed, Batson was nearly ready to go as far as to equate the quest orientation with universal and nonjudgmental compassion (Batson, Eidelman, Higley, & Russell, 2001) until Goldfield and Miner forced him to tone down his enthusiasm. They supported Batson's observation that Christians

with a quest orientation were "more likely to help across a broad range of situations," but they also showed the limits of quest-driven openness, noting that the quest-oriented Christians showed resistance to or prejudice toward religious Fundamentalists, even though they were open to most other traditions (Goldfield & Miner, 2002).

Liberal theologian Walter Rauschenbusch (1907/2007) characterizes the quest orientation. During his ministry, he rejected attempts from Social Darwinists like Andrew Carnegie (discussed below) to address the needs of the poor primarily on the institutional level. Likewise, he rejected the focus on personal salvation rather than on direct service and social reform that he saw from Evangelical traditions. Rauschenbusch was open to other faith traditions—as long as they preached the primacy of direct service to others. He thought Christianity could remake society by substituting love for selfishness, as Jesus did on the cross. He was aware this pursuit would require Christians to reorient themselves from viewing their religious lives from the perspective of individual salvation to viewing them as a charge to build a new society, the Kingdom of God. As Rauschenbusch saw it, Jesus's concern "was not the new soul, but the new society; not man, but Man" (p. 50).

Rauschenbusch (1907/2007) struggled against the social and economic structures that bind humanity in a cycle of domination and subjugation. To him, this cycle parallels the doctrine of original sin. It is a social structural sin, into which we have all contributed. At its center churns *laissez-faire* market capitalism, which draws the poor under its wheels, as if by centrifugal force. The only antidote to these structural sins, Rauschenbusch argued, is selfless love, manifested in direct service to the poor, for the good of society as a whole. This antidote is best achieved in solidarity with the poor and oppressed, serving them and working for justice on their behalf.

America's liberal Christian denominations moderated Rauschenbusch's "social gospel" somewhat by reaffirming the power of sin, or egoism, in our lives and by expressing the need of personal as well as social redemption *among a plurality of religions*. The ambivalence of striving for both personal and social redemption among a plurality of religions might explain data from the 2008 Pew Report that fully 83% of mainline Christians were reluctant to speak of their religious tradition as the only true religion. That reluctance might also explain Batson's observation that quest-oriented Christians seem hesitant to affirm a set body of religious beliefs (Batson & Ventis, 1982).

That reluctance has not diminished liberal mainline Christians' emphasis on the centrality of direct service they find in Jesus's teachings on the Kingdom of God. Jesus commanded his disciples to care for those who do not have the resources to care for themselves. He added the crucial caveat that those who help the poor would enter into the Kingdom of Heaven:

Come, you that are blessed by my Father, inherit the kingdom prepared for you from the foundation of the world; for I was hungry and you gave me food, I was thirsty and you gave me something to drink, I was a stranger and you welcomed me, I was naked and you gave me clothing, I was sick and you took care of me, I was in prison and you visited me. (Matt. 25:34–36)

In this lengthy passage, as Rauschenbusch had noted, there is no mention of a body of knowledge one must possess or of doctrinal purity; there is only a command to care for the poor. Following Jesus's teachings on the Kingdom, liberal mainline denominations have taken on the causes of the poor and defenseless as their central mission as Christ's church.

Beginning with an Evangelical resurgence in response to liberalism and the social gospel, conservative denominations—with their emphasis on evangelism—have seen significant growth, whereas the liberal mainline denominations—who do not share the same emphasis on evangelism—have experienced a sharp decline in numbers. Those trends have intensified over the past decade (Pew Report, 2008). "The result for charitable activities has been mixed," Robert Wuthnow (1990, p. 18) noted. "Liberals have continued to work for social justice and broad humanitarian concerns; conservatives have focused efforts on evangelism, missions, and family issues; and competition between the two factions has sometimes invigorated both" (p. 18). Yet the competition has tended to drain both groups of resources and to deplete liberal mainline denominations' numbers.

Secular Religion and Altruism

Rauschenbusch came onto the scene during a time when urbanization and industrialization had ravaged American societies and had left untold thousands poor and destitute. Following the lead of the Young Women's Christian Association (YWCA), the Young Men's Christian Association (YMCA), and the Salvation Army, Rauschenbusch pushed direct service to the poor and resistance to the industrial machine that had created the crisis in his attempt to resolve the problem. But theirs were not the only voices working against poverty; theirs was not the only strategy.

Social Darwinist (positivist) and industrialist Andrew Carnegie argued against advocates of direct service that it merely creates a welfare society. "One of the serious obstacles to the improvement of our race is indiscriminant charity" (Carnegie, 1889, p. 662). He was convinced that human society had come to a crossroads in its evolution and that it was the responsibility of "men of means" to flourish the institutions that could lift and inspire human society into a new bloom of prosperity and cooperation between employers and their employees. "The best means of benefiting the community is to place within its reach the ladders upon which the aspiring can rise—parks, and means of recreation,

by which men are helped in body and mind; works of art, certain to give pleasure and improve the public taste, and public institutions of various kinds, which will improve the general condition of the people" (p. 663). Social psychologists will find it challenging to categorize Carnegie's religious orientation, which seems to be an admixture of extrinsic (he liked to see his name on buildings) and quest (he was open to any perspective that helped him move his philanthropic industry along, but he was utterly closed to notions of direct service).

Alongside—and sometimes in competition with—the likes of the Rockefellers, Carnegie (1889) followed the best practices of science and industry to modernize philanthropy with "scientific" efficiency by means of foundations. "The best minds will thus have reached a stage in the development of the race" (p. 664), he argued, where they could clearly see their function was to put their excess wealth to use for the common good. The ultimate goal of scientific philanthropy, he firmly believed, was world peace, a lasting testament to this penultimate stage of human evolution, in which Carnegie and other "men of means" would build the infrastructure for a lasting peace.

Carnegie's religion was a form of scientific humanism, Comte's positivism, with its complementary foci on living for others and social progress. A religion in every way but the spiritual, it helped Carnegie formulate his own "gospel of wealth," through which he finally understood what he and other people of means should do with their great wealth. It was incumbent on the wealthy to serve as trustees for the poor, administering their funds for the good of the community—far better than the community could have done for itself, he argued. To this end, Carnegie shifted the model for charitable giving closer to a corporate structure, moving it from inefficient and subjective attempts to discern the needs of individuals to a systematic analysis of "the *eligibility* of individuals for assistance" (Hall, 1990, p. 42). Because the stakes are so high, Carnegie warned, "The man who dies thus rich dies disgraced."

Carnegie's scientific philanthropy may have seemed dispassionate, as he scrutinized people and programs as if they were investment vehicles (Hall, 1990), but his understanding of philanthropy mimicked the business world he already knew. Perhaps the comfort level he found in philanthropy as another industry explains the draw his scientific philanthropy had on the Rockefellers, even though they had been devoted to the social gospel of Rauschenbusch. They understood how to build wealth through industry, so they could use the same model to give it away, seeking the same levels of calculable results they sought in industry. This approach permitted them to see on a ledger sheet of inputs and outcomes what their wealth had accomplished in ways direct service could not.

Today, Warren Buffett and Bill and Melinda Gates seem to have taken hold of the same scientific approach to philanthropy. Based on comments Buffett and Bill Gates have made about their religious inclinations in the past, they may also share some level of the secular humanism found in Carnegie. But, more to the point, their wealth is too vast for them to get caught up in direct service, so they have built foundations that focus on the meta-issues, the major social and institutional problems that only vast wealth can tackle. Agencies who approach the Gates Foundation for funding should expect to produce a ledger showing inputs and outcome expectations.

Love and Altruism

Carnegie's mode of altruism would never meet the definition of *agape* that philosophers and theologians bandy about, as if philanthropy is only valid if it shows no hint of self-interest. Agape, selfless and unconditional love, is an ideal that few can hope to attain more than a few times in their lives, precisely because many scholars believe this absolute form of love must be sacrificial without being introspective. Commenting on altruism, which he defined as a selfless act of agape, love for the benefit of another, Colin Grant argued that the act must be spontaneous and unintentional to be authentic. "Unintentional altruism is most natural for the transcendent sponsorship of the religious level, where we are delivered from ourselves" (Grant, 2001, p. 248). As he saw it, we diminish the validity of our agapic acts the moment we reflect on them, because any reflection on them invariably brings self-interest into the blend. At the moment of introspection, according to his understanding, it ceases to be true altruism.

It is difficult to know how far one can push Grant's view, since the premier theological exemplar of agape is Jesus who willingly and with due introspection at Gethsemane sacrificed himself for humanity. It was Jesus, after all, who commanded his followers to love their neighbors as themselves (Matt. 22:39). Jesus used the same verb here that he had used when he commanded his followers to love God (Matt. 22:37). The agape, or love, of which he spoke is normally selfless and unconditional, but it is also reflective, and it can be directed at the self. There are times when this love demands introspection, as it did prior to Jesus's supreme sacrifice. Introspection does not always lead to selfishness. So it seems that there comes a point at which the *concept* of agape has outgrown the highest expressions of it.

Grant is correct that acting with authentic agape in ways that are truly selfless and unconditional is difficult for us. The Apostle Paul thought it was nearly impossible, because our wills—the internal center in each of us that governs our choices and actions—are bound up in the appetites of our senses (his version of egoism). His insight is consistent with the findings of evolutionary biology that our bodies as biological organisms work continuously for self-interest. "I find it to be a law that when I want to do what is good, evil lies close at hand. For I delight in the law of God in my inmost self, but I see in my members another law at war with the law of my mind, making me captive to the law of sin that dwells in my members" (Romans 7:21–23). Self-interest is always close at hand, and it can diminish the good we want to do.

However, Paul does not rest agape on the human will, where the appetites of our senses can control them. Agape and the altruistic acts that move through it are spiritual qualities, which are bound up in God's grace. According to Paul, grace gives humans the capacity to transcend selfish impulses. Wuthnow identified this capacity as "a higher state of existence" and a "qualitatively better orientation." Grace is "a power that operates in distinct opposition to the natural self-centeredness of humanity in its fallen condition" (Wuthnow, 1993, p. 346). What theologians call human *fallen condition* parallels what evolutionary biologists would call, more simply, the uninhibited biological drive for survival and self-interest. Through the transcendent power of grace, true altruism, an introspective act of selfless love is possible.

All the same, agape might not be the best standard for studies of the altruistic impulse. If our best explanation of the altruistic impulse at this time hangs on our understanding of empathy and on a religious orientation that resembles Batson's quest orientation, future research in this area will need to rethink how human love influences, or at least describes, human altruism. The debates over the character of *eros*, or "desire," have contaminated that term sufficiently that it is useless for studies of altruism, even though eros may well explain many benevolent actions. On the other hand, *philia* (φιλια), which we typically define as "brotherly love," shows promise.

According to Gerhard Kittel, "Φιλια . . . means the love which embraces everything that bears a human countenance. . . . It is not an . . . intoxication which overcomes man, but an order or task which he may evade" (Stauffer, 1964, p. 36). Kittel expands the definition elsewhere: Philia represents the characteristic of "sharing in the lot of a friend, especially when it is hard. . . . [Philia] means service, concern, and sacrifice even to the point of life itself" (Stählin, 1974, p. 161). In philia, we have a theological term that may roughly approximate what Batson et al. labeled the quest orientation. Philia is an order of love that we may evade, yet it prompts us to act for another's benefit, even though that act could mean the supreme sacrifice.

Philia does not require complete selflessness, yet it is always other oriented and seeks what is best for the other. Like agape, philia reflects a willingness to sacrifice one's needs, even one's life, for another. It is the word Jesus finally settled on when he asked Peter three times whether he "loved" him. When Peter answered that he did love (philia) him, Jesus charged him to feed his sheep (John 21:17). At its heart, the word *philia* implies an active orientation toward others.

Social psychologists have shown that one key to understanding the altruistic impulse might be human empathy, a quality reflected in philia in ways agape does not reflect. Perhaps this aspect of philia explains why the ancient

Greeks coined the word *philanthropy* rather than *agapanthropy*. Both words were possible, but only one of them includes the aspect of empathy—what ancient Greeks called *sympathy*—to express such a lofty virtue. The ancient Greeks were less concerned with unintentional self-interest than they were with interest in others and with the capacity to identify with other peoples' emotional states. Philia gives humans a sense of kinship or "friendship" with people we may have never met.

It gives humans a stake in the good of the *polis*—the "public good." *Philia* comprises in its root meaning the two general principles Payton and Moody (2008) suggest are crucial to determine whether an act serves the public good: (1) The act relieves the suffering of others "for whom one has no formal or legal responsibility," and (2) it improves "the quality of life in the community, however one defines that idea" (p. 28). The question of incidental self-interest is unnecessary to the debate, whereas empathic kinship with the unknown other and the desire to improve one's community stand at its heart.

Under most circumstances, our other-oriented benevolent acts will be mingled with self-interest, and they will still be philanthropic, unless self-interest becomes the dominant interest. Recent data suggest that Americans are becoming increasingly narcissistic, so they may "have neither the motivation to become involved in charitable activities nor the familiarity with needs and opportunities for involvement" (Wuthnow 1990, p. 19). The 2008 Pew Report shows a corresponding demographic shift among Americans under the age of 30 from their affiliation with an organized spiritual tradition to unaffiliation, agnosticism, and atheism that could explain this trend.

If Haidt (2007) is correct that the moral systems embedded within our religious traditions evolved to suppress or regulate selfishness to make human life within societies possible, the numerical losses experienced by our nation's religious institutions, which carry our moral systems, could have serious prosocial implications for an entire generation of Americans. Among other things, our religious traditions (spiritual or secular) are the rehearsal stage for human empathy and other prosocial behaviors. Without the ready influence of these institutions, we have fewer means to inhibit our selfishness and fewer opportunities to rehearse prosocial behaviors in community.

Anecdotal evidence suggests that many of the young Americans who have shifted away from organized religious traditions could be gravitating in large numbers toward their own antisocial and egoistic in-groups, bound once again to the laws of self-interest and biological survival in competition with all other groups. Perhaps we see in this shift of orientation what sociobiologist Samuel Bowles (2006) meant when he argued that group-selection theory among humans works better when the groups are in open competition. Then altruistic acts, such as food sharing within groups, could have a broader effect. So many members within these groups find themselves as "couch surfers," moving among friends to meet each other's most basic needs. Members of these groups care for each other to ensure the survival of the group, but they show little interest for the needs of nongroup members.

Future research on the human philanthropic impulse will need to test the anecdotal evidence seen in the rise of gangs, in their apparent in-group altruism, and in the implications of the rise of gangs and other, more loosely knit groups, which try to bind themselves to more altruistic lifestyles. This study must be in search of remedies to repair a social tear that could be riding a phenomenon of global overpopulation. The search for remedies will require the best efforts of evolutionary biologists, social scientists, philosophers, and theologians working in unison and with less concern for disciplinary turf boundaries.

In the meantime, the results from two recent studies shine a small ray of hope on our subject, as they offer some concluding insights into the altruistic impulse: (1) The 2001 Independent Sector report showed that 71% of all Americans who volunteered in the year 2000 *had been asked to do it*, whereas only 29% of all Americans who volunteered that year had not been asked to do it. There is an important equilibrium between egoism and altruism within us: Sometimes, we want to know that others value our capacity for philanthropy enough to ask us to help. (2) The same study shows that Americans who became involved with giving and volunteering before the age of 18 maintained that involvement into adulthood. Considering the number of public and private schools that have begun to require service learning and to offer service opportunities to young students, this trend shows promise (Independent Sector, 2001). Finally, (3) a 2008 Gallup poll showed that Americans who volunteered for at least one charitable cause gave significantly more money to charitable causes than those who have never volunteered (Saad, 2008). The complementary tasks appear to reinforce one's philanthropic impulse to engage in the other. The key may be to ask others to volunteer.

References and Further Readings

Batson, C. D., Duncan, B. D., Ackerman, P., Buckley, T., & Birch, K. (1981). Is empathic emotion a source of altruistic motivation? *Journal of Personality and Social Psychology, 40*, 290–302.

Batson, C. D., Eidelman, S. H., Higley, S. L., & Russell, S. A. (2001). "And who is my neighbor" II: Quest orientation as a source of universal compassion. *Journal for the Scientific Study of Religion, 40*, 9–50.

Batson, C. D., Schoenrade, P., & Ventis, W. L. (1993). *Religion and the individual*. Oxford, UK: Oxford University Press.

Batson, C. D., & Shaw, L. L. (1991). Evidence for altruism: Toward a pluralism of prosocial motives. *Psychological Review, 2*(2), 107–22.

Batson, C. D., & Ventis, W. L. (1982). *The religious experience: A social-psychological perspective.* New York: Oxford University Press.

Bowles, S. (2006). Group competition, reproductive leveling, and the evolution of human altruism. *Science* (New series), *314*(5805), 1569–1572.

Brown, P. (2002). *Poverty and leadership in the later Roman Empire.* Hanover, NH: University Press of New England.

Carnegie, N. (1889, June). Wealth. *North American Review, 391*(148), 653–664.

Clutton-Brock, T. H. (2002, April 5). Breeding together: Kin selection, reciprocity and mutualism in cooperative animal societies. *Science, 296*, 69–72.

Comte, A. (1851–1854). *Système de politique positive.* Paris: Les Presses Universitaires de France.

Darwin, C. (1871). *The descent of man.* New York: Appleton.

Dawkins, R. (1989). *The selfish gene.* Oxford, UK: Oxford University Press. (Original work published 1976)

Dawkins, R. (2003). *A devil's chaplain: Reflections on hope, lies, science and love.* London: Orion.

de Chardin, P. T. (1959). *The phenomenon of man.* New York: Perennial Library.

Demerath, N. J., III. (2002). A sinner among the saints: Confessions of a sociologist of culture and religion. *Sociological Forum, 17*(1), 1–19.

de Waal, F. B. M. (2008). Putting the altruism back into altruism: The evolution of empathy. *Annual Review of Psychology, 59*, 279–300.

Dovidio, J. (1991). The empathy-altruism hypothesis: Paradigm and promise. *Psychological Inquiry, 2*(2), 126–128.

Durkheim, É. (1995). *The elementary forms of religious life* (K. E. Fields, Trans.). New York: Free Press. (Original work published 1912)

Goldfield, J., & Miner, M. (2002). Quest religion and the problem of limited compassion. *Journal for the Scientific Study of Religion, 41*(4), 685–695.

Grant, C. (2001). *Altruism and Christian ethics.* Cambridge, UK: Cambridge University Press.

Haidt, J. (2007). The new synthesis in moral psychology. *Science* (New series), *316*(5827), 998–1002.

Hall, P. (1990). The history of religious philanthropy in America. In R. Wuthnow, V. Hodgkinson, et al. (Eds.), *Faith and philanthropy in America* (pp. 38–62). Washington, DC: Jossey-Bass.

Hamilton, W. D. (1964). The genetical evolution of social behaviour I and II. *Journal of Theoretical Biology, 7*, 1–52.

Independent Sector. (2001). *Giving and volunteering in the United States* [Computer file]. Washington, DC: Author.

Ji, C.-H., Pendergraft, L., & Perry, M. (2006). Religiosity, altruism, and altruistic hypocrisy: Evidence from Protestant adolescents. *Review of Religious Research, 48*(2), 156–178.

Lack, D. (1966). *Population studies of birds.* Oxford, UK: Clarendon Press.

Moe, H. (1961). Notes on the origin of philanthropy in Christendom. *Proceedings of the American Philosophical Society, 105*(2), 141–144.

Nash, J. (1950). Equilibrium points in n-person games. *Proceedings of the National Academy of Sciences in America, 36*(1), 48–49.

Newport, F. (2008, March 21). *Easter season finds a religious, largely Christian North.* Retrieved April 26, 2010, from http://www.gallup.com/poll/111013/worldwide-highly-religious-more-likely-help-others.aspx

Payton, R., & Moody, M. (2008). *Understanding philanthropy: Its meaning and mission.* Bloomington: University of Indiana Press.

Pelham, B., & Crabtree, S. (2008, October 8). *Worldwide, highly religious more likely to help others.* Retrieved April 26, 2010, from http://www.gallup.com/poll/111013/worldwide-highly-religious-more-likely-to-help-others.aspx

Pew report: U.S. religious landscape survey. (2008). *The Pew forum on religion & public life: A project of the Pew Research Center.* Available from www.pewforum.org

Piliavin, J. A., & Charng, H.-W. (1990). A review of recent theory and research. *Annual Review of Sociology, 16*, 27–65.

Rauschenbusch, W. (2007). *Christianity and the social crisis in the 21st century* (P. Raushenbush, Ed., Expanded with notes). New York: HarperOne. (Original work published 1907)

Ricoeur, P. (1977). *The rule of metaphor.* Toronto, ON: University of Toronto Press.

Rigby, P., & O'Grady, P. (1989). Agape and altruism: Debates in theology and social psychology. *Journal of the American Academy of Religion, 57*(4), 719–737.

Saad, L. (2008, December 19). Despite economy, charitable donors, volunteers keep giving [Gallup poll]. *Gallup Daily News.* Available from http://www.gallup.com/poll/113497/despite-economy-charitable-donors-volunteers-keep-giving.aspx#2

Smith, M. J. (1964). Group selection and kin selection. *Nature, 201*, 1145–1147.

Stählin, G. (1974). φίλος, φίλη, φιλία [friend; dear; friendship]. In G. Kittel (Ed.), G. W. Bromiley (Trans.), *Theological dictionary of the New Testament* (Vol. 9, pp. 146–171). Grand Rapids, MI: Eerdmans.

Stauffer, E. (1964). ἀγαπάω, ἀγάπη, ἀγαπητός [to love; love; beloved]. In G. Kittel (Ed.), G. W. Bromiley (Trans.), *Theological dictionary of the New Testament* (Vol. 1, pp. 21–55). Grand Rapids, MI: Eerdmans.

Thielicke, H. (1980). Out of the depths (G. W. Bromiley, Trans.). In *A Thielicke trilogy.* Grand Rapids, MI: Baker Books. (Original work published 1962)

Trivers, R. (1971). The evolution of reciprocal altruism. *Quarterly Review of Biology, 46*, 35–57.

Watson, P. J., Morris, R. J., & Hood, R. W., Jr. (1984). Religious orientation, humanistic values, and narcissism. *Review of Religious Research, 25*(3), 257–264.

Williams, G. C. (1966). *Adaptation and natural selection.* Princeton, NJ: Princeton University Press.

Wuthnow, R. (1990). Religion and the voluntary spirit in the United States: Mapping the terrain. In R. Wuthnow, V. Hodgkinson, et al. (Eds.), *Faith and philanthropy in America.* Washington, DC: Jossey-Bass.

Wuthnow, R. (1993, September). Altruism and sociological theory. *Social Service Review, 67*, 344–357.

Wynne-Edwards, V. (1962). *Animal dispersion in relation to social behavior.* London: Oliver & Boyd.

86

THE CHARITABLE SPIRIT

Tapping Into Altruism to Achieve the Nonprofit Mission

ROBB SHOAF

United Methodist Church in Madison

While altruistic behavior and nonprofit mission need not be opposed, a definition of each is needed to reveal the differences so that a better understanding of collaboration may emerge. To begin with, altruism is a behavior, and nonprofit mission is the expression of a structure within society that exhibits certain behavior. The present chapter is to show that altruism and the nonprofit sector must be understood independently to better understand the collaboration or, put another way, how altruism may be tapped for nonprofit missions.

Altruism may be defined as unselfish behavior that seeks the good of the other as of primary importance and ahead of personal interests. It may be individual or collective in nature, meaning it may involve the actions of one individual, those of a group, or society as a whole.

A nonprofit organization on the other hand is a societal entity that has certain characteristics that clarify its role in a culture. One of the primary characteristics is the fact that profits within the not-for-profit organization are not distributed to stockholders. Overall, there is the perception that a nonprofit embodies behavior that focuses primarily on the public good rather than individual or corporate gain.

This definition may be too broad because governmental structures and for-profit structures (i.e., private business and corporations) may also claim to seek the common good. Yet the nonprofit is not a public entity and is not primarily responsive to the impulses of market forces (i.e., profitability). In fact, nonprofits are often seen as intermediary organizations that operate at the boundaries where market and/or government have failed. It is where producer and consumer cannot meet equitably. Therefore, the presence of soup kitchens, homeless shelters, and other charitable agencies and organizations fill the gaps in society left by this particular failure that is not met by capitalist means or governmental provisions.

In "Part 1: The Nature of Altruism," there will be a closer examination of a behavior understood in terms of various motivational factors. Different perspectives reveal different understandings of altruism as an end in itself, a means to another end, or a by-product of other behaviors, forces, or institutions. "Part 2: The Form of Altruism" will explore ways in which altruism as understood will be a resource for nonprofit organizations. It will take into account various ways in which the nonprofit mission may be enhanced by a proper understanding of some of the complexities of its motivation and character.

Part 1: The Nature of Altruism— Perspectives on Altruistic Behavior

Religious and Philosophical

All major religious traditions have provisions for behavior that is altruistic in nature. Each tradition has within it a set of beliefs and moral guidelines for living individually and within the larger community. Whether it is the *Bhagavad Gita*, the Koran, or the Hebrew or Christian scriptures, each presents instruction on living.

Western cultures have been dominated by the Judeo-Christian heritage with a growing influence from the Islamic tradition. All three have a common source tracing their beginnings to the faith exhibited by Abraham. It is at this juncture that the tradition puts great emphasis on the social nature of behavior. The reason is simply that as a nomadic people, social cohesion is of the utmost importance, and therefore, individualism is limited in scope and importance.

Altruism, though understood as the will of God to care for thy neighbor, had a very practical purpose. Here social cohesion is critical, because the strength of the weakest link may well determine the survival of the group. Within the Jewish tradition, altruistic behavior is represented by the Year of Jubilee. This celebration is based on the forgiveness of debt and the release of slaves that are to occur every 7 years and every 7 cycles of 7 years. This is corporate altruism, once again, seen as the will of God but also having a practical benefit to the society as a whole.

Within the Christian (New Testament) tradition, altruism is given a new twist. Through the teachings of Jesus of Nazareth, selfless behavior and love are measured in terms of self-love, therefore the command to love one's neighbor as oneself. Yet such behavior is not always self-reflective, for example, in the command to turn the other cheek or to go a second mile when only one mile is required. Here, altruism is not based on an egoistic sense or regard for the self but rather focuses simply on the need of the other.

The third great Abrahamic tradition is that of Islam. It formally emerged later than Christianity and follows the teachings of the prophet Mohammed. The tenets of the Islamic tradition are embodied in the Five Pillars of Faith. One of these five is the practice of almsgiving. It is an obligation for Muslims and is based on the requirement to give away a portion of accumulated wealth. Once this requirement is satisfied, there is a continued emphasis on giving, which is not a matter of obligation but is left to the discretion of the individual and is voluntary.

While the Buddhist tradition is traced back to Siddhartha Gautama, the Hindu tradition has no specific founder. Both, as Indian religions, have a component of religious living and behavior called the *dharma*. Here, as in the religious traditions previously mentioned, is an emphasis on altruistic behavior embedded within a philosophical cosmology. A central tenet of this understanding of the cosmos is the recognition of the reality of suffering and the human need to both recognize and seek to bring an end to suffering.

These religious traditions share a common concern for the individual or group as an end in itself. By contrast, the ancient philosophical tradition is more complicated as the sharp edges of means and ends are not as distinct—this blurring seen in the master works of perhaps the greatest of the Greek philosophers: Plato (428–348 BCE). Born to a wealthy family at the end of the 5th century BCE, he was both a student of Socrates and teacher to Aristotle. In Plato's masterpiece, *The Republic*, the state is elevated

above the individual; therefore, the other as a target of altruistic behavior—unlike in religious traditions—is secondary. This is not a result of simply placing greater value on the society but arises from an undemocratic view of the Republic itself. Plato, coming from a well-to-do family, kept the hope of the aristocracy alive and hopes for a city-state led not by the masses but by the elite, and for Plato, that meant those specifically gifted and trained as philosophers.

While Plato's student Aristotle directs his attention to moral behavior in *The Nichomachean Ethics,* he too places greater emphasis on the good of the state ahead of that of the individual. Again, altruistic behavior is seen in the context of the common community.

The question of altruistic behavior as an end in itself, a means to an end, or a by-product of other behavior will continue throughout history and across disciplines. Different perspectives may also arise within a single tradition. Aristotle, for example, set happiness as the central goal of life. Altruistic behavior may be interpreted as taking part in this quest for happiness. There have been times in history where a curious blending of traditions has provided new ways of examining personal beliefs and understanding behavior. During the Middle Ages, it was Thomas Aquinas, called the father of Catholic theology, who placed his *Summa Theologica* within a framework based on the philosophy of Aristotle and its emphasis on human happiness. Here, we find a strange combination of religious and philosophical traditions.

The idea of altruism as being directly or indirectly focused on the other or the neighbor and as an end in itself or a means to another end changes through history depending on the social, religious, and cultural realities of the day. With the collapse of authority occurring within the 18th century, in particular with the American and French Revolutions, a new age dawned. It was the Enlightenment. Philosophically, it reached its apex in the thought of Immanuel Kant. His masterpiece, *Critique of Pure Reason*, carefully examines the boundaries or limits of reason itself. This leads to other major works: *Critique of Practical Reason* and *Critique of Judgment* where issues of morals and taste are explored—all within a rational framework.

Kant, in the *Critique of Practical Reason,* explores altruistic behavior and morals as the reasonable result of one's sense of duty. It is not linked to personal goals or happiness but rather is part of his philosophical system based on the very nature of reason. He first begins to explore his concept of this moral attitude in *Groundwork for the Metaphysics of Morals*, which leads to one of his most famous maxims: the categorical imperative that we should act as though our action would become a universal law. Again, the devotion to altruism as an end itself is restored as a matter of both individual and social responsibility. This is obvious in the U.S. Declaration of Independence's holding truths that are self-evident regarding the sanctity and rights of all human beings regardless of race, class, culture, or belief.

Scientific/Behavioral

The Enlightenment planted seeds spawning modern scientific endeavor and discovery. One of the most significant works is that of Charles Darwin, who in 1859 published *On the Origin of Species*. This work emphasizes a common ancestry of all living things, which, besides its religious implications in questioning the nature and timetable for creation, has a profound effect on understanding the nature of human behavior. Specifically, introducing the concept of natural selection creates controversy with regard to altruistic tenets and beliefs. Natural selection, presented before the discovery of genetics, posits how individual traits that are favorable to species survival are passed on to succeeding generations.

The implications of such a concept continue to unfold. One of the most controversial refers to social engineering and is directly related to altruism. If altruistic behavior is directed to those in need, it stands to reason that many of those considered less fortunate by circumstances or their own behavior would be considered less robust than others in the culture or society. From a natural selection perspective, such individuals possess traits that weaken rather than strengthen the species. Therefore, considering the good of the group, in this case the species, altruistic behavior may be discouraged.

Another challenge comes with the birth of psychology and its various branches where Darwinian influence on behavior continues to be felt. Sigmund Freud, as the father of psychoanalysis, and his followers understood behavior as a combination of instinct and unconscious drive. As a result, study of altruistic behavior when reduced to components of traits and instincts begins to lose its motivational capacity. After all, if the human is no more than a bundle of instincts and drives at one extreme or an automaton at the other, what is the nature of motivation for altruistic behavior?

In 1937, the psychologist Gordon Allport published an article titled "The Functional Autonomy of Motives." His purpose was to argue that while instinctual drives were active, personal motives had a great and lasting impact on behavior. The study of motivation continues to be of primary importance in understanding general behavior and altruistic behavior in particular.

Modern genetics has brought a further confirmation of Darwinian theory. Having given genetics an anthropomorphic title in his work *The Selfish Gene*, Richard Dawkins (2006) looks at altruistic behavior strictly as a behavioral phenomenon, and as his title suggests, his lowest common denominator for natural selection is the gene.

What becomes of interest for our purposes is Dawkins's excursion into the area of social phenomenon that plays a part in the process. His discussion of cultural practices and ideas, or memes, has provided a new area of study, one closely paralleling that of social psychology and sociology. A particular development in the understanding of altruistic behavior has come with *game theory* as reflected in the writings of Dawkins and others such as Robert Axelrod in *The Evolution of Cooperation*. Again, the discussion of game theory in its different formations (e.g., *prisoner's dilemma*) examines implications of the combination of different behaviors that vary in terms of selfish and selfless behavior in anticipation of the responses of others. Therefore, in one scenario, the altruistic or selfish behavior of an individual will be guided by the expectation of the behavior of another. With the use of computer programs, various mathematical models have looked at this phenomenon as it plays through a series of decisions made over time. It has provided a better understanding of the effect decisions have on the behavior of individuals as applied to organizations, institutions, and states.

Part 2: The Form of Altruism: Social Structure's Effect on Altruism

Social Structure

The effects of evolutionary theory continue to be far-reaching. While altruism to this point has been treated by and large as an individual phenomenon, this microperspective expands in the 19th century, taking on a different form and perspective. It is with the birth of sociology that this paradigm begins to frame social behavior. As the development and evolution of species began with Charles Darwin, it expands beyond a biological paradigm to a social one with the work of Herbert Spencer.

It is with Émile Durkheim (1858–1917) that social facts are treated as social realities and society itself as an organic entity. His most famous work in this area is *The Division of Labor in Society* (1893). It is here he makes a separation between the solidarity of societies in the past and those of the present. The former were defined by social bonds and common interests, which Durkheim identified as mechanical in nature. In the 19th century, these bonds change with, among other factors, the division of labor, which gives a specialized function to members of society where he refers to the bonds of solidarity as organic. It is the welfare of the whole that is important because integration and cohesion define the nature of society itself. Durkheim went on to write *Suicide* (1897/1951), which links suicide inversely to social integration where altruism may involve sacrifice of the individual for the larger group.

It is Max Weber (1864–1920) who explores the rational structure of society as a means of carrying out social action. For Weber, bureaucracy was the end result of a legal, rational society. Altruism is an indirect result of the motivation stemming from religious convictions and ideals particularly within the Protestant tradition. His work, *The Protestant Ethic and the Spirit of Capitalism* (1905), identifies the mutual interdependence between the Protestant religious tradition and the economic realities of individual prerogatives that define capitalism.

Institutional Structures

While philosophical, psychological, and sociological theories debate the nature of altruism from the standpoint of motive and form, it is within institutional structures that altruism is embedded and/or excluded. Within most forms of government, the motivation for altruistic behavior is prescribed as a requirement of law. Governments have some type of requirement that makes provision for others that is to some extent sacrificial in nature. The system of taxation is the most obvious example and in the United States provides for different forms of social welfare. There are some who benefit from their own contributions: those who pay taxes and receive direct benefits (e.g., direct government subsidies). These are private benefits. Public benefits on the other hand are distributed equally but are independent of the level of personal contributions (e.g., a local police force or the military). The nature of government provisions and their interpretations may make a great difference in the resulting altruistic behavior of individuals and groups within society. There is more on this later.

A second form of altruistic behavior is evident as a byproduct of economic activity. This is witnessed in forprofit activity and outlined in the work of Adam Smith in *The Wealth of Nations* (1776). Smith believed a market system based on supply and demand is a force that regulates behavior and is based not on altruistic behavior but on self-interest. Members of a society perform best individually if and when they pursue their own interests. In the end, this individual behavior through the natural workings of the market or by an invisible hand benefits not simply the individual but society as a whole. With Smith comes the advent of economics as a discipline and with it an understanding of altruism as a by-product of self-interest.

The nonprofit sector, or third sector, also has a place within the provision of social benefits. One of the primary tasks of the nonprofit organization is to act as an intermediary in instances when there is government or market failure. Often, it is the nonprofit sector that is able to move among and between the other sectors. It shares connections both with the public and for-profit sector. As with government, it is to provide benefit for the common good. Yet as with a for-profit, the not-for-profit organization must operate as a business, for its function depends on supply and demand for its services.

The structure of the nonprofit sector has a unique place in the history of the United States. Perhaps the most insightful analysis of America in its infancy came not from an American but rather a Frenchman—Alexis de Tocqueville (1805–1859). Tocqueville came to the United States from his native France in 1832 to study the American penitentiary system. The result of his trip was the publication of his masterpiece *Democracy in America* (1835, 1840/1994) in two volumes. It is through his travels around the fledgling nation that he notices the strong effect of individualism and the pursuit of self-interest. Yet there is a difference. He notices a strong tendency within communities to gather together and establish associations. The association is an independent organization that along with religious institutions gives birth to the nonprofit sector. Here, self-interest, rightly or properly understood, provides the insight that one's service to others is also essential to one's self-interest. In fact, it is through associational meetings that goods and services may be better distributed. Also, the authority of the government is less centralized but distributed more equitably throughout society. Tocqueville believes that these associations are not only beneficial but also critical to the proper functioning and flourishing of a democracy.

Understand the Organizational Polity

The Downside of Selflessness and the Upside of Selfishness

The first point to be made is that selfless behavior is not always the only means for mission. In some cases, it may impede the goals of the organization. And that is why not only the nature and mission of the organization but also the environment in which the organization operates must be recognized and understood. No organization exists in a vacuum but rather succumbs to influences and forces within and beyond its walls, circumstances within and beyond its control. A rational evaluation is needed before the altruistic impulse is tapped. This both looks for an understanding of the organization systemically within a larger system and also avoids sentimentalism as the only motivator for altruistic behavior.

Let us take the example of a nonprofit that makes low-interest loans to those in need. An example may be the Grameen Bank. The sentiment of altruism may lead an individual to provide a loan based on emotional considerations. That is, those with the most compelling story may receive the least restriction on their loan. To take it one step further, the guidelines and rules of this nonprofit would be superseded by the emotional state of the donor in charge. It is obvious the results would most likely be catastrophic. We know that economic demands place responsibility on a rational deliberation in establishing rules and a faithful objective adherence to those rules in order for the organization to function. Otherwise, the bank fails, and no one is helped. Here, the altruistic impulse is tempered by a greater goal objectively established.

If altruism by definition must be a self-sacrificial act, where one must give up something for another to gain, then its effectiveness will be reduced. Over the years in the United States, one aspect of charitable contributions is favorable tax benefits. Whether it is a tax credit or exclusion, the point is that these economic factors may be motivators for personal giving. The recipient's benefit does not need to be proportional to the donor's cost. Again, how one defines altruistic behavior will have an effect on the decision to contribute time or talent to a particular endeavor. Therefore, to take a phrase from Tocqueville, self-interest, rightly understood, may again apply. Altruism, well understood, may indicate the recipient's gain does not necessarily require the donor's loss.

Egoism and Altruism Are Not Mutually Exclusive

In the previous example, a single nonprofit organization is considered. It is viewed from a motivational perspective that is kept in check by a rational understanding of the nonprofit and its environment and also the mission and goals of the organization. Such scenarios are not uncommon considering nonprofits and altruism by definition seek to provide for public welfare.

While the for-profit institution by definition seeks the benefit of stockholders, its goals may seem removed from altruistic endeavors. Again, the issue here is not only the direct mission of the organization but also the benefits it provides. These benefits may, under certain circumstances, meet the needs of for-profit and nonprofit or, simply put, the egoist and the altruist.

Cross-sector collaboration provides examples of such a process where egoism and altruism are not antithetical but mutually beneficial. In 2000, James E. Austin at Harvard University published *The Collaboration Challenge*. Austin's focus is on collaborations that bridge the nonprofit and for-profit sectors. While these collaborations vary in depth of relationship, Austin recognizes three different types of partnerships: philanthropic, transactional, and transformational. The nature of the partnerships ranges from simply providing a gift (philanthropic) to establishing mutually beneficial interchange (transactional) to forming mutually beneficial organizational change (transformative). What is important is that self-interest properly understood has the potential for not only satisfying the mission of each organization but also (in some circumstances) for providing a transformation that is greater than either organization would achieve by itself. For the latter, he provides the case of a collaboration between Georgia Pacific, a forest products company, and the Nature Conservancy, one of the largest environmental organizations. What makes this case interesting is the fact not only that the organizations are from different sectors but also that the two organizations seem to have opposing purposes and missions.

The point is that altruism, if it is narrowly defined, will be self-limiting. If the focus is only on behavior that is self-sacrificial in nature and has no interest in personal gain or profit, there will be lost opportunities. Altruism, more broadly defined and properly understood, will play a much better role in the organization's purpose if there is an understanding of its place in the process. Altruism may or may not be the motive to provide altruistic results. This occurs through recognition of the organization's polity and the environment in which it finds itself.

Incorporating the Altruistic Impulse

Altruism Seeks Relationship

Having examined how altruism may function within the mission and organizational structure of the nonprofit alone and in collaboration with other organizations, it is important to look again closely at the nature of the altruistic impulse itself. Thus, as a matter of definition, altruism must not simply be broadly conceived but also deeply understood. Above all else, altruism arises out of human desire. Further, it is a desire or orientation to and for another. Whether the result is impersonal, as in making a donation, or personal, as in donating personal service, the impulse is the same. It simply varies in intensity. The important point is that it seeks a relationship and needs to be personal in nature. Many institutions that seek donor support make a distinction between regular donors and those benefactors who make large contributions. The level of personal attention is proportional to the size of the donation. It is not because there is a qualitative difference in donors but rather because the organization has limited resources, and while giving attention to all donors is not practically possible, attention is given to those who provide large gifts and bring in the greatest revenue. It is not a difference in the nature of the gift as much as it is the use of the organization's resources.

It is important to recognize the altruistic impulse in whatever form it takes. Most nonprofits measure donations and success in terms of financial contributions. The point is that other metrics are also needed to locate and take advantage of the altruistic impulse. A financial metric is important but too narrow to include all the benefits of altruistic behavior. Time and volunteer service are also important measures of contributions that are made to the organization's mission. They, too, are responses to the altruistic impulse and need to be valued in the contribution they make to mission.

Social Capital: The Measure of Relationship

The importance of interpersonal relationships cannot be overestimated. While volunteer activity may be quantified, for example, in giving a monetary value to volunteer time served, human interaction is harder to objectify. Still, sociological literature and political science literature have made use of a term that, while not new, has only come into wide use in the past few years: *social capital*. It refers to the nature of relationships that enable a community or society to function together. It involves the qualities of openness, trust, benevolence, and altruistic behavior, to name a few. It was Robert Putnam's (1995) article "Bowling Alone: America's Declining Social Capital" that drew attention to a phenomenon occurring at the end of the 20th century. This was the discovery that civic associations were decreasing in number and influence—exemplified for Putnam, for instance, in the decrease in the number of bowling leagues since the 1960s. While as many people if not more people are bowling today, there is a reduction in the associational nature of bowling. This and other examples led Putnam to the conclusion that civic engagement is declining in the United States.

The point to be made is that the importance of relationships has been validated with the inclusion of social capital in the lexicons of sociology, economics, and political science. The understanding of altruistic impulses and behavior is shaped by differing perspectives through the centuries. Whether it is identified with the political goals of the state, part of our genetic makeup, a by-product of the quest for happiness, or merely a quality of the capital of relationships, each perspective puts its particular stamp on the understanding of the qualities that define the quest for the common good.

Altruism as Self-Expression and Creative Design

The Charitable Spirit

Up to this point, a rather static view has been taken with regard to altruism. Its operation has been defined in relation to the structure of the human organism, both individual and corporate. We have looked at the structures in society to which it must adapt. As we weave our way through the complexities of social existence, we realize the various ways in which the charitable spirit, the altruistic impulse, may be harnessed and used for the benefit of all.

Throughout this discussion, ideas and paradigms changed drastically. The understanding of human nature changes. The understanding of human communities changes. Our ability to isolate and examine individual components of behavior and motivation increases. The scientific study of behavior with advances in statistical analysis and computer modeling has revealed much about the meaning of human behavior patterns.

Throughout this discussion, what has not changed is the essence of the charitable spirit. It is the same today as it was in the days of Plato's *Republic*. The charitable spirit is found in the Buddha, Abraham, and Jesus. It can be found in corporate America and in small villages in Zimbabwe. It may simply take a bit more digging to find it in the former than in the latter.

The point is, the charitable spirit, must also be considered on its own terms. What is at the heart of the charitable spirit? The first point to be made, which was mentioned previously, is the desire for connection—for relationship. It is connectional in nature, and that is fairly obvious. What is not so obvious is the fact that the charitable spirit is a driving force toward self-expression and creative design. It is important to understand how the spirit of altruism may be channeled according to individual and communal wants and desires, but alone, that misses the organic quality of altruism and its creative nature.

Creative Altruism

The study of altruism and its effectiveness in understanding, predicting, and shaping charitable behavior has been and will continue to be of interest to sociologists, psychologists, and political scientists. The discoveries and insights continue to inform the work of nonprofit organizations. Yet understanding altruism is as much an art as a science, and the balance between the two approaches is necessary and difficult to maintain.

Pitirim Sorokin (1889–1968) was instrumental in establishing the department of sociology at Harvard University. He is responsible as well for establishing the Harvard Research Center in Creative Altruism in 1949. Sorokin was a controversial figure and found no lasting success with his center at Harvard, even though he had many supporters in the area of research on altruism and altruistic behavior, notably Gordon Allport and Abraham Maslow. Although research on altruism continues to be popular today, Sorokin felt a certain prejudice against its study and felt that while crime and hatred were often subjects of objective analysis, altruism and emotive studies on love were considered less robust and not worthy of careful examination.

The creative nonprofit organization is in the position to take advantage of the multidisciplinary research on altruism but is not bound or restricted by any specific discipline. The research itself is a means to an end and that end is the mission of the nonprofit. The link between the research and the mission is the area of creative altruism. That is the area of free exploration and expression.

Altruism as an Aesthetic Process

Understanding the positive determinants of behavior without allowing the expression of that behavior is pointless for the nonprofit. To function, the organization must depend on not only rational determinants of altruistic behavior but also on the emotive elements that drive people to volunteer and serve. This is an aesthetic process, meaning it is grounded in experience. It begins and ends in experience. The altruistic motive, whether internal or external is experienced even if it is the experience of an idea. The response is experiential as well.

It is an expressed impulse, desire, or idea.

If the altruistic response is experiential in nature, then the freedom of expression is critical to the benefit derived not only by the volunteer or donor but also by the nonprofit. The challenge for the nonprofit is to be able to define the mission succinctly enough that it provides understandable and measurable goals and objectives while at the same time is broad enough to allow individual freedom of expression. This is in line with the work of Abraham Maslow and his pyramidal hierarchy of needs, the highest point being self-actualization. This is a creative, as well as an aesthetic, process.

The challenge for the nonprofit is to beware of a narrow view of both its mission and the manner in which that mission can be achieved. Altruism is not only relational in nature but also creative. It is a topic of study but organic in nature. Making use of altruism and altruistic behavior is for the nonprofit both a science and an art.

Summary: Telling, Hearing, and Sharing "The Story"

Altruism by definition is relational. The relationship may be direct, when the donor is known, but also indirect, when the donor prefers anonymity. The point is, in each case, there is a desire to make a connection of one type or another. It is critical that the nonprofit organization recognize, engage, and develop this very human impulse. This is the role of the nonprofit leader whose challenge and charge may be summed up as telling, hearing, and sharing the story. Whether it is a board of directors, volunteers, or donors themselves, the leader needs to engage them all. While each set of constituents has different responsibilities regarding the nonprofit, there are certain characteristics all share in common—most importantly, all constituents are involved because of their commitment to the mission of the organization.

The first challenge is to tell the story. It is not at first the story of the organization; it is the story about those the leader is addressing. They first need to know that their behavior is not simply a matter of doing but a matter of showing forth the fullest expression of what it means to be human. The leader needs to recognize this is primary, that the value of fullest expression comes before any appeals to the needs or mission of the organization. At this stage, it is already assumed there is buy-in to the mission; otherwise, the constituents would not be involved.

The constituents also need to know that historically they stand in good company. This article has been an attempt to show just that—the greatest minds, the most courageous individuals, the greatest leaders have recognized the centrality of altruism and societies and cultures have achieved their greatest success and richness when this fact has been accepted and celebrated. The effective leader can lift up the fact that altruistic behavior is not limited to great minds or courageous leaders but rather is part and parcel of the human experience.

So at first, the leader must appeal to all stakeholders within and outside the organization appealing to each at his or her own place but to all on the same level. Their value is not in how much they contribute, who they know, or what position they hold. Rather, it is an appeal to the common core of beliefs and abilities they share that gives them equal footing and a voice to be heard. And this is the key—creating the environment where they can be heard. So at this stage, the leader is challenged to establish a space of openness and trust where each person is not simply told she or he has a place; each must witness it in the behavior of others, and that is validated by the leader.

The second talent of the nonprofit leader is the ability to hear the stories. So much of the work of nonprofits depends on nonmonetary rewards; therefore, the greatest gift the nonprofit leader may give any constituent is the gift of honest time and presence. Donors, workers, and volunteers have all heard from management. They are told what to do and directed in how to do it, but the importance of worker and volunteer feedback begins to address the importance of listening on the part of the leader. The benefits are many. As a creative enterprise, altruism is developed and strengthened as it is shared—in the act as well as in its recollection. Listening to constituents and stakeholders tell their stories, a leader not only validates their work but also exhibits her or his altruistic behavior—for the leader steps aside out of the limelight and lets others be heard.

That is not all. Such sharing provides not only motivation for others to do the same but also offers new ideas in a public forum that supports the organization. This creates a gift economy where there is no competition because one idea is not valued to the exclusion of another. All too often, this occurs only in a limited way at annual banquets or award ceremonies. An annual event may be costly and time-consuming; thus, the focus is thinly spread to cover recognition, award presentations, fundraising, and reportage. Those events are important, but more important is an ongoing practice where small celebrations can take place throughout the year that allow the telling and listening that engages, inspires, and empowers the organization.

Finally, the leader is responsible for summing up the witnessing of constituents in such a way that the organization itself is perceived as a logical expression of the altruistic impulse. As mentioned earlier, the nonprofit organization is to give structure to the expression of experience. This is the time and the place where the burden of proof is reversed. No longer are the donors, volunteers, and staff called on to align themselves with the organization; instead, the organization is to prove itself worthy of the constituents' efforts. This is a matter of order and alignment. Putting first things first, the leader will value the stakeholder, recognizing the stakeholder drives the organization and not the other way around.

Make no mistake; this is a challenge to the nonprofit leader. She or he will face enormous pressures from all sides with differing concerns and needs from various stakeholders; therefore, he or she will need a variety of skills to address them. As the leader calls others to the centrality of mission through recognition of what is most basic and human, so she or he must remain aware of his or her own motives and impulses that provide meaning and purpose. This, too, can and must be shared with the organization. For some leaders, it may be one of the greatest challenges they will face, but it is the foundation of true and lasting success.

References and Further Readings

Austin, J. E. (2000). *The collaboration challenge: How nonprofits and businesses succeed through strategic alliances.* San Francisco: Jossey-Bass.

Cook, W. R. (2004). *Tocqueville and the American experiment: Part II* [Audio CD]. Chantilly, VA: Teaching.

Dawkins, R. (2006). *The selfish gene* (30th Anniversary ed.). New York: Oxford University Press.

Dewey, J. (2005). *Art as experience.* New York: Penguin Group. (Original work published 1934)

Durkheim, É. (1951). *Suicide: A study in sociology* (J. A. Spaulding & G. Simpson, Trans.). Glencoe, IL: Free Press. (Original work published 1897)

Hughes, G. J. (2001). *Routledge philosophy guidebook to Aristotle: On ethics.* London: Routledge.

Joseph, J. (2005). *Social theory: A reader.* Edinburgh, UK: Edinburgh University Press.

Kant, I. (1998). *Groundwork of the metaphysics of morals* (M. Gregor, Ed. & Trans.). Cambridge, UK: University of Cambridge Press. (Original work published 1785)

Knowles, J. G., & Cole, A. L. (Eds.). (2008). *Handbook of the arts in qualitative research: Perspectives, methodologies, examples, and issues.* Thousand Oaks, CA: Sage.

Levinson, J. (Ed.). (2001). *Aesthetics and ethics: Essays at the intersection.* Cambridge, UK: Cambridge University Press.

Maslow, A. (1999). *Toward a psychology of being* (3rd ed.). New York: John Wiley & Sons.

Mason, D. E. (1996). *Leading and managing the expressive dimension: Harnessing the hidden power source of the nonprofit sector.* San Francisco: Jossey-Bass.

Pharr, S. J., Putnam, R. D., & Dalton R. J. (2000). Trouble in the advanced democracies? A quarter-century of declining confidence. *Journal of Democracy, 11*(2), 5–25.

Plato. (2004). *Republic.* New York: Barnes & Noble Classics. (Original English work published 1871)

Powell, W. W., & Steinberg, R. (Eds.). (2006). *The nonprofit sector: A research handbook.* New Haven, CT: Yale University Press.

Putnam, R. D. (1995). Bowling alone: America's declining social capital. *Journal of Democracy, 6*(1), 65–78.

Salamon, L. M. (1999). *America's nonprofit sector: A primer* (2nd ed.). New York: Foundation Center.

Salvati, A. (2008). *Altruism and social capital.* Boca Raton, FL: Universal.

Schön, D. A. (2007). *The reflective practitioner: How professionals think in action.* Farnham, UK: Ashgate.

Sober, E., & Wilson, D. S. (1998). *Unto others: The evolution and psychology of unselfish behavior.* Cambridge, MA: Harvard University Press.

Sorokin, P. A. (1998). *In on the practice of sociology* (B. V. Johnston, Ed.). Chicago: University of Chicago Press.

Tocqueville, A. de. (1994). *Democracy in America.* New York: Alfred A. Knopf. (Original work published 1835, 1840)

Weeden, C. (1998). *Corporate social investing: The breakthrough strategy for giving and getting corporate contributions.* San Francisco: Berrett-Koehler.

87

Philanthropic Motives

Who Gives and Volunteers, and Why?

Seong-gin Moon

Inha University

Matthew Downey

Grand Valley State University

During the past 2 decades, nonprofit organizations have increasingly expanded their roles in dealing with policy problems in areas that have been traditionally left to the function of government, such as health, education, and social services. Among the major challenges these expanding roles present is the need for increased financing and volunteer support. Two major concurrent trends in the United States are attributed to these challenges (Salamon, 2002). First and most importantly, despite the increase in total individual giving over the last several decades, individual giving as a share of personal income has been falling. The percentage of total nonprofit revenues attributed to private charitable giving has been in steady decline from 37% in 1943 to 18% in 1992 (Hodgkinson, 2002, p. 393). This trend of diminishing generosity is a serious concern, considering the importance of individual contributions to nonprofit organizations in terms of sustaining the financial resources that are essential to building strong and healthy organizations. Individual donations account for about 80% of all philanthropic giving compared to corporate contributions, which account for less than 5% (Mathur, 1996). The recent decline in the share of benevolent giving is related to a continuing decline in civic engagement and values in the United States as a representation of people's interest in promoting community and social welfare (Putnam, 1995). Generally speaking, it is now much harder than it has been in the past for nonprofits to obtain support from individuals.

This challenge will likely continue, despite the recent surge in volunteering among young people (Hodgkinson, 2002).

Emerging in the early 1980s was a second trend that further intensified the fiscal constraint on nonprofit organizations: market competition from private organizations for government service provision and contracts (Salamon, 2002). The market competition during this period started with a shift in the form of public sector support to nonprofit organizations. As a part of an effort to push forward a policy of fiscal restraint, the federal government funneled aid directly to consumers through subsidies in the form of vouchers and tax credits rather than through service providers, such as nonprofits, in the form of grants and contracts. This change naturally forces nonprofits to compete with private sector entities for consumers in a market that had been traditionally considered their domain (Salamon, 2002). A serious consequence of this new competition led to a sharp decline in market share that many nonprofits enjoyed in fields like health care and social services.

To summarize, the declining trends of nonprofits' financial base, largely due to the drop in personal generosity, public disinterest in civic engagement, and competition for public service provision, have been continuous and have caused widespread concern among nonprofits, particularly in the midst of increasing public service demands. Responding to this challenge, both nonprofit professionals and scholars are increasing efforts to better understand private philanthropic behavior. For nonprofit professionals, this understanding of the behavior offers an important step toward the development of sophisticated fundraising strategies to solicit philanthropic support and promote civic engagement. What is more, a theoretical exploration of philanthropic motives offers intriguing insights into human behavior since it is contradictory to the assumption of classic microeconomics that views human beings as selfish and utility maximizers.

This chapter addresses two important questions. The first question concerns why people give money and volunteer their time. More specifically, why do individuals act against their own welfare for the sake of others? To answer this question, multiple perspectives that are grounded in different academic disciplines are adopted, such as economics, psychology, sociology, and biology. Building on these theoretical explanations of individuals' philanthropic impulses, a second question is addressed that explores the common attributes of individuals who demonstrate these philanthropic behaviors. To identify the likely donors and volunteers, a review of philanthropic research literature is offered. The research explored in this chapter identifies the major determinants for philanthropic behavior, identifying an individual donor's or volunteer's characteristics and background, such as education, gender, religiosity, marital status, age, and income. Finally, this discussion is concluded by summarizing the major findings and offering suggestions for future research.

Why Give and Volunteer?

To start, it is important to define what constitutes individual philanthropic behavior. First, philanthropy entails actions that promote others' welfare (Monroe, 1994). Good intention or well-meaning thought is one of the important components for altruism but is not the defining factor. In other words, positive attitudes toward helping others must lead to actions, in this case, donations and volunteering, to be considered philanthropic behavior. The second important criterion for philanthropic behavior is that philanthropic actions always demand some sacrifice of the actors' welfare, typically in the form of either money or time, on behalf of others (Monroe, 1994). The action that benefits others without costing some of the actor's own welfare is not defined as philanthropic behavior. While the first element is related to an action, the second element describes a motive for the action.

The complete understanding of individual philanthropic behavior, however, would be challenging since philanthropy occurs as the complex form of behavior that is closely aligned with "personality, bursting with idiosyncratic visions, unsupported claims, and deeply held passions" (Frumkin, 2006, p. 253). Private volunteering and motives for giving are personal with multiple purposes and causes (Frumkin, 2006). Accordingly, there are multiple explanations as to why individuals act charitably, ranging from "joy of giving" and "public recognition" to "desire to help the needy" (Mount, 1996).

To reflect the complex nature of private philanthropic behavior, multiple perspectives that are founded on different academic disciplines, such as economics, psychology, biology, and sociology, are adopted. Different perspectives illustrate distinctive aspects of philanthropic behavior. Economic perspectives are associated with individual interests to obtain economic benefits from philanthropic activity, psychological perspectives with understanding individual charitable behavior in complex psychological frameworks that describe the mental status of individuals, and sociological perspectives with emphasizing the social frameworks that define social norms and expectations as a motivation driver for individuals' helping behavior.

Other important variants include evolutionary biology perspectives that emphasize the importance of biological and genetic makeup to explain philanthropic activity, and perspectives of social cognitive perception that focus on social learning to define moral values and standards. Unlike other perspectives that begin with the assumption that individuals serve their own interests, social cognition perspectives start from the assumption that charitable behavior is an altruistic and compassionate act that emanates from an individual's worldview and self-perception in relation to others, respectively (Monroe, 1994).

Economic Perspectives

The main thrust of the economic perspective is to promote economic benefits and material interests through philanthropic activity. Philanthropic activity is considered one of the strategic means to maximize individual utility. *Reciprocal donation*—what is offered in return for charitable actions—is the most important consideration in this perspective. The economic return that donors realize can be "the recognition granted by the recipient organizations in the forms of a name placed on a plaque or building . . . [or] an invitation to serve on an influential nonprofit board . . . [or] an invitation to a special gala celebration" (Frumkin, 2006, p. 261). Other individual economic benefits from charitable activity include the promotion of favorable publicity and stronger connections with customers.

In addition, private philanthropy is promoted through the U.S. income tax system by providing incentives for donors to deduct charitable gifts from their gross income. This deduction is believed to be an effective means to encourage giving. The incentive effect of the tax deduction on giving by individuals is explained by *price* (or net cost) of giving, which is $1 minus the marginal tax rate. For example, the price for individuals who are subject to a 30% marginal tax rate would be 70 cents per $1 of giving. When marginal tax rates are increased, the price of giving decreases, which in turn encourages individuals to make a charitable gift (Clotfelter, 1997). Conversely, the opposite effect can occur when marginal tax rates are cut, thereby increasing the cost of giving. The effect of such a change is historically noted by changes in giving behaviors between the years 1986 and 1987, corresponding with the enactment of the Tax Reform Act of 1986, a measure that essentially reduced the marginal tax rate for itemizers. According to itemized deductions in 1986, charitable giving peaked that year. Researchers attribute this increase to tax-payer anticipation to changes in the tax code, which were to go into effect beginning with the 1987 tax year. Therefore, in 1987, the first official year of the new tax code and the point at which giving became more expensive, giving dropped sharply by 10% (Brown, 1999). In the economic model, Brown suggests that upper-income donors are generally more sensitive to changes in the tax code than lower income donors.

Psychological Perspectives

The principles of psychological perspectives reflect views held by economists who accept self-interest as an underlying premise of philanthropic acts. Psychologists understand the act of helping others as a way to obtain psychic gratification; making others happy brings happiness and pleasure to philanthropic actors in return (Monroe, 1994). Basically, philanthropic behavior is a purposeful action to satisfy psychological and emotional needs. Three major traits that lead individuals to develop helping behaviors are common among philanthropic donors (Frumkin, 2006). The first trait is related to empathy. It involves the ability of individuals to place themselves in others' deprived situations. This emotional awareness of others' needs is possible through imagination and sympathy (Adam Smith, 1976). Such empathy is often highly developed in women, which suggests reasons why women are generally more generous than men (Mesch, Rooney, Steinberg, & Denton, 2006). This will be explained in more detail in the next section.

The second trait is obligation that arises from a sense of duty or moral binding that manifests in individuals as a strong feeling toward helping others. Philanthropic practices are one of the practical forms of expressing such feeling. The last important trait is a prosocial value that refers to the emotional desire to be part of a community and connected to others. Giving or volunteering becomes a means to connect with others who have similar values and purposes and the social networks through which they belong.

Other psychological expectations that individuals hope to meet through philanthropic activity could be career advancement, enhancement in self-esteem, and a deeper understanding of one's community (Clary & Snyder, 1995). Volunteering and giving experiences offer a feeling of reward. Volunteering for charitable organizations can provide experiences that would benefit one's career while giving can offer social contacts that are useful to one's career. Participation in philanthropic endeavors that helps others and promotes a worthy cause may serve to increase feelings of self-esteem and self-worth (Clary & Snyder, 1995). Finally, contributing and volunteering can provide individuals with opportunities to learn more about the cultural life of the community and better understand the world around them (Clary & Synder, 1995).

Social Learning Perspectives

The social learning perspective is a theoretical variant of the psychological perspectives that define individuals as self-interested beings who help others to make them feel good about themselves (Frumkin, 2006; Monroe, 1994). From this perspective, building on studies of social cognition that examine how people process information necessary for social interaction, it can be argued that charitable acts are altruistic and compassionate behaviors activated by individuals' moral standards and values about caring for others' welfare, not from the desire to satisfy personal psychic needs (Monroe, 1994). This ethical system is internalized through social learning by people observing and emulating a critical role model, particularly in early childhood. Education, religion, and parents play an important role for social learning. Specifically, this perspective is well suited to explaining empirical findings on philanthropic behavior, suggesting that the likelihood of being generous to others increases with higher levels of educational attainment, religious affiliation, and positive parental role modeling. In short, the moral and ethical systems built through social learning processes, not the benefits from the action, trigger individuals to act charitably. This altruistic behavior is evidenced in cases where some donors do not disclose their names and maintain a distance from the beneficiary.

Evolutionary Biology Perspective

The biological perspective emanates from evolutional biology that defines helping behavior as a "built-in evolutionary mechanism" to enhance the chance of survival for a group—group individuals have a strong bond based on (1) common community interest or similarity in nature; and (2) kinship, or sharing a genetic pool (Monroe, 1994; Wilson, 1975). Basically, helping behavior is a natural phenomenon to enhance the chance of group members' survival in the process of natural selection.

Engaging in this helping behavior is commonly found in the human and natural world. First, individuals are willing to sacrifice for those who may be needy or sick or people with whom they have close relationships—friends, for example—as well as to forgo their own welfare for the sake of future generations—environmental protection, for example (Arrow, 1972). The second case is evidenced in humans' (and animals') willingness to sacrifice themselves for the sake of their offspring (Wolfe, 1998). One good example is found in informal philanthropic giving and volunteering where individuals donate their money and time to their family, relatives, and close friends without expecting reciprocity.

Sociological Perspectives

The social perspectives viewpoint offers an understanding of private philanthropic behavior as a by-product of social pressure and expectations that occur in social contexts in which individuals interact with others. Individuals are generally expected to follow norms, traditions, and practices defined by social contexts. The failure to conform to social expectations brings about social punishment in the form of embarrassment and negative distinction.

Helping others through charity is not so different from individual behaviors that are subject to social norms (Frumkin, 2006). The failure to give may result in gendering an ill-perceived image of individuals or even embarrassment, particularly in highly socialized settings, such as peer groups, religious organizations, or traditional society.

As much as social punishment pressures individuals to give or volunteer, social rewards play a significant role in promoting such charitable acts. Among the rewards is the expansion of one's social network, as well as access to elite networks. First, philanthropic behavior forges a social tie among donors, the recipient(s), and the community that individuals belong to (Mount, 1996) as well as connects donors who share common interests and a desire to improve others' welfare. This positive interaction is more likely to lead to other social opportunities that share philanthropic work and activity. As to accessing elite groups, charitable giving offers "entrée into social groups and communities that have social prestige, political power, or business ties" (Frumkin, 2006, p. 258). The amount of giving that demonstrates social position and power is often used to determine membership for elite groups.

Who Gives and Volunteers?

Who gives and volunteers? Obviously, it is not easy to answer the question since the philanthropic decision is convoluted with private motives, visions, and purposes. As such, it is important to link philanthropic behavior to individuals' lifestyle choices that describe who they are, how they spend their time, and what is important to them (Heidrich, 1990). Building on theoretical perspectives of philanthropic motives and philanthropic literature, a number of factors can be seen as influencing an individual's decision to participate in charitable activities and provide an explanation for why. The determinants include age, marital status and relationship, education, religiosity, and income. Although the determinants are interactive and all contribute to the donative decision as a whole rather than individually, each determinant is described as an individual unit for analysis. The possible interactions between these determinants are also addressed in the concluding discussion.

Age

Does age matter in terms of philanthropic motivations? Several studies suggest that older adults tend to be more active in giving and volunteering than younger people (Nichols, 1992; Putnam, 2000). In addition, they are reported to be the largest contributors to charitable organizations (Mathur, 1996), and among them, people aged 50 to 64 are the most active givers (Edmondson, 1986). Some people may argue that the greater likelihood of giving among older adults is simply related to the fact that they tend to have more money to give away than younger people. To address this concern, Steinberg and Wilhelm (2003) statistically controlled the impact of wealth on the giving behaviors among the three adult generations: prewar (born 1945 or earlier), baby boom (born 1946 to 1964), and generation X (born 1965 and after). According to the study, there are significant differences in generosity between generations. Specifically, the younger generations are about one third less generous than those of the prewar group. Likewise, the baby boomers appear more generous than gen-Xers in terms of total giving.

What explains this decline in charitable participation that occurs from one generation to the next? The appropriate answer may be related to the decline in social capital, the accumulation of social interactions and relationships, which is known to be the vital ingredient for trust and civic engagement and actions toward promoting common purposes and interests (Brown & Ferris, 2007; Putnam, 2000). Another plausible answer would be related to the fact that older adults are more likely to be affiliated with religious organizations. Religious affiliation encourages one to develop moral and ethical systems to value helping others as well as offers associational networks where such actions are encouraged.

Religiosity

It is not hard to connect religiosity with individual generosity as numerous studies indeed suggest that people who identify as having a religious affiliation tend to be more generous with their giving not only to religious organizations but also to nonreligious organizations (Clotfelter, 1997; Hodgkinson & Weitzman, 1996). One of the reasons for this is that religion and religious organizations serve both as a source of learning about generosity and social responsibility and as a point of mobilization for congregants around various charitable endeavors (Frumkin, 2006). People in religious organizations are more likely to understand the importance of being generous to others and to be encouraged to act on this understanding. A charitable action is easier to mobilize in religious communities since they serve as social epicenters for people to meet and interact with others who hold similar values. In this setting, people are more likely to be asked to engage in philanthropic activities.

However, providing a complete explanation as to how religiosity contributes to charitable actions is difficult since the relationship is more indirect than direct (Powell, 1998). Moreover, as much as religion offers learning opportunities and associational networks through which individuals are encouraged to participate in charitable activities, education seems to offer a similar positive effect.

Education

How does the level of educational attainment influence an individual's decision to participate in charitable activities? Studies suggest that a positive relationship exists between educational attainment and philanthropic involvement (Brown, 1999; Gittell & Tebaldi, 2006). Specifically, Gittell and Tebaldi find that U.S. states with higher levels of educational attainment among residents, particularly adults with a master's or a doctorate-level degree, have higher levels of giving: "A 1% increase in the adult population with a graduate degree increases average giving per tax filer by about $30.10" (2006, p. 731).

Although several explanations can be provided for this behavioral pattern of philanthropy, social learning and sociological perspectives seem the most convincing. Education helps individuals to be more cognizant about their world or community, which allows them to recognize the importance of others' well-being and to value charitable causes. As for the sociological explanation, education provides individuals with access to social groups in which they are more likely to be exposed to appeals for civic and social obligations (Brown, 2001). One major difference in the charitable activities between higher educational achievers and religiously affiliated individuals would be their charitable preferences. The high educational achievers tend to focus on social causes, such as the arts or higher education. Conversely, the religiously affiliated individual's preference, to a large extent, is directed to his or her affiliated religious organizations and the nonreligious organizations that share the same set of values.

Marital Status

Does marital status have any effect on charitable giving? According to a number of studies, it apparently does. Married couples are not only more likely to make charitable gifts than single people, but also they are more likely to contribute significantly more than singles when they do give (Mesch et al., 2006). When the giving behaviors of married couples, single men, and single women are compared as three separate groups, single men are the least likely to participate in charitable activities. Bryant, Jeon-Slaughter, Kang, and Tax (2003) conclude that the explanation for this phenomenon lies in the sociological

perspectives on charitable giving. People who are single or divorced have smaller social networks than people who are married. In other words, married couples share each other's networks. As we have addressed earlier, social networks serve as a primary source of encouragement to participate in philanthropic endeavors.

In addition to marital status, the role of marriage and the relationship dynamics between the married partners impact giving in three distinct ways: (1) whether or not they decide to make a gift, (2) the amount of their giving, and (3) which types of causes they decide to support (Andreoni, Brown, & Rischall, 2003). More specifically, the individual in the relationship who is the dominant wage earner tends to be the primary decision maker when it comes to charitable giving, although many couples claim to make charitable decisions jointly. Thus, when the male plays the dominant role, the giving tends to be more strategic and concentrated on fewer charities; conversely, when the female plays the dominant role, the giving tends to be spread among a number of different charities, making smaller gifts to each. This distinctive style of giving is related to gender-specific traits. (A more in-depth discussion of gender is provided in the following section.) Where couples make the charitable decisions jointly, the giving tends more to reflect the male's interests and preferences.

Similarly, understanding who in the relationship plays the dominant role can also serve as a predictor for which types of organizations married couples support (Andreoni et al., 2003). For example, in couples where the female partner plays the dominant role, the likelihood is significantly higher that they will choose to support health, education, or religious organizations. In couples where the male plays the dominant role, adult recreation organizations tend to be significantly favored. Support for other types of organizations such as human services, environment, youth development, or private community foundations receive no preferential treatment according to which member of the couple plays the dominant role. Further, married couples tend to give more when they jointly make their charitable decisions (Brown, 2006).

Important to note is the fact that, over time, women's influence in charitable decision making has steadily increased; this is largely explained by their increased roles in the labor market and their resulting increased financial position within married couples. This trend is expected to continue; thus, charities may want to consider this as they develop and refine solicitation strategies for married couples (Brown, 2006).

Gender

How does gender play a role in philanthropic activities? Gender matters when it comes to giving. Several researchers report that single women are significantly more generous than single men, even after controlling for differences in income and education (Mesch et al., 2006).

Why does the difference in giving between genders exist? The answer is related to how men and women process and exhibit charitable activity. Helping behavior is a more highly developed trait in women than it is in men. Women feel a greater sense of empathy toward others, while men are more self-serving and strategic (Brown, 2006; Mesch et al., 2006; Mills, Pedersen, & Grusec, 1989).

While these differences are rather complex to fully comprehend, a better understanding can be achieved by comparing the different giving patterns exhibited between genders. For example, women tend to make smaller-sized gifts than men do, even when they earn similar salaries; women often require some financial education before they are comfortable making substantial gifts; and women tend to take more time between the moment they are asked for a gift and the point at which they offer a positive or negative response (Hall, 2004).

Similarly, when contemplating a financial contribution, men more than women tend to take into account tax benefits or the price of giving (Andreoni et al., 2003). Also, when determining the size of a gift, men are more sensitive to variations in their own personal income. Women, on the other hand, often spread out their giving among many organizations in smaller denominations, whereas men will make larger gifts to fewer charities. This can be explained through the fact that women, on average, still earn somewhat lower salaries than men, and women tend to live longer thus requiring that their financial resources be sustained for more years as older adults (Hall, 2004). What this means to charitable giving is evidenced in women's participation in planned giving; they often wait until their end of life to make their largest, most significant charitable gifts (Brown, 2001; Hall, 2004).

This discussion of the various charitable giving determinants relates to how income affects the donor's propensity to participate in charitable giving. This is not a surprise, given the fact that one's ability to give, determined by income and/or wealth, is a critical beginning point for charitable decision making. Moreover, it is well understood that discretionary resources must be present before a donor is willing to offer any donation at all (Schervish & Havens, 1997).

Income

The propensity to make charitable contributions increases with income level (Andreoni, Gale, & Scholz, 1996; Brown, 2001). Households with higher incomes have a greater likelihood not only of participating in charitable giving but also of making larger gifts on average when they do give. To clarify, although the extent of giving is directly associated with the size of the donors' income, the decision to make a charitable donation is not (Frumkin, 2006); rather, it is the result of a combination of factors merely relevant to the level of income, such as education and external pressures from social groups. More

interestingly, however, is that the effect of income on the size of giving is minimal when giving as a share of personal income is considered (Schervish & Havens, 1995). Similarly, a temporary change in income does not necessarily affect the extent of giving (Brown, 2001). These results suggest that the variation of the effect of income level on the amount of giving depends on the data used to measure income level (temporary income versus income over a longer time period) and giving (giving as a total amount versus giving as a share of personal income). Caution should be paid as to the choice of the data and the implication on empirical findings.

Another interesting area concerns the giving styles of individuals who hold great wealth. As income levels increase, donors' attention shifts from religious to nonreligious charities. Studies have found that wealthier donors tend to direct their support to higher education and arts organizations. Additionally, wealthy donors will often make large gifts to the causes they are most enthusiastic about. They do this not just because they can but also because they seek to make a significant impact with their giving rather than merely offering a small token of support (Brown, 2001; Clotfelter, 1997; Schervish, 2005).

Summary and Future Study

This chapter examined what leads people to engage in philanthropic activities and who most frequently demonstrates them. The approach to understanding private philanthropy is multidimensional; perspectives of several academic disciplines, including economics, psychology, social cognition, evolutionary biology, and sociology, are adopted to highlight different aspects of charitable giving and volunteering. Each of these perspectives is founded on its academic principles and traditions and contributes to a unique understanding of the underlying motives for private philanthropy. All perspectives, except the social learning perspectives, explain private philanthropic behavior as a means for fulfilling the donor's self-interests, desires, and needs but not pure altruism per se. More specifically, the economic perspectives pay attention to economic returns, both monetary (e.g., tax deduction) and nonmonetary (e.g., favorable publicity and recognition, improved customer relations), whereas the psychological perspectives put their major emphases on psychic gratification and emotional needs, such as a desire to help, a need to be connected with others, and an advancement in self-esteem. In addition, the sociological perspectives shed light on the important role of the expectations and group norms for giving that emerge from the community networks with which one is affiliated and the desire many individuals have to expand their social ties and to access elite social groups who demonstrate prestige and political power.

When it comes to the evolutionary biology perspectives, the explanations are found in evolutionary mechanisms that increase the chance of survival for the group with which charitable donors share community interests or have a familial relationship. Separated from the other perspectives that lay their foundations on the premise of self-serving individuals to explain philanthropic behavior, the social learning perspectives shed a more positive light on giving by recognizing that it is a critical function of the moral standards and values that individuals build on and internalize through social learning (e.g., observing and imitating a critical role model).

In addition, the key demographic groups and the patterns of their charitable giving behavior are explored. Theoretical perspectives are particularly useful to explain the rationales behind the philanthropic actions of various groups of people. Six major determinants for philanthropic activities are identified, including age, gender, marital status, educational attainment, religiosity, and income. First, there is a pattern of philanthropic behavior that suggests a greater tendency to give and volunteer among individuals with higher social status (age, education, and income) and religious affiliations. The appropriate reason for this tendency is well explained by the sociological perspectives that highlight the important role of associational networks that social status brings from philanthropic acts (Frumkin, 2006); in the networks, individuals are more likely to be asked and encouraged to give and volunteer. In addition, the perspectives that highlight the importance of social learning seem effective to explain the influence of educational attainment and religiosity on charitable actions. Education and churches can provide individuals with social learning opportunities to build moral standards and ethical values, which is an important ingredient for charitable activities.

Second, gender matters when it comes to giving. Women are more likely to give than men. The psychological perspectives that highlight this personal trait among women, who have a greater ability to identify with others' feelings and difficulties than men do, serve well to explain this giving pattern. Finally, we cannot ignore the economic aspect of philanthropy; people donate their time and money in return for their own personal gains, either material (e.g., tax deduction) or nonmaterial (e.g., reputation enhancement, improved customer relations) as manifested in reciprocal giving.

To further our understanding of private philanthropic behavior, scholars need to pay more attention to the following areas. First, there has been a lack of effort to understand philanthropic behavior among diverse ethnic populations that represent distinctive cultural backgrounds and traditions, such as Asian American, Hispanic, and African American. Of course, philanthropic behavior is expected to be as diverse as the various ethnic groups, such as differences among Chinese, Filipino, Japanese, and Korean. Individuals with different countries of origin have their own cultural heritage that affects their perception toward helping others, although the level of influence would vary with levels of acculturation and Americanization as well as between different generations. In other words, individuals who are more acculturated are less likely to be influenced by their own cultural heritage that defines what is most appropriate and valuable in relation to being generous to others. Similarly, third-generation immigrants are more likely to be acculturated than first- and second-generation immigrants; thus, their definition of what is moral and ethical is less influenced by their cultural heritage but more subjected to the mainstream culture where they have grown up.

References and Further Readings

Andreoni, J., Brown, E., & Rischall, I. (2003). Charitable giving by married couples: Who decides and why does it matter? *Journal of Human Resources, 38*(1), 111–133.

Andreoni, J., Gale, W. G., & Scholz, J. K. (1996). *Charitable contributions of time and money* (University of Wisconsin–Madison Working Paper). Retrieved January 21, 2009, from http://econ.ucsd.edu/~jandreon/WorkingPapers/ags-v8.pdf

Arrow, K. A. (1972). Gifts and exchanges. *Philosophy and Public Affairs, 1*(4), 343–362.

Brown, E. (1999). Patterns and purposes of philanthropic giving. In C. T. Clotfelter & T. Ehrlich (Eds.), *Philanthropy and the nonprofit sector* (pp. 212–230). Bloomington: Indiana University Press.

Brown, E. (2001). *Making philanthropy work: Social capital and human capital as predictors of household giving* (Working Papers 2001-37). Pomona, CA: Claremont Colleges.

Brown, E. (2006, Winter). Married couples' charitable giving: Who and why. *New Directions for Philanthropic Fundraising, 50*, 69–80.

Brown, E., & Ferris, J. M. (2007). Social capital and philanthropy: An analysis of the impact of social capital on individual giving and volunteering. *Nonprofit and Voluntary Sector Quarterly, 36*(1), 85–99.

Bryant, W. K., Jeon-Slaughter, H., Kang, H., & Tax, A. (2003). Participating in philanthropic activities: Donating money and time. *Journal of Consumer Policy, 26*(1), 43–73.

Clary, E. G., & Snyder, M. (1995). Motivations for volunteering and giving: A functional approach. *New Directions in Philanthropic Fundraising, 8*(Summer), 111–123.

Clotfelter, C. T. (1997). The economics of giving. In J. W. Barry & B. V. Manno (Eds.), *Giving better, giving smarter: Working papers of the National Commission on Philanthropy and Civic Renewal* (pp. 31–55). Washington, DC: National Commission on Philanthropy and Civic Renewal.

Clotfelter, C., & Ehrlich, T. (2001). *Philanthropy and the nonprofit sector in a changing America.* Bloomington: Indiana University Press.

Dawkins, R. (1976). *The selfish gene.* Oxford, UK: Oxford University Press.

Edmondson, B. (1986). Who gives to charity? *American Demographics, 8*(11), 45–49.

Frumkin, P. (2006). *Strategic giving: The art and science of giving.* Chicago: University of Chicago Press.

Gittell, R., & Tebaldi, E. (2006). Charitable giving: Factors influencing giving in U.S. states. *Nonprofit and Voluntary Sector Quarterly, 35*(4), 721–736.

Hall, H. (2004). Gender differences in giving: Going, going, gone. *New Directions in Philanthropic Fundraising, 41*(Spring), 71–81.

Heidrich, K. W. (1990). Volunteers' life styles: Market segmentation based on volunteers' role choices. *Nonprofit and Voluntary Sector Quarterly, 19*(1), 21–31.

Hodgkinson, V. A. (2002). Individual giving and volunteering. In L. M. Salamon (Ed.), *The state of nonprofit America* (pp. 387–420). Washington, DC: Brookings Institution Press.

Hodgkinson, V. A., & Weitzman, M. (1996). *Giving and volunteering in the United States.* Washington, DC: Independent Sector.

Mathur, A. (1996). Older adults' motivations for gift giving to charitable organizations: An exchange theory perspective. *Psychology and Marketing, 13*(1), 107–123.

Mesch, D. J., Rooney, P. M., Steinberg, K. S., & Denton, B. (2006). The effects of race, gender, and marital status on giving and volunteering in Indiana. *Nonprofit and Voluntary Sector Quarterly, 35*(4), 565–587.

Mills, R. S., Pedersen, J., & Grusec, J. E. (1989). Sex differences in reasoning and emotion about altruism. *Sex Roles, 20*(11/12), 603–621.

Monroe, R. M. (1994). A fat lady in a corset: Altruism and social theory. *American Journal of Political Science, 38*(4), 861–893.

Mount, J. (1996). Why donors give. *Nonprofit Management & Leadership, 7*(1), 3–14.

Nichols, J. E. (1992). Targeting aging America. *Fund Raising Management, 23*(3), 38–41.

Powell, W. (1998). *Private action and the public good.* New Haven, CT: Yale University Press.

Putnam, R. D. (1995). Bowling alone: America's declining social capital. *Journal of Democracy, 6*(1), 65–78.

Putnam, R. D. (2000). *Bowling alone: The collapse and revival of American community.* New York: Simon & Schuster.

Salamon, L. M. (2002). *The state of nonprofit America.* Washington, DC: Brookings Institution Press.

Schervish, P. (2005). Major donors, major motives: The people and purposes behind major gifts. *New Directions in Philanthropic Fundraising, 2005*(47), 59–87.

Schervish, P., & Havens, J. J. (1995). Major factors influencing giving, wherewithal and beneficence: Charitable giving by income and wealth. *New Directions in Philanthropic Fundraising, 1995*(8), 81–109.

Schervish, P. G., & Havens, J. J. (1997). Social participation and charitable giving: A multivariate analysis. *Voluntas, 8*(3), 235–260.

Smith, A. (1976). *The theory of moral sentiments.* Oxford, UK: Clarendon Press.

Steinberg, R., & Wilhelm, M. (2003). Tracking giving across generations. *New Directions in Philanthropic Fundraising, 42*(Winter), 71–82.

Wilson, E. O. (1975). *Sociobiology.* Cambridge, MA: Harvard University Press.

Wolfe, A. (1998). What is altruism? In W. Powell (Ed.), *Private action and the public good* (pp. 36–46). New Haven, CT: Yale University Press.

88

MAINTAINING PERSONAL BALANCE AS A LEADER OF A NONPROFIT ORGANIZATION

MONIKA L. HUDSON

University of San Francisco

The best part of our life is disappearing into the john to sneak a smoke, or staring at screaming non-stop mills, our eyes unfocused, or standing judging whose sick joke is sickest. Yet nothing you could do could break our silence. We are a check. Do not expect a balance.

Joshua Mehigan (2008)

The expression "work-life balance" was first used in the United Kingdom during the late 1970s to describe individuals' attempts to better manage the amount of time they spent on professional versus personal life tasks ("Work-Life Balance Defined," n.d.). Over the years, as technology and other changes have narrowed the distinction between work and home life, the concept has become even more relevant. How might the conflict between having a successful work and personal life impact nonprofit leaders? Is it different from what business leaders experience as they confront these challenges?

This chapter examines the ways leaders attempt to create equilibrium between the amount of time spent on work versus nonwork activities within nonprofit organizations. It begins with a short review of the literature associated with nonprofit leadership and work-life balance. Next, it discusses what it means to be a nonprofit leader in the 21st century, where helping create workplace environments that allow organizational members to balance work and home life is just another chief executive responsibility. It then identifies a set of practices that nonprofit executives can use as they weave a balanced work-life perspective into their leadership toolkit. Finally, the chapter concludes with a list of additional readings and strategies individuals can consider if they want to more naturally implement personal and professional life balance.

The Nonprofit Sector and Leadership

The Sector

To begin to understand what work-life balance means for nonprofit leaders, it is important to first distinguish between the differing end goals of the for-profit and social sectors. Fundamentally, nonprofit organizations are established "to meet social objectives, human needs and national priorities that *cannot* be priced at a profit" (Collins, 2005, p. 19). What this means is that the measure of successful performance in the nonprofit arena is mission achievement rather than financial return (Collins, 2005), which is fundamentally different from what has come to count in the private sector. The differences in each sector's bottom line are incorporated into the component parts of what gets labeled as appropriate organizational leadership.

Nonprofit Leadership

The literature defines leadership as a set of activities that articulate an organization's vision and ensure that its stakeholders support the same. It commonly defines management as "activities required to ensure than an organization will reliably produce results" (Kotter, 1990, p. 4.) The inevitable tension between leadership and management is usually resolved by identifying a second-in-command individual who manages internal operations. This leaves the organizational leader free to work with the board of directors to develop a clear organizational strategy, precisely articulate it, anchor the strategy in a few key metrics, and build and align an organizational team to refine and implement the evolving strategy—the general purview of an organizational leader.

Crutchfield and Grant (2008) answered the question "what makes great nonprofits great" by stating that it was about having a great nonprofit chief executive. The authors define great chief executives as persons who act as leaders rather than managers and concurrently know how to share organizational power and leadership.

Most scholars have found that while the definition of what constitutes leadership or management tend to be similar, the practice of leadership often differs depending on whether one is examining the nonprofit or for-profit sector. For example, Crutchfield and Grant's findings regarding the importance of nonprofit leadership power sharing are captured in the concept of the *level 5 legislative leader* developed by Collins (2005). Collins's defining research regarding the dynamics of great for-profit firms was modified as he subsequently studied the nonprofit sector, and his level 5 leadership definition arose out of this difference. Collins stated that level 5 leaders are ambitious "first and foremost for the cause, . . . the mission . . . —not themselves—and they have the will to do whatever it takes to make good on that ambition" (p. 10). He noted that effective nonprofit leaders have to employ level 5 legislative strategies even as they face governance and power structures that render private sector, executive-style leadership tactics impractical. What Collins labeled as level 5 leadership, others have come to call the *female management style*. A key feature of this female management style is the notion of working smarter, not harder.

Work-Life Balance

The term *leadership* is not defined in the same ways in the social sectors as it is in the business world. What constitutes work-life balance is also characterized differently. In the 1970s and 1980s, the words *work-life challenge* were used as shorthand to refer to the fact that men and women had begun to prioritize career goals over family, friends, community affairs, and leisure activities. Today, technology extends this challenge further by connecting employees with their jobs on a 24-hour, 7-day basis. Joe Robinson, founder of Work to Live (www.worktolive.com), in a March 2009 note on his blog indicated that "a Boston College study found that 32% of employees and 58% of managers worked on 'vacation.' Many were wired for business on their time off via assorted laptops, cell phones and, most ominously, BlackBerrys. The e-mail pager's street handle—CrackBerry—testifies to the operative dynamic."

General impressions about what makes for equilibrium between work and personal life have also changed over the last 30 years. A 2007 annual survey conducted by the Kenexa Research Institute (KRI) evaluated the perceptions of 10,000 U.S.-based male and female workers about work-life balance. KRI found that women are more positive than men as to their feelings about organizations' efforts to help them weigh work and home life responsibilities. These results indicate that people's perceptions about the need for work-life balance have changed significantly over the last decade. Traditionally, it was women who stated that it was more difficult to balance competing pressures at work and demands at home. Now, men are also finding that their lives are more consumed with family and other personal responsibilities and interests. To attract and retain employees, organizations of all types find they must formally develop ways of supporting equilibrium between the work and home fronts.

Multigenerational thinking is also coming into play as the new wave of *millennials*—the 25- to 35-year-olds, who have been labeled as the next great group of social innovators and leaders—enters the workforce. Research indicates that millennials' mastery of the emerging social and technological networked systems and their idealistic and energetic problem-solving approaches are transforming the nonprofit landscape (Hensen, 2008). The new skill sets of the incoming millennial wave, coupled with baby boomer retirements, are causing 21st-century nonprofit executives to necessarily broaden their leadership perspectives to include the notion that making the world a better place is more than about just competitive positioning or successful fundraising. Rather, by necessity, it must incorporate a perspective that weaves the so-called personal and professional together in a seamless pattern. The millennials don't "turn off" when they leave the workplace. Incorporating work-life balance becomes challenging when employees and their leaders are committed to the organization, its goals and values on a "24-7" clock. When not punching in or out is the norm, how can nonprofit leaders create environments that minimize burn-out and maximize performance-oriented cultures that respect a person's need to find balance, even when the lines of what constitutes work and life aren't clearly articulated by the individual?

Achieving Work-Life Balance

The best nonprofit leaders have a mind-set that focuses on strategic mission clarity, strategy articulation, performance metrics based on mission, shared leadership, and team alignment with organizational mission. The relevant performance metrics for a nonprofit leader relate to mission achievement, irrespective of bottom-line profits generated for shareholders. Does such a leader approach the question of work-life balance any differently than one of the captains of more traditional industries?

In their examination of work-life balance, Muna and Mansour (2007) point out that effective leaders concurrently juggle more than one task yet distinguish between issues that are urgent and those that can be held off for a more opportune time. The authors note that recognized business executives often indicate that the act of balancing work, family, and personal life is a skill that these individuals wished they had managed better. These leaders stated that despite being proficient in effectively addressing short- and long-term issues in their organizations, they spent little time on planning and executing actions that would improve their personal lives.

Clearly, nonprofit leaders need to learn from the private sector and not simply repeat their mistakes. So, what is going to make for a more effective 21st-century-nonprofit leader? One answer lies in encouraging more of what might be called a *millennial mind-set*. This more balanced sense of work-life relationships was described by researcher Nippert-Eng (2005) as an *integrationalist approach*, where the mental, physical, behavioral, and interpretive boundaries between the home and work worlds are completely diffuse.

To be classified as "excellent," nonprofit executives must incorporate a millennial or integrator mode of networked thinking into their leadership repertoire. Work and life are now seen as part of an interwoven continuum rather than separate and distinct spheres. This leadership perspective is designed to countermand myopic "readings of life and work that overlook work as a source of satisfaction and life as encompassing more than just childcare" (Warhurst, Eikof, & Haunschild, 2008, p. 2). Excellent nonprofit leaders are now modifying their respective organizational environments to create standard policies that allow employees to take sabbaticals, job share, arrange for child or eldercare leave, work from home, or work fewer or part-time hours. This new way of thinking is creating a more "virtual" workforce that closely mirrors the evolving wireless technology web. These leaders also recognize that measuring performance is a more valuable metric than measuring "face-time."

Millennials desire to make a difference, and their belief that social and environmental justice are not just ideals also influences the ways that perceptive nonprofit leaders see themselves as organizational players. In some ways, the call to *make the ideal real* supports the preexisting notion of chief executive as power center. On the other hand, the so-called ideal-real perspective is antithetical to the business notion of emphasizing only metrics that demonstrate financial gain. Research indicates that the private sector is learning from the nonprofit world. When long-term sustainability is part of the equation, all 21st-century organizations—private, public, or nonprofit—find nonsustainable work environments block performance achievement. Effective leaders are aware that work-to-family conflicts as well as family-to-work conflicts affect the mental and physical health of working men and women (Muna & Mansour, 2007), which leads to an inherently untenable proposition.

Future Directions

Being an effective leader in an organization requires the use of various strategies and behaviors. Kouzes and Posner (2008) outlined five practices or behaviors that people can use if they want to be effective leaders and achieve stellar performance. Their book cites a number of private sector leaders, although they interviewed managers and leaders from a wide variety of organizations. The results of their findings were used to identify best practice leadership behavior in general. Applying these concepts to the nonprofit world, particularly to address work-life conflict, serves a strategic purpose. The nonprofit executive who implements these practices gains personal and institutional advantages. The sense is that these leadership practices can both help change organizational cultures and result in more work-life friendly environments.

Kouzes and Posner's five practices include (1) challenging the process, (2) inspiring a shared vision, (3) enabling others to act, (4) modeling the way, and (5) encouraging the heart. If nonprofit leaders are serious about incorporating more balance into their personal and professional lives, these principles provide a framework for moving from theory to practice.

Challenging the process, the first practice, enables nonprofit leaders to put Collins's (2005) previously referenced notion of level 5 leadership into practice. This type of leadership involves exploration, experimentation, and risk taking, characteristics that typify the emerging millennial population. When routine procedures are challenged on a regular basis, the problem-solving skills and creativity reserves of individuals tend to engage to achieve success. Research indicates that leaders have to exercise their risk-taking skills on a routine basis to keep their *opportunity eyes* sharp so they can take advantage of small windows of chance as they appear (Muna & Mansour, 2007).

The joy and energy that comes from creative exploration, experimentation, and risk taking typically makes the heart beat faster; it's what allows people to push themselves to the limit. Katherine Graham, the first female CEO of the *Washington Post*, famously said, "to love what you do and feel that it matters—how could anything be more fun?" (Barsh, Cranston, & Craske, 2008). These remarks came as this leader allowed her editor and two unproven reporters to continue to investigate allegations against the then president of the United States, while she experienced the withering pressure of being labeled an "un-American"! Research has found that leaders who challenge the way often have a feeling of transcendence because contributing to something larger than themselves generates a deeper sense of meaning and purpose. As Carole St. Mark, who began her career as a human resource manager, stated, "Because I was put in jobs where I didn't have the technical training, . . . I just did what made sense to me. And that usually worked better than trying to apply a theory" (Swiss, 1996, p. 84). That willingness to use practical thinking along with theory is a mark of the millennial nonprofit leader.

The second practice, *inspiring a shared vision*, merely requires that nonprofit executives do what they are already hired to do: enlist other individuals in mission achievement. The intent is to leverage the capacity of the group to accomplish the goals of the nonprofit organization, recognizing that group outcomes usually exceed those that can be accomplished by one or two individuals operating alone. This practice also engages fellow workers to share in the process of identifying organizational goals and values knowing that this participation can lead to greater commitment and an associated desire to implement activities that are designed to reach such mutually developed goals. Proactive millennial leaders sometimes choose to exercise this practice by gathering coworkers in their home to seek input on important organizational strategies. They indicate that their fellow employees remark that "the connection makes it more pleasant to work together" (Swiss, 1996, p. 27).

Another way to inspire a common vision is for optimistic, millennial leaders to encourage coworkers to engage in what is called *positive framing*. Research has shown that optimists actually see life more realistically than pessimists do (Barsh, Cranston, & Craske, 2008). This ability arises from the fact that optimists are confident that they can both manage life's challenges and move to action. Pessimists, on the other hand, are more likely to feel helpless and consequently get stuck in downward spirals of rumination.

Proactive nonprofit executives distinguish between positive framing and positive thinking on a personal and organizational level. Positive thinking merely replaces adversity with positive beliefs, while positive framing counters adversity with action. Research indicates that people can only temporarily "self-talk" themselves into a view that is actually contrary to the facts; however, they have a longer-term capacity to overcome negative self-talk when they take affirmative action. Thus, when negative events occur, millennial leaders and their fellow employees conduct quick postmortems, seek interpersonal support, and develop action plans that allow for energy restoration—such as collectively engaging in a service activity. All of these activities help the organization as a whole inspire shared vision.

Enabling others to act is the third practice. This concept reminds successful leaders that they are one point of power: When they work with followers and promote coworkers' leadership, only then can long-term organizational success be ensured. Enabling others to act requires that leaders provide their followers with the tools, resources, and permission giving necessary for followers to take ownership of their goals and perform. This is an area of vulnerability for many leaders because the scarcity of time, people, and money often makes it easier to simply complete assignments rather than create the space to train and develop others. Millennial leaders know that they gain in the long run when they either directly empower coworkers to make decisions or provide them with tools (e.g., laptops and cell phones) that enable alternative job arrangements designed to meet the needs of each worker.

The fourth principle of *modeling the way* encourages executives to remember that their behaviors impact coworkers. Modeling the way requires that nonprofit leaders affirm their values and then align their behaviors with these values. The authors note that by demonstrating personal values through consistent action, executives create a more authentic leadership identity. So there is the example of Dr. Muhammad Yunus, of whom the 2006 Nobel Peace Committee declared, "he has shown himself to be a leader who has managed to translate visions into practical action for the benefit of millions of people, not only in Bangladesh, but also in many other countries" (Nobel Peace Committee press release, Oslo, October 13, 2006. p. 1). Dr. Yunus has subsequently inspired not just members of his various organizations but spurred the growth of U.S.-based microfinancing organizations, such as Kiva, whose millennial founder cites the values–action alignment of Grameen Bank and Dr. Yunus as one of the reasons he was attracted to microlending.

The final practice is titled *encouraging the heart*. While this principle is part of the definition of great leadership, it is often not acted on in real-life situations. Chief executives must remember that what inspires and nurtures them as nonprofit leaders also motivates others. By consciously moving into the role of passionate cheerleaders, nonprofit leaders enable their coworkers to see their work sites as places where they can "live to work" rather than simply "work to live." Recognizing performance and hard work in the nonprofit world, while a sign of great leadership, is even more meaningful when recognition is given to those who have overcome work-life challenges and still have the energy to provide 110%.

The application of the five Kouzes and Posner practices, in any order, provides a framework for an operative work-life friendly environment. The five practices represent a useful way to reflect on key personal and professional leadership and balance issues. Implementing new strategic directions, such as enabling millennials to work in new and different ways, requires leaders to behave in ways that enable high performance cultures. Using the five practices, for example, encourages nonprofit executives to apply networked and sustainable thinking on a day-to-day basis. They must, in Kouses and Posner's terms, "challenge the process" every day and look toward the needs and values of the workforce they will manage.

What needs to be challenged? How is networked thinking different in the nonprofit versus the for-profit world? With a goal orientation focused on mission accomplishment rather than financial rates of return, nonprofit leaders often get caught in what gets called the *trade-off* cycle. Under the trade-off way of thinking, time is a commodity that is doled out on a personal versus professional basis. Therefore, when a leader spends time fundraising or cultivating donors outside of the traditional 9-to-5 schedule, these hours are calculated and stored for subsequent "borrowing against" for personal activities. One hears this in the routine conversations of these chief executives—one "takes" compensatory time to attend a child's school activities against so-called overtime hours worked that one has "banked" from preparing a grant application during a prior time period.

When leaders are operating in the previously described mode, they engage in reactive thinking. The premise is the act of valuing time only as a commodity of exchange places the nonprofit leader in an if–then situation that trickles down to organizational employees. The *seamless perspective*—one where mission achievement is the intended outcome—views life as a means to an end, where the personal and professional are merged and both are aligned toward the same goal. Thus, time with family is concurrently an opportunity to use Twitter or LinkedIn to network online with professional colleagues; a nonprofit chief executive coshares housing to support a household on a less-than-corporate salary. Leaders who have the latter perspective are engaging in what could be called proactive millennial thinking. Figure 88.1 details some key differences between millennial and traditional thinking as they relate to the ways that nonprofit executives view their own leadership, donors, volunteers, and employees and organizational consumers, clients, and the community at large. At every step, millennial leaders take an integrative perspective that empowers others by valuing their role in fulfilling organizational mission.

This millennial perspective encompasses a way of thinking that embodies continual renewal, innovation, and rebirth. It moves away from the life span notion of "birth—mid-life—death" to what Gardner (1996) calls the *total system* approach—one where things are being born, flourishing, and dying, but the system, as a whole, continues.

These types of total-system, millennial-oriented nonprofit leaders ask their organizations to periodically revisit and reaffirm core values and implementing behaviors. They encourage benchmarking and so-called best-practice initiatives that raise the bar. An example of this is within the Baptist Health Care organization, where all employees are encouraged to look until they find "the best of the best" in their area of expertise and benchmark against it (Stubblefield, 2005, p. 23).

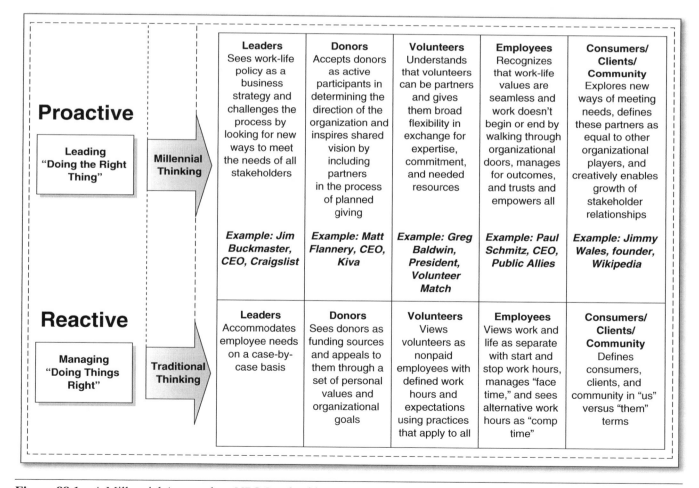

Figure 88.1 A Millennial Approach to NPO Leadership

SOURCE: Chart originally created by Monika Hudson in April 2009 as a way of demonstrating how the Kouzes and Posner concepts can be applied to each of the key constituents that most nonprofit leaders have to work with. Comments on the developing chart were provided by Dayle M. Smith, University of San Francisco.

Summary

This chapter began by reviewing the nonprofit sector, leadership, and work-life balance literature and by distinguishing between leadership and work-life balance in the nonprofit and private sectors. It continued by discussing several concepts that 21st-century nonprofit leaders want to consider as they frame their environment—networked thinking, sustainability, enacting ideals. The chapter concluded with some suggestions for one or two tools that interested individuals can use to enhance their leadership skills, whether or not they are considering nonprofit employment. The intent is to encourage leaders to strive for an authentic sense of self that integrates work with family, friends, community service, spiritual activities, physical exercise, and whatever else matters in their lives (Muna & Mansour, 2007).

Toward that end, it is suggested that readers identify leadership assessment tools and exercises that can support better self-knowledge, the practice of personal and professional leadership principles, the building of personal and organizational support teams, and general work-life integration. One place to begin may be a reference cited in this chapter. The evidence-based website, the Student Leadership Challenge (www.leadershipchallenge.com), contains assessments, journal exercises, and related tools developed by authors Kouzes and Posner (2008). It is a useful place to start identifying other resources available to assess personal and professional leadership capacity. These suggestions are offered understanding that, in the 21st century, successful nonprofit leaders and employees do not have the luxury of viewing success in the workplace and a fulfilling successful personal life as mutually exclusive options.

References and Further Readings

Barsh, J., Cranston, S., & Craske, R. A. (2008). Centered leadership: How talented women thrive. *McKinsey Quarterly*. Retrieved March 24, 2009, from www .mckinseyquarterly.com/article_print.aspx?L2=18&L3=31 &ar=2193

Bolman, L. G., & Deal, T. E. (1997). *Reframing organizations: Artistry, choice and leadership* (2nd ed.). San Francisco: Jossey-Bass.

Brock, B. L., & Grady, M. L. (2002). *Avoiding burnout: A principal's guide to keeping the flame alive*. Newberry Park, CA: Corwin.

Caproni, P. J. (2004). Work/life balance: You can't get there from here. *Journal of Applied Behavioral Science, 40*(2), 208–218.

Chung, R. G., & Lo, C. L. (2007). The relationship between leadership behavior and organizational performance in non-profit organizations, using social welfare charity foundations as an example. *Journal of American Academy of Business, Cambridge, 12*(1), 83–87.

Cohen, L., Duberley, J., & Musson, G. (2009). Work-life balance? An autoethnographic exploration of everyday home-work dynamics. *Journal of Management Inquiry, 18*(3), 229–241.

Collins, J. (2005). *Good to great and the social sectors* [Monograph, ISBN 13-978-0-9773264-0-2, published by author].

Crutchfield, L. R., & Grant, H. M. (2008). Forces for good: The six practices of high-impact nonprofits. San Francisco: Jossey-Bass. Review (L. Zumdahl) obtained from *ABI/INFORM Global: Social Work & Christianity, 35*(3), 346–349.

Dubrin, A. J. (2007). *Leadership: Research findings, practice and skills* (5th ed.). Boston: Houghton Mifflin. Review (J. L. Morrison) obtained from *ABI/INFORM Global: Journal of Education for Business*, 2007, September/October, 52–53.

Fisher, A. (2009, May 25). When gen X runs the show. *Time, 173*(20), 48.

Fitzpatrick, L. (2009, May 25). We're getting off the ladder. *Time, 173*(20), 45.

Friedman, S. (2008). *Total leadership: Be a better leader, have a richer life*. Boston: Harvard Business. Review (S. R. Ezzsdeen) obtained from *ABI/INFORM Global: Personnel Psychology*, 61(4), 936–938.

Gardner, J. W. (1996). Self-renewal. *Futurist, 30*(6), 9–12.

Gortner, D. T. (2009). Looking at leadership beyond our horizons. *Anglican Theological Review, 91*(1), 119–142.

Grant, H. M., & Crutchfield, L. (2008, Spring). The hub of leadership: Lessons from the social sector. *Leader to Leader, 48*, 45–52.

Green, L., Conners S. E., Green, S., & Mick, M. (2008). Put a leader on that horse (association), *Journal of the International Academy for Case Studies, 14*(4), 27–29.

Heifetz, R. A., & Linsky, M. (2002). *Leadership on the line: Staying alive through the dangers of leading*. Boston: Harvard Business School Press.

Hensen, J. C. (2008, Fall). A renaissance in nonprofit leadership. *Leader to Leader*, (50), 15–20.

Hillman, B. (1997). Time problem. *Poetry*. Retrieved March 13, 2009, from http://www.poetryfoundation.org/archive/poem.html

Jager, U., Kreutzer, K., & Beyes, T. (2009). Balancing acts: NPO-leadership and volunteering. *Financial Accountability & Management, 25*(1), 79–97.

Kopp, W. (2009, May 25). *Time, 173*(20), 54.

Kotter, J. (1990). *A force for change*. New York: Free Press.

Kouzes, J. M., & Posner, B. Z. (2008). *The student leadership challenge*. New York: John Wiley & Sons. Review (C. McPherson) obtained from *Planning for Higher Education*, 37 (2), 73–74, retrieved March 15, 2009, from http://0-proquest.umi.com.ignacio.usfca.edu/pqdweb?index=0&did=1620108151&SrchMode=2&sid=2&Fmt=3&VInst=PROD&VType=PQD&RQT=309&VName=PQD&TS=1237129606&clientId=16131

Mehigan, J. (2008, July/August). Work song. *Poetry*. Retrieved March 13, 2009, from http://www.poetryfoundation.org/archive/poem.html?id=181696

Muna, F. A., & Mansour, N. (2007). Balancing work and personal life: The leader as acrobat. *Journal of Management Development, 28*(2), 121–133.

Myners, P. (2008, September). Toughing it out at the top. *Management Today*, p. 29.

Nippert-Eng, C. E. (1995). *Home and work*. Chicago: University of Chicago Press.

Osif, B. A. (2009). Work/life balance. *Library Leadership & Management, 23*(1), 42–46.

Premeaux, S. F., Adkins, C. L., & Mossholder, K. W. (2007). Balancing work and family: A field study of multi-dimensional, multi-role, work-family conflict. *Journal of Organizational Behavior, 26*(6), 705–727.

Quackenbush, M., Bird, M. E., & Klein, S. J. (2008). Bill Kane: Passionate practitioner. *American Journal of Public Health, 98*(11), 1949–1952.

Robinson, J. (2003). *Work to live*. New York: Perigee.

Santora, J. C., & Sarros, J. C. (2008). Interim leadership in a nonprofit organization: A case study. *Business Review, Cambridge, 11*(2), 66–70.

Sherlock, J. J., & Nathan, M. A. (2007). Nonprofit association CEOs: How their context shapes what, how and why they learn. *Nonprofit Management & Leadership, 18*(1), 19–39.

Shipman, C., & Kay, K. (2009, May 25). Women will rule business. *Time, 173*(20), 48.

Stid, D., & Bradach, J. (2009). How visionary nonprofit leaders are learning to enhance management capabilities. *Strategy & Leadership, 37*(1), 35–40.

Stubblefield, A., & Lencioni, P. (2005). *The Baptist health care journey to excellence: Creating a culture that wows!* New York: John Wiley & Sons.

Sturges, J., & Guest, D. (2004). Working to live or living to work? Work/life balance early in the career. *Human Resource Management Journal, 14*(4), 5–20.

Swiss, D. (1996). *Women breaking through: Overcoming the final 10 obstacles at work*. Princeton, NJ: Pacesetter Books.

Tappin, S., & Cave, A. (2008). *The secrets of CEOs: 150 global chief executives lift the lid on business, life and leadership*. Boston: Nicholas Brealey.

Van Buren, J. (2004). *Everywhere except on top: Women executives in the nonprofit sector*. Unpublished manuscript, Case Western Reserve University, Cleveland, Ohio.

Warhurst, C., Eikof, D. R., & Haunschild, A. (Eds.). (2008). *Work less, live more? Critical analysis of the work-life boundary*. Basingstoke, NY: Palgrave Macmillan.

Work-life balance defined. (n.d.). Available from www.worklife balance.com

89

Professionalization of Leadership and the Rise of Formal Management and Leadership Education

Karabi Chaudhury Bezboruah

University of Texas at Arlington

The leadership of nonprofit organizations plays an important role in defining and furthering the mission and vision of the organization through exceptional management and leadership functions. In recent years, the traditional nonprofit management system has encountered serious challenges in the manner they have been operating. This challenge has come from the burgeoning focus on greater accountability and maintaining sustainability of the organization following several instances of transgression by nonprofit leadership. Well-known cases of misdeeds include fraud and tax evasion by the president of United Way of America in 1992, embezzlement by the chief executives of New Era Foundation in 1995 and American Parkinson's Disease Association in 1996 respectively, and mishandling of funds by the Red Cross in the scandal after September 2001, among many.

There was, concurrently, an evolving interest among entrepreneurs and leaders from the private for-profit world in the functions and operations of nonprofit organizations. These leaders believed in the inculcation of professionalized managerial and leadership skills in nonprofit administration. Due to this foray of for-profit management principles, the traditional form of nonprofit leadership is gearing up to meet this challenge. Professional leadership is an essential requirement for professional management of nonprofit organizations. The primary functions of nonprofit management include planning, clearly defining roles and responsibilities, budgeting, accurate accounting and reporting, tracking performance and evaluating results and outcomes, and collaborating, coordinating, and networking with external agencies including donors and the community. By performing the aforementioned functions properly, nonprofit executives can become professional leaders and further sustain the mission and future of their organizations.

This chapter examines the professionalization of leadership in nonprofit organizations by focusing on the need and growth of *professionalization*. Why did the need for professionalization arise? Was there anything wrong or ineffective in the way nonprofit organizations were led and managed earlier? What factors led to the increased demand for professionalization? By emphasizing professional leadership, are nonprofit scholars trying to implant concepts of the corporate for-profit world into the nonprofit world?

This chapter begins by examining the meaning of professional leadership followed by a discussion on its development. The succeeding section talks about the findings from the empirical research on how for-profit corporations decide on which nonprofit organization to select for support among many. One important finding of this research is the need for professionalism in the operation and administration of nonprofits. This finding leads the readers to the challenges in the next section. The challenges outlined point to the need for professionalization of leadership in this sector. Certain mechanisms have evolved in response to these challenges. Summary and conclusions and directions for future research then follow a discussion on professionalization of leadership.

Understanding the importance of professional leadership of nonprofit organizations is timely as well as significant for students who are likely to be practitioners in this area. Knowledge and awareness about professional leadership would assist in upholding the same. Although, historically, the nonprofit sector did not like the concept of management as it was considered to be a jargon of the for-profit corporate world, lately the blurring of the sectors have encouraged certain practices traditionally belonging to the corporate world to be adapted and emulated in the nonprofit world. Professionalism is one of them. Professional leadership by the chief executive, executive director, or the board of nonprofit organizations would only enhance the reputation and sustainability of the organization.

Professional Leadership Defined

Leadership in nonprofit organizations consists of the board and the chief executive. Hierarchically, the board is at the top followed by the chief executive; functionally, the board (comprised of voluntary members) defines the mission, implements policies, and steers the organization in the manner that ensures mission fulfillment. The chief executive, hired help, assists the board in their functions. Papandreou (1952) described the chief executive as the one figure at the helm of an organization that is responsible for managing the multiple conflicting demands with a "sense of the whole" (p. 190). Herman and Heimovics (2005) argue that this conventional model of board centrality, which is found in most normative literature on nonprofit leadership, falls short in the actual performance of boards. They cite Middleton's (1987) work on how nonprofit boards do not always fulfill their duties. Being at the head of an organization, the chief executive performs most of the managerial and leadership functions in conjunction with the board. Further, the chief executive implements the vision of the board. Although hierarchy exists in the organizational structure, when it comes to managing and leading, both the board and chief executive play equally important roles.

Nevertheless, the chief executive's role is very significant because this office supports the board in its functions, serves as the interface between the board and staff, and creates and sustains the mission and strategy for the organization. In addition to the aforementioned roles, certain other duties include overseeing the programs and service delivery, managing the available resources while scouting and seeking additional ones, maintaining documentation, and communicating and portraying the organization to its stakeholders. Only someone who is motivated and believes in the mission of the organization can perform this multiplicity of responsibilities. By serving the mission of the organization, the executive is serving the community while at the same time leading the organization toward its goals. This approach reflects the servant leadership style where a person serves first and then leads (Greenleaf, 1977).

The primary motivation of servant leaders is the desire to serve others. The chief executive of a nonprofit is a servant leader because the person serves the individuals of the organization and the community in the course of fulfilling the organizational mission, and is not influenced by money or power. This leadership style, however, is not an exception, and complements and enhances other leadership models (Senge, 1995). Further, servant leadership style is more appropriate for nonprofit managers because it matches the contemporary social, political, and economic conditions. This leadership style is considered more open, that is, more participatory with shared decision making. In addition, leaders following this style are also capable of maximizing opportunities and optimizing resources available to them. The open style, often practiced by nonprofit managers, allows them to rise to the top and lead the organization while serving the mission of the organization.

Senge (1995) stated that in the traditional perspective, a leader has the ability to establish direction, possesses decision-making authority, and takes responsibility for followers, which essentially reflects the individualistic view of the Western culture. Leaders, according to Senge (1995), need to be stewards of the organization, and the servant leadership style is well suited to organizations because of its focus on relationships and serving others. A chief executive of a nonprofit organization can be referred to as a steward because this executive, as mentioned earlier, serves the mission by steering the organization and the community in the direction of the mission. Based on Larry Spears's characterization of the servant leader's qualities, namely, listening, empathy, healing, persuasion, awareness, foresight, conceptualization, commitment to growth, stewardship, and focus on community, Carroll (2005) argued that servant leadership is ideal for nonprofit managers. Hunter's (2004) assertion that a servant leader consciously chooses to lead through the provision of services to others is also consistent with and reflects a nonprofit manager's role and function.

The leadership of a nonprofit organization consists of the board and management. The chief executive is both a manager and a leader. Although the prominent literature highlights the differences between leaders and managers, a nonprofit manager is atypical in the sense that the person who holds this position is required to manage as well as lead the organization. The internal and external demands and pressures from stakeholders on nonprofit managers are increasing at a rapid pace. Balancing of these complex and sometimes contradictory demands require an adroitness and professionalism that may have not received due credit. Moreover, rather than transforming the organization with their leadership, most nonprofit managers try through their service to meet the demands of leading the organization.

Schon (1983, p. 21) states that professionals are different from others in the sense that they possess a set of distinct "instrumental problem solving" skills. Therefore, by employing professionals to manage an organization, their expertise at tasks and control over decision making will very likely promote organizational competence. Research also suggests that professional values and norms lead to organizational transformation (DiMaggio & Powell, 1983). Application of these values enhances trust among the stakeholders resulting in organizational effectiveness and sustainability.

Application of private-sector management practices to the public sector for improved effectiveness and efficiency of public services delivery is an impetus for the focus on professionalization of leadership. This is because service provision by nonprofit organizations needs to be comparable with services provided by the for-profit organizations operating in the same industry. Moreover, with the public and the for-profit sectors forming alliances and partnerships with the nonprofit sector, the call for professional leadership has increased. Nonprofit organizations are not only becoming more businesslike in their revenue generation but also becoming increasingly led by trustees and executives who have been recruited from businesses.

Nonprofit managers are increasingly becoming more professional in terms of education since the mid-1980s. The growing number of universities offering courses in nonprofit management explains the focus on professionalized nonprofit leadership. The number of professional degree programs has increased exponentially during this period, and the number of nonprofit managers with degrees in programs such as MBA (master of business administration), MPA (master of public administration), MNM (master of nonprofit management), MFA (master of fine arts administration), MSW (master of social works), and various professional certificate programs have also increased. Moreover, in some subsectors, executives are paid as much as for-profit corporate executives (Ott, 2001). Professional leadership is leadership informed and enriched through education and training in one's area of passion and through the practice and application of the training in a vocation stemming from personal choice. Such educational programs provide understanding of pertinent management and leadership concepts, and qualify the person for a position in an organization. In short, formal education endorses the legitimacy of a person's capabilities.

The Rise of Professional Leadership

Salamon (2002, 2005) stated that the nonprofit sector in America became more professional in the past couple of decades and considered this change to be in response to the legitimacy challenges faced by the sector. This challenge is based on the "unrealistic expectations" of the public and lies in the criticisms by conservatives about just another "special interest." Professionalization started with charitable fundraising as reflected in the numerous specialized fundraising organizations that emerged and grew since the 1960s. Fundraising became a profession that used marketing concepts of the for-profit sector in attracting philanthropists and encouraging charitable interests. The use of the latest technology and innovative tools to solicit grants and donations and for informational purposes deserves a noteworthy mention in the professionalization of the nonprofit sector.

In addition, the chief executive or the executive director wears several different hats and performs several different functions from meeting the expectations of the stakeholders, forming alliances, building networks, managing the organization, and being accountable to furthering the mission of the organization. These multiple functions enhance the need for professional leadership—one that leverages education, knowledge, skills, and expertise for the purpose of the organization. It must, however, be noted that not all chief executives or executive directors of nonprofit organizations are skilled or equipped to perform the multiple functions expected of that position. Anecdotal evidence suggests that most chief executives do not possess prior experience in management. Persons hired or promoted to the top position have previously worked and excelled in fields such as counseling, fundraising, preaching, and teaching, that is, nonmanagement fields. As Block (2001) maintains, they were hired on "the basis of their programmatic skills and not on their qualifications as executive managers" (p. 101). Chief executives ascended or attained their positions because of their competency and excellence in one or more fields. However, competence in certain areas such as budgeting or counseling may not be relevant or adequate for the policymaking and implementation that is required of the top management or leadership of nonprofit organizations. This issue is widespread in the nonprofit sector especially among smaller nonprofit organizations and a cause of concern. A case in point is the example of a small nonprofit organization that rehabilitates persons with addictions and substance abuse. This nonprofit is led by a former substance abuser who is currently a strong proponent of treatment and rehabilitation of former addicts and managed by a former high school teacher. Neither of them, however, have any previous experience in leading or managing an organization.

The Peter Principle appropriately describes this problem where competent people are promoted to positions where their skills might be insufficient in relation to what is expected of that position. This principle states that people rise in their careers in their organization to the level of their own incompetence. Peter and Hull (1969) maintained that those employees who have not yet reached their level of incompetence accomplish most of the work in organizations. This is because people are promoted to higher positions because of their competence and excellence in their current positions. Once they ascend to a position where their skills and expertise do not adequately match the position, they become incompetent. Most nonprofit managers face this problem. They are competent in their own areas, but when elevated up the hierarchy, their skills fall short of meeting the expectations. As mentioned earlier, nonprofit managers wear several different hats and perform a variety of functions that may not be within their competency levels. Although this problem persists in nonprofit organizations, lately, there has been an increasing interest among nonprofit managers to undergo training in management and leadership skills.

The following section discusses the empirical research that forms the basis for the need for professionalization of nonprofit leadership. Field survey points to the heightened need for professional leadership of nonprofit organizations and its importance irrespective of the educational qualifications of the chief executive.

Findings From Empirical Research

The author studied 10 corporate grant-giving programs in the north Texas region (Bezboruah, 2009). The participants are executives of corporations in the north Texas region who are involved in philanthropic decision making. The selection of the corporate executives was based on accessibility and personal contacts within the corporations. The selection of companies was primarily based on the snowball sampling technique whereby an interviewee would suggest and refer another executive from a different organization as a plausible subject for interview. This special nonprobability method of sampling was used because the respondents were extremely difficult to locate, approach, and interview. The 10 corporations varied in size and ownership as well as in industry. Their sizes, based on their annual revenues, range from small to medium to large, and the industries to which they belong are semiconductor manufacturing, telecom, software services, banking, book retail, and media. The data were derived from in-depth interviews with corporate executives, annual reports, company websites, and observations made by the researcher in the course of the interviews. A major conclusion is that professional administration of nonprofit organizations was a prime concern among most corporate donors. Due to this concern, many corporations refrain from contributing directly to nonprofit organizations. This has led to the emergence and growth of several intermediary nonprofit organizations with operating models similar to that of the United Way.

Based on the empirical findings and literature review, the next section describes the challenges faced by nonprofit organizations followed by arguments on how professional leadership can overcome these challenges.

Challenges

In addition to the resource scarcity faced by most nonprofit organizations, there are other critical challenges that deserve attention in order to appreciate the need for professionalism.

Inadequate Reporting

Most corporate executives involved in grant-giving decisions were concerned about the reporting frequency and standards regarding the use of funds by recipient nonprofit organizations. The performance of a program or project for which the corporate grant was used was not adequately reported to the grantor company nor accounted for in a timely manner. Corporate grantmakers considered such behavior amateurish and unprofessional. If approached for grants again, these grantmakers would most likely refuse. This could have serious impact on the nonprofit organizations especially the smaller ones. Being accountable for the resources received signals the sincerity, earnestness, and honesty of the nonprofit leaders. Their trustworthiness among the funders heightens, which could result in creating a positive image of the organization. In addition, funding sources could increase because funders are continuously looking for competent and accountable organizations that can make the best and most use of the funds granted. However, as the next section explains, the major constraint of finding and keeping talented and trained individuals to lead the organization acts as a major deterrent in implementing adequate accountability measures. Staffs of most nonprofit organizations spend a major part of their time scouting for grants and funds that are very vital for providing essential services. Timely and adequate reporting of the use of funds is another area in which most nonprofits fail. Case studies (Bezboruah, 2008) revealed that grantors highly value periodic reporting by grant recipients, and reporting is also considered to be a long-term benefit for nonprofits.

Human Capital

Most nonprofits do not have the resources to hire employees for various functions. As a result, they resort to contracting of employees, employ part time, or depend on volunteers to work on various functional areas. In short, nonprofits use temporary employees to overcome the labor shortage. Contingent employment practices have been growing in popularity in the United States since the 1980s, and this popularity is likely to continue (Allan, 2002; Houseman, 2001; Wise, 1994) because of the predicted shortages of professional labor (Karoly & Panis, 2004) and nonprofit leaders (Bell, Moyers, & Wolfred, 2006). Having contract or part-time workers serve in staff and leadership positions cannot be the solution if this sector is to maintain its services. This is because these employees come with the additional baggage of low-quality services (Akingbola, 2004). In addition, they may have differences in work aspirations and goals compared to permanent employees (Tschirhart & Wise, 2007). Even if they act professionally, the temporary nature of their employment might not be conducive for maintaining similar standards once their contracts are over.

Moreover, attracting the talented and educated, especially those trained in management schools, is a problem faced by most nonprofit organizations; the salary expectations will be higher than for professionals without management degrees. Most nonprofit organizations, including the larger ones that constitute about 6% of the organizations, have issues in recruiting talented individuals from diverse backgrounds in leadership positions. The smaller nonprofit organizations constituting 83% of the nonprofits have very small budgets of usually under $1,000,000. It is not surprising that with such a budget they have very little capacity to hire talented individuals. Due to the small budgets, additional human resource systems, such as standard hiring practices, comprehensive benefits, and performance management tools, are rarely followed.

Intermediate Nonprofit Organizations

There has been an increase in the emergence and growth of intermediary nonprofit organizations since the 1990s, which work as a medium between grantmakers and recipient nonprofit organizations. The objective is to create awareness, raise funds, and match grantmakers with prospective nonprofit organizations. These organizations broker between foundations, corporations, and wealthy individuals on one hand, and nonprofit organizations on the other. Notable examples are the United Way, the International Youth Foundation, and the Philanthropic Initiative. Each of these nonprofit organizations matches worthy nonprofit organizations with funders. However, nonprofit organizations need to meet the standards determined by these intermediate organizations in order to receive the benefits of the partnership. These standards include but are not limited to performance measurements, adequate accounting and reporting practices, and use of funds to further the mission of the nonprofit.

Because of the credibility ensured by these intermediary nonprofit organizations, grantmakers choose to donate resources through them. This saves them the resources required for due diligence before selecting a nonprofit for support. Because of the scarcity of resources and cost effectiveness, contributing through intermediary organizations is a better choice. New intermediary organizations have developed over the past few years in response to accountability pressures from the grantmakers. In the Dallas–Fort Worth region, organizations such as Dallas Social Venture Partners (DSVP) and Entrepreneurs Foundation of North Texas (EFNT) have emerged that try to match donors with eligible nonprofit organizations. This matchmaking process follows scrutiny of the nonprofit by the intermediary on its ability to maintain and sustain its mission as well as on its accounting practices. A nonprofit that succeeds in this review is then matched with an individual or corporate donor.

Venture Philanthropy

Another development in the philanthropic sector that provided the impetus for professional leadership is venture philanthropy. Also referred to as highly engaged philanthropy, reengineering of philanthropy, and social entrepreneurism, this model applies the techniques of the venture capital model of the corporate for-profit world. In this model, there is a deeper interaction between the donors and the recipients, with the donors playing an active role in overseeing how their donations are spent by emphasizing outcome measurements. The donors—entrepreneurs, venture capitalists, trusts, and corporations—look for social returns on their investment and focus on the performance and outcomes of the organization. With the surge in personal wealth during the economic boom of the 1990s, new philanthropists emerged who gave philanthropy a different meaning. The emergence of new philanthropic models coincides with the emergence of new philanthropic leaders, such as Bill Gates and Ted Turner, who are highly interested and involved in seeking the best methods in the delivery of services for the most effective social changes.

Proponents of this approach (Letts, Ryan, & Grossman, 1997) emphasize the risk-taking nature of these philanthropists who develop close relationships with organizations, invest for the long term, and monitor performance through agreed on measures. In their study on for-profit and nonprofit leaders, Morino and Shore (2004) found that nonprofit leaders have bold ambitions that do not find any outlet. Access to capital via the investment relationship with funders enables these nonprofit leaders to be strategic and opens up new possibilities. Other themes emphasized were strong professional leadership, importance of the public sector role in the form of garnering public will and political support, and leveraging the funders' network by the nonprofits. Social entrepreneurship models have been used by successful national organizations, such as Teach for America and America's Promise. These organizations also benefit from federal grants and support from affiliation with former first lady Laura Bush and Colin Powell.

Responses

The challenges outlined in the preceding section can be addressed by the following responses that have emerged over the years. Below are some developments that can assist in instilling professionalism in nonprofit leadership.

Management Education

A little over a decade ago, Wish and Mirabella (1998) found that over 70 colleges and universities had graduate degree programs that focused on nonprofit organizations. A more recent count puts the number at 255 colleges and universities who offer courses in nonprofit management. This includes graduate and undergraduate credit courses, noncredit courses, certificate courses, and continuing education. Program variations include specialized courses on fundraising, managing nonprofit organizations, governance, strategic planning, human resource management and financial management, and generic programs on nonprofit management with financial management and leadership courses.

The targeted audiences are a varied lot too. Some programs were targeted at undergraduates as careers with youth and human service agencies through affiliation with American Humanics while others catered to nonprofit managers, fundraising professionals, and researchers. Wish and Mirabella's (1998) research shows that the goal of these programs is to train people with practical knowledge and skills necessary to lead organizations and to have adequate understanding of the external environment to form partnerships. Graduate degrees in business or public administration increase scholastic, social, and cultural capital (Baruch, Bell, & Gray, 2005; Tschirhart, Reed, Freeman, & Anker, 2009). According to these researchers, such education improves knowledge, leadership, and analytic and strategic skills, as well as instills specialized knowledge about the sector. Whether the growth of nonprofit management education helps create a more professionalized sector remains to be seen. The aim of these programs is to provide understanding of the theories of the origin and existence of the sector and to provide the financial and managerial skills for managing an organization. Professionalism need not necessarily be an outcome of education and training, but it assists in inculcating this characteristic. Moreover, education also helps in creating awareness about the problems and opportunities in this sector and assists nonprofit leaders in finding effective ways to fulfill their organizational mission.

Recruiting Practices

Nonprofit leadership consists of the board and the executive director. The boards consist of individuals from various backgrounds who voluntarily participate in and pool their knowledge, skills, and networks to further the mission of the organization. There is a greater likelihood of an individual accepting an offered board seat if the board is in the same sector as his or her employment (Tschirhart et al., 2009). They can use their contacts with people from their respective fields through employment, professional associations, and networks with former classmates. Further, by drawing the board members from a variety of management educational backgrounds, the organization can benefit in terms of knowledge, skills, and networks associated with the individual. Tschirhart et al. (2009) also suggest that nonprofit staffs should give recent graduates with lesser experience a chance at serving on nonprofit boards instead of focusing on individuals with established careers.

The chief executive or the executive director through his or her able management and leadership skills accomplishes most of the work of a nonprofit organization. Hence, recruitment of a competent person is an essential requirement. Some of the competencies outlined by Block (2001) are informational, interpersonal, and decisional.

However, in the continuum of skills required of the chief executive, the boundaries of the aforementioned competencies often blur. Therefore, recruiting a person that is competent and skillful in leading a nonprofit and able to perform multifaceted roles and responsibilities is challenging. Most nonprofits have the Peter Principle problem when it comes to recruiting the chief executive. The size of the organization's budget, mission, geographic location, and reputation are important factors in a person's decision to apply for a chief executive's position. Further, a potential chief executive needs to be aware of the skills and competencies expected of the role and have experience in organizational management techniques.

Training Practices

Over the years, training for nonprofit managers has increased significantly. The fact that executives and managers have access to academic programs and practitioner-oriented workshops on leadership and professional development has helped in providing training and development opportunities. There are avenues such as memberships in professional associations that assist in building networks and alliances with executives and scholars from various fields within the sector. Some of the important associations are the Association for Research on Nonprofit Organizations and Voluntary Action (ARNOVA), the International Society for Third Sector Research (ISTR), and the Association of Chief Executives of National Voluntary Organizations (ACENVO). These associations have focused on the professional development needs of chief executives through mutual assistance. Further, scholarly publications in the form of journals (*Voluntas, Nonprofit and Voluntary Sector Quarterly*, and *Nonprofit Management and Leadership*), regular and electronic newsletters on the current nonprofit information, and websites dedicated to resources on grantmakers, nonprofit research statistics, and legal and financial counseling services expose nonprofit leaders to a wealth of knowledge that contributes to their professional development.

Discussion: The Call for Professionalization

The attention and demands on quality, efficiency, effectiveness, and economy of services and the focus on accountability and sustainability of the organization, have increased the need for professional leadership of nonprofit organizations. Only a professional would be able to meet these needs while at the same time perform several different functions in managing the organization. In an era of globalization, where information about the performance of nonprofit sectors across the globe is easily available, a nonprofit leader cannot remain isolated from the developments elsewhere. Researchers in several nonprofit journals have lauded and repeatedly highlighted best practices by nonprofit organizations to meet these challenges. Professionalization is considered one of the best practices. This is because a professional would be able to meet the demands of the stakeholders adequately, maintain the good faith, create credibility, and work toward the vision of the organization.

This raises concern about the way nonprofit organizations have been traditionally administered. The constituent needing the service was the primary focus because the nonprofit sector grew to address the gap between government provision of services and the market provision of services. While governments were concerned with uniform and equitable service provision, the market focused on revenue generation and the ability to pay for services. In these two extremes, certain sections of the society were overlooked. Their needs did not fall under the category of government services because the provision of these needs was not equitable or uniform. These needs were very specific and varied with subsections of the society. The market did not meet these needs because the people needing them did not have the means to pay for the services, and the services did not generate enough revenues to be considered. Scholars have formulated theories that explain the formation of the nonprofit sector. Weisbrod (1975) stated that government addresses the demands of the median voter but leaves other sections dissatisfied with government provisions thus forcing the other sectors to seek alternative avenues such as private service providers or formation of voluntary agencies to provide collective goods.

In the United States, the nonprofit and voluntary sector is as old as the nation. Historically, people often helped each other through informal associations. With formal organization and structure of nonprofit organizations, leading the organization became a key issue. Nonetheless, nonprofit organizations were successful in meeting the demands of its constituents. Soup kitchens were able to serve food to several poor people. Homeless shelters were able to provide shelter to homeless, and hospices were able to provide medicine and treatment to those without insurance. As Ott (2001) pointed out, many nonprofit organizations that resemble large businesses started out as small voluntary associations. Ott cites the examples of Blue Cross Blue Shield and credit unions. The evolution of these organizations speaks of their effectiveness.

The majority of nonprofits in the United States, however, are small with less than $25,000 in annual income. These organizations also have severe resource constraints including limited capacity to support adequate investments in technology or management. Volunteers run most of them. They are the leaders who need the qualities to be effective in service delivery while at the same time accountable to the stakeholders. Their belief in the cause and their dedication to serve people in need becomes more important than keeping track of the numbers served or their performance. Irrespective of the size of the organization, what is important is the satisfaction of the multiple stakeholders. This means the task of addressing the social issue through effective service delivery and at the same time being accountable to stakeholders' demands. The trust and credibility enjoyed by nonprofit organizations will increase substantially when they achieve this task. Further, such credibility will ensure flow of resources to the organization.

To be professional, management education and academic degrees help but are not the necessary factors. Management education can definitely educate and instill executives with certain important leadership skills and skills such as budgeting or planning that can be very beneficial for the organization. Professionalism is a quality that is beyond management skills. Leaders of nonprofit organizations, especially the executive director or chief executive, wear several different hats and perform several functions. Similarly, board members govern the organization, steer it toward the vision, and provide regulatory and oversight functions. These leaders bring forth professionalism by performing their functions with utmost dedication and empathy toward the community, addressing the needs of their constituents adequately and maintaining high standards in accounting and reporting practices. Because the nature of the nonprofit sector is different from other sectors, it is crucial for nonprofit organization leadership to maintain the trust of their stakeholders and those who share their beliefs in the cause.

Professionalism, therefore, is the ability to address the concerns and needs of the stakeholders and maintain their trust while furthering the mission of the organization. It is the administering of management practices that accomplishes routine functions and upholds the standards by which an organization is ranked by external constituents. Professionalism is very important in a nonprofit organization—behavior of the staff toward clients or customers, attitudes toward each other, and so forth. Leaders especially need to demonstrate exceptional professionalism not only to enhance the image but also to maintain the sustainability of the organization.

There are critics (McKnight, 1995), however, who are apprehensive that the overprofessionalization of the nonprofit sector might lead to diagnosing of human issues as problems thereby distancing the service providers from their constituents and the community. It can also drive out other service providers and organizations considered to be less effective. Most nonprofit service providers work in this sector because of their interest in helping the poor and disadvantaged sections of the society. This represents their altruistic behavior. Lubove (1965) argues that if a professional applies expert knowledge in providing solutions and receives compensation for that service, whereas an altruist on the other hand responds out of unrestrained generosity, then how is it possible to have a professional altruist? An altruist would work irrespective of the monetary reward. In addition, professionalism can also have attributes of the mechanistic corporate world with a fixation for efficiency and effectiveness and therefore have a corporate bias, while the nonprofit sector is supposed to be more humane. While efficiency is not harmful, it should not be at the cost of quality and effective service provision. Salamon (2002) cites the example of the Bush administration's 2001 preference in selecting faith-based charities in the distribution of federal assistance. The idea was to replace formal professionalized nonprofit organizations with informal faith-based groups that relied primarily on volunteers.

Future Directions

Emergence and increase of formal management education is to a great deal in response to the increasing focus on professionalization of nonprofit leadership. Although it is commonly believed that management education can help sharpen the skills of executives, empirical research could further the understanding of the relationship or correlation between management education and higher professionalization. This could also help in explaining why some nonprofit organizations reimburse the tuition of their executives enrolled in MBA, MPA, and other such programs. Further, research could also help in furthering the explanation of those successful nonprofit organizations that are not led by executives trained in management. This of course leads to the question of the importance of values to management education.

Summary

Nonprofit organizations are often criticized for being unprofessional in their activities. Leaders of these organizations are the ones facing the majority of these criticisms for not being able to instill professionalism in their organizations. Empirical research showed that due to unprofessionalism demonstrated by nonprofit executives in accounting and reporting practices, grantmakers are apprehensive about giving grants directly to nonprofit organizations. This fear that the money contributed for projects would not be accounted for is in part responsible for the emergence and growth of several intermediary nonprofit organizations. The primary role of these organizations is to pool resources, monetary and human, and identify eligible nonprofits to receive these resources. To be a recipient and part of the network of the intermediary organization, nonprofits need to maintain high standards of professionalism in terms of management and accounting. The credibility of the intermediary organizations is reflected on the nonprofits that are agencies or a part of the network. Association with these intermediaries also ensures adherence to professional management and leadership principles. Those nonprofit organizations that are not a part of the network have to set their own operating norms and standards and strive to accomplish them. Professionalism becomes paramount in achieving those standards. Moreover, wealthy individuals and successful entrepreneurs from the corporate world have also been important for beckoning and encouraging professionalism in nonprofit leadership and in making certain that the resources invested in the social causes they believed in are well spent. They further try to professionalize the management of the organizations to make them self-sustaining. The emergence of nonprofit management programs in universities is also an attempt to enhance the skill sets and make nonprofit leadership more professional.

In sum, professionalization of leadership of nonprofit organizations ensures successful accomplishment of the mission of the organization while addressing the multiple demands of the stakeholders.

References and Further Readings

Akingbola, K. (2004). Staffing, retention, and government funding: A case study. *Nonprofit Management and Leadership, 14*(4), 453–465.

Allan, P. (2002). The contingent workforce: Challenges and new directions. *American Business Review, 20*(2), 103–110.

Baruch, Y., Bell, M., & Gray, D. (2005). Generalist and specialist graduate business degrees: Tangible and intangible value. *Journal of Vocational Behavior, 67*(1), 51–68.

Bell, J., Moyers, R., & Wolfred, T. (2006). *Daring to lead 2006: A national study of nonprofit executive leadership.* San Francisco: Compass Point.

Bezboruah, K. (2009). *For profit organizations for social change: Understanding corporate philanthropic decision-making.* Saarbrücken, Germany: VDM (Verlag Dr. Müller).

Block, S. R. (2001). Executive director. In J. S. Ott (Ed.), *Understanding nonprofit organizations: Governance,* *leadership, and management* (pp. 100–107). Boulder, CO: Westview Press.

Carroll, A. B. (2005). Servant leadership: An ideal for nonprofit organizations. *Nonprofit World, 23*(3), 18.

DiMaggio, P., & Powell, W. (1983). The iron cage revisited: Institutional isomorphism and collective rationality in organizational fields. *American Sociological Review, 48*(2), 147–160.

Greenleaf, R. K. (1977). *Servant leadership.* Mahwah, NJ: Paulist Press.

Herman, R. D., & Heimovics, D. (2005). Executive leadership. In R. D. Herman et al. (Eds.), *The Jossey-Bass handbook of nonprofit leadership and management* (2nd ed., pp. 153–170). San Francisco, CA: Jossey-Bass.

Houseman, S. N. (2001). Why employers use flexible staffing arrangements: Evidence from an establishment survey. *Industrial and Labor Relations Review, 55*(1), 149–170.

Hunter, J. C. (2004). *The world's most powerful leadership principle: How to become a servant leader.* Colorado Springs, CO: WaterBrook Press.

Karoly, L. A., & Panis, C. W. A. (2004). *The 21st century at work: Forces shaping the future workforce and workplace in the United States.* Santa Monica, CA: Rand.

Letts, C. W., Ryan, W., & Grossman, A. (1997). Virtuous capital: What foundations can learn from venture capitalists. *Harvard Business Review, 75*(2), 36–44.

Lubove, R. (1965). *The professional altruist: The emergence of social work as a career.* Cambridge, MA: Harvard University Press.

McKnight, J. (1995). *The careless society: Community and its counterfeits.* New York: Basic Books.

Middleton, M. (1987). Nonprofit boards of directors: Beyond the governance function. In W. W. Powell (Ed.), *The nonprofit sector: A research handbook* (pp. 141–153). New Haven, CT: Yale University Press.

Morino, M., & Shore, B. (2004). *High-engagement philanthropy: A bridge to a more effective social sector.* Retrieved September 27, 2007, from www.vppartners .org/learning/reports/report2004/report2004_essay.pdf

Ott, J. S. (2001). *The nature of the nonprofit sector.* Boulder, CO: Westview Press.

Papandreou, A. G. (1952). Some basic problems in the theory of the firm. In B. F. Haley (Ed.), *A survey of contemporary economics* (pp. 183–219). Homewood, IL: Irwin.

Peter, L. J., & Hull, R. (1969). *The Peter Principle: Why things always go wrong.* New York: Morrow.

Salamon, L. (2002). *The state of nonprofit America.* Washington, DC: Brookings.

Salamon, L. (2005). The changing context of American nonprofit management. In R. D. Herman et al. (Eds.), *The Jossey-Bass handbook of nonprofit leadership and management* (2nd ed., pp. 81–101). San Francisco: Jossey-Bass.

Schon, D. A. (1983). *The reflective practitioner: How professionals think in action.* New York: Basic Books.

Senge, P. M. (1995). Robert Greenleaf's legacy: A new foundation for twenty-first century institutions. In L. C. Spears (Ed.), *Reflections on leadership: How Robert K. Greenleaf's theory of servant leadership influenced today's top management thinkers* (pp. 217–240). New York: John Wiley & Sons.

Tschirhart, M., Reed, K. K., Freeman, S. J., & Anker, A. L. (2009). Who serves? Predicting placement of management graduates in nonprofit, government, and business boards. *Nonprofit and Voluntary Sector Quarterly, 1.* doi: 10.1177/0899764008327244.1

Tschirhart, M., & Wise, L. R. (2007). U.S. nonprofit organizations' demand for temporary foreign professionals. *Nonprofit Management and Leadership, 18*(2), 121–140.

Weisbrod, B. A. (1975). Toward a theory of the voluntary nonprofit sector in a three-sector economy. In S. R. Ackerman (Ed.), *The economics of nonprofit institutions* (pp. 21–44). New York: Oxford University Press.

Wise, L. R. (1994). Rethinking public employment structures. In P. Ingraham, B. Romzek, et al. (Eds.), *New paradigms for government* (pp. 239–258). San Francisco: Jossey-Bass.

Wish, N. B., & Mirabella, R. M. (1998). Curricular variations in nonprofit management graduate programs. *Nonprofit Management and Leadership, 9*(1), 99–109.

90

Nurturing the Next Generation of Philanthropic Leadership

Pier C. Rogers

The Axelson Center for Nonprofit Management, North Park University

The world of philanthropy, a vital segment of the nonprofit sector, encompasses foundations of every sort and, like the sector as a whole, is at a crossroads. Philanthropic institutions are facing criticisms that were unknown decades ago. They are also confronting the same challenge faced by the rest of the nonprofit world—the need to attract and retain young people and to prepare that next generation to assume leadership positions.

As the baby boomer generation enters the period in which many are moving toward retirement, researchers have conducted studies to determine the impact of their retirement on the nonprofit sector as a whole and have also considered the more specific implications for the philanthropic subsector.

The 2006 Compass Point study (Bell, Moyers, & Wolfred, 2006) called attention to the stark reality that the baby boomer generation would begin retiring in the upcoming 5 years, thus increasing the demand for new leaders. The study also reported that the pipeline of younger generation, or NextGen individuals, was insufficient to fill those positions that would become vacant in the nonprofit sector. And it appears that the philanthropic subsector would have an even greater challenge, since it has even greater barriers to entry.

Twofold Approach to "Nurturing the Next Generation of Philanthropic Leadership"

The concept of nurturing the NextGen of philanthropic leadership will be discussed—from the vantage point of preparing young people for careers in the nonprofit sector in general and more specifically for careers in philanthropy. The point will be raised that attracting and retaining for employment within the field of philanthropy is not enough and that a new paradigm for philanthropy is required.

The traditional approach to this topic would be simply to discuss strategies that should be pursued to attract, prepare, and retain NextGen individuals for careers within the philanthropic sector. Instead, this article will go further to address various critiques of the philanthropic sector and will address some of the suggestions for improvements to the sector that may link with some of the values and interests that are said to belong to NextGeners. The twofold approach will be to examine both the issues involving the need to and the best ways to

1. nurture the younger generation—to encourage interest in philanthropic careers and to consider this group as listeners and change agents for philanthropy, and

2. improve the philanthropic arena—to make it more attractive and meaningful for the next generation. There is an opportunity for the next generation to make significant changes in the way that philanthropy is done.

Definitions

There are several terms that require clarification in order to explore the topic of nurturing the next generation of philanthropic leadership.

The term *philanthropic* refers to professional philanthropy, or the work of foundations that disburse resources to support or impact various causes. For some, philanthropy is intended to help the common good.

In this article, *nonprofit sector* includes all charitable section 501(c) organizations.

The term *nurture* means to encourage somebody or something to grow, develop, thrive, and be successful, according to the Encarta Dictionary (n.d.). What is meant here is to facilitate the professional development of NextGen individuals to prepare them for leadership within the philanthropic sector.

Leadership is used here in a broad sense in terms of cultivating the ability to guide, direct, or influence people, according to the Encarta Dictionary (n.d.). Leadership within the philanthropic sector is not only limited to the highest staff position, but also includes work at various levels of decision making.

The term *NextGen* is broadly meant to include up-and-coming generations who may be preparing to enter the workforce and planning their careers. (They are likely under 40 years old.)

The term *subsector* is used with *philanthropic* and is understood as being a part of the larger nonprofit sector—all 501(c) organizations.

Foundation refers to institutions that are formally established with an endowment fund and support work to advance a particular cause or mission.

About Foundations

Foundations are created in various forms. The basic types include private, public, corporate, community, and operating foundations. There are also family foundations, which are private, but most often involve at least some members of the donor family in the leadership and decision making of the foundation.

Foundations are often referred to as *elite* institutions. They arose out of the interests of men of great wealth who wanted to do some good with their riches during the gilded age of the Industrial Revolution in the United States. Those who created foundations with a charitable purpose were not required to pay federal income taxes, so they also benefited personally from creating a foundation to contribute to the betterment of society at large.

Some foundations employ professional staff to help them operate. In 2007, only 17.2% of U.S. foundations (those with at least $1 million in assets and grants of $100,000 or more, which is 20,641 foundations in number) had staff. Of the 19,027 total staff positions, 47% were full-time professional positions (http://www.foundation center.org/findfunders/statistics). This suggests that there are actually only a few professional employment opportunities in foundations and even fewer openings at any given time. If those openings are considered first for those already in foundation work, there are even fewer available opportunities. However, this should not be a deterrent to those interested in philanthropic careers.

Foundations are reputed to be rather closed to those outside of their circles. It is often the case that there are individuals who wish to work in foundations but never seem able to gain access. Those who do gain access to working in foundations often make lateral moves and work in various foundations over the course of their careers. This further limits the employment openings for others to enter philanthropy as a career option, as openings are often filled by existing philanthropy professionals rather than by new entrants to the field.

Traditional Approaches to Recruit and Retain Younger People

Recruiting and retaining NextGeners to leadership in philanthropy will be discussed from the perspective of the seasoned professional seeking to prepare the way and from the viewpoint of offering direct career guidance for the next generation.

Advice for the Seasoned Philanthropy Professional

If seasoned professionals in the field of philanthropy are interested in encouraging younger generations to become involved in philanthropy careers, there are several issues they should consider.

One issue is that there are a number of traditional routes through which young people seek to enter a new field of nonprofit endeavor. Some become volunteers and become more involved over time. They connect with someone in the field who becomes a sponsor or advocate. They may do a "cold search"—and apply for a job that they find listed on a website. Inadvertently, they fit some criteria for a position at a particular foundation—for example, a volunteer with experience in early childhood, who lives in a particular community that the foundation serves. The young person may be an alum of the same institution as the foundation or head-hunting firm representative and thus taps a connection that may be unknown to the young person. A young person may be a passionate employee at an organization in a certain field (X) whose work comes to the attention of the foundation. Because of that young person's ability, passion, and work on issue X, he or she becomes known to the foundation supporting that work. The foundation representative gets to know the person and helps to bring the young person in on the occasion of a professional-level opening in the given foundation. Not to be forgotten, the Internet in general and other social networking tools of technology have become a staple for younger generations in their overall employment search strategies.

Another issue to be considered by the seasoned professional who wants to encourage NextGeners is to recognize that many individuals may prefer to work directly with those who benefit. Philanthropic work generally means working from a distance; it is not direct hands-on work with clients. It is, however, work that enables organizations that serve the various constituencies to do their work, through the provision of some of the necessary financial resources. Philanthropic work can also provide an opportunity to become involved in influencing research or policies related to particular fields of study or causes. The tangible benefits of philanthropic work are not always immediately obvious for those who may seek hands-on involvement. However, those who seek involvement at the systems level may be attracted to the world of philanthropy.

Nurturing as mentoring should be another area of concern for the seasoned philanthropy professional. It is important to examine some of the elements that comprise nurturing new leaders. If mentoring is intended, then there are strategies to help engage NextGeners and provide them with one-on-one interactions with senior-level foundation professionals so that they can learn more about the philanthropic world from the inside.

The seasoned philanthropy professional might also consider looking *inside* the organization for potential new NextGen philanthropic leaders. Bonner and Obergas (2008) conducted a study of 36 human service organizations, and developed a practical model for internal leadership development. NextGeners who are already in a philanthropic organization could benefit by the sort of attention that these authors propose. The following summarizes that model and what current organizational leaders should do:

- Identify the challenges and strategies that will impact the organization over the next 5 years.
- Create the model of a core set of leadership competencies and behavioral characteristics that will be needed to overcome the challenges and execute the strategies.
- Identify a possible pool of high potential successors for the job in question.
- Use the competency model to assess the leadership potential of each person in the high potential pool.
- Using the results of these assessments, identify who is *ready now*, *ready in 2 to 4 years*, or in some cases who will be *better as individual contributors* rather than leaders of others.
- Create a tailored development program for each individual to improve his or her abilities and close the gaps in the competencies. Ensure that measures of success are embedded in the program. Measure progress frequently and provide useful feedback to the individual. Use this pool of talent to fill positions when they become available.

This model for developing leadership from within offers an alternative in light of the finding that "fewer than a third of nonprofit chief executives are internal hires" (Bell et al., 2006, p. 26). This figure compares with "for-profit companies [that] fill 60–65 percent of their senior management positions by hiring from within" (Tierney, 2006, p. 16).

Advice for the NextGeners on a Nonprofit Career Search

NextGeners might consider basic nonprofit sector career guidance provided by Shelly Cryer in a 2008 publication. She provides a set of key issues to be addressed in

a nonprofit career search that are easily relevant for philanthropic employment as well (p. 168):

- Understand yourself.
- Consider what issues you care about.
- Determine what type of work you've enjoyed.
- Assess your strengths and weaknesses.
- Consider how and where you choose to live.

Cryer (2008) offers numerous other suggestions—direct from interviews with nonprofit leaders in a host of different fields, organizations, and positions. She offers practical tips on the job search itself. Her book is written to be accessible for those seeking to enter the nonprofit sector and who may enjoy the wide variety of approaches in the advice that is offered.

Career Preparation Tips for a Foundation Candidate

There are two major skill-set tracks that NextGeners might consider for entry into the world of foundations: as a generalist bringing written, verbal, and analytical skills; or as an expert in a given program area. Additional tips to follow in pursuing a foundation professional position might include the following:

- Know the organization—mission, vision, history.
- Get to know the culture—what is important there, how people treat one another, the leaders' priorities, how grantees are talked or written about.
- Know your strengths—address the fit of your strengths with the organization's needs; make the case for what you will do for the organization.
- Learn about the family's history and values if it is a family foundation—determine if you are a fit, what role family members play in decision making, how outsiders' views are regarded in the decision-making process.
- Learn about some of the key funds if it is a community foundation—address how you might be an asset in working with a particular strategic area.

Taking these steps and preparing oneself as suggested above are necessary but not sufficient. There is a need to look deeper. Nurturing is the focus here, which suggests a caring effort and one that will be long lasting. If impact is sought, then it is necessary to look at the context into which those NextGen leaders will be placed. Changes in the philanthropic environment itself will be needed if those NextGen leaders will feel they have a stake, that they can be effective and really make a difference. The discussion about changes for the overall philanthropic context will follow in the second half of this article.

Cultivating Helpful Relationships

Another basic career search tip for NextGeners is to develop a *personal board*—that is, those who will encourage and critique his or her professional development. To develop such a board and ensure that it is well-rounded, it is important to bring in people from different backgrounds and experiences. Carla Harris (2009), in her recent book, *Expect to Win: Proven Strategies for Success From a Wall Street Vet,* offers advice that can easily be adapted for the NextGener seeking to enter and become successful in the philanthropic arena. Ms. Harris says that one should cultivate three key relationships: a mentor, an adviser, and a sponsor to advocate on your behalf. These individuals and others on a personal board can serve as a sounding board and offer advice on the politics of an organization and the underlying meanings that are often critical to success. Many assume that the nonprofit and the philanthropic worlds are noncompetitive and that passion for the work, even in a foundation, is sufficient. That is an unrealistic perspective, particularly given the economic downturn of the third quarter of 2008 and early 2009, when holding a job of any sort is no longer taken for granted.

What Else NextGen Leaders Need for Philanthropic Careers

Beyond the skills and experiences cited earlier that a NextGener might bring to a foundation, there is a whole host of other skills and experiences that are often valued but not necessarily discussed outright.

One important skill is sensitivity to different communities. Society has become increasingly complex, and different groups present a variety of needs for programs and services. It is standard practice to create more customized approaches to program development rather than any "one size fits all" model of programming. As a result, it is imperative that foundation professionals learn to deal with differences—of every sort imaginable. Racial-ethnic, gender, gender-orientation, age, disabilities, religious, and geographic differences and more must be acknowledged and considered in programming and funding.

Another skill area that foundation professionals need to cultivate is value for collaborative work to solve problems and address challenges. Sandra Guthman, president of the Polk Brothers Foundation, commented in a 2009 presentation that their foundation culture is a collaborative one. There is a firm belief embodied in their work that the foundation staff is in partnership with the communities they serve to address the challenges faced by those communities. That perspective is one that moves away from the more traditional assumption that the grantmaker is the only one who brings knowledge and expertise to the grantmaking relationship.

Another important skill for NextGen foundation professionals to gain is suggested by Bonner and Obergas (2008), who conclude in a report that "the role of the nonprofit leader today and in the foreseeable future will be one of mastering fluidity, complexity and turmoil. . . . To be successful, individuals will need to develop both technical skills and leadership competencies" (p. 4).

Resources for NextGeners

There are existing career preparation programs for foundation professionals that might be helpful for NextGeners. One such group, Emerging Practitioners in Philanthropy (EPIP), was formed "to strengthen the next generation of grantmakers, in order to advance effective social justice philanthropy" (http://www.epip.org/about.php). EPIP has developed programming that offers networking opportunities for their constituents both locally and nationally and cultivation of leadership and analytical skills for their members to facilitate their effective work in philanthropy. The group also strives to strengthen the role and voice of advocacy to transform philanthropy and encourage and enable younger generations to enter careers in social change philanthropy. Leaders of EPIP attribute its development to a felt need to provide nurturing and professional development to the younger generations of nonprofit professionals who were brought into the philanthropic arena during the growth of foundations in the 1990s but were left to drift on their own without adequate support.

There are fellowship programs that currently exist to prepare individuals for philanthropy careers. Several are mentioned on EPIP's website. Another example is one offered by the Associated Grantmakers of Massachusetts—the AGM Diversity Fellowship Program. "This fellowship program aims to inspire the next generation of philanthropic leaders among people of color by offering training and support to a select group of passionate, emerging professionals. We strive to increase the number and proportion of people of color as staff—and executives—in the field of philanthropy" (www.agmconnect.org, n.d., "Diversity Fellowship Program").

Many general networking groups exist to bring together NextGeners who work in the nonprofit sector. Young Nonprofit Professionals Network (YNPN) has chapters around the country. The Chicago chapter strives to "strengthen the nonprofit community by providing accessible professional development, resources and networking opportunities for young professionals involved in the Chicago-area nonprofit sector" (http://www.ynpnchicago.org).

Changing the Way Philanthropy Is Done

The topic of nurturing the next generation of philanthropic leaders has been explored from several points of view. Several critiques of philanthropy, as well as a discussion of the opportunities to improve how philanthropy is done as a strategy to more effectively attract NextGeners into the world of professional philanthropy, will be offered.

Timely New Opportunities for the Philanthropic Sector

If the focus is only to nurture the next generation to encourage its interest and readiness for leadership in philanthropic organizations, then the outcome will be limited. In that case, the following would be assumed:

- There is only the need to attract and retain the next generation—to attain sufficient numbers of NextGen employees.
- There is only the need to pursue the same recruiting strategies from the past and be successful.
- NextGeners will look at the sector without any criticism and want to belong—that is, they will offer no critique that might cause them to lose interest and deter them from seeking entry.
- The existing barriers to entry will not deter them.
- Other professional options will be less attractive.

The reality is that the philanthropic sector requires examination and improvement itself. There is an opportunity now, more so than in the past, to pursue actions that impact the sector in positive ways. Professionals can now choose to move the philanthropic sector closer toward its intention to serve the common good.

In retrospect, it is apparent that the U.S. society as a whole has become self-interested and self-absorbed. There are many examples that indicate individual and organizational choices have been made primarily based on self-aggrandizement and self-enrichment—even in the charitable and philanthropic arenas. At this point in time, there are two major events that should exert some influence on U.S. society's self-absorption. One is the economic downturn of 2008 to 2009 that has reached every individual from Fortune 500 CEOs to the average homeowner. The second is the election of a president of the United States whose vision is to renew the democratic promise of this society and engage and empower all Americans. The convergence of these two events offers a rare opportunity for the NextGeners. This means that NextGeners, newly empowered due to their role in the nationwide engagement of individuals to participate in the democratic process, may go further and insist on change at every level—even in the world of philanthropy—before they become enmeshed in status quo philanthropy.

Criticisms of Traditional Philanthropy

In an effort to enhance the attractiveness of the field of philanthropy for younger generations, some of the problems and criticisms of traditional philanthropy will be examined. This discussion will include views of the philanthropy professional, the power dimension emerging from the structure of philanthropy, and other criticisms.

Who are philanthropy professionals? Historically, they are gatekeepers. In almost any role involving applicant organizational contact, a philanthropy professional is helping to admit or reject the applicant organization. In the gatekeeper role, there is a choice to make: Will the philanthropy professional perpetuate the institution and its (often exclusive) norms or choose to be more inclusive and strengthen accountability to the community served. The

notion of accountability here goes beyond that owed to the institution whose funding the philanthropy professional is entrusted to administer, for it extends to those the foundation serves—that is, the organizations and communities that receive the foundation's resources.

In some communities, foundations are viewed as institutions that are historically white and inherently racist. The view of the institution as racist pertains to the exertion of power that is discharged in a manner that often discriminates (even unintentionally) against people according to race. This perspective of institutional racism is akin to *structural racism* and has been addressed in literature on community change.

> Structural racism refers to a system in which public policies, institutional practices, cultural representations, and other norms work in . . . reinforcing ways to perpetuate racial group inequity. It identifies dimensions of our [U.S.] history and culture that have allowed privileges associated with "whiteness" and disadvantages associated with "color" to endure and adapt over time. (Lawrence, Sutton, Kubisch, Susi, & Fulbright-Anderson, 2004, p. 11)

The point in offering a perspective of foundations as institutions that embody structural or institutional racism is to generate thoughtful critique of foundation practices and their differential impacts in the context of different communities.

The philanthropy professional is often unwittingly caught in a position of dealing with applicant organizations in a manner that may be uncomfortable—for both. When the foundation has resources and sits in the seat of power over organizations who seek those resources to implement programs, the professional working inside that foundation may feel conflicted. The professional may feel bound to the foundation's formal position toward an applicant organization but have other feelings (e.g., a sense of inequity according to race) on a personal level.

In fact, the traditional complicated nonprofit sector's *threefold relationship* is the overall context in which the foundation professional also must operate.

In that threefold traditional nonprofit relationship, there is a client who often does not pay for the service, the agency that provides the service but needs resources from others, and the funder. Note that those making the decisions are not always the funders; those receiving funds are not always the decision makers or those with the resources. There is an obligation to respect that balance and figure how to best serve those who are on the receiving end of the funds and services.

From the perspective of philanthropy, the relationship becomes fraught with a power dimension and another, deeper aspect. The funder provides resources to solve problems or address the common good. However, in the process, the funder assumes control, and "does unto." The recipient of philanthropic largesse often is viewed as passive, and the foundation can be viewed as patriarchal. The service agency is the intermediary and is expected to implement programs to ensure that common good is addressed along the programmatic lines that are prescribed by its mission, and the funding agreement.

In addition, in today's climate, philanthropy must now compete with other models for doing good in the world—to get the best and the brightest to work in the sector. There are many more choices now to do good through for-profit social enterprises, microfinance, and other organizational configurations outside of the traditional nonprofit charitable models.

Disparity Between Grantee Expectations and Realities

Another criticism of traditional philanthropy deals with the communication between the funder and grantee. It is often viewed by the grantee as inadequate, and sometimes as misleading. If foundation professionals engaged in an exercise to imagine themselves on the other side of the table in the grantee's "shoes," they might gain valuable insights into the entire grantor/grantee relationship. In the following, the vantage point of a prospective grantee will be presented to illustrate possible lessons and identify some communication problems to funders.

The grantee may have limited knowledge of foundations. Research indicates that with the "right" cause and a great proposal—there is an opportunity to receive funding. The grantee may also assume that

- all one needs to know about the application process is found on the website or in materials supplied by the organization;
- when one writes a proposal that adheres to the guidelines the foundation provides, there is a fair chance to be funded;
- the funder cares and will be respectful of the applicant organization and of those served through the organization's programs;
- the timing will be reasonable between application, decision, and receipt of a check; and
- the funder will provide notice of any problems with the application that are outside of the obvious criteria, so they can be corrected in a timely fashion.

Many organizations' experience with foundations does not fit these assumptions. In fact, some organizations' experiences include the following:

- A sense that the funder does not care about the organization or the people and communities it serves
- A sense that the funder will only support organizations with personal connections (either with the foundation board members, senior staff, or program officers)
- An applicant organization that may submit an application and never receive any response
- An applicant organization that may experience a complex web of interactions with the foundation professionals that cause the organization to conclude that dealing with foundations is not worth the trouble

Foundation Bureaucracy Gone Awry

Another problem can arise where a grantee's experience with the foundation becomes enmeshed in the foundation's bureaucracy. Whatever the cause, the resulting convoluted process can further confuse grantees. The following story illustrates such a situation.

Agency ABC had a board member who knew the president of Foundation X, and they talked over an idea. The foundation president said to submit the idea for joint funding. Agency ABC had already secured funding for the project from another foundation. ABC submitted the required information and met with the new program officer (PO) at Foundation X. The PO was not especially impressed with the idea and suggested withdrawing the proposed concept. ABC board member went back to Foundation X's president to discuss the issue. The president intervened. The PO called ABC representatives back for a meeting and shared his concerns. He also offered an alternative idea and said he would basically ensure funding of the alternative idea. ABC representatives revised the proposal, submitted it, and worked with the PO to comply with all his requirements. The new project was funded, and the check was received. Agency ABC had kept the first foundation informed and now went back to ask if they would still agree to fund half of the new project. They took 2 months to respond. Then, they said no—it was not their original agreement and did not meet their goals. Agency ABC called Foundation X again to relay the news, since X's funding was not sufficient to support the entire "new" project. Foundation X's PO said, "Oh, I was going to call you. Instead of funding the new project, I have an opportunity to support the original project—it fits within the scope of another collaborative initiative that I'm supporting. Get me a letter, and we'll change the focus back to the original project."

This feedback was a surprise to Agency ABC. They were shocked at the way all of these events had transpired. They were happy to gain support for the original project. They just could not believe the process they had experienced.

This story involved seasoned professionals in Agency ABC who were experienced in dealing with foundations. They did not take any of this process personally. In fact, they knew that they were treated better than many applicants because their board member had a personal friendship with the foundation president.

It should be considered, though, if Agency ABC were a small, community-based group with no experience dealing with foundations, it might have interpreted the events in a completely different way. The agency could have concluded that foundations as a whole were not welcoming and not interested in serving anyone beyond a closed circle of their friends.

Taking the perspective of the grantee when viewing the work of foundations can offer a sobering look at reality for incoming foundation professionals. It is a viewpoint that can help in the preparation process as well.

Additional Critiques of Philanthropy

A number of perceptions that might negatively impact the desire of NextGen folks to enter the world of philanthropy are presented in the following:

The Aspen Institute engaged Mark Rosenman to conduct a study of philanthropy—the elements that foundation leaders believed needed to change—to better position the world of philanthropy "to more effectively promote social change" (2010, p. 1). This fits with the vision of changing philanthropy to more fully focus on the "common good," as was its earliest intention.

There were four criticisms of philanthropy that emerged in interviews and focus group discussions with over 100 foundation and nonprofit organization professionals in this study:

> Recently . . . policymakers have questioned whether foundations adequately benefit society and those in greatest need, given the public cost of the tax-exemptions and other special treatment extended to them. (Rosenman, 2010, p. 7)

There is a widely accepted rationale for foundations' existence—to serve the common good.

> Often center-left foundations and nonprofit organizations hesitate to question the larger values context in which they operate, and seem more comfortable when they restrict themselves to the realms of supposedly value-free emotions and intellectualized ideas. (Rosenman, 2010, p. 11)

> Many interviewees stated their conviction that foundations tend to reflect the wider society's inequitable power relations in their grantmaking, and have organizational cultures, staffs and boards that serve to direct resources inordinately to "mainstream" institutions, organizations and programs. (Rosenman, 2010, p. 12)

> Foundation funding practices have helped create silos in the nonprofit sector where . . . problems are broken down into fragmented issues with groups specializing in narrow approaches to their resolution. Funding too often is done by program areas that cast problems in ways that are simplistic, mechanistic and isolated from the interrelated and intertwined aspects of an individual's or a community's life and the realities in which most organizations work. (Rosenman, 2010, p. 15)

These criticisms of foundation work are not meant to minimize a great deal of overall positive impact. The comments offered in this study are intended to catalyze action to make improvements in philanthropy. They are offered here as instructions to future philanthropic leaders—to help them understand some of the criticisms offered that they may have opportunities to address and change. Other criticisms are offered in the same spirit in the following paragraphs.

Rob Reich (2007) talked about the connection between philanthropy and liberty as well as equality. However, he argues

that philanthropy is not always a friend of equality, can be indifferent to equality and sometimes even a cause of inequality. When philanthropy causes or worsens inequality, it can be harmful and at odds with social justice. . . . But when philanthropic activity actually worsens inequality, any justification for the state's provision of special tax treatment to philanthropic organizations is considerably weakened, and perhaps entirely eroded. (p. 2)

Another view is offered by Ira Silver (2007), where he argues that alternative philanthropy models also mirror the very class distinctions that it criticizes and purports to rise above in its grantmaking. He says,

> Foundations are instrumental in reproducing the class privilege of elites. Since the 1970s, a cluster of "alternative" foundations has responded to this critique in two ways: (1) By distributing grants to recipients largely overlooked by mainstream philanthropy: marginalized groups organizing for progressive social change, and (2) By making grant decisions in ways that explicitly aim to challenge the class power foundations traditionally exercise. (p. 537)

The method for accomplishing this alternative grant decision process, Silver (2007) explains, simply reinforces class distinctions because donors are either excluded from the decision-making process or put together with community activists to make allocation decisions in a collaborative manner. If we consider the coproduction model, it becomes apparent that the alternative foundations still are not including the client who is the service recipient. Instead, he argues that the alternative foundations have chosen other community representatives to speak on behalf of the clients—who remain disempowered in the process.

New Philanthropic Solutions

In an article, David Boyle (n.d.) commented that public policy failures (pertaining to welfare) are the result of an inability of those public institutions (philanthropy included) to work alongside those who seek or need help (p. 3). Boyle refers to a term that encompasses many social experiments taking place under this rubric of working together—*Co-production*—first coined, Boyle says (p. 2) by Edgar Cahn:

> Put simply the Co-Production idea means that—if they're going to succeed in the long-term—welfare programs, policing or health, need to be equal partnerships between professionals and clients. . . . On the one hand, the "consumers" of justice, mental health services or health insurance are involved with professionals in a whole new series of reciprocal partnerships. (pp. 2–3)

This view of philanthropy is emerging from various segments, and NextGeners are suggesting similar ideas. The concept of co-production is gaining broad legitimacy—both in new conceptions of philanthropy and broadly in the views about public services.

Stewart Wallis (2004), in the preface to a book on co-production made the following comments:

> There are two headline concerns in public service delivery today: money . . . and choice. But there is a third issue, vitally important and yet largely ignored: the powerful potential to improve public services by enabling people to use their skills and capabilities to the fullest . . . by people I do not just mean the doctors, nurses and teachers but also patients, students and the wider community.
>
> The delivery of public services should not just be about one set of people doing something to another passive receptive group but about everyone working together to attain far better, and further-reaching outcomes. . . . The two-way approach to public services generates a wide range of positive effects in terms of sense of self-worth and overall well-being. What we are talking about here is not a feel-good "add-on," to be considered when there is spare capacity, but a vital component in understanding how to organize public services in the future—"co-production." (p. 5)

Implications for Nurturing Philanthropic Professionals

Co-production suggests a different paradigm for training new philanthropic professionals. Instead of learning for new philanthropic professionals that focuses primarily on the grantmaking process—procedures, needs assessments, outcome measures, analyses of proposals, and similar techniques, other skills will be required. There will be a shift necessary in the way philanthropy views the clients and communities who are served. There will be a need to shift away from the view that the individual or institution with financial resources is at a higher level in a hierarchy and possesses all knowledge and skill to solve the problems at hand.

Instead, a new perspective for philanthropy should consider that everyone has something to give, and professionalism does not mean that only professionals have knowledge and expertise to share. In addition, the future philanthropy professional should

- be able to deal with "deep diversity" (Mead & Capek, 2006),
- advocate for change,
- believe in strengths-based approaches to support, and
- always be willing to question one's own individual and institutional perspective.

There are other dimensions of being a philanthropy professional that could be considered by an aspiring young leader in light of other philanthropic institutional realities. The place of the philanthropic professional can be complex and challenging. The philanthropic professional can bring elements to the complex relationship (between funder and grantee) that will move away from the status quo

and offer other important qualities. Some of those elements needed in the future might include

- ethical leadership;
- focus on mission and positive outcomes for those served;
- consideration of the consequences of all actions and decisions, not just the intent; and
- a sense of connectedness with the world and people in it—a global perspective.

The Source of New Leaders Can Offer Another Solution for Philanthropy

A number of career strategies were offered earlier for individuals interested in nonprofit careers. Additional ideas were presented that were specifically connected to careers in the philanthropic sector.

There is another issue here. It has to do with the *source* of philanthropy professionals. As stated earlier, studies indicate that the pipeline of potential nonprofit leaders for the future is inadequate; this suggests that potential leaders for the philanthropic subsector are in even shorter supply.

However, another perspective is possible. Consider the traditional sources for foundation professional staff:

- Recent college grads
- Former grantees who are experts in particular program areas
- Consultants who worked with the foundation
- Foundation professionals making lateral moves from other foundations

When searching for staff primarily from these more traditional sources, the possibility exists for regenerating the status quo of who is involved in philanthropic work and their perspectives on that work. It is possible that there are other, overlooked sources. Some of these include young nonprofit professional groups and young community leaders engaged in advocacy and other work; associations of individuals in different lines of professional work like social workers, black MBAs, and others; fraternal associations (i.e., fraternities and sororities); and university alumni groups. Also to be considered are numerous other groups of young people involved in volunteer work in their communities, religious institutions, and schools whose experiences are preparing them for leadership. Additionally, there are nontraditional groups—including various immigrant groups and communities and colleges and universities that serve primarily immigrants and people of color.

Summary

In this entire discussion, several key issues have been approached from different points of view. Future generations of young people can be guided toward an interest in the nonprofit sector and more specifically the philanthropic subsector through many routes—both traditional and newer alternative routes. They can come from traditional sources and those that are nontraditional. It is imperative to realize that they may question the value of careers in the philanthropic sector; they may want to drastically change the way foundations conduct business and interact with society as a whole.

This article considers ways to cultivate those future leaders for the philanthropic sector—by discussing the career trajectory and by examining the philanthropic world itself. The examination of philanthropy as a career magnet has been done by providing a sampling of the critiques offered. It is assumed here that the positive outcomes that occur as a result of the world of philanthropy stand on their own. It is less often that some of the frank questions are raised. If there is concern about the thorough preparation of future leaders for the philanthropic sector, criticisms of the sector should be part of their education as well. Future leaders have a special opportunity to bring about change within philanthropy at a level never before considered.

Some lessons bear repeating for NextGen philanthropic leaders. As NextGeners consider their work in philanthropy, which often engages with individuals and groups from various communities, they should remember the following:

- Be open or transparent.
- Realize that time and money are limited resources for nonprofits.
- Be alert to race or class issues.
- Remember that one is providing a service and not dispensing one's personal assets.
- It is a two-way transaction. The grantee has a resource also—the services that will be provided with the assistance of the foundation's resources.

- Realize prospective grantees may be afraid of asking the wrong question for fear of how it may influence their chance at funding. The foundation has the power on its side.

Finally, at a Council on Foundations conference some years ago, Dr. Roy Menninger (1981) spoke about the "God complex"—a phenomenon that still causes concern for foundation staff:

Staff members sometimes find it hard to remain properly humble when they believe they are probably brighter, and certainly wiser, than either the board or the seekers. Succumbing to the seductions of the God complex is a real occupational hazard. Having money to give away and the power to decide whom to give it to is intoxicating, and foundations can be irritating examples of the "narcissism of the righteous."
. . . On the other hand, foundation staff who are committed to do good have to be careful of the personal costs that might be incurred in their determination to do good. The desire to do good, can come into conflict with the desire to be liked and to be viewed as helpful, and manifest itself in self-doubt, and even over-identification with the grantee. This personal conflict can become paralyzing, to the extent that the foundation representative . . . overreacts in the opposite direction, at which stage they seem curt, cold, and withdrawn. (p. 5)

In the spirit of Dr. Menninger's remarks from several decades ago—NextGeners can help keep themselves immune to the God complex by becoming connected in the nonprofit world through volunteer work outside of any foundation job duties and where their foundation role is unknown and by involving themselves with friends and other networks outside of philanthropy where their foundation work will not be elevated into near sainthood. Staying grounded is key for a productive and effective career in philanthropy.

References and Further Readings

Associated Grantmakers of Massachusetts. (n.d.). *Diversity fellowship program.* Retrieved from http://www .agmconnect.org/diversity

Bell, J., Moyers, R., & Wolfred, T. R. (2006). *Daring to lead 2006: A national study of nonprofit executive leadership.* Washington, DC: CompassPoint & Meyer Foundation.

Bonner, L., & Obergas, J. (2008, October). *Nonprofit leadership development: A model for identifying and growing leaders within the nonprofit sector* (Report, p. 3). Pittsburgh, PA: Looking Glass Institute &Dewey & Kaye Nonprofit Consultants. Available from wwww.deweykaye.com/dewey/ nonprofit.php

Boyle, D. (n.d.). *The new philanthropy* (p. 3). Available at http://www.timebanks.org/documents/NewPhilanthropywco ver.pdf

Chambers, E. G., Foulon, M., Handfield-Jones, H., Steven, M., Hankin, S. M., & Michaels, E. G., III. (1998). The war for talent. *McKinsey Quarterly, 1*(3), 44–57.

Cornelius, M., Covington, P., & Ruesga, A. (2008). *Ready to lead: Next generation leaders speak out.* San Francisco: CompassPoint Nonprofit Services, Annie E. Casey Foundation, Meyer Foundation, & Idealist.org.

Cryer, S. (2008). *The nonprofit career guide: How to land a job that makes a difference.* St. Paul, MN: Fieldstone Alliance.

Encarta Dictionary. (n.d.). *Leadership.* Available from http:// encarta.msn.com/encnet/features/dictionary/DictionaryResults .aspx?lextype=3&search=leadership

Encarta Dictionary. (n.d.). *Nurture.* Available from http://encarta .msn.com/encnet/features/dictionary/DictionaryResults.aspx? lextype=3&search=nurture

Guthman, S. (2009, February 15). *Strategic philanthropy* [Speech]. Chicago: Polk Brothers Foundation, Chicago Wellesley Club.

Harris, C. (2009). *Expect to win: Proven strategies for success from a Wall Street vet*. New York: Hudson Street Press.

Lawrence, K., Sutton, S., Kubisch, A., Susi, G., & Fulbright-Anderson, K. *Structural Racism and Community Building*. (2004). Aspen Institute Roundtable on Community Change. Washington, DC: Aspen Institute. Available from http://www.aspeninstitute.org/publications/structural-racism-community-building

Mead, M., & Capek, M. E. (2006). *Effective philanthropy: Organizational success through deep diversity and gender equality*. Cambridge: MIT Press.

Menninger, R. (n.d.). *Foundation work may be hazardous to your health* (Adapted from a speech). Annual conference of the Council on Foundations, Philadelphia, May 1981. Available

from http://www.grantcraft.org/index.cfm?fuseaction=Page.ViewPage&pageId=1112

Reich, R. (2007). *Philanthropy and its uneasy relation to equality*. Available from http://www.law.ucla.edu/docs/philanthropyequalityucla.pdf

Rosenman, M. (2010, March). *Caring to change: Foundations for the common good*. Aspen Institute. Available from http://www.caringtochange.org/images/stories/C2C_Foundations_for_the_Common_Good.pdf

Silver, I. (2007). Disentangling class from philanthropy: The double-edged sword of alternative giving. *Critical Sociology, 33*(3), 537–549.

Wallis, S. (2004). Preface. In S. Burns & K. Smith (Eds.), *Co-production works* (p. 5). London: New Economics Foundation.

91

GROWING YOUR CAREER

MICHAEL MEYER AND JOHANNES LEITNER
WU Vienna University of Economics and Business

Careers are always careers in context. Being central to individuals, organizations, and society, they cannot be restricted to the narrow view of individuals moving up corporate or professional hierarchies (Mayrhofer, Meyer, & Steyrer, 2007). The nonprofit sector presents a specific mix of forms of organizing. It combines both traditional organizations with strong hierarchies (e.g., Red Cross, hospitals) and project-based employment (e.g., cultural projects or relief organizations). Somewhat counterintuitively, these specific forms of organizing do not necessarily imply specific forms of careers. Rather, careers in the nonprofit sector tend to oscillate between different forms of organizing, for example, working for an established social care organization may be one career step and participating in a drug prevention project the next. A common and crucial feature throughout the sector, though, is that funding limits employment contracts—even in traditional organizations.

From an individual point of view, the nonprofit sector thus constitutes a career field in which many jobs have an expiration date. Furthermore, we find a specific structure of human resources (HR) in nonprofit organizations (NPOs): Persons regularly employed work together with volunteers, members of religious orders, and civil servants. The share of part-time employees is considerably high. A career field with such characteristics is interesting for two reasons:

1. In the future, career fields are unlikely to present the either–or of project careers or organizational ones (e.g., the film industry as opposed to public administration [Jones, 1996]). It is rather more likely that in the majority of cases, permanent and temporary forms of organizing will coexist. The nonprofit sector can be studied as a testing ground of such forms of organizing society.

2. With around 10% of the average Western economy's workforce employed in the nonprofit sector, this sector already constitutes a career field of considerable economic importance and academic interest. In spite of that, careers in the nonprofit sector have not been systematically researched so far.

Two Faces of Success

Career research has distinguished between an objective and a subjective career (Hughes, 1937): The former is defined as directly observable, measurable, and verifiable by an impartial third party when looking at attainments such as pay, promotions, or occupational status. The latter is experienced directly only by the person and defined by an individual's reactions to his or her unfolding career experiences. In other words, the subjective career is "the moving perspective in which the person sees his life as a whole and interprets the meaning of his various attributes, actions and the things which happen to him" (p. 63).

Thus, careers and career success are Janus-like: There is an objective (or external) dimension, often measured by salary levels, rank of promotion, and occupational status (Judge, Higgins, Thoresen, & Barrick, 1999); as well, there is a subjective (or internal) side, for example, expressed in career satisfaction (Gattiker & Larwood, 1986). For a particular work context, industry, and strata of the workforce, certain objective criteria of success apply. All these measures are somehow linked with an individual's contribution to the success of the organization, be it through sales, production, cost saving, or innovation. Controllers and HR departments alike spend time devising meaningful measures to design remuneration and incentive packages. Consequently, objective career success is largely determined through what the particular organization or industry considers successful: In the business world, income is a key measure; among academics, publications or impact points serve a similar function, while the tennis sport community uses the Association of Tennis Professionals (ATP) rankings to measure success. The following measures regularly appear in order to make this objective career success operational (Childs & Klimoski, 1986): earnings, prestige, budget responsibility, career identification, problem-solving effectiveness, job effectiveness, numbers supervised, peer rate, and progress.

However, this narrow definition of career success reveals some major problems. A purely objective notion of career success ignores the fact that careers have the two aspects mentioned above, and it stands to reason as to which is the more important one. It also ignores different organization and career contexts in which these measures make more or less sense. But if every career also has a subjective element, then subjective, psychological, or intrinsic success will be something that, while it cannot be separated from the objective element of an individual's career is still the individual and subjective interpretation of just those events. One doctor might be frustrated because the war interrupted his career and seriously hindered his chances for advancement, whereas another will rejoice because war afforded him the chance to do what he has always wanted to do, namely, to help people (Pellegrin & Coates, 1957).

Most studies that refer to subjective career success use career satisfaction as the core metrics. But it is doubtful whether career satisfaction can be clearly distinguished from job satisfaction. Consequently, career satisfaction might be high due to a motivating job but not necessarily due to the perception of success. Arthur and Rousseau (1996) found that the majority of career-related studies focused on objective perspectives. Since then, however, subjective criteria have increasingly been adopted (Arthur, Khapova, & Wilderom, 2005). Yet there is no consensus on how to measure this multifaceted construct, which comprises satisfaction, subjective perception of success, work-life/private-life balancing, and so forth.

So how are career success and overall happiness related? There is much evidence that many people are objectively successful but unsatisfied with both their careers and the rest of their lives (Reichel et al., 2006). This can be due to a number of reasons: because the demands of the job and those of the rest of life are conflicting, because one's expectations for job and career remain unmet, because the individual senses a lack of control over his life, or because he has stronger affiliated needs than are satisfied at work. *Work centrality*, measured by the weekly working hours and the subjectively invested share of life-energy into the job, contributes significantly to both subjective and objective career success (Mayrhofer, Meyer, Schiffinger, & Schmidt, 2008). Finally, as one progresses through life's stages and one's choices narrow, the objective success can often feel shallow.

Objective success seems to increasingly cost much more in terms of personal life sacrifices (Evans & Bartolomé, 1981): In the United Kingdom, 1.65 million people work more than 60 hours a week in 2003, and they take fewer holidays than before; stress-related absence from work costs British industry £370 million a year. All this indicates that being successful in one's career does not necessarily square with being successful overall or with feeling successful. In fact, there is evidence that managerial lifestyles often inhibit people from doing what they really want to do (Linder, 1970).

But career practice still upholds the notion that the less of a life outside the job one has, the better and the more useful one is to the organization (de Graaf, 2003). However, this is not necessarily true. There lies great potential in actually trying to set up the work situation so that family life can be well-lived out (Mulgan & Wilkinson, 1995). But to reap these benefits, one needs to recast the view as to what constitutes an ideal employee. Empirical evidence suggests that the greater an individual's perceived work-family conflict, the lower his or her career success (see also Mayrhofer et al., 2008). This effect is stronger for women than for men, for the elder than for the younger. Consequently, we also have to take into consideration work-private-life balance to establish comprehensive measures of career success, which should cover at least four dimensions: (1) objective career success and the rewards by which that is measured, since subjective career success is in part a processing and a reaction to those rewards; (2) job satisfaction, that is, how the job itself is going; (3) career satisfaction, which deals not only with the job at hand, but also with the more long-term prospects of work and development; and (4) finally, life satisfaction. Life satisfaction and job satisfaction overlap and so do career satisfaction and job satisfaction, but they are not the same. Subjective career success overlaps with both of those terms but is broader. On the other hand, since it is an evaluation of objective career experiences, it overlaps as well with objective career success.

Moreover, career success definitions will vary according to gender, culture, and career context, and according to personality and motivational makeup. This allows us now to define career success as follows: Objective career success is the outcome of one's career as measured against objective criteria, such as income, span of control, and hierarchical advancement. Subjective career success is the evaluation of one's career according to personal criteria. To illustrate what elements go into that evaluation, see Figure 91.1. This includes, on the one hand, evaluations of the job itself, the career, and one's life as impacted by the career. On the other hand, these evaluations are made in comparison with different personal standards, which include self- and other-referent elements. It is a multidiscrepancy process in which one compares the status quo

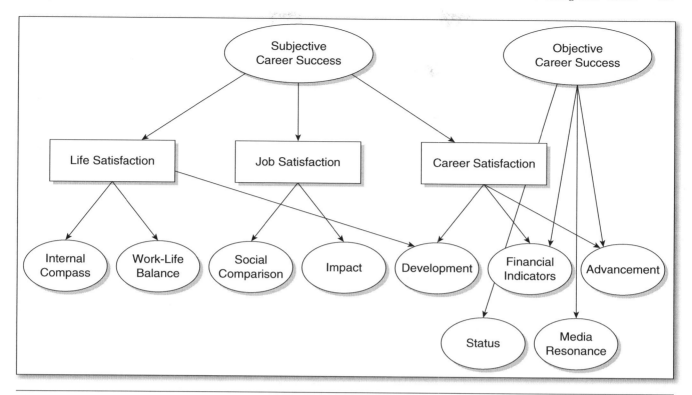

Figure 91.1 Subjective and Objective Career Success

SOURCE: Steinbereithner, 2006.

with various reference points. What weight (if any) each of these referents play depends largely on personality, gender, culture, and career context. This means that subjective career success is a composite construct. How the various elements interact and what weight each of them has depends on personality, gender culture, and career context.

Influencing Factors: The Importance of Career Capitals

Within the practice-theoretical framework of late French sociologist Pierre Bourdieu (see Bourdieu, 1977), individual actors are understood as producers of social practices. Social practices comprise all enactments that can be observed and attributed to an individual. Such practices can be not only concrete decisions and (inter)actions in work life, for example, staffing decisions or contract negotiations, but also everyday activities, such as shopping or traveling, and habitual features, such as gestures, language, or clothes. Individuals produce these practices drawing on a portfolio of resources, which consists of different forms of capital. Bourdieu (1986) distinguishes four forms of capital: (1) *economic capital*, that is, monetary income and wealth in a general sense; (2) three forms of *cultural capital* including (a) incorporated cultural capital—roughly an individual's capabilities resulting from education and

upbringing, (b) objectivized cultural capital—material objects that represent accumulated knowledge or competencies, and (c) institutionalized cultural capital—the legitimized form of incorporated cultural capital as represented in degrees, diplomas, and titles; (3) *social capital*, which consists of the resources that can be mobilized due to membership in a specific group. These three forms of capital provide basic resources for all types of social action. Actors either acquire economic, cultural, and social capital by themselves, for example, during socialization, or inherit it from their parents and ancestors. Inherited capitals, for example, in the form of wealth, education, and social networks, significantly facilitate further capital acquisition; (4) *symbolic capital*, which can best be understood as a "state of aggregation" of the other three forms of capital, depending on the mechanisms that generate field-specific reputation. Specific social fields evaluate different combinations of economic, cultural, and social capital in a specific way. In the nonprofit field, for instance, successful careers depend on specific sets of capitals.

Depending on the social context, all forms of capital can take a particular shape, which is particularly recognized within this context and symbolizes wealth, social status, or success, for example. Each individual draws on a specific portfolio of these forms of capital to produce social practices. In work contexts, for example, individuals can use private contacts (social capital) to facilitate business contracts, or they can use titles (cultural capital in its institutionalized, symbolic form) to signal status and influence. During most of their work time, though, individuals use their knowledge and creativity (incorporated cultural capital) to earn economic capital. The transformation of capital into concrete (work) practices is mediated by what Bourdieu calls *habitus* (see Bourdieu, 1977). Habitus works as an internal framework, which influences how individuals perceive the world and how they (re)act within it. It is not determined but essentially shaped by an individual's position in society. Individual actors produce practices within social fields. According to Bourdieu, a field is a patterned set of practices that suggests competent action in conformity with rules and roles as well as a playground or battlefield in which actors, endowed with a certain field-relevant capital, try to advance their position. As such, they constitute a network of positions, a playground where actors try to follow individual strategies. If you act according to the rules of the game as defined by the specific set of capital most valuable for holding power within the field, you will also contribute to the reproduction of the fields.

These fields include business, culture, politics, or academia. In the business field, investment of economic capital will produce the most benefit, while in the cultural field, specific forms of cultural capital will be most beneficial. In the field of politics, likewise, social capital works very productively. Other field characteristics include the number and type of actors involved and the typical trajectories within a field. We have used this framework to analyze the nonprofit sector as a career field (Iellatchitch, Mayrhofer, & Meyer, 2003). From a work and employment perspective, the nonprofit sector can be understood as a network of positions provided by different forms of organizing, in which individuals work and between which they move. These moves are subject to specific "rules of the game," and thus, some social practices and the investment of specific forms of capital are rewarded more positively than others. Further on, we will detect which forms of capital are most important for a career in the nonprofit field. Those forms of capital that are most valued in a given career field can be called career capital.

While the prior sections introduced theoretical concepts explaining career success and career capitals, the following sections deliver an empirically based insight. Reference is also given to differences between nonprofit and business leaders.

Career Capitals in the Nonprofit Field

If career success factors were the same for different career fields, one might assume that sector shifts between the nonprofit and the business sector occur frequently. It has been shown, however, that despite many proclamations transitions across sectors are very rare (Tschirhart, Reed, Freeman, & Anker, 2008). Their quantitative study among 688 alumni revealed that respondents remained in their initially preferred sector for two main reasons: first, because of perceived competence in the sector and, second, because of career values. The perceived competence in the sector is greatly influenced by the education background the individuals show. For instance, master of business administration (MBA) graduates are more prone to pursue a career in the business sector while master of public administration (MPA) graduates tend to opt for a nonprofit career opportunity (Tschirhart et al., 2008). Career values are shaped through ideas that either focus on helping others or earning a high salary. Consequently, graduates who expect their future career to allow for helping others opt primarily for the nonprofit sector; those who place greater importance on earning a high salary chose the business sector. Moreover, career values are more similar between the public and the nonprofit sector (LeRoux & Sneed, 2006), and thus, more transitions might occur between these sectors—partly because of the strong relationships (e.g., government contracting, accountability) between these two sectors.

Sector boundaries seem to be rigid and stable over an individual's career path, which makes movements across sectors unlikely. Thus, different success factors and career capitals might differ in their impact between the business and the nonprofit sector. Applying the career capital concept, a number of plausible differences between nonprofit executives and business managers emerge (Aghamanoukjan, Leitner, Meyer, Steinbereithner, & Eikhof, 2008; Meyer, Aghamanoukjan, Eikhof, Leitner, & Steinbereithner, 2006):

1. For careers in the nonprofit sector, economic capital is far more important than for business executives.

2. Social capital especially drives business managers.

3. Cultural capital is important in the nonprofit and in the business sector.

4. Business managers are keener to translate their capitals into symbols, namely, status symbols and prestigious items.

Economic Capital: Money Makes Careers Go Round

Probably the most counterintuitive result of our research is the overwhelming importance of economic capital in the nonprofit sector compared to the for-profit sector. This is surprising only at first glance. In the interviews, economic capital, or more prosaically money, is mainly mentioned in the form of organizational income. It is this organizational funding rather than personal income that is mostly precarious for careers in NPOs: called to work but not for profit?

Especially for founders of NPOs, though, boundaries between personal and organizational economic capital are blurred. Rather, both forms are strongly intertwined; they would measure organizational success in monetary terms—relating to the acquisition of public funds, for example. Organizational success, in turn, often enables personal career steps. Whenever economic career capital appears in nonprofit narratives, it is mentioned because of its absence, which is perceived as a career barrier. However, the permanent shortage of money and the resulting necessity to cope without economic capital is important in the nonprofit sector.

Another major reason for the importance of economic capital for nonprofit careers is that many NPOs are project based: Funding is project-oriented and short-termed, and thus, employment and careers are tied to projects with often unknown duration. It is also striking that the perceived stability of organizations has a remarkable impact on the perceived importance of economic capital: Executives from large and well-established NPOs often fail to mention both the organizational and the personal income. In contrast, for executives from small and comparably young organizations, funding and personal income is a major topic.

A further factor impacting the perception of economic capital is the low degree of internal specialization in many smaller NPOs. Managers of pioneer NPOs have to be all-rounders; they are in charge both of operative business and of management tasks, such as finance, HR, and leadership. Needless to say that in bigger organizations functional differentiation increases. In small and project-oriented NPOs, every member feels him- or herself responsible for funding issues. This perceived responsibility corresponds also with the specific ideal of democratic participation in many small grassroots NPOs.

In business organizations, too, organizational structure and size influence the perception of economic capital: Managers in the company world (cf. Iellatchitch, 2003) take financial security for granted; they are proud to be in a position to afford something—that is, transformation of economic capital into symbolic capital is stressed. On the other hand, for the self-employed, economic capital is as much a precondition for career success as it is for our nonprofit sample—the boundaries between organizational and personal income are blurred. Yet economic capital is not nearly as important as it is to their NPO counterparts. Money is not so important for nonprofit executives because it's everywhere in the NPO world but because it is not.

Social Capital: Don't Burn Bridges

The notion of social capital refers to all resources derived from membership in specific groups or networks or from social relations in general. The distinction between formal and informal relationships, friendships, and loose contacts within the organization or beyond is important. In the nonprofit field, networks and loose contacts are much more important than friendships. Likewise, the social capital actors draw mostly on results from relationships beyond

organizational boundaries—which differ significantly from business executives: Most of them rely much more strongly on internal social capital. This difference can be pinpointed using a distinction of different forms of social capital employed by Putnam (1995): Nonprofit careers rely more on what he calls *bridging social capital* than on bonding social capital. Whereas in many business companies it is contacts within the corporation that are perceived as essential for careers, nonprofit executives use focus on interorganizational networks (though this might also be due to different size and structure of business organizations and NPOs). Blurring of the boundaries between private and professional relationships is common and positively valued in the nonprofit field. This is very different from the business field where actors exert considerable effort in separating their work from their private life and preventing their private spheres from occupational spillovers. Nonprofit executives do not distinguish between working hours and leisure time so sharply, and their professional identity dominates their private spheres, too.

Cultural Capital: Learning, and Even More Learning

Cultural and educational capital might appear in different forms: Most generally, it means all knowledge and capabilities. Some of them are (a) specifically incorporated (embodied). Some part of cultural capital is (b) objectivized cultural capital, that is, material objects that represent accumulated knowledge or competencies (e.g., libraries, information technologies [IT]). Finally, some aspect of educational capital is highly visible in the form of (c) institutionalized cultural capital, the legitimized form of incorporated cultural capital as represented in degrees, diplomas, and titles. For most nonprofit executives, cultural capital seems to be the most important form of capital for a career in the nonprofit field.

Further education and training play an important role in context with management and leadership competencies. A permanent search for complementary competencies is a striking feature of many nonprofit executives. For instance, social workers thrive for management competencies, nurses for educations in coaching, administrative staff looks for education in the psychosocial field, and so forth. Trainings in management are attended when career steps require them. A typical career path in the nonprofit sector is often accompanied by different trainings and educational courses: mediation, coaching, leadership, and so forth.

Executives of NPOs are mainly intrinsically motivated to do this continuing education; most of them cover some of the costs from their personal funds. Like the notion of voluntary and conscious self-exploitation for the sake of the NPO, the idea of thriving for permanent personal development and qualification seems to be integral to the NPO executives' self-perception. Unlike nonprofit representatives, business executives are mainly extrinsically motivated when opting for further education.

Despite the fact that the nonprofit sector comprises a large number of professions with a highly specialized training (e.g., nurses, therapists, doctors, and administration specialists), this career field requires more universal or key competencies for a career as an executive, partly because of the rather diffuse requirements and volatile career trajectories. To be as broadly qualified as possible and to be able to react quickly to changes in the organization (i.e., when a project ends), employees provide themselves with many different competencies.

Career paths for managers in the nonprofit field neither provide well-defined entry points nor specify degrees, as is the case in the traditional professional field, for example, for medical doctors, legal professions, and even for business managers. Vocational identity of nonprofit managers arises during their careers and is not created by a specific education.

But it is not just about learning and training that sheds a light on the differences between business and nonprofit leaders. Emotional Intelligence (EI) is an increasingly recognized factor in leadership studies (Morehouse, 2007). While intelligence traditionally has been measured only in its cognitive dimension, the emotional dimension of intelligence found its path into empirical studies within the last decade (Mayer & Salovey, 1993). EI is defined as

> the ability to perceive accurately, appraise, and express emotion; the ability to access and or generate feelings when they facilitate thought; the ability to understand emotion and emotional knowledge; and the ability to reflectively regulate emotions in ways that promote emotional and intellectual growth. (Mayer & Salovey, 1997, p. 23)

Put differently, EI comprises all personal qualities that enable an individual to interact effectively with other people in daily life. EI is recognized to be a crucial success factor and an indicator for identifying top performers in a work environment (Morehouse, 2007).

An investigation among business and nonprofit leaders found that nonprofit managers showed significantly higher scores on the EI scale than did their business counterparts (Morehouse, 2007, p. 303). Three reasons may explain these differences. First, a strong relationship between EI and career choice exists, which reasons that emotionally intelligent employees choose their occupations such as social work, teaching, and so forth according to their emotional disposition. Second, emotional intelligence implies a high level of stress resistance. Stress is, for instance, a typical characteristic of most social work and health care duties. Third, EI also comprises high degrees of adaptability, which is finding ways to cope with everyday difficulties. Again, nonprofit workplaces frequently require adaptability to adverse environmental situations.

Symbolic Capital: My Reputation Is My Organization

Symbolic capital is best understood as a different state of aggregation of economic, social, and cultural capital: According to the rules of a career field, specific combinations of these basic capitals are transformed into symbolic capital thus representing reputation and the image of individuals (e.g., money transformed into expensive office furniture is regarded as a sign for career success). For executives from the nonprofit field, conventional symbolic capital is less important than for those from the business field. Symbols of status, which are quite common in the business field (ranks and position titles, large offices and their furniture, business-class flights, cars, etc.), hardly play a role. Rather, it is the reputation of their organizations that makes nonprofit managers proud. Business managers more frequently refer not only to ranks and titles and office and furniture but also to social relations with key customers as leading to high reputations and thus constituting their symbolic capital. On the whole, symbolic capital seems to be less important for careers in the nonprofit sector than in the for-profit sector.

Indicators for Career Success in the Business and the Nonprofit Sector

The nonprofit career field differs from the business field not only in terms of career capital but also in terms of indicators applied by executives to consider themselves successful in what they do. From the range of indicators as introduced in section 2: "The Importance of Career Capitals" above, two are particularly interesting: (1) *financial indicators*, for example, personal income as well as the financial performance of the organization, and the (2) *internal compass,* which embraces manifold references not only to personal attitudes, values, and standards but also to intrinsic motivations, such as vocation or calling.

These indicators somehow represent two major types of career success criteria conceptualized theoretically by Peter Heslin (2005). Second, the very few pieces of empirical research on careers in the nonprofit sector show that the internal compass, a calling orientation, a "for love, not money" choice, and a total commitment is most important within the career aspirations of CEOs in the third sector (Harrow & Mole, 2005). These categories polarize and sharply distinguish business careers from management careers in civil society.

Financial Indicators

Business Managers—Trapped by Comparisons

For managers in the business world, both for employed and for self-employed—personal income is a crucial indicator for career success—insofar as the prejudice is true, though there are various facets to be found. It is not about the absolute level of personal income. It is, on the one hand, the steady growth of income that matters and on the other hand, a specific lifestyle people get used to, enjoy, and finally perceive as a symbol of their success. Furthermore, this need for a steady growth of income introduces a monetary aspect as core criterion for career transitions: Decisions for change despite financial losses are rare. Sometimes, changes to self-employment, that is, transitions between different career fields, are motivated financially: Business graduates are ready to take even higher risks to significantly raise their income in the long run. It is the best paid job that is seen as the fast lane for social advancement.

What is most striking with financial success indicators in the business world is the omnipresence of comparison processes, that is, to construct criteria in the objective/other-relevant domain (Heslin 2003, 2005). The other type of comparison is the relation between work effort and payment—in line with J. Stacey Adams's (1963) equity theory and more recently, among others, with Janssen (2001). *Money* is the sharp side of all these comparisons: Work-life balance, personal development, social status, having fun, and so forth always remain opaque. Money is often regarded as a means for social status: to acquire a status symbol and independence. Thus, these financial indicators for career success are a picture puzzle with many different aspects. And—you always need a little more than you have (Schor, Jhally, & Alper, 2003). Furthermore, personal income is also seen as a metric for competence.

Nonprofit Managers:
It's the Organization That Counts

In the nonprofit sector, financial indicators are also important for the perception of success, but it is mostly the organization's financial performance that counts. Getting money for the organization becomes a core indicator of personal success, too. As in the business world, personal income is seen in a trade-off relation with work-life balance, but unlike in the business world, managers of nonprofits emphasize the trade-off with their internal compass, their calling, and the impact of their work. Whereas business managers compare themselves in terms of income, work effort, and social status—but not with people from the nonprofit sector—the business world and its managers' income is a constant point of reference for nonprofit executives. Nevertheless, financial issues are not very relevant for career transitions; nonprofit managers decide to change jobs and organizations even despite a lack of money and a decrease in salary.

To get comparatively little pay is regarded as a metric for idealism—which in the long run also contributes to social status, especially if it results in perceiving credits thus gaining influence in political decision making. Unlike

in the business world, it is not a comfortable personal lifestyle that serves as an argument for personal income but rather basic needs. Maybe increasing personal income is also a kind of taboo in nonprofits, which rely on donations and voluntary work. Money is seen rather as a means for organization goals than as an end. Nevertheless, nonprofit managers appreciate a stable and basic personal income for employees as a multiplier for organization effectiveness.

Also in the course of time, personal income might become an indicator for recognition—this is different in the business world where this is true starting from earlier career stages. Managers who have moved from the business to the nonprofit sector suffer most from the restrictions in personal income. Financial indicators are not less important for nonprofit executives, but they have a completely different status: They are somehow taboo, unless it is the financial success of the organization itself, or they are argued with reference to basic needs.

Internal Compass

Business Managers: Intrinsic
Motivation and Quality Standards

The internal compass as a criterion for career success is less important in the business world; however, the internal compass of business managers mainly consists of individual values. Managers refer to self-commitment and the aspiration to "prove myself." Besides quality standards, autonomy and independence—and beyond the emotional evaluation of specific jobs—change and risk taking are highly valued criteria for success. And there are a few hedonistic and ethical elements within the internal compass: to have fun on the one hand and to be able to look oneself in the mirror and to stay authentic on the other hand. Altogether, these specifications cast a poor light on modern managerialism, as they are completely decoupled not only from specific products and services but also from stakeholders (customers, coworkers) and even (mostly) from specific technical competencies.

Nonprofit Managers: More Ethics,
Altruism, and Professional Identity

The picture emerging for the internal compasses of nonprofit managers is much more colorful. First of all, it is the identification with the job itself that seems to be a major success indicator. Not only altruism but also principles, morals, ethics, and maxims play a crucial role. Compared with business executives, vocation and calling play a more prominent role for nonprofit executives. It is important to "put your heart in the job." Hereby, altruism is central and often mentioned, for example, to use one's competencies for the benefit of others. Nonprofit managers refer also to the fit between their self-concepts (e.g., in the form of professional identities, such as social workers, therapists) and their jobs as a criterion for career success. Much more, as mentioned by business managers, it is also thrills and challenges that matter in various ways, but especially to be different from others.

Besides these very specific elements, there are also aspects that resemble those mentioned with business managers: Nonprofit executives want to reach a self-defined degree of professionalization. They thrive on and strive for autonomy, they search for or already enjoy authenticity, and they permanently switch their enthusiasm from one field to the other—that is, they are motivated by permanent change. It is also important to realize their own ideas and to develop their own personalities. This compensates the lack of income.

Make Your Career Grow in the Nonprofit Sector

Civil society as a sphere beyond market and public bureaucracy contributes significantly to the governance of modern societies all over the world. Nonprofit organizations are not only core actors within civil society, but also they yield more trust than business corporations and public agencies. Thus, they have established an attractive career field for many, especially for younger cohorts. Most obviously, for many young people, NPOs offer brighter conditions for a person-organization-fit (Bretz & Judge, 1994) than other organizations, and they provide alternative modes of occupational and organizational socialization. Thus, despite shady prospects for individual wealth and power, the nonprofit sector has established itself as an interesting career field for graduates.

Our research has revealed some empirical evidence that executive careers in the nonprofit sector conform to specific rules: Money is extremely important for nonprofit careers—definitely not as a metrics of personal career success but rather as a prerequisite for attractive and stable jobs. And in higher ranks, it is the NPO's income that counts. Social networks, especially those bridging organizational boundaries are very important, too. Much more than in other fields, further education in terms of professional development beyond one's basic competencies seems to be crucial. To make a career as a nonprofit executive successfully grow, an internal compass based on a strong intrinsic motivation to change things is a major driving force. However, nonprofit executives are not do-gooders but realistically judge the opportunities and limits of their influence.

These career-field rules match harmoniously with theories of intrinsic motivation and value-based leadership. In terms of motivation, careers in NPOs are much more strongly driven by intrinsic than by extrinsic motivation (Lawler & Hall, 1970; Leete, 2000). Thus, remuneration systems in NPOs have to prevent cautiously crowding out effects (e.g., Deci, Koestner, & Ryan, 1999): Too much extrinsic motivation might harm the inner compass. In terms of leadership, research points toward the specific relevance of transformational leadership behavior in NPOs (Lowe, Kroek, & Sivasubramiam, 1996): Leaders have to act in a charismatic, considerate, stimulating, and value-based way.

So what is it finally all about? Beyond research, there is a whole bulk of articles targeted to practitioners giving advice on how to start a career in the nonprofit sector (e.g., Brandel, 2001). Anyone considering a career with a nonprofit organization needs to realize that the organization's mission and values are of great importance. Consequently, the nonprofit's mission, goals, and values should match one's own values and interests. According to this fit, successful nonprofit executives are prepared to develop a strong professional and organizational commitment, which often results in blurring boundaries between their professional and private lives.

This alone certainly does not guarantee job satisfaction if the actual position one finds oneself in does not meet expectations regarding growth potential, daily activities, and so forth. To be quite sure, one has to check this fit between job, organization, and individual values and motives. Volunteering provides this opportunity to get to know the management, decision making, and organizational culture of a particular NPO very well even before deciding to pursue a full-time job there. Volunteer positions providing a broad insight into the organization are especially rewarding since the volunteer gets acquainted with different organizational units and managers.

References and Further Readings

Adams, J. S. (1963). Toward an understanding of inequity. *Journal of Abnormal and Social Psychology, 67,* 335–343.

Aghamanoukjan, A., Leitner, J., Meyer, M., Steinbereithner, M., & Eikhof, D. R. (2008). *Courtier or pirate, knighted or beheaded? The various shades of success aspirations of CSO managers.* The 24th colloquium of the European Organisation Studies Group (EGOS), Amsterdam, The Netherlands.

Arthur, M. B., Khapova, S. N., & Wilderom, C. P. M. (2005). Career success in a boundaryless career world. *Journal of Organizational Behavior, 26*(2), 177–202.

Arthur, M. B., & Rousseau, D. M. (1996). Introduction: The boundaryless career as a new employment principle. In M. B. Arthur & D. M. Rousseau (Eds.), *The boundaryless career* (pp. 3–20). New York: Oxford University Press.

Bourdieu, P. (1977). *Outline of a theory of practice* (R. Nice, Trans.). Cambridge, MA: Cambridge University Press.

Bourdieu, P. (1986). The forms of capital. In J. G. Richardson (Ed.), *Handbook of theory and research for the sociology of education* (pp. 241–258). New York: Greenwood Press.

Brandel, G. A. (2001). The truth about working in a not-for-profit. *CPA Journal, 71*(10), 13.

Bretz, R. D., & Judge, T. A. (1994). Person-organization fit and the theory of work adjustment: Implications for satisfaction, tenure, and career success. *Journal of Vocational Behavior, 44*(1), 32–54.

Childs, A., & Klimoski, R. J. (1986). Successfully predicting career success: An application of the biographical inventory. *Journal of Applied Psychology, 71*(1), 3–8.

Deci, E. L., Koestner, R., & Ryan, R. M. (1999). A meta-analytic review of experiments examining the effects of extrinsic rewards. *Psychological Bulletin, 125*(6), 627–668.

de Graaf, J. (2003). *Take back your time—fighting overwork and time poverty in America.* San Francisco: Berrett-Koehler.

Evans, P., & Bartolomé, F. (1981). *Must success cost so much?* New York: Basic Books.

Gattiker, U. E., & Larwood, L. (1986). Subjective career success: A study of managers and support personnel. *Journal of Business and Psychology, 1*(2), 78–94.

Harrow, J., & Mole, V. (2005). "I want to move once I have got things straight": Voluntary sector chief executives' career accounts. *Nonprofit Management & Leadership, 16*(1), 79–100.

Heslin, P. A. (2003). Self- and other-referent criteria of career success. *Journal of Career Assessment, 11*, 262–282.

Heslin, P. A. (2005). Conceptualizing and evaluating career success. *Journal of Organizational Behavior, 26*, 113–136.

Hughes, E. C. (1937). Institutional office and the person. In *Men and Their Work* (pp. 57–67). Glencoe, IL: Free Press.

Iellatchitch, A., Mayrhofer, W., & Meyer, M. (2003). Career fields: A small step towards a grand career theory? *International Journal of Human Resource Management, 14*(5), 728–750.

Janssen, O. (2001). Fairness perceptions as a moderator in the curvilinear relationships between job demands, and job performance and job satisfaction. *Academy of Management Journal, 44*(5), 1039–1050.

Jones, C. (1996). Career in project networks: The case of the film industry. In M. B. Arthur & D. M. Rousseau (Eds.), *The Boundaryless Career* (pp. 58–75). New York: Oxford University Press.

Judge, T. A., Higgins, C. A., Thoresen, C. J., & Barrick, M. R. (1999). The big five personality traits, general mental ability, and career success across the life span. *Personnel Psychology, 52*(3), 621–652.

Lawler, E. E., & Hall, D. T. (1970). Relationship of job characteristics to job involvement, satisfaction and intrinsic motivation. *Journal of Applied Psychology, 54*(4), 305–312.

Leete, L. (2000). Wage equity and employee motivation in nonprofit and forprofit organizations. *Journal of Economic Behavior & Organization, 43*(4), 423–446.

LeRoux, K., & Sneed, B. G. (2006). The convergence of public and nonprofit values: A research agenda for the intersectoral study of representative bureaucracy. *International Journal of Organization Theory and Behavior, 9*(4), 537–556.

Linder, S. B. (1970). *The harried leisure class.* New York: Columbia University Press.

Lowe, K. B., Kroek, K. G., & Sivasubramiam, N. (1996). Effectiveness correlates of transformational and transactional leadership: A meta-analytic review of the MLQ-literature. *Leadership Quarterly, 7*(3), 385–425.

Mayer, J. D., & Salovey, P. (1993). The intelligence of emotional intelligence. *Intelligence, 17*, 433–442.

Mayer, J. D., & Salovey, P. (1997). What is emotional intelligence? In P. Salovey, & D. J. Sluyter (Eds.), *Emotional development and emotional intelligence: Educational implications* (pp. 3–31). New York: Basic Books.

Mayrhofer, W., Meyer, M., Schiffinger, M., & Schmidt, A. (2008). The influence of family responsibilities, career fields and gender on career success: An empirical study. *Journal of Managerial Psychology, 23*(3), 292–323.

Mayrhofer, W., Meyer, M., & Steyrer, J. (2007). Contextual issues in the study of careers. In H. Gunz & M. Peiperl (Eds.), *Handbook of career studies* (pp. 215–240). Thousand Oaks, CA: Sage Publications.

Meyer, M., Aghamanoukjan, A., Eikhof, D. R., Leitner, J., & Steinbereithner, M. (2006). *Called to work but not for profit? Careers in the nonprofit sector between various forms of organising.* The 21st colloquium of the European Organisation Studies Group (EGOS), Bergen, Norwegen, July 5–7.

Morehouse, M. M. (2007). An exploration of emotional intelligence across career arenas. *Leadership & Organization Development Journal, 28*(4), 29.

Mulgan, G., & Wilkinson, H. (1995). Well-being and time. *Demos Quarterly, 5*, 3ff.

Pellegrin, R. J., & Coates, C. H. (1957). Executives and supervisors: Contrasting definitions of career success. *Administrative Science Quarterly, 1*(4), 506–517.

Putnam, R. D. (1995). Bowling alone: America's declining social capital. *Journal of Democracy, 6*(1), 65–78.

Reichel, A., Schiffinger, M., Chudzikowski, K., Demel, B., Mayrhofer, W., Schneidhofer, T., & Steyrer, J. (2006). *Organising career success. An exploratory study of individuals' configuration of objective and subjective career success.* The 21st colloquium of the European Organisation Studies Group (EGOS), Bergen, Norwegen, July 5–7.

Schor, J., Jhally, S., & Alper, L. (2003). *The overspent American: Why we want what we don't need* [Video]. Northampton, MA. Retrieved June 15, 2010, from http://www.youtube.com/watch?v=_nk2_rk0FLw

Steinbereithner, M. (2006). *Career success in not for profit organizations.* München, Germany: Hampp.

Tschirhart, M., Reed, K. K., Freeman, S. J., & Anker, A. L. (2008). Is the grass greener? Sector shifting and choice of sector by MPA and MBA graduates. *Nonprofit and the Voluntary Sector Quarterly, 37*(4), 668–688.

Work-life balance. (2003, March). *BMI Voyager*, 40–44.

PART VIII

ETHICS AND SOCIAL RESPONSIBILITY IN THE NONPROFIT WORLD

92

FUNDRAISING ETHICS

MELISSA MORRISS-OLSON

Bay Path College

According to the Ethics Resource Center's "2007 National Nonprofit Ethics Survey" (2007), more than half of the 450 nonprofit executives polled reported having witnessed unethical fundraising behavior over the course of their careers. More than 90% of these leaders cited the need for education about ethical fundraising. While ethical challenges arise at all levels in all types of organizations, the impact of such challenges can be especially troublesome for nonprofits. A 2006 Harris poll reported that only 1 in 10 Americans strongly believe that charities are honest and ethical in their use of donated funds. Approximately one third of U.S. adults have less than positive feelings toward America's charitable organizations, and the same number think that the nonprofit sector in America has "pretty seriously gotten off in the wrong direction" (Harris Interactive, 2006, "Non-profits Developing a Bad Reputation"). For organizations that depend on public support and private funding for their livelihood, these sentiments are problematic.

This chapter begins with a review of the concepts that inform and shape the context in which fundraising takes place. Organizational dynamics unfold in unique ways in the nonprofit world and set the stage for particular kinds of ethical issues. In this chapter, we examine those fundraising areas wherein ethical lapses are most likely to occur. Awareness of the potential for ethical issues is an important first step in avoiding ethical lapses. In some situations, these issues are easily resolved with clear-cut right or wrong decisions. Other situations are more difficult to resolve, such as when the issue involves deciding between two alternatives and neither is decidedly right or wrong. This chapter concludes with a review of ethical models for decision making, which can be useful in such situations.

Ethical Context for Fundraising

Nonprofits face a unique set of ethical challenges. Why is it important for nonprofit organizations and their leaders to pay attention to ethical issues, generally? Why is ethics in fundraising important, specifically? While the answers to these questions may seem obvious, a review of basic concepts provides a fuller understanding of the ethical context for fundraising.

Organizational Context

As professionals who do their work within an organizational context, fundraisers must be aware of both the rights and responsibilities that ground their work. Nonprofit organizations benefit in significant ways from our nation's tax structure. In exchange, nonprofits are expected to serve the public good as made explicit by section 501(c)(3) of the Internal Revenue Code. The "nondistribution" clause included here has particular relevance for fundraisers as it makes clear the expectation that nonprofits operate for the public good and that nonprofit employees and board members will avoid self-dealing. Ethical lapses in the nonprofit context are viewed as especially troublesome precisely because of the special trust that has been vested in nonprofits as agents of the public good.

As fundraisers working within this context, ethical practice is extremely important. "The essential test of ethical behavior is 'obedience to the unenforceable,' originally described by England's Lord Justice of Appeal John Fletcher Moulton 65 years ago as obedience to self-imposed law" (Independent Sector, 2002a, p. 8). As fundraisers, this means complying with legal requirements, such as the "nondistribution" clause, as well as upholding ethical practices, which reflect well on the organization. In 2002, The Independent Sector drafted its "Statement of Values and Code of Ethics for Nonprofit and Philanthropic Organizations," which outlines the ethics and values that nonprofits are expected to observe:

1. Commitment beyond self

2. Obedience to the laws

3. Commitment beyond the law

4. Commitment to the public good

5. Respect for the worth and dignity of individuals

6. Tolerance, diversity, and social justice

7. Accountability to the public

8. Openness and honesty

9. Responsible stewardship of resources

Importance of Trust

Not only are fundraisers concerned with maintaining the public trust, but they are also concerned with trust building on an individual level. Nearly all of the fundraising literature in recent years promotes the importance of relationship building as an enduring principle. Indeed, fundraisers are expected to build and maintain positive relationships with a variety of constituencies including donors, volunteers, colleagues, board members, and community members. Trust is a critical ingredient for such relationships; donors must be able to trust that fundraisers will be honest and will act with their best interests at heart. Albert Anderson (1996, p. 75) provides helpful guidelines for building trustworthy relationships:

Truth telling: Communicate, convey, and record information truthfully, accurately, and completely; avoid misleading or deceiving.

Promise keeping: Make and keep promises, agreements, and contracts that are consistent with organizational purposes.

Accountability: Be accountable for the stewardship of donated and organizational resources, and be open to scrutiny by appropriate constituents.

Fairness: Seek fairness and objectivity in arrangements that require the sharing of benefits and burdens and privileges and responsibilities.

Fidelity of purpose: In all relationships, be faithful to bona fide professional and organizational purposes; avoid or disclose apparently conflicting interests, inconsistency, and hypocrisy.

Trust is also an important theme in "The Donor Bill of Rights," created jointly by the Association of Fundraising Professionals (AFP), the Association for Healthcare Philanthropy (AHP), the Council for Advancement and Support of Education (CASE), and the Giving Institute: Leading Consultants to Non-Profits (see Box 92.1). Widely endorsed by numerous organizations, this statement serves as a reminder for all fundraisers about the broader purposes of philanthropy.

Box 92.1 The Donor Bill of Rights

Philanthropy is based on voluntary action for the common good. It is a tradition of giving and sharing that is primary to the quality of life. To ensure that philanthropy merits the respect and trust of the general public, and that donors and prospective donors can have full confidence in the nonprofit organizations and causes they are asked to support, we declare that all donors have these rights:

I. To be informed of the organization's mission, of the way the organization intends to use donated resources, and of its capacity to use donations effectively for their intended purposes.

II. To be informed of the identity of those serving on the organization's governing board, and to expect the board to exercise prudent judgment in its stewardship responsibilities.

III. To have access to the organization's most recent financial statements.

IV. To be assured their gifts will be used for the purposes for which they were given.

V. To receive appropriate acknowledgment and recognition.

VI. To be assured that information about their donation is handled with respect and with confidentiality to the extent provided by law.

VII. To expect that all relationships with individuals representing organizations of interest to the donor will be professional in nature.

VIII. To be informed whether those seeking donations are volunteers, employees of the organization, or hired solicitors.

IX. To have the opportunity for their names to be deleted from mailing lists that an organization may intend to share.

X. To feel free to ask questions when making a donation and to receive prompt, truthful, and forthright answers.

Fundraising as Servant of Philanthropy

Philanthropy is the context, development is the process, fundraising is the result.

Albert Anderson, *Ethics for Fundraisers*, 1996

Clearly, fundraising does not happen in a vacuum. Instead, the processes of gift making and gift receiving are rooted in a deeper sense of meaning, both for the fundraiser and the donor. A donor's reasons for giving are typically complex and multifaceted. Ideally, the gift is freely given without expectation of anything in return other than the government-authorized tax deduction. In reality, and as Joseph Mixer (1993) points out, donors receive any number of important values in exchange for their gifts, ranging from a sense of belonging and social recognition to a feeling of having made a difference. This voluntary exchange—in which the organization receives value from the donor's gift and the donor receives personal value through the process of giving—broadens the meaning of fundraising and gives it a purpose greater than itself.

As a values-based exchange, fundraising draws its meaning from the cause that it seeks to advance; hence, ethics must guide the fundraising process. Accordingly, Hank Rosso (2003) describes ethical fundraising as "the prod, the enabler, and the activator" of the gift-making process as well as "the conscience to the process" (p. 19). As organizations raise funds from the perspective of what best serves the donor's needs and values, fundraising is enacted with the spirit of philanthropy at its core. This contrasts sharply with the notion that some have of fundraising as nothing more than a self-seeking, quid pro quo exchange.

Professionalism and Personal Integrity

Commonly accepted characteristics of a profession include such things as a specialized body of knowledge, a set of skills, a group mission or identity, and standards of behavior and practice. As evaluated against this framework, fundraisers are clearly part of a profession, albeit an emergent one (Levy, 2004). A quick scan of the numerous educational fundraising programs that now exist yields an apparently common understanding about important knowledge and skills for professionals. For example, most programs include content about the history and philosophy of philanthropy, the legal and financial context, and specific skill-based courses, such as annual giving, grantwriting, and donor behavior. The AFP was established in 1960 to promote a common mission and identity for fundraisers. According to its website, AFP now "represents more than 30,000 members in 200 chapters throughout the world, working to advance philanthropy through advocacy, research, education and certification programs." Its mission focuses on the "development and growth of fundraising professionals and promotion of high ethical standards in the fundraising profession" (www.afpnet.org/About).

In 1964, AFP became the first international organization to codify its understanding about the role of ethics in fundraising. According to its "AFP Code of Ethical Principles and Standards" (2004), fundraisers are obligated to place the interests of others above their own and to practice with the highest level of personal integrity and trust (see Box 92.2).

Box 92.2   Association of Fundraising Professionals (AFP): Code of Ethical Principles and Standards (adopted 1964; amended September 2004)

The Association of Fundraising Professionals (AFP) exists to foster the development and growth of fundraising professionals and the profession, to promote high ethical behavior in the fundraising profession, and to preserve and enhance philanthropy and volunteerism.

Members of AFP are motivated by an inner drive to improve the quality of life through the causes they serve. They serve the ideal of philanthropy, are committed to the preservation and enhancement of volunteerism, and hold stewardship of these concepts as the overriding direction of their professional life.

(Continued)

(Continued)

They recognize their responsibility to ensure that needed resources are vigorously and ethically sought and that the intent of the donor is honestly fulfilled.

To these ends, AFP members, both individual and business, embrace certain values that they strive to uphold in performing their responsibilities for generating philanthropic support. AFP business members strive to promote and protect the work and mission of their client organizations.

AFP members both individual and business aspire to:

- practice their profession with integrity, honesty, truthfulness, and adherence to the absolute obligation to safeguard the public trust
- act according to the highest goals and visions of their organizations, professions, clients, and consciences
- put philanthropic mission above personal gain
- inspire others through their own sense of dedication and high purpose
- improve their professional knowledge and skills, so that their performance will better serve others
- demonstrate concern for the interests and well-being of individuals affected by their actions
- value the privacy, freedom of choice, and interests of all those affected by their actions
- foster cultural diversity and pluralistic values and treat all people with dignity and respect
- affirm, through personal giving, a commitment to philanthropy and its role in society
- adhere to the spirit as well as the letter of all applicable laws and regulations
- advocate within their organizations adherence to all applicable laws and regulations
- avoid even the appearance of any criminal offense or professional misconduct
- bring credit to the fundraising profession by their public demeanor
- encourage colleagues to embrace and practice these ethical principles and standards
- be aware of the codes of ethics promulgated by other professional organizations that serve philanthropy

Ethical Standards

Furthermore, while striving to act according to the above values, AFP members, both individual and business, agree to abide (and to ensure, to the best of their ability, that all members of their staff abide) by the AFP standards. Violation of the standards may subject the member to disciplinary sanctions, including expulsion, as provided in the AFP Ethics Enforcement Procedures.

Member Obligations

1. Members shall not engage in activities that harm the members' organizations, clients, or profession.

2. Members shall not engage in activities that conflict with their fiduciary, ethical and legal obligations to their organizations, clients or profession.

3. Members shall effectively disclose all potential and actual conflicts of interest; such disclosure does not preclude or imply ethical impropriety.

4. Members shall not exploit any relationship with a donor, prospect, volunteer, client or employee for the benefit of the members or the members' organizations.

5. Members shall comply with all applicable local, state, provincial, and federal civil and criminal laws.

6. Members recognize their individual boundaries of competence and are forthcoming and truthful about their professional experience and qualifications and will represent their achievements accurately and without exaggeration.

7. Members shall present and supply products and/or services honestly and without misrepresentation and will clearly identify the details of those products, such as availability of the products and/or services and other factors that may affect the suitability of the products and/or services for donors, clients, or nonprofit organizations.

8. Members shall establish the nature and purpose of any contractual relationship at the outset and will be responsive and available to organizations and their employing organizations before, during, and after any sale of materials and/or services. Members will comply with all fair and reasonable obligations created by the contract.

9. Members shall refrain from knowingly infringing the intellectual property rights of other parties at all times. Members shall address and rectify any inadvertent infringement that may occur.

10. Members shall protect the confidentiality of all privileged information relating to the provider/client relationships.

11. Members shall refrain from any activity designed to disparage competitors untruthfully.

Solicitation and Use of Philanthropic Funds

12. Members shall take care to ensure that all solicitation and communication materials are accurate and correctly reflect their organizations' mission and use of solicited funds.

13. Members shall take care to ensure that donors receive informed, accurate, and ethical advice about the value and tax implications of contributions.

14. Members shall take care to ensure that contributions are used in accordance with donors' intentions.

15. Members shall take care to ensure proper stewardship of all revenue sources, including timely reports on the use and management of such funds.

16. Members shall obtain explicit consent by donors before altering the conditions of financial transactions.

Presentation of Information

17. Members shall not disclose privileged or confidential information to unauthorized parties.

18. Members shall adhere to the principle that all donor and prospect information created by, or on behalf of, an organization or a client is the property of that organization or client and shall not be transferred or utilized except on behalf of that organization or client.

19. Members shall give donors and clients the opportunity to have their names removed from lists that are sold to, rented to, or exchanged with other organizations.

20. Members shall, when stating fundraising results, use accurate and consistent accounting methods that conform to the appropriate guidelines adopted by the American Institute of Certified Public Accountants (AICPA)* for the type of organization involved. (* In countries outside of the United States, comparable authority should be utilized.)

Compensation and Contracts

21. Members shall not accept compensation or enter into a contract that is based on a percentage of contributions; nor shall members accept finder's fees or contingent fees. Business members must refrain from receiving compensation from third parties derived from products or services for a client without disclosing that third-party compensation to the client (for example, volume rebates from vendors to business members).

22. Members may accept performance-based compensation, such as bonuses, provided such bonuses are in accord with prevailing practices within the members' own organizations and are not based on a percentage of contributions.

23. Members shall neither offer nor accept payments or special considerations for the purpose of influencing the selection of products or services.

(Continued)

(Continued)

24. Members shall not pay finder's fees, commissions, or percentage compensation based on contributions, and shall take care to discourage their organizations from making such payments.

25. Any member receiving funds on behalf of a donor or client must meet the legal requirements for the disbursement of those funds. Any interest or income earned on the funds should be fully disclosed.

SOURCE: © 1964, Association of Fundraising Professionals (AFP), all rights reserved. Reprinted with permission from the Association of Fundraising Professionals.

Ethical Issues and Dilemmas

Ethical issues can arise in almost any aspect of a fundraiser's daily work. There are six areas in particular where one is most likely to encounter ethical dilemmas: fundraiser relationships, privacy and confidentiality, tainted money, compensation, conflicts of interest, and transparency and disclosure.

Fundraiser–Donor Relationships

As fundraisers develop close relationships with their donors, it is easy to forget who ultimately owns the relationship. A first critical issue for fundraisers arises then in relation to the question of donor relationship ownership. Fundraisers should never benefit personally from their relationships with donors; any benefit from this relationship should accrue first and foremost to the organization. Donors frequently develop strong feelings of affection for the fundraisers with whom they work, sometimes to the point of giving gifts to the fundraisers as a means of expressing their feelings. If fundraisers are serving their organization's interests above all others, it is difficult to imagine a situation wherein it would be appropriate to accept a personal gift from a donor, for any reason. A second source of tension arises when fundraisers move from one organization to another and are tempted to take their donors with them. Given that the donor relationship exists only because of the organization and presumably the donor's commitment to the mission of that particular organization, the relationship must remain with the organization. For a fundraiser to do otherwise is a violation of the trust that the organization has placed in him or her.

Privacy and Confidentiality

Several professional codes explicitly address the importance of privacy and confidentiality including the AFP's "AFP Code of Ethical Principles and Standards" referenced above. The Association of Professional Researchers for Advancement (APRA) begins its code of ethics with the statement, "advancement researchers must balance an individual's right to privacy with the needs of their institutions to collect, analyze, record, maintain, use, and disseminate information." The code goes on to make explicit the profession's commitment to ensuring confidentiality in the handling of all forms of information about constituents (donors and nondonors), as well as confidential information of the institution, to "foster a trusting relationship between the constituent and the institution" (2009, "Statement of Ethics").

Even still, ethical issues arise in this area due largely to the fact that our notion of privacy is fluid and still evolving. Since 9/11 and the introduction of the USA Patriot Act, our country's legal definition of privacy has become increasingly murky. As the APRA's ethics code makes clear, most issues that fundraisers encounter in this area arise from the questions surrounding the individual constituent's right to privacy versus the organization's need to know. Indeed, most of these issues are not as much about the legal right to privacy as they are about the ethics of privacy. The explosion of the Internet and ever-increasing access to web-based search engines that allow one to quickly obtain information about individuals and organizations further complicates an already thorny issue.

When a donor makes a gift, such gifts must be recorded, reported, and acknowledged, meaning information about the gift needs to be made available to others within the organization as well as to external sources through the Internal Revenue Service (IRS) 990 form. Likewise, good fundraising practice dictates keeping careful records of all contacts with constituents. What specific information should be collected and recorded? How widely should this information be shared? Who within the organization really needs to know, and what specific information do they need to know? How does the organization protect the security of its information and donors and other constituents? How does the organization handle anonymous gifts? Should the organization rent or sell its donor lists without first asking permission of the individuals on these lists? These are just a few of the many questions that need to be carefully thought through to avoid potential ethical lapses. The APRA, among other professional associations, recommends establishing clear, detailed policies, procedures, and controls regarding the use and dissemination of constituent information. The ePhilanthropy Foundation has established a code of ethics governing the use of the Internet for philanthropic purposes (www.fundraising123.org/article/network-good-acquire-ephilanthropy-foundation).

Tainted Money Gifts

Tainted money is commonly understood to connote donations that raise questions of propriety for an organization due either to the source of the funds or the circumstances surrounding the donation. Tainted gifts can take different forms. Perhaps the least complicated form of tainted gift is that which comes from illegally obtained activity or sources such as theft, corporate crime, or the sale of illicit drugs. As the Independent Sector's "Statement of Values and Code of Ethics for Nonprofit and Philanthropic Organizations" (2004) makes clear, nonprofits must first and foremost be obedient to the law; hence, it is never appropriate for a fundraiser to knowingly accept a gift that is funded through illegal activity of any kind.

The second type of tainted gift is that which comes through seemingly legal means at the time of the donation but is later questioned due to circumstances surrounding the donor. For example, A. Alfred Taubman, the former chairman of Sotheby's currently serving a prison sentence for price-fixing, gave millions to Harvard University, Brown University, and the University of Michigan at Ann Arbor prior to his arrest and conviction (Maynard, 2001). When tainted gifts lead to the naming of organizational buildings or other visible features as happened with Taubman, they become even more problematic. While a handful of organizations have opted to return such gifts or to remove the name of the tainted gift donor, most nonprofits are reluctant to go this route, choosing instead to avoid controversy.

A third type of tainted gift involves legitimate gifts made by donors who expect to get something in return for their gift. For example, if a board member makes a gift to a nonprofit with the expectation of being advantaged in a business bidding process with the nonprofit, this potentially constitutes a violation of the IRS intermediate sanctions legislation. This law explicitly prohibits individuals from benefiting in their transactions with nonprofits with which they are associated (Independent Sector, 2002b). A less clear-cut example is when donors try to control their gift. If a naming donor for a new science center requests to be involved in the hiring of the center's director, this violates the notion of giving as a voluntary exchange.

While illegal gifts are clearly the most obvious type of tainted gift, these other forms are more common and less straightforward to resolve. In many cases, tainted gifts represent a value conflict between the donor and the nonprofit. When the Florida chapter of the Salvation Army turned down a six-figure gift from a lottery winner, it affirmed its belief that gambling leads to homelessness and poverty and is at odds with its core organizational values (Tubbs, 2003). Nearly all tainted gifts involve trade-offs for the organization,

the donor, and/or the fundraiser. Eugene Tempel (2008, pp. 67–68) offers a series of questions that fundraisers should ask in resolving tainted money dilemmas:

- Will taking money from a donor provide short-term benefits to our clients but risk long-term damage to the reputation of our organization and decrease services to our clients in the long run?
- If we turn down the money, what will be the short-term impact? What services will we not be able to offer?
- What are the various ways in which accepting a potentially tainted gift can affect the organization?
- Would the gift offend key stakeholders or damage long-term relationships with other donors?

Fundraiser Compensation

Ethical issues in this area most often arise over questions about the appropriateness of paying fundraisers on a commission basis or paying external professional solicitors to obtain funds for the nonprofit. Regarding the first, most major fundraising associations view commission-based pay for fundraisers as unethical. The "AFP Code of Ethical Principles and Standards" (2004) has five standards devoted exclusively to the topic (see standards 21–25 above). Taken together, the AFP standards clearly prohibit percentage, or commission-based pay, for fundraisers. According to AFP's former president, Paula V. Maehara (2008), this restriction is grounded in the belief that ethical fundraising must be supported in an environment wherein serving the public good is paramount and free of improper motives, unmerited rewards, or personal gains (p. 94). At the same time, AFP's standards do not prohibit performance-based pay and bonuses for excellent performance.

Regarding the appropriateness of hiring an external party to raise funds on behalf of the nonprofit, the answer is less clear. On one hand, many nonprofits, especially smaller ones with small staff, routinely hire external professional solicitors to conduct their fundraising campaigns, viewing the practice as both efficient and productive. And in some cases, this may be the only fundraising means available to the nonprofit. As long as the practice is free from fraud, paid solicitation is considered by most to be a legal and acceptable fundraising strategy. Many states hold the view shown by the Indiana Attorney General's Office on its website:

Many charitable organizations use professional solicitors to raise money on their behalf. The fact that a charity uses a paid solicitor does not mean that you should not contribute to the charity. However, it is something for you to take into account when you are considering making a donation. (Indiana Attorney General Consumer Division, 2009)

Fundraisers should be aware of the laws that govern the solicitation of funds by paid, professional solicitors. In addition, fundraisers should be mindful of the issues that might arise when a significant portion of funds raised are returned to the solicitor instead of directly benefiting the charity. As with all fundraising practices, nonprofits should assess their use of paid solicitors in light of its impact on public trust. If donors feel that their gifts are not being used wisely or for the purpose given, then their trust will diminish and the practice of using professional solicitors might prove costly.

Conflicts of Interest

Conflicts of interest can arise in various situations and can exist even in the absence of unethical or improper behavior. A conflict of interest typically arises in situations wherein individuals or organizations have competing personal or professional interests. In the nonprofit context, conflicts of interest can emerge when board members do business with the organizations on whose boards they sit. The intermediate sanctions law referenced above makes clear the obligation that nonprofits and their board members have to ensure that such dealings be conducted with the highest level of transparency possible and be subject to the same rules (e.g., bidding processes) as all other transactions.

Conflicts of interest can also arise when a fundraiser has the opportunity to benefit from a donor's philanthropic decisions or personal situation. For instance, it is not uncommon for donors to ask a fundraiser with whom they have developed a close relationship to act as executor for their estate. Even while this may be perfectly legal, others may perceive a conflict of interest based on personal self-interest on the part of the fundraiser. Likewise, a fundraiser who is pressed to meet revenue goals might be tempted to take advantage of an elderly donor who is lonely. Avoiding even the appearance of impropriety is an important standard for fundraisers who aspire to practice in accordance with the ethical principles discussed earlier.

Transparency and Full Disclosure

As the "Independent Sector Statement of Values and Code of Ethics for Nonprofit and Philanthropic Organizations" (2004) makes clear, organizations that seek and use public or private funds and claim to serve the public good have a particular obligation to be open and honest in their reporting, fundraising, and relationships with all constituencies. This means that nonprofits and their fundraisers should give constituents adequate and truthful information about their organizations to ensure well-informed and appropriate giving decisions. Fundraisers should avoid "sugarcoating" or "stretching" the facts about their organizations just to get the gift or to curry favor with a constituent. This also means that organizations should use funds consistent with donor intent and comply with specific conditions placed on donations. Honesty with donors is essential for building and maintaining trustworthy relationships.

A clearly published, board-approved gift acceptance policy can help fundraisers maintain discipline in the gift acceptance process, avoid accepting inappropriate gifts, and ensure full disclosure about the organization's handling of gifts. Such policies typically define the types of assets that are acceptable gifts, the forms of gifts that are acceptable, and the organization's role in the giving process.

Ethical Frameworks for Decision Making

Some situations are easily resolved by referring to clear-cut legal requirements or universally held ethical standards. For example, it is clearly wrong to tell a donor that her gift is tax deductible when, in fact, the organization does not have tax-exempt status. The "rightness" of other situations is not as clear such as whether or not to accept a donation from a longtime supporter whose reputation has been tarnished. Such dilemmas involve choosing between two alternatives—neither of which is decidedly right or wrong. Robert L. Payton (1988) observes that "there are no ethical answers; there are only ethical questions" (p. 123). This chapter concludes with a review of ethical models for decision making, which can provide helpful guidance for those situations wherein answers don't come easily.

Independent Sector Levels of Ethical Behavior

The Independent Sector recommends examining all ethical issues against a three-tiered framework. This can be a helpful starting point in clarifying the potential significance of the behavior as well as identifying appropriate means of resolution. According to the statement outlined in *Ethics and the Nation's Voluntary and Philanthropic Community: Obedience to the Unenforceable* (2002a), the first level of ethical behavior is concerned with the law. From a fundraising practice perspective, some behaviors are clearly illegal and decisions about their rightness are very easy to make. The second level includes those behaviors where one knows the right thing to do but is nevertheless tempted to do otherwise. Behaviors at this level are clearly unethical and as with the first level, the decision about their rightness should be fairly easy to make. The third level of ethical behavior involves conflicting options wherein there is no clear-cut right or wrong choice; instead, one may be left with options that both seem right. This level includes what we know typically as ethical dilemmas. Decision making at this level is difficult at best as the situation usually involves competing "goods" or conflicting values.

Fischer's Framework of Ethical Decision Making

In *Ethical Decision Making in Fund Raising* (2000), Fischer proposes that ethical fundraisers must consider three basic value commitments: organizational mission, relationships, and personal integrity. As nonprofits, the mission provides the raison d'être and is an essential element in ethical decision making. Alternative outcomes for a particular situation should be reviewed in light of their impact on the organization's mission. For example, to what extent will a particular option help advance the mission? Outcomes that hinder or diminish the mission should be rejected. As discussed earlier, fundraisers work within complicated relationship webs. Fischer's second value commitment is concerned with the character and quality of these relationships. Specifically, decision alternatives should be considered according to their potential impact— positive or negative—on this network of relationships. The end goal is to maintain healthy relationships whenever possible. The third value commitment entails one's own personal sense of integrity. Fischer urges fundraisers to consider each ethical dilemma or decision as an opportunity to sharpen one's own ethical character. Each situation should be viewed from an end-of-life perspective and according to whether a particular decision will result in a life well lived.

To assist fundraisers in becoming more ethical decision makers, Fischer (2000) developed a chart using these three basic value commitments. This chart leads one through the ethical reflection process described earlier, organizing the various alternative decisions according to how each might impact the three value commitments and helping the fundraiser ask "good enough questions" (p. 24). Fischer suggests including at least one obviously unethical alternative among your options to prompt less obvious insights and solutions. Asserting that "there is no one single formula which, if applied correctly, will yield an 'ethically correct' decision" (p. 25), Fischer suggests that the real value of this chart lies in helping ferret out the wrong answers:

> There are plenty of wrong answers, and the hope is that after reflection, the wrongness of the wrong answers will be clear. One will be able to choose among the others with sensitivity and good judgment. If an alternative supports all three basic value commitments, you can be assured that it is ethically sound. (p. 26)

Josephson's Pillars of Character

The Josephson Institute has developed a model for ethical decision making that, while not designed specifically for fundraisers, complements Fischer's framework and offers valuable guidance for professionals. Both the Independent Sector and Josephson models are premised on the notion that ethical conflicts and dilemmas can best be resolved by referencing and clarifying the values and beliefs that underlie particular options. In "The Six Pillars of Character" (2002b), Michael Josephson suggests judging options against a series of virtues, which include the following:

1. Trustworthiness (honesty, integrity, promise-keeping, loyalty)

2. Respect (autonomy, privacy, dignity, courtesy, tolerance, acceptance)

3. Responsibility (accountability, pursuit of excellence)

4. Caring (compassion, consideration, giving, sharing, kindness, loving)

5. Justice and fairness (impartiality, consistency equity, equality, due process)

6. Civic virtue and citizenship (law abiding, community service, protection of the environment)

Once the values are identified, Josephson (2002a) recommends a seven-step resolution process for resolving ethical issues:

1. *Stop and think*—Recognizing that many bad decisions are made in haste, this first step entails taking adequate time to think through all aspects of a situation before forming any conclusions.

2. *Clarify goals*—In this second step, practitioners are urged to determine precisely what must be decided as well as all alternatives. All stakeholders should be identified as well as all potential risks. This step also involves considering the short-term and long-term impacts of various alternatives.

3. *Determine the facts*—This third step asks decision makers to clarify what they know and what they need to know to reach a sound decision. Assessing the credibility of information sources and determining what information is most valid is an important part of this step.

4. *Develop options*—In the fourth step, decision makers should identify as many potential options as possible.

5. *Consider the options*—The fifth step involves referencing the six values discussed above to consider and assess each option. Impact on stakeholders is an especially important consideration.

6. *Choose*—In the sixth step, the decision maker chooses an option for implementation. Various criteria might be applied to one's choice including the golden rule test: If you were on the receiving end of this option, how would it feel?

7. *Monitor and modify*—The final step is perhaps the most important part of this process as it requires decision makers to remain vigilant in monitoring the impact of choices. "Since most hard decisions use imperfect information and 'best effort' predictions, some of them will inevitably be wrong. Ethical decision makers monitor the effects of their choices. If they are not producing the intended results or are causing additional unintended and undesirable results, they reassess the situation and make new decisions."

Anderson's Model of Ethical Decision Making

In *Ethics for Fundraisers* (1996), Albert Anderson suggests that most of the decisions faced by fundraisers can be resolved by turning to one of two major theoretical frameworks. The first framework, attributed to John Stuart Mill, is the Utilitarianism approach. According to this framework, the end result matters most: "Any action that on balance is an effective means to a satisfying end, generally 'the greatest good for the greatest number,' is ethically appropriate" (p. 39). Fischer's model discussed above is a good example of this approach.

The second framework (Anderson, 1996), the formalist approach, is attributed to Immanuel Kant and is based on the notion that there are certain moral rights or imperatives that should be followed regardless of the context. "To be morally worthy we must do our duty for its own sake, truly free of every other motivation, even the very strong feelings of sympathy and self-love" (pp. 40–41). Determining one's ethical responsibility depends on whether an action meets the "would it be right for everyone?" test. Anderson offers the example of a fundraiser who is considering deceiving a donor about her organization's plans in order to get a gift. If one turns the deception into a universal law, such as "always deceive others when it serves one's personal agenda," it is readily apparent that the fundraiser's intention is not ethically appropriate.

Based on his primary ethical domains of respect, beneficence, and trust, Anderson suggests that fundraisers should assess alternatives against three core principles: (1) Respect the essential worth and well-being of every person, (2) develop beneficence, and (3) build enduring, trustworthy relationships. After considering these principles, Anderson advises that the right course of action can be determined by applying three key questions to each alternative:

1. What seem(s) to be the ethical issue(s); that is, what does one judge to be right or wrong in this situation?

2. What action(s) would seem to make the situation right; that is, what ought we to do?

3. What ethical principle(s) and ultimate governing framework would justify the action(s)?

Summary and Future Directions

While the ethical codes and statements referenced in this chapter provide a common understanding about important ethical principles for fundraising, the Harris poll findings suggest that nonprofits still have a ways to go in shoring up public confidence. Clearly, the promotion of ethics as a guiding force for fundraising practice is a critical agenda item. Finding ways to more prominently integrate ethics into the education and training of fundraisers should be an important priority for the profession and for the organizations that hire fundraisers. Given the organizational context in which fundraising takes place, institutionalizing a culture of ethics and integrity is an important mandate for nonprofit leaders at all levels. Privacy issues will become increasingly complicated as nonprofits expand their use of social media and other forms of new technology to raise funds and reach out to their constituents. Fundraisers must take a leadership role to ensure that their organizations find the right balance between their need to know and the donors' right to privacy. In this age of mounting donor sophistication, the question, How much donor involvement is too much? is one that many fundraisers are already grappling with. Helping donors find an appropriate level of involvement while giving in the true spirit of philanthropy will be an increasingly crucial challenge for fundraisers going forward. And perhaps most essential, fundraisers must remain diligent in advocating for transparency and full disclosure. Fundraisers should take a proactive role in educating donors and the public about the real costs of fundraising and the need for an adequate fundraising infrastructure. They must lead the way in building and maintaining honest, trustworthy relationships with constituents. Nonprofits cannot fully or effectively realize their missions without the trust of the public they serve. The practice of ethical fundraising is a decisive factor in gaining and preserving this trust.

References and Further Readings

Anderson, A. (1996). *Ethics for fundraisers*. Bloomington: Indiana University Press.

Association of Fundraising Professionals (AFP). (2004). *AFP code of ethical principles and standards*. Available from http://www.afpnet.org/Ethics/EnforcementDetail.cfm?ItemNumber=3261

Association of Fundraising Professionals (AFP). (n.d.). *The donor bill of rights*. Retrieved May 18, 2009, from http://www.afpnet.org/ka/ka-3.cfm?content_item_id=9988

Association of Professional Researchers for Advancement. (2009). *Statement of ethics*. Retrieved from http://www.aprahome.org/ProfessionalStandards/StatementofEthics/tabid/74/Default.aspx

Ethics Resource Center. (2007). *2007 National nonprofit ethics survey*. Retrieved May 24, 2009, from http://www.ethicsworld.org/ethicsandemployees/nbes.php

Fischer, M. (2000). *Ethical decision making in fund raising*. New York: John Wiley & Sons.

Fogal, R., & Burlingame, D. (1994). *Ethics in fundraising: Putting values into practice*. San Francisco: Jossey-Bass.

Hall, H. (2004, October 14). When gifts get personal. *Chronicle of Philanthropy, 17*, pp. 7–8, 10, 12.

Harris Interactive. (2006, April). *Non-profits developing a bad reputation* (Harris Poll No. 33). Available from http://www.fundraiserhelp.com/nonprofits-bad-reputation.htm or from http://www.harrisinteractive.com/vault/Harris-Interactive-Poll-Research-BBC-2009-Privacy-3.pdf

Independent Sector. (2002a). *Ethics and the nation's voluntary and philanthropic community: Obedience to the unenforceable.* Washington, DC: Author.

Independent Sector. (2002b, October). *Intermediate sanctions.* Retrieved May 23, 2009, from http://www.independent sector.org/PDFs/sanctions.pdf

Independent Sector. (2004). *Statement of values and code of ethics for charitable and philanthropic organizations.* Retrieved May 15, 2009, from http://www.independent sector.org/about/code.html

Indiana Attorney General Consumer Division. (2009). *Information on charitable fundraising.* Retrieved May 22, 2009, from http://www.indianaconsumer.com/ consumer_guide/charitable_info.asp

Internal Revenue Service. (n.d.). *Exemption requirements for charitable organizations.* Retrieved May 14, 2009, from http://www.irs.gov/charities/charitable/article/0,,id=96099, 00.html

Josephson, M. (2002a). *Making ethical decisions.* Retrieved May 1, 2009, from http://josephsoninstitute.org/MED/ index.html

Josephson, M. (2002b). *The six pillars of character.* Retrieved May 1, 2009, from http://josephsoninstitute.org/MED/ MED2sixpillars.html

Levy, J. D. (2004). The growth of fundraising: Framing the impact of research and literature on education and training. In J. P. Ryan & L. Wagner (Eds.), *New directions for philanthropic fundraising special issue: Fundraising as a profession: Advancements and challenges in the field* (pp. 21–30). San Francisco: Jossey-Bass.

Maynard, M. (2001, December 9). If a name is tarnished, but carved in stone. *New York Times,* p. B4.

Maehara, P. V. (2008). Compensation. In J. G. Pettey (Ed.), *Ethical fundraising: A guide for nonprofit boards and fundraisers* (pp. 89–104). Hoboken, NJ: John Wiley & Sons.

McNamara, C. (2000). *Complete guide to ethics management.* Retrieved April 28, 2009, from http://managementhelp .org/ethics/ethxgde.htm

Mixer, J. R. (1993). *Principles of professional fundraising: Useful foundations for successful practice.* San Francisco: Jossey-Bass.

Network for Good. (2008). *ePhilanthropy code of ethical online philanthropic practices.* Retrieved May 5, 2009, from http://www.fundraising123.org/article/ephilanthropy-code-ethics

Payton, R. L. (1988). *Philanthropy: Voluntary action for the common good.* New York: Macmillan.

Pribbenow, P. (2005). Public character: Philanthropic fundraising and the claims of accountability. In L. Wagner & T. L. Seiler (Eds.), *New directions for philanthropic fundraising* (pp. 13–27). San Francisco: Jossey-Bass.

Pulley, J. (2003, January 3). Tainted Gifts. *Chronicle of Higher Education, 49,* pp. A32–34.

Rosen, M. J. (2005, August). Doing well by doing right: A fundraiser's guide to ethical decision-making. *International Journal of Nonprofit and Voluntary Sector Marketing, 10,* 175–181.

Rosso, H. A. (2003). A philosophy of fundraising. In E. R. Tempel (Ed.), *Hank Rosso's achieving excellence in fund raising* (pp. 14–20). San Francisco: Jossey-Bass.

Sczudlo, W. (2003, September–October). Motivation: Mission or money? *Advancing Philanthropy,* 30–32.

Tempel, E. R. (2008). Tainted money. In J. G. Pettey (Ed.), *Ethical fundraising: A guide for nonprofit boards and fundraisers* (pp. 61–88). Hoboken, NJ: John Wiley & Sons.

Tubbs, S. (2003, June 10). Churches at odds over gifts from gamblers. *St. Petersburg Times.* Available from www .sptimes.com/2003/06/10/Floridian/Churches_at_odds_over .shtml

93

ISSUES IN NONPROFIT ETHICS

AUDREY BARRETT

San Diego City College

Ethics exists in a multitude of formats from the philosophical and abstract to the realm of applied contexts defined by statutes and codes. All forms vary in their situational importance and some present as contradictory to each other. Scholars and students often find that ethical studies within a particular field follow a similar developmental pattern of moving from concrete, or black and white, to a more fluid shades-of-gray model. Narrowing the focus to applied, organizational-level ethics in the nonprofit sector we find an emerging body of knowledge that is moving along this developmental continuum.

To advance the reader's understanding of this important subject, this chapter discusses a variety of concepts to provide a foundational understanding of ethics assessment relevant to nonprofit organizations. Discussions about the characteristics of the nonprofit sector, organizational culture, and the value of organizational-level assessment combined with the identification of salient constructs for assessing nonprofit ethics, the introduction of an empirically supported tool for assessing ethics in nonprofit organizations, and proposed future directions for this emerging field serve to accomplish this task.

The Importance of Ethics to Nonprofit Organizations

Ethics plays an integral role in the viability of nonprofit organizations for multiple reasons. Nonprofit organizations serve as stewards of public monies and as a result they receive tax exemption privileges. This benefit comes in exchange for the work and services they provide to the societal common good. Nonprofit organizations historically have filled the gap between (a) the goods and services provided by business and government and (b) the remaining unmet needs of communities. This typically includes the specialized needs of marginalized populations. Since the work of nonprofits receives public scrutiny and often depends on the generosity of donors to continue providing services, nonprofits have a vested interest in maintaining ethical organizations. Even the hint or perception of unethical behavior can destroy a nonprofit entity as donors and community members will typically not support a nonprofit organization labeled as unethical.

Healthy and able nonprofit organizations increasingly recognize the value of periodically assessing their current ethical standing and continuously working to maintain high ethical standards within their organizations. Reviewing the events of the past decade, one can easily see the detriment that ethical lapses can cause when nonprofit agencies fail to maintain ethical organizations. The highly publicized unethical behavior of a few large nonprofit organizations has yielded, by some accounts, a sectorwide negative impact in the form of decreased donor generosity. Donors and the public at large don't appear to trust nonprofit organizations in the wake of ethical problems as evidenced by decreased giving trends.

Organizations seeking to ride out the guilty-by-association phenomena, while maintaining their funding streams and reputations, have needed to take a proactive approach to demonstrating their ethical health during these troubled times. Striving to create an ethical context in which ethical behavior is the default behavior has served as one means of accomplishing this task. Nonprofit leaders can promote a healthy ethical context within their organizations by staying informed and actively promoting ethics within their organizations.

Engaging in regular organizational-level assessment serves as one method for gathering the data nonprofit leaders need to assess the current level of ethical health in their organizations. Working from a data-based vantage point maximizes the opportunity to reinforce a culture supportive of positive ethical behavior. This informed perspective decreases the risk of having an ethical lapse. Thus, a proactive approach to organizational ethics through periodic ethics assessment provides nonprofit leaders with the needed data to inform them about the ethical culture that exists in their organization, so they can best serve their missions and constituents.

Distinctions Between the Nonprofit, Business, and Government Sectors

A plethora of contemporary book titles address the issue of organizational ethics. The wealth of publications, or even a simple Google search, indicates that the assessment of ethics at the organizational level represents a topic of interest to the leaders of all types of organizations—for-profit, nonprofit, and government agencies alike. However, important distinctions exist between the three economic sectors in one arena largely related to the acquisition of resources and regulations around the distribution of profits. Nonprofit entities operate under a nondistribution constraint, which prohibits the distribution of profits to their leadership. This prohibition on the sharing of profits presents in stark contrast to the for-profit model, where shareholders expect to receive a percentage of profits. The nondistribution constraint "provides a clear distinction that affects how the organization obtains resources, how it is controlled, how it behaves in the marketplace, how it is perceived by donors and clients, and how its employees are motivated" (Steinberg, 2006, p. 119). Again, given that philanthropic organizations depend largely on donor generosity, one can see how the perceptions of a nonprofit organization as ethical serve as particularly relevant and directly link with continued viability.

As the nonprofit sector and business sector differ, the nonprofit sector and government sectors also exhibit distinct boundaries between each other and their roles in our economy. Nonprofit scholar Steinberg (2006) notes the government sector serves as a mediator, facilitator, and regulator of both for-profit and nonprofit activities. Steinberg uses the example of governments providing roads and highways, which provide literal access to and between places that members of all sectors use. This supports Steinberg's categorization of government as a facilitator or intermediary. Further, governments provide subsidies to specialized groups as needed, and they fill the gap when for-profit or nonprofit entities breach their contract with the public to provide needed goods and services.

The Need for Specialized Tools

The unique quality of the nonprofit sector, as distinct from its for-profit and government siblings, provides the basis for using tools designed specifically for assessing organizational ethics within nonprofit agencies. The

nuanced, and at times, overt differences between the sectors render tools designed for one sector as insufficient to fully assess the others. Stated another way, it's not that assessment tools cannot be used across sectors with some success, but that the distinctions among the sectors indicate that each warrants instruments designed specifically to meet the needs of that particular sector. The paragraphs that follow further discuss the need for specialized tools to assess nonprofit organizations.

Limitations of Existing Tools From Other Sectors

The business sector, followed by the government sector, has conducted the largest amount of work in the area of assessing and understanding organizational ethics. However, significant criticisms exist regarding this body of literature. The work in both of this milieu has been limited and has often focused on solely one part of the organization: For example, studies tend to highlight the ethics of executive managers or the effect of ethics policies on compliance. Focusing an assessment on one area of an organization can provide detailed information about that department or segment of the organization, but it risks obtaining a false picture of the organization's overall ethical health. As an alternative, organizational-level assessment provides comprehensive data able to inform nonprofit leaders about ethical strengths and weaknesses within the organization and provides a holistic view of the organization.

An additional concern regarding the work on organizational ethics conducted in other sectors grows out of questions surrounding the methodological soundness of those instruments and studies. Specifically, the business literature identifies poor use of instrument pretesting, limited validity and reliability testing, and antiquated practices, among many tools used to assess ethics in the for-profit sector.

In a literature review conducted by Randall and Gibson (1990) on studies of business ethics, an astounding 78% (73% by Barrett's calculation) of the studies they looked at conducted no pretest of their research instruments with a relevant population, and only three researchers received a positive nod for conducting statistical reliability or validity measures. Additionally, 53% (50% by Barrett's calculation) of the studies used new (previously untested) assessment tools without any reported pretesting. This lack of rigor among the testing practices and use of these instruments raises serious questions about the reliability, validity, and the generalizability of these numerous studies to the business sector, let alone to the nonprofit sector.

Limitations of Applying Tools Across Sectors

In addition to recognizing the weaknesses of the existing tools in other sectors, support for using assessment tools designed specifically for nonprofit organizations comes from the growing body of literature that identifies the limitations of applying best business practices to nonprofits with the expectation of achieving similar positive results. In fact, some indication exists that well-intended business practices used in a nonprofit organization may be not only ineffective but also harmful to the organization and its ability to achieve its mission. This may be a result of fundamental differences in organizational purpose between for-profit and nonprofit organizations or a variety of factors. Whatever the cause, it provides more support for using sector-specific tools for assessment and at a minimum informs organizational leaders to proceed with caution when using tools across sectors.

Upon considering the information reviewed above, one can easily appreciate the need for specialized tools given the unique characteristics of the nonprofit sector, the limitations of existing tools in other sectors, and the evidence that applying methods and tools across sectors may not provide the best assessment for organizations outside the original type it was designed to assess. In light of such significant support, one may wonder why the use of specialized tools is not already standard practice. The next section explores the answer to this question.

A Paucity of Specialized Tools

The primary challenge to using instruments designed for the nonprofit sector to evaluate organizations within the sector is the lack of such instruments. Strikingly few empirical studies of organizational ethics in the nonprofit sector exist. Two studies of note constitute the bulk of literature in this area: The *National Nonprofit Ethics Survey* (2008) conducted by the Ethics Resource Center (ERC) and *The Nonprofit Ethics Survey* (Barrett, 2008).

The National Nonprofit Ethics Survey

The *National Nonprofit Ethics Survey* is a specialty report produced from the National Business Ethics Survey (NBES). Since 1994, the ERC has conducted the NBES approximately every 2 years, and many business leaders recognize the NBES as the gold standard for identifying trends in business ethics. The NBES gathers data from employees of all three economic sectors, and in 2008, the ERC produced two specialized reports from the NBES data: the *National Government Ethics Survey* and the *National Nonprofit Ethics Survey*.

The *National Nonprofit Ethics Survey* serves as a practitioner-friendly report of trends in ethical behavior by the employees of nonprofit organizations. The survey clearly identifies the important link between organizational culture, the actions of an organization's leadership, and the presence of a compliance program in supporting organizational ethical health. The survey report also presents a risk index model for nonprofit organizations and compares the ethical behavior of nonprofits to that of the business and government sectors.

The primary critique of the *National Nonprofit Ethics Survey* report is the use of the same instrument for employees of all three sectors. Thus, it too is not tool or study specific to the nonprofit sector. However, the large number of subjects in the study, the methodologically solid survey instrument and survey process, and longevity of the study serve to ameliorate this concern. Additionally, the use of the same survey instrument across sectors in a study with a scope as large as the NBES allows for comparisons between sectors. Now, while the confidence with which one can generalize about results between sectors remains open to further exploration and validation, the survey provides a pioneering attempt at comparing ethical behavior across sectors in a methodologically sound manner.

The Nonprofit Ethics Survey

The Nonprofit Ethics Survey (Barrett, 2008) stands as the only empirically supported survey instrument designed specifically for assessing nonprofit organizational ethics. The survey grew out of a multiyear ethics initiative at the Institute for Nonprofit Education and Research at the University of San Diego and created a methodologically sound, practitioner-friendly instrument.

The "Nonprofit Ethics Survey" instrument assesses ethics at the organizational level by asking all members of the organization the same questions about ethics to provide a snapshot view of the organizations ethical health and to identify any disparities between levels of the organization should they exist. The survey is based on six empirically supported constructs, which are described later in this chapter, and includes a separate section of questions about governance practices asked only of the organization's board members.

To facilitate ease of survey administration, data collection, and interpretation of results, the "Nonprofit Ethics Survey" is an online survey instrument that nonprofit organizations can self-administer. The survey typically takes 10 to 20 minutes to complete depending on the respondent's level of computer proficiency and whether or not the respondent is a board member (board members answer additional questions on the survey about governance issues). Access to the survey is free of charge to any nonprofit organization and available through the Institute for Nonprofit Education and Research website (www.sandiego.edu/npresearch).

The age of the "Nonprofit Ethics Survey" serves as the primary critique of this instrument. The survey was developed and tested in 2008 and has been available to the public via the Internet since late 2009. As greater numbers of organizations use the survey and provide feedback, the level of methodological and positive anecdotal support that already exists for the survey will gather greater depth and fortitude.

Distinctions Between the Surveys

An important distinction exists between the *National Nonprofit Ethics Survey* and the "Nonprofit Ethics

Survey." The *National Nonprofit Ethics Survey* is a *report* of survey data collected by telephone interviews approximately every 2 years using a tool designed primarily for the business sector, but used with employees of all three sectors. The "Nonprofit Ethics Survey" is an online survey *instrument* designed for assessing ethics in individual nonprofit organizations.

The *National Nonprofit Ethics Survey* and the "Nonprofit Ethics Survey" instrument present as complementary in their use to members of a nonprofit organization's leadership, such as an executive director or a board of directors. The *National Nonprofit Ethics Survey* report provides overall data about national trends in nonprofit ethics and the components of ethics programs identified as critical to maintaining an ethical organization. The "Nonprofit Ethics Survey" provides a methodologically sound instrument with which to gather data about the individual organization to assess its current ethical health. Nonprofit leaders using both the report and survey would obtain reliable data about their organization with the opportunity to benchmark its standing against national trends and the known best ethical practices.

As noted, the *National Nonprofit Ethics Survey* and *The Nonprofit Ethics Survey* comprise the bulk of the scholarly literature on nonprofit organizational ethics. Three additional studies exist. However, they focus on a segment of ethics within an organization, not on organizational-level assessment, and as such do not provide a comprehensive evaluation of an organization. Given that five studies comprise the complete body of scholarly literature on nonprofit organizational ethics, the field presents as ripe with empirical research opportunities and in great need of further exploration.

Compliance: Important to Ethics but Not Enough

Separate from the empirical studies conducted in the field of nonprofit ethics, a large body of complementary work has focused on issues of compliance. Compliance typically refers to adherence to laws, policies, or procedures. Checklists represent a useful way to measure compliance by providing recommendations for how things should be in an organization. Primarily, three forms of tools exist in this arena: (a) checklists to determine whether organizations use empirically supported best practices, (b) checklists to measure the level of compliance with regulatory statutes, and (c) voluntary certification programs.

Organizations assessing themselves by compliance standards, such as the three types mentioned above, demonstrate awareness of ethical issues. However, relying on compliance alone has limits. The existence of a policy says nothing about the practical application and use of the policy—specifically, how things actually are in the organization. Further, the literature shows that the most beautifully written, long-established, and formally adopted code,

policy, or procedure within an organization will prove no match for the ethical context of the organization if the code, policy, or procedure conflicts with the ethical context.

This means organizations committed to preventing ethical lapses must focus on creating a culture that fosters an ethical environment. Stated another way, compliance checklists and organizational best practice guidelines provide a good start—but no more—as they ignore the integral role of organizational culture in ethical behavior. If organizations want to decrease their risk of unethical conduct, they must put their energy into building the right culture over building a compliance infrastructure. The ERC explicitly identifies this relationship stating that a well-designed compliance program serves as one component of creating a culture supportive of ethical health within nonprofit organizations. Thus, compliance is integral to ethics but not a stand-alone solution.

The next sections of this chapter further discuss the important role of organizational culture on ethics and compliance. Additionally, information about the comprehensive nature of organizational-level assessment and how this practice gleans information missed by programs based solely on compliance and checklists is reviewed.

The Power of Organizational Culture on the Members of an Organization

All types of organizations create and maintain a unique social context, including nonprofits. Social context, also often referred to as organizational climate or organizational culture, serves as the unwritten code of conduct by which members of an organization abide. The power social context has over the members of an organization to shape and direct their behavior often exceeds the written polices and procedures of the organization. To underscore the singularity and strength of culture, one can best conceptualize opposition to the values and beliefs of an organization's social context as equivalent to swimming against the current of a river, while still heading at a fast pace toward a waterfall. Typically, those who do not comply with the unwritten rules of the organization find themselves faced with the choice of leaving the organization or "going over the falls."

The Role of Individual Ethics

The literature on ethics supports the above claims. To confirm this, let's explore the role of individual ethics within the milieu of the organization and define ethics and ethical behavior. These confirmations will serve to support the connection between organizational social context and organizational ethics. To begin, one must first appreciate that each member of an organization holds personal ethical beliefs. Bowman (1976) defined ethical beliefs as judgments about what represents right or wrong and whether or not those judgments present as bad or good. These beliefs shape the actions or behaviors by the individuals on behalf of the organizations to which they belong. Actions and behaviors by individuals make up *ethical behavior*, which Runes defined in 1964 as the "just" or "right" standards of behavior between participants in a given setting (as cited in Randall & Gibson, 1990).

The Power of Situational Context

However, although personal beliefs play a role in decision making and behavior, the strength of the organizational context significantly affects the ethical behaviors of individuals. The power of situational factors can cause individuals to act in a manner inconsistent with their personal beliefs and in contradiction to known best practices.

The behavior of U.S. military personnel at Abu Ghraib prison in Iraq provides a highly publicized example of the power of situational context, or culture, on individual ethics and behavior. One can reasonably assume that under normal circumstances the U.S. soldiers at Abu Ghraib would not engage in torture. However, we now know that some did and to great extremes. In attempting to understand what happened at Abu Ghraib, scholars have added to our knowledge of the critical link between organizational culture, the actions of administrators that create and reinforce a particular culture, and the behavior of the organization's members. Scholar Reinke (2006) explicitly explored these relationships to highlight the power of organizational culture on individual behavior.

Additional work in this area exists including the Stanford Prison Experiment conducted in 1971 by Philip Zimbardo (2007) and the work of psychologist Stanley Milgram (1974) on obedience to authority. Zimbardo's study tested what happens when "good" people are placed in an "evil" position, and the experiment, originally planned for 2 weeks, ended after 6 days due to the extremely disturbing behavior of participants. Both Zimbardo's and Milgram's research further demonstrate that profound changes in behavior, including unethical behavior and behavior reported as inconsistent with the person's moral and ethical values, does in fact occur when supported by the situation or culture.

Relative Morality and the Importance of Knowing an Organization's Culture

Research on the strength of the situation, or social context, provides some answers and theory to support the concept of relative morality: the thought that individuals will have inconsistent or incongruous ethical responses within different contexts. Given the potential for this ethical fluidity, the leaders of nonprofit organizations have a critical need to know where on the spectrum of ethical support their organization's social context falls. Stated directly, one cannot simply employ ethical employees and expect to have an ethical organization. An organization must maintain an ethical context that both supports and reinforces

ethical behavior, while also upholding accountability to ethical standards at all levels of the organization.

For these complex reasons, it serves as critical for the leadership of nonprofit agencies to periodically engage in organizational-level ethics assessment with statistically sound instruments and to understand the components critical to maintaining ethical health. The next sections of this chapter will discuss organizational-level assessment, the macro-level motivations for nonprofit organizations to embrace organizational-level ethics assessment, and the constructs critical for nonprofit leaders to assess.

What Is Organizational-Level Assessment?

Organizational-level assessment provides a 360-degree view of the organization by engaging all members in the assessment process. Imagine if only one level of the organization, for instance board members, participated in an ethics assessment. The board may falsely believe the organization is ethical, or their knowledge of solely governance issues may blind them from the daily operations in which staff members ignore the policies and procedures that, if followed, would ensure ethical behavior. In this case, by only assessing the board members, the opportunity to identify differences in perception between levels of the organization is lost.

In organizational-level assessment, the unit of analysis is the organization. By asking all members to participate, if disparities exist between the board members and staff or between senior staff and line staff, they will be identified. Identification of varied perceptions helps to ensure an accurate picture of the organization. This accurate information then allows the leadership of the organization, usually the executive director, board members, and in larger organizations, key members of the senior or executive staff to make any needed changes and to work toward creating or maintaining a healthy ethical context.

The potential minimization of positive response bias serves as an added advantage of conducting an organizational-level assessment. Granted, most people have a positive response bias when completing a survey about themselves or their organization, unless things are really bad, but by asking all levels of the organization to participate, even with positive response bias present, a pattern of behavior and norms (whether good or bad) can be more readily identified. To further explore positive response bias, consider our earlier example of assessing only the board members of an organization. In an organization with poor ethical health, if solely the board members are surveyed and the board—through lack of knowledge, denial of problems, or simple ignorance—provides a falsely positive picture of the organization, the credibility of the positive assessment has no basis for evaluation or internal reliability. However, if all levels of the organization participate in the assessment, a falsely positive report by the board members can be challenged by variations in responses at different levels of the organization, even when the variations in response present as subtle.

Drawback to Organizational-Level Assessment

The investment of resources, namely time, presents as one significant drawback to conducting an organizational-level assessment. As all members are requested to participate, the organization must commit the necessary resources to engage all members in the process through paid employee time, volunteer time, and infrastructure support (e.g., computers for online surveys). However, the old adage that anything worth doing is worth doing well may indicate that organizations serious about ethics assessment will consider these costs an investment in the process and well worth the expense.

Taken together, the benefits of organizational-level assessment indicate that it presents a great option for nonprofit organizations who wish to obtain a comprehensive picture of their ethical context. The pro of knowledge gained outweighs the con of expense and the required infrastructure support for forward-thinking, proactive nonprofit organizations.

Motivations for the Nonprofit Sector to Embrace Organizational-Level Assessment

Primary motivations for the nonprofit sector to engage in organizational-level ethics assessment include providing the best possible stewardship of public monies and trust and compliance with governmental regulation. The key elements of these motivations are addressed in the paragraphs that follow to further demonstrate the benefit of organizational-level ethics assessment to nonprofit organizations.

Stewards of Public Monies and Trust

A primary motivation for nonprofit organizations to embrace measures of organizational-level ethics assessment relates to their position as stewards of public monies and trust. Nonprofits seeking to keep the faith of donors and all stakeholders in the organization must regard efforts to build and maintain ethical organizations as critical. Specifically, they must work to maintain public trust. Engaging in comprehensive ethics assessment and applying the knowledge gathered, along with being a learning organization, serve as effective methods to help secure public trust.

Much support exists for the link between ethics assessment and increased levels of public trust. First, the process of conducting an ethics evaluation often raises awareness of ethics simply by virtue of asking members of the organization to think about ethics. Researchers have also found the use of assessments increases the use of recognized best practices within organizations thus leading to more healthy, progressive, and adaptive organizations. Most recently, this has manifested in the form of organizations with greater levels of transparency. Finally, the employment of regular and formalized evaluation also presents as

a trait of *learning organizations,* an organizational type first described by Argyris (1977) and Senge (1990). Learning organizations use evaluation feedback to promote positive growth within their organizations, and scholars report that possessing the traits of a learning organization serves to enhance public trust.

Argyris described organizational learning as a process of identifying and removing barriers to knowledge, and he identified two types of organizational learning: single-loop and double-loop. *Single-loop* learning works in a reactive manner: An organization or system recognizes a problem and then takes steps to correct the problem. Argyris uses a thermostat as an example to describe single-loop learning. Thermostats register if the temperature in a room is too high or too low and then adjust the temperature. However, single-loop learning, like the thermostat, functions only as a reactive response. Single-loop learning provides no opportunity to prevent the problem just simply to fix it once it has occurred. *Double-loop* learning involves an organization or system questioning its policies and procedures and their underlying objectives. Double-loop learning represents a proactive response, and engaging in it can promote an evaluative atmosphere that may prevent problems.

Double-loop learning develops the ethical context of organizations in a positive manner, and it requires self-examination and assessment to provide the data needed for organizational learning. Studies have found that learning organizations have an increased likelihood of ethical integrity as the process of questioning the underlying assumptions that compose the social and ethical context of an organization facilitate transparency. As noted earlier and discussed more fully later in this chapter, organizational transparency plays a key role in organizational ethics.

By examining the links between organizational learning, ethics assessment, and public trust, the value of engaging in comprehensive regular ethics assessments presents clearly. Substantial motivations related to being good stewards of public monies and public trust exist that also relate to organizational-level ethics assessment for nonprofits.

Governmental Regulation

Government regulation serves as the second motivation for nonprofit agencies to embrace organizational-level ethics assessment. Nonprofit organizations have great reason to expect increased governmental regulation soon as the three economic sectors tend to follow the same trends. Following the passage of the Sarbanes-Oxley Act of 2002, which holds businesses to higher accountability standards, a ripple effect occurred in the nonprofit sector. Since 2002, twenty-nine states have put forth similar legislation for nonprofit accountability (National Council of Nonprofit Associations, 2007, http://www.councilofnonprofits.org).

Additionally, the Internal Revenue Service (IRS) has released a significantly revised 990 form with a rolling implementation schedule that commenced with tax year 2008. Larger nonprofits used the revised form effective tax year 2008 while smaller organizations were given a 3-year period to comply with all requirements of the revised form. Nonprofit organizations, those agencies granted tax-exempt status by the IRS, with gross annual receipts of $25,000 or greater, are required to file the 990 form each year. The revisions to the 990 form continue the two historical uses of the form: (1) provide information to the IRS and (2) provide information to the public. However, the new form collects many additional pieces of data and includes a summary sheet that creates a more user-friendly snapshot of the organization. This snapshot perspective can help inform current or potential donors as well as the IRS about the activities of a specific nonprofit agency.

Some additions to information gathered by the 990 form incorporate an element of oversight into the governance of individual nonprofit organizations. This addition can potentially allow an individual outside the organization to assess the relationship between a nonprofit's level of corporate governance and compliance with the tax code (Lewis, 2009). Related to governance, the revised 990 form inquires about the nonprofit's board of directors, the presence of compliance policies including a conflict of interest policy, whistle-blower protection, document retention policies, the use of board meeting minutes, and even bylaw details, such as number of voting board members. Attention to corporate governance by the IRS, via the actions to summarize the information and make it easily accessible, highlight the need for nonprofit leaders to take corporate governance seriously and the continuing trend toward increased organizational transparency.

As a result of this movement toward increased governmental regulation and in the interest of raising the standard of nonprofit operations, nonprofit leaders and advocates have proactively increased the forms and modes of self-regulation within the sector. However, most self-regulatory efforts have focused on compliance, which as discussed previously is necessary but, used alone, insufficient to establish consistently high levels of ethical conduct (Barrett, 2008; Ethics Resource Center, 2008). The next section of this chapter will further explore this issue through a review of some current trends in self-regulation by the nonprofit sector.

Increased Self-Regulation by the Sector

Since the introduction of Sarbanes-Oxley, nonprofits have significantly stepped up their individual and collective efforts at self-regulation. This increase is evidenced by the promotion of published standards for ethics, legal compliance, empirically supported best practices, voluntary certification programs, and sector-wide educational campaigns. Published standards for legal compliance and best practices typically combine the minimum legal standards for nonprofits with the known best practices for governance, transparency, and financial matters. These integrated checklists serve as benchmarks against which to compare organizations. Voluntary certification programs have also emerged as a form of self-governance; they typically require verified compliance with specific published guidelines. With verified compliance from the accrediting body, nonprofit organizations receive certification, sometimes in exchange for a fee.

The rapid increase in the awareness of ethics, transparency, and other related issues throughout the nonprofit sector comes as a secondary benefit of increased government regulation and initial efforts at self-regulation. However, the majority of these efforts focus on compliance. As mentioned previously, while having a well-established compliance program serves as a key component of maintaining an organization with strong ethical health, it works best when paired with a strong cultural emphasis on ethics inclusive of ethical leadership, supervisor reinforcement, peer commitment to ethics, and having ethical values embedded in the organization (Ethics Resource Center, 2008).

At present, many organizations within the nonprofit sector have not yet achieved a state of strong ethical health and the sector at large has only recently adopted sector-wide standards, such as the Panel on the Nonprofit Sector's principles (2007). Additionally, while a plethora of articles discussing self-regulation demonstrate overall support for the standards set forth by the Panel on the Nonprofit Sector, significant and well-founded criticisms of the self-regulation movement also exist. The concerns voiced deem the sector's actions and the Panel on the Nonprofit Sector's principles as too weak. Specifically, some believe the Panel on the Nonprofit Sector's *Principles for Good Governance and Ethical Practice* (2007) represents a missed opportunity to create guidelines with real depth. While the lack of perspicuity may be a result of the diversity of the sector and the panel's attempt to design a one-size-fits-all set of standards, the critique stands.

To the panel's credit, within the guidelines, graduations serve to increase the auditing and recommended regulatory actions based on organizational budget size. However, indication exists that the nonprofit community may view the guidelines as too weak for large organizations and too overbearing for small nonprofits. Potentially in response to these critiques, or at least at the request of nonprofit practitioners grappling with how to practically apply the principles in their organization, Independent Sector (the convener of the Panel on the Nonprofit Sector) working with BoardSource has created the *Principles Workbook* (2009) to assist nonprofit leaders with applying the panel's *Principles for Good Governance and Ethical Practice* guideline. Nonprofit leaders using the workbook are promised clarification of each principle and its underlying issues, as well as an understanding of the relevant compliance components tied to each principle. Finally, in spite of significant critiques, the sector-wide support for the principles created by the Panel on the Nonprofit Sector and the continued focus on ethics represent positive forward movement by the sector. They also provide evidence of movement toward double-loop learning.

Another way to frame the progress of the sector in a positive light—in the presence of credible critiques—comes from considering the reality of a stricter alternative. Juxtaposing the burden of adopting self-imposed standards, such as the Panel on the Nonprofit Sector's principles, with the hypothetical burden of adhering to Sarbanes-Oxley (should similar legislation pass for nonprofit organizations), one begins to view the principles as an important first step. Consider that a 2005 study by the Urban Institute revealed that requiring nonprofit organizations to comply with solely the audit committee provisions of Sarbanes-Oxley would prove a burden for 40% of nonprofits. Taking on the whole of Sarbanes-Oxley's requirements adapted for nonprofits would likely cripple or eliminate smaller nonprofit organizations. This indicates that the sector must make slow progress toward the voluntary ideals set forth by the Panel on the Nonprofit Sector's principles and recognize them as foundational steps toward meeting likely future requirements of governmental regulation.

This section has presented two well-supported motivations for nonprofit organizations to embrace organizational-level assessment: stewardship of public monies and preparation for likely increased regulation. The latter of these motivations can be served by increased self-regulation and informed assessment in three ways. First, successful self-regulation may deter or slow increased governmental regulation. Second, if governmental regulation remains likely, or unavoidable, then proactive movement to self-regulation will ease the burden of compliance when imposed regulation occurs. Finally, the sector can collectively raise the standard of accountability by promoting increased knowledge of empirically supported best practices.

The former of these motivations will serve nonprofit organizations and an increasingly informed and sophisticated public through the attainment of reliable data about individual organizations. Together, these two motivations present compelling support for nonprofit organizations and the sector as a whole to embrace organizational-level ethics assessment.

Incremental Progress and Movement Toward Double-Loop Learning as a Sector

Through the discussion in the previous section, we have chronicled the movement of the nonprofit sector from regulation occurring at various levels within individual organizations to sector-wide self-regulation in compliance with identified standards. It serves as important to remember that the sector's movement along this developmental path can be viewed in a positive or negative light.

Consider compliance in the following example. A valid criticism of the sector can be made by noting that compliance serves as only one element of promoting ethical health in organizations and that an emphasis on compliance represents a reactive approach most characteristic of single-loop learning—creates compliance checklists that

model a thermostat approach: Compares an organization's current activities to a predetermined standard to see how it measures up (e.g., if the room is too hot or too cold). However, the same fact, emphasis within the sector on compliance, represents great progress when one considers that less than a decade ago none of the checklists or standards for accountability existed. Thus, evidence exists that philanthropic organizations (and the sector as a whole) are moving toward double-loop learning. The leaders of nonprofit organizations through their increased interest in ethics have begun to actively assess and question the current state of affairs within their organizations in a sophisticated manner by searching beyond the surface-level policies and procedures to access their underlying objectives. This searching will facilitate the ability to attend to the subtleties of social and ethical context and work toward greater ethical health.

In summary, recognizing the current status of the nonprofit sector as part of a natural progression forward provides a basis for objectively monitoring progress and a source of hope that the sector will ultimately advance toward greater overall ethical health. The next section of this chapter will explore the constructs relevant to assessing the ethical context of nonprofit organizations through the "Nonprofit Ethics Survey," an instrument designed specifically for nonprofits to conduct an organizational-level assessment.

Salient Constructs for Assessing the Ethical Context of Nonprofit Organizations

The identification of constructs salient to assessing the ethical context of nonprofit organizations served as the first step to developing the "Nonprofit Ethics Survey." Through a rigorous methodological process, the constructs were identified, survey questions crafted, and the final instrument tested, revised, and implemented with several nonprofit organizations. This process yielded a statistically reliable and valid instrument based on six constructs critical to assessing the ethical context of nonprofit organizations. Perhaps equally as important, the constructs measured by the "Nonprofit Ethics Survey" resonate with nonprofit practitioners and scholars when applied in nonprofit organizations. The six constructs are organizational transparency, open communication, decision making, accountability, daily-ethics behaviors, and governance. Notably, the most commonly used compliance checklists discussed throughout this chapter have representation of the six constructs embedded in their frameworks. Information about each of the constructs and how it relates to nonprofit ethics follows.

Organizational Transparency

Organizational transparency represents a well-defined and studied concept in the academic literature and numerous researchers have found that transparency promotes good governance in organizations. Transparency calls for allowing access to information about internal processes, policies, and decision making. That said, transparency does not equal full or thoughtless disclosure. Appreciating organizational transparency as a positive characteristic of organizations requires recognizing it as movement from complete containment of information by an organization (the historical business norm) to discretionary release of information in the spirit of openness. Transparency erases the need to assume and instead provides information freely. In exchange for the efforts required to promote transparency within an organization, nonprofits can anticipate increased protection from the threat of corruption, unethical activities, and scandal. Maintaining a transparent organization increases the ethical health of the organization by serving to facilitate and reinforce a culture supportive of transparency and ethical behavior.

Open Communication

Open communication relates to organizational ethics by assessing whether organizations have an environment that promotes or inhibits inquiry and learning. Scholars support a belief that periodic review of the agency's activities and especially mistakes provides an opportunity for increased knowledge. Without a social milieu supportive of dialogue, discussion, and debate, organizations run the risk of falling into an "emperor without any clothes" scenario. In this type of organization, as in the parable, no one speaks the painfully obvious truth. However, in the nonprofit sector (and business world), ethical lapses may secure front-page coverage on the local newspaper. Thus, creating a safe and open atmosphere for discussion can facilitate the discovery and correction of ethical issues—before they make headlines. Open communication and the culture of inquiry also promote double-loop organizational learning.

Decision Making

Decision making exists as a broad organizational concept in the academic literature whose scope narrows for the "Nonprofit Ethics Survey" to interests about whether stakeholder input has been gained at key intervals (e.g., before starting a new program and at stated intervals thereafter), and whether organizations use evidence on which to base their program and agency decisions. Substantial support for the use of data-driven decision-making methods exists in the nonprofit literature. Ethical decision making links closely with organizational transparency as the process of making informed program decisions and gathering stakeholder input constitutes a transparent operation.

Accountability and Daily-Ethics Behaviors

Daily-ethics behaviors encompass the traits and level of communication and the consideration of ethics in daily activities present in the organization. This concept was first identified by the National Business Ethics Survey (NBES) conducted by the Ethics Resource Center (2005, 2007). Daily-ethics behaviors, assessed by the "Nonprofit Ethics Survey," evaluate specific daily activities related to ethics and measure the accountability standards at all levels of the organization. These two constructs in the "Nonprofit Ethics Survey" assess two key areas: (1) Are members at all levels of the organization held equally accountable? (2) Do the actions of members at all levels of the organization set a good example of ethical behavior and communicate a consideration of ethics? These concepts are instrumental to assessing the current ethical culture of an organization. Research has demonstrated that the board of directors and senior management set the ethical tone of organization; thus, understanding how they are perceived by all levels of the organization provides valuable insight into the organizational culture.

Governance

Governance comprises one of the most widely studied concepts in the nonprofit and business literature. Effective best practices for governance shape the ethical context of organizations. As discussed above, ethical *tone at the top* promotes ethical behavior, and maintaining consistent accountability to universal standards throughout the organization serves as critical to developing an ethically healthy organization (Ethics Resource Center, 2005; Seligson & Choi, 2006). Adherence to established best practices for governance also promotes an ethical organizational context and represents some essential practices of effective governance. The "Nonprofit Ethics Survey" serves to assess the knowledge level of board members regarding governance issues that often identify areas that would benefit from further discussion, training, or policy development.

Additional Details and Supplemental Survey Questions

In the case of the "Nonprofit Ethics Survey" the same questions about ethics are asked of the board members, senior staff, line staff, and in some cases, the volunteer members of the organization. This allows the leadership of the organization to identify areas of consistency or discrepancy among respondents. The inclusion of all members of the organization in the assessment serves as a means for obtaining a comprehensive picture of the organization. The governance questions represent the only exception to this practice. Solely the voting members of the board of directors respond to the governance questions in the survey, as typically they are the only ones knowledgeable (or required to be knowledgeable) about those practices.

In addition to questions categorized under the six constructs identified above, the "Nonprofit Ethics Survey" contains supplemental questions to assess the organization's ethical culture from an intuitively supported perspective. An example of a supplemental question is "learning from mistakes is encouraged in our organization" or "we consciously strive for continual improvement in our organization." Neither of these questions fit within the empirically supported constructs of the survey, but use of the survey with nonprofit organizations revealed that the leaders of those organizations found value in knowing how the members of their organization responded to these questions.

Ultimately, the constructs identified as salient to assessing ethics at the organizational level within nonprofit organizations, in combination with the supplemental questions, compose the first (and currently only known) statistically supported survey instrument designed specifically for use with nonprofit organizations. Use of the survey provides a snapshot assessment of a nonprofit organization's current ethical culture. Nonprofit leaders also have the opportunity to use the survey with an organization over time to gather a longitudinal assessment and monitor change. Secondary gains of using the survey may include increased use of empirically supported best practices and a smaller gap between known ethical behaviors and what actually occurs day-to-day.

Future Directions

The field of nonprofit ethics presents as open to exploration on a multitude of levels. First, as a sector, advancements in theory and practice to help move the field from a reactive to a proactive approach will greatly increase overall effectiveness. Increased efficiency will prove invaluable to a sector plagued by endless work with scarce resources. Additionally, the development of a broad range of empirically supported, user-friendly, sector-specific tools for assessment will provide nonprofit leaders with a means to gather needed data. Data will help facilitate informed decision-making processes and encourage double-loop learning by individual organizations and the sector as a whole.

Monitoring studies of the business sector and the impact of Sarbanes-Oxley on ethics, business infrastructure, and compliance will also serve the nonprofit sector well. By understanding the efficacy, or potential ineffectiveness of Sarbanes-Oxley, the nonprofit sector will create an informed platform from which to lobby for helpful legislation and against needless bureaucracy or ineffective and burdensome laws.

Moving from the macro-level to the specifics of the two studies discussed in this chapter, the *National Nonprofit Survey* report will benefit from continued replication to monitor trends in workplace ethics and identify changes in nonprofit-sector ethical behavior over time. Additionally, studies will determine if the comparisons between sectors by the *National Nonprofit Ethics Survey* report are empirically supported and whether use of a universal instrument to assess organizational ethics in all three sectors performs well under scientific scrutiny.

The "Nonprofit Ethics Survey" instrument will benefit from continued use with a greater number of organizations over time. Through anecdotal feedback gained and potentially repeated statistical analysis, the survey can be further strengthened and refined to yield the most parsimonious measure of organizational ethics.

The dynamic state of the nonprofit sector during recent years provides great opportunity for research and theoretical contributions to help advance the field. Nonprofit practitioners, the consumers of nonprofit services, and the public at large have become increasingly sophisticated, and the demand for knowledge about best practices shows no signs of slowing. The sector and field will continue to evolve, and movement that propels the nonprofit sector away from a reactive approach and toward more double-loop learning will benefit all nonprofit agencies.

References and Further Readings

Abraham, A. (2006, September). Financial management in the nonprofit sector: A mission-based approach to ratio analysis in membership organizations. *Journal of American Academy of Business, Cambridge 10*(1), 212–218.

Argyris, C. (1977, September–October). Double-loop learning in organizations. *Harvard Business Review,* 115–125. DOI: 10.1225/77502

Barrett, A. (2008). The nonprofit ethics survey: A contextual approach. *Dissertation Abstracts International, A 69* (5). (ProQuest No. 1549336601)

Berns, P. V. (2007). A missed opportunity to ensure real charity accountability: Panel on the nonprofit sector. *Chronicle of Philanthropy, 20*(2), 47.

Better Business Bureau. (2007). *Wise giving standards.* Retrieved August 23, 2007, from http://www.us.bbb.org/ WWWRoot/SitePage.aspx?site=113&id=4dd040fd-08af-4dd2-aaa0-dcd66c1a17fc

BoardSource. (2007). *Educational materials for nonprofit organizations.* Retrieved August 27, 2007, from www.boardsource.org/Knowledge.asp?ID=1

BoardSource. (2009). *Principles workbook: Steering your board toward good governance and ethical practice.* Retrieved August 2, 2009, from http://www.independentsector.org/ issues/accountability/workbook.html

Bowman, J. S. (1976). Managerial ethics in business and government. *Business Horizons, 19,* 48–54.

Brown, M. E., & Trevino, L. K. (2006). Ethical leadership: A review and future directions. *Leadership Quarterly, 17,* 595–616.

Buckmaster, N. (1999). Associations between outcome measurement, accountability and learning for non-profit organisations. *International Journal of Public Sector Management, 12*(2), 186–197.

Cullen, J. B., Victor, B., & Stephens, C. (1989, Autumn). An ethical weather report: Assessing the organization's ethical climate. *Organizational Dynamics, 18*(2), 50–62.

Ethics Resource Center. (2005). *National business ethics survey: How employees view ethics in their organizations (1994–2005)* (Report). Washington, DC: Author.

Ethics Resource Center. (2007). *National business ethics survey* (Report). Washington, DC: Author.

Ethics Resource Center. (2008). *National nonprofit ethics survey: An inside view on nonprofit sector ethics* (Report). Washington, DC: Author.

Gebler, D. (2006, May). Creating an ethical culture. *Strategic Finance, 87*(11), 28–34.

Hemmelgarn, A. L., Glisson, C., & James, L. R. (2006, Spring). Organizational culture and climate: Implications for services and interventions research. *Clinical Psychology: Science and Practice, 13*(1), 73–89.

Independent Sector. (2007). *Educational publications.* Retrieved August 22, 2007, from www.independentsector.org/pubs_cart.htm

Independent Sector. (2008). *Facts and figures about charitable organizations.* Retrieved January 10, 2008, from www.independentsector.org/facts_figures-2008

Lewis, J. D. (2009). Nonprofits and the new IRS form 990. *Educational publication.* Retrieved July 30, 2009, from http://www.nolo.com/legal-encyclopedia/article-30274.html

Milgram, S. (1974). *The individual in a social world: Essays and experiments.* New York: McGraw-Hill.

Ostrower, F. (2007, June). *Nonprofit governance in the United States: Findings on performance and accountability from the first national representative study.* Retrieved August 3, 2009, from http://www.urban.org/publications/411479.html

Panel on the Nonprofit Sector. (2007, October). *Principles for good governance and ethical practice: A guide for charities and foundations* (Report). Washington, DC: Author.

Powell, W. W., & Steinberg, R. (2006). *The nonprofit sector: A research handbook* (2nd ed.). New Haven, CT: Yale University Press.

Randall, D. M., & Gibson, A. M. (1990, June). Methodology in business ethics research: A review and critical assessment. *Journal of Business Ethics, 9*(6), 457–471.

Reinke, S. J. (2006). Abu Ghraib, a case of moral and administrative failure. *Public Integrity, 8* (2), 135–147.

Seligson, A. L., & Choi, L. (2006). *Critical elements of an organizational ethical culture* (Report). Washington, DC: Ethics Resource Center.

Senge, P. M. (1990). *The fifth discipline: The art and practice of the learning organization.* New York: Doubleday Currency.

Standards for Excellence. (2007). *Standards for excellence: An ethics and accountability code for the nonprofit sector.* Retrieved August 24, 2007, from www.marylandnonprofits.org/html/standards/sfx_intro.asp

Steinberg, R. (2006). Economic theories of nonprofit organizations. In W. Powell & R. Steinberg (Eds.), *The nonprofit sector: A research handbook* (1st ed., pp. 117–139). New Haven, CT: Yale University Press.

Trevino, L. K., Butterfield, K. D., & McCabe, D. L. (1998). The ethical context in organizations: Influences on employee attitudes and behaviors. *Business Ethics Quarterly, 8*(3), 447–476.

Victor, B., & Cullen, J. B. (1987). A theory and measure of ethical climate in organizations. In W. C. Frederick (Eds.), *Research in corporate social performance and policy* (pp. 51–71). Greenwich, CT: JAI Press.

Victor, B., & Cullen, J. B. (1988). The organizational bases of ethical work climates. *Administrative Science Quarterly, 33(1),* 101–125.

Vidaver-Cohen, D. (1998, August). Moral climate in business firms: A conceptual framework for analysis and change. *Journal of Business Ethics, 17*(11), 1211–1226.

Zimbardo, P. (2007). *The Lucifer effect: Understanding how good people turn evil.* New York: Random House.

94

BUILDING AN ETHIC OF SERVICE

CATHERINE McCALL MARSH

North Park University

David Whyte (1994) describes the relationship that many Americans have with work:

> We have been handed an accepted work world in which the things that really matter in human life have been pushed to the margins of our culture. Much of our present struggles with our organizations have to do with remembering what is essential and placing it back in the center of our lives. We stop waiting in quiet desperation for our career rewards to get to the point where they finally make up to us for everything we have lost. (pp. 294–295)

This chapter investigates the power of service as a way of, as Whyte stated, "remembering what is essential and placing it back in the center of our lives" (pp. 294–295). It attempts to answer the question, "How can the nonprofit organization better tap the potential of the ethic of service inherent within its ordination?"

Although Whyte speaks of the corporate workplace, the nonprofit workplace is not exempt from the malaise of brokenness experienced by so many in the workforce. The nonprofit world does, however, have a singular advantage. Nonprofits are born out of human needs. While the for-profit organization spends hours and dollars crafting the perfect mission statement that will motivate its workforce to sacrifice itself in pursuit of altruistic goals undergirded by values that sound as though Mother Theresa were the CEO, the nonprofit organization's mission is clear from the outset. Certainly, that mission statement requires refocusing from time to time, but due to the fundamental nature of the nonprofit, the drive for profit does not distract it from its raison d'être. Master of business administration (MBA) students learn that the fundamental aim of business is to increase value for shareholders; nonprofit students learn

that the fundamental aim of the nonprofit organization is service. Employees of both for-profit and nonprofit organizations, however, according to research conducted by Jurkiewicz, Massey, and Brown (1998), appear to have similar drives and needs and do not have significant differences when rating important motivational factors. The research reported a surprising finding: "Of special note and quite contradictory to previous research is the finding that private sector employees assign a higher rank to 'chance to benefit society'" (p. 236).

In apparent support of the research conducted by Jurkiewicz et al. (1998), on May 30, 2009, the *New York Times* printed an article heralding the ethic of service in the world of profit. It reported on a trend among students of the top tier business schools toward taking an oath to consciously serve the greater good and limit personal ambition:

> Nearly 20 percent of the graduating class (at Harvard) have signed "The M.B.A. Oath," a voluntary student led pledge that the goal of a business manager is to "serve the greater good." It promises that Harvard M.B.A.'s will act responsibly, ethically and refrain from advancing their "own narrow ambitions" at the expense of others. (Wayne, 2009, "A Promise to Be Ethical in an Era of Immortality")

Additionally, the power of service has been acknowledged as numerous corporations turn to providing paid time off to employees for the purpose of volunteering. Employee involvement in volunteering, although initially designed to enhance the corporations' social responsibility profiles, is now understood to enhance overall employee morale (Basil, Runte, Easwaramoorthy, & Barr, 2009).

As the private sector is awakening to the emergent ethic of service, the nonprofit arena struggles to maintain the motivation that attracts its employees to public service. Miech and Elder (1996) discovered in their research, conducted primarily within the public school system, that "the values that shape individuals' career decisions are not necessarily reinforced by subsequent work experience" (p. 237). To understand and reverse this trend will require that the nation's nonprofit leadership examine the power of the ethic of service and learn to leverage that power within their sector. The discussion that follows provides a context for the emergence of service as a guiding workplace ethic, suggests service learning as the method and the learning organization as a venue for leveraging the ethic, discerns the leadership style that is best suited for leading in an era of service, and concludes with suggestions for implementation.

Definition of Terms

Gaining insight on what is meant by the terms *ethic* and *service* and understanding the historical context of each, will help set the stage for the discussion that follows.

Service

The *Oxford English Dictionary* explains that the term *service,* originally associated with servitude or slavery, is the term that more recently has been applied to employment with the military or other public careers. Being "at one's service," implies being in a state of devotion to someone such as a king, a military commander, or even a lover. One of the most common uses of the term, which encompasses all others, explains service as the conduct of helping, or benefiting, the welfare or advantage of another. Service is other centered. When one operates from a perspective of service, one is happy because one is other-directed rather than self-directed; happiness is the result of service to others.

Ethic

In defining *ethic,* the *Oxford English Dictionary* cites Clifford (1879):

> The doctrine of a special kind of pleasure or displeasure which is felt by the human mind in contemplating certain courses of conduct, whereby they are felt to be right or wrong, and of a special desire to do the right things and avoid the wrong ones. ("On the Scientific Basis of Morals")

Also cited is Bentham (1789): "Ethics at large may be defined, the art of directing men's actions to the production of the greatest possible quantity of happiness" ("An Introduction to the Principles of Morals and Legislation"). Although today the term *ethic,* or *ethics,* is often seen as compliance to ethical codes and laws (Hatcher, 2002) and is the focus of many people who see themselves as ethical guardians in the corporate environment, earlier notions of

the terminology were associated with gratifying human wants and needs (Sharp, 1921). When we do good, we feel good; behaving in accordance with our ethic or what we perceive to be ethical creates happiness.

Work Ethic and Consumer Ethic

It follows that exploring specific ethics that have guided workplace behavior, the *work ethic* and *consumer ethic,* may provide insight into America's pursuit of happiness. As noted in research (Lancaster & Stillman, 2003; Marston, 2007; Zemke, Raines, & Filipczak, 2000) conducted on values embraced by new generations of employees as they enter the workforce, the work ethic was a motivational driver throughout much of the 20th century. Americans became known for embracing hard work with a religious zeal that was lauded as the protestant work ethic. Doing good was equated with working hard; happiness was the result of a hard day's work.

Hard work, however, according to the same generational research (Lancaster & Stillman, 2003; Marston, 2007; Zemke et al., 2000), was replaced in the later part of the 20th century with other drivers. One of those drivers has been the consumer ethic. Work became valued not for the virtue of work itself but for what could be purchased with the wages that were provided, and if wages were not high enough, purchases were made on credit, laying claim to future wages. Work became a means to maintaining a lifestyle rather than an end in itself. The ethic governing employment shifted from production to consumption. Doing good shifted away from the work being done and was measured by what could be purchased based on the market value of the job. Happiness was attained through buying and maintaining the lifestyle associated with the brands placed not only on products but also on neighborhoods, schools, and churches. The higher the market valued one's job, the greater the buying power and the greater the happiness.

While some might see the credit crisis of the early 21st century and the collapse of many of the financial institutions that funded consumerism as the beginning of a shift away from the consumer ethic, the discussion began before the turn of the century. At the height of America's prosperity, Firat and Dholakia (1998) discerned that the self-centered nature of modern consumerism had led to "problems with alienation, anomy and oppression" (Bajde, 2006, p. 312). Studs Terkel, in his acclaimed 1972/1990 book *Working,* had a glimmer of the desperation brought on by consumerism:

> Perhaps it is this specter that most haunts working men and women: the planned obsolescence of people that is of a piece with the planned obsolescence of the things they make. Or sell. It is perhaps this fear of no longer being needed in a world of needless things that most clearly spells out the unnaturalness, the sureality of much that is called work today. (p. xxii)

The Emergent Service Ethic

In his observation of the perils of the consumer ethic, Terkel (1972/1990) knew that salvation would not come through a return to the old work ethic. He imagined a new ethic based on concern for others:

> Perhaps it is time the "work ethic" was redefined and its idea reclaimed from the banal men who invoke it. In a world of cybernetics, of an almost runaway technology, things are increasingly making things. It is for our species to go on to other matters. Human matters. (p. xxviii)

The dissatisfaction with the consumer ethic and the desire to do as Terkel suggested and go on to human matters has been documented by Hoar and Kirwan-Taylor (2004) in the annual management agenda survey of 735 employees conducted by the Roffey Park (United Kingdom) management research and training institute. The survey found that 70% of managers are looking for a greater sense of meaning. While the survey had been running for 8 years, recent responses have revealed a growing disillusionment and a desire to do something more meaningful. What was once palatable, due to the associated financial rewards, is no longer seen as tolerable.

Applebaum (1998) suggests that our dissatisfaction with our current work life is partially due to the emergence in 20th-century America of a new ethic, which can make life richer and more fulfilling. While the new ethic is envisioned, however, the older consumer ethic has not yet passed away and living in the transition has created an unresolved tension. Leach (1993) claims that the remnants of the consumer ethic are out of control and running amok, conquering everything in its path. Lansley (1994) fears that people are being haunted by vestiges of consumerism, yet at the same time, he sees that they display an array of concerns for broader issues indicating a growing consciousness of social concerns and the environment.

Similarly, Hatcher (2002) explains that today's complex business problems that arise from our diverse and complicated world, force us to examine new paradigms and further develop our transcendent nature that connects us with others. He states,

> The perspective of work as providing higher meaning or right livelihood to individuals and enhancing society moves beyond traditional ideas of work as means of production dedicated solely to enhancing individual gain or corporate profit. Rather, it recharacterizes work as a concept that the workplace is not separate from, but is interdependent with humans, society, and the environment. (pp. 51–52)

Like Hatcher, Chalofsky (2003) taps into this connection between service to others and spiritual transcendence in his discourse on an emerging construct for meaningful work. He stresses that more work should be undertaken in learning how to tap into intrinsic forms of motivation. Drawing from the Zen Buddhist belief that work and pleasure should be so aligned that they are indistinguishable one from the other, he quotes from *Artful Work: Awakening Joy, Meaning and Commitment in the Workplace*:

> More attention should be paid to our whole selves at work, to admit that some work has no meaning to us and offers no possibility of joy, to examine what work will have meaning to us and seek such work, to meet our co-workers self-to-self, center-to-center, and to stop pretending that our interior lives don't matter. [Only then] will our work become more joyful [and] our organizations will flourish with commitment, passion, imagination, spirit and soul. (As cited in Chalofsky, 2003, p. 80)

Prior to Chalofsky, Senge (1990/2006) spoke of the awakening of the individual to the emerging other-centered ethic:

> Genuine commitment is always to something larger than ourselves and is guided by a sincere desire to serve the world. . . . The will of a person committed to a larger purpose is like a cry from the soul which has been shaken and awakened. (p. 171)

The work ethic gave way to the consumer ethic, which may now be giving way to an ethic based on concern for society and service to others. Whether the cry is one of pain or joy or perhaps both combined, it accompanies the birthing process.

Beyond Capitalism

As the volume and dimension of the cry have increased over recent years, scholars have clamored to understand its growing cadence and predict its impact on our economic system. Bajde's (2006) struggle to make sense of other-centered behavior as a market force may provide insight into understanding what appear to be paradoxical forces at play. He explains,

> The social sciences in general and consumer research in particular have been detrimentally hampered by the presumption of self-interest as an exclusive foundation of human behavior. As a result, conduct that fails to conform to the self-interest paradigm has often been ignored, or worse, grossly twisted to fit the dominant categorizations. (p. 301)

Could the outcome of an ethic of service be a reformed or revitalized version of capitalism, an economic system based on the principle of enlightened self-interest? Bajde (2006) does not believe that concern for others rules out care for oneself; in fact, he opens the way for further discussion on the possibility of an economy based on service to society as being in each member of that society's self-interest—perhaps an evolved conception of the notion of enlightened self-interest. Similarly, Thurow (1983) hints at a new economic paradigm that has its roots in previous forms:

> Societies are not merely statistical aggregations of individuals engaged in voluntary exchange but something much more subtle and complicated. A group or community cannot be understood if the unit of analysis is the individual taken by himself.
>
> A society is clearly something greater than the sum of its parts. (pp. 222–223)

Daly and Cobb (1994) expand on Thurow by indicating that "economics can rethink its theories from the viewpoint of person-in community and still include the truth and insight it gained when it thought in individualistic terms" (p. 8). In the same vein, Bakan (2004) does not see a conflict between self-interest and societal concern and heralds other-interest as a viable economic force. He states,

> Though individualistic self-interest and consumer desires are core parts of who we are and nothing to be ashamed about, they are not all of who we are. We also feel deep ties and commitments to one another, that we share common fates and hopes for a better world. We know that our values, capacities, aesthetics and senses of meaning and justice are, in part, created and nurtured by our communal attachments. (p. 156)

Baptiste (2001) has voiced disagreement with the precepts of our economic system based on self-interest, which "treats humans as lone wolves: radically isolated hedonists, creatures of habit (not intentions) who temper their avarice with economic rationality" (p. 197). He has suggested that "maybe humans are more than fated adapters. Maybe they are capable of becoming creative transformers" (p. 197).

Daly and Cobb (1994) are trusting that humans are more than fated adapters as they sound a wake-up call:

> We humans are being led to a dead end—all too literally. We are living by an ideology of death and accordingly we are destroying our own humanity and killing the planet. Even the one great success of the program that has governed us, the attainment of the material affluence, is now giving way to poverty. The United States is just now gaining a foretaste of the suffering that global economic policies, so enthusiastically embraced, have inflicted on hundreds of millions of others. If we continue on our present paths future generations, if there are to be any, are condemned to misery. (p. 21)

Without rejecting the fundamentals of economic theory, Daly and Cobb (1994) provide a service-based context: "The analysis of the market can continue to play an extremely important role within a context that sees the purpose of the economy as the service of the community" (p. 19).

Perhaps in response to the plea uttered by Daly and Cobb (1994), Korten (1999) describes the postcorporate world that he believes is in its infancy:

> Indeed millions of people, unsung heroes of a new era, are already hard at work constructing building blocks of a post-corporate-post-capitalist civilization. They are demonstrating

alternatives far more attractive and viable than socialism or the failed economic models of the former Soviet Union. The most promising alternatives center on applying the familiar principles of democratic governance and market economics to create societies that function in service to life and treat money as a facilitator, not the purpose, of our economic lives. (pp. 2–3)

Korten's (1999) vision is one of a new economy that is based on healthy markets with a core-defining purpose of serving the needs of all citizens rather than the capitalist outcome of making money for those who have money.

If the transition away from markets based on money to those based on life as described by Korten requires demarcation, the financial crisis from 2008 to 2009 may serve that purpose. Greider (2009) proclaims that the financial crisis can provide a springboard to the future. He indicates that while the pace of the social responsibility movement has been "too slow to attract much political respect, . . . the current crumbling of the old order will clear the way for more dramatic progress."

Greider (2009) lays out his vision based on living more while accumulating less:

> Here is the grand vision I suggest Americans can pursue: the right of all citizens to larger lives. Not to get richer than the next guy or necessarily to accumulate more and more stuff but the right to live life more fully and engage more expansively the elemental possibilities of human existence. That is the essence of what so many now seem to yearn for in their lives.

Greider (2009) goes on to associate the new economic order with an ethic of service. He implores,

> Can we envision an economy designed to serve society, rather than the other way around? Some will say that this is an idle daydream. I say it is our birthright, our inherited privilege. We are Americans. We get to think larger thoughts about our country and ourselves. Daydreams are the seedbed for the possible. We can argue later about how to achieve them.

Before turning to the next section of this chapter, wherein some arguments for micro-level organizational implementation are presented, the overall contribution of capitalism to humanity's ongoing development should be acknowledged. Korten (1999) says it well:

> Just as periods of disease and disability can serve as powerful moments of individual learning, the period of capitalist expansion, for all its tragedy and pain, and violence, has enriched our knowledge and awareness of the whole of the planet and its inhabitants. It has led many of us to establish bonds of friendship and affection that bridge the boundaries of culture, religion, class and geography; helped us realize that all humanity shares a common destiny inextricable linked to the living systems of the planet; and now leaves us poised to move to a new level of self-aware consciousness. Perhaps in this respect, global capitalism merits appreciation for its contribution to creating the potential and the necessity to take this next step to species maturity. (p. 280)

Service Learning

Up to this point, this chapter has provided a context for building an ethic of service by postulating that as the economic system has evolved so too has the guiding ethic for the workforce; the ethic has progressed from a work ethic to the consumer ethic and is now taking on new dimensions of what could be a new ethic that focuses on concern for others as well as concern for self. As the discussion now turns toward implementation, the chapter suggests service learning as a tool for leveraging the service ethic. A focus on learning seems appropriate as a means of accelerating the shift to a paradigm of service in that real learning, according to Senge (1990/2006), allows us to undergo the fundamental change required to transition to a new paradigm. Senge states,

> Real learning gets to the heart of what it means to be human. Through learning we re-create ourselves. Through learning we become able to do something we were never able to do. Through learning we reperceive our relationship to it. Through learning we extend our capacity to create, to be part of the generative process of life. (p. 13)

In determining the learning methodology best suited to leveraging an ethic of service, service learning, due to its focus on experiential learning that is other-focused, appears to be a suitable choice. Service learning is an other-centered approach in that it focuses on what knowledge is gained by the learner and also allows those who are being served to control the service that is provided to them. Hence, the service provided is real and necessary—not just constructed for the purpose of learning (Sigmon, 1979). Perkins (as cited in Bush-Bacelis, 1998) provides one definition of service learning:

> Academic service-learning is a method by which students learn and develop through active participation in thoughtfully organized experiences that meet actual community needs and are coordinated with the academic and local communities to enhance academic course work. (p. 20)

Additionally, Furco (1996) stresses,

> Service-learning programs must have some academic context and be designed in such a way that ensures that both the service enhances the learning and the learning enhances the service. Unlike a field education program in which the service is performed in addition to a student's courses, a service-learning program integrates service into the course(s). (p. 5)

As an experiential approach to learning (Rice, 1994), however, certainly the exploration of service learning as applicable to the workforce in a nonacademic environment deserves consideration. Rather than integrating service into coursework, one might suggest that workforce educators consider integrating some of the intentional academic rigor that accompanies coursework into the ongoing

experience of service that exists in the nonprofit workplace. Experience would become the entry point for the learner rather than something structured in as part of a classroom approach to learning. Experiential learning as an aspect of adult development was touted as early as 1926 when Lindeman (1926/1961) declared that "the resource of highest value in adult education is the learner's experience. If education is life, then life is also education. . . . Experience is the adult learner's living textbook" (pp. 6–7). Another notable authority on adult learning, Knowles (1970/1980), stated, "As people grow and develop, they accumulate an increasing reservoir of experience that becomes an increasingly rich resource for learning" (p. 44). Similarly, Kolb (1984) defined learning, as "the process whereby knowledge is created through transformation of experience" (p. 38). Jarvis (1987) went so far as to claim "all learning begins with experience" (p. 16). Fenwick (2003) said similarly, "all of learning is experience-based" (p. ix).

Building on the notion of experiential learning, Saltmarsh (1997) indicates that service learning is a part of the paradigm of what he calls *connected knowing*. Unlike *separate knowing*, which is based on the specialized knowledge of academic disciplines, connected knowing "integrates thought and action, reason and emotion, education and life," and "does not divorce people from their social and natural contexts" (Martinas cited in Saltmarsh, p. 82). An example of separate knowing that became connected knowing can be found in the research conducted by Beale, Davis, and Chisolm (2008). In their study, they reflected on a service-learning curriculum component of a finance course in which students responded to a community request to gain knowledge about the risks of subprime lending. The researchers reported it was not only that the community residents were served but also that the students were gaining organizational citizenship skills due to their involvement in a natural setting that provided a social context beyond what was available in the classroom. The students improved their technical skills through the process of providing a needed service, but it is possible that the technical skills may have been learned separately through separate knowing that is provided through classroom instruction. The knowing that was grounded in a real-world setting and connected to genuine human needs and then followed by opportunities to reflect on the experience, however, created the connected knowing that allowed the students to develop a new consciousness. While university students must leave the classroom to operate within a natural social context, the workplace provides the venue where employees are able to learn within their ongoing social environment. To fully facilitate the development of connected knowing, however, it is up to workforce educators to operate from an intentional pedagogy that allows employees to not only serve but also to grow as multidimensional human beings as they reflect on their interactions with those being served.

Academics in the field of human resource development (Turnbull & Madsen, 2004) are indeed researching the power of service learning for workforce development. In fact, the continuity of learning provided by a consistent work environment could have a positive impact on learning. Dewey (1938) indicated that if learning from experience is to happen, that continuity of experience and interaction with the environment must be involved. The traditional classroom cannot provide the same continuity of experience and interaction with the environment as the workplace, but it has provided the opportunity for the essential component of reflection-on-experience to take place. If service learning is taken seriously as an aspect of workforce development, however, reflection can intentionally be structured into the service experience. Workforce educators can and do build periods of reflection into their curriculum although significant challenges do exist. Rigg and Trehan (2008) stressed that their research illustrated "difficulties of employing critical reflection within the workplace arising from the more complex power relations between the multiple stakeholders" (p. 374).

One of the multiple stakeholders is the recipient of the service: the stakeholder within the community. Flower (2002) argues that the action side of service learning must be balanced with the reflective side, which includes a true dialogue between those serving and those being served. The resulting intercultural inquiry allows the roles to be reversed and allows the caregiver to be the one receiving care (Coogan, 2005). Two sides of the dialogue come together as colleagues who are partnering in the other's liberation. Lila Watson, an Australian Aboriginal activist is credited with having said, "If you have come to help me, you are wasting your time. But if you have come because your liberation is bound up with mine, then let us work together" (Pate, 2006). Although the actual source of this quote is hard to verify, the words represent well the goal of intercultural inquiry as one aspect of service learning.

Liberation, or empowerment, takes place when real learning occurs, and oftentimes, organizational stakeholders other than the client, the one receiving the service, are not prepared to take on the challenges presented by truly empowered employees. When reflection and action are combined, double-loop learning (Argyris & Schön, 1996), or deep learning (Senge, 1990/2006), occurs. As the skill of reflective thinking is incorporated into the learning cycle, new sensitivity and awareness develops that leads to a change in attitudes and beliefs. It is this deep learning that catapults the learner to the shift in paradigm required to act out of an ethic of service. But once the paradigm has shifted, the employee-learner is no longer content with the status quo, or business as usual, in the traditional organization run by command and control hierarchies. As a result, the organization must change, or the organization experiences a backlash brought about by either an exodus of employees or a group of disenchanted, less-than-productive organizational citizens who show up but whose commitment and passion for the organization's mission no longer motivates them to perform.

The Learning Organization as Vehicle

It follows that when leaders embrace the decision to build an ethic of service through service learning, they will be required to allow organizational transformation to occur. If the organization is to benefit from a move to an ethic of service, one must ponder whether there is potential for the learning organization to serve as a vehicle that will facilitate the integration of the service ethic into organizational life. Senge (1990/2006) defines the learning organization as

organizations where people continually expand their capacity to create the results they truly desire, where new and expansive patterns of thinking are nurtured, where collective aspiration is set free, and where people are continually learning to see the whole together. (p. 3)

Watkins and Marsick (1993) define the learning organization as

one that learns continuously and transforms itself. Learning takes place in individuals, teams, the organization and even the communities with which the organization interacts. Learning is a continuous and strategically used process—integrated with and running parallel to work. Learning results in changes in knowledge, beliefs and behaviors. Learning also enhances organizational capacity for innovation and growth. The learning organization has embedded systems to capture and share learning. (pp. 8–9)

Marquardt (2002) says quite simply, "The new learning organization is able to harness the collective genius of its people at the individual, group and systems levels" (p. 2).

Combing through the above definitions, one can conclude that service learning on the part of individuals in a learning organization could launch a complete transformation within people and systems resulting in an organization whose knowledge, belief, and behaviors are a living demonstration of the ethic of service. In its new form, the transformed organization would be as Whyte (1994) calls it, "the new organization that honors the soul and the soul of the world" (p. 296), in that it is

as much concerned with what it serves as what it is, as much attentive to the greater world as the small world it has become, as much trying to learn from the exquisite patterns that inform that greater world as trying to impose its own pattern on something already complete. (p. 296)

Whyte (1994) further claims that the learning organization may allow us to "join the concerns of our workplace with the concerns of our world" (p. 297). The essential link for Whyte is between what and whom we are serving at work and what and whom we are serving in the rest of our lives. It is this fundamental connection to which Senge (1990/2006), probably the best-known proponent of the learning organization, refers when he says, "through learning we reperceive the world and our relationship to it. Through learning we extend our capacity to create, to be part of the generative process of life" (p. 14).

Whyte (1994) and Senge (1990/2006) give credibility to the association between the learning organization and maximizing an ethic of service, for with service as the dominant workplace ethic, the purpose of the organization's intent must be questioned—meaning or matter? People or profit? Even at the nonprofit level, as discussed by McHargue (2003), is the organization focused on the meaning found through service or in competing with rival nonprofits for publicity and funding as well as clients? Senge (1990/2006) quotes Bill O'Brien, CEO of Hanover Insurance:

> Our grandfathers worked six days a week to earn what most of us now earn by Tuesday afternoon. The ferment in management will continue until we build organizations that are more consistent with man's higher aspirations beyond food, shelter and belonging. (p. 5)

The service ethic, consistent with the higher aspirations mentioned by O'Brien, although inherent within the nonprofit's mission, can get lost as management steers the organization toward the achievement of goals. Shifting the focus toward learning that can tap into employees' higher aspirations rather than simply achieving may be necessary if organizations are to transform themselves to the extent that they are able to benefit from the power of the emerging ethic.

Leadership

If the learning organization is to become the vehicle for operationalizing the service ethic, the burden of its success appears to rely on the commitment of leadership to the transformation process. "Embarking on the journey to become a learning organization is a time- and resource-intensive change process" (Ellinger, Ellinger, Yang, & Howton, 2003, pp. 168–169). But based on the evidence of research, there appears to be a payoff for implementing learning organization initiatives—the payoff is not immediate; a long-term commitment is required. Whitmore (2004) adds to the argument for investing in the long-term process. He concedes that if business leaders understood more fully the power found by exploring processes that bring meaning back into the workplace, they would be providing everything possible so that meaning could be experienced:

> They would build their business structures, ethics, products, and management style on a completely different ethos than that upon which it is currently based; businesses and the economy would then be in service to people rather than people being in service to businesses and the economy. (p. 8)

Senge (1990/2006) outlines three tasks for leaders of learning organizations—design, teaching, and stewardship. Designing is done primarily behind the scenes working with infrastructure and systems that allow for the organization to adapt as its people learn and grow. The leader-designer is unseen; it is those who are successful within the system who receive credit for the excellence of the design. Teaching is accomplished not through masterful lectures or rallying speeches but by facilitating learning environments that encourage risk taking and learning from mistakes. The leader-teacher shows others how to learn by exemplifying the humility of one who never knows everything and is always learning something—he or she models learning. Stewardship is seen through service. The leader-steward serves those he or she would lead; the service is always in pursuit of a larger purpose.

Senge's defining qualities of leadership are other-centered. His focus is on service. Like Senge, Denhardt and Denhardt suggest that if leadership is to guide America into an other-centered future that places value on people rather than things and emphasizes service as its guiding ethic, the leadership theory worthy of the task of transformation is that of servant leadership; leaders who are successful at organizational transformation may be required to shift their leadership paradigm from one of steering to one of serving (Denhardt & Denhardt, 2000). The concept of servant leadership is attributed to Robert Greenleaf, who believed that the leader's major concern should be for the have-nots and he or she should care for and nurture his or her followers, alleviating social inequalities and shifting power to those who are led while providing maximum opportunities to participate in community life (Northouse, 2007). Greenleaf (1996) wrote,

> The servant leader is servant first. . . . It begins with the natural feeling that one wants to serve, to serve *first*. . . . The best test, and the most difficult to administer, is: Do those served grow as persons? Do they, *while being served*, become healthier, wiser, freer, more autonomous, more likely themselves to become servants? *And*, what is the effect on the least privileged in society; will they benefit or at least not be further deprived? (pp. 1–2)

The major difference between servant leadership and other leadership theories is the focus of the leader. Commitment to the organization and its objectives is the focus of many leadership theories. Hence, the leader's behavior motivates the followers toward organizational ends. The servant leader, on the other hand, focuses on the followers themselves with the achievement of organizational objectives as a secondary and subsequent outcome. "The extent to which the leader is able to shift the primary focus of leadership from the organization to the follower is the distinguishing factor" (Stone, Russell, & Patterson, 2004, p. 349). The servant leader focuses on the revolution called for by Whyte (1994), which is a personal one to be carried out through the collective courageous acts of individuals rather than an organized effort for change by the organization itself. He stated, "There is nothing more transforming to the American workplace than the thousands of daily decisions now being made that put soul life above the abstracts of organizational life" (p. 295). According to Banutu-Gomez (2004), if leaders just got out of the way and encouraged self-management in their followers, a personal and organizational transformation would occur.

This shift of attention to the follower is what Margaret Wheatley (2004) indicated is needed if hope and confidence are to be restored to the thousands of employees who have lost confidence in their leaders. She states,

> Servant leadership is not just an interesting idea, but something vital for the world. The concept of servant leadership must move from an interesting idea in the public imagination toward the realization that this is the only way we can go forward. (p. 16)

Moving forward may mean moving in the direction of the emerging ethic of service. This chapter has given a brief depiction of the synergy that is building among theories of the service ethic, service learning, and servant leadership, but the task that remains is to move beyond theory and highlight specific steps that nonprofit leaders can take to leverage the ethic of service in their organizations.

Summary and Future Directions

Much of what has been written in this chapter relies on known theory: service learning, the learning organization, and servant leadership. Theories have been explored as a means to the end of leveraging the ethic of service. To help leaders to bridge the gap between theory and practice, a few suggestions for implementation follow:

1. Take advantage of the power of mission. Mission is the greatest advantage resident in the nonprofit workplace for leveraging and ethic of service. Revisit the organization's mission statement. Does it tap the desire to serve that rests within all employees? Does it speak to everyone in the organization no matter what their role or position in the organization? If not, rewrite and reeducate.

2. Create stakeholder maps for everyone. Allow each employee to understand the impact of his or her job on those who are served by the organization—both internal and external to the organization. Those in administrative functions can lose sight of the mission in the day-to-day difficulties of managing finances, operations, and people, but every job performed moves the organization toward its mission. Clarify the connections between work done and end-service provided.

3. Consider job rotation that puts every employee on the front lines with the client being served. Coming face to face with the recipient of the service provides a powerful reminder of the organization's mission. If it is only one day a month that the clerical or administrative person serves on the front lines, it is still a constant reminder of why they do what they do. Create a schedule and stick with it; there will always be reasons for why there isn't enough time to let go of the office duties for a day.

4. Provide opportunities for service providers to dialogue with the recipients of the service. The end user of the service knows what works and doesn't work and can enhance the employee's ability to make an impact by including them in the loop of continuous improvement that must go on if the nonprofit is to remain viable. Those on the front lines are positioned best to improve the quality of service. By listening and asking questions, knowledge is gained that can improve overall organizational processes that are in place to support the delivery of services.

5. Build reflection time into the work routine by providing structured time for personal and group reflection and discussion. Members of groups can help one another construct meaning from the experience by sharing insights and asking questions of one another. The learning community will continue to build new knowledge and enhance each individual's learning. Personal reflection is good, but the power of feedback that is given and heard out of a stance of openness and trust will allow each individual to grow and improve in their roles.

6. Leadership should be involved with all of the above. Leadership must be visibly committed to the transformation and must be seen not only as advocates but also as active participants in the process. As they experience the pain and joy that comes from fully engaging in service, they will continue to create structures that support serving.

This chapter began with quoting David Whyte (1994):

> We have been handed an accepted work world in which the things that really matter in human life have been pushed to the margins of our culture. Much of our present struggles with our organizations have to do with remembering what is essential and placing it back in the center of our lives. (pp. 294–295)

The for-profit world is learning that providing paid time off for volunteering enhances the well-being of their workforce by paying attention to what matters—in light of an ethic of service. That source of power is resident with the ongoing work of the nonprofit workplace. Nonprofit leaders who understand the power of the service ethic will experiment with ways to tap that power source. Those who do will quite naturally have an advantage over those who do not. The ethic of service does not need to be created; it simply needs permission to grow and flourish in its natural habitat.

References and Further Readings

Applebaum, H. (1998). *The American work ethic and the changing work force: An historical perspective.* Westport, CT: Greenwood Press.

Argyris, C., & Schön, D. A. (1996). *Organizational learning II: Theory, method and practice.* Reading, MA: Addison-Wesley.

Bajde, D. (2006). Other-centered behavior and the dialectics of self and other. *Consumption Markets & Culture, 9*(4), 301–316.

Bakan, J. (2004). *The corporation: The pathological pursuit of profit and power.* New York: Free Press.

Banutu-Gomez, M. B. (2004). Great leaders teach exemplary followership and serve as servant leaders. *Journal of American Academy of Business, 4*(1–2), 143–151.

Baptiste, I. (2001). Educating lone wolves: Pedagogical implications of human capital theory. *Adult Education Quarterly, 51*(3), 184–201.

Basil, D. Z., Runte, M. S., Easwaramoorthy, M., & Barr, C. (2009). Company support for employee volunteering: A national survey of companies in Canada. *Journal of Business Ethics, 85,* 387–398.

Beale, R. L., Davis, J., & Chisolm, L. (2008). Organizational citizenship competency development during college promotes technical competence for corporate experience. *Journal of Academy of Business and Economics, 8*(3), 121–129.

Bentham, J. (1789). An introduction to the principles of morals and legislation. In *Oxford English Dictionary.* Retrieved May 1, 2009, from http://dictionary.oed.com

Bush-Bacelis, J. L. (1998). Innovative pedagogy: Academic service-learning for business communication. *Business Communication Quarterly, 61*(3), 20–34.

Chalofsky, N. (2003). An emerging construct for meaningful work. *Human Resource Development International, 6*(1), 69–83.

Clifford, W. K. (1879). On the scientific basis of morals. In *Oxford English Dictionary.* Retrieved May 1, 2009, from http://dictionary.oed.com

Coogan, D. (2005). Counterpublics in public housing: Reframing the politics of service-learning. *College English, 67*(5), 461–482.

Daly, H. E., & Cobb, J. B., Jr. (1994). *For the common good: Redirecting the economy toward community, the environment, and a sustainable future* (2nd ed.). Boston: Beacon Press.

Denhardt, R. B., & Denhardt, J. V. (2000). The new public service: Serving rather than steering. *Public Administration Review, 60*(6), 549–559.

Dewey, J. (1938). *Experience and education.* New York: Collier Books.

Elinger, A. D., Elinger, A. E., Yang, B., & Howton, S. W. (2003). Making the business case for the learning organization concept. *Advances in the Development of Human Resources, 5*(2), 163–172.

Fenwick, T. J. (2003). *Learning through experience: Troubling orthodoxies and intersecting questions.* Malabar, FL: Krieger.

Firat, F. A., & Dholakia, N. (1998). *Consuming people: From political economy to theaters of consumption.* London: Routledge.

Flower, L. (2002). Intercultural inquiry and the transformation of service. *College English, 65*(2), 181–201.

Furco, A. (1996). Service-learning: A balanced approach to experiential education. In B. Taylor (Ed.), *Boundaries: Serving and learning* (pp. 2–6). Washington, DC: Corporation for National Service.

Greenleaf, R. K. (1996). *On becoming a servant leader.* San Francisco: Jossey-Bass.

Greider, W. (2009, May 25). The future of the American dream. *Nation.* Retrieved May 25, 2009, from http://www.thenation.com/doc/20090525/greider

Hatcher, T. (2002). *Ethics and HRD: A new approach to leading responsible organizations.* Boulder, CO: Perseus.

Hoar, R., & Kirwan-Taylor, H. (2004). Work with meaning. *Management Today,* 44–53.

Jarvis, P. (1987). *Adult learning in the social context.* London: Croom Helm.

Jurkiewicz, C., Massey, T. K., & Brown, R. G. (1998). Motivation in public and private organizations: A comparative. *Public Productivity & Management Review, 21*(3), 230–250.

Knowles, M. (1980). *The modern practice of adult education: From pedagogy to andragogy.* New York: Cambridge. (Original work published 1970)

Kolb, D. A. (1984). *Experiential learning: Experience as the source of learning and development.* Englewood-Cliffs, NJ: Prentice-Hall.

Korten, D. C. (1999). *The post-corporate world: Life after capitalism.* San Francisco: Berrett-Koehler.

Lancaster, L. C., & Stillman, D. (2003). *When generations collide: Who they are. Why they clash: How to solve the generational puzzle at work.* New York: Collins Business.

Lansley, S. (1994). *After the goldrush: The trouble with affluence, consumer capitalism and the way forward.* London: Century.

Leach, W. (1993). *Land of desire: Merchants, power and the rise of a new American culture.* New York: Pantheon.

Lindeman, E. C. (1961). *The meaning of adult education.* Norman, OK: Harvest House. (Original work published 1926)

Marquardt, M. J. (2002). *Building the learning organization: Mastering the 5 elements for corporate learning.* Mountain View, CA: Davies-Black.

Marston, C. (2007). *Motivating the "What's in it for me" workforce: Manage across the generational divide and increase profits.* Hoboken, NJ: John Wiley & Sons.

Martin, J. (1984). *Changing the educational landscape: Philosophy, women and the curriculum.* New York: Routledge.

McHargue, S. K. (2003). Learning for performance in nonprofit organizations. *Advances in the Development of Human Resources, 5*(2), 196–204.

Miech, R. A., & Elder, G. H., Jr. (1996). The service ethic and teaching. *Sociology of Education, 69,* 237–253.

Northouse, P. G. (2007). *Leadership: Theory and practice* (4th ed.). Thousand Oaks, CA: Sage.

Pate, K. (2006, February 28). "If you have come here to help me . . .": Why women are in Canadian prisons. *Canadian dimension: For people who want to change the world.* Retrieved June 1, 2009, from http://canadiandimension.com/articles/1870

Perkins, D. F. (1994). Why community service and service learning? Providing rationale and research. *Democracy and Education, 9,* 11–15.

Rice, D. L. (1994). *Service learning faculty manual.* Ypsilanti: Eastern Michigan University.

Rigg, C., & Trehan, K. (2008). Critical reflection in the workplace: Is it just too difficult? *Journal of European Industrial Training, 32*(8), 374–384.

Saltmarsh, J. (1997). Ethics, reflection, purpose and compassion: Community service learning. *New Directions for Student Services, 77*, 81–93.

Senge, P. (2006). *The fifth discipline: The art and practice of the learning organization* (Rev. ed.). New York: Currency Doubleday. (Original work published 1990)

Sharp, S. C. (1921). Hume's ethical theory and its critics. *Mind, 30*(17), 40–56.

Sigmon, R. L. (1979, Spring). Service-learning: Three principles. *Synergist* (National Center for Service-Learning), *8*(1): 9–11.

Stone, G. A., Russell, R. F., & Patterson, K. (2004). Transformational versus servant leadership: A difference in leader focus. *Leadership & Organization Development Journal, 25*(3–4), 349–361.

Terkel, S. (1990). *Working.* New York: Ballantine. (Original work published 1972)

Thurow, L. G. (1983). *Dangerous currents.* New York: Random House.

Turnbull, O., & Madsen, S. R. (2004). Academic service-learning in the HRD curriculum. *Proceedings of the 2004 Academy of Human Resource Development International Conference,* Austin, TX, 989–996.

Watkins, K., & Marsick, V. (1993). *Sculpting the learning organization: Lessons in the art and science of systemic change.* San Francisco: Jossey-Bass.

Wayne, L. (2009, May 30). A promise to be ethical in an era of immorality. *New York Times.* Retrieved May 30, 2009, from http://www.nytimes.com/2009/05/30/business/30oath.html

Wheatley, M. (2004). Servant leaders. *Executive Excellence, 21*(7), 15–16.

Whitmore, J. (2004). Something really has to change: "Change management" as an imperative rather than a topic. *Journal of Change Management, 4*(1), 5–14.

Whyte, D. (1994). *The heart aroused: Poetry and the preservation of the soul in corporate America.* New York: Doubleday.

Zemke, R., Raines, C., & Filipczak, B. (2000). *Generations at work: Managing the clash of veterans, boomers, xers, and nexters in your workplace.* New York: AMACOM, A division of American Management Association.

95

CROSS-CULTURAL MANAGEMENT AND NGO CAPACITY BUILDING

TERENCE JACKSON AND FREDERIK CLAEYÉ
Middlesex University Business School

This chapter outlines the necessity of integrating a cross-cultural management perspective into the management of nongovernmental organizations (NGOs) and the importance of developing leadership and organizational capacity in this kind of organization. It considers why management and leadership are important to NGOs, and particularly why a consideration of cross-cultural management is so important. It asks how cross-cultural theory might address practical NGO management and leadership issues, focusing first on the different levels of cross-cultural interaction and how we might understand cultural differences. In particular, it highlights the importance of the way human beings in organizations are valued differently in Western and non-Western cultures, explaining why uncritically exporting the concept of human resource management (HRM) from the private sector or public administration to the nonprofit sector is inappropriate both in many developed countries and in developing countries. The example of NGO management and leadership in Africa is used to illustrate this point. The chapter discusses the hybridization (i.e., cross-fertilization of ideas and practices from Western and non-Western countries or from the private sector and public administration) of organizations and management through cross-cultural interactions and why this process is so important to building NGO capacity. Here, the discussion mainly addresses NGO managers as leaders, tending to use the term interchangeably but distinguishing between these terms in the text as appropriate. While we primarily focus on Africa to illustrate our point, much of what we say might also be useful in NGOs working, for example, with minority groups in the United States or other developed and developing countries.

Management and Leadership

The idea of managing NGOs has only recently come to the attention of practitioners and academics. Academics in the field of development studies who have shown an increasing interest in analyzing NGO management have often been ill equipped for the task. Opinions among people working in NGOs seem to run from complete dislike of anything to do with managerialism to the uncritical acceptance of Western management and leadership principles. Lewis (2007) shows that techniques and principles such as strategic planning that were being ditched by commercial-sector managers during the 1990s were happily being adopted by NGOs as quick fixes. In addition, it seems that some development academics (including Lewis, 2007) have discovered Hofstede's (2001) theory, which has dominated cross-cultural management studies, just at a time when it is being heavily criticized by the international management academic community.

So why should the development community be more aware of current issues and competencies in management studies, and why should NGOs be developing management and leadership capacity? As Jackson (2004) argued, "good organizational management is essential for the well being of human kind. . . . Effectively managing resources would seem a logical way of alleviating human hardship and poverty, and ensuring the welfare and dignity of all people" (p. xi).

Yet to develop successful international and indigenous NGOs, their global and multicultural operating contexts must be a central consideration if capacity building and organizational impact are to be successful and appropriate.

Why a Cross-Cultural Approach?

Despite the fact that the daily work of many NGOs involves working across cultures (not only in Africa but also in multicultural societies like the United States or the United Kingdom), the growing literature on NGO management rarely mentions the word *culture*. Where culture or a cross-cultural perspective is discussed, it is seen as an additional factor that should be considered rather than an integral part of our understanding of NGO capacity building (such as in the otherwise useful introduction to NGO management of Lewis, 2007). Few organizations operating in the modern globalized world can remain untouched by cross-cultural considerations.

When NGOs claim that their comparative advantage is in their closeness to the people, local responsiveness, social focus, and cultural sensitivity to peoples' needs and the appropriateness of interventions, it is difficult to argue that cross-cultural perspectives are not central to NGO management and leadership. For example,

- the way knowledge, technology, and best practices are transferred from one country to another may be problematic without considering the cross-cultural implications;
- the way change should be managed in hierarchical, uncertainty avoiding, or communalist cultures may be substantially different from Western textbook methods;
- appropriate styles and methods of leadership may differ substantially from one culture to another;
- Western-style participatory decision-making processes developed in individualistic cultures may be entirely inappropriate in community-based cultures; and
- concepts of ethics differ substantially across cultures— including values relating to people, relationships, exclusion, gender, and power—and cross-cultural sensitivities as well as principles and mechanisms to manage these differences need to be developed. These aspects may have consequences for the way NGOs import foreign management principles (e.g., staff selection methods) as well as the way organizational and project impact is assessed.

How Can Cross-Cultural Theory Address Practical Issues of NGO Management and Leadership?

The recent discovery of cross-cultural management theories, particularly those of Geert Hofstede (2001), by the academics and the development community in general and those addressing NGO management in particular (e.g., Lewis, 2007), has not helped in addressing many of the issues. They only highlighted some of the problems. For example, such theories rarely address issues of leadership across cultures and neglect many cross-cultural dynamics, including power relations and processes of how hybrid forms of organization develop. It is important to understand how these dynamics affect various ways of leading nonprofit organizations working with minorities in the United States or working in the context of sub-Saharan Africa. More important now is to ask the question, How can this be used now to contribute to successful and appropriate leadership capacity building for NGOs operating in a context where different cultures and subcultures interact?

The first stage is to consider the complexity and dynamics of cross-cultural influences on NGO leadership capacity building. This involves understanding the different levels of cross-cultural interaction, and the dynamics of cultural crossvergence and organizational hybridization.

Levels of Cross-Cultural Interaction

Levels of cross-cultural interaction can be understood as follows:

Intercontinental level focuses on the dynamics of interaction of Western and indigenous cultures and leadership styles. The appropriateness of leadership principles and the transfer of knowledge surfaces when considering this level. Hybridization takes place through historical and current foreign and indigenous influences with the potential of developing ways of leadership that are highly adaptive to their environments.

Cross-border level focuses on interaction between countries (e.g., between the United States and Mexico or between African countries). In the case of Africa, this interaction was discouraged under colonial rule and is now becoming more important in economic cooperation within regional associations, particularly for the commercial sector. Northern-southern NGO interaction may undermine cross-border interaction and cross-fertilization of ideas and technologies and can support the argument that such relationships perpetuate former relationships between colonizer and colonized. A consideration of cultural differences and similarities is important at this level of analysis.

Interethnic level focuses on day-to-day issues of conflict, harmony, and power relations among ethnic groups as well as raises questions in Africa of the virtual and political nature of ethnic groupings and, for example, the extent to which tribes were colonial creations.

These three levels of cross-cultural interaction affect all development of NGOs. Northern NGOs import assumptions and methods to developing regions. Southern NGOs often have dependency relations with the North and adopt these imported assumptions uncritically. Cross-fertilization of ideas and technologies are important across borders in the South, and cross-cultural differences should be taken into account at the cross-border level. Finally, interethnic interactions are often prominent within southern NGOs (where they are not, exclusion may be taking place where employees are recruited predominantly from one ethnic group), and often with and among local clients. All this has profound implications for managers and leaders operating in NGOs in the context of developing countries and equally so for NGOs working with minorities in the United States or other countries.

Understanding Cross-Cultural Differences

For NGOs working, for instance, with minority groups in the United States, interethnic considerations might be more important, while for developing countries, differences appear to be most fundamental at the intercontinental level. Both levels should be considered when looking at the transferability of leadership principles. Of primary importance in understanding these cross-cultural differences between Western and non-Western cultures is the concept of *locus of human value*. Although this concept seeks to assess the appropriateness of people management approaches, it is also useful for understanding differences in approaches to leadership between, for example, Africa and the West.

Western management (American, French, Scandinavian, etc.) encompasses many different approaches to managing people and organizations. Culturally, these approaches appear to be linked by an *instrumental* view of people in organizations as a means to an end. This distinguishes them from non-Western views that see people as an end in themselves. Concepts such as viewing human beings as *resources* reflect the Western view.

The predominance of the phrase *human resource management* throughout the world, including within the NGO sector, reflects the (uncritical) influence of this view although, for example, the term *people management* is only now gaining currency in South Africa. In cultures that stress the value of persons in themselves (and often as part of a wider social collective), imposing a perception of persons as having a value only in what they can do for the organization (a resource)—rather than valuing them for who and what they are—runs contrary to many non-Western cultural value systems. It is no wonder that many interviewees in Africa explained that when they went in to work in the morning, they were stepping outside their culture and when going home at night, they were stepping back into it.

There is a danger that the NGO sector is adopting the idea of human beings as a resource quite uncritically and culturally insensitively. This may well be in line with their humanitarian mission (the task and results on which they are focused causing them to see staff as a means to achieving this), but may well be at odds with their humanitarian values—which logically should also apply to their staff.

The project detailed in *Management and Change in Africa* (Jackson, 2004) identified locus of human value as an important factor in understanding the different management systems in Africa, their appropriateness, and how they often combine in hybrid forms in individual organizations. We now focus on those different forms of management and explain their significance to understanding the cross-cultural context of managing NGOs.

How Can NGO Leadership Be Understood in the Cross-Cultural Context of Developing Regions?

Appropriate leadership varies across nations and continents. NGO managers cannot just "pick up" a technique or a principle from a textbook and apply it anywhere. What may look like a quick fix may be entirely inappropriate, particularly within a southern context, as we saw with the concept of HRM above. Therefore, the first step is to understand the different management systems and the associated assumptions on leadership operating within the South. During the above-mentioned research project, the following were identified as *ideal types* (in the Weberian sense) in sub-Saharan Africa.

"Postcolonial" Management

When management academics look at management in developing countries, they see and describe *postcolonial* management and leadership systems without identifying these as such: hierarchical, centralized, authoritarian or at best paternalist, rule bound, lacking in flexibility, distrustful of employees. Management in developing countries is thus seen in this pejorative sense. The obvious solution within this *developing-developed* world paradigm is to move toward a Western approach: results and market focused, leadership often consultative and participative, and task and people focus balanced using a *contingency* approach. Multinational corporations as well as agencies such as the World Bank and International Monetary Fund (IMF) are urging this movement. This uptake of Western principles also applies to NGOs operating in developing countries. Yet this represents a similar dynamic to that which created postcolonial systems.

Dia (1996), among others, puts forward the disconnect thesis: Institutions were imposed on communities during the colonial era. This gave rise to the systems of management and control that have continued to be seen as "African"—because, after all, African chiefs were dictatorial, authoritarian, and nonconsultative, weren't they? Yet these postcolonial systems continue to actually alienate African employees.

So, are so-called Western (or more accurately Anglo-American) management systems any more appropriate in Africa and other developing regions?

Western or "Postinstrumental" Management

It is difficult to argue that mature, modern HRM systems in Western countries reflect a *hard instrumentalism*, which overly emphasizes people as being mere resources. These modern systems have adopted a *softer form of instrumentalism* by incorporating the contingency principle that uses task- and people-focused approaches. However, there is evidence to suggest that where Western HRM methods have been adopted in emerging economies, such as the former Soviet countries, they have taken the harder forms. This is also evident in Africa. Participation and empowerment are part of the discourse of contingency instrumental approaches rather than part of a humanist approach that values people as ends in themselves.

In the commercial sector in countries such as South Africa, they are often being used on a tactical basis at an operational level of the organization (where the objective and task are provided to a work team that can then implement the decision in any way it wishes within budgetary and other constraints) leaving strategic decision-making processes within the sphere of the organization's (often-foreign) elite, and without reference to a wider stakeholder base.

Humanist ("African Renaissance") Management

Humanist approaches to management are being articulated within Africa. This is particularly manifest in South Africa through the concept of *ubuntu,* from a Xhosa (one of the local South African languages) saying that means "people are only people through other people." A number of public and commercial-sector organizations have implemented management development programs based on these principles that seek to capture indigenous African values.

It would be wrong, however, to suggest that this approach has had a tremendous and profound effect on management and approaches to leadership in South Africa. Yet it serves as an ideal, and may well represent an approach that is more in line with African employees' values of a person and a humanist locus of human value. However, evidence from other organizations in countries that have not necessarily come into contact with ubuntu principles from South Africa are attempting to reintroduce African values. Consider, from a group interview with key managers in Afriland First Bank in Cameroon, the following quote on indigenous approaches to leadership (Jackson, 2004):

> In our traditional culture it isn't the chief who makes the decision. Every stone is turned, by bringing people together. With individual decision-making there is a chance that you will make a mistake. So decisions are taken at the group level. We are like an African family that is trying to ensure our stability for the longer period. But in our family the chief cannot always see that he is doing wrong. . . . In the north of the country you have isolated big trees in savannah areas. So people gather around the tree. They solve community matters, preventing small problems becoming destructive. This is the model here. Every month people gather without consideration of rank, to discuss internal matters. There is no general manager present. We look at good news. We discuss things that are not right. We ask people what they think and to decide upon the issue in respect to their individual operating unit. (p. 227)

Leadership Approaches and NGOs

Although there is a growing literature on how NGOs should be managed (often within a Western framework), there has been little research undertaken on the role of NGO leaders and how NGOs are actually managed. There is isolated evidence that postcolonial systems may be a feature in some southern NGOs or that Western approaches may nowadays be used uncritically. When reviewing the available literature on leadership in nonprofit organizations, Hailey (2006) discerned four types of NGO leaders: paternalist, activist, managerialist, and catalytic leaders. Paternalist leaders, he argues, typically demonstrate a patriarchal or matriarchal style of leadership, which is often rooted in relationships of kin. While this closeness may result in greater loyalty of the employees toward their manager, to outsiders, this type of leadership may seem rather autocratic and top-down. We can relate this type of leadership quite easily to the ideal type of postcolonial management outlined above. Activist leaders, Hailey continues, are highly motivated, often charismatic, leaders and typically focus actively on a single issue like advocacy or lobbying work. Although their managerial and organizational skills are not always the most effective, through their charisma, they often have the ability to instill motivation in their employees. In contrast, managerialist leaders seem to score higher where activist leaders score lower. As Hailey argues, they typically demonstrate an instrumental ability to manage organizations and can effectively establish reliable systems and appropriate structures as well as manage a diverse workforce. Catalytic leaders, Hailey finally argues, in their capacity as effective networkers demonstrate an ability to take a longer-term strategic and holistic approach to managing organizations effectively. They have the ability to promote and implement change. Their success as change agents rests on their ability to delegate work well, to build and maintain relationships with the various stakeholders, and to balance tough decisions—for example, strategic priorities with the values and identity their organization wants to carry out.

Similarly, some researchers make reference to the fact that NGOs need to relate to their local clientele in a way that reflects local values and practices but say little on the way that internal management reflects humanist and communalist values. It is more likely that NGOs, just like organizations in other sectors, have got to adapt and develop hybrid organizations that are effective within the context in which they operate. This aspect is considered next.

Why Are Cultural Crossvergence and Hybridization Important to NGO Management?

Although the three ideal type systems are unlikely to be found in Africa (or other developing regions) in any pure form, they represent historical and current cultural influences on modern-day management and leadership practices in various hybrid forms of organization across sectors. There may be other systems. For example, Japanese management may be seen as an alternative to Western principles. Rather, these ideal types are used as a device, or metaphor, to conceptualize and analyze the different influences on management in Africa. They are seen as content components in the process of cultural cross-fertilization and hybridization of management systems and approaches to leadership.

There is a tendency in the international management literature either to accept the *convergence* thesis that, due to globalization, cultures are coming together—often through the economic power and hegemony of American influence—or the *divergence* thesis that (national) cultures—although changing—remain essentially different from each other and that these differences should be taken into consideration when managing across cultures. A third thesis is becoming more current: *crossvergence*. This suggests that through different cultural influences, hybrid forms of management and leadership are developing, with some highly suitable to their operating environment, with some less suitable. This has been increasingly studied in Hong Kong; it has also been used to develop systems of people management such as in the case of Indian HRD, which brings together Western and Indian influences.

However, these theories do tend to miss out on the importance of power and ideology in the development of hybrid forms. For example, the power of development agencies and donors and the influence of Western management textbooks and courses undoubtedly have a substantial impact on the type of hybrid management forms operating within development NGOs. Yet Western management and leadership principles should not be immediately dismissed. It may also be a fact of life that African organizations cannot simply go back to supposed management methods that existed before colonial times. History perhaps cannot be defied. However, the process of hybridization can be managed. The complexities of the operating environment can be understood and redefined. Different stakeholders' inputs can be facilitated. Appropriate leadership can be developed. Motivation and commitment can be attuned to local conditions. And

multiculturalism and multiple influences of culture can be used as an advantage, not a disadvantage.

International and indigenous NGO capacity building should be grounded in solid empirical research, which itself should be based on cross-cultural principles. No organization on the globe today can ignore cross-cultural management issues. Development NGOs are no exception to this. Cross-cultural management is absolutely central to their raison d'être, and to their own sustainable development. We now look at the processes involved in this.

How Can Leadership Capacity Be Built Through Cross-Cultural Management?

We now focus on the way NGO capacity may be built effectively and appropriately through cross-cultural management. Drawing on the concept of cultural crossvergence, we can discuss how the process of hybridization might be managed to develop organizations that are highly adaptive to their environments. Crossvergence draws on the findings of the research project detailed in the book by its name, *Management and Change in Africa: A Cross-Cultural Perspective* (Jackson, 2004), and looks at the importance of developing capacity in the following areas:

- Managing complexity and uncertainty in the development context
- Managing decision-making processes through multiple stakeholders
- Using appropriate leadership and management styles
- Motivating and rewarding managers
- Gaining employee commitment through work attitudes and organizational climate
- Managing multiculturalism and developing managers

Box 95.1 outlines the main findings from the above-mentioned project that surveyed managers in 15 sub-Saharan countries from the commercial, public, and third sectors and that focused on specific organizations in South Africa, Cameroon, Nigeria, and Kenya. These findings are now discussed in relation to development NGOs and how capacity might be built.

Box 95.1   Management and Change in Africa—Key Results

Managing Complexity and Uncertainty in the African Environment

The way the operating environment is seen in terms of constraints and opportunities is important to successful and appropriate organizational management.

Understanding how perceptions of uncertainty and ambiguity are culturally formulated is important to how managers act toward the operating environment.

An ability to "capture" the wider societal collectivism, humanism, and entrepreneurial flair in Africa may all be key to organizational success.

(Continued)

(Continued)

The capability to develop cultural synergies and include different and wider stakeholders is a prerequisite to making appropriate decisions—through a more thorough understanding of the operating environment—helping to reduce uncertainty and including multiple stakeholders.

Managing Decision Making

Understanding the influences of cultural differences on decision making and managing different value systems is important in developing decision processes and in transferring knowledge and decision systems from other cultures.

As above, effective and appropriate decision making should be based on the inclusion of a wider stakeholder base, and some organizations are beginning to recognize this in part.

However, current participatory and empowerment management, transferred from Western systems, is gaining in importance in Africa but is mostly "tactical" at the implementation level and based on contingency principles, leaving strategic decisions to top management—and often by foreign boards, with little or no wider stakeholder involvement.

Using Appropriate Leadership and Management Styles

There are a variety of hybrid management systems operating in Africa, some highly adaptive to the operating environment—and successful—some maladaptive.

These can be described by reference to three "ideal type" management systems: *postcolonial* (based on coercive leadership and alienative involvement), *postinstrumental* (based on remunerative reward and contractual involvement), and *African renaissance* (based on normative leadership and moral involvement).

African management systems appear currently to be predominantly *results* and *control* oriented (postinstrumental and postcolonial), with some country differences: Democratic Republic of Congo is more *control* oriented; Mozambique and Rwanda are more *people* (normative) oriented.

There is a general desire among managers to be more *people* and *results* oriented (particularly Burkina Faso and Botswana); but *people* orientation is not reflected in managers' projections of the future of their organizations, whereas a higher emphasis on *results* is.

Motivating and Rewarding Managers

Locus of control, the extent to which managers perceive that events can be controlled by them (internal locus) or are outside their control (external locus), has implications for motivational systems, such as results-driven reward systems. Generally, this was found to be moderately "internal" (contrary to general assumptions)—with managers in Botswana, Ghana, Republic of South Africa (RSA), and Zambia more internal than in other countries and among cultural groups within RSA more differences than in other countries.

Security needs, which affect the "hygiene" nature in motivational systems of a steady and secure job appear to be higher in Kenya, Ghana, and Zambia and lower in RSA, Botswana, and Zimbabwe.

Managers generally report a preference to work as part of a team, but they see this tendency as being lower in others.

Work centrality is generally low: Family and life outside work is more important.

Gaining Employee Commitment: Work Attitudes and Organizational Climate

Humanist and communalist attitudes are prominent.

There is a need for stability, and employees have expectations of loyalty from their employer.

Employees report a moderately high loyalty to the organization yet a moderately low work centrality.

There is a separation between home-community life and work life.

Reported levels of coercive control (postcolonial management systems) seem too high.

Employees appear to be team workers.

Managing Multiculturalism: Developing Managers

Difference in learning styles may suggest that Anglo-Saxon teaching methods with a focus on process may be inappropriate.

Also questioned is the appropriateness of the "organizational learning" concept that is being introduced into organizations in Africa with very little thought.

Consideration of the points above indicate management development and organizational capacity building should include the following areas: understanding constraints and uncertainty, accommodating interests of multiple stakeholders, developing decision processes that give voice to those interests, motivating and gaining commitment by reconciling home-community and work life, assessing appropriateness of management principles and practices, and managing multiculturalism and cross-cultural development.

SOURCE: From Jackson, T. (2003). *Cross-Cultural Management and NGO Capacity Building: How Can Capacity Be Built Through Cross-Cultural Management?* (Intrac Praxis Note 2), available online at www .intrac.org/resources.php?action=resource&id=111.

Managing Complexity and Uncertainty

The context of developing countries is often uncertain, risky, and complex. Add to this the overall operating context of NGOs whose management has

> to balance the needs of local communities, with complex financial and operational considerations, and the demands of government and aid donors' and . . . face the challenge of working with some of the most vulnerable and disadvantaged people in the world today in a range of projects. (Hailey, 2002, p. 2)

Now, one has an idea of the scale of challenge for NGOs operating in developing regions, such as sub-Saharan Africa. Compounding this complexity and uncertainty is the mission of most NGOs to make fundamental changes to the way things are. Yet the way the context is perceived may be culturally influenced and shaped by power relations; the way that uncertainty is perceived has been shown to be influenced by culture; and the way that change is managed in the West may be entirely inappropriate in cultures that are more hierarchical and uncertainty avoiding.

Perception of Constraints and Opportunities

Some authors have argued that some bodies, including the World Bank, have interests entrenched in an African crisis; their importance, the resources they command, perhaps even their very existence, depend on a perceived need to rescue Africa from disaster. We might extend this to include the African elite who might have a vested interest in an Africa crisis. This is not to pour scorn on the work of

agencies and NGOs but to prompt NGO managers to make a proper assessment of the way constraints and opportunities are seen in relation to their work. The interviews conducted with managers in Africa over a broad range of sectors indicated large variation among organizations in the degree to which managers saw opportunities positively, made a realistic assessment of constraints, and developed strategies for overcoming constraints.

Perception of Uncertainty and Ambiguity, and the Management of Change

Two factors, which vary across cultures, especially appear to influence the perception of uncertainty and ambiguity and therefore the way that change can be managed in a complex environment, such as sub-Saharan Africa.

Uncertainty Avoidance

There is some evidence that African cultural groups are less tolerant of uncertainty than, for example, white settler groups in South Africa. Change management processes that seek to empower lower-level staff members to take ownership of change may only worsen the perception of uncertainty and may be seen as the "boss not managing" in a culture that is more hierarchical.

Locus of Control

There is evidence that African groups may have a perception of not being able to control external events (compared with Western groups who appear to have a higher internal locus of control). This factor, which concerns the way people act toward their environment should be taken into account when NGO leaders seek to develop methods of managing change in the organization. In times of adversity, for example, this external locus of control manifests itself in the perception of NGO staff and managers that many outcomes are beyond their personal control.

Managing Decision-Making Processes Through Multiple Stakeholders

One way in which uncertainty may be effectively managed within a change process is through the inclusion of multiple stakeholders in the decision-making process. Evidence in Africa (Jackson, 2004) suggests that a wide stakeholder base is important to managing in an uncertain and complex context and indeed to organizational performance and impact. This is no less important in the NGO sector (see Edwards, 2002, on NGOs in South Asia). Yet while some enlightened (commercial) organizations are tempted to involve a wider stakeholder group, most organizations appear to be introducing more participative, empowering approaches purely on a tactical basis and not involving wider stakeholder groups in strategic decision making. Strategic decisions, often made at head offices, may not be appropriate to the needs of the wider stakeholder base and may not enable organizations to effectively adapt to and manage their operating environment. Hailey (2001) suggests how the formulaic approaches to participation in the work of NGOs may be not only culturally inappropriate but also culturally more ominous as part of the agenda of donor agencies. He describes approaches of community networking within a wide stakeholder base that may be more appropriate in south Asia.

There is therefore a need to look at participation in the decision-making process in terms of both the cultural context (what type of participation is culturally appropriate and why?) and in terms of the power relations between, for example, northern and southern NGOs, or donor agencies and development NGOs. It is likely, certainly in the contexts of sub-Saharan African countries, that wider stakeholder involvement in decision-making processes is both more appropriate in the communalist oriented cultures, and more effective in making appropriate organizational decisions for sustainable development and capacity building.

Using Appropriate Leadership and Management Styles

Previously we discussed the different ideal type management systems operating in Africa as well as other developing regions:

- *Postcolonial* systems are based on coercive leadership and alienative involvement of employees.

- *Postinstrumental* systems are based on remunerative reward, where leadership is task and results driven and staff has a contractual involvement with the organization.
- *African renaissance (humanist)* systems are based on normative, often value-driven leadership, and moral involvement of people within the organization.

Lewis (2007) appears to align coercive-alienative leadership with public-sector management, remunerative-contractual leadership with commercial-sector management, and normative-moral leadership with NGO management. Although this may have a ring of logic, it may be altogether too simplistic. Evidence from the Management and Change in Africa project suggests that organizations across sectors still retain strong elements of coercive leadership yet also have a results focus (for *control* and *results* orientation, see Box 95.1). Yet they have a low *people* (or normative) orientation with a desire, as indicated by a survey of managers, for a stronger *people* as well as *results* focus.

Organizations in sub-Saharan Africa (and other developing regions) across sectors are developing numerous hybrid management systems. There are tremendous pressures, from multinational organizations on local subsidiary organizations and from World Bank and IMF on public-sector organizations and on donor agencies on NGOs, to adopt more Western approaches and hence more instrumental focus where leadership employs a contingency approach, balancing between task focus and tactical participatory focuses. Western management education and textbooks reinforce these pressures. NGOs, like public and private-sector organizations, must be mindful of the appropriateness of leadership styles and methods and, in particular, to be aware of the cultural embeddedness of leadership and management styles that have implications, among other aspects, for management and staff motivation.

Motivating and Rewarding Managers

There may be a temptation to downplay the role of motivating and rewarding managers in NGOs. Such managers may be seen to be motivated by higher ideals, such as contributing to social change. Yet as Fowler (2002) points out, this attitude may well be changing, as NGOs became more businesslike and market-driven during the 1990s, the sector enlarged, and the need increased for good managers and staff from other NGOs and from donor agencies. There are increasing market-driven pressures to focus more on the way managers are motivated and rewarded. There may also be movement of managers from one sector to another. Commercial managers from the private sector may need attracting. Poaching from the public sector may also be a factor. NGOs appear to be less immune from motivational and reward considerations. Factors that appear to play a part in considering this (from evidence in Africa) are the following:

- Locus of control plays a part in the extent to which reward systems should be results driven, as this may influence the extent to which managers feel they can control outside events and to achieve the results they are targeted on. This aspect seems to vary across sub-Saharan countries (Box 95.1).
- Security needs appear to be important. A job that motivates through higher ideals may be no good if it cannot guarantee ongoing and secure employment.
- Feeling part of a team appears to be important rather than being motivated and rewarded as an individual (as is often the emphasis in Western reward systems).
- Work centrality appears to be generally low in Africa. This may be because of the community and family emphasis in many developing countries. This may be a particularly important factor in motivating managers in NGOs, where there is a need to have a closer integration of community and NGO.

Gaining Employee Commitment Through Work Attitudes and Organizational Climate

Staff commitment is another area that appears to have been neglected in the literature, and has not been approached from a cross-cultural perspective. This is surprising in view of the often large staffs of many development NGOs, often working within different cultural contexts. When staff commitment is treated in the literature, it is often linked with the question of participation (i.e., high levels of participation are related to high staff morale and commitment). Yet lack of hierarchy, structure, and a perceived authority may actually militate against employee morale and commitment.

Results from interviews in South Africa, Cameroon, Nigeria, and Kenya for the Management and Change in Africa project, suggest that

- communalist and humanist leadership attitudes are important within organizations across sectors;
- employees expect both stability in their jobs and loyalty from their employers;
- work is by no means central in people's lives, yet there is still a moderately high level of loyalty shown to the organization (which may be dependent on loyalty being shown to the employee);
- employees appear to be team players rather than individualists; yet
- these aspects appear not to be fully realized as there seems to be a separation between home-community life and the world of work and also a perception by employees that levels of control are too high.

The extent to which Western principles of participation and individual incentives are appropriate must be questioned. NGO leaders may find that building loyalty may be more usefully seen as a longer-term reciprocal process of joint loyalty building through stability in employment,

integration of community and work life in both attitudinal forms, for example, by adopting a more communalistic or humanistic leadership attitude, and actual reciprocal involvement of community and organization and focus on incentives for teams.

Again, as an approach to leadership, participation could more usefully be seen as including a range of stakeholders, including those within the community. Yet the above does not rule out more paternalistic ways of managing or more authoritarian and hierarchical organizational structures and processes. However this is in common with the areas discussed above, an important area for future research.

Managing Multiculturalism and Developing NGO Leaders

Management training and development in a multicultural context (involving the three levels of cross-cultural dynamics, i.e., intercontinental, cross-border, and interethnic discussed above) involves both *process* (how do we do it?) and *content* (what do we do?). Process can further be considered in terms of individual learning and organizational leaning.

Learning as a concept varies across cultures—so much so that the Anglo-Saxon notion of learning is difficult to translate even into other European languages. Such a concept is learner centered and process focused. The emphasis is on process, or how to learn, rather than on the content, or what you know. Many other non-Anglo-Saxon approaches to teaching are content focused, such as the French approach. This also seems to be the case in many African cultures with an emphasis on observation and an oral tradition of knowledge transmission and memorization. Lecture methods may be far more appropriate for individual learning than workshop methods, for example. Furthermore, knowledge is highly respected, highly valued, and almost feared where the learner becomes dependent on the trainer as a source of knowledge and wisdom. The idea of the *independent learner* does not appear to be appropriate.

The Anglo-Saxon concept of the *learning organization* may also be inappropriate in a developing country context. First, it relies heavily on the idea of experiential learning and learning as a process, which may be at variance to, for example, African notions. Second, it relies on the perception of organizations as *open systems* that pursue the executive goals of the organization, are instrumental, and use learning to fulfill executive goals. This also touches on the discussion above about the narrowly defined and tactical nature of participation. To be successful, organizational learning for NGOs working in developing countries should be more inclusive of a wider stakeholder base. At both the individual and organizational levels, management learning and development should include the following aspects that have been discussed above:

- Awareness among the management team of the broader operating constraints (political, economic, legislative, social, and cultural) within a complex operating environment and how these may be turned into opportunities
- Incorporation of the interests of multiple stakeholders including employees and their representatives, managers, community, government, suppliers, and clients as well as donor agencies in its strategic objectives
- Development of real and effective internal means for incorporating the perceptions, expectations, strengths, and interests of stakeholders and different cultural and gender groups in the decision-making process and the management of change through active and wider (rather than simply tactical) participation
- Obtaining commitment and motivation by developing understanding of the relationship between community-family life and work life and the way this relationship is differently perceived by different cultural perspectives

- Maintenance of a high level of awareness of the contributing factors to the way the organization is managed through principles, policies, and practices and their appropriateness to the sociocultural contexts within which the organization operates
- Conscious management of the dynamics of multiculturalism in order to develop strengths and synergies from these, including the management of equal opportunities of individuals from different ethnic and gender groups to influence the direction of the organization

Many of these aspects of management and leadership development and organizational capacity building involve a consideration of the transfer of knowledge and best practices from one organization to the other and from one culture to another. This involves issues of management and organizational learning, of the nature of leadership and decision making, and of the way that change is managed as well as ethical issues involved in decision making and the adoption of management practices (see Box 95.2).

Box 95.2 Developing Cross-Cultural Leadership Skills in Practice: Cultivating Cultural Intelligence

We discuss here some ways in which one might put the theoretical insights outlined above to practice. We use the concept of *cultural intelligence* (drawn here mainly from Thomas et al., 2008) to highlight how this might be done. In essence, cultural intelligence comes down to the ability to interact effectively with people from different cultural backgrounds. This includes ways of managing and leading effectively across cultures. We discuss here three aspects of cultural intelligence that students aspiring to lead NGOs in multicultural environments might benefit from: cultural knowledge, mindfulness, and cross-cultural skills.

Developing Cultural Knowledge

This refers to developing an understanding of what makes people from other cultures both different and similar to us. It refers both to understanding the content (e.g., knowledge about one's own and other cultures) and process (e.g., knowing that people's behavior is influenced by their cultural norms and values). In practice, this means that understanding other cultures also involves understanding one's own culture. Therefore, it is important that we also know who we are and where we come from (i.e., what shapes our *own* cultural values, attitudes, and behaviors). This requires people to be willing to look themselves in the mirror and question if what they do and how they do it is the *only right* way of doing things. For example, to use a simple analogy, opening a document in the Microsoft Word software program can be done by clicking on the file one wishes to open in the "My Documents" folder. The same document, however, can also be opened from within Microsoft Word by clicking on *Open* in the *File* tab. Is one way "better" than the other? No, both produce the same end result. Thus, acquiring cultural knowledge involves learning from specific experiences of dealing with people from different cultures and is the result of reflection on one's own behavior and the behavior of others. Understanding differences and similarities (both in terms of content and process) is a first step toward culturally sensitive leadership.

Mindfulness

Mindfulness refers to an active awareness of the differences and similarities among cultures and processes and forms the link between cultural knowledge (discussed above) and action (which we will discuss in the next section). If we are mindful of what we know about, for instance, a Hispanic subculture, then this can help us to act or lead in a more culturally sensitive way. Therefore, mindfulness includes being aware of our own assumptions, norms, and values and of the ways in which *we perceive* other cultures. It also relates to understanding others not only by focusing on what we see but also by understanding the context (i.e., the values and norms shaping their behavior). This requires an open mind and empathy toward others by trying to put ourselves in other persons' shoes in order to better understand the situation and the ways in which they act. Therefore, mindfulness is both an awareness of the differences that may divide us and the similarities that may bring us closer together, and it is a way of putting that knowledge to action in a culturally sensitive way.

Developing Cross-Cultural Leadership Skills

Developing cross-cultural intelligence implies learning from specific cross-cultural experiences. This means paying attention to what makes leadership practices across cultures different and similar. Two important dimensions of leadership that may differ across cultures are a focus on the task at hand (getting things done) and a focus on relationships (getting on with people). Developing cross-cultural leadership skills that balance both dimensions requires a certain amount of open-mindedness, flexibility, and empathy toward other ways of leading (nonprofit) organizations. However, if we wish to be good cross-cultural leaders, we need also to be able to adapt our style of leadership based on what we have learned about and from other cultures. This means we need to be able to integrate cultural knowledge and mindfulness to develop new attitudes and behaviors that balance tasks and relationships differently. This does not necessarily mean we need to adapt completely to other cultures. Cross-cultural leadership is not about forgetting our own culture but about learning how to make best use of the differences and similarities that may exist to achieve the organizational goals. It is about finding the right balance between a focus on tasks and relationships. As we discussed earlier, this implies developing hybrid ways of leading organizations that incorporate elements from different cultures to produce new approaches to leadership that might be more appropriate when we operate in a multicultural environment.

As the above shows, cross-cultural leadership involves understanding what makes us different and similar and using this diversity to the advantage of the organization. Reflecting on our own culture and the cultures of others as a way to develop cross-cultural intelligence is central to this.

Summary

In this chapter, we argued that in the context of developing countries, management and leadership of NGOs cannot but take cross-cultural issues into account (the same can be said about NGOs dealing with minorities in the United States or other developed countries). As NGO leaders and managers operate in an environment in which people from different continents, cultures, and ethnicities are required to work together in order to achieve the goals the NGO has set for itself, they need to be not only aware of cultural differences, but also, more importantly, able to manage and lead the organization in effective and culturally appropriate ways.

We argued that management and leadership in Africa can be understood by using three ideal types to describe the different ways in which organizations are organized. Postcolonial systems are based on coercive leadership and tend to alienate employees. Postinstrumental systems are based on remunerative reward, where leadership is task and result driven, and staff has a contractual involvement with the organization. It tends to have a flatter hierarchy than we find in postcolonial systems and tends to be more open to participative leadership styles. African renaissance (humanist) systems are based on normative, often value-driven, leadership and moral involvement of people within the organization. An activist or charismatic leadership approach seems to answer to this profile.

Even though each of these ideal types might not exist in their pure form in local NGOs, one can identify the main assumptions guiding management and leadership approaches through these three ideal types. This leads us to identify hybridization or cultural crossvergence as a way to understand the complex interactions and the power dynamics between the stakeholders in and around nonprofit organizations shaping the emergence of hybrid ways of leading and managing NGOs.

Understanding the above is key if we wish to proceed toward building management and leadership capacity within organizations operating in this complex and uncertain environment and to gain employee commitment. Hence, we argued that management learning and development needs to build on an awareness of this environment. Simultaneously, it needs to incorporate the interests of various stakeholders by developing the internal means of drawing them into the decision-making process and the management of change to motivate staff and obtain commitment. This all requires managers and leaders to adequately manage the dynamics of multiculturalism.

References and Further Readings

Dia, M. (1996). *Africa's management in the 1990s and beyond.* Washington, DC: World Bank.

Edwards, M. (2002). NGO performance: What breeds success? New evidence from South Asia. In M. Edwards & A. Fowler (Eds.), *The Earthscan reader on NGO management* (pp. 275–292). London: Earthscan.

Fowler, A. (2002). Human resource management. In M. Edwards & A. Fowler (Eds.), *The Earthscan reader on NGO management* (pp. 441–455). London: Earthscan.

Hailey, J. (2001). Beyond the formulaic: Process and practice in south Asian NGOs. In B. Cooke & U. Kothari (Eds.), *Participation: The new tyranny?* (pp. 88–101). London: Zed Books.

Hailey, J. (2002). *Development leaders: Issues in NGO leadership.* Paper presented at the EIASM Workshop on Leadership Research, Said Business School, Oxford, UK, December 2002. Oxford, UK: INTRAC.

Hailey, J. (2006). *NGO leadership development: A review of the literature* (Praxis Paper No. 10). Oxford, UK: INTRAC.

Hofstede, G. (2001). *Culture's consequences: Comparing values, behaviors, institutions, and organizations across nations* (2nd ed.). Thousand Oaks, CA: Sage.

Jackson, T. (2004). *Management and change in Africa: A cross-cultural perspective.* London: Routledge.

Lewis, D. (2007). *The management of non-governmental development organizations* (2nd ed.). London: Routledge.

Thomas, D. C., Elron, E., Stahl, G., Ekelund, B. Z., Ravlin, E. C., Cerdin, J., et al. (2008). Cultural intelligence: Domain and assessment. *International Journal of Cross Cultural Management, 8*(2), 123–143. doi: 10.1177/1470595808091787

96

MAKING THE CASE FOR WORKPLACE DIVERSITY

JASMINE MCGINNIS

Georgia State University and Georgia Institute of Technology

Open any recent nonprofit trade journal, and there are a number of reports detailing the lack of staff and board diversity in the sector. Despite the common perception that nonprofit organizations are and *should* be representative of the constituents they serve, an Annie E. Casey Foundation study finds that 84% of nonprofits are led by whites, while 58% of these same nonprofits serve racial and ethnic minority communities (Tempe & Smith, 2007). Along similar lines, another study finds that within foundations, only 6% of CEOs and 10% of foundation board members are racial and ethnic minorities (Burbridge, 2002). Additionally, statistics on nonprofit senior managers and CEOs often reveal that a "glass ceiling" exists for women (Odendahl & O'Neill, 1994). Although women make up the majority of nonprofit employees across many occupations, when it comes to management and senior-level positions, men are significantly overrepresented (Odendahl and O'Neill, 1994).

Of particular mention here is the unique demand placed on nonprofit managers to better understand the term *diversity* within the sector. For example, understanding what it means for a nonprofit organization to have a diverse workforce in terms of gender is especially unique. The concept of gender diversity in the nonprofit workforce may require understanding why women (who constitute the majority of the nonprofit workforce) still do not constitute the majority of nonprofit managers (Odendahl & O'Neill, 1994). Additionally, in particular nonprofit subsectors, male staff members would be considered a "minority" group. Again, both a true understanding of the definition of diversity and its nuances within the nonprofit sector along with a better understanding of the connection between diversity and an organization's performance are necessary components of making a case for diversifying the nonprofit workforce.

However, the number of reports and studies detailing the lack of diversity within the nonprofit sector seem to have an underlying assumption that increasing the diversity of an organization's board or staff members would improve organizational performance. Yet unlike the growing evidence and research conducted in the business and public sectors examining the connection between workforce diversity and performance, similar research in the nonprofit sector is sparse and not well known. Oftentimes, when reading a research report on the lack of diversity within the nonprofit sector, underlying assumptions about the impact of diversity appear anecdotal or normative, without providing evidence of how diversity can impact nonprofit organizations or clients.

Examples of this normative evidence can be seen in the reasoning given for why diversity is important in the nonprofit sector. A 2007 *Nonprofit Times* article states that a lack of workforce diversity "puts the sector at risk of losing touch with the populations nonprofits are organized to serve" (Tempel & Smith, 2007, "Nonprofits Have a Spotty Record"). Other reports suggest that board and staff diversity allow nonprofits to both better represent the constituents they serve and be more innovative with their solutions to social problems (John, 2008). But the real question we must begin to ask ourselves is whether or not these statements are true? How do we know that increasing diversity in the nonprofit sector will allow nonprofits to better serve their clients? Because the literature examining this topic within nonprofit research is sparse, what previous research can we use from the business and public sectors to better understand the link between workforce diversity and organizational or client performance within the nonprofit sector? And finally, will the relationship between workforce diversity and organizational or client performance be any different in the nonprofit sector than in the business and public sector?

This chapter explores these questions and others, going beyond common writings about workforce diversity, which typically either emphasize descriptive statistics of the nonprofit workforce or provide suggestions on how to best manage diversity within an organization. This chapter will seek to enhance the understanding of the connection between diversity and performance to create more informed advocates and ambassadors who understand why having a diverse workforce is important. First, an overview of the research conducted in the business and public sector examining the relationship between workforce diversity and performance measures is provided. Second, this chapter presents an overview of research conducted examining the relationship between diversity and performance in nonprofit literature. In fact, the latter can be grouped into two distinct bodies of literature. There is quantitative research that examines the relationship between *board* diversity and *organizational* outcomes and qualitative research that examines the relationship between *workforce* diversity and *client* outcomes.

Finally, a few strategies are presented that can be used by any nonprofit employee who works in an organization where diversity training and/or education has not been incorporated into that organization's culture and work environment. But most importantly, the aim of this chapter is to provide an initial starting point to begin discussions in the nonprofit organization's individuals may work in. At the end of this chapter, each reader will have a better understanding of the empirical research connecting workforce diversity and organizational or client performance rather than anecdotal statements that diversity is necessary and important. Furthermore, for future managers in the nonprofit sector, this research creates a discourse of the components necessary in an organization's environment and culture to best support diversity initiatives within their organization, as both the workforce and community demographics of those served by nonprofits is continually changing.

Defining Terms

For the purpose of this chapter, *diversity* is being defined as the U.S. Equal Employment Opportunity Commission (EEOC) defines *protected classes*, which includes a person's race, color, religion, sex (including an unborn child's during pregnancy), national origin, age (40 or older), disability, or genetic information (http://www.eeoc.gov/eeoc/index.cfm). This specific definition of diversity is used rather than much broader definitions of diversity (which can include categories like values, personality types, etc.; for a broad

discussion of the term *diversity* and the multiple viewpoints about how diversity should be defined, please see Carrell, Mann, and Honeycutt Sigler, 2006). The EEOC's definition is similar to the perspective of scholars in this arena such as Carmines and Stimson who write that "one of the most enduring relationships is the impact of race and ethnicity on values" (as cited in Meier, Wrinkle, & Polinard, 1999, p. 1026).

Performance measures are defined here as the umbrella concept under which outputs and outcomes are classified. Scholars in different areas of research (for-profit, public, and nonprofit sectors) use different performance measures both within and across sector research. It is worth taking time then to define outputs and outcomes, as some studies use outputs as a measure of an organization's performance while others use outcomes. Poister (2003) defines outputs as "the immediate products or services produced by public and nonprofit organizations" (p. 99). Organizational outputs have primarily been the focus of work in nonprofit literature examining the relationship between board diversity and performance. Most of this work focuses on outputs such as financial performance (i.e., funds raised for the organization) or other organizational performance metrics (such as board effectiveness and/or board performance).

Some scholars examine the connection between diversity and performance, which evaluate the impact of diversity on outcomes. Outcomes are defined as the results an organization produces (Poister, 2003). Additionally, distinctions are often made between different types of outcomes: short-term, intermediate, and long-term outcomes. Yet most scholars conducting research examining diversity's impact on performance do not denote whether they are measuring short-term, intermediate, or long-term outcomes. For a rich discussion of outcome measurement in nonprofit organizations, please see the Urban Institute's Outcome Indicators Project webpage (http://www.urban.org/center/cnp/projects/outcomeindicators.cfm).

The next section explores research conducted in the private sector that examines the connection between workforce diversity and performance. It will be important to keep in mind the definitions provided above regarding the difference between outputs and outcomes. In particular, the private sector researchers typically examine the connection between workforce diversity and financial outputs of an organization.

Private-Sector Research: Diversity's Impact on Organizational Performance

During the 1990s, the phrase "making a business case for diversity" was commonly used throughout the private sector and even found its way into public conversation and mainstream news sources. The business case for diversity was often used to justify an assumed belief or value held by many managers throughout the for-profit sector that diverse groups and teams had a positive impact on achieving a business's objectives. A number of studies emerged measuring the relationship between workforce diversity and operational or administrative outputs of a business. These outputs were often operational in terms of increased profits, less employee turnover, the creation of more innovative goods and services, and higher stock prices (Fernandez & Barr, 1993; Jackson, Joshi, & Erhardt, 2003; Kochan et al., 2003; Mannix & Neale, 2005; Robinson & Dechant, 1997).

Yet over time, studies of the relationship between workforce diversity and organizational performance in the private sector had different, conflicting, or inconclusive results. Some studies that were conducted indicated that diverse teams and organizations have positive impacts on various measures of organizational performance, while other studies found either negative relationships or none at all between workforce diversity and performance (Jackson et al., 2003; Kochan et al., 2003; Milliken & Martins, 1996; Richard, 2000).

Recent work conducted in the private sector introduces two concepts of organizational context and group-team processes to better understand the casual mechanisms that occur between workforce diversity and organizational performance. Kochan et al.'s (2003) work embodies the aims of current research in the private sector: They find that to empirically examine the relationship between workforce diversity and organizational performance both an organization's context and group-team processes need to be measured. Understanding an organization's culture and the group-team processes involved in the work often serve as antecedent and intervening variables, which are necessary when measuring the relationship between workforce diversity and performance. These authors define *organizational context* as a number of different factors that are important to measure, as neither diversity nor organizational performance exists "in a silo." Organizational context is defined as organizational culture, business strategy, and human resource policies and practices (Kochan et al., 2003). This same study defines group-team processes as a number of different variables that likely impact organizational performance, such as communications, conflict, cohesion, information, and creativity. Jackson et al.'s (2003) work provides a survey of literature conducted in the private sector examining the relationship between diversity and performance and finds that there are four contextual elements that have been used throughout many studies. These four contextual factors include the task characteristics of work, the organizational culture, and the strategic and temporal context of the work.

This research indicates that although diversity studies have shown a variety of often conflicting or inconclusive results, diversity's impact on organizational performance can primarily be observed by better understanding an organization's context (Jackson et al., 2003; Kochan et al., 2003; Mannix & Neale, 2005; Milliken & Martins, 1996; Richard, 2000; Robinson & Dechant, 1997). Kochan et al. (2003) argue that many of the reasons why researchers

have inconclusive or negative results is because the effects of diversity have not been measured within the context of where and how work takes place.

Private-sector researchers have truly led the efforts to empirically measure the impact of workforce diversity on organizational performance while using theories to guide and frame their research. Private-sector scholars also established a precedent of the critical need to make operational, observe, and measure both antecedent and intervening variables to accurately examine the relationship between workforce diversity and performance.

Overall, in private-sector research, we can identify a long tradition of not only understanding diversity as a complex concept (often measured in terms of cultural and demographic diversity) but also observing a commitment from researchers to examine the entire organization as well as the group-team processes that can affect the potential impacts of workforce diversity and organizational performance. In the public sector, we also observe a similar tradition of examining the complexities of the impact of workforce diversity on organizational performance. Yet organizational performance is made operational and conceptualized differently than performance used in private sector research (such as employee turnover, growth of profits, etc.). Instead, organizational performance is evaluated in terms of client outcomes, which are primarily found in the research of representative bureaucracy. This literature attempts to understand the relationship between public-sector organization workforce diversity and the outcomes of clients that use these services. Below is an overview of this literature, which again has some similarities to the research conducted by private-sector scholars but conceptualizes the performance measures very differently.

Public-Sector Research: Diversity's Impact on Client Outcomes

In 1944, Kingsley published one of the first works examining the concept of representative bureaucracy in public-sector organizations. He was one of the first scholars to examine the relationship between the demographics of the public-sector workforce and the outcomes of the clients that organizations serve. Since that time, a number of scholars have conducted rigorous empirical work on this same concept and are seeking to further understand how representation affects the public good (Hindera, 1993; Keiser, Wilkins, Meier, & Holland, 2002; Meier et al., 1999; Pitts, 2005).

Mosher's (1982) research distinguished between two different types of representation, *passive* and *active* representation. Passive representation is defined as the relationship between the demographics of an organizations workforce matching the demographics of the clients the organization serves. On the other hand, active representation is defined, "wherein an individual (or administrator) is expected to press for the interests and desires of those whom he is presumed to represent, whether they be the whole people or some segment of the people" (as cited in Dolan and Rosenbloom, 2003, p. 20).

One particular study of note that explores the concept of workforce diversity and its impact on client outcomes within a public-sector organization is demonstrated in Selden's (1997) research on the Farmers Home Administration. This study provided a unique analysis of representative bureaucracy as "the FmHA is not normally thought of as an agency with a mission emphasizing minority representation, despite the direct relevance of its programs to minority communities" (p. 66). This study focused on county supervisors who were responsible for providing loans to low-income residents in rural counties for housing purchase and repair. Selden finds a positive relationship between passive and active representation and also finds a positive relationship between an administrator's perception of himself or herself as an advocate of minority interests and active representation. She writes, "The extent to which a county supervisor perceived his or her role as an advocate of minority interests significantly influenced the percentage of eligibility decisions favoring minorities and the extent to which the supervisor publicized the loans program in the minority community" (p. xiv).

Researchers Thielemann and Stewart (1996) conducted another interesting study examining passive representation. Thielemann and Stewart surveyed 510 people living with AIDS to determine whether people living with AIDS, who receive services necessary for their survival, would care about the demographics of the employees that they interact with and receive services from? The results from their study indicate that clients do have a preference for working with service providers who are demographically similar to themselves. Thielemann and Stewart write, "A clear majority of each group—at least three-fourths of the African-American and Hispanic respondents and slightly over three-fifths of the Anglos—care if they received their services from people of the same ethnic group" (p. 171). Another surprising finding from this study is that the higher level bureaucrats in this service organization are "faceless" and unimportant to the citizens being served by this organization.

Unlike research done in the private sector focusing on the relationship between workforce diversity and organizational performance, public-sector scholars are primarily concerned with discerning the relationship between workforce diversity and client outcomes. Yet similar to private-sector researchers, public-sector scholars have found that organizational context and group-team processes within an organization *matter*. Concepts such as administrative discretion, attitude congruence with minorities, critical mass, and organizational strategies have all been identified as important variables that should be measured in public-sector research examining the relationship between workforce diversity and client outcomes (Andrews, Boyne, Meier, O'Toole, & Walker, 2005; Bradbury & Kellough, 2007;

Dolan & Rosenbloom, 2003; Meier et al., 1999; Selden, 1997). Again, public-sector scholars also realize that workforce diversity and client outcomes don't operate in a vacuum, and it is important to examine the complete picture of an organization when evaluating the impact of diversity on performance.

Nonprofit Research: Board Diversity's Impact on Organizational Outputs

Unlike research in the public and private sectors, the nonprofit research conducted on this subject primarily focuses on the link between board diversity and performance. There is a small amount of literature (primarily qualitative research) that examines the relationship between workforce diversity and client outcomes. Although the majority of nonprofit literature does not explicitly examine workforce diversity, we can certainly learn from previous research as to the potential impacts of a diverse nonprofit workforce and organizational outputs and/or client outcomes. This section describes a number of different studies conducted across different subsectors of nonprofits examining the impact between board diversity and organizational outputs.

The majority of nonprofit research examining the relationship between diversity and organizational outputs focuses on the diversity of nonprofit boards. This is not surprising since board members of nonprofits are especially important as they often bring new resources to nonprofits (often financial), which ultimately impact the operational, administrative, and financial outputs of the organization (Siliciano, 1996; Zald, 1969). Similar to work conducted in the private sector, nonprofit researchers define diversity as a multidimensional concept. In much of this research, a board member's occupation, race, sex, age, gender, and/or socioeconomic status is used to create an index of diversity.

Zald (1969) is one of the earliest authors to examine the relationship between board diversity and organizational outputs (which he defines as board effectiveness). Zald (1969) conducted a survey of 37 departments in Chicago-area Young Men's Christian Associations (YMCAs). He created an index of performance measures of board effectiveness through four separate indicators:

1. Financial contributions of board members

2. Participation of board members in programs

3. Board attendance

4. Ratings of departmental effectiveness

Zald (1969) found that YMCAs with board members who were not local community residents were able to secure more resources and operate more efficiently.

Bradshaw, Murray, and Wolpin (1996) conducted a similar study but primarily focused on the relationship between gender diversity within nonprofit boards and organizational performance measures. The organizational outputs examined are focused on the connection between gender diversity and board performance—operative as both board and organizational effectiveness. Bradshaw et al. (1996) conducted this research on 417 nonprofit organizations in Canada. They found no significant relationships between the percentage of women as board members or CEOs of nonprofits and organizational effectiveness, in either subjective or objective operations of this variable. However, a positive relationship was found between the percentage of women on boards and the degree of board formalization, board attendance, and the CEOs' satisfaction with board performance.

Siliciano (1996) used a multidimensional concept of diversity to understand the relationship between board diversity and organizational outputs, focusing on the link between gender and occupational diversity and an organization's performance. Siliciano defined organizational performance as a combination of both client focused outcomes (such as ability of a nonprofit to fulfill its mission) and organizational outputs (such as fiscal performance). Surveying a sample of 240 YMCA organizations, Siliciano found that the occupational diversity of board members had a positive relationship with both organizational and fiscal performance measures. Siliciano also found that a higher proportion of women on a nonprofit board of directors was positively associated with the organization's ability to fulfill its mission but negatively associated with levels of donations.

In 2002, Brown was one of the first researchers to examine the relationship between the *racial-ethnic* diversity of the board and organizational outputs (which Brown measured in terms of board performance). Brown also follows in the tradition of most researchers from the private and public sector examining the relationship between diversity and organizational outputs, as he takes into account both the organizational context and group-team processes that exist within an organization. His research used survey data from 121 executive directors in two metropolitan cities to examine the relationship between board diversity, attitudes about diversity, and an organization's recruitment practices on board performance. Board performance was measured using a modified version of the Board Self Assessment Questionnaire (which assesses the characteristics of effective boards) revealing a moderate relationship between the board's racial-ethnic diversity and board performance. Additionally, Brown (2002) found that diversity recruitment strategies and the board's attitudes about diversity were positively associated with higher levels of board performance. This finding is similar to both private and public sector findings as the organization's culture and its ability to manage diversity *well* within an organization serves as an intervening variable impacting an organization's performance.

In addition to the quantitative studies that primarily focus on the relationship between board diversity and

organizational performance, there is a small body of literature that examines the relationship between workforce diversity and client outcomes (along the lines of what is researched in public sector research) within the nonprofit sector. Below is an overview of this research to provide a better understanding of the research that's been conducted examining this topic on nonprofit organizations but more importantly on how measures of client outcomes are made operational within this research arena.

Nonprofit Research: Workforce Diversity's Impact on Client Outcomes

There is another group of literature that examines the intersection of workforce diversity and an organization's cultural responsiveness to its clients. This research posits that nonprofit organizations engage in human resource practices to be inclusive in order to both recruit a diverse workforce and be responsive to the diverse clients they serve. Because this research is mostly qualitative, many of the contextual factors (human resource practices, organization strategy, and group-team practices) that both private- and public-sector researchers examine are included in these studies. Similar to work in the public sector, which makes a distinction between passive and active representation, scholars in this research arena make a distinction between first and second order changes. The findings from this research are similar to the findings of public-sector researchers who examine representative bureaucracy. First order changes (hiring more diverse staff members) does not impact organizational or client outcomes but second order changes (managing diversity within an organization's environment) have the most impact on performance measures (Hyde, 2003; Hyde & Hopkins, 2004).

Hyde (2003) conducted a qualitative study of 20 nonprofit managers in the New England area examining the values, goals, and attributes that both initiated and resulted in an organization's diversity practices. Most managers reported that they initiated human resource practices and strategies of hiring diverse staff members either to be more responsive to their clients or to assist in recruiting other diverse staff members. Allison's (2001) study describes the relationship between a nonprofit's workforce and an organization's responsiveness to clients, as he found that less diverse workforces affected clients adversely. Allison examined youth-related nonprofit agencies in a qualitative study and found that in those nonprofit organizations with less diversity, staff members believed it negatively impacted their ability to recruit and/or serve diverse clients or establish community partnerships.

The reviews of this literature allow us to hypothesize that there are many positive benefits when the workforce of a nonprofit organization is diverse. Furthermore, the benefits resulting from a diverse workforce can be both quantitative and qualitative, focused on outputs or outcomes, or focused on clients or organizational performance.

However, these potential benefits will only be realized when an organization's culture is supportive of these practices. Examining the impact of staff diversity across for-profit, public, and the nonprofit sectors certainly indicates not only that context matters but also that increasing staff diversity without taking into account how this diversity can be integrated into an organization's culture and group-team work processes is imperative. Below, possible strategies to incorporate more inclusive practices into their nonprofit organizations are suggested for employees beginning their first nonprofit jobs. Whether someone identifies as a minority or not, the knowledge gained from this chapter indicates that understanding strategies on how to potentially enhance these diversity-related benefits will affect the work and the impact an organization has.

Summary

In considering a career in the nonprofit sector, a person must first consider how he or she can determine if an organization has a commitment to inclusive hiring practices. When interviewing and reviewing an organization's material, one must pay particular attention to its human resource policies and discrimination policies. These documents should indicate whether or not this organization recognizes the potential benefits from having an organizational culture that is supportive of a diverse workforce or if it relies on more anecdotal and normative beliefs concerning the relationship between diversity and performance. If an organization's human resource policies are not clear, take a look at the statements the organization makes on its website, brochure, and other public relations material to determine its commitment to serving a diverse clientele. An example could be an organization that has its forms and information translated into a second language so that it can be responsive to an increasingly diverse clientele. Other examples could include organizations that have explicit and clear statements made available to the public about their commitments to nondiscrimination. If these documents are not clear, employees should feel free to approach the human resources manager or direct supervisor to suggest implementing human resource policies or nondiscrimination statements that not only suggest that the nonprofit is supportive of incorporating more diverse staff members into its organization but also indicate that the organizational culture is supportive of and recognizes the potential benefits of diversity.

Another important question concerning nonprofits is to ask what sort of diversity training and/or education programs the organization has in place. Does the organization provide diversity training annually or only once when an employee is hired? Are there opportunities for additional training or education programs for managers or supervisors to support diversity initiatives? If the organization has a diverse clientele, what sort of training for employees will it implement in order to adapt to an increasingly diverse clientele? Additionally, is diversity training and education something that is recognized as important by all employees or just management? What is the organization's definition of diversity, and is this explicitly stated in the diversity training materials? It is also important to understand the procedures set in place for reporting incidents of intolerance or discrimination.

One can also imagine a situation where individual employees may serve as ambassadors or advocates for increasing the diversity and training-education materials in an organization, if some of these questions remain unanswered or are not made clear in existing materials. Organizing a monthly potluck where staff members bring dishes that are representative of their heritage or background could be a great start for an organization that is beginning discussions around the importance of having a diverse workforce. Another way to highlight the importance of diversity could be in organizing a day of service for the employees within an organization whose principles stress tolerance and justice.

It is important to recognize the connection that exists between workforce diversity and performance. Nonprofit employees should take a particular interest in serving as an ambassador or advocate for diversity-related benefits that may enhance the performance of an organization. In this era of changing demographics and increased reliance on nonprofit organizations to provide many basic social and human services, recognition of the relationship between workforce diversity and performance will lead to a generation of nonprofit employees who serve as both advocates and ambassadors for diversity.

References and Further Readings

Allison, M. (2001). Diversity issues and challenges facing youth-related nonprofit agencies (Report). *Center for Nonprofit Leadership and Management, 6*, 8.

Andrews, R., Boyne, G., Meier, K., O'Toole, L., & Walker, R. (2005). Representative bureaucracy, organizational strategy, and public service performance: An empirical analysis of English local government. *Journal of Public Administration Research and Theory, 15*(4), 489–504.

Bradbury, M., & Kellough, J. (2007). Representative bureaucracy: Exploring the potential for active representation in local government. *Journal of Public Administration Research and Theory, 18*(4), 697–714.

Bradshaw, P., Murray, V., & Wolpin, J. (1996). Women on boards of nonprofits: What difference do they make? *Nonprofit Management and Leadership, 6*, 241–254.

Brown, W. (2002). Racial diversity and performance of nonprofit boards of directors. *Journal of Applied Management and Entrepreneurship, 7*(4), 43–57.

Burbridge, L. (2002, May). *Diversity in philanthropy: The numbers and their meaning, meaning and impact of board and staff diversity in the philanthropic field.* Available from http://www.philanthropy.iupui.edu/Millennium/usefulInformation/The%20Meaning%20and%20Impact%20of%20Board%20and%20Staff%20Diversity%20in%20the%20Philanthropic%20Field.pdf

Carrell, M., Mann, E., & Honeycutt Sigler, T. (2006). Defining workforce diversity programs and practices in organizations: A longitudinal study. *Labor Law Journal, 57*(1), 5–12.

De Vita, C. J., & Roeger, K. L. (With assistance of Max Niedzwiecki). (2009, November). *Measuring racial ethnic diversity in California's nonprofit sector.* Available from http://www.urban.org/uploadedpdf/411977_CA_Diversity.pdf

Dolan, J., & Rosenbloom, D. (2003). *Representative bureaucracy: Classic readings and continuing controversies.* Armonk, NY: M. E. Sharpe.

Fernandez, J., & Barr, M. (1993). *The diversity advantage: How American business can out-perform Japanese and European companies in the global marketplace.* New York: Lexington Books.

Hindera, J. (1993). Representative bureaucracy: Further evidence of active representation in the EEOC district offices. *Journal of Public Administration Research and Theory, 3*(4), 415–429.

Hyde, C. A. (2003). Multicultural organizational development in nonprofit human service agencies: Views from the field. *Journal of Community Practice, 11*(1), 39–59.

Hyde, C., & Hopkins, K. (2004). Diversity climates in human service agencies: An exploratory assessment. *Journal of Ethnic and Cultural Diversity in Social Work, 13,* 25–44.

Jackson, S., Joshi, A., & Erhardt, N. (2003). Recent research on team and organizational diversity: SWOT analysis and implications. *Journal of Management, 29*(6), 801–830.

Jehn, K., Northcraft, G., & Neale, M. (1999). Why differences make a difference: A field study of diversity, conflict, and performance in workgroups. *Administrative Science Quarterly, 44*(4), 741–763.

John, L. (2008, August 13). Board and employee diversity in the philanthropic sector: A landscape analysis. Available from http://www.onphilanthropy.com/site/News2?page=NewsArticle&id=7577

Keiser, L., Wilkins, V., Meier, K., & Holland, C. (2002). Lipstick and logarithms: Gender, institutional context, and representative bureaucracy. *American Political Science Review, 96*(3), 553–564.

Kochan, T., Bezrukova, K., Ely, R., Jackson, S., Joshi, A., Jehn, K., Leonard, J., et al. (2003). The effects of diversity on business performance: Report of the diversity research network. *Human Resource Management, 42*(1), 3–21.

Mannix, E., & Neale, M. (2005). The promise and reality of diverse teams in organizations. *Psychological Science in the Public Interest, 6*(2), 31–55.

Meier, K., Wrinkle, R., & Polinard, J. (1999). Representative bureaucracy and distributional equity: Addressing the hard question. *Journal of Politics, 61*(4), 1025–1039.

Milliken, F. J., & Martins, L. L. (1996). Searching for common threads: Understanding the multiple effects of diversity in organizational groups. *Academy of Management Review, 21*(2), 402–433.

Mosher, F. (1982). *Democracy and the public service* (2nd ed.). New York: Oxford University Press.

Odendahl, T., & O'Neill, M. (1994). *Women and power in the nonprofit sector.* San Francisco: Jossey-Bass.

Pitts, D. (2005). Diversity, representation, and performance: Evidence about race and ethnicity in public organizations. *Journal of Public Administration Research and Theory, 15*(4), 615–631.

Poister, T. (2003). *Measuring performance in public and nonprofit organizations.* San Francisco: Jossey-Bass.

Richard, O. (2000). Racial diversity, business strategy, and firm performance: A resource-based view. *Academy of Management Journal, 43*(2), 164–177.

Robinson, G., & Dechant, K. (1997). Building a business case for diversity. *Academy of Management Executive, 11*(3), 21–31.

Selden, S. (1997). *The promise of representative bureaucracy: Diversity and responsiveness in a government agency.* Armonk, NY: M.E. Sharpe.

Siliciano, J. I. (1996). The relationship of board member diversity to organizational performance. *Journal of Business Ethics, 15*(12), 1313–1320.

Tempel, E., & Smith, L. (2007, February 26). Nonprofits have a spotty record on diversity. *Nonprofit Times.* Available from http://nptimes.com/07Feb/news-070226-1.html

Thielemann, G., & Stewart, J., Jr. (1996). A demand-side perspective on the importance of representative bureaucracy: AIDS, ethnicity, gender, and sexual orientation. *Public Administration Review, 56*(2), 168–173.

Wilkins, V. M., & Williams, B. (2008). Black or blue: Racial profiling and representative bureaucracy. *Public Administration Review, 68*(4), 654–664.

Zald, M. N. (1969). The power and functions of boards of directors: A theoretical synthesis. *American Journal of Sociology, 75*(1), 97–111.

Websites

Best practices in achieving workforce diversity, http://govinfo.library.unt.edu/npr/initiati/benchmk/workforce-diversity.pdf

Urban Institute. *Outcome indicators project,* http://www.urban.org/center/cnp/projects/outcomeindicators.cfm

U.S. Equal Employment Opportunity Commission: http://www.eeoc.gov/index.cfm

Workforce diversity and inclusion committee (American Humanics), http://www.humanics.org/site/c.omL2KiN4LvH/b.2157037/k.2110/Workforce_Diversity_and_Inclusion_Committee.htm

Appendix A

Print Resources on Nonprofit Leadership

Books on Nonprofit Leadership

Anheier, H. K., & Hammack, D. C. (2010). *American foundations: Roles and contributions.* **Washington, DC: Brookings Institution Press.**

This book attempts to assess the impact and significance of philanthropic foundations in the United States. Over the course of 3 years, the authors Helmut Anheier and David Hammack gathered leading researchers to examine the work of foundations across a broad spectrum of fields including education, health care, social welfare, and the arts and culture. The research sought to address a number of compelling questions: Is American society different because of the existence of foundations? What roles have foundations played in the history of the United States? What roles do they fill now, and what roles are they likely to fill in the future? See also other books by Hammack: *Making the Nonprofit Sector in the U.S.* and *Nonprofit Organizations in a Market Economy: Understanding New Roles, Issues, and Trends* (with Young).

Bennis, W. G. (2009). *On becoming a leader.* **New York: Basic Books.**

Warren G. Bennis is a university professor and founding chairman of the Leadership Institute at the University of Southern California. He is also chairman of the Center for Public Leadership at Harvard's Kennedy School and Distinguished Research Fellow at the Harvard Business School and the author of numerous articles and books on leadership. This book explores the qualities that define leadership and those who exemplify those qualities. It explores the strategies that make leaders successful and provides guidance for those wishing to excel in leadership positions.

Bennis, W. G., & Nanus, B. (1985). *Leaders: Strategies for taking charge.* **New York: HarperCollins.**

Warren G. Bennis is a university professor and founding chairman of the Leadership Institute at the University of Southern California. He is also chairman of the Center for Public Leadership at Harvard's Kennedy School and Distinguished Research Fellow at the Harvard Business School and the author of numerous articles and books on leadership. Burt Nanus is professor emeritus of management at the University of Southern California and founder of the university's Center for Futures Research. In this text, the authors argue that the most pressing issue facing corporate America is leadership. They address what they see as the four key principles of management: attention through vision, meaning through communication, trust through positioning, and the deployment of self. This book is of interest to any person in a position of leadership or any student of leadership theory.

Boris, E. T., & Steuerle, C. E. (Eds.). (2006). *Nonprofits and government: Collaboration and conflict.* **Washington, DC: Urban Institute Press.**

This collection of 10 essays considers the relationship between government and the nonprofit sector. It attempts to address such critical issues as the role that tax breaks should play in charitable giving and whether nonprofits can fill the gaps in public service created by cuts in government spending over the last 3 decades. This should be of interest to researchers or policymakers, as well as to those directing or working within nonprofit institutions or foundations.

Bremner, R. (1988). *American philanthropy.* **Chicago: University of Chicago Press.**

Robert Bremner, the author of several books on philanthropy, is professor emeritus at Ohio State University. This book, which Bremner admits is not meant to be encyclopedic, offers a history of philanthropy in America from the country's founding to the present. New chapters in the book cover the last quarter century and the radical changes in tax law that have dramatically altered how money and resources are given, by whom, and to whom. The book includes a substantial bibliographic essay offering suggestions for further reading in the field. The book serves as an excellent introduction to the study of philanthropy in America.

Brest, P., & Harvey, H. (2008). *Money well spent.* **New York: Bloomberg Press.**

Paul Brest is President of the William and Flora Hewlett Foundation. Before joining the Hewlett Foundation, he was a professor at Stanford Law School, serving as dean from 1987 to 1999. Hal Harvey is founder and President of the ClimateWorks Foundation. Previously, he directed the Hewlett Foundation's Environment Program. This book argues that strategy is the critical factor in successful philanthropy. It provides foundations and philanthropists with a road map for developing strategies to achieve their missions and philanthropic goals.

Brinckerhoff, P. C. (2009). *Mission-based management: Leading your not-for-profit in the 21st century.* **Hoboken, NJ: John Wiley & Sons.**

Peter C. Brinckerhoff is a trainer, author, and consultant to nonprofit organizations, working to help them become more mission capable. This book provides ideas and criteria for success in today's competitive nonprofit sector. Written with nonprofit managers and leaders in mind, it addresses their unique concerns, providing a list of core characteristics of successful nonprofits and tools for using technology to improve mission outcome

Bryson, J. M. (2004). *Strategic planning for public and nonprofit organizations* **(3rd ed.). San Francisco: Jossey-Bass.**

The book is about the set of concepts, tools, and designs leaders need to develop to cope with the changing environment. The leader will need to decide and develop a coherent organizational vision of success, using strategic identifications and approaches. The book features the strategy change cycle, a proven planning process used by a large number of organizations. It also offers detailed guidance on implementing the planning process and specific tools and techniques to make the process work in any organization. Leadership, management, and strategic planning are blended together in alignment with trends in the field. Practitioners, nonprofit managers, board leaders, students, and fundraisers will benefit from the broad range of topics covered, including strategy, mapping, stakeholder analysis, and strategic management.

Burlingame, D. (Ed.). (1992). *The responsibilities of wealth.* **Bloomington: Indiana University Press.**

This collection of essays questions both the tradition and current state of philanthropic giving in the United States. It begins with Andrew Carnegie's "The Gospel of Wealth" (1889) and uses that as a frame to explore the philosophical basis for charitable giving: Who should give? In what context? What should be the relationship between the donor and recipient? What should be given? The collection considers the more practical side of philanthropy but is primarily concerned with the fundamental questions underpinning charity and whether the wealthy have a responsibility to share with those less fortunate. See also *Critical Issues in Fund Raising; Philanthropy Across the Generations: New Directions for Philanthropic Fundraising; Philanthropy in America: A Comprehensive Historical Encyclopedia; Taking Fund Raising Seriously: Advancing the Profession and Practice of Raising Money* (with Hulse); and *Corporate Philanthropy at the Crossroads* (with Young).

Burlingame, D. (Ed.). (1997). *Critical issues in fund raising.* **New York: John Wiley & Sons.**

This collection of 16 pieces has its roots in the "Think Tank on Fund-Raising Research" and presents a wide-ranging consideration of the most fundamental questions facing philanthropical organizations today. The ethics of philanthropical giving are considered, as are the patterns of giving in Europe and how those might help organizations in America. One paper looks at current research in donor motivation, while another tackles the role of the government in regulating charitable fundraising. This collection, given its scope, should appeal both to fundraising professionals and academics, board members and consultants. See also other books by Burlingame: *The Responsibilities of Wealth; Philanthropy Across the Generations: New Directions for Philanthropic Fundraising; Philanthropy in America: A Comprehensive Historical Encyclopedia; Taking Fund Raising Seriously: Advancing the Profession and Practice of Raising Money* (with Hulse); and *Corporate Philanthropy at the Crossroads* (with Young).

Burlingame, D. (Ed.). (2004). *Philanthropy across the generations: New directions for philanthropic fundraising.* **San Francisco: Jossey-Bass.**

This is the 42nd issue of the quarterly report series *New Directions for Philanthropic Fundraising,* representing the

16th Annual Symposium on Philanthropy, held in August 2003. The nine chapters in this volume consider such questions as whether or not altruism is an evolutionary adaptation, how to resolve potential moral ambiguities in philanthropical giving, the potential for transforming the roles of "fundraising practitioners" in the future, and the critical value of the estate tax. See also other books by Burlingame: *The Responsibilities of Wealth; Critical Issues in Fund Raising; Philanthropy in America: A Comprehensive Historical Encyclopedia; Taking Fund Raising Seriously: Advancing the Profession and Practice of Raising Money* (with Hulse); and *Corporate Philanthropy at the Crossroads* (with Young).

Burlingame, D. (Ed.). (2004). *Philanthropy in America: A comprehensive historical encyclopedia.* Santa Barbara, CA: ABC-CLIO.

This is a three-volume set. The first two volumes have 250 entries that document the history, the major figures, the important events, and the prominent organizations of American philanthropy. The third volume supplements those entries with 75 primary source documents that range from Aristotle's consideration of charity to a 2003 Supreme Court case. The encyclopedia considers America's history of not only philanthropy but also the roots of that history, tracing, for example, the institutionalization of charity in 14th-century England. See also other books by Burlingame: *The Responsibilities of Wealth; Critical Issues in Fund Raising; Philanthropy Across the Generations: New Directions for Philanthropic Fundraising; Taking Fund Raising Seriously: Advancing the Profession and Practice of Raising Money* (with Hulse); and *Corporate Philanthropy at the Crossroads* (with Young).

Burlingame, D., & Hulse, L. J. (Eds.). (1991). *Taking fund raising seriously: Advancing the profession and practice of raising money.* San Francisco: Jossey-Bass.

This book is a compilation of papers originally presented at a 1990 symposium held at the Indiana University Center on Philanthropy. The papers not only look at the critical role that nonprofit organizations play in American society but also question the potential public misconceptions of nonprofit fundraising. Along with the history of nonprofits, the authors also consider the ethics of public fundraising. Individual papers address current changes in the structure and leadership of nonprofit organizations. This collection is aimed at those interested in distinct individual views on the history, ethics, and future of public fundraising. See also other books by Burlinghame: *The Responsibilities of Wealth; Critical Issues in Fund Raising; Philanthropy Across the Generations: New Directions for Philanthropic Fundraising; Philanthropy in America: A Comprehensive Historical Encyclopedia;* and *Corporate Philanthropy at the Crossroads* (with Young).

Burlingame, D., & Young, D. (Eds.). (1996). *Corporate philanthropy at the crossroads.* Bloomington: Indiana University Press.

This collection of papers, from academics and volunteers, business people and students, considers the future of corporate philanthropy as it moves from a "do what is right" model toward a "consider only the bottom line" model. The papers are heavily research driven and are geared toward fundraisers as they think about the future of their organizations and potential corporate donations. They may also be of interest to academics working in corporate philanthropy. See also other books by Burlingame: *The Responsibilities of Wealth; Critical Issues in Fund Raising; Philanthropy Across the Generations: New Directions for Philanthropic Fundraising; Philanthropy in America: A Comprehensive Historical Encyclopedia;* and *Taking Fund Raising Seriously: Advancing the Profession and Practice of Raising Money* (with Hulse).

Canfield, J., Hansen, M. V., Oberst, A., & Boal, J. (2002). *Chicken soup for the volunteer's soul: Stories to celebrate the spirit of courage, caring and community.* Deerfield Beach, FL: Health Communications.

This collection of stories is designed to inspire community involvement and social engagement. The individual stories highlight Habitat for Humanity, Big Brothers/Big Sisters, the Peace Corps, the Red Cross, and many other nonprofit organizations. A constant theme is that the individual who volunteers tends to discover something important or unique about him- or herself. It should be of interest to those who volunteer or those considering giving time or money to volunteer organizations.

Carnegie, A. (2008). *The gospel of wealth.* Gloucester, UK: Dodo Press.

Andrew Carnegie was a businessman, a major philanthropist, and the founder of the Carnegie Steel Company, which later became U.S. Steel. This book is an essay he wrote in 1889 describing the responsibility of philanthropy by the new upper class and arguing for the superiority of the American system of republican government to the British monarchical system. He argues that the wealthy entrepreneurs must accept the responsibility of giving money in the most effective manner possible.

Carver, J. (2006). *Boards that make a difference: A new design for leadership in nonprofit and public organizations.* San Francisco: Jossey-Bass.

This author considers the variety of different boards and the difficulties they tend to face. Based on these difficulties, Carver argues for new principles of governance and approaches to policymaking for boards. He argues for new approaches to board-staff relationships, as well as the role of the chief executive. The book addresses performance monitoring and virtually every aspect of the board-management relationship. The author also recognizes the importance of keeping the mission of the organization in front. The book is of particular interest to those serving on boards, or those who work with nonprofit boards.

Clifton, D. O., & Rath, T. (2004). *How full is your bucket?* **New York: Gallup Press.**

This brief book contains helpful and simply offered information on how the smallest interactions can affect your relationships, health, and productivity. Based on the simple metaphor of a bucket and a dipper, the authors' theory states that everyone has an invisible "bucket" that is constantly being filled or emptied depending on what others say or do to other people. This book would resonate well with all those wishing to learn how they can better motivate and encourage as well as show their appreciation to others. Teachers, parents, managers, coaches, and so on would benefit from the information in this book.

Clinton, B. (2007). *Giving: How each of us can change the world.* **New York: Alfred A. Knopf.**

This book, by the former president of the United States, considers via personal stories and anecdotes from Oseola McCarthy, Andre Agassi, Oprah Winfrey, and others how individual acts of charity and giving can change the world for the better. In chapters on "Giving Money," "Giving Time," "Giving Things," and "Giving Skills," Clinton encourages individuals to ask what they have to offer the public sector and then offer it. More an inspirational collection than an academic work, it should be of interest to anyone working in, or considering getting involved in, the nonprofit sector.

Collins, J. (2001). *Good to great: Why some companies make the leap . . . and others don't.* **New York: HarperCollins.**

Jim Collins is known for his work examining enduring companies—how they grow, how they attain superior performance, and how good companies can become great ones. He founded a management laboratory where he conducts multiyear research projects and works with executives from the private, public, and social sectors. This book outlines the results of a 5-year research project comparing companies to identify what makes a company likely to progress from good to great. This book discusses concepts like level 5 leadership, first who (first get the right people on the bus, then figure out where to drive it), and the flywheel. See also Collins's *Good to Great and the Social Sectors: Why Business Thinking Is Not the Answer—A Monograph to Accompany Good to Great.*

Collins, J. (2005). *Good to great and the social sectors: Why business thinking is not the answer—A monograph to accompany good to great.* **New York: HarperCollins.**

Jim Collins is known for his work examining how enduring companies grow, attain superior performance, and become great. This brief monograph, originally intended as a new chapter in future editions of *Good to Great: Why some Companies Make the Leap . . . and Others Don't*, is based on interviews and workshops with over 100 social sector leaders. Collins examines the concepts of good to great and their meaning and applicability within the public sector. The monograph addresses such issues as how to define *greatness* for the public sector and how to recruit and retain the right people. See also Collins's *Good to Great: Why Some Companies Make the Leap . . . and Others Don't.*

Compton, D. W., Baizerman, M., & Stockdill, S. H. (Eds.). (2002). *The art, craft and science of evaluation capacity building.* **San Francisco: Jossey-Bass.**

This book defines evaluation capacity building (ECB) and provides a practical framework for understanding its core elements. The book examines four case studies that demonstrate ECB's complexity and the variation that can occur within organizations. Using the guidance and information presented in this literature, an organizational ECB checklist can be developed for organizational use. The purpose of the book is to help develop a general understanding of ECB and how it can be conducted and implemented in an organization; accordingly, the book is meant for students and those entering the nonprofit sector, as well as working professionals in the private and public sector.

Cortes, M., & Rafter, K. M. (Eds.). (2007). *Nonprofits and technology: Emerging research for usable knowledge.* **Chicago: Lyceum Books.**

This book is a collection of 10 research papers regarding the challenges facing nonprofits when investing in new technology. The papers were originally presented and debated in a symposium of technology adaptation in 2004 in the Institute for Nonprofit Organization Management at the University of San Francisco. The book explores how nonprofit organizations are using technology, the problems they encounter, and how technology can be used to its full potential to advance their goals and mission. Contributing authors include both scholars and practitioners, presenting information in a number of ways, including both in-depth case studies and large data sets of 1000s of surveys. This book would be of interest to students, nonprofit staff, and funders.

Drucker, P. F. (2005). *Managing the nonprofit organization: Principles and practices.* **New York: HarperCollins.**

Peter F. Drucker is the author of over 35 books, including many on business management and economics. In this book, he considers the management skills that are necessary to managing any operation and those especially unique to the nonprofit sector. He offers "dos" and "don'ts" for truly effective leadership, suggestions for fundraising, possible methods for evaluating success, and models for developing successful staff and donor relationships. This book is of most interest to managers of nonprofit organizations but also of interest to those who study the nonprofit sector.

Eisenberg, P. (2004). *Challenges for nonprofits and philanthropy: The courage to change—Three decades of reflection* **(S. Palmer, Ed). Lebanon, NH: Tufts University Press.**

Pablo Eisenberg is a senior fellow at the Georgetown University Public Policy Institute. He is also the leader of the Center for Community Change and founder of the National Committee for Responsive Philanthropy. This book is a collection of his speeches and articles spanning nearly 3 decades. The works address both American and global philanthropy in terms of their challenges, responsibilities, successes and failures, accountability, and leadership. He also speculates on what the future might hold as the United States moves toward the greatest transfer of intergenerational wealth in the country's history. This collection would be of interest to nonprofit leaders, donors, grantmakers, those involved with poverty-fighting organizations, and faculty members and researchers who study nonprofit organizations.

Ellis, S. J. (1999). *From the top down: The executive role in volunteer program success.* **Philadelphia: Energize.**

Susan J. Ellis is president of Energize, Inc., a training, consulting, and publishing firm specializing in volunteerism. She has authored and coauthored many books on the topic of volunteer recruiting and from 1981 to 1987 served as the editor in chief of the *Journal of Volunteer Administration.* This book is unique in its focus on the top decision-maker's roll in a volunteer program. With the intent of explaining how to structure a successful volunteer program, the author explores issues such as including an overall vision, policy questions, budgeting, staffing, employee-volunteer relations, the role of the board of directors, and assessing the impact of volunteer contributions. She also addresses dealing with risk management, and legal and insurance issues. See also Ellis's *Volunteer Recruitment and Membership Development* (3rd ed.).

Ellis, S. J. (2002). *Volunteer recruitment and membership development* **(3rd ed.). Philadelphia: Energize.**

Susan J. Ellis, president of Energize, Inc., a training, consulting, and publishing firm specializing in volunteerism, has authored and coauthored many books on the topic of volunteer recruiting. This book provides recommendations on the subject of volunteer recruitment, addressing how an organization's image can impact recruitment success and where to find the most qualified individuals. It includes a 2002 Appendix update, "Outreach in Cyberspace," exploring how to use the Internet and social media to their full potential as recruitment tools. See also Ellis's *From the Top Down: The Executive Role in Volunteer Program Success.*

Esposito, V. M. (Ed.). (1999). *Conscience and community: The legacy of Paul Ylvisaker.* **New York: Peter Lang.**

This is a collection of essays, speeches, and articles by Paul Ylvisaker on philanthropy, education, urban issues, and community. Paul Ylvisaker made a profound contribution to the American people through his philanthropic works and his commitment to public service. The writings span a period of 30 years, addressing critical issues and movements such as the war on poverty, the environmental movement, the meaning of public service, and education reform. See also Ylvisaker's *Family Foundations Now—and Forever? The Question of Intergenerational Succession.*

File, K. M., & Prince, R. A. (1994). *The seven faces of philanthropy: A new approach to cultivating major donors.* **San Francisco: Jossey-Bass.**

Karen Maru File is associate professor of marketing at the University of Connecticut at Stamford. Russ Alan Prince is president of Prince & Associates, a consultancy in the private wealth field. This is primarily a book about identifying what the authors refer to as the "seven types of major donors." File and Prince offer strategies on how to approach these different types of donors, with the notion that knowing the different types can help nonprofits tailor their marketing to best appeal to its target audience. Any person responsible for fundraising will be interested in this book.

Fleishman, J. L. (2007). *The foundation: A great American secret: How private wealth is changing the world.* **New York: Public Affairs.**

Joel L. Fleishman is a philanthropist and a professor of Law and Public Policy at Duke University and serves as a director of Boston Scientific. In this book, he traces the history of private foundations in America, covering philanthropists from Andrew Carnegie to Bill Gates, and he looks closely at contemporary private foundations that collectively are responsible for giving away over $32 billion each year. He uses 12 individual case studies—Children's Television Workshop, for example—to ask why some succeed, why some fail, and what can and should be done to improve private foundations in the future.

Flynn, P., & Hodgkinson, V. A. (Eds.). (2001). *Measuring the impact of the nonprofit sector.* New York: Klewer Academic/Plenum.

The 16 papers collected in this text were written in an attempt to assess the current methods of studying the efficacy of nonprofit organizations. The early sections are primarily concerned with general methodology ("Concerns of Measurement and Evaluation"); later sections are more concerned with the various subsectors of the nonprofit world ("Measuring the Impact of Various Subsectors and Special Populations"). Throughout, the focus remains on the question of how to effectively study and evaluate the effectiveness of nonprofit organizations. It is primarily of interest to those studying the nonprofit sector or those involved in evaluating the efficacy of individual nonprofit institutions.

Friedman, L. J., & McGarvie, M. (Eds.). (2003). *Charity, philanthropy and civility in American history.* New York: Cambridge University Press.

Lawrence J. Friedman is professor of History and Philanthropic Studies at Indiana University. Mark McGarvie is the Gotlieb Fellow in Legal History at New York University School of Law. This collection of papers provides surveys of the history of philanthropic giving in America, as well as various theories seeking to explain the role of philanthropy in that history. Individual essays cover such topics as Protestant missionaries, post–Civil War Reconstruction, American philanthropy abroad, Catholic charities, the civil rights movement, and the welfare state. Both historians and those working within philanthropic institutions should find this book of interest.

Frumkin, P. (2005). *On being nonprofit: A conceptual and policy primer.* Cambridge, MA: Harvard University Press.

Peter Frumkin is professor of Public Affairs at the Lyndon B. Johnson School of Public Affairs, and director of the RGK Center for Philanthropy and Community Service. This concise book provides insight into the

conceptual and policy terrain of the nonprofit sector. The book is divided into six chapters: "The Idea of a Nonprofit and Voluntary Sector," "Civic and Political Engagement," "Service Delivery," "Values and Faith," "Social Entrepreneurship," and "Balancing the Functions of Nonprofit and Voluntary Action." This book will be of value both to those new to public-sector work and experts in the field. See also Frumkin's *Strategic Giving: The Art and Science of Philanthropy.*

Frumkin, P. (2006). *Strategic giving: The art and science of philanthropy.* Chicago: University of Chicago Press.

Peter Frumkin is professor of Public Affairs at the Lyndon B. Johnson School of Public Affairs, and director of the RGK Center for Philanthropy and Community Service. This book, first and foremost, attempts to place philanthropic giving on a philosophical or theoretical scale. Frumkin argues that philanthropy should be seen not only as a way to meet the needs of society but also as a way of conveying personal beliefs. In searching for a theoretical framework for philanthropy that will accomplish both of those goals, he identifies what he insists all donors must consider, including how much engagement is sought, the purpose of the gift, and the time frame for the donation. This text should be of interest to those considering establishing a foundation or donating to an existing foundation, as well as to any student of philanthropy. See also Frumkin's *On Being Nonprofit: A Conceptual and Policy Primer.*

Galaskiewicz, J., & Bielefeld, W. (1998). *Nonprofit organizations in an age of uncertainty: A study of growth and decline.* New York: Walter de Gruyter.

Joseph Galaskiewicz is a professor of Sociology and Strategic Management/Organization at the University of Minnesota. He is the author of several books, and his research has focused on the role of informal social structures in explaining business organizations and on organizational change. Wolfgang Bielefeld is associate professor of Sociology and Political Economy in the School of Social Sciences at the University of Texas in Dallas. His research has focused on the relations between organizations and their environments and the dynamics of nonprofit sectors. This book is a study of organizational change using data from a panel of public charities in the Minneapolis–St. Paul metropolitan area from 1980 to 1994. It focuses on why some nonprofits survived and why others did not during that period of time, specifically on the strategies that were employed and the consequences for the nonprofits as a result of those strategy choices. The first two chapters in the book introduce the research program, the next three chapters provide the empirical results, and the final chapter draws conclusions from the research data.

Galston, W. A. (Ed.). (2005). *Community matters: Challenges to civic engagement in the 21st century.* **Lanham, MD: Rowman & Littlefield.**

This collection of essays, the fourth volume in a series from the Institute for Philosophy and Public Policy Studies, addresses the challenges of making a citizen, how citizens are to agree or disagree, and the rights and responsibilities of citizenship. Galston explores the underperformance of schools in terms of their civic missions, the critical process of decision making in a community while avoiding violence and maintaining a sense of unity, and the arguments surrounding compulsory military service.

Gardner, J. W. (1993). *On leadership.* **New York: Free Press.**

John Gardner served as secretary of Health, Education, and Welfare under President Lyndon Johnson. He also created Common Cause, the first nonprofit public interest group in the United States. In this book, he explores leadership theory, and through using historical figures as examples of the tremendous public energy and potential that can be tapped by effective leaders, he argues that the greatest problem facing the country is a lack of leadership. He challenges current leaders to rededicate the country to its ideals of freedom and justice and to develop and refine a vision of the country's vast potential. The book is of interest to any person in a position of leadership or any student of leadership theory. See also Gardner's *Self-Renewal: The Individual and the Innovative Society.*

Gardner, J. W. (1995). *Self-renewal: The individual and the innovative society.* **New York: W. W. Norton.**

John Gardner served as Secretary of Health, Education, and Welfare under President Lyndon Johnson. He also created Common Cause, the first nonprofit public interest group in the United States. Originally published in 1963, this book explores why some individuals and societies are capable of renewal and innovation while others fall into stasis and decay. He argues that the attributes of the "self-renewing" individual—independence, motivation, self-knowledge, and flexibility—are the same for organizations and societies. Organizations and societies that possess these attributes will flourish; those that don't possess them most likely will not. This book is of interest to those interested in motivational theory, as well as those serving in positions of power within organizations. See also Gardner's *On Leadership.*

Gast, E. (2005). *Community foundation handbook: What you need to know.* **Washington, DC: Council on Foundations.**

This text provides an overview of community foundations. It includes chapters on accountability, management and finance, grantmaking, donor relationships, and marketing. It is written primarily for foundation staff, but it will also be of interest to board members and volunteers.

Gerston, L. N. (2002). *Public policymaking in democratic society: A guide to civic engagement.* **Armonk, NY: M. E. Sharpe.**

In this book, Larry Gerston, a professor of political science at San Jose Sate University, provides an overview of the American political process as it relates to making policy. He covers the process from identifying an issue to implementation and evaluation, providing the tools and information a citizen needs to participate fully in policymaking. It will be of most interest to students, interns, those participating in service-learning opportunities, and anyone attempting to both inspire citizens to participate in their government and teach them how to participate in that government effectively.

Goldberg, G., Pittelman, P., & Resource Generation. (2006). *Creating change through family philanthropy: The next generation.* **New York: Soft Skull Press.**

This book is based on the work and experience of the Resource Generation, a nonprofit institution that works with wealthy young people. The book offers an introduction to family foundations and explains how such foundations work. The authors argue that family foundations can legitimize social issues, and as such, those with wealth are in a unique position to define what issues are important. In that context, the book is a resource for creating and managing family foundations. Young people interested in philanthropical giving might find this of most use, but philanthropical advisers and nonprofit fundraisers should also find it interesting.

Greenleaf, R. K. (1998). *The power of servant leadership.* **San Francisco: Berrett-Koehler.**

This collection of nine essays by the late Robert K. Greenleaf examines the theory behind and practice of servant-leadership as a model for business leaders. When Robert K. Greenleaf retired from AT&T in 1964, where he had worked in management, research, development, and education, he began a new career as a speaker, writer, and consultant. He coined the term "servant-leadership," emphasizing an approach to leadership that puts serving others, including employees, customers, and the community, first. These essays explore the nature and practice of servant-leadership, interweaving issues of spirit, wholeness, and vision.

Grimm, R. (Ed.). (2002). *Notable American philanthropists: Biographies of giving and volunteering.* Westport, CT: Greenwood Press.

This book is a collection of 78 profiles of individuals and families who have made significant contributions to the history of American philanthropy through voluntary service or charitable donations. The profiles cover both men and women from different time periods, of varying race and ethnicity, and from differing social strata. The profiles follow the same general format, examining the individual's early years, education, career, and philanthropic philosophy and actions. The profilers go on to examine the individual's motivations and justifications for philanthropy. Individuals profiled include Clara Barton, Andrew Carnegie, Cesar Estrada Chavez, the Guggenheim Family, and Booker T. Washington. The contributing authors have all done significant work related to specific philanthropists or related to American philanthropy in general.

Hall, P. D. (1992). *Inventing the nonprofit sector and other essays on philanthropy, voluntarism, and nonprofit organizations.* Baltimore: Johns Hopkins University Press.

Peter Dobkin Hall is a cultural historian and a Leonard Bacon Research Scholar in the Yale University Program on Non-Profit Organizations. He teaches in the Divinity School at Yale University. Through this collection of his essays, he describes and analyzes the development of the fastest growing institutional sector in the United States. The essays explore the historical, religious, cultural, managerial, and public policy aspects of philanthropy and volunteerism. The book concludes with an essay exploring the near future of the nonprofit sector in the aftermath of the "me generation."

Hammack, D. C. (Ed.). (1998). *Making the nonprofit sector in the U.S.* Bloomington: Indiana University Press.

This book is a collection of essential documents, including interpretations and critiques by recent scholars on the origins and evolution of the nonprofit sector in the United States. This anthology is divided into four primary sections: British and Colonial Patterns, The American Revolution: Sources of the Nonprofit Sector, Uses of Nonprofit Organizations, and Nonprofit Structures for the Twentieth Century. Each section is divided by chronology and subject matter and explores why the United States has funneled most of its formal

religious activity through the nonprofit sector. See also Anheier and Hammack's *American Foundations: Roles and Contributions*, and Young and Hammack's *Nonprofit Organizations in a Market Economy: Understanding New Roles, Issues, and Trends.*

Harkavy, D. (2007). *Becoming a coaching leader: The proven strategy for building your own team of champions.* Nashville, TN: Thomas Nelson.

The information in this book revolves around Harkavy's "Core Four Success Puzzle" of developing leaders. Beginning with an in-depth explanation of "what is a coach?" the author then dives into the Core Four and how you can develop as well as inspire others to create their plan. This book would resonate well with anyone who is striving to achieve more success and satisfaction in both their personal and professional lives. Individuals in leadership-management positions would find this book helpful as it serves as a guide to transform the lives of the people they lead and serve.

Hodgkinson, V., & Foley, M. (Ed.). (2003). *The civil society reader.* Hanover, CT: University Press of New England.

This book is an anthology on civil society comprised of 24 readings from individuals who helped shape and define the civil society tradition in Western political thought. The introduction provides a foundation for understanding the complexities of the debate over the conditions of citizenship and the defining qualities of a good society. Writings include excerpts from Aristotle's *The Politics*, Thomas Paine's *Rights of Man*, Peter L. Berger and Richard John Neuhaus's *To Empower People*, and Jean L. Cohen and Andrew Arato's *Civil Society and Political Theory*. See also Schervish, Gates, and Hodgkinson's *Care and Community in Modern Society: Passing on the Tradition of Service to Future Generations*, and Wuthnow and Hodgkinson's *Faith and Philanthropy in America: Exploring the Role of Religion in America's Voluntary Sector.*

Houle, C. O. (1997). *Governing boards: Their nature and nurture.* San Francisco: Jossey-Bass.

Cyril O. Houle is a senior consultant for the W. K. Kellogg Foundation and professor emeritus at the University of Chicago. He has served on more than 30 boards and has written many books. This book serves as a basic yet comprehensive manual for boards. It addresses issues such as the underlying concept behind boards; how to determine, structure, and organize board membership; board procedures and accountability; and external board relationships. It provides insight into how to successfully manage the full range of challenges facing board members.

Illchman, W. F., Katz, S. N., & Queen, E. L., II (Eds.). (1998). *Philanthropy in the world's traditions.* **Bloomington: Indiana University Press.**

The 20-odd contributors to this collection argue that far from being a particularly Western phenomenon, philanthropy is a tradition with a worldwide scope, encompassing many different cultures and traditions. Individual essays consider such diverse topics as "Reciprocity and Assistance in Precolonial Africa," "Generosity and Service in Theravada Buddhism," and "The Origins of Modern Jewish Philanthropy." Also addressed are Native Americans, 17th-century China, Islamic philanthropy, and the Serbian Orthodox Church. The collection should be of interest to any student of philanthropy.

Ingram, R. (2009). *Ten basic responsibilities of nonprofit boards.* **Washington, DC: BoardSource.**

This book explores both the fundamental responsibilities of nonprofit boards and the challenges that those nonprofits and their boards face today. Individual issues considered include determining the board's mission, selecting the chief executive, monitoring programs and services, ensuring adequate financial resources, protecting assets, ensuring legal and ethical integrity, and enhancing the organization's public standing. This is of particular interest to board members and executives.

Jeavons, T., & Basinger, R. B. (2000). *Growing givers' hearts: Treating fundraising as a ministry.* **San Francisco: Jossey-Bass.**

Thomas H. Jeavons is general secretary of Philadelphia Yearly Meeting of the Religious Society of Friends and was the founding director of the Center on Philanthropy and Nonprofit Leadership at Grand Valley State University. Rebekah Burch Basinger is an independent consultant in fundraising and stewardship education. This book is based on a 3-year study of Christian organizations that have been successful in raising funds and material resources and in encouraging spiritual development in their donors. This book is written primarily for Christian development staff, executives, and board members.

Karoff, H. P. (Ed.). (2004). *Just money: A critique of contemporary American philanthropy.* **Boston: TPI Editions.**

H. Peter Karoff is the founder of The Philanthropic Initiative and a senior fellow at Tufts University

College of Citizenship & Public Service. This book collects the experience and insight of 10 former leaders of large philanthropic foundations, national, community, and corporate. While the experience reflected in these 10 pieces is diverse, the lessons learned and the wisdom gained return again and again to the same ideas: Not only can money be used to do good, but it also can be used to do good well. As a resource to better management of foundations in the future, the book is of most interest to those working with philanthropic organizations.

Karoff, P., & Maddox, J. (2007). *The world we want: New dimensions in philanthropy and social change.* **Lanham, MD: AltaMira Press.**

Peter Karoff founded the Philanthropic Initiative (TPI) to help donors increase the impact of their philanthropy and at the same time make "giving" more meaningful in their own lives. President of TPI from 1989 to 2002, he is a senior fellow at the College of Citizenship and Public Service at Tufts University. Jane Maddox is an editor and writer at TPI who has worked to help public agencies, companies, and nonprofits communicate their missions, programs, and ideas. This book presents a vision for an ideal work through personal reflections and conversations with more than 40 social entrepreneurs, activists, nonprofit leaders, and philanthropists. It focuses on the value of human connection, the capacity for caring, and citizen engagement.

Kass, A. A. (Ed.). (2008). *Giving well, doing good: Readings for thoughtful philanthropists.* **Bloomington: Indiana University Press.**

This anthology explores the enterprise of philanthropy and serves as a sequel to Amy A. Kass's first edited anthology of writings on philanthropy, *The Perfect Gift.* It brings together critical texts from the classic to the contemporary and includes speeches, foundation documents, and writings of poets and novelists. Each reading provides guidance to current and prospective donors, trustees and professional staffs of foundations, and leaders of nonprofit organizations. The book is organized thematically, focusing on goals and intentions; gifts, donors, and recipients; grants, grantors, and grantees; bequests and legacies; effectiveness; accountability; and leadership.

Katz, S. N. (2000). *Colonial America: Essays in politics and social development.* **New York: McGraw-Hill.**

This is an anthology of readings by some of the most highly regarded scholars in the field of early American history. It focuses on the British colonies in North

America, presenting current research from colonial historians on topics ranging from abortion and gender roles and social and political organization to early religion and early contact with Native Americans.

Kim, D., & Cory, D. (2004). *It begins here: Organizational learning toolkit.* **Singapore, Republic of Singapore: Cobee Trading.**

It Begins Here provides an overview of several useful tools divided into four sections. The Organizing Framework section includes two tools that can be used to describe the organization's theory of success and its capabilities to support organizational learning. The Aspiration section discusses the Creative Tension Model and the Hierarchy of Choices Model, which help to discuss personal mastery and shared vision. In the Generative Conversation section, 11 different models are demonstrated to facilitate the understanding of mental models and team learning. Finally, the Understanding Complexity section discusses 11 models to further systems thinking. This book is for nonprofit leaders from executive directors and board members to program staff that desire to better understand how their nonprofit can engage in organizational learning.

Kleiner, A., Roberts, C., Ross, R., Roth, G., Senge, P., & Smith, B. (1999). *The dance of change: The challenges to sustaining momentum in learning organizations.* **New York: Doubleday.**

This book can be considered a follow-up to the 1990 bestseller *The Fifth Discipline* in which Peter Senge brought to light the concept of the *learning organization* and how personal mastery and systems thinking are vital to the success of an organization. This book dives deeper into the concept by explaining how to sustain the changes described in *The Fifth Discipline.* The authors outline potential obstacles to organizational learning and propose ways to turn these obstacles into sources of improvement. This book would resonate well with management wanting to drive and sustain positive change within their organization to make it a more worthwhile place to work.

Knowlton, L., & Phillips, C. (2009). *The logic model guidebook.* **Thousand Oaks, CA: Sage.**

The Logic Model Guidebook offers a thorough description of the various thinking and planning skills needed for the logic modeling process. The authors examine the structures and the processes of logic modeling. This serves as an instrument to develop and implement change in programs within a variety of organizational

contexts. By offering step-by-step guidance and visual examples of how to develop, design, and revise logic models, the authors prepare students, researchers, and practitioners to critically think about the programs and initiatives that their organizations are conducting. This guidebook serves as a great tool to increasing the efficiency of programs and services that nonprofit organizations are performing.

Kunreuther, F. (2008). *Working across generations: Defining the future of nonprofit leadership.* **Hoboken, NJ: John Wiley & Sons.**

This book specifically deals with the nonprofit sector and the generational workforce phenomenon. Kunreuther offers insight on how to communicate across generations and ensure that organizations make a smooth leadership transition. The author also provides good context for the differences about generations and why organizations will change based on these differences.

La Piana, D. (2000). *Nonprofit mergers workbook: The leader's guide to considering, negotiating, and executing a merger.* **Saint Paul, MN: Amherst H. Wilder Foundation.**

This text walks nonprofits through mergers from the earliest stages of planning through implementation and funding. It includes chapters on internal self-assessment for nonprofits, assessment of potential partners, potential difficulties associated with mergers, and negotiation strategies. Also included are case studies, checklists, resources, and decision trees. This text is of interest, especially, to those working within nonprofits who might consider or who might benefit from a merger with another organization. See also La Piana's *Nonprofit Strategy Revolution: Real-Time Strategic Planning in a Rapid-Response World.*

La Piana, D. (2008). *Nonprofit strategy revolution: Real-time strategic planning in a rapid-response world.* **Saint Paul, MN: Fieldstone Alliance.**

David La Piana is an expert on partnerships among nonprofit organizations, known for his work to improve leadership and management practices throughout the nonprofit sector for greater social impact. This book introduces the concept of real-time strategic planning, a fluid, organic process that engages staff and board in a program of systematic readiness and continuous responsiveness. It provides readers with the tools to clarify competitive advantages, develop criteria for evaluating strategies, handle big issues effectively, develop and test strategies, and implement and adapt strategies on a continuous basis. See also *La Piana's Nonprofit Mergers*

Workbook: The Leader's Guide to Considering Negotiating and Executing a Merger.

Light, P. C. (2002). *Pathways to nonprofit excellence.* Washington, DC: Brookings Institution.

Paul C. Light is a professor at New York University's Wagner School of Public Service, a senior fellow at the Brookings Institution, and a former grantmaker and presidential adviser. This volume is the fourth in a series of reports regarding the changes in what public service means both within the government and the nonprofit sector. It is based on interviews with 250 leaders on philanthropy, scholarship, and consulting and interviews with 250 executive directors from some of the most effective nonprofits in the United States. The author argues that higher performance can be achieved using one of several strategies and that every nonprofit organization can improve how they are currently performing.

Lohmann, R. A. (1992). *The commons: New perspectives on nonprofit organizations and voluntary action.* San Francisco: Jossey-Bass.

Roger A. Lohmann is a professor and director at West Virginia University–Nova Institute. He formerly served as the editor in chief at Nonprofit Management & Leadership. This article presents the concepts of "commons" and common goods as having critical multidisciplinary implications. Commons refers to uncoerced participation, mutuality, and shared purposes and resources.

Mahwah, B., & Avolio, J. (2005). *Leadership Development in Balance: Made/Born.* Mahwah, NJ: Lawrence Erlbaum.

A valuable contribution to the field of leadership development—the book is a good reflective piece for practitioners. The author notes how leadership development happens within one's life and is often facilitated by "trigger events." He encourages a process of Advanced Action Review (AAR), that is, reflection or personal debriefing on the effects of one's actions. He defines leadership as "influencing people to achieve some particular targeted objective." He shows how the leader may tend to use one of four lenses to view these events: control, quid pro quo, stakeholder, and transformation. There is material on trust building, "e-leadership," measuring the impact of leadership programs, and distinguishing among passive-avoidant, corrective, transactional, and transformational leadership. His model of leadership development asserts the need for leaders to grow in self-awareness, self-regulation, and self-development.

Maxwell, J. C. (1991). *The 21 irrefutable laws of leadership: Follow them and people will follow you.* Nashville, TN: Thomas Nelson.

The book will help you understand that leaders are made. The 21 laws will help you become a person people want to follow. The author also uses some examples of leaders' intriguing stories about their leadership experiences, such as Princess Diana, Ray Kroc, and Theodore Roosevelt, who used these leadership principles to achieve great success in their lives and had a major impact on the lives of many other people. Leadership in this book is made simple, but its powerful effect is demonstrated through these illustrations. It is full of direction and encouragement and the hope that with these procedures, students and professionals may learn and apply these timeless principles.

Maxwell, J. C. (1998). *Developing the leaders around you.* Nashville, TN: Thomas Nelson.

This book is about helping others reach their potential. Developing a leader means knowing the leadership within you. John Maxwell shows how to train and develop an eye for potential leaders. The message of the book is for any person—an individual can't lead alone. If a person really wants to be a leader, that is, to have power to influence others, he or she must develop other leaders around him or her by establishing a team. The author details how to help others reach their full potential and how to identify and train potential leaders in order to get a personal vision seen. Leaders are made, not born. Maxwell also indicates that leadership grows from mentoring relationships and helping others.

McCarthy, K. (2009). *The on-purpose person—Making your life make sense.* Winter Park, FL: On-Purpose Publishing.

This book is for anyone who has ever felt like his or her life is being pulled in too many directions. The content presents principles that are easy to apply to everyday life in short story format that is entertaining to read. Various topics include how to feel satisfied rather than stressed out at the end of the day, finding meaningful personal time, and managing hurdles and setbacks in a positive light as well as how to tap into your highest potential. This book would resonate with all who feel as though their personal and professional schedule-calendars are out-of-control and who need additional focus in their lives to accomplish more of what is important to them. This book would be particularly helpful for managers who have an overwhelming amount of work on their plate and have difficulty maintaining a work-life balance.

McNamara, C. (2003). *Field guide to leadership and supervision for nonprofit staff.* **Minneapolis, MN: Authenticity Consulting.**

This is a guide that offers advice for how to recruit the best staff and volunteers for a nonprofit, as well as for how to work with a board. It considers the role of a nonprofit leader and looks at the day-to-day challenges typically faced in such a position. It offers instruction for how to lead, how to collaborate, and how to manage your staff and yourself. It is of particular interest to founders, executive directors, and managers of nonprofits. See also McNamara's *Field Guide to Developing, Operating and Restoring Your Nonprofit Board* and *Field Guide to Nonprofit Program Design, Marketing and Evaluation.*

McNamara, C. (2008). *Field guide to developing, operating and restoring your nonprofit board.* **Minneapolis, MN: Authenticity Consulting.**

This text offers guidelines and advice for planning, starting, and maintaining nonprofit boards. Issues considered include marketing, staffing, finances, fundraising, evaluations, transparency, sustainability, and lobbying. The author specifically addresses ways to detect and fix broken boards, as well as how to define how much board members should be involved in management, whether or not committees should be used, how to establish appropriate goals for committees, and how to ensure ethical behavior of board members. This is of interest to those who manage or serve on boards. See also McNamara's *Field Guide to Leadership and Supervision for Nonprofit Staff* and *Field Guide to Nonprofit Program Design, Marketing and Evaluation.*

McNamara, C. (2008). *Field guide to nonprofit program design, marketing and evaluation.* **Minneapolis, MN: Authenticity Consulting.**

This book provides guidelines for designing, marketing, and evaluating a nonprofit program. In addition to the guidelines, the book includes worksheets to help a nonprofit develop marketing, advertising, promotion, fundraising, and business plans. It includes a section on how to conduct market research and how to analyze the data collected. It is of interest to managers of nonprofits, members of boards of nonprofits, and those who donate to nonprofits. See also McNamara's *Field Guide to Leadership and Supervision for Nonprofit Staff* and *Field Guide to Developing, Operating and Restoring Your Nonprofit Board.*

Nielsen, W. A. (1996). *Inside American philanthropy: The dramas of donorship.* **Norman: University of Oklahoma Press.**

In this book, an analysis of American philanthropic institutions, the author looks at both historical and contemporary philanthropists from Andrew Carnegie to Bill Gates and from Warren Buffett to small family foundations. He also considers what he calls "The Forgotten History" and devotes an entire chapter to "Women in Philanthropy." As he argues for the true importance of individual organizations' founders and the deeply personal factors that drive their charitable decisions, he points out the numerous ways foundations have both succeeded and failed, the common pitfalls and the inspirational triumphs. The book will be of interest to both established donors and potential foundation creators, as well as nonprofit advisers and fundraisers.

Nielsen, W. (2002). *Golden donors: A new anatomy of the great foundations.* **New Brunswick, NJ: Transaction.**

Waldemar Nielsen is a counselor on philanthropy policy. He has served as an adviser to individuals such as John D. Rockefeller III and to major corporations and foundations. This book updates his study of the 36 largest private foundations in the United States. For each foundation, he provides information on the donor as an individual, the foundation's management, and the development of the foundation's mission and programs. The stories about each foundation provide insight into which foundations have been successes and which have failed in recent years and into how the federal government and administrations are helping or hindering their success.

Noonan, W. R. (2007). *Discussing the undiscussable: A guide to overcoming defensive routines in the workplace.* **San Francisco: Jossey-Bass.**

There has been significant research around how well-meaning, smart people can create vicious cycles of defensive behavior to protect themselves from embarrassment and threat, particularly by well-known author Chris Argyris. This book dives deeper into Argyris's work by providing a set of "how to" exercises for detecting, surfacing, and discussing organizational defensive routines in a safe and productive way. This book would resonate with individuals working in a "defensive environment" where addressing challenging issues is an uncomfortable and, in some cases, nonexistent, process.

Northouse, P. G. (2004). *Leadership: Theory and practice.* **Thousand Oaks, CA: Sage.**

The author defines leadership as "a process whereby an individual influences a group of individuals to achieve a common goal." The book offers a good review of 10 theoretical approaches to analyzing leadership: trait, skills, style, situation, contingency, path-goal, leader-member exchange, transformation, team, and psycho-dynamic. Northouse also discusses gender factors and the ethics of leadership useful for today's managers, practitioners, researchers, and students.

O'Connell, B. (1987). *Philanthropy in action.* **New York: Foundation Center.**

This text considers American philanthropical institutions and individuals and assesses what they have done, as well as the manner in which they have done it. Although he labels and addresses nine different goals of philanthropical activity, including to improve communities and to honor the deceased, he argues, ultimately, for the primacy of two: to maximize human potential and to relieve human misery. The book is simultaneously a defense of and celebration of philanthropy in America. See also O'Connell's *Powered by Coalition: The Story of Independent Sector, Civil Society: The Underpinnings of American Democracy,* and *Fifty Years in Public Causes: Stories From a Road Less Traveled.*

O'Connell, B. (1997). *Powered by coalition: The story of independent sector.* **San Francisco: Jossey-Bass.**

In this book, activist, professor, and author Brian O'Connell recounts the founding of Independent Sector, a huge coalition of over 800 foundations, institutions, philanthropic organizations, and corporate giving programs. In addition to the story of how the coalition came together, the challenges overcome in order to remain together, and what it managed to accomplish through cooperation and collaboration, O'Connell also considers the current and future threats to the independent sector in America and includes lessons in building and maintaining large, diverse coalitions. This book will be of interest to those in positions of power within volunteer organizations or coalitions of such organizations, as well as those who study such coalitions. See also O'Connell's *Philanthropy in Action, Civil Society: The Underpinnings of American Democracy,* and *Fifty Years in Public Causes: Stories From a Road Less Traveled.*

O'Connell, B. (1999). *Civil society: The underpinnings of American democracy.* **Hanover, CT: University Press of New England.**

In this book, activist, professor, and author Brian O'Connell argues that active citizen participation is essential to a strong democracy. Such active citizen participation creates what he calls *civil society,* a society that shares power and responsibility between communities, government, businesses, and volunteer organizations. Civil society, according to O'Connell, is threatened—by government action, by increasing wealth disparity, and by elected officials more attune to lobbyists and special interest groups than their constituents. O'Connell presents solutions to these problems and steps to strengthen civil society, including educating the country's youth on citizens' rights and responsibilities and drawing on the country's tradition of service. Those working in community organizations or serving as elected officials or studying the current state of civil society, will find this book of interest. See also O'Connell's *Philanthropy in Action, Powered by Coalition: The Story of Independent Sector* and *Fifty Years in Public Causes: Stories From a Road Less Traveled.*

O'Connell, B. (2005). *Fifty years in public causes: Stories from a road less traveled.* **Lebanon, NH: Tufts University Press.**

In this memoir, activist, professor, and author Brian O'Connell writes of his life in philanthropy, public work, and civic action. He includes stories from his time as head of the Mental Health Association and the Independent Sector, a coalition he cofounded with John W. Gardner that advocated for voluntary initiative and philanthropy. In addition to the stories of how much can be accomplished by motivated, dynamic individuals and organizations, O'Connell includes what he sees as the important lessons to pass on to the next generation of activists, organizers, and volunteers. See also O'Connell's *Philanthropy in Action, Powered by Coalition: The Story of Independent Sector,* and *Civil Society: The Underpinnings of American Democracy.*

Odendahl, T. J., Boris, E. T., & Daniels, A. K. (1985). *Five experienced grantmakers at work.* **New York: Foundation Center.**

This book presents the results of a study regarding the career paths of foundation employees and is a valuable primer on the various levels of grantmaking jobs. It provides an overview of the roles, responsibilities, and career paths and explores the culture of various foundations with a particular focus on a comparison between men and women working in the field.

O'Leary, R.. (2006). *The ethics of dissent: Managing guerrilla government.* **Washington, DC: CQ Press.**

The author composes a compelling synthesis of the effect of guerrilla government on democracy by analyzing case studies and delving into this under the discussed topic of managers. This is a great contribution to public administration to help better understand the distinction between dissent and commitment to public service. This author gives a glimpse of what happens in the real working world. The book is most interesting when she combines theory and practice. It also provides a list of professional workplace ethical standards. This is eye opening and compelling not only for students and managers of both public and private organization but also for political figures.

O'Neill, M. (1989). *The third America: The emergence of the nonprofit sector in the United States.* **San Francisco: Jossey-Bass.**

This book explores the major nonprofit subsectors and describes the concerns, trends, funding and policy issues, and historical context and development of each. Chapters address the role of various institutions in the nonprofit sector, including religion, health care, education, arts and culture, and legal services. This book would be of value to both scholars in the field, interested in a clear synthesis of academic developments, and students, teachers, and those new to the field, who will find clear, concise information on key nonprofit sector issues. See also O'Neill's *Nonprofit Nation: A New Look at the Third America.*

O'Neill, M. (2002). *Nonprofit nation: A new look at the third America.* **San Francisco: Jossey-Bass.**

This book attempts to provide a complete guide to understanding the public sector. O'Neill looks at the different nonprofit subsectors—social services, religious organizations, and health care, for example—and considers their influence on government, business, and society. After considering the public sector in its contemporary context, O'Neill presents possibilities for the role and growth of nonprofits for the next 25 years. This should be of interest to those who study the nonprofit sector, as well as to those who work within the public sector and are considering how to maintain and grow their organizations. See also O'Neill's *The Third America: The Emergence of the Nonprofit Sector in the United States.*

Orosz, J. J. (2000). *The insider's guide to grantmaking.* **San Francisco: Jossey-Bass.**

Joel Orosz is the senior program director in the Philanthropy and Volunteerism programming area of the

W. K. Kellogg Foundation in Battle Creek, Michigan. In this guide, he provides a practical overview of the necessary skills for successful and ethical grantmaking. It provides a history of public foundations, as well as their function in society. It also looks at the day-to-day activities of program officers and offers advice on the wide variety of challenges they face. It's written primarily for this audience but is also of great value for other grant seekers. See also Orosz's *Effective Foundation Management: 14 Challenges of Philanthropic Leadership— And How to Outfox Them.*

Orosz, J. J. (2007). *Effective foundation management: 14 challenges of philanthropic leadership—And how to outfox them.* **Lanham, MD: AltaMira Press.**

In *Effective Foundation Management,* the author presents "seven challenges" and "seven dilemmas" facing contemporary nonprofit foundations. It considers, for example, the problem of a lack of ideological cohesion within a foundation's staff and lack of an accepted body of good practices within a foundation. It also attempts to respond to questions foundations might face such as whether to be expert based or community based, or whether to be high profile or low profile, or whether a foundation's energy should be turned toward innovation or implementation. The book is especially helpful for foundation managers, but anyone working within the nonprofit sector should find it of value. See also Orosz's *The Insider's Guide to Grantmaking.*

Pallotta, D. (2008). *Uncharitable: How restraints on nonprofits undermine their potential.* **Hanover, CT: University Press of New England,**

Dan Pallotta founded Pallotta Team-Works, the for-profit company that created the AIDS Rides and Breast Cancer 3-day events, which raised over half a billion dollars and netted $305 million in 9 years. This book is the author's response to media reports and other attacks questioning the act of spending so much money to raise money and the violation of the premise behind charitable organizations: low profile, low budget, and little or no profit. The book calls into question the fundamental canons of charity and argues that nonprofits must be allowed to use the tools of commerce to thrive and accomplish their missions.

Payton, R. L., & Moody, M. P. (2008). *Understanding philanthropy: Its meaning and mission.* **Bloomington: Indiana University Press.**

Robert L. Payton served as the first director of the Center on Philanthropy at Indiana University. Michael Moody is assistant professor in the School of Policy,

Planning, and Development at the University of Southern California. Together, they have written a book that explores both why philanthropy exists and what place it has in society. They draw on a wide range of examples, from the Good Samaritan to contemporary student volunteers, to make their case that philanthropy is action, voluntary moral action. The book also serves as an argument for further study of philanthropy and the incorporation of philanthropy into college curricula. The book will be of interest to both students of philanthropy and professionals, and grant seekers and grantmakers alike.

Peters, T., & Waterman, B. (2001). *Disney Institute "Be our guest"—Perfecting the art of customer service.* **New York: Disney Editions.**

This book outlines the various principles and processes on which the Disney company has built its worldwide empire, specifically around perfecting the art of customer service. The strategies, tactics, and real-life examples presented are geared toward helping an organization focus its vision and assemble its people and systems with a cohesive strategy that focuses primarily on the concept of "exceptional customer service." This book would resonate with managers or leaders wishing to enhance the understanding and implementation of superior customer service.

Putnam, R. D. (1993). *Making democracy work: Civic traditions in modern Italy.* **Princeton, NJ: Princeton University Press.**

Putnam, a Harvard professor, asks in this book why some democratic governments succeed while others fail. To answer his question, he addresses a 1970 experiment in which Italy created new governments for each of its regions. His findings are far-reaching: A strong democratic government depends on a solid civic community and a virtuous citizenry; weak governments tend not to create wealth but to preserve poverty. He argues that civic community is created more by "secondary associations" and not so much by the central government. This book will be of interest to those studying the creation and preservation of democracy. See also Putnam's *Bowling Alone: The Collapse and Revival of American Community.*

Putnam, R. D. (2000). *Bowling alone: The collapse and revival of American community.* **New York: Simon & Schuster.**

Harvard professor Robert Putnam argues in this book that Americans since 1960 have become increasingly disconnected from one another and their communities.

Drawing on surveys and interviews, Putnam explores the various ways in which civic involvement in America has changed over the last quarter century. He argues that social engagement is a cause of, not a result of, social circumstances. In the second half of the book, Putnam addresses the negative consequences of America's social disengagement and concludes by looking at the large social movements of the early part of the 20th century and considering what the country needs to restore a sense of social engagement and community. This book will be of interest to sociologists and academics studying patterns of social engagement, community activism, and philanthropy. See also Putnam's *Making Democracy Work: Civic Traditions in Modern Italy.*

Pynes, J. E. (2004). *Human resources management for public and nonprofit organizations* **(2nd ed.). San Francisco: Jossey-Bass.**

Human resources are essential to any organization, and understanding this field better will promote a more successful organization. Joan Pynes describes how strategic human resource management is critical to the ever-changing environment that nonprofits face. This edition offers guidance on budgeting and compensation. It also assists practitioners in navigating the current legal and technological challenges.

Quinn, R. E., Faerman, S. R., Thompson, M. P., McGrath, M., & St. Clair, L. S. (2007). *Becoming a master manager: A competing values approach* **(4th ed.). Hoboken, NJ: John Wiley & Sons.**

The book emphasizes the importance of managerial skills, which are imperative in the diverse situations and challenges we face in the organization. It also focuses on the management practices and organization of those practices in a theoretically valid framework of managerial competency with the knowledge and application of the four critical actions: compete, collaborate, control, and create. Students in nonprofit and public administration as well as students of business administration, will find tools to assist them in understanding their competing values by learning the eight interactive learning modules covering different leadership roles, including director, producer, mentor, facilitator, coordinator, monitor, innovator, and broker.

Reinelt, C., Foster, P., & Sullivan, S. (2002). *Evaluating outcomes and impacts: A scan of 55 leadership development programs.* **Brookline, MA: Development Guild/DDI.**

The authors present a typology of outcomes for leadership development programs, including outcomes at the individual, organizational, community, field, and systemic levels. They present a range of methods and approaches for conducting program evaluation, sources of information for evaluations, and challenges faced by evaluators. Over 54 leadership programs were evaluated. Not only practitioners and managers in private corporations but also students in public administration will be benefitted by this book.

Robbins, D. (2009). *Understanding Research Methods: A Guide for the Public and Nonprofit Manager.* **Boca Raton, FL: CRC Press.**

Many leaders in organizations are faced with quickly reviewing large amounts of information and are asked to use what they learn to make informed decisions. These decisions may have lasting implications for organizations. Learning how to quickly and thoroughly go through massive amounts of information is a skill that leaders need to learn. Discerning valuable information is a vital skill of decision making. This useful text can be used by students and professionals in the nonprofit, public, and private sectors.

Rosso, H. A. (1991). *Achieving excellence in fund raising: A comprehensive guide to principles, strategies, and method.* **San Francisco: Jossey-Bass.**

Henry A. Rosso is the founder of The Fund Raising School, a program of the Center on Philanthropy at Indiana University. This is a guide to successful fundraising. The author considers each step in a successful fundraising cycle: assessing needs, setting goals, researching markets, soliciting new donors, and encouraging repeat donors. At every step, Rosso considers the reasoning behind the strategies and the principles behind the techniques. This book will be of interest to anyone involved in public-sector fundraising. See also *Rosso on Fund Raising: Lessons from a Master's Lifetime Experience.*

Rosso, H. A. (1996). *Rosso on fund raising: Lessons from a master's lifetime experience.* **San Francisco: Jossey-Bass.**

Henry A. Rosso is the founder of The Fund Raising School, a program of the Center on Philanthropy at Indiana University. In this book, Rosso identifies the five essential steps of fundraising: analysis, planning, execution, control, and evaluation. Considering case studies and real-life examples, Rosso offers insights from his five decades of experience fundraising for nonprofits. It should be of interest to anyone involved in public-sector fundraising. See also Rosso's *Achieving Excellence in Fund Raising: A Comprehensive Guide to Principles, Strategies, and Methods.*

Salamon, L. M. (1999). *America's nonprofit sector: A primer.* **New York: Foundation Center.**

Lester M. Salamon is the director of the Johns Hopkins Center for Civil Society Studies. In this book, Salamon considers the structure, scope, and the evolving role of nonprofits in society. By putting the nonprofit sector in context with the government and business sector, he shows how the nonprofit sector has changed over time. He looks at the role of nonprofits in health care, education, legal service, international aid, recreation, advocacy, and social services. He also includes material on different types of tax-exempt institutions and foundations. This book is of interest to anyone working within or interested in the nonprofit sector. See also Salamon's *The Resilient Sector: State of Nonprofit America.*

Salamon, L. M. (2003). *The resilient sector: State of nonprofit America.* **Washington, DC: Brookings Institution Press.**

Lester M. Salamon is the director of the Johns Hopkins Center for Civil Society Studies. In this book, Salamon assesses the state of nonprofit institutions today—their significance, impact, health, and future—and considers the changes that might be necessary to ensure the long-term security of those institutions. In considering the challenges that nonprofits face today, Salamon discusses competition, the fiscal health of nonprofits, staffing issues, and the effect on nonprofits of evolving technology. In considering achievements and opportunities, Salamon looks at overall nonprofit sector growth, the dramatic changes in charitable fundraising over the last 2 decades, and the influence of market culture on nonprofit institutions. This book is of interest to both academic students of the nonprofit sector and nonacademic participants in that sector. See also Salamon's *America's Nonprofit Sector: A Primer.*

Schein, E. H. (2004). *Organizational culture and leadership.* **San Francisco: Jossey-Bass.**

This book focuses on the crucial role that leaders play in helping to implement the principles of culture in order to reach organizational goals. The author goes on to show readers how to identify, nurture, and shape the culture of their organizations at any stage and thus presents new practices and information from the field. Key focus areas are understanding team and organizational dynamics, influence of new technology, managing cross-cultural boundaries as well as data relative to overcoming resistance to internal change. This content would be informative to anyone in a leadership position who desires to create and maintain a strong organizational culture that rewards and encourages the collective effort.

Schervish, P. G. (Ed.). (1994). *Wealth in Western thought: The case for and against riches.* **Westport, CT: Praeger.**

This text is based on a series of discussions held at an interdisciplinary seminar at Boston College in 1989 and 1990. These essays explore America's contemporary "doctrine of wealth" by considering such diverse source material as Ancient Greece, the New Testament, and modern philanthropical organizations. Together, the individual essays, and the collection as a whole, attempt to frame a new debate on wealth and the wealthy in America. See also other books by Schervish: *Taking Giving Seriously: Beyond Noble Intentions to Responsible Giving* (with Dean and Sherman); *Care and Community in Modern Society: Passing on the Tradition of Service to Future Generations* (with Gates and Hodgkinson); *Gospels of Wealth: How the Rich Portray Their Lives* (with Lewis and Coutsoukis); and *Wealth and the Will of God: Discerning the Use of Riches in the Service of Ultimate Purpose* (with Whitaker).

Schervish, P. G., Dean, P., & Sherman, L. (Eds.). (1993). *Taking giving seriously: Beyond noble intentions to responsible giving.* **Bloomington: Indiana University Center on Philanthropy.**

In this collection of academic and personal essays, authors consider how to share resources—money and time, for example—wisely and justly. See also other books by Schervish: *Wealth in Western Thought: The Case for and Against Riches; Care and Community in Modern Society: Passing on the Tradition of Service to Future Generations* (with Gates and Hodgkinson); *Gospels of Wealth: How the Rich Portray Their Lives* (with Lewis and Coutsoukis); and *Wealth and the Will of God: Discerning the Use of Riches in the Service of Ultimate Purpose* (with Whitaker).

Schervish, P. G., Gates, M., & Hodgkinson, V. (Eds.). (1995). *Care and community in modern society: Passing on the tradition of service to future generations.* **San Francisco: Jossey-Bass.**

This is a collection of 22 essays by scholars and practitioners regarding how the traditions of a caring society are transferred to future generations. It explores how people become involved and committed to caring for others and the impact such care has on our civic, ethical, and spiritual traditions. Contributors represent a cross-section of disciplines including psychology, religious studies, and public policy and leadership from within community organizations, youth groups, and the government. The essays examine topics such as involving children in philanthropy and volunteerism, an exploration of leadership education in the United States, and how institutions impact the evolution of a caring society. This book would be of interest to scholars, nonprofit executives, fundraisers, and students. See also other books by Schervish: *Wealth in Western Thought: The Case for and Against Riches; Taking Giving Seriously: Beyond Noble Intentions to Responsible Giving* (with Dean and Sherman); *Gospels of Wealth: How the Rich Portray Their Lives* (with Lewis and Coutsoukis); and *Wealth and the Will of God: Discerning the Use of Riches in the Service of Ultimate Purpose* (with Whitaker).

Schervish, P. G., Lewis, E., & Coutsoukis, P. E. (Eds.). (1994). *Gospels of wealth: How the rich portray their lives.* **Westport, CT: Praeger.**

This collection of essays attempts to develop a new sociology of wealth, one that goes beyond traditional theories. Its individual chapters allow 12 different Americans to explore, relatively directly, how their financial and spiritual lives intertwine. Chapters such as "What It's Really Like to Be Born Rich" and "Them With the Gold Makes the Rules" offer opportunities for academics in sociology, philanthropy, economic life, and cultural studies to consider a new theoretical framework for understanding wealth and the wealthy. See also other books by Schervish: *Wealth in Western Thought: The Case for and Against Riches; Taking Giving Seriously: Beyond Noble Intentions to Responsible Giving* (with Dean and Sherman); *Care and Community in Modern Society: Passing on the Tradition of Service to Future Generations* (with Gates and Hodgkinson); and *Wealth and the Will of God: Discerning the Use of Riches in the Service of Ultimate Purpose* (with Whitaker).

Schervish, P. G., & Whitaker, A. K. (2010). *Wealth and the will of God: Discerning the use of riches in the service of ultimate purpose.* **Bloomington: Indiana University Press.**

Schervish and Whitaker, professors at Boston College, consider in this book the various Christian spiritual resources that might aid in reflection on wealth and charity. The text begins with Aristotle before moving on to early Christian thinkers, as well as Luther, Calvin, and Jonathan Edwards. The individual chapters should inspire contemporary readers to consider the purpose of love, charity, friendship, and human life. It also looks at ways to connect what we can know about the spiritual foundations of charity with contemporary social needs. See also other books by Schervish: *Wealth in Western Thought: The Case for and Against Riches; Taking Giving Seriously: Beyond Noble Intentions to Responsible Giving* (with Dean and Sherman); *Care and Community in Modern Society: Passing on the Tradition of Service to Future Generations* (with Gates and Hodgkinson); and *Gospels of Wealth: How the Rich Portray Their Lives* (with Lewis and Coutsoukis).

Senge, P. M. (1990). *The fifth discipline: The art and practice of the learning organization.* **Garden City, NY: Doubleday.**

Peter Senge is the founder of the Center for Organizational Learning at MIT's Sloan School of Management. In this book, he explains methods for converting companies into "learning organizations." He covers the "five disciplines" of such organizations, including "personal mastery," "team learning," and "systems thinking" (the fifth discipline itself). He also explores the problems currently facing companies and their employees and covers his "eleven laws of the fifth discipline," including his assertions that behavior may grow worse before it grows better and that, sometimes, the cure is worse than the disease. It will be of interest to executives of both nonprofit and for-profit organizations looking for new ways to understand their organizations' habits, performance, and future.

Shafritz, J. M., Ott, J. S., & Jang, Y. S. (2005). *Classics of organization theory* **(6th ed.). Belmont, CA: Harcourt College.**

The *Classics of Organization Theory* is a collection of important works in organization theory written by some of the most influential authors in the field. Within this compilation are works that have stood the test of time and that tell the history of organization theory through the words of great theorists. It is meant to help those new to the field of organization theory understand and appreciate the important themes and perspectives that these theories present. Every chapter focuses on one major perspective or "school" of organization theory. This helps readers learn the theories one perspective at a time. This is a reader-friendly book of theories that have been not only shortened from previous editions but also edited to help readers focus on the central ideas that make these works classics. *The Classics of Organization Theory* is meant for students, those new to the field, and people who want to be refreshed in the organization theory classics.

Simmons, A. (2006). *The story factor—Inspiration, influence, and persuasion through the art of storytelling.* **New York: Perseus Books Group.**

In this revised edition of the original 2001 version, the author revisits with readers her concept that "the oldest tool of influence is also the most powerful." The book showcases over 100 examples of effective storytelling drawn from business and governmental sectors as well as myths, fables, and parables from all over the world. The author uses these examples to show how the story can be used to persuade, motivate, and inspire in ways that cold facts, bullet points, and directives cannot. The book's step-by-step storytelling guide reveals how an ancient art can achieve very modern goals in today's society. Key bits of information included in the book's content include the definition of a story, how to tell a good story, story listening as a tool of influence, storyteller dos and don'ts, and story thinking as a skill. This book would assist anyone interested in learning about unique and creative ways to influence, motivate, and inspire, specifically through the act of storytelling.

Steinberg, R., & Powell, W. (Eds.). (2006). *The nonprofit sector: A research handbook.* **New Haven, CT: Yale University Press.**

Walter Powell is professor of education and organizational behavior, sociology, and communications at Stanford University. Richard Steinberg is professor of economics, philanthropic studies, and public affairs at Indiana University–Purdue University Indianapolis. This collection of papers and articles addresses the history and scope of the nonprofit sector, the relationship between nonprofits and the marketplace, key roles played by nonprofits in society, who participates in nonprofits and why, and the mission and governance of nonprofits. The book is of interest to anyone involved in managing a nonprofit or engaged in research on nonprofits.

Summerville, B., & Setterberg, F. (2008). *Grassroots philanthropy: Field notes of a maverick grantmaker.* **Berkeley, CA: Heyday Books.**

Bill Summerville is the founder of Philanthropic Ventures Foundation. Fred Setterberg has coauthored several books on philanthropy. In this book, Summerville, with Setterberg, argues for a new approach to philanthropy. He urges a drastic reduction in the bureaucracy that tends to bog down so many foundations. He asks why, instead of having to climb the mountains of paperwork that characterize traditional philanthropical organizations, philanthropists cannot simply engage with their communities, find individuals who are doing recognizably great work, and fund those projects. He argues that foundations need to stop summing up what's wrong and start acting, quickly, efficiently, and decisively, to create what's right. This book is of interest to community leaders and activists and philanthropists.

Tempel, E. R. (Ed.). (2002). *Understanding donor dynamics: The organizational side of charitable giving: New directions for philanthropic fundraising.* **San Francisco: Jossey-Bass.**

The individual chapters in this collection cover consideration of such topics as how to build a donor-focused community foundation, how to increase donor loyalty, and the major waves of change affecting philanthropy in the United States. Together, they reflect a concern with the wants and needs of donors, the growth of philanthropy in the late 20th century, and the evolution of economic theory as it relates to philanthropy. This should be of interest to those studying American philanthropy, as well as nonprofit fundraisers, or those serving as executive officers for philanthropical institutions.

Tempel, E. R. (2003). *Hank Rosso's achieving excellence in fund raising* (2nd ed.). (2003). San Francisco: Jossey-Bass.

Fundraising is a critical component to supporting a successful nonprofit organization. *Hank Rosso's Achieving Excellence in Fund Raising* provides a conceptual foundation for the fundraising profession. This book examines the profession's strategies, principles, and methods and provides advice and tips guided by the fundraising master, Henry A. Rosso. Meant for students interested in fund development, current and potential professionals within the field, and nonprofit organizations, this book is filled with strategies for a vast array of fundraising activities. Providing information on topics such as developing a case for support, approaching donors, managing campaigns, and practicing stewardship, this is a tool that will help professionals develop better fund-development techniques. This book is easy to read and navigate, making it a valuable resource to many current and potential fund-development professionals and nonprofits in the sector.

Tocqueville, A. de. (2000). *Democracy in America: The complete and unabridged volumes I and II.* New York: Bantam Classics.

Democracy in America, first published in 1835 and based on de Tocqueville's travels through the United States in the 1830s, is a study of the national character and government of the early 19th century. He writes of the significant effect of majority rule on the rights and liberties of the individual, as well as the need for elected officials to be not only responsible to their constituents, but also moral and virtuous toward them. Students and scholars of American democracy and the American character will be interested in this collection.

Van Til, J. (2000). *Growing civil society: From nonprofit sector to third space.* Bloomington: Indiana University Press.

Jon Van Til is professor of Urban Studies and Community Planning at Rutgers University. In this text, Van Til argues that the "third space," the part of society occupied by volunteer organizations and the various individuals and groups that work together for the good of that society, is, has been, and will be critical in furthering the common good. Van Til considers the ways

these nonprofit (and typically nongovernmental) organizations contribute to the common good and the role he sees them playing, potentially, in the future. See also Van Til's *Mapping the Third Sector: Voluntarism in a Changing Social Economy.*

Van Til, J. (2000). *Mapping the third sector: Voluntarism in a changing social economy.* New York: Foundation Center.

Jon Van Til is professor of Urban Studies and Community Planning at Rutgers University. He attempts, in this book, to define the field of voluntarism in contemporary society and explore the relation of voluntary action to the business sector, the government, and modern households. He recognizes that American society is changing, that the social economy is changing, and attempts to grapple with those changes as they relate to voluntarism. The book will be of most interest to academics in the field. See also Van Til's *Growing Civil Society: From Nonprofit Sector to Third Space.*

Warwick, M. (2008). *How to write successful fundraising letters* (2nd ed.). San Francisco: Jossey-Bass.

Fund development is an important task for nonprofit organizations and Warwick offers advice on how to get results. This book is meant for students wanting to learn about fund development, new professionals in the field, and those wanting to be refreshed on the fundamentals of fundraising. Warwick outlines how to plan campaigns; how to compose, phrase, and punctuate appeals; and how to conduct follow-ups. Providing a vast array of examples and case studies, he offers solid advice and analysis. In addition, Warwick supplies a variety of thank you letters and solicitation letters. This is an effective and easy-to-follow overview of fund development and the steps needed to become successful in fundraising.

Weisbrod, B. A. (2000). *To profit or not to profit: The commercial transformation of the nonprofit sector.* New York: Cambridge University Press.

The book is a great contribution to understanding the trend in nonprofit organizations of adopting the model of for-profit private firms and the consequences of commercialization, including acknowledging the often unseen harmful effects. Nonprofits are becoming increasingly like private firms and the growing financial dependence is moving from charitable donations to commercial sales activity. This book is a coordinated set of studies of the growing tendency of the third sector on user fees and revenue from ancillary activities that do not contribute directly to the organizational mission.

Weisbrod has brought attention to important research that will help us define and understand these new relationships. The book concludes with recommendations for research and public policy.

Wholey, J. S., Hatry, H. P., & Newcomer, K. E. (2004). *Handbook of practical program evaluation* **(2nd ed.). San Francisco: Jossey-Bass.**

The ability for nonprofit organizations to demonstrate results is increasing in importance to funders. This book offers economical and efficient methods for assessing program results and helps to identify approaches to improve program performance. The handbook is meant for students, professionals in the private, public, and nonprofit sectors, or for those simply wanting to learn more about how to effectively analyze programs. Including methods for analyzing evaluation data, the handbook covers how to select and train evaluators, the standards and ethics involved in evaluation work, and the steps to increasing the usefulness of the evaluation results for program improvement. The handbook also informs the reader on selecting appropriate evaluation designs, how to select data procedures, and the future trends in program evaluation. This is a thorough overview of evaluation and how it can be used.

Wooster, M. M. (2007). *The great philanthropists and the problem of "Donor intent."* **Washington, DC: Capital Research Center.**

This book addresses the continuing importance of the issue of donor intent and provides insight into how those who create charitable foundations can ensure that their wishes are carried out after their death. The author examines the entrepreneurship and charity of some of the best and least known founding fathers of philanthropy in the United States, including Andrew Carnegie, John D. Rockefeller, and Henry Ford. The book follows those cases in which donor intent was upheld and those in which it was not, including a number of cases in which donor intentions were completely violated. The executive summary provides a concise overview of the book.

Wuthnow, R. (1993). *Acts of compassion.* **Princeton, NJ: Princeton University Press.**

Robert Wuthnow is Andlinger Professor of Social Sciences and Director of the Center for the Study of American Religion at Princeton. Wuthnow presents case studies and anecdotes from over 2,000 adults he surveyed across the country as he attempts to answer the question of why Americans volunteer. It is neither a history of philanthropy nor an argument for how to improve the function of philanthropical organizations

but, instead, an honest attempt to understand different Americans' motives for volunteering their time, energy, and money. It should be of particular interest to students of philanthropy and those active in volunteer work. See also Wuthnow's *Learning to Care: Elementary Kindness in an Age of Indifference.*

Wuthnow, R. (1995). *Learning to care: Elementary kindness in an age of indifference.* **New York: Oxford University Press.**

Robert Wuthnow is Andlinger Professor of Social Sciences and Director of the Center for the Study of American Religion at Princeton. In this book, Wuthnow asks how we learn to care and how we can inspire caring in others, especially in the young and especially when so many problems seem too vast for an individual to make a difference. In answering his questions, he draws on interviews and national surveys and presents his argument that compassion is learned. As such, he argues that it is through opportunities to volunteer to serve, whether through schools or through religious institutions, that young people develop a sense of the value of service. It is of particular interest to those working within volunteer organizations that work with young people. See also Wuthnow's *Acts of Compassion.*

Wuthnow, R., & Hodgkinson, V. A. (Eds.). (1990). *Faith and philanthropy in America: Exploring the role of religion in America's voluntary sector.* **San Francisco: Jossey-Bass.**

This collection of essays, originating in a conference sponsored by the Independent Sector, will be of most interest to leaders of nonprofit associations, both religious and secular, as well as to scholars studying such organizations. The collection was written as an attempt to correct what is seen as a flaw in nonprofit study—that is, the general failure to include religious institutions in serious academic considerations of nonprofit institutions. The individual essays cover tax law, history, current case studies, and the potential future of religious nonprofits in order to argue that the theoretical divide between religious and secular nonprofit associations is only that: purely theoretical. See also Hodgkinson and Foley's *The Civil Society Reader,* and Schervish, Gates, and Hodgkinson's *Care and Community in Modern Society: Passing on the Tradition of Service to Future Generations.*

Ylvisaker, P. (1991). *Family foundations now—and forever? The question of intergenerational succession.* **Washington, DC: Council on Foundations.**

This text is a resource that provides models for the successful operation of family foundations. It also provides different models for how families can negotiate intergenerational succession by considering the roles succeeding generations can play in the administration of a family foundation. It is of particular interest to those within such family foundations or those interested in setting up a multigenerational family foundation. See also Esposito's *Conscience and Community: The Legacy of Paul Ylvisaker.*

Young, D. R. (2003). *Effective economic decision-making by nonprofit organizations.* **New York: Foundation Center.**

This book is the first publication of the National Center on Nonprofit Enterprise (NCNE). Dennis R. Young is the director of the Nonprofit Studies Program at Stanford University and a former president and founding CEO of NCNE. The book provides practical guidelines for helping nonprofit managers to further their organization's mission while balancing the often competing interests of trustees, funders, government, and staff. It explores different factors of economic decision making including pricing, employee compensation, outsourcing, fundraising costs, investment and expenditure, commercial ventures, institutional collaboration, and Internet commerce. Chapters are based on the work of a task force that deliberated before the NCNE inaugural conference.

Young, D. R. (Ed.). (2006). *Financing nonprofits: Putting theory into practice.* **Lanham, MD: AltaMira Press.**

This book represents the culmination of 3 years original research and thinking. It is based on the premise that nonprofit finance is fundamentally different than corporate or public-sector finance. It presents the work of many authors, identifying trends and underlying theories in the forms of support available for nonprofits, from individual contributions to debt financing. The editor, Dennis R. Young, director of the Nonprofit Studies Program at Stanford University and a former president and founding CEO of the National Center on Nonprofit Enterprise, weaves these writings together into a comprehensive theory of nonprofit finance and offers a set of principles for guiding the development of nonprofit portfolios. This book will be of interest to nonprofit CEOs, CFOs, trustees, and to scholars and students of nonprofit finance.

Young, D. R., & Hammack, D. C. (Eds.). (1996). *Nonprofit organizations in a market economy: Understanding new roles, issues, and trends.* **Hoboken, NJ: John Wiley & Sons.**

This collection of essays explores nonprofit organizations and how they function in a market economy. Contributors address topics such as nonprofit organizations as alternatives and complements in a mixed economy, trade associations in the American political economy, how and why nonprofit organizations obtain capital, and what nonprofits and businesses can learn from each other. The target audience for this work includes administrators and policymakers. See also Anheier and Hammack's *American Foundations: Roles and Contributions* and Hammack's *Making the Nonprofit Sector in the U.S.*

Journal Articles on Nonprofit Leadership

Clegg, S. R. (1992). Postmodern management? *Journal of Organizational Change Management, 5,* 31–50.

"Postmodern Management?" is a contextual and cross-cultural look at organizational structures and methods for dealing with change in Japan in comparison to the Western world. It claims that the Western world is centered in a modernist organizational structure that emphasizes unified theories rooted in class struggle, market forces, and classism while the Japanese model can be described as postmodern, focusing more on economic calculation, worker-centered strategy, and long-term goal investment. While the West is focused on growth and strategy, Japan, the author argues, is more focused on the organization as a learning collective worth investing in for core competency over capital gains. The article is written in a typically postmodern style with cultural references and wide historical scope. Its usefulness is in the depth of its cross-cultural analysis as a method of exploring alternatives to Western institutional paradigms.

Cline, K. D. (2000). Defining the implementation problem: Organizational management versus cooperation. *Journal of Public Administration Research and Theory, 10,* 551–571.

Tackling the area of public policy implementation, Cline analyzes two implementation models to determine which strategy is best for nonprofits and how this affects the way change is approached. Using Goggin and colleagues' communication model, which focuses on the organization management side of strategy, and the implementation regime framework, which prizes achieving cooperation, Cline evaluates implementation strategy based on 4 criteria. These include top-down versus bottom-up structure, the role of communication, level conflict or cooperation, and applicability to networks. His results show that the cooperation model works better in the nonprofit sector. Without a systematic understanding of the implementation of change, nonprofits will be blocked from moving forward with policies and programs. This article provides insight into the ways in which implementation studies can streamline the process.

Ferres, N., & Connell, J. (2004). Emotional intelligence in leaders: An antidote for cynicism towards *change?* *Strategic Change, 13,* 61–71.

Ferres and Connell focus on the emotional intelligence needed by leaders to reduce the level of employee cynicism and resistance to organizational change. They take a historical approach, summarizing challenges to change in organizations over the last 100 years. This is followed by a survey of employees to test the hypothesis that managers who are emotionally intelligent have reduced levels of change cynicism among their staffs. They define emotional intelligence using Goleman's ideas, stating that it is characterized by self-awareness, emotional recognition, self-regulation, motivation, and empathy. There results show that their hypothesis was correct and provides important information for people looking to find ways to manage change, increase leadership capabilities, and understand organizational relationships and culture.

Grant, H. M., & Crutchfield, L. R. (2007, Fall). Creating high-impact nonprofits. *Stanford Social Innovation Review,* 32–41.

Grant and Crutchfield outline six major myths about nonprofit management that are assumed to be necessary for success. These myths include perfect management, brand-name awareness, new ideas, textbook mission statements, good statistical standing, and large budgets. They counter these myths by describing the six services of high-impact nonprofits. These are service and advocacy, making markets work, inspiring evangelism, nurturing and cooperation with other nonprofits, adaptation, and sharing leadership. The authors then analyze 12 nonprofits that show outstanding effectiveness and exhibit these nontraditional characteristics. Their writing provides insight into innovative changes in the nonprofit sector and is a useful guide to changing long-held ideas about the necessity for an organization to be competitive and successful.

Hoag, B. G., Ritschard, H. V., & Cooper, C. (2002). Obstacles to effective organizational change: The underlying reasons. *Leadership & Organizational Development Journal, 23,* 6–15.

This article is a summary of research methods and results for an exploratory survey conducted by the authors at a conference for the Chartered Institute of Personnel and Development and the Institute of Management. The article begins with an explanation of existing research indicating that the factors most often blamed as obstacles for organizational change are external issues (cost, workload-staff, legislation). Their survey methods are explained and the results are described, showing that the most frequently cited impediments to organizational change are not external but rather internal structural issues including problems with leadership and management. This article shows that what we accept as "common knowledge" in the field of organizational management may, in fact, be part of the underlying structural faults themselves. Any study of changing trends in public administration would benefit from this article and its clear explanation of perceptions of barriers to change on the part of employees and the ways that those perceptions of poor leadership and noncommunicative management prevent smooth organizational transitions.

Kong, E. (2007). The strategic importance of intellectual capital in the non-profit sector. *Journal of Intellectual Capital, 8,* 721–734.

Eric Kong provides a discussion of the need for strong strategic management concepts that take into account the unique properties of nonprofit organizations. His article carefully examines the foundations and pros and cons of several of the most common of these concepts including resource-based view, balanced scorecard, and intellectual capital among others. He argues that given the need for nonprofits to be both competitive and operate under nontraditional business structures, it is intellectual capital (IC) that best serves the sector as a management strategy. IC uses nonfinancial indicators to measure the possibility of future successes, making nonprofits able to include their volunteer base, talent, donations, and so on in describing their prospective financial success. Kong provides a clear description of management concepts and shows clearly how each would function in a nonprofit context.

Lemak, D. J. (2004). Leading students through the management theory jungle by following the path of the seminal theorists: A paradigmatic approach. *Management Decision, 42,* 1309–1325.

In his article, Lemak explains the three major barriers to teaching organizational management (OM) and the problems with current teaching methods and proposes his solution to this problem. He states that the barriers are the amount and rapid pace of the body of knowledge in OM, the gap between practitioners and scholars, and the increasing diversity of the student body. It is his opinion, derived from Koontz, that we need to develop a paradigmatic approach to teaching OM, with an emphasis on context and history rather than chronology (which makes theory seems outdated and therefore of lesser value) and schools of thought (which provide little context or applicability). He attempts to structure this new approach around the ideas of natural law in the "hard" sciences, with a goal of reaching underneath what has changed over the years and finding what common threads exist. By using clear, simple language and avoiding jargon and arcane references, Lemak provides insights that would be valuable both to the organization management teacher but also to the struggling student who wishes to understand more about the epistemological practices of the discipline.

Luthens, F. (2002). The need for and meaning of positive organizational behavior. *Journal of Organizational Behavior, 23,* **695–706.**

In this article, Luthens discusses new trends in positive psychology and the implications of new research in this field for application in organizational behavior theory. Luthens argues that, like psychology, organizational behavior theory has focused too heavily on the negative aspects of organizational change including leadership dysfunction and employee resistance. A discussion of new characteristics and states of being are described, and the development of a new model for studying organizational change is explained. The CHOSE model focuses on these new characteristics (confidence, hope, optimism, subjective well-being, and emotional intelligence) in order to establish new criteria for studying qualities that lead to successful change within organizations as a way of identifying who may be adaptable to transition. This article provides a counterpoint to the large body of work in organizational management theory focusing on the negative aspects of organizational structure-culture that inhibit change. It is a valuable article for showing new insights and point of views in how we view the development of methods for analyzing the likely success of implemented change.

Norman, S., Luthans, B., & Luthans, K. (2005). The proposed contagion effect of hopeful leaders on the resiliency of employees and organizations. *Journal of Leadership & Organizational Studies, 12,* **55–64.**

Norman and the Luthans build on the work of Fred Luthans and begin to shape the possible implications of positive organizational behavior theory. They suggest that there is a positive correlation between leadership that possesses the skills of hope and confidence and employees that are resilient and content during organizational transition periods. They claim that change is happening so rapidly and constantly now that we must develop new ways to think about coping skills in an institutional setting. They caution against superficial "theories" presented by the new genre of popular psychology management books but stress the need for solid research into ways of defining hope and resiliency in an effort to discover functional methods for creating it in an organizational environment. Their research is a straightforward discussion of new possibilities in the field of organizational management and an excellent starting point for those looking for ways to effectively implement change.

Service, R. W. (2006). The development of strategic intelligence: A managerial perspective. *International Journal of Management, 23,* **61–77.**

While there is much discussion of emotional intelligence in modern organizational theory, Service chooses to focus on strategic intelligence. The author asserts that while strategic planning may be commonplace in organizations, strategic thinking requires training and is far rarer. Even strategic thinking is only a stepping-stone on the path to strategic leadership. He argues for a move away from the "mechanical process" of planning and introduces ways to develop it into a more human-focused skill. He describes a lengthy list of strategic commandments followed by a discussion of ways in which one can begin to hone the skills necessary to move from vision to situational success. This article, while not highly accessible, is useful for those who want to take a deeper look at the actual actions of planning and implementing goals within an organization.

Bibliography

The insights from the chapter authors in this handbook on nonprofit leadership are supported by generations of insight, research, and experience from scholars and reflective practitioners working to understand and improve both the philanthropic sector and the craft of leadership. You will find these references at the ends of each chapter, and I would encourage the reader to "dig deeper" by going to some of these sources directly. The following lists a few of the key readings mentioned across the chapters that can assist a nonprofit leader in the further understanding of the work of leading a third-sector organization. The list is only a very, very small sampling of the writings of individuals who care deeply and approach thoughtfully the ideas of leadership in the civil society sector. As you complete the readings in this handbook, you may wish to continue your investigation of the sector by delving into these works.

Adizes, I. (1988). *Corporate lifecycles: How and why corporations grow, die and what to do about it.* Englewood Cliffs, NJ: Prentice Hall.

Andreasen, A. R., & Kotler, P. (2003). *Strategic marketing for nonprofit organizations* (6th ed.). Englewood Cliffs, NJ: Prentice Hall.

Anheier, H. K. (2005). *Nonprofit organizations: Theory, management, policy.* New York: Routledge.

Argyris, C. (1993). *Knowledge for action: A guide to overcoming barriers to organizational change.* San Francisco: Jossey-Bass.

Atkinson, R. (1997). Theories of the federal income tax exemption for charities: Thesis, antithesis, and syntheses. *Stetson Law Review, 27,* 395–431.

Auerswald, P. (2009). Creating social value. *Stanford Social Innovation Review, 7*(2), 50–55.

Avina, J. (1993). The evolutional life cycle of nongovernmental development organizations. *Public Administration and Development, 13*(5), 453–474.

Axelrod, N. (2005). Board leadership and development. In R. Herman et al. (Eds.), *The Jossey-Bass handbook of nonprofit leadership & management.* San Francisco: Jossey-Bass.

Barry, B. W. (2001). *Strategic planning workbook for nonprofit organizations* (Rev. ed.). St. Paul, MN: Amherst H. Wilder Foundation.

Bass, B. M. (2008). *The Bass handbook of leadership: Theory, research, & managerial applications.* New York: Simon & Schuster.

Bass, B. M., & Riggio, R. E. (2006). *Transformational leadership* (2nd ed.). Mahwah, NJ: Lawrence Erlbaum.

Behrens, T., & Kelly, T. (2008). Paying the piper: Foundation evaluation capacity calls the tune. *New Directions for Evaluation, 2008*(119), 37–50.

Bell, J., Moyers, R., & Wolford, T. (2006). *Daring to lead: A national study of nonprofit executive leadership.* Available from http://www.compasspoint.org/assets/194_daring tolead06final.pdf

Bellah, R. N., Madsen, R., Sullivan, W. M., Swidler, A., & Tipton, S. M. (1985). *Habits of the heart: Individualism and commitment in American life.* Berkeley: University of California Press.

Bennis, W. (1994). *On becoming a leader.* Reading, MA: Addison-Wesley.

Bennis, W. (1996, July 1). Lessons in leadership from superconsultant Warren Bennis. *Bottom Line Personal.*

Bennis, W. G. (2004, January). The seven ages of the leader. *Harvard Business Review,* pp. 46–53.

Bennis, W. G., & Thomas, R. J. (2002). *Geeks and geezers: How era, values, and defining moments shape leaders.* Boston: Harvard Business School Press.

Bernholz, L., Fulton, K., & Kasper, G. (2005). *On the brink of new promise: The future of U.S. community foundations.* San Francisco: Blueprint Research & Design.

Berry, J. M., & Arons, D. F. (2003). *A voice for nonprofits.* Washington, DC: Brookings Institution Press.

Bielefeld, W. (2009). Issues in social enterprise and social entrepreneurship. *Journal of Public Affairs Education, 15*(1), 69–86.

Blanchard, K. (2007). *Leading at a higher level.* Upper Saddle River, NJ: Prentice Hall.

Block, P. (1996). *Stewardship: Choosing service over self-interest.* San Francisco: Berrett-Koehler.

Block, S. R. (2003). *Why nonprofits fail: Overcoming founder's syndrome, fundphobia and other obstacles to success.* San Francisco: Jossey-Bass.

BoardSource, (1999). *Starting a nonprofit organization.* BoardSource E-Book series. Available from www.board source.org

Bolman, L., & Deal, T. (1997). *Reframing organizations: Artistry, choice and leadership.* San Francisco: Jossey-Bass.

Boris, E. (2000). Nonprofit organizations in a democracy: Roles and responsibilities. In E. Boris & C. E. Steuerle (Eds.), *Nonprofits and government: Collaboration and conflict* (pp. 1–35). Washington, DC: Urban Institute Press.

Bothwell, R. O. (2001, September). Trends in self-regulation and transparency of nonprofit organizations in the U.S. *International Journal of Not-for-Profit Law, 4.*

Bremner, R. H. (1988). *American philanthropy.* Chicago: University of Chicago Press.

Brest, P., & Harvey, H. (2008). *Money well spent: A strategic plan for smart philanthropy.* New York: Bloomberg Press.

Brilliant, E. (2000). *Private charity and public inquiry.* Bloomington: Indiana University Press.

Brinckerhoff, P. (2000). *Mission-based management.* New York: John Wiley & Sons.

Brinkerhoff, P. C. (2002). *Mission-based marketing: Positioning your not-for-profit in an increasingly competitive world.* Hoboken, NJ: John Wiley.

Bryson, J. M. (2005). The strategy change cycle: An effective strategic planning approach for nonprofit organizations. In R. D. Herman & Associates (Eds.), *The Jossey-Bass handbook of nonprofit leadership and management* (2nd ed., pp. 171–203). San Francisco: Jossey-Bass.

Burlingame, D. F. (2002). *Taking fundraising seriously: The spirit of faith and philanthropy: New directions for philanthropic fundraising* (J-B PF Single Issue Philanthropic Fundraising). San Francisco: Jossey-Bass.

Burns, J. (1978). *Leadership.* New York: Harper & Row.

Carnegie, A. (2001). The gospel of wealth. In J. S. Ott (Ed.), *The nature of the nonprofit sector.* Boulder, CO: Westview Press.

Carver, J. (1990). *Boards that make a difference: A new design for leadership in nonprofit and public organizations.* San Francisco: Jossey-Bass.

Carver, J. (2002). *John Carver on board leadership.* San Francisco: Jossey-Bass.

Collins, J. (2001). *Good to great: Why some companies make the leap and others don't.* New York: Harper Business.

Collins, J. (2005). *Good to great and the social sectors* [Monograph, ISBN 13–978–0–9773264–0–2, published by author].

Covey, S. R. (1996). Three roles of the leader in the new paradigm. In F. Hesselbein, M. Goldsmith, & R. Beckhard (Eds.), *The leader of the future* (pp. 149–159). San Francisco: Jossey-Bass.

Crutchfield, L. R., & Grant, H. M. (2008). *Forces for good: The six practices of high-impact nonprofits.* San Francisco: Jossey-Bass. Review (L. Zumdahl) obtained from *ABI/INFORM Global: Social Work & Christianity, 35*(3), 346–349.

Dartmouth College (n.d.). *History.* Available from http://www .dartmouth.edu/home/about/history.html

De Pree, M. (1992). *Leadership jazz.* New York: Dell.

De Pree, M. (1997). *Leading without power: Finding hope in serving community.* Holland, MI: Shepherd Foundation.

De Pree, M. (2004). *Leadership is an art.* New York: Doubleday.

Dewey, J. (1991). *Lectures on ethics.* Carbondale: Southern Illinois Press. (Original work published 1900–1901)

DiMaggio, P., & Powell, W. (1983). The iron cage revisited: Institutional isomorphism and collective rationality in organizational fields. *American Sociological Review, 48*(2), 147–160.

Dobkin Hall, P. (1990). Conflicting managerial cultures in nonprofit organizations. *Nonprofit Management & Leadership, 1*(2), 153–165.

Drucker, P. (1985). *Innovation and entrepreneurship: Practices and principles.* New York: HarperCollins.

Drucker, P. (1990). *Managing the nonprofit organization: Principles and practices.* New York: HarperCollins.

Drucker, P. F. (1993). *The effective executive.* New York: HarperCollins.

Drucker, P. F. (2003). *The new realities.* New York: Transaction.

Drucker, P. F. (2006). *Managing the nonprofit organization: Practices and principles.* New York: HarperCollins.

Edie, J. A. (2001). *First steps in starting a foundation* (5th ed.). Washington, DC: Council on Foundations.

Etzioni, A. (1993). *The spirit of community.* New York: Crown.

Fleishman, J. (2007). *The foundation: A great American secret.* New York: Public Affairs.

Foundation Center. (2002). *The foundation directory, 2002 edition.* New York: Author.

Friedman, T. (2008). *Hot, flat and crowded.* New York: Farrar, Straus & Giroux.

Fromm, E. (1955). *Man for himself.* New York: Rinehart.

Frumkin, P. (2002). Civic and political engagement. In P. Frumkin, *On being nonprofit: A conceptual and policy primer* (pp. 29–63). Cambridge, MA: Harvard University Press.

Gardner, J. W. (1990). *On leadership.* New York: Free Press.

Gardner, J. W. (1996). Self-renewal. *Futurist, 30*(6), 9–12.

Greenleaf, R. (1977). *Servant leadership: A journey into the nature of legitimate power and greatness.* New York: Paulist Press.

Greenleaf, R. K. (1978). *Servant, leader, & follower.* New York: Paulist Press.

Greenleaf, R. K. (1996). *On becoming a servant leader.* San Francisco: Jossey-Bass.

Greiner, L. (1998, May). Evolution and revolution as organizations grow. *Harvard Business Review,* 37–46.

Hammack, D. C. (Ed). (1998). *Making the nonprofit sector in the United States.* Bloomfield: Indiana University Press.

Heifetz, R. A., Grashow, A., & Linsky, M. (2009). *The practice of adaptive leadership.* Boston: Harvard Business Press.

Hersey, P., & Blanchard, K. H. (1977). *The management of organizational behaviour* (3rd ed.). Upper Saddle River, NJ: Prentice Hall.

Hodgkinson, V. A. (2002). Individual giving and volunteering. In L. M. Salamon (Ed.), *The state of nonprofit America* (pp. 387–420). Washington, DC: Brookings Institution Press.

Houle, C. O. (1989). *Governing boards.* San Francisco: Jossey-Bass.

Hoyt, C. (1998). Tax-exempt organization. In J. S. Ott (Ed.), *The nature of the nonprofit sector* (pp. 148–151). Boulder, CO: Westview Press.

Ilchman, W. F., Katz, S. N., & Queen, E. L. (Eds.). (1998). *Philanthropy in the world's traditions.* Bloomington: Indiana University Press.

Joseph, J. A. (1995). *Remaking America. How the benevolent traditions of many cultures are transforming our national life.* San Francisco: Jossey-Bass.

Josephson, M. (1992). *Ethics in grantmaking & grantseeking: Making philanthropy better.* Marina Del Rey, CA: Joseph & Edna Josephson Institute of Ethics.

Josephson, M. (2002). *Making ethical decisions.* Retrieved May 1, 2009, from http://josephsoninstitute.org/MED/index.html

Josephson, M. (2002). *The six pillars of character.* Retrieved May 1, 2009, from http://josephsoninstitute.org/MED/MED-2sixpillars.html

Karl, B. D., & Katz, S. (1981). The American philanthropic foundation and the public sphere: 1890–1930. *Minerva: A Review of Science, Learning & Policy, 19,* 236–270.

Katz, D., & Khan, R. L. (1966). *Organizations and the system concept: The social psychology of organizations* (pp. 14–20). New York: John Wiley & Sons.

Kidder, R. M. (2009). *How good people make tough choices: Resolving the dilemmas of ethical living* (2nd ed.). New York: Harper.

Knowlton, L. W., & Phillips, C. C. (2009). *The logic model guidebook: Better strategies for great results.* Thousand Oaks, CA: Sage.

Kohlberg, L. (1971). Stages of moral development as a basis for moral education. In C. M. Beck, B. S. Crittenden, & E. V. Sullivan (Eds.), *Moral education.* New York: Newman Press.

Kretzmann, J. P., & McKnight, J. L. (1993). *Building communities from the inside out: A path toward finding and mobilizing a community's assets.* Evanston, IL: Institute for Policy Research.

La Piana, D. (2008). *Nonprofit strategy revolution: Real-time strategic planning in a rapid response world.* Saint Paul, MN: Fieldstone Alliance.

Light, P. C. (2000). *Making nonprofits work: A report on the tides of nonprofit management reform.* Washington, DC: Brookings Institution Press.

Light, P. C. (2002). *Pathways to nonprofit excellence.* Washington, DC: Brookings Institution Press.

Lohmann, R. A. (1992). *The Commons: New perspectives on nonprofit organizations and voluntary action.* San Francisco: Jossey-Bass.

Maslow, A. (1943). A theory of human motivation. *Psychological Review, 50,* 370–396.

Nanus, B., & Dobbs, S. M. (1993). *Leaders who make a difference: Essential strategies for meeting the nonprofit challenge.* San Francisco: Jossey-Bass.

Nielsen, W. A. (1972). *The big foundations.* New York: Columbia University Press.

Nielsen, W. A. (2001). *Golden donors: A new anatomy of the great foundations.* Piscataway, NJ: Transaction.

Northouse, P. G. (2007). *Leadership: Theory and practice* (4th ed.). Thousand Oaks, CA: Sage.

O'Connell, B. (1993). *Origins, dimensions, and impact of America's voluntary spirit.* Washington, DC: Independent Sector.

O'Connell, B. (1999). *Civil society: The underpinnings of American democracy.* Medford, MA: Tufts University Press.

Odendahl, T. (1990). *Charity begins at home: Generosity and self-interest among the philanthropic elite.* New York: Basic Books.

O'Neill, M. (1989). *The third America: The emergence of the nonprofit sector in the United States.* San Francisco: Jossey-Bass.

O'Neill, M. (2002). *Nonprofit nation.* San Francisco: Jossey-Bass.

Orosz, J. J. (2000). *The insider's guide to grantmaking: How foundations find, fund, and manage effective programs.* San Francisco: Josey-Bass.

Orosz, J. (2007). *Effective foundation management.* New York: AltaMira Press.

Payton, R. L. (1988). *Philanthropy: Voluntary action for the common good.* New York: Macmillan.

Payton, R. L., & Moody, M. P. (2008). *Understanding philanthropy: Its meaning and mission.* Bloomington: Indiana University Press.

Plato. (2004). *Republic.* New York: Barnes & Noble Classics. (Original English work published 1871)

Powell, W. W., & Clemens, E. S. (1998). *Private action and the public good.* New Haven, CT: Yale University Press.

Powell, W. W., & Steinberg, R. (2006). *The nonprofit sector: A research handbook* (2nd ed.). New Haven, CT: Yale University Press.

Putnam, R. (2000). *Bowling alone: The collapse and revival of American community.* New York: Simon & Schuster.

Rifkin, J. (1995). *The end of work: The decline of the global labor force and the dawn of the post-market era.* New York: Tarcher/Putnam.

Rinehart, S. T. (1998). *Upside down: The paradox of servant leadership.* Colorado Springs, CO: NavPress.

Salamon, L. M. (1987). Partners in public service. In W. W. Powell (Ed.), *The nonprofit sector: A research handbook* (Chap. 6, pp. 99–117). New Haven, CT: Yale University Press.

Salamon, L. (1999). *America's nonprofit sector.* New York: Foundation Center.

Salamon, L. M. (Ed.). (1999). *Global civil society: Dimensions of the nonprofit sector* (Vol. 1). (Johns Hopkins Center for Civil Society Studies). Bloomfield, CT: Kumarian Press.

Salamon, L. (2002). *The state of nonprofit America.* Washington, DC: Brookings Institution Press.

Schervish, P. (2005). Major donors, major motives: The people and purposes behind major gifts. *New Directions in Philanthropic Fundraising, 2005*(47), 59–87.

Senge, P. (1990). *The fifth discipline: The art and practice of the learning organization.* New York: Doubleday.

Senge, P. M. (1995). Robert Greenleaf's legacy: A new foundation for twenty-first century institutions. In L. C. Spears (Ed.), *Reflections on leadership: How Robert K. Greenleaf's theory of servant leadership influenced today's top management thinkers* (pp. 217–240). New York: John Wiley & Sons.

Steinberg, R. (2006). Economic theories of nonprofit organizations. In W. Powell & R. Steinberg (Eds.), *The nonprofit sector: A research handbook* (1st ed., pp. 117–139). New Haven, CT: Yale University Press.

Tempel, E. R., & Burlingame, D. F. (2001). *Understanding the needs of donors: The supply side of charitable giving: New directions for philanthropic fundraising* (J-B PF Single Issue Philanthropic Fundraising). San Francisco: Jossey-Bass.

Tocqueville, A. (1972). *Democracy in America* (H. Reeve, Trans., F. Bowen & P. Bradley, Eds.). New York: Random House. (Original work published 1840)

Van Til, J. (1988). *Mapping the third sector: Voluntarism in a changing social economy.* New York: Foundation Center.

Van Til, J. (2000). *Growing civil society: From nonprofit sector to third space.* Bloomington: University of Indiana Press.

Wheatley, M. (1992). *Leadership and the new science.* San Francisco: Berret-Koehler.

W. K. Kellogg Foundation. (2001). *Logic model development guide.* Available from www.wkkf.org/Pubs/Tools/Evaluation/Pub 3669.pdf

Wuthnow, R. (1990). Religion and the voluntary spirit in the United States: Mapping the terrain. In R. Wuthnow, V. Hodgkinson, et al. (Eds.), *Faith and philanthropy in America.* Washington, DC: Jossey-Bass.

Wuthnow, R. (1993, September). Altruism and sociological theory. *Social Service Review, 67,* 344–357.

Ylvisaker, P. (1991). *Family foundations now—and forever?* New York: Council on Foundations.

APPENDIX B

Online Resources in the Nonprofit and Philanthropic Sector

Journals and Publications

Chronicle of Philanthropy
(http://www.philanthropy.com)

The *Chronicle* is published every other week and is a news source for people involved in the philanthropic enterprise. The website offers a summary of the contents of the current issue, a list of forthcoming conferences and workshops, job opportunities in the nonprofit world, and other relevant philanthropic information.

Contributions Magazine
(http://www.contributionsmagazine.com)

This magazine is designed for those working or volunteering at charitable organizations in the United States. Its mission is to give helpful resources on all the sides of fundraising and organizational management. This magazine is published bimonthly (once every 2 months); however, users can find archived copies of past issues on the magazine website.

Don Kramer's *Nonprofit Issues*
(http://www.nonprofitissues.com)

Nonprofit Issues is a national electronic newsletter of "Nonprofit Law You Need to Know." It uses current federal and state cases to show readers the issues of critical importance to nonprofit executives and their advisers. Topics can range from federal tax, employment law, volunteer law, and board liability to corporate governance, foundation rules, charitable giving, insurance, and copyright and trademark.

Foundation Review (http://www.foundationreview.org)

The *Foundation Review* is the first peer-reviewed journal of philanthropy, written for and by foundation staff and boards. The mission is to "share evaluation results, tools, and knowledge about the philanthropic sector in order to improve the practice of grantmaking, yielding greater impact and innovation." The *Foundation Review* is published quarterly and is a product of The Dorothy A. Johnson Center for Philanthropy at Grand Valley State University.

International Journal of Nonprofit and Voluntary Sector Marketing (http://www3.interscience.wiley.com/journal/110481870/home)

This journal is designed to be an international forum for peer-reviewed papers and case studies on the latest techniques, thinking, and best practices in marketing for the not-for-profit sector. The main sectors covered in this publication are the marketing of goods and services, fundraising, advertising and promotion, branding and positioning, campaigns and lobbying, ethics and fundraising, information technology and database management, sponsorship, public relations, and events management.

Leader to Leader (http://www3.interscience.wiley.com/journal/73505673/home)

This quarterly report is published on behalf of the Leader to Leader Institute (formerly the Drucker Foundation) and Jossey-Bass. Their purpose is to provide insight into what top executives and thought leaders are planning for, what they see as the major challenges ahead, and how they are dealing with current changes.

Nonprofit and Voluntary Sector Quarterly
(http://nvs.sagepub.com)

The *Nonprofit and Voluntary Sector Quarterly* is an international, interdisciplinary journal dedicated to the study of nonprofit organizations, philanthropy, and voluntary action. This journal works to enrich the knowledge of nonprofit organizations, philanthropy, and voluntarism. It is published by Association for Research on Nonprofit Organizations and Voluntary Action (ARNOVA).

Nonprofit Quarterly
(http://www.nonprofitquarterly.org)

This journal is designed to strengthen the role of nonprofit organizations to promote democratic values. The journal publishes management information and proven practices for nonprofits. Users can receive the quarterly journal report or can also sign up for a free e-newsletter.

Nonprofit Times (http://www.nptimes.com)

This publication is designed to be an online newspaper for people working in nonprofit management. It is a monthly publication that targets all issues of nonprofit management along with global current events and how they relate back to the nonprofit world.

Nonprofit World Magazine (http://www.snpo.org)

This magazine is published six times a year by the Society for Nonprofit Organizations. Its target is to provide hard-working nonprofit leaders with concise and practical articles that can be easily implemented into any nonprofit organization. In addition to current issues, members also have access to an online archive of over 700 printable articles.

Philanthropy Journal
(http://www.philanthropyjournal.org)

The *Philanthropy Journal* is designed to help people understand, support, and work in the nonprofit and philanthropic world, while also assisting them to recognize and solve social problems. The journal offers a daily website and a free, weekly e-mail bulletin, which contains nonprofit news, resources, announcements, and job listings. The *Philanthropy Journal* is a program of the Institute for Nonprofits at North Carolina State University in Raleigh.

Philanthropy Journal Online
(http://www.pnnonline.org)

This online journal delivers news, information, and resources to all segments of the nonprofit world to help staff members better achieve their organization's goals. New content is featured each day on the website, along with a highly active job postings service.

Stanford Social Innovation (http://www.ssireview.org)

The journal's mission is to frontier the search for new and better ways of improving the world as a whole. The goal is to share substantive insights and practical experiences that will help those whose mission it is to improve society to perform even better.

Third Sector (http://www.thirdsector.co.uk)

This publication is for all people who like to be aware of all the changes in the voluntary and not-for-profit sector throughout the United Kingdom. The publication offers a weekly print version and an online newspaper for UK charities.

VOLUNTAS: International Journal
of Voluntary and Nonprofit Organizations
(http://www.springerlink.com/content/104985)

This is the official interdisciplinary international journal of the International Society for Third-Sector Research. It aims to be the central forum for worldwide research in the area between the state market and household sectors by presenting leading-edge academic arguments in a style that is accessible to both practitioners and policymakers. *VOLUNTAS* is essential reading for all those engaged in research into the Third Sector (voluntary and nonprofit organizations).

Blogs and Forums and Wikis Discussing Volunteer Leadership

Blogs are, by their nature, personal musings by the individuals who start them, but they can be excellent sources of useful information and new perspectives. This is particularly true if the person writing the blog has significant experience in the field and/or works in a position where he or she has an unusual opportunity to observe and reflect. Wikis are sites that engage visitors in collaborative writing and exchange, while Forums provide a more organized and often linear sharing of ideas among participants who sign on to be a part of the forum discussion.

Acronym (http://blogs.asaecenter.org/Acronym/volunteer_management)

From the American Society of Association Management, "a veritable alphabet soup of ideas for the association community."

AL!VE: Association for Leaders in Volunteer Engagement (http://www.volunteeralive.org)

This forum serves to enhance the character of volunteer meetings in America by promoting collaboration and networking and professional development and by providing advocacy for leaders involved in community engagement. The website features numerous updates and reports published by AL!VE.

Association for Research on Nonprofit Organizations and Voluntary Action (ARNOVA) (http://www.arnova.org)

This forum is dedicated to strengthening the research community in the emerging field of nonprofit and philanthropic studies. The organization brings together both theoretical and applied interests while providing access to research that professionals can use to improve the quality of life for their communities. Major activities of this organization include an annual conference, publications, electronic discussions, and special interest groups.

Association Forum of Chicagoland (http://www.associationforum.org/resources/digital-forum.asp)

The forum was founded in 1916. Today, it serves 47,000 Chicagoland association professionals whose efforts serve 37 million members and 9 million donors. This forum is designed to advance the professional practice of association management.

Association of Volunteer Managers (http://www.volunteermanagers.org.uk/blog)

This blog is maintained by the Association of Volunteer Managers (AVM). This association is an independent body that aims to support and represent people who manage volunteers in England regardless of field, discipline, or sector.

Care2 Community (http://www.care2.com/community)

This website contains blogs that are posted by different volunteers who engage in green causes throughout the world. The website has over 10 million contributing members.

Chronicle of Philanthropy—"Give and Take" (http://philanthropy.com/giveandtake)

This newspaper is a popular news source for nonprofit leaders, fundraisers, grantmakers, and other people involved in the philanthropic enterprise. The paper is available in print form and an online form. The online blog section of the online form, or e-newspaper, includes a lengthy list of blogs about the nonprofit world, many of which include volunteer-related issues.

"Conversations From the Field of Volunteer Management" (http://www.volunteermaine.org/blog)

This blog is written by various contributors from the VolunteerMaine Partnership and Maine Commission for Community Service. The Partnership was created to be an important vehicle in solving challenges faced by Maine's volunteer sector.

Energize Book Blog (http://www.energizeinc.com/blog)

This book blog was coordinated to give colleagues in the volunteer sector the opportunity to learn about and suggest management books.

Engaging Volunteers (http://blogs.volunteermatch.org/engagingvolunteers)

This blog is for organizations that wish to recruit and partner with volunteers to reach their organizations' missions. The blog contains many articles that help organizations more effectively recruit and manage volunteers.

Everyday Giving Blog (http://everydaygiving.typepad.com)

This blog is all about different ways of giving to help others and impacting the world to make it a better place. The blog is published and maintained by Roger Carr.

Have Fun—Do Good Blogspot (http://havefundogood.blogspot.com)

This blog is a resource for people who want to give back and "do good" in their communities and throughout the world while also having fun.

IdealistNews (http://www.idealistnews.com)

This blog is a free "social news" service for nonprofits. Users can vote on news links to decide which links are the most relevant and important for nonprofit organizations.

Inside GOOD Blogspot (http://theinsidegoodblog.blogspot.com)

This blog is a place for employees, interns, volunteers, and donors of nonprofit organizations. Users can rate their experiences working with, or donating to, nonprofits. The blog also discusses the trends in ratings of nonprofits, expert opinions, and more.

Jayne Blog (http://blogs.forumer.com/jcravens)

This was one of the nonprofit field's first blogs. It is run by Jayne Cravens, who is an expert in online volunteering. The blog offers information on volunteerism, as well as nonprofit technological issues.

JFFixler Blog (http://www.jffixler.com/blog)

This blog is written by Jill Fixler and others in her firm. The main focus is to help nonprofit organizations achieve excellence in volunteer engagement, strategic planning, and board and organizational assessment and development.

New York Nonprofit Press—Volunteer Management Blog (http://www.nynp.biz/index.php/community-forums/234-alexandra-collier)

This blog is written by experienced volunteer administration practitioner Alexandra Collier to explore challenges to the field and new program ideas.

Nonprofit Commons Project (http://npsl.wikispaces.com)

This is a virtual place of practice for nonprofits to explore the opportunities and benefits of using Second Life. This wiki provides documentation and other information not only for NP Commons tenants, but also for any nonprofit that is interested in learning about the different uses of Second Life.

Nonprofit News and Comment (http://hausercenter.org/npnews)

This blog from the Hauser Center for Nonprofit Organizations at Harvard University surveys major newspapers and periodicals for important stories and links to a wide range of nonprofit news.

Points of Light Blog (http://www.pointsoflight.org/blog)

This blog is maintained by the Points of Light Institute and focuses on blogging about service and civic engagement.

Realizing Your Worth (http://realizedworth.blogspot.com)

This site is about helping business and nonprofits create and implement volunteer programs. The blog specifically focuses on corporate social responsibility and corporate volunteering.

ServiceWire (http://servicewire.org/wire)

This tool from Youth Service America is for accessing current news, information, and grant opportunities from the service-learning and youth service fields.

Social Citizens Blog (http://www.socialcitizens.org/blog)

This blog is for people who consider themselves to be "social citizens," which are those people who use technology as a gateway to make changes in and throughout their communities.

Tactical Philanthropy (http://tacticalphilanthropy.com)

This is the blog of Sean Stannard-Stockton, director of Tactical Philanthropy at Ensemble Capital Management. It is an open space for discussion of philanthropy and a chronicle of "The Second Great Wave of Philanthropy," including some volunteer issues.

Urban Survival Project (http://urbansurvivalproject.blogspot.com)

This blog focuses on social networking to achieve a socially beneficial outcome while also charting the journey of a social idea from conception to reality.

Volunteer Manager (http://volunteermanager.wordpress.com)

This is a blog for "all volunteers and volunteer managers" started in September 2006 by Greg Colby. It is a place where people can come to blog about issues or opinions and receive advice from others in the sector.

Volunteer's Guide to Changing the World (http://howtorelay.blogspot.com)

This blog is maintained by Mark Horoszowski and is based out of Seattle. It is a blogspot for volunteers to visit and receive assistance throughout the volunteer sector.

Wendy Biro-Pollard's Volunteer Management Blog (http://wendybiro-pollard.com/category/volunteer-management)

This website contains articles and insights from Wendy Biro-Pollard, a trainer and certified volunteer administrator with over 25 years of experience. The blog section focuses on helping those within the volunteer management field.

World Volunteer Web Blog (http://www.worldvolunteerweb.org/join-the-network/blogs/volunteer-blog.html)

Part of the excellent World Volunteer Web website, this blog offers a forum for both volunteers and managers. It contains information and resources linked to volunteerism that can be used for campaigning, advocacy, and networking.

APPENDIX C

Nonprofit Organizations

National Organizations

Association for Research on Nonprofit Organizations and Voluntary Actions (http://www.arnova.org)

The Association for Research on Nonprofit Organizations and Voluntary Actions is involved in advancing research and research practices in nonprofit and philanthropic studies. The mission of ARNOVA is to foster, through research and education, the creation, application, and dissemination of knowledge on nonprofit organizations, philanthropy, civil society, and voluntary action. Its website features its publications, the *Nonprofit and Voluntary Sector Quarterly* and *ARNOVA News*, as well as a discussion forum.

Association of Fund-Raising Professionals (http://www.afpnet.org)

The Association of Fund-Raising Professionals embodies more than 30,000 members in 206 chapters throughout the world. The association works to evolve the philanthropy field. It works to do this through advocacy, research, education, and certification programs.

GuideStar (http://www2.guidestar.org)

GuideStar collects and maintains records of nonprofits to facilitate engagement among nonprofits and the public, as well as collects vital information that is matched with other sources to form comprehensive nonprofit information. Participating organizations are able to use its website to update organizational information that is reflected in its reviews and publications. In addition to data collection and analysis tools, the website contains publications on the nonprofit sector, as well as current news and trusted blogs.

Independent Sector (www.independentsector.org)

Independent Sector is composed of nearly 600 organizations that seek to fulfill the mission of advancing the common good by leading, strengthening, and mobilizing the charitable community. Its website features independent work that highlights major areas within the nonprofit sector such as giving and volunteering, annual reporting and auditing, financial responsibility, ethics, and bylaws. Member organizations can use Independent Sector's resources to further their advocacy missions, collaborate on key issues facing the nonprofit sector, and inform their organizations' work.

National Association of Volunteer Programs in Local Government (NAVPLG) (http://www.navplg.org)

NAVPLG focuses primarily on the unique needs of volunteer programs within the structure of local, city, and county governments. The organization strives to provide resources and promote ways in which volunteerism can strengthen government programs at the local, city, and county levels.

National Council of Nonprofits (www.nycon.org)

The National Council of Nonprofits is a network of state and regional nonprofit associations working together to initiate greater change with a more unified voice. Local organizations not only have easier access to national audiences, but also are aided in management, policy, and many other areas through this collaborative, nonprofit sector council. The website features links to individual states' nonprofit associations, as well as links to nonprofit resources representing the best practices in key areas, such as administration and management, marketing, fundraising, governance, and policy.

National Organizations Volunteerism Network (NOVN) (http://www.nassembly.org/nassembly/novn.htm)

This is an online network for volunteer management professionals that are part of the nation's nonprofits in the fields of health, human and community development, and human services. The network is an opportunity for users to share knowledge and expertise about their work in the nonprofit health sector.

Nonprofit Technology Network (NTen) (http://www.nten.org)

This organization is a membership organization for nonprofit technology professionals. Its mission is to help all nonprofits use technology more efficiently and effectively in their organizations. NTen networks nonprofits with one another and facilitates programs and discussions for nonprofit technology professionals.

Urban Institute (http://www.urban.org)

The Urban Institute analyzes policies, evaluates programs, and informs community development to improve social, civic, and economic well-being. The Urban Institute's main webpage provides information on current projects, recent publications, and special events and provides research resources to foster sound public policy and effective government. In addition, the Urban Institute provides in-depth state, regional, and national reports and statistics on advocacy, charity, community, service, and faith-based nonprofits.

State Associations

Alliance of Arizona Nonprofits
(www.arizonanonprofits.org)

Arkansas Coalition for Excellence
(www.acenonprofit.org)

California Association of Nonprofits
(www.canonprofits.org)

Center for Non-Profit Corporations (New Jersey)
(www.njnonprofits.org)

Colorado Nonprofit Association
(www.coloradononprofits.org)

Connecticut Association of Nonprofits
(www.ctnonprofits.org)

Delaware Association of Nonprofit Agencies
(www.delawarenonprofit.org)

Donors Forum
(www.donorsforum.org)

Hawai'i Alliance of Nonprofit Organizations
(www.hano-hawaii.org)

Idaho Nonprofit Center
(www.idahononprofits.org)

Iowa Nonprofit Resource Center
(nonprofit.law.uiowa.edu)

Louisiana Association of Nonprofit Organizations
(www.lano.org)

Maine Association of Nonprofits
(www.nonprofitmaine.org)

Maryland Association of Nonprofit Organizations
(www.marylandnonprofits.org)

Massachusetts Council of Human Service Providers
(www.providers.org)

Michigan Nonprofit Association
(www.mnaonline.org)

Minnesota Council of Nonprofits
(www.mncn.org)

Mississippi Center for Nonprofits
(www.msnonprofits.org)

Montana Nonprofit Association
(www.mtnonprofit.org)

New Hampshire Center for Nonprofits
(www.nhnonprofits.org)

New York Council of Nonprofits
(www.nycon.org)

Nonprofit Association of Oregon
(www.nonprofitoregon.org)

Nonprofit Association of the Midlands
(www.nonprofitam.org)

Nonprofit Coordinating Committee of New York
(www.npccny.org)

Nonprofit Leadership Initiative
(www.kynonprofits.org)

Nonprofit Resource Center of Alabama
(www.nrca.info)

North Carolina Center for Nonprofits
(www.ncnonprofits.org)

North Dakota Association of Nonprofit Organizations
(www.ndano.org)

Northwest Nonprofit Resources
(www.nnr.org)

Oklahoma Center for Nonprofits
(www.oklahomacenterfornonprofits.org)

Pennsylvania Association of Nonprofit Organizations
(www.pano.org)

South Carolina Association of Nonprofit Organizations
(www.scanpo.org)

Texas Association of Nonprofit Organizations
(www.tano.org)

Utah Nonprofits Association
(www.utahnonprofits.org)

Virginia Network of Nonprofit Organizations
(www.vanno.org)

Wisconsin Nonprofits Association
(www.wisconsinnonprofits.org)

Grantmaking Foundations: National Organizations and Resources

Association of Small Foundations (http://www.smallfoundations.org)

The Association of Small Foundations (ASF) serves the needs of foundations and grantmaking organizations with few or no staff. As a membership organization, the association provides its constituents with targeted resources, trainings, peer-learning opportunities, and ongoing support. With over 3,000 foundation members, they are currently the largest foundation-support organization in the country.

Council on Foundations (http://www.cof.org)

The Council on Foundations (COF) is a national nonprofit association comprised of grantmaking foundations and corporations. COF provides its members with services, publications, and resources related to all aspects of foundation management on a national and international level. The council operates on principles of stewardship, accountability, transparency, diversity and inclusiveness, governance, and respect.

Dorothy A. Johnson Center for Philanthropy at Grand Valley State University (http://www.gvsu.edu/jcp/)

The Dorothy A. Johnson Center for Philanthropy at Grand Valley State University (GVSU) (JCP) is a university-based academic center on philanthropy with programs in undergraduate and graduate education in nonprofit leadership, nonprofit professional development, applied social research and mapping, and professional resources for grantmakers. The professional grantmaker resources include the Grantmaking School (a series of professional development workshops), the Foundation Review (a national peer-reviewed journal for grantmakers), and the Frey Chair in Family Foundations and Philanthropy.

Forum of Regional Association of Grantmakers (http://www.givingforum.org/s_forum/index.asp)

The Forum of Regional Association of Grantmakers is a national network of regional associations from across the United States. The forum provides support and resources to regional associations of grantmakers to ensure that they fulfill their missions and promote their growth and effectiveness. Additionally, the forum provides training and workshops for its members, as well as identifying giving trends in the sector.

Foundation Center (http://foundationcenter.org)

The Foundation Center was founded in 1956 and is a leading authority in the philanthropic and nonprofit sector. Its audiences include grant seekers, grantmakers, researchers, policymakers, the media, and the general public. The center maintains a comprehensive database on U.S. grantmaking organizations and their grants; issues a wide variety of print, electronic, and online information resources; conducts and publishes research on trends in foundation growth, giving, and practice; and offers an array of training and educational programs.

GrantCraft (http://www.grantcraft.org)

A project of the Ford Foundation, GrantCraft has been providing grantmakers with resources and publications since 2001. Drawing on the expertise, opinions, and experiences of hundreds of grantmakers, GrantCraft has developed a series of materials around topics such as evaluation, equity and social change, personal strategy, and much more. GrantCraft resources are available as online downloads, printed guides, videos, and workshops.

Grantmakers for Effective Organizations (http://www.geofunders.org)

Grantmakers for Effective Organizations (GEO) promotes grantmaking practices that help to build stronger nonprofits and improve results. Based in Washington, D.C., this membership-based coalition of over 350 grantmakers provides resources, publications, professional development opportunities, and a biennial national conference. GEO's priorities include learning strategies, leadership development, financial sustainability, and stakeholder engagement.

Grantmaking School (http://www.grantmakingschool.org)

The Grantamaking School is the first university-based, professional development program for advanced grantmakers. Offerings include Advanced Proposal Analysis and Advanced Grant Portfolio Management courses focused on developing and improving on key skill sets in grantmaking. The Grantmaking School's courses are designed to address the complex work of foundation grantmaking professionals who are central to their organization's effectiveness. The Grantmaking School is a program of the Dorothy A. Johnson Center for Philanthropy at Grand Valley State University.

National Center for Family Philanthropy
(http://www.ncfp.org)

The mission of the National Center for Family Philanthropy is to promote philanthropic values, vision, and excellence across generations of philanthropists and their families. The center's work is based on the fundamental belief in the value of philanthropy and the ongoing participation of the donor and the donor's family. The National Center was founded in response to the need for a full-time national resource dedicated to serving the needs of families in philanthropy. The center's staff has expertise in governance, grantmaking, planning, evaluation, and more.

Grantmaking Foundations: State and Regional Associations

Arizona Grantmakers Forum
(http://www.azgrantmakers.org)

Associated Grant Makers
(http://www.agmconnect.org)

Association of Baltimore Area Grantmakers
(http://www.abagmd.org)

Colorado Association of Funders
(http://www.coloradofunders.org)

Conference of Southwest Foundations
(http://www.c-s-f.org)

Connecticut Council for Philanthropy
(http://www.ctphilanthropy.org)

Council of Michigan Foundations
(http://www.michiganfoundations.org)

Council of New Jersey Grantmakers
(http://www.cnjg.org)

Delaware Valley Grantmakers
(http://www.dvg.org)

Donors Forum
(http://www.donorsforum.org)

Donors Forum of South Florida
(http://www.donorsforumsf.org)

Donors Forum of Wisconsin
(http://www.dfwonline.org)

Florida Philanthropic Network
(http://www.fpnetwork.org)

Grantmakers Forum of New York—Rochester
(http://www.grantmakers.org)

Grantmakers of Oregon and Southwest Washington
(http://www.gosw.org)

Grantmakers of Western Pennsylvania
(http://www.gwpa.org)

Indiana Grantmakers Alliance
(http://www.indianagrantmakers.org)

Iowa Council of Foundations
(http://www.iowacounciloffoundations.org)

Maine Philanthropy Center
(http://www.mainephilanthropy.org)

Minnesota Council on Foundations
(http://www.mcf.org)

New Mexico Association of Grantmakers
(http://www.nmag.org)

Northern California Grantmakers
(http://www.ncg.org)

Ohio Grantmakers Forum
(http://www.ohiograntmakers.org)

Philanthropy New York—New York City
(http://www.philanthropynewyork.org)

Philanthropy Northwest
(http://www.philanthropynw.org)

San Diego Grantmakers
(http://www.sdgrantmakers.org)

Southeastern Council on Foundations
(http://www.secf.org)

Southern California Grantmakers
(http://www.socalgrantmakers.org)

Washington Regional Association of Grantmakers
(http://www.washingtongrantmakers.org)

Western New York Grantmakers Association—Buffalo
(http://www.wnygrantmakers.org)

Council on Foundations: Grantmaker Affinity Groups

Africa Grantmakers' Affinity Group
Phone: 540–878–5015
Fax: 540–347–3405
http://www.africagrantmakers.org
info@africagrantmakers.org

Asian Americans/Pacific Islanders in Philanthropy
Phone: 415–273–2760
Fax: 415–273–2765
http://www.aapip.org
aapip@aapip.org

Association of Black Foundation Executives
Phone: 646–230–0306
Fax: 212–747–9320
http://www.abfe.org
stoomer@abfe.org

CFLeads (Community Foundations Leading Change)
Phone: 800–292–6149
Fax: 816–468–1698
http://www.cfleads.org
martha@cfleads.org

Communications Network
Phone: 630–328–2857
Fax: 917–677–4769
http://www.comnetwork.org
info@comnetwork.org

Consortium of Foundation Libraries (CFL)
Phone: 317–278–2329
http://www.foundationlibraries.org/
bburk@iupui.edu

Disabilities Funders Network
Phone: 703–795–9646
Fax: 804–794–7852
http://www.disabilityfunders.org
khutchinson@disabilityfunders.org

Environmental Grantmakers Association
Phone: 646–747–2655
Fax: 646–747–2656
http://www.ega.org
ega@ega.org

Funders' Committee for Civic Participation
Phone: 503–724–2922
http://www.funderscommittee.org
dross@publicinterestprojects.org

Funders Concerned About AIDS
Phone: 718–875–0251
http://www.fcaaids.org
info@fcaaids.org

Funders for Lesbian and Gay Issues
Phone: 212–475–2930
Fax: 212–475–2532
http://www.lgbtfunders.org
info@lgbtfunders.org

Funders' Network for Smart Growth and Livable Communities
Phone: 305–667–6350
Fax: 305–667–6355
http://www.fundersnetwork.org
info@fundersnetwork.org

Funders Network on Population, Reproductive Health & Rights
Phone: 301–294–4157
Fax: 301–294–4158
http://www.fundersnet.org
info@fundersnet.org

Funders Together to End Homelessness
Phone: 617–236–2244
http://www.funderstogether.org
jason@melvilletrust.org

Grantmakers Concerned With Immigrants and Refugees
Phone: 707–824–4374
http://www.gcir.org
info@gcir.org

Grantmakers for Children, Youth & Families
Phone: 301–589–4293
Fax: 301–589–4289
http://www.gcyf.org
info@gcyf.org

Grantmakers for Education
Phone: 503–595–2100
Fax: 503–595–2102
http://www.edfunders.org
information@edfunders.org

Grantmakers in Aging
Phone: 937–435–3156
Fax: 937–435–3733
http://www.giaging.org
cfarquhar@giaging.org

Grantmakers in Film + Electronic Media
Phone: 410–675–4024
http://www.gfem.org
info@gfem.org

Grantmakers in Health
Phone: 202–452–8331
Fax: 202–452–8340
http://www.gih.org
info@gih.org

Grantmakers in the Arts
Phone: 206–624–2312
Fax: 206–624–5568
http://www.giarts.org
gia@giarts.org

Grants Managers Network
Phone: 202–329–7670
Fax: 504–837–4274
http://www.gmnetwork.org
info@gmnetwork.org

Grassroots Grantmakers
Phone: 361–798–1808
http://www.grassrootsgrantmakers.org
info@grassrootsgrantmakers.org

Hispanics in Philanthropy
Phone: 415–837–0427
Fax: 415–837–1074
http://www.hiponline.org
info@hiponline.org

International Funders for Indigenous People
Phone: 518–358–9500
Fax: 518–358–9544
http://www.internationalfunders.org
ifip@internationalfunders.org

International Human Rights Funders Group
Phone: 212–609–2631
Fax: 212–609–2633
http://www.ihrfg.org
info@ihrfg.org

Jewish Funders Network
Phone: 212–726–0177
Fax: 212–594–4292
http://www.jfunders.org
jfn@jfunders.org

Native Americans in Philanthropy
Phone: 612–724–8798
Fax: 612–879–0613
http://www.nativephilanthropy.org
info@nativephilanthropy.org

Neighborhood Funders Group
Phone: 202–833–4690
Fax: 202–833–4694
http://www.nfg.org
nfg@nfg.org

Peace and Security Funders Group
Phone: 434–989–1514
http://www.peaceandsecurity.org/
kmagraw@peaceandsecurity.org

Philanthropy for Active Civic Engagement
Phone: 303–765–3411
http://www.pacefunders.org/
cgates@pacefunders.org

Technology Affinity Group
Phone: 610–688–6832
http://www.tagtech.org
info@tagtech.org

Women's Funding Network
Phone: 415–441–0706
Fax: 415–441–0827
http://www.wfnet.org
info@wfnet.org

Nonprofit Academic Centers Council (http://www.nacccouncil.org)

"The Nonprofit Academic Centers Council is a membership association comprised of academic centers or programs at accredited colleges and universities that focus on the study of nonprofit organizations, voluntarism and/or philanthropy. Established in 1991, NACC is the first group entirely dedicated to the promotion and networking of centers that provide research and education in philanthropy and the nonprofit sector" (NACC website).

Available on the website are the *Curricular Guidelines for Graduate and Undergraduate Study in Nonprofit Leadership, the Nonprofit Sector and Philanthropy.* Also available is *Indicators of Quality in Nonprofit Academic Centers.* The public portion of the site also lists the member academic centers with links to their home pages.

University Nonprofit Academic Centers

Arizona State University, ASU Lodestar Center for Philanthropy and Nonprofit Innovation

Baruch College, City University of New York, Center for Nonprofit Strategy and Management

Boston College, Center on Wealth and Philanthropy

Case Western Reserve University, Mandel Center for Nonprofit Organizations

DePaul University, School of Public Service

George Mason University, Nonprofit Management Studies

Georgetown University, Center for Public and Nonprofit Leadership—Georgetown Public Policy Institute

Georgia State University, Nonprofit Studies Program—Andrew Young School of Public Policy Studies

Grand Valley State University, Dorothy A. Johnson Center for Philanthropy

Harvard University, Hauser Center for Nonprofit Organizations

Indiana University, The Center on Philanthropy at Indiana University

Johns Hopkins University, Center for Civil Society Studies

Louisiana State University—Shreveport, Institute for Human Services and Public Policy—College of Liberal Arts

New School, Graduate Management Programs—Nonprofit Management Program

New York University, Public and Nonprofit Management & Policy Program—Robert F. Wagner Graduate School of Public Service

New York University School of Law, National Center on Philanthropy and the Law

North Park University, Axelson Center for Nonprofit Management

Northwestern University, Center for Nonprofit Management—Kellogg School of Management

Portland State University, Institute for Nonprofit Management, Mark O. Hatfield School of Government

Regis University, Nonprofit Management Program

Seattle University, Center for Nonprofit and Social Enterprise Management

Seton Hall University, Center for Public Service

Texas A&M University, Program in Nonprofit Management—Bush School of Government and Public Service

University at Albany-SUNY, Center for Women in Government & Civil Society—Rockefeller College of Public Affairs and Policy

University of California-Berkeley, Center for Nonprofit and Public Leadership

University of California-Los Angeles, Center for Civil Society

University of Delaware, Center for Community Research & Service

University of Michigan, Nonprofit and Public Management Center, School of Social Work

University of Minnesota, The Public and Nonprofit Leadership Center, Humphrey Institute of Public Affairs

University of Missouri-Kansas City, Midwest Center for Nonprofit Leadership—Henry W. Bloch School of Business and Public Administration

University of Missouri-St. Louis, Nonprofit Management and Leadership Program

University of Pennsylvania, Center for Community Partnerships—Penn Program for Public Service

University of San Diego, Institute for Nonprofit Education and Research

University of San Francisco, Institute for Nonprofit Organization Management

University of Southern California, Center on Philanthropy and Public Policy

University of Texas at Austin, RGK Center for Philanthropy and Community Service

University of Washington, Nancy Bell Evans Center on Nonprofits and Philanthropy

University of Wisconsin-Milwaukee, Helen Bader Institute for Nonprofit Management

Virginia Tech, Institute for Policy and Governance

Australia

Queensland University of Technology, Centre of Philanthropy and Nonprofit Studies

Canada

Mount Royal College, Institute for Nonprofit Studies

York University, Nonprofit Management & Leadership Program—Schulich School of Business

London, England

City University London, Centre for Charity Effectiveness—Cass School of Business

Virgin Islands

University of St. Thomas, Center for Nonprofit Management

University Students: Nonprofit and Philanthropic Websites

American Humanics (http://www.humanics.org/ site/?c=omL2KiN4LvH&b=1098773)

American Humanics is a national academic program designed to prepare students for entry-level professional positions in nonprofit organizations. The certificate that the student receives is awarded by American Humanics, Inc., a national organization of over 70 collaborating universities and national nonprofit organizations. On this website, you will find current information on their national nonprofit and affiliated academic partners and student information. From the main page, you can link to subsections including the NextGen scholarship program, the Management Institute, the listing of affiliated campus programs, and the listing of academic campus directors.

AmeriCorps/VISTA (http://www.americorps.gov)

See Federal Support for Volunteer Service.

Campus Compact (http://www.compact.org)

Campus Compact is a national coalition of over a 1,000 college and university presidents. The main intent of the organization is to use school heads to promote public and community service by incorporating community-based learning into college curricula. The website provides many faculty and student resources that help facilitate implementation and ensure successful relationship ties with local communities. Campus Compact also supports affiliated groups on university campuses to further their work at the state level. State Campus Compacts work with colleges and universities in their states to promote community service and community-based learning among students.

Emerging Practitioners in Philanthropy (http://www.epip.org/index.php)

Emerging Practitioners in Philanthropy (EPIP) strives to strengthen the next generation of grantmakers, with an emphasis in advancing social justice philanthropy. EPIP members primarily consist of foundation staff and trustees, donors, philanthropic support organizations, and graduate students in philanthropy under the age of 40. The organization provides opportunities for its members through networking, leadership, and advocacy programs. EPIP has chapters in the San Francisco Bay Area, Boston, Indiana, Los Angeles, Michigan, Minnesota, New York, Philadelphia, Seattle, and Washington, D.C. and is a recognized affinity group of the Council on Foundations.

Idealist (http://www.idealist.org/en/resources.html)

Idealist.org not only offers a fast and easy way to locate volunteer and employment opportunities, but it also offers a variety of resources for individuals, nonprofit organizations, and government agencies. The site offers information on various topics ranging from volunteer management to planning and assessing programs to human resource management. Individuals interested in learning more about the nonprofit sector, how to obtain

a graduate degree, and transitioning mid-career will also find this website useful. It also provides tips and advice on volunteering internationally. Additionally, it answers questions about nonprofit organizations and connects people around the world through their interactive capabilities. Idealist is a unique website that offers opportunities for individuals and organizations to become better versions of themselves through the various resources, advice, and materials that they offer.

Peace Corps (http://www.peacecorps.gov)

See Federal Support for Volunteer Service.

Young Nonprofit Professionals Network (http://www.ynpn.org/s/936/start.aspx)

The Young Nonprofit Professionals Network is dedicated to helping young nonprofit professionals gain entrance into, and be successful within, the nonprofit sector. YNPN aims to fulfill its mission of promoting an efficient, viable, and inclusive nonprofit sector through strengthening career support and professional development, advocating on behalf of young professionals, and by building organizational capacity. Its website features more information about getting involved in YNPN, as well as resources on the sector's best practices.

Federal Support for Volunteer Service

AmeriCorps/VISTA (http://www.americorps.gov)

AmeriCorps VISTA is the national service program designed specifically to fight poverty. It was founded as Volunteers in Service to America in 1965 and incorporated into the AmeriCorps network of programs in 1993. VISTA has been on the front lines in the fight against poverty in America for more than 40 years helping to establish important programs such as Head Start, Upward Bound, and the American system of credit unions. The VISTA website includes state-specific information about how to get involved, as well as information about other AmeriCorps programs. VISTA is a program of the Corporation for National and Community Service, a federal agency created to connect Americans of all ages and backgrounds with opportunities to give back to their communities and their nation.

Corporation for National and Community Service (http://www.nationalservice.org)

The Corporation for National and Community Service is the federal umbrella for a large number of volunteer and service programs supported with government funding.

These include AmeriCorps; Learn & Serve America; VISTA; older Americans' programs, such as ACTION, RSVP, Foster Grandparents, and Senior Companion. Information is also available from 1201 New York Avenue, NW, Washington, DC 20525. Tel: (202) 606–5000. TTY: (202) 606–3472. Email: info@cns.gov

Peace Corps (http://www.peacecorps.gov)

Originally established in 1960 under President John F. Kennedy, the Peace Corps challenges everyday Americans to serve their country in the cause of peace by living and working in developing countries. Since that time, Peace Corps has had over 200,000 Peace Corps volunteers serve in 139 host countries across the globe. The website includes information about the Peace Corps, its history and current operations, instructions for applying, and resources for Peace Corps members and their families.

Points of Light Institute (http://www.pointsoflight.org)

In 2007, the Points of Light Foundation and the HandsOn Network merged to become the Points of Light Institute, an organization supporting the work of volunteerism and community and civic engagement across the nation. On the website, you will find information about its major programs including the HandsOn Network, MissionFish, and The Civic Incubator. The site also includes information about how to get involved, access to its blog, service-related media, and other resources for Americans who want to be more civically engaged.

Senior Corps (http://www.seniorcorps.gov)

Along with programs of interest to college students, the Corporation for National and Community Service offers support to older Americans. New nonprofit leaders may want to tap into these resources. Senior Corps is a national service program specifically designed for Americans over 55 with a lifetime of experience to share and the desire to make a real difference in their world. Senior Corps connects its members with people and organizations that need them most. Senior Corps members serve as mentors, coaches, or companions to people in need, or contribute their job skills and expertise to community projects and organizations. The Senior Corps website includes information about how to become involved as a Senior Corps member, history and background about the program, information for local nonprofit organizations who want Senior Corps members as part of their working staff, as well as information on other national service programs.

APPENDIX D

Civic Ideals and the Giving Society

Connecting Social Studies and
Philanthropy for Grades 9–12

Project Director

Joseph P. Stoltman

Learning to Give Director

Kathryn A. Agard

Project Coordinators

Barbara Dillbeck
Rita Higgins

Editors

Diane Cottrell
Jennifer Matteson
Evelyn Nash

CONTENTS

Introduction to Philanthropy

Joseph P. Stoltman

People often ask questions when they begin a journey. What will I see? Who will I visit? What should I pack? How will we travel? Those questions help us to prepare for new and different things.

People also ask questions when they discover new ideas in their lives. Is it a good idea? What makes it good for me? Is it good for other people? Is it good for my future and the future of others?

In this book you will take a journey of discovery about philanthropy, an old idea, but new to many people. It is one of those ideas that people ask questions about. In this book, you will learn about how philanthropy works. You will have the chance to look at philanthropy in several different ways. You will look at the history, geography, and economics of philanthropy, as well as philanthropy's role in democracy.

What Is Philanthropy?

But first, what is philanthropy? Figure D.1 helps to answer that question. The definition of *philanthropy* is: *giving, serving, and private citizen action intended for the common good.* The common good (also called the public good) refers to the improved condition of society in general. For example, a society that is able to improve the care and education of children has improved its general condition. A society that is able to provide adequate housing for its people has improved its general condition. Improving the conditions that make up the common good is philanthropy's goal.

What kinds of activities does philanthropy include? The three columns of Figure D.1 address this question. Listed are the three general activities, with specific examples, included in philanthropy: giving money, giving goods, or giving service. For example, giving service could involve repairing someone's home or serving as a monitor in a five-mile walk to raise funds to aid cancer patients. It might involve a person using their special skills as a doctor, carpenter, or teacher, to help others. Giving involves individuals and organizations.

Figure D.1: What Is Philanthropy?

Look at some of the specific volunteer actions shown in the first column. How do these actions help promote the public good? Let's consider two examples. People volunteer to deliver "meals on wheels" to elderly people. This act of service helps the common good by making certain that the elderly have proper and adequate diets. Student organizations volunteer to plant flowers on the school grounds. Flowers growing at school make the school grounds look nice, and people enjoy viewing them. Students take pride in their school. The more attractive school grounds improve the common good.

Philanthropy begins when a person or group of people recognize a need. If a person is ill, then people may join together to help that person. If a new community center needs to be constructed, people may volunteer to work together to build and equip it. If a family loses their home to fire, then people may help them repair and refurnish items that were lost in the fire. Each is an act of philanthropy.

Who Participates in Philanthropy?

Individuals have been giving for the common good for a very long time. Giving is evident across the ages and among all cultural groups. Individuals living at different

Giving *SERVICE*	Giving *GOODS*	Giving *MONEY*
Specific examples of giving service	Specific examples of giving goods	Specific examples of giving money
Reading to children	Donating food to a food drive	Giving money to the fund for new books at the local library
Delivering meals to elderly people	Giving good, used items to a charity	Pledging to a telethon raising money for medical research
Tutoring immigrants learning English	Giving needed food and other items for a family in need	Donating to organizations doing disaster relief
Helping at an animal shelter	Donating medical supplies after a natural disaster	"Adopting" a child through an organization that helps children in developing countries
Planting flowers on the school grounds	Giving computers to a school	Donating money for a new building on a university or college campus
Helping build affordable housing		

Figure D.1 Philanthropy Is Giving, Serving, and Private Citizen Action Intended for the Common Good

times in history have participated in philanthropy. People who volunteer to improve the common good live in many different places. They usually do not know one another. They have different types of jobs or careers. However, all of them are connected by the shared commitment to voluntary giving. They believe in giving to others.

People around the world give to assist others. They give special types of skills, from cooking and reading to helping inspire others to succeed in their lives. They sometimes give money, but often they volunteer their time and talents. In each case, they are people who help people so that their community, region, and world become better places. They believe that society is improved when people give to help one another.

Who are some of those people who have volunteered for the public good? Sarah Jones is a high school student who volunteers at a community center. She helps children learn to express their feelings through art. Benjamin Franklin gave money to begin a technical school in Boston. The city and its people greatly benefited from this gift. Matel Dawson worked hard and saved money during his life. He left his money for scholarships that would help high school graduates attend a university. Sojourner Truth devoted her life to helping African Americans escape to freedom before the Civil War. After the Civil War, she fought for civil rights for African Americans.

Jackie Joyner-Kersee is one of the world's greatest athletes. She uses her fame and skills to help others improve their lives. Eleanor Roosevelt gave time and money to improve the lives of people in many parts of the world. As First Lady, she was able to encourage many others to give. Russell Mawby became President of the W. K. Kellogg Foundation. The founder of the breakfast cereal company started the Foundation, which has many resources to use to help others. Dr. Mawby was responsible for helping make wise choices for philanthropy.

What Needs Do Volunteers Meet?

Millions of people across the world volunteer to help others. They may volunteer as part of a group. They may volunteer for individual tasks. They may volunteer in their community. They may volunteer to work in other parts of the country or the world. Each believes there is a need for their volunteer giving. None expect to receive payment for their work. What are some of the needs they observe that encourage people to take action to improve the public good? Here are several examples.

Giving to improve the common good often begins in the community where a person lives. Communities are where people spend most of their time. Communities may also include diverse populations. They may have buildings that were once new, but have aged and need repairs. Often community groups volunteer to help repair a house. It will then look better from the outside, and provide a better home for the people who live there.

People also volunteer their time across the United States. Nationwide programs connect people with specific needs to people and organizations that have resources. When a natural disaster, such as a hurricane, tornado, or earthquake occurs, volunteers respond. They help people recover from the damage. The help may be in the form of money, food, or time spent rebuilding damaged homes and buildings. People of all ages will assist in the clean up and rebuilding.

Philanthropy reaches great distances. For example, students in the United States participate in money-raising activities. They may include school programs, trips, and other special school events. Those same students may also partner with a community and its school in another part of the world. They collect money, books, and other goods and donate them to meet the needs in another school. They are taking action to improve the common good by helping that faraway community improve its school. Sometimes there is no school, and students have to attend class without desks or other materials. Philanthropy may provide a means for the students in those places to have a school. Donating time, money, and special skills may play a big part to improve the common good for students and their community.

Philanthropy is a way to improve the common good. Recognizing the need is the first, very important step.

Providing the volunteer giving to meet the need is the next big step.

How Will We Learn More About Philanthropy?

Using this book, you will be taking the perspective of several subjects that you study in school. They are civics, geography, history, and economics. Each of those subjects brings a special point of view to philanthropy. Each demonstrates how individuals can participate in philanthropy. Each provides some examples of how we might include giving in our everyday lives. Each provides an example of how philanthropy extends from the decisions we make in our local communities to the rest of the United States and to the world.

Philanthropy is similar to a journey. As the journey unfolds, you will observe the needs of people and communities. You will also develop ideas about how to meet those needs. You can apply those ideas now as well as later in your life as you participate in philanthropy.

1. PHILANTHROPY, CIVIL SOCIETY, AND DEMOCRACY IN AMERICA

JOHN J. PATRICK

After America was attacked, it was as if our entire country looked into a mirror and saw our better selves. We were reminded that we are citizens, with obligations to each other, to our country, and to history. We began to think less of the goods we can accumulate and more about the good we can do. . . . In the sacrifice of soldiers, the fierce brotherhood of firefighters, and the bravery and generosity of ordinary citizens, we have glimpsed what a new culture of responsibility could look like. We want to be a nation that serves goals larger than self. We have been offered a unique opportunity, and we must not let this moment pass.

In his 2002 State of the Union Address, President George W. Bush praised Americans for their charitable behavior following the terrorist attack against the United States on September 11, 2001. Like leaders throughout history, the President recognized philanthropy as civic duty.

Philanthropy includes three types of charitable behavior: giving money; donating goods, such as food, clothing, shelter, and blood; and giving time, such as volunteering to help others. In response to the tragedy of 9/11/01, Americans donated huge amounts of money, time, and services. The emotion-packed response involved people, concerned about helping others. It involved taking action for the common good. On a daily basis, Americans give in many ways to help others.

Americans give as a way of taking action for the common good. They support relief during natural disasters, carry out community projects, and help meet individuals' needs. Philanthropy has greatly contributed to a healthy democracy in America, and it continues to do so.

This chapter examines the important relationship between philanthropy and civil society. It includes the topics of (a) philanthropy and civil society within American democracy; (b) trends and patterns of philanthropy and civil society in American democracy; (c) promising programs and practices for strengthening connections

between philanthropy, civil society, and democracy, and (d) reflections on education for philanthropy, civil society, and democracy in America.

Philanthropy and Civil Society Within American Democracy

Philanthropy—giving, serving, and private citizen action intended for the common good—is strongly related to the traditional American understanding of democracy. What is that relationship? Before answering this question, let's explore American democracy.

In America there is a simple way to judge whether people practice democracy. That is, do the people regularly select their representatives in government in free, fair, open, and contested elections? If they do, then government is by the consent of the governed, and the people's representatives are accountable to them. Government in the United States, the world's oldest existing democracy, has more and more fit this definition throughout its history.

Yet a full democracy does more than meet this minimal standard. It also provides constitutional guarantees for the rights that are enjoyed equally by all individuals. Such a

John J. Patrick is Professor of Education and Director of the Social Studies Development Center at Indiana University.

democracy has, in the words of Abraham Lincoln, "government of the people, by the people, for the people."

This democratic government both gets its power from and is limited by the Constitution. The Constitution protects people's rights to think, speak, and assemble with others. It protects their rights to influence the policies and actions of government. It provides the rights needed to act for the common good of the community. Yet it also protects the rights of a minority of persons who disagree with the policies and actions of the majority.

Is democracy practiced perfectly in America? Perhaps not, but it does fit James Madison's observation, "No government of human device and human administration can be perfect. . . . That which is the least imperfect is therefore the best government."

The long success of constitutional democracy in America is the result of reasonable decisions and actions by citizens. Citizens make decisions and take action on elections, public policy issues, and serious social problems. Citizens must balance their own private interests, as well as public interests, for democracy to thrive. The freely made choices of citizens in a democracy start civic virtue in motion. *Civic virtue* requires putting the common good of the community ahead of immediate, personal concerns.

What does civic virtue look like? For a high school student, practicing civic virtue might mean volunteering at a local day care center rather than hanging out with friends after school. It might also mean trying to change an attendance policy that is unpopular but will, in your opinion, be better for your school. Or it might mean donating your hard-earned savings to a food bank rather than spending it on a new pair of shoes.

At its best, being a virtuous citizen in a democracy involves philanthropy. Philanthropy includes voluntary service, where citizens give freely to promote the well-being of people and the community. A huge financial donation by wealthy persons is a characteristic of philanthropy in the United States. But most philanthropy involves small-scale civic giving by ordinary people through regular participation in civil society.

Civil society is the network of voluntary groups that act on their own or as partners with state agencies. This independent sector is not part of the government and must obey the laws. The independent sector, created and operated by private individuals, is an important part of civil society. Examples of organizations that are a part of civil society are labor unions, faith-based groups, human-rights groups, environmental-protection organizations, support groups providing social welfare services to needy people, independent newspaper and magazine publishers, independent and private schools, community service clubs, and professional associations. A person may belong to many independent sector organizations during a lifetime. Americans, for example, have a long tradition of numerous memberships in voluntary, nongovernmental organizations.

Participating in charitable nongovernmental organizations opens up opportunities for philanthropy. In America, citizens who participate in the groups that are part of civil society are much more likely to give time, goods, and money to worthy causes than those who are not.

Citizen participation in civil society builds social capital. *Social capital* is the ability of people to act together to meet community needs, solve public problems, and improve community life. The information network that brings a group of volunteers together to perform a community service is an example of social capital. Without the network, the service work might never occur. The network owns no buildings or equipment, but has value because it helps people to organize and do the work.

In doing philanthropic work, people need civic skills. They include the skills to organize others, become informed, vote, petition, discuss, write persuasive letters, and identify goals that are possible to achieve. Those skills are critical to social capital.

Social capital provides benefits in many ways. It results in improved neighborhoods, better schools, and services to people in need. Social capital benefits government as well. Civic participation by citizens makes government officials accountable. Citizens become responsible for activities, such as a community food bank, and government is able to focus on other community needs. Giving money, services, and time to the community adds to the common good for all citizens.

Philanthropy by citizens for the common good is a key element of a vibrant civil society. Without it, the chance of building and maintaining democracy and freedom are not good. By contrast, in totalitarian or despotic systems, citizens depend upon the government to solve all social and economic problems. Philanthropy is largely missing; if practiced, it must be hidden from governmental officials.

In contrast, constitutional democracy enables the people to protect individual rights to speech, assembly, and association. Those rights are necessary for philanthropy to be useful. Thus, a constitution protects civil society by guaranteeing the rights of individuals to join and operate nongovernmental or private sector organizations.

Democracy in America also receives bottom-up ("grassroots") support from community nongovernmental organizations acting for the public good. Civil society organizations are public guardians through which citizens take responsibility for their rights and hold public officials responsible. Through participation in organizational activities, members also acquire the knowledge, skills, and virtues that keep philanthropy and democracy going. Thus, community-based, independent sector organizations are places where citizens learn how to practice philanthropy and democracy in America.

Trends and Patterns of Philanthropy and Civil Society in American Democracy

Imagine traveling through another country noticing how its citizens participate in civil society. Then imagine that your observations are read and reread for nearly 200 years because they provided such thoughtful insights on civil society and government. This may seem far-fetched, but that is how the observations of Alexis de Tocqueville, a French visitor to the United States, have been seen since the 1830s. Tocqueville observed and praised Americans' philanthropic and democratic participation in civil society organizations, in his book *Democracy in America.*

Tocqueville saw civil society as the collection of voluntary groups of citizens that assisted individuals in interactions with their government. He saw that this network of groups cooperated among themselves to achieve worthy public purposes. He emphasized the public good achieved by people acting together in a lawful and civic manner in voluntary, community-based organizations. Americans, he believed, showed the world how to make democracy work for both the community and the individual through the interactions of civil society and government.

Tocqueville noted the fundamental place of philanthropy in American life through the voluntary associations. In 1831–1832, he observed,

Americans of all ages, all conditions, and all dispositions constantly form associations. They have not only commercial and manufacturing companies in which all take part, but associations of a thousand other kinds, religious, moral, serious, futile, general or restricted, enormous or diminutive. The Americans make associations to give entertainments, to found seminaries, to build inns, to construct churches, to diffuse books, to send missionaries to the antipodes; in this manner they found hospitals, prisons, and schools. If it is proposed to inculcate some truths or to foster some example, they form a society. Wherever at the head of some new undertaking you see the government of

France, or a man of rank in England, in the United States you will be sure to find an association.

According to Alexis de Tocqueville, citizens in the American democracy readily used their constitutionally protected rights to participate in and contribute to the political and civic life of the community. He called this "self-interest rightly understood." It was through freely made, voluntary contributions to the good of the community that citizens helped one another to maintain the public well-being needed to pursue personal and private interests. Tocqueville wrote, "The principle of self-interest rightly understood is not a lofty one, but it is clear and sure.... Each American knows when to sacrifice some of his private interests to save the rest."

According to Tocqueville, the success of American democracy was due to the "enlightened self-interest" of citizens who regularly and freely contributed to the common good.

Civic giving certainly has been a long-time tradition in America. Throughout the 19th, 20th, and 21st centuries, philanthropy was much greater in America than in any other country. In recent years, more than two thirds of households in the United States annually made financial contributions for the welfare of their community; the average contribution in 2009 was $2,000. Types of contributions and percentages of households contributing to them are shown in Figure D.2.

More than 65 percent of adult Americans contribute voluntary service annually. The total value of this volunteered time is estimated to be $225.9 billion.

As in Tocqueville's time, philanthropy in America today is strongly related to participation in civil society. There are more than 1.4 million independent sector organizations in America, including faith-based institutions; clubs, such as Rotary International, and service organizations, such as Food Bank. More than 80 percent of the members of those organizations give to their communities each year. By contrast, fewer than 40 percent of people who do not belong to independent sector organizations give to community causes. Further, members of civil society or independent sector organizations are ten times more likely to give to community causes than nonmembers. Social capital is very strongly reflected by community service, even more so than is financial capital.

Long ago, Tocqueville noticed the connection between faith-based organizations and philanthropy. Today, persons who attend faith-based institutions regularly are more likely to give to community causes than those who do not. For example, among those who attend faith-based services regularly, 54 percent volunteer, in contrast to only 32 percent of those who do not attend regularly. Further, those who attend faith-based institutions contribute 70 percent of the hours given each month to voluntary community service. This illustrates social capital. People in social networks, such as faith-based organizations, are more likely to be asked to give.

Persons involved in faith-based organizations more often give to community causes (see Figure D.3). This supports Tocqueville's claim that the success of civil society depends upon a high level of morality among the people. So democracy in America requires civic morality.

Social Categories of Giving Category	Percentage of Giving to Particular Category
1. Arts, culture, humanities	4
2. Education	13
3. Environment/Animals	2
4. Health	7
5. Human services	9
6. International affairs	3
7. Gifts to foundations	10
8. Unallocated giving	10
9. Faith-based organizations	33
10. Public-society benefit	8
11. Foundation grants to individuals	1

Figure D.2 Households and Philanthropy, 2009

SOURCE: From *Giving USA Foundation Annual Report*, 2010, Washington, DC.

Other factors related to civic giving are education, income, and age. Persons with higher levels of education and income give more. As Figure D.4 shows, people in their middle years, 35 to 54 years of age, are more likely to volunteer through associations and be philanthropic than persons in younger or older age groups.

Although giving in America remains high compared to other countries, it has decreased during the past 40 years. Giving has declined gradually among members of both faith-based and secular organizations. Volunteer service by young Americans (18–25 years of age) is strong. Young people are more likely to volunteer, but they avoid government and political issues to a greater degree than older Americans. Yet they tended to be disinterested in politics, government, and civic affairs.

During the past ten years, civic leaders have expressed great concern about civic and political apathy in the United States, especially among young Americans. A report of the National Commission on Civic Renewal, for example, warned, "In a time that cries out for civic action, we are in danger of becoming a nation of spectators." Others have agreed that the civic condition of the United States is weaker than it was and needs to be improved. Participation of citizens in their civil society and government has steadily declined.

Robert D. Putnam's book, *Bowling Alone: The Collapse and Revival of American Community,* makes a convincing case about the decline of civic and political participation in

Age Group	Percentage of Group in Voluntary Activity
1. 18–24	22.0%
2. 25–34	23.5%
3. 35–44	31.5%
4. 45–54	30.8%
5. 55–64	28.3%
6. 65+	23.9%

Figure D.4   Relationship of Age Group to Voluntary Community Service

SOURCE: From *Bureau of Labor Statistics,* 2009, Washington, DC: U.S. Government.

the United States. Putnam concludes, "Americans are playing virtually every aspect of the civic game less frequently today than we did two decades ago."

The continuing strength of democracy in America depends upon involving citizens in both political and civic life. Community service without commitment to and participation in government is not sufficient to maintain democracy. The political alternatives to democracy, as we know it, are not likely to encourage a free and open society in which individuals join together to solve their problems. Civic engagement and philanthropy go together in a healthy democracy. What can be done to strengthen the connections of philanthropy, civil society, and democracy in 21st century America? The next section of this chapter looks at some promising ideas.

A. All Households	Giving to Religious and Secular Organizations
1. Households Giving to Faith-Based Organizations	60.6%
2. Households Giving Only to Secular Organizations	27.7%
3. Nongiving Households	11.7%
Total	100.0%

B. All Charitable Contributions	Annual Giving to All Causes by Source
1. Households Giving to Faith-Based Organizations	87.5%
2. Households Giving Only to Secular Organizations	12.5%
Total	100.0%

Figure D.3   Philanthropy and Membership in Religious Organizations

SOURCE: Adapted from *Faith and Philanthropy: The Connection Between Charitable Behavior and Giving to Religion,* by Christopher Toppe et al., 2002, p. 9, www.Independentsector.org.

Promising Approaches for Strengthening Philanthropy and Democracy in 21st-Century America

In recent years, the U.S. government has established programs for civic renewal through voluntary public service. In various public statements, Presidents William J. Clinton, George W. Bush, and Barack Obama have called upon the American people to be civically involved and philanthropically committed to community service and the common good. President Bush, for example, challenged all Americans to give at least two years or 4,000 hours, during their lifetimes, in service to others.

The federal government has several programs that promote civic involvement and community service. These programs are AmeriCorps, Senior Corps, and Learn and Serve America. The programs are run by the Corporation for National and Community Service.

AmeriCorps programs support more than 75,000 persons each year in service to meet needs in education, the environment, public safety, homeland security, and other areas of public concern. In return for a year of full-time service, AmeriCorps members receive living expenses and a $4,725 education award to help pay for post-high school education.

An example of AmeriCorps voluntary service is provided by Justin Ceniceros of Texas. He worked to restore meadows in Fairfax, Virginia; to rehabilitate and repair a broken-down neighborhood in Philadelphia, Pennsylvania; and to tutor children in Washington, D.C. Thinking about his experiences, he wrote,

> AmeriCorps gave me the initiative to do things I never thought I could do, to be the person I always wanted to be. It's made me realize that life is what you make of it. When you take responsibility and grab initiative, you can make things happen.

Senior Corps is a set of three federal programs that use the skills of Americans age 55 or older to handle community problems and needs. Older citizens volunteer from a few hours a week to nearly full time. RSVP (Retired and Senior Volunteer Program), the largest of the three Senior Corps programs, connects older volunteers to various opportunities for service in their own communities, such as delivering hot meals to others, tending neighborhood gardens, or teaching English to immigrants. The Foster Grandparent Program involves older volunteers in one-on-one work with needy children, while the Senior Companion Program provides opportunities for older volunteers to help home-bound seniors meet their daily needs. Foster Grandparents and Senior Companions volunteer 15 to 40 hours a week and receive a small stipend for their service; RSVP volunteers can serve from just a few hours a week to nearly full time, depending on their preference.

Learn and Service America supports service-learning programs in schools, universities, and communities. Opportunities are provided for more than a million young Americans to connect community service with academic learning in schools. They build feelings of responsible citizenship. Community service includes education, public safety, human welfare services, and the environment.

The three major domestic programs—AmeriCorps, Senior Corps, and Learn and Serve America—are conducted in the spirit of an older international service program, the Peace Corps. Launched by President John F. Kennedy in 1961, the Peace Corps has sent American volunteers to more than 139 countries in all parts of the world. These volunteers have served teaching children, providing health care, digging wells, working on farms, and doing many other necessary jobs that help people improve their lives.

Shortly after the September 11, 2001, terrorist attacks, President George W. Bush called upon every American to get involved in strengthening America's communities and sharing America's compassion around the world. He called on every American to dedicate at least two years over the course of their lives to the service of others. He created the USA Freedom Corps to help Americans to answer his call. As a Coordinating Council housed at the White House, USA Freedom Corps is working to strengthen our culture

of service and help find opportunities for every American to start volunteering.

While the national programs in civic involvement and service are large and well publicized, most philanthropy in the United States goes on in local communities. Organizations like the Rotary Club, Kiwanis Club, Lions Club, and the League of Women Voters are engaged. Extensive and various services are provided through faith-based organizations. The United Way provides opportunities for philanthropy in communities across the country.

Much philanthropy involves ordinary people providing service to improve their communities. The efforts of such people are described in a book titled *Local Heroes Changing America.* Photographers and interviewers for The Indivisible Project fanned out across the country to find and tell the stories of people working together to improve their communities. For example, the project reported on volunteer anticrime patrols in Delray Beach, Florida. These patrols have changed a crime-ridden and depressed community into a haven of safety, security, and prosperity. Farm workers in San Juan, Texas, founded a community association to help low-income families move from substandard housing to higher quality houses. The project's cameras also recorded the civic renewal achieved by voluntary civil associations in a rural community, Marshall, North Carolina, and in an inner-city neighborhood in Philadelphia, Pennsylvania. The common theme captured in those pictures is volunteers acting philanthropically to contribute to the common good.

School-based programs throughout the United States are important sources of community service.

More than 50 percent of the country's public and private schools provide community service opportunities for students from grades 6 through 12. In many public school districts across the nation, community service is an integral part of the curriculum. In the state of Maryland, students must perform approved community service to meet high school graduation requirements.

In many public and private schools, lessons on philanthropy and citizenship in a democracy are included in the curriculum. Some students may experience a few lessons on philanthropy while others take part in multi-lesson units or entire courses of instruction.

The Council of Michigan Foundations has produced another highly regarded philanthropy education program. The program for kindergarten through grade 12 is called *Learning to Give.* It includes lessons on the relationships between philanthropy, responsible citizenship, civil society, and democracy in America (see sample materials below). According to its program developers, *Learning to Give* is "designed to encourage young people to take positive action in their own lives, become involved in community initiatives, embrace ownership of their democratic society, and aspire to do good."

Learning to Give stresses learning by doing. Knowledge, skills, and attitudes about the connections of philanthropy, civil society, and democracy in America are taught through lessons that combine knowledge with experience of civic education.

Learning to Give: Philanthropy and You

An introductory lesson in the *Learning to Give* curriculum presents several sources, including those on the following pages, and asks students to develop a personal definition of philanthropy based on these materials. Do you think this is a good way to introduce the concept of philanthropy? How would you define the term based on these materials?

Philanthropist

A poem by Valerie Belay, *Learning to Give* Founding Teacher, 1997:

Philanthropist
Helper, giver, server, volunteer
Brother of humanity
Lover of the poor, the homeless and the sick
Who feels compelled, compassionate and driven
Who needs no thanks, flowers or tax credits
Who fears others' losses, hunger pangs and pain
Who gives time, money and service
Who would like to see an end to
Poverty, sickness, and undereducated children
Resident of my community
You

Definitions of Philanthropy

From Dr. Robert Payton, Richard Bentley, and Luana G. Nissan, Center on Philanthropy at Indiana University:

- The giving of one's time, talent, or treasure for the sake of another or for the common good.
- Voluntary action for the public good.
- Voluntary giving, voluntary service, and voluntary association primarily for the benefit of others.
- Giving and serving.
- Active efforts to promote human welfare.

Information About Philanthropy

- Philanthropy is an individual responsibility. Only 25% of America's philanthropy is from corporations and foundations. About 75% is from individuals.
- Philanthropy is practiced three ways: monetary contributions, volunteer activities, and in-kind contributions such as office space, transportation, etc.
- Major contributions of philanthropy have been in areas of benefiting others such as the women's movement, environmental movement and civil rights movement.
- Examples of nonprofit operations frequently supported by philanthropic giving are hospitals, faith-based organizations, schools, the Red Cross, and Girl Scouts.
- Philanthropy is learned behavior that has a benefit for all, can provide job skills, help build a resume, can be done at any age with any amount of money and time, and can be fun!
- No matter how little you have, you can always give—almost everyone in a civil society has given to others.

Conclusion

Civic education that stresses philanthropy is key to a strong democracy in the United States. If the United States is to have a healthy constitutional democracy in the 21st century, then young people must learn how to practice philanthropy in civil society. Students must learn what philanthropy and civil society are, why they are important in a democracy, and how they depend upon civic participation by citizens. Further, they need to increase their knowledge and skills by working successfully with others in civil associations and volunteering to improve society. Finally, students in schools must develop civic attitudes favoring philanthropy in order to maintain and improve democracy.

Education about philanthropy in civil society should not end in the 12th grade. If democracy is to be strengthened, then adults must also participate in learning about the connections between philanthropy, civil society, and democracy. Adult education for democracy is most easily and practically experienced through participation in the voluntary associations of civil society, such as labor unions, professional associations, community service clubs, and faith-based organizations.

Alexis de Tocqueville noted the importance of formal and informal education of Americans for responsible citizenship in democracy. He identified the important role of civic knowledge and skills. However, he viewed civic morality, or commitment to do what is "right and just," as the most important characteristic to be learned by citizens. Tocqueville wrote,

It cannot be doubted that in the United States the instruction of the people powerfully contributes to the support of the democratic republic; and such must always be the case, I believe, where the instruction which enlightens the understanding is not separated from the moral education which amends the heart.

Tocqueville stressed that a good constitution, good institutions of government, and good laws are necessary. However, they are not enough for a healthy democracy. Tocqueville concluded that strong moral qualities or "habits of the heart" were essential for citizens to practice philanthropy. Let us, then, resolve to revitalize and renew democratic citizenship in America through life-long civic education that stresses the morality of public action for the common good. Public action for the common good, Tocqueville's "habits of the heart," is the solid foundation for philanthropy in a free and open society that will nourish democracy and freedom in the United States.

References

Bureau of Labor Statistics. (2009). Economic News Release: Volunteering in the United States. Retrieved July 28, 2003, from www.bls.gov/news.release/volun.toc.htm

Bush, George W. (2002, January 29). State of the Union Address. Retrieved July 28, 2003, from www.whitehouse.gov/news/releases/2002/01/20020129-11.html

Bush, George W. (2002, April 19). A Proclamation by the President of the United States of America in Recognition of National Volunteer Week. Retrieved July 28, 2003, from www.whitehouse.gov/news/releases/2002/04/20020419-6.html

Center on Philanthropy at Indiana University. (2002). *The America Gives Report*. Indianapolis: Indiana University-Purdue University at Indianapolis. Retrieved July 28, 2003, from www.philanthropy.iupui.edu/AmericaGivesReport.htm

Eisenstadt, S. N. (1995). Civil society. In Seymour Martin Lipset (Ed.), *The Encyclopedia of Democracy*, Vol. 1 (pp. 240–242). Washington, DC: Congressional Quarterly, Inc.

Gibson, Cynthia, and Levine, Peter. (2003). *The Civic Mission of Schools*. New York: Carnegie Corporation.

Giving USA Foundation. (2007). Annual Report. Retrieved July 28, 2003, from www.aafrc.org

Giving and Volunteering in the United States. (2001). Washington, DC: Independent Sector. Retrieved July 28, 2003, from www.independentsector.org/programs/research.gv0l.main.html

Huntington, Samuel B. (1991). *The Third Wave: Democratization in the Late 20th Century*. Norman: University of Oklahoma Press.

Just the Facts. (Spring 2002). *For the Common Good: Notes from Learning to Give 3* (2). Retrieved July 28, 2003, from www.learningtogive.org./newsletter/newsv3n2/Common Good.pdf

Koch, Adrienne. (1961). *Powers, Morals, and the Founding Fathers*. Ithaca, NY: Cornell University Press.

Ladd, Everett Carll. (1991). *The Ladd Report*. New York: The Free Press.

Lincoln, Abraham. (1863/1992). Gettysburg Address. In Andrew Delbanco (Ed.), *The Portable Abraham Lincoln*. New York: Viking.

Member stories. Washington, DC: Americorps. Retrieved July 28, 2003, from www.americorps.org/joining/memberstories/member2.html

National Commission on Civic Renewal. (1998). *A Nation of Spectators: How Civic Disengagement Weakens America and What We Can Do About It*. College Park, MD: Institute for Philosophy and Public Policy at The University of Maryland.

The New Nonprofit Almanac and Desk Reference (2003). Washington, DC: Independent Sector. Retrieved July 28, 2003, from www.independentsector.org/media/NA01PR.html

Putnam, Robert D. (1993). *Making Democracy Work: Civic Traditions in Modern Italy*. Princeton, NJ: Princeton University Press.

Putnam, Robert D. (1995, January). Bowling alone: America's declining social capital. *Journal of Democracy 6*, 65–78.

Putnam, Robert D. (2000). *Bowling Alone: The Collapse and Revival of American Community*. New York: Simon & Schuster.

Rankin, Tom, Ed. (2000). *Local Heroes: Changing America*. New York: W. W. Norton. Retrieved July 28, 2003, from www.wwnorton.com/catalog/fall00/005028.htm

Tocqueville, Alexis de. (1835/1945). *Democracy in America*, Vol. 1 (Phillips Bradley, Ed. and Trans.). New York: Alfred A. Knopf.

Tocqueville, Alexis de. (1839/1945). *Democracy in America*, Vol. 2 (Phillips Bradley, Ed. and Trans.). New York: Alfred A. Knopf.

Toppe, Christopher, et al. (2002). *Faith and Philanthropy: The Connections Between Charitable Behavior and Giving to Religion*. Washington, DC: Independent Sector. Retrieved July 28, 2003, from www.independentsector.org/programs/research/faithphilanthropy.html

2. CIVIC AND PHILANTHROPIC ACTION ON A GLOBAL SCALE

JON VAN TIL

Philanthropy has developed into a global activity. Regions of the world that knew very little of organized giving have developed deep commitments to supporting nonprofit and philanthropic organizations. They have had to develop a national philanthropic "habit of mind." Some countries lacked a philanthropic "habit of mind" because the government wanted to provide all the necessities of living. In other countries the government did little, and nonprofit and volunteer organizations took on great influence, becoming more important than local and national government in the process. International philanthropy is an interesting balance of too much versus too little. This chapter uses several case studies to explore both the emergence and the growth of philanthropy as a *social and civic responsibility*, which is the ability and means among individuals and groups to take action in a positive manner for the common good.

Philanthropy in a Global Society

Will the civic/philanthropic sector continue to find a place in the new global society in spite of national economic issues and the emergence of the global economy? One expert who believes so is Lester Salamon, a leader in the study of international philanthropy. He says that the death of this sector has "been greatly exaggerated." Salamon claims the international philanthropic sector "remains a major presence in virtually every country of the world. Whether measured by what it does, or in more traditional economic terms, this set

of institutions is a major force in our social and economic life" (Salamon and Anheier, 1997, p. 23).

How are global changes reflected in 21st-century economics and civic forces? Paul Cantor has studied the changes and concludes:

In the face of global economic forces, individual nation[s] are increasingly compelled to allow markets to dictate their policies, rather than dictating policies to markets. . . . As economic organization progressively takes the form of globalized free markets, nation[s] begin to lose much of their reason for existence and also find the scope of their authority greatly reduced. (Cantor, 2001, p. 197)

Thus, during the 20th century attention was focused on independence for former colonies in Africa and Asia. Great efforts were made to help these governments function for their citizens and to increase their citizens' feelings of social responsibility. The 21st century began with the focus on global mega-corporations rather than national governments. National governments have often been challenged with problems of divisions in the country and cultural conflicts (Barber, 1996). Solving those conflicts and building social responsibility presents challenges to international philanthropy.

Philanthropy for a *civil society* is the work of individuals, families, corporations, and governments in every country of the world. *Civil society* is the network of voluntary groups. They act on their own or as partners with state agencies. Civil society is a public domain or independent

---

Jon Van Til is Professor of Urban Studies and Community Planning at Rutgers University, Camden, New Jersey.

sector created and operated by private individuals. In some countries, philanthropy is mainly the result of individuals giving time and resources. In other countries, large businesses and individuals are giving. Governments that encourage philanthropy also gain from it through public participation. In this chapter we look closely at two cases: Northern Ireland and Hungary. Recent experiences in these two places show us the ways in which national and global societies have changed.

Northern Ireland (1968–1998): Weak Government and Strong Civic Sector

If Americans have heard of Northern Ireland, chances are they have an image of violence between Catholics and Protestants. To be sure, in the 30 years from 1969 through 1998, a time the Northern Irish recall as "The Troubles," more than 3,000 individuals were killed in political violence (O'Leary and McGarry, 1996, p. 36).

Northern Ireland, despite its name, is not a part of the Republic of Ireland, though it is located on the northeastern corner of the island of Ireland (Eire). Northern Ireland is a province of the United Kingdom, which also includes Wales, Scotland, and England.

The conflict between Catholics and Protestants in Northern Ireland goes back well over 400 years. While it would take a book in itself to explain that conflict, the issue is this: Northern Ireland's 1.5 million people include a large group who believe strongly that they should be part of the Republic of Ireland. The Republic of Ireland gained independence from Britain in the 1920s. Most of these protesters are Catholics. They call themselves "Nationalists" or "Republicans" (that is, loyal to the Republic of Ireland, which is mainly Catholic). Most Protestants, on the other hand, consider themselves "Unionists" or "Loyalists" and wish to remain united to Britain and loyal to the Queen of England.

Confusing? Well, just imagine that a large minority group in the United States made it clear that its members did not want to vote in American elections or even consider themselves Americans. Moreover, some of them felt so strongly about their views that they were willing to organize themselves into paramilitary forces. They revolted against those who disagreed with them, including the police and the army. Such problems clearly would give rise to "Troubles," and so it was in Northern Ireland.

After years of violence, the two sides agreed in 1998 to settle their grievances peacefully. The "Good Friday" agreement reduced the level of violence in Northern Ireland. A major effort at civic cooperation has led to a shared power arrangement within government. The result

has been a greater sense of peace and security. Yet there is still much work to do.

A look at the four sectors of society in Northern Ireland—families, businesses, government, and voluntary organizations—provides an interesting picture. We see a society in which family life has been strong and businesses have allowed a decent standard of living. But it is a society that has failed to build a government under whose rule the greatest number of citizens are willing to live. When governments fail, much of the responsibility falls on the shoulders of organizations and people participating in civic and philanthropic activity. This is the case in Northern Ireland.

The lives and work of many individuals in Northern Ireland show the power of civic and philanthropic activity. They have helped reshape Northern Ireland for the benefit of its people.

Dr. Arthur P. Williamson is one such individual. Born to Protestant parents in the Northern Irish City of Armagh, Williamson is a historian who has studied civic organizations in Northern Ireland. He also established the Centre for Voluntary Action Studies at the University of Coleraine.

Dr. Williamson has demonstrated that research can bring people of differing backgrounds together. He has made detailed notes of people's actions. Studying civic and voluntary action in its many forms, he observes that in Northern Ireland the separate groups have performed many of the functions that government would normally provide. Since Northern Ireland's government has often been challenged by the very different views of its Protestant and Catholic leaders, finding ways to live and work together has frequently become the task of civic and philanthropic organizations.

In his community life, Arthur Williamson has also shown how local organizations can meet important human needs. He is a cofounder of the Sandel Community Association. This association brings persons of different backgrounds together for nondenominational worship, socializing, and service to the broader community.

Karen Johnston is a generation younger than Williamson. She grew up in Derry, a lovely walled city that has often been a battleground for opposing forces. The River Foyle divides the city into Waterside, a largely Protestant area, and Cityside, the historical city center.

Like Karen Johnston, *Glen Barr* was born in the Waterside area of Derry, and he still works there as the Chief Executive Officer of the Ebrington Maydown Corporation. Glen did well in high school, but his family lacked the resources to send him to college. He became an electrician and an active member in the labor union at a large power plant. One day the managers of the plant were to hold a meeting and they needed a room. The workers' break room was taken for the meeting. The

In Her Own Words: Karen Johnston

Interviewed by Jon Van Til in Derry, May 2002

I grew up in the Waterside area of Derry. My family was Catholic, but we also had some Protestants in our background. My family's house was in a Loyalist (Protestant) area. I first understood that there was a difference between the two communities when I learned that my best friend would not be going to the same school as me. Because of the way things are here, she went to what you would call a public school, and I was sent to a parochial school.

I wasn't the brainiest in the class, but I was above average. I was sort of a tom-boy and participated in a lot of sports. I was lucky enough to be chosen in a cross-community project, "Water Under the Bridge," that took up two years of my life. Twenty were selected for this program, ten from the Catholic community and ten from Protestants. We raised our own money to go on a sports holiday in the south of France.

I don't like to be told what to do, so I chose to go to a technical high school in Limavady, a largely Protestant town. My parents supported me in this, seeing that I was willing to take a 40-minute bus trip each way to get to and from school. I liked it there, because people didn't know who I was or where I was from. I did well enough to go to college and majored in leisure studies and began to work with youth groups in Derry.

I began to work with young people who fell through the net in school. I worked with them in groups, helping them develop skills and improving their view of life. It's been an amazing learning experience for me to be able to do this work. I've learned that it doesn't matter to a young person what side of the fence they are on—there are still health and employment issues.

My present task is to develop a "shadow (city) council" here in Derry. There will be 39 young people, ages 16 to 22, who will be named to this group. It will have its own constitution and will meet bi-monthly in council chambers. It's going to be formal, and last for two years. It will be the first time in our city that there will be a structured body of young people taking the responsibilities of council. They will set their own agenda.

Sometimes people are too quick to blame young people for a whole series of problems. These young people will all represent different areas and problems. The whole idea was developed by young people themselves; they brought it to City Council for their approval.

My job is to help make it work. It's new and challenging. Sometimes it's frustrating, because it isn't the top priority of Council. But they have their job to do, and so do I. And the energy of the young people is terrific: They say, "It's about time we have a voice."

tables normally used for the morning tea break were placed in the men's restroom. That was more than Glen and his colleagues could take, and they organized a strike to protest their working conditions.

As union influence grew and complaints about management increased, the union became powerful enough to shut down electrical power to all of Northern Ireland. As a result of his union leadership, Glen assumed an advisory role with a paramilitary organization called the Ulster Volunteer Force (UVF). The UVF members armed themselves. They believed they had to defend their community from an armed Catholic paramilitary group in a nearby community.

As the conflict between groups in Northern Ireland grew more serious, Glen realized that violence was not the answer to solve deep-seated social problems. His ability to be persuasive is shown in his group leadership. Working with a number of supporters, he founded what has become a major social agency to provide jobs, job training, and hope to the Waterside community. The Ebrington Centre now has a theater, a health club, a restaurant and pub, and other facilities to serve the needs of residents. Over the years, hundreds of Derry youth, both Protestant and Catholic, have learned useful construction and office skills at the Ebrington Centre.

Paddy Doherty, another Derry citizen, was an outstanding elementary school student. But his family did not have enough money to buy the books and uniforms required for high school attendance. While still a teenager, Paddy had to leave school. He became a carpenter. After he married, he was informed by local officials that a young Catholic father like him would have to wait many years for a housing unit. At that news, Paddy joined with other people to set up Derry's first credit union. When conflict between Catholics and Protestants increased, Paddy became the principal spokesperson for what became known as "Free Derry."

The Free Derry movement intended to provide the community with social responsibility. Bogside neighborhood declared itself an independent political entity. Derry police units were not permitted to enter. Free Derry helped the neighborhood develop its own civic structure, including government, police, and court systems. Few other civic enterprises have been so bold. The net effect was to win the attention and finally the support of the British government, which was responsible for developing a civil society in Northern Ireland. Though just one neighborhood, Free Derry, had accomplished that goal with the leadership of Paddy and others.

Like Glen Barr and his union's triumph, Paddy Doherty recognized that his long-term contribution would come from

In His Own Words: Paddy Doherty

Interviewed by Jon Van Til, March 21, 2002

In school I was an avid reader and a good student. But I was out of books and there was a scholarship at the local school and my father went up to see the headmaster and he said, "Look, you're wasting your time. On a docker's wages you could not buy his books. You might get a scholarship, but you'd have to buy his books, you'd have to buy his clothes. No use. Get him out and get him a job." I was at the top of my class. Maybe I resented that but looking back I might have ended up as a teacher. Which is what I tried to do.

There was arrogance in me that I could do almost anything. I became a carpenter because there was nothing else to do. When I didn't want to be a carpenter, I became a foreman for six months. I could've been a scientist. I was good at mathematics. I could've been a surgeon. I was good with my hands, any of those things. But those opportunities were blocked so I had to find a way around them in order to express myself.

When I met Eileen, I'd saved to get married. We had no house, no place to live. I said, "Let's get married first, that's the important thing, we're going to get married." She said, "But we've nowhere to live." I said, "God will provide. We will get married." And then I went looking for a house and I couldn't get one. And I said, "If I can't rent one, I'll build me one." They wouldn't even put me on the housing list then. At that time there were just no houses. It took me two years to build the house.

In 1960 we started what became the biggest community credit union in the world. We started with nine pounds sixteen shillings (less than $20). This year, we are having our building refurbished for the cost of two million pounds; our membership has twenty-four million pounds (about $50 million) on deposit.

I see apathy as frozen violence. You can sit on the people for so long but eventually they blow just like a volcano. So, I came up with the idea of setting up a community bank. We got one expert to come to advise us and he had all these books and he said, "You'll be breaking the Banking Act and all of these credit acts." And I said, "Is there anything wrong with me loaning money to my friend?" "No, no," he said. "Nothing wrong at all." So, we set up and it took ten years for the government to catch up with us and make us get registered. But that's all the money we had that night, nine pounds sixteen.

Later on, to rebuild the city of Derry was my vision. And it wasn't just about the building of the city, it was about the politics, it was about a whole range of stuff. There was an establishment to deal with.

I've learned that a tree will grow if it has proper soil, if it has proper sunlight, if it has proper water, all of that. Human beings are the same. They won't grow unless the atmosphere is correct for them. A tree won't grow in the desert without water. So, what you have to do is get the people involved in creating jobs for themselves, seeking education in every form, working together in groups.

building programs rather than protesting governmental policy. After a few years abroad, Paddy returned to Derry and found the city had been burned by protest fires and bomb explosions during the Troubles. Paddy would not give up. He developed the Inner City Trust, a nonprofit civic and philanthropic organization that he now directs. The trust has rebuilt dozens of historic buildings, created a thriving tourist and shopping area, and recently opened a magnificent new hotel. Of Paddy Doherty it can truly be said, "If you seek his monument, just walk around his city."

Arthur Williamson, Karen Johnston, Glen Barr, and Paddy Doherty are examples of citizens taking responsibility for their own peace and tranquility. In most countries, government provides those services. Citizen action cannot accomplish everything that governments can provide. Citizens who organize into paramilitary forces are not providing a civil solution. Citizens who separate their communities from the larger civil society do not provide a civil solution. Long-lasting solutions that allow people to live together peaceably and productively are needed.

Arthur Williamson has several recommendations for voluntary organizations in Northern Ireland:

It is also essential that the many voluntary and community organizations that constitute the sector continue vigorously to represent disadvantaged sections of the population, provide appropriate and effective services, assist with building social infrastructure and community relations, and contribute to the social and economic development of the region. (Birrell and Williamson, 2001, pp. 217–218)

Dr. Derick Wilson (2001) is a leading figure in Northern Irish youth development. He is former director of the Corrymeela, a cross-community rural-based organization. Corrymeela permitted him to observe that conversations usually focused on sports or the weather rather than real issues. Real issues are job opportunity, equal rights, and social justice.

Progress occurs when positive and lasting relationships between individuals, families, and groups develop. This requires safe spaces that promote confidence between persons of differing backgrounds. Trust is the main ingredient for social progress in Northern Ireland. Building trust requires a vision of fairness, diversity, and interdependence. The civic and voluntary sectors can play a key role in achieving such a vision.

Hungary (1949–1989): Strong Government and Weak Civic Sector

Hungary throughout much of the 20th century faced just the opposite problem from the one that faced Northern

Ireland. Totalitarian governments ruled Hungary during the 1930s and 1940s, and from 1949 to 1989 it had a Communist government. Leaders in those governments were in complete control of society, and civic action and philanthropy were not permitted. Several generations of Hungarians were born and raised with no knowledge of philanthropy—the organized giving of time, resources, and money. The government provided everything.

Democratic government returned to Hungary in 1989. Since then, individuals in the country have developed a civil society through civic and philanthropic action. One person in particular has taken a leading role: *George Soros*. Soros made a career for himself in financial investment, becoming one of the richest people in the world. His real passion, however, involved giving, and he became one of the world's most famous philanthropists.

According to a story in a Budapest newspaper, from December 23, 1939, young George, then a fourth-grader, showed up at the newspaper offices due to its appeal for donations for people in Finland. At the time, the Finns were resisting invasion by the Soviet Union. George opened his pencil case and retrieved two ten-pengo notes from among his belongings. When the editor questioned where George had gotten the money, he explained that he earned it by publishing a newspaper while on summer vacation and wished to donate it to the Finnish people (Kaufman, 2002, pp. 25–26). Thus, Soros began practicing philanthropy early.

Much later in his life, Soros founded the Open Society Institute. He has supported dozens of valuable individual and community programs in many countries of the world. One of the most imaginative programs involved sending several hundred photocopy machines to Hungary for use by students, researchers, writers, and scientists. Government officials had previously been able to prevent people from obtaining research papers, letters, and newspaper clippings. After the introduction of the machines, information moved much more swiftly among individuals and organizations. Soros's act of philanthropy changed one of the prime laws under totalitarianism, the control of information. Philanthropy made it possible for Hungarian society to create a more open government (Kaufman, 2002, p. 197).

Gabor Hegyesi was born in 1949, the year the Communists took control of Hungary. A sociologist by training, he joined his colleagues in the 1980s to found a voluntary organization to provide help for families in desperate need. The organization was called "Laresh," and its services were made available when a parent or child was hospitalized or otherwise disabled. Hegyesi believed it was foolish to believe the government could solve all of a country's problems.

The government was critical of the work by Gabor and his colleagues. Under communism, government officials declared that all needs were met. Convincing the government to license their civic work was difficult.

In His Own Words: Gabor Hegyesi

Interviewed by Jon Van Til, May 16, 2002

My father was forced to serve in the "Jewish Army" in World War II. They were pushed through the fields where there may have been land mines. If they stepped on one, they would be blown up. After the Jewish army went through to clear the fields in this cruel fashion, the regular Hungarian army could then follow.

My father survived because he escaped. My grandmother hid him in a place under the floor of her house during 1944–1945. Jews during that time who were discovered by the fascist Hungarian government were taken to the banks of the Danube River and shot. Their bodies were then floated down the river.

I finished my undergraduate work in 1973 and went to work in a sociological research institute. By that time, we were no longer ruled by a fascist government; the Communists had taken over after World War II.

Then came the late 1970s, a very exciting time in Hungary. A list began to circulate expressing opposition to the government. This petition had begun in Czechoslovakia with the name "Charta '77." It was a kind of declaration of independence. At my office, I was the first to sign it; ultimately, 11 more of the 40 people there did so. Overall, 302 people in Hungary signed.

All of us were interviewed by the police and many were expelled from their jobs or even the country. I was one who was removed from his job. But at that time, four of us had started to work on developing Laresh. So I took a part-time job as a social worker with Laresh in 1982.

One of our founding group worked for the government, where she tried to undermine the system from the inside. We tried to make alliances between the "internal opposition" and the "external opposition" to the way things were going.

We came up with the idea of offering home services to families with special needs. At that time there was a reform movement in Hungary to create "socialist enterprises" that would provide some social services. We met with a governmental official in charge of licensing these new efforts. We proposed Laresh as one such enterprise and developed its mission statement, structure, and plan for its support.

We then took our plan to the Ministry of Finance, to the Director of Services. She rejected the plan, arguing that the Hungarian government was already providing all these services. But while these discussions were going on, two things were happening in her family. At the very same time, both her father-in-law and her husband became sick and were placed in different hospitals. She was faced with the problem of how to care for her preschool child in the face of this family crisis. They lived in the country, had no close ties with her neighbors, and no other family in the area. She faced a crisis in how to cope.

By the second day of this crisis, she was really going crazy. She called Laresh to ask for help. Of course, we pretended to be very official and told her that we had been told that the government provided all the needed services. We asked her: "Why don't you go to the local government for help?" She broke out laughing. "You are absolutely right. I went to the local government and they told me they couldn't help in this situation. I was told it was my private responsibility. And I certainly was not ready to leave my child with a babysitter I found in the telephone book." After that, she gave us her support. She had learned that government can't do it all, that citizen action and volunteering to help each other when people are in need are also important.

Being able to provide voluntary service to families, however, did not create all the change Gabor Hegyesi desired. He publicly supported the growth of democratic rights and practices in Hungary. After the fall of the Communist government, Gabor became the leading force in support of voluntary and civic action in Hungary. Today he directs an important university program that educates and trains people to become leaders of civic and philanthropic organizations.

Another leading Hungarian civic activist, *Nilda Bullain,* was a high school student when the Communist government fell in 1989. Nilda's parents and grandparents were all active politically. As a teenager, Nilda campaigned in Hungary's elections following the fall of communism. Strongly motivated to spread social justice, she knew that Hungary's future would require strong civic and philanthropic action. As a young adult, she entered law school and became active in a number of feminist and community organizations. Her present position is as Executive Director of the International Center for Nonprofit Law.

In Her Own Words: Nilda Bullain

Interviewed by Jon Van Til, August 13, 2002

My mother is a leading scholar and activist in social development in Hungary. She was part of the team of academics who fought to introduce social policy and social work into higher education institutions in Hungary in the early 1980s. Until then, under the official socialist ideology, there could not be social problems in the country and therefore there was no need for social policy or social work in addressing them. So my mother's success also meant that the socialist state acknowledged that they were struggling with unemployment, poverty, and discrimination just as western countries.

In my teenage years I often accompanied my mother to blighted areas of Hungary; I saw impoverished regions, gypsy colonies, destroyed nature, and destroyed lives. Much of what I saw was not known for an average Hungarian adult, let alone a teenager from a middle-class family.

Based on this experience it was inevitable that I became involved in alternative movements at the time of the change of the political system (1988–1989). These were groups that organized themselves around alternative values as they did not want to follow the course of either socialism or capitalism. The membership consisted of anarchists, feminists, and environmentalists—perceived as radicals by the society at that time. It was from this movement that the first women's organization was formed in 1991, called the Feminist Network, of which I was a founding member as well.

I experienced in the Network that while we wanted to achieve a lot of important things, we did not have enough skills and expertise to effectively reach our goals. There was some element missing that I could not define until I came across an initiative by American citizens who were doing research on the development of democracy in Eastern Europe. They pointed out in their findings that while many NGOs (nongovernmental or civil society organizations) have been formed after the collapse of socialism, they lack the management know-how to make their work effective. This was how I started to work with the Civil Society Development Foundation (CSDF) Hungary, to build the capacity of Hungarian and East European NGOs so that they can better achieve their goals.

My work in CSDF Hungary contributed to the development of professional know-how among the NGOs. Professionalism in NGOs is needed to ensure that they can achieve the changes they set out to accomplish. For example, the Feminist Network actually fell apart after a few years due to the lack of management capacity. It gave way to several new and successful women's organizations that had already learned how to set up their structures, plan their projects, raise funds for their programs, communicate about what they do, etc. Ultimately, my work and the Foundation's work helped strengthen democracy through strengthening the NGOs that help control government and perform a lion's share of public services in Hungary today.

Giving by individuals is the major source of philanthropy. Private companies and governmental agencies support philanthropic organizations. Civil societies, in order to grow and function properly, need a balanced approach to philanthropy. The goal is to meet more fully the needs of the country. In Hungary, balancing nongovernmental with governmental action in support of the civil society did that.

Working for a Civil Society in Other Places

Philanthropy occurs in other parts of the world as well. It exists in almost every culture and often in very advanced forms. Among the Yoruba peoples of southwestern Nigeria, for instance, giving involves a complex set of obligations. If a Yoruba receives a gift from someone, the recipient is obliged to give something back in return. The act of giving not only helps someone in need, but it also links the receiving person more closely to the giver. The person receiving is also a giving person. The individuals are then on equal terms, since both have given and both have received. Similar traditions of giving are widely observed among many ethnic and cultural groups.

Just as faith-based beliefs are important to philanthropy in Northern Ireland, they are also important in Africa. In Islamic regions of West Africa, the religious leader, or imam, usually directs philanthropy. The imam receives gifts in the form of a tax from all Muslims and then redistributes the gifts (Feierman, 1998).

Archbishop Desmond Tutu provides another African example of philanthropy. Reverend Tutu has given considerably to promote a civil society, devoting his life to helping others. First, he served as a teacher in a Bantu school in South Africa. He next studied to be a minister and rose through the church ranks to become Archbishop and later the Secretary General of the South African Council of Churches. Through his opposition to apartheid and his efforts to promote a civil society in South Africa, he gained national and international fame.

In 1995, South African President Nelson Mandela gave Archbishop Tutu a major assignment: heading the Truth and Reconciliation Commission. The Commission examined the large number of human rights violations committed in South Africa between 1960 and the election of the black majority government. Service on the Commission required Archbishop Tutu to call on his years of service to others, his commitment to social justice, and his commitment to the civil society (Desmond Tutu Peace Foundation USA, 2002).

Philanthropy is equally important in Asia, which provides two outstanding 20th-century examples. The first was Mohandas Gandhi as leader of the Indian independence movement. He took traditional Hindu religious concepts and transformed them into social and political ideas. Giving by all Indians to help build a democratic society based on participation was one of the building blocks of independence.

The second example of giving in India was the result of cultural pluralism, the mixing of traditions from several different cultural and ethnic groups. Agnes Gonxha Bojaxhiu was born in Skopje, Macedonia, in 1910. At the age of 18, she joined the Sisters of Loretto, a Catholic order. She took the name "Teresa" after St. Teresa of Lesiux, patroness of the Missionaries. She became known as Sister Teresa and became one of the world's most revered women for her personal gifts and sacrifices to help the poor and ill of India and other countries.

In Calcutta in 1950, she formed a Catholic order of nuns called the Missionaries of Charity. This order began with 12 Catholic sisters in India. It has grown to include more than 3,000 sisters in 517 missions throughout 100 countries worldwide. In 1979 the woman known worldwide as *Mother Teresa* received the Nobel Peace Prize for her lifetime of giving to others (Catholic.net, 2004).

Meeting the Challenges of Global Society

George Soros, the Hungarian-born philanthropist, believes that global society can work effectively if it is an "open" society. What would that involve? He recommends:

1. An informed and active citizenry comes first. All of us should vote intelligently, express our thoughtful opinions, and join with others in organizations and actions.

2. When we act together, civic/philanthropic/voluntary associations will be formed. These organizations will be able to give a voice to many groups in society.

3. These organizations are not enough to build the civil society. Government and business must also play their roles—assuring justice, a fair distribution of work and resources, and peace among persons, groups, and countries.

Increasingly, countries like Northern Ireland and Hungary are linked in a variety of ways with other countries. Hungary is part of the European Union (EU), which spans the European continent. Northern Ireland is also a member of the EU. Programs supported by the EU are designed to address social justice and peace. The EU focus on civil society allows philanthropy to assume an important role.

Contacts between community and philanthropic organizations that cross national borders have also increased. Philanthropic organizations like Habitat for Humanity, Heifer International, and Amnesty International operate on a global, rather than a national level. Individuals in many countries join in such international activity. Together, their philanthropic activity permits people to learn from each other and to work together to improve the world. It also enables them to build on special resources and experiences that people in various parts of the world may have.

One doesn't have to be rich or well connected to participate actively and effectively in global philanthropic activity. For example, students at Rutgers, the State University of New Jersey, participate in a ten-day study course in Northern Ireland. They listen to lectures from academic and organizational leaders, visit with community organizations, and share ideas with people in other places on how to improve the world.

Each year several guests who have developed important programs of community and philanthropic action in the United States join the Rutgers group. Among these individuals have been the leaders of the Center for Youth as Resources (CYR), an organization that supports more than 90 organizations in three countries. CYR enables young people to play full and important roles in developing their own programs of philanthropic action. The young people create activities to make their communities better places. But that is not all they do: they also serve as members of the board of directors of the program; they join with adults to raise funds to pay for programs they develop; and they select proposals for projects that seem most worthy of support.

When Rutgers students travel to Northern Ireland, they visit with young people to work actively on problems that trouble their communities. In 2003, for instance, one group of students met with leaders of youth-serving organizations. The goal was to provide opportunities for youth to leave paramilitary organizations that rule many of their ghetto communities. Those conversations among students will someday soon allow Northern Irish youths caught up in gangs to experience new ways to address issues. Some will visit the United States to observe community philanthropy.

Many people help with international philanthropy. Student groups, members of faith-based organizations, members of service organizations, and individuals all participate. Philanthropy involves changing the world on a person-to-person basis. As the old expression goes: Try it, you will like it!

Conclusion

This chapter illustrated some important ideas by people who have sought to enhance civic action and philanthropy in other countries. In brief, the lessons are:

1. Civic action and philanthropy are not just American ideas. The actions and organizations represented by civic action and philanthropy are found in every culture. In Northern Ireland and Hungary, they have proven to be critically important.

2. Civic action and philanthropy do not substitute for the workings of government. Instead, a strong commitment to civic participation is necessary. Democratic institutions are needed for a balanced and effective "open society." Too much government prevents civic participation, but civic action alone cannot guarantee stability and peace.

3. What is true for the relationship between civic action and government is also true for relations with economic and family organizations. "Free market capitalism" needs a thriving democratic government and vital civic activity if the needs of citizens are to be met. Families can only support their members if opportunities exist for each to grow and develop, find employment, and actively participate in governmental and civic life.

A modern society resembles a table with four legs. Each of the legs is necessary to support the entire table, but each leg must have enough strength to support its role, or the table will topple. Think of each leg as one of the following: family, government, civic/philanthropy, and business. Each leg needs to be the right size for the society to be able to support its population. All are necessary, and none by itself is sufficient (Van Til, 2000). There is no escape from the necessity of balanced social development in our global society. Philanthropy has a critical role to play as the future unfolds for people in many regions of the world.

References

Barber, B. R. (1996). *Jihad vs. McWorld: How globalism and tribalism are reshaping the world.* New York: Ballantine.

Birrell, D. & Williamson, A. (2001). The voluntary-community sector and political development in Northern Ireland, since 1972. *Voluntas, 12*(3), 217–218.

Cantor, P. (2001). *Gilligan unbound: Pop culture in the age of globalization.* Lanham, MD: Rowman and Littlefield.

Catholic.net. (2004). *Mother Teresa of Calcutta.* New Haven, CT: Catholic.net. Retrieved January 22, 2004, from www.catholic .net/hope_healing/template_channel.phtml?channel_id=22

Desmond Tutu Peace Foundation USA. (2002). *Archbishop Tutu profile.* New York: Desmond Tutu Peace Foundation USA.

Retrieved February 17, 2010, from www.tutufoundation-usa.org/about.html

Feierman, S. (1998). Reciprocity and assistance in precolonial Africa. In W. Ilchman, S. Katz, & E. Queen (Eds.), *Philanthropy in the world's traditions.* Bloomington: Indiana University Press.

Kaufman, M. T. (2002). *Soros.* New York: Knopf.

O'Leary, B. & McGarry, J. (1996). *Politics of antagonism: Understanding Northern Ireland.* London: Athlone Press.

Salamon, L., & Anheier, H. (1997). *Defining the nonprofit Sector: A cross-national analysis* (Johns Hopkins Non-Profit Sector Series 3). Baltimore, MD: Johns Hopkins University Press.

Van Til, J. (2000). *Growing civil society: From nonprofit sector to third space.* Bloomington: Indiana University Press.

Wilson, D. (2001, March). Presentation to Rutgers University Study Group, Portstewart, Northern Ireland.

3. Geography of Philanthropy in the United States

Mark Wilson

Philanthropy and geography are connected. *Philanthropy* is the voluntary giving of money, services, and time. Philanthropy is provided by many *nonprofit* and *nongovernmental* organizations. Those organizations may work with government, but they are not a part of local, state, or national governments.

The local community is a place where philanthropy begins. The community's geography is based on its cultural groups, economic activities, and environment. Many examples of philanthropy can be found in almost all places. Every community that has a United Way is a location with philanthropy. Every community that has a service club, such as Rotary or Kiwanis, is a site for philanthropy.

Some communities get much attention for their philanthropic activities. Santa Barbara, California, for example, is a place where philanthropy makes front-page headlines because of who participates in philanthropic activities in that city. A newspaper report about an event to raise funds for philanthropy highlighted an appearance by Oprah Winfrey, the television talk show host, author, and Hollywood celebrity (Overend, 2003).

While Santa Barbara is home to many rich and famous people, it also is home to many people whose families have lived there for several generations. It is a small city located on the California coast about 90 miles north of Los Angeles. It has museums and a symphony orchestra, both supported by donations. It has homeless shelters, groups that work to protect the environment, and community education programs that offer lifelong learning opportunities to residents. Those programs are also supported by donations. While the rich and famous attract the headlines, most residents of Santa Barbara give money, services, and time as a way to develop civic pride and responsibility within the community.

Not all communities are exactly like Santa Barbara in terms of the people who live there or its location along the Pacific Ocean. However, people in most communities recognize the importance of philanthropy and participate in giving time, services, and money. They view philanthropy as a way to improve civic life in the place where they live.

Local philanthropy affects the daily lives of most people. You may not recognize it in your own community, but *nonprofit, nongovernmental organizations* help make most communities function successfully. Nonprofit organizations obtain funds through donations and the services they are paid to provide. Many nonprofit organizations invest their money and earn interest or dividends. As we think about it, the name nonprofit may seem incorrect. However, for-profit and nonprofit organizations are quite different. The nonprofit must spend its earnings on the programs it offers. For-profit organizations can spend their income in many ways. Nongovernmental organizations are not a part of local, state, or national government. Sometimes they work with governmental agencies, and at other times they are entirely separate.

When people are considering visiting a museum, they usually want to know "where" it is located and "what" is there. For example, people from all over the world visit the Field Museum in Chicago. The museum was a gift from Marshall Field, a businessperson and philanthropist during the early 20th century. Visitors need to know "where" the museum is and "what" they will find there. Think about museums, sports facilities, medical centers,

Mark Wilson is Associate Professor of Urban Planning and Geography at Michigan State University, East Lansing, Michigan.

or recreational or school programs you have visited. Some may have been close to where you live. Visiting others may have required you to travel across town or to another city or state. In each case you were interested in knowing "where" the facility was located and "what" was there.

Geographers are interested in philanthropy for some of the same reasons. For example, geographers can discover much about a *place* by studying the "where" and "what" of the philanthropy at that place. Place refers to the human and physical features at a location that makes it different from all other places. Characteristics of place include culture, climate, land use, and natural hazards, among other features. The name of a place (e.g., Chicago, Michigan, or the Southwest United States) is also an important characteristic of the place.

Think about Santa Barbara as an example. The city has characteristics, such as museums, homeless shelters, and symphony orchestras, that give it civic qualities. Of course, not every place is like Santa Barbara. Towns and cities across the United States have differences. But they also have some similarities. While not every place has Oprah Winfrey, the people in most places practice philanthropy. They give to help others.

Another reason geographers study philanthropy is to determine what giving occurs in a county, a state, and a country. Some places have large amounts of philanthropic benefits and others have fewer. Mapping and analyzing the patterns of giving in the United States helps explain where and why giving occurs and who benefits.

Geographers use maps in the study of philanthropy. Maps are useful tools for presenting the "where" and "what" information. When geographers study philanthropy, they

1. use maps that show nonprofit activity at the national, state, city, and local levels;

2. observe patterns of philanthropic and nonprofit activity that reveal the importance of location;

3. compare the activities of nonprofit organizations with other parts of the economy; and

4. apply methods of geographic analysis to explain the patterns of philanthropy and nonprofit activities.

A Geographic Perspective on Philanthropic and Nonprofit Activities

Philanthropy at the National Scale

Philanthropic giving and nonprofit action occur in many forms, from one person helping another to large organizations contributing money, supplies, and services in many places in the United States. Much of the giving that occurs is not measured or widely publicized. Only those persons or organizations involved and the people receiving the benefits know they have made a difference. Yet this type of giving is good for society because it builds on the *civility* between individuals and groups that a democratic society requires. Civility means treating others with respect, as persons worthy of regard whether or not you agree with their positions on issues. What is the effect of giving money, services, and time on the common good?

Geographers use several ways to study the philanthropic and nonprofit sector in the United States. One approach is to study the reports of nonprofit organizations. Nonprofit organizations are registered with the Internal Revenue Service (IRS). IRS data tells where the nonprofit organizations are located, but the list is very long, so analyzing it would take a long time.

A map is a better way to show the information. Figure D.5 shows nonprofit organizations by state. By looking closely at the map, you can identify whether nonprofits are distributed evenly across the United States and, if not, which places have more nonprofits than others.

As you look at the map, imagine that you are looking for a job with a nonprofit organization. Are some states likely to have more jobs in the nonprofit sector than other states? How would the map help you make a decision about where to look for work? The job search could be in a specific state or in a region of the country, such as the northeast, southeast, west, etc.

You prefer living in Idaho to living in New York. Based on the map, what are the opportunities going to be in these two states? In frustration, you throw up your hands and ask: "Why are nonprofits more concentrated in some states and regions than in others?" What might the answer be? How could you investigate this question?

To answer such questions, researchers often look for another geographic distribution that they think may provide the reason. For example, population distribution may be important. You could ask: "Is there a relationship between the distribution of nonprofits and the population of the states?" A map showing the population distribution by state may provide the answer (Figure D.6).

How does the distribution of nonprofit organizations compare with population by state? The states and regions with the most nonprofit organizations also have higher population densities. The patterns on the maps suggest that there are more nonprofit organizations where there are more people. This is a positive relationship between population density and nonprofit organizations. Nonprofit organizations are located where there is a larger population to be served, as well as a larger number of people who give.

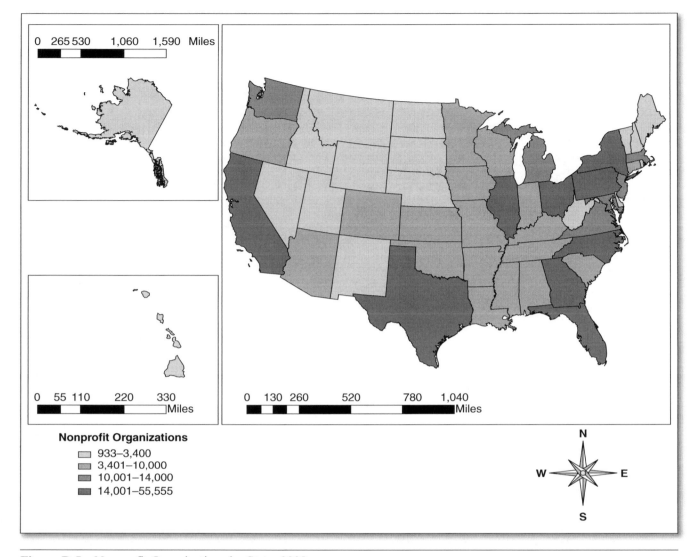

Figure D.5 Nonprofit Organizations by State, 2008

SOURCE: Map created by Jeremy Pyne from ESRI data, National Center for Charitable Statistics.

We now have some general information about the geography of philanthropy for the United States. We might ask how much money is spent per person per year in each state by nonprofit organizations? This is called expenditure per capita, which means per person. The total amount spent in a state is divided by the number of people in the state to develop this measure, expenditure per capita. The pattern on the map presenting this data (Figure D.7) is different from the two prior maps.

Figure D.7 is useful because it tells how much, on average, was spent on philanthropy for each person in your class and in your school. No, not everyone received that amount of money. Some people received more and others less. The per capita figure provides an easy way to compare the common good provided by philanthropy in each state. It states the value in dollars; people can compare $100 with $1,000 per capita and recognize the difference.

Philanthropy at the State Scale

The United States has 50 states, as shown on the prior maps. Geographers often change the scale of their analysis to focus on a single state. Changing the *scale* permits studying a particular state in greater detail. Small-scale maps show little detail, and usually show the world or a country. Large-scale maps show more detail. The neighborhood or community is shown with streets and buildings.

Using Michigan as a case study, Figure D.8 shows that nonprofit and philanthropic organizations are located in many cities and counties in the state. The map shows the locations of nonprofit organizations by county in the state. Counties are a useful political unit for mapping information.

In Grand Rapids, nonprofit and philanthropic organizations are concentrated near the center of the

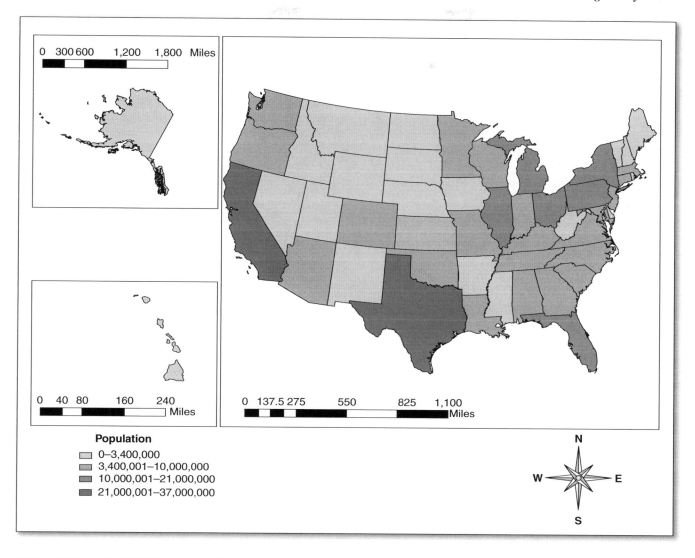

Population
- ☐ 0–3,400,000
- ☐ 3,400,001–10,000,000
- ☐ 10,000,001–21,000,000
- ■ 21,000,001–37,000,000

Figure D.6 Estimated Population of United States, by State in 2008

SOURCE: Map created by Jeremy Pyne from ESRI data, National Center for Charitable Statistics.

city, also referred to as the downtown. Organizations often choose a downtown location because it allows them to serve the entire city from one central location. The map also shows that some parts of the city have very few organizations. Nonprofit and philanthropic organizations in an urban area like Grand Rapids serve many people and other organizations. They often decide on their location in the city based on the services they provide. A homeless shelter will most likely be located within easy walking distance of locations where homeless people gather. The League of Women Voters may have their offices in a suburb since they rely on telephone, mail, and community meeting centers to provide services. For someone in high school, would it matter where nonprofit and philanthropic organizations are located? Should nonprofit organizations serving young adults, such as the YMCA or YWCA, be located downtown or in the suburbs?

Philanthropy at the Local Community Scale

The information at the scale of the state provided more detailed information than the national scale. A map at the scale of the city provides even more. Grand Rapids, the second largest city in Michigan, provides an example of philanthropy at the city scale. Figure D.9 shows in great detail the location and distribution of nonprofit and philanthropic organizations in Grand Rapids.

At the scale of the neighborhood, nonprofit and philanthropic organizations are often located on major streets, in commercial districts such as mini-malls, and at community centers. The locations at the neighborhood scale reflect two things.

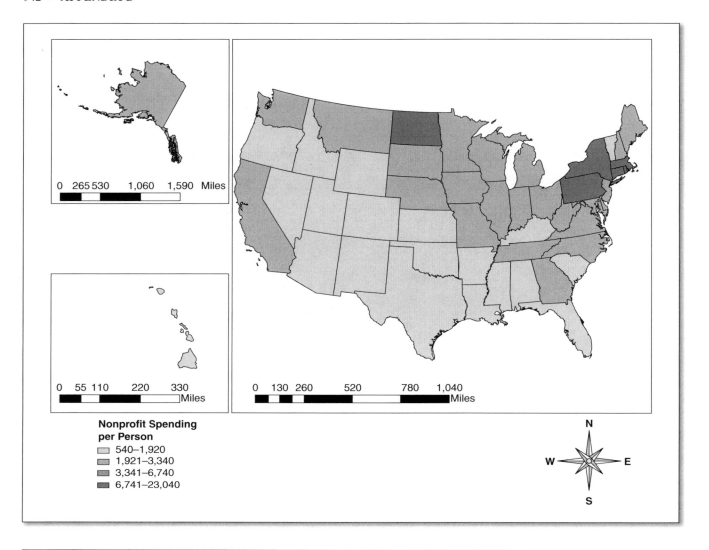

Figure D.7 Nonprofit Spending per Person in 1999

SOURCE: Map created by Jeremy Pyne from ESRI data, National Center for Charitable Statistics.

First, the history of the neighborhood as it relates to the nonprofit organizations is important. Were the nonprofits at that location for a long time? In the southeast region of Grand Rapids, organizations that operate from faith-based institutions and their properties are most common. In most instances, urban faith-based institutions have been located there for many years. In addition, they are often located near one another. A cluster of such institutions is not uncommon. Second, local zoning regulations set up by the city government help decide where nonprofits will be located. Decisions about zoning and land use should result in a common good. For example, educational and health services located where people can reach them easily contribute to the common good.

Philanthropy at the Neighborhood Scale

We have mapped the geography of nonprofit and philanthropic organizations at the national, state, and city levels and seen how changes in scale increase the information. One important map remains. For most people, the geographic scale they use most often is the neighborhood. Nonprofits and philanthropic organizations also operate at the neighborhood scale. Neighborhood residents see and can visit them each day; neighborhood nonprofits and philanthropic organizations may be where parents, relatives, and people in the neighborhood work.

Let's look into a Grand Rapids neighborhood. It is the southeast region of Grand Rapids, shown by Figure D.10. The map shows the distribution of religious, education, arts, and environmental organizations that provide services to this neighborhood. The services they provide may also be offered to people in other neighborhoods in the city.

The map of Michigan shows us that nonprofit and philanthropic organizations are found in every county of the state. However, they are not evenly distributed.

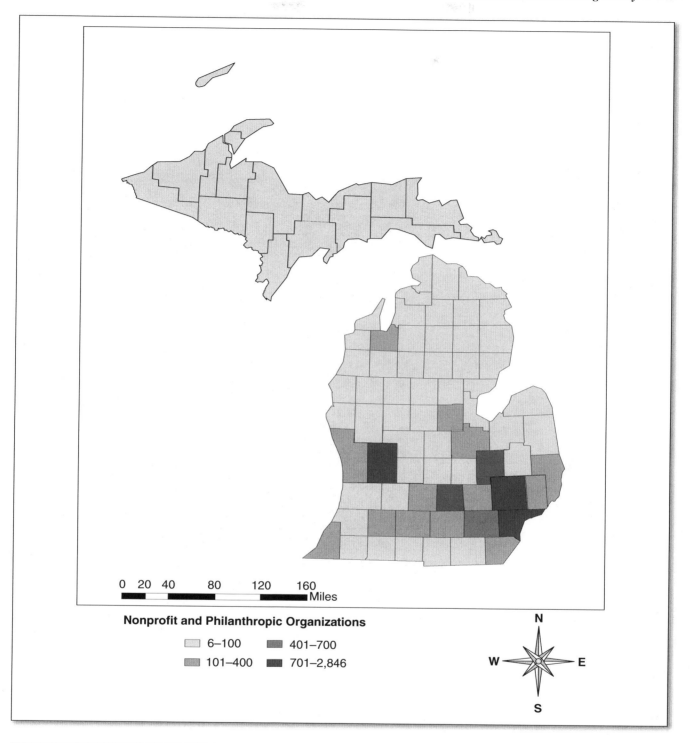

Figure D.8 Nonprofit and Philanthropic Organizations by County in Michigan in 2008

SOURCE: Map created by Jeremy Pyne from ESRI data, National Center for Charitable Statistics.

Instead, they are concentrated mainly in the southern part of the Lower Peninsula, where the population is greatest.

The number of nonprofit or philanthropic organizations is positively related to overall population, as is seen by examining the locations of cities. As the city size increases, so does the number of nonprofit organizations. There are several explanations for this. First, more resources are available in areas with more people. For example, there are more volunteers to provide services and more financial resources to pay for programs that

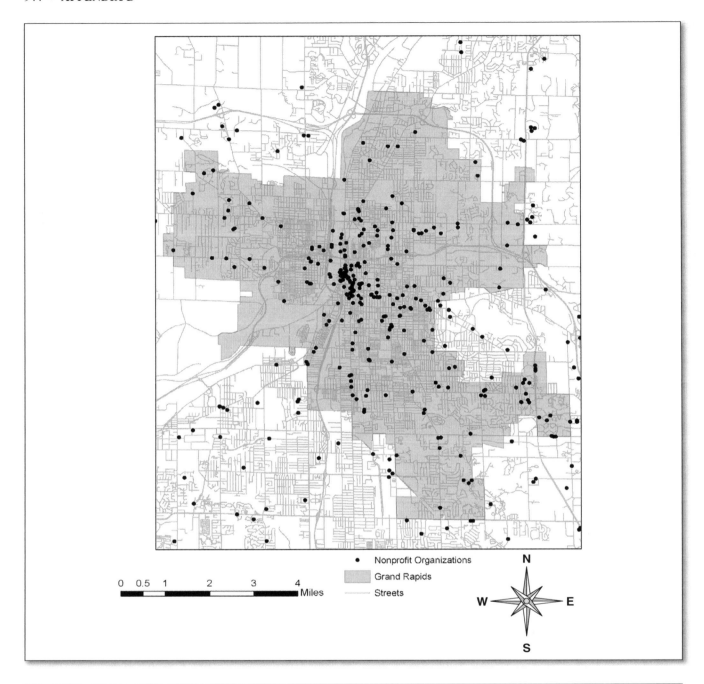

Figure D.9 Nonprofit and Philanthropic Organizations in Grand Rapids, Michigan, in 2006

SOURCE: Map created by Jeremy Pyne from ESRI data, National Center for Charitable Statistics.

organizations sponsor. Second, a larger population means greater demand for the services that are provided. For example, larger numbers of homebound people require more "meals on wheels" delivered, home cleaning and repairing services, and visiting health care workers.

The relationship between urban regions and philanthropy is usually clear. In other cases, zip code regions outside cities have quite a large number of nonprofit organizations. Think about the state where you live. What patterns would you expect to find? The

National Center for Charitable Statistics provides information about the number of organizations by county for every state. It is an excellent data source for researching philanthropy in your state and local area (www.nccs.urban.org). People who work in philanthropy (such as directors of planned giving, United Way officials, etc.) and those who study philanthropy (geographers, historians, economists, government officials, etc.) use data and geographic information to draw and analyze maps such as those in this book.

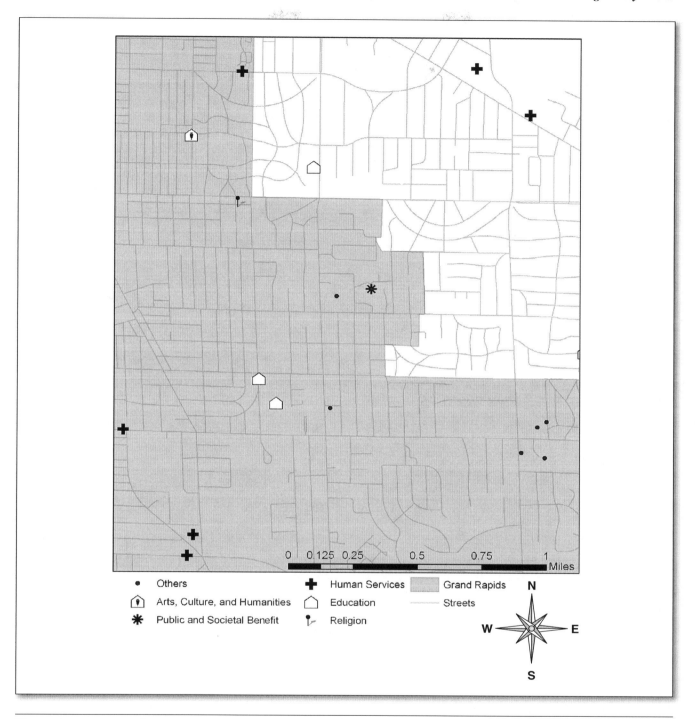

Figure D.10 Nonprofit and Philanthropic Organizations in Southeast Region of Grand Rapids, Michigan, in 2006

SOURCE: Map created by Jeremy Pyne from ESRI data, National Center for Charitable Statistics.

Summarizing the Patterns on the Maps

The information presented on the maps allowed us to make some generalizations about philanthropy in the country, the state, the city, and the neighborhood. We concluded that nonprofit and philanthropic organizations tend to cluster in populated areas. This is called the spatial relationship between organizations and population density.

Knowing where nonprofits are located is important. Imagine that a Goodwill Industries store is located in a neighborhood with high unemployment. A map of employment patterns and the location of the store may be mapped. A geographic analysis of the map will indicate where Goodwill can find people looking for work. Maps provide a way for nonprofit and philanthropic organizations to analyze the characteristics of the local area. By doing so,

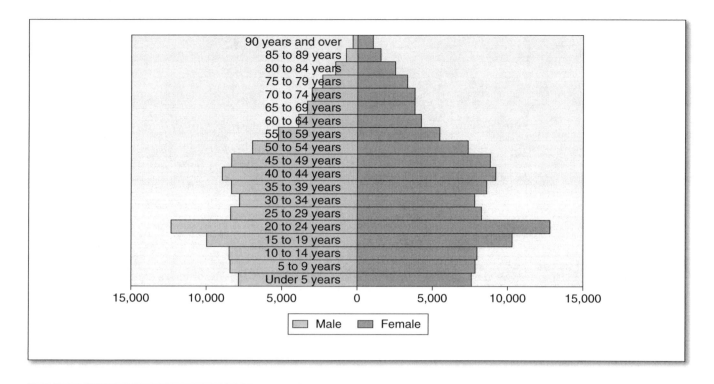

Figure D.11   Population Pyramid of Kalamazoo County, Michigan, in 2000

SOURCE: U.S Bureau of Census, 2000.

they learn who may need their services. Maps will also inform them of where they may obtain volunteers to donate time, people with special services, and the ability of the local population to give money to support civic projects.

Exploring a Community's Population

Nonprofit and philanthropic organizations need information about the populations they are serving. Are there many elderly people in the community? How many children are there and what are their ages? How many people in the community are able to volunteer time and services?

Those questions may be answered in part by examining a population pyramid of a community. Figure D.11 shows population data for Kalamazoo County, Michigan. This population pyramid shows the population of females and males in each age group from birth (0) to 90 plus years.

The population pyramid provides information about a community, the needs it may have, and the resources it may provide. Nonprofit and philanthropic organizations rely on such information to inform them

about the population geography of the communities they serve. The population pyramid also informs those organizations about the giving and volunteering they might expect from a community. Knowing the number of people who live there and their age and gender is important in planning and providing services. For example, a large number of young people ages 15 to 24 live in Kalamazoo County. Many of these young people are students attending Western Michigan University, Kalamazoo College, and Kalamazoo Valley Community College; others are high school students and young adults not in college. This group is usually not able to donate large amounts of money to nonprofit and philanthropic organizations. However, they do have time. Volunteer time to help others is important social capital for the community. Nonprofit organizations may invite that large population of young adults to volunteer.

Employment by Nonprofit and Philanthropic Organizations

Employment opportunities and where they are located are both important geographic questions. In the United States

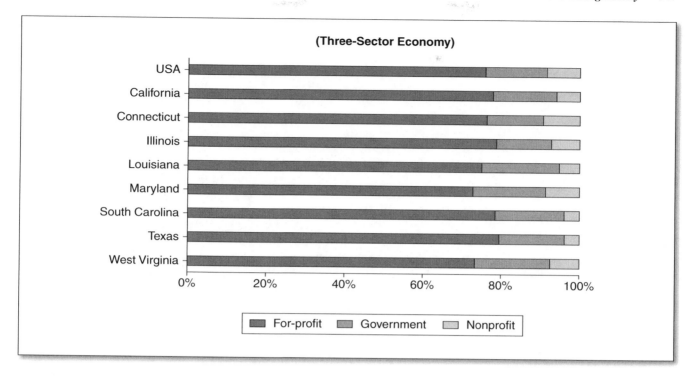

Figure D.12   Employment by Sector in Selected States in 2001

SOURCE: Created by Jeremy Pyne from ESRI data, National Center for Charitable Statistics.

in 2001, total employment of 129.6 million workers was divided between for-profit firms (98.4 million workers), government (20.3 million workers), and nonprofit organizations (10.9 million workers). In other words, for-profit firms employed 75.6% of the workforce, followed by government with 15.6%, and the nonprofit sector with 8.4%.

All 50 states can be compared in a table or graph. However, it is sometimes more revealing to examine a smaller number of states that have major differences. The sampled states can also represent different regions of the country. The sample of states may then be used to determine why differences occur. The pattern of employment in nonprofit organizations in the sample of states may then be compared to other states or to other regions.

Figure D.12 provides data on a sample of eight states in different regions of the United States. Looking at this data will allow us to see if the pattern of employment in nonprofits is the same or different from state to state.

The graph shows that the percentage of employment in the nonprofit sector is larger than the national average in Connecticut, Maryland, and West Virginia. Nonprofit employment is lower than the national average in California, Louisiana, South Carolina, and Texas.

Reasons for the Locations of NonProfit and Philanthropic Organizations

The location of nonprofit and philanthropic organizations in the United States is the result of many influences over the past two centuries. The major forces that have decided where nonprofits are located include (1) the early presence of the philanthropic organization at an ideal location, (2) resources, and (3) leadership.

Initial Presence

The presence of nonprofit and philanthropic organizations can often be traced to historic advantages at the place they were founded. Organizations that were started many years ago—some in the 1800s—are well established today. These organizations had the advantage of being first and were able to meet local needs. For example, Pittsburgh was the home of Andrew Carnegie, and the Carnegie Foundation had an early interest in improving life in Pennsylvania. The Kellogg Foundation was started in Battle Creek, Michigan, in 1934. One of its initial projects was the Michigan Community Health Project. The Kellogg Foundation set up health programs in rural southwestern Michigan counties. Public health departments were opened in locations that other organizations, including the government, believed were too small in population. The Kellogg Foundation proved that the common good was served by providing health services in those communities.

When a large philanthropic organization gave attention to a local area, other organizations that might have considered offering similar goods and services at that location were discouraged because needs were already being met. The early nonprofit and philanthropic organizations could meet local needs. For example, during the 18th and 19th centuries, education was not a government concern. The most likely source of education was through faith-based schools. Beginning in the latter part of the 19th and early 20th centuries, government took on increased responsibility for education since it served the common good. Today, some regions of the United States, such as the Northeast, have both public and faith-based school systems. The faith-based system operates on donations and fees for service instead of taxes.

Resources

Nonprofit and philanthropic organizations need resources to provide services. Resources may come from donations or fees for services. Places that lack donors or have many low-income residents may not be able to support those organizations. Even though the need may be great, the organizations lack the resources needed to carry out their nonprofit and philanthropic missions. Some regions of the United States, therefore, have difficulty creating new nonprofit organizations. They are unable to obtain local resources or attract donations from other parts of the United States. Without these resources, it is impossible to begin helping people. In the South there is a high proportion of giving among the population. However, much of the giving is directed to faith-based programs. New nonprofit organizations receive less compared to the faith-based programs, which often have a local focus and involve local people. The philanthropy, both giving and receiving, occurs only within their clearly defined group.

When nonprofit and philanthropic organizations are well established, but the need is greater than can be met, the government may provide resources directly to those organizations rather than providing the service itself.

Leadership

An important element of nonprofit and philanthropic success is entrepreneurship—the leadership skills necessary to attract resources and allow production. If there are few persons with the talent or willingness to build organizations, then organizations will not be created. Without organizations, production of goods and services by the nonprofit and philanthropic sector will not occur, or will occur at a slower rate. Also, in some parts of the country with a strong governmental sector, public-spirited persons may work for government rather than for nonprofit and philanthropic organizations. In Santa Barbara they rely on people whose families have lived there for generations as well as the new rich and famous residents. Most communities do not rely on celebrities. They rely on local leaders to improve philanthropic "habits of mind" among the residents. Such leadership may come from a school principal, a teacher, a well-known business person, a community son or daughter, or a committee of dedicated, hard-working local people. Their common efforts usually result in amazing successes as they build civic participation and the common good.

Conclusion

The landscape of nonprofit and philanthropic activities is not the same across the United States. It is different in different places. Santa Barbara, California, is quite different from Kalamazoo, Michigan. However, both places have strong community foundations. Different people have been involved during different periods of time, but both places share a common vision for a civil society involved in giving to help others.

What about the nonprofit organizations in your community? The locations and spatial distribution of nonprofit organizations and the goods and services they provide are a good indicator of the "geography of giving" in a community. Giving involves not only money or other resources, but also volunteering time to assist someone in need. The spatial distribution of nonprofit and philanthropic organizations in a community is usually explained by the combination of three factors:

1. What organizations were first to provide those services at a location?

2. What resources are available at the location?

3. What leadership was available to get the organizations working successfully?

Those are the important parts of the "philanthropic landscape" in a community. Each informs us about people giving money, services, and time to help others.

Acknowledgments

The Nonprofit Michigan Project at Michigan State University and the Dorothy A. Johnson Center for Philanthropy at Grand Valley State University generously provided data for this chapter. Jeremy Pyne of the Johnson Center and Fitria Wahid, Western Michigan University, prepared the maps.

References

Bielefeld, W. (2000). Metropolitan nonprofit sectors: Findings from NCCS data. *Nonprofit and Voluntary Sector Quarterly 29*(2), 297–314.

Overend, W. (2003, September). Charity must be in the water. *Los Angeles Times*. Retrieved July 28, 2004, from www.sbrm .org/LATimes.html.

Weisbrod, B. A. (1988). *The nonprofit economy.* Cambridge, MA: Harvard University Press.

Wolpert, J. (1993). *Patterns of generosity in America: Who's holding the safety net?* New York: Twentieth Century Fund Press.

4. Geography and International Philanthropy

Joseph P. Stoltman

Introduction

A recent high school graduating class decided to leave a lasting legacy to their school. No, it was not brightly painted goal posts on the football field. It was not a flower garden that future students could care for and cultivate. The class raised a significant amount of money and donated it to build and equip an elementary school in a developing country. Is it a lasting legacy? Yes, it is, and from two points of view. First, many students in the developing country will attend the new school. Some who attend may become teachers, public health workers, or business people. The education they receive will enable them to become productive members of a civil society.

Second, the legacy does not stop with the students who raised the money. They have challenged the next graduating class from the high school to match or exceed the contribution they made. Each new senior class will elect a committee to decide on their project, which can be in any country in the world. The plan is for each future class to make the same challenge to the students who follow. Thus, this year's high school class has left a legacy of giving to everyone who will graduate from their high school in the future.

What BIG idea is the senior class passing along to students in the future? It is "international philanthropy." The legacy has two benefits. One benefit is to the recipients of a new school in a developing country. The other is to the students who are giving. The intended outcome is to promote a civil society among people in both places.

International philanthropy occurs in many different ways. It occurs at different times, in different places, and in different political situations. In some places, local families and villages provide philanthropy for their own people. In other places

philanthropy comes from outside the country, as with the example of the high school students presented above. This chapter will enable you to find out what "international philanthropy" does and how it happens in different places.

Geographers and Philanthropy

In their professional work, geographers are interested in the study of international philanthropy for two reasons. First, cultural geography (also called human geography) focuses on the distinct traditions that people have developed in particular places and regions. The traditions include social systems, such as the family, and economic systems, such as food production. Cultural traditions also include people's commitment to such ideas as the common good and helping one another, which are both important in philanthropy. Thus, study of philanthropy is a comfortable subject in cultural geography.

Where are things located? Why are they there? These are two questions that geographers ask. They use maps to show where things are located. They research the way things, such as money, services, and ideas, move from one location to another. International philanthropy is the movement of money, services, and ideas from one place or country to another. The purpose is to provide assistance so people can improve their condition of life. The assistance may include health services, food, basic education, or skills for jobs.

Where are volunteer resources available? Where are resources needed? How do we get resources from the location where they are available to where they are needed? The high school graduating class described earlier moved resources from where they were available to where they were needed. In geography, that process is called *spatial analysis,* or studying

Joseph P. Stoltman is Professor of Geography at Western Michigan University, Kalamazoo, Michigan.

where things are on the Earth's surface, why they are there, and the ways they move from one location to another. Geographers' interest in *spatial analysis* is the second reason that they find philanthropy an interesting topic of study.

In this chapter, we examine international philanthropy as geographers do, using cultural geography and spatial analysis questions.

Philanthropy and Culture

Soccer, often referred to as the world's most popular team sport, is played in many countries. People in South America, Asia, Africa, and Europe follow soccer clubs and teams, becoming devoted supporters of "their team." Aldo Panfichi is a supporter of the Alianza Lima soccer club in Lima, Peru. His account of attending a soccer match with some of his friends appears below.

Mr. Panfichi's experience led him to think about the actions of the young soccer fans he encountered that day. The crowd used up a huge amount of energy, but not in a positive manner. He found that soccer is often linked to violence in places where it is played. His own experience playing soccer was that the sport is generally nonviolent. Players are seldom injured seriously as a result of the game. Soccer follows basic rules of democracy, and the authority of the referees and the rules of fair play are widely respected. People of all economic, ethnic, social, and national groups either play or are spectators. Soccer is played in parks, stadiums, and other public places, even in the streets. In Latin America, soccer is so much a part of the culture that soccer clubs are an important part of their society. The clubs are geographically linked with specific cities, barrios, or ethnic or social groups (Panfichi, 2002). How, he wondered, could the vibrant cultural and social energies he observed that day be put to good use?

Aldo Panfichi faced a dilemma. What could be done to capture the motivation and energy of soccer fans in Lima and redirect them to positive purposes?

Mr. Panfichi recognized that the "solidarity between individuals of different social classes organized around a given club" was a valuable resource. He and his co-workers at a local university decided to take action. With the help of the AVINA Foundation, a Swiss philanthropic organization, they started a program to build youth leadership in the communities (barrios) that were geographically and culturally linked with soccer clubs and teams. It was called "Soccer and Barrios: Youth as Promoters of Local Development" (*Futbol y Barrios: Jovenes Gestores de Desarollo Local*). The leadership program has four main activities.

1. Learning a trade or technical occupation that will allow the youths to be better prepared to join the labor market.

2. A civic training workshop that seeks to make the youths conscious of their natural leadership skills, but also of their rights and obligations as citizens.

3. Communications training to help these youths develop a voice of their own that can be heard by society.

4. Local community development, in which the barristas, or neighborhood organizations, propose projects that benefit their neighborhoods. (Panfichi, 2002, p. 4)

This example from Lima, Peru, shows how a person who observes a need in the community can take action. Local human resources were combined with funds from a Swiss foundation. Will the youth leadership program stop all the problems associated with the energy of soccer fans? Probably not, but it has prompted a large number of rowdy fans to consider their rights and responsibilities as citizens of their barrio, the city of Lima, and Peru. From a geographic perspective, the program developers relied on soccer as the common cultural tradition. The neighborhood, city, and country will all be positively affected by the successes of Futbol y Barrios.

Philanthropy and International Borders

Globalization means looking at economic and human topics from a worldwide viewpoint rather than that of a single

---

In His Own Words: Aldo Panfichi

It's Sunday at 2 p.m. in Lima, Peru. My friends and I meet to go to the stadium, as we always do on weekends. Nobody has watches or wallets, only the white and blue striped t-shirts we have worn since we were kids. We decide to take one car to avoid being trapped by the heavy traffic, the *barras bravas* (violent fans), and the human sea that converges from different districts of the city on to the stadium. Taking a short cut, we suddenly face exactly what we feared: a crowd of ragged looking youths, jumping and singing fanatically, war paint on their faces and flags waving in the wind. They surround us in a threatening manner and rock the car as though trying to overturn it. We lower the windows and despairingly show them the team colors on our chests and begin to sing together, loud, ever louder, until little by little they move aside, forming a corridor of bodies and songs that we urgently pass through. The mounted police arrived late but nevertheless violently crush the young crowd. We arrive on time to the stadium, but in the streets the game had already begun. (Panfichi, 2002, p. 1) country. At one time economic and humanitarian ideas traveled at the speed of sailing ships and camel caravans. That is no longer the case. A newly released popular music recording from the Philippines is heard across the globe instantly via satellite radio, television, cell phone, and Internet. The moment it is created, the newest hairstyle can be viewed on the World Wide Web, satellite television, or digital photography in other parts of the world. Early morning or late night editions of big city newspapers no longer require a walk to the newsstand or a wait for paper delivery. They can be viewed in electronic form the moment they are printed.

As globalization has continued to change the cultures and geography of places, another change has been occurring in many countries of the world: the rise of democratic government. Like globalization, democracy has been here for a very long time. It was practiced in early Greece and Rome, but probably occurred in other ancient locations as well. In the 20th century, and especially in the 1990s, progress toward a civil society and full participation by citizens in democratic government were characteristics of that time.

Democracy requires hard work and positive results. Newly emerging democracies give people a far greater voice in how and where they live, where they work, and how their government is run. Citizen participation is necessary for a democratic form of government to survive and thrive. In a democracy, people must make choices, and they must interact with each other in order to make informed choices.

How have globalization and democracy affected international philanthropy? Newly formed democratic governments often recognize that the task ahead of them is huge. The government may need to provide such public services as schools, hospitals, and public utilities (e.g., water and electricity). They sometimes cannot do all of this work on their own (Hodgkinson, 2001). When that happens, governments turn to international philanthropic organizations for assistance.

This assistance often requires citizen involvement to meet needs. The process builds mutual trust and a positive working relationship between the citizens and those donating time and resources. Trust and working relationships are part of the *social capital* that philanthropy tries to develop. *Social capital,* as defined by Robert Putnam, refers to features of social life-norms and trust that enable people to act together more effectively to pursue shared objectives.

The Geography of International Philanthropic Organizations

Many international organizations operate philanthropic and nonprofit activities. Figure D.13 is a partial listing of philanthropic, nonprofit, and nongovernmental organizations that span the globe with their activities. The figure includes organizations that provide various kinds of services.

Many of the organizations listed in Figure D.13 have outreach programs that cross international borders. They usually accomplish *three missions.*

1. They provide aid and lend support to groups of people and countries that are in need.

2. They work with the local people and their government to begin projects that enable those people and governments to help themselves.

3. They empower the population to bring about positive changes in the future that will help them in the long-run.

Let's take a closer look at several international philanthropic organizations.

Case Study 1: The Federation of Red Cross and Red Crescent Societies

Among the best-known organizations is the International Federation of Red Cross and Red Crescent Societies. Founded in 1919, the Federation is the world's largest humanitarian organization and provides international assistance without regard to nationality, race, religious beliefs, class, or political opinions. In 2009, the Federation had 186 member Red Cross and Red Crescent societies. There were 60 field offices and delegations to support activities around the world.

The Red Crescent is the symbol of the Federation in Islamic countries; the Red Cross is used in other member countries. While not yet a Federation member, Israel has asked to use the Star of David to designate its humanitarian missions once it becomes a member.

While "giving blood" may be the only contact most people have with the Red Cross and Red Crescent Societies, the Federation's philanthropic activity is truly international. Each of the member societies also has a national or regional relief program. In the United States, it is the American Red Cross; states, counties, and cities may each have a Red Cross chapter.

From its main office in Geneva, Switzerland, the Federation has responded to appeals from the regions of the world shown in Figure D.14. Those appeals have been for different types of relief (Figure D.15). The figures list the "where?" and the "why?" of international calls for help.

The Federation has responded to approximately 22 appeals per year since it was founded in 1919. The appeals have come from every region of the world in response to humanitarian needs ranging from disaster relief to food and nutrition. The appeals resulted in money, hospital supplies, clothing, medical equipment, vaccinations, and seeds for crops, to name a few. Volunteers willing to donate their time were available. The immediate results have been the rebuilding of communities and people's lives. The long-term goal is to build a civil society in which members of the global community respect and care for one another.

Case Study 2: Oxfam Philanthropy and Civic Principles

Oxfam, an organization started in Oxford, England, during the 20th century, is recognized internationally for its

Organization	Location
ACCORD: African Center for the Constructive Resolution of Disputes	Mount Edgecombe, South Africa
Lawyers' Environmental Action Team	Tanzania, Africa
International Institute for Sustainable Development	Manitoba, Canada
Philanthropy Australia	Melbourne, Victoria, Australia
The Regional Environmental Center for Central and Eastern Europe	Szentendre, Hungary
The Indian National Trust for the Welfare of Tribals	Delhi, India
Economic Research Forum	Cairo, Egypt
The Abraham Fund for Education for Co-Existence	Jerusalem, Israel
Federation of Red Cross and Red Crescent Societies	Geneva, Switzerland
Ashoka	Arlington, VA, United States

Figure D.13 International Philanthropic Organizations

Region	(CHF millions)
Africa	361.0
North and South Americas	148.6
Asia and Pacific	890.1
Europe	37.3
Global	152.5
Total	1,589.5

Figure D.14 Donor Response to Programs/Appeals 2006 to 2010

SOURCE: Adapted from *Red Cross and Red Crescent Societies,* Geneva: International Federation of Red Cross and Red Crescent Societies, 2010. Retrieved February 19, 2010, www.ifrc.org.

Category of Aid	(CHF millions)
Disaster Management	1,003.1
Health & Social Services	360.6
National Society Development	94.0
Principles & Values	23.7
Coordination	108.1
Total	1,589.5

Figure D.15 Donor Response by Sector, 2006 to 2010

SOURCE: Adapted from *Red Cross and Red Crescent Societies,* Geneva: International Federation of Red Cross and Red Crescent Societies, 2010. Retrieved February 18, 2010, www.ifrc.org.

work in famine relief. When the two words, Oxford and famine, are placed side by side, a shortened, combined version of both becomes Oxfam. People in many countries of the world recognize Oxfam for its philanthropic and non-profit activities. Oxfam International is made up of affiliated organizations that support the overall mission. Figure D.16 shows where Oxfam works around the world.

The mission of Oxfam is to help people become empowered through greater knowledge and information about economic and social justice. In order to achieve its mission, Oxfam performs many other activities. It provides financial and material support to communities, individuals, schools, hospitals, and in-country volunteer groups, as well as its own volunteers. It also promotes ideas, values, and sustainable methods of producing food and other goods to improve the lives of people.

Oxfam has based its philanthropic program on the ideas of global citizenship and economic justice. It focuses on human rights, women's rights, international debt relief for poor countries, banning of landmines, and holding those who commit genocide legally responsible. It is the philanthropy of ideals and human values that Oxfam has supported most directly. Nearly every philanthropic organization has those values in its mission. For Oxfam, it is a major part of the mission.

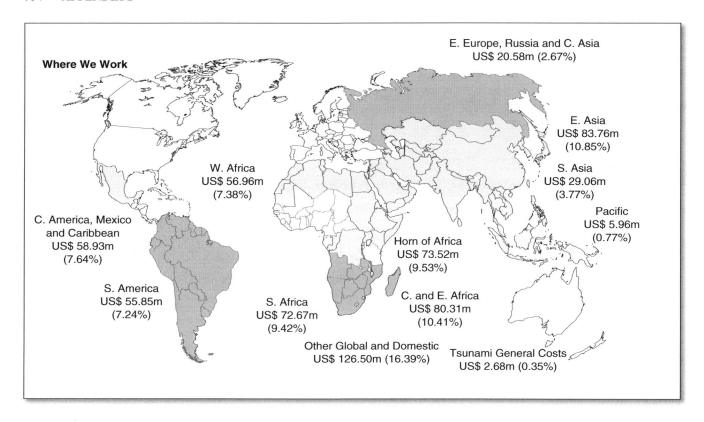

Figure D.16 The Global Geographic Distribution and Percent Expenditures of Oxfam's Activities

SOURCE: From p. 17 of *Oxfam International Annual Report 2008–2009,* Oxford, UK: Oxfam, 2009.

Oxfam's view of global citizenship has a very practical meaning. People should know how their daily activities and choices affect other people, whether geographically far or near.

Oxfam believes that global citizens have the responsibility to examine:

1. How we learn about other peoples and their cultures.

2. The daily choices we make as shoppers, vacationers, and investors.

3. How we welcome strangers and refugees and question stereotypes.

4. How we react to humanitarian crises in countries far away from our own.

5. The attitudes we communicate to our children, colleagues, neighbors, and friends.

6. The political choices we make as citizens. (Oxfam, 2009)

Does a civil society result when people are able to discuss issues and exchange ideas? In a civil society, do people need the freedom to openly support the plan or person they think will help solve the issues or problems they face? If you believe these actions are important to a civil society, then you must also recognize that other people will feel quite different about the same issues. These differing views will cause tension within society. Some citizens support one idea, while others are opposed to it. That tension is part of the culture that geographers look for in a place. It is the political and social culture that allows people to disagree with one another, but still be civil toward each other. It is that level of civility that volunteers and supporters of organizations like Oxfam believe is important to global citizenship and democratic government.

Expenditures by Oxfam reflect the underlying values of the organization (Figure D.17). The two categories with the largest funding are life and security, and livelihoods. Life and security refers to food, medical treatment, and sanitation. Livelihood activities help people earn a living and include job training. Basic social services, which are third, include hospitals, schools, and public health. Everyone agrees those are very important to a civil society.

The two remaining categories, the right to be heard and gender and diversity, are also important, but are very different. They focus on ideals rather than services or material goods. They are values supported by democratic societies. Countries should be helped to build a society based on civility, trust, and giving. The acceptance of both material assistance and values of a civil society are cultural considerations. The way those values are viewed will vary from place to place as the cultural geography varies.

Category of Support	Percentage of Funding
Livelihoods	25.88%
Basic Social Services	13.56%
Life and Security	31.94%
Right to Be Heard	14.48%
Gender and Diversity	14.13%

Figure D.17 Percentage of Oxfam Funding Going by Category of Support

SOURCE: From p. 17 of *Oxfam International Annual Report 2008–2009,* Oxford, UK: Oxfam, 2009.

Geographic Analysis of International Philanthropic Organizations

The importance of culture in philanthropy is clearly seen in the questions asked during a geographic analysis: What are the cultural practices of the people in a place? How will they react to the services, material goods, and volunteers from our organization? Will they accept the ideas of civility, women's rights, and ethnic diversity that our organization supports? The answers to those geographic questions are important to the long-term success of international philanthropy. The answers depend on information about locations, people, and environments on Earth.

The map and tables showing the activities of the International Federation of the Red Cross and Red Crescent Societies and Oxfam are also important in geographic analysis of international philanthropy. Those data provide information about the locations where assistance has been provided, such as the country or world region; the kind of philanthropic assistance that has been provided, such as education, health, water supplies, etc.; and how much has been provided, such as the percentage of total assistance that has gone to a country or region.

A geographic analysis of Figure D.14 informs us that the Asia/Pacific region has had the greatest number of responses to programs and appeals for assistance since 2006. We would next ask the questions: What type of assistance was provided and what percentage of the total appeals for assistance has gone to the Asian/Pacific region? With that information, a comparison may be made with other regions, such as Africa, which is second in total number of appeals, or Europe, which is third. Important geographic questions must be asked in order to determine the problems and the changes in the number of problems over time in a region. If, for example, the problem of food security is worsening, then increased food production may require more funding. A geographic analysis of the data tells philanthropic organizations about changes so they may develop effective policies and plans.

A geographic analysis of the information in the two case studies supports these conclusions. First, knowledge of cultural geography informs us that the Red Cross and Red Crescent Societies will have programs in Africa south of the Sahara. There are Islamic, Christian, and traditional societies in the region. While both Red Cross and Red Crescent would respond to needs, there is an important cultural tie to the symbolism of the Cross and Crescent, based on religion.

Oxfam International is also active in the region, providing approximately one-third of its available resources for Africa. Why is Africa in such great need?

In recent decades, Africa has been a region of warfare and conflict. It is also a region where the population suffers from malaria, AIDS, and polio. Serious droughts have caused crops to fail. The result has been large migrations of rural people to look for work in urban centers.

The presence of philanthropic organizations provides several ways to bring about change. One alternative is to enable people in the region to solve the conflicts, perhaps drawing on philanthropic help that is made available. Another is to wait for military conflict to end. Then social, economic, and political order may be reestablished and the door will be opened for help from international organizations. Philanthropic organizations will be ready to assist in rebuilding people's lives and their property. The problems that caused regions of Africa to have conflicts, human suffering, and economic problems must also be addressed. Giving food, medicine, and sending medical teams provides relief. It often does not, however, solve the larger problems countries in the region face. Those include governmental corruption, dictatorial governments, and lack of economic opportunity for the people. Philanthropy must address the urgent concerns, but it also must promote a civil society based on democratic ideals and human rights.

Purchasing Crafts From Other Countries: Is It International Philanthropy?

Can people be philanthropic when they buy material goods that they enjoy? Let's consider a group of people living in a country or region of a country who produce some interesting crafts. However, they have no way to market the products; even if they were able to do so, they have little information about the international consumers who would purchase them. They have the option to sell their crafts to a local trader, who would then resell them to a larger export company. Eventually the products would reach boutiques and shops in London, Chicago, Paris, Tokyo, and other large cities. If they were popular with consumers, then they would be purchased quickly at quite a high price. However, the people who handcrafted the products received a very low price. They have no way of knowing that the products sold for a high price in the international market. When this happens, the artists or crafts persons are left with little profit. Most of the profit goes to persons and companies who exported, imported, and retailed the crafts.

Does it always have to work this way? No, it does not, but a change requires both organizations willing to help and awareness from consumers who eventually purchase such handcrafted items. The consumers may display a *philanthropic habit of mind* by buying from a store or organization that returns a fair market price to the person who produced the item.

One organization that addresses this problem is *Ten Thousand Villages*. In 1946, the Mennonites, a faith-based group, began working with people in several countries to give them a "fair price" place to sell their products. Fair price means that the person who produced the craft is paid an amount that fairly rewards the time, materials, and skills invested. The project has grown to include nearly 100 *Ten Thousand Villages* stores in the United States and Canada. Crafts and cultural products are imported mainly from countries in four regions—Africa, Latin America/Caribbean, Southeast Asia, and South Asia (Figure D.18).

Artisans who are unemployed or find it difficult to market their crafts in their country make most of the products. They live in locations that are difficult to reach, they have little capital to pay for exporting their products, or they do not have the marketing skill necessary to obtain the best price. The local artist who sells products to *Ten Thousand Villages* gets a "fair market" price and receives the money promptly to help pay for food, education, health care, and housing. To keep the cost of operating the *Ten Thousand Villages* stores low, the nonprofit organization relies on thousands of people in Canada and the United States volunteering at stores in their home communities.

Ten Thousand Villages, a nonprofit organization, has several values, principles, and goals that guide their activities. Among them are the following:

1. Handicrafts reflect and reinforce rich cultural traditions; they are environmentally sensitive.

2. Honor the value of seeking to bring justice and hope to the poor.

3. Make payments promptly and consistently for handicrafts and artistic work at a fair trade price.

4. Use resources carefully and value the volunteers who work in the North American operations. (Ten Thousand Villages, 2009)

Most people agree with the values, principles, and goals of the organization. But not all people agree that shopping at Ten Thousand Villages is a form of philanthropy. They argue that consumers are receiving material goods through their purchases and, thus, this is not philanthropy at all.

Does this value issue (donation versus purchase) create a tension regarding the way that international philanthropy is viewed? Can philanthropy be both direct and indirect? Direct philanthropy is a donation of time or other resources. Indirect philanthropy occurs when there is a positive benefit, but not as a donation of time and resources. Are organizations being philanthropic when they provide "fair market" outlets for crafts from poor regions of the world? Is the consumer who pays a slightly higher "fair market" price at such a store compared to the cost of a similar product at another store being a philanthropist?

The issue goes beyond crafts. For example, the more developed countries are a very large market for coffee. Much of the coffee is grown in less developed countries. On some farms the tropical forest is removed so coffee trees can be planted. On other farms the coffee is grown in the shade of large tropical forest trees. Shade-grown coffee does not require all the tropical forest to be cleared and helps save the environment. Is drinking only shade-grown coffee a means to show environmental philanthropy?

These are some of the questions we should think about as socially and economically conscious consumers. Where would you buy crafts? What kind of coffee would you buy? How would you justify your decision regarding those decisions?

Some Geographic Reasons in Support of International Philanthropy

International philanthropy is successful. Important knowledge and ideas spread from one geographic region to another. During the 20th and 21st centuries, global improvements in the quality of life were caused by philanthropy. They included the end of smallpox, fewer cases of polio, increased food production due to the Green Revolution, the introduction of democratic ideals to many countries, environmental stewardship and protection, and better nutrition for children.

Is international philanthropy always successful? Success is measured in different ways, but warning signs indicate when problems exist. For example, if a group of people becomes dependent on international philanthropy, then overall success has not occurred. International philanthropy is usually concerned with "teaching people to provide for themselves so they someday will not require assistance." Corrupt governments and international philanthropy often work in the same places. Supplies, medicine, food, and equipment are sometimes stolen and resold before they get to the people who need them. When that happens, the success of international philanthropy is greatly reduced.

Philanthropy pursues investment to improve the capacity of people to achieve long-term benefits. There are great differences geographically between poor and rich regions of the world. Philanthropy makes social and cultural investments in people and organizations in poor regions to improve the quality of life. Their successes often benefit other people in the region and the world. The rise of civil societies that share democratic ideas has long-term benefits to the international community.

Philanthropy is a powerful global force socially, economically, and politically. Cooperation is most successful when international borders are ignored. The combined efforts of international philanthropic organizations to collaborate on

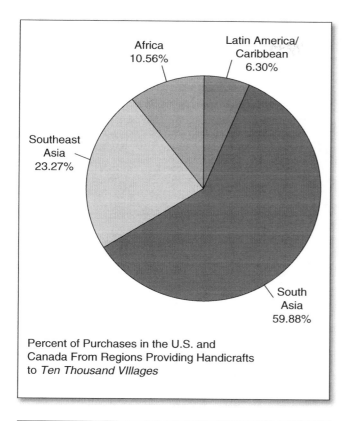

Figure D.18 2009 Purchases by Region

SOURCE: Adapted from *Ten Thousand Villages U.S. Annual Report,* New Hamburg, ON: Ten Thousand Villages, 2009. Retrieved February 18, 2010, www.villages.ca.

issues such as human rights, hunger, poverty, the environment, and population are enormous. As a group, philanthropic organizations have great influence in countries and regions of the world. They not only provide time, services, and money, but they plant ideas that support the growth of civil societies.

International philanthropy increases contacts between individuals and groups. The cultural differences between the group that is giving and the group that is receiving sometimes creates tensions. Does the donor group expect the receiving group to change some part of their cultural tradition? Being informed about public health or vaccinations is change at one level. Converting to a different faith belief is quite a different expectation. International philanthropy can exert great pressure for changes that the receiving group may not want to accept. How do you think tensions could be avoided?

International philanthropy promotes democratic ideals. The geographic spread of ideas about democracy is important. Newly emerging democratic governments are fragile. Tensions both within countries and with neighboring countries test the will of democracies. International philanthropy provides resources and volunteers to help strengthen civic ideals and participation.

International philanthropy enables people from diverse backgrounds and regions of the world to participate in global development. The world's cultural geography is diverse. Philanthropic organizations have shown that there is more than one way to enable people to improve their quality of life. Culture has a strong influence on how natural landscapes and resources are seen. One culture views a forest as a source of seeds and fruit; another perceives it as lumber for buildings. Philanthropic organizations use their skills in resolving those different views of the same environment. The results are often a healthy environment and a sustainable quality of life for both groups of people despite their conflicting views.

International philanthropy benefits everyone, both donors and recipients. Because of the geography of Earth most people live on a relatively small percentage of the land surface. Thus, people are more and more in contact with others. Many people consider giving of time, services, and money as the most rewarding activities they carry out during their lives. Local faith-based organization members may volunteer to help build homes in a community in Belize. A newly graduated student may volunteer for the Peace Corps and spend time in Africa teaching children to read, teaching young mothers about childhood nutrition, or digging wells to provide a safe water supply. Whatever the activity, in doing the work, each person builds a bond with others that is based on respect, giving, and civility. Perhaps without realizing it, that person is also growing in global citizenship.

Geography of Philanthropy: The Spread of Giving and Civic Ideals

At the beginning of this chapter we explained that a geographic point of view includes two parts: cultural geography and spatial analysis (where things are located and why they are there). The geographer uses maps and information to study the culture of human groups and to show distributions, or where things are located. We stated that a geographic perspective is important to knowing about and participating in international philanthropy.

You began by reading about Aldo Panfichi, an avid soccer fan in Peru. The culture of soccer presented a conflict for society. On the one hand, it was a terrific social and sporting event that demonstrated many strong elements of civic participation. On the other hand, the poor social behavior caused by fans of opposing teams presented difficult problems. Capturing the fans' energy and converting it into meaningful civic action was the issue that Mr. Panfichi faced.

You then examined two international philanthropic organizations, The International Federation of Red Cross and Red Crescent Societies and Oxfam. Both organizations are international, providing aid to similar regions of the world. The Federation responds to needs and serves largely to provide disaster relief, but also works on social and economic needs. Oxfam works in many of the same areas, providing social and economic assistance. However, Oxfam takes a proactive role in promoting social justice, equity, women's rights, and the rights of ethnic groups. The Federation and Oxfam are both engaged in philanthropy in the same regions of the world, but meet different needs and have different goals. Both organizations demonstrate that philanthropy includes giving material goods and financial assistance. They also believe civic ideals and democratic values are important to the quality of life.

The third example you studied, Ten Thousand Villages, presented a value question for those in the developed countries. As consumers, they can purchase from an entire range of goods, from crafts to mass-produced items. People working for low wages make some products in sweatshops; the consumer can buy them for low purchase prices. Other products are produced in places where a fair wage is paid, and a fair price is asked of the consumer. What are the civic issues a consumer faces as a member of the global society when confronted with such choices?

The patterns of giving and the flow of funds and assistance from donor to recipient can be geographically analyzed. Geography enables you to inform yourself about other peoples and their cultures so that you can make informed decisions about the world beyond your community. More importantly, it allows you to consider what you can do individually to promote civility in society, both at home and in other parts of the world.

References

Hodgkinson, V. (2001). *The roles and contributions of volunteers globally: Passing on the tradition to future generations*. Washington, DC: Center for the Study of Voluntary Organizations and Service. Retrieved February 18, 2010, from www.democracycollaborative.org/publications/hodgkinson.pdf

International Federation of Red Cross and Red Crescent Societies. (2009). *Red Cross and Red Crescent Societies*. Geneva: International Federation of Red Cross and Red Crescent Societies. Retrieved February 18, 2010, from www.ifrc.org

Oxfam (2009). *Annual report*. Oxford, UK: Oxfam. Retrieved February 18, 2010, from www.oxfam.org

Panfichi, A. (2002). Soccer and youth leadership in Peru. *Harvard Review of Latin America*. Retrieved February 18, 2010, from www.fas.harvard.edu/~drclas/publications/revista/Volunteering/tcontent.html

Ten Thousand Villages. (2009). *Ten Thousand Villages U.S. annual report*. New Hamburg, ON: Ten Thousand Villages. Retrieved February 18, 2010, from www.villages.ca

5. THE HISTORY OF PHILANTHROPY IN THE UNITED STATES: 1620 TO 2010

JOEL J. OROSZ

Leisure is time for doing something useful.

Benjamin Franklin

The story of philanthropy in the United States includes both continuity and change. There was philanthropy in what is now the United States before European settlers arrived. Other giving traditions came with those settlers. Thus, the existence of philanthropy provides continuity to the story.

Philanthropy has changed over time, however. Social changes have created new needs to be addressed. For example, huge numbers of immigrants came to the United States in the late 1800s. At the same time, more and more people were living in cities. Both of these factors created new needs that philanthropic groups tried to meet. Philanthropy also changed during the Great Depression, a time when needs were high. The New Deal, a government effort to deal with these enormous needs, changed the way people think about the role of government in solving social problems. Thus, it changed how philanthropy and government worked together.

This chapter examines philanthropy throughout U.S. history. As you read, look for examples of continuity and change in the history of philanthropy. Try to identify periods in history when American philanthropy changed in important ways.

The Colonial Period: Social Advancement in a New Land

As sailing ships approached the shores of North America in the 1600s, the passengers were about to find two things: hard work and opportunity. Often the immigrants arriving had no housing, no ready or reliable source of food, and no sponsorship. How were they to survive?

From the very early periods, the people in the colonies relied upon philanthropy. On November 11, 1620, the adult passengers of the *Mayflower* agreed to certain principles of civic responsibility and signed the following Social Compact:

> . . . covenant and combine ourselves together into a civil Body Politick, for our better Ordering and Preservation, and Furtherance of the Ends aforesaid; And by Virtue hereof to enact, constitute, and frame, such just and equal Laws, Ordinances, Acts, Constitutions and Offices, from time to time, as shall be thought most meet and convenient for the General good of the Colony; unto which we promise all due submission and obedience. *The Mayflower Compact*, 1620.

Underlying the social compact was the belief that those who gave time and services to help others might benefit

---

Joel J. Orosz is a Distinguished Professor of Philanthropic Studies and Director, Philanthropic and Nonprofit Knowledge Management Initiative at the Dorothy A. Johnson Center for Philanthropy at Grand Valley State University, Grand Rapids, Michigan.

themselves another day. There was no telling when someone might need help. Life in the colonies was often difficult, and philanthropy was both welcome and necessary. People worked together in quilting bees and house and barn raisings; they pitched in to help neighbors with harvests and heavy jobs.

As Europeans settled North America, they encountered many groups of Native Americans who had an established tradition of philanthropy (Berry, 1999). The Puritans met Squanto, whose Native American name was Tisquantuminn. Squanto served as a friend and interpreter for the Puritans as they made contact with Native American groups. He arranged for other Native Americans to help the Puritans learn skills and find resources necessary to live in New England.

Squanto's gifts to the Puritans were important. He helped the Puritans plant corn, showed them the best fishing grounds, and helped them trade with other American natives. If not for his help, it is believed that many more Puritans would have died from the harsh life in the colonies. It is also believed that Squanto used his connections with the Puritans to his own benefit. He is accused of taking bribes and requiring a payment for trade agreements he arranged. His final service to the Puritans was as the guide and interpreter on William Bradford's expedition around Cape Cod. He contracted smallpox and died in 1622.

The help and giving demonstrated by Squanto was practiced among other Native American groups as well. The celebration of giving in the Pacific Northwest, called the potlatch, was a form of philanthropy. Social status and sharing one's wealth were important ideas among many Native American groups. Gift giving was common, and the person receiving the gift was often expected to pass it along to another person. Giving helped create harmony within the Native American group. However, traditional giving among Native Americans was quite different from what the European settlers practiced. It is described as sharing the wealth provided by nature, compared to the European idea of redistributing wealth from rich to poor to improve living conditions.

Philanthropy in all its early forms had a common mission: *social advancement*, that is, the improvement of quality of life including social, economic, psychological, spiritual, and physical well-being for people. Early philanthropy aimed to advance or improve the quality of life (Bremner, 1988). That goal was not just an idea in the minds of colonists: it was an everyday reality. Two indicators reflected the philanthropic spirit in the early colonies. First was the establishment of faith-based institutions. These institutions provide a means of religious expression, an important core value for the English colonies. They provided a way to gather resources and give them to people most in need in the congregation or community.

The establishment of schools was a second important indicator of philanthropy. Schools made it possible for young people to read and write. For philanthropy to grow and succeed, the public must be informed of how philanthropy improves the quality of life. Literacy is thus important to the growth of philanthropy. Both are needed to develop a civil society.

Such early colonial leaders as John Winthrop in New England and William Penn in Pennsylvania believed that giving was essential. They combined faith-based beliefs and personal beliefs to form a philanthropic tradition. Another colonial leader was Cotton Mather. He became a major supporter of philanthropy. He arranged for parcels of land to be given to immigrants, helped build faith-based institutions in new communities, and organized people to give their time for important causes. He called the attention of the rich in Massachusetts Colony to the poor, encouraging the rich to share their wealth. He said, "Let us try to do good with as much application of mind as wicked men employ in doing evil" (Bremner, 1988, p. 14). Mather's role in the Salem Witch Trials often gets the greatest attention in history books. Yet Mather's ideas about service continue to form the basis for philanthropy in the United States to the present.

Case Study: Good Ben and Philanthropy

Among the leaders who encouraged the idea of philanthropy in colonial America was Benjamin Franklin. In Philadelphia, he assisted in starting a volunteer fire department and developed the means to have garbage collected and to have streets cleaned and lighted. Improvements to the quality of life in cities were his passion. That included hospitals, schools, and a university.

Many of Franklin's ideas had been included in his book, *Poor Richard's Almanack*. One of his most interesting acts of philanthropy was to leave a special bequest in his will. A gift of 1,000 pounds sterling (British currency) was made to the citizens of both of the cities of Boston and Philadelphia. The money was to be loaned out to young workers starting their careers. After 100 years from Franklin's death in 1790, the two cities could use three-quarters of the money to build museums and undertake other civic projects. Then, the remaining one-quarter was used for loans for another 100 years. Finally, in 1990, Franklin's will directed that the money be distributed for charitable purposes. The Boston money was spent on a number of projects, but Philadelphia decided to use their dollars to start a scholarship fund for students studying trades and crafts (Grimm, 2002). This act of colonial philanthropy is but one example of the tradition that continues today in the United States. Social advancement remains an important reason for this tradition.

A New Country and Expanded Philanthropy

The Declaration of Independence and the Constitution of the United States are the nation's founding documents. Both have become living documents forming the basis for civic behavior. For example, statements in the Constitution are reinterpreted and reflected upon by the Supreme Court. Thus, the documents, especially the Constitution, come to life as the law of the land. Evidence of philanthropy in either document is scanty and open to interpretation. For example, the Declaration refers to the "public good" in its first grievances against the King of England. The Preamble to the Constitution includes the phrase "promote the general welfare." Both statements are open to interpretation but seem to suggest that the writers and signers of both documents supported the idea of one's responsibility to the community.

Even if philanthropy was not on the minds of the nation's early leaders, they made it possible in Amendments I and X of the Constitution. Amendment I protects the freedom of religion; the freedom to uphold personal faith-based beliefs. The organizations that have sprung as a result of these beliefs have, and continue to play, a major role in philanthropy. The Amendment also protects the right to assemble, which is important to the existence of nonprofit groups. Amendment X reserves certain rights of government to the states. Most philanthropic organizations in the United States are chartered and operate within a state, either at the community, county, or statewide level. The founding documents made philanthropy possible within the governmental structure of the newly established United States.

Philanthropy: Emerging Patterns in the Independent United States

The early 19th century saw many changes in the United States. The population began to increase rapidly. This growth was mainly the result of the arrival of thousands of new immigrants. Many of these immigrants settled in Eastern cities: Savannah, Charleston, Baltimore, New York, and Boston. Other immigrants moved to rural farmlands, since land held a promise of security many did not experience in Europe. Forced immigration of enslaved Africans and an agricultural system based on slave labor, while morally unacceptable to many, also contributed to population growth.

Faith-based organizations were important and financially strong. Their members, as well as businesses donated to these organizations. Remember, at the time the government provided little or no assistance to those in need. Social security, welfare, and governmental assistance did not exist. People relied on private help, such as that given by faith-based organizations. These organizations offered programs to assist people with food, housing, and medical care. Churches ran Sunday schools, elementary and high schools, and social clubs for making clothing, serving food, and job training. Religious organizations believed their philanthropy carried moral and spiritual messages.

People experiencing poverty also received assistance from women's organizations, a trend that began in the center for Quaker beliefs, Philadelphia. For example, the Female Society for the Relief of the Distressed offered food, clothing, bedding, medicine, and firewood. The New York Free School Society was funded by the city to run schools for the poor (Gross, 2003).

Philanthropy was widely performed within African American communities at the time. The philanthropy of both free and enslaved African Americans came from religious and social organizations as well as from each other. The tradition of giving was as old as African civilization. It was brought to the New World just as music, language, and traditional religious beliefs were. Despite the immoral and inhuman conditions of slavery, African Americans found ways to help each other.

David Walker, an African American abolitionist, founded the Massachusetts General Colored Association, which became a forceful voice for all abolitionists. Walker's Appeal was circulated to African Americans and whites in both the North and the South. It spoke out strongly against slavery and its injustices. Possession of Walker's book, by those held in slavery, led to some states enacting stronger laws against teaching slaves to read and the distribution of inflammatory written materials (Walker, 1820). The educational benefits that philanthropy provided became a threat within the slave-holding regions of the country.

Controversy arose around philanthropy's aims with another philanthropic organization in the early 1800s. The American Colonization Society was founded in 1817 and was supported by many of the moral reform groups of the time. The Society collected funds in both the North and South to buy land in Africa where returning and freed slaves could settle. A delegation of officials and 88 black emigrants traveled to the west coast of Africa in 1820. The officials concluded:

> The surpassing fertility of the African soil, the mildness of the climate during a great part of the year, the numerous commercial advantages, the stores of fish and herds of animals to be found here, invite her scattered children home. (*Afro American Almanac,* 2004)

A large parcel of land in West Africa was purchased and a colony was started. Between 1822 and 1860, nearly 11,000 freed slaves emigrated to Africa. The colony developed with philanthropy became the country of Liberia in 1847.

There was much disagreement about the colonization plan. Some people from the southern states saw it as a way to return those who were freed from slavery to Africa. Once out of the United States, they would not be able to influence people still held as slaves. Northern donors saw the plan as a means to return African people who were being held as slaves in the South to their homeland. One side saw an opportunity to strengthen slavery by removing the opposition of freed slaves, and the other saw an opportunity to free slaves in the South by permitting them to return to

Africa. Others concluded it was a plan to decrease the number of African Americans in the United States. As a result, some people who had supported the American Colonization Society withdrew their support.

Various philanthropic organizations helped African Americans prepare for citizenship through free education. Others helped freed black people and those fleeing from slavery to establish new lives in the North and in Canada. By the mid-1800s, these relatively modest beginnings led to the much larger abolitionist movement.

Colleges received large financial gifts during the Age of Benevolence in the early 1800s. Private colleges such as Oberlin, Amherst, Williams, Andover, and Harvard received large endowments and gifts. Those colleges and universities continue to benefit from these gifts nearly 200 years later.

Philanthropy for education extended beyond formal schooling. People of wealth became interested in the public understanding of science. Money was directed to museums and other public education activities during that time. One such gift to establish a national, landmark museum was quite unexpected.

James Smithson, a British chemist, died in 1829 and left approximately $500,000 to a relative. He stated that if the relative died childless, the entire estate should be given to the U.S. government. That occurred in 1835. The will required that an educational institution be built and equipped in Washington, D.C. Former President John Quincy Adams was in favor of the federal government becoming active in education and research, and Congress voted to accept the gift in 1836. After much political debate and financial difficulties in preserving the gift, the Smithsonian Institution was begun in 1846. It is called the Smithsonian Institution in honor of James Smithson. Without the philanthropy of this British chemist, the United States might not now have one of the world's most popular scientific and educational museums.

Case Study: Benevolence and Abolitionism

Slavery was one of the great social issues of the 18th and 19th centuries. The abolitionists wanted to end slavery. They used many different tools in their efforts to end slavery. Philanthropy was one of the tools. Money was needed, and faith-based organizations, individuals, and private businesses contributed funds to end slavery. Money was not enough, however, and the abolitionists gave time and effort, endangering their safety and their very lives.

Harriet Tubman escaped from slavery. However, she continued to travel to southern states and assist other enslaved people to reach safety in the North. A network of volunteers who risked arrest and jail to help fugitive slaves operated the Underground Railroad. The Railroad helped runaway slaves escape and make their way to Canada. Charles Torrey, a northern preacher, was arrested for helping African Americans escape and died in a southern jail. Lawyers donated time and money to defend escaped slaves who were caught. Ministers not only preached against slavery but encouraged members of their churches to contribute funds to abolish it. The abolitionists included many people from different walks of life. They were determined to end slavery, and devoted money, services, and time until the Civil War made it possible to end slavery in the United States.

Philanthropy During the Civil War

Women in the United States were involved in a wide range of philanthropic activities during the Age of Benevolence. Their contributions were often overlooked, however. The Civil War changed that situation. As the war began, the need for supplies, medical aid, and attention to disabled veterans increased rapidly. People in both the North and South responded to the need, but women especially rose to the challenge.

Dorothea Dix organized more than three thousand nurses to serve with the Union Army. Almost every town and city in the North began an aid society to help soldiers and their families. Women ran the aid societies. Volunteers during the war included Louisa May Alcott, a nurse who later became a widely read American author. Harriet Tubman was a nurse and served as a spy behind enemy lines. She was African American, knew the lay of the land as a result of her work on the Underground Railroad, and was skilled at avoiding capture. Clara Barton was not a nurse, but she excelled at organizing relief supplies and getting them to where they were needed. After the Civil War, Barton organized the American Red Cross. Women in the South also organized aid societies to help the families of soldiers. They provided medical care near the battlefields and took the wounded into their homes. Giving and caring during wartime influenced the way that relief would be administered in later conflicts, especially World War I. Those wartime lessons carried over to relief from earthquakes, volcanoes, hurricanes, and other natural disasters. Philanthropy was meeting more needs than ever before.

Philanthropy, the Rise of Industrial America, and the Progressive Response

The Civil War resulted in a major increase in industry in the United States. The Industrial Revolution was taking place.

Industry needed labor, and labor was located in cities. The result was a rapid growth in urban centers. The major cities, mainly in the North, became home to waves of immigrants. Many of those arriving in the United States were poor and faced wretched conditions in American cities.

Within those economic and social conditions, a new type of philanthropy began. It was called *scientific philanthropy.* The aim of scientific philanthropy was to improve the quality of life by addressing the root causes of poverty and developing preventive measures and self-help programs to eradicate it. It was scientific because it had well-established rules. It required visitation, inspection, and advice to those receiving relief services. Charities and aid associations applied the scientific rules. Orphanages, schools, mental hospitals, and shelters for the homeless were inspected. Children in homeless shelters were to be placed in foster homes and sent to public schools. The scientific check list of what to look for and how to respond became part of a larger progressive movement in society. The needs of each person were decided in a scientific manner. Philanthropy was given out in a more efficient manner using the scientific approach. If the rules were followed, then there would be positive results. Critics of scientific philanthropy, though, said that it was "all head and no heart"—that the scientific philanthropists were so efficient that they sometimes lost sympathy for human suffering.

The latter years of the 19th century also saw American tycoons emerge. Andrew Carnegie became rich beyond belief, in part from the toil of workers in iron ore mines, steel mills, and coal mines. He was ruthless in both business and labor management. In his later years, however, he became one of the country's best-known philanthropists. His wealth was used to start universities and build public libraries, concert halls, and museums. Carnegie believed that only a few people should accumulate wealth, which should then be redistributed to the needy. He believed that in "bestowing charity, the main consideration should be to help those who will help themselves" (Carnegie, 1889). That philosophy of giving was published in a small booklet, "Carnegie's Gospel of Wealth," which was widely discussed among people working in philanthropy.

Carnegie's was not the only philosophy regarding how philanthropy should be handled. Other people believed in ending poverty and suffering for every individual, not just "those who will help themselves." They were followers of the *Progressive Movement.*

The *Progressive Movement* lasted from 1900 to about 1920. Progressives believed that irresponsible actions by the rich were corrupting both public and private life. Presidents Theodore Roosevelt, William Howard Taft, and Woodrow Wilson were supporters of the Progressive Movement. Jane Addams, a noted Progressive, believed that making direct connections between the wealthy and the poor was an important step. She began a series of settlement houses in poor sections of cities. Hull House in Chicago became the best known. The settlement houses enabled educated young people to experience the poor living conditions and needs of their neighbors. The benefits would be twofold. First, the conditions of the urban poor would be recognized. Second, progressive methods for helping the urban poor would be identified and tried.

Increased Philanthropy in the New Century

The 20th century saw a rapid increase in philanthropic opportunities, especially for people who did not have great wealth but did have some money available. The tradition of volunteering and lending a helping hand in times of need continued. However, a new, more distant philanthropy also developed. Old and new organizations entered into what became known as retail philanthropy. *Retail philanthropy* was the new practice of asking donors for funds—any amount was accepted—through magazine and newspaper ads and through the U.S. mail. Donations were sent to locations distant from the local community and were often used in places even farther away. Many new organizations, as well as established groups, asked for donations on a national basis. Figure D.19 lists several of the new organizations, but there were hundreds more. Philanthropy in the Progressive Era was a growing industry.

World War I brought attention to the American Red Cross. Medical and hospital supplies were sent to Europe. While many organizations provided relief, President Woodrow Wilson officially recognized the American Red Cross. He worked to increase funds for the Red Cross and to widen its mission to assist the U.S. military. The Red Cross provided ambulance crews, nurses, and health officials. The military depended on the Red Cross to distribute supplies and get information and aid to families. The Red Cross also provided food, clothing, and medical aid to civilians in Europe, as they suffered greatly during the war.

The war and its aftermath increased the need for international philanthropy. In 1920–1921 schoolchildren, community chest organizations, and religious groups raised funds for European relief. Europe faced many difficulties, but the United States was about to enjoy nearly a decade of economic prosperity.

Philanthropy increased during the 1920s. Wealthy people continued to give money. The middle class gave money, service, and time to their favorite philanthropic activities while poorer people often contributed service and time. The choices were many. African Americans and whites contributed to educational funds for minority students. Community-chest organizations collected money and provided help to people within the community and for local projects. Giving became more organized. Mail requests became the favored way to ask for funds. Professional fundraisers worked with and for many organizations. It was a decade of philanthropy on a grand scale. Despite increased amounts given, the amount needed to help the needy was even greater. States began programs of public assistance using tax money. These programs helped educate blind and deaf children and provided public health, public hospitals, and family welfare.

Organization	Year Established
Goodwill Industries	1902
National Tuberculosis Association	1904
American Association for Labor Legislation	1905
Lighthouse	1905
National Child Labor Committee	1907
National Association for the Advancement of Colored People (NAACP)	1909
Boy Scouts	1910
National Urban League	1911
Girl Scouts	1912
American Cancer Society	1913

Figure D.19 New Organizations in U.S. Philanthropy in the Early 20th Century

The Great Depression of the 1930s created immense needs across the country. Tension developed between those who believed people with money should meet the needs of the homeless, unemployed, and hungry and those who believed the government must play a role in providing widespread assistance. President Herbert Hoover believed local people should contribute to local community chest campaigns to raise money to help those in need. In 1931, he endorsed a major effort through the Unemployment Relief Organization. Its members included the leaders of major corporations and businesses. The Association of Community Chests and Councils carried out the fundraising. While considerable money was raised, the amount fell far short of what was needed for relief. The policy of depending on private donors rather than government to solve major national problems was about to change.

Government Philanthropy and World War II

The social welfare problems during the Great Depression were so large that only government could address them. When President Franklin Roosevelt took office in 1933, he had a very different approach from President Hoover. President Roosevelt's programs allowed government to provide assistance. This was a new type of philanthropy—government philanthropy. The federal government used New Deal programs to lessen unemployment through public works such as the Civilian Conservation Corps (CCC) and the Work Progress Administration (WPA).

Would private philanthropy survive the Great Depression and the New Deal? Government programs were replacing smaller community programs. While the government contributed major funding, private philanthropy continued to provide aid. At times, private and governmental programs cooperated. In 1937, for example, the Red Cross and the federal government joined to help flood victims along the Mississippi and Missouri rivers. The federal government also encouraged private philanthropy. The Revenue Act of 1935 permitted corporations to deduct 5 percent of their charitable giving from their taxable income. The federal government was thus granting a tax incentive for giving. Yes, philanthropy would survive. There was plenty of work for both government and private philanthropy.

World War II philanthropy dealt with military conflict and its outcomes. In 1941, the Red Cross established its blood donation program, which continues today. Many relief groups organized to assist military personnel, their families, and war refugees, and to make preparations for rebuilding after the war ended. Due to the war, giving was so great that it was very difficult to coordinate successfully. Every community in the country wanted to help with the war effort. A major coordination effort was necessary to collect items of clothing or food from several thousand towns and cities. The items then needed to be sorted, packaged, shipped to another country, and delivered into the hands of the people who needed them. Programs during the war needed approval from governmental agencies. The philanthropic spirit was at work, but the difficulties were great. Despite the problems, philanthropic organizations in the United States sent huge amounts of money and goods to the war zones (Bremner, 1988).

The need did not end with the war. Beginning in 1946, packages from the Cooperative for American Remittances to Europe (CARE) were sent to Europe in large numbers. They were prepared and sent by American schoolchildren, factory workers, and faith-based groups.

During the Depression and World War II, philanthropy had gone through a change. From a mainly private activity, philanthropy had also become a major activity of federal and state governments. The federal government worked at two levels—within the United States and internationally. In the United States there were major public works projects and social programs in education and health care. Outside the United States there was the Marshall Plan in Europe and international assistance to developing countries. The United States was a founding member of the United Nations (UN), which supported educational, social, and cultural programs in countries around the world. Developing countries in Asia, Africa, and Latin America needed agriculture, health, and social services. The United States assisted directly and indirectly through the UN and other international organizations. The U.S. government had become a major donor at home and in other countries.

Late 20th-Century Philanthropy

In his 1961 inaugural address, John F. Kennedy stated, "that the torch has been passed to a new generation of Americans." Government at the state and federal levels reassessed the needs of the country. Not since the New Deal had there been such an increase in programs to assist people at home and abroad. One of President Kennedy's programs, the Peace Corps, was begun in 1961. Thousands of volunteers went to Africa, Asia, Latin America, and the Pacific Islands to assist local people in improving their lives. They taught in schools, dug wells for drinking water, introduced new methods of farming, and improved public health. The Peace Corps continues today (Peace Corps, 2003).

Government programs during Lyndon Johnson's presidency continued to grow, with a strong focus on needs in the United States. The War on Poverty allowed federal and state governments to address social and economic issues. Tax dollars poured into government programs. The amount of money collected and distributed by philanthropic organizations was less than that spent by governmental agencies. Was traditional philanthropy, as it had developed since the time of Cotton Mather and Benjamin Franklin, still needed? Although the great increase in direct government funding for social and economic assistance created tension between philanthropic organizations and the government, several public policy changes provided support for philanthropy. First, government agencies gave money to community service organizations to provide services and assistance. Voluntary agencies began using government funds to carry out their work. The result was a new policy in which private resources supplemented public funds to improve the quality of life.

Second, tax policies were changed to encourage philanthropy. The 1969 Tax Reform Act included major changes in how foundations were managed and increased tax benefits to individuals who gave to charitable organizations. The new tax law rewarded individuals who gave money. Individuals gave 80 percent of the funds donated in the 1960s. About half of those funds went to faith-based institutions (Bremner, 1988).

Yet another important change was occurring in the United States during this period. Wealth was increasing. People earned higher wages and had more money to spend. Investment and retirement funds grew. Would that be reflected in giving by individuals? Despite concerns that governmental programs would end philanthropy, the total amount of funding has increased steadily from 1962 to the present. The total giving in current dollars has increased in every year except 1987 and 2009. Adjusted for inflation, giving typically increases in non-recession years and stays flat or falls in recession years. During the 1973–1975 recession, inflation-adjusted giving declined 9.2%. In 1987, it declined 4.8%. For 2009, the inflation-adjusted estimate of decline in giving was 3.2%.

How is the donated money distributed and used? The pattern has not changed very much over the past forty years. Faith-based organizations receive the most contributions, but contributed funds meet many needs. According to Giving USA, religious organizations received 33% of the contributions in 2009. The next largest funding recipients in 2009 were education (13%), grantmaking private, community, and operating foundations (10%), and human services (9%). Other recipient types include arts, culture, and humanities (4%), environment/animal-related organizations (2%), health organizations (7%), international affairs organizations (3%), gifts to foundations (10%), unallocated giving (10%), and public-society benefit such as United Ways, Jewish federations, and free-standing donor-advised funds (8%). Individuals received an estimated 1% of the dollar value of charitable contributions, mainly in the form of medicines supplied by the operating foundations sponsored by pharmaceutical companies.

Political Leaders' Views of Philanthropy

The final two decades of the 20th century saw many political leaders in the United States focus the country on philanthropy. President Jimmy Carter and Mrs. Rosalynn Carter began working with Habitat for Humanity in 1984. Habitat builds houses for people who are poor in the United States and in other countries of the world. Observing a past president and his wife volunteer their time and labor inspired many others to participate.

President George H. W. Bush used the phrase a "thousand points of light" in his speech at the 1988 Republican National Convention. He was referring to the thousands of volunteers and organizations in the United States that give to help others. During his presidency, the Points of Light Foundation was formed. It coordinates community service through a partnership with the Volunteer Center National Network.

President Bill Clinton gave personal support to volunteer action. In numerous public speeches he stressed the importance of people helping people. In January 2001, an earthquake in India killed more than 20,000 people. President Clinton asked India's Prime Minister how he might use his influence to address the crisis. The result was the America India Foundation, which organized relief for victims of the earthquake, assisted in reconstruction of houses and community buildings, and helped with food and health care. Since the earthquake, the Foundation continues to provide funds and volunteers to assist with projects in India (Global Giving Matters, 2002). In this case, one phone call from the president resulted in many people joining the effort to help.

A major government-sponsored project to increase and focus the efforts of millions of volunteers in the United States was approved in 1993. Called the Corporation for National and Community Service, its mission is to provide opportunities for Americans of all ages and backgrounds to engage in service that addresses the nation's educational, public safety, environmental, and other human needs to achieve direct and demonstrable results and to encourage all Americans to engage in such service. In doing so, the Corporation will foster civic responsibility, strengthen the ties that bind us together as a people, and provide educational opportunity for those who make a substantial commitment to service. (Corporation for National and Community Service, 2003, p. 1)

The Corporation operates three main programs. Senior Corps was designed to use the skills, talents, and experience of more than 500,000 Americans age 55 and older. These Americans serve as foster grandparents, offer companionship to homebound adults, and perform such other services as conducting safety patrols for local police, participating in environmental projects, and responding to natural disasters.

Through the second program, AmeriCorps, fifty thousand Americans serve their communities 20 to 40 hours a week. Most AmeriCorps members work through local and national nonprofit organizations such as Habitat for Humanity, the American Red Cross, City Year, Teach for America, and Boys and Girls Clubs of America, and small community organizations, both secular and faith-based. Volunteers can be paid living expenses and receive an education award after completing two years of service.

The third program, Learn and Serve America, provides grants to schools, colleges, and nonprofit groups. These grants support efforts to engage students in community service linked to academic achievement and development of civic skills. This type of learning, called service-learning, improves communities while preparing young people for responsible citizenship.

In 2002, President George W. Bush placed the Corporation for National and Community Service and Peace Corps under the umbrella of the USA Freedom Corps, continuing the tradition of presidential leadership for service. Of course, the support of Congress for such programs is also necessary.

Issues related to philanthropy can still cause controversy. One of the tensions within American government has been the separation of church and state. During the presidency of George W. Bush, this tension arose in the context of philanthropy. President Bush proposed that faith-based organizations be given greater opportunities to gain governmental funding. This proposal was referred to in the media as the Faith-Based Initiative, and debates, discussions, and both organized support and protests followed. Whether this idea violated the First Amendment's prohibition of government-established religion was the question.

One of the important achievements of democratic government was realized. A compromise was reached. In 2003 the Congress passed The Charitable Tax Act of 2003 (Congressional Budget Office, 2003). The act increased the tax benefits for individuals who donate money to philanthropic organizations. We can be sure, however, that the debates regarding the relationship between government and philanthropy will continue.

Looking to the Future

Just as philanthropy has carved a major place in American society in the past, its importance is expected to increase in the future. Two reasons are given for this prediction. First, future trends are often related to the past. The growth of giving between 1962 and 2002 may be used to predict giving in future years. While the exact amount cannot be predicted, the general trend of increased giving will probably continue.

Second, each generation of Americans—whether the Great Depression Generation, the Baby Boom Generation, or Generation X—has its own personal and social history. Members of the generation that were involved in World War II, sometimes called the "Greatest Generation" because of their sacrifices during the war, are now 75 years or older. More and more of them are dying each year. With their passing, the wealth they accumulated is passed to a new generation. The children of the "Greatest Generation" are the "Baby Boomers." The oldest members of that generation are in their 60s. Part of the wealth of those two generations will be left to children and other family members. However, the trend over the past several decades has been that more and more people are leaving all or part of their wealth to philanthropy. Predictions are that total giving will increase with the passing of the Baby Boom Generation.

Conclusions

Philanthropy and giving were among the core values that immigrants practiced in Colonial America. With the founding of an independent country, the principles of giving became increasingly important. The young United States was viewed as a country of helpers and givers. Communities responded to the needs of others in very basic and practical ways. In the African American community, giving was based on African traditions and was an important way to withstand the brutal institution of slavery. Across the country, people helped one another in many different ways. That tradition continues today.

In the 21st century, giving is organized differently. Organizations like the United Way, St. Jude's Children's Research Hospital, Toys for Tots, and hundreds more pursue different goals. However, they represent an umbrella of giving that permeates all of American society. Giving money, services, and time to participate in improving the quality of life has been and continues to be a core value of American society.

Note

Giving USA is a public outreach initiative of Giving USA Foundation™. The foundation, established by Giving Institute: Leading Consultants to Non-Profits, endeavors to advance philanthropy through research and education. The Center on Philanthropy at Indiana University is a leading academic center dedicated to increasing the understanding of philanthropy and improving its practice worldwide through research, teaching, training, and public affairs programs in philanthropy, fundraising, and management of nonprofit organizations. The complete *Giving USA 2010* report, with data covering 2009 giving, is available at www.givingusa2010.org, at www.givingusa.org, and at www.philanthropy.iupui.edu.

References

Afro American Almanac. (2004). The American Society for Colonizing the Free People of Color of the United States. Retrieved February 23, 2004, from www.toptags.com/ aama/events/acs.htm

American Association of Fund Raising Counsel. (2003). *Giving USA: 2008.* Indianapolis, IN: American Association of Fund Raising Counsel Trust for Philanthropy.

Berry, M. L. (1999). *Native American philanthropy: Expanding social participation and self determination.* Council on Foundations. Retrieved February 19, 2010, from www.cof .org/files/Documents/Publications/Cultures_of_Caring/native american.pdf

Bremner, R. H. (1988). *American philanthropy* (2nd Ed.). Chicago: University of Chicago.

Carnegie, A. (1889). *Gospel of wealth.* Retrieved November 20, 2003, from wps.prenhall.com/wps/media/objects/107/109902/ ch17_a2_d1.pdf

Congressional Budget Office. (2003). *The Charitable Giving Act of 2003.* Retrieved November 25, 2003, from www.cbo.gov/ showdoc.cfm?index=4555&sequence=0

Corporation for National and Community Service. (2003). *Mission statement.* Retrieved November 25, 2003, from www.nationalservice.org

Global Giving Matters. (2002). *American India Foundation long distance philanthropy brings donors closer to home.* Retrieved February 19, 2010, from www.synergos.org/ globalgivingmatters/features/0201aif.htm

Grimm, R. T., Jr. (2002). Benjamin Franklin (1706–1790). In R. T. Grimm Jr. (Ed.), *Notable American philanthropists: Biographies of giving and volunteering.* Westport, CT: Greenwood Press.

Gross, R. A. (2003). Giving in America: From charity to philanthropy. In L. Friedman & M. McGarvie (Eds.), *Charity, philanthropy, and civility in American history* (pp. 29–48). Cambridge, UK: Cambridge University Press.

The Mayflower Compact. (1620). Society of Mayflower Descendants in the State of North Carolina. Retrieved February 19, 2010, from www.law.ou.edu/hist/mayflow .html

Peace Corps. (2003). *Peace Corps history.* Retrieved February 19, 2010, from http://peacecorpsonline.org/messages/messages/ 2629/3988.html

Smithsonian Institution. (2003). *James Smithson's gift.* Retrieved February 19, 2010, from www.150.si.edu/smithexb/start.htm

Walker, D. (1829). *David Walker's appeal.* S. Railton and the University of Virginia. Retrieved February 18, 2010, from www.iath.virginia.edu/utc/abolitn/walkerhp.html

6. PHILANTHROPY IN WORLD HISTORY AND CULTURE

KATHRYN ANN AGARD

W orld history, even when limited to the period after human beings arrived on the scene, covers a vast amount of time. Thus, in writing about a topic within world history, such as philanthropy, a clear focus is needed. To select a focus for this chapter, we asked the question: What were the major relationships providing knowledge about philanthropy throughout history? Two influences are especially important. One is language, which holds the record of philanthropic deeds or patterns among a group of people. The second is religion, the source of many ideas and concepts that have become part of various groups' cultures. Therefore, in this chapter we first examine the role of language in studying philanthropy. We then focus on the role of philanthropy within major religions.

Using Language as a Clue to Study Philanthropy

Imagine that you have been asked to reconstruct a period of history that occurred before there were written records. What would you do?

Consider the many groups of people in East Africa who developed civilizations before there were written records. They were known as Bantu peoples because most of them spoke a similar language. The language developed in Central Africa and spread east and south as people migrated to new agricultural and hunting grounds. The language of those early peoples has been reconstructed. It is called proto-Bantu because it is a model of what the language was probably like several thousand years ago. It is based on evidence found in the

languages of people across the region today (Feierman, 1998).

You are researching whether the early Bantu-speaking peoples had the practice of giving to one another. Today, we call this practice philanthropy, giving to improve others' quality of life. As you review words in the proto-Bantu language, you discover the word gab. It has several different meanings (Figure D.20). What would you conclude if you were researching the idea of "giving" and discovered the word gab?

A second ancient word, -kúmú (Figure D.20), refers to a person who is rich, has honor, and is a leader. If the two proto-Bantu words are used together, then it suggests a very old pattern of giving as a means to build leadership. While no written accounts are available, the language handed down across the centuries reveals patterns of giving very early in African history.

The language of a group of early North Americans also reveals the concept of giving. The Ojibway lived in the Great Lakes Region around 500 years ago. They moved regularly, spreading their influence along the Mississippi Valley and west of the Great Lakes Region. They left no written record of their culture. However, they did leave evidence of their presence in mounds that they constructed. The mounds were large piles of earth that had religious importance to the Ojibway. Scientists examining the mounds have found such artifacts as tools, carvings, and trade items from distant locations.

Two words from the Ojibway language suggest that giving was a part of religious ceremonies. The term *mide* means "the sound of the drums." The word *wiwin* is translated to mean "doings." The *midewiwin* was a story of the migration of the Ojibway people. It told of the strong sense of community among the people. It also told of the redistribution of

Kathryn Ann Agard is founder and served as Executive Director of *Learning to Give* from 1996 to 2004.

goods given as gifts. Those who have studied the language of the Ojibway suggest the "common good" was an important value (Grim, 1998).

In Southwest Asia about 4,000 years ago, Hammurabi ruled as King of Babylonia. His empire extended from the Persian Gulf through the Tigris and Euphrates river valleys

Words	Meanings
gab	a. to divide b. to give away c. to distribute d. to help or provide services
-kúmú	a. a rich man b. someone who has honor c. leader

Figure D.20   The Proto-Bantu Language and Philanthropy

(Mesopotamia and present-day Iraq) and westward to the coast of the Mediterranean Sea. He was very successful at protecting his lands from enemies and fostering prosperity. Throughout his long reign, he personally supervised many projects to improve the "common good." These included navigation on the rivers, irrigation, agriculture, and tax collection.

Hammurabi is remembered for establishing codes, or laws, that he expected would result in a civil society. Hammurabi's "civil society" must be considered in historical context. There were enslaved people, a class system, and harsh penalties for breaking the codes. However, many of the codes were directed toward the "common good." For example, arrangements were made to protect widows and children. The codes did not specify giving money, services, or time to assist others, but did present a philosophy of helping others (Hammurabi, c. 1700 BCE).

Most cultures that have been researched include the concept of generosity. Across the sweep of world history, that generosity reveals itself in various forms because of the cultural and historical conditions in which it occurred. Cultures having few material goods may have given encouragement or time. Cultures that developed considerable wealth may have given huge monuments and buildings as gifts to a society. However, the underlying desire to give was present across time and place (Anderson, 1998).

The most common word in English that describes this pattern of giving and serving is "philanthropy." The word is rooted in the Latin language from the Greek-based words philanthropos meaning loving people combined with anthropos meaning human being. In Western civilization the word for giving and serving, philanthropy, means quite

literally the love of human beings (Merriam-Webster, 2009).

The Connections Between Religion and Philanthropy

Generosity, giving, and service to others have often sprung from a religious system or philosophy. The love of human beings, philanthropy, describes the religious beliefs in a higher being's love for people. For example, the Ojibway concept of common good was a result of that group's religious practices. The Ojibway religion, while not one of the world's major belief systems, provided a means to focus on the well-being of others in the community.

The world's current major religions have been the basis for much individual and group philanthropy throughout world history. Secular, or nonreligious, organizations emerge in the 19th century as participants in philanthropy and individuals began to be noted for philanthropy not tied to any religion. Thus, the world's religions hold much of the early historical record of giving. In order to examine the role of religion, we will look at the importance of philanthropy within several religious perspectives.

Hinduism and Philanthropy

Hinduism is believed to be among the oldest of the world's religions. It differs from other religions in several ways. First, it does not have a known founder. Second, it does not have one main religious organization. Hinduism consists of hundreds of religious groups that have developed in India over approximately 4,000 years.

The precise year in which Hinduism began is not known. Historians have found evidence that it dates to about 6800 BCE. Much of the early information about the religion was passed from person to person by the spoken word. Some things are known about Hinduism's early period. For example, Greek historians in about 300 BCE wrote that the Hindu people of western India had a record of past kings and events that can be dated to about 6800 BCE. In 6000 BCE people in settlements in Rajasthan, in present-day western India, were growing barley and raising animals. The evidence suggests that Hinduism as a belief system has existed in South Asia for a very long time.

Much of the Hindu belief system is recorded in an ancient written language called Sanskrit. Sanskrit was the basis for many of the world's present languages in the Indo-European family of languages, including English. Today the written form is used for research and the spoken form mainly for religious and scholarly activities. One term in the Sanskrit texts is *dāna*. No English word has exactly the same meaning, but several are close (Figure D.21).

The language provides evidence that generosity and philanthropy had important roles in early Hinduism. The *dāna* has been an important part of Hindu belief. Hindu books such as the *Bhagavad Gita* also provide evidence of generosity.

Philanthropy is deeply embedded within the Hindu religion. However, there is a tension. On the one hand, it is the individual's duty to give. On the other hand, one must decide who is needy and deserves support.

The teachings to humanity about the principles of *dāna* state:

Give. Give with faith. Do not give without faith. Give with sensitivity. Give with a feeling of abundance. Give with right understanding.

The *Bhagavad-Gita* teachings dwell on the ethical and moral imperatives of practicing philanthropy: "The meaning of giving is that which is given without any expectations of return and without any strings attached." *Datavyamiti yaddaram diyate anupakarine (dāna.).*

Kabir (c.1398–1470), one of the great mystics and critics of religion and morality, challenges human beings saying:

"You came into this world with fists closed and you go away with open palms. So even while living stretch your hand open and give liberally." *Mutti bandhe aye jagat me hat phasare jaoge bhai.*

Historically, giving within Hinduism has many aspects. The caste system (which is no longer legal) decided the role of people in society. The Brahmin was the highest level in the Hindu caste system. The Brahmins' special role in society was to pass along knowledge and learning. The Brahmins were given gifts by people in the lower castes.

India is often described as a country that makes guests feel welcome. In earlier times the welcoming of guests was a duty and responsibility. It was a part of the Hindu act of giving. That act of giving to strangers remains a part of Indian culture. The philosophy that the individual is responsible for the well-being of others has been the basis for generosity within Hinduism.

Buddhism and Philanthropy

Buddhism is both a religion and a philosophy of life. It provides a guide to a caring and nonviolent life. It is one of the world's oldest religious faiths, beginning in India about 2,500 years ago. Studying Buddhism is somewhat like studying philanthropy. An individual who gave up wealth and status in order to serve others started the religion. Today more than 500 million people in the world follow Buddhism.

A son named Siddhartha was born to a wealthy ruler of a small kingdom in northern India. The year was 563 BCE. The Guatama family was able to give their son all of the fine things in life. He married at age 16. Siddhartha's father wanted him to become King and rule the kingdom. The

family's wealth protected Siddhartha from the daily problems earning a living.

Siddhartha's life from this time forward is not well recorded. Legend and historical record have been woven together to explain Guatama's role in the development of Buddhism. After living a rather lavish life, the young Guatama reportedly decided to leave the palace, his wife, young son, parents, and servants. He decided to search for the cause of suffering and do something to overcome it. He gave up his way of life to help others.

Sanskrit Word	English Translation
dāna	1. gift 2. charity 3. donation 4. grant 5. alms 6. benefice

Figure D.21   Translations From Sanskrit

Guatama developed his belief system through personal suffering and sacrifice. He starved himself until near death. During one close call with starvation, Guatama saw an image of a lute, a three-stringed instrument. If the strings were too loose, they made no sound. If they were too tight, they broke. The strings must be just right to produce a musical sound. That vision led Guatama to a period of meditation, or deep, quiet thought. In meditation he saw his true nature and the nature of all living things. At the conclusion of this meditation, he became known as Buddha.

Buddha and the monks and nuns who followed him were traveling teachers of the religion. They relied upon gifts of food and shelter, on the faith that people would welcome and take care of a stranger. Each carried a begging bowl. Food given to the monks and nuns in the streets was also shared with poor people. Almsgiving, or giving food to poor people, thus developed as an important shared belief within the religion. Donations were also used to build rest houses for travelers and monasteries.

Buddhism in modern society involves generosity and giving. Buddhism exercises three strong influences on people's desire to give. First, Buddhism expects that followers will participate in socially important acts of charity, including almsgiving of food and money. It also includes voluntary service as gifts of time and energy in service to the poor.

Second, Buddhism expects its followers to perform acts of mercy. The goal is to recognize suffering among all living things and provide relief. Third, Buddhism provides the gift of education to all who want to learn. Learning, the highest gift, enables the mind to expand, meditate, and reflect in the very way that Buddha did 2,500 years ago (Guruge et al., 1998).

During the past 2,500 years, Buddhism has spread across the world. Every inhabited continent has followers of Buddhism. The largest numbers of followers are in Asia in a wide arc stretching from Myanmar to Sri Lanka to Japan. Northern India, where Buddhism began, is no longer a major center for Buddhism, and the Buddhist population is a minority. The region does retain its importance as the historical site where the religion began. One of the most prominent followers of Buddhism is the Dalai Lama. He is the spiritual leader of Tibetan Buddhists (Tucci, 1980).

Buddhist societies have organized in all parts of the world to encourage charitable and philanthropic activities among followers. The religion has been important in the philanthropic history of the world. Buddha laid down the philosophy for generosity and giving that has influenced and assisted others.

Judaism and Philanthropy

There are many references to philanthropy within Judaism from its early-recorded history. The Torah, the Jewish holy written word, contains many indications of charitable deeds and giving. The Talmud, scholarly writings about the religion, represents more than 2,000 years of recorded Jewish history. Judaic scholars believe that, while philanthropy was part of the religion, it was also necessary for survival (Penslar, 1998). Jewish philanthropy focused largely on the family and the Jewish community. Judaic scriptures make reference to the gabbai, people similar to social workers who worked to help poor people in the Jewish community.

In Genesis, the Jewish people are guided by the words: "I will make you into a great nation and I will bless you; I will make your name great, and you will be a blessing. I will bless those who bless you, and whoever curses you I will curse; and all peoples on earth will be blessed through you."

Moses Maimonides (1135–1204) is one of Judaism's most revered rabbis (teachers). "He speaks of eight levels of tzedakah, a term often translated as "charity" but perhaps better translated as "righteousness" or "equity" (Kass, 2002). In the Mishneh Torah he noted eight levels of giving, each more virtuous than the previous. These are giving

1. reluctantly;

2. less than one should, but cheerfully;

3. enough, but only after being asked directly;

4. before being asked;

5. in a way so the giver doesn't know who receives the tzedakah;

6. in a way so the receiver doesn't know who gave the tzedakah;

7. in a way that neither knows who the other was; and

8. in the form of providing work or money so the receiver will not need tzedakah again.

The Middle Ages began in about 500 CE and extended to 1500 CE. This era began with the decline of the Roman Empire. It ended with the period of enlightenment, in which European developments in science and technology emerged.

Jewish people in the Middle Ages lived mainly in the growing cities of Europe and Southwest Asia. They lived within sections of the cities called the Jewish ghetto. Often Jews were forced to live in certain areas of the city by the governing authorities. During the Middle Ages, Jews were not permitted to belong to guilds. Guilds were organizations of merchants and skilled workers who decided who could and could not belong. The guilds and the Christian communities were the major providers of charity, and Jews belonged to neither. The ruling authorities expected that Jewish people with more financial resources would care for the poor in their community. A sense of obligation to giving thus developed within the Jewish communities and later became a part of the religion.

The first Jewish orphanage was started in Amsterdam in 1648 (Penslar, 1998). Philanthropy to aid the Jewish community included many of the same services provided by philanthropy in other religious communities. Another important philanthropic activity for Jews was sending funds to the Holy Land. The funds were to help Jews who were preserving the Jewish presence and culture in the region.

During this period, disputes occurred between the two major European religions of the time—the Roman Catholics and the Protestants. The disputes reached their peak in the "Thirty Years War" (1618–1648), which destroyed much of Europe. People lost their homes. Armies occupied regions and people were forced to migrate. Jews became scapegoats based on poverty and their country of origin. Jews from Germany and Poland were especially affected and fled to communities in other parts of Europe. The Jewish community reacted by helping immigrants learn trades and find employment.

The 200 years between the end of the Thirty Years War and the mid-1800s witnessed a steady increase in both the need for and the response by philanthropy within the Jewish community (Penslar, 1998). B'nai B'rith was established in 1843 as an international philanthropic organization. The organization was founded on the religious obligation to give. It provides relief largely, but not exclusively, to Jewish communities and individuals. It continues to be very active and has become a powerful voice for Jewish philanthropy throughout the world. In the second half of the 20th century it assisted in many countries, providing disaster relief, senior housing, and community projects such as health and education.

An organization called the Duetsch-Israelitischer Gemeindebund (DIGB) was started in Germany in 1872 to help homeless and poor Jews. DIGB built and ran hospitals, retirement homes, orphanages, schools for girls, and workers' dormitories.

The growth of Jewish philanthropy during the 20th century was affected by the Jewish diaspora. A diaspora is the settling of national or ethnic groups far from their homelands. The migration of Jews from the Holy Land and Eastern Europe was a *diaspora*. It was the result of persecution of Jews over the centuries culminating in the Holocaust during World War II.

Throughout history, Jewish philanthropy has focused on three aspects of giving. First, in Hebrew, giving is called Tzedakah and is believed to be the necessary and right thing to do. While there is a long history of Jews giving within their communities, giving now extends to other communities.

Second, giving is focused on strengthening the cultural, ethnic, and religious identity of the Jewish community worldwide. Education, Jewish holidays, Hebrew language, and synagogues are supported to assure that the religion and culture continue.

Third, Jews have suffered greatly as a result of persecution during the 20th century. Entire families and communities of people were exterminated during the Holocaust. Philanthropy has been used to help Jews in unsafe situations. An example is the rescue of Jews from the former Soviet Union in the 1980s and 1990s. At the same time, Jews in Ethiopia were experiencing discrimination and extreme poverty as civil war engulfed that country. Major programs were undertaken to deliver Jews in life-threatening situations to safety in Israel or another welcoming country.

Christianity and Philanthropy

The practice of giving was an early part of the beliefs of Christianity. Three main divisions of Christianity are: Catholics, Protestants, and Orthodox. In turn, there are subdivisions within each of the three groups. For example, Protestants include Lutherans, Presbyterians, Methodists, Baptists, and many more.

As a written document, the Bible provides much information about philanthropy and its beginnings in Christianity. The story of the "Good Samaritan" has been repeated many times; present-day headlines often refer to someone who has done a good deed as a Samaritan. While the Bible contains many references to "giving," several are widely recognized:

2 Corinthians 9:7 — God loves a cheerful giver.

Acts 20:35 — It is more blessed to give than to receive.

Luke 12:33 — Sell your possessions and give to the poor. Provide purses for yourselves that will not wear out, a treasure in heaven that will not be exhausted, where no thief comes near and no moth destroys.

The biblical references to philanthropy have undoubtedly influenced many individuals to participate in giving. Giving of one's personal time and services in direct ways came to be viewed as the most meaningful act of Christian philanthropy (Oates, 2003).

Philanthropy among Christians was both institutional and individual. It was institutional because Christian communities actively encouraged charity for the poor. In Christian Europe during medieval times, the churches and monasteries were economic as well as religious organizations. They owned and controlled large areas of land and natural resources, allowing them to provide help to the poor, the homeless, the sick, and the pilgrims who sought shelter during their journeys to holy sites in Jerusalem.

The Christian church relied on *tithes*, or donations of money, from people who lived nearby or who attended the church. Tithes were given freely by individuals, but were expected by the church if one was to show true Christianity. Rich landlords and noblemen also funded the building of shelters, hospitals, and the care of orphans. Alms boxes were also common inside churches where gifts could be left for the poor.

Giving to the church in Medieval times did have some advantages for the donor. Those receiving aid often were required to pray for the donor's soul! When the Black Death (The Plague) struck in the 1340s, the poor and homeless were affected most. They, therefore, were seen as less desirable residents of communities. The charity they once received from the church was discouraged in hopes they would move.

The increasing population in Europe in the late 1500s, especially in such urban areas as London, Paris, and Amsterdam, raised many concerns about how to care for people in need. The main economic practice was *mercantilism,* a system based on accumulating valuable metals, creating colonies, and building industry to make products for export. European governments believed they should export goods and build up reserves of precious metals, mainly gold and silver. The workers who produced the goods were often poor. The result was an increase in philanthropic activity to provide services such as schools, hospitals, and housing for the poor. Fortunately, the rise of mercantilism increased the food and supplies available to churches to assist the poor.

Population growth in cities put faith-based philanthropy at a disadvantage in the 1700s. Cities like Amsterdam, Paris, London, and Nuremberg attracted more people than the churches could assist. This resulted in an important change in European philanthropy. City authorities took responsibility for providing assistance. People were taxed to provide for the sick and the poor. Government care for the poor through both donations and taxes became common.

The Age of Exploration that began around 1500 and the colonies that resulted from the explorations made it possible for the idea of Christian charity to be exported to other parts of the world. Members of the Christian churches joined or followed the explorers to North and South America, Africa, and East Asia. In Central and South America, the major force was the Catholic Church. In Africa it was a mix of Protestant and Catholic, depending upon whether the colonizers were French, Belgian, Portuguese, and Spanish Catholics, or English and Dutch Protestants. In Asia, Islam, Buddhism, Hinduism, and the teachings of Confucius in China met the Christian religious groups.

While there were conversions to Christianity among the local people, most continued to follow their traditional religion. The major exceptions were French Indo-China (present-day Vietnam, Laos, and Cambodia), where the Catholic Church gained a foothold during the colonial period. In China, Hong Kong was the exception, with the Church of England becoming prominent. In North America, the French Catholics settled in Quebec, and the American colonies included Puritans, Quakers, Catholics, and Church of England (which later became the Episcopal Church in the United States).

One of the most active Christian philanthropic organizations was the Sisterhood of Holy Charity, begun in 1727 in Latin America. Rich landholders provided money and land. The Catholic Church provided people to run the charities. The charities provided food, housing, medical assistance, and education to the poor. The Sisters of Charity provided an opportunity for women to enter the public world. The Sisters served as nurses, social workers, and public health teachers. For most women, there were barriers to entering the workforce. Those who did work did so out of economic necessity and were restricted to jobs as domestic servants. The Sisters returned the philanthropic gifts of wealthy landowners by assuring a steady supply of healthy workers. In an economic system based largely on plantation agriculture, healthy workers were critical (Thompson et al., 1998).

Beginning in 1776 in North America, in the 1820s in South America, and during the 20th century in Africa and Asia, there was a movement away from colonialism. While the end of the colonial era still continues today, earlier changes had a major impact on philanthropy. Welfare, social services, health care, and education were often viewed as the responsibilities of the newly formed governments that emerged from the former colonies. Taxes or other government revenues were used to provide support for people who could not support themselves.

Often faith-based institutions were the only organizations that had experience with philanthropy. Organizations that could manage funds, services, and time from volunteers to help people in need were set up in a number of different ways. Sometimes immigrants from a particular region formed an ethnic association, such as the Polish American Society. In some cases philanthropy was based on trade unions, with each member of the union expected to donate a certain amount from each paycheck. The donations went to support health care, job training, schools, holiday camps, and other services.

Many of the early Christian traditions of philanthropy remain strong today. Christian societies and organizations operate in many countries of the world. They are built on long traditions of service.

Islam and Philanthropy

The Islamic religion was founded in the seventh century. Its followers are referred to as Muslims. The term Muslim means that a follower of Islam has submitted to the will of Allah (God) and is a believer. Muhammed was the central figure in the rise and spread of Islam. Following his death in 632 CE, the followers of Islam collected Muhammed's philosophical statements and beliefs in a book called the Koran (Qur'an). The Koran became the holy book for followers of Islam.

Muhammed was born in Mecca in 570. Mecca was a great trade city in what is now Saudi Arabia. It was an important crossroads for camel caravans linking Southwest Asia, North Africa, and Europe. The busy trade of the city drew people of all races and religions, from many different countries. The people of Mecca had a commitment to provide for the "common good" among the city's many residents and visitors.

The religious belief system for Islam is based on five pillars that guide individuals. The first pillar insists that all Muslims recite the profession of faith, "There is but one God and Muhammed is His prophet. Allah is great and Muhammed is His prophet." The second pillar is participation in the public prayers that occur five times a day. The third pillar is the payment of the *zakat,* a tax to help the poor. The fourth pillar requires fasting from daybreak until sunset during the month of Ramadan. The fifth pillar requires a *hajj,* or pilgrimage, to the holy city of Mecca.

An important idea in Islam is *altruism,* concern for the welfare of others. Islam, within its basic beliefs, stresses altruism. The Qur'an makes many references to service to humanity, philanthropy, and charity. Muhammed displayed altruism on many occasions. In one instance he nursed an elderly woman who was a non-Muslim. Muslims are encouraged to follow the path of altruism (Bhuiya et al., 2003, p. 18). The widely respected books of Islamic Law (*fiqh*) also describe the obligations to giving and the common good.

Know that whatever of a thing you acquire, a fifth is for Allah, for the Messenger, for the near relatives, the orphans, the needy, and the way-farer.

Qur'an 8:41

Islam has more than one billion followers, living in a large number of the world's countries. In some countries, like Saudi Arabia and Iraq, the people have followed Islam since it spread from the region where it began. Other countries, such as Germany and the United States, have seen large numbers of Muslims immigrate and become citizens. Other individuals have converted to Islam, such as the Black Muslims in the United States. Each group is a religious society based on Islam, but its members are also German, American, Egyptian, Turkish, etc., depending on the larger society in which they live.

Islamic philanthropic traditions mainly involve giving to support social welfare within the Muslim community. Donations are traditionally made either directly to persons in need or through Islamic social welfare institutions. Within Islam, the goal for philanthropy is to achieve *social justice*. Social justice is defined as the protection of universal human rights. Those include civil, political, economic, social, and cultural rights. In addressing social justice issues, there should be no discrimination on such grounds as religion, sex or gender, race or ethnicity. The goal of social justice in the broadest context is similar to the philanthropic goals of other religions.

The Qur'an states that the most important direction in which the (free choice of mankind) can lead is to free the oppressed, relieve the hunger of the uncared for and those who are so destitute as to be reduced to grinding poverty. Those who choose this path, embody the highest values of compassion and caring (Nanji, 1995).

Yet Islamic philanthropy reflects the diversity of Muslim societies around the world. Some employ a rigid interpretation and application of Islamic teachings in philanthropic activities. Others believe that philanthropy should be a nonpublic activity, known only to the person giving. Still others believe that designated public organizations should be responsible for philanthropy (Center for Languages and Culture, 2002).

In spite of differences within Islamic societies about how giving is carried out, several basic principles guide Islamic philanthropy:

1. Charity has to be from lawfully earned money; no concept of Robin Hood-like acts exists in Islam.

2. The concept of ownership of wealth in Islam is that all wealth, after necessary personal and family expenses, belongs to Allah. It is up to the individual to decide how much of this excess wealth he should give back to the cause of Allah; if none is given, it is claimed by Satan.

3. All philanthropy should be for the pleasure of Allah alone. (Shahid, 1997)

Islamic law defines traditional charity that is expected of Muslims. The first type is zakah, a required tax. Every Muslim is obliged to give. Within Islamic law, zakah is the legal right of the poor to the wealth of the rich. The zakah must amount to 2.5 percent of the year's savings. Zakah means purification, and the purpose of giving is to purify a person's wealth.

Another form of charity is sadaqah. This is voluntary giving that depends on both the need to give as well as the amount of excess wealth one owns. Within Islamic beliefs, philanthropy should not be used as a tax shelter or to win personal recognition. It is to be used strictly for the love of Allah.

Recent History of Global Philanthropy

Three important changes have recently occurred in the history of world philanthropy. First, in 1945, delegates of 51 countries meeting in San Francisco established the United Nations. Its Charter provides for the UN to monitor human rights, to provide relief and assistance, and to create programs to improve the human condition. Second, the number of nongovernmental organizations has increased rapidly as well as the donations of money and volunteer time they receive. These organizations provide a variety of assistance to people in many countries. Third, since the 1980s there has been a steady increase in the number of wealthy individuals who have given large amounts of wealth for international philanthropy. Those gifts make headline news, but are only a small part of overall contributions, mostly made by people who do not have great wealth.

The United Nations

The United Nations (UN) was established to preserve peace through international cooperation and collective security. At the beginning of 2004, 191 countries belonged to the UN. Figure D.22 lists UN agencies providing aid to people in various parts of the world. These agencies give money, services, or time in ways that will help people worldwide.

UNICEF, the first agency in Figure D.22, has a major role in meeting the needs of children worldwide. For example, within 48 hours of a major earthquake in Iran in

UNICEF	United Nations Children's Fund
UNESCO	United Nations Educational, Science, and Cultural Organization
ILO	International Labor Organization
FAO	Food and Agriculture Organization
WHO	World Health Organization
WB	World Bank
IMF	International Monetary Fund
UNHCR	Office of the United Nations High Commission for Refugees
WFP	World Food Program
UNEP	United Nations Environmental Program

Figure D.22 United Nations Philanthropic Agencies

2003, UNICEF flew in "40 tons of much-needed medical supplies, blankets, water tanks, and material for building makeshift shelters" (UNICEF, 2003). The agency also provided experts to assist local authorities with their efforts to recover from such events.

Member nations contribute funds to the United Nations. UN agencies then redistribute the funds through programs. The contributions are examples of philanthropy by countries to help other countries.

Nongovernmental Organizations

A nongovernmental organization (NGO) is any nonprofit, voluntary citizens' group. It may be organized on a local, national, or international level. NGOs are supported by individuals, corporations, international organizations such as the World Bank, and governmental agencies that provide international aid.

A large number of important philanthropic projects are undertaken by NGOs. Some address specific issues, such as health or the environment. Others focus on the establishment of community gardens in poor neighborhoods. Many work with agencies of the United Nations. Since the end of the colonial period in Africa and Asia, NGOs have increased their role in providing international philanthropy (Knickerbocker, 2001).

The Internet and World Wide Web have aided the development of NGOs. They have enabled NGOs to coordinate their activities more effectively and efficiently. Money can be donated electronically, large numbers of members can be alerted to lobby governments and corporations, and information about their work can be sent to many people. People from different places can be recruited to volunteer time and skills. More people are able to communicate and take an active part in decision making.

The 1992 United Nations Conference on the Environment and Development (the "Earth Summit") in Brazil was an example of the power of NGOs. Their views on the environment were often opposed to the views of the 100 governmental delegations at the conference. Because of pressure from volunteers, the NGOs were able to participate in the debates.

NGOs from 23 countries greatly influenced an international treaty banning the manufacture, distribution, and use of landmines. In 1997, Jody Williams, a leader in the U.S.-based International Committee to Ban Landmines, was awarded the Nobel Peace Prize for their accomplishments. In receiving her award, she stated her main resource in bringing pressure to ban landmines was e-mail from the millions of people who supported the ban.

Finally, NGOs have had an impact on the thinking of international business leaders. Nike, the maker of sporting equipment, was convinced to improve working conditions for its workers in many countries. Home Depot was convinced to consider the effects of deforestation and now certifies its lumber products as harvested "sustainably." The World Wildlife Fund has influenced Chevron Oil Company in its worldwide program to protect the environment.

Wealthy Individuals as International Philanthropists

At the beginning of and during the 20th century a number of wealthy persons gave their fortunes to philanthropy. They included Andrew Carnegie, W. K. Kellogg, Eli Lilly, John D. Rockefeller, Charles Stewart Mott, Henry Ford, Madame C. J. Walker, John D. and Catherine T. MacArthur, as well as others.

At the end of the 20th century, a new group of wealthy individuals entered international philanthropy. Ted Turner, the head of Turner Broadcasting, pledged one billion dollars to the United Nations. George Soros, an investment entrepreneur, founded the Open Society Institute. Bill and Melinda Gates of Microsoft started the Bill and Melinda Gates Foundation.

The Soros-funded Open Society Institute has been very effective in starting programs to improve democratic government and civil society in Eastern Europe and Russia. The Turner grant to the United Nations will be used for a number of international programs. The Gates Foundation is supporting projects mainly in health and education. One example is a project to develop a vaccine against malaria. Thus, these large sums of money donated by wealthy individuals are having an impact on specific problems.

Conclusion

As far as we know, philanthropy, or giving to help others, has been present for all of human history. Philanthropy is often viewed as one thing that makes people uniquely human. There is satisfaction in helping others, and in some cultures it is an expected part of traditions. Families, villages, extended families, cultural groups, and even complete strangers give willingly of their money, services, and time.

Individuals of modest or little means give most of the world's philanthropy. Most of the philanthropy given is time and service. People provide service to their communities and to each other each no matter where they live. Religious traditions inform us that this has been going on for at least three millennia.

Religious faith brought people together who focused on their right to exist beyond the power of the state or crown to control. "Such groups insisted, in the name of all that was holy, that no one could prevent them from joining together 'for religious and charitable purposes.' In the name of God, they claimed the right to be, to organize, to care for the neighbor, and to set forth their views publicly" (Stackhouse, 1990).

This organization around principles of faith has carved out a "social space" in many nations that has become the philanthropic sector. Philanthropy continues to play an important role in the civil society of the newest millennium.

References

Anderson, L. (1998). Contextualizing philanthropy in South Asia: A textual analysis of Sanskrit sources. In W. Ilchman, S. Katz, & E. Queen (Eds.), *Philanthropy in the world's traditions* (pp. 57–78). Bloomington: Indiana University Press.

Bhuiya, K. W. (2003). Islam on philanthropy. *The Independent.* Retrieved February 18, 2010, from www.independent-bangladesh.com/news/oct/24/241020003lt.htm#A3

Center for Languages and Culture. (2002). *Penelitian tentang philantropi Islam (Islamic philanthropy).* Jakarta, Indonesia: Author. Retrieved January 2, 2004, from www.pbb-iainjakarta .or.id/newsDetail.cfm?News=7

Feierman, S. (1998). Reciprocity and assistance in precolonial Africa. In W. Ilchman, S. Katz, & E. Queen (Eds.), *Philanthropy in the world's traditions* (pp. 3–24). Bloomington: Indiana University Press.

Grim, J. (1998). A comparative study in Native American philanthropy. In W. Ilchman, S. Katz, & E. Queen (Eds.), *Philanthropy in the world's traditions* (pp. 25–53). Bloomington: Indiana University Press.

Guruge, A., & Bond, G. (1998). Generosity and service in Theravada Buddhism. In W. Ilchman, S. Katz, & E. Queen (Eds.), *Philanthropy in the world's traditions* (pp. 79–96). Bloomington: Indiana University Press.

Hammurabi. (c. 1780 BCE). Hammurabi's Code of Laws. *Exploring Ancient World cultures.* Retrieved December 1, 2003, from www.eawc.evansville.edu/anthology/hammurabi .htm

Knickerbocker, B. (2000). Non-governmental organizations are fighting—and winning—social, political battles. *Christian Science Monitor Service.* Retrieved February 18, 2010, from www.scj.org/scj_homp/conference-generale-2000/monitor-12022000.html

Oates, M. J. (2003). Faith and good works: Catholic giving and taking. In L. Friedman & M. McGarvie (Eds.), *Charity, philanthropy, and civility in American history* (pp. 281–299). Cambridge, UK: Cambridge University Press.

Penslar, D. (1998). The origins of modern Jewish philanthropy. In W. Ilchman, S. Katz, & E. Queen (Eds.), *Philanthropy in the world's traditions* (pp. 197–214). Bloomington: Indiana University.

Shahid, A. (1997). Islamic philanthropy: For the love of Allah. *Islamic horizons: Islam in America.* Retrieved January 2, 2004, from www.islam-usa.com/e90.htm

Sicherman, H. (2003). Victory over terrorism: Strategies for donors. *The philanthropy roundtable.* Retrieved January 3, 2004, from www.philanthropyroundtable.org/magazines/2003/current/victory.html

Thompson, A., & Landim, L. (1998). Civil society and philanthropy in Latin America: From religious charity to the search for citizenship. In W. Ilchman, S. Katz, & E. Queen (Eds.), *Philanthropy in the world's traditions.* Bloomington: Indiana University Press.

Tucci, G. (1980). *The religions of Tibet* (G. Samuel, Trans.). Berkeley: University of California Press.

UNICEF. (2003). *Iran—country in crisis.* New York: Author. Retrieved January 7, 2004, from www.unicef.org/emerg/iran/index_emergency_supplies.html

7. The Economics of Philanthropy: Do We Give Until It Hurts, or Does It Hurt Until We Give?

Robert B. Harris and Richard Steinberg

Economics as Decision Making

People often think of giving to charity strictly in terms of sacrifice; of course, giving does mean sacrificing something. However, the explanation is more complicated than that. Donors give because they want to contribute, and their motives are varied. Economists assume that people are rational, which means that they make decisions that improve their lives, rather than making themselves worse off. That doesn't mean that the gain has to be financial or even that people are selfish. It means that philanthropy occurs because people are happier giving than not giving—and there are many reasons why being charitable makes people happy.

Economics is the study of how individuals and societies make choices regarding the use of scarce resources. Economics helps us understand why people choose to share their resources (wealth, time, products) with others.

Economics concerns the difficulty of making choices when resources are scarce. Philanthropy fits squarely in economics because there are more worthy causes than there are resources to address them. Donors and volunteers must choose who to help first and how far down their list they want to go.

Types of Economic Systems

Every economic system faces the same basic economic question: How do we satisfy the most wants with our limited resources? Some societies depend on a command economy, or government control, to make their decisions. Others follow tradition, making decisions because "that's the way we have always done it." The most common economic system today uses the market to make decisions. However, all real-world economic systems use a mix of *command, tradition,* and *market principles.*

A *command economy* is an economic system in which the basic economic questions (what to produce, how to produce it, and for whom it is produced) are answered primarily by government. North Korea is an example of a largely command economy.

A *traditional economy* is an economic system in which decisions about the use of resources are made primarily through reliance on tradition or culture. For example, some isolated rural areas in Vietnam and China are still largely traditional economic systems.

A *market economy* is an economic system in which the basic economic questions are answered through buyers and sellers interacting in the marketplace. In many ways, the 19th century United States was primarily a market economy with little interference by government.

Even the United States, which is considered by many to be a free enterprise or market system, is actually a mixed economic system, relying on a combination of markets, government, and tradition.

Consider farming, which is often used as an example of free enterprise. The decision to become a farmer is

Robert B. Harris is Professor of Economics and Director, Center for Economic Education, Indiana University-Purdue University, Indianapolis (IUPUI), Indianapolis, Indiana.

Richard Steinberg is Professor of Economics, Philanthropic Studies, and Public Affairs, Indiana University-Purdue University, Indianapolis (IUPUI), Indianapolis, Indiana.

influenced by many things. We know that market influences are important; for more than a century, low farm prices have pushed most of those in agriculture into other jobs. However, tradition remains strong in agriculture. Many people continue to farm rather than move to the city for higher pay because farming is more than a job. It is a way of life. Government uses command powers to slow the movement of people out of farming. Government price supports for farm products have made it easier for some people to remain in farming.

The story is similar in other countries. The People's Republic of China has had a command economy since 1949. In recent times it has become more of a market economy. Government policy was changed to permit capitalists (those who supply financial resources to businesses) to join the Communist Party. That important change showed a willingness to accept the role of markets in this supposedly command economy.

There are also modern and market-driven sides to China's economy (for example, Shanghai). One of the most rapidly growing parts of the city is Pudong, a highly modern urban landscape that thrives on a market economy.

In some isolated rural areas in China, economic activity is decided mainly by tradition. One such place is Luobo, in northern Sichuan Province. This mountaintop village has little to do with the outside world. Consequently, laws and regulations from a distant government have little to do with daily life. There is little trade with the outside world, so nearly all economic decisions are based on traditions in the village. People use barter, shared ownership, and a village market square to sell surplus crops. It is hard to imagine the great distance geographically, culturally, and economically between this village and Pudong, Shanghai.

The Central Asian country Kyrgyzstan is another largely traditional economy, somewhat like Luobo. Economic activities are determined mainly by culture and tradition. However, changes are occurring quite rapidly. When Kyrgyzstan gained independence in 1991, the economy officially changed from a command system to a market economy. Still, for people living a nomadic life as herders of cattle, sheep, and goats, the economic system changed very little. Tradition directed the economy, along with some market activity and command decisions by government. Kyrgyzstan is strongly influenced by tradition. The yurt, or traditional tent, is still used by Kyrgyz nomads. These rural nomads must be able to follow their herds of livestock to new pastures and their yurts are moved easily. This yurt, however, has found a useful role in the growing market economy in the capital city of Bishkek. Shop owners locate them where business is good, such as near a city square. They may also move them to another location later that day or on another day if business appears to be better elsewhere.

The examples from China and Kyrgyzstan demonstrate that, in practice, economies are generally a mix of the three main economic systems: market, command, and traditional. If we examine agricultural subsidies (financial aid) in the United States and France (as well as other countries), then we find a combination of command and market systems. Even in countries that have a strict command economy, there is nearly always a strong underground economic system that operates on the principles of supply and demand. Therefore, modern economic systems are hybrids, or combinations of economic systems that are successful.

The Significance of Economics for Nonprofit Organizations

People often believe that economics is less important for nonprofit organizations than it is in the business world. Nothing could be further from the truth. Resources are scarce, and so nonprofit organizations have to decide how to use them to best further their mission. Some of these resources are unpriced (volunteer time and services are provided at no charge). Economics provides tools that aid decision making even for unpriced resources.

Let's look at an example. Imagine a $75/hour professional person taking time off work to volunteer cleaning up trash in a local park. The city could have hired someone for $5/hour, but now they can have the park cleaned for "free." Or is it? Surely it is cheaper for society to have professionals work where they are most valuable. In economic terms, we would say that the professional persons have a comparative (relative) advantage at doing their own work, and a less-skilled worker has a comparative advantage at cleaning the park. People tend to understand this instinctively, which is why professional people are more likely to donate money than time.

It's the Thought That Counts

Is it really the thought that counts? Have you ever received a gift that you didn't really like? People tend to buy things they like, but other people do not necessarily care for the same things.

Holiday gift-giving is a major economic activity. It is estimated that there is a "remorse loss" to the economy. When people receive items they do not want or need, this "remorse loss" is known more formally as a *social loss*. Social loss is measured as the excess that gift givers paid compared to the value that recipients placed on their gifts. Think about it for a moment. The giver pays $100 for the necklace, but the recipient only values it at $20! The $80 difference is the social cost to the economy. Has it ever happened to you as either a giver or a receiver of gifts?

Perhaps that's why some people have stopped trying to find the ideal gift and settled for gift certificates. Of course, that ignores the old saying, "It's the thought that counts." People enjoy giving and receiving apart from the value of the gifts themselves. Thus, you sometimes have to keep telling yourself that the ugly sweater was really a sweet thought, and the thought was what counted.

Why do people give? Is it because they expect something in return? Or is it because they get satisfaction from making others happy? Or perhaps they want to be liked and loved? Is giving rational? Understanding people's motives for giving is crucial to making sense of the role of philanthropy in the economy. Economists think of charitable giving the same way that they treat other activities—people do things that make them feel better.

Economists argue that people give because it is satisfying for them to contribute. That is especially obvious in the case of gifts within a family, but it is also true of gifts to strangers. Helping the poor may relieve guilt about one's good fortune. It may express sympathy for the less fortunate, or it could reflect a sense of a social contract. Some may think, "If I give to the poor, then I will also receive support if my luck changes." It's sort of an insurance policy without a formal contract.

People often recall reading the children's book, *The Giving Tree,* by Shel Silverstein, or the short story, "The Gift of the Magi," by O. Henry. Both stories are about giving and receiving. Both demonstrate unselfish love, although in different ways. *The Giving Tree* follows a young boy from childhood into old age, and a tree gives him support in various ways while he goes through life. "The Gift of the Magi" is about a young couple so poor that they cannot afford to buy each other gifts. Each ultimately gives up his or her most prized possession out of unconditional love for the other—long, beautiful hair for her, and a pocket watch for him. He sells his pocket watch to buy her a lovely clasp for her beautiful long hair. Ironically, she has cut and sold her hair to buy a gold chain for his watch. After the initial shock, they both seem to find a deeper meaning in the gifts—a meaning that goes beyond the materialistic or physical. The stories are entertaining, but they also raise important questions about why people give.

Economic Concepts and Philanthropy

Several ideas explain the role of philanthropy within the U.S. economic system. Remember, the economic system in the United States is mainly a free market. However, some elements of both command and traditional economies also play important roles. Following are several basic economic concepts that are important in explaining philanthropy.

1. *Scarcity:* Society, as well as individuals, must make choices: we cannot have everything that we want, no matter how rich we are. We sometimes hear people say that the United States "cannot afford" to pay for a public policy such as cleaning up the environment or making highways safer. What those people mean is that we cannot improve the environment and make highways safer and continue doing everything else that we want to do as a country with the funds we have to spend. Funds, or resources, are limited, which is the same as saying they are scarce.

2. *Opportunity cost:* Closely related to scarcity is opportunity cost. Every choice requires giving something up. This is called a lost opportunity. This loss is true even when the resources used were donated. In the case of the professional person donating time for community cleanup, the opportunity cost to both the person and to society is the lost output of their professional services. The value of the work was $75 per hour, which is what society was willing to pay for the professional person's work. Volunteer work does have a cost to society. Thinking in economic terms, both the professional person and a nonprofit organization would be better off if the professional donated $75 cash instead of an hour's work. The nonprofit could then hire perhaps five or six hours of a worker's time with the cash contribution.

3. *Efficiency:* Efficiency is defined as getting the greatest value from a set of resources. This occurs when resources are not wasted in poor production techniques or in producing the wrong things.

4. *Comparative advantage:* Comparative advantage occurs when one person or region can produce a good or service at a lower opportunity cost than another. The professional person in the opportunity cost example has a comparative advantage at their professional work, but not at cleanup tasks. Specializing according to comparative advantage leads to efficiency because it increases production of valued services. The professional person's donation of money, for example, provides more hours of cleanup services than if the professional did the cleanup.

5. *Market failure:* Markets do not always perform efficiently. Markets are inefficient when decision-makers do not bear all of the costs, or gain all of the benefits, of their actions. Action by government and nonprofits can sometimes correct for market failures. For example, education has benefits outside the market system for people other than the students (the consumers in economic terms). It is widely accepted that better educated citizens make better political decisions, commit fewer crimes, and contribute in many other ways. Those contributions do not always return financial rewards to the individual. Similarly, a person who imposes costs on others, such as driving a car that gives off oil fumes, does not take those costs into account when oil is regularly added to the engine. The cost of the pollution to society will be realized only when the car's exhaust is monitored and the car's owner is required to repair the car or is fined for pollution.

6. *Public goods:* Public goods are an example of market failure. Public goods are those goods for which it is difficult to prevent nonpayers' use and one person's consumption doesn't interfere with another's. In such cases, the market fails to provide the socially desired level of provision. For example, the benefits one person gets from police protection do not reduce the protection another person receives when the police patrol through the neighborhood.

Spending (Cost)	Donations (Benefit)	Marginal Cost (per $100)	Marginal Benefit (per $100)	Net Benefit	Benefit/Cost
$100	$1,000	$100	$1,000	$900	10.0
$200	$1,500	$100	$500	$1,300	7.5

Figure D.23 Example of Marginal Thinking

Therefore, it makes sense for people to share police protection. The question is: How do we pay for this service? If I hire and pay for private security to patrol the street, my neighbors also benefit, even if they refuse to help me pay for it. How can we avoid *free riders* in such a case? Even though we all benefit, no single consumer is willing to pay the cost without others also paying their share. The group agrees to contribute to the common good. Social services such as public health are provided through taxation even though not everyone pays the same amount in taxes.

7. *Thinking at the margin:* This "economic way of thinking" means looking at the *marginal cost* and *marginal benefit* in making any decision. Efficiency (getting the most from our scarce resources) requires that we increase production of any good or service whenever marginal benefit exceeds marginal cost, stopping when the two marginal values are equal. This principle is true for individuals, organizations, and societies. Consider the case of a nonprofit fundraising campaign that can spend nothing, $100, or $200 with returns given in Figure D.23.

Marginal cost is the additional cost associated with the production or consumption of an additional unit of a good or service.

Marginal benefit is the additional value associated with the production or consumption of an additional unit of a good or service.

Thinking on the margin will lead you to the correct solution—the charity should spend $200 because the marginal benefit of the second $100 is greater than its marginal cost. This is in contrast to the benefit/cost ratio, which wrongly suggests the charity should only spend $100.

Nonprofit Organizations Compared With Business and Government

Economic concepts are used everyday by decision-makers in *nonprofit organizations, government agencies,* and *for-profit businesses.* How are the decisions made in those three types of organizations similar? How are those decisions different? Nonprofit organizations make some economic decisions that are similar to those made in government agencies and others that are similar to decisions in for-profit businesses.

Both nonprofit and for-profit business organizations must do several things. Both must pay their bills for operating, such as rent, employees' wages, telephone, office equipment, etc. Neither can deficit spend or raise taxes like government. Finally, both are managed by private citizens rather than public officials. However, nonprofits differ from for-profits in two ways. First, for-profit businesses are expected to increase in value over time, unlike nonprofits. Second, nonprofits receive donations and grants, unlike for-profits.

Like governmental organizations, nonprofits have a public or collective mission. Neither government agencies nor nonprofit organizations can legally distribute any surplus funds or profits to their owners or managers.

Government treats nonprofit and for-profit organizations differently. Nonprofit organizations are exempt from many taxes that for-profit organizations must pay. Government subsidizes donations to many nonprofit organizations by offering tax breaks to donors.

Key Terms

A *Nonprofit Organization* is one that cannot distribute any financial surplus to stockholders, board members, or anyone else that controls the organization. Rather, surpluses must be used for expanding services, reducing prices, or making grants to other nonprofit organizations.

A *For-Profit Business* is an organization with private owners that have the right to keep any financial surpluses (profits) generated by the organization.

A *Government Agency* is an organization owned by the public and its elected representatives. Elected officials are prohibited from receiving the agency's financial surpluses, which must be used for expanding government, reducing taxes, or reducing the deficit.

The nonprofit part of the economy of the United States provides between 5 and 10 percent of the country's economic output and employment. The exact size of the nonprofit sector is difficult to measure because of the hidden costs. Those costs include the use of volunteers, and the true value of donated time, services, and equipment is difficult to determine. Nonprofits are nearly the only providers of some services (such as houses of worship or symphony orchestras). In other areas (including hospitals and nursing homes), nonprofits provide the majority of services, in competition with for-profit firms and government agencies. In still other areas (day care or higher education), nonprofits provide a substantial minority share of services.

The degree to which nonprofits interact with other sectors of the economy is striking. Often, nonprofits deliver public services paid for by government. For example, Meals on Wheels delivers cooked food to people who would have trouble cooking for themselves. The program is paid for by government, but nonprofit workers and volunteers do the cooking and deliver the meals.

For-profit and nonprofit organizations also work together at times. For-profit businesses donate money, products, and expertise to nonprofits. Sometimes they work as partners. For example, for-profit banks and nonprofit charities form partnerships to provide low-income housing opportunities. Nonprofit universities and for-profit firms form partnerships to research, develop, and deliver new medicines or new computing technologies. Finally, for-profits outsource some of the services they provide for their employees to nonprofit organizations. For example, nonprofits may provide employees with training programs, family counseling, and day care services for their children. In short, nonprofits are highly inter-dependent with the government and business sectors.

Nonprofits in the U.S. Economy

Clearly, nonprofits are an important part of the mixed market economy in the United States. Nonprofits serve a valuable role in two ways. First, they are an efficient way to make goods and services available that are under-provided by the market and government. This is the *public goods theory* of the role of the nonprofit sector. Second, they are more trustworthy than for-profits about some matters that cannot easily be written into a contract, the *contract failure theory* of nonprofits.

Government agencies provide public goods whenever there is sufficient political agreement about the amount to spend and the way to spend it. Those who hold a point of view different from the majority opinion can work together through nonprofits to achieve their goals. Thus, the public goods theory asserts that nonprofits are a response to diversity of opinion, to causes that are very important to specific groups but not to a majority of the population. Parochial schools that provide a religious alternative to public schools are a good example of how nonprofits respond to diversity.

Habitat for Humanity provides another example of public goods theory in action. Habitat uses volunteers to help build housing for low-income people. The volunteers and contributors who support Habitat for Humanity do not think government does enough to provide low-income housing. Because they are unable to persuade voters and lawmakers to spend more public money on this cause, they take matters into their own hands, supporting a private nonprofit alternative. Similarly, contributors to the *Nature Conservancy,* which buys land to protect it from development, seem to desire more wilderness areas than the typical taxpayer or consumer is willing to pay to protect. In such cases, it is not possible to reach an agreement needed for government to take action. When government does not or cannot address an issue, individuals can work together through nonprofits to achieve their goals.

Sometimes, an idea is too new to attract widespread public support, and then nonprofits may be the pioneers. This was the case for pre-Kindergarten educational programs for disadvantaged youths. Nonprofits proved the concept, and the government took over later. This is where *Head Start* programs came from.

Nonprofits rely mainly on volunteer workers. This fact suggests that there are subgroups of the population in the

---

Key Terms

The *Public Goods Theory* of the role of nonprofit organizations states that nonprofits correct market failures that result in the underprovision of public goods. Government also provides public goods, but only to the extent there is a political will to do so. Citizens support nonprofits by donating and volunteering when they are dissatisfied with the quality or quantity of government provision.

Contract Failure Theory states that nonprofits are more trustworthy than for-profits about some hard-to-observe aspects of product quality. When quality cannot be observed easily, guarantees and contract terms about quality cannot be enforced. This means for-profits have the motive and opportunity to shortchange the consumer. Nonprofits lack the profit motive to shortchange customers, and so are more trustworthy.

United States that put a high value on services not provided by the business or government sectors. Staff members at nonprofits tend to work for less than those who do the same job in business and government. This suggests that they work not just for financial gain, but for the satisfaction achieved by working toward the nonprofit's mission.

Finally, nonprofit community groups can provide a mix of services that varies from community to community. Locally, people may want to choose where they live knowing which community services are available. A new resident may refer to a telephone directory to locate where particular services are available. Maps of health care providers, Goodwill stores, libraries with volunteer reading programs, etc. may be important and helpful to individuals. Knowledge of the location of nonprofit services relative to where one lives in the state, county, community, and neighborhood may prove to be important to individuals who want to give as well as those in need of services. That important relationship is discussed and analyzed in Chapter 3, "Geography of Philanthropy."

Contract Failure Theory

Contract failure theory suggests that nonprofits arise in situations where trust is important, for example where the customer is vulnerable and cannot speak up for himself such as nursing homes or child care. The contract failure theory asserts that for-profit firms have both the motive and the opportunity not to deliver on their contract with the customer. We don't mean to suggest that for-profit firms always fail to deliver quality to their customers. For-profits can be trusted about many things because they care about their reputation, offer guarantees, and can be sued if they mislead customers about the quality of the services they sell. However, if a firm knows it will never get caught shortchanging customers, there exist economic reasons why cost-saving short cuts might be taken in a situation where a company will not suffer a loss of reputation, customers won't ask for their money back, and nobody will sue the firm. Contract failure applies to cases where the quantity or quality of the product cannot be objectively verified so those who cut corners will not be caught. It is called contract failure because one cannot write an enforceable contract regarding matters that can't be observed.

In a hypothetical example, it is hard to know whether a nursing home is properly administering sedatives to its residents. Some residents genuinely need sedatives for medical reasons, but it is not obvious to the outside observer whether sedatives are needed at any given moment. A facility that administered more sedatives than necessary would need less staff to provide recreational opportunities and to supervise residents' care. With lower costs, a facility that used more sedatives than necessary

would have higher profits than their more trustworthy competitors. The owners of for-profit firms get to keep these profits, and this could tempt them to change how they deliver service. Nonprofit owners do not keep the surplus, so, according to contract failure theory, they may be less likely to cut corners in this way.

Contract failure matters for private consumers, insurers, and government agencies. When the government pays a private agency to provide foster care and adoption placements for orphans, it would like the children to be well cared for. It wants children placed with the most compatible families. These aspects of quality cannot be written into contracts in any meaningful way, so the government might prefer to work with a nonprofit foster care agency. Similarly, when the government or a private insurer pays for medical care, billing procedures are so complex that it is hard to be sure there is no overbilling. For this reason, governments and private insurance companies may prefer to do business with nonprofit health care providers.

Contract failure theory is controversial for three reasons. First, nonprofits have other, nonfinancial reasons to cut corners in serving their customers and donors in some cases. Second, it is hard to enforce the nondistribution of profits, so that some organizations pretending to be nonprofit may actually be for-profit. Third, for-profit hospitals, day care centers, and nursing homes continue to prosper despite competition from supposedly more honest nonprofits. Nonetheless, contract failure theory remains a popular explanation of the role that nonprofits actually play (or should play) in our mixed economy.

The Future of Nonprofits in the United States

Although fairly small compared to the government and business sectors, the nonprofit sector is growing in importance and is even dominant in some industries. This trend is likely to continue, as businesses and government look for additional ways to increase efficiency. Each of the sectors will continue to specialize according to their comparative advantage. As they specialize, they will have all the more reason to partner with nonprofits that bring a different mix of specialized skills to their projects.

Economic and financial considerations are important when government and for-profit businesses consider working with nonprofit organizations. In some cases the advantages are obvious. Nonprofits may have expertise in providing home care services; government health agencies may not have the specifically trained professionals required to provide this service. Providing these services through private business would cost more since nonprofits have volunteers to do many of the necessary jobs. The economics of nonprofits enable them to work closely with both government and for-profit organizations in achieving their goal within a community.

References

Boris, E. T. (1999). The nonprofit sector in the 1990s. In C. T. Clotfelter & T. Ehrlich (Eds.), *Philanthropy and the nonprofit sector in a changing America.* Bloomington: Indiana University Press.

Burlingame, D. F. (2004). *Philanthropy in America: A comprehensive historical encyclopedia.* Santa Barbara, CA: ABC-CLIO, Inc.

Council of Economic Advisers. (2000). *Philanthropy in the American economy.* Washington, DC: Author. Retrieved July 28, 2004, from http://clinton4.nara.gov/media/pdf/philanthropy.pdf

Foundation for American Communications. (2002). *Journalist's guide to economic terms.* Pasadena, CA: Author. Retrieved July 28, 2004, from www.facsnet.org/tools/ref_tutor/econo_term/glossary.html#

Mings, T., & Marlin, M. (1999). *The study of economics.* Guilford, CT: Dushkin.

O'Herlihy, M. A., Havens, J. J., & Scherviah, P. G. (2006). Charitable giving: How much, by whom, and to what? In W. W. Powell & R. Steinberg (Eds.), *The nonprofit sector: A research handbook* (2nd ed.). New Haven, CT: Yale University Press.

Weisbrod, B. A. (1988). The nonprofit economy. Cambridge, MA: Harvard University Press.

Young, D. R., & Steinberg, R. (1995). *Economics for nonprofit managers.* New York: Foundation Center Press.

INDEX

NOTE: Main topics and their page numbers are in **bold.** Page numbers referring to figures and tables are followed by (fig.) and (table), respectively.